AFFECT REGULATION
AND THE ORIGIN OF THE SELF

The Neurobiology of Emotional Development

AFFECT REGULATION AND THE ORIGIN OF THE SELF

The Neurobiology of Emotional Development

ALLAN N. SCHORE
Department of Psychiatry and Biobehavioral Sciences
University of California at Los Angeles School of Medicine

LAWRENCE ERLBAUM ASSOCIATES, PUBLISHERS
1994   Hillsdale, New Jersey   Hove, UK

Lawrence Erlbaum Associates, Inc., Publishers
365 Broadway
Hillsdale, New Jersey 07642

Library of Congress Cataloging-in-Publication Data

Schore, Allan N., 1943-
    Affect regulation and the origin of the self : the neurobiology of
emotional development / Allan N. Schore
        p.   cm.
    Includes bibliographical references and indexes.
    ISBN 0-8058-1396-9 cloth: (alk. paper) ISBN 0-8058-3459-1
    (pbk: alk. paper)
    1. Emotions in infants--Physiological aspects.   2. Self in
infants--Physiological aspects.   3. Socialization--Physiological
aspects.   4. Developmental neurology.   5. Mother and infant.
I.. Title.
    [DNLM: 1. Affect–in infancy & childhood.   2. Affect–physiology.
3. Learning–physiology.   4. Child development.   5. Ego. WL 103
S374a   1994]
BF720.E45S36   1994
155.42'224–dc20
DNLM/DLC
for Library of Congress   93-40228
                                                                    CIP

Books published by Lawrence Erlbaum Associates are printed
on acid-free paper, and their bindings are chosen
for strength and durability.

Printed in the United States of America

10 9 8

To my mother and father,
Barbara and George Schore

and to my wife
Judith

Contents

PART V: CLINICAL ISSUES

List of Illustrations

Foreword

James S. Grotstein
University of California, Los Angeles

Maturation, with its achievements and failures, is fundamentally determined—and altered—by a vast array of carefully timed neurodevelopmental processes that can now be conceived of, thanks to the explosion of new interdisciplinary data, as occupying vaster and more complex, as well as more intricately timed and sequenced scenarios than we could have ever imagined. These developmental sequences are determined by a fantastic, almost surrealistically complex choreography that integrates postnatal neural anatomic and neurochemical development so that they unfold in an intricately coordinated series of contacts with the maternal–social environment—all in an orchestration of specifically timed phases of availability to a holding environment of appropriate, mediating caregiver functions that at first soothe, validate, and confirm, and then stimulate, challenge, and encourage, the sequential interventions that appear to be absolutely necessary for neural development—and, as a consequence, the roots of the infant's emotional development—to occur. Upon this depends the unfolding of the neural anatomy of the affect regulatory centers of the brain, particularly the right hemispheric orbitofrontal cortex, which apparently becomes the control center for the regulation and mediation of affect, social relations, and emotional balance, to name just a few of its functions. Put another way, if I read Dr. Schore correctly, it is the prefrontal cortex generally—and the right hemispheric orbitofrontal cortex specifically—that is most responsible for the establishment and mediation—and even development of the *humanness* of the infant!

In this remarkable and unique integrative contribution on socioaffective ontogeny, Dr. Schore has assembled an incredible array of data that spans virtually the length and breadth of modern science, including neurobiology, developmental neurochemistry, behavioral neurology, evolutionary biology, sociobiology, developmental psychology, developmental psychoanalysis, and infant psychiatry. His aim in this work is to construct an interdisciplinary model for the attainment of optimum integration from all these disciplines so that we see a more transcendent picture of the emerging human infant as a neurobiological-social-emotional *self*. I believe that he has achieved his aim and, in so doing, he has lifted our neurobiological "hardware" into a unique costarring role with our mental (cognitive/affective) software and has highlighted how our neurons become key players in the formation of our personalities. We can almost now see brain and mind in a paradoxically discontinuously continuous Möebius strip connection.

Dr. Schore portrays a series of contrasting scenarios of ontogenesis that are both Cartesian in their definitive oppositions with each other and yet, at the same time, holistic in terms of their origins, cycles, and ground plan. When the Cartesian (particulate) and the holistic are put together, we can comprehend a transcendent dialectic hologram as the ultimate ground plan for neural organization, which I shall elaborate upon later. Perhaps we can begin to understand this complex and intricate choreography if we employ the dual-track theory, a concept that I have proposed elsewhere (Grotstein, 1980, 1993). This theory suggests that all living organisms develop, mature, and exist along dialectical-dialogical lines. Dialectics apply to closed systems, whereas dialogic characterizes the interaction in open systems (Bakhtin, 1981). Neural development occurs in a closed system with the environment; whereas normal, mature interactions and adult discourse occur in a dialogically open system. Freud was not fully aware that each of his successive theories of psychoanalysis was dialectical. The concept of the relationship of consciousness to unconsciousness, of primary process to secondary process, and of psychic conflict are but instances of oppositionalities of qualities that, by opposing one another, consequently differ with one another yet declare that they belong to one another, and therefore *define* one another. Dr. Schore has given us ample evidence that dialectics is one of the irreducible principles involved in the infant's neurodevelopmental progression as the outcome of a series of oppositional interactions between genotype and phenotype, that is, selected, evolving cortical neurons in the infant, first with each other for "Darwinian" neuronal survival,[1] then neuronal systems agonist-antagonist expression/inhibition—and then in dialectical relationships with the skilled, empathic, attuned presence of his/her mother, first as caretaker and later as social interactor, stimulator, "transformational object" (Bollas, 1987), or "existential coach" (Grotstein, 1993).

The history of modern clinical neurology has also been characterized by a dialectical tension, especially, for example, when a brain lesion occurs; emphasis is generally placed on its specific localization while oftentimes the overall effect

---

[1]Gerald Edelman (1987, 1989) has already addressed the "Darwinian survival" issue of neuronal group selection, and his views help in preparing the way for Dr. Schore's pivotal contribution.

on the level of functioning of the central nervous system is ignored. The "Broca" specificity school was countered by the concept of ascending hierarchical levels of cerebral organization developmentally and descending levels of organizational functioning occurring with brain lesions. J. Hughlings Jackson (1879, 1931) and Freud (1891) were prominent in the latter category. It is of no small interest, parenthetically, that Freud himself never gave up the idea of ultimately uniting psychoanalysis with neurology (Amacher, 1965; Freud, 1895/1950).

An additional aspect of the concept of the dual-track may be of help in comprehending the complex choreography that informs this vast array of developmental research. I am referring to the concept of *holography*, to which I have alluded earlier and which I now wish to use as a metaphor to understand the unique complexity of these developmental sequences. With the concept of holography we can picture both the overall holistic unity of the developmental genetic plan in operation *and* the dialectical, particulate, individual aspects as subsumed within the holistic aspects. Holography subtends holism and individualism, in other words. Thus, a new dialectic emerges that juxtaposes the unified holistic perspective with the linear, sequential, particulate perspective, both within the overall holographic choreography.

Dr. Schore's (1991) involvement with this vast project began with his earlier work on the phenomenon of shame, which offered a template for the unfolding of his integrative ideas that link psychoanalytic metapsychology and infant development with a vast array of neurobiological and sociobiological research. He brought to our attention there the unusual importance of a particular stage of infancy, 10–12 to 16–18 months, the practicing subphase of separation and individuation (Mahler, 1968), a period of heightened activation of the sympathetic aspects of the autonomic nervous system, and the need for the mother to attune properly to the infant's excitement at that time. Failure for her to do so results in the premature activation of the parasympathetic nervous system, which results in the phenomenon of excessive shame to counterbalance the now-found-to-be-dangerous excitement of the early practicing period. Thus, he postulated that in the early practicing subphase normal excitement evolves and has to be properly attuned. Then, in the later aspects of practicing, the parasympathetic system comes into play becoming a normal neurobehavioral "antagonist" to its predecessor so as to mediate and regulate its expression. This correlation between neurobiology, psychoanalysis, infant development theory, and attachment theory was to become the embryo for this larger work.

Speaking as a psychiatrist and psychoanalyst, I shall convey what I believe to be some of the more salient findings and conclusions from Dr. Schore's work that bear upon psychoanalysis, psychotherapy, and infant development. The infant brings inherent, constitutional givens (genotype) to the birth situation, which continue to unfold for a considerable length of time past birth. These genetic endowments are partially open to environmental modification (phenotype) and are also partially closed. To the extent that they are open they are acted upon, modified, completed, and developed in a continuous dialectical interaction with primary caregivers. What psychoanalytic theory had speculated upon from its very beginning now turns out to be truer than had been anticipated. As in chaos theory, which states in part that there occurs *an unusual sensitivity to initial conditions*, the role of the mothering person with her offspring, which had been all but neglected in the dawn of psychoanalysis, especially by "orthodox psychoanalysis," began to become recognized by object relations theorists (Ferenczi, Hermann, Klein, Fairbairn, Winnicott, Balint, etc.) and ego psychologists (Erikson, Jacobson, Hartmann, etc.), especially in the latters' concept of adaptation. Nobody then anticipated *how* dependent the infant's *brain* was on the mother's caregiving and social interaction as a *releasor* moiety to her infant's inherent and evolving brain structures, structures that emerge slowly, discontinuously, in momentary "niches" that must be optimalized or forfeited in a timely way—while, at the same time, an overabundance (because of an overproduction) of neurons is being selectively and skillfully decimated so that an evolving neurobehavioral-affective-social *self* can emerge. Furthermore, Freud's concept of drive theory, one of discharge, has become superseded by an object-relations concept; thus, the drives, like the affects, and even like nerves, can now be seen to *communicate* by signals, and later, signs and symbols. The brain, like the mind, is first and foremost an information-seeking and -functioning organ, not primarily a tension-reducing one.

Perhaps the most salient aspects of the author's work lie in its clinical applications. Neurobiology has recently been knocking harder and harder on the doors of psychoanalysis and psychotherapy, but, until recently, we therapists did not know how to forge a connection except in terms of using medication (reluctantly) to deal with dysfunctional mental states that seemed to be clearly "organic" in their origin—and which did not yield—or easily yield—to interpretive interventions. As a result of Dr. Schore's contribution we now have many more overarching bridges between neurobiological psychiatry and psychoanalytic psychology that are "user-friendly" and "user-relevant" for psychotherapists. One immediately thinks of developmental psychopathology, insecure attachments and their neuropsychological consequences, affect dysregulation, the onset of personality disorders, and vulnerability to somatization disorders. Developmental psychopathology, which is rapidly becoming a field unto itself, can certainly be understood in no small measure by the concept of the "failed appointment," that is, failure, whether by chance, trauma, neglect, or inherent genetic programming, for the key neuronal connections to have been evoked at the proper time by the mother-as-appropriate-selfobject at the appropriate time.

One certainly must now view such disorders on the anxiety spectrum, such as the disorders of anxiety, panic, phobias, hypochondria, and such trait–state disorders as borderline personality, the obsessive-compulsive disorders, affect dysregulation (the manic-depressive-dysthymic spectrum disorders), schizophrenia, and many others as being deeply rooted in one or another form of a neurobiologically induced disorder of regulation. Joseph Palombo (1993), who works with the neuro-perceptual-cognitive aspects of developmental disorders of child-hood, including the childhood borderline syndrome, calls attention to the pres-ence in these impaired children of a discrepancy between their private, personal selves and their shared selves in terms of a lack of ease in communication. Put another way, these damaged children seem to sense that there is something neurodevelopmentally wrong with them, and they feel a deep sense of shame about themselves as a result. One of the consequences of this awareness is alienation and withdrawal. Another is the development of a true-self/false-self dichotomy (Winnicott, 1960).

Insecure-avoidant attachments are yet another aspect of clinical relevance. Certainly Bowlby's (1969, 1973, 1981) concept of attachment and bonding has turned out to be one of the most suitable and overarching theories that lends itself to the interdisciplinary paradigm. From one point of view one can consider all psychopathology as due to the failure, to one degree or another, of proper attachment and bonding. Hofer (1983, 1984) even talks of the hidden biological regulators that mother's body offers her newborn in terms of body heat, heart rate, sleep/wake cycle, and central nervous system neurotransmitter regulation.

Yet another aspect of this work that deserves mention is the recognition and importance that the author gives to the new concept of *self-regulation theory*. This concept has begun to have importance for infant development research (Stern, 1985) and for psychosomatic theory and practice (Grotstein, 1986; Krys-tal, 1988; Taylor, 1993). In terms of Dr. Schore's thesis, one can say that self-regulation corresponds to *neurodynamics*, which conceptually parallels *psycho-dynamics*.

I am also reminded, in reference to some clinical applications, of Tustin's (1990) findings that infant's fear ecstacy, as well as tantrums, and need the mothering person to help them regulate the excesses of these passions. The author's emphasis on the adaptive function of early exploratory experiences brings to mind Winnicott's (1971) concept of "playing," in which the infant must be induced to produce illusions that he or she has created the object *at the same time as the mother proffers the object to be discovered*. Winnicott, the master of dialectics and paradox, can be seen to have anticipated the interactive principle of ontogenetic unfolding that runs like an Ariadne's thread through Dr. Schore's work.

How do these new awarenesses clinically affect our psychoanalytic and psy-chotherapeutic understanding of our patients? First of all, the very awareness of the complexity of nature's neuropsychical choreography makes us even more humble as therapists than we were before. Second, we are challenged to develop a new found respect for "neurotransmitter psychology," in the context of disor-ders of self-regulation, as a significant organizer of experience and particularly as an organizer of the mental and emotional development and maturity with which we continue to organize and reorganize the narratives of our ongoing experiences. We must learn to consider that the very phenomenon of psycho-analytic and psychotherapeutic transference constitutes a repetition of the archival history of our patients' attempts to attach to their mothers and fathers and also a record of how mothers and fathers bonded to them. We can clinically observe and/or intuit a great deal of this in how our patients are able to problem solve, soothe themselves, and tolerate shame, anxiety, frustration, absences, etc. We need to go beyond the mere psychodynamic formulation of the key fantasy involved in the patients' associations. We must alert ourselves to *how* our patient's are processing, visualizing, hearing, and organizing their associative thoughts and feelings and try to intuit the neural bias of the lens through which they inform themselves and us of their feelings.

We must rethink our conceptions about the holding (bonding and attachment) aspects of treatment and its dialectical relationship to those interventions, such as confrontative interpretations, that bespeak "weaning." In other words, maybe some patients who have had subtle or overt developmental disorders may need more "holding" rather than premature analytic releasing into the void of unintentional neglect. We need, in short, to be deeply immersed in the truth of the biopsychosocial paradigm rather than pay lip service to it.

Let me give an example of how this contribution has affected my thinking. I have been attempting to define a syndrome that seems to occur quite often but has hitherto remained unnoticed. This syndrome includes patients suffering from overt and especially covert agoraphobia, social phobia, schizoid personality, and shy–avoidant personality. I have also linked them with Michael Stone's (1988) concept that inherent and/or acquired hyperirritability is the "red thread" running through the borderline disorder. My own hypothesis is as follows: The patients that I believe belong to the syndrome suffer from the consequences of unbearable anxiety, particularly separation, "geographic anxiety," and neophobia. They seem to curtail and constrict their lives in narrower and narrower perimeters because of the fear of involvement and commitment. They are pathologically self-reflective (self-conscious and susceptible to intense shame) and cannot play or explore. The syndrome is due, I believe, to the interaction of heredity and sensitization at key points in development, particularly to the practicing subphase of separation and individuation. In particular, they are sensitive to and sensitized by separation anxiety and later by stranger anxiety. Developmentally informed clinical intervention could be thought of as advisable for the children who are to become these patients. During the practicing subphase, trained professionals could help in diagnosis and intervention prophylaxis so that these infants could be more optimally validated during their phases of enthusiastic self-expression.

What I have alluded to here constitute mere desultory comments upon a rich tapestry of intricate interdisciplinary threads. This is a pioneering work that holds considerable promise for everyone in the behavioral sciences. It fundamentally alters our traditional, fundamentalistic, cyclopean psychodynamic way of viewing infants and patients and dramatically informs a newer and much needed interdisciplinary perspective.

REFERENCES

Amacher, P. (1965). *Freud's neurological education and its influence on psychoanalytic theory. Psychological Issues, 4* (Monograph 16).

Bakhtin, M. (1981). *The dialogic imagination: Four essays of M.M. Bakhtin* (C. Emerson & M. Holquist, Trans.). Austin: University of Texas.

Bollas, C. (1987). *The shadow of the object.* London: Free Associations Press.

Bowlby, J. (1969). *Attachment and loss: Vol. 1. Attachment.* New York: Basic Books.

Bowlby, J. (1973). *Attachment and loss: Vol. 2. Separation, anxiety and anger.* New York: Basic Books.

Bowlby, J. (1981). *Attachment and loss: Vol. 3. Loss, sadness and depression.* New York: Basic Books.

Edelman, G.M. (1987). *Neural Darwinism: The theory of neuronal group selection.* New York: Basic Books.

Edelman, G.M. (1989). *The remembered present: A biological theory of consciousness.* New York: Basic Books.

Freud, S. (1891). *Zur Auffassung der Aphasien, eine kritische Studie* [*On aphasia*]. Leipzig: F. Deuticke.

Freud, S. (1966). Project for a scientific psychology. In J. Strachey (Ed. and Trans.), *The standard edition of the complete psychological works of Sigmund Freud.* London: Hogarth Press. (Original work published 1895)

Grotstein, J.S. (1980). A proposed revision of the psychoanalytic concept of primitive mental states: I. Introduction to a newer psychoanalytic metapsychology. *Contemporary Psychoanalysis, 16,* 479–546.

Grotstein, J.S. (1986). The psychology of powerlessness: Disorders of self-regulation and interactional regulation as a newer paradigm for psychopathology. *Psychoanalytic Inquiry, 6,* 93–118.

Grotstein, J.S. (1993). *The dual track theorem: A newer paradigm for psychoanalytic theory and technique.* Manuscript in preparation.

Hofer, M. (1983). On the relationship between attachment and separation processes in infancy. In R. Plutchik & H. Kellerman (Eds.), *Emotion: Theory, research, and experience* (Vol. 2, pp. 199–219). New York: Academic Press.

Hofer, M. (1984). Relationships as regulators: A psychobiologic perspective on bereavement. *Psychosomatic Medicine, 46,* 183–197.

Jackson, J. H. (1879). On affections of speech from diseases of the brain. *Brain, 2,* 203–222.

Jackson, J. H. (1931). *Selected writings of John Hughlings Jackson* (Vols. I and II). London: Hodder and Stoughton.

Krystal, H. (1988). *Integration and self-healing: Affect-trauma-alexithymia.* Hillsdale, NJ: The Analytic Press.

Mahler, M.S. (1968). *On human symbiosis and the vicissitudes of individuation.* New York: International Universities Press.

Palombo, J. (1993). Neurocognitive deficits, developmental distortions, and incoherent narratives. *Psychoanalytic Inquiry, 13,* 85–102.

Schore, A.N. (1991). Early superego development: The emergence of shame and narcissistic affect regulation in the practicing period. *Psychoanalysis and Contemporary Thought, 14,* 187–250.

Stern, D.N. (1985). *The interpersonal world of the infant.* New York: Basic Books.

Stone, M.H. (1988). Toward a psychobiological theory on borderline personality disorder: Is irritability the red thread that runs through borderline conditions? *Dissociations, 1,* 2–15.

Taylor, G.J. (1993). Clinical application of a dysregulation model of illness and disease: A case of spasmodic torticollis. *International Journal of Psycho-Analysis, 74,* 1–12.

Tustin, F. (1990). *The protective shell in children and adults.* London and New York: Karnac Books.

Winnicott, D.W. (1965). Ego distortion in terms of true and false self. In *The maturational processes and the facilitating environment* (pp. 37–55). New York: International Universities Press.

Winnicott, D.W. (1971). *Playing and reality.* London: Tavistock.

Preface

Over the past two decades, a diverse group of disciplines have suddenly and simultaneously intensified their attention on the scientific study of internal processes. The nature of the covert mechanisms that underlie overt behaviors were, for much of this century, deemed to be outside the domain of prevailing psychological models and existing research methodologies. The remarkable productivity of investigations of various cognitive operations has demonstrated the accessibility of internal processes to both qualitative and quantitative analyses, and has legitimized a shift from the formal study of the exterior and observable to the interior and hidden, yet substantive, aspects of human functioning. Even more recently, a sudden surge of multidisciplinary activity, at quite different levels of analysis, has initiated a deeper exploration into another class of internal processes, that of emotional states.

This acceleration of research into affective phenomena has been paralleled by an explosion in the number of studies of early human structural and functional development. Developmental neuroscience is now delving not only into early cognitive and memorial processes, but also into the ontogeny of hierarchically organized brain systems that evolve to support the psychobiological underpinnings of socioemotional functioning. Studies of the infant brain demonstrate that its development occurs in stages over critical periods, and that its maturation is influenced by the environment and is experience dependent. Concurrent developmental psychological research dramatically emphasizes that the infant's emerging socioaffective functions are fundamentally influenced by the dyadic transactions the child has with the primary caregiver. In these fast acting, "hidden" communications, the mother senses and modulates the nonverbal and affective expressions of her infant's psychobiological states. In other words, the experiences that fine-tune brain circuitries in critical periods of infancy are embedded in socioemotional interchanges between an adult brain and a developing brain. In line with these findings, developmental studies are revitalizing contemporary psychoanalysis. This observational data strongly suggests that the mother's regulatory functions not only modulate the infant's internal state, but also indelibly and permanently shape the emerging self's capacity for self-organization. Studies of incipient relational processes and their effects on developing structure are thus an excellent paradigm for the deeper apprehension of the organization and dynamics of affective and affect-regulatory phenomena.

The purpose of this book is to integrate two rapidly converging streams of developmental research: psychological studies of the critical interactive experiences that influence the development of socioemotional functions and neurobiological studies of the ontogeny of postnatally maturing brain structures that come to regulate these same functions. A triad of fundamental assumptions underlies this work on the neurobiology of emotional development—that the compelling questions of human emotion and motivation can only be understood in terms of structure–function relationships, that the primordial conditions in which these evolve occur in the context of the caregiver–infant interaction, and that an understanding of the principles of human developmental psychobiology is a prerequisite and powerful impetus to the elucidation of the dynamic mechanisms of all later socioemotional phenomena.

This volume addresses the fundamental problems of how and why early events permanently affect the development of the self. Drawing upon current findings in infant research and neurobiology, a central hypothesis is proposed—that the infant's affective interactions with the early human social environment directly and indelibly influence the postnatal maturation of brain structures that will regulate all future socioemotional functioning. This principle of the experience-dependent development of self-regulatory structures and functions is supported by multidisciplinary evidence from a spectrum of developmental sciences. Furthermore, the structural characteristics and the dynamic functional properties of such a system are identified to be mediated by the orbitofrontal cortex, the major cerebral system involved in social, emotional, motivational, and self-regulatory processes. This cerebral structure is hidden in the anterior undersurface and interior of the cortex, and is especially developed in the right hemisphere. Due to its unique and extensive interconnections with a number of subcortical systems, it represents the hierarchical apex of the limbic system. A critical period for the maturation of this prefrontal structure exactly overlaps the temporal interval extensively investigated by both attachment and psychoanalytic researchers. An understanding of the caregiver-influenced development of this corticolimbic structure elucidates the unique role of the early maturing right hemisphere in affective processes and in the regulation of internal states.

More than just a review of several literatures, the studies cited in this work are used as a multidisciplinary source pool of experimental data, theoretical concepts, and clinical observations that form the base and scaffolding of an over-arching heuristic model of socioemotional development that is grounded in contemporary neuroscience. This psychoneurobiological model is then used to generate a number of heuristic hypotheses regarding the proximal causes of a wide array of affect-related phenomena. The keystone of this model is the principle of the development of self-regulation. An emergent property of hierarchically organized cortical–subcortical systems is the capacity to regulate the transitions between various internal states that support affect, cognition, and behavior. A current common focus on the adaptive regulatory processes of living systems, from the molecular up through the social levels, highlights the unique explanatory power of this central linking concept to organize what on the surface appear to be disparate bodies of knowledge and to reveal many of the "hidden" mechanisms of development. My intention in writing this volume is to demonstrate that a deeper understanding of affect regulation and dysregulation can offer penetrating insights into a number of affect-driven phenomena—from the motive force that underlies human attachment to the proximal causes of psychiatric disturbances and psychosomatic disorders, and indeed to the origin of the self.

Allan N. Schore
Northridge, California

Acknowledgments

I would like to express my appreciation to Dr. Paul Gilbert, not only for his stimulating and encouraging response to my work, but also for his concrete suggestions about how to transform a theoretical-clinical treatise into a book. I have greatly valued the ongoing conversations I have had with Dr. James Grotstein, whose creative mind and extraordinarily penetrating intellect have been an inspiration to me. I am also grateful for his allowing me to present, over a series of meetings, a number of the ideas in this book to the Interdisciplinary Group for Advanced Studies in Psychosis. That feedback not only forced me to sharpen and focus my theoretical ideas, but also challenged and motivated me to more directly link these to clinical issues. Similarly, my interactions with Dr. Henry Krystal have deepened my appreciation of the unique and direct relevance of infant studies to the study of adult psychopathology. I am most thankful for his invitation to present my ideas on infant shame experiences and affect regulation to his Colloquium on Early Development of Affect and Mental Structures at the American College of Psychoanalysts.

I especially want to thank my patients, who have taught me much about their/my emotional inner world, and have been a source and testing ground for many of the clinical hypotheses outlined in this work. In addition, numerous child and adult neuropsychological assessments have afforded me invaluable clinical opportunities to learn not only about brain–behavior relationships, but also about the social and emotional consequences of impaired brain systems to self-organization.

A number of people have been instrumental to the evolution of this volume. Judith Amsel was most helpful to me in my initial contacts with LEA and in the transformation of the early manuscript. Amy Pierce has been accessible, responsive, and informative throughout the process. I am particularly indebted to Sondra Guideman for the considerable amount of time and effort it took to edit this volume. She has taught me a great deal not only about the complex skills required for the production of a book, but also how a professional assiduously attends to high standards of excellence in her work. Her contributions to the coordination of text and illustrations in this volume were invaluable. Along this line, I would also like to thank the following for providing me with original materials: Professors Rolf Dermietzel, Harry B. Uylings, Noburo Mizuno, Andries Kalsbeek, Ernest Martin, Susan Sesack, and Dean Falk.

But by far the greatest influence on my work, and indeed in my life, has come from my wife, Judith. She has continually encouraged and indeed enabled me to follow what has at times been a solitary path—to be led into a variety of scientific domains, different than those in which I was trained, by nothing more than my curiosity. Although I had some idea of the intellectual demands of this task, I could not anticipate the emotional demands of working objectively, and by necessity subjectively, with internal affective processes. In order to pursue the rather large time commitment to engage in independent research, she has taken upon herself a few "minor" roles, like rearranging income responsibilities, guiding me through the rocky shoals of treacherous computer problems, setting forth the expectation that I improve my writing skills, carefully proofreading numerous drafts of the text, and providing a spectrum of invaluable and complex "secretarial" skills that merely constitute the structural integrity of the book. Most importantly, through her intellectual keenness and emotional honesty, she continues to reflect and reveal to me those essential reciprocal emotional processes that are, willingly and unwillingly, most clearly exposed in an intimate human relationship.

BACKGROUND AND OVERVIEW

1 Introduction

The understanding of early development is one of the fundamental objectives of science. The beginnings of living systems set the stage for every aspect of an organism's internal and external functioning throughout the lifespan. It is often not appreciated that an individual's genetic inheritance which encodes the unvarying sequence of development is only partially expressed at birth. Genetic systems that program the evolution of biological and psychological structures continue to be activated at very high rates over the stages of infancy, and this process is significantly influenced by factors in the postnatal environment. Of special importance are the incipient interactions the infant has with the most important object in the early environment—the primary caregiver. Events that occur during infancy, especially transactions with the social environment, are indelibly imprinted into the structures that are maturing in the first years of life. The child's first relationship, the one with the mother, acts as a template, as it permanently molds the individual's capacities to enter into all later emotional relationships. These early experiences shape the development of a unique personality, its adaptive capacities as well as its vulnerabilities to and resistances against particular forms of future pathologies. Indeed, they profoundly influence the emergent organization of an integrated system that is both stable and adaptable, and thereby the formation of the self.

The principle that the early events of development have far-reaching and long enduring effects is one of the very few elemental and overarching postulates that is shared by all disciplines studying living organisms. We now know that the concept of "early experiences" connotes much more than an immature individual being a passive recipient of environmental stimulation. Rather, these primordial events represent active transactions between the infant and the first external

3

environment. Yet despite their fundamental importance, the scientific study of these phenomena has, perhaps until recently, been far from a unified pursuit. Each separate discipline contains a split-off "developmental" branch, and the transfer of information between these bodies of knowledge, especially those at different levels of analysis, has been quite restricted. The recent explosion of infant research has emphasized the essential importance of a multidisciplinary perspective, but it should be remembered that this field spans the gamut from developmental neurochemistry and neurobiology through developmental psychology to developmental psychoanalysis and infant psychiatry. And yet these seemingly disparate fields share the common assumption that the deeper apprehension of the individual's early development can elucidate the mechanisms of all later function and dysfunction. A powerful impetus towards an integrated multilevel approach has come from recent studies which demonstrate that the early transactions with the social environment are "hidden" within the dyadic relations between mother and child, and that in this dialectic the mother acts as a crucial regulator of the child's development. The characterization of these hidden processes is now a major focus of study, since it has been demonstrated that not only the infant's overt behavior but its covert physiology and thereby its internal state are directly regulated by the mother. The consequences of these revolutionary findings to preexisting theory are turning out to be profound.

Perhaps the best way to give the reader a sense of the state-of-the-art, as it were, of current developmental knowledge is to briefly outline some of the major questions that are being addressed by contemporary multidisciplinary researchers. The nature of the problems that are presently being explored reflects a confidence in the rapidly expanding and exciting field of infant research. Questions that have been up until recently considered as outside of scientific exploration are now being translated into testable hypotheses.

1. How do early experiences induce the growth of structure in the developing human infant?
2. What internal and external factors influence development, and how exactly do these factors interact?
3. What kind of psychobiological mechanisms mediate the regulation of developmental processes by these internal and external factors?
4. How does the variation of these influences shape the organism's inherited genetic contributions? What processes transform genotype into phenotype?
5. Because it is now known that the expression of inherited genetic information is not completed at birth but continues at high rates in infancy, what common fundamental gene-environment processes operate both pre- and postnatally?
6. How does the primary caregiver influence genetically programmed mechanisms that are responsible for the infant's growth?

7. What essentially is the early environment, and what part does the organism's contacts with its mother play in establishing the child's social environment?
8. How do various stresses influence the course of development?
9. Why does development occur in stages?
10. What mechanisms regulate the onsets and offsets of critical periods for the maturation of particular structures and functions?
11. Why are early critical periods of development so important to the functioning of the individual throughout the rest of the lifespan, and why and how do the events of early childhood imprint permanent effects?

In addition to these questions about the general nature of development, more specific ones arise from the study of human socioemotional development.

1. What part do early social-affective experiences play in the postnatal maturation of the human brain?
2. How does the infant's early social environment influence the growth of structural systems involved in emotional functioning that are maturing in infancy?
3. How does the earliest relationship with a specific human being, the attachment to the primary caregiver, permanently influence the individual's capacities to enter into all later relationships ?
4. What psychobiological mechanisms underlie the attachment process?
5. What is the role of emotional communications in the child's continuing dialectic between himself and the social environment?
6. How does the child respond to the changes in the social environment that occur over the stages of infancy, and how do these changes effect the course of socioemotional development?
7. How does the developing child retain continuity and self-regulate as it traverses these changes?
8. What factors facilitate or inhibit the emergence of the adaptive capacity for self-regulation?
9. What is the relationship among failures of development, impairments of adaptive capacities, and psychopathology?
10. How can an elucidation of the events of infancy, especially early socioemotional transactions, lead to a deeper understanding of adult normal and abnormal phenomena?
11. How can developmental knowledge be utilized to formulate heuristic strategies toward the treatment of psychological developmental disorders?
12. What defines a self, and how does it evolve?
13. How do early events influence the development of consciousness?

I believe that the answers to the foregoing questions—which are further addressed in subsequent chapters—will not come from single or even multiple discoveries within any one discipline. Rather, an integration of the findings of many related fields is essential to the ultimate creation of a heuristic model of development that can accommodate interdisciplinary data, and can freely shift back and forth between their different levels of analysis.

A primary purpose of this volume is to bring together and to present in one place the latest observations, data, and concepts from the developmental branches of various disciplines. Such an integrative approach prescribes that the reader is presented with a number of different bodies of current literatures. It is difficult enough to keep up to date within one's own area of study, let alone to be aware of the newer concepts in related fields. Nevertheless, this is an absolute necessity in light of the current emphasis on multidisciplinary research. To that end, a major goal of this study of socioemotional development is to supply psychological researchers and clinicians with relevant up-to-date developmental neurobiological insights and findings, and to expose neuroscientists to recent developmental psychological and psychoanalytic studies of infants. Contemporary infant research is now directed towards much more than merely describing the development of overt behaviors. Over the past 2 decades a paradigmatic shift away from the narrow constraints of a strict behaviorism has occurred in all areas of psychology. This has allowed for a sanctioning of the scientific study of internal states, and has created an environment that supports the generation of new methodologies that more directly access the proximal internal causes of overt behavior. As a result the developmental sciences have produced a large amount of information about the ontogeny of both cognitive and affective internal processes. This approach is paralleled by the rapidly expanding intense interest in the covert, hidden aspects of the relationship the growing child has with a changing environment.

Another fundamental intention of this work is to focus specifically on social and emotional development, particularly as it occurs in the human infant. Much of the data from developmental neuroanatomy and neurochemistry comes from animal research, yet these studies uniquely reveal the biological and chemical changes that comprise the internal processes underlying the complex affective and cognitive capacities that come to be so highly developed in humans. It is now very clear that well before the advent of language the baby's capacities to interact with the social and physical environments, functions supported by these internal processes, are extremely complex and sophisticated. The fast acting, psychobiological mechanisms that mature in early and late infancy continue to operate throughout life. Indeed they serve as the keystone of all future human intraorganismic, intrapsychic, and interpersonal functioning, as the manifestation of all later developing capacities is contingent upon their initiatory expression.

Many of the latest findings are quite unexpected in terms of the predictions of older theories, and each field is now radically altering the fundamental assumptions that lie at the core of its conceptions of development. Although their methodologies are quite different, the data emerging from what appear to be distantly related fields are converging on certain common conclusions.

One such finding that appears again and again is the interactive nature of development. Development essentially represents a number of sequential mutually driven infant-caregiver processes that occur in a continuing dialectic between the maturing organism and the changing environment. It now appears that affect is what is actually transacted within the mother-infant dyad, and this highly efficient system of emotional communication is essentially nonverbal. Human development, including its internal neurochemical and neurobiological mechanisms, cannot be understood apart from this affect-transacting relationship.

A second fundamental conclusion is that the study of development must include more than just a documentation of changing functions. The problem of the maturation of structures responsible for the onset of new functional capacities must also be simultaneously addressed. In fact, development can only be understood in terms of a progression of structure-function relationships, since structure, by definition, is continually organizing, disorganizing, and reorganizing in infancy. Changes in the child's behavior (studied by developmental psychology) or in the child's internal world (studied by developmental psychoanalysis) can only be understood in terms of the appearance of more complex structure that performs emergent functions. At this stage of our scientific knowledge, any discipline that theorizes about *structure* needs to evaluate its models against what is now known about the veritable characteristics of biological structure as it exists in nature. This brings psychology back to biology, and emphasizes the importance of developmental neuroscience.

A third crucial finding is that we now know that the early environment is fundamentally a social environment, and that the primary social object who mediates the physical environment to the infant is the mother. Through her intermediary action environmental stimulation is modulated, and this transformed input impinges upon the infant in the context of socioaffective stimulation. The mother's modulatory function is essential not only to every aspect of the infant's current functioning, but also to the child's continuing development. She thus is the major source of the environmental stimulation that facilitates (or inhibits) the experience-dependent maturation of the child's developing biological (especially neurobiological) structures. Her essential role as the psychobiological regulator of the child's immature psychophysiological systems directly influences the child's biochemical growth processes which support the genesis of new structure.

And fourth, the concept of regulation is one of the few theoretical constructs that is now being utilized by literally every developmental discipline. The current focus on adaptive regulatory phenomena, from the molecular to the social levels, represents a powerful central linking concept that could potentially elucidate the "hidden" processes in development and thereby organize what appear to be disparate bodies of developmental knowledge. With respect to socioemotional ontogeny, it is now established that the infant's affect is initially regulated by the mother, but over the course of development it becomes increasingly self-regulated. The elucidation of the psychobiological mechanisms that underlie the experience-dependent maturation of a structural system that can adaptively auto-regulate affect is a very active area of current multidisciplinary research.

2 General Principles of Growth of the Developing Brain

Current biological concepts focus on the organizational properties of living organisms. . . .The central question then becomes how organized systems retain continuity while changing in response to developmental and environmental pressures.

—Virginia Demos and Samuel Kaplan (1986)

The development of social behavior can be understood only in terms of a continuing dialectic between an active and changing organism and an active and changing environment, with cause and consequence closely interwoven. The most important part of that environment are the interactions and relationships that the child has with others. . . .

—Robert A. Hinde (1990)

[T]he idea of developmentally regulated shifts in sensitivity to various aspects of the environment is absolutely central to the study of ontogenesis.

—Susan Oyama (1979)

The relationship between the dynamics of early interactional development and the ontogeny of the emergent function of self-regulation is perhaps the most fundamental problem of development. Although investigators of socioemotional development are using diverse biological and psychological models to study this problem, there is general agreement that the maturation of the capacity for regulating emotion and social interactions (Campos, Barrett, Lamb, Goldsmith, & Stenberg, 1983) and the ontogenetic attainment of the capacity for the "self-regulation of affect" (Krystal, 1988) are critical to the adaptive functioning of the individual throughout the lifespan. Developmental studies from the rapidly expanding field of infant research are valuable sources of clues in this pursuit, since "the ontogeny of self-regulation provides an entree to the ontogeny of psychic structures" (Sander, 1977b, p.29). In other words, the structural maturation of the brain in infancy and childhood essentially represents the ontogenetic development of more complex autoregulatory functional systems.

It has been said that the study of the developing brain may uniquely forge a link between basic and clinical research (Himwich, 1975). I would add that the integration of neurobiological with psychological perspectives, of structure-function relationships, is absolutely essential to a deeper understanding of early development. Extrapolations from neonatal to mature psychological functioning (and vice versa) can be misleading, since the immature central nervous system is an entirely different brain from that of the adult. Noebels (1989) points out that the electroencephalogram of the human in the first month of life if derived from the scalp of an adult, would be considered "sufficiently abnormal to indicate imminent demise" (p. 152). Electrophysiological studies of animal models of cerebral development show that compared to adults, the higher centers of young brains are able to treat only a small amount of information per unit of time, and this occurs in circuits that function more slowly than those of adults (Scherer, 1967). In addition, developmental neurophysiological research demonstrates that the neonatal cerebral metabolic rate that sustains early cortical function is very low (Thurston & McDougal, 1969). An essential question then is how does the orderly sequence of interactions between the genome and the environment produce the transmutation of an immature into a mature brain? In this chapter I give a brief introductory overview of four basic principles of the structure-function relationships of the postnatally developing brain that are extracted from the currently expanding knowledge base of the developmental sciences. In later chapters I expand on these principles in some detail and present extensive multidisciplinary evidence to support an emergent overarching theory of the development of self-regulation.

PRINCIPLE 1: THE GROWTH OF THE BRAIN OCCURS IN CRITICAL PERIODS AND IS INFLUENCED BY THE SOCIAL ENVIRONMENT

At present there is considerable interest in the neurosciences in the search for the specific brain structures that support self-regulatory function, as the more precise characterization of their structure-function relation may be relevant to the elucidation of mechanisms underlying normal and pathological development. Any understanding of the ontogeny of autoregulatory systems and indeed of development *per se* must be anchored in the fact that structure is literally being built on a daily basis during the time of accelerated and continuing brain growth in infancy.

Lecours (1982) points out that the stupendous growth rate of the first year of life is reflected in the increase of brain weight from 400g at birth to 1000g at 12 months. Furthermore he notes that the accelerated growth during this "critical period" is influenced by "social forces." The human brain growth spurt, which is at least 5/6 postnatal (Dobbing & Sands, 1973), continues to about 18-to-24-months-of-age (Dobbing & Smart, 1974) (see Fig. 2.1). During the postnatal period those brain regions in most rapid growth are most susceptible (Winick, 1976) or sensitive (Almi & Finger, 1987) to external stimulation. Late maturing cortical areas, which differentiate after subcortical brainstem areas, are particularly sensitive to postnatal influences.

The concept of critical or sensitive periods is one of the most enduring constructs in biology. The original hypothesis, formulated at the end of the last and beginning of this century (Dareste, 1891; Stockard, 1921), stated that in the maturing organism developmental processes in different areas proceed at different rates. During these periods of intensified growth and differentiation, the organism is subject to environmental conditions, and if these are outside the normal range a permanent arrest of development occurs. Later work revealed that

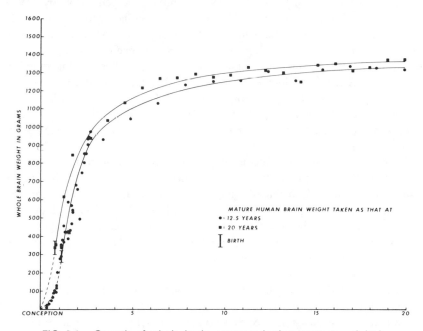

FIG. 2.1. Growth of whole brain compared when mature weight is taken at 12.5 years and at 20 years. From Himwich (1975). Forging a link between basic and clinical research: Developing brain. *Biological Psychiatry, 10.* Reprinted by permission of Plenum Publishing Corporation.

each developing organ or even parts of an organ passes through an individual critical period of accelerated growth and differentiation during which it is sensitive to conditions in the external environment (Arey, 1962). This concept has also been adopted by neurobiology. Developmental brain research has revealed that different regions of the infant's nervous system mature at different periods (Anders & Zeanah, 1984), and that different neurological systems may underlie different sensitive periods (Greenough, Black, & Wallace, 1987). Indeed, neuroanatomical studies have demonstrated that even the individual layers of different areas in each cerebral lobe have their own developmental rate (Rabinowicz, 1979).

The critical period concept also connotes that "specific critical conditions or stimuli are necessary for development and can influence development only during that period" (Erzurumlu & Killackey, 1982, p. 207). We now know that during early critical periods brain structural development is sensitive not only to abnormal or injurious environmental influences but also to all types of environmental stimulation (Diamond, 1976). Even more specifically, rapidly growing tissues or systems are particularly sensitive to changes in the amounts and types of environmental stimulation (Riesen, 1961; Scott, 1979b). The development of late-maturing control systems is of special importance, and Bowlby (1969) points out that their ontogeny may be open to the influence by the particular environment in which development occurs. Greenspan (1981) refers to growth-promoting and growth-inhibiting environments influencing the ontogeny of homeostatic self-regulatory and attachment systems. In light of the more extended ontogenetic development of prefrontal structures, cortical systems that perform control and regulatory functions, Goldberg and Bilder (1987) propose, "Critical periods for pathogenic influences might be prolonged in these more slowly maturing systems, of which the prefrontal cortex is exemplary" (p. 177).

Thus, the vast majority of the development of axons, dendrites, and synaptic connections that underlie all behavior is known to take place in early and late human infancy. Indeed, increased synaptic production has been used to anatomically define a critical period (Greenough & Black, 1992). The fact that this growth occurs during the period of close mother-infant interaction suggests both that the organism's postnatal environment acts as a regulator of brain development (Haracz, 1985) and that postnatal stages of brain development may provide an explanation for how early experience affects later behavior (Kolb, 1989). There is now no doubt that that the dendritic growth and synaptogenesis of the postnatally developing brain is "experience-sensitive" (Greenough, 1987) and "experience-dependent" (Aoki & Siekevitz,1988), yet the exact nature of such "experience" is still vaguely defined. It should be emphasized that the primary caregiver is the most important source and modulator of stimulation in the infant's environment and the primal wellspring of the child's experience. Hinde (1990) articulates the principle that the most important parts of the environment are the interactions and relationships that the child has with others. Indeed, Scheflen (1981) argues that the neurodevelopmental processes of dendritic proliferation and synaptogenesis which are responsible for postnatal brain growth are critically influenced by events at the interpersonal and intrapersonal levels. Hofer (1983) asserts that the mother specifically serves as an external regulator of the neurochemistry of the infant's maturing brain. These interactive psychoneurobiological processes may mediate the fundamental mechanism of action of early "environmental regulators of development" (Sameroff, 1989).

The maturation of the prefrontal cortex, the largest area in the human cerebral cortex (Uylings & Van Eden, 1990), is essentially postnatal. A period of dendritic and axonal development in this cortex occurs in the first year of infancy, and a second period marked by further histogenetic changes occurs in the second year of human life (Mrzljak, Uylings, Van Eden, & Judas, 1990). There is now strong evidence suggesting that the major structural and histochemical reorganization of the prefrontal region that occurs in the first 2 years of infancy is "open to interactions with the external world" (Kostovic, 1990, p. 233). In accordance with this experimental work, Winson (1985) concludes:

> the neurons of all of the neocortex, the prefrontal cortex included, are in an immature state at birth. Their dendrites and axons grow during the first few years of life, making interconnections which are affected by environmental stimuli during the critical period and then become largely permanent. (p. 219)

In future chapters I propose that a critical period of synaptic growth and differentiation of an affect regulating limbic structure in the prefrontal cortex of the right hemisphere commences at the end of the first year, and that this developmental process is significantly influenced by the stimulation embedded in the infant's socioaffective transactions with the primary caregiver.

PRINCIPLE 2: THE INFANT BRAIN DEVELOPS IN STAGES AND BECOMES HIERARCHICALLY ORGANIZED

Most workers in the neurobiological sciences would now agree that the brain develops in discrete stages (Jackson, 1931; Pandya & Barnes, 1987; Martin et al., 1988), that the sequential process of development is not continuous and linear, but rather reflects the effects of the steps of neural maturation that bring about the transition from one stage to the next (Plooij & van de Rijt-Plooij, 1989, Wiggins, 1985). Experimental studies in this area have revealed that stages of neuroanatomic maturation are correlated with "time-linked sequences of normal development" (Adams & Victor, 1989).

At the end of the last century the discovery that the brain evolves in stages was part of an overarching model of brain development and organization proposed by John Hughlings Jackson (1931). Based on both evolutionary theory and on his neuropathological investigations that laid the groundwork of modern neurology, Jackson proposed that the brain is hierarchically organized into horizontal levels. Over discrete stages of development, each higher level re-represents and expands at a more complex level of organization those functions present in the previous, more primitive level of organization. In this hierarchical model of the caudal to rostral ontogeny of the brain, later developing higher cortical levels come to inhibit earlier developing lower subcortical levels. Jackson's illuminating insights were further advanced in this century by Luria (1980), who established both that the highest level of organizational complexity occurs in the prefrontal cortex, and that this cortex performs an inhibitory function. Most importantly, Luria argues that the development of this structure occurs postnatally and is influenced by the social environment. In recent work, Martin et al. (1988), Mrzljak et al. (1990) and Thatcher (1991) provide evidence to show that the maturation of the last parts of the human cerebral cortex to develop, the frontal lobes, also occurs in stages (see Fig 2.2).

This leads to the next question: What factors influence the change from one stage to the next? The fundamental biochemical causes of the accelerated growth of specific brain areas in particular stages is thus an important area of inquiry. The growth and function of the brain, perhaps more than any other organ, are highly dependent upon the continued availability of energy substrate. Yet there are some important biochemical differences between the immature and mature brain. In classical work, Himwich (1951) demonstrated the fundamental biochemical principle that the brain's production of energy shifts from anaerobic to aerobic metabolism in early stages of development. The onset of aerobic oxidative metabolism, which results in significantly increased energy output, continues to occur in the postnatal period of mammalian infancy (Himwich & Fazekas, 1941). Guroff (1980) notes that:

> During the development of the animal, the reliance on anaerobic pathways seems to change. The immature brain has a low energy requirement and is relatively insensitive to anoxia. The energy requirement rises as the brain matures and the cells differentiate and form connections. (p. 293)

Indeed the dramatic transformations of energy production which occur in specific portions of the maturing nervous system during specific postnatal temporal intervals may represent the physiological basis of developmental stage and critical period phenomena (Meier, Nolan, Bunch, & Scheidler, 1960). These authors suggest that such transformations allow for the onset of increasing complexity of structure and efficiency and integration of function. They also posit that postnatal

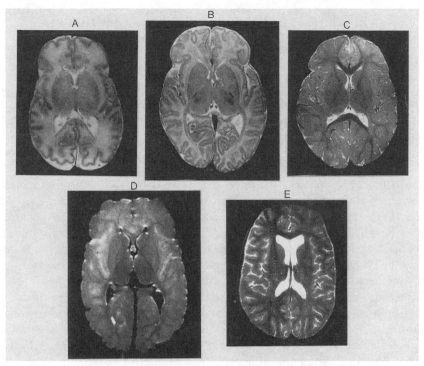

FIG. 2.2. Axial magnetic resonance (MR) image of infant brains showing stages of myelination. (A) Boy, birth, no myelin visible in frontal cortex. (B) Boy, 1 month, beginning myelination in frontal cortex. (C) Girl, 3 months, transient pattern of frontal myelination. (D) Child, 14 months, continued transient myelination. (E) Girl, 2 years, adult frontal myelination pattern. From Martin, Kikinis, Zuerrer, Boesch, Briner, Kewitz, and Kaelin (1988). Developmental stages of human brain: An MR study. *Journal of Computer Assisted Tomography, 12,* 917–922. Reprinted by permission of Raven Press Ltd.

brain development can be characterized as a family of curves representing particular structures undergoing principal development during a stage, "generally alike but each with a different time scale".

In later chapters I propose that a local metabolic transition enables the maturation of a specific cortical area essential to social functioning during a developmental stage which onsets at the end of the first year and offsets in the middle of the second year of human life. This late maturing higher cortical structure is situated at the apex of the limbic system, and its hierarchical dominance over lower subcortical limbic structures accounts for its preeminent role in socioemotional development.

PRINCIPLE 3: GENETIC SYSTEMS THAT PROGRAM BRAIN DEVELOPMENT ARE ACTIVATED AND INFLUENCED BY THE POSTNATAL ENVIRONMENT

It is now accepted that early postnatal development represents an experiential shaping of genetic potential. Genetic effects do not exert their total influence at birth but are amplified during periods of stepwise maturational progressions of development, and in fact several different and specific gene-environment interactions are thought to occur over the course of development (Kendler & Eaves, 1986; McClearn, 1970). Increased levels of both brain DNA (Benjamins & McKhann, 1981; Winick, Rosso, & Waterlow, 1970) and RNA (Cummins, Loreck, & McCandless, 1985) synthesis continue from birth through the second year. In fact the human cerebral cortex adds about 70% of its final DNA content after birth (Howard, 1973). Both the diversity of RNA sequences (Grouse, Schrier, Letendre, & Nelson, 1980) and the amount of protein (Renner & Rosenzweig, 1987) in the postnatally expanding brain are directly influenced by early environmental enrichment and social isolation experiences.

Genetic material is composed of nucleic acids, and their biosynthesis is mediated by a unique series of biochemical reactions known as the hexose monophosphate shunt. Also known as the pentose phosphate pathway, this cycle of carbohydrate metabolism is very active in the postnatal period (O'Neill & Duffy, 1966; Winick, 1974), a time of intense RNA and DNA biosynthesis (Winick & Noble, 1965). In fact, one of the major biochemical differences between the neonatal and the adult brain is the high levels of the hexose monophosphate shunt found in the infant brain (McIllwain, 1966). The activity of this pathway that converts 6-carbon sugars such as glucose to 5-carbon sugars such as ribose may account for the bulk of the enormous increased glucose metabolism that is found uniquely in the first 2 years of life (Chugani, Phelps, & Mazziotta, 1987). The end product of the pentose shunt is ribose-5-phosphate, and this extremely versatile metabolite is used for phospholipid and therefore membrane synthesis, ATP generation, as well as for ribonucleic acid synthesis (Stryer, 1981). Very high levels of ribose-5-phosphate are found in the postnatally developing brain (Tofts & Wray, 1985). Figure 2.3 shows the nuclear magnetic resonance spectra of a neonatal human brain (Cady et al., 1983). This technique can identify individual molecules, and the very prominent peak 7, a constituent that is involved in the rapid growth of the brain, is attributed by the authors to ribose-5-phosphate. The hexose monophosphate shunt thus biochemically mediates the brain growth spurt, and its activity has been implicated in the understanding of critical period phenomena.

> The developing nervous system has critical periods of RNA and lipid synthesis, and thus brain development may be reflected in patterned development of the pentose phosphate pathway. (Cummins et al., 1985, p. 168)

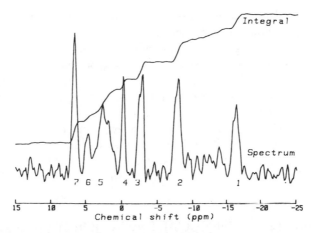

FIG. 2.3. Nuclear magnetic resonance spectroscopy of human neonate (17 days). From Cady et al. (1983). Reprinted by permission of
Williams and Wilkins.

According to Guroff (1980) this pathway that generates the raw materials of
biosynthesis is responsive to "developmental stimuli."

The onset and offset of sensitive periods are now attributed to the activation
and expression of specific genes at particular times in development (Bateson &
Hinde, 1987). Maturational neurogenetic discontinuities reflect the fact that families of programmed genes synchronously turn on and off during infancy, thereby
controlling the transient enhanced expression of enzymes of biosynthetic pathways regulating protein and lipid synthesis which allow for growth in particular
brain regions. The activation of timed gene-action systems that may program the
sequential caudal to rostral structural development of the brain has been proposed
to account for the chronological appearance of emergent functions over successive developmental stages (R.S. Wilson, 1983).

Developmental genetic research reveals that certain genetically programmed
"innate" biological structural systems that support adaptive psychological functions require particular early developmental environmental input to be manifest
(experience-dependent development). In other words, the expression of hereditary influences require transactions with the environment (Plomin, 1983), especially during sensitive periods, bounded temporal intervals that constitute
"unique windows of organism-environment interaction" (Bornstein, 1989).
Maternal behavior itself is thought to be an external environmental event that
mediates genetic differences (McClearn & De Fries, 1973). Developmental psychobiological studies are now revealing that during the earliest organismic-
environmental transactions, infant-maternal dyadic interactions, the mother
serves as a hidden regulator of the infant's endocrine and nervous systems

(Hofer, 1984a, 1990). In the latest neurochemical models of critical period events, "external influences" are understood to mediate alterations in a hierarchy of internal regulatory signals—neurohormones and neurotransmitters—that act as internal clocks to coordinate the timing of developmental processes (Lauder & Krebs, 1986). It is well known that hormones regulate gene transcription (Anderson, 1984). In this manner, external relations with the mother could regulate internal genetic events.

In upcoming chapters I present evidence to argue that the infant's interactions with the mother directly elicit psychoendocrinological changes that influence the biochemical activation of gene-action systems which program the critical period growth and differentiation of a corticolimbic structure responsible for self-regulation.

PRINCIPLE 4: THE SOCIAL ENVIRONMENT CHANGES OVER THE STAGES OF INFANCY AND INDUCES THE REORGANIZATION OF BRAIN STRUCTURES

Studies of the developing nervous system and behavior now reveal that each stage in development is viewed as functional in its own right, and that some structures and functions are transient and adaptive only for a restricted period of development. The developmental biological concept of "ontogenetic adaptation" (Oppenheim, 1980) emphasizes the unique adaptive characteristics of emerging developmental responses in early environmental niches that exist for a limited period of time. This concept has also been embraced by developmental psychology, where it is now held that "many qualities seen early in development may be temporary adaptations to that particular stage of growth" (Kagan, 1986, p. 71). The companion concept of "ontogenetic niche" refers to a set of social and physical environmental circumstances that specifies the behavioral adaptations of the developing child and parent (West & King, 1987). Parental behavior is now considered to be an important component of the ontogenetic niche. This model is now being applied to the understanding of postnatal development which is characterized by Alberts (1987) as:

> a sequence of stages of adaptive organization, functionally articulated in relation to the ontogenetic niche. During the perinatal period, these niches tend to be dramatically different, and the adaptive adjustments displayed by the infant are correspondingly stunning. (p. 18)

The principle of ontogenetic adaptation is also applicable to the infant's maturing socioaffective learning and adaptation to unique "social environmental niches" which vary over different early periods, that is, the ontogenetic adaptive responses to the changing nature of the infant's object relations with primary attachment figures over the first years of life. Hinde (1990) asserts that

The development of social behavior can be understood only in terms of a continuing dialectic between an active and changing organism and an active and changing environment. (p. 162)

The social environment changes dramatically over the stages of infancy, especially between early infancy in the first year and late infancy in the second year. During this time the mother's role shifts from primarily caregiving to socialization. This transition represents a stress for the dyad, as earlier ontogenetic adaptations are no longer quite as adaptive in the new socioaffective environment. Lazarus (1993) asserts that stress defines an unfavorable person-environment relationship, and that its essence is process and change. Sroufe (1989b) argues that although relationship systems require stabilization they must also change in response to both internal demands and external challenges; adaptation is a balance between stability and change.

Neurobiologists have pointed out that successful stagewise transitions that depend on coordinated and integrated readjustments (Alberts, 1987) are specifically manifest in both the disappearance of ontogenetic adaptations specific for early stages (Prechtl, 1982) and the appearance of new adaptive functions. Oppenheim (1980) points out that ontogenetic adaptations require the creation of structures and functions that are adaptively suitable at one stage but which may be not quite as necessary for adaptations at later stages. This requires a mechanism whereby the earlier characteristics and structures can be eliminated, suppressed, or reorganized. Such a mechanism exists in a "parcellation" process, a competitive elimination of excess axons and pruning of overproduced synapses which occurs during the postnatal development of the cerebral cortex (Rakic et al., 1986). Parcellation has been implicated in the mechanism by which the developing nervous system becomes increasingly complex, and involves the selective loss of connections and redistributions of inputs that allow for the appearance of an emergent function (Ebbesson, 1980). There is now a large body of evidence to support the general principle that cortical networks are generated by initial overabundant production of synaptic connections, which is then followed by a process of competitive interaction to select those connections that are most effectively entrained to environmental information (Tucker, 1992). Changeux and Dehaene (1989) point out that the selective stabilization of synapses that have functional significance in a particular environment occurs in cortical areas during postnatal sensitive periods. This "Darwinian" psychobiological process is "activity dependent." Weiss (1969) emphasizes that an activity of an organism is in essence an interaction with the environment.

The experience-dependent neurodevelopmental processes of synaptic overproduction, parcellation, and programmed cell death and the evolutionary biology concept of ontogenetic adaptation point to a number of important axioms concerning the growth of the developing brain. It is now thought that the study of development requires both a theory of transition which can account for transient structures that are only adaptive for a restricted phase of development and at the same time an explanation of how earlier functions are transformed into more mature functions (Hopkins & Butterworth, 1990). The facts that the infant brain contains from 15% to 85% more neurons than the adult brain (Joseph, 1982) and that a large number of these neurons die (Hamburger & Oppenheim, 1982) and/or their processes are retracted in the early years of life (Cowan, Fawcett, O'Leary, & Stanfield, 1979) must be included into any conception of the genesis of biological structure. Early functional development cannot be understood without reference to epigenetic structural maturation, and pre- and postnatal brain development are both characterized as a process of organization, disorganization, and reorganization. The continuity of development does not imply a simple progressive pattern of increments but changes in organization. Scott (1979b), who defines development as change in the organization of living systems which allows for increasing complexity, stability, and adaptivity, asserts the general principle that "there can be no reorganization without disorganization" (p. 233). These precepts apply equally well to psychoanalytic conceptions of the development of psychic structure.

In the following sections of this book, I contend that heightened levels of positive affect and play behavior represent ontogenetic adaptations at the end of the first year of infancy. The emergence of these functions occurs at the outset of a stage of development associated with the appearance of upright locomotion, and they reflect a maturational advance of the prefrontal cortex. An important change in the ontogenetic niche occurs later in this same stage of infancy, in the second year when the mother's role shifts from caregiver to socialization agent. This alteration of the infant's social environment specifically induces a diminution of the former socioaffective adaptations. The dyad's response to this stressful alteration of the relationship is instrumental to the final structural maturation of an adaptive cortical system that can self-regulate emotional states. This maturation specifically involves a reorganization of the circuits of the orbitofrontal areas of the cerebral cortex.

3

Recent Advances in the Multidisciplinary Study of Emotional Development

No one is fitted to begin the materialistic study of the brain unless he has a good knowledge of psychology.

—John Hughlings Jackson (1931)

All our provisional ideas in psychology will presumably some day be based on organic substructure.

—Sigmund Freud (1914/1957)

The study of the psychology of emotions has only recently become a "legitimate" area of "hard" scientific research. As recently as 1989, Skinner admitted ". . . It has always been difficult to do much with feelings and states of mind because of their inaccessibility" (1989, pp. 73-74). Despite this, almost singlehandedly, Tomkins (1962, 1963), some thirty years ago, investigated the unique characteristics of specific negative and positive affects. The robust findings of these pioneering studies are only now being appreciated. Over this time period, although important contributions have been made by personality theorists (Lazarus, 1968) and developmental psychologists (Izard, 1977), perhaps the most intense focus on emotional processes has been from psychoanalysts. Indeed, the newer conceptions of affective processes are now revolutionizing psychoanalysis. In addition, over the last decade the neurosciences have begun to shift away from an almost exclusive focus on the neurobiology of cognition to a growing interest in the neurobiology of emotion. In this chapter I discuss some recent advances in our understanding of the development of emotional processes and the brain structures which underlie them.

THE EMERGENCE OF SOCIOEMOTIONAL FUNCTIONS
IN SEQUENTIAL STAGES

At present, and for some time now, the investigation of socioemotional development has lagged far behind research in cognitive development. Strongly influenced by the enormous contributions of Piaget, developmental researchers have focused on cognitive ontogeny, and the stage concept emphasized by Piaget is now routinely utilized in the study of the growth and transformations of cognitive processes (Fischer & Silvern, 1985; Tamis-LeMonde & Bornstein, 1987) where Mounoud (1982) refers to "revolutionary periods of early development." Sroufe (1979) has proposed that the ontogenesis of emotional systems parallels changes in Piaget's sensorimotor stages and is intimately related to the infant's interpersonal relations. In his stage theory, developmental reorganizations which are expressed in affective growth and in qualitatively different transactions with the environment occur during the first 2 years. A similar model of increasingly integrated levels of emotional awareness over Piagetian sequential periods has been offered by Lane and G. Schwartz (1987). Drawing on Harlow's (1965) experimental investigations of a critical period for the development of primate social behavior, Kandel and J. Schwartz (1985) have described an early stage for the development of social competence during which the infant's interactions with the environment produce long lasting imprinting experiences. Although ethological studies have long indicated that there is a restricted period during which imprinting occurs (Gottlieb, 1961), these authors do not specify the time frame of this stage in human infants.

In a landmark review article Campos (Campos et al., 1983) has evaluated the contributions of two other influential theorists in the field of socioemotional development—John Bowlby and Margaret Mahler. Bowlby's work (1969), derived from ethological-evolutionary theory, points out that the infant's early attachment relationships with the mother in the earliest stages of life play a critical role in shaping long-lasting features of personality development. Attachment functions first appear at a particular time, 7 to 8 months, and then organize into stable patterns that can be reliably observed by the end of the first year. Bowlby's model, perhaps in part because it has been translated into an efficient experimental paradigm by Ainsworth (Ainsworth, Blehar, Waters, & Wall, 1978), has influenced research in this area much more than Mahler's. It is important to note that in this methodology Ainsworth has specifically focused on studying the attachment-emotional behavior of 12-to 18-month-old infants. In response to Bowlby's classic volume *Attachment and Loss*, Ainsworth (1969) observed that "In effect what Bowlby has attempted is to update psychoanalytic theory in the light of recent advances in biology" (p. 998). The insightfulness of this early observation has been corroborated by recent work that integrates neuroscience and attachment theory. For example, Field (1985a) proposes that attachment is fundamentally a process of psychobiological attunement, and Trad

(1986) concludes that stable attachment bonds are vitally important for the infant's continuing neurobiological development.

In agreement with the concept of sequential stages of early development propounded in current neurobiological, neurochemical, ethological, embryological, psychological, and biological theory, Mahler (Mahler, Pine, & Bergman, 1975) has proposed specific phases of socioemotional development. As a result of her observational and clinical studies with infants and toddlers, Mahler—who is perhaps the most important impetus to the inception of a program of rigorous developmental psychoanalytic research—characterizes a sequence of universal sequential stages of socioaffective ontogeny. These consist of an earliest postnatal "autistic" phase followed by a "symbiotic" phase, which is itself superceded by a pivotal "separation-individuation" phase. This critical latter stage consists of a "practicing" subphase characterized by an elated mood (divided into an early practicing period and a practicing subphase proper) and a "rapprochement" subphase characterized by a depressive and fearful mood. It is in this period from the latter half of the first to the end of the second year that the "psychological birth of the human infant" takes place. This event is marked by the emergence of a structure that contributes to autonomous emotional functioning, most importantly to the self-regulation of affect.

Although parts of Mahler's work are controversial, her careful description of the ontogenetic adaptation of very high levels of positive hedonic affect which occur in a circumscribed period of infancy, the early practicing period of 10 to 14 months, has been corroborated by other psychoanalytic and nonpsychoanalytic infant researchers (e.g., Emde, 1989; Sroufe, 1979). In fact, a recent neuropsychological study demonstrates that a statistically significant increase in positive emotion occurs over the developmental period of 10 to 13.5 months (Rothbart, Taylor, & Tucker, 1989). The proposal that the practicing phase is a temporally circumscribed stage of affective ontogeny is supported by the finding that major socioaffective transformations occur between 10–12 and again at around 15–18 months (e.g., Emde, 1989; Stern, 1985). This is the same time frame of Piaget's fifth stage of the sensorimotor period in which the infant attains the ability to represent the self. It also exactly corresponds with the interval when Bowlby's attachment patterns are measured. Furthermore, it overlaps critical periods in the first and the second year for the experience-dependent maturation of the prefrontal cortex (Mrzljak et al., 1990), a cerebral structure essential to social and emotional behavior (de Bruin, 1990).

This developmental stage which straddles early and late infancy is a critical period for the development of socioemotional functioning. I shall later present evidence that suggests that at the end of the first year increased and more efficient attachment functioning between mother and child is associated with the appearance of the high levels of positive affect that characterize the early practicing period. These events in turn directly influence the growth of connections between cortical and limbic structures in the infant's developing brain that are associated with attachment function. A significant change in dyadic affective transactions occurring in the late practicing period accounts for a further maturation of these structures. The interval between 10–12 to 16–18 months is a critical period for the final maturation of a system in the prefrontal cortex that is essential to the regulation of affect over the rest of the lifespan. For shorthand purposes, in this book the developmental span marked by these temporal boundaries will be descriptively referred to as the practicing period, without any acceptance or rejection of Mahler's, Bowlby's, or Piaget's interpretations of the underlying mechanisms that are operative during this period.

CONTEMPORARY REVISIONS OF PSYCHOANALYTIC THEORIES OF DEVELOPMENT

Mahler's infant observational research represents a testing and expansion of developmental psychoanalytic theory, the most important advance in psychoanalysis since the introduction of an adaptive perspective into psychoanalytic thinking some 50 years ago (Hartmann, 1939). The essential impetus for this restructuring of the fundamental, basic concepts laid down by Freud derives from the integration of recent information from infant research on socioemotional development into psychoanalytic models of the dynamics of early mental events and the elucidation of the causal factors that influence the development of psychic structure. After an early career in which he made numerous contributions during the "golden age of neurology," Freud (1895/1966) prepared his seminal treatise, the *Project for a Scientific Psychology*, the earliest attempt to comprehensively explain psychological phenomena in terms of neurobiological explanatory models. This work, published after his death, is a source pool from which he later developed the major concepts of his psychoanalytic theory (McCarley & Hobson, 1977). Not surprisingly, Freud's thinking at this transitional point was intensely influenced by his experiences as a neurologist and a research scientist. The "Project" presented a view of early development that remained unchanged throughout all his later writings—that the infant was relatively passive and undifferentiated, and that its primary motivational aims were associated with tension-discharging, drive reducing activities. The infant's awareness of objects was viewed as secondary to the fulfillment of oral needs. This view was first seriously challenged by a stream of British psychoanalysts, beginning with Fairbairn (1941, 1952) who proposed that the infant's behavior is primarily object seeking from the start.

This object relational model has flourished, as its heuristic character has enabled the creation of newer techniques of treatment of early forming socioemotional psychopathologies that are the outcome of developmental structural deficits rather than due to conflict. Instead of focusing on later occurring paternally-influenced Oedipal events, it stresses the long enduring effects of early

maternal-infant relations, and posits that the critical period for personality formation occurs from birth to 3 years, not 3 to 6 years as classical Freudian theory had
proposed (Beit-Hallahmi, 1987). The primary concern of object relations theory
is how individuals develop in relation to the emotional interactions they have
with the people around them (Hamilton, 1989), and the essential question this
developmental theory addresses is, what are the crucial early events that are
necessary for the transformation of the relatively unformed infant to the relatively patterned adult? (Greenberg & Mitchell, 1983). In this model, emotion,
which serves the function of organizing object relations, is seen as developing
within an interpersonal context rather than in terms of the organism's interaction
with the physical environment. Object seeking is defined as the sharing and
communication of affects (Modell, 1975). Affects in general are understood to be
intrinsic to relationship paradigms, and specific affects imply a particular form of
relatedness (Geller, 1984).

Critical early affective transactions with the social environment are mentally
stored in the form of representations of the self emotionally interacting with
significant objects. Horner (1989) explains:

> We use the term "object," rather than "mother" because the particular mental image
> is in part *created by* the child in accord with his or her limited mental capabilities,
> and with his or her own unique experience of the early caretaking environment. In a
> way, the child creates a metaphor or template for the significant other from his or
> her interpersonal experiences. . . . Through its genetically endowed intrinsic cre-
> ative capacities, its inborn intrinsic power, the infant creates an inner image of itself
> as well. "Object relations" refers to the dynamic interplay between the inner images
> of both self and other. (pp. 28–29)

How is this template created? Mutually interactive experiences in the first 2 years
are occurring while various sensory systems are maturing, and,

> the residua of exposure to the environment are internalized as permanent idio-
> syncratic modifications of the nervous system and, therefore, such more or less
> fixed characteristics of the developing individual as the ability to differentiate self
> from nonself, to make internal representations of both self and nonself and to enter
> into object relations. (Freedman, 1981, p. 841)

These mental representations are cognitive-affective units that consist of a configuration of self-representation, object representation, and a linking mediating
affect (Kernberg, 1976). Internal object relations, stored representation of interaction, therefore have emotional energy—an affective charge—impressed upon
them. Furthermore,

> The aim of psychoanalytic phenomenology is to elucidate not only the functional
> significance, but also the developmental origins of subjective representational con-

figurations. This is an imposing task indeed, for it involves the formation of a developmental psychology of the representational world which requires a comprehensive knowledge of both emotional and cognitive development. (Stolorow & Atwood, 1976, p. 186)

Despite the fact that this model now drives more rigorous and formal study of affect development in infancy (Lichtenberg, 1983) and that the significance of this research is being applied to clinical theory and practice (Dowling & Rothstein, 1989; Pine, 1985), aside from a recent seminal interdisciplinary volume (Sameroff & Emde, 1989) much of this work has not crossed into other disciplines.

A second powerful influence on the current revision of the elemental psychoanalytic conceptions of development is from "self psychology," the product of the pioneering work of Heinz Kohut, a psychoanalyst who like Freud also trained in neurology. Self psychology is built upon a fundamental developmental principle—that parents with mature psychological organizations serve as "selfobjects" that perform critical regulatory functions for the infant who possesses an immature, incomplete psychological organization. The concept of the mother-infant pair as a self-selfobject unit emphasizes that early development is essentially characterized as an interdependence between self and objects in a system. Indeed, Kohut (1971, 1977) attributes the crucial maintenance of the infant's homeostatic balance to the infant's continuous dyadic reciprocal interactions with selfobjects, rather than to his monadic efforts of tension reduction through the discharge of drives. Furthermore, Kohut posits that phase-appropriate maternal optimal frustrations of the infant elicit "transmuting internalization," the developmental process by which selfobject function is internalized by the infant and psychological regulatory structures are formed. According to Kohut (1984), Mahler's late symbiotic and early separation-individuation phases are the most critical time for self-selfobject relationships, and these ultimately allow for the maternally-influenced building of structures involved in drive-regulating, integrative, and adaptive functions previously performed by the mother.

The psychobiological significance of the newer psychoanalytic concepts is only now beginning to be explored in the ground-breaking interdisciplinary works of Grotstein (1990a), Gilbert (1989, 1992a), and Taylor (1987). This latter author has extended Kohut's concept in concluding that selfobjects act as external psychobiological regulators. Palombo (1992) asserts that selfobjects facilitate the regulation of affective experience, and Nathanson (1992) describes these as techniques by which the caregiver experiences the affect broadcast by the infant and comes to act as an external modulator of this affect. The child in turn is thus provided with selfobject experiences that directly effect the energic vigor and structural cohesion of the self. According to Wolf (1988):

> The most fundamental finding of self psychology is that the emergence of the self requires more than the inborn tendency to organize experience. Also required is the presence of others, technically described as objects, who provide certain types of experiences that will evoke the emergence and maintenance of the self. (p. 11)

The bulk of contemporary psychoanalytic developmental theory (Emde, 1989; Loewald, 1978; Pine, 1985; Stern, 1985; Wilson, Passik, & Faude, 1990) and research (Beebe & Lachman, 1988a; Lichtenberg, 1983; Mahler et al., 1975) strongly suggests that the infant's early object relations (socioaffective interactions) with the mother are indispensable to the development and organization of psychic structure responsible for self-regulation and adaptation. Thus, the basic theoretical assumption underlying the latest psychoanalytic models of early socioemotional development is in actuality similar if not identical to the conceptualization by developmental neuroscientists outlined previously—that the early critical period growth of structures which subserve self-regulatory functions is profoundly influenced by postnatal social environmental forces.

On the other hand, it should be pointed out that contemporary psychoanalysis does not specify the particular site or characterization of these structures. In fact, recent works in the field are now turning to neurobiology for clues that may elucidate the psychic structural systems alluded to in the psychoanalytic literature (Levin, 1991; Miller, 1991b). Also, despite the fact that psychoanalysis, perhaps even more than other disciplines, is in need of a general theory of affect, in the last 2 decades it has been heavily influenced by developments in cognitive psychology. It is often forgotten that 100 years ago, Freud's "Project" proposed a neurophysiological model of affect generation and a detailed characterization of regulatory phenomena. Many of the regulatory principles outlined in that work of 1895 have been found to be quite compatible with modern control and systems theory (Pribram & Gill, 1976).

Later in this volume I cite evidence to demonstrate that the interconnections between the newer psychoanalytic and neuroscientific concepts are essential to an understanding of the changes in structure-function relationships that characterize early development. The unique contribution of contemporary psychoanalysis to the study of development lies in its emphasis upon and elucidation of the critical "hidden" selfobject regulatory functions that are embedded within dyadic affect transacting object relational processes, since these characterize the form and dynamics of the "social forces" that influence the maturation of regulatory structure within the infant brain in the first 2 years of life. Psychoanalysis also articulates the nature of and emphasizes the importance of internal representations to the individual's adaptive object relational (socioemotional) functioning.

THE RELATIONSHIP BETWEEN THE MATURATION OF CORTICAL AND LIMBIC STRUCTURES AND THE EMERGENCE OF DISCRETE AFFECTS OVER STAGES OF INFANCY

The critical nature of early experiences, stressed by all investigators of socioemotional development, lies in their effects of enhancing or inhibiting the experience-dependent maturation of structural systems which anatomically and physiologically mature during particular sequential periods of infancy. By directly influencing the growth and differentiation of these developing brain systems, such experiences indelibly and permanently affect the subsequent emotional and social attachment functions that these structures will subserve. The fact that discrete emotional expressions and social behaviors appear in an invariant ontogenetic sequence that is dependent on the maturation of brain structures has now been adopted as a fundamental tenet within personality research (Izard, 1977; Plutchik, 1983; Tomkins, 1963), neurobiology (Fox & Davidson, 1984), neurology (Adams & Victor, 1989), and developmental psychoanalysis (Tyson & Tyson, 1990). In light of the well established finding that there are nodal points of development in the maturation of affects (Basch, 1976; Krystal, 1988; Pine, 1980), the maturation of the brain structures associated with emotion must therefore set the limits within which the development of these emotional functions can proceed.

Basch (1976) argues that the earliest forms of affective behavior are general physiologic reactions such as response to stimulation (autonomic reactivity) mediated by the autonomic nervous system; in later development they provide the substrate for all affective experience. Krystal (1988) asserts that all affects evolve out of a state of contentment and a state of distress (pleasure-unpleasure) present in the neonate. Krystal (1978a) also differentiates two lines of emotional development, an infantile nonverbal affect system and a verbal adult system. In a similar conceptualization, Gazzaniga (1985) now proposes a basic primitive affect system and a verbal-conceptual system that are localized in separate hemispheres. Evidence is mounting to show that the right hemisphere mediates pleasure and pain and the intrinsically more primitive emotions (Semenza, Pasini, Zettin, Tonin, & Portolan, 1986). Researchers are now focusing on the unique character of a cluster of biologically primitive emotions (Plutchik, 1980; Tomkins, 1962, 1963). According to Johnson and Multhaup (1992, p. 42):

> These emotions are thought to be evolutionarily old (Ekman, 1984), appear early in an individual's development (Lewis, Sullivan, Stanger, & Weiss, 1989), arise quickly and "automatically" (Berkowitz, 1990), are expressed in universally recognizable configurations of facial movements (Ekman, 1973), are correlated with differentiable autonomic system activity (Ekman, Levenson, & Friesen, 1983), may show subcortical conditioning (LeDoux, 1992), may be disposed to certain stimuli (Ohman, Dimberg, & Ost, 1985), and serve fundamental motivational functions within the individual and communication functions within a social group (Izard, 1977; Plutchik, 1980; Tomkins, 1963).

The mechanisms responsible for the ontogenetic emergence of specific primitive emotions in early periods of development have yet to be elucidated.

Infant researchers have documented that development occurs in "leaps and bounds" and contains significant qualitative shifts (Stern, 1985), and that new integrations consolidate in the relatively quiescent intervals (Lichtenberg, 1989).

Significant organizational shifts occur regularly in development, and these are always signaled by the emergence of new affective behavior (Spitz, 1965). The biobehavioral shifts that are marked by affective changes occur in an invariant sequence in early development, indicating the presence of new levels of organization (Emde, 1989). Indeed, developmental neurobiological studies suggest that critical periods of development associated with significant changes in the emotional repertoire are correlated with shifts in nervous system growth and reorganization (Weber & Sackheim, 1978). The Russian researcher, Bozhovich (1978), drawing upon the concepts of Vygotsky, emphasizes the importance of "crises" occurring at transitions between stages of socioemotional development. According to this author, psychological structures that contain affective and motivational components emerge at the end of each stage and are responsible for new socioemotional needs. Confirming this, Plooij and van de Rijt-Plooij (1989) assert that during postnatal reorganizations of the brain, the organism is in a very labile state in which "very little additional stress is needed to throw the organism completely off balance" (p. 280). Brazelton and Cramer (1990), who refer to stages of mother-infant interaction, describe a similar scenario:

> The central nervous system, as it develops, drives infants towards mastery of themselves and their world. As they achieve each level of mastery, they seek a kind of homeostasis, until the nervous system presses them on to their next level. Internal equilibrium is always being upset by a new imbalance created as the nervous system matures. Maturation of the nervous system, accompanied by increasing differentiation of skills, drives infants to reorganize their control systems. (p. 98)

This last statement about control systems gives some clue as to which specific developing systems involved in affective functions are influenced by interactions with the early environment. Indeed, Bowlby (1969) states that the ontogeny of control systems are influenced by the particular environment in which development occurs. Can such structures be neuroanatomically identified? From the vantage point of infant psychiatry Anders and Zeanah (1984) put forth the argument that the emotion-generating limbic system (Papez, 1937; MacLean, 1958) is the most obvious site of developmental changes associated with the ascendence of attachment behaviors. Neurobiological studies reveal that the dramatic onset of function in the first 18 months of life reflects the immense synaptogenesis that occurs during this period of infancy. Indeed the specific period from 7 to 15 months (roughly Bowlby's period for the establishment of attachment patterns and Mahler's practicing period) has been shown to be critical for the myelination and therefore the maturation of particular rapidly developing limbic and cortical association areas (Kinney, Brody, Kloman, & Gilles, 1988; Yakovlev & Lecours, 1967). Meyersburg and Post (1979) show a general temporal correspondence of postnatal neurodevelopmental myelination cycles, Mahler's stages of infant development, and critical periods of psychosocial maturation. The onset of mature function in these corticolimbic structures is instrumental to the emergence of infant affective, affect regulatory, and cognitive processes. Indeed, limbic areas of the human cerebral cortex show anatomical maturation at 15 months, suggesting that corticolimbic functional activity expressed in "emotional activities and mechanisms of memory" are operating at this specific time (Rabinowicz, 1979). There is now strong evidence indicating that this maturation is experience-dependent and directly influenced by the caregiver-infant relationship (Gilbert, 1989). Indeed, it is now thought that the infant must experience nurturance and affection in order for the limbic nuclei to develop normally (Joseph, 1992).

Of special importance are the connections between cortical areas and subcortical limbic regions. It could be speculated that subcortical limbic and brainstem structures which are expressive in the "domain of affect and motivation" (Nauta, 1979) (e.g., medullary, septal, amygdala, hypothalamic, and upper midbrain systems) underlie the affect components and that inhibitory cortical structures represent the affect regulatory components of all emotional behavior. This reflects the traditional assumption that spontaneous emotional expression is mainly subcortical and that cortical control is inhibitory (Bard, 1934; Monrad-Krohn, 1924). Izard states that "emotion expression changes developmentally as a function of maturation of neural inhibitory mechanisms and experience" (Izard, Hembree, & Huebner, 1987, p. 105). Emotional expression is mediated by the energy-mobilizing sympathetic and energy-conserving parasympathetic components of the autonomic nervous system (Truex & Carpenter, 1964), and these components continue to develop postnatally, at different rates (Hofer, 1984b). Over the course of infancy sympathetic subcortical excitatory systems that are operating at birth are superceded by parasympathetic cortical inhibitory systems. We now know that such inhibitory structures—such as those in the prefrontal cortex—develop more slowly in the postnatal period (Thompson, 1990).

Furthermore, in early infancy the mother is

> an important resource for stimulations which are an essential aid to the infant's still inadequate inhibitory capacities. At birth, the human organism is remarkably ill-equipped to cope with the variations and excitations of its new environment. It is a subcortical creature, which is in danger of going into shock through overreacting to powerful or unexpected stimuli because it lacks the means for modulation of behavior which is made possible by the development of cortical control. The role of the higher structures is played by the mother: she is the child's auxillary cortex. (Diamond, Balvin, & Diamond, 1963, p. 305)

Is it possible to precisely identify the sites of such higher cortical structures? The sides of the frontal lobes between the hemispheres and the pathways between and just under the hemispheres that connect the cortex with the subcortical drive and affective integrative centers are known to subserve unique roles in emotional and social adjustment (Valenstein, 1973). Descending projections from the prefrontal cortex to subcortical structures are known to mature during infancy (Johnson, Rosvold, Galkin, & Goldman, 1976). Infant tomography studies show that glucose utilization in frontal and association cortices, an estimate of their synaptic metabolic activity, first becomes prominent between 8 and 18 months (Chugani & Phelps, 1986). The early maturing (Geschwind & Galaburda, 1987) and "primitive" (Tucker, 1992) right cortical hemisphere, moreso than the left, is particularly well reciprocally connected with limbic and subcortical regions (Joseph, 1982; Tucker, 1981) and is dominant for the processing, expression, and regulation of emotional information (Joseph, 1988). It has been suggested that "investigations into the neural bases for social interaction should focus on the role of the holistic, affective, silent right hemisphere in the mediation of social life" (Barchas & Perlaki, 1986, p. 348).

THE DYADIC ORIGIN OF THE ADAPTIVE CAPACITY TO SELF-REGULATE AFFECT

Although previously overlooked and understudied by developmental psychologists, the important problem of the development of the regulation of emotion is only now becoming the focus of a number of current investigations (Campos, Campos, & Barrett, 1989; Izard, 1990). In a very recent formulation, Cicchetti and Toth (1991) conclude that:

> the concept of experience-expectant and experience-dependent sensitive periods can be viewed as organizing constructs for highlighting the role that caregiving and other environmental factors may play in the ontogenesis of neuroregulatory and self-regulatory processes across the lifespan. (p. 7)

What specific kinds of environmental experiences are these authors referring to? Sander (1980) refers to an epigenetic sequence of adaptive issues which must be negotiated by the caregiver-infant dyad to achieve self-regulation. Of special importance is the mother's participation in "interactive repair" (Tronick, 1989), a regulatory process utilized after her induction of stress in her infant. These dyadic transactions regulate the infant's affect state in the short term and lead to structural changes in the long term. Wilson et al. (1990) assert that secure attachment facilitates the transfer of regulatory capacities from caregiver to infant. Thompson (1990) underscores the cardinal principle that emotion is initially regulated by others, but as development proceeds it becomes increasingly self-regulated as a result of neurophysiological maturation. Such observations suggest that the mother's external regulation of the infant's developing yet still immature emotional systems during particular critical periods may represent the essential factor that influences the experience-dependent growth of brain areas prospectively involved in self-regulation. This growth occurs in stages, and at the end of a stage a more complex structure is capable of a more complex regulatory function. The outcome of effective dyadic affect regulatory transactions is an integration and restructuring of the infant's developing socioemotional system on a higher level of complexity.

Bronson (1965) proposes that early development represents the differentiation over successive critical periods of adaptive mechanisms of increasing complexity which are built upon and yet supercede earlier maturing less complex adaptive mechanisms. In recent psychoanalytic models, development is conceptualized as a progression of stages in which emergent adaptive self-regulatory structures and functions enable qualitatively new interactions between the individual and his environment (Settlage et al., 1988). Applying the biological principle of epigenesis to the study of the development of self-regulatory capacities Wilson et al. (1990) assert that:

> the formation of psychic structure is the result of successive transactions between the organism and the environment; that the outcome of each mode of organization depends on the outcome of each previous mode; and that each new mode integrates the previous modes, has a new level of organization and regulation, and possesses unique "emergent" qualities. (p. 152)

In the case of the development of socioaffective regulation the experience-dependent maturation of cortical and limbic structures is responsible for the appearance of more complex affects that are more autonomously regulated. The frontal lobes are known to develop postnatally in stages (Mrzljak et al., 1990), and the orbitofrontal areas in particular are intimately invoved in social (de Bruin, 1990), emotional (Tranel, Damasio & Damasio, 1988), and regulatory (Kolb, 1984; Luria, 1980) functions.

Developmental psychological research in affect development suggests both that there is a particular developmental period that is most important in the development of emotional regulation (Gottman & Fainsilber Katz, 1989), and that the age at which the infant is capable of regulating emotional expression may differ for each of the discrete emotions (Buechler & Izard, 1983). The emergence of the adaptive capacity to self-regulate affect is reflected in an "expansion in the affect array" (Pine, 1980) and the appearance of more complex emotions (Johnson & Multhaup, 1992) that result from the simultaneous blending of different affects (Hyson & Izard, 1985). Many of these new findings and conclusions obviously fit well with the previously discussed developmental psychoanalytic concepts. Krystal (1988) argues that the development and maturation of affects represents the key event in infancy, and emphasizes the essential adaptive capacity of the self-regulation of affect.

In upcoming chapters, I offer the proposal that by mediating and modulating environmental input, the primary caregiver supplies the "experience" required for the experience-dependent maturation of a structural system responsible for the regulation of the individual's socioemotional function. By providing well modulated socioaffective stimulation, the mother facilitates the growth of connections between cortical limbic and subcortical limbic structures that neurobiologically mediate self-regulatory functions. The dyad's response to stressful transactions, such as occur in socialization experiences in the second year, are particularly instrumental to the final structural maturation of an adaptive cortical system that can self-regulate emotional states. Early object relational experiences thus directly influence the emergence of a frontolimbic system in the right hemisphere that can adaptively autoregulate both positive and negative affect in response to changes in the socioemotional environment. This regulatory capacity allows for a continued expansion of the affect array—the emergence of more intense discrete affects and then a blending of these affects into more complex emotions—over the stages of childhood. The core of the self lies in patterns of affect regulation that integrate a sense of self across state transitions, thereby allowing for a continuity of inner experience. Dyadic failures of affect regulation result in the developmental psychopathology that underlies various forms of later forming psychiatric disorders.

4 Structure-Function Relationships of the Orbitofrontal Cortex

In view of the relationship between emotions and the limbic system, this system would seem an appropriate place to look for developmental changes associated with the rise of attachment behaviors.
—Thomas F. Anders and Charles H. Zeanah (1984)

Increasingly complex self-regulatory structural systems mature during infancy, and their development is a product of early dynamic object relational environmental interactions that shape the outcome of genetic predispositions. The Russian neuropsychologist, Aleksandr Luria, has argued that complex functional brain systems are not ready-made at birth. They do not arise spontaneously in development "but are formed in the process of *social contact* [my emphasis] and objective activity by the child" (1980, p.33). Sixty years ago Luria (1932) proposed that young children are subject to diffuse cortical excitation because they lack higher regulatory function. This function is provided by a late maturing inhibitory structure that is the internalized form of culturally mediated, socially transmitted behavior. Luria was particularly interested in the neuropsychological and neuroanatomic characterization of the cortical system which adaptively modulates lower structures, inhibits drive, and regulates arousal and activity states. His work indicates that postnatally developing prefrontal cortex is the critical cortical regulatory system, especially early maturing orbitofrontal cortex (as opposed to later maturing dorsolateral "nonlimbic" prefrontal cortex) with its unique extensive connections with lower limbic structures in the brain stem, midbrain, and diencephalon and with all other parts of the cerebral cortex. He extensively documents neurological disturbances of the autonomic or-

34

bital frontal regions that elicit gross changes in affective processes in the form of lack of self-control, emotional outbursts and generalized disinhibition. These affective alterations are responsible for an observable disturbance of personality.

The present chapter focuses on the unique structure-function relationships of the orbital frontal cortex (so called because of its relation to the orbit of the eye) that is "hidden" in the interior surfaces of the prefrontal lobe. Its distinctive anatomical locus and its dense reciprocal interconnections with distant sites in both the cortex and subcortex account for its involvement in a number of critical functions, including affect regulation.

FUNCTIONS OF THE ORBITOFRONTAL CORTEX

The orbital region, a phylogenetically older mesocortical area of the "visceral brain" (MacLean, 1949) on the ventral and medial surfaces of the frontal lobe, is especially enlargened in the right hemisphere (Falk et al., 1990). Figures 4.1 through 4.5 illustrate the neuroanatomy and cytoarchitecture of this region of the cerebral cortex. The orbitofrontal cortex is so intimately interconnected into limbic areas that it has been conceived of as an "association cortex" (Martin, 1989; Pribram, 1981) for the limbic forebrain (see Fig. 4.6). This cerebral structure receives multimodal input from all sensory areas of the posterior cortex (Chavis & Pandya, 1976), since axons from the visual, somesthetic, auditory, and olfactory sensory association cortices all converge in this frontolimbic cortex (Yarita, Iino, Tanabe, Kogure, & Takagi, 1980). Along with these cortical connections, the areas of the frontal lobes just under the hemispheres are known to project extensive pathways to subcortical drive and affective integrative centers (Valenstein, 1973). As a result of such widely distributed anatomical linkages, the orbitofrontal cortex occupies a unique position between the cortex and subcortex. Due to its connections with hypothalamic and autonomic areas as well as brain stem neuromodulator systems, this preeminent component of the "paralimbic core of the brain" plays an essential adaptive role in emotional and motivational processes (Tucker, 1992). Indeed, at the orbitofrontal level cortically processed exteroceptive information concerning the external environment is integrated with subcortically processed interoceptive information regarding the visceroendocrine environment (Nauta, 1971). Nauta suggests that prefrontal autonomic control is required for the visceral, interoceptive "gut feelings" that are experienced in response to both real and imagined threats.

Although the finding that the orbital frontal area of the cerebral cortex controls the autonomic nervous system was first demonstrated at the end of the last century (Spencer, 1894) and firmly established by the middle of this one (Fulton, 1949; Kaada, Pribram, & Epstein, 1949), the importance of this is only now

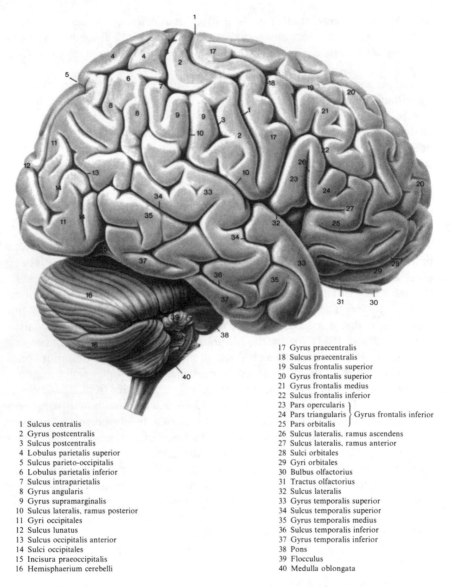

1 Sulcus centralis
2 Gyrus postcentralis
3 Sulcus postcentralis
4 Lobulus parietalis superior
5 Sulcus parieto-occipitalis
6 Lobulus parietalis inferior
7 Sulcus intraparietalis
8 Gyrus angularis
9 Gyrus supramarginalis
10 Sulcus lateralis, ramus posterior
11 Gyri occipitales
12 Sulcus lunatus
13 Sulcus occipitalis anterior
14 Sulci occipitales
15 Incisura praeoccipitalis
16 Hemisphaerium cerebelli

17 Gyrus praecentralis
18 Sulcus praecentralis
19 Sulcus frontalis superior
20 Gyrus frontalis superior
21 Gyrus frontalis medius
22 Sulcus frontalis inferior
23 Pars opercularis ⎫
24 Pars triangularis ⎬ Gyrus frontalis inferior
25 Pars orbitalis ⎭
26 Sulcus lateralis, ramus ascendens
27 Sulcus lateralis, ramus anterior
28 Sulci orbitales
29 Gyri orbitales
30 Bulbus olfactorius
31 Tractus olfactorius
32 Sulcus lateralis
33 Gyrus temporalis superior
34 Sulcus temporalis superior
35 Gyrus temporalis medius
36 Sulcus temporalis inferior
37 Gyrus temporalis inferior
38 Pons
39 Flocculus
40 Medulla oblongata

FIG. 4.1.   Lateral view of the human right cerebral hemisphere. Note the position of the orbital sulci (labeled 28) and gyri (labeled 29) in the frontal undersurface. From Nieuwenhuys et al. (1981). Reprinted by permission of Springer-Verlag.

36

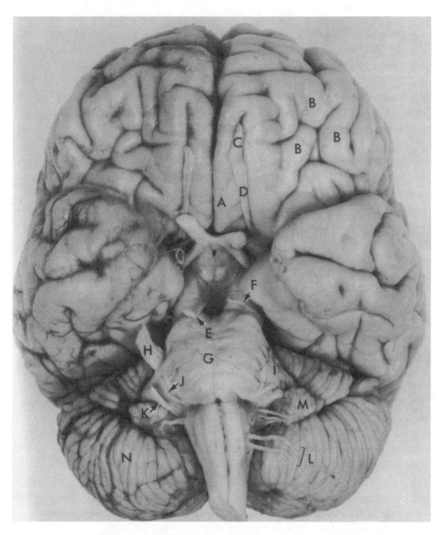

FIG. 4.2. Photograph of the base of the human brain showing orbital gyri and sulci at sites (labeled B). From Watson (1977). Reprinted by permission of Little, Brown and Company.

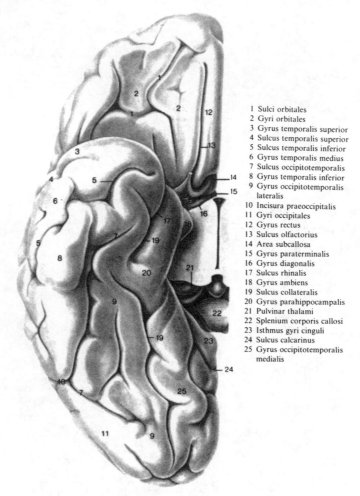

1 Sulci orbitales
2 Gyri orbitales
3 Gyrus temporalis superior
4 Sulcus temporalis superior
5 Sulcus temporalis inferior
6 Gyrus temporalis medius
7 Sulcus occipitotemporalis
8 Gyrus temporalis inferior
9 Gyrus occipitotemporalis
   lateralis
10 Incisura praeoccipitalis
11 Gyri occipitales
12 Gyrus rectus
13 Sulcus olfactorius
14 Area subcallosa
15 Gyrus paraterminalis
16 Gyrus diagonalis
17 Sulcus rhinalis
18 Gyrus ambiens
19 Sulcus collateralis
20 Gyrus parahippocampalis
21 Pulvinar thalami
22 Splenium corporis callosi
23 Isthmus gyri cinguli
24 Sulcus calcarinus
25 Gyrus occipitotemporalis
   medialis

FIG. 4.3. Basal view of the human right cerebral hemisphere. Note orbital sulci (labeled 1) and orbital gyri (labeled 2). From Nieuwenhuys et al. (1981). Reprinted by permission of Springer-Verlag.

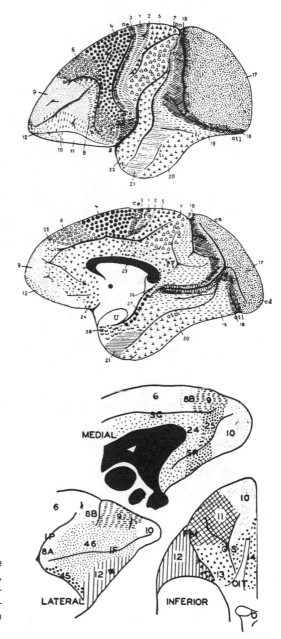

FIG. 4.4. Cytoarchitectonic areas of the primate brain. Note orbito-frontal areas 11, 12, 13, and 14. From Pandya and Barnes (1987). Reprinted by permission of Lawrence Erlbaum Associates.

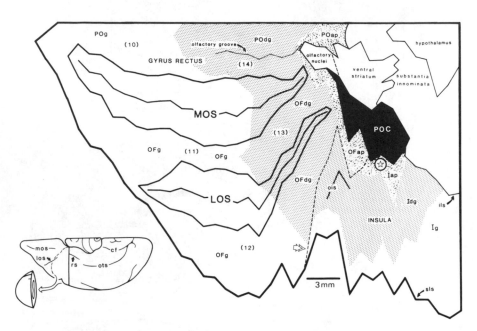

FIG. 4.5. Two-dimensional flattened cytoarchitectonic map of the primate orbitofrontal cortex, identifying medial (MOS) and lateral (LOS) divisions. From Morecraft, Geula, and Mesulam (1992). Cytoarchitecture and neural afferents of orbitofrontal cortex in the brain of the monkey. *Journal of Comparative Neurology, 323,* Reprinted by permission of Wiley-Liss, a division of John Wiley and Sons, Inc.

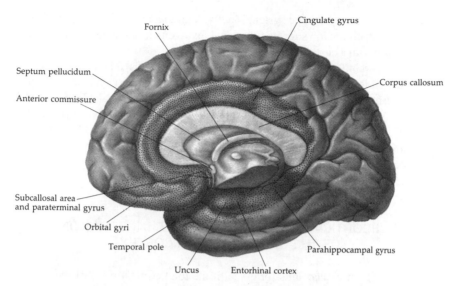

FIG. 4.6. Midsagittal view of the right cerebral hemisphere, with brain stem removed. The limbic association cortex is indicated by the dotted regions. Note the orbital gyri. From Martin (1989). Reprinted by permission of Elsevier.

being appreciated (Neafsey, 1990). The essential involvement of this structure, more than any other site in the higher cortex, in the modulation of the autonomic nervous system is in part due to the anatomical fact that this region of the cerebral cortex sends direct monosynaptic connections to the diencephalic hypothalamus (Nauta, 1972). Its stimulation elicits hormonal and neurohormonal changes. Increases of hypothalamico-pituitary-adrenocortical corticosteroid levels (Hall & Marr, 1975; Kandel & Schwartz, 1985) and alterations in sympathoadreno-medullary catecholamine release (Euler & Folkow, 1958) have both been documented. The frontolimbic cortex is uniquely involved in a number of essential functions. These include: a generalized arousal reaction (Kandel & Schwartz, 1985; Truex & Carpenter, 1964), homeostatic regulation (Kolb, 1984), drive modulation (Rosenkilde, 1979), modulation of ascending excitatory influences (Butter, Snyder, & McDonald, 1970), and the supresion of heart rate (Kaada et al., 1949), behavior (Wilcott, 1981), and aggression (De Bruin, VanOyen, & VandePoll, 1983). Electrical stimulation of certain sites in this cortex elicit parasympathetic decreases in cardiovascular functions, while stimulation of other sites elicits opposite sympathetic responses (Hall, Livingston, & Bloor, 1977). Fuster (1980) concludes that the majority of autonomic effects produced by stimulation of the limbic orbital cortex (e.g., changes in heart rate, skin temperature, blood pressure) "seem to be parasympathetic or the result of inhibitory influences on the sympathetic system" (p. 94), and that the orbital suppression of internal information allows for its functional involvement in the temporal organization of behavior (Fuster, 1985).

Most importantly, recent neuroscience research shows that in the cerebral cortex, the orbitofrontal region is uniquely involved in social (Damasio & Tranel, 1988; de Bruin, 1990; Kolb & Whishaw, 1990) and emotional (Tranel et al., 1988; Yamamoto et al., 1984) behaviors, in the regulation of body (Luria, 1980) and motivational states (Pandya & Yeterian, 1985), and in the adjustment or correction of emotional responses (Rolls, 1986). Indeed, developmental neurobiological studies now indicate that this cortical structure is critically involved in attachment processes (Steklis & Kling, 1985).

SUBCORTICAL CATECHOLAMINERGIC INNERVATION OF THE ORBITOFRONTAL CORTEX

The prefrontal cortex accounts for 30 % of the total cortical mass of the human brain (Uylings & Van Eden, 1990). It contains two major subdivisions, the orbitofrontal and dorsolateral cortices (see Figs. 4.7 and 4.8). The exact anatomi-

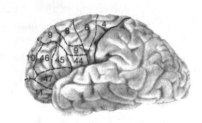

A Lateral View

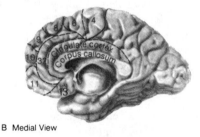

B Medial View

FIG. 4.7. Approximate boundaries of functional zones of the human cerebral cortex, showing the dorsolateral prefrontal areas 9, 10, 45, and 46, and orbital prefrontal areas 11, 13, and 47. From *Fundamentals of Human Neuropsychology,* 3rd edition, by Kolb and Whishaw. Copyright (1990) by W. H. Freeman and Company. Reprinted by permission.

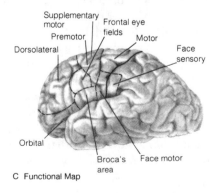

C Functional Map

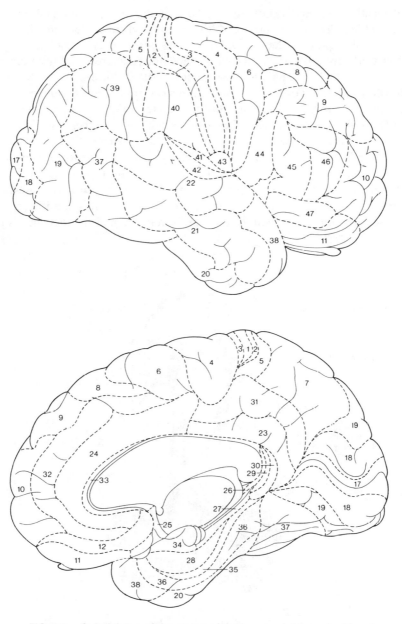

FIG. 4.8.   Subdivision of the cortex of the human right cerebral hemisphere into cytoarchitectonic fields according to Brodmann. Note orbitofrontal areas 11, 12, and 47, and dorsolateral prefrontal areas 9, 10,
and 46. From Nieuwenhuys et al. (1981). Reprinted by permission of
Springer-Verlag.

cal identification and delineation of the subfields of the prefrontal cortex is required in order to more precisely dissociate their distinct functions. However, this technical problem has been difficult and unsolved only until recently. In older work this was done on the basis of the input each received from different areas of the thalamus (Akert, 1964; Leonard, 1969; Rose & Woolsey, 1948). However, as a result of recent technological advances in neuroanatomical visualization methods, it is now thought that the differentiation of the prefrontal cortical areas can more accurately be made on the basis of their innervation by specific subcortical monoaminergic nuclei that are anatomically part of the arousal-generating reticular formation (Thierry, Godbout, Mantz, & Glowinski, 1990) (Fig. 4.9). Indeed, the frontal lobes, especially their basal and medial portions, more than any other part of the cerebral cortex, have the closest connection with the reticular formation (Luria, 1973). It is this specific property that accounts for their central function in the regulation of the individual's psy-

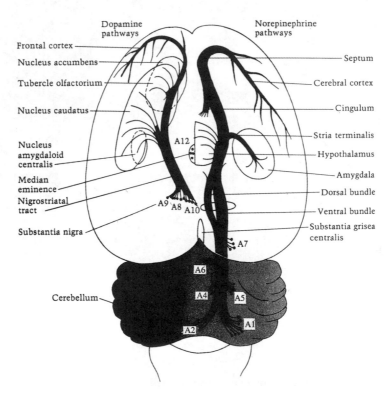

FIG. 4.9. Schematic of dopamine and noradrenaline pathways of rat brain. The numbers refer to defined groups of catecholaminergic neurons. From Bradford (1986); adapted from Ungerstedt (1971). Reprinted by permission of the publisher.

chobiological states. The catecholamines dopamine and noradrenaline (nor-epinephrine), acting as neuromodulators in the nervous system, biochemically mediate states of arousal and integrate metabolism. These bioamines are impor-tant regulators of emotion, attention, movement, and visceral function. The identification of specific behavioral and physiological roles served by individual catecholaminergic pathways is a major theme of current neurochemical research (Nieuwenhuys, 1985; Bjorklund, Hokfelt, & Tohyama, 1992).

It is now well established both that catecholamines are required for neuronal activity in the cerebral cortex and that no catecholamine producing neurons reside in the cortex. All central bioamines are produced in brainstem areas (see Fig. 4.10 regarding the anatomical relation of brainstem areas to the right hemi-spheric orbital cortex), and although catecholamine-containing neurons make up not even 1% of the neurons in the brain (Moore, 1982), their effects are wide-spread and essential to the functioning of all neuronal systems. Biochemical studies reveal that unmyelinated axons containing the catecholamines dopamine and noradrenaline innervate the orbitofrontal cortex (Levitt, Rakic, & Goldman-Rakic, 1984), with a tendency of the former in the deep layers and the latter in superficial layers (Lewis, Foote, Goldstein, & Morrison, 1988; Lewis & Mor-

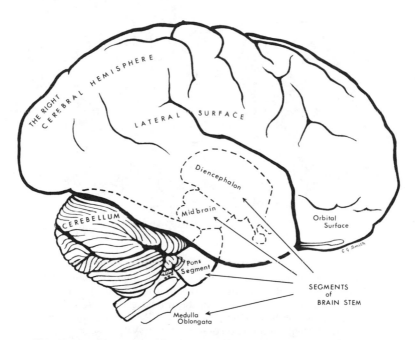

FIG. 4.10.   Relationships of brain stem structures to the orbital surface of the right hemisphere. From Smith (1981). Reprinted by permission of the publisher.

rison, 1989; Seguela, Watkins, & Descarries, 1988) (Fig. 4.11). Terminals of the two neuromodulators are, however, frequently intertwined (Fig. 4.12).

Orbitofrontal cortical columns receive a dense ipsilateral innervation of dopaminergic projections ascending from the A10 ventral tegmental (as opposed to A9 substantia nigral) area in the midbrain (Oades & Halliday, 1987; Porrino & Goldman-Rakic, 1982). These neurons produce the enzymes regulating catecholamine synthesis in their cell body in the brainstem and axonally transport these enzymes a great distance to nerve terminals at distal sites (Figs 4.9, 4.13 and 4.14). There is evidence to show that dopaminergic neurons in the ventral tegmental area of the midbrain project collaterals up the neuraxis to different forebrain areas (Fallon & Loughlin, 1982; Swanson, 1982). The same dopaminergic neuron, for example, innervates the septum and the prefrontal cortex, suggesting a mechanism of functional interrelation between different areas (Lindvall, Bjorklund, & Divac, 1977). The innervation of multiple neuronal regions at various levels of the brain by ascending collaterals of a single neuron has been found in other catecholami-

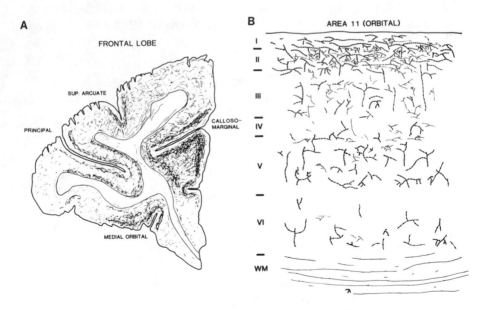

FIG. 4.11.   Schematic line drawing of the catecholamine innervation of the primate frontal lobe. (A) Frontal lobe. Note noradrenaline (heavier lines) and dopamine (thinner lines) axons in the orbital cortex. (B) Catecholamine axon termination in the orbital cortex. From Levitt, Rakic, and Goldman-Rakic (1984). Region-specific distribution of catecholamine afferents in primate cerebral cortex: A flourescence histochemical analysis. *Journal of Comparative Neurology, 227.* Reprinted by permission of Wiley-Liss, a division of John Wiley and Sons, Inc.

FIG. 4.12. (A) Dopamine terminals (arrows) are finer and have
smaller varicosities than noradrenaline terminals (asterisk)
in the orbital frontal cortex. (B)
Another example of delicate dopamine fibers intermixed with
thicker noradrenaline fibers in
the frontal cortex. From Levitt,
Rakic, and Goldman-Rakic
(1984). Region-specific distribution of catecholamine afferents
in primate cerebral cortex: A
fluorescence histochemical analysis. *Journal of Comparative
Neurology, 227.* Reprinted by
permission of Wiley-Liss, a division of John Wiley and Sons, Inc.

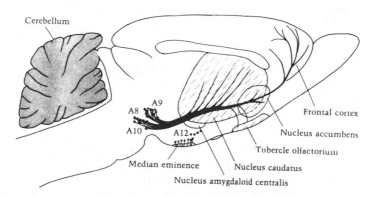

FIG. 4.13. Schematic of dopamine pathways of rat brain. Note position of A10 nucleus in the ventral tegmental area and its innervation of
the frontal cortex. From Bradford (1986); adapted from Ungerstedt
(1971). Reprinted by permission of the publisher.

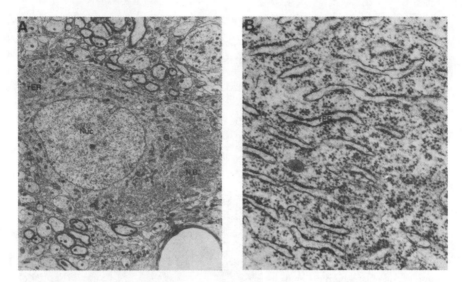

FIG. 4.14. (A) Electron micrograph of a dopamine cell in the ventral tegmental area. Note the large Nissl bodies (NB), rough endoplasmic reticulum (rER), Golgi apparatus (G), and indented nucleus (Nuc). (B) At higher magnification the Nissl bodies are seen as large blocks of well-stacked rER cisternae. Note densely distributed free ribosomes filling much of the cellular spaces. This configuration indicates that the dopamine neuron contains an extremely well-developed protein synthesis mechanism. Reprinted from Domesick, Stinus, and Paskevich (1983). The cytology of dopaminergic and nondopaminergic neurons in the substantia nigra and ventral tegmental area of the rat: A light- and electron-microscopic study. *Neuroscience, 8,* 743–765, with permission from Pergamon Press Ltd, Headington Hill Hall, Oxford OX3 OBW, UK.

nergic neuronal pathways (Steindler, 1981). This property of bioaminergic neurons has important implications for conceptions of brain functioning. It may account for Jackson's (1931) conception of the hierarchical organization of the horizontal levels of the brain, Luria's (1973) principles that the brain is "vertically organized" and that structural systems in the subcortex and brainstem maintain and regulate the tone of the cerebral cortex, and Changeux's model of the coordinated participation of distant subcortical and cortical domains at the "circuit level" of brain organization (Changeux & Dehaene, 1989).

The inclusion of the orbitofrontal region in the ventral tegmental dopaminergic circuit accounts for a number of its important functional properties. The prefrontal "mesocortical" dopamine system is now thought to be specifically associated with the cerebral circuitries of reward and emotionality (Thierry, Tassin, Blanc, & Glowinski, 1978), and mesolimbic dopamine release is a neurochemical correlate of the anticipation of reward (Willner & Scheel-Kruger, 1991). This dopaminergic circuit also supports locomotor and exploratory behavior (Fink & Smith, 1980), and is functionally involved in the initiation of movements to emotional or motivational stimuli (Vertes, 1990). Mesocortical circuits are selectively activated by separation stress (Blanc et al., 1980) and biochemically mediate the regulation of affective responses (Tassin, 1987). These dopaminergic-mediated functions match well with certain observed capacities of the orbitofrontal cortex. This cerebral region not only mediates motivational reward effects (Rolls & Cooper, 1974), it is responsive to changes in reward (Niki, Sakai, & Kubota, 1972), and is also involved in the pleasurable qualities of social interaction (Panksepp, Siviy, & Normansell, 1985). Ventral tegmental dopaminergic innervation has also been shown to be implicated in the major cognitive functional output of the orbital prefrontal cortex, the delayed response function, the cognitive operation that underlies representational processes (Simon, Scatton, & LeMoal, 1980).

In addition to this midbrain dopaminergic input, vagal projections from the reticular formation in the medulla oblongata (see Fig 4.10), a major component of the parasympathetic nervous system which is intimately involved in autonomic regulation, are also known to innervate the orbitofrontal cortex (Encabo & Ruarte, 1967). Korn, Wendt, and Albe-Fessard (1966) have demonstrated that interoceptive visceral information reaches the cortex via vagal inputs to orbital areas. Vagal innervation of the orbitofrontal cortex was demonstated by Bailey and Bremer (1938) over 50 years ago, and stimulation of the vagus nerve has been shown to trigger a cortical evoked response only in the orbitofrontal and adjacent insular areas (Aubert & Legros, 1970; Dell & Olsen, 1951; Hardstaff, Jagadeesh, & Newman, 1973; Korn & Massion, 1964). Electrical stimulation of the vagus nerve or the nucleus of the solitary tract has a synchronizing effect on forebrain EEG activity that long outlasts the stimulus (Kandel & Schwartz, 1985). Orbitofrontal "visceral sensory cortex" has been shown to interconnect with the vagal nucleus of the solitary tract, the medullary source of ascending gustatory and cardiopulmonary autonomic information to the cortical level (Saper, 1982). Cechetto and Saper (1987) have provided evidence to show that this cortex responds to visceral sensory stimuli, and refer to "the specific site in the orbitoinsular cortex responsible for mediating central autonomic manifestations of emotional behavior" (p. 43). The close integration of autonomic activity with emotional states was established in the early part of this century in the classical work of Cannon (Cannon & Britton, 1925). The essential role of feedback from bodily systems, especially facial and postural activity, into the cortex as a neurophysiological mechanism underlying the generation of emotion is a central concept in Izard's (1977) differential emotions theory.

A direct, long-pathway projection from the nucleus of the solitary tract in the hindbrain to forebrain structures (e.g., hypothalamus, amygdala) was first reported by Ricardo and Koh (1978). This pathway, subsequently shown by

Nosaka (1984) to transmit vagal visceral input to forebrain structures, was suggested to "convey ascending viscerosensory information to the 'visceral' forebrain structures, which upon receipt of the input, may regulate either endocrine or autonomic nervous functions" (p. 494). Nosaka, in agreement with Ricardo and Koh, has concluded that A2 catecholamine neurons in the solitary nucleus contribute to the noradrenergic pathway ascending to the forebrain (Fig. 4.15). These medullary neurons give rise to the fibers of the "ventral noradrenaline bundle' (Ungerstedt, 1971) (Fig. 4.9) or "ascending 'ventral' noradrenaline pathway" that passes through the ventral tegmental area and projects rostrally via the medial forebrain bundle (Schofield & Everitt, 1981). The visceral afferent nuclei of the solitary tract (Takahashi, Satoh, Sakumoto, Tohyama, & Shimizu, 1979; Thor & Helke, 1988) and most of the other structures in the core of the lower brainstem (Fritschy & Grzanna, 1990) have recently been shown to contain and to be innervated almost exclusively by these non-locus coeruleus noradrenergic neurons (Kalia, Fuxe, & Goldstein, 1985) (Figs. 4.16 and 4.17). These same monoaminergic neurons are known to be projected upon by vagal afferent fibers (Katz & Karten, 1979). Furthermore, such medullary catecholaminergic neurons are known to possess axon collaterals projecting to different parts of the forebrain (Nosaka, 1984), a property shared by A10 ventral tegmental dopaminergic and locus coeruleus A6 noradrenergic monoamine neurons. The primary function of these A2 neurons which target limbic structures is "to relay visceral information to forebrain sites involved in neuroendocrine and / or emotional control" (Vertes, 1990, p. 58). The nucleus of the solitary tract contains a gustatory zone populated by catecholaminergic neurons (Davis & Jang, 1988). Visceral regulation is a primary function of catecholamines (Coyle & Snyder, 1981).

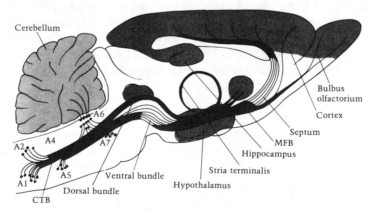

FIG. 4.15.   Schematic of noradrenaline pathways of rat brain. Note position of A2 nucleus in the medulla and the "ventral bundle." From Bradford (1986); adapted from Ungerstedt (1971). Reprinted by permission of the publisher.

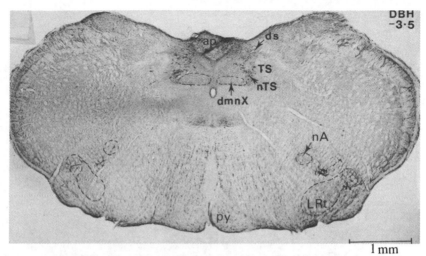

FIG. 4.16.   Low magnification photomicrograph of the rat medulla oblongata showing the location of noradrenergic neurons. Note positions of the nucleus of the solitary tract (nTS), area postrema (ap) and dorsal motor nucleus of the vagus (dmnX). From Kalia, Fuxe, and Goldstein (1985). Rat medulla oblongata. II. Dopaminergic, noradrenergic (A1 and A2) and adrenergic neurons, nerve fibers, and presumptive terminal processes. *Journal of Comparative Neurology, 233.* Reprinted by permission of Wiley-Liss, a division of John Wiley and Sons, Inc.

Thus a noradrenergic neuron in the deep brainstem which receives (Sumal, Blessing, Joh, Reis, & Pickel, 1983) (Fig. 4.18) and is excited by vagal input into its dendrites in the medulla projects its catecholamine releasing axons up the neuraxis into various parts of the forebrain, and this mechanism is proposed to account for the "vagal' innervation of the forebrain orbitofrontolimbic cortex. I propose that the "vagal projections" of the medullary reticular formation to the orbital undersurface of the cortex reflect the lateral tegmental (as opposed to the locus coeruleus dorsal tegmental) noradrenergic (Robbins & Everitt, 1982) innervation of sites in the orbital limbic cortex. I also suggest that medullary noradrenergic neurons are a primary source of the norepinephrine that is found in the deeper layers of the orbitofrontal cortex (Lewis & Morrison, 1989). It should be noted that although it has been established that medullary noradrenaline neurons (Halliday et al., 1988) innervate forebrain regions (Jones, Halaris, & Freedman, 1979), and it has been recently demonstrated both that relatively strong direct reticulocortical projections originate from lower medullary cell groups which are "probably catecholaminergic" (Newman & Liu, 1987) and that projections associated with the "laterodorsal tegmental" area reach the orbitofrontal cortex (Morecraft et al., 1992), a study investigating specific lateral tegmental innerva-

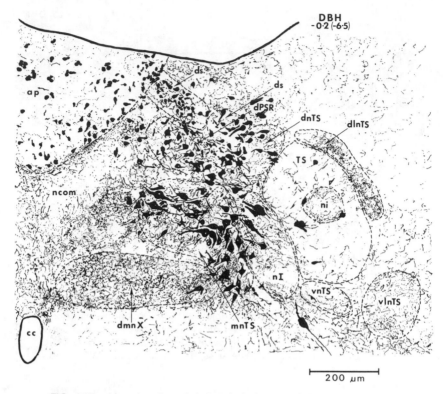

FIG. 4.17.   Line drawing of the exploded rat medulla. Noradrenaline neurons and fibers are shown in the dorsal (dnTS) and medial (mnTS) nucleus of the solitary tract and related structures. From Kalia, Fuxe, and Goldstein (1985). Rat medulla oblongata. II. Dopaminergic, noradrenergic (A1 and A2) and adrenergic neurons, nerve fibers, and presumptive terminal processes. *Journal of Comparative Neurology, 233.* Reprinted by permission of Wiley-Liss, a division of John Wiley and Sons, Inc.

tion of the immature or mature human orbitofrontal cortex, the cortical representation of the "visceral brain," has not, to the knowledge of this author, yet been done.

ORBITOFRONTAL INNERVATION OF SUBCORTICAL CATECHOLAMINERGIC NUCLEI

The orbitofrontal cortex, with its unique chemical neuroanatomy and dual catecholaminergic innervation, relays cortically processed information down to subcortical sites. It sends descending cholinergic projections directly to the amyg-

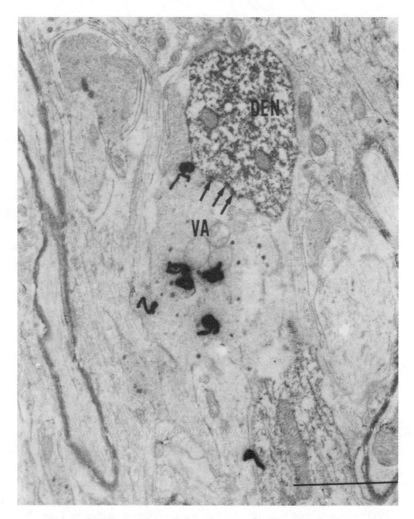

FIG. 4.18.   Synapse between a vagal axon (VA) and a dendrite (DEN) of a catecholamine neuron in the rat solitary nucleus tract. From Sumal et al. (1983). Reprinted by permission of Elsevier.

daloid central nucleus, the septal region, the lateral hypothalamus, and most significantly, to the ventral tegmental area (Kita & Oomura, 1981; Nauta, 1964; Saper, 1982). In very recent work, Sesack and Pickel (1992) have demonstrated that the prefrontal cortex, including the medial orbital cortex, provides direct, monosynaptic input into dopaminergic neurons in the rostral ventral tegmental area of the midbrain (see Fig. 4.19). This cortex also sends direct projections to the nucleus of the solitary tract in the medulla (Reep & Winans, 1982; Saper,

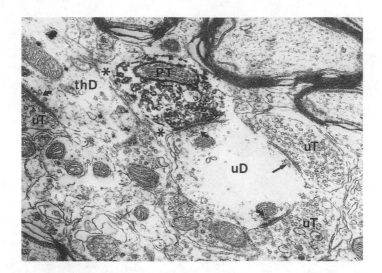

FIG. 4.19. Electron micrograph of a synapse between a prefrontal terminal (PT) and a dendrite (uD) of a dopamine neuron in the rostral ventral tegmental area. From Sesack and Pickel (1992). Prefrontal cortical efferents in the rat synapse on unlabeled neuronal targets of catecholamine terminals in the nucleus accumbens septi and on dopamine neurons in the ventral tegmental area. *Journal of Comparative Neurology, 320.* Reprinted by permission of Wiley-Liss, a division of John Wiley and Sons, Inc.

1982; Shipley 1982; van der Kooy et al., 1982,1984; Yasui, Itoh, Kaneko, Shigemoto, & Mizuno, 1991), the first relay center of the autonomic nervous system in the CNS (see Fig. 4.20). The medullary vagus complex receives sensory projections from various visceral organs (Kalia & Mesulam, 1980). Orbital-medullary connections may thus be involved in the mechanism by which the frontolimbic cortex maintains surveillance over the viscera. Indeed Yasui et al. (1991) now conclude that the orbital cortex subserves a feedback mechanism for controlling or modulating visceral inputs. Orbitofrontal cortex has been characterized as an inhibitory area of respiratory movement and gastric motility, and as a control area of blood pressure, circulatory, and cardiovascular function (Babkin & Kite, 1950; Bailey & Sweet, 1940; Fuster, 1980; Kaada et al., 1949; Sachs, Brendler, & Fulton, 1949). The contribution of visceral sensations as well as respiratory and circulatory alterations to the experience of emotion was emphasized in the last century by William James (1922) and continued in the works of Wenger (1950) and Gasanov (1974).

The direct projections from the orbitofrontal cortex down to the two catecholaminergic nuclei mediate an important mechanism by which this cortex regulates subcortical structures. Mizuno, Sauerland, and Clemente (1968) have

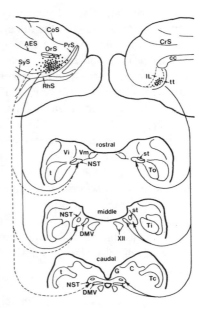

FIG. 4.20. Schematic of direct cerebral projections from the orbital gyrus (OrG) and infralimbic cortex (IL) to the nucleus of the solitary tract (NST) and the dorsal motor nucleus of the vagal nerve (DMV) in the cat medulla. From Yasui et al. (1991). Reprinted by permission of Springer-Verlag.

identified fibers originating in the orbitofrontal cortical region that project to sites in the midbrain and sites in the medullary reticular area in the brain stem, and postulate these perform a cortical suppression of subcortical activity. These orbitofrontal descending projections may specifically mediate the phenomenon of response suppression by a generally acting cholinergic inhibitory mechanism described by Carlton (1969), and may be instrumental to the orbital prefrontal inhibition of subcortical drive, modulation of the reticular formation, regulation of body states, and involvement in affective processes described by Luria. Mesulam and Mufson (1982) now conclude that this paralimbic structure may act as a cortical system that is specialized to regulate autonomic responses to affective cues, according to the prevailing mental state.

ORBITOFRONTAL HIERARCHICAL DOMINANCE
OF DUAL LIMBIC CIRCUITS

Based on his extensive neuroanatomical studies of the limbic system, the neuroanatomist H.J. Nauta now proposes the existence of two limbic forebrain-midbrain circuits, one associated with the dopaminergic ventral tegmental area, and a second with the lateral tegmental area (Nauta & Domesick, 1982). The latter is in "close afferent relationship with the vagus nerve" (p.199). I would speculate that these two catecholaminergic structural systems are associated with the respective dual excitatory and inhibitory functional mechanisms of the limbic system (Stellar, 1982). The ventral tegmental circuit, which originates in A10 dopaminergic neurons in the midbrain, represents an energy-expending component of the sympathetic nervous system. The lateral tegmental circuit, which originates in A2 noradrenergic neurons in the medulla and courses along the ventral noradrenergic bundle, represents an energy-conserving component of the parasympathetic nervous system. The emotion-regulating orbitofrontal cortex is structurally a region in which dopaminergic and noradrenergic fibers are "densely intertwined" (Oades & Halliday, 1987), and functionally a site of convergence of limbic and autonomic connections (Saper, 1982). Anatomical research reveals that the distribution of neurons in the prefrontal cortex, which provides direct connections with the medullary solitary nucleus, overlaps and matches the distribution of the mesocortical dopamine system (van der Kooy et al., 1984). This cortical structure, which influences both sympathetic and parasympathetic activities (Fuster, 1980), is posited to be densely interconnected into these two systems. In fact, this frontolimbic cortex, which represents the apex of the hierarchy of control of autonomic functions (Pribram, 1981), hierachically dominates both limbic circuits.

Each limbic circuit contains a subcortically ascending catecholaminergic element and a cortically descending cholinergic element. I cite evidence later suggesting that in a catecholaminergic-cholinergic circuit the catecholaminergic wiring develops earlier than the cholinergic. Upon completion of development, the two are linked in a closed circuit, and the operation of this subcortical-cortical loop sustains emergent functions. The inceptive event in the creation of these circuits is the maturation of the catecholaminergic innervation of various brain regions. This maturation is reflected in elevated levels of dopamine and noradrenaline and is known to occur primarily in infancy (Herregodts et al., 1990). The most dramatic shifts take place in prefrontal association areas, where both catecholamines increase more gradually than in other cortical areas, corresponding to the more protracted development of prefrontal function (Johnston, 1985). A developmental neurochemistry study by Goldman-Rakic and Brown (1982) indicates that in early postnatal periods prefrontal dopamine levels are higher than noradrenaline, while in late infancy this reverses. A similar early precedence of dopamine over noradrenaline activity in the early postnatal development of the cortex is reported by Von Hungen, Roberts, and Hill (1974). These data suggest an earlier regional maturation of this bioamine, and imply that the ventral tegmental limbic circuit matures earlier than the lateral tegmental.

ORBITOFRONTAL DEVELOPMENT IN HUMAN INFANCY

I propose that the growth, maturation and functional onset of this prefrontal psychobiological structure underlies the emergent psychological affect regulatory function which evolves in the critical period of primary socialization of infancy, the practicing period (10–12 to 16–18 months). The early postnatal growth of the orbitofrontal area, a region known to be involved in homeostatic regulation and attachment functions, is particularly active in the right cerebral hemisphere (Figs. 4.21, 4.22, and 4.23), the hemisphere that is thought to contribute to the develoment of reciprocal interactions within the mother-infant regulatory system (Taylor, 1987). The frontal pole is larger in the human right hemisphere (Weinberger et al., 1982; Weis et al., 1989) and the dense specific interconnections between the orbitofrontal regions of this cortex and the subcortex accounts for the unique properties of this hemisphere. Indeed, it has been suggested that the intimate involvement of the right hemisphcre in emotional functioning is due to its extensive interconnections with subcortical structures (Joseph, 1982). This hemisphere specializes in the processing of social-emotional information (Hellige, 1990), and maintain controls over the autonomic (Heilman, Schwartz, & Watson, 1977) and endocrinological (Wittling & Pfluger, 1990) activities that

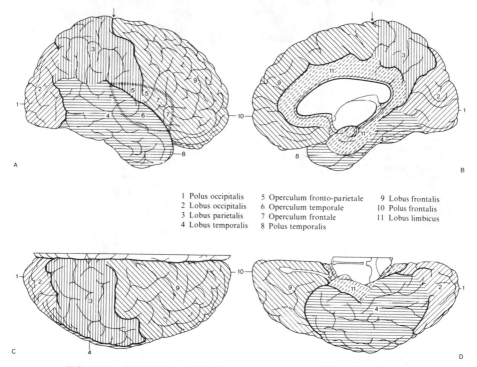

1 Polus occipitalis	5 Operculum fronto-parietale	9 Lobus frontalis
2 Lobus occipitalis	6 Operculum temporale	10 Polus frontalis
3 Lobus parietalis	7 Operculum frontale	11 Lobus limbicus
4 Lobus temporalis	8 Polus temporalis	

FIG. 4.21. Subdivision of the human right cerebral hemisphere into lobes. (A) Lateral view. (B) Medial view. (C) Superior view (C) Inferior view. From Nieuwenhuys et al. (1981). Reprinted by permission of Springer-Verlag.

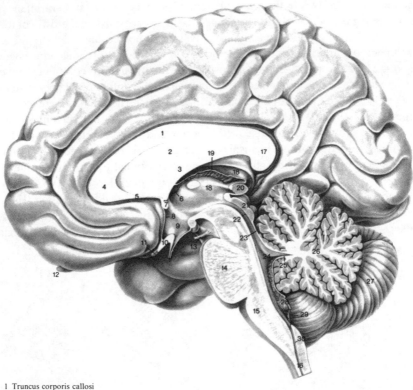

1 Truncus corporis callosi	
2 Septum pellucidum	
3 Fornix	
4 Genu corporis callosi	17 Splenium corporis callosi
5 Rostrum corporis callosi	18 Thalamus
6 Foramen interventriculare	19 Tela choroidea ventriculi tertii
7 Commissura anterior	20 Corpus pineale
8 Lamina terminalis	21 Lamina quadrigemina
9 Hypothalamus	22 Aqueductus cerebri
10 Chiasma opticum	23 Velum medullare superius
11 Nervus opticus	24 Ventriculus quartus
12 Bulbus olfactorius	25 Velum medullare inferius
13 Nervus oculomotorius	26 Vermis cerebelli
14 Pons	27 Hemisphaerium cerebelli
15 Medulla oblongata	28 Tela choroidea ventriculi quarti
16 Medulla spinalis	29 Apertura mediana ventriculi quarti
	30 Canalis centralis

FIG. 4.22. Medial view of the bisected right half of the human brain. Note the position of the hypothalamus (9), pons (14), and medulla (15). From Nieuwenhuys et al. (1981). Reprinted by permission of Springer-Verlag.

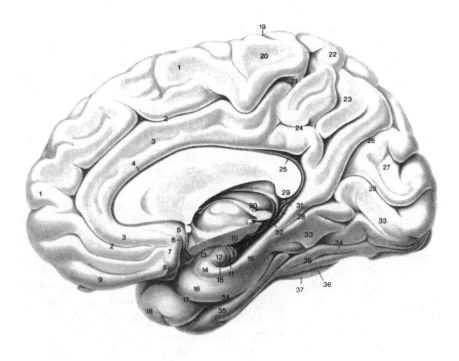

1 Gyrus frontalis superior	19 Sulcus centralis
2 Sulcus cinguli	20 Lobulus paracentralis
3 Gyrus cinguli	21 Sulcus cinguli, pars marginalis
4 Sulcus corporis callosi	22 Lobulus parietalis superior
5 Gyrus par.terminalis	23 Praecuneus
6 Sulcus parolfactorius posterior	24 Sulcus subparietalis
7 Area subcallosa	25 Indusium griseum
8 Sulcus parolfactorius anterior	26 Sulcus parieto-occipitalis
9 Gyrus rectus	27 Cuneus
10 Gyrus intralimbicus	28 Sulcus calcarinus
11 Limbus Giacomini } Uncus	29 Gyrus fasciolaris
12 Gyrus uncinatus	30 Taenia thalami
13 Gyrus semilunaris	31 Isthmus gyri cinguli
14 Gyrus ambiens	32 Gyrus dentatus
15 Incisura unci	33 Gyrus occipitotemporalis medialis
16 Gyrus parahippocampalis	34 Sulcus collateralis
17 Sulcus rhinalis	35 Gyrus occipitotemporalis lateralis
18 Gyrus temporalis superior	36 Sulcus occipitotemporalis
	37 Gyrus temporalis inferior

FIG. 4.23.   Medial aspects of the human cerebral right hemisphere. From Nieuwenhuys et al. (1981). Reprinted by permission of Springer-Verlag.

underlie emotional functions. I present evidence to show that just as the postnatal growth of posterior cortical neural networks underlying developing visual capacity requires appropriate forms of visual stimulation during a critical period (Hubel & Wiesel, 1970; Bronson, 1974), the postnatal emergence of anterior cortical neuronal systems mediating affective processing also requires adequate caregiver-provided intensity and variety of affective stimulation during a time-window of plasticity in early postnatal development. In other words, the mother's role as a selfobject, as a provider of modulated affect, is essential to the development of the child's internal affect regulating system.

In recent work on the neuropsychology of cortical networks and developing emotion, Tucker (1992) proposes that "in early development the factors influencing the child's emotional state will also influence the state of cortical plasticity" (p. 118). Watt (1986), a psychoanalytic theoretician, has recently proposed that prefrontal corticolimbic connections which regulate emotion are "assimilated through experience." Plutchik (1983) asserts that the typical pattern of emotional behavior appears in a certain time sequence in infants and only in an "average, expectable environment." This "average environment" may represent the affective stimulation and modulation provided by the "good-enough mother" (Winnicott, 1966). Even more specifically, in future chapters I argue that the onset of the self-regulation of affect—the orbitofrontal modulation of subcortical activity—is dependent upon different types of critical social-affective stimulation experiences during the early and late phases of the practicing period, 10–12 to 16–18 months.

The psychoneurobiological mechanism underlying this phenomenon may be revealed in studies of environmentally induced brain changes in early experience, which show postnatal "experience-sensitive synaptic plasticity" (Greenough, 1986), and which demonstrate neurons will fully develop only in the presence of adequate amounts of stimulation, that is, under optimal levels of arousal (Cummins, Livesy, Evans, & Walsh, 1977). This, in turn, may reflect the finding in developmental neurobiology that the final stage of neuronal maturation, growth and differentiation, is contingent upon stimulation. Sensory stimulation is required for the maturation of neuronal circuits, and failure of neural maturation is known to occur after sensory deprivation (Jacobson, 1978). Adequate levels of sensory stimulation may be most important to the postnatal maturation of the reticular formation (Yakovlev & Lecours, 1967) and brainstem catecholaminergic neurons (e.g., Nakamura, Kimura, & Sakaguchi, 1987), and therefore of energy-generating catecholaminergic neuronal systems which regulate arousal functions. Catecholamines are known to play an important role in the responsiveness of brain structures to environmental stimulation (Pettigrew & Kasamatsu, 1978).

It is now accepted that there are specific postnatal critical periods and developmental sequences for the appearance of the biogenic amines dopamine and noradrenaline which are responsible for different types of arousal (Jonsson &

Kasamatsu, 1983; Meyersburg & Post, 1979). Optimal levels of stimulation during critical periods thus are required to support the expansion of the circuitry of the biological hardware of arousal, that is, of the bioaminergic "reticular" systems (both medullary and pontine-mesencephalic) which are in an intense state of active growth at this time and whose neurochemical activity is responsible for arousal. Central catecholaminergic neurons undergo an accelerated development in mammalian infancy (Loizou, 1972). These periods are also a time when regional catecholaminergic receptors are amplified (Hartley & Seeman, 1983). The experience-dependent expansion and contraction of particular monoaminergic neuronal systems in specific brain regions is proposed to be a central force which drives brain development and consequent ontogenetic transformations of function. The functional consequence of this process in the orbitofrontal cortex could account for the observation that the infant's ability to tolerate higher levels of arousal and stimulation increases during infancy (Field, 1985a; Fogel, 1982).

5 Overview

The premier developmental question is, of course, the nature of the transition from one developmental stage to another—the emergence of new forms. How does a system retain continuity and yet produce discontinuous manifestations?

—Esther Thelen (1989)

I define science as the organization of our knowledge in such a way that it commands more of the hidden potential in nature.

—Jacob Bronowski (1972)

With this introductory presentation of some of the more recent work on the psychology and neurobiology of emotion in mind, the overarching purpose of the following interdisciplinary theoretical research is to propose a psychoneurobiological model of the ontogeny of emotional self-regulation. The central thesis of this book is that the early social environment, mediated by the primary caregiver, directly influences the evolution of structures in the brain that are responsible for the future socioemotional development of the child. I present evidence to show that progressively more complex affect transacting object relations between the developing infant and the changing socioemotional environment occur over the stages of infancy. The resulting variety of dyadic affective interactions between the caregiver and the infant is imprinted into the child's developing nervous system. Different types of stimulation are embedded in these "hidden" socioaffective interactions, and they elicit distinctive psychobiological patterns in the child. In response to such socioenvironmental experiences, hormonal and neurohormonal responses are triggered, and these physiological alterations are registered within specific areas of the infant's brain which are undergoing a structural maturation during a sensitive period. At the end of the first and through the middle of the second year these psychoneuroendocrinological phenomena are particularly important to the maturation of frontolimbic regions, since these areas, especially in the early developing right hemisphere, are in a state of active growth at this time. The object relational-induced release of growth-promoting (trophic) biogenic amines and neurohormones allows for the experience-dependent critical period growth of connections between subcortical and cortical structural components which neuroanatomically mediate the regulation and expression of emotion.

I further propose that despite the changes in object relations over the stages of infancy, the mother's constant selfobject role as an external regulator of the child's internal affective state is essential in providing the infant's limited nervous system with the modulated stimulation that optimally enhances the growth of its own affect regulating structure. Her active involvement in affective transactions with the infant allows for the internalization of this maternal function, that is, she directly influences the growth and assembly of brain structural systems in the child that perform self-regulatory functions. Experiences with an affect regulating caregiver are generated and stored in these structures. Such enduring prototypical interactive representations can be accessed and regenerated in the future in order to regulate the psychobiological energy transformations associated with discrete affective states, even in the mother's absence. This emergent adaptive function essentially mediates the individual's interpersonal and intrapersonal processes throughout the lifespan. The adaptive capacity to efficiently self-regulate affect thus evolves only in specific early critical periods and in particular environments.

This psychoneurobiological developmental model views the brain as a self-organizing system (Singer, 1986a). It also fits particularly well with a number of essential tenets of nonlinear dynamic systems (chaos) theory. This powerful model is now being utilized in physics, chemistry, and biology to explore the problem of how complex systems come to produce emergent order and new forms. In an innovative exposition of a systems approach to developmental processes, Thelen (1989) asserts that the behavior of a multicomponent, complex system is dynamically assembled as a product of the interactions of the elements in a particular context. A fundamental postulate of this conception is that there is no dichotomy between the organism and the environmental context in which it develops. The physical and social context of the developing human is more than merely a supporting frame, it is an essential substratum of the assembling system. Of particular importance to chaos theory are the transitions from one developmental stage to another, when the organism encounters instability while it shifts from one stable mode to a new mode. Ontogenetic change represents the reorganization of components to meet adaptive tasks. The result of adaptive self-organization is a fundamental property of hierarchically structured biological systems—the capacity to evolve toward a state of higher organization. Self-organization is thus defined as the emergence of pattern and order from the process of the interactions of the components of a complex system. Thelen suggests that in the application of systems principles to the question of development, there ultimately should be an integration of the different levels of description, that the dynamics at the neural level should be coupled to the dynamics at the behavioral level.

The methodology of the theoretical research presented in this book involves the integration of current developmental observations, data, and concepts from various fields that are studying the problem of socioaffective ontogeny—neurobiology, behavioral neurology, evolutionary biology, sociobiology, social psychology, developmental psychology, developmental psychoanalysis, and infant psychiatry. A special emphasis is placed on the application and integration of current developmental data from neurochemistry, neuroanatomy, neuropsychology, and psychoendocrinology into the main body of developmental theory. In contrast to reductionism, this approach is guided by the tenet that:

> Developmental progress can only be explained by studying it simultaneously along several separate but interrelated dimensions ranging from the biological level of organization through the social and cultural-historical levels to the outside physical world. (Hopkins & Butterworth, 1990, p. 22)

In this "decade of the brain" researchers and theoreticians are now appreciating the absolute necessity of utilizing a multilevel integrative approach in studying "social neuroscience" (Cacioppo & Berntson, 1992) and "affective neuroscience" (Panksepp, 1991) phenomena. To my mind, the frontiers of science lie in the borderland between the separate fields of science. The answers to various major unexplained questions about the nature of living systems may be found in the elucidation of the interconnections between the different levels of analysis that are represented in the various scientific disciplines. It is my purpose to show not just that there are commonalities between different fields of study, but that exploring and charting the linking conceptual pathways between them can yield exciting and revealing insights. In light of the fact that the events that characterize the beginnings of living systems uniquely influence all aspects of later life, the essential nature and yet unsolved vital problems of human existence may be more profitably explored by studying the developing human child rather than the completely formed human adult. Although it may appear too obvious and elementary to be a fundamental tenet of human biology, the primordial environment of the infant, or more properly of the commutual psychobiological environment shared by the infant and mother, represents a primal terra incognita of science.

In the course of this book, a sizeable number of studies are presented, not for the sole purpose of an up-to-date review of various literatures, but also as a multidisciplinary source pool of experimental data, theoretical concepts, and observations from which to attempt to begin to frame an overarching heuristic model of socioemotional development which is grounded in contemporary neuroscience. Throughout, I shall attempt to clearly differentiate the presentation of experimental results from the generation of hypothetical models which are based on the extrapolation or linkages between these results. Because different fields utilize their own unique terminology to characterize very similar developmental phenomena, I will try to provide a common language of the most agreed upon and precise concepts shared by various developmental disciplines. I should also mention that the reader will soon observe that some chapters are more heavily laden with information gleaned mostly from a particular discipline, one that may differ from the reader's. Since each chapter contains an introductory overview and a summary of its cardinal points the reader could just refer to these instead of examining a more in-depth presentation of the details of the current findings of a field which appears to be beyond his or her area of interest. I am well aware that on the surface there appears to be an impassable gulf between say, neurochemistry and psychoanalysis. However, a primary goal of this type of integrative theoretical research is to exhort the reader to venture beyond the familiar boundaries of his or her own discipline.

To this point I have presented a review of advances in the conceptualization of socioemotional development and a characterization of the structure and properties of a brain region that matures in infancy which is critically involved in the child's emerging capacities for affect regulation and social behavior. Using these principles as a springboard, in the second part of the book I present evidence to support the proposal that the maturation of this cortical area begins in a specific critical period which commences at the end of the first year of human infancy. It is hypothesized that maternal regulated high intensity socioaffective stimulation provided in the ontogenetic niche, specifically occurring in dyadic psychobiologically attuned, arousal-amplifying, face-to-face reciprocal gaze transactions, generates and sustains positive affect in the dyad. These transactions induce particular neuroendocrine changes which facilitate the expansive innervation of deep sites in orbitofrontal areas, especially in the early maturing visuospatial right hemisphere, of ascending subcortical axons of a neurochemical circuit of the limbic system—the sympathetic ventral tegmental limbic circuit. This imprinting experience initiates the maturation of a frontolimbic excitatory system that is responsible for the ontogenetic adaptations in the inceptive phase of the practicing critical period—behavioral hyperactivity, high levels of positive affect and play behavior, and subsequently the establishment of the capacity to form an interactive representational model that underlies an early functional system of affect regulation.

Part III of the volume focuses on events in late infancy. Evidence is presented to support the hypothesis that an ensuing significant change in the ontogenetic niche occurs in the second year with the onset of socialization procedures. The 14-to 16-month-old infant's psychobiological response to such stressful socializing transactions is frequently a state of hypoarousal. These stage-typical stress states, accompanied by a different pattern of psychoneuroendocrine alterations, serve as an optimal socioaffective stimulus for the expansion of the other limbic circuit, the parasympathetic lateral tegmental limbic circuit. The experience-dependent wiring of this circuit into the orbitofrontal cortex allows for the emergence of an efficient and adaptive inhibitory system. A competition between the sympathetic and parasympathetic limbic circuits underlies a parcellation process that produces a mature differentiated orbitofrontal system at about 18 months, the end of the critical period. This reorganization is responsible for a loss of the earlier ontogenetic adaptations, and the emergence of more complex representational and more efficient affect regulatory functions.

Following these sections of basic theoretical research, later chapters are devoted to the application of this developmental model to a number of current areas of inquiry. Part IV outlines the essential role of affect regulation in a number of phenomena—the dynamics of internal representations, the influence of psychological factors on the operations of the autonomic nervous system, the modulation of rage reactions, and the interactive genesis of early moral development. In Part IV I also present a comprehensive theory of affect, a psychoneurobiological model of the processing of socioemotional information. In Part V I apply the developmental model to a number of clinical issues—the neurobiology of insecure attachments, the clinical psychiatry of disorders of affect regulation, the developmental psychopathology of borderline and narcissistic personality disturbances, the etiology of psychosomatic disease, and the articulation of various principles of psychotherapy of developmental disorders. In the final section, Part VI, I integrate the developmental data from a number of disciplines to stress the importance of early forming right hemispheric language and to propose a theory of self-functioning and the dyadic origin of consciousness. I then utilize data from various levels of analysis, from the molecular through the organismic, to present an overarching conceptualization of development. Finally, I argue that in order to penetrate certain essential questions of human existence it is now expedient and indeed obligatory to forge a rapprochement between psychoanalysis and the other sciences.

In essence, this entire volume is fundamentally an account of the experience-dependent development of the corticolimbic system and the emotional, cognitive, and behavioral advances that result from its maturation. A particular focus is on its role in the ontogenetic expression of psychobiological states and primitive affects. This work also highlights and emphasizes the essential contribution of the experience-dependent maturation of the nondominant right hemipshere to the origins of socioemotional functioning. This hemisphere, although often viewed as *more primitive* than the linguistic left, is actually more essentially involved in the fundamental capacities that define a human self. I show that the development of a capacity to self-regulate psychobiological state transitions parallels the primary caregiver-influenced maturation of the right cortex, and that the understanding of its developing structure-function relationships in the first 2 years of human life can offer penetrating insights into a host of psychobiological affect-driven human phenomena, from the motive force that drives human attachment to the proximal causes of later forming psychiatric disturbance and psychosomatic disorders, and indeed to the origin of the self.

II EARLY INFANCY

6 Visual Experiences and Socioemotional Development

> *The most significant relevant basic interactions between mother and child usually lie in the visual area: The child's bodily display is responded to by the gleam in the mother's eye.*
>
> —Heinz Kohut (1971)

The maturation of the orbitofrontal region, the cerebral cortical structure involved in the regulation of subcortically generated affect, is experience-dependent. This "experience" is specifically affective, or more properly socio-affective, since it is embedded in stimulation provided in the relationship between the primary caregiver and the child. An essential question is therefore precisely what kinds of early stimulation are required for the maturation of affect systems in which specific critical periods? The infant is now conceptualized to be more of a sensoriaffective than a sensorimotor being (Stechler & Carpenter, 1967), and researchers are currently emphasizing the central role of affect in development (Demos, 1988). Emde and Gaensbauer (1981) point out that "all meaningful social relationships are seen to be *affective* " (p. 581; my emphasis).

In this chapter I present multidisciplinary evidence to demonstrate that a particular type of visual information which conveys the primary caregiver's affective response to the infant is critical to the progression of socioemotional development. In sustained mutual gaze transactions, the mother's facial expression stimulates and amplifies positive affect in the infant. The child's internally pleasurable state is communicated back to the mother, and in this interactive system of reciprocal stimulation both members of the dyad enter into a symbiotic state of heightened positive affect. This psychoneurobiological mechanism is essential to an imprinting phenomenon in the child's developing right hemi-

71

sphere, thereby enabling the maturation of limbic areas in this cortex that are involved in socioemotional functions.

THE MOTHER'S FACE AS A PRIMARY SOURCE OF VISUAL STIMULATION

The critical import of visual stimulation to socioemotional development has been stressed by workers in various fields. The salience of the visual information specifically provided by the mother's face is explained by the observations that infants have a fixed accommodative system in which objects that are about 10 inches away are most clearly in focus (Haynes, White, & Held, 1965), and that mother's tend to hold their infants approximately 8 to 10 inches away from themselves (Papousek & Papousek, 1979). In parallel to this, the activity of the infant's eyes is a potent inducer of the forms of maternal behavior that eventuate in an appropriate mother-infant bond (Freedman, 1981). Researchers have found that extremely long gazing periods on the part of the mother towards her infant are a common occurrence (Stern, 1974) and that the infant's gaze reliably evokes mother's gaze (Messer & Vietz, 1984). Sustained facial gazing mediates the most intense form of interpersonal communication (Tomkins, 1963). Spitz (1958) refers to the importance of visual systems functioning in the "dialogue between mother and child." It is now well established that eye-to-eye contact gives nonverbal advance notice of the other (Riess, 1978), and that the temporal structure of gaze, the most immediate and purest form of interrelation, provides clues to the readiness or capacity to receive and produce social information. The visual perception of facial expressions has been shown to be the most salient channel of nonverbal communication (Izard, 1971), and visual modes of communication that precede vocal modes of mutual communication (Schaffer, 1984) are dominant in the forging of preverbal affective ties in the first year of life. These observations may be explained by Conel's (1955) conclusion that the primacy of vision at this time is due to the more advanced maturation of cortical visual over auditory areas at the end of the first year.

Studies of facial-visual signaling in early social development reveal that the maternal face acts as a potent stimulus in the infant's environment (Stern, 1974) and stress the role of eye-to-eye contact on the development of maternal-infant attachment (Robson, 1967). The child's intense interest in her mother's face leads the infant to track it in space (Izard, 1991). Research on face scanning indicates infants are most sensitive to facial affective expressions in which specifically the eyes vary the most (Haith, Bergman, & Moore, 1979). After the second month (the onset of Mahler's symbiotic period), fixation on the mother's eyes increases (Maurer & Salapatek, 1976), and at 17 weeks the eyes are a more salient feature of the mother's face than her mouth (Caron, Caron, Caldwell, & Weiss, 1973). By 2 to 3 months the infant's smile can be induced by a full-faced presentation and a pair of circles painted on a balloon, and can be extinguished by turning of the head so as to present a profile in which the representations of the eyes are eliminated (Spitz, 1965). Sherrod (1981) emphasizes that a particularly animated part of the face, the eyes, draws the infant's attention, thereby setting the stage for the mutual visual regard which mediates social relations. Kohut (1971) refers to the infant-energizing effects of the "gleam" in the mother's eye.

The work of Hess (1975) on the critical nature of pupil size in nonverbal communication may reveal the specific dynamics of mutual gaze and may elucidate the mechanism by which the social environment operates to generate and amplify infant affect. In a series of studies, Hess found that one person uses another's pupil size as a source of information about that person's feelings or attitudes; this process usually occurs at unconscious levels. Dilated pupils occur in states of pleasure and are an indicator of "interest." For example, his experiments showed that women's eyes dilate in response to a picture of a baby (Hess, 1965). Most importantly, Hess discovered that viewing enlarged dilated pupils rapidly elicits larger pupils in the observer. In a developmental study, infants smiled more when a female experimenter's eyes were dilated rather than constricted, suggesting that large pupils act as a "releaser" in infants, triggering a response that is "learned early in life." He also observed that large pupils in the infant release caregiver behavior.

Subsequent developmental research has demonstrated that gaze is a critical regulator of arousal in infant-mother interactions (Brazelton, Koslowski, & Main, 1974; Stern, 1974) and that that the sight of her infant is physiologically arousing to the mother (Wiesenfeld & Klorman, 1978). Adult studies have shown that gaze patterns, which have been conceptualized as external indicants of internal states, trigger physiological arousal, as reflected in EEG changes (Gale, Lucas, Nissim, & Harpham, 1972), and produce alterations in the physiology of another (Mazur et al., 1980). Gaze patterns may act as a "hidden regulator" (Hofer, 1984a) of arousal throughout the lifespan, and may underlie Zajonc's (1965) "social facilitation" effect in which the presence of or observation by another elevates nonspecific physiological arousal levels. Recent psychophysiological studies demonstrate that "mere observation," being the focus of attention of a conspecific, elevates physiological reactivity to environmental changes (Cacioppo, Rourke, Marshall-Goodell, Tassinary, & Baron, 1990).

With respect to Hess' idea that gazing dilated pupils elicits pupillary changes associated with pleasure and interest in the viewer, Tomkins (1962) refers to the facial expressions of the positive affect of interest-excitement, in which the eyebrows are down and the stare fixed on an object or tracking it (Fig. 6.1). Izard (1979) describes the facial indicators of the positive affect of interest in the infant to include eyes (like the mother's) that are widened and rounded. Demos (1988) equates this with a state of alert inactivity in which the eyes are open and have a "bright shiny appearance." Similarly, Brazelton and Cramer (1990) observe an

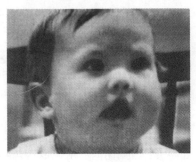

FIG. 6.1. The facial expression of interest in a young infant. From Izard (1991). *The psychology of emotions.* Reprinted by permission of Plenum Press.

awake, alert state, in which the infant's face is inactive, with eyes that are "bright and shining." (In contrast, infants exposed to a non-affectively expressive maternal face, one with no "brightness" in the mother's eyes, express negative affect; Tronick, Ricks, & Cohn, 1982.)

The gleam in the mother's eye thus triggers dilation of the infant's pupils. What psychobiological mechanism could account for this? Pupillary dilation, a central indicator of brain activation, is regulated by sympathetic centers in the hypothalamus (Truex & Carpenter, 1964), as opposed to pupillary constriction which is mediated by parasympathetic centers. The iris muscles, an involuntary muscle system that contains both dilator and constrictor fibers, control the diameter of the pupil (Smith, 1960). Variations in pupillary diameter can produce up to 5-fold changes in the amount of light reaching the retina (Ganong, 1973), and during interactive gaze the mother's facial expression is frequently exaggerated, with the eyes as wide open as possible (Stern, 1977, p. 19). The maternal gleam, a manifestation of the mother's attention-focusing behavior reflecting heightened interest in her infant, may literally be a sparkle, that is, a flash of light processed by and reflected off of the mother's hyper-exposed foveal area of the retina and on to the infant's fovea. Mahler et al. (1975) propose that the mother serves as a "beacon of orientation." In recent conceptualizations, attention has been likened to a "spotlight" (Posner, 1980), and the gleam in the mother's eyes may be isomorphic to the child's activation of her "internal attentional searchlight" (Crick, 1984). This attentional searchlight, activated in the mother's selective attention to the child's pupils, evokes the "brightness" in the child's eyes. In other words her interest kindles his interest. Indeed, optic system structure-function relationships may provide a neurophysiological basis for this "hidden" phenomenon. It is known that "ideoretinal light" represents excitations of optic neurons arising from within the retina without benefit of light from the external world (Horowitz, 1983).

Interestingly, visual flicker producing receptive changes in illumination on the infant's retina has been shown to be a stimulus for imprinting in an early critical period (James, 1960). Electroencephalographic studies have revealed that brief flashes of light produce larger average evoked potentials over the infant's visuo-spatial right (rather than left) hemisphere (Hahn, 1987). Ekman (1993) describes the adaptive value of rapidly transmitted *momentary* facial expressions, so named

> because the information they convey about an emotion can be captured in an instant. Typically, such expressions last a few seconds, but a single frame. A snapshot taken at any point when the expression is at its apex can easily convey the emotion message. (p. 399)

Livingston (1967), in an article on the mechanism of reinforcement, refers to a "Now Print!" mechanism that neuropsychologically preserves a photographic image of a critical event in the brain.

> Following 'Now print!' order, everything that has been ongoing in the recent past will receive a 'Now print!' contribution in the form of a growth stimulus or a neurohormonal influence that will favor future repetitions of the same neural activities. (p. 576)

Early imprinting experiences may represent inceptive "Now Print!" events that are registered in the right cortex. Even more intriguingly, these face-to-face transactions may be registered in long-term memory as inceptive "flashbulb memories" (Brown & Kulik, 1977). According to these authors such memories label events that are consequential for the individual by creating highly visual and detailed remembrances of an important experience. Flashbulb memories occur during high arousal states, and they represent an important adaptive significance to the individual's survival.

CAREGIVER-INFANT GAZE TRANSACTIONS AS AN INTERACTIVE MEDIUM FOR IMPRINTING PROCESSES

The importance of central foveal (as opposed to peripheral) vision to the establishment of a primary attachment to the mother is well established (Bowlby, 1969). Drawing upon ethological studies and applying these to human development, Bowlby suggests that imprinting is the learning process underlying social attachment bond formation. During mutual gaze transactions, the infant, in a state of heightened interest foveates and tracks the caregiver's pupils. The child thus fixates directly on the visible portion of the mother's central nervous system, her eyes, which specifically reflect the activity and state of her right hemisphere, the hemisphere that is known to be dominant for gaze behavior (Meador et al., 1989). Regarding the visual inspection of pupillary changes as a reflection of internal states, Hess (1965) notes, "Embryologically and anatomically the eye is an extension of the brain; it is almost as if a portion of the brain were in plain sight . . . to peer at" (p. 52).

In these exchanges, the infant utilizes the mother's expressed "optimal level of stimulation" (Stern, 1985) as a template for the programming of the optimal level of stimulation for the development of his own evolving brain, specifically his maturing plastic right hemisphere. Imprinting has been described as "template" learning (Staddon, 1983), and neurobiological studies of this genetically controlled process have indicated that the participation of visual signals and forebrain regions are essential (Panksepp et al., 1985). Corter and Fleming (1990) point out that the mother serves to provide adequate stimulation and learning opportunities in order to promote her infant's normal growth, development and socialization, and that visual stimulation uniquely conveys information about physical states independently of movement and behavior. The original concept of critical periods, derived from classical embryology, asserts that during specific stages of ontogeny specific tissues (structures) are susceptible to particular environmental influences (stimulation) at that time and no other, the fate and future of the tissue being fixed thereafter (Spemann, 1938). A neuroanatomic study of avian imprinting shows consequent structural changes (synapse formation) occur very rapidly first in the right hemisphere; then, with further experiences, the left hemisphere "catches up" (Bradley, Horn, & Bateson, 1981).

These fundamental biological principles, applicable to all developing biological systems, can be related to the critical importance of maternal-infant gaze transactions to imprinting processes. In this interactive context the mother's emotionally expressive facial displays provide a rich source of visual stimulation, and this acts as an imprinting stimulus for the continuing development and differentiation of the infant's right hemisphere. The infant's early maturing (Chi, Dooling, & Gilles, 1977; Crowell et al., 1973; Geschwind & Galaburda, 1987; Giannitrapani, 1967; : Hellige, 1993; Schenkenberg, Dustman, & Beck, 1971; Taylor, 1969; Tucker, 1986) right hemisphere is known to be specifically impacted by early social experiences (Denenberg, Garbanti, Sherman, Yutzey, & Kaplan, 1978). This hemisphere is dominant for the processing of visuospatial information (Galin, 1976). The nature of the mother's gaze behavior reflects the functional state of her visuospatial right cortical hemisphere which predominates in the expression and processing of emotional information (Bradshaw & Nettleton, 1983; Hellige, 1990; Natale, Gur, & Gur, 1983) and in nonverbal communication (Benowitz et al., 1983). This cortex is specialized for selectively attending to facial emotion (Etcoff, 1984a).

I propose that during these eye-to-eye transactions the infant's maturing right hemisphere is "psychobiologically attuned" (Field, 1985a) to the output of the mother's right hemisphere. Hughlings Jackson (1879) discovered in the last century that this right hemisphere, moreso than the left, participates directly in perceptual processes and is essentially involved in direct, visual forms of relationships with the outside world. Developmental neuropsychological research now reveals that the infant's right hemisphere is preferentially involved in selective attention (Risberg & Prohovnik, 1983) and in the child's processing of visual emotional information (Saxby & Bryden, 1985). The right cortex is also dominant for the infant's perceptual recognition of the maternal face (de Schonen, Gil de Diaz, & Mathivet, 1986) and arousal-inducing maternal facial affective expressions (Nelson, 1987). Very recent developmental neuropsychological research with young animals suggests that neural structures fed by the left eye—mainly located in the right hemisphere—are better at processing and/or storing the visual information involved in social recognition (Vallortigara, 1992). Other studies have firmly established that this hemisphere is specialized as an "early processor" of incoming low frequency stimulation, as found in visuospatial stimuli (Sergent, 1987), a bias which Hellige (1990) suggests may be related to the fact that in early development the more mature right hemisphere is specifically influenced by incoming lower ranges of visuospatial frequency such as are associated with infant facial recognition processes (de Schonen et al., 1986). In support of this, developmental studies have indeed shown that infant's are responsive to visual stimuli with only low spatial frequencies (Turkewitz & Kenny, 1982).

The classical definition of imprinting implies an irreversible stamping of early experience upon the developing nervous system. In developmental neurobiological investigations of the ontogeny of individual differences in cortical organization, Galaburda, Rosen, and Sherman (1990) posit that "subtle modifications" of visual input in very young individuals lead to very specific changes in cortical cytoarchitecture and connectivity. It is tempting to speculate that with the onset of a discriminate attachment to the primary caregiver at 7 to 8 months, dyadic gaze transactions facilitate the experience-dependent growth and maturation of cerebral cortical temporal polar regions, known to be connected with visual association areas relating to central vision and somatosensory association areas for the face and head representation (Pandya & Yeterian, 1985). The synaptic density of the human visual cortex is highest at 8-to 12-months-of-age and thereafter declines (Huttenlocher, de Courten, Garey, & Van der Loos, 1982). At 8–10 months this rapidly accelerated synaptogenesis reaches rates of 35,000–90,000/mm^3 × hour (Huttenlocher & de Courten, 1987). The anterior temporal cortex, a limbic structure that receives input from the posterior visual cortex, contains neuronal centers that respond specifically to emotionally expressive faces (Hasselmo, Rolls, & Baylis, 1989a; Ojemann, Fried, & Mateer, 1980), particularly to features of the eye region (Perrett, Rolls, & Caan, 1982), and encode "object-centered representations of faces" (Hasselmo, Rolls, Baylis, & Nalwa, 1989b). Clinical neurological studies demonstrate right temporal lobe involvement in facial recognition (Milner, 1968). Most intriguingly, primate studies have shown that the anterior temporal cortex is implicated in maternal behavior (Bucher, Myers, & Southwick, 1970; Franzen & Meyers, 1973). These data support the proposal that the output of the mother's anterior temporal limbic cortex serves as a template for the imprinting of the 8-month-old infant's developing anterior temporal cortex.

VISUALLY-MEDIATED MERGER EXPERIENCES AND
THE INDUCTION OF A DYADIC SYMBIOTIC STATE

In the first chapter I asserted that a number of disciplines are now converging on the centrality of the basic principle that the growth of the brain is dependent upon and influenced by the socioemotional environment, and that for the developing infant the mother essentially *is* the environment. Trevarthen (1989), a neuroscientist, now proposes that "the affective regulations of brain growth" are embedded in early social interactions. He suggests that socialization-induced cerebral hemispheric growth "appears to reside in a mechanism that requires older brains to engage with mental states of awareness, interest, and emotion in younger brains" (Trevarthen, 1990, p. 335). This mechanism involves a coordination between the "motivations" of the infant and the "feelings" of adults. In a similar conclusion, Emde (1988), a developmental psychoanalyst, states "It is the emotional availability of the caregiver in intimacy which seems to be the most central growth-promoting feature of the early rearing experience" (p. 32). In particular, he stresses that positive affect from the caregiver has an enhancing role on developmental epigenesis (R. N. Emde, personal communication, July 16, 1991). Both of these authors emphasize the importance of the mother's availability to engage in emotional transactions with her infant—that is, to act as an affect regulator. Wilson et al. (1990) now propose that in early social development the caregiver who possesses certain advanced psychological abilities regulates and is regulated by the inner world of her child who has less advanced abilities.

The mother's function as an external regulator of the child's internal processes is emphasized in the work of Hofer. In a psychobiological translation of Mahler's concept of symbiosis, Hofer (1990) concludes that in the "symbiotic" state, the adult's and infant's individual homeostatic systems are linked together in a superordinate organization which allows for "mutual regulation of vital endocrine, autonomic, and central nervous systems of both mother and infant by elements of their interaction with each other" (p. 71). Furthermore, Hofer states that:

> In postnatal life, the neural substrates for simple affective states are likely to be present and that the experiences for the building of specific pleasurable states are likewise built into the symbiotic nature of the earliest mother—infant interaction. (p. 62)

Hofer thus offers a psychobiological mechanism by which the caregiver's emotional transactions with the infant can induce the growth of the child's internal affective structures, specifically the maturation of the autonomic nervous system that is responsible for emotional functioning. Indeed, in earlier work (Hofer, 1984a) he provides evidence to show that the mother is *the* regulator of the functioning of the infant's developing autonomic nervous system as well. Symbiotic states are physiologically mediated by the regulation of the infant's immature and developing internal homeostatic systems by the caregiver's more mature and differentiated nervous system. Importantly, a primary function of this symbiotic state is the generation of pleasurable states, that is, states marked by high levels of positive affect.

The importance of affect to symbiotic processes is stressed by Spitz (1965):

> When the infant experiences a need, it will provoke in him an affect that will lead to behavioural changes, which in their turn provoke an affective response and its concomitant attitude in the mother; she behaves "as if she understood" what particular need of the infant causes his affective manifestation. (p. 95)

In order for this linkage of internal states to occur, there must be a psychobiological attunement within the dyad. Stern (1985) suggests that the major indicators of attunement are pleasure and interest. Lichtenberg (1989) points out that in the last quarter of the first year the child's attachment experiences enable him to share an intersubjective affect state with the caregiver. This communicative exchange:

> involves one person, the parent, who possesses the capacity for symbolic representation, and another person, the infant, who possesses the capacity for modal and cross-modal perceptual-action patterns and affective amplification, but not for the symbolic representation until the middle of the second year. (p. 283)

Kohut (1977) describes that as a result of the empathic merger of the child's rudimentary psyche with the maternal selfobject's highly developed psychic organization, the child experiences the feeling states of the selfobject as if they were his own.

In line with Hofer's idea that mutually regulated symbiotic interactions act as a generator of positive states, Stern (1990) concludes that the affect of joy is the product of a mutual regulation of social exchange by both partners. The facial expression of joy is illustrated in Fig. 6.2. I propose that this social exchange

FIG. 6.2.   The facial expression of joy in a young infant. From Izard (1991). *The psychology of emotions.* Reprinted by permission of Plenum Press.

occurs specifically in the context of face-to-face dyadic gaze transactions during "central moments" (Pine, 1985) of the growing infant's day. Pine, a developmental psychoanalyst, holds that these "high intensity" events are "formative in their effect far out of proportion to their mere temporal duration" (1981, p. 25). As previously mentioned, this visual dialog between the mother and child, the most intense form of interpersonal communication, acts as a crucible for the forging of preverbal affective ties. The term "imprinting" is derived from the German word *Prägung* which literally means forging or stamping. Petrovich and Gewirtz (1985) state that imprinting involves "synchrony" between sequential infant maternal stimuli and behavior. In synchronized, mutual gaze, a state of "mutually entrained central nervous system propensities" (Horner, 1985) involved in "mutual regulatory systems of arousal" (Stern, 1983a), the infant's postnatally maturing limbic system is exposed to the maternal gleam. This gleam emanates from the eyes of the responsive mother's expressive and highly stimulating face, and mirrors the excitatory activity of her limbic system. The dyad thus creates a symbiotic "merger" experience (Pine, 1986a). In agreement, Kaufman (1989) asserts that merger or fusion occurs principally through the eyes.

In line with the principle that gaze patterns, external indicants of internal states, trigger physiological arousal, I suggest that in the psychobiologically attuned merger or fusion state in which a match occurs not between external behavioral events but between the expression of internal states (Stern, 1985), the child is stimulated into a similar state of heightened catecholaminergic-induced sympathetic arousal as the mother. Elevated sympathetic activity, an accompaniment of dilated pupils, is known to be associated with a positive hedonic state in infants (Lipsitt, 1976). Pine (1981) refers to "supercharged" high intensity moments between mother and infant. Mahler and Kaplan (1977) observe that during the symbiotic through early practicing phases, the "mirroring" caregiver "electrifies" the infant, and Stern (1985) characterizes maternal social behavior that can "blast the infant into the next orbit of positive excitation." Schaffer (1984) describes that soon after the infant gazes at the mother's greeting look of great delight, "then he too stirs into activity." In accord with Hess' findings, Beebe and Stern (1977) report that sustained levels of foveal visual regard can crescendo into positive affect, expressed in the infant's full gape smiles. This interactive process is illustrated in Fig. 6.3.

In perhaps the most detailed experimental study of this phenomenon, Izard (Termine & Izard, 1988) had mother's express the positive affects of joy and interest in close-up face-to-face interactions with their 9-month-old infants (the culmination of Mahler's symbiotic period). Maternal joy expressions induced long periods of infant gaze, and the longer the infant looked at the mother the more joy the infant expressed. Izard concludes that emotion expressions of one member of the mother-infant affective relationship tend to elicit emotions in the other member. The bidirectionality of the attunement process, the communica-

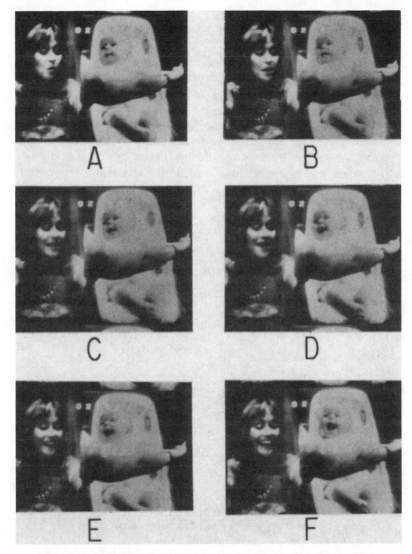

FIG. 6.3. Photographic illustrations of a "mirroring" sequence. Mother and infant are seated face to face, and are looking at each other. At point A, mother shows a "kiss-face," and infant's lips are partially drawn in, resulting in a tight, sober-faced expression. At point B, .54 seconds later, mother's mouth has widened into a slightly positive expression, and infant's face has relaxed with a hint of widening in the mouth, also a slighly positive expression. At point C, .79 seconds later, both mother and infant show a slight smile. At point D, .46 seconds later, both mother and infant further widen and open their smiles. Again at points E, .46 seconds later, and F, .58 seconds later, both mother and infant further increase their smile display. Points E and F illustrate the infant "gape smile." At point F the infant has shifted the orientation of his head further to his left, and upward, which heightens the evocativeness of the gape-smile. From Beebe and Lachman (1988a). Reprinted by permission of Analytic Press.

tive match between internal states, is seen in the infant's stimulation of maternal positive affect. Stern (1985) describes:

> A nine-month-old girl becomes very excited about a toy and reaches for it. As she grabs it, she lets out an exuberant 'aaaah!' and looks at her mother. Her mother looks back, scrunches up her shoulders, and performs a terrific shimmy with her upper body, like a go-go dancer. The shimmy lasts only about as long as her daughter's 'aaaah' but is equally excited, joyful, and intense. (p. 140)

MIRRORING GAZE TRANSACTIONS AND THE DYADIC AMPLIFICATION OF POSITIVE AFFECT

Researchers of the imprinting (stamping) process have found that the stimulation provided by the imprinting object is, like brain self-stimulation, innately reinforcing (Bateson & Reese, 1969; Hoffman & Ratner, 1973). Hunt (1965a) refers to "intrinsic motivation," and Bertalanffy (1968) posits that the endogenously organized response of "primary activity" is central to life. Pavlov (1927) and Skinner (1953) both held that all living organisms are predisposed to react in specific ways to certain classes of stimulation. This unconditioned response to the stimulating face of the imprinting object is independent of prior learning history and is isomorphic with responses to intracranial brain stimulation, the activation of neural pathways subserving the properties of natural reinforcers (Rolls, 1976). Self-stimulation has been utilized to study the "stamping-in mechanism," the neural basis of reinforcement (Huston, 1982). Livingston's (1967) "Now Print!" is a reinforcement mechanism that strengthens the memory of important experiences. In these imprinting experiences the innately reinforcing properties of the mother's gaze that radiates from her animated face triggers an unconditioned response mediated by an activation of reward circuits in the brain. The ventral tegmental dopaminergic limbic circuit is known to be centrally involved in motivational reward processes and in intracranial (Corbett & Wise, 1980) self-stimulation. Furthermore, such a phenomenon may represent a proto-typical example of "biologically prepared learning" (Seligman & Hager, 1972). This form of learning is typically defined as being more easily attached to some type of stimuli than to others, as requiring minimal input in terms of training, and as resulting in very persistent responses that are extremely resistant to extinction.

Dyadic mirroring gaze transactions thus induce a symbiotic, psychobiologically attuned affect-amplifying merger state in which a match occurs between the expression of rewarding, arousal accelerating, positively hedonic internal states. Trevarthen (1979) refers to the critical importance of emotional generation induced by "resonances" to the emergence of "primary intersubjectivity." This process of interpersonal fusion thus generates dynamic "vitality affects" (Stern, 1985). Wright (1991, p. 12) asserts that the mother's face reflects back her baby's "aliveness," and Izard (1991, p. 138) observes that joy enhances a sense of "oneness with the object" and is accompanied by "feelings of strength and vigor." According to Wolf (1988) mirroring selfobject experiences enhance the "energic vigor" of the self. It is now established that infants seek stimulation that arouses, excites, and activates them, and find this state of heightened activation intensely pleasurable (Stern, 1990). In current conceptualizations the mother is understood to act as a highly arousing unconditioned stimulus (Fogel, 1982), and her emotionally expressive facial behaviors act as what ethologists call "key stimuli" (Eibl-Eibesfeldt, 1967). Frijda (1988) proposes that particular states of action readiness, manifest in facial expressions and overt behavior are biological dispositions that need sensory stimuli as their unconditional releasers. In recent developmental psychoanalytic work, Wright (1991) asserts that object seeking specifically revolves around the mother's face, and it is her emotionally expressive face that is searched for and recognized.

In a similar conclusion from developmental neuroscience, Trevarthen (1990) hypothesizes that:

> Adaptation of a given brain to a particular social world depends . . . on a motivated search by the young for certain target experiences (as in) expressing mental or motivational states to others, and getting into contact with their mental states". (p. 335)

Joy (elation) is defined by Frijda (1988) as a state of pleasure plus the urge toward exuberance and contact-seeking. An expression of joy on the face of an infant is known to increase the probability of caregiver interaction (Brazelton et al., 1974). The anticipation and attainment of dyadically induced intensely pleasurable states associated with sustained mutual eye contact may thus represent the target experiences of contacting and sharing the mother's mental state by entering into a "reciprocal reward system" (Emde, 1980a). The motivated search (attachment motivation) for such is understandable in that elation is known to occur when progress toward an important goal is facilitated (Duffy, 1941), and "euphoric states are perhaps the most appetitively compelling experiences available to life forms as so far evolved" (Schwartz, 1990, p. 125). It is now well established that the excitement of seeing mother's face is an affect triggered by responses activated when the attachment motivational system is dominant (Lichtenberg, 1989).

As previously mentioned, this affective response may be psychobiologically mediated by activation of the ventral tegmental limbic circuit. Dopamine is the most important catecholamine involved in reward effects (Wise & Rompre, 1989), and the anticipation of reward and an increase of incentive motivation are neurochemical correlates specifically of mesolimbic dopaminergic activity (Willner & Scheel-Kruger, 1991). The unconditionally rewarding and exciting properties of the mother's gaze in these imprinting experiences are proposed to activate ventral tegmental dopaminergic elation (Kelley & Stinus, 1984) and dopaminergic arousal (Iversen, 1977) in the infant.

Thus, the (emotionally expressive face of the) mother, acting as a powerful reinforcing stimulus, in a heightened state of pleasure and interest triggered by the perception of her infant, stimulates, mirrors, and amplifies positive affect in the child. The mother's face, the child's "emotional" (Searles, 1963) or "biological mirror" (Papousek & Papousek, 1979), reflects back her baby's "aliveness" in a "positively amplifying circuit mutually affirming both partners" (Wright, 1991, p. 12). Izard (1991), in experimental investigations of affective processes, observes that in the experience of joy the object is seen as enhancing the self of the perceiver. Kohut (1971, 1984), in psychoanalytic reconstructions of early experiences, proposes the existence of an essential "mirroring stage" of development. In his model, to be mirrored is to be looked upon with joy and basic approval by a delighted parental selfobject. Winnicott (1971), a pediatrician-psychoanalytic observer of infants, describes the critical developmental process of affective mirroring of the mother, who reflects her delight and pleasure in her infant back to the infant: "the mother is looking at the baby and what she looks like is related to what she sees there" (p. 112). Stern (1990)'characterizes the level of intensity of the joyful, excited infant as attaining extremely high levels of activation, almost maximally tolerable to the developing nervous system:

> Joy is the product of a mutual regulation of social exchange by both partners. Smiling back and forth is the prototypic example; it usually begins at a relatively low level of intensity. Each partner then progressively escalates—kicking the other into higher orbit, so to speak. The exchange occurs in overlapping waves, where the mother's smile elicits the infant's, reanimating her next smile at an even higher level, and so on. These overlapping waves build in intensity, until, most often, simultaneous mutual hilarity breaks forth. (p. 16)

An audience effect, in which the frequency of infant smiles increases in the presence of an other, is specifically observed at 10 months (Jones, Collins, & Hong, 1991).

These congruent findings from neuroscience, infant research, and psychoanalysis have significant and even perhaps radical implications for an overarching conceptualization of the role of affect and motivation in early development. Positive emotions in general play a much larger organizational role in development than previously thought (Emde, 1992), and joy (elation) in particular results from modulated increased and not decreased levels of stimulation. Freud (1955/1920), in *Beyond the Pleasure Principle,* proposed that "unpleasure corresponds to an increase in the quantity of excitation, and pleasure to a diminution" (p. 8). Tomkins (1987), throughout all his writings, also maintained this same notion about the neurophysiological dynamics of pleasure: "If internal or external sources of neural firing suddenly decrease, s/he will laugh or smile with enjoyment" (p. 141).

These views are not supported by recent neurochemical research which indicates that activation and not deactivation of a specific reward circuit, the ventral tegmental dopaminergic system, mediates elation. In contrast to Freud's assertion that pleasure is maintained only in a quiescent state, infant elation is known to be associated with heightened activation of the excitatory, energy-mobilizing sympathetic component of the autonomic nervous system (Lipsitt, 1976), and joy is physiologically accompanied by significant heart rate increases (Izard, 1991). These findings do, however, confirm the developmental conceptualizations offered by two contemporary models derived from classical psychoanalysis, object relations theory which views the infant to be primarily motivated by object seeking rather than tension-discharging activities, and attachment theory which holds that the function of attachment seeking is the generation of pleasurable states. In a chapter in a recent book, *Pleasure Beyond the Pleasure Principle*, Hofer (1990) presents evidence to show that the creation of pleasurable states is built into the symbiotic nature of the mother-infant interaction. In this same volume, Stern (1990) suggests that pleasure is associated with moderate stimulation (excitation) not at a falling or zero excitation, where Freud had placed it.

THE INTERACTIVE PSYCHOBIOLOGICAL REGULATION OF POSITIVE AFFECT

In earlier work, Stern (1983b) emphasized that the infant has optimal levels of stimulation below which more stimulation is sought and above which stimulation is avoided. The psychobiologically attuned mother sensitively dispenses her stimulation; when it is too intense and becomes stressful, the infant gaze averts to self-regulate emotional arousal and she reduces her input so as to provide an optimal level of arousal. Brazelton and Cramer (1990) describe:

> A mother's most effective technique in maintaining an interaction seems to be a sensitivity to her infant's capacity for attention and need for withdrawal—partial or complete—after a period of attending to her. Short cycles of attention and inattention seem to underlie all periods of prolonged interaction. Although there appears to be continuous attention to the mother on the part of the infant, stop-frame analysis uncovers the cyclical nature of the infant's looking and not looking. By looking away, infants maintain some control over the amount of stimulation they take in during such intense periods of interaction. (p. 105)

Psychophysiologically, gaze aversion is a "cut-off" arousal reducing mechanism (Chance, 1962) which discharges an overload of social information processing. Fogel (1982) has demonstrated that due to the infant's very low threshold for arousal, the caregiver must modulate heightened potentially disorganizing states. Tronick et al. (1982) refer to a maternal interactive pattern of "elaboration" in which the responsive mother imitates or exaggerates infant social actions, and "backs off" briefly during infant gaze averts (see Fig. 6.4). In this way

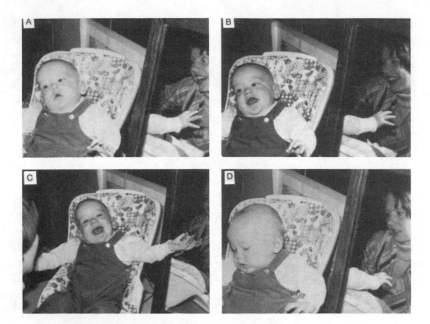

FIG. 6.4. A typical sequence observed during "attuned" interactions of normal infants and their mothers: (A) the infant looks at the mother and the mother shows an exaggerated facial expression (mock surprise); (B) the infant and mother smile; (C) the infant laughs, the mother "relaxes" her smile; and (D) the infant looks away, the mother ceases smiling and watches her infant. From Field and Fogel (1982). Reprinted by permission of Lawrence Erlbaum Associates

the parent facilitates the infant's information processing by adjusting the mode, amount, and timing of information to the infant's actual integrative capacities (Papousek & Papousek, 1984). Penman, Meares, and Milgrom-Friedman (1983) argue that the development of synchronized interactions is fundamental to the healthy affective development of the infant.

> The more the mother 'tunes' her activity level to the infant during periods of social engagement, and the more she allows him to recover quietly in periods of disengagement, the more synchronized their interaction. (p. 1)

Alterations of gaze thus regulate the flow of the dialog, and in order to accomplish this adaptive dyadic temporal coordination the sensitive mother must separate her expectations (based on a monitoring of her own internal rhythms) from her observations of the infant's affective display in order to identify and match the child's internal state. At an optimal level of stimulation the child shares the positive affect state of the caregiver. The differences between attuned (normal) and misattuned (high-risk) dyadic transactions is depicted in Fig. 6.5.

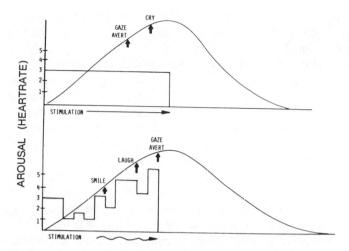

FIG. 6.5.   A schematic representation of differences between the behavioral curves of normal (attuned) and high-risk (misattuned) infant-
mother dyads. The upper curve represents the high-risk dyad, with the
mother stimulating her infant at a level sufficient to maintain her infant's attention but then sustaining that level rather than modulating
stimulation during infant gaze aversion and crying. The lower curve
depicts the normal infant-mother dyad, showing varied or modulated
stimulation by the mother as a function of the infant's affective signals
and a cessation of behavior at infant gaze aversion, with the infant
never reaching a crying state. From Field (1985a). Reprinted by permission of Academic Press.

The mother's role in this face-to-face dialectic is thus to grossly attune and
then by monitoring her infant's response to fine-tune her inputs to the particular
baby's level of communicative capacity. In other words, she initially attempts
to attune to, that is, to match and synchronize to the infant's inner state, but as
his state is dynamically activated (or deactivated or hyperactivated) and expressed in an alteration of gaze and behavior, she fine-tunes, that is adjusts and
corrects the intensity and duration of her stimulation in order to maintain a
positive affect state in the child. In this way she provides optimal "chunking" of
bits of sociaffective stimulation that the child's developing right hemispheric
socioaffective information processing system can efficiently process. The burgeoning capacity of the infant to experience positive "vitality" affects is thus at
this stage of development "externally" regulated by the mother's participation in
the psychobiological attunement process. The reception and expression of these
visuoaffective signals in the child's early maturing right hemisphere, the cortex
that is dominant for the processing of visual emotional information (Saxby &
Bryden, 1985) and nonverbal communication (Benowitz et al., 1983), may re-

veal the mechanism underlying Izard's (1991) observation that long before the infant either comprehends or speaks a single word, it possesses an extensive repertoire of signals to communicate its internal states.

Hofer (1990) suggests that the mother's and infant's endocrine systems that mediate their internal states are mutually linked in symbiotic interactions. Over 15 years ago Klaus and Kennell (1976) hypothesized that extended periods of maternal gaze elicit hormonal changes in the infant which facilitate the affectional bond between mother and infant. What particular kinds of interpersonally induced endocrine alterations might be involved? One class of psychobiological hormonal changes of special importance is maternal-stimulated increases of infant endogenous opioids, the enkephalins and endorphins, which are known to have rewarding properties and to mediate social affect (Herman & Panksepp, 1978). These neurohormones are found in very high concentrations in the dopaminergic ventral tegmental area (Britt & Wise, 1983) and in the anterior temporal cortex (Steklis & Kling, 1985). Ventral tegmental dopamine neurons are activated by opiates (Matthews & German, 1984), and opiates injected into the ventral tegmental area are rewarding (Bozarth & Wise, 1981; Phillips & Le Piane, 1980). Opioid neuropeptides, especially long-lasting endorphins, are involved in the experiencing of positive hedonic affects associated with social contact, and in the modulation of mechanisms underlying social emotion (Oliverio, Castellano, & Puiglisi-Allegra, 1984), thereby contributing to the formation and maintenance of social attachments (Steklis & Kling, 1985). Hoffman (1987) suggests that the imprinting object stimulates the production of opioid peptides in the infant, and that this hormonal alteration psychobiologically mediates attachment processes.

This psychobiological mechanism may be operative during symbiotic merger experiences that involve high intensity visuo-emotional object relations and may physiologically underlie Krystal's (1988) observation that affects are active from the beginning in forming attachments. It may also represent the "neurohormonal influence" that operates in the "Now Print!" neurobiological mechanism that stores emotionally important experiences (Livingston, 1967). These neurophysiological and neurochemical events, which have been suggested to mediate the motivational substrate for imprinting (Hoffman, 1987), may be directly involved in the neuroendocrine linkage described by Hofer in symbiotic transactions. Furthermore, I would argue that this developmental psychoneurochemical mechanism underlies all imprinting phenomena and explains Bowlby's (1969) claim that imprinting represents the learning process which supports all attachment phenomena. On the basis of the foregoing information, I conclude that mutually regulated opioid activity supports the psychobiologically attuned mirroring process, and that the positive affect-amplifying mirroring process supports a neurobiological imprinting mechanism which occurs first in the symbiotic, and then, if so, most intensely in the practicing period. I shall further expand upon these ideas in a later chapter.

THE DEVELOPMENT OF POSITIVE AFFECT
OVER THE FIRST YEAR

A developmental transformation occurs in mutual gaze-generated positive affect: the elicitation of "delight" (Tomkins' enjoyment) in 4-month infants (Beebe & Lachman, 1988a) becomes high intensity elation (Tomkins' joy) in 9-month infants (Termine & Izard, 1988). With respect to the other primary positive affect, an increase in the facial indicators of interest and also in heart rate acceleration in response to the female face has been observed from 2 to 8 months (Langsdorf, Izard, Rayias, & Hembree, 1983). Studies of 3-month-old infants show a significant association of heart rate deceleration and smiling (Brock, Rothbart, & Derryberry, 1986), while 9-month-old babies show heart rate acceleration during smiling (Emde, Campos, Reich, & Gaensbauer, 1978). Heart rate is known to increase in experiences of joy (Izard, 1991). Malatesta (Malatesta, Culver, Tesman, & Shepard, 1989) has demonstrated that as infants mature from $2^1/_2$ to $7^1/_2$ months their interactions with their mothers consist of increasingly positive encounters in which high rates of maternal modeling of joy and interest are associated with increases in infant joy and interest.

Emotions are now considered to have, in addition to a hedonic dimension, an intensity or arousal dimension (Russell, 1980). It is suggested that the high arousal intense positive affect states of elation (joy) and excitement developmentally emerge in the early practicing period of separation-individuation only if the caregiver-infant dyad successfully negotiates the preceding stages. In the orderly, sequential maturation of brain and behavior, "Each developmental step is in some way dependent on a certain degree of maturation of the previous steps." (van der Vlugt, 1979). The psychobiologically attuned mirroring process is proposed to increase to high levels at 9 to 10 months and to represent the mechanism of merger experiences which generate tolerance for the high arousal positive affects of elation and excitement of the subsequent early practicing phase (10 to 12 months). (Although Stern [1985] has pointed out that Mahler's symbiotic period does not represent an entire phase in which only merger transactions occur, the frequency and intensity of daily "central moments" of high energy object relations which mediate these affect amplifying transactions increases dramatically over the period of 2 to 9 months).

Fogel (1982) refers to a major developmental task of the first year to be the evolution of increasing affective tolerance for high arousal; this evolves as a result of early maternal sensitivity to and modulation of the infant's highly stimulated states. Krystal (1978a) notes that an essential function of the mother is to permit the child to bear increasingly intense affective tension, but then to step in and comfort the child before his emotions overwhelm him. McLaughlin (1989) proposes that the mother's prevailing tendency to overshoot, just by a little, her infant's tolerance boundaries induces the infant to stretch and grow.

Continual episodes of sustained eye contact that generate high levels of arousal, a characteristic feature of this period of infancy, may represent a transient ontogenetic adaptation, as at later points of development mutual gaze is brief because its intensity becomes intolerable (Kaufman, 1989). This ontogenetic adaptation is essential to further socioemotional ontogeny; Mahler asserts that a normal symbiotic period is a prerequisite to the favorable onset of the practicing phase at 10 to 12 months.

The practicing period has been operationally defined to begin with the emergence of independent upright locomotion (Mahler et al., 1975), a developmental milestone that is reached at approximately the end of the first year (Forssberg, Stokes, & Hirschfeld, 1992). Mahler (1980) describes that when the infant begins to walk freely with upright posture

> the plane of his vision changes: from an entirely new vantage point he finds unexpected and changing perspectives, pleasures, and frustrations. At this new visual level there is more to see, more to hear, more to touch, and all of this is experienced in the upright bipedal position. How this world is experienced seems to be subtlty related to the mother, who is the center of the child's universe from which he gradually moves out into ever-widening circles. (p. 7)

At 11 months visually distinctive features of objects become more compelling than any other sensory modality, and visual input plays a preeminent directive role in processing environmental information (Bushnell & Weinberger, 1987). It is known that when the infant locomotes more widely in its environment, vision is the primary mode of connection with the mother (Rosenblum, 1987). In this developmental period, an intensified and concentrated version of this dyadic visuoaffective process may be fundamental to coordinated affect-transmitting, attention-focusing, social referencing experiences, known to onset at 10 to 12 months, in which the toddling infant's affect and behavior are regulated by maternal facial expression (Klinnert, 1984). Oatley and Jenkins (1992) note that in social referencing the infant is guided in exploration by the mother's emotional expression, and underscore the importance for the child to "keep an eye on" what mother is feeling.

The socioemotional function of gaze thus emerges in the practicing period, as the appearance of the infant's new cognitive capacity to "read" mother's face coincides in time with the increase in motility (Riess, 1978). In studies of this social referencing phenomenon, Feinman (1982) finds mood modification effects via, for example, dyadic resonance or contagion of positive affect, and Walden and Baxter (1989) observe that infants at 12 months look more often when the parent's face expresses positive affect. Sroufe (1989a) describes the 12-month-old who grasps an object that captures her attention "with widened eyes" and then directly shares her delight with the observing mother, and Emde (1988) characterizes the 12-month-old toddler's "sparkling-eyed pleasure" associated with early mastery experiences which is amplified under the watchful eye of the approving caregiver. By this time caregiver-regulated nonverbal communications enable the child to tolerate amplified levels of arousal, and this dyadic psychobiological mechanism may be responsible for the conversion of the positive affects enjoyment into joy (elation) and interest into excitement. This trend continues in the early practicing period; a statistically significant increase in positive emotion has been documented from 10 to 13.5 months (Rothbart et al. 1989). Such a developmental period of intensified positive affect was referred to by Freud as a phase of "primary narcissism."

In an upcoming section of this work, I contend that the practicing phase represents a critical period for the experience-dependent maturation of the orbitofrontal cortex, a region that is anatomically expanded in the right hemisphere (Falk et al., 1990), the hemisphere that is engaged in the processing of elation affect (Tucker, 1981). This frontolimbic structural system is implicated in attachment processes (Steklis & Kling, 1985) and is composed of neurons that respond to the emotional expressions of faces (Thorpe, Rolls, & Maddison, 1983). Research studies indicate that the activity of this cortex is involved in eye movements (Kaada et al., 1949), pupillary dilation (Okinaka et al., 1960), and in tracking emotionally relevant objects in the extrapersonal space (Mesulam, 1985). The orbitofrontal region is a site of brain-stimulation reward (Clavier & Gerfen, 1979; Mora, Avrith, & Rolls, 1980; Rolls & Cooper, 1974) and is involved in the pleasurable qualities of social interaction (Panksepp et al., 1985), and along with anterior temporal regions contains the highest levels of opioids in the cerebral cortex (Steklis & Kling, 1985).

SUMMARY

Visual stimulation, embedded in mutual gaze transactions between caregiver and infant, is an essential component of a growth promoting environment. The mother's emotionally expressive face is the most potent source of visuoaffective information, and in face-to-face interactions it serves as a visual imprinting stimulus for the infant's developing nervous system. During visual dialogues the primary caregiver is psychobiologically attuned to the infant's internal state, and in these merger experiences she creates and maintains a mutually regulated symbiotic state in the dyad. In mirroring transactions, a dyadic reciprocal stimulating system generates an elevation of regulated sympathetic arousal that supports heightened levels of interest-excitement and enjoyment-joy. This amplification of positive affect is neurochemically mediated by activation of the ventral tegmental dopaminergic system and the stimulation of endogenous opioids in reward centers of the infant's brain. The child's capacity to tolerate higher levels of arousal increases over the first year. These phenomena culminate in very high levels of positive affect at the onset of the practicing phase at the end of the first year.

7 The Practicing Period

During this precious six-to-eight month period, for the junior toddler (ten-twelve to sixteen-eighteen months) the world is his oyster. The child concentrates on practicing his mastery of his own skills and autonomous capacities. He is exhilarated by his own capacities, continually delighted with the discoveries he is making in his expanding world, quasi-enamored with the world and with his own omnipotence.

—Margaret S. Mahler (1980)

When do the proximal essential events critical to the maturation of affect structures and the expansion of socioemotional development take place? The practicing subphase begins at 10–12 months and extends through 16–18 months. Mahler divides it into an early phase at the end of the first year and a late phase which extends into the middle of the second year. The subphase thus straddles both early and late infancy. This developmental period overlaps with Piaget's fifth stage of sensorimotor intelligence which signals the cognitive ability to represent the self and external causation (Lester, 1983). It also is the same developmental interval in which Bowlby's patterns of attachment behaviors can first be reliably observed and measured. The effective vocabulary of the average 12-month-old is 3 words; at 15 months, 19 words (Mussen, Conger, & Kagan, 1969). The infant at this point is essentially preverbal, yet, according to Mahler, it is over this developmental period that the "psychological birth of the human infant" takes place. This event is marked by the emergence, at the end of the practicing period, of a structure that contributes to autonomous emotional functioning, that is, to the self-regulation of affect.

In this chapter I present an overview of the unique affective characteristics, developmental neurobiology, ontogenetic adaptations, and epigenesis of this critical period.

AFFECTIVE CHARACTERISTICS

A major biobehavioral shift occurs at the end of the first year of human infancy, and this developmental thrust is expressed in cognitive, motor, and affective spheres. Infant observers identify an abrupt major maturational behavioral reorganization which occurs at about 12 months (Plooij & van de Rijt-Plooij, 1989). Zelazo's (1982) research indicates that a fundamental change in cognition first appears around 12 months of age, supporting Kagan's (1971) suggestion that the capacity for "active thought" develops towards the end of the first year. The onset of the practicing period is defined by Mahler by rapid changes in motor behavior, that is, of upright posture and locomotion supporting the child's first independent steps, an event paramount in human individuation. Oster (1981) notes that beginning in the latter part of the first year, infants become increasingly mobile and increasingly active in pursuing their mothers. Interestingly, in his ethological work, Hess (1959) states imprinting occurs in an early critical period that is marked by the onset of locomotor activity.

Despite these significant cognitive and behavioral advances, I think, however, that it is the affective characteristics of this period that are unique and definitional. Bowlby (1969) pointed out important affective changes occur when locomotion emerges. Later experimental research has supported this proposal. Bertenthal, Campos, and Barrett (1983) report mobile infants show different types of emotional reactions than prelocomotor infants, and Fox and Davidson (1984) also note tight linkages exist between the onset of locomotion and the occurrence of important changes in affective behavior. These dramatic affective transformations are critical to the establishment of permanent characteristics of the emerging personality. Perhaps more than any other time in the lifespan the individual's internal state is externally observable and susceptible to socioenvironmental influences.

Mahler (1980) describes the practicing junior toddler's omnipotent exhilaration (excitement) and narcissistic elation (joy), and notes that at this time, more than any other in development, "narcissism is at its peak." Freud (1914/1957) originally defined infantile narcissism cognitively, as the sense of being "the center and core of creation." The mother's participation in generating the high levels of positive affect that characterize this narcissistic state has been described earlier. Stern (1985) proposes that attunement with states of enthusiasm promotes desirable and healthy feelings of omnipotence and grandiosity. Developmental psychoanalytic researchers have observed that, "When the love affair with the world begins at approximately 10 or 12 months, narcissism is at its highest peak in the life cycle" (Wagner & Fine, 1981, p. 8), and that "the practicing period offers a release into manic excitement and involvement in a world far more reinforcing than that of the unreliable nurturance offered earlier" (Johnson,1987, p.26).

Social referencing transactions first appear in this period, and in these dyadic mirroring visuoaffective communications positive affect is rapidly and efficiently amplified in the neo-toddler. Pine (1980) observes that elated affect is coupled with boundless energy in the constantly moving toddler. Emde (1989) describes a major transformation in all spheres including the intensification of elated affect at 12 months. The 1-year-old's frequent mood of elation has also been observed by non psychoanalytic observers such as Sroufe (1979). Indeed, 60 years ago Bridges (1932), in a seminal study of emotional development in infancy, recorded that elation first appears at 12 months. These observations have been corroborated in recent studies from workers in two different fields. In a developmental neuropsychological study of infant emotional expression, Rothbart et al. (1989) find a statistically significant increase in positive emotion and decrease in negative emotion over the developmental period of 10 to 13.5 months. And in developmental psychological research, Mayes and Zigler (1992) report that infants aged 9–11 months routinely express positive affective responses (smiling, laughing) while practicing motor tasks (standing with support, taking steps with support). The experience of positive affect remains undiminished, even as the infants continue to practice and master these tasks.

DEVELOPMENTAL NEUROBIOLOGY

It is important to note that the practicing stage-specific hedonic tone of elation (Lipsitt, 1976), high levels of arousal (Field, 1985b), and elevated activity level (boundless energy) (Breese et al., 1973) are all associated with heightened activation of the sympathetic component of the autonomic nervous system. Furthermore, in various animal models, it has been found that young mammals typically pass through a period of midinfancy in which they display a state of organismic hyperarousal and increased energy metabolism, especially when apart from the mother (Reite, Kaufman, Pauley, & Stynes, 1974). This reflects unmodulated excitatory activity of early maturing, reticular formation brain stem systems responsible for arousal (Campbell & Mabry, 1972; Moorcroft, 1971). In late infancy this activity is decreased due to the later onset of forebrain inhibitory systems. Lesions of the forebrain orbital inhibitory system in the infant monkey have been shown to produce hyperactivity manifested when the infant is separated from its mother. Hyperactivity is also seen in lesions of the orbital cortex in adult animals (Kolb, 1974; Ruch & Shenkin, 1943).

Sympathetic and parasympathetic components are known to have different timetables of development, resulting in unique physiological organizations at different stages of postnatal life. Hofer (1984b) has observed high levels of sympathetic activity and high resting heart rates in mid infancy, followed by a reduction in late infancy due to the neural maturation of parasympathetic (vagal) restraint. Thompson (1990) emphasizes the importance of this principle of autonomic nervous system organization to the development of emotional self-regulation. He underscores the principle that sympathetic excitatory processes develop earlier than parasympathetic inhibitory processes, specifically citing the slower postnatal development of parasympathetic activities in the frontal lobes.

Over 100 years ago, the British neurologist Hughlings Jackson (1931) postulated that the infant will pass through an excitable stage in ontogenesis that is diminished by the later functional onset of cortical inhibitory centers, reflecting the sequential caudal to rostral development of the brain. Jackson's astounding insights into the hierarchical organization of the brain greatly influenced Luria's ideas about late maturing prefrontal inhibitory structures that hierarchically regulate early appearing excitation. Luria expanded this concept by proposing that the development of adaptive regulatory structures occurs postnatally and is influenced by the social environment. Other studies in the early part of this century revealed that spontaneous emotional expression is mainly subcortical and that cortical control is inhibitory (Bard, 1934; Monrad-Krohn, 1924). These classical models are now being supported by contemporary research. Recent investigations of the early development of biogenic amine systems, the neurochemical substrates of arousal, reveal an ontogenetic pattern of "inhibitory maturation" which counterbalances the infant's initial excitatory tendencies in motor activity and spontaneous motility (Pradhan & Pradhan, 1980). Furthermore, it is known that essential subcortical limbic system substrates involved in emotional and cognitive behavior postnatally mature earlier than corresponding systems in the cerebral cortex (Meyersburg & Post, 1979).

ONTOGENETIC ADAPTATIONS

According to the developmental biological concept of ontogenetic adaptation developing capacities are adaptive to the period in which they first emerge. I propose that the affective, behavioral, and cognitive aspects unique to the practicing period reflect a biologically timed period of sympathetic-dominant limbic hyperarousal and behavioral overexcitation which have adaptive significance in the practicing socioenvironmental niche. The neo-toddler's hyperactivity and high rates of positive affects that result from this hyperarousal represent such ontogenetic adaptations. Pine's observation of the elated, constantly moving toddler who is filled with boundless energy is a precise definition of infant active play. Kagan (Tulkin & Kagan, 1972) reports that at 10 months fully 90% of maternal physical and verbal behavior consists of affection, play, and caregiving, with only 5% involved in prohibiting the child from ongoing activity. Developmental observers have noted that by 1 year-of-age stimulation-seeking exploratory play time may increase to as much as 6 hours of the child's day. Chisholm (1990) underscores the adaptive aspect of early play: by altering the relationship of the young organism to its developmental environment, play in effect makes the environment an "enriched" one. Play behavior may thus reflect the phase specific heightened activation of an exploratory-assertive motivational system (Lichtenberg, 1989). Indeed, Oppenheim (1980) points out that play behavior qualifies as an ontogenetic adaptation.

I believe that practicing period play experiences are an essential component of a growth-promoting environment (Greenspan, 1981), and that these experiences generate high levels of positive affect that facilitate further structural growth. Isen (1990) asserts that in development positive affect is associated with flexibility in cognitive organization and with broader or more interrelated cognitive structures. Tucker (1992) propounds the general principle:

> The ability to participate in processes of play and affectional interaction may be a key determinant of both information flow and the brain arousal that help to shape developing networks. (p. 80)

Even more specifically, the highly elevated levels of stimulation-seeking exploratory (play) behavior that accompany the onset of upright locomotion may be a behavioral manifestation of the stage-specific increased activity of the mesocortical dopamine system that is known to support locomotion and investigatory exploration behavior (Fink & Smith, 1980). The ventral tegmental dopaminergic limbic circuit may neurochemically mediate the early developing egocentric "landmark" (as opposed to a later developing nonegocentric "relational") knowledge system which the maturing organism uses during exploration in order to gain information about objects and events in the environment (Nadel, 1990). Nadel reports that exploration emerges quite abruptly in development, and suggests that some factor, "a neurotransmitter perhaps," may be responsible for the onset of this function.

A defining characteristic of all ontogenetic adaptations is that they are transient. I show later in some detail that a shift in the ontogenetic niche occurs at about 14 months, the late practicing period. At this time the caregiver's interactions are strongly marked more by socialization prohibitions than by play behavior. These socioaffective transactions, different than those of the early practicing period, induce inhibitory low arousal rather than excitatory high arousal psychobiological states in the infant. They thereby reduce sympathetic-supported ontogenetic adaptations of the early practicing period. These same interactive phenomena facilitate the growth of parasympathetic cortical structures.

EPIGENESIS

According to the principle of epigenesis the outcome of each mode of organization depends on the outcome of each previous mode, and each new level of organization possesses unique emergent qualities (Wilson et al., 1990). Another essential quality of ontogenetic adaptations is that they are provisional (Oppenheim, 1980). In line with these tenets, the ontogenetic adaptation of the ability to experience the practicing high arousal states supporting the positive affects of elation and interest-excitement depends on precedent and continuing successful dyadic psychobiologically attuned visuoaffective (symbiotic "merger") transactions which occur in the previous stage. The infant's capacity to engage in a visually communicating social referencing process with the mother first appears in the practicing period (Klinnert, 1984). The emergence of this attachment process (Bretherton, 1985) that mediates a resonance or contagion of positive affect (Feinman, 1982) requires the dyad's successful passage through the symbiotic stage. The dramatic increases in positive affect-toned play in this period may only fully develop as a result of successfully negotiated dyadic positive affect amplification experiences in earlier pre-practicing periods.

The caregiver-influenced capacity to increase the infant's affective tolerance for high arousal states (Fogel, 1982) and thereby experience these basic positive affects may regulate the intensity and the rate of attachment bond formation, since it now accepted that the the baby becomes attached to the modulating caregiver who maximizes and expands opportunities for positive affect and minimizes the experience of negative affect (Demos & Kaplan, 1986). It is also now well established that the combination of joy and interest motivates attachments (Buechler & Izard, 1983), and that pleasure and interest are the major indicators of affect attunement (Stern, 1985). Psychobiological attunement has been proposed to be the mechanism that drives the attachment process (Field, 1985a). These factors may bear upon the assertion by Brent and Resch (1987) that "The baby's ability to adjust the amount of interaction with mother in accordance with internal states increases with physiological and psychological maturity" (p. 26). In other words, the child's capacity to link her developing homeostatic system into the mother's more differentiated homeostatic system by elements of their interaction with each other—Hofer's (1990) definition of symbiosis—increases in Mahler's symbiotic phase, thereby allowing for transition into the subsequent practicing stage.

Furthermore, although attachment first appears at 7 to 8 months, it is proposed that this subphase of separation-individuation, which begins at 10–12 months with the onset of upright locomotion and ends at about 18 months, represents the critical period of socialization for the formation of enduring attachment bonds to the early primary caregiver. Ainsworth (Stayton, Hogan, & Ainsworth, 1971) notes that attachment forms at about the same time that locomotor exploration appears. Indeed, in the most widely used experimental methodology for studying the genesis of patterns of infant-mother attachments, the "strange situation", devised by Ainsworth (Ainsworth et al., 1978), the earliest age at which attachment functions are sufficiently expressed and measurable is at 12 months, and the latest time of assessment at 18 months. These patterns of attachment guide all future socioemotional functioning.

SUMMARY

The practicing period, 10–12 to 16–18 months, spans early and late infancy. Although its onset is marked by the dramatic appearance of upright locomotion, its unique affective characteristics define the essential role of this stage in socio-emotional development. Social referencing transactions, visuoaffective communications that efficiently and rapidly amplify infant interest-excitement and enjoyment-joy, begin in this period. This dyadic mechanism generates extremely high levels of positive hedonically-toned play behavior in the early practicing infant. As a result, the toddler psychologically experiences a stage-typical narcissistic state of grandiosity and omnipotence. This phenomenological state is psychobiologically supported by a hyperarousal of the sympathetic nervous system, produced by a hyperactivation of the mesocortical component of the ventral tegmental dopaminergic limbic circuit. The epigenetic precursors of this stage occur in visuoaffective merger experiences in the preceding symbiotic stage of development. The practicing phase in which the infant truly becomes a behaviorally and socially dynamic organism represents a critical period for the formation of enduring attachment bonds to the primary caregiver. The nature of the attachment to the mother influences all later socioemotional transactions.

8 The Psychobiology of Affective Reunions

*In stable environments in which mothers allow infants to move from them when the infant feels secure enough to do so and in which **mothers allow infants to return to them freely,** (my emphasis) the infants are able to modulate their arousal levels so as to permit learning of effective responses to the complex physical and social environment in which they and their mothers live.*

—Leonard A. Rosenblum (1987)

Attachment might be viewed as a relationship that develops between two or more organisms as their behavioral and physiological systems become attuned to each other. Each partner provides meaningful stimulation for the other and has a modulating influence on the other's arousal . . . Thus, attachments are psychobiologically adaptive for the organization, equilibrium, and growth of the organism.

—Tiffany Field (1985a)

Where do the essential events critical to socioemotional development and separation-individuation take place? Ainsworth (Ainsworth et al., 1978), studying the dynamics of the attachment process described by Bowlby, has emphasized the importance of "reunion" episodes that occur after periods of separation between the 12-month-old infant and the caregiver. The careful investigation of reunion transactions, especially after periods of stress, is highly informative because it is at these times when high intensity attachment behavior is most likely to be activated. In parallel work, Mahler (Mahler et al., 1975) discovered instances of "emotional refueling," which she conceptualized as an exchange of energy between the partners in the caregiver-infant dyad. Upon return from brief separations, his initial ambulatory attempts to separate himself from his mother in order to explore the larger world (Rheingold & Eckerman, 1970), the practicing toddler frequently is in a "toned-down" state. Mahler (1980) notes this low energy state is rapidly terminated upon reunion with the briefly absent mother: "The wilting and fatigued infant 'perks up' in the shortest time, following such contact, after which he quickly goes on with his explorations, once again absorbed in pleasures in his own functioning" (p. 6).

This chapter contains an analysis of the critical dyadic events that occur during reunions after incipient, brief separations between the emotionally responsive mother and the neo-ambulatory practicing toddler. In these "hidden" visuoaffective transactions the mother's microregulation of the infant's arousal level both sustains the child's current behavior and facilitates his ongoing socioemotional development. These interactive processes support the experience-dependent growth of an internal system that is capable of appraising motivationally significant and emotionally meaningful environmental events.

THE PSYCHOBIOLOGICAL FUNCTION OF REUNION EPISODES

Beginning with the very onset of mobility, the child, in the face of stressful situations, will return to the mother. This reunion behavior is an even more important indicator of the quality of attachment than the child's protest at the point of separation (Ainsworth et al., 1978). It is during these reunion transactions that the attuned caregiver acts to maintain the infant's arousal level (Brazelton, Koslowski, & Main, 1974; Brent & Resch, 1987; Rosenblum, 1987) by constructing a psychobiologically attuned "mutual regulatory system of arousal" (Stern, 1983a) with her infant. These episodes of "microregulation" (Sameroff, 1989) are thus critical moments of emotional reconnection after separations, and involve the practicing infant's reentering into patterned interactive transactions with the caregiver who regulates the infant's arousal, affective, and attentional state. What fast-acting dyadic psychobiological mechanism mediates this process? A clue to the answer to this question lies in Rosenblum's (1987) observation that when the infant locomotes more widely in its environment, vision is the primary mode of connection with the mother. I propose that practicing-onset social referencing experiences (Walden & Ogan, 1988), a special form of attachment behavior (Bretherton, 1985) likened to Mahler's emotional refueling (Emde, 1990), occur during these reunion episodes. In these visuoaffective transactions the mother's facially expressed emotional communications provide the infant with salient maternal appraisals of interactions and events (Hornik, Risenhoover, & Gunnar, 1987) in order to regulate his affect and behavior (Klinnert, 1984).

In an important developmental advance, the neo-ambulatory child now communicates with the caregiver by distal (primarily visual) instead of proximal (tactile) modes of relating (Birch, 1962; Greenspan, 1988). It has been established both that visual stimuli are processed faster than tactual (Lobb, 1965) and that infants process visual stimuli more quickly as they get older (Fagan, 1976). Studies in developmental cognition reveal that the rate of information processing is faster in 12-month than 6-month old infants (Rose, 1990). The efficient reciprocal signaling embedded in social referencing transactions allows the refueled toddler to remain emotionally connected to the mother in "reunions that occur across social space" (Brent & Resch, 1987). Brent and Resch observe a practicing reunion pattern of "vitalizing reciprocity," which they equate with Mahler's refueling. In this transaction the underaroused toddler is energized, is primed by the mother, and unfocused attention and negative hedonic tone is transformed in as little as 10 seconds (!) into focused attention and positive hedonic tone. A description of an early form of this transaction, offered in Brent and Resch's observational research, is presented in Table 8.1.

The rapid speed of this dyadic synchronization is underscored by several researchers. Stern's (1977) asserts that the mother and infant interact in a split-second world, Izard (1991) demonstrates that emotions can be facially expressed

TABLE 8.1
Vitalizing Reciprocity

Before Reunion

Tad has been playing with a plastic toy drum and now sits gazing around the room. His glance shifts from object to object without staying on any one item or even appearing quite to see. His face is drooping, his expression lax, his eyes a bit glazed. His body is slightly slumped and flacid; his movements are slow but without any apparent direction. (His emotion is rated as glum; attention, unfocused; hedonic tone, negative.) 10 sec

Reunion

Tad moves onto all fours and starts crawling. He moves slowly but directly toward his mother who is sitting several yards away on the floor. He touches her arm lightly. She helps him pull to a kneeling position beside her. As Tad continues to pull himself to standing, he smiles slightly and puts his arm around his mother's neck firmly for additional support. Now standing, he touches a nearby chair with his free hand. He stands gazing around the room with a sweet, soft smile on his face. His expression gives the impression that he is quietly pleased with himself and with standing there. He puts his thumb in his mouth momentarily and then turns to his mother, lightly pressing his body into hers in a brief hug. The interaction is tender and quiet. Mother continues holding him for a few moments. Presently she places him on the floor to sit. She hands him a cloth block as she prepares to stand up.

After Reunion

Mother gets up and walks away from Tad to an area behind the couch. Tad watches her movements carefully for some moments, then quite suddenly his body becomes energized as he rolls over onto is stomach. He starts crawling over to the busy box on the floor several feet away. He pulls the busy box onto his lap and looks at it in concentration for a few moments. (His emotion is rated as interest/curiosity; attention, focused; hedonic tone, positive.) 10 sec

From Brent and Resch (1987). Reproduced by permission of Lawrence Erlbaum Associates.

in as little as one-half second, and Schaffer (1984) observes that the average length of gaze of 12-month-old infants directed at the mother in a play situation is only 1.33 seconds. In these mother-infant communications, each partner responds to the other extremely rapidly, in latencies ranging from simultaneous to one-half second (Beebe & Lachman, 1988b). The dyad thus evolves an operative practical system for processing high intensity affective transmissions that rapidly maintains psychobiological attunement and sustains merger states without the need for frequent and prolonged physical (tactile) contact. These episodes of microregulation thus occur at a high rate of speed and without any movement of gross motor systems, and these facts may in part explain the "hidden" nature of the maternal regulation of the infant's nervous and endocrine systems (Hofer, 1990). Such synchronous exchanges serve as a template for imprinting, the very rapid (Hess, 1973) learning process underlying attachment phenomena that involves synchrony between sequential infant-maternal stimuli and behavior (Petrovich & Gewirtz, 1985).

One of the important evolutionary functions of attachment behavior is the protection of offspring from predation. Bowlby (1988a) explains that the emotionally responsive mother creates a "secure base" from which the mobile toddler may sortie to explore the world and then return in the face of physiological need or danger. In social referencing interchanges, the infant, now at greater distances from the mother yet increasingly sensitive to her gaze, keeps an eye on the feelings expressed on the mother's face (Oatley & Jenkins, 1992). The child thereby uses the mother's affective expression as a signal, an indicator of her appraisal of danger or safety in a particular environmental circumstance. However, although the phenomenon may be more covert and subtle, the mother's facially expressed affective transmissions also act as an amplifier of positive arousal, a generator of energy required for further physical explorations of the environment by the infant. This allows for ongoing separations and reconnections that facilitate further growth by enabling the child to be exposed to an "enriched" (Rosenzweig, Bennet, & Diamond, 1972), "growth-promoting" (Greenspan, 1981) environment. Practicing "vitalizing reciprocity" refueling transactions are thus rapidly processed, highly efficient, condensed symbiotic merger experiences that represent a fundamental ontogenetic adaptation, and they allow for the appearance of another ontogenetic adaptation, play behavior. Play transforms an environment into an enriched one (Chisholm, 1990), that is an environment that facilitates the processing of novel information and thereby improves learning capacity. Rose (1972) proposes that merging in order to reemerge may be a part of the fundamental process of psychological growth on all developmental levels.

Furthermore, these reunion episodes, which involve shifts in arousal, affect, and behavior, are stored as a single indivisible unitary chunk of experience in episodic memory, as Stern (1989) suggests. Indeed, these transactions may act as a matrix for the primal generation of the autobiographical experience of episodic memory, which Tulving (1972) describes as memory for real life moments occurring in real time. The enduring effect of early reunion transactions on future socioemotional development is emphasized in the psychoanalytic literature:

> In the further course of development, repeated experiences of separation and reunion are remembered and anticipated, providing the structural basis for progressively more varied and modulated affective responses, whether basically painful or basically pleasurable. (Pao, 1971, p. 788)

REUNION TRANSACTIONS AS SYNCHRONIZED BIOENERGETIC TRANSMISSIONS

Notice that immediately upon returning from each autonomous foray away from the mother and into the novel environment, that is, after each separation, the immature organism seeks to resynchronize the arousal level generated by its nervous system against the reference standard, the template set by the mother's nervous system. Wright (1991) asserts that "the mother's face is the beacon to which the child references back for orientation and reaction" (p. 334). In reunions, the "orientation" function refers to social referencing, in which the child searches the mother's face for emotional information about the physical environment and then follows her gaze (Scaife & Bruner, 1975). But in addition to this her face serves as a stimulus that induces "reaction" in the child. How might this be explained? At the point of reunion the mother's interest and attention is again intensely focused on the face of her returning child. In this manner the psychobiologically attuned mother reads the child's face to appraise his current internal state. This allows her to adjust her output in order to optimally create a "synchrony or mesh among sequential infant maternal stimuli and behavior" (Petrovich & Gewirtz, 1985). By reengaging in rapid synchronized mutual gaze with the emotionally reconnecting toddler she recreates a mutual regulatory system of arousal in which she can modulate the child's current level of arousal. This modulation of the child's psychobiological state causes a "reaction," since the alteration in this organismic state is reflected in a change in affect, behavior, and cognition. Indeed, the caregiver modulates the child's energetic state, as arousal levels are known to be associated with changes in metabolic energy (Gonzalez-Lima & Scheich, 1985). These externally induced changes in metabolic energy may underlie Mahler's description of energy exchanges that occur during episodes of emotional refueling which follow periods of separation. The referencing of reunions thus involve not just an orientation, but also a recalibration of the arousal level produced by the toddler's plastic, developing nervous system against the reference standard of the mother's, which is reflected in her visually communicated facial signals.

In fact, practicing phase refueling reunion transactions involving a pattern of energy transmissions between the mother and the infant may represent the fundamental core of the attachment dynamic. The need of the early organism to enter into psychophysiologically induced matter-energy transformations with the primary caregiver in order to sustain the enormously increasing bioenergetic demands of nervous system-regulated activity and growth may underlie its "biological preparedness for social interactions" (Emde, 1989). Trevarthen (1990) argues that the epigenetic program of brain growth requires brain—brain interaction and occurs in the context of a positive affective relationship between infant and mother, and Trad (1986) observes that stable attachment bonds are vitally important for adequate neurobiological development in the infant. These events may represent the dialectical psychoneurobiological imprinting process by which the mother critically influences the permanent "hard-wiring" of brain regions in human infancy. In developmental psychoanalytic terms, in dyadic reciprocal interactions the maternal selfobject performs regulatory functions which maintain the child's homeostatic balance (Kohut, 1971, 1977). Such refueling experiences (Mahler et al., 1975) facilitate the building of new structure.

Furthermore, this phenomenon may represent the deeper psychobiological mechanism which underlies "the transfer of affect between mothers and infants" (Tronick, Cohn, & Shea, 1986), and which explains the observation that it is the affective state that underlies and motivates attachment behavior (Gaensbauer, Connell, & Schultz, 1983). Mahler's observation of maternal refueling, a function that "perks up" the toddler from a toned-down state to a state of renewed exploratory behavior and pleasure, literally occurs in the form of her triggering infant cardiac acceleration and elation. Her conceptualization of an energy exchange mediated in "refueling looks" (Lichtenberg, 1989) may represent a priming "jump-start" or recharging of psychic energy that activates the attachment and thereby the exploratory motivational systems. This may be reflected in Mahler's and Kaplan's (1977) observation that the "mirroring" caregiver "electrifies" the infant, and Stern's (1985) characterization of a particular maternal social behavior that can "blast the infant into the next orbit of positive excitation."

Indeed, attachment dynamics result in pleasurable states (Reite & Capitanio, 1985) and the intensely positive affect of elation is known to be associated with increased energy levels (Duffy, 1941). The practicing phase reunion pattern of vitalizing reciprocity, in which the psychobiologically attuned dyad's physiological systems are homeostatically coregulated, provides for a fast-acting and efficient amplification of arousal. This high intensity visual affective stimulation may retrigger the onset of the rapidly accelerating high energy vitality affects of interest-excitement and elation. The generation of these positive affects allows the curious child to securely separate from the mother and again venture into a new environment. This biophysical process may be subsumed under the fundamental principle of the first law of thermodynamics which states that the total energy of a system and its surroundings is a constant. Energetic interactions between the infant and the maternal environment thus obey the fundamental principle of physics, the transformation and conservation of energy, in that the total amount of energy within the dyadic system during a transaction remains constant, though it may assume different forms successively. In recent conceptions, living systems are defined as "inherently dynamic energy-transformation regimes that co-evolve with their environments, and that organize and regulate themselves in accord with physical laws" (Schwalbe, 1991, p. 270). A central tenet of dynamic systems theory asserts that during ontogeny "directed flows of energy" allow developing living systems to self-organize and generate emergent functional structures that exhibit pattern and order (Thelen, 1989).

I also suggest that in the energetic transduction of this arousal amplification process, the infant, seeking to replenish energy supplies, initially reconnects in a receptive parasympathetic energy-conserving mode with the mother who is in an expressive sympathetic energy-expending mode. This process is described in Basch's (1976) observation that the language of mother and infant consists of signals produced by the autonomic, involuntary nervous system in both partners. Winnicott (1966) characterizes the mother's willingness and ability "to drain interest from her own self into the baby." I would add that such a transfer of interest occurs in synchronized mutual gaze transactions. The outcome of this form of psychobiological attunement is expressed in the dyadic participation of "mutually entrained central nervous system propensities" (Horner, 1985), in which both are now in an excitatory, sympathetic state. As a result of her engagement in vitalizing reciprocity, the mother induces an arousal amplification in the infant; the previously underaroused toddler is now in an energized state. The caregiver thus facilitates a state transition, manifest in a change in patterns of arousal, energy level, cognitive processing, motor behavior, and particulary an affect shift (Putnam, 1992). Field (1985a) defines psychobiological attunement underlying attachment in terms of the dyad being "on the same wavelength"; this may be more than a metaphor, as it may refer to similar brain and thereby bodily (internal) states. As mentioned, the practicing stage characteristic high level of arousal, elevated activity level and heart rate, and positive affective state of elation are all associated with heightened activation of the sympathetic component of the autonomic nervous system.

A fundamental postulate of biology asserts that each living organism exists within an immediate environment from which it receives matter and energy and to which it returns matter and energy. Schwalbe (1991) notes that: "Dynamical systems are open to continuous interaction with their environments. This interaction involves the input of free energy from the environment and its export in degraded form" (p. 274). As I have previously emphasized the developing infant's encounters with the larger environment are mediated by the mother (Schaffer, 1984) and the maternal face is the most powerful stimulus in the infant's environment (Stern, 1974). In fact the "specifically-experienced environment" of the child is now thought to be contained within the specifically-experienced caregiver relationship (Emde, 1988). It is commonly accepted that the mother, the primary caregiver, is the infant's fundamental source of environmental matter (foodstuffs) required for anabolic processes, especially of lipids and essential fatty acids that sustain the high metabolic demands of the postnatal critical period brain growth spurt (Crawford, Hassam, & Stevens, 1982; Innis, 1991). It is not as well appreciated that she also acts as a primal generator, transducer, and modulator of physical energy (light, sound, pressure, temperature) that reaches the infant. His developing nervous system senses this "free energy from the environment" and responds to these energies, thereby triggering catabolic energy-mobilizing processes. This stimulation also influences brain growth (Cummins et al., 1977; Jacobson, 1978), since it generates the positive affect of interest in the infant. Izard (1991) now contends that in motivating sustained sensory transactions with the environment, the affect of interest functions to promote brain development. Of particular importance would be the experience-dependent development of those structures in the brain that regulate energy transactions between the evolving organism and the "primordial other" of its species in the early protosocial environment.

These dyadic energy transactions occur in great frequency in the critical period of socialization, the practicing period, a time of elevated energy metabolism and heightened elation, a high energy affect. Brazelton and Cramer (1990) note that critical phases are times when energy is high in the infant and the parent for receptivity to each other's cues and for adapting to each other. Egeland and Farber (1984) suggest that the amount of emotional energy the mother has for responding to her infant affects the quality of the infant-mother attachment. Collins (1981) argues that the fundamental purpose of human interaction is that it "serves as a machine for intensifying emotion and for generating new emotional tones and solidarities" (p. 1001). Social transactions act as a medium for the transmission of "emotional energies":

> An individual who is successfully accepted into an interaction acquires an increment of positive emotional energy. This energy is manifested in what we commonly call confidence, warmth, and enthusiasm. Acquiring this in one situation, an individual has more emotional resources for successfully negotiating solidarity in the next situation. Such chains, both positive and negative, extend throughout every person's lifetime (Collins, 1981, p. 1002).

I view this practicing process as an example of the ongoing development of entrained biological rhythms in infancy (Hellbrugge, 1960). Work in this area has emphasized the importance of "social Zeitgebers," that is, psychosocial contacts that critically influence the synchronization of circadian (Ehlers, Frank, & Kupfer, 1988) and ultradian (Anders & Zeanah, 1984) rhythms. The work of Reppert, Duncan, and Weaver (1987) emphasizes maternal influences on the infant's developing circadian system. Reite and Capitanio (1985) suggest that an essential function of attachment is to promote the synchrony or regulation of biological and behavioral systems on an organismic level. Schwalbe (1991) proposes that as a result of the infant's "locking on" to a set of "consistently responsive objects in its environment," the evolving brain modulates and synchronizes the body's rhythmic patterns of energy dissipation. The early practicing caregiver acts as a social Zeitgeber during reunion episodes, acting to shift the infant from parasympathetic-dominant to sympathetic-dominant autonomic nervous system activity. The mother thus functions as a socioaffective stimulus which arouses the infant's nervous system, and with the shunting of blood from the viscera and the periphery to the skeletal muscles, the toddler's new found exhilarated mobility is reestablished. She also acts to modulate nonoptimal high levels of stimulation, thereby down-regulating supra-heightened levels of sympathetic arousal and elevating parasympathetic dominance.

The infant's maturing autonomic nervous system is particulary sensitive to changes in temporal parameters. The mother, through her entrained interactions, directly influences the developing ultradian rhythmic pattern of the child's activity-passivity cycles. In this manner the primary caregiver's unique patterns of psychobiological attunement, misattunement, and reattunement effect the creation of cycles of social engagement and disengagement in the infant. Penman et al. (1983) demonstrate that the neurophysiological capacities of the mother (habituation) and infant (social gaze) determine the cyclical patterns of their synchronized interaction. Anders and Zeanah (1984) conclude that the mother's rhythmic responsiveness regulates the autonomic, behavioral, neurochemical, and hormonal functions of the infant. Hofer (1984a) points out that in early infancy the mother is *the* regulator of the infant's developing autonomic nervous system, and that social interactions may play an important role in the everyday regulation of internal biological systems.

A form of this very same process continues in further development since, Certain social interactions are as essential for physiological and psychological homeostasis among adults as they are among infants (McGuire, Marks, Neese, & Troisi, 1992). Grotstein (1983) suggests that the regulatory selfobject function "never disappears; it only undergoes transformation and maturation" (p. 176). Field (1985a) posits that the psychobiological attunement of attachment occurs in multiple relationships at all stages of the lifespan. Indeed, it is now thought that the operation of the attachment dynamic occurs in adult life. According to Heard and Lake (1986), it involves the activation of an internal system, first developed in early infant-caregiver interactions, that maintains an affective state of well-being, enjoyment, and interest via the exchange of "emotive messages." In experimental work, Krause observes that all social interactions involve regulating processes which operate via the unconscious transmission of nonverbal microbehaviors within dyads—gaze behavior, facial expression, vocal affect signals, on-off patterns and gesticulations (Krause, Steimer, Sanger-Alt, & Wagner, 1989). A number of different disciplines are now converging on this common theme. The psychoanalyst Novey (1961, p. 22) asserts that "no human relatedness is conceivable without affective participation," and Sroufe (1989b, p. 106), a developmental psychologist, concludes "a major function of all close relationships throughout the lifespan is to create or maintain basic patterns of arousal (or affect) regulation." In the sociobiological literature, McGuire and Troisi (1987) note that certain types and frequencies of social interaction are essential to maintain normal physiological function. It is thus imprecise and misleading to posit mutually exclusive biological or social regulatory systems at any point in development.

THE ORIGIN OF THE APPRAISAL OF EMOTIONALLY MEANINGFUL AND MOTIVATIONALLY SIGNIFICANT ENVIRONMENTAL EVENTS

In psychobiologically attuned reunion episodes the mother and her 12-month-old practicing infant maintain a remarkable pattern of interpersonal synchronization in their gaze behavior, so much so that it has been described as a "shared visual reality" (Scaife & Bruner, 1975) and a "shared program" (Schaffer, 1984). In social referencing, an affectively charged dialogic process of the mutually attuned communication of "emotional vision" (Bauer, 1982), the mother induces a mood modification in the infant (Feinman, 1982) and is directly influencing the infant's learning of "how to feel," "how much to feel," and "whether to feel" about particular objects in the environment. According to Mahler et al. (1975) the chief characteristic of the practicing period is the child's great narcissistic investment in his own functions and in "the objects and objectives of his expanding reality." As I previously stressed, the effect of this fundamental psychoneurophysiological process on personality development is profound, since it generates stage-specific increases in enjoyment-joy (elation) and interest-excitement, positive affects that are required for continued socioemotional and cognitive development. Practicing period reunion episodes may therefore establish the parameters of the individual's future "hedonic capacity" (Meehl, 1975), "positive affectivity" (Watson & Clark, 1988), and "affect intensity" (Larsen & Diener, 1987). They also may indelibly influence his positive cathectic ("narcissistic") capacity, which Freud described as the sum of psychic energy or sum of excitation available for the self's investment of internal and external objects with emotion-inducing properties. Indeed, in his last writings, Freud (1940/1964) defined cathexis as physical energy being lodged in or attaching itself to mental structures or processes, analogous to an electric charge.

With regard to the development of interest, curiosity, and "excited anticipation," social referencing maternal attention-focusing strategies may also be essential to the practicing caregiver's enduring effect on the infant's learning of "what to feel" about objects in the social environment (including the mother herself and through her the father and other social objects), and "what to be interested in" amongst the objects in the physical environment. These critical period events may induce "topographic familiarity" and begin to generate "personally relevant" aspects of the individual's world (Van Lancker, 1991). Developmental studies of 12-month-olds support the notion that social referencing accounts for the maternal emotional biasing of infant reactions to novel inanimate objects (Hornik et al., 1987). In other words, these early synchronized visuoaffective attunement experiences influence the development of the child's motivational systems. Of special importance at this time is the development of what Lichtenberg (1989) calls the exploratory-assertive motivational system. I have previously discussed the roles of play behavior as an essential ontogenetic adaptation of the practicing period and as a central component of an enriched environment. Indeed, this developmental period represents Piaget's fifth stage of sensorimotor intelligence, a time of the the first appearance of tertiary circular reactions which enable the toddler to actively and spontaneously explore for newness in the environment. It now appears that this phenomenon is much more dyadic than Piaget thought, as the caregiver strongly influences the cognitions that mediate these circular reactions. The nature of this visuoaffective modulation is revealed in Emde's (1988) description of the 12-month-old toddler's "sparkling-eyed pleasure" associated with early mastery experiences which is amplified under the watchful eye of the approving caregiver, and Sroufe's (1989a) observation of the 12-month-old who grasps a novel object that captures his attention "with widened eyes" and then immediately shares her delight with the observing mother. Futhermore, these experiences are registered in memory. Bauer and Mandler (1992) report that by 1 year-of-age children can accurately remember novel event sequences.

This importance of dyadic visual communicative mechanisms has also been described by other researchers. Between 10 and 13 months "joint visual attention" becomes intensified and the child first exhibits communicative pointing (Butterworth, 1991), a social gesture (Leung & Rheingold, 1981) that occurs in the context of a shared activity (Murphy, 1978). In this sequence, the child points to an object in the environment but also looks at the other to check the person's gaze as well (Masur, 1983). Near the end of the first year, infants also produce preword vocalizations which are directed to persons or objects (Dore, 1985). According to Dore these "proto-communications" begin at about 11 months, and are accompanied by gestures, affectively salient tones, and facial expressions. Such emotional communications occur within the context of dialogic "face-engagements" between mother and child who share "intimate connections." Attuned adults interpret these "as if the infant intended to communicate something; they attribute either some specific internal state or a particular word meaning to the infant" (Dore, 1985, p. 23). Dore concludes that meaning emerges from the process of dialog in which the dyad is intimately engaged.

In the earlier part of this century, Vygotsky (1978) emphasized that the child's discovery of the physical environment is socially mediated. This seminal idea has been incorporated into and expanded upon in the latest models of emotion. Lazarus (1991a) now contends that it is not the physical properties of the environment but the subjective meanings that count in the emotion process. Frijda (1988) holds that emotions "arise in response to the meaning structures of given situations, to events that are important to the individual, and which importance he or she appraises in some way" (p. 349). The emotional communication of social referencing transactions provides access to the mother's appraisal of objects in the animate and inanimate world, and this influences the development of an internalized system in the infant that can appraise the personal emotional meaning of any particular environmental event. Indeed, rapid unconscious appraisals on the basis of the optic stimulus array are now viewed as a necessary and sufficient condition of emotion (Lazarus & Smith, 1988). Emotion is currently understood to involve reactions to fundamental relational meanings that have adaptive significance (Lazarus, 1991b). Infant research now highlights the principle that an event achieves significance when it is amplified by an affective response (Lichtenberg, 1989). Lichtenberg also underscores the important principle that "affects play a major role in amplifying the experience of motivation as they unfold" (p. 6).

What sociobiological learning processes might influence the development of an appraisal system that determines the affective and motivational significance of environmental stimuli? I hypothesize that in this developmental period of elevated excitation, a form of Pavlovian conditioning (e.g., Rescorla, 1981) occurs when the infant accesses the caregiver's affectively-toned appraisals of environmental stimuli. The temporal parameters of this conditioning are prescribed by the synchronized sequences of the attunement process. This conditioning facilitates the experience-dependent growth of the infant's own appraisal system. For example, viewing the mother's smiling face induces a positive hedonic response in the infant, and this may be paired with a neutral novel object, a conditioned stimulus. The result would be the formation of a permanent conditioned response, an "affective set," a positive expectancy towards the object. Rolls (1986) suggests the learning of emotional responses specifically involves a process of "stimulus-reinforcement association" which occurs via the Pavlovian process of classical conditioning. This learning process may be embedded in the mother's "contingent responsivity" to the infant's burgeoning mirroring needs.

The infant's positive hedonic state is known to be associated with sympathetic limbic activity, and the involvement of orbitofrontal and ventral tegmental dopaminergic activity in reinforcement mechanisms has been previously described. Schiff (1982) describes a process of "conditioned dopaminergic activity" in which environmental cues that affect the activity of dopaminergic neurons can act as conditioning signals. The mesocortical dopamine system is a good candidate for emotional conditioning, since it is centrally involved in emotionality (Thierry et al., 1978), in exploratory behavior (Fink & Smith, 1980), and in stimulant and opioid conditioning effects (Stewart, deWitt, & Eikelboom, 1984).

Noting that this system is involved in incentive/reward effects, Fowles (1992) states that incentive motivation refers to the ability of conditioned stimuli or the expectation of receiving a reward to motivate behavior. Panksepp (1986) describes an "expectancy command circuit" that connects higher limbic areas in the orbitofrontal cortex with lower brain stem areas, contains ventral tegmental dopaminergic elements, and supports emotional functions involved in positive expectancy processes. He also suggests that emotive circuits can come under the conditioned control of emotionally neutral environmental stimuli (Pankseep, 1992). Dopaminergic conditioning may thus mediate the expansion of the ventral tegmental system from a dyadic attachment function to a nondyadic exploratory function.

More specifically, this affective-limbic conditioning may pair an interoceptive, autonomic response, such as the maternally induced cardiovascular accompaniment of affective behavior (Spyer, 1989) with an exteroceptive visual input. The involvement of limbic structures in the classical conditioning of heart rate by visual (as well as olfactory and auditory) inputs has been demonstrated in infant mammals (e.g., Sananes, Gaddy, & Campbell, 1988). The result could be a conditioned response of cardiac acceleration, that is, an excited anticipation, a prefrontal "anticipatory set" of emotion-induced selective attention associated with the object. Fox and Davidson (1986) propose that cardiac acceleration can precede positive emotional expression. Zelazo (1982) reports that $11^1/_2$ but not $9^1/_2$ month-old infants show excitement and heart rate acceleration during specific information processing tasks. Kagan (1982) describes a disposition to predict future events which emerges at 10–11 months. Indeed, imprinting phenomena are known to facilitate the establishment of "acquired preferences" and "developing predispositions" (Johnson, Bolhuis, & Horn, 1985).

One example of such a predisposition is an attachment motivation preferentially directed toward the mother. This psychobiological mechanism could thus mediate the conditioned elicitation of a positive hedonic response in anticipation of the actual perception of the mother's smiling face at reunion. Expectations are phenomenologically experienced as imagined scenes amplified by the positive affects of excitement and enjoyment, as images of things desired (Kaufman, 1989). Frijda (1988) characterizes elation as pleasure plus the urge toward contact seeking. It has been observed that at the onset of mobility the infant becomes increasingly active in pursuing the mother (Oster, 1981) and learns to anticipate and search for the "desired object" (Sugarman & Jaffe, 1990). Sroufe (1989a) indicates that a new level of organization of goal directed behavior, based much more on the infant's appraisal of both internal and external parameters, is attained at 12 months.

If these dyadic psychobiologically synchronized reunion transactions do influence the structural development of the child's appraisal system, where is this important structure located? The most parsimonious answer to this question is suggested by neuropsychological studies that indicate that orbitofrontal activity is involved specifically in the functions of appraisal (Pribram, 1987), attention (King, Corwin, & Reep, 1989), motivation (Pandya & Yeterian, 1985), and reward (Mora et al., 1980). This cortex, which both supports attachment functions (Steklis & Kling, 1985) and plays an essential role in tracking emotionally relevant objects in space (Mesulam, 1985), is suggested to be critical to the indelible formation of selective attention to motivationally significant stimuli in the early practicing period. Physiological studies show that this cortical area uniquely co-processes autonomic interoceptive and exteroceptive information (Rosenkilde, Bauer, & Fuster, 1981). Scott (1958) has found that during the sensitive period for the development of social responses, changes in heart rate occur which indicate the establishment of neural connections between the cortex and hypothalamus. It is well established that the hypothalamus is the hub of the motivational systems (Hadley, 1989). Anatomic studies reveal the orbitofrontal cortex sends direct projections to the hypothalamus (Nauta, 1972). I suggest that the formation and imprinting of these and other subcortical-cortical connections may represent the expansion and activation of the ventral tegmental "expectancy command circuit" into the orbitofrontal cortex. In the next chapter I present evidence to show that the early practicing phase is a critical period for this growth. Indeed, dopaminergic innervation acts as a trophic stimulus for the growth of this frontolimbic cortex.

SUMMARY

With the onset of independent upright locomotion in the early practicing period, the neo-toddler is able to separate himself from the mother in order to begin to explore the nonmaternal environment. The caregiver regulates this process by allowing the child to emotionally reconnect with her in reunion transactions. The child's sorties into the world occur under the watchful eye of the caregiver, but at the point when he returns to the secure base the mother's attention to the child's emotionally expressive face intensifies. With these facial cues the psychobiologically attuned mother is now able to appraise the child's internal state, and on the basis of this she reengages in synchronized patterns of visuoaffective communication. The returning toddler, in social referencing transactions, attentively responds to the stimulation emanating from the mother's emotionally expressive face. In these dyadic interchanges the mother regulates the child's internal state of arousal. In a reunion pattern of vitalizing reciprocity, she triggers a rapid arousal amplification in the infant by inducing a psychobiological state transition. By promoting a symbiotic entrainment of her mature and his immature nervous systems, the child shifts from a parasympathetic dominant energy-conserving mode into a similar state as the mother, a sympathetic dominant energy-expending mode. This external activation of the child's sympathetic nervous system generates elevated levels of arousal, regenerated positive affects, and heightened levels of activity and mobility which enable the reenergized toddler to go back out into the world.

Practicing period reunion transactions also have long-term enduring effects. In addition to their impact on attachment dynamics, these visuoaffective transactions influence the formation of an exploratory motivational system which is developing at this time. Indeed, the dyadic psychobiological experiences that occur during early reunions serve as imprinting events for the experience-dependent maturation of a structural system that for the rest of the lifespan appraises the affective and motivational significance of environmental stimuli. A central component of this system resides in the orbitofrontal cortex, and the critical period for its physiological maturation occurs in the practicing phase.

9 Early Imprinting

The term critical period should not be used unless it is accompanied by (a) an approximate onset and terminus of the period, (b) the most exact specification of the critical period stimulus to which the organism is most sensitive, and (c) a correspondingly exact specification of the critical system that will be affected later on by exposure to, or deprivation of, the stimulus during the period.

—John Columbo (1982)

What developing brain structures which potentially regulate socioemotional functioning and motivational states are permanently imprinted by dyadic socio-affective experiences in the early phase of the practicing period? Developmental psychoanalytic researchers are now finding that the emotional availability of the caregiver in intimacy is the central growth-promoting feature in the developing infant's environment (Emde, 1988). This principle is also being articulated by neuroscientists who propose that the development of cerebral cortical circuits, which undergo their greatest transformations in infancy, occurs in the context of an intimate affective relationship (Trevarthen, 1990). Although infant investigators have not agreed upon the specific nature of the mother's "intimate affective availability," I have suggested that at the end of the first year this refers to her involvement in mutual gaze, the most intense form of human communication (Tomkins, 1963). I have also presented evidence that indicates that the high intensity visuoaffective transactions of the early practicing phase are imprinted into limbic structures which are undergoing a critical period maturation. Winson (1985) points out, "The critical period coincides with the time period during which the neocortex develops anatomically, and it may be related to this develop-

114

ment" (p. 162). An integration of such data suggests that in this time frame intimate object relations with the mother influence the structural maturation of cortical circuits in developing prefrontal cerebral areas. In a review of the critical period literature, Columbo (1982) proposes that the development of the prefrontal cortex may specifically provide a useful model for elucidating the phenomena and underlying mechanisms of postnatal development.

In earlier chapters I proposed that maternally regulated high intensity affective stimulation, particularly visual stimulation, provided in psychobiologically attuned, arousal-amplifying, synchronized face-to-face transactions, generates and sustains high levels of positive affect and activity in the infant. In this chapter I present extensive evidence that suggests that this socioaffective input supports the experience-dependent growth of ventral tegmental mesocortical dopamine terminals into orbitofrontal regions. The early phase of the practicing period (10–12 to 14–16 months) serves as a critical period for the early maturation of this structure. In the course of presenting this model, I outline, in some detail, the developmental biochemical and anatomical events that are involved in this maturational process.

PROPOSAL: THE ONSET OF A CRITICAL PERIOD FOR THE MATURATION OF THE ORBITOFRONTAL CORTEX OCCURS AT THE END OF THE FIRST YEAR

Luria (1973) reports that in the first and second years of human life the prefrontal areas of the cortex are in a state of rapid growth. Animal ablation (Goldman, 1971; Nonneman, Corwin, Sahley, & Vicedomini, 1984) and anatomical (Corwin, Leonard, Schoenfeld, & Crandall, 1983; Van Eden & Uylings, 1985a) research indicate that the maturation of the structurally primitive orbitofrontal cortex begins early in infancy and precedes the maturation of the other prefrontal system, the dorsolateral cortex. Studies of prefrontal cytoarchitecture also demonstrate that the orbital surfaces develop in more primitive stages and precede dorsolateral maturation which occurs in later stages of ontogeny (Pandya & Barnes, 1987). Indeed, it has been concluded that the prefrontal delayed response function in the infant must be mediated by regions other than the dorsolateral cortex (Nonneman et al., 1984). This adaptive capacity, unique to prefrontal areas, allows the individual to react to situations on the basis of stored or internalized representations, rather than on information immediately present in the environment. Both comparative neuropsychological (Mishkin, 1964; Niki, Sakai, & Kubota, 1972) and neurological (Freedman & Oscar-Berman, 1986) investigations demonstrate that the orbitofrontal cortex functionally mediates delayed response processing.

Goldman (1971) has found that the orbitofrontal cortex undergoes a significant developmental shift in functional organization in early infancy. A study of the role of frontal involvement in emotion expression in 10-month-old infants suggests that functional differentiation among various cortical regions "increases developmentally" (Fox & Davidson, 1987). Fox (1991) now postulates that in the first year of life individual differences in patterns of frontal activity associated with the generation of emotion "may be susceptible to both maturational and environmental influences" (p. 870). Just prior to 10 months infants perform poorly on a Piagetian object permanence task involving delayed recall of recently experienced stimuli (Schacter & Moscovich, 1984), a finding attributed to the lack of frontal lobe anatomical maturation to this point of development (Diamond & Goldman-Rakic, 1983). However, by 11 to 13 months children show ordered recall after a delay for both familiar and new events (Mandler, 1990). Recent neuropsychological research reveals functional evidence of a major maturational change in the prefrontal cortex of the human infant at 10 to 12 months (Diamond & Doar, 1989). I contend that this change is facilitated by imprinting experiences that occur at this time.

The mechanism of imprinting, a very rapid form of learning which underlies attachment bond formation, has been understood to involve an irreversible stamping of early experience upon the developing nervous system. Staddon (1983) refers to "template learning," and Ainsworth (1967) asserts that attachment is internal, "being built into the nervous system, in the course of and as a result of the infant's experience of his transactions with the mother" (p. 429). The dyadic experiences which build attachment into the nervous system are embedded in practicing maternal-infant visuoaffective mutual gaze transactions, which provide a "synchrony or mesh among sequential infant maternal stimuli and behavior" (Petrovich & Gewirtz, 1985). In these episodes of "mutually entrained nervous system propensities" (Horner, 1985) the infant's differentiating orbitofrontal cortex, which contains neurons that track emotionally relevant objects in the interpersonal space (Mesulam, 1985) and respond to the emotional expressions of faces (Thorpe, Rolls, & Maddisson, 1983), is exposed to the output of the mother's orbitofrontal cortex. This adult frontolimbic cortex, which has been shown to be implicated in maternal behavior (Raleigh, 1977), eye and head movements (Pribram, 1987), and motor responses of the face (Sugar, Chusid, & French, 1948), thus serves as a template for the structural imprinting of the infant's orbitofrontal cortex and its function in attachment processes (Steklis & Kling, 1985).

The onset of the practicing period—the time at which the child first demonstrates upright posture and the independent locomotion that enables her to explore her surroundings—thus represents the beginning of a critical period for the maturation of the paralimbic core of the brain, an adaptive system which controls "postural and affective states" (Tucker, 1992). The capacity of locomotion requires not only control but the capability to adapt to the changing surroundings (Forssberg, Stokes, & Hirschfeld, 1992). The latter authors conclude that the maturation of human locomotion involves a process whereby spinal circuits become progressively influenced by higher brain centers. A direct projection from the orbitofrontal cortex to the corticospinal tract has now been identified in neonates (Van Eden, Kros, & Uylings, 1990).

In the latter part of the first year the increasingly mobile human infant begins to actively pursue the mother (Oster, 1981). In classical ethological work, imprinting is associated with the onset of locomotor activity (Hess, 1959). Developmental psychobiological research demonstrates that during an early critical period of infancy for the development of approach behavior, levels of catecholamine-generated arousal are elevated (Kovach, 1970). Rauschecker and Marler (1987) conclude that a stimulus which elicits a high level of catecholamine-generated arousal enables the imprinting process and evokes attachment. "There is an increased probability that stimulation experienced in an aroused state or accompanied by stimuli that induce arousal will exert an undue influence on neural and behavioral development" (p. 360). Fuster (1985) reports that the functional activity of prefrontal neurons is dependent upon the level of arousal, and that these neurons, rare outside the frontal cortex, increase their activation in anticipation of a motor response "and may be attuned to the particular movement the cue calls for" (Fuster, 1991, p. 210). Such properties could mediate the involvement of prefrontal cortex in psychobiological attunement processes and elucidate the importance of the mother's face as an arousal-generating cue for attachment behavior. Most importantly, I posit that the arousal associated with the imprinting of this cortex is specifically dopaminergic arousal (Iversen, 1977).

PROPOSAL: MESOCORTICAL DOPAMINE ACTS AS A TROPHIC STIMULUS FOR PREFRONTAL DEVELOPMENT

I have presented multidisciplinary evidence that suggests that modulated high intensity visual and auditory affective stimulation provided in psychobiologically attuned, arousal-amplifying, synchronized face-to-face transactions generates and sustains high levels of positive affect and activity in the infant. I now propose that these maternally regulated affective experiences act as a growth-promoting influence by inducing endocrine alterations that activate and support the experience-dependent growth of ventral tegmental mesocortical dopamine terminals into orbitofrontal regions. The commencement of the practicing critical period of hyperarousal at 10 to 12 months is suggested to be inaugurated by the innervation of deep cortical sites in the orbitofrontal association cortex by ascending collateral sprouting axons terminals of diffusely projecting mesocortical dopamine neurons in the mesencephalic ventral tegmental area (Gilad & Reis, 1979), thereby initiating a localized orbital growth spurt in the furthest terminus of this circuit. The ventromedial mesencephalic tegmentum, the source of dopaminergic neurons which project to the orbitofrontal cortex via the mesocortical pathway, is known to be composed of various subnuclei. The work of Porrino and Goldman-Rakic (1982) with primates suggests that its medial component nuclei project to the ventral prefrontal cortex. The research of Tork (Halliday & Tork, 1986; Scheibner & Tork, 1987) (Fig. 9.1) with humans implies that the rostral linear nucleus in particular most massively projects collaterals to and between different cortical areas. This nucleus, in humans, contains a total of only 17,000 neurons. From these facts I deduce that the dopaminergic innervation of the orbitofrontal region derives from the arrival and sprouting of axons of specifically rostral linear ventral tegmental dopamine neurons into the deep layers of this prefrontal cortex. Paralimbic areas are known to show a predominance of deep cortical layers (Pandya & Yeterian, 1985).

Significant alterations in the number, shape, and form of dopaminergic axons projecting to the developing orbitofrontal cortex have been observed during mammalian infancy. The postnatal appearance of "adult morphology" of these fibers—very thin axons with irregularly spaced varicosities—is believed to signal the onset of dopaminergic innervation (Kalsbeek, Voorn, Buijs, Pool, & Uylings, 1988) (Fig. 9.2). In a recent study of the ontogeny of dopaminergic function in the frontal cortex during a postnatal stage of development, Noison and Thomas (1988) suggest that a developmental "cross talk" occurs in which increases in presynaptic dopamine synthesis produces a postsynaptic increase in dopamine receptor formation. Dopamine is known to stimulate incorporation of

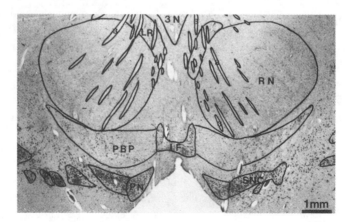

FIG. 9.1. Photomicrograph of the human ventromedial mesencephalic tegmentum (VMT). Note location of the rostral linear nucleus (LR) and the substantia nigra pars compacta (SNC). From Halliday and Tork (1986). Comparative anatomy of the ventromedial mesencephalic tegmentum in the rat, cat, monkey and human. *Journal of Comparative Neurology, 252.* Reprinted by permission of Wiley-Liss, a division of John Wiley and Sons, Inc.

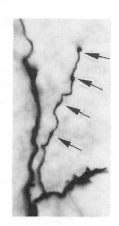

FIG. 9.2. Photomicrograph of a growing dopaminergic axon and growth cone in the postnatal prefrontal rat cortex. Arrows point to dopaminergic varicosities. From Kalsbeek, Voorn, Buijs, Pool, and Uylings (1988). Development of the dopaminergic innervation in the prefrontal cortex of the rat. *Journal of Comparative Neurology, 269.* Reprinted by permission of Wiley-Liss, a division of John Wiley and Sons, Inc.

inorganic phosphate into phospholipids at receptor sites during postnatal brain development (Deskin, Seidler, Whitmore, & Slotkin, 1981). Deskin also observes that the formation of dopaminergic receptors in the postnatal brain depends on the maturation of their presynaptic terminals.

These findings suggest that the increases in presynaptic dopamine terminals in this cortex are matched by the postnatal amplification of dopamine-sensitive adenylate cyclase (D1) receptors (Richfield, Young, & Penney, 1989) that have been identified in the deep layers of this prefrontal cortex (Savasta, Dubois, & Scatton, 1986). D1 dopamine receptors are defined as the receptors for dopamine linked to stimulation of adenylate cyclase (Kebabian & Caine, 1978), and these receptors are important for a variety of behavioral functions mediated by dopamine (Waddington & O'Boyle, 1987). Adenylate cyclase is responsible for the formation of cyclic $3',5'$-adenosine monophosphate (cAMP), and this "second messenger" that translates the extracellular messages of neurotransmitters and hormones into an intracellular response is fundamentally involved in the regulation of biochemical responses of cells and organs to external stimuli (Robison, Butcher, & Sutherland, 1971). Cyclic AMP is also known to induce the morphological maturation of brain cells (Lim, Mitsunobu, & Li, 1973). The developmental period of heightened spontaneous activity has been specifically associated with the postnatal appearance of high levels of dopamine-sensitive adenylate cyclase receptors in the forebrain (Gelbard, Teicher, Faedda, & Baldessarini, 1989). Environmental factors have been suggested to influence the components of newly formed receptors at various stages in early development (Hill, Mistretta, & Bradley, 1986), both in terms of types of receptor molecules and ion transport channels involved in transduction (Heck, Mierson, & DeSimone, 1984; Kashiwayanagi, Miyake, & Kurihara, 1983). Indeed, another class of catecholamine receptors, beta adrenergic receptors, are known to show changes in postnatal development (Hatjis & McLaughlin, 1982).

Cell culture experiments demonstrate that dopamine regulates the outgrowth of axons and growth cones (McCobb, Haydon, & Kater, 1985; Norman, Earl, & Bird, 1991). Stimulation of D1 receptors by dopamine in an early developmental period leads to a large increase in cAMP. This biochemical alteration in the dopamine receptor is accompanied by an inhibition in the outgrowth and motility of neuronal growth cones (Lankford, DeMello, & Klein, 1988) (Fig. 9.3). This signal could facilitate adhesive cell-cell contacts of nascent junctions. Lankford presents this as evidence that dopamine acts as a morphogenetic growth regulator in the developing nervous system. Neuroanatomists have come to a similar conclusion. The early postnatal maturation of mesocortical dopaminergic projections has been suggested to provide a "trophic" function in prefrontal development (Schmidt, Bjorklund, Lindvall, & Loren, 1982). Indeed Kalsbeek et al. (1987) have specifically demonstrated a growth-promoting neurotrophic role for dopamine produced by ventral tegmental neurons in the early postnatal development of this association cortex. How could this neurotransmitter induce brain growth?

The answer to this question may lie in the functional properties of catecholamines to stimulate various glucose-related biochemical processes. All known biosynthetic processes require the biochemical sugar, glucose, the primary carbon source for brain amino acid synthesis and energy production. Neurochemical studies demonstrate that dopamine agonists increase glucose metabolism in prefrontal areas (McCulloch, Savaki, & McCulloch, 1982). Various imprinting experiences have been shown to elicit increased glucose uptake in rostral forebrain regions (Maier & Scheich, 1983). Imprinting also triggers a biochemical cascade of intracellular processes culminating in genomic activation, and this means that nucleic acids, the macromolecules that carry genetic information, are formed. All nucleic acids contain a backbone of sugars and a sequence of bases. Neurochemical studies reveal that during the imprinting pro-

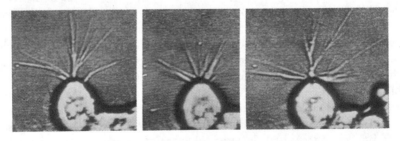

FIG. 9.3.   Micrograph of dopamine-induced neurite retraction and recovery. (Left) Cell immediately before dopamine addition. (Center) Cell 10 min after dopamine addition. (Right) Cell 10 min after return to control medium. From Lankford et al.(1988). Reprinted by permission of the publisher.

cess the base uracil is incorporated into nucleic acid (RNA), and that this nucleic acid synthesis occurs in anterior forebrain regions (Bateson, Rose, & Horn, 1973).

This genomic activation may specifically occur in the nucleolus, a primary site of production of nuclear RNA, especially ribosomal RNA (rRNA), the major component of ribosomes. Dramatic changes in nucleolar morphology associated with increasing levels of metabolism in the growing neuron are known to occur in differentiating pyramidal cells of the frontal cortex during early postnatal development (Buschmann & LaVelle, 1981). The progressive morphological changes in the neuronal nucleus that occur during a postnatal critical period of growth are illustrated in Fig. 9.4. A remarkable increase in the volume of the neuronal nucleus occurs during postnatal development (Crespo, Viadero, Villegas, & Lafarga, 1988), and this increase is associated with changes in cellular metabolism and activity (Hildebrand, 1980). Temporally coordinated nucleolar changes in cells in a particular brain region may contribute to the phenomenon of "critical periods of RNA synthesis" that are observed in the postnatally developing brain (Cummins et al., 1985). In a later chapter I show that genomic activation is regulated by circulating gonadal steroids (McEwen, 1989), and that these hormones specifically produce changes in the nucleolus (Cohen, Chung, & Pfaff, 1984).

RNA that is manufactured in the nucleus is subsequently transported into the cytoplasm (Fawcett, 1981), and in this way the nucleolus plays a central role in ribosome biogenesis (Sommerville, 1986) and in the control of cellular protein synthesis (Hadjiolov, 1985). Ribosomes, the site of RNA translation and the biosynthesis of cellular proteins, are found postnatally on the spines of growing dendrites, where they are thought to be involved in synapse construction (Steward, 1983). They have been observed to be disaggregated and therefore very active during critical period intervals of the cerebral cortex (Garey & Pettigrew, 1974). This disaggregation is specifically mediated by dopamine (Weiss, Munro, Ordonez, & Wurtman, 1972). It is thought that unattached ribosomes seen in immature neurons are associated with the synthesis of proteins needed for growth (Lavelle, 1973). One type of cellular protein that is of particular importance in brain development are glycoproteins, since these are involved in neuronal differentiation (Richter-Landersberg & Dukain, 1983) and interneuronal communication (Barondes, 1970). These macromolecules are localized in developing dendrites and axons (Dyson & Jones, 1976; Morgan & Winick, 1981) and are utilized in synaptic membranes (Burgoyne & Rose, 1980). Imprinting experiences have been demonstrated to increase the biosynthesis of sugar containing glycoproteins (Rose, 1989) in, for example, the forebrain region of the right hemisphere (Lossner & Rose, 1983). Cell surface carbohydrates play an important functional role in postnatal synaptic transmission and memory formation, and their production in early development is influenced by environmental stimulation (Morgan & Winick, 1980). Intriguingly, dopamine and cyclic AMP have

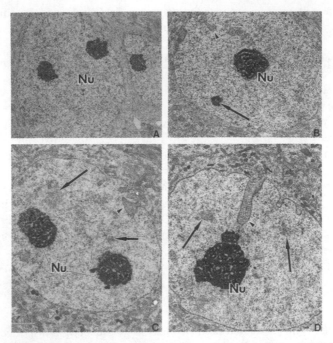

FIG. 9.4.   Nuclear changes during the growth period of hamster facial neurons. (A) The small nucleus from a 14-day fetal neuron is devoid of nuclear invaginations, has a homogenous nucleoplasm, and contains 2 immature nucleoli (Nu). (B) The nucleus from a postnatal day 1 neuron has a shallow nuclear invagination (arrowhead), a clump of heterochromatin (arrow), and a nucleolus. (C) The nuclear invaginations of the postnatal day 5 neuron are more elaborate (arrowhead), and the nucleoplasm has some accumulation of interchromatin granules and fibers (arrows). Multiple nucleoli are still common. (D) By postnatal day 13, the nuclear invaginations are much deeper (arrowhead). The nucleoplasm contains interchromatin granules and fibrils (arrows) and a single prominent nucleous. Adapted from Clark, Jones, and La Velle (1990). Ultrastructural and morphometric analysis of nucleolar and nuclear changes during the early growth period in hamster facial neurons. *Journal of Comparative Neurology, 302.* Reprinted by permission of Wiley-Liss, a division of John Wiley and Sons, Inc.

been specifically demonstrated to mediate increased glycoprotein synthesis associated with early experience in the postnatal period (Lossner, Jork, & Matthies, 1981; Jork, Lossner, & Matthies, 1982).

A major biochemical function of catecholamines is to degrade glycogen—a readily mobilized storage form of carbohydrate (Fig. 9.5). It is broken down to yield glucose, which then is used to provide energy or to supply short-chain carbon skeletons that are reused in the synthesis of various basic components of the cell (Fawcett, 1981). Within various types of cells glycogen is concentrated

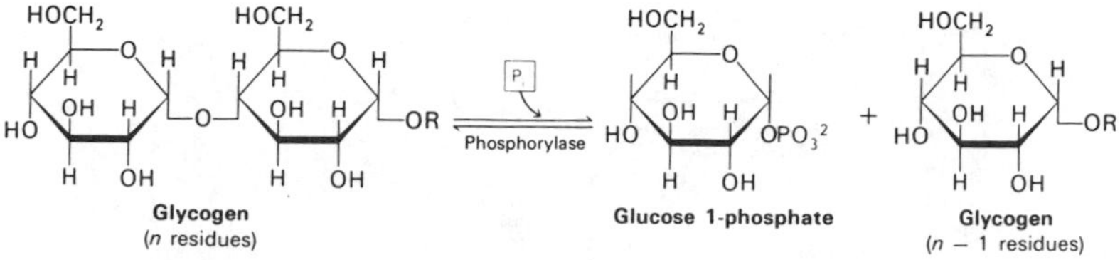

FIG. 9.5.   Glycogen cleavage. From Stryer (1981). Reprinted by permission of W. H. Freeman.

in the smooth endoplasmic reticulum (Fawcett, 1981), and this organelle which can extend to the surface of the neuron (Rosenbluth, 1962) has been suggested to play a role in glycogenolysis (Porter & Bruni, 1959). The smooth endoplasmic reticulum is also thought to be an important site for the synthesis of glycoproteins and their transport to synaptic sites (Koenig, di Giamberardino, & Bennett, 1973). The neonatal brain contains very high levels of glycogen, and this is sharply reduced in the postnatal period (Kohle & Vannucci, 1977). In electron microscopic studies, large quantities of granules containing glycogen have been seen in astroglia and neurons of immature brain (Phelps, 1972) and in the growing tips of dendrites (Peters, Palay, & Webster, 1991). It is now thought that dopamine, like noradrenaline, activates the decomposition of glycogen by an adenylate cyclase-catalyzed cyclic AMP reaction that acts on glycogen phosphorylase (Clarke, Lajtha, & Maker, 1989). Dopamine-sensitive adenyl cyclase activity that stimulates cAMP has been found in the postnatal cerebral cortex (Von Hungen, Roberts, & Hill, 1974).

The end product of catecholamine regulated glycogenolysis, glucose 1-phosphate, is readily converted by the enzyme phosphoglucomutase into glucose 6-phosphate, the entry molecular substrate of the pentose phosphate pathway (Stryer, 1981) (Figs. 9.6 and 9.7). The oxidative branch of this pathway, also

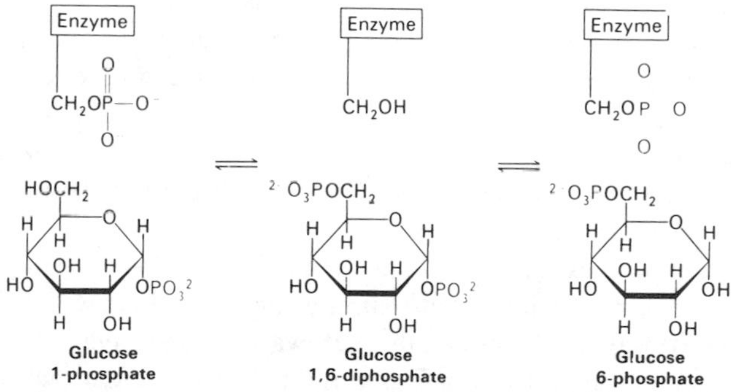

FIG. 9.6.   The conversion of glucose 1-phosphate into glucose 6-phosphate. From Stryer (1981). Reprinted by permission of W. H. Freeman.

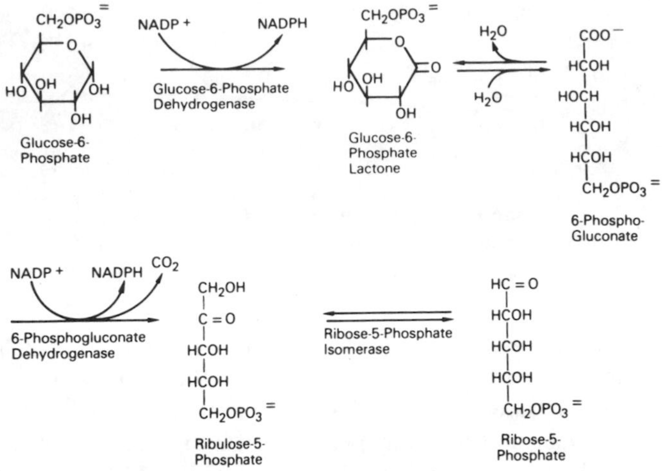

FIG. 9.7. The intermediates and enzymes of the of the oxidative arm of the pentose phosphate pathway. From *Developmental Neurochemistry,* edited by Wiggins, McCandless and Enna. Copyright (1985). Reprinted by permission of the University of Texas Press.

known as the hexose monophosphate shunt, which mediates biosynthetic processes, is very active in the postnatal period (O'Neill & Duffy, 1966; Winick, 1974). Its series of biochemical reactions uniquely convert 6-carbon sugars (hexoses) such as glucose, into 5-carbon sugars (pentoses) such as ribose. The latter is the form of sugar used in ribonucleic acids that transmit genetic information. Studies of the developing brain reveal that this pathway plays a major role in making ribose equivalents available for RNA synthesis (Burt & Wenger, 1961). The pentose shunt thus supplies ribose 5- phosphate molecules for nucleic acid synthesis and reducing equivalents for phospholipid synthesis (Stryer, 1981). Neurochemical research has indeed demonstrated that the catecholamines dopamine and noradrenaline stimulate the pentose phosphate pathway (Appel & Parrot, 1970; Brannan, Maker, & Karp, 1982; Tabakoff, Groskopf, Anderson, & Alivisatos, 1974). Dopaminergic activation of this pathway has been specifically observed in the postnatal brain (Hothersall, Greenbaum, & McLean, 1982). The resultant enhanced focal biosynthetic metabolism supports a critical period of growth of the orbitofrontal cortex. "Trophic" agents in the brain (such as catecholamines) specifically increase the activity of this "ancillary pathway of energy metabolism" (Cummins et al., 1985).

Experimental studies show that this route of metabolism in the cortex is intensified by electrical stimulation (Kimura, Naito, Nakagawa, & Kuriyama, 1974). Guroff (1980) concludes that this pathway is responsive to "developmental stimuli," and is important "during certain developmental periods." These properties suggest to me that the temporal interval during which this biochemical pathway is elevated in a particular brain region may fundamentally define a "critical period". In fact there may be a simultaneous increase of pentose shunt biosynthetic metabolism in brain vascular endothelial cells and glial cells, as well as different types of neurons. This coordinated process may take place within cortical columns in a specific brain region, such as the yet undifferentiated areas of the orbitofrontal cortex. The result is a critical period local expansion of vasculature, a multiplication and production of myelin by glia, and a growth spurt of neuronal dendrites and axons. Increased pentose phosphate-driven lipid synthesis in oligodendroglia accounts for the myelination that is typical of critical periods (Guroff, 1980). This pathway is also active in synapses (Appel & Parrot, 1970), a finding that may explain the heightened levels of synaptogenesis that occurs in critical periods.

The enhancement of such biosynthetic events may be more extensive in the "primitive right hemisphere" that expresses an increased emphasis on paralimbic networks (Tucker, 1992). The right cortex has a greater metabolic activity (Glick, Meibach, Cox, & Maayani, 1979), and is larger (Nonneman & Whishaw, 1982) and heavier than the left (Broca, 1885; Diamond, Johnson, & Ingham, 1975; Kertesz, Polk, Black, & Howell, 1992; Schwartz et al., 1985). The early maturing (Geschwind & Galaburda, 1987; Tucker, 1986) right cortical hemisphere is known to be specifically impacted by early social experiences (Denenberg et al., 1978). It is critically involved in the infant's recognition of the mother's face (de Schonen et al., 1986) and in the perception of arousal-inducing maternal facial expressions (Nelson, 1987). It is thus uniquely suited to process imprinting stimuli. The hypothesis of a postnatal practicing period expansion of the right orbitofrontal cortex is supported by the findings of a human study which demonstrate that the right frontal pole is known to develop earlier than the left (Thatcher, Walker, & Giudice, 1987), and of animal studies which report that the infant right orbitofrontal cortex is larger than the left (Van Eden, Uylings, & Van Pelt, 1984). Anatomical (Hadziselomovic & Cus, 1966; Weinberger et al., 1982; Weis et al., 1989) and tomographic (LeMay, 1982) (Fig. 9.8) studies reveal that the human adult right frontal pole is longer, wider, and larger than the left.

Most intriguingly, Falk et al. (1990) have recently demonstrated that the

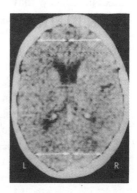

FIG. 9.8. Computerized axial tomogram of a brain showing the right hemisphere frontal region to protrude further forward and to be wider than the left. From LeMay (1982). Reprinted by permission of Elsevier.

FIG. 9.9. Asymmetrical features of the primate frontal
lobe, left lateral see through
view. Dashed features in right
hemisphere, solid lines from
left hemisphere. The right lateral orbital (lo) sulci are significantly longer than the left. From
Falk et al. (1990). Reprinted by
permission of Elsevier.

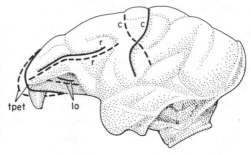

primate right hemisphere contains an enlargened orbitofrontal structure (see Fig.
9.9). This is due to an expansion of area 12, the lateral orbital area (see earlier
Fig. 4.5) in the right cortex. Falk notes that the lateral orbital area is concerned
with memory for visual information, and suggests that this right prefrontal anatomical feature may account for the dominance of the right hemisphere in the
processing of visual and emotional information. This conclusion is supported by
a recent neurochemical study that shows that the lateral orbital area contains
large amounts of the D1 dopamine receptor, a protein found throughout the
limbic system and thought to be very important in mediating functions associated
with memory, learning, and cognitive processing (Huang et al., 1992). Again, I
am suggesting that the ontogenetic expansion of this lateral orbitofrontal area
involved in the processing and storage of visual information occurs in the practicing critical period, and is induced by visuoaffective stimulation emanating from
the mother's face.

THE DEVELOPMENTAL BIOCHEMISTRY OF THE
ORBITOFRONTAL SUBPLATE ZONE

The mechanism underlying the onset of maturation of this prefrontal area at this
time in infancy may involve the activation of the "subplate zone," which is
directly beneath the developing prefrontal cortex (Mrzljak, Uylings, Kostovic, &
Van Eden, 1988; Van Eden & Uylings, 1985a) (Fig. 9.10). This transient developmental structure serves as an anatomical substrate for cortical differentiation.
It is sequentially innervated first by monoaminergic neurons in the brain stem
(Lidov, Molliver, & Zecevic, 1978), known to be amongst the earliest forming
neuronal populations in the brain (Lauder, 1983), and then by cholinergic subcortical projections. Tyrosine hydroxylase, the rate limiting enzyme of dopamine
(and noradrenaline) biosynthesis, has been suggested to exert an inductive influence on the development of the cerebral cortex (Coyle & Axelrod, 1972). This
enzyme is specifically found in axonal pathways in the subplate zone beneath the

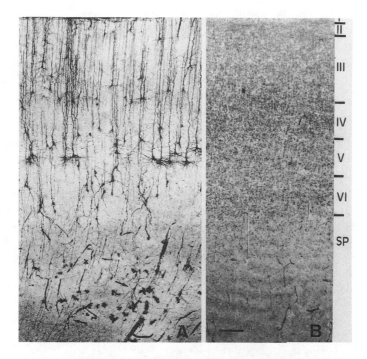

FIG. 9.10. Golgi-rapid-impregnated and Nissl-counterstained section of the human neonatal prefrontal cortex. Arrows point to the neurons in the persisting subplate zone below layer VI. The border between layer VI and the subplate is not sharp. From Mrzljak, Uylings, Kostovic, and Van Eden (1988). Prenatal development of neurons in the human prefrontal cortex: I. A qualitative Golgi study. *Journal of Comparative Neurology, 271.* Reprinted by permission of Wiley-Liss, a division of John Wiley and Sons, Inc.

cortical plate in late prenatal ontogeny (Specht, Pickel, Joh, & Reis, 1981). In the early postnatal period the vast majority of catecholaminergic axons within the subplate remain confined to the subplate "waiting compartment" (Molliver & Kristt, 1975). Thus, developing axonal systems do not directly innervate the cortical plate, but wait for varying periods of time within the subplate before finally growing into the overlying cortex. The growth of axons out of the subplate and into the cortex occurs at a later time, during a postnatal critical period, and this growth is associated with the maturation of the cortical area that lies above it. Kostovic and Rakic (1990) suggest that the subplate zone's "pattern of subcortical axonal bundles plays an active role in the formation of cerebral surface configuration" (p. 467).

Which specific axons are responsible for initiating the onset of the critical period maturation of the orbitofrontal cortex? And what signal causes the axons waiting in the subplate to grow into that overlying cortex? Ventral tegmental dopaminergic neurons are the most likely source of such axons, since they are present in the subplate and are known to play a trophic role in prefrontal development (Kalsbeek et al., 1987; Schmidt et al., 1982). The best candidate for the signal for axonal growth would be a neurotrophic molecule, since these agents specifically induce axonal growth (Lander, 1987; Snider & Johnson, 1989). Hyman et al. (1991) have recently discovered that brain-derived neurotrophic factor (Leibrock et al., 1989) is a trophic factor for mesencephalic dopamine neurons. BDNF has been identified, in low amounts, in the prenatal orbitofrontal cortex (Huntley, Benson, Jones, & Isackson, 1992) (Fig. 9.11), but its peak expression is known to commence at a postnatal stage when connections are established (Friedman, Olson, & Perrson, 1991). Like nerve growth factor (NGF) it is a member of the neurotrophin family (Thoenen, 1991). In addition to promoting axonal growth, neurotrophic factors also enhance the activity of the pentose phosphate shunt (Benjamins & McKhann, 1981) and induce the synthesis of tyrosine hydroxylase (Hendry & Iversen, 1971) and glycoproteins (Stallcup, Beasley, & Levine, 1985). Nerve growth factor and nerve growth factor-like

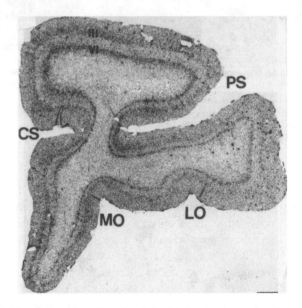

FIG. 9.11. Autoradiogram of a late fetal primate prefrontal cortex showing the distribution of BDNF mRNA in the medial orbital (MO) and lateral orbital (LO) sulci. From Huntley et al. (1992). Reprinted by permission of Elsevier.

molecules are known to play a dynamic role in the developing nervous system, and NGF has recently been shown to modulate the expression of NGF receptors in the postnatal forebrain (Fusco et al., 1991). It is thought that BDNF binds to the same receptor as nerve growth factor (Rodriguez-Tebar, Dechand, & Barde, 1990). Receptors for NGF are now known to exist in cortical subplate neurons (Allendorfer, Shelton, Shooter, & Shatz, 1990) during specific postnatal developmental stages (Eckenstein, 1988) and in prefrontal cortical neurons (Bandtlow et al., 1990). Most importantly, NGF is seen as participating in the developmental processes that give rise to the structure of the adult cortex (Allendorfer et al., 1990).

It has recently been suggested that BDNF plays an essential role in the formation of prefrontal cortical connectivity (Huntley et al., 1992). On the basis of these facts I suggest that the dopaminergic axonal terminals which innervate the deep layers of the orbitofrontal cortex (Lewis et al., 1988) at the onset of the practicing period derive from brain-derived neurotrophic factor-activated dopaminergic axons in the prefrontal subplate waiting compartment. This neurotrophic factor would also induce tyrosine hydroxylase (Fig. 9.12) and thereby dopamine production, and in such a manner the concentration of this trophic catecholamine increases in a localized region of late-developing cerebral cortex. The activation of "waiting" ventral tegmental axons occurs postnatally, and it triggers the onset of a critical period in the maturation of the orbitofrontal cortex. (I later show that this localized sprouting of dopaminergic axons is also influenced by circulating sex steroids, since these agents are known to induce neurite outgrowth in mesencephalic neurons and to modify postsynaptic dopaminergic sensitivity.)

The critical role of dopamine in the development of the orbitofrontal cortex is also indicated in recent research on DARPP-32, a dopamine and cyclic AMP—

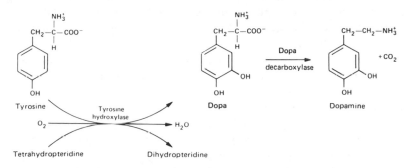

FIG. 9.12. Tyrosine hydroxylase, the rate-limiting enzyme in dopamine synthesis. From Guroff (1980), pp. 179–181. Reprinted by courtesy of Marcel Dekker, Inc.

regulated phosphoprotein associated with D1 receptors (Walaas, Aswad, & Greengard, 1983). This protein, whose distribution corresponds to the terminal fields of dopamine neurons, has been identified in layers V and VI of postnatal orbitofrontal association cortex (Berger, Febvret, Greengard, & Goldman-Rakic, 1990). These authors contend that DARPP-32 plays a significant role during the postnatal development of cerebral cortical areas. In contrast to its transient appearance in most cerebral areas, its expression, which undergoes "important developmental changes," is specifically continued in mature orbital (but not dorsolateral) prefrontal cortex.

Although most of the neurons in the subplate zone undergo programmed cell death (Valverde & Facal-Valverde, 1988), the surviving ones (Woo, Beale, & Finlay, 1991) (presumably at BDNF and DARPP-32 orbitofrontal sites) become part of the future layer VIb in the deep cortex at the cortico-subcortical junction, where they are thought to "undergo significant changes in morphology during later postnatal life" (Kostovic & Rakic, 1990, p. 465). Synapse formation of subplate neurons lasts through early postnatal development (Friauf, McConnell, & Shatz, 1990), at a time when synaptogenesis occurs in the cortex itself (Rakic et al., 1986). Indeed neurons in the deep layers of the frontal polar regions of the human cortex are known to mature at 1-year-of-age (Rabinowicz, 1979), and synaptic excess has been observed to onset in the human prefrontal cortex at the end of the first year of life (Huttenlocher, 1979). The subplate zone, thought to be critical to the developmental plasticity of the cerebral hemisphere (Kostovic et al., 1989), reaches its maximal size in human association cortex. Prefrontal subplate programmed cell death is not seen in early postnatal human development (Mrzljak et al., 1988), in line with a later postnatal maturation of prefrontal cortex. BDNF, a neurotrophin that prevents naturally occurring cell death (Hofer & Barde, 1988), is found in low quantities in the prenatal orbitofrontal cortex (Huntley et al., 1992). Kostovic and Rakic (1990) have recently concluded that the postnatal shaping of the frontal lobe is associated with the more prolonged existence of this region in human infancy. Indeed, even in the adult primate orbitofrontal cortex, the deep cortical layers are not well demarcated from the subcortical plate (Morecraft et al., 1992).

These events in the orbitofrontal subplate represent an expansion of the ventral tegmental dopaminergic limbic circuit into the prospective frontolimbic cortex. Further evidence for this assertion is suggested in the finding that limbic system—associated membrane protein (LAMP), a surface antigen expressed on developing limbic system axons and growth cones, is found in subplate and deep cortical sites of the postnatal prefrontal cortex (Horton & Levitt, 1988). Its reputed function as a receptor for diffusable trophic agents and in "pathway formation" and the establishment of "connections between limbic regions" indicates a critical role in the ontogeny of the dopaminergic ventral tegmental forebrain—midbrain circuit.

THE EXPANSION OF THE VENTRAL TEGMENTAL
LIMBIC CIRCUIT AND THE EMERGENCE OF
ORBITOFRONTAL FUNCTION

Hofer's work (1983) demonstrates that the mother serves as an external regulator of the neurochemistry of the infant's maturing brain. It is now being appreciated that "parenting . . . and other experiences in a child's life in interaction with biological endowment may lead to temporary or prolonged alterations in neurotransmitter metabolism" (Cohen, Shaywitz, Young, & Shaywitz, 1982, p. 216). During critical periods, monoamine neurotransmitters and neurohormones regulate the temporal framework of developmental brain growth as well as mediate the effects of external influences on this process (Lauder & Krebs, 1991). Foote and Morrison (1987) conclude that monoamines influence the ontogeny of cortical circuitry and have "complex, long-lasting effects on postsynaptic biochemical processes which might mediate developmental influences" (p. 418). It is now known that neurotransmitters control the development of the neural circuits in which they later participate, and that brain function can alter brain structures through changes in transmitters (Mattson, 1988). Bioaminergic and peptidergic neuromodulators have been specifically shown to render new pathways accessible in physically defined networks (Kavanau, 1990). Johnston (1985) cites a "general theme in neurotransmitter development—that segments of multineuronal circuits have distinct developmental timetables" (p. 211).

The most distal segment of the mesocortical dopaminergic ventral tegmental forebrain-midbrain circuit is thus constructed in the orbital cortex, the "association cortex" of the limbic forebrain. The completion of this limbic circuit involves the addition of its final component in the frontolimbic cortex, and this occurs in the practicing period. In a psychopharmacological study, Holson, Ali, and Scallet (1988) find that infant animals reared in isolation during a period from weaning to 90 days show reduced levels of prefrontal mesocortical dopamine activity, with no changes in other mesolimbic dopamine-rich forebrain regions outside of the prefrontal cortex. This implies that the increases in dopaminergic activity in this postnatal period are localized to prefrontal segments of the ventral tegmental limbic forebrain-midbrain circuit, and that social stimulation is required for this increase. It is well known that stimulation (external influence) is required for the maturation of neural circuits (Jacobson, 1978) and that optimal levels of arousal are necessary for neuronal development (Cummins et al., 1977). This limbic circuit is proposed to be especially developed in the right cerebral hemisphere, the cortex that contains expanded paralimbic networks (Tucker, 1992). There is now extensive evidence for a right hemispheric lateralization of the catecholaminergic systems which are the neurochemical substrates of cortical arousal (Robinson, 1979; Tucker & Williamson, 1984). Manipulation of the prenatal environment results in long-term changes in right and not left prefrontal dopamine activity (Fride & Weinstock, 1988).

With the physical establishment of this limbic circuit, it can now begin to contribute to the emergent functions of the orbitofrontal cortex. Earlier, evidence was presented to show that the same dopaminergic neuron innervates two components of the ventral tegmental circuit, the lateral septum and the orbital cortex (Lindvall, Bjorklund, & Divac, 1977). This suggests that mesocortical dopamine, which is known to be associated with the cerebral circuits of reward and emotionality (Thierry et al., 1978), exerts the same excitatory effect on orbitofrontal neurons that it has been shown to have on septal neurons (Assef & Miller, 1977). This is supported by a very recent study of dopaminergic innervation of the cortex which concludes that dopamine modulates excitatory input (Smiley, Williams, Szigeti, & Goldman-Rakic, 1992). Orbitofrontal involvement in the pleasurable qualities of social interaction (Panksepp, Siviy, & Normansell, 1985) is neurochemically mediated by intensified dopamine-mediated elation (Kelley & Stinus, 1984), and this is responsible for the increase in positive and decrease in negative emotion observed from 10 to 13.5 months, the span of the early practicing period (Rothbart et al., 1989). (This may explicate Freud's description of an early period of heightened pleasure and "primary narcissism.")

The highly elevated levels of stimulation-seeking exploratory (play) behavior that accompany the onset of upright locomotion also reflect the increased activity of the mesocortical dopamine system that is known to support locomotion and investigatory exploration behavior (Fink & Smith, 1980). Indeed, Oppenheim (1981) has suggested that play may represent an ontogenetic adaptation of a particular stage of development. Play behavior transforms the physical environment into an enriched environment (Chisholm, 1990), and the changes in cortical synaptic development associated with exposure to enriched environments has been attributed to elevated arousal (Walsh & Cummins, 1975). Play also enhances behavioral flexibility through an increase in neural interconnectivity (Fagen, 1977). All these observations may reflect the stage-specific expansion of this mesocortical dopaminergic system.

Other ontogenetic adaptations that emerge in the practicing period can also be understood to result from the maturation of this limbic circuit. The intensification of attachment behavior at the end of the first year, reflected in the infant's increasingly active pursuit of the mother, is mediated by the increased activity of this dopamine system which serves to "initiate movements to emotional or motivational stimuli" (Vertes, 1990, p. 74). This specifically occurs in the orbitofrontal region, the frontolimbic structure critically involved in attachment behavior (Steklis & Kling, 1985), motivational (Pandya & Yeterian, 1985), and postural-affective states (Tucker, 1992).

Furthermore, Kalsbeek now postulates:

the mesocortical dopamine system exerts a general activating influence on the whole prefrontal cortex . . . what the ascending reticular activating system does for the whole cortex, the mesocortical system does for the prefrontal cortex . . . this activating influence is mediated by dopamine. (Stam, de Bruin, van Haelst, van der Gugten, & Kalsbeek, 1989, p. 330)

Dopaminergic stimulation of D1 receptors positively coupled to adenylate cyclase is known to modulate waking and sleep states (Ongini & Trampus, 1992) and to regulate EEG activity related to behavioral arousal (Ongini, Caporali, & Massotti, 1985) (Fig. 9.13). These authors document that various sensory stimuli elicit this same EEG desynchronization, and the resultant arousal is behaviorally expressed in a "raising of the head" and a "widening of the eyes." (Recall that Izard [1979] describes the facial indicator of the positive affect of interest in the infant to include eyes that are widened and rounded.) Activity in the mediobasal cortex accompanies a change in the state of the organism associated with the development of an arousal reaction (Luria, 1980). Behavioral EEG arousal and cortical desynchronization are both known to reflect activity of the energy-

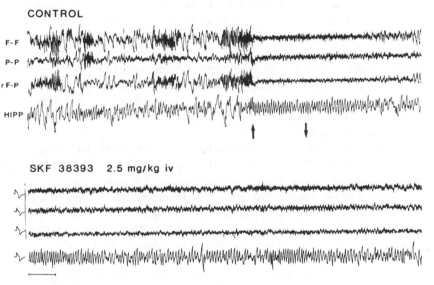

FIG. 9.13. Activation of the D-1 receptor by the dopamine agonist SKF 38393 produces desynchronization of the EEG activity in the rabbit. Reprinted from Ongini, Caporali, and Massotti (1985). Stimulation of dopamine D-1 receptors by SKF 38393 induces EEG desynchronization and behavioral arousal. *Life Sciences, 37,* 2327–2333, with permission from Pergamon Press Ltd, Headington Hill Hall, Oxford OX3 OBW, UK.

mobilizing, sympathetic-dominant, ergotropic system in the brainstem (Gellhorn, 1970). These findings suggest that in the early practicing period the increase in dopamine-mediated general arousal (Iversen, 1977) produces an energy-expending increased excitability of the orbitofrontal cortex. This results in an imbalance in total brain functioning between excitation and inhibition. The resultant state of Pavlovian over-excitation is reflected in the hyperarousal and high activity level typical of this developmental period.

SUMMARY

A developmental shift in the orbitofrontal cortex occurs at the end of the first year of human infancy. This shift reflects the onset of a critical period for the postnatal maturation of this cortex. During this period, the infant is most sensitive to high intensity stimulation emanating from the mother's emotionally expressive face. Maternal socioaffective stimulation induces heightened levels of arousal in the infant, and the resultant amplified levels of arousal act as a signal for the imprinting of new circuits in the orbitofrontal cortex. This arousal specifically induces the experience-dependent sprouting of dopamine-releasing axon varicosities in the deep layers of the prefrontal cortex. These axons in the far anterior forebrain represent the terminals of A10 catecholaminergic neurons whose cell bodies lie in the rostral ventral tegmental area of the midbrain. Dopaminergic axons, in a "waiting compartment" in the subplate zone immediately beneath the orbitofrontal cortex, are activated by BDNF, a neurotrophic agent that induces axonal growth in mesencephalic dopamine neurons. The growth of these dopaminergic axons is matched by an intensified synthesis of dopaminergic (D1) receptors.

Increased levels of dopamine trigger a local growth spurt in the blood vessels, neurons, and glia of this prefrontal cortex, especially in the early maturing right hemisphere. The neurotrophic action of this catecholamine is mediated by its biochemical action of degrading glycogen to glucose and of converting glucose to sugars that are specifically used in biosynthetic processes. The expansion of the mesocortical dopamine system into the orbitofrontal cortex represents the maturation of the ventral tegmental forebrain-midbrain circuit. Anatomical connections between subcortical limbic regions and this prefrontal cortical area account for the emergence of the unique functional properties of this frontolimbic cortex. These emergent functions—hyperarousal, hyperactivity, high levels of exploratory behavior and positive affect—are first expressed in the early practicing period.

10 Imprinting Neuroendocrinology

So far as is present known, the way in which attachment behavior develops in the human infant and becomes focused on a discriminatory figure is sufficiently like the way in which it develops in other mammals and birds, for it to be included, legitimately, under the heading of imprinting.
—John Bowlby (1969)

According to Bowlby (1969) imprinting is the process that underlies human attachment bond formation. The term imprinting is derived from the German word Prägung which literally means forging or stamping. The mechanism of this process has been understood to involve an irreversible stamping of early experience upon the developing nervous system. Hofer's work (1990) demonstrates that an essential characteristic of the child's early experience is that the mother acts as a "hidden" regulator of the infant's immature endocrine and nervous systems. In line with these principles, I have proposed that maternally regulated high intensity stimulation provided in synchronized, face-to-face affective interactions induces physiological alterations that directly influence the imprinting of corticolimbic areas of the infant's postnatally maturing nervous system. Mutually regulated neuroendocrine activity biochemically supports the dyadic amplification of the positive affects of excitement and joy, and in these refueling transactions the psychobiologically attuned mirroring process drives the attachment mechanism. These psychoneuroendocrinological events occur frequently and at rapid rates in the context of visuoaffective social referencing communications of the practicing period, a critical period of growth of the orbitofrontal cortex. The next question is, then, what is the specific nature of these endocrine alterations? This problem has been addressed in the research of H.S. Hoffman (1987). His

135

work suggests that the imprinting object stimulates the production of opioid peptides in the infant, and that endogenous opiates play a special role in mediating the neurochemistry of the attachment process.

In the following pages I shall integrate data from various disciplines in order to present a model that explains how maternally induced endocrine changes directly influence the growth of the infant's brain. The child's perception of the mother's positive emotional facial expression triggers an elevation of opioid peptides. These endorphins physiologically activate ventral tegmental dopamine neurons and trophically regulate orbitofrontal development.

MATERNAL STIMULATION OF OPIOID PEPTIDES AND THE IMPRINTING OF THE ORBITOFRONTAL CORTEX

In addition to neurotransmitters, neurohormones are essential to critical period events, as these agents act to biochemically mediate the effects of external influences on developmental processes (Lauder & Krebs, 1986). Again, it is important to emphasize that the primary caregiver is the major external influence on the child's developmental processes. Neuroendocrinological research of early postnatal periods reveals that during ontogeny, the organism passes through a number of periods at which time various developing or differentiating systems are especially sensitive to the presence of specific hormones in the circulation (Schapiro, 1968).

> Hormonal and/or neural control of sensitivity offers the advantage of being able— through slight temporal changes of local specialization in particular loci of the brain—to serve the needs for increases and declines in specific sensitivities to the environment without affecting the gross course of development. (Immelman & Suomi, 1981, p. 402)

In the early practicing period, what particular developing brain sites are sensitive to which specific hormones? Hormones that influence the metabolic activity of catecholaminergic neurons and their receptors, which are in active growth at these times, would be important candidates. Opioid peptides are found in very high concentrations in the dopaminergic ventral tegmental area (Britt & Wise, 1983). In the cerebral cortex the highest levels are found in the anterior temporal and orbitofrontal regions (Steklis & Kling, 1985), limbic areas that both contain neurons that respond to emotional facial expressions (Hasselmo et al., 1989a; Thorpe et al., 1983). In accord with Hoffman's results, I offer the proposals that the emotionally expressive face of the imprinting object stimulates infant opioid production, and that this psychoendocrinological alteration mediates the imprinting of brain sites involved in attachment processes. More specifically, in the early practicing period maternally regulated hormonal events influence the development of the prefrontal area that is undergoing a critical period growth spurt at the end of the first year. This orbitofrontal structure comes to mediate attachment functions (Steklis & Kling, 1985).

In order to understand the unique role endogenous opioids play in the development of orbitofrontal structure and its attachment function it is necessary to review the properties of these neuropeptides. Both the neurohormone adrenocorticotropin (ACTH) and the opioid peptide beta endorphin belong to a peptide family that is synthesized from a common precursor (Mains, Eipper, & Ling, 1977). The synthesis of both ACTH and beta endorphin occurs in the same cells in the anterior pituitary, and their production is controlled by the same regulating factor, corticotropin releasing factor (CRF) (Brownstein, 1989; Makara, 1985). CRF is produced only by paraventricular neurosecretory neurons in the neighboring hypothalamus (Vale, Spiess, Rivier, & Rivier, 1981). Axons of these neurosecretory neurons terminate adjacent to portal capillaries in the median eminence of the hypothalamus, and here they release CRF into the portal vasculature which then travels in the circulation to the anterior pituitary (see Fig. 10.1). By way of this hypothalamohypophyseal portal system (Makara et al., 1981) CRF reaches cells in the anterior pituitary, where it then stimulates the synthesis of ACTH and the endogenous opioid beta endorphin. Pituitary cells then secrete these neuropeptides into the general circulation (Guillemin et al., 1977) where they then travel back into distant sites in the brain and the peripheral nervous system. Three such brain sites are the orbitiofrontal and anterior temporal areas of the cortex, and the ventral tegmental area in the midbrain.

In addition to containing opiate receptors (Wise & Herkenham, 1982) (Fig. 10.2), relatively large numbers of CRF-immunoreactive cells and fibers (Lewis

FIG. 10.1. Control of anterior pituitary function. Releasing hormones are secreted into portal capillaries in the zona externa of the median eminence of the hypothalamus. The hormones travel to the anterior pituitary; there they act on tropic hormone producing cells. These cells secrete into the general circulation; tropic hormones may also travel back to the brain through the portal vessels. From Brownstein (1989). Neuropeptides. In Siegel, Agranoff, Albers, and Molinoff (Eds.), *Basic neurochemistry* (4th ed., pp. 287–309). Reprinted by permission of Raven Press Ltd.

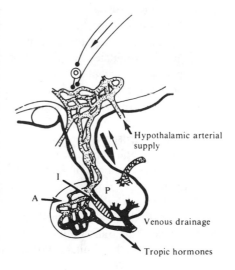

Hypothalamic arterial supply

Venous drainage

Tropic hormones

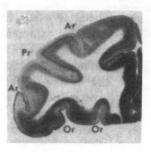

FIG. 10.2. Autoradiograph showing opiate receptors in the primate orbital frontal cortex (Or).
From Wise and Herkenham
(1982). Copyright (1982) by the
AAAS. Reprinted by permission.

et al., 1989; Swanson, Sawchenko, Rivier, & Vale, 1983) and CRF receptors (Aguilera et al., 1987) are found in orbital prefrontal areas. These CRF receptors are coupled to adenylate cyclase (Aguilera et al., 1987), the enzyme responsible for the synthesis of cyclic AMP, the cellular mediator of the action of many hormones. Neurophysiological studies show that CRF acts as an excitatory neurotransmitter which activates certain hypothalamic, limbic, and cortical neurons (Aldenhoff et al., 1983). Indeed, CRF activates the ventral tegmental dopaminergic system (Kalivas, Duffy, & Latimer, 1987) and induces increases in dopamine metabolism in the prefrontal cortex (Dunn & Berridge, 1990), properties relevant to practicing period dopaminergic activity. In fact, CRF is known to increase exploratory behavior (Britton, Koob, & Rivier, 1982), behavioral activation, and emotionality (Sutton et al., 1982)—all heightened in the practicing period. These relations account for the observation that this peptide plays an important role in the regulation of higher-order information processing of association and limbic regions (Lewis et al., 1989). With respect to developmental observations, CRF has recently been demonstrated in GABAergic interneurons in the prefrontal cortex from the right hemisphere of infant rhesus monkeys (Lewis & Lund, 1990).

Such findings suggest that the emotionally expressive face of the practicing mother elicits hypothalamic activation of the regulatory peptide CRF, which consequently stimulates the production of the anterior pituitary opioid peptide beta endorphin. Receptors for both of these biochemical agents exist in the frontolimbic cortex, and its development and functioning are thereby influenced by these subcortically manufactured neuropeptides. I propose that early in this developmental critical period CRF synthesis is heightened in hypothalamic paraventricular neurosecretory neurons. As a result, elevated concentrations of ACTH and the opioid peptide beta endorphin are expressed in the circulation and sensed in different areas of the ventral tegmental forebrain-midbrain limbic circuit. In support of this proposal, studies have demonstrated that high levels of ACTH selectively activate mesocortical dopamine synthesis in the frontal cortex (Bannon & Roth, 1983) and facilitate imprinting (Martin, 1978). Dopamine, in turn, increases the transcription of the gene that encodes the precursor of ACTH and endorphin in the pituitary (Pritchett & Roberts, 1987). Increased amounts of endogenous opioids would therefore also be found in the circulation during the critical period, and these would also be sensed by and then trigger metabolic effects in limbic and frontolimbic areas. Endorphin levels and opiate receptor binding are known to be highest during early development (Maseda, Aguado, Mena, & de Yevenes, 1983).

Extensive work by Zagon (Zagon & McLaughlin, 1988) reveals that endogenous opioids act as trophic regulators of neural development. In recent work (Hauser, McLaughlin, & Zagon, 1989) Zagon concludes that these opioids determine "the temporal course and magnitude of cytoarchitectonic expression in the developing neuraxis." The developmental endocrinological research of Bartolome indicates that the endorphinergic control of postnatal development is mediated by its inhibition of DNA synthesis and cellular proliferation (Bartolome, Bartolome, Lorber, Dileo, & Schanberg, 1991). This effect in turn may be due to the biochemical actions of opioids, namely their action as a regulator of glucose and insulin homeostasis (Bartolome, Bartolome, Harris, Pauk, & Schanberg, 1989). The orbitofrontal cortex, which contains the highest levels of opioids in the cortex (Steklis & Kling, 1985), has been shown to be specifically responsive to glucose (Nakano et al., 1984) and insulin (McGregor & Atrens, 1991) concentrations. Elevated levels of opioids in the circulation during this hormone-sensitive period of orbitofrontal cytoarchitectonic differentiation could thus support locally enhanced glucose utilization in the pentose phosphate shunt which mediates biosynthetic growth processes.

ORBITOFRONTAL CONTROL OF CORTICOTROPIN RELEASING FACTOR AS A MECHANISM OF REGULATION OF SYMPATHETIC AND PARASYMPATHETIC ACTIVITIES

In addition to the finding that CRF acts on higher centers in the brain (Brownstein, 1989) and thereby regulates the activity of higher-order limbic structures, other research shows that the production of CRF is itself controlled by higher cortical areas via pathways passing through structures of the limbic system (Martin, 1977). Brownstein (1989) points out that the neuroendocrine system is a hierarchy with higher centers regulating lower ones, and that a change related to neuroendocrine activity is detected by "a control center." These facts lead me to believe that the "higher cortical areas" that act as a "control center" to regulate CRF are in the corticolimbic orbitofrontal cortex. I have previously argued that the orbital cortex hierarchically dominates subcortical limbic activity. Evidence consistent with this implication is found in Okinaka et al.'s (1960) demonstration that activation of the orbitofrontal cortex triggers a sharp and transient rise in ACTH, and Pribram's (1981) conclusion that orbitofrontal activity increases the secretion of endorphins. What is more, in line with Hoffman's findings, the stimulation that triggers orbitofrontal activation emanates from the face of the emotionally stimulating caregiver. It is known both that facial emotional expressions induce a firing of orbitofrontal neurons (Thorpe, Rolls, & Maddisson, 1983) and that the tracking of emotionally relevant objects in the extrapersonal space involves the activation of the orbitofrontal cortex (Mesulam, 1985).

As previously mentioned, the orbitofrontal cortex has direct connections with dopamine neurons in the ventral tegmental area via a mesocortical pathway. A mesodiencephalic pathway between ventral tegmental dopamine neurons and hypothalamic nuclei is also known to exist (Oades & Halliday, 1987). Indeed, hypothalamic neurosecretory nuclei receive a substantial dopaminergic innervation (Lindvall, Bjorklund, & Skagerberg, 1984), and paraventricular hypothalamic areas contain dense numbers of D1 dopamine receptors (Huang et al., 1992). Lipovits and Paull (1989) report that "the paraventricular nucleus receives a selective dopaminergic innervation and these dopaminergic axons might influence the function of the pituitary and adrenal glands via the hypothalamic corticotropin releasing hormone system" (p. 119). A direct descending input from the hypothalamic paraventricular nucleus to sympathetic preganglionic neurons in the spinal cord has also recently been demonstrated (Hosoya et al., 1991). Ventral tegmental dopamine neurons that directly innervate the paraventricular hypothalamus may thus be involved in functions of the sympathetic nervous system. As previously mentioned, the neurons in the orbitofrontal area of the cerebral cortex send direct projections down to dopamine neurons in the ventral tegmental area of the midbrain. These anatomical linkages could allow for the orbitofrontal regulation of the final common pathway for the central control of ACTH release from the anterior pituitary, and could mediate the known "cognitive influences" (Swanson, 1991) on CRF and ACTH secretion.

The orbitofrontal cortex also sends direct connections to the hypothalamus (Nauta, 1972), and the connections between the cerebral cortex and the hypothalamus have been suggested to occur during the sensitive period for the development of social responses (Scott, 1958). The activation of this pathway could trigger anterior hypothalamic neuroendocrine secretion into the portal system, which in turn may elicit sympathetic adrenal medullary (Mason, 1968) release of catecholamines into the circulation. Adrenal catecholamines are known to produce energy mobilization, alterations in blood flow, increased perfusion of the brain and heart, inhibition of gastrointestinal function, facilitation of motor activity, and elevated arousal. Orbital stimulation is known to cause alterations in sympathoadrenomedullary catecholamine release (Euler & Folkow, 1958), and this effect may be mediated by direct orbitofrontal-hypothalamic connections since stimulation of particular hypothalamic sites also activates adrenal catecholamine release (Folkow & Euler, 1954). Hypothalamic CRF stimulates sympathetic nervous system activity (Brown et al., 1982b), significantly increases plasma concentrations of norepinephrine (Irwin, Hauger, Brown, & Britton,

1988) and glucose, elevates oxygen consumption (Brown et al., 1982a), and increases arousal in stress (Shibasaki et al., 1991). Aguilera et al. (1987) state that CRF "results in activation of the hypothalamic-pituitary-adrenal axis and the sympathetic nervous system, with consequent visceral, metabolic and behavioral responses" (p. 55). This corticolimbic structure could thus mediate higher influences on the activity of the sympathetic nervous system, and represent the elusive "central origin" (Fox & Fitzgerald, 1990) of the sympathetic nervous system.

A major physiological role of adrenal catecholamines in relation to carbohydrate metabolism is to trigger the delivery of elevated levels of glucose into the bloodstream under conditions of intense effort and emotion (West & Todd, 1962). Henry and Stephens (1977) propose that sympathetic-adrenomedullary function, associated with an accelerated metabolic rate due to the increased expenditure of energy in the body, is activated during active coping. The orbitofrontal area of the cerebral cortex may therefore be intimately involved in the activation of adrenal noradrenaline in response to emotional stress (Ganong, 1973). Emotional stimulation of adrenal sympathetic activity was first observed by Cannon (Cannon & de la Paz, 1911). I would speculate that this energy-mobilizing, arousal-elevating sympathetic hypothalamic-adrenomedullary system that generates circulating noradrenaline is regulated by the orbitofrontal cortex. This catecholamine, travelling in the brain vascular system, could act at noradrenaline receptors to trigger cAMP and calcium-regulated glycogenolysis (Quach, Rose, & Schwartz, 1978), thereby releasing glucose for increased local energy demand. Furthermore, it is tempting to speculate that this represents the physiological substrate of the affect of interest-excitement.

Along with connections into the sympathetic nervous system, paraventricular hypothalamic neurons also directly innervate key autonomic elements of the parasympathetic nervous system. Paraventricular neurons project to (Saper, Loewy, Swanson, & Cowan, 1976; Sawchenko & Swanson, 1982) and inhibit medullary cardioinhibitory neurons, thereby producing increases in heart rate (Ciriello & Calaresu, 1980), that is, tachycardia mediated by a decrease in vagal tone. CRF receptors are found in the medullary nucleus of the solitary tract, and the vagus nerve has been implicated in the effects of CRF on parasympathetic function (Dunn & Berridge, 1990). A central autonomic modulation of cardiac baroreflex by CRF has recently been demonstrated (Fisher, 1989). Paraventricular neurons that react to external stimuli by emitting CRF are known to be implicated in autonomic and stress reactions (Lewis, Foote, & Cha, 1989) and to be involved in the pituitary-adrenal response to stress (Ixart et al., 1982). These relationships may reflect the reputed role of CRF in autonomic and neuroendocrine homeostatic control (Swanson & Sawchenko, 1980), in the control of central autonomic function and mediation of the visceral and behavioral responses to stress (Aguilera, Millan, Hauger, & Catt, 1987), in the initiation of biological actions within the brain in response to stress (Lenz, Raedler, Greten,

& Brown, 1987). The production of this regulatory neurohormone by hypothalamic neurons, influenced by higher structures in the brain, thus activates
sympathetic and deactivates parasympathetic components of the ANS. The increased stimulation of CRF by expanding mesocortical dopamine-innervated
orbitofrontal sites may account for the dominance of sympathetic over parasympathetic brain states in the early practicing period.

OPIATE-DOPAMINERGIC INTERACTIONS AND THE
EMERGENCE OF ORBITOFRONTAL FUNCTION

According to Hoffman (1987) the imprinting object stimulates an increase of
opioids in the infant, and this hormonal alteration influences the attachment
process. What neurochemical and neuroanatomical mechanisms might mediate
this phenomenon? In Chapter 6 I postulated that the emotionally expressive face of
the mother stimulates, mirrors, and amplifies positive affect in the child. The
caregiver, in a heightened state of pleasure and interest triggered by the perception
of her infant, induces a similar state of sympathetic arousal in the infant's nervous
system. Such an amplification of positive affect is a prerequisite of attachment
bond formation. I also suggested that these events are psychobiologically mediated by the activation of the ventral tegmental dopaminergic system and the
stimulation of reward centers in the child's brain by endogenous opioids.

Opiate reward is currently thought to be mediated by the ventral tegmental
dopaminergic system (Bozarth, 1986; Phillips, Le Plane, & Fibiger, 1983; Wise,
1988), a circuit involved in reward and emotionality (Thierry et al., 1978).
Opiates injected into the ventral tegmental area are rewarding (Bozarth & Wise,
1981; Phillips & LePiane, 1980). The dopamine neurons in this site are known to
be activated by opiates (Matthews & German, 1984) and to be more sensitive to
the stimulatory effects of opioids than are nigral dopamine neurons (Bozarth,
1988). (Conversely, opioid peptides inhibit the release of noradrenaline; Nakamura, Tepper, Young, Ling, & Groves, 1982.) Opiate receptors, associated
with adenylate cyclase (Loh & Smith, 1990), have been identified at both mesolimbic dopamine cell body regions and their terminal fields (Pollard, Llorens,
Boneet, Costentin, & Schwartz, 1977). The euphorigenic effects of opiates
(Katz, 1988) and the rewarding properties of opioid-enhanced dopaminergic
neurotransmission would together account for the stage-typical elation of the
early practicing period. The suggestion that endogenous opioids are elevated in
this developmental period of behavioral overactivity is supported by the pharmacological evidence that opiates applied directly to ventral tegmental dopamine
neurons causes increased locomotion (Joyce & Iversen, 1979) and that endorphins activate the ventral tegmental dopaminergic system and produce hyperactivity (Stinus, Koob, Ling, Bloom, & Le Moal, 1980).

These opiate-dopaminergic interactions neurochemically underlie the socioemotional effects of endogenous opioids. The interrelationships between these

two neurohormonal and neurotransmitter systems become more intertwined in the practicing period. Opioid activity, which is sensitized during key periods of social development (Zagon, McLaughlin, Weaver, & Zagon, 1982), is known to mediate social affect (Herman & Panksepp, 1978), kin selection (D'Amato & Pavone, 1993), imprinting (Hoffman, 1987), attachment (Steklis & Kling, 1985), play (Panksepp, Siviy, & Normansell, 1984), and exploration (Katz, 1988) processes. In a review of the role of opioid mechanisms in social interaction and attachment, Benton and Brain (1988) conclude that social emotion is modulated by endorphinergic mechanisms.

Almost 25 years ago, Klaus and Kennell (1976) hypothesized that extended periods of maternal gaze elicit hormonal changes in the infant which facilitate the development of the bond between mother and infant. This assertion has been expanded upon by Hoffman (1987). His work suggests that in the critical period for social attachments, certain distinctive features of the mother, such as her face, come to elicit pleasurable responses that are mediated by the production of endorphins. These hormonal alterations influence the attachment process. In a further elaboration of these ideas, I am contending that the developing orbital cortex, a cortical structure critical to attachment behavior, is a primary site of action of these hormonal effects. The importance of central foveal (as opposed to peripheral) vision to facial perception and to the establishment of a primary attachment to the mother is emphasized by Bowlby (1969). The majority of neurons in the orbitofrontal cortex receive direct projections from posterior visual areas (Squatrito, Galletti, Maioli, & Battaglini, 1981) and have been shown to possess the unique feature of having receptive fields that specifically include the central area of the visual field (Mucke, Norita, Benedek, & Creutzfeldt, 1982). Indeed, prefrontal neurons are known to be activated during gaze (Suzuki & Azuma, 1977) and paralimbic neurons in the visually responsive orbitofrontal cortex are known to be involved in eye movements (Kaada, Pribram, & Epstein, 1949) and in tracking emotionally relevant objects in the extrapersonal space (Mesulam, 1985). Stimulation of particular neurons in this area induces pupillary dilation (Okinaka et al., 1960; Sachs et al., 1949) and increases opioid release (Pribram, 1981).

The orbitofrontal region, which is intimately involved in the pleasurable qualities of social interaction (Panksepp et al., 1985), contains the highest levels of opioids in the cerebral cortex (Steklis & Kling, 1985). This structure possesses an anti-nociceptive function (Cooper, 1975). Noting that responses to pain are altered by stimulation of anterior orbitofrontal but not posterior parietal cortex, Pribram (1981) proposes that stimulation of this frontolimbic forebrain area increases the local and perhaps general secretion of endorphins (a contraction of the words "endogenous" and "morphine"). These structure-function relationships would be first observed in the practicing phase, a critical period for the maturation of this prefrontal cortex, and they contribute to the explanation for the decrease in negative emotion and increase in positive emotion over the developmental period of 10 to 13.5 months (Rothbart et al., 1989). Intriguingly, Mahler et al. (1975) observe that practicing age toddlers show a "great imperviousness to knocks and falls and other frustrations."

THE DEVELOPMENTAL NEUROCHEMISTRY OF PRACTICING PERIOD REUNIONS

An integration of the information presented in this and previous chapters produces the following account of the psychobiology of practicing reunion transactions, points of emotional reconnection following inauguratory separation events. Upon return from his first toddling exploratory forays into the physical environment, the early practicing infant's incipient upright locomotor skills and competent transactions with the environment evoke high intensity affective responses in the emotionally reactive proud mother. Affect theory now defines pride as enjoyment/ excitement affect invested in self or accomplishments of the self (Nathanson, 1987b). Kaufman (1989, p. 79) asserts that a parent's pride is expressed in "the gleam in the parent's eyes along with the smile on the mother's face," which reveals her "deepening enjoyment." The mother thus mirrors this positive affect of pleasure and excitement back to the neo-toddler in animated facial displays and in high intensity visuoaffective stimulation behaviorally expressed in foveal transmissions via her "maternal gleam," which she transmits in her "widened eyes." In this "hidden" maternal regulatory function, the junior toddler's "sparkling-eyed pleasure" associated with important early mastery experiences is amplified under the watchful eye of the approving caregiver (Emde, 1988). Such practicing experiences are early building blocks of the child's emerging sense of "competence" (White, 1960). White holds that the earliest competence experiences are associated with "pleasure in function." Mears (1978) proposes that the pleasure of self-motion play—the motion of the whole body through space—is associated with the infant's developing sense of competence.

These external visible events reflect the significant psychobiological state changes that are occurring internally. The rapid psychoneuroendocrinological elevation of opioid peptides in the infant following the perception of the imprinting object's emotional face, especially her eyes in mutual gaze transactions, may mediate the amplification of positive affect in social referencing mirroring experiences. Embedded in rapid communications between each partner's eyes is the "hidden maternal regulation" of the infant's endocrine and nervous systems in symbiotic interactions (Hofer, 1990). This dyadic interactive phenomenon may underlie the involvement of endorphins in the experiencing of positive affects associated with social contact (Oliverio et al., 1984), specifically joy (elation), and also CRF in the generation of excitement affect. The increased levels of circulating endogenous peptides stimulated by the positive emotional face of the mother could be taken up in ventral tegmental dopaminergic neurons, which are known to contain high concentrations of endogenous opioids (Britt & Wise, 1983).

The endorphinergic activation of ventral tegmental dopamine neurons (Stinus et al., 1980) may support and signal the outgrowth of dopaminergic axons which mediate a neurotrophic role in the postnatal maturation of the orbital frontolimbic cortex (Kalsbeek et al., 1987). Opioid peptide uptake would also occur in dopaminergic axon terminals in the orbitofrontal subplate, specifically promoting local axonal sprouting. As a result, externally regulated opioids acting as "trophic regulators" in a critical period for orbitofrontal maturation would influence its "cytoarchitectonic expression" (Hauser et al., 1989). In such a manner maternally induced endocrine changes directly influence the growth of the infant's brain. This psychoendocrinoneurobiological mechanism may define an essential developmental sociobiological process by which socialization induces growth of the cortical hemispheres (Trevarthen, 1990), and may mediate the imprinting of early experience with the mother upon the infant's developing orbitofrontal cortex, a cortical area implicated in attachment functions (Steklis & Kling, 1985).

SUMMARY

Opiates play a unique role in socioemotional, imprinting, and attachment developmental processes. In face-to-face affective interactions, the emotionally expressive face of the imprinting object, the mother, induces alterations in opioid peptides in the child's developing brain. The mechanism of this psychoendocrinological process involves the caregiver's regulation of the infant's hypothalamic production of corticotropin releasing factor (CRF). This neuropeptide activates the sympathetic and deactivates the parasympathetic components of the autonomic nervous system. CRF controls the synthesis of ACTH, a hormone known to facilitate imprinting.

CRF also regulates the production of beta endorphin by the anterior pituitary, another neuropeptide that has been implicated in imprinting processes. Secretory cells in the pituitary release the endogenous opiate into the circulation, where it travels both to the peripheral nervous system and back into the brain. Dopamine neurons in the ventral tegmental area are specifically activated by opioids, and their roles in reward functions, locomotion, and nociception are a result of interactions between this neurotransmitter and this neuropeptide system. Uptake of neurotrophic endorphins by dopaminergic axons in the developing orbitofrontal cortex promotes the structural maturation of the frontolimbic cortex. This development allows the frontolimbic cortex to itself regulate hypothalamic CRF production, and thus to hierarchically control the sympathetic and parasympathetic nervous systems.

11 Socioaffective Influences on Orbitofrontal Morphological Development

Many physiological factors govern the adequate development of the central nervous system. Those critical factors which limit this process may determine the level of cerebral functioning achieved. The high requirement of cerebral tissue for glucose and oxygen make it likely that one such limiting parameter may be the rate at which nutrients are supplied to the brain by the vascular system . . . maintenace of optimal cerebral vascular supply may be dependent on a patterned sensory input to the brain.

— Stephen C. Bondy and Beatrice S. Morelos (1971)

It would seem that the sufficiency of the mother-child relationship . . . has important effects on the maturing nervous system. In other words, neuro-connections made during maturation (especially in the limbic system) are very much influenced by the interactions a child has with its mediators.

— Paul Gilbert (1989)

In accord with the general principle that maternally induced neuroendocrine changes influence the growth of the child's brain, I have suggested that the mother acts as a biotrophic regulator of the biochemical and anatomical maturation of the 1-year-old's orbitofrontal cortex. Just as certain forms of early stimulation determine the tuning curves of neurons in the visual cortex (Blakemore, 1974) and auditory cortex (Clopton & Winfield, 1976), the high intensity socioemotional stimulation in the early practicing phase sets the structure-function relationships and the firing patterns of neurons in the orbitofrontal cortex, a structure involved in the processing of social and emotional information. In line with the principle that early experience alters brain plasticity (Wilson, Willner, Kurz, & Nadel, 1986), imprinting experiences may modify the responsiveness (influence the plasticity) of a population of maturing neurons in orbitofrontal association areas. This would occur by the experience-dependent induction of the interdependent processes of dendritic growth and synaptogenesis (Jacobson, 1978), the responses to "environmental enrichment" found in the early postnatal development of other visually responsive cortical systems (Rosenzweig et al., 1972). Cortical synaptic density has been shown to be influenced by early environmental conditions (Turner & Greenough, 1985).

Studies of the human infant reveal that regional differences in the time course of cortical synaptogenesis exist (Huttenlocher, 1990), and that the metabolic activity that underlies regional cerebral function is ontogenetically highest in the posterior sensorimotor cortex and only later rises in anterior cortex (Chugani & Phelps, 1986). Indeed, although a period of synaptic excess occurs at 4 months in visual cortex, a similar process does not onset in the prefrontal anterior cortex until the end of the first year of human life (Huttenlocher, 1979). The volume of the mammalian orbitofrontal cortex increases significantly above adult values in early postnatal development (Van Eden & Uylings, 1985b). Indeed, the cause of volumetric expansion, synaptic overproduction, has been used to anatomically define a critical period (Greenough & Black, 1992).

What specific changes occur in the orbitofrontal cytoarchitecture as a result of practicing critical period experiences? This prefrontal area, like other cortical regions, is organized into cortical columns or processing modules (Mountcastle, 1978) which consist of groups of vascular, neuronal, and glial cells. The specific nature of the early social environment has been shown to permanently influence the growth of and the interrelationships between these cellular elements. In this chapter I describe the morphogenetic responses of orbitofrontal vascular, dendritic, and axonal elements to socioaffective stimulation at the end of the first year.

VASCULAR MORPHOGENESIS

In order for tissue to grow it must receive a supply of vital nutrients and of oxygen, "the engine of morphogenesis" (Forster & Estabrook, 1993), and it must be able to remove metabolic waste products. In the case of brain tissue, extensive growth is expressed not so much in the enlargement of the neuronal cell body as in the expansion of and differentiation of dendrites and axons. This allows for the formation of synaptic connections between the cytoplasmic processes of different neurons, and it is this interconnection that is responsible for nervous system function. Yet before such events can occur, a microvascular system must be created that can deliver and remove the metabolic substrates that provide for growth and resultant function. It is now commonly accepted that the protein metabolism that is responsible for the growth and function of the neuron is dependent upon the activity level of its inputs (Hyden, 1943). However, it is often overlooked that the metabolic support that is essential for the cellular processing of these inputs, the capacity for synaptic function, is derived from the local brain vasculature (Greenough & Black, 1992). Indeed, there is evidence to show that the effects of early critical period experiences are mediated by stimulation-induced increases in regional blood flow which result in a localized enriched nutritional environment that enhances the dendritic growth required for synaptogenesis (Schapiro & Vukovich, 1970). The association between the vascularity of a brain region, its synaptic structures, and its functional capacities has been known for some time.

The major anatomical organization of the capillaries of the mammalian cerebral cortex occurs postnatally (Caley & Maxwell, 1970; Donahue & Pappas, 1961), with little change beyond this period. In earlier research, Diamond, Krech, and Rosenzweig (1963) demonstrated that an enriched postnatal environment induces an increase in the number and size of cortical vessels. Recent studies reveal that early environmental conditions influence the organization of the brain vasculature, including both the volume of blood vessels in the developing cortex (Black, Sirevaag, & Greenough, 1987) and the number of vasculature-associated glial astrocytes (Greenough & Black, 1992). During the postnatal period astroglial elements differentiate in coordination with the development of the brain parenchyma (Dermietzel & Krause, 1991). Figure 11.1 portrays a diagrammatic representation of the relationships between the brain capillaries,

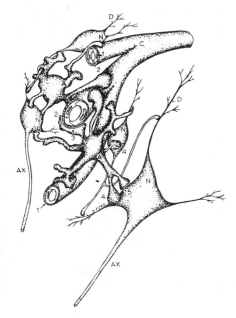

FIG. 11.1. A diagrammatic representation of the relationship between brain capillaries (C), astrocytes (A), and neurons (N). Axons are indicated by AX, dendrites by D. 1, Basement membrane of the capillary; 2, Endothelial cells of the capillary; 3, Astrocyte foot processes in apposition with the capillary basement membrane; 4, Astrocyte foot processes in apposition to the neuron. From Kaplan and Ford (1966). Reprinted by permission of Elsevier.

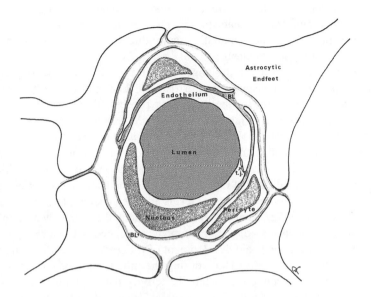

FIG. 11.2.   Schematic representation of the essential structural elements constituting the blood-brain barrier. The "tight" segment of cerebral microvessels possesses an endothelium which exhibits tight junctions (t.j.). Note astrocyte endfeet surrounding the capillary. From Dermietzel and Krause (1991). Reprinted by permission of the publisher.

astrocytic glial cells, and neurons. Brain capillaries are almost completely enveloped by astrocytic processes (Goldstein & Betz, 1986) (Fig. 11.2), suggesting a functional synergism between these two components. Based on their studies, Greenough and Black (1992) now conclude that "regional variations in human brain vasculature might exist as a function of experiential history" (p. 188).

What psychobiological mechanism might mediate the effects of the postnatal environment on the organization of the microvasculature? Animal studies indicate that certain types of early learning experiences associated with new levels of arousal lead to rapid increases in the volume of hemispheric blood flow (Bondy & Harrington, 1978), and that increases of blood flow occur in the cortex and limbic system during the emotional processing of environmental stimuli (LeDoux, Thompson, Iadecola, Tucker, & Reis, 1983). In human infants such learning experiences are mediated through dyadic face-to-face socioemotional transactions that generate heightened levels of infant arousal. The socioaffective stimulation provided by the mother's emotionally expressive face that amplifies the child's physiological state thus elicits an increased blood supply to particular regions of the developing cerebral cortex. Such a sequence of emotional imprinting events is consonant with Zajonc's (1985) vascular theory of emotion, in which he proposes that facial action in emotional expressions regulates blood supply to the brain. This mechanism may also explicate Rauschecker and Marler's (1987) proposition that stimulation that induces arousal exerts a significant influence on neural development.

Bondy has proposed that a prolonged elevation of blood flow, as produced in early experiences of visual attention (Bondy, Lehman, & Purdy, 1974), is an underlying requirement for the imprinting process (Bondy & Purdy, 1976). Both imprinting (Kohsaka, Takamatsu, Aoki, & Tsukada, 1979) and arousal (Gonzalez-Lima & Scheich, 1985) are associated with increased metabolic activity. During the period of postnatal brain maturation, blood flow, known to correlate with changes in arousal level (Obrist, Thompson, Wang, & Wilkinson, 1975), and to be an indicator of regional oxidative metabolism (Fox et al., 1986; Raichle et al., 1976), rises to maximal levels and then declines (Kennedy, Grave, Jehle, & Sokoloff, 1972). Kennedy et al. suggest that the peak elevation in early infancy reflects the increased energy demands associated with biosynthetic processes essential for growth and development of differentiating cortical structures and their emergent functions. Thus, during the initial phase of intense growth, cortical depth is maximum and metabolic activity that supports this growth is heightened. In support of this, developmental neuroanatomical studies demonstrate that localized expansions in the postnatal cortical mass are associated with postnatal changes in cortical vascularity (Rowan & Maxwell, 1981).

What biochemical signals could trigger such arousal-associated metabolic changes in the developing orbitofrontal cortex? The postnatal mammalian cortex receives a major innervation from monoaminergic neurons, and this brainstem input has been suggested to exert a trophic influence on cortical differentiation (Coyle & Molliver, 1977). Tyrosine hydroxylase, the rate limiting enzyme of dopamine (and noradrenaline) biosynthesis, is known to exert an inductive influence on the development of the cortex (Coyle & Axelrod, 1972). Dopamine, a neuromodulator which increases arousal (Iversen, 1977), has been shown to specifically increase prefrontal metabolism (McCulloch, Savaki, & McCulloch, 1982). These findings suggest that the initial increased energy demands of growing prefrontal cortical tissue are met by localized dopamine-enhanced uptake of glucose, some of which is utilized in the oxidative arm of the pentose phosphate shunt (Hothersall et al., 1982), the biochemical pathway that supports biosynthetic processes. Indeed, catecholamines have pronounced effects on cerebral oxidative metabolism and blood flow, especially in areas with an "imperfect" blood-brain barrier (Berntman, Dahlgren, & Siesjo, 1978). Dopamine, in particular, functionally increases blood flow in various brain areas (Ekstrom-Jodal, Elfverson, & Von Essen, 1982; Von Essen, 1974), including a brain region with an incomplete barrier (choroid plexus; Townsend, Ziedonis, Bryan, Brennan, & Page, 1984). In addition, the catecholaminergic regulation of the permeability of water into this local brain region via its effects on the rate of cerebral blood flow (Raichle, Eichling, & Grubb, 1974) may allow for the transport of an optimal amount of water into the developing parenchyma that facilitates cell growth and differentiation and thereby synaptogenesis.

The elevation in prefrontal blood flow and increase in energy metabolism in the practicing period may reflect the ongoing postnatal construction of an operational blood-brain barrier (Bradbury, 1979; Johanson, 1989) (see Fig. 11.2). This important interface between circulating blood and brain is located in the endothelial cell lining of cerebral blood vessels, which is only one cell layer thick (Reese & Karnovsky, 1967). These brain capillary endothelial cells are "metabolically active" during the postnatal period (Goldstein, Wolinsky, Csejtey, & Diamond, 1975). The local establishment of the barrier is initiated by vascular proliferation, and the maximal increase in the number of endothelial cells in the brain occurs postnatally (Robertson, Dubois, Bowman, & Goldstein, 1985). The developing brain produces an angiogenesis factor (Gospodarowicz, Chang, Lui, Baird, & Bohlen, 1984; Risau, 1986) a peptide growth factor that influences the vascularization of the nervous system (Gospodarowicz, Massoglia, Chang, & Fujii, 1986) and promotes the growth of dopaminergic (Engele & Bohn, 1991) and cerebral cortical (Morrison, Sharma, De Vellis, & Bradshaw, 1986) neurons. Active capillary sprouting and branching is observed postnatally in the cerebral hemispheres (Bar & Wolff, 1972). By the end of the first year the capillary density of the human cortex doubles (Purves, 1972). A significant increase in the number of "seamless" endothelia asociated with capillary branching are seen in areas of the cerebral cortex during postnatal development (Wolff & Bar, 1972). Sprouting may also occur in the highly branched vasculature of the subplate (Mrzljak et al., 1990) and in the middle cerebral artery which irrigates the lateral parts of the orbitofrontal cortex and/or the anterior cerebral artery which supplies the medial portions of the orbitofrontal cortex (Damasio, 1983; Truex & Carpenter, 1964) (see Fig. 11.3). High levels of vascular endothelial growth factor, an endothelial cell mitogen (Levy, Tamargo, Brem, & Nathans, 1989) that induces vascular permeability (Keck et al., 1989), have been found in postnatal brain (Breier, Albrecht, Sterrer, & Risau, 1992).

Indeed, vessel proliferation in the postnatal cerebral hemispheres is known to be associated with high levels of nonspecific permeability (Stewart & Hayakawa, 1987), and neurotrophic peptides such as CRF, neurotrophins, and glucose-regulating endorphins which do not cross the mature blood-brain barrier would have access to developing orbitofrontal parenchyma through this permeable vasculature. The postnatal reduction of permeability (Tuor, Simone, & Bascaramurty, 1992) is associated with a developmental "tightening" of the blood-brain barrier (Stewart & Hayakawa, 1987), the creation of high-resistance, tight junctions between the endothelial cells of the cerebral microvasculature (Fig. 11.4). Maturation of developing human brain capillaries is associated with changes at the cytological level (Hauw, Berger, Escourolle, 1975). During the postnatal period the endothelial cells become thinner and drawn out (Donahue & Pappas, 1961). These phenomena may be time limited to a critical period. Figure 11.5

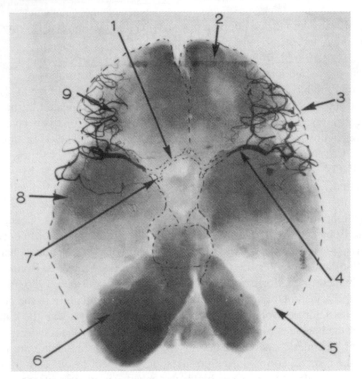

FIG. 11.3. The ventral aspect of the human brain showing the distribution of the orbitofrontal branches of the middle cerebral artery. 1, Anterior cerebral artery; 2, Frontal lobe; 3, Cortical network of the orbitofrontal vessels; 4, Middle cerebral artery; 5, Occipital lobe; 6, Cerebellum; 7, Internal carotid artery; 8, Temporal lobe; 9, Cortical-orbital branches. From Kaplan and Ford (1966). Reprinted by permission of Elsevier.

shows a comparison between a permeable, immature vessel of the cortex of early infancy and a vessel of a mature blood-brain barrier of late infancy. Compare Fig. 11.6 a capillary from fetal frontal lobe, with Fig. 11.7, capillary from postnatal cortex.

The local maturation of the microvasculature undergoes regional development in neonatal periods (Saunders, 1977), and this process occurs latest in the cortex in the prefrontal area (Tuor et al., 1992). Intriguingly, endothelial cells of brain capillaries are known to contain enzymes for dopamine metabolism (Owman & Rosengren, 1967), and the major sources of dopamine metabolites are enzymes located extraneuronally (Kopin, 1985). Cerebral capillaries are known to be rich in adenylate cyclase (Baca & Palmer, 1978; Joo & Toth, 1975). Postsynaptic dopamine receptors are found in the vascular beds of various organs of the body,

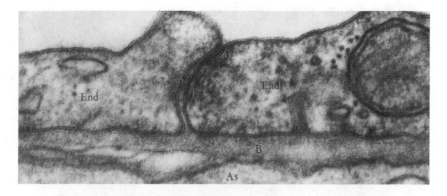

FIG. 11.4. Electron micrograph of a tight junction (J) between the endothelial cells of the cerebral microvasculature. From Peters et al. (1991). Reprinted by permission of Oxford University Press.

and these receptors, linked to adenylate cyclase, exhibit considerable similarity to the D1 receptors in the brain (Goldberg, Volkman, & Kohli, 1978). Importantly, it has been observed that many dopaminergic varicosities in the deep layers of the orbitofrontal cortex lack a synaptic specialization, suggesting that dopamine exerts its effects at sites other than traditional neuronal presynaptic-axonal, postsynaptic-dendritic contacts (Seguela, Watkins, & Descarries, 1988)

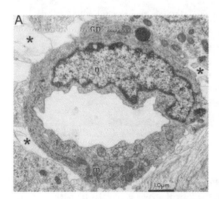
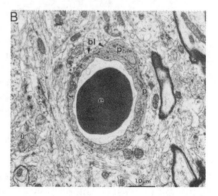

FIG. 11.5. (A) Vessel from day-5 mouse cerebral cortex. The vessel is large and thick-walled. The endothelial cell contains a large nucleus (n), numerous mitochondria (m) and abundant ribosomes. The typically large extracellular space of immature brain is shown (asterisks). (B) Vessel of 6 week cortex. The vessels are smaller and thinner-walled than at 5 days. Erythrocyte (e); pericyte (p); basal lamina (bl). From Stewart and Hayakawa (1987). Reprinted by permission of Elsevier.

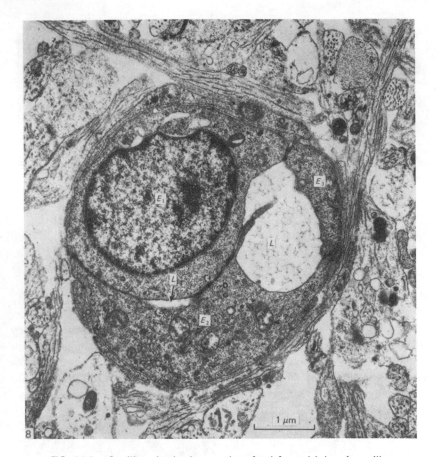

FIG. 11.6. Capillary in the human late fetal frontal lobe. A capillary formed by three endothelial cells (E1, E2, and E3). From Allsopp and Gamble (1979). Reprinted by permission of Cambridge University Press.

(see Fig. 11.8). In fact, Descarries asserts that these nonjunctional dopaminergic varicosities act in a "diffuse and/or long-lasting manner on vast neuronal ensembles implicated in 'state'-dependent activities" (p. 20). Dopamine produces a significant increase in blood flow in the cerebral cortex, including the frontal cortex, and this has been suggested to reflect the activation of specific receptors located on endothelium (Tuor, Edvinsson, & McCulloch, 1986). As previously mentioned, D1 dopamine receptors linked to adenylate cyclase are found in in the deep layers of the orbitofrontal cortex (Savasta, Dubois, & Scatton, 1986). Brain receptors for dopamine are amplified in postnatal periods (Hartley &

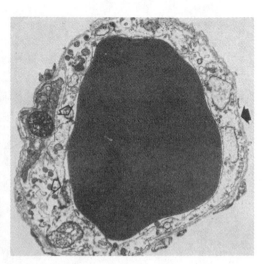

FIG. 11.7. Capillary from postnatal rat cortex. A red blood cell is entrapped in the lumen. Tight junctions (open arrows) between the endothelial cells are present. Reprinted from Goldstein, Wolinsky, Csejtey, and Diamond (1975). Isolation of metabolically active capillaries from rat brain. *Journal of Neurochemistry, 25, 715–717*, with permission from Pergamon Press Ltd, Headington Hill Hall, Oxford OX3 OBW, UK.

Seeman, 1983), and environmental factors influence receptor formation in these periods (Hill et al., 1986).

Integrating these findings, I propose that an amplification of endothelial dopamine receptors in the orbitofrontal microvasculature occurs in the practicing critical period, and that this allows for a subcortical dopaminergic regulation of the local cortical blood-brain barrier. This event may be associated with a tightening of the endothelial junctions in the orbitofrontal microvasculature. In such a manner, this catecholamine comes to influence the maturation and function of the "dynamic regulatory interface" (Cornford, 1985) of the blood-brain barrier. This establishment of a functional blood-brain barrier that acts as "a homeostat between the brain-body interface" (Dermietzel & Krause, 1991) enables the onset of parenchymal aerobic oxidative metabolic processes that are required for the maturation and differentiation of local brain regions. These latter authors conclude that:

> If one considers the blood-brain barrier as a homeostat that provides for specific, blood-borne substrates which are necessary for maintaining brain metabolism, the closure of the blood-brain barrier during development is, consequently, indicative of the differentiation processes occurring in individual brain cells. (pp. 92–93)

Brain capillaries, which constitute only 0.1% of the brain mass (Bar, 1980), are responsible for the transport of glucose for the entire brain. Glucose is the prime energy substrate utilized by the high metabolic demand of the immature brain, as its metabolism accounts for the bulk of the brain's oxygen metabolism. It is the blood-brain barrier that regulates the transport of glucose from blood to brain (Fuglsang, Lomholt, & Gjedde, 1988; Lund-Anderson, 1979).

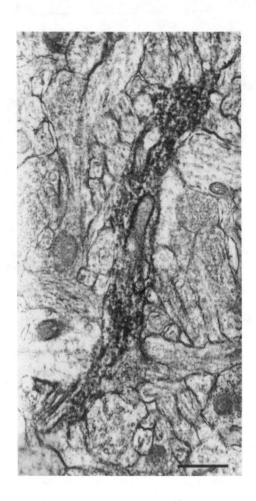

FIG. 11.8. Nonjunctional dopaminergic terminal in deep orbital
layers. The axon bears two slightly beaded varicosities containing
aggregated synaptic vesicles. No
part of this profile exhibits any
membranous differentiation sug-
gestive of a synaptic junction.
From Seguela et al. (1988). Reprinted by permission of Elsevier.

Observers have noted that stimulation of the brainstem reticular formation influences cerebral blood flow and oxygen consumption (Meyer, Nomura, Saka-moto, & Kondo, 1969), that highly branched fibers originating in brainstem catecholaminergic neurons innervate blood vessels in widely dispersed areas of the brain (Swanson & Hartman, 1975), and that catecholamines regulate vascular permeability and influence blood flow in the cerebral microcirculation (Raichle et al., 1975). Catecholaminergic modulation of microvascular transport of glu-cose from the circulation into orbitofrontal columns would represent a control mechanism by which oxygen, energy substrate, and catalytic hormonal factors would be more efficiently delivered into the expanding orbitofrontal neuropil. The anatomical maturation of this subcortical-cortical system could support emergent functions that result from more complex synaptic events. According to Hartman and Udenfriend (1972) the innervation of the brain vasculature by

156

distant catecholaminergic neurons operates as a regulator that responds to the local needs of brain regions. I suggest that this underlies the mechanism whereby subcortically manufactured biogenic amines regulate the biochemical response of an individual cerebral cortical cholinergic synapse (Shimizu, Creveling, & Daly, 1970) and by which a single dopamine axon can modulate a large number of cortical pyramidal cells (Smiley et al., 1992). The monoaminergic control of brain microvascular systems thus mediates an essential homeostatic role.

It is now established that biogenic amines play an essential role in microcirculatory homeostasis (Schayer, 1970). Indeed, this neurobiological mechanism may underly Cannon's (1939) concept of homeostasis. Cannon described the maintenance of the internal milieu by control systems that regulate the functioning of the organs and tissues. This conception expanded upon the pioneering work of Bernard, the physiologist who first described the concept of biological regulation. According to Bernard (1930) the cells of the body live and grow in an internal environment, the extracellular fluid, which he termed the milieu interieur:

> The living organism does not really exist in the milieu exterieur (the atmosphere, if it breathes air; salt or fresh water, if that is its element), but in the liquid milieu interieur formed by the circulating organic liquid which surrounds and bathes all the tissue elements; this is the lymph or plasma, the liquid part of the blood. (p. 281)

In brain regions, the establishment of the stability of the internal milieu occurs with the maturation of a local blood-brain barrier, since "the cerebral endothelium assists in the integration of brain and body functions by transmitting metabolic and homeostatic information bidirectionally" (Dermietzel & Krause, 1991, p. 59). This structural development is influenced by the child's social matrix, a dominant component of the milieu exterieur. In fact, Hofer (1983) has demonstrated that "the regulation of the infant's milieu interieur is partially delegated to processes within the relationship with its mother" (p. 61).

The emergence of this mature microvascular system may be associated with a postnatal regional shift from anaerobic to aerobic oxidative metabolism that supports a significantly increased energy output (Farkas-Bargeton & Diebler, 1978; Guroff, 1980; Himwich, 1951) of the orbitofrontal cortex. The transformation of energy production in a specific region during a postnatal interval has been suggested to mediate critical period phenomena (Meier et al., 1960). In light of the facts that synaptic overproduction operationally defines a critical period and that brain vasculature is intimately involved in the metabolic and functional support of synapses, experience-dependent regional blood flow events, influenced by subcortically exported catecholamines, may thus be a critical regulating factor in the development of regional differences in the time course of human cortical synaptogenesis. Indeed, ontogenetic catecholamine-microvasculature interactions may represent a fundamental mechanism by which core brain regulatory system neuromodulator projection pathways exert an organizing influence on cortical differentiation. This property lies in the unique role that central catecholamine neurons play in the cerebral circulation (Yokote et al., 1986).

The blood-brain barrier is now thought to represent not simply an impermeable protective barrier but a critical site of blood-brain interfaces where bidirectional exchange processes occur (Dermietzel & Krause, 1991). Critical period events may establish a microvasculature that is able to handle the increased metabolic load associated with higher levels of neural activity. It is now known that the capillary network in a region is directly correlated with the region's oxygen consumption (Cragie, 1945), that regional blood flow and regional metabolism are coupled to local synaptic activity (Greenberg, Hand, Sylvestro, & Reivich, 1979), and that differences between blood flow and oxygen consumption exist not at the macroregional but at the microregional level (Reivich et al., 1977). Brain areas are known to differ in capillary form and blood flow function (Fenstermacher et al., 1988). The lateral parts of the orbital gyri are irrigated by the middle cerebral artery, an important artery that also nourishes the motor and premotor areas, the somesthetic and auditory projection areas, the lateral gyri of the occipital lobe, and the higher receptive association areas (Truex & Carpenter 1964) (see Fig. 11.9). Its occlusion, when not fatal, produces an inability to distinguish between different intensities of stimuli and a hemiplegia of the face. Dopamine has been demonstrated to produce a vasoconstriction of this specific artery (Tuor et al., 1986). The medial portion of the orbitofrontal cortex is supplied by the anterior cerebral artery, an artery that is peculiar in having both a cortical and a central distribution. The sympathetic innervation of the right branches of both of these cerebral arteries is known to continue in stage-like fashion during postnatal developmental periods (Handa, Nojyo, Tamamaki, Tsuchida, & Kubota, 1993).

In fact, the microvascular patterns of this cortex are unlike those of the rest of the cortex (Lorente de No, 1983). Its unique structural aspects are seen at the cytological level. For example, Weibel-Palade bodies are only found in endothelial cells (Gospodarowicz, Brown, Birdwell, & Zetter, 1978) and are very rarely seen in the normal, mature human brain (Hirano, 1974). These unusual cytoplasmic inclusions are observed in human fetal brain capillaries (Bauer & Vester, 1970), and are thought to be an indicator of increased metabolic activity or proliferation of endothelial cells (Phillips, Kumar, Kumar, & Waghe, 1979). Figure 11.10 shows Weibel-Palade bodies in the endothelial cell of a capillary in the mature human orbital cortex. The unique functional capacities of orbital microvasculature, on the other hand, may underlie the "hyperfrontal" distribution of elevated blood flow and metabolic activity that is known to support the mature prefrontal anticipatory programming of behavior (Ingvar, 1979). Practicing imprinting experiences may influence the emergence of the anterior cortical blood-brain barrier which allows for the emergence of this function.

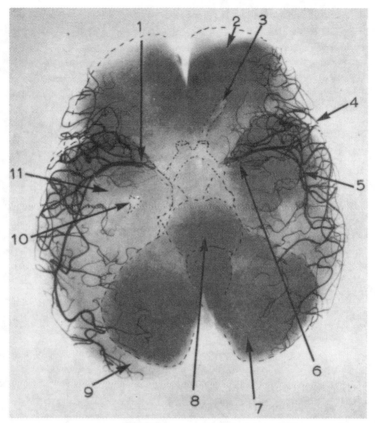

FIG. 11.9. The ventral aspect of the human brain showing the branches of the middle cerebral artery. 1, Anterior cerebral artery; 2, Frontal lobe; 3, Anterior horn of the lateral ventricle; 4, Cortical branches of the middle cerebral artery; 5, Cortical branches of the middle cerebral artery over the insula; 6. Lenticulostriate vessels; 7, Cerebellum; 8, Pons; 9, Occipital lobe; 10, Tip of the inferior horn of the lateral ventricle; 11, Temporal lobe. From Kaplan and Ford (1966). Reprinted by permission of Elsevier.

DENDRITIC MORPHOGENESIS

In discussing the anatomical development of the prefrontal cortex, Goldman-Rakic asserts that "the character of the postnatal environment" influences both synaptic density and dendritic growth (Goldman-Rakic et al., 1983). Similarly, Winson (1985) asserts that during the first years of human life, the growth of prefrontal dendrites is affected by environmental stimuli. In the altricial human infant especially, these environmental stimuli are primarily social. In fact,

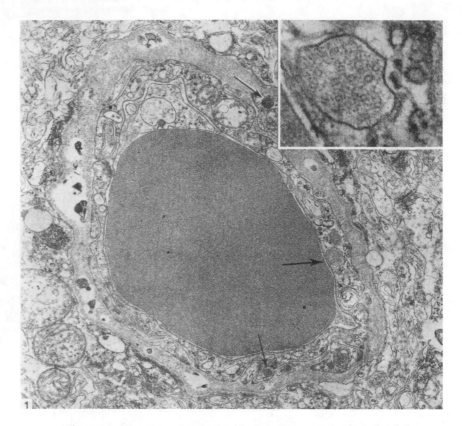

FIG. 11.10.   Capillary of the orbital cortex. Three Weibel-Palade bodies are arrowed. Inset: Higher magnification of one body showing microtubules in a matrix. From Herrlinger et al. (1974). Reprinted by permission of Cambridge University Press.

Greenough and Black (1992) are very specific about the nature of such environmental stimuli; they posit "much of the sensory input that shapes . . . dendrites probably arises from contact with the mother during nursing and other interaction" (p. 165). These data support Scheflen's (1981) conclusion that the neurodevelopmental processes of dendritic proliferation and synaptogenesis which are responsible for postnatal brain growth are critically influenced by events at the interpersonal and intrapersonal levels. A period of dendritic development is known to occur in the prefrontal cortex in the first year of infancy (Mrzljak et al., 1990). Social imprinting may thus be a special form of environmental stimulation, a socioaffective stimulation, which induces dendritic growth particularly in the orbitofrontal cortical region. In recent neuropsychological work on the development of cortical networks involved in early emotion, Tucker (1992) proposes that factors influencing the child's emotional state also influence cortical plasticity.

Imprinting and the development of cortical plasticity have been suggested to involve the same sort of neural mechanisms (Rose, 1981) and to reflect the expression of a common developmental process (Bischoff, 1983). Kellaway (1989) asserts that the incomplete differentiation of neuronal and glial cells for a finite period after birth is the basis of plasticity that permits modification of protein synthesis, neural circuitry, and electrical activity by the sensory periphery. In an analogy with embryologic development, Lorenz (1970) refers to the imprinting of the final character of cells by the local environment. Studies of the developmental neuroanatomic correlates of the imprinting process have revealed significant morphological changes in neurons in a forebrain area implicated in the long-term storage of information acquired through the imprinting experience. These include an increase in the size and arborization of terminal branches, the length of the synaptic apposition zone (postsynaptic density) (Bradley, Horn, & Bateson, 1981), and the number of cholinergic receptor sites (Bradley & Horn, 1981). Increases in the number of synapses and the density of synaptic vesicles (Stewart, Csillag, & Rose, 1987) and in the number and structure of dendritic spines (Patel & Stewart, 1988) have also been reported. This latter effect is especially important, since dendritic spines play a role in modulating synaptic efficiency (Perkel & Perkel, 1985), and alterations in the shape of dendritic spines result in changes in neuronal information processing (Erulkar, 1989). Spine formation has been shown to be influenced by visual information embedded in social interactions (Coss & Globus, 1978).

Noison and Thomas (1988), studying the ontogeny of dopaminergic function in the postnatal frontal cortex, conclude that environmental stimuli regulate the anatomical, cellular, and even molecular organization of the developing nervous system. In research on biochemical changes that occur in response to early experiences, Aoki and Siekevitz (1988) find a specific activation of microtubule-associated protein (MAP2), a structural protein which is located in dendrites. Critical period stimulation triggers the catecholamine-mediated dephosphorylation of this organic molecule, causing a dynamic change in the shape and branching patterns of dendrites and inducing the growth of dendritic spines which are potential sites of synaptic contact. Early visual stimulation induces an alteration in the biological activity of MAP2, and this modification of its functional activity is necessary for the dendritic reception of external information. These cyto-architectural changes influence the cell's future ability to respond to incoming signals and may underlie the "experience-dependent synaptic changes" which are responsible for final postnatal wiring patterns. Although their studies are on the effects of early visual stimulation on development of the posterior visual cortex, these authors suggest that the activity-dependent biochemical changes in MAP2 play an important role in plasticity and stabilization and in critical period onset and offset in regions throughout the brain. I deduce that a similar alteration of dendritic biochemistry, mediated by dopamine, occurs in the synaptic microenvironment of anterior orbitofrontal dendrites. This proposal is supported by the findings that during early postnatal visual experiences, the enhancement of glycoprotein into newly forming synapses is biochemically mediated by dopamine and cyclic AMP (Jork, Lossner, & Matthies, 1982; Lossner, Jork, & Matthies, 1981), and that dopamine is thought to modulate the activity of cortical distal dendrites (Smiley et al., 1992).

In discussing his work on the induction of cortical structure by early experience, Greenough (1987) finds a common pattern—dendritic growth followed by exuberant synaptogenesis followed by synaptic pruning and preservation. With regard to this last step, he refers to an "activity-dependent selective preservation of synapses." Rosenzweig et al. (1972) also report that cortical development involves an initial period of increased growth followed by a dimunition in cortical depth. This ontogenetic decline in cortical depth is influenced by environmental stimulation-induced neural activity (Cummins, Livesey, & Bell, 1982). It is important to note that imprinting-influenced expansive changes coincide with a selective degeneration of other local neural systems (Wolff, 1979), that imprinting involves the construction of some new synapses and the elimination of other previously existing ones (Horn, Bradley, & McCabe, 1985; Patel, Rose, & Stewart, 1988). Changeux and Dehaene, (1989) describe the essential developmental phenomenon of the activity-dependent Darwinian elimination and selective stabilization of synapses. This adaptive process occurs, for example, in developing cortical association areas (Price & Blakemore, 1985) during postnatal imprinting sensitive periods. Huttenlocher (1990) emphasizes that there is a very significant loss of cortical synapses in the postnatal period, and that cortical synapse elimination plays an especially important role in the development of complex systems. I shall further discuss the importance of these mechanisms to the final maturation of the orbitofrontal cortex in an upcoming chapter.

The imprinting-induced amplification of cholinergic receptors on dendrites in the deep layers of the orbitofrontal cortex would allow for an increased number of synaptic connections with incoming axons. The next question is, what sites are delivering axons to these prefrontal dendrites? In other words, what kinds of connections need to be made in order to sustain mature function? Subcortical input from the magnocellular portions of the mediodorsal nucleus of the thalamus (Corwin et al., 1983; Leonard, 1969; Rose & Woolsey, 1948) and regions of the amygdala (Porrino, Crane, & Goldman-Rakic, 1981) and hippocampus (Morecraft et al., 1992) are known to be delivered to this cortex. Ingrowing axons to deep orbital neurons are also derived from the lateral, medial, and posterior regions of the hypothalamus (Morecraft et al., 1992). It should be remembered that these orbitofrontal columns receive the convergent input of processed sensory information (olfactory, somesthetic, visual, and auditory) from all cortical association cortices (Yarita et al., 1980).

I surmise that these inputs into orbitofrontal dendrites occur sequentially in ontogenesis, beginning with subcortical olfactory-gustatory inputs. The very first imprinting experiences that begin immediately after birth involve the stamping in of axonal pathways that deliver olfactory and somesthetic inputs provided by the mother into the orbitofrontal cortex. This imprinting experience may produce the first representations of the mother in the form of olfactory-tactile-thermal models. The orbitofrontal processing of olfactory stimuli (Yarita et al., 1980) which allows for complex olfactory discriminations (Eichenbaum, Clegg, & Feeley, 1983) thereby mediates the earliest expression of the specific recognition of the mother. Neuropsychological research now reveals that the human orbitofrontal area in the right and not left cortex is activated in odor discrimination (Zatorre, Jones-Gotman, Evans, & Meyer, 1992). Neurobiological studies have established the important role of this frontal cortex in the regulation of skin temperature changes (Blass, 1969; Delgado & Livingston, 1949; Fairman, Livingston, & Poppen, 1950). Newborn mammals born with closed eyelids use olfactory and thermal sensory cues provided by the mother in "homing behavior" (Freeman & Rosenblatt, 1978). Indeed, MacFarlane (1977) has documented that 6-day-old infants can reliably discriminate the scent of their mother's breast pad from that of another woman. Although these inputs are initiated soon after birth, by the end of the first year, the beginning of the practicing period, the predominant input into these prefrontal dendrites is from visual processing areas.

In addition to subcortical inputs, posterior cortical sensory inputs are delivered into and synapse upon dendrites in this anterior association cortex. For example, with the emergence of upright locomotion that signals the onset of the practicing period, orbital neurons may simultaneously receive afferent input from both posterior parietal (Cavada & Goldman-Rakic, 1989) areas that provide an image of the position of the body in space with respect to objects in the surrounding space (Hecaen & Albert, 1978), and input from posterior visual areas (Squatrito, Galletti, Maiali, & Battaglini, 1981). This combination would allow for this prefrontal structure to play an essential role in "recording movements of the visual environment relative to the body" and in "the adjustment of motor behavior to such movements" (Mucke et al., 1982). These specific connections enable the orbital regulation of visual guidance of upright locomotion. Studies of 13- to-16 month-old infants show that visual-proprioceptive information is specifically utilized in the earliest attempts to maintain stable standing posture (Lee & Aronson, 1974).

Furthermore, orbital prefrontal neurons receive a convergent multimodal input from all sensory areas of the posterior cortex (Chavis & Pandya, 1976; Jones & Powell, 1970) and are involved in the formation of cross-modal associations between stimuli of different sensory modalities (Benevento, Fallon, Davis, & Rezak, 1977; Thorpe et al., 1983; Watanabe, 1992). Cross-modal transfer is a cognitive process that contributes to the development of abstraction and representational abilities (Rose, 1986). Anatomical connections between the anterior and posterior cortex in the early practicing period may be primarily responsible for the significant cognitive advances that emerge at the end of the first year. The developing nervous system thus acquires its rapidly expanding capacity to process and integrate complex multisensory information by increasing the number of subcortical-prefrontal and cortical-prefrontal connections, and this property is reflected in the appearance of emergent capacities that involve the transfer of learning between modalities over stages of infancy.

CHOLINERGIC AXONAL MORPHOGENESIS

In addition to this organization of dendritic inputs, there is also a critical period expansion of the axonal output system of orbital neurons, especially those in cortical layers V and VI. These deep layers receive dopaminergic innervation (Lindvall, Bjorklund, Moore, & Stenevi, 1974), and the axons in these layers that descend into the subcortex towards the ventral tegmental area represent "non-dopaminergic" components of the mesocortical system (Thierry, Deniau, Herve, & Chevalier, 1980). Anatomical research suggests that dopaminergic afferents exert a modulatory effect on the cortico-subcortical projecting neurons which are known to be located in these deeper layers (Berger, Trottier, Verney, Gaspar, & Alvarez, 1988). As previously mentioned, prefrontal subplate neurons that survive programmed cell death, presumably DARPP-32 associated neurons identified in deep orbitofrontal layers, become part of layer VIb in the deep cortex and undergo morphological changes in postnatal periods. De Carlos and O'Leary (1992) have reported that subplate cells constitute the first axonal projections growing out of the cortex. Shatz has recently concluded that the axon pathways formed by subplate neurons are essential to the normal development of descending cortical-subcortical projections (McConnell, Ghosh, & Shatz, 1989). Berger et al. (1990) have proposed that DARPP-32 is associated with long-projecting pyramidal neurons which are involved in "corticosubcortical projections" and in "specific anatomical circuits." Orbitofrontal-subcortical cholinergic projections, which deliver cortically processed information directly to underlying limbic structures responsible for affect and drive, are known to mature and functionally onset in mammalian infancy (Johnson, Rosvold, Galkin, & Goldman, 1976). Johnston (1985) has concluded that the cholinergic links in dopaminergic-cholinergic circuits develop later than the dopaminergic components.

This expansion specifically involves the oligodendroglial myelination and growth of descending axons to (nicotinic?) cholinergic receptors in anterior temporal (Moran, Mufson, & Mesulam, 1987) and other "upstream" sites of the ventral tegmental limbic circuit (e.g., the central amygdaloid nucleus, the lateral septum, areas of the hypothalamus, and especially the ventral tegmental area itself). A high density of cholinergic receptors has been observed in the vicinity of ventral tegmental dopamine cells (Paxinos & Watson, 1982). The dendrites of these catecholaminergic neurons may receive the descending fast-conducting cholinergic axons with a short refractory period that are known to synapse on the dopaminergic neurons of the ventral tegmental area (Wise, 1983). This cholinergic fiber system runs in a rostro-caudal direction opposite to unmyelinated dopaminergic axons, and is thought to activate the ascending ventral tegmental reward system (Bozarth, 1988). Such descending orbitofrontal axons may also synapse upon other components of the ventral tegmental circuit. Mature prefrontal cortical regions are known to contain branched neurons in the deep layers which send axon collaterals to multiple subcortical areas (Thierry, Chevalier, Ferron, & Glowinski, 1983). These cortical-subcortical projections may act to facilitate frontolimbic mesocortical and inhibit subcortical hyper-excitatory mesolimbic dopaminergic activity.

In support of these proposals, Sesack and Pickel (1992) have very recently demonstrated that the prefrontal cortex, including the medial orbital and ventral infralimbic subdivisions, sends direct, monosynaptic projections to subcortical nuclei and to dendrites of dopaminergic neurons in the rostral ventral tegmental area (Figs. 4.19 and 11.11). Their research produces three major findings: that these descending projections mediate a predominantly excitatory influence on ventral tegmental dopamine neurons, that the excitatory amino acid glutamate is the major transmitter in this pathway, and that dopaminergic neurons are activated by stimulation of glutamate receptors. (The importance of glutamate to orbitofrontal function is explained in the next chapter.) Other research reveals that glutamate is present in prefrontal cortical fibers (Fonnum, Soreide, Kvala, Walker, & Walaas, 1981) and that layer V of the prefrontal cortex contains mesocortical dopamine terminals and glutamatergic pyramidal neurons (Mora & Cobo, 1990). These data suggest that the socioaffective experience-dependent growth of axons from neurons in the deep layers of the orbitofrontal cortex to subcortical sites, especially to rostral nuclei of the ventral tegmental area, represents the emergent maturation of the nondopaminergic mesocortical component of Nauta's ventral tegmental limbic forebrain-midbrain circuit.

It is also now known both that the mesocortical subcircuit shows a higher dopamine turnover and faster firing rates than subcortical limbic subcircuits, and that prefrontal cortical systems modulate subcortical dopaminergic activity (Bannon & Roth, 1983). This may reflect the specific orbitofrontal activation of the ventromedial rostral linear subnucleus which innervates the cortex at the expense of other noncortically projecting mesencephalic A10 subnuclei. In this way, the mesocortical dopamine subcircuit may be preferentially activated over the mesolimbic and mesodiencephalic ventromedial subcircuits. This represents a hierarchical dominance of the mesocortical circuit over other subcortical ventral tegmental circuits. Sesack and Pickel (1992) now conclude that the excitatory monosynaptic feedback from the prefrontal cortex may explain the unique physiological and pharmacological properties of mesocortical dopaminergic neurons. Indeed, the prefrontal mesocortical system is known to function in the regulation of affective responses (Tassin, 1987). This mechanism may be involved in the orbitofrontal modulation of ascending excitatory influences (Butter, Snyder, &

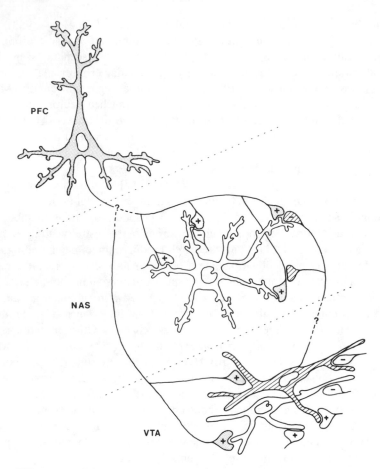

FIG. 11.11.   Schematic drawing of synaptic connections between projections from the prefrontal cortex (PFC) and dopaminergic neurons in mesolimbic circuitry. PFC neurons and their axon terminals are indicated by shading, while dopaminergic cells and terminals are depicted with hatch marks. PFC projections to the nucleus accumbens septi (NAS) are also shown. PFC projections to the ventral tegmental area (VTA) make monosynaptic contact with the dendrites of dopaminergic cells. From Sesack and Pickel (1992). Prefrontal cortical efferents in the rat synapse on unlabeled neuronal targets of catecholamine terminals in the nucleus accumbens septi and on dopamine neurons in the ventral tegmental area. *Journal of Comparative Neurology, 320.* Reprinted by permission of Wiley-Liss, a division of John Wiley and Sons, Inc.

McDonald, 1970) and drive (Rosenkilde, 1979), and in its action as a regulatory influence on the sympathetic nervous system (Fuster, 1980). In the development of this frontolimbic cortex, its direct affect regulatory role as a modulator of activity of the sympathetic component of the ANS thus ontogenetically precedes its function as a modulator of activity of the parasympathetic component. In upcoming chapters I show that the direct modulation of the parasympathetic nervous system by the orbitofrontal cortex does not begin until the final maturation of this cortex in the late practicing period.

SUMMARY

Socioaffective stimulation at the end of the first year induces permanent morphological changes in each of the cellular components of the orbitofrontal cortex. The heightened levels of arousal associated with imprinting experiences lead to rapid increases in regional blood flow and the establishment of a local blood-brain barrier. The vascular delivery of vital nutrients and oxygen sustains the increased energy demands of biosynthetic processes in the growing brain tissue. Dopamine, in its role of regulating vascular permeability, elevates blood flow and metabolism in the developing prefrontal cortex. The maturation of the microvasculature is associated with a critical period shift from anaerobic to aerobic regional metabolism, and this transition makes possible the rapid and exuberant growth and differentiation of orbitofrontal dendrites. These dendrites can now receive axonal input from various subcortical and cortical areas, and it is these varied interconnections that underlie the unique functional capacities of this prefrontal cortex. The growth of frontolimbic cholinergic axons back down the neuraxis towards the dopaminergic neurons in the midbrain represents the final maturation of the ventral tegmental forebrain-midbrain circuit.

12 The Emotionally Expressive Face

A . . . consequence of the infant's attachment to the mother is that the infant develops a finely articulated schema for his mother, especially her face. It is assumed that the infant acquires a mental image of the person who is the object of attachment.
—Paul H. Mussen, John J. Conger, and Jerome Kagan (1969)

[F]acial recognition is not merely a cognitive or perceptual phenomenon, but also an act of utmost emotional and relational significance. In other words, the eye-to-eye relationship—and, perhaps more importantly, its internalized psychic representation—is a form of dialogue essential for psychic development . . .
—Moshe Halevi Spero (1993)

The orbital prefrontal cortex is a convergence point of various subcortical and cortical inputs, and it is this anatomical property that accounts for its central role in the organism's adaptive functions. As opposed to other synaptic linkages, perhaps the most important prefrontal-cortical connections specifically contributing to imprinting and attachment phenomena are between the orbitofrontal cortex and another member of the ventral tegmental limbic circuit, the anterior temporal cortex. It is known that visual information about the mother is processed in the anterior temporal cortex, an area that responds specifically to emotionally expressive faces (Hasselmo, Rolls, & Baylis, 1989a; Ojemann, Fried, & Mateer, 1980), especially to features of the eye region (Perrett, Rolls, & Caan, 1982), and encodes "object-centered representations" of faces (Hasselmo, Rolls, Baylis, & Nalwa, 1989b). This information is then delivered to orbitofrontal association areas which receive the input (Thorpe, Rolls, & Maddison, 1983), categorize, abstract, and store it in memory.

In this chapter I present evidence that supports the idea that the onset of connections between right hemispheric neuronal centers in the superior temporal polysensory area of the anterior cortex and the orbitofrontal cortex occurs in the early practicing period. The coordinated activity of these two cortical limbic components is expressed in a visuolimbic pathway which enables the infant to efficiently process and regenerate an image of the mother's face, even in her absence.

THE VISUOLIMBIC PATHWAY AND MATERNAL FACIAL RECOGNITION

The infant's functional capacity to process more and more complex visual information emanating from the caregiver's face develops over the first year. Soon after birth the neonate preferentially perceptually attends to the human face (Fantz, 1963). At 2 to 7 weeks she orients towards her own mother's face longer than to a stranger's (Carpenter, 1974), and at 6 months she can recognize differences between female and male faces (Fagan & Singer, 1979). At 7 months she can categorize certain facial changes expressing affect (Nelson, Morse, & Leavitt, 1979), a skill that markedly improves through the 9th month (Caron, Caron, & Myers, 1985). However, it is not until 10 months that the infant is able to construct abstract prototypes of human visual facial patterns (Strauss, 1979). Nelson and Ludemann (1989) pose the cental question of how the structures responsible for face perception change across the lifespan, and whether the mechanisms mediated by these structures change as well. The structures which analyze emotional expression must be capable of processing the invariant patterns of change and movement in the facial musculature, voice, and body.

Structures in the temporal lobes of the cerebral cortex are part of a system involved in such functions, as temporal polar regions are connected with the somatosensory association areas for the face and head representations, with the visual association areas relating to central vision, with auditory association areas, and with the orbitofrontal regions (Pandya & Yeterian, 1985). The growth of deep layer orbitofrontal dendrites in this critical period allows for synaptic connections with axons from the superior temporal polysensory area which transmit visual information regarding the mother's face. Dopamine is now thought to modulate the activity of cortical neurons in layers V and VI that participate in cortico-cortical connections (Berger, Gaspar, & Verney, 1991). Both anterior temporal and orbitofrontal association cortices show the highest concentration of dopamine (Brown, Crane, & Goldman, 1979) and opioid peptides (Steklis & Kling, 1985) in the cerebral cortex, are innervated by the mesocortical dopamine circuit, and are DARRP-32 immunoreactive sites (Berger et al., 1990). These areas share cytoarchitectural similarities to limbic cortex (MacLean, 1954) and are reciprocally connected to each other and other limbic structures (Seltzer & Pandya, 1989). They are both components of the paralimbic cortex whose structure surrounds the more medial and basal areas of the limbic forebrain and whose function involves the tracking of emotionally relevant objects in the extrapersonal space (Mesulam, 1985). In addition, both share the common functions of acting as sensory convergence areas (Benevento et al., 1977; Hikosaka, Iwai, Saito, & Tanaka, 1988) and processing the social signals necessary for the initiation of social interactions and affiliative behaviors (Raleigh & Steklis, 1981).

Rolls (1986) describes these neuronal components, which are involved in the emotional and social responses to faces, as "part of a system that has evolved for the rapid and reliable identification of individuals from their faces, because of the importance of this in primate social behavior" (p. 131). It is noteworthy that imprinting has been defined as the rapid learning process by which developing individuals come to identify members of their own species, a capacity that is certainly adaptive. In discussing the preferential connections between orbital and temporal cortices, Pandya and Barnes (1987) point out that "by virtue of interconnections among evolutionarily related regions in a given stage, a unit is formed that may subserve an individual function" (p. 68) (Fig. 12.1). Bear

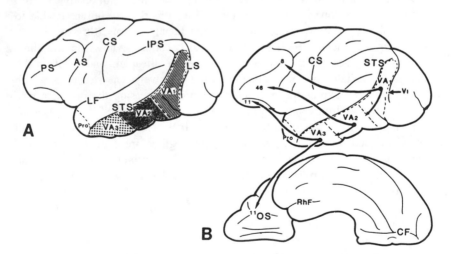

FIG. 12.1.   Diagrams showing the three major subdivisions of the visual association areas of the primate occipitotemporal cortex (A) and their frontal lobe connections (B). Note the third-order visual association area, VA3, connects with Area 11 of the orbitofrontal cortex. From Pandya and Barnes (1987). Reprinted by permission of Lawrence Erlbaum Associates.

(1983) proposes that the interconnected anterior temporal lobe and orbital frontal cortex are both elements of a phylogenetically older visuolimbic pathway which functions in drive-relevant responses in central foveal vision and in acquisition and storage of visuoemotional associations. Figure 12.2 shows the anatomical relationships of the eye, visual sensory area, and orbitofrontal cortex in the medial right hemipshere.

In light of the general neurobiological principle that the pattern of interconnections between neurons depends on experience (Kandel & Schwartz, 1985), the caregiver-infant psychobiologically attuned, arousal-amplifying, visuoaffective phenomena in practicing phase social referencing face-to-face transactions may specifically indelibly imprint orbitofrontal-anterior temporal mesolimbocortical circuitry. The socioaffective stimulation produced by the mother's face facilitates the experience-dependent growth and stabilization of synaptic connections between these two circuit components of the infant's growing right hemisphere, allowing for the functional onset of the visuolimbic pathway. Face selective neurons in the visual association cortex, which exhibit a tuning of neuronal responses by experience so that an ensemble of neurons provides a "long-term representation of familiar faces," are known to send "outputs to multimodal

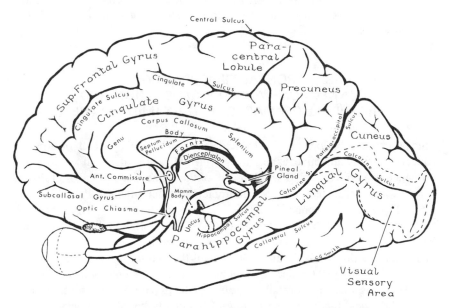

FIG. 12.2.   Schematic representation of the medial apect of the right hemisphere showing the position of the eye and the optic chiasm. Note location of the orbital prefrontal area, so called because of its relation to the orbit of the eye. From Smith (1981). Reprinted by permission of the publisher.

structures" (Rolls, Baylis, Hasselmo, & Nalwa, 1989). These outputs of the posterior cerebral cortex are delivered to temporal and prefrontal association areas of the anterior cortex for further processing. The converging input of all sensory modalities processed in various areas is known to occur through the common nodal link of the orbital region. However, the visuo-perceptual stimulation and information provided by the mother's emotionally expressive face, initially processed by occipitoparietal sensory regions in the right posterior cortex and subsequently delivered and further processed in the right temporal and orbitofrontal multimodal cortices, is of special importance to the ontogeny of socioemotional and attachment functions. The frontal lobe of the nondominant hemisphere is known to be more critical to the processing of emotional information than any other area of the cerebral cortex (Kolb & Milner, 1981).

Diamond and Carey (1977) suggest the development of face recognition should be placed in the context of the development of other visuospatial right hemispheric functions. In discussing the right hemispheric appreciation of the identity of human faces, Hecaen and Albert (1978) note:

> The question must be asked, then, whether or not a mechanism exists that may be activated, created, developed, or liberated by perceptual inputs, if these inputs are presented at a critical period of cerebral development, and that orients subsequent learning activity according to individual experience but in a direction prescribed by an innate apparatus. (p. 241)

ORBITOFRONTAL-TEMPORAL CORTICAL CONNECTIONS AND THE GENERATION AND RETRIEVAL OF IMAGES OF THE FAMILIAR FACE

This psychoneurobiological model elucidates a mechanism by which information concerning early affective experiences with the postnatal social environment influences the critical period development of the connections of the orbitofrontal cortex with anterior temporal corticolimbic and other subcortical limbic structures. These synaptic connections result in an expansion of the limbic system in the cerebral cortex. They also produce a prefrontal corticolimbic structure that hierarchically dominates limbic system involvement in face recognition, attachment, and emotional functioning. The face of the imprinting object is easily the most familiar and most expected stimulus in the infant's environment. Pribram (1987) asserts that "the orbital contribution to psychological processes is to provide a critical facility to the feeling of familiarity based on processing both interoceptive and exteroceptive inputs" (p. 19). Nauta (1971) concludes that at the orbitofrontal level re-representations of the external world in the anterior temporal region are integrated with subcortical information regarding the internal visceroendocrine environment. This operational circuit is a cortical subcircuit of

Nauta and Domesick's (1982) ventral tegmental limbic forebrain-midbrain circuit and is biochemically activated by the mesocortical dopamine system (Bannon & Roth, 1983). It is also identical to Panksepp's (1986) "expectancy command circuit" that connects higher limbic areas in the orbitofrontal cortex with subcortical limbic areas, contains ventral tegmental dopaminergic elements, and supports emotional functions involved in positive expectancy processes.

The emergent function of this cortical-subcortical circuit is essential to the memorial mechanism by which an early imprinted external social stimulus becomes familiar, meaningful, personally significant, and attractive (or aversive) with experience. In this way a particular environmental stimulus is capable of inducing positive anticipation and selective attention. This circuit also is involved in a memorial mechanism by which an exciting social source of stimulation comes to arouse internal emotion. Nothing fits this description as well as the mother's face, the most potent stimulus in the infant's environment. Early social experiences specifically impact the development of the right hemisphere, and this cortex comes to plays a special role in establishing, maintaining, and processing personally relevant aspects of the individual's world (Van Lancker, 1991). It is predominantly involved in selective attention (Posner & Petersen, 1990; Risberg & Prohovnik, 1983), and an area within the frontal lobe of the right hemisphere is known to be important for the regulation of sustained attention (Whitehead, 1991). The orbitofrontal cortex, expanded in this hemisphere, is an important component of a cortical circuitry of directed attention (King et al., 1989). Experimental studies have revealed that the paralimbic orbitofrontal association cortex receives "highly coded sensory information about rewarding and aversive stimuli" (Thorpe et al., 1983, p. 113).

Pandya and Yeterian (1985) note that incoming sensory information is integrated with information about the internal state emanating from the limbic system at the level of the orbital cortical region: "Such integration might provide a way whereby incoming information may be associated with motivational and emotional states to subserve processes such as selective attention and memory formation and retrieval." (p. 51) A recent neuropsychological study shows a specific coactivation of right hemispheric orbitofrontal and basal temporal limbic regions during the mental generation of images of faces (Goldenberg et al., 1989). This circuit may specifically function to couple an emotion with a mental image, thereby producing what Izard (1991) calls an "affective-cognitive structure": "An affective-cognitive structure can be very simple, as when it is the positive feeling of a young infant that has been linked to an image of its mother's face" (p. 15). Such images of the mother's face are visual, and they first appear at the end of the first year in the form of abstract prototypes of human facial patterns that are described by Strauss (1979).

It is now accepted that memory traces are stored in the same neural systems that are involved in the perception, processing, and analysis of the corresponding sensory inputs, and that information must be processed by the limbic system in order to be retained in the cortex (Squire, 1986, 1987). These systems also include subcortical reticular formation components, as the activity of such structures is required for short- and long-term memory processes (Kesner & Conner, 1973). Memory can be described as a multidimensional collection of relatively independent attributes that represent both internal and external aspects of the environment noticed at the time the memory was acquired (Spear, 1978). Based on memory research, Hasher and Zacks (1979) conclude that humans automatically process place, temporal, and frequency information about naturally occurring environmental events. This proposal has been recently confirmed in very young infants, even before hippocampal maturation, suggesting to the authors that an alternate structure is responsible for encoding and maintaining environmental information in early development (Hayne, Rovee-Collier, & Borza, 1991).

The orbital prefrontal region co-processes interoceptive and exteroceptive information (Rosenkilde, Bauer, & Fuster, 1981) and regulates autonomic responses to affective cues (Mesulam & Mufson, 1982). Its unique functional activity in the storage of early visuoemotional associations would allow for the ability of the visual memory (internal image) of the expressive face of the imprinted object to trigger the infant's interoceptive, autonomic reaction to this input, thereby enabling an attentional-emotional response in the absence of the direct perception of the object. From the perspective of neuroscience, Roitblat (1982) points out that conceptually there is no qualitative difference between environmental and internal generated stimuli. This equivalence is also implied by the psychoanalyst Basch (1988) who describes that as a result of development:

> No longer is affect mobilized only by external stimuli: it is now also possible for signals originating from within the cortex to stimulate the limbic system of the subcortical brain as one recalls past experiences. . . .(p. 102)

In recent work in the cognitive sciences, Mandler (1990) defines the bringing into awareness of information about something that is not perceptually present as recall, and asserts that recall can specifically take the form of imagery. Using a nonverbal measure of recall, she demonstrates that by 11 months infants can recall event experiences.

A fundamental functional characteristic of an internal representation is that it allows an organism to have access to information about an environmental event, even in its absence. In contemporary psychoanalytic terminology, the child can now access an internalized object relation, defined as a template for the significant other (Horner, 1989). These cognitive-affective units (affect-laden images) are stored representations of the self emotionally interacting with a significant object. The unique salience of visual sensory input to the emergence of internal representations is demonstrated in developmental psychoanalytic studies of congenitally blind infants. As they develop, children deprived of early visual sensory stimulation, but not congenitally deaf infants, frequently show impairments in representational and affective functions that are responsible for severe emotional problems (Freedman, 1981).

It is now well established that imagery evokes the same pattern of physiology as found in the actual situation (Cuthbert, Vrana, & Bradley, 1991) and that activated visual images possess the capacity to potently trigger emotional and physiological changes (Paivio, 1973) . At the beginning of the century Freud (1915/1957) posited: "Affectivity manifests itself essentially in motor (secretory and vaso-motor) discharge resulting in an (internal) alteration of the subject's own body without reference to the external world" (p. 179). Schwalbe (1991) has recently proposed that as development proceeds, the internal representation of an external object who consistently responds to the infant's impulses in a stimulating manner can be accessed in memory in order to functionally modulate these impulses, even when the object is not present.

SUMMARY

At the end of the child's first year, socioaffective transactions with the primary caregiver facilitate the growth and stabilization of the interconnections between the anterior temporal and the orbitofrontal cortices. With this linkage, a visuo-limbic pathway is established, and this circuit functions in the identification of the faces of familiar individuals. The patterns of these connections are imprinted in face-to-face transactions with the mother. As a result, the infant creates a schema of the face of the attachment object. This representational model contains a permanent abstract prototype of the mother's emotionally expressive facial expressions that is linked to the child's interoceptive response to this input. This internal affect-associated image (internalized object relation) can be accessed even in the mother's absence, and is therefore an important mechanism in attachment functioning.

13 The Neurochemical Circuitry of Imprinted Interactive Representations

This capacity [representational memory] may be considered a building block, if not a cornerstone, of cognitive development in man. Moreover, "object permanence"—the recognition that an object has continuity in time and space when not in view—*must depend on the elemental capacity to form representations of the outside world and to base responses on those representations in the absence of the objects they represent.*
—Patricia Goldman-Rakic (1987a)

The neocortex of the young mammal is in a flexible state. There is a genetically given structure but also coded in the genes is the capability of the neocortex to respond to and be molded in a long-lasting fashion by early experience. This capability allows the formation of neural circuits which are best suited to extract information from the environment and to establish patterns of behavior that are suitable for survival.
—Jonathan Winson (1985)

With the imprinting of a representational model (Miller, Galanter, & Pribram, 1960; Piaget & Inhelder, 1956; Young, 1964) of the primary attachment figure affective responses to a person or object can be maintained even in their absence. The exact same mechanism may be involved in the attainment of object constancy. Goldman-Rakic (Goldman-Rakic, Isseroff, Schwartz, & Bugbee, 1983) points out that the "delayed response," the defining cognitive operation of the orbitofrontal cortex (Goldman, 1971; Lawicka, Mishkin, Kreiner, & Brutkowski, 1966; Niki, Sakai, & Kubota, 1972), resembles Piaget's object permanence task. The presence of this capacity indicates that the individual has attained the concept that an object exists continuously in time and space. It is now accepted that the delayed response function underlies the individual's ability to guide his behavior, initiating certain responses and inhibiting others, by stored information, that is, by internalized representational memory (Fuster, 1980). Representational memory, a capacity that depends on limbic substrates (Post, 1992), is fundamentally involved in a critical adaptive function, the regulation of behavior (Goldman-Rakic, 1987b). This conclusion is similar to Schwalbe's (1991) proposal that the internal representation of an external object can be accessed in memory in order to functionally modulate impulses, even when the object is not present.

A developmental progression of object constancy occurs between 7^1/$_2$ and 12 months (Diamond & Doar, 1989). This same period is known to be a watershed in the development of infant memory (Rovee-Collier & Fagan, 1981; Schacter & Moscovich, 1984). I suggest that this cognitive progression is associated with a structural reorganization of the orbitofrontal frontal cortex which allows for a functional advance in its delayed response function. The initiation of prefrontal structural maturation at the beginning of the practicing period is responsible for the functional transformation of representational memory and inhibitory control, and the emergence of these capacities are central to the cognitive and attentional changes that are observed at the end of the first year (Zelazo, 1982).

In the first part of this chapter I discuss the role of the orbital prefrontal cortex in generating affect regulating interactive representations, also known as internal working models of attachment relationships. Later in the chapter I present recent neurochemical information on the imprinting of the dynamic circuits that under-lie these models.

THE ORBITOFRONTAL GENERATION OF AFFECT REGULATING INTERNAL REPRESENTATIONS

Major changes in cognition have been documented in the 12 month-old infant (Kagan, 1971; Zelazo, 1982). Kagan (1986) suggests that the enhancement in retrieval memory in this time frame derives from "maturational events in the central nervous system as long as children are growing up in environments containing people and objects" (p. 73). This maturation specifically occurs in the orbitofrontal cortex, and is reflected in an increased efficiency of its delayed response function. In the first year of life the prefrontal cortex is "susceptible to both maturational and environmental influences" (Fox, 1991). I previously cited developmental cognition research that indicates that before 10 months infants perform poorly on an object permanence task involving delayed recall of recently experienced events (Schacter & Moscovitch, 1984), but by 12 months infants are capable of recall after a delay (Mandler, 1990). Recent developmental neuropsy-chological research reveals functional evidence of a major maturational change in the prefrontal cortex at 10 to 12 months (Diamond & Doar, 1989).

The orbitofrontal cortex is known to subserve cognitive and memory functions (Stuss et al., 1982; Thorpe et al., 1983) and to generate mental images of faces (Goldenberg et al., 1989). A major function of prefrontal circuits is to access and "hold on line" representational short-term knowledge of the outside world (Goldman-Rakic, 1987b). These functional capacities enable it to be fundamentally involved in the generation of internal representations of the self interacting with the "outside world," especially the "primordial other" who mediates the social world. Internal representations of relationships are now being defined as abstractions that average various internal subjective experiences and corresponding interactional behaviors (Zeanah & Barton, 1989). The concept of internal representations of external object relations, of models of the nascent self interacting with the early social environment, is now being utilized by a number of different disciplines. In the developmental psychoanalytic literature Stern (1985) describes "representations of interaction that have been generalized" (RIGS), in current psychiatric writings Heard and Lake (1986) refer to "internal representational models of experiences in relationships," and in experimental psychological work Forgas (1982) speaks of "internal representations of social interactions that guide interpersonal behavior." All of these conceptions stress the interactive nature of such representations, but I would add that since they arise in visuoaffective face-to-face social interactions they have a particularly visual quality. Horowitz (1983) concludes that representations with visual sensory quality uniquely:

> allow immediate depiction of objects in relationship due to the simultaneous organization of information in a single image. We usually characterize the objects of greatest emotional importance as self and other. Even a single image can initially show self and other in some kind of transaction. (p. 87)

Thus, such internal representations of the self-in-interaction-with-other are more precisely abstractions of the infant's autonomic physiological-affective responses to the visual perception of the emotionally expressive face of the attachment object. By the last quarter of the first year the infant is capable of constructing abstract prototypes of facial patterns that it visually perceives (Strauss, 1979).

On the basis of experimental studies, Beebe and Lachman (1988a) conclude that at the end of the first year representations of the relationship of "self-with-other" first appear. This emergent function of recognizing and storing patterns from experience as a "presymbolic representational capacity" is a substratum out of which "abstracted prototypes" are formed. Research on perceptual and cognitive development reveals that at 10 months, and not before, infants can generate an abstraction of invariant relations from a category set of discriminable stimuli and a subsequent generalization to a novel stimulus (Younger & Cohen, 1983, 1986). At 12 months cross-modal transfer from tactual to visual (Gottfried et al., 1977) and visual to tactual (Rose, Gottfried, & Bridger, 1981) modalities occurs, and this capacity has been suggested to contribute to the development of abstraction and representational abilities (Rose, 1986).

In a paper integrating evolutionary biology and psychoanalytic conceptions of adaptive representational phenomena, J. Jacobson (1983) emphasizes the importance of imprinting events and asks if humans have "constraining timetables for crucial representational world developmental steps" (p. 55). Horner (1989), an investigator of psychoanalytic object relations theory, a theory that is fundamentally a psychology of internal representations of self and significant others, offers the proposal that the mental image of the object (mother) is "created by the child in accord with his or her limited mental capacities" (p. 28). The fact that these capacities are expanding over the stages of the growth spurt of the brain suggests to me that these representations become more complex. Horner (1989) further concludes that: "The patterning of the mental schema we call "self" and the patterning of the mental schema we referred to as the "object" take place in predictable, hierarchical stages" (p. 28). Blatt, in experimental object relations research, demonstrates that object representations develop epigenetically through successive developmental stages, and that these stages can also be considered as stages of object constancy (Blatt, Quinlan, & Chevron, 1990). Trad (1986) asserts that developmental gradations of representational capacity, reflected in a progression of object constancy over stages of ontogeny, are known to have important implications for affective development. (This progression continues in the late practicing period. At 18 months, a more complex representational system that programs symbolic evocative memory emerges.)

In the attachment literature internal representations are referred to as "internal working models." According to Bowlby (1973) these models of attachment relationships first emerge at about 12 months, the early practicing period. The internalization of the affective and cognitive characteristics of relationships, whereby interactive experiences become mentally represented, operationally defines the construction of internal working models (Pipp & Harmon, 1987). These models of the infant's interactions with the attachment figure are formed in imprinting experiences. The resultant stored mental representations contain affective as well as cognitive components (Main, Kaplan, & Cassidy, 1985), and are accessed and utilized in the generation of coping strategies of affect regulation (Kobak & Sceery, 1988). This most important regulating attribute of representations is also stressed by Schwalbe (1991) and Goldman-Rakic (1987b). In developmental psychoanalytic observational research, Settlage et al. (1988) conclude that beginning in the first year the mother's regulatory functions are internalized.

In a study of infant emotional development at the end of the first year, Fox (1991) documents that the frontal region is involved in important integrative functions related to affective and cognitive behaviors, and is responsible for the articulation of coping responses and planful behavior. Muller (1985) refers to the prefrontal generation of "internal models, concerning outside world and own identity." Similarly, imprinting experiences that establish the formation of attachment bonds have been proposed to induce the development of a "neuronal model" of certain classes of stimulation (socioemotional stimulation), such as those provided by the imprinting object (Hoffman & Ratner, 1973). The imprinting process that underlies attachment bond formation involves an irreversible stamping of early experience upon the developing nervous system. What do we know about the neurochemistry of this psychoneurobiological etching process?

THE NEUROCHEMICAL CIRCUITRY OF A NEURONAL MODEL OF THE FACE OF THE ATTACHMENT OBJECT

During critical periods specific neuronal circuits which are the building blocks of neuronal models may be formed by synaptic facilitation,

> a process whereby passage of a signal along a particular circuit via particular synapses makes a later passage of a signal along the same circuit easier; therefore a later signal is more likely to flow through this facilitated circuit than through an alternate one. (Winson, 1985, p. 178)

Ciompi (1991) emphasizes that

> an 'affective imprint', mediated through the limbic system and its neurotransmitters, is needed both for the fixation and for the activation of the extended neuronal pathway representing memory storage. (p. 101)

Rauschecker and Marler (1987) point out that imprinting occurs under high levels of catecholamine-generated arousal and that stimuli that induce arousal will exert an enduring influence on neural development. The neurophysiological process of synaptic facilitation which mediates permanent imprinting effects occurs under heightened levels of arousal and is identical to a potentiation of catecholaminergic pathways in the limbic system following their repetitive activation during a critical period. This activity may occur in high arousal episodes which activate a neuropsychological "Now Print" mechanism that favors future repetition of the same activity (Livingston, 1967).

It is well known that electrical activity plays a major role in sculpting circuits in the nervous system. Imprinting experiences have been shown to produce long-term electrophysiological effects on the spontaneous neuronal activity of different regions of the brain (Payne & Horn, 1982, 1984). I have suggested that socioaffective imprinting events at the end of the first year facilitate the establishment of new synaptic connections between subcortical and cortical components of the ventral tegmental limbic circuit. Dopaminergic neurons in the ventral tegmental area of the midbrain project collaterals up the neuraxis to different forebrain areas, and in the practicing period the growth and functional activity of axon collaterals and their receptors are amplified in the prefrontal cortex. The sequential firing of neuronal groups along this cortical-subcortical axis, including the enduring excitatory reverberations of the mesocortical dopaminergic circuit of the visuolimbic pathway in the orbitofrontal and anterior temporal cortices, represents a cell assembly (Hebb, 1949). This system is capable of long-term memory processing, as it is known that long-term storage involves neuronal contributions from various cortical and subcortical areas (Penfield, 1968). Such a circuit neuronally encodes "flashbulb memories" (Brown & Kulik, 1977), very clear, long-lasting visual memories of consequential events. The stored image of the mother's face, distributed in part over the visual processing areas of the cortex, represents a prototypical primordial flashbulb memory.

This cortical input into the limbic circuit would trigger electrochemical events in the subcortical elements of the circuit. However, input at any point within the cell assembly activates the entire assembly through their mutually excitatory connections, thereby allowing for a reverberating (self-re-excitational) neural circuit—a self-contained neuronal network which sustains a nerve impulse by channeling it repeatedly through the same network (Rosenzweig & Leiman, 1968). In this vertically organized system, neurons at one level of the ventral tegmental limbic circuit are interconnected with neurons at another level which share the functional properties of selectively responding to complex social stimuli embedded in faces (Hasselmo, Rolls, & Baylis, 1989a; Sanghera, Rolls, & Roper-Hall, 1979; Thorpe, Rolls, & Maddison, 1983), and of participating in the acquisition of stimulus-reward associations. The common involvement of orbital, temporal, and amygdala neurons in the processing of sensory (particularly visual) information of emotional significance has suggested that they "may form part of a specialized neural system for the processing of social stimuli" (Steklis & Kling, 1985, p. 129). The furthest terminus of this circuit, the orbitofrontal cortex, represents the hierarchical apex of this system. This is functionally expressed in its unique capacity to categorize, abstract, store, and regulate the practicing infant's emotional responses to the face of the attachment figure. In line with the proposal of orbitofrontal maturation at 10–12 months, distinct patterns of infant facial expressions, indicators of motor responses to emotion, are first reliably coded at the end of the first year (Malatesta et al., 1989). This dynamic intergrated circuit operationally functions as a neuronal model of the child's interaction with the maternal object. More precisely, this circuit encodes the child's affective response to the visual perception of the emotionally expressive face of the primary attachment object.

A model of the neural mechanism of imprinting, very similar to this one, has been propounded by Horn and McCabe (1984). Citing the research of Perrett et al. (1982) on the neurobiology of facial recognition, they propose that an object that resembles the species elicits a powerful central nervous system response. This effect is specifically expressed in high levels of activity in certain neurons that selectively respond to faces. These authors suggest that such visual input would concurrently excite neurons that are components of an integrated neural network. Referring to the seminal research of Hebb (1948), Horn and McCabe further hypothesize that:

> If the neurons are interconnected the probability of conjoint firing would be high. The interconnections might undergo rapid modification and hence the network would form an assembly representing the stimulus. (p. 291)

In a continuation of this work, the same authors have determined that the functional alterations of synaptic transmission and recognition memory which result from imprinting experiences (McCabe & Horn, 1991) are associated with an increase in N-methyl-D-aspartate (NMDA) receptor binding of the excitatory amino acid L-glutamate (McCabe & Horn, 1988). They suggest the agent that activates these NMDA receptor channels:

> is effective in opening the channels only under certain conditions. One possibility is that the channels are gated by the depolarizing actions of neurons the activity of which is controlled by the attentional or affective state of the animal or by input from neuronal assemblies representing these memories. (p. 2853)

Interestingly, Knapp, Schmidt, and Dowling (1990) report that under the exposure of dopamine, cells become more responsive to L-glutamate; that dopamine enhances the glutamate mediation of fast excitatory neurotransmission; and that this effect involves an increase in the frequency of channel openings. Activation of NMDA receptors induces dephosphorylation of DARPP-32 (Halpain, Girault, & Greengard, 1990), a protein associated with dopamine receptors that plays a significant role in postnatal development and in the genesis of specific anatomical circuits (Berger et al., 1990). Dopamine and NMDA exist in the same layers in the prefrontal cortex (Mora & Cobo, 1990), an area that contains the highest density of NMDA receptors in the entire cerebral cortex (Cotman, Monaghan, Ottersen, & Storm-Mathisen, 1987).

Cline, Debski, and Constantine-Paton (1987) conclude that the activation of NMDA receptors during periods of postnatal experience-dependent differentiation of the brain "suggests a general mechanism for the development and maintenance of neural maps in the vertebrate central nervous system based on a scheme originally proposed by Hebb" (p. 4345). Cotman, Monaghan, and Ganong (1988) discuss the importance of the relationships between excitatory amino acid neurotransmission, NMDA receptors, and Hebb-type synaptic plasticity. Greenough and Black (1992) propose that the NMDA receptor requires both activation by neurotransmitter and activation of the postsynaptic cell before it can become active, a property of Hebbian synapses that allows for a synapse that fires synchronously with a large number of others. They believe that the NMDA's receptor characteristics make it an excellent candidate by which early experiences organize the developing brain.

In support of these assertions, it is now established that sensory stimulation specifically activates NMDA receptors in the developing neonatal cortex (Fox, Sato, & Daw, 1989; LoTurco, Blanton, & Kriegstein, 1991; Tsumoto, Hagihara, Sato, & Hata, 1987), and that NMDA receptor numbers peak above adult levels in developing brain areas (Insel, Miller, & Gelhard, 1990). Glutamate responsive NMDA receptors are known to be selectively associated with postsynaptic densities that provide a framework for the attachment of transmitter receptors (Fagg & Matus, 1984), and to be involved in establishing synaptic plasticity during a critical period of postnatal cortical development (Tsumoto, Hagihara, Sato, & Hata, 1987). Such receptors have been implicated in cortical plasticity during critical periods of early development (Artola & Singer, 1989). Activation of the NMDA receptor is thought to lead to an alteration of synaptic number and postsynaptic thickening length (Brooks, Petit, LeBoutillier, & Lo, 1991), an increase in dendritic branching (Brewer & Cotman, 1989), and a selective stabilization of coactive synapses (Rabacchi, Bailly, Delhaye-Bouchard, & Mariani, 1992).

The central importance of this receptor, known to play a major role in brain synaptic transmission (Watkins & Evans, 1981), long-term potentiation (Collingridge & Bliss, 1987), and learning, memory, and behavior (Morris, Anderson, Lynch, & Baudry, 1986), is due to its critical function in modulating the biochemistry of the neuron—glutamate activation of the receptor allows calcium ions to flow into the cell. Due to the state of the blood-brain barrier in the early stages of development, very high concentrations of glutamate gain access to the brain (Tuor et al., 1992). Excitatory neurotransmitters regulate postsynaptic calcium influx in developing neocortex (Yuste & Katz, 1991) and glutamate acting at NMDA receptors increases intracellular calcium in neurons (Burgoyne, Pearce, & Cambray-Deakin, 1988), which, if uncontrolled, leads to intracelluar damage or cell death (Garthwaite & Garthwaite, 1986). Calcium ions regulate important neuronal functions, such as neurite elongation and growth cone movement (Mattson & Kater, 1987) and neurotransmission at synaptic junctions (Erulkar, 1989). Stimulation of postnatal NMDA receptors leads to morphological changes in neuronal neurites within minutes, and this rapid effect has been suggested to result from calcium, cAMP, and the induction of the immediate-early response proto-oncogene c-fos (Rashid & Cambray-Deakin, 1992).

Indeed, activation of NMDA receptors is known to induce c-fos mRNA expression (Herrera & Robertson, 1990; Sonnenberg et al., 1989; Szekely, Barbaccia, Alho, & Costa, 1990). Intriguingly, the c-fos gene is also induced by dopamine D1 receptors that are linked to adenylate cyclase (Robertson, Peterson, Murphy, & Robertson, 1989; Young, Porrino, & Iadarola, 1991) and by calcium and cAMP (Morgan & Curran, 1988). In fact dopamine and glutamate act cooperatively to induce c-fos protein in neurons expressing DARPP-32 (Berretta, Robertson, & Graybiel, 1992). Stress has been shown to cause the induction of c-fos protein in the paraventricular hypothalamic neurons that produce corticotropin-releasing factor (Ceccatelli, Villar, Goldstein, & Hokfelt, 1989), and CRF is known to activate the ventral tegmental dopaminergic system (Kalivas et al., 1987) and to induce elevations in dopamine metabolism in the prefrontal cortex (Dunn & Berridge, 1990). It has been reported that an increase in c-fos mRNA precedes an increase in the mRNA of BDNF, the trophic factor for mesencephalic dopamine neurons (Zafra, Hengerer, Leibrock, Thoenen, & Lindholm, 1990). Importantly, the induction of c-fos occurs in specific pathways in the CNS, and this leads to an anatomical spreading of a "memory trace" (Post, 1992). This alteration of c-fos gene transcription is responsible for its role in the genetic regulation of adaptive neuronal change (Yang & Koistinaho, 1990) in the brain, specifically for the long-term modification of the output of a circuit that underlies learning and memory (He & Rosenfeld, 1991; Morgan & Curran, 1989; Sheng & Greenberg, 1990). A rapid form of learning occurs in long-lasting imprinting events, and c-fos gene expression occurs in the postnatal forebrain in response to early experience (Anokhin, Mileusnic, Shamakina, & Rose, 1991). On the basis of these findings I suggest that this circuit is specifically the dopaminergic ventral tegmental limbic forebrain-midbrain limbic circuit. Thus events at this particular receptor channel trigger the cascade of biochemical processes that are essential for the permanent imprinting of developing brain circuitry, the modification of neural connections during growth, and the ensuing alterations in synaptic transmission that produce stabilized Hebbian assemblies. I also speculate that the early, fast-acting neurochemical modifications that are initiated by socioemotional transactions are etched into long-term storage by late acting biochemical processes that continue in infant sleep states that follow these events.

In a discussion of the experience-dependent stabilization of excitatory Hebbian synapses in the postnatal cortex, Singer (1986b) concludes:

> The activity-dependent modifications follow rules that allow them to stabilize selectively pathways between neuronal elements that have a high probability of being active at the same time. Hence, this selection process has an associative function, coupling preferentially those cells with each other that share particular functional properties. This selection process could, therefore, serve to develop assemblies of cooperating neurons whose coherent and—if reciprocally coupled— reverberating responses could represent the neural code for particular patterns of activity at the sensory surfaces. (p. 291)

nger further suggests that these experience-dependent processes rely both upon rtical sensory processing of information from the "outer" world, and on inter- lly generated signals involving catecholamines from the reticular formation ich reflect the central state of the organism. As previously mentioned this tical-subcortical junction point is at the level of the orbitofrontal cortex, since cortex uniquely processes and integrates exteroceptive information concern- the external environment with subcortically processed interoceptive informa- regarding the internal environment (Nauta, 1971). In socioaffective contexts, er's sensory "patterns of activity" in the "outer world" represent arousal-generating stimulation transmitted in visually perceived patterns of movement of the mother's facial muscles. Neurons at different levels of the brain which share the functional property of firing in response to her emotionally expressive face are coupled preferentially.

Fuster (1991) now proposes that the unique functional capacities of the prefrontal cortex are supported by its reciprocal interactions with cortical association areas and subcortical structures through the neural reverberations of a Hebbian network. Building upon this principle, I propose that with the developmental expansion of the ventral tegmental limbic circuit into the frontolimbic cortex, direct orbital connections into subcortical mesencephalic dopamine neurons can now trigger a reverberating cortical-subcortical loop. Orbitofrontal cholinergic axons synapsing on dopaminergic dendrites in the rostral nuclei of the ventral tegmental area may release the excitatory transmitter L-glutamate which would activate NMDA receptors at these dendritic sites. This excitatory cortical input into a group of subcortical catecholaminergic neurons would elicit further dopamine release for cortical consumption. A number of recent findings support this model—descending orbitofrontal glutaminergic projections mediate an excitatory influence on ventral tegmental dopamine neurons (Sesack & Pickel, 1992), NMDA receptors are found in the ventral tegmental area (Seutin, Verbanck, Massotte, & Dreese, 1990), L-glutamate acting at NMDA receptors has been demonstrated to stimulate dopamine release from these neurons (Mount, Quirion, Chaudieu, & Boksa, 1990), and glutamate has been shown to regulate the mesocorticolimbic dopamine system (Kalivas, Duffy, & Barrow, 1989). Furthermore, Johnson, Seutin, and North (1992) propose that the frontal cortex sends a major excitatory amino acid-containing input to ventral midbrain dopamine neurons. This NMDA releasing cortical pathway controls burst firing in these neurons, an activity correlated with behavioral arousal. I interpret these data to mean that such a cortical regulatory input into ventral tegmental arousal-generating catecholamine neurons mediates the cortical regulation of subcortical affect patterns. These anatomical connections account for the affect regulating properties of early interactive representations.

In a recent formulation, Schwalbe (1991) has proposed a model of the development of internal representations of external objects—such as faces—that consistently provide stimulating responses to the infant. The elements which mediate this function are found in a "neural network or connection matrix," and the creation of the architecture of this network depends upon pulses of electrochemical energy through the infant's brain "at critical developmental junctures."

As these pulses flow through the brain, synaptic connections are established and strengthened and the firing rates of groups of neurons are set. The result is that certain kinetic pathways are established, making it more likely that these patterns will guide energy flows in the future . . . The initial configuration of the matrix may influence the possibility of capturing certain kinds of information later; its initial form may affect the vividness and completeness with which different kinds of imagery (visual, tactile, olfactory, auditory) can be captured. (p. 280)

This captured imagery, which "works in the same way as cognitive schemas" enables the brain to "regulate and maintain a regular pattern of information flow within itself" (Schwalbe, 1991, p. 283).

SUMMARY

At the end of the first year the anatomical maturation of the orbitofrontal cortex allows for a developmental advance in cognitive and memory functions. The increased functional efficiency that results from such experience-dependent structural development also enables this cortex to generate abstract mental images of faces. As a result, this prefrontal system can now generate interactive representations, or internal working models of the infant's affective interactions with the primary attachment figure. Such internal representations encode the infant's physiological-affective responses to the emotionally expressive face of the attachment figure. They can be accessed for regulatory purposes, even in the mother's absence.

These models are anatomically expressed in dynamic cortical-subcortical neuronal circuits that are imprinted in high arousal socioaffective face-to-face transactions. The growth of dopaminergic axon collaterals in the orbitofrontal cortex represents an expansion of the ventral tegmental forebrain-midbrain limbic circuit, so that it now includes the frontolimbic cortex. The process of synaptic facilitation produces linkages between the components of this circuit at different levels, thereby forming a stabilized Hebbian network. This allows for a reverberating, self-excitational circuit. Components of this circuit, at different levels of the nervous system, contain neurons that respond to faces. The orbitofrontal cortex is anatomically situated at the hierarchical apex of this circuit, and as such it categorizes, abstracts, stores, and ultimately modulates the infant's emotional reponses to the face of the mother. The excitatory neurotransmiter, L-glutamate, plays an important role in the development and operation of this circuit. Its action at sites of connections between descending orbitofrontal axons and ventral tegmental dopaminergic dendrites mediates a mechanism by which the cerebral cortex regulates affect.

14 The Regulatory Function of Early Internal Working Models

> *It has seemed to me that the face stands in a pivotal position at every point along this developmental pathway. At the very beginning—before separation, before there is an object at all—the mother's face is already there, as that which mediates attachment behavior and perhaps also as the first visual form of an early blissful experience. A little later, though still part of the attachment process, there develops that interactive smiling and looking between faces, the conversation of gestures between infant and mother, which I have suggested is important in laying the foundations of the self. As separation gets under way and the child begins to circle out from the mother, the mother's face is the beacon to which the child references back for orientation and reaction, and the conversation of smiles and other visually perceived facial expressions becomes the means of keeping in touch and making the distance tolerable.*
>
> —Kenneth Wright (1991)

The preeminent role of the face in early development is characterized in the foregoing extraordinarily comprehensive and concise manner by Wright (1991). Wright further concludes that the mother's face, which fosters and modulates the attachment process, eventually becomes a "proto-symbol" through which the object can be represented: "The unique configuration of the mother's face is a complex configuration that comes to represent the mother" (p. 355). Ultimately the remembered image of the mother's face acquires a representational function of anticipating a repeated experience with the object after a delay. Bowers et al. (1991) describe long-term visual representations of prototypes of facially expressed emotion that activate "face-icons." Kraemer et al. (1991) characterize the internalized regulatory capacities of the infant that develop in relation to the mother as a "mother icon" that acts as a "neurobiological guidance system." Schwalbe (1991) suggests that internal representations of external objects, such as faces, allows the brain to regulate and maintain a regular pattern of information flow within itself.

In previous chapters I have proposed that internal representations of self-in-interaction-with-other are fundamentally abstractions of the infant's autonomic physiological-affective response to the visual perception of the emotionally expressive face of the primary attachment object. Such representations of the relationship of self-with-other developmentally emerge at the end of the first year and make available to the infant "abstracted prototypes" that allow for the emergence of a "presymbolic representational capacity" (Beebe & Lachman, 1988a). The structural affective-cognitive schemas embedded in these interactive representations perform regulatory functions. In this chapter I shall integrate the material presented up to this point to propose a psychoneurobiological model by which such inceptive representations regulate the processing of facially expressed socioaffective information between the infant and caregiver. More specifically, the Jacksonian principles of the hierarchical organization of the brain into horizontal levels and the rerepresentation and expansion of function from lower to higher levels may elucidate the dynamic activity of the ventral tegmental limbic structural circuit that biochemically mediates these events.

THE HIERARCHICAL PROCESSING OF FACIALLY EXPRESSED SOCIOAFFECTIVE INFORMATION ALONG THE VENTRAL TEGMENTAL LIMBIC CIRCUIT

We now know that the infant functions as a registrar and comparator of images (Basch, 1975; Lichtenberg, 1983). Sherrod (1981) asserts that early experiences of scanning the internal features of the mother's animated face "pushes" the infant towards a "global" scanning style which focuses attention to the "holistic" properties of social stimuli. In the "split-second world" of mother-infant interactions (Stern, 1977) incoming information concerning the external social environment, specifically transmitted in an emotionally expressive face, is initially processed and encoded in posterior occipitoparietal sensory areas of the "holistic" (Bever, 1975; Bradshaw & Nettleton, 1983) right hemisphere. It is now well established that very briefly presented spatial information and holistic perception compel a visual mode of encoding compatible with right hemispheric information processing (Barchas & Perlaki, 1986), and that such input can be encoded in the form of higher order visual representation (Kemp & Haude, 1979). A corpus of neuropsychological studies shows that the visuospatial processing capacity of this right cerebral posterior cortex is essential to the recognition of familiar and ambiguous faces (Lezak, 1976). Auditory information emanating from the mother's face, embedded in the affective tone of her emotionally expressive voice, is known to be processed in the right parietotemporal cortex (Ross, 1983). Posterior parietal areas have recently been shown to send direct input to the orbitofrontal cortex (Cavada & Goldman-Rakic, 1989). Neuropsychological studies now reveal that the right hemisphere contains neural representations of species-typical facial expression, prosodic contours, and gestures (Blonder, Bowers, & Heilman, 1991).

Neuroanatomical studies of the cerebral cortex have underscored the fact that in order to adaptively respond to an environmental stimulus, an accurate perception of the stimulus is required. In line with the principle that information is processed in stages (Sternberg, 1969), this involves the sequential processing of the individual sensory modalities in the primary and association cortices for the specific senses, and then subsequent processing of input from the various senses in multimodal association cortex. The final steps in the discrimination of an incoming stimulus pattern takes place in multimodal or paralimbic association areas in the temporal and frontal cortices (Pandya & Yeterian, 1985), which register the motivational significance of the stimulus. In this manner, the emotional significance of a perceived stimulus is attached only after the cortical recombination of all of its processed sensory processes (Krushel & van der Kooy, 1988). In the case of socioaffective stimuli impinging on the infant, activated multimodal perceptual input, especially changes of stimulation emanating from the caregiver's eyes and face, is delivered to and thereby "primes" the anterior orbital frontal cortex, the apex of the limbic system, where rapid cognitive appraisals of this optic stimulus array are performed. Emotion expression that "fleets across the face" of the mother (Wright, 1991) is thus searched for and recognized, and these sensory patterns are set over against abstracted prototypes of the face that are generated by orbitofrontal presymbolic representational capacity.

Experimental studies reveal that the scanning of a face in order to interpret the meaning of a facial expression provides information that is matched against previously stored abstract structural codes that are held in face-recognition units (Bruce & Young, 1986). The primal encoding of information emanating from the mother's emotionally expressive face occurs during practicing period face-to-face socioaffective transactions and produces the imprinting of abstract prototypes of visual facial patterns. It is known that encoding is not a simple reproduction of information about an object taken in by the perceptual system, but a conceptual redescription (representation) of this information into symbolic terms, so that the information can be accessible (as a prototype) at a later time when the object is not perceptually present (Mandler, 1990). Mandler (1992) refers to the infant's formation of image-schemas, and these "conceptual primitives" that are analogical representations grounded in the perceptual world enable preverbal thought. It is now thought that the right hemisphere contains an analogical representational system (Tucker, 1992) and a "lexicon," long-term memory representations, of various facial emotions (Bowers, Blonder, Feinberg, & Heilman, 1991). This corticolimbic appraisal operation involves match-mismatch comparisons which are read out against templates of prototypical memorial representations of the maternal face stored in internalized working models, thereby computing the affective significance and valence of the particular socioemotional stimulation emanating from a facial display at a specific point in time. At the beginning of this century Titchener (1916) posited that recognition of faces can be "wholly a matter of the feeling" (p. 408).

This same prefrontally processed input, a "hot cognition" (Greenberg & Saffran, 1984), is subsequently synaptically relayed down the visuolimbic pathway via fast-conducting branched cholinergic axons from neurons in deep orbitofrontal layers to be matched against stored representations of the face of the imprinting object distributed at different lower levels of the nervous system—anterior temporal cortex, amygdala and so on, down to the hypothalamus. This cortical-subcortical connection closes and thereby activates a reverberating neural circuit, and such re-excitational activity allows for the "persistence" of a memory trace. In recognition processes, "psychological material which persists 'matches' some immediately present sensing pattern" (Bartlett, 1967, p. 196). The hierarchical processing of this information, mediated by descending cholinergic projections of the ventral tegmental limbic circuit, occurs sequentially along the upstream components of the mesocorticolimbic system. The measure of the degree of matching of different Jacksonian levels of representations could thus influence the activation of subcortical limbic activity underlying an affective response. More specifically, high degrees of matching could "amplify" the initial cortical signal by activating subcortical elements of the ventral tegmental reward system, such as the septal area, an area known to be associated with pleasurable emotional states (Heath, 1964; Olds & Milner, 1954), as this and other subcortical components of the mesocorticolimbic circuit could also deliver excitatory feedback into arousal generating ventral tegmental dopamine neurons. Amplification sites in the anterior temporal pole, amygdala, etc., areas known to contain neurons that selectively respond to human faces, thus process "representations of the mother's face."

This descending corticosubcortical information, via orbital-hypothalamic (and orbital-kindled anterior temporal-hypothalamic, amygdala-hypothalamic, septal-hypothalamic, etc.) connections determines which particular modular hypothalamic motivational system and thereby which emotion-specific action tendency is activated by the external, environmental socioaffective stimulus change. Ensuing hypothalamic activation of neuropeptide (pituitary endorphin) release into visceroendocrine circulatory systems would directly influence ventral tegmental activation. This in turn elicits dopamine release back up the circuit (which may entail catecholamine release of varicosities of the same neuron at different levels). Resultingly, arousal increases are triggered up this limbic neuraxis that ultimately affect the highest hierarchical levels of cortical information processing and response systems. These arousal increases mediate the amplification of the intensity of an affect. At the end of the last century Freud (1895/1966) proposed that affect is initiated by environmental stimulation but is augmented and supported by the resulting endogenous excitation.

It is now accepted that the autonomic nervous system plays a central role in amplifying and sustaining emotion (Izard, 1977) and in modulating the intensity of emotion experiences (Chwalisz, Deiner, & Gallagher, 1988). Sroufe (1979) points out that the amplification and exaggeration of behavior is a prominent function of infant affects, and Young (1979) describes learning as a process of selection and amplification. Thus, orbital-hypothalamic-orbital interactions would determine which motivational system is activated and expressed in a particular facial expression, while orbital-ventral tegmental-orbital interactions would influence the intensity and duration of a specific motivational system expressed in an affect display. In such a manner subcortical internal states are manifest in the infant's subsequent facial expressions and overt behavior in response to recognition of the arousal-influencing maternal face. These mechanisms would determine, for example, whether positive affect, practicing period typical elation, or negative affect, separation protest, the dominant negative emotional response to brief separation in 13-month-old infants (Shiller, Izard, & Hembree, 1986), is generated.

In line with the principle that the infant's tolerance for more intense arousal increases over the first year (Fogel, 1982), it was earlier suggested that heightened arousal amplification resulting from regulated mutual gaze transactions in the last quarter of the first year specifically activates the imprinting and maturation of the orbitofrontal cortex. The experience-dependent maturation of this cortical-subcortical system may account for the observed orbitofrontal capacity to modulate arousal mechanisms in late infancy (Bowden, Goldman, Rosvold, & Greenstreet, 1971). Importantly, the arousal regulating (or dysregulating) function of the mother directly influences the developing capacity of the infant's maturing orbitofrontal cortex, at the supraordinate level of the hierarchy, to mentally generate images of faces (Goldenberg et al., 1989), specifically visual representations of the mother's face. Ultimately these representations are stored in the right cerebral hemisphere. Burton and Levy (1991) have recently discussed the relationship between levels of arousal and the hierarchical processing of information embedded in the human face:

> the right hemisphere's capacity for configurational representation of faces is realized only when the relative level of its arousal is sufficient. It is reasonable to imagine that there is a hierarchy of processing operations in which neural integration over progressively larger networks increases with ascent of the hierarchy. At lower levels, processing can be conducted by relatively confined and small networks that must be integrated into a higher-order network at the next step of the hierarchy. Possibly, the integrative capacities are determined by the arousal resource available, and if this is low, full integration at the top of the hierarchy, cannot be attained. In consequence, representations are more piecemeal and primitive than would be possible if the arousal level were higher. (p. 104)

Tucker (1992) suggests that when processing in the limbic hierarchy is highly constrained by primitive networks, the representational function of the hierarchy degrades. These ideas suggest that higher levels of arousal are required for orbitofrontal generation of images of the face than for structures lower in the neuraxis which also code facial representations. The mother's arousal regulating function may support higher optimal levels of dopaminergic arousal (Iversen, 1977) at higher levels of the limbic hierarchy, that is in the frontolimbic cortex. If the mother does not provide this function, and instead frequently serves a primary source of arousal dysregulation, this system may not evolve. It is important to keep in mind that maternal overstimulation also can produce arousal dysregulation in the form of inducing supra-heightenend levels of arousal in the child. I shall later discuss that this is a condition that supports infantile rage responses, since removal of the mature orbitofrontal cortex results in rage behavior (Kennard, 1945; Kolb, 1984) and an increase of aggressive interactions (Raleigh, Steklis, Ervin, Kling, & McGuire, 1979). The dominance of the activation of primitive subcortical over cortical representations and the loss of mesocortical regulation of lower mesolimbic excitatory activity may be behaviorally expressed in extended protest or rage reactions. "Primitive" representations may reflect the hyperactivity of neurons in, for example, the amygdala which selectively respond to human faces (Sanghera, Rolls, & Roper-Hall, 1979). Unmodulated subcortical activity and primitive representations may thus drive infant narcissistic rage, (Kohut, 1978b), equated with Bowlby's bitter separation protest, the heightened frustration-triggered aggression that is common in this developmental period (Fox, 1977; Kagan, 1976).

THE AFFECT REGULATING FUNCTIONS OF INCEPTIVE RIGHT HEMISPHERIC INTERNAL WORKING MODELS

In discussing the infant's information processing system responsible for the recognition of specific persons, Olson (1981) refers to the central role of the "monitor," a control system which utilizes information from perceptual analysis and regulates the storage of new information in order to determine the types of internal states involved in responding to the environment. In recent work on facial expressions and the regulation of emotions, Izard (1990) asserts that:

> In early development, an internal or external emotion-eliciting event triggers the neural processes of affective evaluation that lead directly to an expression and a congruent experience or feeling state. . . . (p. 492)

Pribram (1987) proposes that the ventrolateral cortex, acting in an "evaluative" or "appraisal" capacity, functions to "refine" emotions in keeping with current sensory input. The early practicing experience-dependent development of the mesocortical neuronal circuit, especially prefrontal descending cholinergic projections which modulate subcortical dopaminergic activity (Bannon & Roth, 1983) and thereby act as a regulator of sympathetic affective states (Fuster, 1980), mediates its earliest affect regulatory function. The orbitofrontal cortex is known to be involved in the modulation of ascending excitatory influences (Butter, Snyder, & McDonald, 1970). Indeed, it is documented that the prefrontal mesocortical system is associated with the cerebral circuitry of emotionality (Thierry et al., 1978) and is involved in the regulation of affective responses (Tassin, 1987). The activity of subcortical mesolimbic dopamine neurons increases in the anticipatory phase of behavior (Schultz & Romo, 1990), and is known to be associated with the incentive of motivation that leads to the motor output of behavior (Willner & Scheel-Kruger, 1991).

The mesocortical dopamine system is also implicated in cognitive representational processes (Simon, Scatton, & LeMoal, 1980). Izard (1990) states that in order to modulate an emotion expression through cognitive processes, the infant must comprehend the meaning and anticipate the effects of the eliciting event. This anticipatory function is performed by the orbitofrontal cortex, a component of an "expectancy-based memory system" (Kesner, 1986) and a dopaminergic "expectancy command circuit" (Panksepp, 1986). Recent cognitive research is now characterizing special "dynamic mental representations" that contain expectancy effects and represent real time change analogically (Freyd, 1987). The capacity to formulate and utilize dynamic mental representations that code a temporal dimension in which "time goes forward" (Freyd, 1987) appears at the end of the first year, the period when the child is first capable of predicting future events (Kagan, 1982) and is able to generate internal working models that are used as a guide for future actions (Bowlby, 1981). Internal representational functions are fundamentally involved in the modulation of impulses (Schwalbe, 1991). The incipient capacity for self-initiated and self-modulated emotion manifest in involuntary spontaneous facial expressions also emerges at about 1 year-of-age (Izard, 1990).

It is now accepted that regulation of spontaneous facial expression and spontaneous emotional expression depends on functional activity at the cortical level (Borod & Koff, 1984; Sackeim & Gur, 1983). Goldman-Rakic now concludes that the regulation of behavior by mental representation requires the collaboration of a large set of both cortical and subcortical structures (Goldman-Rakic, Funahashi, & Bruce, 1990). Pandya and Yeterian (1985) emphasize that the execution of behavior depends on the integration of activity at various different levels of the central nervous system. Hecaen and Albert (1978) have described the much overlooked importance of vertical corticosubcortical functional systems:

> Cortical neural mechanisms of one hemisphere would be responsible for a particular performance, and subcortical structures connected to these cortical zones would

participate in the realization of the performance, creating a complex, corticosubcortical functional system specific to each hemisphere. (p. 414)

The right, and not left hemisphere has been demonstrated to gain inhibitory control over subcortical facial displays in the last quarter of the first year (Rothbart, Taylor, & Tucker, 1989).

A functional maturation of prefrontal cortex occurs at 10–12 months (Diamond & Doar, 1989), the same time period in which the infant gains the capacity to abstract prototypes of human visual facial patterns (Strauss, 1979). This is also the identical time frame in which the first internal working models appear. The activity of the frontolimbic orbital cortex underlies the formation of nonverbal internalized cognitive-affective working models of attachment that organize the individual's construction of subsequent attachment relationships. Its functional capacities support their production—this cortex is uniquely involved in attachment (Steklis & Kling, 1985) and emotional (Yamamoto et al., 1984) behavior, in the identification of individuals from their faces and the monitoring of emotional responses to environmental stimuli (Rolls, 1986), in the mental generation of images of faces (Goldenberg et al., 1989), and in the mediation between the internal milieu and the external environment (Mesulam & Mufson, 1982). This working model, the product of an orbitofrontal control system which hierarchically dominates the activity of the dopaminergic ventral tegmental limbic forebrain-midbrain circuit (Panksepp's "expectancy command circuit") acts as a regulator of subcortical generated affect via its mesocortical delayed response function. This proposal fits the general cybernetic principle that the inclusion of a dynamic internal model of the outside world in a control component of a feedback regulator is responsible for internal stability and output regulation (Wonham, 1976).

The developmental psychologists Kobak and Sceery (1988) argue that working models are "styles of affect regulation" which are utilized as "strategies for regulating distress in situations that normally elicit attachment behaviors" (p. 136). Stern, an infant researcher, describes representations of interactive history (Stern, 1989), mentally represented generalized episodes of interactive experience which are related to the affective aspects of episodic memory (Stern, 1985). Tomkins (1979), a theoretician of affect phenomena, characterizes "nuclear scenes" as affectively charged episodic memories which become cognitively interconnected to form dominant life themes. Similarly, Forgas (1982), an experimental social psychologist, refers to "episode cognitions" which function as highly salient integrative schemata in the representation of social information. These internal representations contain a strong affective component and are used as interaction routines that guide interpersonal behavior. Lichtenberg (1989), a developmental psychoanalyst, asserts that the record of early lived experience persists in representations of "model scenes" which are nonlinear and contain visual, action, auditory, and especially affective components. These precipitate around affect-laden situations conveyed by facial expressions and auditory tone, are associated with transitions of enhanced states of vitality, and are stored in episodic memory, memory for real life moments occurring in real time (Tulving, 1972).

I conclude that the early maturing (Giannitrapani, 1967; Taylor, 1969) visuospatial (Galin, 1976) right hemisphere, which is known to contain an expanded orbitofrontal structure (Falk et al., 1990) and an enlargened frontal lobe (Weinberger et al., 1982; Weis et al., 1989), and to be densely interconnected with subcortical systems (Joseph, 1982), is a storage site for these inceptive internal working models. This hemisphere is active in the perception of arousal-inducing maternal facial expressions (Nelson, 1987), is essential to the perception of the communicative content of nonverbal expressions directly from facial and prosodic stimuli (Blonder et al., 1991), and is dominant for the processing, expression, and regulation of emotional information (Joseph, 1988). The right cortex is implicated in the memorial storage of emotional faces (Suberi & McKeever, 1977) and is now thought to contain an analogical representational system (Tucker, 1992) based on self-and-object images (Watt, 1990). Further evidence for this assertion is found in studies that indicate that the right hemipshere is instrumental in processing personally relevant aspects of the individual's world (Van Lancker, 1991), is activated during the recall of early childhood memories (Horowitz, 1983), and is involved in autobiographical (Cimino, Verfaellie, Bowers, & Heilman, 1991) and personal episodic (Knapp, 1983) memory.

SUMMARY

By the end of the first year the neo-toddler truly becomes a social being. At this time the infant possesses a rather complex psychobiological mechanism to process socioaffective information. Toward this end the child compares a current perceptual socioemotional input against stored interactive representations, physiological-affective responses to various emotional facial expressions of the attachment figure. These internal working models that guide interpersonal behavior and regulate affect are stored in the orbitofrontal cortex of the right hemisphere. This system of affect regulation involves orbitofrontal regulation of the mesocortical dopamine system, especially subcortical components which contain neurons that selectively respond to faces, that is, encode representations of the emotionally expressive face. The sequential processing of socioemotional information occurs along the ventral tegmental limbic forebrain-midbrain circuit by neuronal centers at various hierarchical levels of the cortex and subcortex.

In line with the principle that information is processed in stages, the entire temporal sequence involves sensory-perceptual encoding of a socioaffective facial stimulus in the posterior cortex, cognitive appraisal in the frontolimbic anterior cortex, amplification of the signal during cortico-subcortical transmission along the visuolimbic pathway, activation of hypothalamic motivational systems which influence internal states and generate emotion-specific action tendencies, activation of the ascending ventral tegmental mesocortical dopamine circuit, and finally activation of prefrontal areas and frontal cortical motor regions responsible for facial and body emotion response expression.

This early system of affect regulation involves the corticolimbic regulation of the ventral tegmental limbic circuit. The mesocortical dopamine system neurochemically supports affect regulating cortical representational processes, and these operations are performed in the orbitofrontal cortex in the right hemisphere. The frontolimbic system in the right cerebral cortex stores cognitive-affective schema of styles of affect regulation, that is, inceptive internal working models.

In the second year, as we shall soon see, the orbitofrontal cortex is innervated by the lateral tegmental limbic circuit and achieves its final maturation. This allows for its hierarchical dominance of the two limbic circuits, and the generation of even more complex internal representations that mediate affect regulatory functions. A psychoneurobiological model of the dual limbic component processing of socioemotional information is presented in a later chapter.

III LATE INFANCY

15 The Onset of Socialization Procedures and the Emergence of Shame

Socialization training during the second year is generally focused on the inhibition of undesirable behaviors—that is, parents begin to impose restrictions on activities that are unacceptable but that the child normally finds pleasurable; they demand that he inhibit certain kinds of behavior that he enjoys. . . .Toilet and cleanliness training, and the tasks of curbing tantrums, destructive activities, and unrestricted exploration and wandering are generally initiated when the child is between 12 and 18 months of age.
　　　　　—Paul H. Mussen, John J. Conger, and Jerome Kagan (1969)

Yet for the human brain, the most important information for successful development is conveyed by the social rather than the physical environment. The baby brain must begin participating effectively in the process of social information transmission that offers entry into the culture.
　　　　　—Don M. Tucker (1992)

I presented evidence earlier to support the proposal that dyadic socioaffective experiences directly and specifically influence the development of the orbitofrontal cortex, an affect regulating cerebral structure, at the end of the first year of human infancy. Early practicing high levels of attachment and locomotor exploratory behavior, elated affect, and positive expectation were conceptualized as ontogenetic adaptations to the ontogenetic niche which generates elevated levels of socioaffective stimulation. West and King (1987) assert that parental behavior is an important component of the ontogenetic niche, and at the beginning of the practicing period 90% of maternal behavior consists of affection, play, and caregiving while only 5% is involved in prohibiting the junior toddler from

199

ongoing activity (Tulkin & Kagan, 1972). The ensuing state of increased arousal is accompanied by neuroendocrine changes that facilitate the expansion of neurotrophic mesocortical axons of the ventral tegmental limbic circuit into this frontolimbic cortex whose emergent function is responsible for the ontogenetic adaptations of this time.

The ontogenetic niche changes in early development, eliciting adaptive adjustments in the infant (Alberts, 1987). Observational studies show that 12-month-olds receive more positive responses from mothers, while 18-month-olds receive more instructions and directions from both parents (Fagot & Kavanaugh, 1993). The mother of the 11-to 17-month-old toddler expresses a prohibition on the average of every 9 minutes, thereby placing numerous demands on the infant for impulse control (Power & Chapieski, 1986). In this chapter I describe how the socioaffective environment changes from the last quarter of the first to the first quarter of the second year. The transition from the early to the late practicing period represents the progression from early to late infancy. With the onset of socialization procedures in the second year, the emotional climate between the senior toddler and mother that generates high levels of pleasurable affect is stressed. As originally discussed by Freud (1905/1953), in the course of the child's cultural and moral education, shame (and disgust) comes to function as a prohibitive, inhibitory, and reactive counterforce to the pleasure principle. I argue that the process of socialization, usually conceptualized behaviorally or cognitively, is transmitted affectively, and that shame is the essential affect that mediates this socializing function. Specifically, the mother utilizes facially expressed stress-inducing shame transactions which engender a psychobiological misattunement within the dyad. Such visuoaffective communications trigger an inhibition of the infant states of hyperarousal that support positive affect.

THE SOCIOAFFECTIVE ENVIRONMENT CHANGES
IN THE SECOND YEAR

As the practicing period proceeds into the second year the "social environmental niche" of the caregiver-infant dyad changes dramatically. In their classic text on child development, Mussen, Conger, and Kagan (1969) point out that the onset of the process of socialization occurs in the second year, and that during this time the mother's role in relation to the child now begins to change. Her increased expectations which demand the "delay" of behaviors that are inherently gratifying to the child may be a major source of intense friction within the dyad. Hoffman (1975a) notes that in contrast to the dyadic interactions of early infancy:

> Sometime in the second year, owing mainly to a rapid increase in cognitive and neuromuscular development and gross motor activity, the child begins frequently to get into things and behave in other ways at variance with parental desires. Something distinctly new then begins to characterize far more interactions than previously: the parent's frequent attempts to change the child's behavior against his will,

and the child's attempts to have his way despite knowing what his parent wants. The stage is thus set for sustained conflicts of will and the parent's role makes a dramatic shift from primarily a caretaker to primarily a socialization agent. (p. 236)

Maccoby and Martin (1983) point out that soon after the onset of upright locomotion, the toddler becomes willful, negation emerges in speech, and parental socialization focuses on discipline in addition to nourishing functions. Spitz (1957) describes severe maternal restrictions to volition peak at about 15 months, especially in relation to socialization of body function. At about this time the mother introduces the word "No" into her object relations with the active ambulatory toddler, pushing the child back from activity into inactivity. Spitz (1965) asserts:

Whether she forbids him some activity, or he is prevented from achieving a thing which he desires; whether one disagrees with the manner in which he wishes to conduct his object relations-it always will be the instinctual drives which will be frustrated. (p. 185)

White (1985) describes the intensification of negativism at around 14 months, and stresses a crucial element of social development involves the parents' communicating to the child that "he is terribly important: his needs and interests are special, but he is no more important than any other person in the world, especially his parents" (p. 181). Johnson (1987) points out that from the practicing phase onward, the caregivers must supply repeated but supportive and not humiliating frustration of the child's illusion of grandiosity. It is proposed that this stressful stimulation is a critical experience for triggering further orbitofrontal structural development which is required for an ontogenetic progression to occur.

THE EMERGENCE OF SHAME IN THE LATE PRACTICING PERIOD

A number of authors have emphasized the growth-facilitating importance of small doses of shame in the socialization process of the infant (Broucek, 1982; Kohut, 1971; Nathanson, 1987a). In recent work on emotion socialization, Malatesta-Magai (1991) concludes that even the most benign parenting involves some use of mild shaming procedures to influence behavior, and the extensive use of shame as a socializing technique is only now being appreciated (M. Lewis, 1992; A. Miller, 1981). In fact, this "attachment emotion" (H.B. Lewis, 1980), which has been described as "the primary social emotion" (Scheff, 1988), makes its initial appearance in the practicing period (Schore, 1991). In developmental research, Amsterdam and Leavitt (1972, 1980) note that embarrassment (a component of shame) is completely absent before 12 months and is first observed at 14 months. Plutchik (1983) concludes that between 12 and 18 months affects such as "shame, defiance, and negativism" first appear. Pine (1980) comments that certain affects "are first born at later stages in the developmental process when the psychological conditions for their emergence are met" (p. 232), and Spitz (1965) proposes that significant organizational shifts occur in development which are signalled by the emergence of new affective behavior.

Earlier, a typical early practicing reunion was described in which the caregiver-induced a parasympathetic to sympathetic transition and a rapid energization of the infant. This effect was proposed to be mediated by a psychobiologically attuned elevation of sympathetic-driven arousal, reflected physiologically in cardiac acceleration and psychologically in elated affect. These interactive episodes were suggested to be a matrix for the ontogeny of the positive affects of joy (elation) and interest, and for the generation of excited, positive anticipatory states. Mahler (1979, p.63) observes that the early practicing toddler, absorbed in his own narcissistic pleasures, upon mastery of some autonomous function, becomes aware of his need for his mother's acceptance and renewed participation. Parens (1980, p. 108) describes the typical late practicing reunion behavior in which the 16-month-old toddler brings the things he or she is exploring and attempting to master to the mother's vicinity.

However, at this point of social development the nature of the reunion exchanges is altered in that they now more than any time previously also engender intense arousal dysregulation and stress. Mahler notes that at 15 to 16 months specifically, the practicing toddler's narcissism is "particularly vulnerable to the danger of deflation" (Mahler et al., 1975). The returning toddler, in a hyperaroused state of excited anticipation, eagerly looking forward to to the expected satisfaction of "the need of the budding self for the joyful response of the mirroring selfobject" (Kohut, 1977, p. 788) (mutually attuned elation) is suddenly and unpreparedly confronted with the "unexpected noncooperation of the mirroring object" (Kohut, 1978a, p. 655). Izard (1991) observes that face-to-face encounters that at one time elicited only joy become the principal context for shame experiences. Shame, a visual, nonverbal affect (Erikson, 1950) typically associated with an "unexpected" onset (Lynd, 1958) and triggered by an appraisal of a disturbance in facial recognition (Izard, 1977) arises:

> in the infant's contacts with mother at those moments when mother becomes a stranger to her infant. This happens when the infant is disappointed in his excited expectation that certain communicative and interactional behavior will be forthcoming in response to his communicative readiness. . . .shame arises from a disturbance of recognition, producing familiar responses to an unfamiliar person, as long as we understand the "different" mother to be the unfamiliar person. That a mother (even a 'good enough' mother) can be a stranger to her own infant at times is not really surprising since the mother's moods, preoccupations, conflicts and defenses will disturb her physiognomy and at times alter her established communication patterns. (Broucek, 1982, p. 370)

Tomkins (1963) posits that shame is a:

> specific inhibitor of continuing interest and enjoyment . . . any barrier
> exploration which partially reduces interest or the smile of enjoyment wil
> the lowering of the head and eyes in shame and reduce further exploration or self-
> exposure powered by excitement or joy. Such a barrier might be because one is
> suddenly looked upon by one who is strange, or because one wishes to look at or
> commune with another person but suddenly cannot because he is strange, or one
> expected him to be familiar but he suddenly appears unfamiliar, or one started to
> smile but found one was smiling at a stranger. (p. 123)

Guided by the principles that affects develop within an interpersonal context
and that specific affects imply a particular form of relatedness, I have recently
proposed a prototypical model of shame that is based on an analysis of incipient
shame experiences (Schore, 1991). As in the early practicing period, the late
practicing toddler, in an activated, hyperstimulated, high arousal state of stage-
typical ascendant excitement and elation, exhibits itself during a reunion with the
caregiver. Despite an excited expectation of a psychobiologically attuned shared
positive affect state with the mother and a dyadic amplification of the positive
affects of excitement and joy, the infant unexpectedly encounters a facially
expressed affective misattunement, thereby triggering a sudden shock-induced
deflation of narcissitic affect. The infant is thus propelled into an intensified low
arousal state which he cannot yet autoregulate. Shame represents this rapid
transition from a preexisiting high arousal positive hedonic state to a low arousal
negative hedonic state.

This model articulates "the interplay between attachment and shame" (G.
Kaufman, personal communication, October 1, 1991). The fundamental import
of this attachment emotion is that it represents the proximate organismic response
to the primary caregiver's frustration of the infant's expectation that the attachment need will be gratified. It is now known that when combined with joy,
interest motivates attachments (Buechler & Izard, 1983) and that pleasure and
interest are major indicators of affect attunement (Stern, 1985). Psychobiological
attunement drives the attachment process by acting as a mechanism that maximizes and expands positive affect and minimizes and diminishes negative affect
(Field, 1985a). Shame occurs only when the individual is experiencing interest-
excitement or enjoyment-joy (Izard, 1991). This negative affect, a specific inhibitor of activated ongoing positive affects (Tomkins, 1963), is thus the infant's
immediate phenomenological, physiological-emotional response to an interruption in the flow of an anticipated maternal regulatory (selfobject) function, psychobiological attunement which generates positive affect, and to the maternal
utilization of misattunement as a mediator of the socialization process. It is well
known that attachment bond disruptions precipitate an imbalance in the regulation of affect (Reite & Capitanio, 1985). The misattunement in shame, as in other
negative affects, represents a regulatory failure, and is phenomenologically expe-

rienced as a discontinuity in what Winnicott (1958b) called the child's need for going-on-being and Kestenberg (1985) refers to as dead spots in the infant's subjective experience.

This intense psychophysiological state of shame distress, a "decrescendo" (Stern, 1985) affective response to a sudden alteration of the familiar "average expectable environment," subjectively experienced as a "spiraling downward" (Kaufman, 1989), is proposed to represent a sudden shift from sympathetic- to parasympathetic-dominant autonomic nervous system activity. The conscious experience of this "primitive, biologically based" affect (Broucek, 1982) reflects a rapid switch from sympathetic predominant "ergotropic" arousal to parasym-pathetic predominant "trophotropic" arousal (Scherer, 1986). Indeed, Buss (1979) has demonstrated that shame represents parasympathetic arousal. This shift from an active arousal to a passive arousal state is equated with a transition from a hyperaroused state to a hypoaroused state. Negative emotions are known to differ in level of arousal (Mandal, Tandon, & Asthana, 1991), and shame (like disgust and sadness) is associated with a state of low arousal.

This arousal state transition is reflected in the toddler's overt behavior—his motionless headhang and body posture due to a reduction in tonus of the neck and body muscles, his decreased tonus of facial muscles causing a loss of the social smile, his averting the eyes, and the hallmark of shame, blushing, (which is known to be absent in early infancy). Blushing, the end product of the physi-ological discharge of shame (J.P. Miller, 1965), is a parasympathetic function (Knapp, 1967) caused by reduction of sympathetic vasoconstrictor tone and onset of vasodilatation (Drummond & Lance, 1987). The parasympathetic-dominant affect of shame has been suggested to reflect the action of an intrinsic neuro-humoral vasodilator (Nathanson, 1987a). Mahler (1979) observes a practicing "low keyed" state of slowed motility and diminished interest in the environment; she specifically equates this with a parasympathetic state of "conservation-withdrawal" (Kaufman & Rosenblum, 1967, 1969). This state occurs in helpless and hopeless stressful situations in which the individual becomes inhibited and strives to avoid attention in order to become "unseen" (Powles, 1992). Mahler's observations have been corroborated by Beebe and Lachman (1988b), who de-scribe a stressed-induced "inhibition of responsivity" in which a sudden total cessation of infant movement accompanies a limp, motionless headhang.

According to Joseph (1992) parental disapproval, an important mediator of the socialization process, is expressed nonverbally in, for example, "looks of embarrassment". Such shame messages are "keenly observed by the right half of the brain" of the child. In discussing the mother's signaling of "visual" prohibitions to the hyperactively locomoting toddler during the first several months of the second year, Riess (1978) describes:

> The child's greater potential responsiveness to his mother's signalling messages can therefore be put in the service of the necessary curbs and restrictions of the roaming

toddler who is in constant danger of hurting himself. It must be assumed that mothers react to many and varied methods of dealing with a newly locomoting "practicing" toddler with a penchant for impulse-ridden independent action. One possible method may be the facial display of approval and disapproval . . . mothers may . . . use the visual mode, i.e., facial expressiveness, as an educational or socializing tool. (p. 385)

Freud (1905/1953) states that as a result of education, shame acts as a psychic "dam" to the child's instinctual life. Knapp (1967) points out that shame curbs "dangerous arousal," restrains active mobilization, opposes general activation, and initiates a "slowing effect." The affect of "visual shame" (Erikson, 1950) that induces hypoactivation (Ferguson, Stegge, & Damhuis, 1991) thus acts as a countervailing force to the hyperactivity and hyperarousal of mammalian midinfancy (Reite, Kaufman, Panky, & Stynes, 1974) and to the "boundless energy" of the constantly moving practicing toddler (Pine, 1980).

Over 60 years ago MacCurdy (1930) proposed that the blushing and immobility seen in shame are due to a shift in balance in the autonomic nervous system, with an offset of sympathetic activity and an onset of vagal activity, leading to cardiac deceleration and a fall in blood pressure. As opposed to the attuned state, shame elicits a painful infant distress state (Broucek, 1982), manifest in a rapid inhibition of excitement and a sudden decrement in mounting pleasure (Tomkins, 1963), and cardiac deceleration (Buck, Parke, & Buck, 1970) by means of vagal impulses (Knapp, 1967). Heart rate deceleration is also seen in infants who are approached by "real" strangers (Bohlin, 1987), supporting the idea that the mother is perceived as a stranger in early shame transactions. Izard (1991) has pointed out that the quality of a specific emotion feeling is identical from infancy throughout the rest of the lifespan. The prototypical conscious subjective experience of shame is psychobiologically mediated by a sudden shift from sympathetic-dominant to parasympathetic autonomic nervous system activity. Throughout the rest of the lifespan it is phenomenologically experienced as a blockage of vitality affects, a sharp gradient of change of emotion, a rapid, unexpected, uncontrollable transition from a "crescendo" to a "decrescendo," an "animate" to an "inanimate" (Stern, 1985) feeling state, a switch from an attachment-affiliation or exploratory-assertive to an aversive motivational functional system (Lichtenberg, 1989). This sudden emotional transformation has been described as a "flight from positively experienced exhibitionism to negatively experienced shame" (Miller, 1985).

SHAME AND DYADIC VISUOAFFECTIVE PROCESSES

Specific emotions are now understood to involve a distinctive "core relational theme" which describes an essential person-environment relationship (Lazarus, 1991b), and to be elicited by an appraisal of actual or expected changes in events that are important to the individual (Frijda, 1988). These principles apply to an understanding of the essentially visual object relation of shame. Reciprocal gaze behavior, the most intense form of interpersonal communication (Tomkins, 1963), acts as a powerful mediator of affect attunement, but it can also transmit misattunement, since "this visual feedback system carries within it the potential of mutual gratification as well as frustration" (Riess, 1978, p. 382). The activation of this need for dyadic psychobiological attunement in which positive affect is maximized and expanded and negative affect is minimized is expressed in a state of "communicative readiness" (Broucek, 1982). The experience of shame is associated with unfulfilled expectations (Wurmser, 1981), and the practicing toddler's attentive focus on the mother's eyes and the frustration of the child's expectation of her participation in foveal eye-to-eye contact and visuoaffective communication may be the key visual cue triggering the shame state. Shame is experienced as an interruption, and it functions to impede further affective resonance (Nathanson, 1992) and communication (Kaufman, 1989).

Amsterdam and Leavitt (1980) point out that the mother's gleam is specifically absent in the shame transaction, and Hess (1965) notes that constricted pupils occur when a person views something that is distasteful or unappealing. The impediment to anticipated positive affect is specifically a perception of (or later an activated stored internal image of) a facial display which signals the absence of the maternal gleam, which may mirror instead disgust, and which precedes a sudden unanticipated break in social referencing, a process now considered to be a form of attachment behavior. Lewis (1992) points out that a disgusted face is widely used in the socialization of children, though parents are often unaware that they are producing it:

> This expression might appear only briefly, but children do perceive it. When they see a disgusted face they turn sharply away and seem inhibited for a moment. It is likely that such behavior reflects shame. The disgusted face is effective in socialization through shaming as well as informing the child not to repeat the action. (p. 111)

Disgust, like shame, has a unique and distinctive facial expression (Ekman & Friesen, 1975; Izard, 1971), first recognized by Darwin (1872) as deriving from closing off the nostrils to avoid unpleasant odor and opening the mouth to expel its contents. It elicits a characteristic action tendency of distancing the self from an offensive object, and triggers a distinctive physiological manifestation (nausea) and feeling state (revulsion) (Rozin & Fallon, 1987). These latter authors describe this emotion as a type of rejection motivated by ideational factors. Tomkins (1987) proposes that dissmell and disgust function in motivation and as a signal, both to the individual who emits this signal and to the one who receives it, of feelings of rejection. "The object of disgust is the prototypical ambivalently held object, attractive and desirable enough to be brought into close contact but then rejected as noxious" (Broucek, 1991, p,. 113). Kaufman (1989) describes:

The face pulls away in dissmell from the offending, "bad-smelling" other, and in disgust the face spits out the "bad-tasting" other . . . the parent similarly rejects the child as if it, too, were bad-smelling or bad-tasting, pulling away in dissmell or spitting out in disgust. (p. 40)

Izard (1991) implicates disgust (dissmell) in rejection and avoidance behaviors.

Lewis also refers to another maternal facial expression, a contemptuous maternal face which blends disgust with anger/rage. Cross-cultural studies have shown that the facial expression of contempt is universal (Ekman & Friesen, 1986; Izard & Haynes, 1988). Izard (1991) notes that to be chronically held in contempt is to be shamed or to anticipate shame. It is suggested that parental facial dissmell/disgust elicits infant shame, while contempt—angry rejection— triggers humiliation and "shame-rage" (H. B. Lewis, 1987). The latter, also entitled "humiliated fury" by Lewis is equated with Kohut's (1978b) "narcissistic rage." Weil (1978) emphasizes that maternal shame when compounded with rejection results in an especially hostile object relationship. As opposed to the elevated parasympathetic autonomic component which always accompanies shame, humiliation involves an elevated parasympathetic plus a heightened sympathetic reactivity. Tomkins (1963) refers to shame-humiliation, the former a low intensity affect, the latter high intensity. Psychophysiologically this may represent, respectively, a state of activated trophotropic arousal versus an intensely stressful state of trophotropic combined with ergotropic arousal.

It is well known that direct gaze can mediate powerful aggressive messages (Ellsworth, 1975), and this would occur in instances when a the child witnesses the mother's narcissitic rage. The mother's hypersympathetic state would be expressed in her hyperdilated pupils. Peto (1969), in a child psychoanalytic study of "terrifying eyes," describes how the infant's gazing upon the "red-glow that glares up" in the adult's pupils triggers "a corresponding fire of shame (humiliation) in the child." Studying a nonclinical sample, Malatesta-Magai (1991) concludes, "we have rarely seen parents use contempt with very young infants and it appears to be used sparingly with older infants" (p. 219). However, Gaensbauer and Mrazek (1981) have recorded observations of a provocative, "teasing" mother who intensified her toddler's anger into a state of rage. Early unregulated contempt-humiliation exchanges may be a common form of practicing dyadic pathology and an important source of transmission of severe emotional disorders associated with the under regulation of aggression. For example, there is now strong clinical evidence that shame-humiliation dynamics always accompany child abuse (Kaufman, 1989; M. Lewis, 1992). Narcissistic personality disorders who have difficulty modulating rage typically present a background with a parent who humiliates the child by "harsh, continuous, or massive exposure" (Johnson, 1987). In later chapters I cite evidence that indicates a prominent role of early unregulated visual shame in the etiology of various primitive psychopathologies.

The failure of expressed communicative readiness to achieve the expected amplification of a positive affect state and the break of social referencing mutual foveal gaze-mediated visuoaffective transmissions is reflected in the descriptions of shame as a sense of exposure (Kaufman, 1989). The eye is the prevailing organ of shameful exposure (Thrane, 1979), and shame first appears in the context of a developmental transaction between the infant's face and the mother's face:

> Shame is originally grounded in the experience of being looked at by the Other and in the realization that the Other can see things about oneself that are not available to one's vision. (Wright, 1991, p. 30)

What is not available to the infant's vision is his own face and the emotion being expressed on it, one that differs from the one expressed in and reflected by the child's emotional mirror, the mother's face (Searles, 1963). This misattuned relational transaction triggers gaze aversion (Tomkins, 1963), a response of hiding the face "to escape from this being seen or from the one who sees" (Wright, 1991, p. 30), and a state of withdrawal (Lichtenberg, 1989). Under the lens of a "shame microscope" which amplifies and expands this negative affect (Malatesta-Magai, 1991), visible defects, narcissistically charged undesirable aspects of the self, are exposed (Jacobson, 1964). "It is as though something we were hiding from everyone is suddenly under a burning light in public view" (Izard, 1991, p. 332). Shame throws a "flooding light" upon the individual (Lynd, 1958), who then experiences "a sense of displeasure plus the compelling desire to disappear from view" (Frijda, 1988, p. 351), and "an impulse to bury one's face, or to sink, right then and there, into the ground" (Erikson, 1950, p. 223) which impels him to "crawl through a hole" and culminates in feeling as if he "could die" (H.B. Lewis, 1971, p. 198). The sudden shock-induced deflation of positive affect which supports grandiose omnipotence has been phenomenologically characterized as a whirlpool—a visual representation of a spiral (Potter-Effron, 1989) and as a "flowing off" or "leakage" through a drain hole in the middle of one's being (Sartre, 1957, p. 256). The individual's subjective conscious experience of this affect is thus a sudden, unexpected, and rapid transition from what Freud (1914/1957) called "primary narcissism"—a sense of being "the center and core of the universe," to what Sartre (1957) described as a shame triggered "crack in my universe."

Late practicing period shame transactions thus specifically communicate to the child that "he is no more important than any other person in the world, especially his parents" (White, 1985). In contrast to affect attunement that promotes omnipotence and grandiosity (Stern, 1985), the visually transmitted misattunement of shame during reunions after early separation events uniquely and specifically acts as a brake on the developing child's narcissistic desire to be constantly at the center of his parents' attention. Shame stress experiences puncture the "practicing illusion" of a grandiose cognition "that the mother is constantly available in her mirroring function" (Sherwood, 1989, p. 15). These

affect socializations thus function to terminate the attachment need
the high arousal positive affects of elation and interest-excitement tha
ticing omnipotence and grandiosity.

THE INTERNALIZED INTERACTIVE REPRESENTATION OF INCIPIENT SHAME TRANSACTIONS AS AN ONTOGENETIC ADAPTATION

As previously mentioned, current psychobiological research has demonstrated
that the developing organism occupies a distinct sequence of postnatal niches
(Alberts, 1987). The postnatal "specifically-experienced environment," contained in the relationship with the caregiver (Emde, 1988), which is not static and
constant but fluid and changing, is thus in actuality a series of early environments. The fact that development represents social experience-dependent structural growth and functional adaptation through a sequence of environmental
niches which are constructed out of the changing nature of the mother's interactions with the child emphasizes the need to elucidate "the qualities and the
changes in the mother that allow her to meet the developing needs of her infant"
(Emde, 1990, p. 885). "The responses of the 'optimal' mother of the symbiotic
period, it is clear, are not those of the 'optimal' mother of the practicing period,
and they must again be modified with the onset of rapprochement" (Greenberg &
Mitchell, 1983, p. 280). The optimal "good enough" mother (Winnicott, 1971)
of the late practicing period is thus one who can tolerate inducing stressful
socialization transactions in her infant.

Winnicott (1958a, p. 246) points out that the attuned, mirroring function of
the early mother gives way to maternal "graduated failure of adaptation," and
that this is essential to the development of the child's capacity to separate and
differentiate himself from the mother. Hunt (1965b) has suggested that regularly
sheltering children from stressors is counterproductive for optimal emotional
development. Stress is defined as a change or a threat of change demanding
organismic adaptation (Schneiderman & McCabe, 1985). The increasing expectations of the socializing mother elicit alterations in the growing toddler's perception of social contingencies, since "the nature of the social stimulation that it
receives changes substantially, that is, the contingencies themselves to which it is
exposed change as it grows older" (Suomi, 1981, p. 192). The mother's changes
are matched by ontogenetic adaptations on the part of the maturing infant.
Tronick (1989) has demonstrated that the interactive stress of dyadic mismatches
allow for the development of interaction and self-regulatory skills. Cairns asserts
that periods of severe environmental challenge represent opportunities for the
potential of achieving new patterns of social adaptation (Cairns, Gariepy, &
Hood, 1990). Settlage argues that a "developmental" challenge of previously
adequate adaptive functioning, in the form of a new "environmental expecta-

tion," activates a developmental process which may lead to an advance in adaptive and self-regulatory capacities (Settlage et al., 1988).

In line with the well established observations that visual stimulation is the primary type of external sensory input that generates shame (Izard, 1991), and that internally generated shame is directly related to visual imagery, the internalization of the shame core relational transaction in the form of a stored image of an interactive pattern that is imprinted with shame affect may represent such an ontogenetic adaptation, an advance in self-regulatory function. Kaufman (1989) underscores the principle that "what is internalized are images or scenes that have become imprinted with affect" (p. 59). Although the origin of shame is dyadic and external—"the experience of being looked at by the Other" (Wright, 1991)—under optimal conditions it is internalized as "the eye of the self gazing inward" (Morrison, 1987). Now the elicitation of this affect which is ontogenetically inhibitory and prohibitive (Freud, 1905/1953) does not require the presence of an external person. In line with the well established observation that visual imagery possesses a potent capacity to elicit physiological changes (Zikmund, 1975), the mental image of the misattuned face of the mother engenders a rapid brake of arousal and the onset of an inhibitory state.

Indeed, at 18 months an internal signaling system emerges, in which affect can be used as a signal function (Greenspan, 1988). In signal shame, internal mentation alerts the individual to the possibility that a particular external circumstance may evoke an intense experience of this painful affect in a fully developed state. The operational message of the signal function of shame has been interpreted as "Stop. You are no good" (M. Lewis, 1992) and "If you do this or that, you may be looked at and despised" (Fenichel, 1945, p. 139). These principles may underlie the description by Horowitz (1983) of an emergent inhibitory mechanism:

> A child wanted some candy that he had been emphatically told not to touch. As he tentatively reached for it with one hand, he made a stern reproving face and stopped his reaching with the other hand. The gesture and facial expression represent a train of thought: I want it, mother would say no, better not. The mimicry of the mother's facial expression adds emotive power to the restraining ideas. (p. 79)

The capacity to access this stored representation enables the child to regulate impulsive behavior by anticipating the mother's emotional response to it. Schwalbe (1991) describes that in the first two years "imagery begins to modulate impulsive behavior" (p. 284). Izard (1971) argues that shame comes to play an adaptive central active role in the regulation of (impulsive) emotional expression, and therefore for more effective social interaction.

Nathanson (1987a) argues that shame acts as a major force in shaping the infantile self. Kohut (1971, 1977) proposes that phase-appropriate, maternal shame-induced empathic failures and frustrations serve as a stimulus for the establishment of adaptive internal self-regulatory structures. Kaufman (1989) states that graded and appropriately timed frustrations often stimulate positive change. The Shame results from the mother's frustration of the child's expectation that an upcoming dyadic visuoaffective communication will gratify his attachment need for a psychobiologically attuned amplification of positive affect. Shame stress, an essential affective mediator of the socialization process (Thrane, 1979) which is associated with an interactive misattunement and unfulfilled expectations (Wurmser, 1981) induces a lapse in smooth physiological (psychobiological) functioning (Nathanson, 1987a). In the physiologically hyperactive state of shame (Darwin, 1872/1965), an affect that elicits a greater awareness of the body than any other emotion (Izard, 1991), the individual experiences an influx of autonomic proprioceptive and kinesthetic feedback into awareness (H.B. Lewis, 1971). The heightened autonomic reactions in shame have been likened to the infantile preverbal psychosomatic state (Anthony, 1981), and psychophysiological experiments have demonstrated that shaming conditions specifically induce a psychophysiological stress reaction (Buck et al., 1970).

Stress has been conceptualized as the occurrence of an asynchrony (misattunement) in an interactional sequence (Chapple, 1970), and asynchronies between individual-psychological and cultural-sociological sequences have been specifically proposed to define developmental crises which are a major source of further development (Riegel, 1976). Maternal gradual failures of adaptation which mediate the socialization of body function and emotion in the late practicing period elicit a caregiver-induced shame stress state in the infant. The induction of a stress state at this point is understandable in that "stress is defined as a change or a threat of change demanding adaptation by an organism" (Schneiderman & McCabe, 1985, p. 13). Indeed, shame socialization events trigger an adaptation syndrome (Selye, 1956), and serve as a stimulus for a further ontogenetic progression. The adaptation syndrome involves the sympathomedullary and especially the parasympathetic hypothalamico-pituitary-adrenocortical neuroendocrine systems, which are critical to organismic development and maturation (Timiras, 1989) and are interactive with orbitofrontal cortex (Euler & Folkow, 1958; Hall & Marr, 1975). Failure of expectancy (Levine, Goldman, & Coover, 1972) (as in the frustration of expectation in shame) and strangeness (Levine, 1985) (as in the mother's strange face in the practicing socializing shame transaction) are known to activate the parasympathetic hypothalamico-pituitary-adrenocortical stress system as expressed in elevated corticosteroid levels. The physiological concomitants of shame are associated with the onset of vagal activity (MacCurdy, 1930; Knapp, 1967). Vagal projections are known to innervate the orbitofrontal cortex (Encabo & Ruarte, 1967). These stage-specific dyadic events may serve as stress-induced signals that trigger neuroendocrine responses which facilitate the experience-dependent development of the frontolimbic structure essential to socioemotional and affect regulatory functioning.

SUMMARY

In the second year the mother's role undergoes a substantial shift from caregiver to socialization agent, a change that produces an alteration in the dyadic affective relationship. She now utilizes facially expressed shame induction in order to impose an inhibition of activities that the toddler finds pleasurable. These events occur during late practicing reunion transactions. Upon return from exploratory forays, the senior toddler, in a high arousal state of stage-typical excitement and elation, exhibits itself to the caregiver. Despite an excited expectation of a psychobiologically attuned shared positive affect state with the mother and a dyadic amplification of the positive affects of excitement and joy, the infant unexpectedly experiences a misattunement communicated in the mother's facial expression of disgust. This break in an anticipated visuoaffective transmission triggers a sudden shock-induced deflation of narcissistic affect. The infant is thus propelled into an intensified low arousal state which he cannot yet autoregulate. In this shame state, the preexisting activated affects of interest-excitement and enjoyment-joy are suddenly inhibited, and the self exposure and exploration powered by these positive affects are reduced. The psychobiological state of shame distress represents a sudden shift from sympathetic-predominant ergotropic arousal to parasympathetic-dominant trophotropic arousal. The mother thereby engenders in the infant a rapid brake of arousal and an inhibitory state of conservation-withdrawal.

The incipient core relational shame transactions that occur throughout the late practicing period are stored in interactive representations imprinted with shame affect. These internalized visuoaffective images can be accessed, even in the mother's absence, in order to automodulate impulsive behavior. Such an advance represents an ontogenetic adaptation, as it mediates further socioemotional development. Socialization shame transactions induce a stress state, and the concomitant elevation of corticosteroid levels and parasympathetic vagal activity specifically facilitates further maturation of the orbitofrontal cortex.

16 Late Orbitofrontal Development

> *Diffuse excitatory processes—such as those related to the sympathetic nervous system and subcortical structures—are functionally active from birth, partly because of their relevance to organismic survival. But many of the more finely tuned inhibitory systems—which include parasympathetic nervous system activity and higher—order cortical processes, especially in the frontal lobes—are slower to develop and myelinate, and their influence emerges more slowly in the postnatal period.*
> —Ross A. Thompson (1990)

> *The ultimate function of the neurons in the prefrontal cortex is to excite or inhibit activity in other parts of the brain.*
> —Patricia Goldman-Rakic (1992)

According to Freud, the fundamental dynamic alteration of the socialization process is the adaptive maturational transformation of "primary" to "secondary narcissism," and of the pleasure into the reality principle. I have previously characterized the early practicing period, a developmental stage of heightened pleasurable affect that fuels infantile grandiosity, as a phase of primary narcissism. Changes in the socioemotional environmental niche, in the object relations between mother and toddler, occur in the late practicing period, and are manifest in dyadically regulated socializing shame stress transactions that rapidly transform positive into negative affect. Such events in this critical period for socialization deflate grandiosity and induce the infant's reluctant departure from primary narcissism. It is known that critical periods represent windows of time during which the sensitivity of developing systems to environmental experiences is augmented (Aslin, 1981) and that rapidly growing systems are particularly sensitive to conditions of changing environmental stimulation (Scott, 1979a). In the latest neurochemical models of development, a critical period is characterized as an early interval in which:

> a hierarchy of internal regulatory signals, provided by neurotransmitters, neurohumors (neuronal substances such as peptides) and hormones is superimposed upon basic ontogenetic events. It is suggested that these internal humoral and hormonal signals can mediate the effects of external influences on developmental processes. . . .(Lauder & Krebs, 1986, p. 120)

Socializing procedures represent important "external influences" in the second year of human life.

The socialization process is essentially socioemotional conditioning that is mediated by negative affect generating shame transactions, and shame distress is triggered by the infant's recognition of the caregiver's unexpected break in participation in dyadic foveal gaze (social referencing) transactions and an interruption of the dyadic regulated visuoaffective stimulation of positive affect. This latter event leads directly to specific endocrinological alterations, and these hormonal alterations facilitate the experience-dependent maturation of limbic structure. In this chapter I document how such visually-induced, shame-mediated neurohormonal signals are registered in the orbitofrontal cortex, known to contain neurons with the unique feature of having receptive fields that specifically include the central area of the visual field (Mucke, Norita, Benedek, & Creutzfeldt, 1982) and which are highly responsive to visual changes that are motivationally relevant (Mesulam, 1985).

PROPOSAL: SHAME STRESS DEACTIVATES THE VENTRAL TEGMENTAL AND ACTIVATES THE LATERAL TEGMENTAL LIMBIC CIRCUITS

The psychobiological mechanism underlying socialization events is embedded in dyadic shame transactions that stressfully reduce positive affect. This involves stressing the mesolimbocortical ventral tegmental system associated with narcissistic, pleasurable qualities of social interaction, thereby reducing dopamine- and endorphin- regulated positive hedonic affect. Such a psychoneurochemical effect explains the assertion that "both neurologically and psychologically, shame is more closely associated with the positive emotions than any of the other negative emotions" (Izard, 1991, p. 337). This prefrontal biochemical system is known to be specifically activated by stress (Thierry, Tassin, Blanc, & Glowinski, 1976). The maternal stress of the early practicing onset mesocortical system may define the optimal socioemotional stimulation required for further structural growth of the orbitofrontal cortex. It has been suggested that high levels of endogenous endorphinergic activity "might leave an individual psychologically immature as a consequence of failure to fully benefit from social experiences" (Benton & Brain, 1988, p. 230).

Shame stress represents a sudden rapid transition in the toddler from what Lundberg and Frankenhauser (1980) call a "joyous happy state" of "effort without distress"—accompanied by sympathetic-mediated catecholamine secretion and corticosteroid suppression, to a helpless, depressed state of "distress without effort"—characterized by elevated cortisol levels produced by the pituitary-adrenocortical system activated conservation-withdrawal response. This interactive stress, a form of hypostimulating "solitary" or "social isolation" stress, thus deactivates the sympathetic and activates the parasympathetic systems, as reflected in decreased opioid and increased corticosteroid levels in the circulation. An identical psychoendocrinological pattern has been observed in attachment bond interruptions (Trad, 1986). Increased corticosteroid levels are also found in 12-month old practicing infants under separation stress from the mother (Tennes, Downey, & Vernadakis, 1977).

The negative affect of shame that mediates socialization procedures is behaviorally expressed in the avoidance of mutual facial gazing (Kaufman, 1989), and the consequent reduction in reciprocal mirroring transactions results in a diminution of psychophysiologically-responsive opioid peptide levels. As a result of these psychobiologically-driven neurohormonal changes, the early practicing period of overexcitation is followed by the subsequent development of forebrain inhibition in the late practicing period. Stearns (1982) describes "developmental switches" expressed in "discrete plasticity" that are triggered by unpredictable and discontinuous socioecological changes. Different catecholamines are known to be critically involved in local plasticity phenomena (Aoki & Siekevitz, 1988). I suggest that in the late practicing period, lowered opioid levels in the circulation lead to a reduced growth of the sympathetic excitatory mesocortical dopamine system.

PROPOSAL: MEDULLARY NORADRENALINE AND ADRENAL CORTICOSTEROIDS INDUCE THE EXPANSION OF THE LATERAL TEGMENTAL LIMBIC CIRCUIT IN THE ORBITOFRONTAL CORTEX

At the same time that ventral tegmental dopaminergic growth is reduced, there is an intensive expansion of the innervation of the orbitofrontal association cortex by the parasympathetic lateral tegmental noradrenergic system of the lower brain stem medullary reticular formation (see Figs. 4.11 and 4.12). This vagal catecholaminergic (A2 noradrenergic) (Figs. 4.9 and 4.15) system has been previously described to arise in the solitary nucleus (Figs. 4.16 and 4.17) and to ipsilaterally (Riche, de Pommery, & Menetrey, 1990) project axon collaterals up the neuraxis via the ventral noradrenaline pathway (Olson & Fuxe, 1972) to higher forebrain regions (see Fig. 4.15). It is now accepted that axonal growth is enhanced under optimal levels of stimulation (Cummins et al., 1977). I deduce that growth of ventral tegmental dopaminergic axons is optimal under high levels of stimulation, while lateral tegmental noradrenergic axonal growth is facilitated under low intensity stimulation. In shame states the individual reduces sensory input, especially visual input, by gaze aversion. Low arousal shame states are neurophysiologically induced by vagal impulses (Knapp, 1967), and vagal activation is known to elicit a cortical evoked response in the orbitofrontal cortex (Dell & Olson, 1951; Siegfried, 1965). Such a proposal fits well with the concepts that different types of stimulation have a facilitating effect on developmental processes (Riesen, 1961), and that specific neurochemical groups in the brain which exhibit differences in temporal sequences of development and divergent functional properties are subject to different forms of environmental regulation (Noison & Thomas, 1988). It is also consonant with the observation that the maturation of the activity of the other noradrenergic system, the dorsal tegmental A6 neurons of the locus coeruleus, is intimately related to sensory input during an early postnatal stage of brain development (Nakamura, Kimura, & Sakaguchi, 1987).

Furthermore, alterations of circulating stress-induced corticosteroids and ACTH are logical candidates for mediating the activated and deactivated growth of these two catecholaminergic systems. It has been established that corticosteroids suppress ACTH (Kraicer & Milligan, 1970) and CRF (Yates & Maran, 1974) release into the circulation. This would reduce opioid peptide (endorphin) activation of ventral tegmental dopaminergic systems (Stinus et al., 1980). The subcortical plate beneath the postnatally developing orbitofrontal cortex is an attractive possible site of action of stress-associated alterations of steroids and peptides, since the extracellular milieu of the subplate mediates a unique set of interactions that are required for the development of the cerebral cortex (Chun & Shatz, 1988). During critical periods developing systems are especially sensitive to circulating hormones (Schapiro, 1968) which regulate developmental brain growth (Lauder & Krebs, 1986). It is known that corticosteroids are selectively retained by limbic structures (McEwen, Weiss, & Schwartz, 1968), that glucocorticoid receptors are located within layer VI of the cerebral cortex (Fuxe et al., 1985), and that early postnatal experiences alters the number of glucocorticoid receptors in the frontal cortex (Meaney et al., 1985).

Stress-induced adrenocortical steroids which are known to influence brain growth and neurotransmitter synthesis (Meyer, 1985) may also act directly on dopaminergic neurons in the medial portion of the ventral tegmental area, since these neurons that project to the orbital prefrontal cortex (Porrino & Goldman-Rakic, 1982) contain the greatest amounts of glucocorticoid receptors in the entire A10 group (Harfstrand et al., 1986). High concentrations of corticosteroids, known to reduce levels of nerve growth factor (Simonoski, Murphy,

Rennert, & Heinrich, 1987) and to inhibit fiber outgrowth of catecholaminergic sympathetic neurons (Unsicker, Krisch, Otten, & Thoenen, 1978), may impair growth of mesocortical dopaminergic terminals. Elevated levels of corticosterone have been shown to decrease glutamate binding in the limbic system (Halpain & McEwen, 1988), and may thus depress glutamate activation of NMDA receptors that stimulates mesencephalic dopamine release.

It should be noted that the heuristic proposal of the postnatal medullary noradrenergic innervation of the orbitofrontal cortex, although not yet looked for nor experimentally demonstrated in the infant or adult human, is suggested by the following data. Dopamine and noradrenaline are known to innervate the deep and superficial layers, respectively, of the adult orbital (Lewis et al., 1988; Lewis & Morrison, 1989) and neonatal frontal (Loren, Bjorklund, & Lindvall, 1976) cortex; in pre- and postnatal ontogenesis, deep layers of the cortex ontogenetically mature earlier than superficial layers (Marin-Padilla, 1970), a principle demonstrated in developing human prefrontal cortex (Mrzljak, Uylings, Kostovic, & Van Eden, 1988; Rabinowicz, 1979); prefrontal dopamine levels reach peak concentrations earlier in development than noradrenaline (Goldman-Rakic & Brown, 1982); although the bulk of the noradrenergic innervation of the entire cortex arises from the locus coeruleus, a smaller yet constantly observed amount of cortical noradrenaline does not derive from this source (Gaspar et al., 1989); the noradrenaline terminals that innervate the orbitofrontal cortex (Levitt et al., 1984) are thick, like those from the medullary pathway, while locus coeruleus terminals are fine (Olson & Fuxe, 1972) (see Fig. 4.12); medullary noradrenaline neurons are known to innervate forebrain regions (Jones, Halaris, & Freedman, 1979); catecholaminergic axons from the solitary nucleus in the medulla project axon collaterals up the neuraxis to different parts of the forebrain (Ricardo & Koh, 1978); orbital neurons are known to send direct connections to the solitary nucleus (Saper, 1982), and all other limbic structures which project to this brain stem area and process similar information have reciprocal connections with it (Riche, de Pommery & Menetrey, 1990; van der Kooy et al., 1984).

In addition, current conceptions of the limbic system and the autonomic nervous system also suggest the above developmental model: orbitofrontal cortex is the major cortical component of limbic circuitry (MacLean, 1954); two limbic-forebrain-midbrain circuits exist, one originating in the ventral tegmental, the other in the lateral tegmental areas (Nauta & Domesick, 1982); limbic function contains excitatory and inhibitory mechanisms (Stellar, 1982); orbitofrontal cortex plays a functional role in "selective activation and inhibition" (Muller, 1985); sympathetic and parasympathetic components develop postnatally, at different rates, with early maturing sympathetic-dominant activity being followed by parasympathetic, inhibitory, vagal restraint (Hofer, 1984b); and perhaps most relevantly, parasympathetic autonomic inhibitory systems in the frontal cortex which underlie emotional regulation develop more slowly in the postnatal period than sympathetic autonomic excitatory systems (Thompson, 1990).

Furthermore, according to Hofer (1983a) the mother "serves as an external regulator of the infant's behavior, its autonomic physiology, and even the neurochemistry of its maturing brain" (p. 199). I have implied that it is important to specify which neurochemical systems are directly influenced by the social environment at what particular points in time. Tucker (1992) now proposes that brain stem regulatory systems, acting through neuromodulator projection pathways, exert an organizing influence on cortical differentiation and on the specification of network structure in the early years of life. Similarly, Trevarthen (1990) holds that far-reaching ipsilateral connections from relatively few brain stem reticular neurons which later regulate emotion and motivation act as sources of trophic substances that influence cerebral morphogenesis and differentiation.

> Core regulatory neuron activities set the condition for the responses of cortical cells to stimuli from the world outside the body. They also control how new nerve network associations grow and how mechanisms for perceiving goals and for acting on them are coupled in development and learning. (p. 335)

We now appreciate that there are a number of anatomically and neurochemically distinct reticular neuronal populations, and that each may be a source of innervation to the prefrontal cortex. Kostovic (1990) concludes that:

> current evidence supports the idea that changes in the distribution and chemical properties of the subcortico-cortical pathways play a significant role in the perinatal reorganization of the prefrontal cortex in man. (p. 232)

Changes in neurotransmitters are known to be associated with alterations in brain structure (Mattson, 1988).

Like the other catecholamine, dopamine, noradrenaline is known to serve a neurotrophic role in the postnatal development of the cortex (Felten, Hallman, & Jonnson, 1982). Brain stem noradrenergic neurons innervate cerebral microvasculatures (Hartman, Zide, & Udenfriend, 1972) and this bioamine exerts a moderating effect on resting cerebral blood flow (McCalden, Benjamin, & Eidelman, 1976; Onesti, Strauss, Mayol, & Solomon, 1989). Stimulation of the dorsal medullary reticular formation elicits noradrenergic-induced alterations in blood flow in the cortex, including prefrontal areas (Iadecola, Lacombe, Underwood, Ishitsuka, & Reis, 1987). Noradrenaline stimulates the incorporation of phosphorous into membrane phospholipids of the cerebral cortex (Hokin, 1969). It also activates the pentose phosphate shunt (Brannan et al., 1982; Hothersall et al., 1982), the biochemical pathway that is utilized in cellular biosynthetic activities such as oligodendroglial myelin formation. In early postnatal development, this bioamine has been shown to influence the development of cortial circuitry (Foote & Morrison, 1987) and synaptic plasticity (Bear & Singer, 1986), properties that I have earlier suggested are due to the unique role that central catecholamine neurons play in modulating cerebral circulatory systems (Yokote et al., 1986). The increase in noradrenergic terminals in the orbitofrontal cortex is matched by the development of noradrenergic receptors (Deskin, Seidler, Whitmore, & Slotkin, 1981). This leads to further development and reorganization of orbital columns, including the expanded dendritic reception of known multimodal inputs from all sensory areas of the posterior cerebral cortex (Chavis & Pandya, 1976; Jones & Powell, 1970). Studies have also demonstrated that noradrenaline facilitates the normal maturational changes in receptive field properties of cortical neurons of infants (Daw, Rader, Robertson, & Ariel, 1983), and plays an important role in the responsiveness of the cortex to environmental stimulation during an early critical period (Pettigrew & Kasamatsu, 1978).

Increased growth of orbital (muscarinic?) cholinergic projections back down to subcortical sites in the diencephalon, midbrain, and especially the nucleus of the solitary tract in the brain stem would also occur at this time. Orbitofrontal projections to subcortical regions are known to mature in infancy (Johnson, Rosvold, Galkin, & Goldman, 1976), and synaptic development of the medullary solitary nucleus has been shown to continue to develop postnatally (Miller, McKoon, Pinneau, & Silverstein, 1983). Neurons in the solitary tract undergo a dramatic morphological change during early mammalian infancy, and this rapid maturation in an early critical period is influenced by "appropriate environmental signals" (Kalia, Schweitzer, Champagnat, & Denavit-Saubie, 1993). The maturation of descending regulatory fibers allows for the onset of an even more efficient orbitofrontal Jacksonian control of spontaneous activity (Lynch, 1970), manifested in the curtailment of practicing behavioral hyperactivity. Mizuno et al. (1968) have posited the morphological substrate for the cortical suppressor influence on subcortical activity resides in fibers originating in the orbitofrontal region which project to brain stem sites in the pons and medulla oblongata. Newman and Wolstencroft (1959) have presented neurophysiological evidence suggesting the existence of descending fiber connections between the orbital cortex and the medulla; these cortical projections directly influence medullary activity.

This complete neurochemical circuit, with both an ascending catecholaminergic and a descending cholinergic link, is identical to Nauta and Domesick's (1982) lateral tegmental limbic forebrain-midbrain circuit.

DESCENDING PROJECTIONS FROM NORADRENERGIC INNERVATED ORBITOFRONTAL SITES MEDIATE THE ONSET OF AN INHIBITORY STATE

The hierarchical dominance of the orbitofrontal cortex over the lateral tegmental limbic circuit allows for a critical ontogenetic progression. The growth of axons from noradrenergic innervated sites in the orbitofrontal cortex to subcortical targets allows for its role in "vagal restraint" and in the energy-conserving inhibition of autonomic function (Kaada et al., 1949). Stimulation of particular orbitofrontal sites triggers an almost instantaneous inhibition of gastrointestinal motility, respiratory movements of inspiration, and somatic locomotor activity, and a dramatic precipitous fall in blood pressure (Kaada, 1960). The involvement of vagal-orbitofrontal connections in shame is suggested by the "active restraining quality" of this affect which brakes arousal and triggers a "partial paralysis of outer activity" (Knapp, 1967). With respect to the sudden motionless headhang and body posture reflecting a reduced tonus of neck and body musculature seen in shame, this rapid onset of vagal inhibition of responsivity is caused by the activation of the orbitofrontal cortex, known to inhibit muscle tone and brain stem regulated somatic relexes (Sauerland, Knauss, Nakamura, & Clemente, 1967). This function accounts for the influx of autonomic proprioceptive and kinesthetic feedback into awareness that occurs in shame (Lewis, H.B. 1971). Orbital cortex also regulates the motility of the proximal and distal part of the gastrointestinal tract, and information from the gastrointestinal tract is communicated by the vagus nerve to the nucleus of the solitary tract (Sirotin, 1961; Zhang, Fogel, & Renehan, 1992), itself a target of orbitofrontal axons (Yasui et al., 1991).

Primary visceral interoceptive information also is received in a medullary structure adjacent to the nucleus of the solitary tract, the area postrema (Figs. 4.16 and 4.17). Since these two areas show similarities in anatomical connections, receive input from vagal fibers onto noradrenergic neurons, and share common neural and hormonal afferent sources, it is thought that they serve closely related functions. The area postrema specifically acts as a chemoreceptor trigger zone in the induction of emesis (Borison & Brizzee, 1951), a natural behavioral response to ingested toxins, as it transmits its input to a localized integrative circuitry for vomiting (Wang & Borison, 1950). Shapiro and Miselis (1985) conclude that this medullary area is centrally involved in ingestion and emesis, and that its connections allow for a confluence of gustatory input and interoceptive influence in the adjacent nucleus of the solitary tract and for a modulation of ascending interoceptive information. It is suggested that in the late practicing period descending information, especially visual information embedded in the mother's emotionally expressive facial display of disgust (M. Lewis, 1992), is delivered from the orbitofrontal areas that process gustatory stimuli (Rolls, Yaxley, & Sienkiewicz, 1990), to the area postrema. As a result of this subcortical processing, its modulation of ascending information is expressed in an increase of medullary noradrenaline in the orbitofrontal cortex. Activation of the anterior ventrolateral cortex is known to produce tongue protrusion (Whishaw & Kolb, 1989), a prominent component of the universal facial expression of disgust (Izard, 1991).

Tomkins (1987) points out that disgust is an innate defensive response. Food is tasted, and if offensive is spit out; if swallowed and it is toxic it produces nausea and is vomited out. Importantly, disgust evolves from an ejecting drive reducing function of turning off the hunger drive to a signal and motivational function. Nathanson (1987a) echoes this:

When we reject with disgust a person or relationship previously found pleasing, a mechanism initially functioning as a drive auxiliary—protecting us from unselective hunger—now functions as an affect and turns off the relationship. (p. 13)

Disgust is a response "to a bad other and the termination of intimacy with such a one is assumed to be permanent unless the other one changes significantly" (Tomkins, 1987, p. 149). The functional similarity of shame and dissmell-disgust in beaking attachment bonds is thus related to structural similarity of the orbitofrontal-medullary mechanisms that underlie them.

Saper (1982) has demonstrated a direct connection from this "visceral sensory cortex" to the nucleus of the solitary tract (NTS) in the medulla, a component of the brain stem vagal complex which receives distinct patterns of sensory and motor projections from cardiac, laryngeal, tracheobronchial, pulmonary, and gastrointestinal visceral organs (Kalia & Mesulam, 1980) and a substantial somatosensory input from the spinal cord for somatovisceral activation (Menetrey & Basbaum, 1987). Similarly, Shipley (1982) has found direct connections from this cortex to the solitary nucleus and brain stem visceromotor regions. van der Kooy et al. (1984) have characterized the same prefrontal structure that sends direct monosynaptic inputs to the nucleus of the solitary tract as a cortical component of a "visceral forebrain system," which may influence cardiovascular, respiratory and other autonomic functions that are processed in the NTS. Yasui et al. (1991) (Fig.4.20) have recently observed that axons from layer V of the orbital cortex terminate in the rostral two-thirds of the nucleus of the solitary tract bilaterally, with an ipsilateral predominance. These authors refer to this orbital-medullary connection as a cerebral cortical control mechanism upon visceral systems. Pribram (1981) has stressed the important fact that this frontolimbic cortex represents the apex of the hierarchy of control of autonomic functions.

Neurons in the deep layers of the orbitofrontal cortex thus send direct projections to the vagal nucleus of the solitary tract, the medullary source of cardiopulmonary autonomic function (Saper, 1982). Catecholaminergic neurons in the solitary nucleus (and area postrema; Pickel, Chan, Joh, & Beaudet, 1983) are known to directly receive vagal afferent fibers (Sumal et al., 1983), including primary cardiovascular afferent fibers such as those from aortic baroreceptors (Katz & Karten, 1979). Over 40 years ago prefrontal stimulation was shown to increase baroreflex sensitivity (Rinkel, Greenblatt, Coon, & Solomon, 1947). In more recent work van der Kooy et al. (1984) have suggested that prefrontal afferents to this medullary nucleus play a significant role in modulating the baroreceptor reflex and other cardiovascular functions. The experience-sensitive postnatal myelination and maturation of descending cholinergic orbitofrontal axons to the medulla that modulate cardiac vagal discharge could provide a route for cortically processed signals to reach this area of the brain stem which controls cardiovascular function and is involved in the cardiovascular features of affective behavior.

It is known that parasympathetic cardioinhibitory neurons in the medulla mediate vagal bradycardia (Nosaka, Yamamoto, & Yasunaga, 1979; Thomas & Calaresu, 1974). Hardy and Holmes (1988) show that low levels of stimulation of rodent lateral prefrontal cortex (the homolog of primate orbitofrontal cortex; Sarter & Markowitsch, 1984) elicits bradycardia, a finding earlier demonstrated by Kaada (1960) and later by Buchanan, Powell, and Valentine (1984). It is suggested that a centrally-induced heart rate deceleration follows activation of an orbitofrontal-vagal pathway and that this descending system which projects to the brain stem serves a parasympathetic function. Indeed, this mechanism may underlie Fuster's description of orbitofrontal control of parasympathetic function, and it may contribute to the cortical modulation of the cardiovascular aspects of emotion. Vagal tone, which indexes tonic levels of activation of the parasympathetic branch of the ANS (Porges, 1984), has been suggested to represent the physiological basis for the development of emotion regulation ability (Gottman & Fainsilber-Katz, 1989). Respiratory sinus arrhythmia, an index of parasympathetic nervous system cardiac vagal tone that is sensitive to noradrenergic activty, is now being used to study emotion induction (Grossman, Stemmler, & Meinhardt, 1990). The developmental onset of this parasympathetic modulation may account for the observation that elevated infant heart rates begin to decrease at 13 months (Kagan, 1982), a phenomenon attributed to the maturation of parasympathetic, vagal restraint (Hofer, 1984b), and for the observed maturational increases in vagal tone (Porges & Fox, 1986). These events may reflect the postnatal maturation of inhibitory parasympathetic systems in the frontal lobes discussed by Thompson (1990).

Furthermore, this later maturing parasympathetic orbitofrontal inhibitory system may in part suppress heart rate (Kaada et al., 1949) and behavior (Wilcott, 1981) via its regulation of noradrenaline release by neurons in the medulla oblongata that specifically influence parasympathetic hypothalamico-pituitary-adrenocortical corticosteroid levels. Neurons in deep orbital layers project their axons to dendrites of neurons in the solitary nucleus, thereby providing a modulating, controlling function (Yasui et al., 1991). In turn, the solitary tract nucleus sends direct projections to hypothalamic paraventricular (and supraoptic) nuclei (Ter Horst, De Boer, Luiten, & van Willigen, 1989; Weiss & Hatton, 1990). Even more specifically, adrenergic neurons in the solitary nucleus in the medulla send axons to various hypothalamic regions (Nosaka, 1984), including paraventricular nuclei (Al-Damluji, 1988). Noradrenaline infused into the paraventricular hypothalamus reduces energy expenditure and motor activity (Siviy, Kritikos, Atrens, & Sheperd, 1989). It has been suggested that cortisol is controlled by a pathway dependent upon alpha adrenergic activity in the hypothalamus (Depue & Kleiman, 1979), and more recent studies have demonstrated that noradrenergic A1 and A2 (and not A6 locus coeruleus) fibers mediate the stimulation of corticosterone secretion (Feldman, Conforti, & Melamed, 1988). Medullary noradrenaline neurons of the solitary nucleus contain a very high number of glucocorticoid receptors (Harfstrand et al., 1986). I interpret this anatomical data to mean that this pathway is the medullary lateral tegmental noradrenergic system, which is known to innervate the hypothalamus (Robbins & Everett, 1982).

In a study demonstrating noradrenergic input from A2 neurons in the nucleus of the solitary tract specifically into regions of the paraventricular hypothalamus which contain CRF neurosecretory neurons, Cunningham and Sawchenko (1988) suggest:

> A more direct role for the noradrenergic cells in the medial NTS may lie in the regulation of the hypothalamo-pituitary-adrenal axis. The medial part of the NTS, including the general region of the A2 cell group, is known to play a role in the control of cardiovascular homeostasis (Palkovits & Zaborszky, 1977), perturbations of which have been shown to influence peripheral levels of both ACTH and glucocorticoids, as well as portal blood levels of CRF. (p. 74)

Indeed, it is also now known that a noradrenergic system inhibits ACTH release (Jones et al., 1982). Again, I suggest this is the medullary noradrenergic system.

THE FINAL MATURATION OF THE ORBITOFRONTAL CORTEX AND THE REGULATION OF THE HYPOTHALAMO-PITUITARY-ADRENAL AXIS

The orbitofrontal cortex hierarchically dominates the hypothalamo-pituitary-adrenal axis. Its stimulation has been shown to elicit increased corticosteroid levels (Hall & Marr, 1975; Kandel & Schwartz, 1985). Consequent high levels of circulating adrenocortical steroids are taken up at various sites in the neuraxis. Of special importance, however, would be uptake by the corticosteroid receptors of corticotropin releasing paraventricular cells (Agnati et al., 1985; Cintra et al., 1987; Meyer, 1985), since this inhibits CRF expression (Sawchenko, 1987). Fuxe et al. (1985) report that the paraventricular hypothalamic nucleus contains an overlap between glucocorticoid and CRF receptor sites, and suggest glucocorticoids regulate CRF secretion by an action at this level. The CRF receptor is known to be coupled to adenylate cyclase (Aguilera et al., 1987), and corticosteroids specifically modulate cyclic AMP systems (Harrelson & McEwen, 1987). Indeed, it is now established that glucocorticoids regulate negatively paraventricular hypothalamic neuropeptides that in turn regulate ACTH (Swanson, 1991) and that high circulation levels of cortisol inhibit release of CRF (Yates & Moran, 1974) and ACTH (Davidson, Jones, & Levine, 1968). Frontolimbic controlled cortisol production may thus block CRF release and CRF increases in heart rate and sympathetic activity (mediated by hypothalamic CRF regulated release of adrenal medullary noradrenaline into the circulation).

As previously mentioned, these paraventricular neurons also receive a dopaminergic innervation which has been proposed to directly influence CRF release (Lipovits & Paull, 1989) and thereby pituitary and adrenal sympathetic activity. CRF secretion is known to be mediated by brain catecholamines (Guillaume et al., 1987), and A2 noradrenaline and A10 dopamine may specifically play a predominant role in the expression of this regulating factor. These catecholamines, themselves regulated by the orbitofrontal cortex, could fundamentally influence the hypothalamo-pituitary-adrenal axis in different ways.

These proposals are in line with recent evidence suggesting that cortisol secretion associated with stressful emotionally-laden situations is under cortical control (Wittling & Pfluger, 1990). They may also explain the psychobiological mechanism by which the shame imprinted image of the misattuned face of the mother triggers a rapid brake of arousal. It is now established that cortisol plays a role in human memory (Carpenter & Grune, 1982) and that glucocorticoids are involved in the retrieval or expression of the immobility response (Mitchell & Meaney, 1991). Shame, a sudden switch from sympathetic-dominant to parasympathetic-dominant ANS activity which accompanies immobility (MacCurdy, 1930), induces corticosteroid production and cardiac deceleration, opposes and restrains "mobilization for excitement" (Knapp, 1967), and inhibits activated and ongoing interest-excitement, an affect earlier proposed to be mediated by the sympathetic hypothalamic-adrenomedullary system. In referring to central representations of the parasympathetic branch of the ANS which are associated with shame triggered cardiac deceleration, Knapp (1967) describes:

> In the important function of cardiac regulation inhibiting mechanisms appear to be represented in progressively more complex and far reaching integrations as we ascend in the brain. As such they are progressively more open to symbolic influences. (p. 530)

In addition to cortical-medullary connections, direct orbital-hypothalamic connections would allow for cortical regulation of hypothalamic regions which, in turn, are known to influence cardiovascular reflexes at the medullary level (Gebber & Snyder, 1970). This effect may be relevant to the known orbitofrontal inhibitory influences on the sympathetic system (Fuster, 1980). Even more specifically, this function may be mediated by orbitofrontal projections that have been shown to have inhibitory effects on the hypothalamic ventromedial nucleus (Ohta & Oomura, 1979), a sympathetic structure known to be involved in cardiac acceleration (Gellman, Schneiderman, Wallach, & LeBlanc, 1981), vagal suppression, and affective states (Colpaert, 1975). Kita and Oomura (1981) have demonstrated other direct connections between the orbital prefrontal cortex and the lateral hypothalamus, a structure that continues to develop in a postnatal critical period (Fisher & Almli, 1984). These orbitofrontal-hypothalamic connections may mature in the second year. In support of this, Scott (1958) has reported that during the sensitive period for the development of social responses, changes in heart rate occur which reflect the establishment of neural connections between the cortex and the hypothalamus.

The experience-dependent maturation of these specific orbitofrontal-subcortical connections in the middle of the second year may allow for the appearance of the emergent adaptive function of visually triggered conservation-withdrawal, a primary regulatory process for organismic homeostasis (Engel & Schmale, 1972) characterized by heart rate deceleration, low levels of activity (McCabe & Schneiderman, 1985), and a lowered metabolic rate (Powles, 1992). Administration of norepinephrine directly into the paraventricular hypothalamus induces a hypometabolic effect (Siviy, Kritikos, Atrens, & Sheperd, 1989), and infusion of this catecholamine into the orbitofrontal cortex also elicits autonomic effects, specifically a hypometabolic alteration of energy balance and a reduction in energy expenditure (McGregor, Menendez, Atrens, & Lin, 1991). Orbital outflow has been shown to modulate both behavioral and autonomic homeostatic changes (McGregor & Atrens, 1991). van der Kooy et al. (1984) suggest that the forebrain system which provides direct inputs into the medullary solitary nucleus functions to "override brain stem homeostatic mechanisms during periods of stress or emotional activity" (p. 23).

Thompson (1990) concludes that the growth of cortical inhibitory control over subcortically mediated excitatory processes which underlies the regulation of emotional arousal does not become functional "until long after birth." Orbital prefrontal cortex, with its reciprocal interactions with the reticular activating system, is known to modulate arousal mechanisms in late infancy (Bowden, Goldman, Rosvold, & Greenstreet, 1971). This system which controls the excitability of the cortex has been characterized as a "nonspecific system governing internal inhibition" (Velasco & Lindsley, 1965) underlying the Pavlovian process. Its functional onset thereby alters the excitatory-inhibitory balance in the prefrontal system, modulating the earlier excitatory-dominant system. The ontogenetic establishment of corticolimbic links between the orbital cortex and the brain stem lateral tegmental monoamine system may account for the "inhibitory maturation" of monoamine systems which counterbalances the infant's initial excitatory tendencies in spontaneous motility and motor activity (Pradhan & Pradhan, 1980) and for the maturation of a forebrain inhibition system which can modulate the excitatory activity of early maturing reticular brain stem systems responsible for behavioral arousal (Moorcroft, 1971).

The late practicing onset of orbitofrontal regulation of hypothalamic and medullary autonomic centers is responsible for the functional emergence of an environmentally attuned prefrontal cortical system which can rapidly uncouple arousal and switch off sympathetic cardiac acceleration and switch on parasympathetic cardiac deceleration. In this way, this structure acts as a cortical system which regulates autonomic responses to affective cues (Mesulam & Mufson, 1982). Stimulated activity of orbital cortex is known to produce cardiac output adjustments (Hall, Livingston, & Bloor, 1977). Such a corticolimbic system represents an environmentally sensitive cortical mechanism which regulates the reciprocal changes in the activity of the sympathetic and parasympatheic components of the ANS in response to environmental demands. This orbitofrontal system is expanded in the right hemisphere, the cerebral hemisphere that is differentially involved in the bilateral regulation of arousal (Heilman & Van Den Abell, 1979), is closely associated with heart rate regulation (Lane et al., 1988) and neuroendocrine control (Wittling & Pfluger, 1990), and is responsible for maintaining important controls over autonomic activities (Heilman et al., 1977). Kinsbourne and Bemporad (1984) argue that the right frontotemporal cortex specifically exerts inhibitory control over intense emotional arousal.

PROPOSAL: THE OFFSET OF A CRITICAL PERIOD FOR THE MATURATION OF THE ORBITOFRONTAL CORTEX OCCURS IN THE MIDDLE OF THE SECOND YEAR

I propose that in the late, as opposed to the early practicing period, circulating levels of endogenous endorphins and ACTH are decreased and corticosteroids are increased. In contrast to the early practicing infant's imperviousness to frustrations (Mahler et al., 1975), the late practicing infant readily shows "pained," "hurt feelings" in response to shaming prohibitions of the parents, especially when these are delivered in an angry tone (Emde, 1988). Recent work on brain opioids and social emotion suggests visceral pain and the affective response to social isolation share common neurochemical substrates (Panksepp, Siviy, & Normansell, 1985). A reduction in pituitary ACTH has been proposed to be an important factor in ending the sensitive period of socialization (Martin, 1978). Corticosteroids are taken up by limbic forebrain structures (McEwen, Weiss, & Schwartz, 1968; Meyer, 1985), and low doses of cortisol administered directly into the hypothalamus are known to suppress both basal secretion of ACTH and stress-induced increases in the secretion of this hormone (Davidson et al., 1968). Animal studies show that an elevated adrenal corticosteroid level in the blood is found at the end of the socialization critical period (Weiss, Kohler, & Landsberg, 1973).

In a review of developmental psychoendocrinological research, Trad (1986) identifies a correlation of elevated cortisol and diminished endogenous opioids with interruptions of the attachment bond. Late practicing period alterations in the maternal social environment, especially socializing shame transactions, induce orbitofrontal associated increases in corticosteroid levels. Elevated levels of plasma corticoids, a physiological concomitant of Seyle's adaptation syndrome (Levine & Treitman, 1969), are expressed in a state of "distress without effort" (Lundberg & Frankenhaeuser, 1980) and in the emotional state of frustration when there is an absence or delay of expected reward (Goldman, Coover, & Levine, 1973). These conditions characterize shame experiences that mediate socialization learning. High corticosteroid concentrations are known to facilitate extinction and relearning (Van Wimersma Greidanus & De Wied, 1977). It is now well established that glucocorticoids play an important role in learning and memory, especially in avoidance learning (Ogren, Archer, Fuxe, & Eneroth, 1981). As mentioned earlier, avoidance is a primary component of shame-driven behavior.

Increased levels of corticoids have also been demonstrated to alter mood states and be associated with depression (Rubin et al., 1987; Rubinow et al., 1984) and fearfulness (Fredrikson, Sundin, & Frankenhaeuser, 1985), and to depress sensory detection activity in each of the sensory modalities (Henkin, 1974). These orbitofrontal-regulated neurochemical changes may signal the end of the practicing period, characterized by intense sensory inspection of the mother's face, elated mood and excited exploratory behavior. They may also be instrumental to the onset of the ensuing rapprochement period. Mahler et al. (1975) characterize the affective tone of this stage to be a depressive mood and an intensification of fear and separation anxiety. This developmental progression may represent a shift from stage-typical positive to negative expectation and the predominance of an avoidant-withdrawal negative affective bias, an aversive motivational system (Lichtenberg, 1989). Animal studies show that fear and avoidance reactions onset at the end of the critical period of socialization imprinting (Hess, 1973; Scott, 1962), leading Colombo (1982) to conclude that the emergent fear/adrenocortical system signals the terminus of the critical period for social imprinting. Indeed current theory in infant psychiatry now holds that fearful responses bring the period of attachment to an end (Anders & Zeanah, 1984).

Mahler et al. (1975) observe that at the stage transition from practicing offset to rapprochement onset the toddler's elated preoccupation with locomotion and exploration begins to wane. Importantly, the loss of elated mood may represent a disappearance of an earlier ontogenetic adaptation, as may the curbing of early practicing hyperactive locomotor behavior via a shame system which induces a hypoactivation (Fergusson, Stegge, & Damhuis, 1991) and "slowing effect" that produces a "paralysis of outer activity" (Knapp, 1967). These overt behavioral changes reflect an internal alteration from an increased to a reduced state of organismic arousal. It is now thought that the time course of a sensitive period is modified by the organism's state of arousal (Kellaway, 1989).

ORBITAL PREFRONTAL CONTRIBUTIONS TO THE DIMINUTION OF ORAL ACTIVITY AND THE ONSET OF BLADDER AND BOWEL REGULATION

The orbital cortex is known to suppress orality and oral tendencies (Butter, McDonald, & Snyder, 1969), and its maturation, reflected in the inhibition of the exploring of environmental objects in the toddler's mouth, may mark the end of the oral stage of development which Freud claimed ends at 18 months. Developmental research has demonstrated that:

> In general, it seems that in the first year or two of life, children will put almost anything that fits into their mouths and that much of what they learn in the first years of life is what *not* to eat. (Rozin & Fallon, 1987, p. 34)

This cortex, due to its medullary connections, has previously been suggested to activate disgust, a state that discourages ingestion and opposes a positive attraction related to the prospect of consuming an appealing object (Rozin & Fallon, 1987). Over 40 years ago MacLean (1949) observed the specific association of orbitofrontal activity with oral dependent impulses and behavior. Experimental research implicates the unique contribution of this cortex in appetite and the control of food intake (Kolb, Whishaw, & Schallert, 1977; Rolls, Yaxley, & Sienkiewicz, 1990) which is mediated by its connections with the "gustatory subdivision" (Whitehead, 1993), of the nucleus of the solitary tract.

Furthermore, the ensuing rapprochement phase, which onsets at 16–18 months, is complementary to Freud's anal stage of development. With the introduction of the socialization procedure of toilet training the mother's role shifts from a caregiver to one who holds an expectation that her infant will withhold elimination. This social learning is shame associated (Erikson, 1950; Tomkins, 1987), especially through nonverbal maternal facial expresions of dissmelldisgust. In a classical psychoanalytic conceptualization, Jones (1948) proposed that the toddler's tendency, if unconstrained, is to play with excreta "as a token of affection and pleasure, a demonstration usually misinterpreted by the recipient" (p. 424). Recall the prototypical object relation of shame, in which the toddler exhibits himself in an excited expectation of a psychobiologically attuned pleasurable affect state with the mother, suddenly encounters a misattunement appraised in the maternal facial expression. Although the early infant's attitude toward feces is positive (Freud, 1905/1953), by 14 months children appreciate that disgust substances such as feces have special significance to adults (Dunn, 1986), and feces become the first external object of disgust to appear in development (Rozin & Fallon, 1987). These latter authors propose that the creation of primary disgust during the enculturation process involves a process of transmission from adult to child through nonverbal facial expressions.

Toilet training, a voluntary control over an involuntary process which requires the child to associate a pattern of interoceptive cues (bowel and bladder tensions) with exteroceptive cues (the bathroom), is not ordinarily possible until the child is about 18 months old (Mussen, Conger, & Kagan, 1969). Greenspan (1979) posits that specifically at 18 months the child has a "vastly enhanced capacity for experiencing the internal milieu." The phenomenology of shame is associated with an intense awareness of the body (Izard, 1991) and an influx of proprioceptive and kinesthetic signals into consciousness (Lewis, 1971). Interoceptive abdominal visceral information is known to reach the cortex via vagal innervation of the orbital cortex (Korn, Wendt, & Albe-Fessard, 1966), a cortical region which processes "sensations from the internal milieu" (Krushel & van der Kooy, 1988) and modulates visceral input (Yasui et al., 1991). At about 18 months the toddler can now experience a heightened awareness of the body image and pressure in the body (Mahler et al., 1975). Lichtenberg (1989) asserts the general principle that the combination of self-awareness of bodily indicators and coordination between mother and infant provides for the foundation of successful regulation. Neurobiological studies have shown that orbitofrontal function is involved in the regulation of bladder capacity (Gjone & Setekleiv, 1963; Rinkel, Solomon, Rosen, & Levine, 1950; Strom & Uvnas, 1950) and that individual orbital neurons respond to the "biologically significant" odors of urine and feces (Onoda, Imamura, Obata, & Iino, 1984). I deduce that the emergent function of bladder and bowel regulation involves the operation of an evolved orbitofrontal system, especially in the right hemisphere, the hemisphere that is known to be dominant for the analysis of information received by the individual from his own body (Luria, 1973) and for the generation of internal images of (disgust-signaling) faces, at the end of the practicing period.

The dramatic developmental advances in socialization seen at this time are mediated by the experience-dependent maturation of the frontolimbic cortex. This affective experience is supplied in shame transactions, and these transactions are stored in shame imprinted interactive representations that are distributed along the lateral tegmental limbic circuit. The parasympathetic dominant affect of shame has been defined as a signal to the individual that whatever he is doing is not working and should be stopped (Basch, 1992). The growth of orbitofrontal connections into parasympathetic structures allows for a more efficient cortical modulation of hypothalamo-pituitary-adrenocortical activity (Hall & Marr, 1975). Gilbert (1989) emphasizes the adaptive function of this system:

> Although the HPAC system may be a system mediating stop behavior, it could also be seen as a physiological component of disengagement from incentives which helps to reduce the purposeless pursuit of unobtainable incentives and clears the way for new learning. (p. 112)

These structural mechanisms allow for the Freudian transformation of the pleasure to the reality principle as the essential internal event of socialization. The frontolimbic cortex has been designated as the site of a "stop" mechanism that deals with emotions (Pribram & McGuiness, 1975). Indeed, mature orbital function has been described as enabling the organism to "withhold non-reinforced responses and to steer ongoing behavior to more reinforcing consequences" (Rosenkilde, Bauer, & Fuster, 1981, p. 391), and as "functioning to balance internal desires with external reality" (Jouandet & Gazzaniga, 1979, p. 35).

SUMMARY

Incipient shame transactions in the late practicing period induce hormonal and neurohormonal alterations in the infant's developing brain. These affect mediating socializing transactions deactivate the ventral tegmental dopaminergic and activate the lateral tegmental noradrenergic limbic circuits. Low levels of endorphin and high levels of corticosteroids in the orbitofrontal subplate facilitate the growth of ascending catecholaminergic axons of noradrenaline neurons whose cell bodies are in the medullary nucleus of the solitary tract. The sprouting of these parasympathetic terminals into the overlying cortex allows for delivery of noradrenaline, and this bioamine acts to trophically induce a further maturation of orbitofrontal regions. The mother, the primary provider of affective socialization experiences to the child, thus directly influences the growth of prefrontal axons back down the neuraxis onto subcortical targets. These connections complete the organization of the lateral tegmental forebrain-midbrain limbic circuit.

The hierarchical dominance of the frontolimbic cortex over this limbic circuit allows for the emergence of a number of adaptive functions. Stimulation of particular areas of the orbitofrontal cortex serves to brake arousal and rapidly trigger the onset of an inhibitory state of conservation-withdrawal. This control of the viscera is expressed, for example, in the induction of a heart rate deceleration in response to certain environmental cues. Orbital-medullary and orbital-hypothalamic pathways deactivate sympathetic and activate parasympathetic functions in the ANS.

The maturation of the orbitofrontal cortex begins in the early practicing period and concludes in the late practicing period. Dyadic shame transactions involve the infant's interoceptive inhibitory responses to the exteroceptive input of the mother's disgusted face. These stored interactive representations are distributed along the lateral tegmental limbic circuit. By the middle of the second year these neuropsychobiological advances enable the automodulation of hyperactive behaviors and hyperaroused states. The orbital frontolimbic structural system is intimately involved in the socialization-induced diminution of oral activity and appearance of bladder and bowel regulation that are seen at this time.

230

17 Orbitofrontal Versus Dorsolateral Prefrontal Ontogeny

> *Early maturation of the right hemisphere would be consistent with the importance of emotional communication in early life. In the second year, the child's increasing motor competence and rapid development of language skills suggests a major transition in brain maturation, with a shift toward left hemisphere dominance. . . .This may reflect a shift from close attentional as well as emotional dependence on the social environment, mediated by the right hemisphere, toward increasing articulation of cognitive and motor control, and increasing emotional and attentional autonomy, as the functional role of the left hemisphere is established.*
> —Don M. Tucker (1992)

Mahler asserts that the practicing period ends at about 16 to 18 months. This temporal interval represents a transition into the next developmental stage, the rapprochement period. As previously mentioned, significant affective alterations occur at this time. Mahler observes that the affective climate changes from an elated to a depressed and fearful mood. Stern (1985) also reports a major socio-affective transformation occurs at around 15 to 18 months. These functional transformations reflect the important structural transmutations that have occurred. In this same time frame corticolimbic areas show anatomical maturation (Kinney et al., 1988), and this allows for advances in emotional activities and memory mechanisms (Rabinowicz, 1979). In line with the neurobiological principles that neural structural maturation is responsible for the transition of one stage to the next, that the frontal lobes develop in stages, and that a major maturation of the prefrontal cortex occurs in the second year of life, I have argued that the end of the practicing period represents the offset of a critical period for the maturation of the orbitofrontal cortex.

In a review article, Columbo (1982) concludes that the end of a critical period for the development of any particular system has been regularly found to be due to the beginning of the maturation of some other system. What other system could be initiating a structural maturation in the middle of the second year? In this chapter I offer the suggestion that as the orbital prefrontal growth spurt finalizes, a critical period is initiated for the maturation of the other major prefrontal division, the dorsolateral cortex. This transitional event also represents a shift in growth from the early maturing right cortex to the later maturing left hemisphere.

PROPOSAL: THE CRITICAL PERIOD OF MATERNAL ATTACHMENT OFFSETS AND PATERNAL ATTACHMENT ONSETS IN THE MIDDLE OF THE SECOND YEAR

A significant developmental transformation, signaled by affective changes, occurs in the middle of the second year (Emde, 1989), practicing offset and rapprochement onset. In the psychoanalytic infant literature this portal into the next stage of socioemotional development is referred to as the "rapprochement crisis." Bozhovich (1978) observes "crises" occurring at transitions between stages of socioemotional development. Infant researchers report the common observation of an upsurge of oppositional behavior (Escalona, 1973) and age-appropriate negativism (Wenar, 1982) at 15 to 18 months. In this period the child engages in dramatic fights with the primary caregiver, and this phenomena is interpreted as a "disidentification" from the mother (Mahler et al., 1975). The child's behavior during the crisis is described as ambivalent, since she or he shows increased dependence towards the mother while separated, but increased aggression upon reunion. (The successful resolution of this ambitendence represents the "rapprochement" between the mother and child.) The child continues to pursue the mother during periods of distress, but now the toddler actively gravitates and seeks out the father with a new intensity and purpose. Mahler et al. (1975) reports:

> The child's desire for expanded autonomy not only found expression in negativism toward mother and others, but also lead to active extension of the mother-child world: primarily to include father. Father, as a love object, from very early on belongs to an entirely different category of love objects than mother. In the children in our study we could observe that from about 16–17 months on, they liked to

spend increasingly long periods away from their mothers in the toddler room, and that boys and girls alike began to seek out observers, every so often the male observers, and to form quite close attachments to them. (p. 91)

Mahler further states that in this period the father remains uncontaminated by the intense ambivalence that effects the child's relationship with the mother, and that he plays an indispensable role in the resolution of that emotional ambivalence. In fact, the father's burgeoning role as an affect regulator places him on a par with the mother as an emotional object. The effect of this is momentous, as it signals the shift in the infant, at 18 months, from predominantly dyadic to triadic object relationships (Hadley, 1992; Tyson & Tyson, 1990).

This phenomenon has also been identified from the perspective of attachment theory. In the middle of the second year attachment ties with the mother are observed to loosen (Galenson & Roiphe, 1976), reflecting the end of the period of maternal imprinting. Concurrently, the formation of a second attachment system to the father becomes apparent (Schaffer & Emerson, 1964), as the child now expresses a separation response to the absence of either parent. Developmental psychological studies have shown that the quality of the toddler's attachment to the father is independent of that to the mother (Main & Weston, 1981). At 18 months both a "mother attachment system" and a "father attachment system" are operational (Abelin, 1971). It is now thought that the father at this point takes over from the early mother some significant portions of infantile attachment emotions (Blos, 1984). What has been called "father thirst" (Abelin, 1971) or "father hunger" (Herzog, 1980) (increased paternal attachment activation) has been observed in rapprochement age children who are deprived of contact with father.

Field (1985a) offers the intriguing proposal of serial attachments in which the mother initially serves both stimulation and arousal modulation functions, while the father subsequently serves the child's stimulation needs. It is well established that during early critical periods brain structural development is sensitive to various types of environmental stimulation (Diamond, 1976). I have previously argued that in the first year the mother is the major source of the environmental stimulation that facilitates (or inhibits) the experience-dependent maturation of the child's developing biological (especially neurobiological) structures. In the second year, however, the father now becomes an important source of arousal induction and reduction, and his modulation of stimulation will influence formation of those neural structures that are entering into a critical period of growth. In other words, in the middle of the second year the structural development of the child's brain is shifting from a maternal experience-dependent maturation of one postnatally developing cortical system to a paternal experience-dependent maturation of an even later developing cortical system. The question then is what brain region could be beginning to mature at this time?

PROPOSAL: THE OFFSET OF THE ORBITAL AND THE ONSET OF THE DORSOLATERAL PREFRONTAL CRITICAL PERIODS OCCUR IN THE MIDDLE OF THE SECOND YEAR

I suggest that these events represent a major developmental discontinuity, and that the offset of the maternal attachment-regulated orbital frontal critical period is followed by the onset of a paternal attachment-regulated critical period for the maturation of the other prefrontal system, the dorsolateral prefrontal association cortex. This region (see previous Fig. 4.7) develops later than the orbitofrontal (Nonneman et al., 1984; Van Eden & Uylings, 1985a), is the slowest to myelinate in the cortex, and is the last area of the brain to attain functional maturation (Fuster, 1980; Stuss & Benson, 1986). Unlike the orbital system it is innervated by nigral dopaminergic neurons (Porrino & Goldman-Rakic, 1982) and both receives (Morrison, Molliver, & Grzanna, 1979) and sends direct connections to locus coeruleus dorsal tegmental noradrenergic neurons (Arnstein & Goldman-Rakic, 1984).

Rosvold (1972) has demonstrated different subcortical counterparts of the two prefrontal systems. An orbital system includes the orbitofrontal cortex, ventrolateral caudate, medial pallidum, centromedian nucleus, hypothalamus, and septal nucleus. The dorsal system consists of the dorsolateral prefrontal cortex, anterodorsal caudate, lateral pallidum, subthalamic nucleus, and hippocampus. (Hippocampal postnatal development is known to be influenced by the environment; Jones & Smith, 1980; Wilson et al., 1986). Similarly, Bear (1983) differentiates two circuits—a ventral system including the orbitofrontal cortex, temporal lobe, amygdala, and hypothalmus, and a dorsal system, with such components as the dorsolateral prefrontal cortex, inferior parietal lobule, cingulate gyrus, and the locus coeruleus. Studies of neurological pathology of the two prefrontal areas have long described dissociable "personality syndromes." Orbitofrontal patients show sexual disinhibition, inappropriate social behavior, impulsiveness, a self-indulgent attitude, explosiveness, and increased motor activity, while dorsolateral patients manifest little overt emotion, depression, and reduced spontaneity of behavior (Stuss & Benson, 1983). Notice the similarity of these to the affective characterizations of the practicing and rapprochement periods.

The activity of coeruleal catecholaminergic neurons is immature in the early postnatal stages of brain development, and peripheral sensory input is required to elicit mature noradrenergic electrical activity (Nakamura et al., 1987). Although studies have yet to be done, I would think that extensive axonal sprouting of locus coeruleus catecholaminergic axons is initiated in the dorsolateral prefrontal cortex in the second half of the second year. The high levels of circulating corticosteroids in this period may influence this process. Indeed, the finding that cells of the locus coeruleus bind corticosterone during the postnatal period has been interpreted as demonstrating a direct role for glucocorticoids in the develop-

234

ment and functional activity of this noradrenergic cell group (Lauder & Krebs, 1986). It is well established that locus coeruleus noradrenergic neurons innervate brain microvessels (Kalaria, Stockmeiser, & Harik, 1989). Following this innervation, a noradrenergic trophic effect may induce the growth of cholinergic axons in deep layer dorsolateral neurons down toward sites on dendrites of locus coeruleus noradrenergic neurons in the midbrain. The critical period for the maturation of dorsolateral-coeruleal and dorsolateral-nigral connections may extend into early childhood. However the final maturation of this cortex, including the overproduction, pruning, and presevation of dorsolateral-cortical connections may be quite extended, perhaps into adolescence. Huttenlocher et al. (1982) have found that synaptic loss in the human frontal cortex continues until age 14. Diamond (1990) has suggested that the dorsolateral prefrontal cortex may not fully mature until puberty, an idea recently confirmed in a study by Segalowitz, Unsal, and Dywan (1992), and Thatcher (1991) has demonstrated that corticocortical connections with frontal regions occurs through age 16.

Arnstein and Goldman-Rakic (1984) have revealed a dissimilarity in afferent and efferent projections of the orbital and dorsolateral cortices, and suggest that this structural differentiation underlies the observed functional differences of these two prefrontal systems. The facts that the orbital system alone directly projects to the ventral tegmental area, hypothalamus and medullary dorsal vagal complex, and that the dorsolateral cortex alone projects to the (A6) noradrenergic neurons in the locus coeruleus (as opposed to the lateral tegmental [A2] noradrenergic neurons in the medulla) and (A9) dopaminergic neurons in the substantia nigra, are significant. The experience-dependent growth of descending fibers to the locus coeruleus from this later maturing prefrontal cortex occurs in the rapprochement period (end of the second and into the third year), thereby allowing for an arousal regulating function of this cortical structure. Gray (1982) identifies a noradrenergic pathway originating from the locus coeruleus as the physiological substrate of anxiety. A number of studies indicate that cell bodies in the locus coeruleus increase noradrenaline release during stress (Stone, 1975). Malloy (1987) argues that the modulation of limbic anxiety arousal is due to "descending dorsolateral inhibitory influences" (p. 210). Kagan (Kagan, Reznick, & Snidman, 1990, p. 223), in studying temperamental traits of inhibition and anxiety in 21-month-old infants (Mahler's rapprochement period), suggests an underlying "enhanced reactivity of the locus coeruleus." Kagan thus may be studying dorsolateral prefrontal ontogeny, specifically the inefficient capacity of this cortex to project to the locus coeruleus and thereby modulate locus coeruleus-generated anxiety (Redmond & Huang, 1979).

Thayer (1989) differentiates "tense arousal," associated with feelings of anxiety and fearfulness, that is located in a brain system separate from "energetic arousal," reflected in sensations of energy and vigor. The former covaries with negative affect, the latter with positive affect. (Energetic arousal may reflect the activity of mesolimbic dopaminergic neurons.) Tucker and Williamson (1984) propose that a dopaminergic tonic activation system associated with nigrostriatal (and not mesolimbic) dopaminergic projections involved in motor readiness is a neural substrate of anxiety. Heightened stimulation of this system that is involved in the regulation of movement may account for the elevated striate muscle activity that accompanies high levels of anxiety (Fridlund, Hatfield, Cottam, & Fowler, 1986). Gilbert (1989) refers to a defense system in the lower brain concerned with the avoidance of threat, injury, and attack; the psychobiology of this primitive escape system that detects danger arousal is prominent in phobias and panic disorders. I suggest that the ontogenetic formation of an internal anxiety regulating system, located in dorsolateral prefrontal—locus coeruleus connections, is influenced by the child's rapprochement phase experiences with the father. Herzog (1980) has reported that paternal absence in boys aged 18 to 28 months is associated with night terrors. Blos (1984) points out that "early experience of being protected by the father and caringly loved by him becomes internalized as a lifelong sense of safety" (p.3).

PROPOSAL: THE EXECUTIVE FUNCTIONS OF THE RIGHT AND LEFT HEMISPHERES ARE RESPECTIVELY MEDIATED BY THE ORBITOFRONTAL AND DORSOLATERAL PREFRONTAL CORTICES

The "nonlimbic" dorsolateral system, which is contiguous (Morecraft et al., 1992) yet functionally dissociable from the "limbic" orbital cortex (Kolb & Nonneman, 1975; Rosvold, 1972), utilizes a prefrontal circuitry based on dorsal tegmental (as opposed to lateral tegmental) noradrenergic and nigral (in lieu of ventral tegmental) dopaminergic neurons. (The dopamine-norepinephrine inter- actions of these two catecholamine groups are also known to be oppositional; Antelman & Caggiula, 1977). This system would be responsible for a prefrontal delayed response function with different operational characteristics and biases than the orbital system, and may be associated with left hemispheric onset and language maturation. The left cortical hemisphere is known to have its own mode of information processing, qualitatively different from the earlier forming right hemisphere (Gazzaniga & LeDoux, 1978). The fact that the "executive, control function" (Stuss & Benson, 1987) of the left hemisphere may be dominated by the dorsolateral prefrontal cortex versus the executive function of the right hemi- sphere by the orbital prefrontal cortex could account for the observed differential capacities of the hemispheres to assimilate information from the environment (Nichols & Cooper, 1991). Hecaen and Albert (1978, p. 414) have suggested that each hemisphere is involved in its own unique corticosubcortical functional system. Tucker (1992) argues that a neuropsychological theory of early emotion- al development needs to explain how each hemisphere interacts with subcortical mechanisms. It is now clear that while the right hemisphere is particularly well connected into the limbic system (Bear, 1983), the left is specialized for nonlimbic connections and operates at a distance from adaptive limbic constraints (Tucker, 1992).

Allen (1983) offers the hypothesis that hemispheric specialization may be a product of the existence and operation of smaller neural processing entities that differ in distribution and function within the hemispheres. The orbital prefrontal cortex is especially enlargened in the right hemisphere (Falk et al., 1990). Although the right hemisphere develops in carliest infancy, the growth spurt of the human left hemisphere does not begin until the latter part of the second year (Thatcher, Walker, & Giudice, 1987). An expansion of intracortical connections in the left hemisphere occurs at ages 1.5 to 3.0 years (Thatcher, 1992). These data suggest to me that the development of hemisphericity and cerebral dominance over the first years of life may reflect the differential ontogenetic emergence and operational capacities of the orbital and dorsolateral prefrontal hemispheric regulators. Their callosal connections may be centrally implicated in interhemispheric relationships. It is now established that the two hemispheres have different critical periods (Tucker, 1992) and exhibit differential developmental features (Thatcher, 1991), and that social development occurs independent of language development (Bretherton & Bates, 1984). The differences in the ontogeny of these two prefrontal systems may reflect the succession of more complex Jacksonian hierarchical cortical systems in development. These characterizations may describe the central nervous system events which have been suggested to underlie the observed major discontinuity in the development of mental abilities that occurs at 15—18 months (Lewis, Jaskir, & Enright, 1986), a period contemporaneous with the end of the first postnatal growth spurt of the brain (Epstein, 1978).

PROPOSAL: THE TWO PREFRONTAL SYSTEMS ARE RESPONSIBLE FOR THE HEMISPHERIC LATERALIZATION OF EMOTIONS

Speech production, long considered a product of the "verbal" left hemisphere, is particularly dependent upon prefrontal functioning. Recent tomographic and blood flow studies reveal that verbal fluency is specifically associated with an increase in metabolic activity of the left dorsolateral prefrontal cortex (Frith, Friston, Liddle, & Frackowiak, 1991; Warkentin et al., 1991). This prefrontal area is operative in the analysis of sequences of phonemes (Alexander, Benson, & Stuss, 1989). However, the orbital cortex is also known to be implicated in auditory functions (Fallon & Benevento, 1978). In fact, Ross (1983) points out the often overlooked finding that the right hemisphere is centrally and uniquely involved in the recognition and expression of the prosodic, affective components of language. It is now thought that the two hemispheres contain unique representational systems, affective-configurational in the right, and lexical-semantic in the left (Watt, 1990). Bruner (1986) postulates a narrative form of thought which arises earlier than a paradigmatic form is associated with autobiographic self-in-interaction-with-other experiences and is heavily affectively charged. Vitz (1990) concludes narrative thought is expressed in intonation and emotion-associated images, and is characterized as "language in the service of right hemisphere cognition." I shall expand on the importance of the child's affective relationship with the mother to the development of one word speech (Dromi, 1986) in later chapters. For now, I suggest that the child first imprints the developing right hemisphere to affective interchanges with the mother, thereby constructing non-verbal working models. This is followed in later infancy by the imprinting of his or her left hemisphere to affective transactions with the father, thus initiating the construction of verbal internal working models.

Krystal (1978a) differentiates two lines of emotional development, an infantile nonverbal affect system and a verbal adult system, and Gazzaniga (1985) now proposes a basic primitive affect system and a verbal-conceptual system which are localized in separate hemispheres. Research on the hemispheric lateralization of emotions reveals the existence of dual affective systems, a right hemisphere system dominant for the expression of nonverbal mood and affect, and a left hemisphere system involved in verbally mediated affective and mood states (Silberman & Weingartner, 1986). Wexler's investigations reveal that the right hemisphere responds to emotion-evoking stimuli out of conscious awareness, while the left responds more to conscious processing of emotional material (Wexler, Schwartz, Bonano, Warrenburg, Jammer, & Michaelis, 1989). Ohman's (1986) studies demonstrate two dissociable modes of processing of affective information, a rapid unconscious preattentive analysis of an emotional stimulus followed by a later conscious assessment of the relevance of the same emotional stimulus. The later forming, later acting dorsolateral system may be involved in left hemispheric function in verbally mediated affective states such as anxiety (Tyler & Tucker, 1982) and guilt (Bear, 1979; Joseph, 1992) (both of which are not considered to be "primitive" affects), as opposed to the earlier maturing, earlier acting orbitofrontal, right hemispheric dominance for nonverbal mood and affect such as elation (Joseph, 1988; Tucker, 1981), disgust (Davidson, 1992), and shame (Schore, 1991).

SUMMARY

In the middle of the second year a major transition in development occurs. During the progression from the end of the practicing to the beginning of the rapprochement stages the child's affective transactions with the mother become ambivalent and colored by negative affect. At this same time the father first begins to become an emotional object on a par with the mother, thereby shifting the infant from primarily dyadic to triadic object relations. His increasing role in arousal modulation and stimulation influences the experience-dependent growth of cortical areas that are structurally maturing at this time. In terms of socioemotional functioning, the movement from the practicing to the rapprochement phases represents the offset of the critical period for orbitofrontal growth and the onset of the critical period for the growth of the dorsolateral prefrontal cortex. The inceptive experience-dependent maturation of the dorsolateral system is suggested to be significantly influenced by the child's dyadic affective transactions with the "preoedipal" father.

This later maturing dorsolateral prefrontal cortex contains a set of subcortical connections that are distinct from the orbitofrontal cortex. This accounts for functional operations and capacities that are dissociable from the orbital and medial prefrontal regions. The orbital prefrontal cortex performs an executive control function in the right hemisphere, while the dorsolateral cortex performs such a role in the left hemisphere. The unique anatomical and functional properties of the two prefrontal systems account for the hemispheric differences in the lateralization of emotions.

The Dyadic Origin of Internal Shame Regulation

> [T]he child's excited response to a wide variety of stimuli will inevitably
> generate behavior that will be seen by parents, other adults, or children
> as inappropriate or wrong. From the child's vantage point, she is not
> really indecorous, she is merely indulging in natural self-expression; yet
> she is shamed. Children's great capacity for excitement and joy and the
> activity that these emotions generate greatly increases the range of possi-
> bilities for censurable behavior. The importance of a positive and non-
> punitive socialization of shame is evident.
>
> —Carroll E. Izard (1991)

The socialization of shame is an essential task of socioemotional development,
since this affect uniquely promotes sociability by acting as a restraint on self-
centeredness and egotism. This occurs in the late practicing period, a time in
which the caregivers supply repeated but supportive and not humiliating frustration of the child's illusion of grandiosity. In optimal situations this deflation
should be gradual and not precipitous and overwhelming; the nascent self is
plastic, yet fragile. White (1985) emphasizes that for continuing optimal socioemotional growth, the parents must communicate to the toddler the dual seemingly paradoxical messages that he is important and his needs and interests
special, and yet he is no more important and his needs and interests no more
paramount and unique than those of others. It is proposed that these are both
transmitted affectively and mainly nonverbally in the late practicing period. The
former is communicated in dyadic psychobiologically attuning mirroring experiences which amplify positive affect by stimulating higher levels of endorphin and
ventral tegmental dopaminergic activity. Elation and excitement fuel the height-

240

ened pleasure, grandiosity, and sense of specialness associated with narcissistic states. Misattunement-triggered shame stress socializations, which terminate the attachment need and inhibit the high arousal positive affects of enjoyment-joy and interest-excitement, are proposed to deflate primary narcissism and thereby mediate the latter message.

In this chapter I trace the dyadic events that facilitate the growth of an internal system that can adaptively regulate the duration and intensity of shame affect. The practicing caregiver's instigation of interactive repair transactions is instrumental to the child's psychobiological recovery from the stressful shame state. The internalization of this mechanism is critical to the individual's affect regulating capacities for the rest of the lifespan.

THE DYADIC REGULATION OF SOCIALIZING SHAME TRANSACTIONS IN THE PRACTICING CRITICAL PERIOD

Practicing period shame experiences facilitate socioemotional development. The adaptive psychophysiological function of this trophotropic low arousal affect is to act as an inhibitor, a counterforce to ongoing ergotropic high arousal which supports positively toned hedonic states. In direct contrast to the psychobiologically energized state, shame, an acutely painful stress-associated affect (Buck et al., 1970), triggers a rapid de-energizing state in the infant in which the deflated self, depleted of energy (Morrison, 1983) withdraws (Lichtenberg, 1989), recoils, and attempts to disappear from view from significant objects (Levin, 1967). As opposed to processes that promote and prolong contact and facilitate "merging with sources of satisfaction" in order to generate euphoric emotions and pleasurable activity, shame induces "ending contact and halting arousal" (Knapp, 1967). The sudden onset of shame distress reflects a rapid transition from a sympathetic-dominant state which sustains high levels of arousal (Field, 1985b), activity (Breese et al., 1973), and elation (Lipsitt, 1976) to a parasympathetic-dominant (Buss, 1979), low energy state. Physiologically, this represents an offset of ventral tegmental dopaminergic and an onset of lateral tegmental noradrenergic circuits and a reduction of endorphin and elevation of corticosteroid neurohormonal activty. The acute termination of the mesocortical dopamine system accounts for the "sudden decrement of mounting pleasure" (Tomkins, 1963), (the reduction in narcissism) observed in shame.

Fast (1984) observes that the child's emergence from the early state of infantile narcissism is marked by a sense of injury. Despite the trophic effects of this negative affect, the intensity and duration of this painful state must be regulated. Malatesta-Magai (1991) points out that the potent negative affect of shame is "too toxic an affect for older infants to sustain for very long" (p. 219). Moreover, the infant at this point cannot autoregulate this distress state without the cooperation of the caregiver. Demos and Kaplan (1986) articulate the central developmental principle of the dyadic regulation of infant negative affects:

> Although infants possess some capacity to modulate their negative affect states at a low level of intensity, they tend to continue to escalate, thereby compounding intensity with duration and producing a high density of affect. Infants are therefore dependent on caregivers to modulate, soothe, and maintain them at more moderate or optimal density levels. (p. 175)

Shame acts as "a powerful modulator of interpersonal relatedness" (Nathanson, 1987a), and indeed it ruptures the dynamic attachment bond between individuals. The sundering of this emotional connection triggers an internal experience of an "intersubjective disjunction" (Stolorow, Brandchaft, & Atwood, 1987). Although the individual has "broken a desired bond with another" (Basch, 1976), "the individual wishes to resume his or her commerce with the exciting state of affairs, to reconnect with the other, to recapture the relationship that existed before the situation turned problematic" (Tomkins, 1987, p. 144). Shame leaves the individual "turned in on himself, communicating to the world a greater or lesser degree of helplessness and entreaty" (Knapp, 1967, p. 522). This is most clearly observed in the nonverbal communicative behavior of the toddler. Tolpin (1986) describes a "self-righting" tendency in the infant which follows a deficient experience; the baby attempts to rebound from a deficit by looking up at and reaching toward the caregiver. This tendency represents the child's attempt to restore a secure attachment. Kaufman (1989, p. 36) states that after a shame-induced breach of the "interpersonal bridge," the preverbal child longs for reunion and reaches upward, expressing a spontaneous request to be held, an "attempt to reaffirm both self and the ruptured relationship, to feel restored and secure." Stern (1985) points out that the child uses facial behavior to invite higher levels of stimulation from the caregiver when the level of excitation has fallen too low. It has long been known that disorganization of emotional response occurs at very low, as well as very high energy levels (Duffy, 1941).

Thus the parents' active participation in regulating the child's shame state is critical to enabling him to shift from the negative affective state of deflation and reduced importance to the reestablished state of positive affect which underlies the narcissistic sense of specialness described by White. This transition involves and highlights the central role of stress recovery mechanisms in affect regulation. Stress has been defined as the occurrence of an asynchrony in an interactional sequence; further, "a period of synchrony, following the period of stress, provides a "recovery" period" (Chapple, 1970, p. 631). Aversive responses, such as the withdrawal of shame, provide signals to the caregivers to relieve distress (Lichtenberg, 1989). The overt behavior of the toddler, his facial expression of shock, his motionless headhang and body posture due to a reduction in tonus of the neck, body, and facial muscles causing a loss of the social smile, his averting the eyes, and the hallmark of shame, blushing, act as a signal to the attuned mother of his internal state of distress. Postural responses are known to serve communicative functions (Riskind, 1984). If the caregiver is sensitive, responsive, and emotionally approachable, especially if she initiates and reenters into arousal-inducing affect regulating mutual gaze visuoaffective (as well as tactile and auditory affect modulating) transactions, the dyad is psychobiologically reattuned, the object relations link (attachment bond) is reconnected, the arousal deceleration is inhibited, and shame is metabolized and regulated. These events define what Izard (1991) calls a positive socialization of shame.

THE PSYCHOBIOLOGY OF SHAME RECOVERY

The conscious experience of this decrescendo affect is psychophysiologically characterized as a rapidly amplifying negative affect state associated with an acute corticosteroid elevation of a hypothalmo-pituitary-adrenocortical stress response. Developmental psychobiological studies have demonstrated that the infant's glucocorticoid stress response is modulated by maternal cues (Stanton & Levine, 1990). In longer delays of parental responsiveness to this state of plummeting arousal, in extended periods of a loss of visuoaffective communication, the toddler's appeal turns to despair. At this point of more severe arousal dysregulation social referencing visuoaffective input may have to be supplemented by tactile-kinesthetic stimulation in the form of contact comfort (Harlow, 1958). Arousal modulation through tactile stimulation may be a component of "containing" or "holding" behaviors, a complex of emotional and physical maternal functions which the available "good enough mother" utilizes in the face of her infant's emotional/impulsive expressions (Winnicott, 1971).

Developmental endocrinological studies have shown that increased levels of touch and other somesthetic sensory modalities have both immediate and enduring effects (Denenberg & Zarrow, 1971). The short-term effects are demonstrated in the observations that maternal contact inhibits the infant's pituitary-adrenal response to stress (Stanton, Wallstrom, & Levine, 1987), and that subsequent to "handling stimulation" the infant's mobile exploratory behavior increases (Weinberg, Krahn, & Levine, 1978). The long-term effects are reflected in the facts that early postnatal handling alters glucocorticoid receptor concentrations in the frontal cortex that are expressed in adulthood (Meaney et al., 1985), and that glucocorticoid-sensitive neurons are involved in terminating the adrenocortical stress response (Sapolsky, Krey, & McEwen, 1984). As a result of these critical period experiences, in the face of a subsequent novel stimulus the infant shows a lesser corticoid output (Levine, Haltmeyer, Karas, & Denenberg, 1967), a more rapid return of corticosterone to baseline levels (Hess, Denenberg, Zarrow, & Pfeifer, 1969), and an increased level of hypothalamic corticotropin releasing factor (CRF) (Zarrow, Campbell, & Denenberg, 1972).

CRF is known to increase exploratory behavior (Britton, Koob, & Rivier, 1982), to produce behavioral activation and an increase in emotionality (Sutton et al., 1982), and to play an important role in the regulation of higher-order information processing of association and limbic regions (Lewis et al., 1989). The autonomic dysregulation in shame may thus be attenuated by CRF, a neurohormone which plays an important role in the "control of central autonomic function" and in "mediating visceral and behavioral responses to stress" (Aguilera, Millan, Hauger, & Catt, 1987). Aguilera et al. state that CRF "results in activation of the hypothalamic-pituitary-adrenal axis and the sympathetic nervous system, with consequent visceral, metabolic and behavioral responses" (p. 55). The recovery from shame states of interpersonal stress that accompany attachment breaks may be psychobiologically mediated by CRF. The stimulation of sympathetic nervous system activity by hypothalamic CRF (Brown et al., 1982a,b) may account for the resumption of sympathetic arousal and activity, and the regulation of endorphin production by CRF (Vale et al., 1981) may activate positive affect required for stress reduction. It was proposed earlier that the visual perception of positive affect in the facial display of a mirroring other stimulates opioid peptide production. Opiate activity has been associated with the operation of a safety system associated with positive affectivity within the individual (Gilbert, 1989). This psychobiological mechanism may act throughout the lifespan, and may underlie the assertions by social support theorists that a supportive other tranquilizes the nervous system and makes the individual less reactive to perceived stress (House, 1981), and that positive feeling states enhance one's capacity to adapt to stress (Cohen & Syme, 1985).

This stress regulating reparative reunion pattern is equivalent to "vitalizing reciprocity," a practicing refueling transaction in which the underaroused infant is energized by the mother, thereby transforming negative into positive hedonic tone and unfocused into focused attention in as little as 10 seconds! (Brent & Resch, 1987). The socializing mother's shame stress-triggering actions rapidly shift the hyperaroused practicing infant in a sympathetic-dominant state to a hypoaroused parasympathetic-dominant state, from sympathetic predominant "ergotropic" to parasympathetic predominant "trophotropic" arousal (Scherer, 1986). Her subsequent shame stress-regulating interventions induce a psychobiological state transition, the reignition of the child's sympathetic activity which can support higher levels of arousal. Tomkins (1962, 1963) notes that shame is activated when one expects another to be familiar but the other suddenly appears unfamiliar. He also posits that negative emotion in the infant is displaced by the "sudden appearance of the familiar mother," and that the cessation of the negative affect of shame activates the positive affects of joy and interest. Izard (1991) observes that

> During the experience of joy all of our internal systems function easily and smoothly, and both our mind and body have time for recuperation or recovery from periods of stress and strain. (p. 139)

This is biochemically mediated in the adaptive resumption of endogenous CRF influenced endorphin production and reactivation of the ventral tegmental, meso-cortical dopamine system which is responsible for the reinstitution of arousal, activity, and joy associated with positive affective states. Such a mechanism may account for the observations that laughter is associated with the reduction of shame and that laughter is physiologically antagonistic to shame (M. Lewis, 1992).

The caregiver's affect regulating activity thus enables the infant to transition from a low energy, low-keyed state of low interest (Mahler, 1979) to a reen-ergized state of "alert inactivity" (Beebe & Lachman, 1988a), that is, activated interest, and to switch from negative/passive to positive/active mood. The infant thus psychobiologically cycles from a pre-shame state of elation and excite-ment—of "alert activity" (Nathanson, 1987a), to a shame state of passive, "fro-zen inactivity" (Knapp, 1967), and thence to a post-shame state of "alert inac-tivity." Regulatory activities that generate modulated interest are adaptive, since Izard (1991) emphasizes that interest is the affect that operates most frequently in guiding attention, and that moderate levels of this positive affect organize suffi-cient energy to sustain behavior over long periods of time. The caregiver's dual function in arousal reduction and induction facilitates the establishment of a moderate level of infant arousal, a state known to be associated with focused attention and positive affect (Malmo, 1959).

The mother and infant thus dyadically negotiate the state transition of affect, cognition, and behavior that occurs in shame transactions and breaks of attach-ment. Sroufe (1989b) has emphasized the principle that in order to meet the changing needs of the developing child the relationship system must change in response to both internal demands and external challenges. Sander (1988) refers to an infant internal state of "regulatory equilibrium" which occurs when infant and caregiver are in a state of coordination and harmony of regulation, and which is critical to the early organization of psychic structure. Malatesta-Magai (1991) concludes that "the process of reexperiencing positive affect following negative experience may teach a child that negativity can be endured and conquered" (p. 218). Demos (1991) characterizes infant resilience as the capacity of the child and the parent to transition from positive to negative back to positive affect.

THE INTERNALIZATION OF INTERACTIVE REPAIR
TRANSACTIONS

This recovery mechanism is proposed to underlie the phenomenon of "interactive repair" (Tronick, 1989) in which participation of the caregiver is responsible for the reparation of dyadic misattunements. (It is now established that although infants engage in social play with fathers, when stressed they seek the primary caregiver—the mother—for relief from distress; Lichtenberg, 1989.) In this process the mother who induces interactive stress and negative emotion in the infant is instrumental to the transformation of this affect into positive emotion. Tronick holds that under the aegis of a caregiver who is sensitive and cooperative in this reparative process, the infant develops an internal representation of himself as effective, of his interactions as positive and reparable, and of the caregiver as reliable. Similarly, Lamb (1981) argues that salient "distress-relief sequences" initiated by the accessible mother facilitate a transition in the infant to a state of controlled arousal, quiet alertness, and responsiveness. This allows the infant to recover from negative affect states, to construct a multimodal nonverbal concept of the caregiver as predictable, and permit him to develop the capacity for anticipation of relief and a sense of his own efficacy. The same concept is presented by Gilbert and Trower (1990) who emphasize the immense developmental importance of parental "reassurance signals" after agonistic encounters. Winnicott (1971) describes the "good enough" mother's "holding" or "containing" function as the capacity to "stay with" the child through its emotional/impulsive expressions, "to hold the situation in time." Pine (1986b) notes that "it is in these moments of delay in the face of beginning distress, as well as in contented and quiescent periods, that much of learning and the moves toward higher order functioning takes place" (p. 453).

These communications from the emotionally responsive mother follow in a timely fashion misattuned shame socialization transactions which interrupt the flow of a communicative tie to anticipated regulatory functions. Dyadic reparative socioaffective transactions that occur after shame regulatory failures and which provide comfort and arousal regulation allow for a resumption of close proximity, affiliative, and exploratory behaviors in the short term, and build a positive schemata of the self and an autoregulatory recovery capacity to cope with future socioaffective stress in the long term. Most importantly, this reparative system allows for the essential adaptive capacity to reactivate the attachment system and reform the attachment bond after the affective object relations link has been transiently severed. Izard (1991) refers to "the effort to repair and strengthen the self after experiencing intense shame" (p. 344).

Settlage asserts that the mother-child relationship is temporarily disrupted by the stress of maternal limit setting, protective, or disciplinary intrusions on the behavior of the 16 month-old toddler. His research (Settlage et al., 1990) reveals that intrusion stress (like Ainsworth's "strange situation" separation stress) elicits a distress reaction which represents a failure of self-regulation in the child. Consequently, the toddler initiates an "appeal" toward the mother to enter into an "interactional phase." During this interaction the attuned mother accepts and assuages the child's feelings, thereby enabling him to reestablish emotional regulation and return to autonomous activity. This work emphasizes the important fact that the attuned bond of the relationship can be stressed and degraded by the mother even when she is in close proximity and not physically separated from the child. Maternal-instigated breaks in attuned attachment, infant distress, and initiation of an appeal to enter into reunion affect regulating transactions occur regularly in the proximate relations of the dyad, and not [...] physically separated. Most importantly, Settlage argues tha[...] sent repeated circumscribed units of developmental interac[...] nalized and which mediate the formation, integration, and [...] chic structures that support developing self-regulation an[...] manner the mutual regulatory function of the child-pare[...] second year serves as a model for identification in the child's development of self-regulation (C.F. Settlage, personal communication, August 10, 1989).

The frustrative state of shame and the mother's response to this particular affect expression are stored as a unitary "interactive representation" (Beebe, 1986), allowing for the developmental transition of external to internal regulation via increasing levels of internalization (McDevitt, 1980). From a psychoanalytic viewpoint, Loewald (1970) has emphasized the important principle that what becomes internalized are not objects but interactions and relationships. Non-psychoanalytic workers now also propound that the child internalizes both his role and aspects of the caregiver's role in the child-parent relationship (Sroufe & Fleeson, 1986). Wilson (Wilson et al., 1990) concludes that the experience of being with a self-regulating other is incorporated into an interactive representation. The critical importance of the mother's affective response to the reengaging toddler at reunions after attachment breaks has been detailed by this author in an earlier work (Schore, 1991). These practicing period events are critical to the future development of an internalized shame affect regulator. In that work, I also presented evidence to show that the child's experiencing of an affect and the caregiver's response to this particular affect are internalized as an affect regulating interactive representation. Under the aegis of the mother's regulation of practicing shame states, shame comes to play an adaptive central active role in the regulation of emotional expression, and therefore for more effective social interaction (Izard, 1971).

On the other hand, without the mother's modulation of prolonged socialization-associated shame distress states, without her participation in shame stress-regulating interactive repair, an enduring sensorimotor self-concept is created in which "one's affective needs generally are somehow unacceptable and shameful" (Basch, 1985, p. 35). Without access to the mother's affect regulating function, the child remains stuck fast for long periods of time in a parasympathetic-dominant state of conservation-withdrawal, a state in which dysphoric cognitive-affective patterns color all subjective experience (Powles, 1992). This strategy is utilized, according to Powles, in overwhelming interpersonal situations such as humiliation, rejection, and abandonment which elicit "the cognitive estimate that the self is helpless and the future hopeless" (p. 418).

Helplessness, whose origin and quality is in the experience of the abandoned 1-to 2-year child, and which can be equated with despair, relates to the dependency of young children and their need for help and protection. In helplessness, the distressed person depends (unsuccessfully) on the environment for relief, and feels personally powerless to change matters . . . the child who learns hopelessness comes to believe that the self is inadequate, that one's deficiencies are to blame for one's powerlessness, and that there is no hope that others will come to the rescue. (Powles, 1992, p. 416)

M. Lewis (1992) concludes that failure in the parent-child relationship leads to pathology through an enduring disposition to shame. The "ubiquitous and unrelieved" experience of of shame, "one of the least tolerable affects for humans" (Malatesta-Magai, 1991), therefore becomes associated with an expectation of a painful self disorganizing state which cannot be interpersonally nor intrapersonally regulated, and therefore is consciously avoided or "bypassed" (H. B. Lewis, 1971).

When shame is not acknowledged, it is almost impossible to mend the bond. In itself, unacknowledged shame creates a form of self-perpetuating entrapment in one's own isolation. If one hides this sense from the other due to shame, it creates further shame, which creates a further sense of isolation. (Retzinger, 1989, p. 5)

The central role of early unregulated shame experiences in the etiology of all primitive psychopathologies and psychosomatic diseases will be greatly elaborated in future chapters.

SUMMARY

In practicing period socializing shame transactions the mother induces a stressful state of hypoarousal in the infant. The child can not autoregulate this negative affect, and nonverbally appeals to the mother to reinstigate psychobiologically attuned object relations. This reattunement is mediated by the mother's reinitiating dyadic visuoaffective transactions that regenerate positive affect in the child. Her shame stress-regulating interventions allow for a state transition in the infant—the parasympathetic dominant arousal of the shame state is supplanted by the reignition of sympathetic-dominant arousal that supports increased activity and positive affect. The latter effect is neurochemically mediated by a resumption of CRF-inducing endorphin production and a reactivation of the ventral tegmental dopaminergic limbic circuit.

The interactive repair transactions of this critical period have not only short-term but also long-term effects on the child's developing socioemotional capacities. The experience of being with a regulating (or dysregulating) other is incorporated into an enduring interactive representation. Such representations can be accessed in the future in order to autoregulate shame states. On the other hand, without the mother's responsive cooperation in shame repair, the infant remains in lingering parasympathetic-dominant states of anaclitic depression. These early unregulated shame experiences lie at the core of various developmental psychopathologies.

19 Socialization and Experience-Dependent Parcellation

Ontogenetic adaptations may require the creation of structures and functions that are adaptively suitable at one stage but which may be unnecessary for or incompatible with adaptations at later stages. This requires a mechanism whereby the earlier characteristics can be eliminated, suppressed, or reorganized.

—Ronald W. Oppenheim (1980)

In its strictest evolutionary form, the perspective of ontogenetic adaptation is based on the assumption that natural selection can operate on each point in development. This is an important idea because it directs our attention to specialized responses of the organism to specific environmental challenges.

—Jeffrey R. Alberts (1987)

The quality and quantity of the caregivers' mirroring, shame inducing, and especially shame regulating transactions which facilitate interactive repair are critical to the loss of ontogenetic adaptations and the emergence of new function the end of the practicing period. Kagan (1986) asserts the principle that each developmental phase can be characterized by both gains and losses with respect to adaptation to that period. Early practicing high levels of locomotor exploratory behavior, positive emotion, and elated mood were previously conceptualized as ontogenetic adaptations to the ontogenetic niche which generates elevated levels of socioaffective stimulation. This stimulation facilitates the growth of mesocortical axons into the orbitofrontal cortex, and trophic factors induce its early structural maturation. The expansion of the ventral tegmental limbic circuit into

249

this frontolimbic cortex is responsible for its involvement in the "pleasurable qualities of social interaction" (Panksepp, Siviy, & Normansell, 1985).

Oppenheim (1980) points out that the stage-associated decline of functional ontgenetic adaptations implies a mechanism whereby structure is progressively eliminated or reorganized. In this chapter I suggest that this mechanism involves a *parcellation* process, a competitive elimination of excess axons and pruning of overproduced synapses that occurs during postnatal development of diverse regions of the cerebral cortex (Rakic et al., 1986). More specifically, I contend that practicing socialization experiences induce a Darwinian parcellation of the orbitofrontal cortex. This allows for its final dual-circuit anatomical maturation and the onset of emergent adaptive functions in the second half of the second year.

THE PARCELLATION OF THE ORBITOFRONTAL CORTEX

Parcellation involves the selective loss of connections and redistributions of inputs in the developing nervous system. This process has been implicated in the mechanism by which brain areas become increasingly complex, thereby allowing for the appearance of an emergent function (Ebbesson, 1980). Ebbesson specifically notes that this type of rewiring may occur in imprinting phenomena, the irreversible stamping of early experience on the developing nervous system. Huttenlocher (1990) finds a very substantial loss of cortical synapses occurs in the postnatal period, and concludes that cortical synapse elimination plays an especially important role in the development of more complex systems. The ontogenetic decline in cortical depth is influenced by environmental stimulation-induced neural activity (Cummins et al., 1982).

The same developmental remodeling mechanism is described by Prechtl (1982), who emphasizes that a reduction in the number of axons is mostly expressed in the partial elimination of collateral axon sprouts. Purves and Lichtman (1980) present evidence to show that the reduction of axons may be a general feature of neural development. Cowan (Cowan, Fawcett, O'Leary, & Stanfield, 1984) concludes that the programmed retraction of axon collaterals in early life is critical to "fine-tuning" adjustments of the circuitry of the developing nervous system. Similarly, Stanfield (1984) states that axon collateral elimination occurs in the infant primate's cortex, and that such alterations in the patterns of neural connections that occur during postnatal development are responsible for adaptive developmental changes.

I have suggested that at the end of the first year an excess of ventral tegmental dopaminergic axon collaterals exists in the orbitofrontal cortex. This presynaptic amplification is matched by a postnatal increase in D1 dopamine receptors (Richfield et al., 1989) in the deep layers of this prefrontal cortex. The expansion of the dopaminergic ventral tegmental limbic circuit and mesocortical dopamine into the frontolimbic cortex is responsible for the ontogenetic adaptations of the early practicing period. A retraction and degeneration of orbitofrontal dopaminergic axons in the late practicing period is postulated to underlie the disorganization of excitatory synapses at this time. In fact, a decline of D1 dopamine receptors positively coupled to adenylate cyclase has been observed to take place in the "early stages" of human infancy (Cortes, Gueye, Pazos, Probst, & Palacios, 1989).

I have also argued that due to the action of mesocortical dopamine and other neurotrophic factors, an amplification of orbitofrontal cholinergic synapses occurs in the early practicing period. Catecholamines are known to be critically involved in "experience-dependent synaptic changes" and in local plasticity and stabilization phenomena (Aoki & Siekevitz, 1988). Indeed, a period of maximum synaptic excess is known to occur in the human prefrontal cortex at the end of the first year and subsequently declines (Huttenlocher, 1979). It is now accepted that "early regressive changes in the nervous system constitute fundamentally important mechanisms in the ontogeny and regulation of behavior" (Carlson, Earls, & Todd, 1988, p. 20). Indeed, synapse elimination is an integral process of normal cortical development (Huttenlocher et al., 1982). In the latest conceptualization of developmental synaptology, Edelman, Gall, and Cowan (1987) propose, "In postnatal life, the responses of networks and a major part of their historical alteration by behavior depend upon how synapses are altered" (p. 303). Such alterations of early developing synapses are known to be related to their functional use/disuse (Ruijter, Baker, de Jong, & Romijn, 1991). Greenough (1987) refers to the "activity-dependent preservation of synapses."

SHAME SOCIALIZATION AND THE REWIRING OF
ORBITOFRONTAL LIMBIC CIRCUITRY

In the progression through the practicing stage, the social environmental niche of the caregiver-infant dyad changes. Imprinting-influenced expansive changes are known to coincide with selective degeneration of other local neural systems (Wolff, 1979). Evidence was previously presented to support the assertion that a major response to the alteration of the socioemotional niche in the late practicing period is the reduced growth of the excitatory ventral tegmental mesocortical dopaminergic and the intensified expansion of the lateral tegmental noradrenergic innervation in the orbitofrontal cortex. The changes in the socioaffective niche, reflected in the changes in dyadic object relations, are critical to the experience-dependent expansion and retraction of the two competing catecholamine systems which innervate and neurotrophically regulate the synaptic relations and the final maturational profile of the orbitofrontal cortex. The role of competitive processes in establishing neural structure is a general organizing principle for brain development (Greenough & Black, 1992). There is now a large body of evidence to support the general principle that cortical networks are achieved "first by overabundant production of synaptic connections, then by a process of competitive interaction to select those connections that are effectively entrained to environmental information" (Tucker, 1992, p. 75). In developing orbitofrontal cortex the competitive interaction is between the two catecholamines of the ventral and lateral tegmental limbic circuits that regulate growth and mediate environmental influences, and the environmental information refers to changes in the socioaffective environment.

Shame stress, which functions as a first central step in the socialization process (Thrane, 1979), triggers a sudden offset of sympathetic and onset of parasympathetic vagal activity (MacCurdy, 1930; Schore, 1991) and an influx of autonomic proprioceptive and kinesthetic feedback into awareness (Lewis, 1971). Orbitofrontal regulated parasympathetic autonomic effects (Fuster, 1980) are expressed in its control of vagal tone (Porges, 1984). Shame inducing transactions trigger an elevated corticosteroid level in the infant's brain, and this would suppress CRF production (Yates & Moran, 1974) and thereby reduce sympathetic nervous system activity (Brown et al., 1982b) and endorphinergic activation of the ventral tegmental dopamine system (Stinus et al., 1980). In Chapter 16 I suggested that critical period growth of ventral tegmental dopaminergic axons is optimal under high levels of stimulation, while lateral tegmental noradrenergic axonal growth is facilitated under low intensity stimulation. I also offered the proposal that variations in orbitofrontal subplate biochemistry determine the growth behaviors of the different local catecholaminergic circuitries. The competitive dominance of parasympathetic lateral tegmental over sympathetic ventral tegmental growth during the late practicing period and the socioaffective experience-dependent competitive elimination of excess dopaminergic axons and overproduced synapses (parcellation) account for the shame-induced loss of the ontogenetic adaptation of high levels of locomotor exploratory behavior and of heightened positive emotion which underlies the elated mood of the early practicing period. The socioemotional experience-dependent degeneration and disorganization of earlier imprinted limbic circuit patterns which produces a rewiring of orbitofrontal columns may thus be the neurodevelopmental mechanism responsible for the disappearance of transient neural, physiological, and hormonal phenomena (Oppenheim, 1981) that support previous ontogenetic adaptations.

Dyadic shame regulating transactions in the practicing critical period also generate permanent effects in the frontolimbic cortex. The interactive regulation of this negative affect state has been proposed to be mediated by the psychobiological resumption of hypothalamic CRF production. Infantile handling, tactile stimulation associated with comforting "holding" and "containing" experiences provided by the mother, induces long-lasting changes on the glucocorticoid receptors concentrations in the adult frontal cortex (Meaney et al., 1985) and permanent modifications of later hypothalamic CRF levels (Campbell, Zarrow, & Denenberg, 1973). These same experiences produce structural changes specifically in the early maturing right hemisphere (Denenberg et al., 1978). This hemisphere is known to be specialized for tactile perception on both sides of the body (Boll, 1974; Carmon & Benton, 1969) and for the perception and recall of spatial patterns of touch in nonverbal memory (Milner & Taylor, 1972). CRF is known to induce the release of pituitary ACTH and beta endorphin (Vale, Spiess, Rivier, & Rivier, 1981), and endorphins act as trophic regulators of neural development (Zagon & McLaughlin, 1988) and along with CRF (Kalivas, Duffy, & Latimer, 1987) activate the ventral tegmental dopamine system (Stinus, Koob, Ling, Bloom, & LeMoal, 1980). Since shame regulating interactive repair transactions involve reactivation of ventral tegmental activity, this maternal function may be important to the maintenance and preservation of mesocortical dopamine axons which innervate the right cortex during the late practicing period and therefore to the final wiring patterns of this limbic circuit in the mature orbitofrontal cortex. The completed orbitofrontal mesocortical dopamine innervation pattern may regulate the future trajectory of the child's evolving attachment-affiliative and exploratory-assertive capacities.

PROPOSAL: THE PRIMARY CAREGIVER FUNCTIONS AS AN AGENT OF NATURAL SELECTION THAT INFLUENCES THE STABILIZATION OR ELIMINATION OF PERMANENT ORBITOFRONTAL-LIMBIC CONNECTIONS

Changeux and Dehaene (1989) point out that the selective stabilization of synapses which have functional significance in a particular environment occurs in cortical association areas. During postnatal sensitive periods this preservation of synaptic connections is an "activity dependent," "Darwinian" process. Edelman (1987) has recently emphasized that the concept of organismic competition for survival also applies at the neuronal level, a principle earlier promulgated by Jacobson (1978), Ramon y Cajal (1929/1960), and indeed Darwin (1888). It is commonly accepted that the fundamental process of natural selection occurs in the context of the interaction of the developing organism and its surrounding environment. Hofer (1990) refers to the neonate's "inherited environment of the mother's body," and Emde (1988) emphasizes the salient point that the infant's environment "is contained within the specifically-experienced caregiver relationship." It is now thought that early postnatal development represents an experiential shaping of genetic potential and that specific gene-environment interactions occur over the course of development (Kendler & Eaves, 1986). An important finding of recent quantitative genetic research demonstrates the importance of "nonshared" (individual, unique) environmental influences which are expressed in "differential parental treatment" (Plomin, Rende, & Rutter, 1991). Thus different children of the same mother experience unique early interactions with her. This principle is also emphasized in the current psychoanalytic literature:

> If a mother has eight children, there are eight mothers. This is not simply because of the fact that the mother was different in her attributes to each of the eight. If she could have been the same with each . . . each child would have had his or her own mother seen through individual eyes. (Winnicott, 1986, p. 40)

Stern (1985) refers to the importance of selective attunement in the process described by Lichtenstein (1961) as "the infant becoming the child of his particular mother." Similarly, Papousek et al. (1991) point out that parental interventions which mediate preverbal affective communication "may appear finely adjusted to each infant in individual cases."

In referring to the importance of "the information ecology of early life," Tucker (1992) stresses that the most important information for ongoing development is conveyed by the social environment. Schaffer (1984) describes:

> A large part of early stimulation is of a social nature: the mother is still the singlemost frequent stimulus the infant meets, and even his encounters with the rest of the environment are largely mediated by the mother. (p. 52)

Parental behavior is now conceptualized as a most important source of stimulation in the child's ontogenetic niche (West & King, 1987), and a dramatic alteration of ontogenetic niches accompanied by infant adaptive adjustments is known to occur in postnatal development (Alberts, 1987).

> Ontogenetic adaptation is easily appreciated by considering an organism's progress through developmental stages to be a sequence of adaptations, shaped by natural selection, by which the myriad proximate adjustments are made to changing habitats so that the organism can survive and reproduce. The emphasis here is on the sequence of requirements imposed by the developmental milieu. (p. 459)

Alberts adds that a series of environmental changes in the social surround necessitates sudden adaptive shifts. According to Lewontin (1978), "The concept of adaptation implies a preexisting world that poses a problem to which an adaptation is the solution" (p.213). In a recent paper on the emergent discipline of evolutionary psychology, Tooby and Cosmides (1989, p. 30) assert that "natural selection defines information processing problems the organism must be able to solve (in a given adaptive context)." This principle also applies to the processing of social information. I propose that the mechanism of natural selection is operative during times of reorganization in critical periods when new adaptations are required in response to the stress of changing socioemotional environmental conditions.

In the first year of life the most significant environmental challenge the human infant faces is the establishment of a dyadic system with the mother, which can process synchronous and asynchronous socioaffective information and higher levels of arousal. In other words the challenge of the first year is to form an attachment to the mother, that is, to enter into psychobiologically attuned trans-actions with her at higher and higher levels of social stimulation. This socioaffec-tive stimulation facilitates the experience-dependent brain growth spurt of the first year, since "it is the social environment that calls forth and acts on the developing nervous system, exploiting what plasticity there is" (Gilbert, 1992a, p. 135–136). Anders and Zeanah (1989) posit the importance of attachment relates to the immaturity of the infant's nervous system and "the evolutionary advantage of allowing environmental circumstances to influence postnatal devel-opment" (p. 61). Ainsworth (1967) underscores the fact that attachment is essen-tially internal, that it is built into the developing infant's nervous system as a result of his transactions with his mother. I have suggested that such attachment experiences specifically and directly influence the early maturation of the orbit-ofrontal cortex, a corticolimbic structure that is critically involved in attachment processes (Steklis & Kling, 1985).

In the last quarter of the first year, these experience-dependent attachment episodes culminate in the formation of an efficient communicational system in the early practicing period which can rapidly generate high levels of enjoyment-joy and interest-excitement. Izard (1991) posits that "In evolutionary perspec-tive, joy complements the emotion of interest in guaranteeing that human beings will be social creatures" (p. 149). Positive affect is a prerequisite for the child's emergent ability to form social bonds with other members of the species, and this in turn enables the individual to later enter into intimate sexual interactions through which it can pass on its genome. It is said that natural selection favors characterisitics that maximize an individual's contribution to the gene pool of succeeding generations. In humans this may entail not so much competitive and aggressive traits as an ability to enter into a positive affective relationship with a member of the opposite sex. MacLean (1958) has stressed the unique import of the limbic system to the preservation of the species. In addition, the capacity to regulate positive affect underlies the capacity to securely explore the physical environment. Early practicing period transactions may therefore significantly influence the trajectory of "positive affectivity," a measure of the individual's capacity to experience joy and pleasure and of one's general engagement in the world (Watson & Clark, 1988). It is quite apparent that by any Darwinian standard, these capacities are adaptive!

With the onset of socialization in the second year, the socioaffective environ-ment changes dramatically, and the caregivers' increased expectations require another adaptive shift in the toddler. The socializing, emotional stress-inducing late practicing mother continues to act as the primary evolutionary agent of Darwinian natural selection. Cairns et al. (1990) emphasize that periods of severe environmental challenge represent opportunities for the potential of achieving new patterns of social adaptation. These challenges include the more demanding caregiver expectations that are embedded in socialization experiences. Spitz (1965) argues that frustration is built into development and is the most potent catalyst of evolution at nature's disposal. Davidson (1991) holds that "certain types of environmental challenges presented at the appropriate point of development may have long-term consequences on asymmetric brain function" (p. 127). More specifically, maternal stress and stress regulating object relations transactions, which significantly change over the course of the practicing period, act as a selection pressure to critically shape the activity-dependent Darwinian process of the selective stabilization and elimination of specific dual subcortical catecholaminergic connections with the anatomically maturing orbitofrontal cortex. Gilbert (1992a) describes that the interaction the child has with its mediators influences the maturation of connections within his developing limbic system. In other words, the primary caregiver is potently involved in the critical period imprinting of the dual limbic circuits in the infant's maturing right frontolimbic cortex. This area of the cerebral cortex is critically involved in the adaptive capacities of regulating social behavior (de Bruin, 1990; Kolb & Whishaw, 1990) and monitoring emotional responses to environmental stimuli (Rolls, 1986). In very recent work on developing emotions and cortical networks Tucker (1992) concludes that cortical paralimbic networks are formed through "ontogenetic plasticity, that is, through a natural selection of those connections that match the data in the environment."

In his current work, Galaburda is directly addressing the important question of how individual patterns in cortical structural organization and their eventual relationship to function develop. In this attempt to more fully understand and precisely specify the principles which elucidate the ontogeny of anatomical variations and individual differences in brain organization, he points out that both heritable and environmental factors influence developmental plasticity. In discussing extant experimental explorations of the effects of environmental influences on the development of brain morphology, he notes:

> For instance, the exact topography and size of distinct architectonic areas in the cortex reflect, at least in part, inputs from the periphery that can be environmentally modified. Although the environmental manipulations have thus far been severe. . . .in very young animals, it is possible that more subtle modifications of the visual input lead to limited cortical changes as well. Together with shifts in cytoarchitectonic topography and size, there may be accompanying changes in cortical connectivity. (Galaburda, Rosen, & Sherman, 1990, p. 530)

I suggest that this "subtle" modification of visual input includes variations of visuoaffective input from the primary source of emotional stimulation in the child's environment, and that the resultant changes in cytoarchitectonic topography and connectivity which take place at this time occur in maturing orbitofrontal areas in the anterior cortex that are highly responsive to visual changes that are motivationally relevant (Mesulam, 1985).

In light of Hofer's (1983) assertion that the mother regulates the neurochemistry of the infant's maturing brain, dyadic affect transactions may specify the nature of the activity of "activity-dependent selective preservation of synapses" (Greenough, 1987) which imprints the connectivity of the frontolimbic cortex. Kaas (1987) has propounded the principle that:

> The apparent importance of self-organizing processes in development, based on activity patterns, suggests that some specific features of cortical organization, such as the topographic details of sensory and motor representations, the border alignment of fields, and types of modular grouping of neurons, could be side products of timing sequences in the building of brains. (p. 149)

These "timing sequences" are defined in specific ordered critical periods of regional growth and maturation. Stage-specific socioaffective imprinting experiences activate neurochemical internal regulatory signals that act as internal "clocks" to coordinate the timing of developmental processes (Lauder & Krebs, 1986), thereby driving the mechanism by which the synaptogenesis responsible for postnatal brain growth is critically influenced by events at the interpersonal and intrapersonal levels (Scheflen, 1981). These psychoneurobiological events lead to the establishment of a differentiated dual component orbital frontolimbic system.

Tucker (1992) refers to the developmental phenomenon of "ontogenetic sculpting, as information-dependent competitive elimination provides an epigenetic articulation of the genetic plan." Carlson et al. (1988) emphasize the importance of "psychological" factors in the "pruning" or "sculpting" of neural networks, as in the postnatal frontal, limbic, and temporal cortices, which support the developmental emergence of specialized and adaptive behavioral functions. Gelb (1989) points out that during the course of ontogeny the "social-interpersonal experience of the individual" produces "changes in the number, interrelationships, and integrity of cells and ultimately even structural changes such as the size of the brain and its ventricles" (p. 549). During the critical period for socialization, "psychological," "object relational" experiences thus permanently influence the printing and fine-tuning of emotion regulating limbic circuits in the developing cerebral cortex. Shame socialization transactions intensify parasympathetic activity and support the vagal innervation of orbitofrontal cerebral areas. Vagal tone has recently been demonstrated to directly affect the emergent capacity for social responsivity (Campos, Campos, & Barrett, 1989; Fox, 1989; Gotteman & Fainsilber Katz, 1989). The developmental reorganization of this frontolimbic structure involves its progression from single to dual limbic circuit operations. The ontogeny of these structure-function relationships may account for the Freudian characterized adaptive maturational transformation of "primary" to "secondary narcissism," and of the pleasure into the reality principle, the fundamental dynamic alteration of the socialization process according to Freud.

IMPLICATIONS FOR DEVELOPMENTAL THEORY

Perhaps most significantly, the experience-dependent neurodevelopmental processes of synaptic overproduction, parcellation, and programmed cell death and the evolutionary biology concept of ontogenetic adaptation point to a number of important principles which need to be incorporated into the main body of general developmental theory. At the core of the latest biological, psychological, and psychoanalytic models of development is an epigenetic principle which stresses the interactive nature of development, the continuing dialectic between the developing organism and its changing environment. In a recent paper on causes of development—the explanation of developmental change—Hopkins and Butterworth (1990) propose that the study of development requires both a theory of transition which can account for transient structures that are only adaptive for a restricted phase of development and, at the same time, explain how earlier functions are transformed into more mature functions. The facts that the infant brain contains from 15% to 85% more neurons than the adult brain (Joseph, 1982) and that a large number of these neurons die (Hamburger & Oppenheim, 1982) and/or their processes are retracted in the early years of life (Cowan et al., 1979) are generally not appreciated by most developmental and behavioral researchers. The maturation of the brain is not simply an accretive process, but rather a winnowing of surplus circuitry, a mechanism analogous to natural selection (Changeux, 1985; Young, 1979). Indeed, the finding that programmed cell death ("apoptosis") plays a crucial role in the early development and growth regulation of living systems (Gerschenson & Rotello, 1992) has not been incorporated into the main body of the psychological sciences.

Early functional development cannot be understood without reference to epigenetic structural maturation, and pre- and postnatal brain development are both characterized as a process of organization, disorganization, and reorganization. Lichtenberg (1989) correctly points out that continuity of development does not imply a simple progressive pattern of increments but changes in organization. Carlson et al. (1988) state that regressive changes in the developing brain are related to progressive changes in the growth of personality. In a paper on critical periods in organizational processes, Scott (1979b), who defines development as change in the organization of living systems which allows for increasing complexity, stability, and adaptivity, asserts the general principle that "there can be no reorganization without disorganization" (p. 233). He further proposes: "The central problem now becomes one of empirically determining the time relationships between the organizing processes of growth and behavioral development, and the nature of the interactions between the systems produced by each" (p. 225). From a biological perspective Goodwin (1990) points out that an explanation of biological form (structure) and transformation "requires a theory of organization, of how the constituents are ordered in space and time" (p. 53). These phenomena elaborate the dynamic processes which drive the stage-dependent maturation and differentiation of brain (Martin et al., 1988) and particularly frontal (Thatcher, 1991) structure that account for sequential stages of early development. Furthermore, the same principles apply equally well to psychoanalytic conceptions of the development of "psychic structure'.

In pursuit of this, an appreciation of the developmental timetables, dynamic organization, and experience-dependent interactions between postnatally active subcortical structures, both deep brain stem and hypothalamic, and subplate zones directly subadjacent to the orbitofrontal cortex, is essential to an understanding of developmental structure-function relationships since they contain the system which generates the psychological structures responsible for the onset of emergent socioemotional functions over the stages of infancy. The cardinal features of early human development, unvarying sequence, lawful order, relatively enduring change, and organization (Blasi, 1976) reflect the fact that the maturation of the frontal lobe in the first years of life occurs in invariant stages (Thatcher, 1991).

SUMMARY

The child's socioemotional environment changes from the early to the late practicing period. The socialization experiences of the second year induce a parcellation, a selective loss and redistribution of connections, in the orbitofrontal cortex. Critical period inceptive shame transactions trigger an onset of parasympathetic and offset of sympathetic activities, ultimately producing a competitive elimination of excess mesocortical dopaminergic axons. This prefrontal regressive change is responsible for the loss of the ontogenetic adaptations of the early practicing period. Shame transactions facilitate the expansion of the lateral tegmental limbic circuit in this cortex. Shame regulating transactions and continuing attuned mirroring processes preserve the ventral tegmental limbic wiring of the frontolimbic cortex.

In both phases of this critical period of orbitofrontal maturation, the active expression of genetic systems that program prefrontal anatomical development is directly influenced by the social environment. The environmental challenge of socialization, mediated by maternal stress and stress regulating transactions, induces an adaptive change in the toddler. Maternal object relations thus act as a selection pressure that critically shapes the activity-dependent Darwinian process of the selective stabilization and elimination of specific dual subcortical catecholaminergic connections with the anatomically maturing orbitofrontal cortex. The resultant transformation from a single to a dual limbic circuit system defines the final maturation of this frontolimbic cortex. This structural reorganization is responsible for the emergence of new more complex functions at the end of the critical period.

20 The Origins of Infantile Sexuality and Psychological Gender

The lifelong effects of early exposure to sex hormones are characterized as organizational, because they appear to alter brain function permanently during a critical period.

—Doreen Kimura (1992)

Steroid-induced changes in neuronal metabolism during the critical period might express themselves morphogenetically in differences in the development or rate of development of the individual components of neural circuits, the end result of which could produce the observed instances of sexual dimorphism in the adult.

—C. Dominique Toran-Allerand (1978)

The dramatic changes in behavior that occur over the developmental stages of infancy reflect the maturation of brain circuits which subserve more complex functions. The invariant order of both the ontogenetic maturation of brain structures and the connections between these structures into functional circuits reflects the activation of timed gene action systems that encode a timetable of emergent capacities (R. S. Wilson, 1983). Genetic systems responsible for more complex structure-function relations are sequentially activated in postnatal development. These hereditary expressions require transactions with the environment (Plomin, 1983), and in fact different and specific gene-environment interactions occur over the course of development (Kendler & Eaves, 1986). What biological mechanism could mediate the postnatal environmental activation and repression of specific neurogenetic programs?

It is now thought that in early development, the action of gonadal steroid hormones links the genome of brain cells with the environment through the process of variable genomic activity (McEwen, 1989). According to this fundamental principle the organism's interactive experiences with the environment, including the psychosocial environment, trigger hormone secretion, and these hormones, sensed by receptors in brain cells, subsequently act on genome systems. Steroid hormones regulate gene expression, and, depending upon the cell type, induce or repress sets of genes (Anderson, 1984; Beato, Arnemann, Chalepakis, Slater, & Wilman, 1987). They thereby act as an essential link between "nature and nurture" (McEwen, 1988). This mechanism mediates a process by which "developmental accommodations become assimilated into the genetic program" (Cairns et al., 1990), that is by which psychoneuroendocrinological changes during critical periods can initiate permanent effects at the genomic level. The final developmental outcome of early endocrine-gene interactions is expressed in the imprinting of evolving brain circuitry.

An impressive body of evidence now indicates that the postnatal maturation of the cerebral cortex (MacLusky, Naftolin, & Goldman-Rakic, 1986) and the development of cerebral asymmetry (Diamond, 1987) and lateralization (Gordon & Galatzer, 1980) are significantly influenced by circulating gonadal steroids in infancy which produce a permanent sexual dimorphism in cortical structure and function. Sex steroids are known to play an important role in the hormonal organization of neural circuits. In this chapter I outline a model by which gonadal steroids influence the morphological development of orbital frontolimbic and frontocortical circuits. I contend that the sexual dimorphism of this corticolimbic structure is responsible for various documented gender differences in affect, cognition, and behavior.

THE EFFECTS OF GONADAL STEROIDS ON DEVELOPING ORBITOFRONTAL CIRCUITRY

It is now established that during critical postnatal periods, sex steroids organize developing neural circuits by altering their morphology (Arnold & Breedlove, 1985), specifically by modulating dendritic growth (DeVoogd & Nottebohm, 1981; Toran-Allerand, 1983), by influencing the formation of synaptic contacts (Clark & Goldman-Rakic, 1989) and the localization of synaptic terminals (Raisman & Field, 1973), and by protecting developing circuits from programmed cell death (Breedlove, 1984; Nordeen et al., 1985). These permanent influences on developing brain structure are mediated through the genome. Gonadal steroids bind to a receptor complex, which then stimulates the protein synthetic capacity of the cell. This in turn provides for the increased production of cytoskeletal elements and membrane components that is responsible for neuronal growth.

Such effects are also seen in catecholaminergic systems. Loy and Miller (1980) suggest that the sprouting of catecholaminergic axons is influenced by local sex steroids. Neurochemical studies indicate that sex steroids induce neurite growth in mesencephalic dopamine neurons (Reisert et al., 1987) and modify postsynaptic dopaminergic sensitivity (Nausieda, Koller, Weiner, & Klawans, 1979), factors essential to dopaminergic synaptology. The close interaction between this catecholamine and sex steroids is also reflected in the finding that dopamine activates the human gonadal steroid (and not glucocorticoid) receptor (Power, Mani, Codina, Conneely, & O'Malley, 1991). I have previously suggested that catecholaminergic terminals in the orbitofrontal subplate would be an important site of action of steroid effects. In fact, transient estrogen receptors are located in the the upper parts of cortical layers 5 and 6 (Sheridan, 1979), supporting the conclusion that sex hormone effects are prominent during early periods of development (Kolodny, 1984). Gonadal steroids acting in an early critical period of development are known to exert a permanent influence on the long term control of dopamine functions (Vaccari, Brotman, Cimino, & Timiras, 1977; Vadasz, Baker, Fink, & Reis, 1985). Estrogen induces an increased sensitivity in dopamine receptors (Hruska & Silbergeld, 1980). A regional sexual dimorphism in the amount of dopaminergic innervation has been demonstrated (Simerly, Swanson, & Gorski, 1985), and Vadasz et al. (1988) refer to a "feminized' or "masculinized" dopaminergic regional brain pattern. The noradrenaline synthesizing neurons of the locus coeruleus also show a dimorphic pattern (Luque, de Blas, Segovia, & Guillamon, 1992). Specific gender differences of another monoamine, serotonin, has recently been reported in the orbitofrontal cortex (Arato, Frecska, Tekes, & MacCrimmon, 1991).

Genital-sexual behavior and reproductive tract differentiation are currently understood to be a function of a sexually dimorphic preoptic region of the hypothalamus (e.g., Gorski, Harlan, Jacobson, Shryne, & Southam, 1980), an area that receives direct projections from the prefrontal cortex (Damasio, 1979). This dimorphism is reflected in sex differences in dendritic patterns in this area (Greenough, Carter, Steerman, & DeVoogd, 1977). A sexual dimorphism that is dependent on sex hormone levels during a postnatal period of brain differentiation has been found in another later maturing limbic structure, the medial and central amygdala (Dorner, 1980; Mizukami, Nishizuka, & Arai, 1983; Nishizuka & Arai, 1983). This developmental anatomical event has been suggested to be in part responsible for sex differences in a nonreproductive function, social play (Meaney, Dodge, & Beatty, 1981). Still another anatomical sexual dimorphism has been identified in the postnatally developing orbitofrontal cortex by Van Eden et al. (1984). Recently, both estrogen (MacLusky, Naftolin, & Goldman-Rakic, 1986) and androgen (Clark, MacLusky, & Goldman-Rakic, 1988) receptors have been discovered in the postnatally developing orbitofrontal association cortex (as well as in later differentiating dorsolateral prefrontal cortex). Most interestingly, Clark and Goldman-Rakic (1989) have found that a critical period for sex steroid effects on sexual differentiation of the orbitofrontal cortex occurs in early postnatal life.

These data suggest that the amounts of circulating estrogen and androgen occurring during the practicing period of orbitofrontal maturation, a time when this differentiating structural system is responsive to these gonadal steroids, would profoundly and irreversibly affect the mature sexually dimorphic structure and function of this frontolimbic system. Toran-Allerand (1978) notes that during critical periods steroids influence the rates of development of the components of neural circuits. The orbitofrontal cortex hierarchically dominates both limbic circuits. The dual excitatory-sympathetic and inhibitory-parasympathetic components of the orbitofrontal system, each with its own timetable of development, would be influenced by levels of circulating sex steroids in the early and late practicing period, respectively. It is known that estrogens tend to increase activation and decrease inhibition of neural systems (Broverman, Klaiber, Kobayashi, & Vogel, 1968). For example, estrogen has a stimulatory effect on neurons in the medial amygdala (Scheiss, Joels, & Shinnick-Gallagher, 1988). In fact, orbitofrontal neurons in the adult show increased bursting activity in response to the odor of estradiol sex steroid hormones (Onada et al., 1984).

Fox (1975) proposes that the effects of gonadal hormones on emerging brain structure may lie in the hormone balance or ratios of estrogens and androgens occurring at a particular period of development. This balance may affect the critical period maturation of the orbitofrontal system by influencing the parcellation of orbitofrontal columns, specifically through gonadal steroid hormonal influences that enhance or protect orbital circuit synaptology from programmed cellular degenerative processes. Sex steroids thus may hormonally mediate the "activity-dependent selective preservation of synapses" (Greenough, 1987). The gonadal steroid influenced parcellation process may be relevant to the chemoarchitectural organization of the final, mature distribution patterns of dopaminergic and noradrenergic innervation of the various cortical layers of orbitofrontal columns. Such a developmental psychoneurochemical mechanism could produce an enduring feminized or masculinized catecholaminergic orbitofrontal brain pattern and an anatomical sexual dimorphism reflected in sex differences in the dendritic patterns of this frontolimbic cortex.

Sex steroids that regulate cell growth and cell death phenomena could thus determine the final dual complementary (Lewis & Morrison, 1989) catecholaminergic innervation pattern of orbitofrontal columns, and emphasize either early practicing, excitatory, ventral tegmental dopaminergic or late practicing, inhibitory, lateral tegmental noradrenergic inputs, thereby influencing the permanent structure and functional capacities of this prefrontolimbic regulatory system. These steroids could also effect the growth patterns of descending cholinergic axons of neurons in the deep layers of orbitofrontal columns (the site of gonadal steroid receptors) which project to subcortical sites and modulate subcortical activity. Furthermore, it is speculated that as in the ontogenetic development of the most studied sexually dimorphic system (Jacobson, Shryne, Shapiro, & Gorski, 1980), orbitofrontal differentiation and growth will stabilize earlier in females than in males. In a developmental study demonstrating orbit-ofrontal cortex functionally matures according to different timetables in females and males, Goldman et al. (1974) conclude: "A sex-dependent difference in the development of cortical regions could have major implications for the formative years and quite possibly for behavioral differences that outlast those years" (p. 542). Indeed, D. Taylor (1969) presents evidence suggesting that cerebral matu-ration as a whole is more rapid in human females than in males, a finding also corroborated in animal studies (Gregory, 1975). This developmental neuro-biological phenomenon may help elucidate the observation that early experience differentially impacts females and males (Juraska, 1984).

ORBITOFRONTAL INVOLVEMENT IN INFANTILE
SEXUALITY AND PSYCHOLOGICAL GENDER

Recent investigations with primates differentiate genital from behavioral non-reproductive sex differences, with the latter referred to as "gender role identifica-tion" effects (Goy, Bercovitch, & McBriar, 1988). This work corroborates a large body of human research on "psychological masculinity and femininity" (Spence & Helmreich, 1978). Psychological gender is known to be firmly and irreversibly established within the first 18 to 24 months of human life (Money & Ehrhardt, 1968). These latter researchers find a crucial developmental divide at 18 months (practicing offset and rapprochement onset); sex reassignment is impossible after this critical period. The critical variable in determining gender identity is known to be postnatal learning experience, specifically the sex in which the infant is raised in the first 2 years. It should be remembered that the gonadal steroid-influenced parcellation process responsible for differentiated prefrontal structure is also influenced by the environment, that is, by the socioaffective imprinting influences earlier described. Developmental neurobiological studies of sex differ-ences in brain and behavior clearly show that the presence of neural sex differ-ences is dependent on the rearing environment (Juraska, 1986). Psychological studies confirm this—social stimulation and imprinting experiences in the early psychosocial environment critically and permanently shape psychological gender (Money, Hampson, & Hampson, 1957). The imprinting that occurs during the critical period when orbitofrontal maturation is sensitive to gonadal hormones will thus effect its permanent dimorphic structure and function. It is therefore misleading to ask whether behavioral sex differences subserved by these struc-tures are due to social-cultural or biological-genetic factors.

What specific kinds of critical period environmental stimulation and social imprinting experiences could influence the emergence of psychological sexuality in the second year? In discussing the beginning of gender identity, Mahler ob-serves that the child's attainment of upright posture facilitates genital explora-tion, an experience accompanied by "unmitigated pleasure" (Mahler et al.,

1975). Izard (1991) proposes that "children's low threshold for interest-excitement and consequent exploratory activity almost inevitably lead them to visual and tactual exploration of their sex organs" (p. 349). An intensification of pleasurable endogenous genital stimuli has been observed at 18 months, when male toddlers become interested in satisfying self-stimulation of their genitals (Kleeman, 1966). It is now thought that the genital sensory system is not maturationally functional until about 18 months of age, and that full genital responsivity with masturbatory excitability develops at this time (Hadley, 1992). Tabin (1985) proposes that the toddler's experiencing of genital excitement in the presence of the opposite gender parent at this specific time is instrumental to the formation of gender identity.

Freud's (1905/1953) original conceptualization of shame was that it acted as a counterforce to the child's exhibitionistic sexual excitement and overstimulation. Tomkins (1963) expanded upon this, and asserted that the function of shame is to be the inhibition of interest-excitement and enjoyment-joy. Amsterdam and Leavitt (1980) note that a major shame transaction in the second year involves "the negative reaction of a parent who looks on the infant anxiously when the child is engaged in genital exploration or play" (p. 78). They further conclude that the parental response to the rapprochement onset upsurge in genital sexuality is critical to developing shame affect. Nathanson (1987a) points out that "the earliest manifestations of genitality and gender identity are exactly contemporaneous with the period during which shame takes on its deepest significance in terms of the self" (p. 39). The unique and critical import of shame socialization experiences to the imprinting and emergence of gender identification processes has been discussed by this author in a previous publication (Schore, 1991).

Thus, the caregivers' shame-socializing regulation of the late practicing toddler's genital play (Kaufman, 1989) and the critical period for gender role imprinting (Money & Ehrhardt, 1968) both occur during the critical period for orbitofrontal development. The differential parental responses to the child's inceptive sexual exhibitionistic behavior are imprinted into the prefrontal area that coprocesses exteroceptive and interoceptive information. Sexual arousal involves more than sexual anatomy, it also is asociated with the activity of the neocortical structures responsible for awareness, memory, and fantasy, and the affect system (Nathanson, 1992). The frontolimbic system stores representations that integrate external environmental responses (images of parental facially expressed affective responses to the child's sexual exhibitionistic display) with interoceptive responses (pleasurable sexual arousal). These shame-imprinted interactive representations can be internally accessed for their inhibitory function. It is well established that shame is a basic component of the normal homeostatic mechanisms regulating the sexual drive (Levin, 1967). Indeed, experimental and clinical studies indicate that this frontolimbic system is involved in homeostatic regulation (Kolb, 1984) and in the regulation of sexual drive and behavior (Grafman et al., 1986; Sapolsky & Eichenbaum, 1980).

The storage of such representations in the orbital cortex in the form of internal working models of femaleness and maleness mediates the internalization of gender. The final structural maturation of this cortex at 18 months accounts for the observed irreversible determination of gender identity at this time. This reflects its socioaffective-dependent final maturation into a feminized or masculinized dimorphic organization at the end of the critical period. Indeed, at around the second half of the second year the child is capable of identifying self and others as to femaleness and maleness (Fast, 1984). Furthermore, deprivation or alteration of the social imprinting experiences with each parent that are required for its experience-dependent development in the second year may be instrumental to the more precise understanding of the etiology of gender disturbances of "psychosocial" etiology (Socarides, 1982; Stoller, 1968) and the infantile origins of disturbances of sexual identity (Roiphe & Galenson, 1984).

Clark and Goldman-Rakic (1989) suggest the sexual dimorphism of the prefrontal orbital cortex accounts for documented sex differences in orbitofrontal regulated cognitive and behavioral abilities (Goldman, Crawford, Stokes, Galkin, & Rosvold, 1974). I would expand this and propose that sex differences in cognitive abilities (Maccoby & Jacklin, 1974), spatial capacities (Caplan, MacPherson, & Tobin, 1985), cerebral lateralization (Gordon & Galatzer, 1980), hemispheric asymmetry (McGlone, 1980), and particularly in the regulation of emotionality and aggression, which in large part account for psychological gender differences, indeed reflect the sexually dimorphic functioning of the orbital limbic cortex. In addition, the gonadal steroid influenced sexual differentiation of the earlier maturing sympathetic and later maturing parasympathetic orbitofrontal components is proposed to be definitional to the excitation-inhibition autonomic balance (Grings & Dawson, 1978) of this prefrontal system which regulates emotional responses (Rolls, 1986). Gender differences in the regulation of emotional behavior will be expressed in the practicing phase, a period in which orbitofrontal systems mature. In support of this, Malatesta (Malatesta, Culver, Tesman, & Shepard, 1989) has recently reported the important developmental observation of a dimorphism in emotional behavior during reunion episodes in the second year of life.

The sexual dimorphism of emotional function reflects a sexual dimophism of the limbic structures responsible for such function. In other words, the sexes may differ in the experience-dependent patterns of the wiring of the limbic system. Gender differences in the regulation of emotional behavior may be neurobiologically mediated by sexually dimorphic patterns of descending orbitofrontal cholinergic axons, which project to subcortical sites and modulate subcortical catecholaminergic and hypothalamic neuroendocrine activity. The critical role of the hypothalamus (e.g., the paraventricular and ventromedial nuclei) in sexual motivation has long been known (Grossman, 1967), and orbitofrontal projections to such diencephalic regions (Nauta, 1972) could mediate a cortical influence on the expression of sexual behavior. For example, direct orbitofrontal projections could regulate the production of gonadotropin-releasing hormone (GnRH) by the hypothalamus, which stimulates the secretion of luteinizing hormone (LH) and follicle-stimulating hormone (FSH). These hormones, in turn, regulate the secretion of the gonadal estrogenic and androgenic steroid hormones. The "rapid membrane effects" of gonadal steroids allows for changes in mood states to occur within minutes (Schumacher, 1990). The action of these steroid hormones in the brain has been associated with the neurobiological mechanisms of sexual motivation and a variety of sociosexual behaviors (Pfaff, 1982). The structural completion of this frontolimbic circuit, in which higher orbital systems hierarchically regulate lower limbic components associated with sexual functioning, is manifest in the functional onset of what Lichtenberg (1989) calls the sensual-sexual motivational system.

Finally, the sexual differentiation of the orbitofrontal system that takes place during the practicing period mainly under the aegis of the maternal attachment object may account for the proposition, now accepted in gender research, that both sexes contain a feminine (and masculine) component of the personality (Spence & Helmreich, 1978; Stoller, 1968). This principle is also promulgated in the most recent conceptualizations of gender identity offered by developmental psychoanalytic theory (Fast, 1984). It should be pointed out that the dorsolateral prefrontal cortex, which also binds gonadal steroids in early life, may, along with orbital prefrontal systems, be involved in gender differences. It is hypothesized that the onset of a "paternal attachment system" at 18 months, the rapprochement stage, would significantly influence the differentiation of the late maturing dorsolateral cortex and thereby the gender identity of both sexes. Gender biases in orbitofrontal versus dorsolateral prefrontal development may psychobiologically underlie documented sex and hemipheric differences in access to imagery codes versus verbal codes for processing emotional expressions (Safer, 1981).

SUMMARY

During early critical periods the infant's experiences with the environment trigger genomic activity in brain cells, thereby producing permanent effects on evolving brain circuitry. In an earlier chapter I discussed how imprinting experiences activate the cell's genetic systems and increase nucleic acid synthesis. This process is critically influenced by gonadal steroids, hormones that specifically regulate gene expression. Sex steroids play an important role in the postnatal maturation of the cerebral cortex and in the organization of brain circuits, including those of the developing orbitofrontal region. A critical period for the sexual differentiation of this cortex exists in early postnatal life. Gonadal steroids influence the parcellation and resultant sexual dimorphism of this frontolimbic structure, and are thus responsible for the ontogeny of its permanent feminized or masculinized circuitry.

The action of sex steroids on brain structures psychobiologically underlies the developing child's sexual motivation and behavior. In the second year an upsurge of genital excitement, associated with the onset of a sensual-sexual motivational system, accounts for the emergence of infantile sexuality. Parental affective responses to the toddler's exhibitionistic sexual displays are imprinted into the maturing orbitofrontal cortex, a structure that comes to function in the regulation of sexual drive. These shame transactions critically influence gender identification processes that emerge in the middle of the second year. The sexually dimorphic maturation of the orbitofrontal cortex is responsible for observed sex differences in structure (cerebral lateralization, hemispheric asymmetry) and function (cognition, spatial perception). Even more specifically to socioemotional function, steroid-induced feminized and masculinized wiring patterns of the frontolimbic cortex produce gender differences in affect regulation.

21

The Onset of Dual Component Orbitofrontal Mature Structure and Adaptive Function

Human cerebral hemispheres gain anatomical and functional definition by a process of education, immature and mature brains entering into a long program of communication that is directed by a transforming complex of emotions.

—Colwyn Trevarthen (1990)

The process of an individual's education and maturation can be seen as the establishment of plans and actions and responses that are influenced by basic drives, but guarantee that the related goals are achieved through socially acceptable means. The orbital and lower mesial cortices and their subadjacent white matter may be the structure in which most such patterns of behavior are inscribed, and through which most of the pertinent information traverses.

—Paul J. Eslinger and Antonio R. Damasio (1985)

During the practicing period, the critical period for socialization, caregiver-infant affective transactions permanently imprint frontolimbic circuits in the cerebral cortex. The patterns of interconnections within the limbic system, responsible for socioemotional functioning, are influenced by the interactions a child has with its mediators (Gilbert, 1989). This principle has far-reaching implications. In psychoanalytic terms, object relations facilitate the growth and nature of developing psychological structure. In neuropsychological conceptualizations, complex functional brain systems are formed in the process of social contact and activity by the child (Luria, 1980). Tucker (1992) asserts that social interaction which promotes brain differentiation is the mechanism for teaching "the epigenetic patterns of culture," and that successful social development requires a high

269

degree of skill in negotiating emotional communication, "much of which is nonverbal." He also states that the important brain systems in such functions are those that are involved in affective communication processes and mediate socialization. Tucker concludes that such emotional information engages "specialized neural networks in humans, within the right hemisphere." Similarly, Trevarthen (1990) now posits that "cultural transmission" (socialization), mediated by the coordination of the infant's motivations and the feelings of the caregiver, is a central force in facilitating the "growth and education" of the cerebral hemispheres. Eslinger and Damasio (1985), in neurological research, suggest that orbitofrontal structures are critical to the incorporation of "social impulses into the total personality structure.'

The experience-dependent maturation of cerebral structures in the practicing critical period is expressed in the fact that a "very important moment in cortical maturation" onsets at about 15 months, "a period at which almost all the layers reach, for the first time, a similar state of maturation" (Rabinowicz, 1979, p. 122). Indeed in the middle of the second year anatomical maturation occurs in the frontal lobe, the motor areas of speech, the auditory projection area, the visual association area of the occipital cortex, the anterior temporal lobes, and, significantly, the anterior and posterior limbic areas of the cortex involved in emotional activities and mechanisms of memory. The developmental appearance of emergent function is supported by the anatomical connections between these areas as these units become increasingly related to each other.

In this chapter I present evidence to demonstrate that the experience-dependent final differentiation of the frontolimbic cortex is expressed in its hierarchical involvement in both limbic circuits, and that this structural maturation enables the functional maturation of its adaptive capacities. I also trace the ontogeny of both individual temperamental features of personality and shared cultural emotional biases.

THE MATURATION OF DUAL CATECHOLAMINERGIC CIRCUITS AT THE END OF THE CRITICAL PERIOD OF ORBITOFRONTAL GROWTH

In a review of the relevance of the critical period literature to neurobiology, Erzurumlu and Killackey (1982) conclude that a more precise elucidation of the general mechanisms of critical period events contributes to our understanding of the underlying developmental principles and the functional organization of the nervous system:

> The development of the nervous system is a heterogeneous process that involves complex biochemical mechanisms, operating at different times and rates in different parts of the system. This process can be characterized by well-ordered se-

quences of organizational mechanisms in which timing is crucial and the operation of which are dependent on the entire sequence of related preceding events. Furthermore, various regulatory mechanisms exert their control over this process of organization. (p. 218)

The regulatory neurotrophic catecholamines, acting sequentially in ontogenesis, are responsible for the transmutations, the successive changes of form, of the orbitofrontal cortex from the early to the late practicing critical period. This transmutation of structure is paralleled by a transformation of function, as the single circuit wiring and subsequent dual circuit rewiring enables more complex "wiring diagrams" of the prefrontal delayed response capacities (Goldman-Rakic, 1987a). The mature prefrontal catecholaminergic pattern, unique in the cerebral cortex, in which dopamine innervates the deep layers and noradrenaline the superficial layers (Lewis, Foote, Goldstein, & Morrison, 1988; Lewis & Morrison, 1989), is thus proposed to be the outcome of a practicing period parcellation process which allows for the appearance of an emergent function (Ebbesson, 1980), the onset of mature, that is, more complex and efficient delayed response capacities. In their discussion of prefrontal ontogeny, Pandya and Barnes (1987) conclude that each stage of development is marked by a more differentiated cytoarchitecture and a new set of connections, which together subserve a new, and more advanced, behavior.

I suggest that the psychoneurobiological mechanism that mediates this ontogenetic progression involves a socioemotional stimulation-dependent competition between the two catecholaminergic limbic circuits for orbitofrontal innervation sites. The psychoneurobiological events in the early and late phases of this critical period also account for the observation that experience-dependent orbitofrontal functional maturation is associated with an initial increase in orbitofrontal volume above adult values, followed by a later decrease in volume of orbital tissue, reduced plasticity, reduction of collaterals, and stabilization of connections (Van Eden & Uylings, 1985b). This same pattern is seen in the development of other limbic structures, and the hard-wiring and functional responsiveness of their pathways is now also thought to be influenced by the postnatal environment (Rosselli-Austin, Hamilton, & Williams, 1987). Socioaffective stimulation-dependent parcellation processes occurring in imprinting experiences of "template learning" (Staddon, 1983) in this critical period would thereby fine tune, would imprint, would etch into frontolimbic regions the template, the cytoarchitectonic domains of the two circuits of the limbic system. At the end of the critical period, the resulting dual component orbitofrontal system is capable of adaptive autoregulatory functions. In regard to the maturation of evolutionary adaptive prefrontal regulatory functions, Muller (1985) describes: "an ontogenetic development which depends not only on biological factors but also on individual experience (learning), to make the function more (or sometimes less) competent to deal with changing requirements" (p. 433).

Parcellation, the environmentally sensitive fine-tuning of maturing structural systems, may be essential to the developmental process of differentiation. In proposing a model of the evolution of frontal brain structure, Goldberg (1987) refers to "the concept of progressive differentiation of a neural system archetype from uniform simplicity to parcellated complexity and compartmentalization occurring in evolution as well as ontogeny" (p. 274). The experience-dependent transmutation in the structure-function relationships of this cortical regulatory system may be characterized as an ontogenetic progression. Werner's (1957) orthogenetic principle states that "wherever development occurs it proceeds from a state of relative globality and lack of differentiation to a state of increasing differentiation, articulation and hierarchic integration" (p. 126). This transformation from a homogeneous to a heterogeneous condition may reflect the transition from a purely dopaminergic to a mature dual dopaminergic-noradrenergic innervation of the orbitofrontal cortex and the formation of a developmentally organized compartmental architecture.

Almi and Finger (1987) suggest that the ending of a critical period is regulated by bioamine systems and is anatomically identifiable when competitive synaptogenesis diminishes and stabilizes. The cessation of intensive catecholaminergic-driven orbitofrontal expansion and differentiation and ensuing loss of plasticity may define the terminus of the critical period. The end of the practicing period may be associated with the ontogenetic disappearance of the transient orbitofrontal subplate zone, a developmental structure that is critical to the postnatal shaping of the frontal lobe (Kostovic & Rakic, 1990), and an intensification of regressive changes in its active synaptic circuitry. The activity-dependent Darwinian process of selective elimination of specified catecholaminergic collateral sprouting axon terminals and the stabilization of the dual catecholaminergic patterns would thus produce a transmuted, reorganized, and more complex system of orbital columns, and this emergent structure would be responsible for the adaptive affective, cognitive, and behavioral changes that are supported by mature delayed response functional capacities at the end of this critical period.

> Typically, increases in complexity of structure and function and in efficacy of action are related to increases in complexities of behavior need satisfaction and/or the number of environments compatible to the organism. (Meier et al., 1960, p. 4)

Compatability between the adaptive capacities of the individual and the demands and expectations of the environment is now considered to be fundamental to recent definitions of *healthy* development and functioning (Chess & Thomas, 1986).

The original embryological concept of critical periods connoted bounded times in development when a rapidly growing tissue in the developing organism is most vulnerable to alterations by external factors. In seminal works, Stockard (1921) proposed that during these times a particular structure develops at a rate entirely in excess of the general developmental rate of the maturing organism, and Child (1921) concurrently showed these most rapidly growing areas of the developing nervous system are most vulnerable to toxic agents of any sort. Thirty years ago, Arey (1962) argued that the nature and scope of embryology extends to include a cummulative progression of form and function which occurs in prenatal *and* postnatal periods. Since that time it is now appreciated that "the human brain growth spurt is very much more postnatal than had previously been supposed" (Dobbing, 1974, p. 5). Tucker (1992) refers to the concept of "psychological embryology," and points out that the long period of nurturance and social interaction provided human children allows "the life experience of other individuals to serve as epigenetic determinants of brain differentiation and intelligence" (p. 122).

The practicing critical period is thus defined specifically in terms of the original embryological concept—the final weaving together of the differentiating vascular, neuronal, and glial elements of orbitofrontal histology occurs at 12 to 18 months in the human, in accord with the principles that different regions of the infant's brain mature at different periods (Anders & Zeanah, 1989) and that segments of multineuronal circuits have developmental timetables (Johnston, 1985). (It is speculated that although future orbital-cortical connections can be made, reciprocal orbital-subcortical growth terminates at the end of the critical period.) This experience-dependent anatomical maturation allows for permanent connections to be made within and between this structure that concenters subcortical and cortical inputs. Nadel (1990) articulates the general ontogenetic axiom:

> During development, an increasing proportion of the connection-paths through the structure become functional, and at a certain point, enough connectivity has been established so that the structure as a whole can begin to do its job. (p. 621)

Almli and Finger (1987) propose a concordant principle:

> The perceived relation between rapid growth and susceptibility to external stimulation suggests that a critical period may be a time of enhanced neurobehavioral plasticity, related to emergent functional maturation or growth of neurobehavioral systems. This would mean that the onset of a critical period could be related to, and signaled by, the achievement of some level of development and functional maturation, and that the critical period could end when a higher level of growth and maturation is achieved. (p.126)

THE ONSET OF MATURE ORBITOFRONTAL FUNCTION IN THE SECOND HALF OF THE SECOND YEAR

After the first postnatal year the pyramidal neurons of layer three of the prefrontal cortex begin to mature (Kostovic, 1990). These neurons are the major sources of associative and commissural projections (Schwartz & Goldman-Rakic, 1984), important neuronal elements that underlie prefrontal cognitive processing. This specific neurodevelopmental process is suggested to be instrumental to the dramatic emergence of cognitive functions in the second year of human life (Kostovic, Skavic, & Strinovic, 1988). Goldman (1971) reports that the delayed response is the definitional cognitive operation of the orbitofrontal cortex, and that this cortex undergoes a postnatal developmental shift in functional organization. The delayed response function is now understood to underlie internalized representational memory (Fuster, 1980). Representational memory, a capacity that depends on limbic substrates (Post, 1992), is fundamentally involved in a critical adaptive function, the regulation of behavior (Goldman-Rakic, 1987b). Trad (1986) proposes that there are developmental gradations of representational capacity, and that these critically influence affect development and the ability to tolerate disruptions in affective states (affect regulation). Beebe and Lachman (1988a) observe that representations of interiorized interactions begin at the end of the first year and undergo a major reorganization at 18 months. Plooij and van de Rijt-Plooij (1989) describe a hierarchical reorganization of the CNS at 18 months in which one type of control system supercedes an earlier one. I suggest that these characterizations describe the late practicing period experience-dependent maturation of orbitofrontal dual circuit neuronal operations that generate a more efficient delayed response function. This developmental prefrontal cognitive advance, in turn, provides for more complex representational capacities than in the early phase of the critical period. Indeed, it is known that presymbolic representational capacity emerges at 12 months (Beebe & Lachman, 1988a), while symbolic representation appears in the middle of the second year (Blum, 1978; Lester, 1983; Lichtenberg, 1989). More complex representations provide even more efficient affect regulatory functions.

In discussing the development of emotional regulation, Thompson (1990) notes that "the postnatal period is one of progressive consolidation and integration of excitatory/inhibitory processes" (p. 419). Gardner (1969) proposes that mental processes described as "alert wakefulness" (alert inactivity) reflect activation of higher hierarchical levels and regulation by fine controls of facilitation and inhibition. Thus a mature, dual component orbitofrontal system that contains both excitatory and inhibitory mechanisms to homeostatically autoregulate arousal systems functionally matures at the end of the practicing period in the middle of the second year.

> Regulated sensory stimulation supplied through dyadic interaction is necessary for the development of neural mechanisms that modulate and control central nervous system arousal and for the development of consistent neural responses necessary for the processing of sensory stimulation. (Anders & Zeanah, 1984, p. 65)

This socioaffective sensory stimulation effects the growth of descending frontolimbic axons that target the arousal-generating catecholamine neurons at the source of the two limbic circuits. These bioaminergic-cholinergic limbic circuits are proposed to respectively underlie the orbital frontolimbic role in "selective activation and inhibition" (Muller, 1985), to be critical to the excitatory and inhibitory functional mechanisms of the limbic system (Stellar, 1982).

It is now accepted that excitatory and inhibitory neurotransmitters interact to produce a net effect on neuronal structure, and that a balance between these inputs is important in maintaining neuronal circuits (Mattson, 1988). In recent explorations of the dynamics of microcircuitry, Marder, Hooper, and Eisen (1987) demonstrate that the output of a model neuronal system which contains two circuits that share the same space in the neuropil is modulated by a diversity of aminergic and peptidergic neurotransmitters. Not only the output of each circuit, but also the interaction between the circuits is influenced by one or more monoaminergic inputs, thereby allowing for an adaptive flexible control of multiple output patterns or states. They conclude that in complex nervous systems, bioaminergic neurotransmitters, acting over large distances, provide a mechanism for the production of multiple outputs of a single neural network.

This general principle may be applied to the effects of catecholamines on the dynamics of orbitofrontal network structure and function. Dopaminergic and noradrenergic projections from the brain stem not only have different trophic effects on the developing structure of prefrontal columns, but also "may have different, and in some cases complementary, influences on the activity of prefrontal cortical columns" (Lewis & Morrison, 1989). Studies of the neuronal activities underlying the output of orbitofrontal networks—the delayed response function—reveal two types of neuronal responses: an "expectancy unit" which fires several hundred msec in advance of the response, and a "delay unit" that fires during the delay interval (Kubota & Niki, 1971). A more recent study of single unit activity in orbitofrontal cortex reveals one cell type shows descending firing in the course of delay, while another type increases firing as the delay progresses (Rosenkilde, Bauer, & Fuster, 1981). The involvement of arousal-generating catecholamines in this process is supported by Fuster's assertions that the activity of prefrontal cells during the delay is dependent on the overall level of arousal (Fuster, 1985), and that units related to reward are more common in the orbital (as opposed to dorsolateral) cortex, reflecting the fact that this prefrontal area is densely connected to limbic structures and thus presumably related to the motivational substrate (Fuster, 1987).

Indeed, activation of the mesolimbocortical dopamine system is associated with initiation of "movements to emotional or motivational stimuli" (Vertes, 1990, p. 74) and the incentive of motivation and the anticipation of reward (Willner & Scheel-Kruger, 1991). Ventral tegmental dopamine neurons are involved in the orbitofrontal delayed response function (Simon, Scatton, & LeMoal, 1980) and the activity of prefrontal neurons during the delay interval is now thought to depend on "input from the ventral tegmental area, most likely dopaminergic input" (Stam, de Bruin, van Haelst, van der Gugten, & Kalsbeek,

1989, p. 32). Stimulation of dopamine-sensitive adenylate cyclase receptors is known to regulate the state of arousal (Ongini, Caporali, & Massotti, 1985). It is important to point out that a large body of evidence argues against a unitary conception of arousal. Therefore, I suggest that lateral tegmental noradrenergic activity mediates a local low arousal state in the orbitofrontal cortex, and that this system also operates during the delayed response function. I further propose that the complementary influence of the two catecholamines on prefrontal columns reflects the excitatory activity of orbital dopamine receptors that are positively coupled to adenylate cyclase while inhibitory vagal noradrenergic receptors are uncoupled to adenylate cyclase, and that orbitofrontal stimulation of the ventral tegmental dopamine receptors decreases the responsiveness of lateral tegmental noradrenaline receptors and vice versa.

There is now an extensive literature to show that brain stem neurons modulate forebrain learning mechanisms (Gabriel, Poremba, Ellison-Perrine, & Miller, 1990) and play a fundamental role in the elaboration of adaptive behaviors (Berntson & Micco, 1976). In line with the principle that brain stem and subcortical structures are responsible for maintaining the "tone" of the cerebral cortex (Luria, 1973), these two bioamines which have different modes of operation and functional roles in the anterior cortex (Audet, Doucet, Oleskevich, & Descarries, 1988) may induce different tones, different subcortical "priming" of the orbitofrontal cortex. Tucker (1992) describes "convergence zones" in the paralimbic cortex. Oades and Halliday (1987) also refer to the prefrontal cortex as a "convergence zone" which, as a result of its position in receiving diverse inputs and its role in reciprocal dialog with monoaminergic nuclei, functions in the modulation of information processing. They further propose that "dopamine activity is responsible for increasing the probability of switches between sources of input competing for the control of the input of the convergence zones" (p. 150). Marder et al. (1987) assert that particular neuromodulatory bioaminergic inputs elicit unique "operational states" of specific neural networks. Their suggestion that single networks program numerous outputs may be reflected in different orbitofrontal delayed response functions depending on which catecholamine is dominant in response to a particular environmental condition.

The ability to shift between the two limbic circuits and transition between low and high arousal operational states in response to stressful alterations of external environmental conditions may fundamentally define adaptive affect regulatory function. Functionally this may be manifested as a shift of "prefrontal sets" designed to process an anticipated quality and quantity of socioemotional information. The salience of "set" for efficient problem solving has a long tradition in psychology (Gibson, 1941), and set-shifting is a known expression of orbitofrontal activity (Passingham, 1972). The capacity of attuning specific internal psychobiological states to different environmental conditions neurobiologically mediates the unique role of the orbitofrontal cortex in social (Damasio & Tranel, 1988) and emotional (Tranel et al., 1988) behaviors, and in the adjustment or correction of emotional responses (Rolls, 1986). Such frontolimbic functions are essential to socioemotional learning, the incorporation of social impulses into the personality structure, and to the individual's achievement of goals through socially acceptable means (Eslinger & Damasio, 1985).

THE EMERGENCE OF ENDURING TEMPERAMENTAL FEATURES OF PERSONALITY

The maturation of the two cortical-subcortical limbic circuits allows for the emergence of a truly autoregulated dynamic limbic system that cycles between psychobiological states of activity and inactivity. In recent models a dynamic system is described as a series of interrelated subsystems that function in a rhythmic manner over time (Weiner, 1989). The infant's specific rhythmic autonomic patterns of cycling between these limbic circuits is established in the relationship with the mother, and in such a manner she influences the establishment of the child's "autonomic balance" (Grings & Dawson, 1978). The developing individual's particular socioaffective imprinting-dependent parcellation process fine-tunes the final, mature distribution of the innervation pattern of orbitofrontal columns, emphasizing either early practicing, sympathetic, excitatory, ventral tegmental dopaminergic inputs, or late practicing, inhibitory, parasympathetic, lateral tegmental, noradrenergic inputs, thereby influencing the excitation-inhibition balance of the prefrontolimbic regulatory system. The excitatory and inhibitory modes of the limbic system physiologically represent the two dimensions of autonomic patterning that determine infant temperament, "reactivity" (excitability/arousability) and "self-regulation" (inhibition) (Rothbart & Derryberry, 1981). Fox (1989) proposes that "differences in reactivity are present early in the first year, but that regulation of reactivity develops more slowly" (p. 365). In recent work (Fox, 1991) he concludes that frontal EEG asymmetry may be an early psychophysiological marker of temperamental predispositions.

Infant temperament is now being defined as individual differences in tendencies to express the primary emotions (Goldsmith & Campos, 1982). The expression of emotion depends on both the sympathetic and parasympathetic components of the autonomic nervous system, and these branches of the ANS are known to have different timetables of development. Thompson (1990) points out that parasympathetic inhibitory systems, such as in the frontal lobes, develop more slowly than sympathetic excitatory processes. Carlson et al. (1988) have recently suggested that "postnatal developmental regressive changes resulting in a structural reorganization of the brain may be a fundamental mechanism in determining the final appearance of stable characteristics in normal temperament" (p. 14). Citing studies that demonstrate a temporal correlation between the emergence of enduring temperamental features of personality and regressive changes in the organization of neural connections during a critical period in the second year of life, these authors propose "the molding of temperamental traits into stable characteristics of personality is a transformation occurring in frontal, temporal or limbic cortical areas" (p. 14). Prefrontal cortex is known to be involved in personality factors (Markowitsch, 1988), and these developmental psychoneurobiological phenomena may contribute to the genesis of individual differences in normally distributed characteristics of affective behavior, that is, personality differences.

The study of personality differences in the psychophysiological expression of emotional behavior can be traced back to the work of Eppinger and Hess (1915) who discovered that individuals fall into two broad category types with regard to their psychopharmacological response to sympathetic vs. parasympathetic drugs, thereby differing in their physiologic response to autonomic stress. A "sympatheticotonic" type was characterized by a dominance of sympathetic reaction such as rapid heart beat, enlargened pupils, and excitable temperament. A second "vagotonic" pattern reflected a heightened readiness to respond (a bias) with the vagus nerve and the parasympathetic branch of the autonomic nervous system, reflected in low heart rate and small pupils. Contemporary research has shown mixed patterns of sympathetic and parasympathetic dominance (Grings & Dawson, 1978) and has related specific autonomic imbalances to various psychopathologies (Porges, 1976). I suggest that these essential typologies are first established in the early sympathetic-dominant and late parasympathetic-dominant practicing subphases, and that they reflect the functional status of each member of the dual component orbitofrontal affect regulatory structural system, which is critical to the determination of autonomic balance. Sympathetic-dominant and parasympathetic-dominant frontolimbic patterns may respectively underlie undercontrolled and overcontrolled developmental psychopathology (Lewis & Miller, 1990) and underregulation vs. overregulation regulatory disturbances (Emde, 1990), and their etiology traces back to early and late practicing period circuit imprinting events.

In addition to prefrontal cortical-subcortical connections, prefrontal-posterior cortical connections are also involved in socioemotional information processing. Thatcher (1991, 1992) demonstrates that the establishment of corticocortical connections with regions of the human frontal lobes occurs sequentially and dominates postnatal cerebral development. The functional result of this developmental process is that local neural networks in posterior cortical regions are brought under increasing control of frontal regions. This anterior cortex receives multimodal input from all sensory areas of the posterior cortex (Chavis & Pandya, 1976), and, especially in the right hemisphere, sends a significant number of cholinergic projections back to sensory areas in the posterior cortex (Pandya, Seltzer, & Barbas, 1988) that deliver information flow from anterior limbic to posterior sensory cortex (Tucker, 1992). Pandya and Yeterian (1985) conclude that the integration of external sensory information with information about the internal state that takes place at the orbital cortex provides a route by which incoming information becomes associated with motivational and emotional states.

With respect to ongoing socioemotional development, the growth spurt of the orbitofrontal axons described by Pandya into various sensory (e.g., kinesthetic, visual, auditory) cortices may occur in the late practicing period. As a result of the critical period information-dependent ontogenetic sculpting of these anterior-to-posterior cortical connections, particular patterns of frontolimbic-sensory cortical innervation are imprinted. Consequently, this prefrontal cortex may now perform an executive control over operations in the right posterior cortex, which are associated with the recognition of emotion (Fox & Davidson, 1986). Dyadic affective experiences in this critical period may permanently influence the types of information channels and the specific patterns of input used by a particular personality organization to receive and recognize idiosyncratically meaningful socioaffective signals that trigger particular motivational systems. Gilbert (1989) asserts that "feature detectors" sample information embedded in nonverbal communication, that social information processing is multichannelled and concerned with a variety of biosocial goals, and that biosocial goals give rise to motivational systems necessary for interpersonal interaction.

Thus, the experience-dependent maturation of orbitofrontal-subcortical and orbitofrontal-cortical circuits in the practicing critical period is responsible for the development of temperamental predispositions that underlie personality styles. In support of this model of the ontogeny of individual differences in the processing of socioemotional information, Emde (1983) has identified the primordial central integrating structure of the nascent self to be the emerging "affective core," which functions to maintain positive mood and to regulate the infant's interactive behavior. (This central integrating structure is proposed to be identical to Ledoux's [1989] "core of the emotional system" that computes the affective significance of environmental stimuli, to Tucker's [1992] frontal networks of the "paralimbic core" that function in the evaluation of information for adaptive significance and in corticolimbic self-regulation, and to Joseph's [1992] "childlike central core," localized in the right brain and limbic system that maintains the self image and all associated emotions, cognitions, and memories that are formed during childhood.) The infant's biologically organized affective core "becomes biased with tendencies toward certain emotional responses, depending on early experiences in the caregiving relationship" (p. 50). Malatesta proposes that emotion biases in personality, which first appear in the second year of life, may be due to the fact that certain neurophysiological and neuroanatomical emotive circuits may become more readily activated than others (Malatesta et al., 1989). These biases may reflect the predominance of one of the forebrain-midbrain limbic (emotive) circuits, the ventral tegmental or lateral tegmental (Nauta & Domesick, 1982), reflecting a predispositional emphasis on either the excitatory or inhibitory limbic mechanisms (Stellar, 1982) under particular stress conditions. They are responsible for psychobiological differences in childhood stress responses (Boyce & Jemerin, 1990).

Tronick (Tronick, Cohn, & Shea, 1986) emphasizes that "The affective core biases the infant's evaluation of a new situation and his interactive patterns even before the information arising from the situation has been processed" (p. 23). The prefrontal orbital region, a component of a cortical circuit of directed attention (King et al., 1989) is suggested to mediate the preattentive analysis which triggers a fast and automatic affective reaction to the emotionally expressive face (Ohman, 1986). This system, which directly interacts with both ventral tegmental and vagal limbic circuits, and whose unique connections allow for the individual to consider both complex sensory data and motivational factors prior to executing a motor act (Pandya & Yeterian, 1985), is involved in attentional and affect regulatory processes. The psychobiological development of the catecholaminergic innervation and neurotrophic maturation of this cortical structure which projects directly into the sympathetic and parasympathetic branches of the autonomic nervous system may be relevant to the elucidation of how the biological affective core becomes biased by early infant-caregiver experiences.

THE DYADIC GENESIS OF UNCONSCIOUS AFFECT AND CULTURAL EMOTIONAL BIASES

This psychoneurobiological mechanism may be ontogenetically involved in determining whether the individual's future processing of specific types of socioemotional information is biased to generate particular affect states that are consciously of unconsciously experienced. In other words, early affective experiences critically and permanently influence the development of the psychic structures that process unconscious information. Visual information contained in faces is processed in the right posterior occipitoparietal cortex (Bradshaw & Nettleton, 1983) and auditory information emanating from the face is processed in the right parietotemporal cortex (Ross, 1983), and the activity of each of these areas is controlled by the orbitofrontal cortex, a structure that controls "the allocation of attention to possible contents of consciousness" (Goldenberg et al., 1989). Winson (1985) suggests that during the critical period environmental stimuli influence the formation of permanent interconnections of the limbic-prefrontal system, a cortical structure which processes unconscious information. These early experiences mold "the formation of neural circuits which are best suited to extract information from the environment" (p. 178). Edelman (1989) now proposes that the right hemisphere, including anterior prefrontal and posterior sensorimotor cortical systems, mediates "primary consciousness."

Bowlby (1984) asserts that prolonged and repeated frustration of early attachment behavior leads to a "defensive exclusion" of processing of information that would reactivate attachment motivation. Neurobiologically, this represents an inhibition of the onset of ventral tegmental limbic circuit activity. This selective exclusion from conscious awareness of emotions is here equated with what is known in the psychoanalytic literature as passive primal repression (Frank, 1969), the predominant form of defensive activity in the earliest mode of functioning (Gedo & Goldberg, 1973). I have earlier proposed that the most powerful elicitor of affect is information emanating from an emotionally expressive face, and the specific information that is excluded also emanates from the human face. This exclusion could be mediated by continual and regular infant gaze aversion of particular dysregulating maternal emotional facial displays. Extended periods of conservation-withdrawal would be accompanied by long-term states of inhibition associated with prolonged activation of the parasympathetic, lateral tegmental limbic circuit. These experiences would permanently shape the final critical period maturation of the dual circuit orbitofrontal cortex and thereby indelibly influence its appraisal capacities and the types of socioaffective stimuli to which it selectively attends or excludes.

Taylor (1987) suggests that deficiencies of reciprocal interactions within the mother-infant regulatory system can cause the child to fail to develop a capacity to be "in tune" with himself. This growth inhibiting environment produces an individual with high levels of inhibited, repressed, and therefore unconscious affect. These experiences may interfere with the development of prefrontal autonomic control that is required for the experiencing of visceral, interoceptive "gut feelings" in response to both real and imagined threats (Nauta, 1971). In later chapters, I argue that this requires a reciprocal relationship between the two limbic circuits, and that to the contrary, both are activated in enduring states of unconscious affect, a phenomenon stressed in psychoanalytic conceptions of affect (Emde, 1980b; Pulver, 1971). Emotion biases towards the unconscious experiencing of particular affects may be identical to psychoanalytic "ego defensive organizations" that trigger unconscious "transferential reactions" throughout the lifespan. Gergely (1992) presents evidence from developmental psychology and developmental psychoanalysis which supports the idea that representational systems that perform defensive operations become established by the time the infant is between 12 and 18 months old. According to Mahler (1968), repressions of the discharge of asocial instinctual reactions appear as early as 15 months. Greenspan (1979), another developmental psychoanalytic researcher, concludes that the dynamic unconscious first emerges at 18 months.

The socioaffective experience-dependent sculpting of subcortical-frontolimbic and frontolimbic-corticocortical connections in the practicing period could generate not only individually unique but also culturally shared patterns of recognition and expression of salient affects. This psychoneurobiological process may underlie the mechanism of the child's induction into an "emotional culture," by which the child constructs out of social interaction "a molar or complex unit of prototypical components for each emotion identified by the culture" (Gordon, 1989, p. 323). Izard's (1971) work indicates that cultures differ in their attitudes toward fundamental emotions and therefore in the frequency with which certain emotions interact with others. In the process of early socialization the developing child learns "certain affective states which represent a selection from the entire potential range of interpersonal and emotional experiences" (Geertz, 1959, p. 225). This education may occur much earlier than is currently thought, and it may be mediated more by nonverbal-affective than verbal-cognitive communications. Cultural emotional biases result from the imprinting of emotive circuits, the same inscribed orbital circuits, described by Eslinger and Damasio (1985), through which social information traverses.

SUMMARY

An anatomical maturation of the connections between limbic areas in the frontal lobe and other areas of the cortex occurs in the middle of the second year. In the same period permanent interconnections between the frontolimbic cortex and subcortical limbic sites are also established. The experience-dependent imprinting of these circuits is influenced by the child's affective experiences in dyadic infant-caregiver interactions during the early and late practicing period. By the end of the critical period, a socioaffective stimulation-dependent parcellation process has etched the ventral and lateral tegmental limbic circuits into orbitofrontal regions. This differentiated, dual circuit system is capable of an ontogenetic progression, the generation of a more efficient delayed response which supports symbolic representational capacity and a more complex affect regulatory function.

The developing infant's particular socioaffective experience-dependent parcellation process emphasizes either early practicing, sympathetic, excitatory, ventral tegmental dopaminergic inputs, or late practicing, inhibitory, parasympathetic, lateral tegmental, noradrenergic inputs. Both of these subcortical catecholaminergic systems modulate the tone of the orbitofrontal cortex and the operational characteristics of its delayed response function. The ability to shift between internal low and high arousal psychobiological states in response to alterations of external socioaffective conditions essentially defines the adaptive capacity of affect regulation. The caregiver influences the parcellation of the two limbic circuits in the infant's maturing orbitofrontal cortex, and thereby the permanent excitation-inhibition (autonomic) balance of his prefrontolimbic regulatory system. This dyadic psychoneurobiological mechanism ontogenetically sculpts the enduring temperamental features of the child's emerging personality. It also generates emotional biases that determine whether an individual's or a culture's processing of a particular affect will generate a conscious or unconscious emotional state.

IV

APPLICATIONS TO AFFECT REGULATORY PHENOMENA

22

A Psychoneurobiological Model of the Dual Circuit Processing of Socioemotional Information

Emotions may be considered the most complex of mental states or processes insofar as they mix with all other processes (usually in a very specific way, depending on the emotion).

—Gerald M. Edelman (1992)

A theory of emotion is, in effect, a theory of how motivation and cognition produce emotions in adaptationally relevant encounters . . . Without some version of a motivational principle, emotion makes little sense, inasmuch as what is important or unimportant to us determines what we define as harmful or beneficial, hence emotional.

—Richard S. Lazarus (1991a)

To accomplish various age-specific tasks, the brain must be able to shift from one state of functional organization to another and thus form one mode of information processing to others within an essentially modular structure. These organized states constitute an important component of motivational systems, and they can be considered to provide the neural substrates of affect—both the internal experience of affect and the communicative aspects that are embedded in the form and patterning of the behavior that is produced during these states.

—Myron A. Hofer (1990)

In Chapter 14, I presented a model that outlined the sequential processing of socioemotional information along the ventral tegmental limbic forebrain-midbrain circuit. This ontogenetically earliest appearing system of affect regulation emerges at the end of the first year. The initial structural maturation of the orbitofrontal cortex culminates in its hierarchical dominance over neuronal cen-

285

ters at lower levels of this limbic circuit, specifically lower structures that contain neurons that selectively respond to faces, that is, encode representations of the emotionally expressive face. The cortical regulation of subcortical components of this sympathetic circuit, especially dopaminergic neurons in the ventral tegmental area and neuroendocrine neurons in the hypothalamus, is biochemically mediated by the orbitofrontal control of the mesocortical dopamine system. The experience-dependent maturation of this frontolimbic system continues in the second year, as this visceral sensory cortex also interconnects with the second limbic circuit, the parasympathetic lateral tegmental limbic circuit, thereby allowing for its role in mediating the central autonomic manifestations of emotional behavior. Indeed, human facial expressions are also registered in the noradrenergic medullary nucleus of the solitary tract (Steiner, 1979). The final maturation of the orbitofrontal cortex occurs at 18 months, and by this time the frontolimbic cortex now hierarchically dominates both limbic circuits which may operate singularly or concurrently.

Although the functional ramifications of the progression from a single to a dual circuit system are profound, the cortical-subcortical sequence of hierarchical interactions which regulates spontaneous emotion in a dual circuit system is, however, identical to a single circuit system. This temporal sequence begins with an encoding of socioaffective environmental cues via posterior cortical processing of peripherally sensed incoming visual and auditory stimulation emanating from an emotionally expressive face, appraisal by a "primed" anterior cortex—a cognitive evaluation of changes in the socioaffective significance of an environmental signal, amplification of the signal during cortical-subcortical transmission, induction of modular hypothalamic neuroendocrine and ascending brain stem catecholaminergic arousal systems responsible for the generation of central states, and finally, activation of cortical prefrontal and frontal areas involved in facial and body emotion expression. The very rapid unconscious processing of socioemotional information in sequential stages or steps in which each output is an input for a subsequent operation reflects the reprocessing of information at different hierarchical levels of the brain.

The structural development of this dual limbic circuit system that processes socioemotional information provides important clues towards the creation of an overarching theory of affect. There is now strong evidence for a psychobiological universal basis for the emotion mechanism (Scherer, 1993). In this chapter I outline in some detail a psychoneurobiological model of the dual component processing of socioemotional information. This model rests upon five fundamental assumptions. First, the neural representations of emotions are distributed throughout the subcortical and cortical regions of the limbic system. Second, subcortical limbic and brainstem structures underlie the affect components and cortical structures mediate the affect regulatory components of all emotional behavior. Third, the limbic system is not unitary, but is composed of two circuits. Fourth, the orbitofrontal cortex, expanded in the right hemisphere, hierarchically dominates both limbic circuits. And fifth, socioemotional information is processed in discrete temporal stages at various hierarchical levels of the neuraxis.

POSTERIOR CORTICAL-ORBITOFRONTAL
TRANSMISSIONS AND APPRAISAL PROCESSING

In very recent definitions, emotion is characterized as a "response to events that are important to the individual, and which importance he or she appraises in some way" (Frijda, 1988, p. 349) and as "processes of establishing, maintaining or disrupting the relations between the person and the internal or external environment, when such relations are significant to the individual" (Campos, Campos, & Barrett, 1989, p. 395). Socioemotional stimuli, especially patterns of change in visual and auditory stimuli emanating from an emotionally expressive face, must be evaluated in terms of their significance to the particular individual. The importance of appraisal processing has long been emphasized by affect theoreticians. In classical work, Duffy (1941) asserted that emotion involves an internal adjustive change in the reactivity and energy level of the individual in response to an environmental situation, which he interprets as having marked significance for himself. Fifty years later, Lazarus underscores the importance of rapid unconscious appraisals of harm or benefit to the individual, done automatically on the basis of the optic stimulus array. In fact, he views appraisal as both a necessary and sufficient condition of emotion (Lazarus & Smith, 1988). Le Doux (1989) now holds that "the core of the emotional system is thus a mechanism for computing the affective significance of stimuli" (p. 271). Gilbert (1992a) observes that affects serve the critical adaptive function of informing the individual who is tracking biologically relevant goals.

Both the structures and the functional operations of this dynamic process have been investigated. Ohman (1986) describes a very quick, involuntary, unconscious and holistic "preattentive stimulus analysis" of an emotionally expressive face, Broadbent (1977) refers to a "hidden preattentive process" of analysis of incoming emotional stimuli, and Zajonc (1984) describes an early, fast evaluation which computes the affective significance of an external stimulus. It is now well established both that emotional stimuli are processed unconsciously (Wexler et al., 1989, 1992), and that recognition of familiar faces occurs without awareness (De Haan, Young, & Newcombe, 1987). Izard's work (1991) demonstrates that adult facial expressions can last as little as a half of a second. Socioaffective stimuli, especially patterns of change in visual and auditory stimuli emanating from an emotionally expressive face, are processed in the right posterior occipitoparietal (Bradshaw & Nettleton, 1983) and right parietotemporal (Ross, 1983) association cortices, respectively. This processed information is delivered to the orbitofrontal cortex (Chava & Pandya, 1976) to be matched against practicing period-imprinted abstract facial patterns stored in this structure that functions in the mental generation of images of faces (Goldenberg et al., 1989). Mesulam

(1985) cites evidence to show that orbitofrontal areas are involved in tracking emotionally relevant objects in the extrapersonal space. Pribram (1987) proposes that the ventrolateral cortex, acting in an "appraisal" or "evaluative" capacity, functions to refine emotions in keeping with sensory input. Luria (1980) refers to the participation of the frontal lobes in determining the "regulatory significance" of stimuli that reach the organism.

Appraisal represents an evaluation of the personal significance of what is happening in an encounter with the environment (Lazarus, 1991b). In this process, match-mismatch readouts of incoming current environmental socioemotional information, processed in the right posterior cortex (Fox & Davidson, 1986), are computed against paralimbic templates (internal working models) of predispositional, affect-associated interactive representations. Such templates contain prototypes of attuned and misattuned facial emotional expressions. These frontolimbic templates which operationally manifest "expectancy priming of certain schemata for matching with potential patterns" (Horowitz, 1983, p. 248) activate or deactivate the two limbic circuits that are hierarchically dominated by the frontolimbic appraisal system. The orbitofrontal cortex is functionally involved in affect-associated expectancy processes (Panksepp, 1986) and is a central component of an expectancy based memory system (Kesner, 1986). According to Tucker (1992), representations in paralimbic networks that function in adaptive evaluation support "novelty orientation and hedonic response" and "characterize the emotional significance of events." In this manner the paralimbic orbitofrontal cortex performs a "valence tagging" function, in which perceptions receive an affective charge of a positive (pleasurably toned, idealized) or negative (unpleasurable, dysphoric) hedonic quality (Watt, 1990). This process, reminiscent of Freud's idea that perception can be endowed with psychic energy, may account for the generation of "hot cognitions."

The development of this function was earlier shown to be provided by and subsequently influenced and shaped by maternal appraisals in social referencing emotional communications. In these visuoaffective transactions the mother's facially expressed emotional communications provide the infant with salient maternal appraisals of interactions and events (Hornik et al., 1987) in order to regulate his affect and behavior (Klinnert, 1984). By accessing the mother's emotional facial display that occurs in a particular environmental context, the infant re-calibrates the emotional arousal level generated by its nervous system against the reference standard set by the mother's nervous system. Such critical period transactions not only teach adaptive socioemotional skills, but serve as imprinting experiences of "template learning" (Staddon, 1983). The mother's frontolimbic output is providing a standard which directs the imprinting of templates within the child's developing orbitofrontal cortex. These templates, inscribed in the early and late practicing critical period, contain a lexicon of abstract prototypes of the caregiver's facial patterns that can be referenced in future appraisal processing. These representations are identical to object representations described in contemporary psychoanalytic theory as templates for the significant other that are created by the child's mental capabilities in response to his interpersonal experiences (Horner, 1989). They contain "face-recognition units" that structurally encode an invariant representation of the face which fire when current input generates an image corresponding to the stored representation (Bruyer, 1991). Previous authors have suggested that there is a constancy of appraisal processing—objects evoke the same appraisal "for all time to come" (Arnold, 1960), and that "developmentally earlier templates allow for the activation of affects in new situations " (Watt, 1990, p. 511).

Bogen (1969) asserts that the unique "appositional" capacity of the right hemisphere, expressed in terms of apposing or comparing percepts or perceptual constructs that defy verbal description, is operative in the identification and remembering of familiar faces. Bowers et al. (1991) present experimental evidence to show that the right cortex contains a lexicon of internal representations of facial emotions, and Etcoff (1984b) demonstrates that this hemisphere is superior for the perceptual and conceptual organization of facial emotions. Tucker (1992) emphasizes that right hemispheric representations are analogical, an analog of the perceptual experience, and have an affective immediacy. The right cerebral cortex has been suggested to be specialized for initial orienting to novel information (Goldberg & Costa, 1981; Regard & Landis, 1989), holistic processing (Bradshaw & Nettleton, 1983; Lezak, 1976), memorial storage of emotional faces (Suberi & McKeever, 1977), and autobiographical memory, which is "invariably emotional" (Cimino, Verfaellie, Bowers, & Heilman, 1991). As opposed to the left, this hemisphere has extensive reciprocal connections with subcortical and limbic areas (Joseph, 1982; Tucker, 1981), an anatomical property which accounts for its central involvement in emotional functioning. Orbitofrontal cortex, the "association cortex" for the limbic forebrain (Pribram, 1981), known to be expanded in this hemisphere (Falk et al., 1990) is densely interconnected into various subcortical systems. Tucker (1992) points out that:

> In functional terms, the right hemisphere's importance to understanding and expressing emotional communications may occur because its representations are more integrated with paralimbic networks than those of the left hemisphere. (p. 121)

ORBITOFRONTAL CORTICAL-SUBCORTICAL TRANSMISSIONS AND AMPLIFICATION PROCESSES

Alterations in socioaffective input excite an emotional resonance within groupings of orbital neurons that selectively respond to the stimulation emanating from the faces of social objects, that is, they trigger firing patterns in enduring orbitofrontal neuronal models that code internal representations of images of emotional faces. Watt (1990) describes:

When the current situation fits (presumably in a "good enough" fashion) with an internally stored template of self and object, it is as though an internal switch flips, a circuit is completed, and the current flows (affect is felt). (p. 506)

As a result of posterior cortical priming of anterior orbital areas, orbital-subcortical transmissions are induced along the descending cholinergic axons of one or both of the two limbic circuits. The neurochemical-neurophysiological connections between cortical and subcortical components of the limbic circuits are enjoined, and this linkage initiates reverberating, reexcitational activity along the circuit. This creates a corticosubcortical system (Hecaen & Albert, 1978) in which reciprocally coupled assemblies of neurons at different hierarchical levels of the limbic neuraxis concurrently process the same information, thereby producing an adaptive emergent function, the amplification of an emotional reaction in response to a particular environmental condition. The neurochemical mechanism of the amplification of the affective signal during cortico-subcortical transmission through different limbic levels was discussed in a previous chapter.

Izard (1990) asserts that cognitive processes that occur during the delay between evaluation of the eliciting event and the onset of expressive behavior regulate subsequent emotion experience and expression. The rapid unconscious right hemispheric corticolimbic appraisal of actual or expected changes in favorable or unfavorable environmental conditions thus initiates and controls the processing of socioaffective information by regulating the onset of subcorticolimbic amplification processes. In other words, when an event is appraised to be emotionally meaningful, the specific affects embedded in the input are amplified. The explanation of the observation that representations activate affect lies in the capacity of this frontolimbic system to act as a limbic affect generator by inducing excitatory reverberations within either or both of the two forebrain-midbrain limbic circuits. Bertalanffy (1974) asserts that a small change in an anterior "higher" controlling center "may by way of amplification mechanisms cause large changes in the total system. In this way a hierarchical order of parts or processes may be established" (p. 1104). Similarly, Schwalbe (1991) concludes that "small fluctuations in energy flows through one part of the system can sometimes be radically self-amplifying such that discontinuous changes in system states can occur" (p. 275).

In his forward-looking *Project for a Scientific Psychology* Freud (1895/1966) deduced that although affect is initiated by environmental stimuli, it is augmented by the resulting excitation. This principle has been validated in a large body of contemporary research. The activity of the autonomic nervous system is now known to play an essential role in amplifying and sustaining emotion (Izard, 1977). Bear (1983) argues that extensive direct corticolimbic connections of the right hemispheric "ventral pathway," which includes orbitofrontal and anterior temporal components, are responsible for its function in enabling a heightened autonomic response and an immediate, powerful affective reaction to particular stimuli. Ohman (1986) observes that the fast appraisal of an emotionally relevant stimulus "primes" autonomic and skeletal responses. Tomkins (1984) character- izes affect as an "analog amplifier," in that affect amplifies and extends the duration and impact of whatever activates it.

Psychological researchers of infant affective functioning also emphasize the importance of affect amplifying processes. Stern (1985) states that unique dy- namic accelerating or decelerating "vitality affects" are associated with "changes in motivational states" (p. 54). Lichtenberg (1989) suggests that "affects play a major role in amplifying the experience of motivation as they unfold, providing experiential targets for motivational aims" (p. 6), and Tomkins (1987) asserts that affect is "the primary innate biological motivational mechanism" (p. 137). Fox (1991) speaks of appraisals of changes in conditions which generate "emotion- specific" motivational tendencies. Similarly, Sandler (1987) proposes that "stim- uli arising from the external world" and "influences arising within the body" (p. 296) both exert their effects on motivation through changes in feelings.

Neuroscience investigators are now identifying the primary structural system that performs this affect-regulating, motivation-inducing function. Pandya and Yeterian (1985) conclude that the integration of external sensory information with information about the internal state that takes place at the orbital cortex provides a mechanism by which incoming information may be associated with emotional and motivational states. Indeed, the orbitofrontal system is known to play a critical role in the establishment and maintenance of motivational states (Eslinger & Damasio, 1985; Pandya & Yeterian, 1985). Falk et al. (1990) con- clude that "directional asymmetries of the frontal lobe that favor the right hemi- sphere may also be concerned with emotional or motivational factors" (p. 43).

THE CORTICAL TOP-DOWN INDUCTION OF
SUBCORTICAL CENTRAL STATES

Subcortical limbic events are known to be modulated by cortical "top-down" controls (Tucker, 1992). Over 50 years ago, Papez (1937) suggested that emo- tions were subcortically mediated and that cortical cognitive processes have top-down influences on lower structures. Recent research has confirmed this. It is now well established that the instantaneous cognitive appraisals that yield information about the relationship of the environmental stimulus to the individual result in the generation of central states in the brain responsible for an emotional expression (Ledoux, 1989). States consist of "a constellation of certain patterns of physiological variables and/or patterns of behaviors which seem to repeat themselves and which appear to be relatively stable" (Emde, Gaensbauer, & Harmon, 1976, p. 29). The nature of these central states may vary. Frijda (1988) describes states of action readiness that correspond to general activation (facil- itation) or deactivation (inhibition) modes and physiologic and hormonal patterns. Putnam (1992) refers to discrete behavioral states that reflect specific co-occurring patterns of physiological and psychological (psychobiological) activity that are stable and enduring over time.

Transitions from one discrete state to another are manifest by nonlinear (chaotic, discontinuous) changes in the patterns of arousal, energy level, cognitive processing and motor activity, and are associated with affect shifts. These states are ubiquitous background phenomena, and switches are usually "contextually appropriate." Gilbert (1989) offers interesting proposals regarding "the psychobiology of changing states." The importance of these transitions has also been appreciated in psychoanalytic investigations, where Lichtenberg (1989) characterizes microshifts between motivational systems with unique neurobiological bases and "transitions from motivational dominance by one system to another" (p. 260). In psychobiological research, Hofer (1990) refers to the concept of "state organization" and concludes that the brain's shifting between different modes of information processing is an important component in the generation of motivational states. I propose that neurochemically induced "switches" in prefrontal convergence zones (Oades & Halliday, 1987), especially orbitofrontal areas involved in motivational states (Pandya & Yeterian, 1985), regulate transitions in psychobiological brain states. How do these switching mechanisms originate?

In early childhood (before prefrontal areas mature) transitions between states and disruptions of ongoing states are modulated by parents (Putnam, 1992). The relationships between the nonlinear dynamical aspects of behavioral states, state transitions, and the expression of emotion in early infancy have been studied and described in a recent work of Wolff (1987). In a previous chapter this regulatory function of the responsive caregiver was shown to be expressed in her psychobiological attunement to the child's internal state by appraising his facial displays. In doing so, she matches and then activates and amplifies the child's state. If the intensity and rate of her socioaffective stimulation is too high or too low and the infant is in a hyper- or hypoaroused distress state, she reattunes and modulates her input in order to allow the child to switch back into a positive affective state. As a result of practicing period events, these dyadic transactions are stored in an interactive representation in which the infant represents the expectation of "participating in the state of the other" (Beebe & Lachman, 1988a). This representation is a "dynamic mental representation" that specifically encodes information about transitions between states (Freyd, 1987) and generates cognitive expectations (Intraub & Richardson, 1989). Putnam (1992) concludes that as a result of parental state modulation the infant is able to utilize "the ability to bring forth an appropriate behavioral state for a given situation" (p. 101).

How might the shifting between the psychobiological states of different motivational systems be accomplished? Developmental data may give clues to this question. Developmental psychoanalysts are now focusing on the emergence of motivational systems in the first 1½ years of life (Lichtenberg, 1989). Emde (1990) has recently stressed that:

Early-appearing motivational structures are strongly biologically prepared in our species, develop in the specific context of the infant-caregiver relationship, and persisit throughout life. (p. 883)

I suggest that as a result of the experience-dependent maturation of dual component orbitofrontal convergence zones and their cortical and subcortical connections, the infant can now access in memory (in the absence of the caregiver) interactive representations—identical to Hofer's (1984a) internal representations of human relationships that serve as "biological regulators" by influencing physiological processes. Hofer points out that in early infancy the mother is *the* regulator of the infant's developing sympathetic and parasympathetic components of the autonomic nervous system. However, as this system matures, especially its hierarchically dominant cortical constituent, the child is increasingly capable of self-modulating a spectrum of internal states and the transitions between these states.

Luria (1980) concludes that the orbitofrontal areas participate in "the regulation of the body state and reflect changes taking place in that state" (p. 262). Frontolimbic-generated interactive representations may thus be fundamentally responsible for the adaptive capacity to shift back and forth between excitatory sympathetic and inhibitory parasympathetic arousal limbic circuits that generate different psychobiological states in response to environmental alterations. In other words, stored orbitofrontal representations alter internal motivational states in response to unexpected changes of visual and auditory affective stimulation emanating from the face of an other who is appraised to be emotionally significant. Tucker (1992) states that the "paralimbic core of the brain," due to its connections with hypothalamic and autonomic areas and brain stem neuromodulator systems, plays a central adaptive role in emotional and motivational processes.

The role of the limbic circuits and paralimbic cortex in psychological function is a crucial one for neuropsychological theory because these structures seem to combine the control of motivation with the control of memory. (p. 105)

The orbitofrontal cortex directly innervates the hypothalamus (Nauta, 1972), the major subcortical center which regulates the sympathetic and parasympathetic components of the autonomic nervous system (Truex & Carpenter, 1964), and which has long been considered to be the hub of motivational systems (Hadley, 1989). Adaptive orbitofrontal appraisal of the nature of a particular environment generates information that is directly relayed to the hypothalamus. This input determines which particular modular hypothalamic motivational system and thereby which emotion-specific state of action readiness, is activated by an external, environmental socioaffective stimulus change. A particular internal state is behaviorally manifest in overt behavior and in facial expressions of affect

(Frijda, 1988) and phenomenologically experienced as moods that "maintain a distinctive readiness" (Oatley & Jenkins, 1992). In this way motivation plays an important role in the generation of emotion expression (Campos, Campos, & Barrett, 1989). In very recent work Swanson (1991) is studying the biochemical switching in hypothalamic circuits mediating responses to stress. He concludes that alterations in neurotransmitter and neuropeptide levels may represent "the substrate for biochemical switching of information flow in what could be anatomically fixed circuitry, and that it could represent a strategy used in many other parts of the brain" (p. 196).

This principle may indeed apply to various levels of the brain, including circuits in the orbitofrontal cortex that hierarchically dominate the limbic system and regulate hypothalamic activity. This "top-down" cortical psychobiological modulation of hypothalamic motivational systems would recruit action tendencies that determine and organize approach and avoidance (e.g., fear-flight; anger-fight) behaviors. Lazarus (1991b) proposes that specific emotions generate a particular action tendency, a psychophysiological response pattern "as preparation and sustenance for what must be done about the person-environment relationship" (p. 823). In a neuropsychological conceptualization of the adaptive function of the paralimbic core, Tucker (1992) describes, "As behavior unfolds, processing involves negotiating between the environmental influence and the adaptive core" (p. 102). In psychoanalytic terminology, this psychic mechanism would appraise and organize which basic mode of relating to other humans— moving toward, moving away from, and moving against others (Horney, 1945)— is adaptively utilized in a particular object relational context.

ASCENDING SUBCORTICAL-CORTICAL EVENTS AND THE BOTTOM-UP CONTROL OF ORBITOFRONTAL AND OTHER CORTICAL AREAS

In discussing the mechanism which mediates the regulatory function of paralimbic networks, Tucker (1992) concludes:

> If the extensive networks of the cortex are to self-regulate effectively they may need to call up the modulatory influences of the brain stem projection systems, through communication channels gated by paralimbic network representations. (p. 104)

This cortex uniquely sends direct monosynaptic projections to both ventral tegmental dopaminergic and lateral tegmental noradrenergic neurons. Orbitofrontal appraisal of a particular object relational transaction would induce specific patterns of transmission down the two limbic circuits, and these patterns would depend on the the specific emotional content of an appraised affective signal. These transmissions would differentially excite (amplify the activity of) ventral tegmental dopaminergic and/or medullary noradrenergic limbic nuclei, which in turn would release catecholaminergic neurotransmitter back up the neuraxis and into orbitofrontal columns. Fuster (1980) points out that inputs from the brainstem and subcortical regions convey to the prefrontal cortical regions information related to basic arousal states. In addition to frontal lobe presetting of limbic structures (Nauta, 1971), limbic structures may preset and reset frontal structures, thereby allowing for "bottom-up" as well as "top-down" (Tucker, 1992) control.

This psychobiological mechanism directly influences the excitatory or inhibitory tone of the paralimbic cortex. The prefrontal cortex, in a state of sympathetic predominant "ergotropic" or parasympathetic predominant "trophotropic" arousal, would differentially activate motor regions in the frontal cortex, especially the more ventral areas of the primary motor cortex which are known to control face, head, and neck movements associated with orientation to sensory stimuli (Barbas & Pandya, 1989). Orbital activity is known to elicit eye and head movements (Pribram, 1987) and motor responses in the face (Sugar, Chusid, & French, 1948). Importantly, these orbitofrontal-frontal connections would therefore mediate motor activity reponsible for facial, vocal, and body emotion response expression. Orbital-hypothalamic-orbital interactions determine which motivational system is activated and expressed in a particular emotional expression, while orbital-ventral tegmental-orbital and orbital-lateral tegmental-orbital interactions influence the intensity and duration of a specific motivational system expressed in an affect display. In such a manner internal states are manifest in specific emotional expressions and overt behavior in response to a particular environmental context.

In line with Marder's (Marder et al., 1987) principle that specific neuromodulatory bioaminergic inputs elicit unique "operational states" of specific neural systems, the "state organization" of the orbitofrontal convergence zone may be switched in a modular fashion depending on the which ascending catecholaminergic circuit—associated with sympathetic or parasympathetic arousal—is providing more input to orbital columns. A switch in orbitofrontal tone in response to a change in socioaffective environmental conditions is neurochemically mediated by an alteration of the proportion of ventral tegmental dopaminergic versus lateral tegemental noradrenergic input to orbital columns. This psychobiological mechanism would adaptively reset the frontolimbic appraisal-expectancy mechanism in preparation for an organismic response to anticipated upcoming high or low levels of stimulation, that is, it would "re-prime" the orbitofrontal cortex. The dual component cortical affect regulatory system which mediates between the internal milieu and the external environment acts to monitor, adjust, and modify emotional reactions in response to hypostimulating ("deprivational," "solitary") and hyperstimulating ("social") stressful socioenvironmental conditions. This capacity may define the essence of its adaptive function.

Exposure to more drastic environmental changes—"chronic stressors"—over longer periods of time could trigger substantial alterations of subcortical hormonal neuromodulators that produce enduring alterations of orbitofrontal tone and an impairment of the adaptive function of shifting between sympathetic and parasympathetic states. For example, although both parasympathetic medullary noradrenaline and parasympathetic hypothalamo-pituitary-adrenocortical neuroendocrine systems provide an inhibitory function, Gilbert (1989) proposes that the former is a short-term "stop" mechanism, the latter long-term. In line with his suggestion that the cortisol system is more involved in inducing and maintaining long-term states, adrenal alterations may be primarily responsible for persistent parasympathetic-dominant orbitofrontal states.

In bottom-up control, subcortical neuromodulators alter cortical activity. In addition to the two catecholaminergic nuclei, hypothalamic hormonal output also influences the "tone" of this prefrontal cortical regulator. Leshner (1978) asserts the general principle that baseline hormonal states that exist before an organism encounters a stimulus influence the responsiveness of neural mediating mechanisms to that stimulus. Gellhorn (1967) describes the influence of the hypothalamus and brain stem in inducing cortical activity or inactivity. Glassman and Wimsatt (1984) propose that the hypothalamus is a source of an excitatory or inhibitory diffuse "bias" on cerebral areas that process sensorimotor information. Hypothalamic neuropeptides and peripheral hormones and adrenal neurotransmitters and neurohormones regulated by these neuropeptides are sensed in the orbitofrontal circulation, and in this circulatory communication channel the paralimbic cortex is provided with continuous information about internal bodily states (Mesulam & Mufson, 1982). These signals are biochemically active in the paralimbic microvasculature, and act as neuromodulators of populations of paralimbic neurons, thereby altering local columnar activity.

In altering the firing patterns of orbitofrontal neurons, the output of these columns to other cortical regions is also influenced. Prefrontal neurons are known to manifest executive control (Stuss & Benson, 1987) over cerebral cortical areas. Orbitofrontal neurons transmit information from the anterior limbic to the posterior sensory cortex via direct cholinergic projections (Pandya, Seltzer, & Barbas, 1988). In this manner, hypothalamic motivational systems, acting through cortical paralimbic structures, could influence sensory receptor activity in the posterior cerebral cortex. Such an effect is reported by Beagley and Holley (1977), who demonstrate that hypothalamic stimulation leads to changes in cortical visual processing. Panksepp (1992) maintains that subcortical emotive circuits change the sensitivities of sensory systems. Motivation has been defined as "activity of central origin that sets the state of information pickup, and an underlying form, pace, and direction of activity in relation to which sensory afference becomes informative" (Trevarthen, 1990, p. 340). Local orbitofrontal adrenocorticoids also would influence this activity, since glucocorticoids are known to depress sensory detection activity for each of the sensory modalities (Henkin, 1974). Gilbert (1989) points out that internal physiological states bias attentive and response systems, and Putnam (1992) suggests that discrete behavioral states, reflecting enduring patterns of physiological and psychological variables, act as "nonlinear transforms for sensory information" (p. 99).

Blood flow studies show that posterior cortical activity in each particular sensory area is coupled with activity in a corresponding frontal area (Roland, 1985), suggesting a "functional tuning of posterior activity by frontal areas" (Tucker, 1992, p. 114). Prefrontal cortex sends "corollary discharge" output to sensory structures, inducing a "prefrontal sensory set" that prepares posterior cortical structures for the anticipated effects of actions (Fuster, 1991). This operation may be involved in the "imaging" or "imagining" of the emotional expression of a face that will be perceived at some future time, that is, a rehearsal of an anticipated, upcoming reunion transaction with an emotionally significant object. Prefrontal connections to posterior sensory association cortex have been suggested to mediate visuospatial working memory (Goldman-Rakic, 1988), and this working memory may operate in facial emotional imaging to act as a motivational bias to search for expected particular emotional expressions, either positive or negative. Goldman-Rakic's proposal is supported by Jonides et al. (1993), who report positron emission tomography (PET) studies of human regional cerebral blood flow that reveal activation in right hemisphere prefrontal, occipital, parietal, and premotor cortices accompanying spatial working memory processes. Most importantly, in this study of the circuitry of working memory, the activated prefrontal region, area 47, is part of the orbitofrontal cortex (see Figures 4.7 and 4.8), and is in the right and not left hemisphere.

In a recent study of the generation of facial emotion imagery, Bowers et al. (1991) propose that long-term memory visual representations of prototypes of facially expressed emotion activate spatially arranged "face-icons" in a "visual buffer" for visuospatial processing "where they could be pictured in the 'mind's eye'." The result is a consciously experienced short-term image of a facial emotion that the authors equate with an "emotion representation." Although they don't identify the locus of the storage of facial emotion protoypes, this should be the orbitofrontal cortex, which is known to be involved in the generation of images of faces (Goldenberg et al., 1989), and the visual buffer should be in the right posterior cortex, the site of the visuospatial processing of faces (Lezak, 1976). This posterior cortical—prefrontal—subcortical limbic—prefrontal—posterior cortical loop would activate a reverberating (self-reexcitational) circuit that mediates a long-term memory function. In other words, a match transforms short-term working memory, mediated by prefrontal-posterior corticocortical connections into long-term memory, mediated by cortical-subcortical transmissions.

It is tempting to speculate that this operation may underlie the phenomenological experience of a feeling state that is anticipated to be present in a desired face-to-face transaction—an interpersonal need. The psychoanalytic concept of "need" has been defined by Sandler (1987) as a represented wish, one that includes the desired or expected response of the significant other, that is the response of the object to this wish. In an affectively-tinged motivational state the image of an anticipated emotionally expressive face of an "imagined other" (Shulman, 1987) that amplifies an ongoing positive affective state could be consciously experienced as an emotionally charged interpersonal fantasy, known in the psychoanalytic literature as a "symbiotic wish" (Horner, 1992). If an external array matches or attunes to this face icon (if an interpersonal expectation is met) a match readout to a prefrontal prototype or template occurs in the form of a posterior-anterior corticofrontolimbic transmission. This activates orbitofrontal columns and triggers descending messages to subcortical amplification sites along the ventral tegmental limbic circuit, thereby increasing the imprinting of an affective charge onto the representation. Furthermore, this dynamic mechanism accounts for the phenomenological experiencing of emotion "intrapsychically," that is in the absence of any interpersonal contact. Basch (1988) asserts that as a result of development affect is mobilized by recall as well as by external stimuli, and that cortical signals are capable of stimulating subcortical limbic structures. Lang (1979) argues that emotion imagery can trigger the physiological response in emotion—metabolic support for a context-specific action preparatory set.

In addition to prefrontal sensory sets, Fuster (1992) further proposes that a preparatory "prefrontal motor set" operates "in anticipation of movement." Tucker (1992) concludes that paralimbic networks control "postural" and affective states. Particular body movements are associated with specific emotions (Sogon & Masutani, 1989), and postural adjustments are known to vary across emotions and serve adaptive functions (Riskind, 1984). Corticolimbic connections into the motor areas of the frontal cortex may specify the forms of motor responses that define the individual's characterological approach and avoidance behaviors. Pandya and Yeterian (1985) point out that the unique structural connections of the orbitofrontal cortex allow for the individual to consider both complex sensory data and motivational and emotional factors prior to executing a motor act. Ingvar (1979) concludes that hyperfrontality, high resting anterior cortical blood flow, enables a prefrontal "simulation of behavior," that is, an anticipatory planning of motor and behavioral responses. I would add that this prefrontal mechanism also supports an anticipatory planning of an expected emotional response to an upcoming social situation. It is now thought that appraisal refines emotions so that they are more in keeping with current sensory input and with the consequences of actions (Pribram, 1987), and takes place in relation to an individual's concerns and coping potential (Fox, 1991). Nauta (1971) suggests that the frontal lobe may preset limbic structures according to the expected outcome of a behavioral plan, thereby inscribing affective monitoring mechanisms that guide behavior.

One particularly important orbitofrontal set or primed state of action readiness (expectancy) is "communicative readiness" (Broucek, 1982), in which the individual anticipates certain rewarding communicative and interactional (attachment) behaviors. Horner (1992) describes the symbiotic wish as the essential subjective condition that drives the organism to seek object relationships. This state may represent a predominance of dopaminergic orbitofrontal circuitry, since the mesolimbocortical dopamine system is known to be functionally involved in the anticipation of reward (Willner & Scheel-Kruger, 1991) and the initiation of movements to emotional or motivational stimuli (Vertes, 1990). Such a "prefrontal set" is physiologically supported by the activation of Panksepp's (1986) expectancy command circuit which contains ventral tegmental dopaminergic elements and maintains emotional functions involved in positive expectancy processes. On the other hand, a predominance of the lateral tegmental activation of the orbitofrontal cortex would be found in nonobject seeking modes.

According to Fuster (1991) columns or modules of prefrontal cortical systems are critically involved in the cybernetic cycle of influences from the environment being directed through sensory receptors, to motor effectors, to the environment, and back to sensory receptors, thereby acting to adaptively regulate an orderly sequence of behavior. Tucker (1992), like myself, expands this loop to include subcortical circuits. He presents a hierarchical model of the dynamic bidirectional processing of emotional information by paralimbic networks. These networks may be "prepared beforehand" to organize representations cascading up and down different levels of the hierarchy:

> A stimulus is represented initially in the differentiated outer cortex, then as representations cascade down toward the limbic core they become increasingly evaluated for adaptive significance, conjoined with visceral states and motor impulses. Through progressive organization back toward the outer surface, the adaptive urges and dispositions of the paralimbic cortex are increasingly articulated into a motor plan that becomes integrated within the differentiated environmental interface. (p. 101)

I suggest that this cascading effect is directed along both the lateral tegmental limbic circuit that is involved in visceral functions and the ventral tegmental circuit whose activity is associated with motor functions.

As a result of reciprocal interactions with both cortical and subcortical structures, prefrontal systems perform, in addition to a retrospective function, a prospective, future related function involved in planning (Fuster, 1991). Fuster equates the function of the prefrontal set with Ingvar's (1985) "memory of the future." The frontal cortex and its connections with various posterior structures is known to be involved in the processing of second-order representations (Frith & Frith, 1991), and these "representations of representations" are now thought to be implicated in thinking about hypothetical and future states and events (Perner, 1991). At the orbitofrontal level re-representations of the external world are integrated with subcortical information regarding the visceroendocrine environment (Nauta, 1971), thereby allowing for its essential function in affective processes. The frontolimbic cortex is thus instrumental to the temporal properties of emotion. Wiener and Graham (1989) emphasize that emotions influence future plans and function to "bridge between the past and future" (p. 401).

SUMMARY

Any theory of affect must be grounded in the operations of the brain structures that perform this function. The limbic system, the cortical-subcortical system that processes socioaffective information, consists of two circuits. The ventral tegmental forebrain-midbrain limbic circuit represents the widespread domain of axons of dopamine neurons in this area of the midbrain. The activity of neurons at various levels of the mesolimbocortical circuit is responsible for the locomotor and reward functions of emotion. The second circuit, the lateral tegmental limbic circuit, originates in noradrenergic neurons in the medulla, and its activity accounts for the autonomic-visceral aspects of emotional functions. These two circuits constitute the essential wiring of the sympathetic and parasympathetic components of the autonomic nervous system in the CNS. By the middle of the second year, the latest maturing elements of both circuits are functionally operational in the orbitofrontal cortex, and these frontolimbic areas of the cerebral cortex hierarchically dominate both limbic circuits.

Both of these circuits are responsive to changes in socioaffective information emanating from an emotionally expressive face. These visual and auditory signals are centrally processed in the posterior regions of the right hemisphere. This environmental input is forwarded to the orbitofrontal cortex, where it is appraised for its adaptive relevance to the individual. Match-mismatch readouts are computed against paralimbic templates of prototypical facial emotional expressions. As a result of the comparison of a representation of the current socioenvironment against stored dynamic interactive representations, corticolimbic networks at the apogee of the limbic circuits are resonantly excited, and fire synchronously.

Since the orbitofrontal regions lie at the common boundary of the cortical and subcortical areas of the brain, the cortical signal, a "hot cognition," is transmitted down the neuraxis towards the catecholaminergic cores of the two limbic circuits. Reprocessing of this signal at various hierarchical levels of the dual component limbic system that encode neural representations of the emotionally expressive face amplifies the signal. As this amplified signal reaches the arousal-generating catecholaminergic neurons and the hypothalamic neuroendocrine neurons, it now may induce a transition in the central state produced by these subcortical systems.

The specific patterns of these top-down cortical-subcortical transmissions are embedded in the amount of activation of one or both limbic circuits triggered by the current socioenvironment. This cortical output serves as an input to various hypothalamic nuclei, and determines which particular hypothalamic motivational system(s) is activated in response to the environmental change. Inputs into the two catecholaminergic groups influence the activation of arousal systems. In this way affectively significant input from the external environment establishes, maintains, or disrupts the individual's internal environment. Dopamine and nor-adrenaline release back up the circuits would produce an ergotrophic versus a trophotropic predominant local arousal of the orbitofrontal cortex.

In such bottom-up control, subcortical neuromodulators influence the excita-tory or inhibitory tone of the prefrontal cortical regulator. The output of the orbitofrontal cortex is delivered by direct projections to the motor cortex that control eye, head, and face movements. This information then triggers the facial and vocal expressions of emotion. This pathway also is responsible for a prefron-tal motor set, an anticipatory planning of an expected emotional response to an upcoming social transaction. Direct connections to posterior cortical areas also induce a prefrontal sensory set, in which the sensory perceptual system is biased to search for the image of a particular facially expressed affective display.

The higher and lower components of the two limbic circuits thus reciprocally influence each other. The essential role of the orbitofrontal cortex in affect regulation and in the adjustment or correction of emotional responses derives from its unique anatomical location between the cortex and subcortex. This structural property allows it to integrate external sensory information with infor-mation about the internal state, and thereby provides a mechanism by which incoming information becomes associated with motivational and emotional states. The switching of psychobiological states in response to specific socioen-vironmental conditions that are significant to the individual represents the essen-tial adaptive function of emotional behavior.

23

Cross-Modal Transfer and Abstract Representations

Apprehending any object (external or body part) simultaneously in various modalities, such as touching or manipulating it while also looking at it, prompts a more distinct awareness of the thing or its properties than is possible through a single modality.

—Sybil K. Escalona (1963)

An identical, amodal description of an object perceived through two different modalities may be possible because the object eventually stimulates a group of cells that receive input from more than one modality. These cells, however, might not be active or developed at birth; response to amodal properties across systems would not be possible, then, until the appropriate neural substrate had developed.

—Susan A. Rose and Holly A. Ruff (1987)

The anatomical convergence of different sensory afferents in the frontal lobe has been corroborated by several physiological and behavioral studies and may be the morphological basis for intermodal and cross-modal exchange of information.

—Deepak N. Pandya and Clifford L. Barnes (1987)

Developmentally mature orbital prefrontal columns receive a convergent multi-modal input from all sensory areas of the posterior cerebral cortex (Chavis & Pandya, 1976; Jones & Powell, 1970), specifically from their association systems related to the olfactory-gustatory, somesthetic, visual, and auditory sensory modalities (Yarita et al., 1980). These same neurons send intracortical axons back to sensory areas (Pandya et al., 1988), and the functional consequence of this developmental process is to bring local posterior cortical neural networks under increasing control of frontal regions (Thatcher, 1992). These anatomical properties, in addition to their direct connections into both catecholaminergic regulated limbic circuits, enables them to act as a cerebral hemispheric regulator. Increased orbitofrontal activity is associated with a lower threshold for awareness of sensations of both external and internal origin (Goldenberg et al., 1989). This emergent structural system allows the preverbal child to process, store, and integrate exteroceptive information from several modalities with interoceptive autonomic information via critical period imprinting-generated neuronal models, thereby acting as a central mechanism that coordinates information from cortical and subcortical levels.

The development of the direct interconnections between the orbitofrontal and posterior sensory cortices takes place in the first two years of life. In this chapter I suggest that this particular expansion of prefrontal connections produces new functional capacities in the child's expanding cognitive, behavioral, and affective repertoires. Of particular importance is the capacity for cross-modal transfer, a cognitive function that underlies the organization of abstract representations.

MATERNAL SENSORY STIMULATION AND THE DEVELOPMENT OF POSTERIOR SENSORY ASSOCIATION CORTICES

The adaptive ability to acquire knowledge about the world rests upon the capacity of the individual's various perceptual systems to tune in to information about the self in the environment (J.J. Gibson, 1966). The development of such systems depends on environmental "affordances" (E.J. Gibson & Spelke, 1983). Each system is sensitive to a different form of energy, and each has unique peripheral receptors and central pathways. According to Turkewitz and Kenny (1982), human infant sensory systems develop in an invariant sequence at different rates, and the interaction and competition between sensory systems at different stages of development result in a disruption of stabilized organization and provide the basis for a more advanced reorganization of function.

> In our view, the normal course of ontogeny, entailing as it does unequal rates of development of sensory systems, serves to modulate and orchestrate the competitive relationships among sensory systems and so make possible an optimal or at least highly functional sharing of neuronal space. (p. 362)

Although these authors don't identify the site of this neuronal space, it is logical to assume that it lies in the orbitofrontal cortex, which receives sensory input from every sensory modality. This competition may refer to a sensory experience-dependent parcellation of this cortex, and disruption may describe the selective loss of connections and redistribution of cortical inputs, specifically in terms of the posterior cortical projections entering into this prefrontal structure. The neurobiological mechanism underlying this cortical remodeling, studied by Cowan (1984), Prechtl (1982), and Stanfield (1984), has been described in chapter 19.

The early environment, mediated and modulated by the mother, provides different forms and intensities of sensoriaffective stimulation that serves as the "experience" that induces the "experience-dependent" maturation of the orbitofrontal areas, the cortical system centrally involved in homeostatic regulation (Kolb, 1984). Kraemer (1992) notes that "the mother appears to provide a multimodal set of sensory stimuli (thermal, olfactory, somatosensory, visual) that selectively regulate an equally broad and multimodal physiological and behavioral homeostatic system in the infant" (p. 498). He further suggests that the topographical representation of sensorimotor systems in brain regions depends on competition for synaptic space. Competition is associated with developmental status and individual experience, and reflects the way the organism incorporates features of its environment.

The "changes in the social environmental niche" over the course of infancy may be expressed in the primary caregiver's supplying higher, yet regulated and therefore optimal, levels of stimulation of a particular sensory modality in a particular critical period. This stimulation, which occurs in the context of an afffective dyadic transaction, influences the final growth and maturation of the posterior cortical area that processes such modality-specific information throughout the lifespan. I propose that the final maturation of a particular sensory association cortex involves its establishing structural and therefore functional interconnections with anterior prefrontal regions. I also suggest that growing axons from posterior sensory areas reach orbitofrontal dendrites in an invariant sequence: olfactory-gustatory, somesthetic-thermal, visual, and then auditory.

In the first postnatal period, birth until the second month, olfactory-gustatory stimulation is the primary form of sensory stimulation provided in dyadic transactions with the mother, and somesthetic-thermal inputs are secondary. Schaal (1986) observes olfactory exchanges between the mother and neonate in the immediate postpartum period allow for mutual recognition. In a study of early human olfactory communication, Russell (1976) demonstrates that at 6 weeks, infants will orient toward the maternal breast odor and produce sucking movements in response to it, and not to the odor of another mother. Animal studies show that there is a sensitive period for the development of olfactory imprinting in the first week (Woo & Leon, 1987). The anterior ventrolateral cortex is known to receive direct projections from subcortical regions that are involved in olfactory processing (Groenewegen, Berendse, Wolters, & Lohman, 1990). This olfactory tract projects to the posterior orbitofrontal cortex, and this region, in the right hemisphere, plays a predominant role in human odor memory (Jones-Gotman & Zatorre, 1993). Neurons in the solitary nucleus are the first-order relay for visceral information (van der Kooy et al., 1984), and show a gustatory sensitivity (Travers & Smith, 1979; Travers, Pfaffman, & Norgren, 1986). It is suggested that this represents a critical period for the maturation of subcortical olfactory bulb—cortical orbitofrontal circuits (see Fig. 4.1). Olfactory-tactile associative learning processes have recently been demonstrated to involve the ventrolaterlal prefrontal cortex (Whishaw, Tomie, & Kolb, 1992).

At the end of this period olfactory stimulation is reduced and tactile increases. The neonate's tongue is extremely sensitive to pressure changes (Thatch & Wiffenbach, 1976), and the earliest form of prominent tactile sensitivity is "oral touch." Rochat (1983) finds developmental changes in oral discrimination between 1 and 4 months, including an increase in oral exploratory behavior. Following this, tactile sensitivity of the fingers and hands increases. During this period of maturation of the association areas of the parietal cortex (Chugani et al., 1987), centrally involved in the processing of tactile (cutaneous) and kinesthetic (deep muscle and joint) sensation (Luria, 1980), high levels of tactile stimulation are provided by the maternal environment, with visual input secondary. This may be specifically expressed in the sensory characteristics associated with maternal contact comfort that releases early attachment behavior (Harlow, 1958). In psychoanalytic theoretical work, Bick (1968) discusses the unique role the skin plays in early object relations. The infant actively seeks to adhere to as much an area of skin surface on the mother's body as possible. Kohut (1971) postulates that the ability to regulate skin temperature and to maintain a feeling of warmth is acquired by the internalization of the mother's function of providing physical warmth. Taylor (1987) notes, "The sensations impinging on the infant's skin presumably help regulate aspects of the infant's behavior and physiology" (p. 164).

These proposals are supported by recent neurobiological research which indicates that "in early postnatal life, maintenance of critical levels of tactile input of specific quality and emotional content is important for normal brain maturation" (Martin, Spicer, Lewis, Gluck, & Cork, 1991, p. 3355). The sensory input derived from contact with the mother during nursing has been suggested to shape dendritic growth (Greenough & Black, 1992). In light of the fact that the maturation of brain and body tissues are temperature dependent, psychobiological regulation of maternal tactile input at this stage may also mediate the known critical role the mother plays in infant thermoregulation (Schwartz & Rosenblum, 1983; Stone, Bonnet, & Hofer, 1976). This may involve the maternal regulation of the infant's sympathetic nervous system thermogenesis functions. Stroking reduces the body and brain temperatures of infant mammals (Sullivan, Shokrai, & Leon, 1988; Sullivan, Wilson, & Leon, 1988). Such a function may be "internalized" in the maturation of a higher structural system that can autoregulate skin temperature changes. Indeed, neurobiological studies have established the important role of the orbital frontal cortex in the thermoregulation of skin temperature changes (Blass, 1969; Delgado & Livingston, 1948; Fairman, Livingston, & Poppen, 1950). By 2 to 3 months, infants show tactile recognition of shape and tactual intermodal transfer (Streri, 1987), and at 6 months tactual recognition of temperature (Bushnell, 1986). In the middle of the first year infants are mastering the use of their hands as tools for exploration, and are engrossed with "tactually capturing" objects (Bushnell, Shaw, & Strauss, 1985).

By 10 to 12 months the predominance of visual over kinesthetic processing is well established, as relected in the findings of the preeminent directive role of visual input (Bushnell & Weinbeger, 1987) and the faster speed in encoding visual over tactual information (Rose, Gottfried, & Bridger, 1983) observed at this time. At 7 to 9 months tactile stimulation is the major source of the positive affect of joy (expressed in laughter), while at 10 to 12 months visual stimuli predominate (Sroufe & Wunsch, 1972). Between 10 and 11 months acoustic stimuli, in contrast to visual stimuli, only begin to acquire representational significance (Freedman, 1981). Towards the end of this practicing period visual processing decreases (through shame transactions) and auditory increases. Thus, there is a shift from emphasizing olfactory-gustatory and tactile to visual and then auditory inputs from early to late infancy, and such shifts cause changes in ontogenetic adaptations. These sensory inputs influence the maturation of the various posterior cortical association areas that process modality-specific information and the growth of their corticoprefrontal axons that communicate this information to the regulatory anterior prefrontal cortex.

The myelination of these axons into the orbitofrontal cortex occurs sequentially in ontogenesis, beginning with subcortical olfactory-gustatory inputs, followed by the maturation of posterior parietal association areas and connections delivering processed somesthetic information, occipital corticofrontal connections delivering visual information, and finally, input from superior temporal auditory areas. Axons that deliver information from different information-processing domains would compete for sites on the dendrites of maturing orbitofrontal pyramidal neurons, and those pathways that are underutilized in a later stage of development would be subject to a partial elimination of axon collaterals that is responsible for the loss of an earlier ontogenetic adaptation. In contrast, those sensory channels that are actively used in a particular period would undergo an "activity dependent preservation" of corticoprefrontal synapses. Of particular importance would be the delivery of input from different posterior sensory areas onto the same orbital neuron.

During this critical period of orbitofrontal maturation, prefrontal axons would grow back towards targets in the different posterior sensory association areas. In this manner, multiple working memory "centers," each dedicated to different information processing domains (Goldman-Rakic, Funahashi, & Bruce, 1990) equated with multiple memory systems, each characterized by fundamentally different rules of operation (Sherry & Schacter, 1987), are created. In psychoanalytic terminology, this may represent a developmental advance in ego functions. The supplanting of earlier maturing proximal (olfactory and tactile) sensory systems allows for a distal (visual, auditory) sensory hierarchical dominance, and the integration of these sensory inputs under orbitofrontal control results in the appearance of new functions. These phenomena may account for the basic developmental observations that at 11 months visually distinctive features are more compelling than tactually distinctive features (Bushnell & Weinberger, 1987), and that at 12 (versus 6) months, the eye processes information faster than the hand (Rose, 1990). It is suggested that these emergent functions result from the experience-dependent maturation of synaptic connections, rewiring, and fine-tuning of connections in the orbitofrontal cortex.

ORBITOFRONTAL-POSTERIOR CORTICAL CONNECTIONS AND CROSS-MODAL TRANSFER

These unique temporally programmed anatomical relationships allow for the development of important functional advances. Greenough and Black (1992) conclude that development allows "information from a more mature modality (e.g., touch) to help integrate and organize input from a newly developing modality (e.g., vision)" (p. 169). At 12 months, infants show cross-modal transfer from tactual to visual modalities (Gottfried, Rose, & Bridger, 1977). This is expressed in the infant's selectively fixating novel stimuli presented visually following familiarization to the same stimuli presented tactually. The mother's critical role in this process is to provide appraised novel stimuli to her infant via social referencing (Klinnert, 1984) experiences that produce dyadic episodes of psychobiologically attuned (Field, 1985a) "joint visual attention" (Butterworth, 1991). These transactions amplify interest, the positive affect that keeps attention moving from one feature of an object to another long enough to see its unity (Izard, 1991) and that facilitates intersensory coordination (B. White, 1985). The transferring of information across sense systems defines sensory integration. As a result of the emergence of cross-modal transfer, "Although physically different input is being received about the object from the separate sense systems, the infant can nonetheless recognize similarities and perhaps equivalence between these inputs" (Rose, Gottfried, & Bridger, 1978, p. 643). This allows for the adaptive capacity to recognize the identity of an object in the face of change in sensory input.

The recognition of "equivalence" or detection of invariant features may specifically refer to a similarity of affect that accompanies the inputs of different sensory modalities. Marks (1978) posits a doctrine of equivalent information, which states that each unique sensory modality can inform about the same features of the external world. Rose (1990) points out that amodal (supramodal) properties cut across different sensory modalities; in addition to intensity and duration she lists "hedonic tone," and refers to "cross-modal equivalence in physiological arousal." Social referencing-induced cross-modal learning may also be involved in the organization of socioemotional object constancy; touching the face of the playful mother, seeing her smiling face, and hearing her excited, laughing voice all elicit the pleasurable affect of joy. In light of Rose's (1986) conclusion that cross-modal processes contribute to the development of abstraction and representational abilities, this integration may allow for the creation of complex, affect-laden abstract representations of the mother. Scott (1969) proposes that the attributes of objects or images are integrated and grouped according to their affective relevance to the individual. Maternal representations may be grouped in terms of positive or negative affect, and could exist as representations of an arousal regulating "good mother" and an arousal dysregulating "bad mother." These ideas also strongly suggest that the facilitation of cross-modal learning by dyadic social referencing socioaffective transactions that create a psychobiologically attuned state in the mother and infant may represent the mechanism by which the child's discovery of the physical environment is socially mediated and may describe the hidden dynamics of the "processes that are currently in a state of formation" in the "zone of proximal development" (Vygotsky, 1978).

The structure-function relationships which support cross-modal transfer, the transfer of information across modalities, are at present unknown. In pursuit of the solution of this problem, it should be mentioned that it is now thought that hemispheric limbic structures are critical to the transfer of learning between modalities (Trevarthen, 1990). Due to its involvement in many modality-specific processes, the right hemisphere is preferentially involved in establishing the "personal relevance" of stimuli (Van Lancker, 1991). This hemisphere, with dense reciprocal interconnections with limbic and subcortical structures (Tucker, 1981), is specialized to regulate arousal (Levy, Heller, Banich, & Burton, 1983) and to integrate perceptual processes (Semmes, 1968). Semmes concludes that the diffuse organization of the right hemisphere underlies "specialization for behaviors requiring multimodal coordination, such as various spatial abilities" (p. 11). Indeed, it contains larger cortical areas than the left of intermodal associative zones that integrate processing of the three main sensory modalities (Goldberg & Costa, 1981). The onset of right hemispheric specialization for tactual processing, as reflected in cross-modal transfer, occurs between the first and second year (Rose, 1984). Active touch exploration of extrapersonal space, in both right- and left-handed humans, is associated with the functioning of the parietal cortex of the right hemisphere (Dewsmedt, 1977). This right hemisphere, moreso than the left, is structurally specialized for greater cross-modal integration (Chapanis, 1977; Tucker, 1992), perhaps due to the facts that it contains more myelinated fibers that optimize transfer across regions than the left (Gur et al., 1980), and that it is specialized to represent multiple information channels in parallel (Bradshaw & Nettleton, 1981).

The observed greater width of the right frontal lobe (Galaburda et al., 1978) has been suggested to reflect the expansion of multimodal association areas (Tucker, 1992), and the large right frontal region has been demonstrated to show a high degree of intrinsic connectivity (Tucker, Roth, & Bair, 1986). These connections within the right frontolimbic area may represent interconnections between the various sites in the orbitofrontal cortex that receive olfactory, somesthetic, visual, and auditory sensory input and mediate intersensory communication. Rose and Ruff (1987) speculate that, "It is possible that the final abstract description is represented in the same parts of the brain or by the same mechanism regardless of the system that responded to the input in the first place" (p. 320). Indeed, the anatomical convergence of the various sensory afferents in the prefrontal cortex has been proposed to be the morphological basis for the intermodal and cross-modal exchange of information (Petrides & Iversen, 1976). The functional output of prefrontal cortical systems, the delay function, is characterized by supramodality—it is influenced by somesthetic, visual, and auditory cues—and cross-modality (Fuster, 1991). Cross-modal transfer has been suggested to involve the development or operation of a "mediator" that integrates information from the various senses (Rose et al., 1978), and the mediating process that supports equivalences serves to "bridge a gap that exists between the two modalities" (Rose & Ruff, 1987, p. 319). Prefrontal structures play an essential role in "bridging temporal gaps" (Fuster, 1991, p. 201).

Most importantly, studies have shown that the orbitofrontal (Benevento et al., 1977; Thorpe et al., 1983) and not the dorsolateral (Azuma & Suzuki, 1984) prefrontal cortex is involved in the formation of cross-modal associations. In a very recent investigation of polymodal prefrontal, including lateral orbital, cortex, Watanabe (1992) concludes that this cortex "plays important roles in the crossmodal coding of the associative significance of the stimulus" (p. 244). These findings suggest that the right orbitofrontal cortex, which performs an essential role in the regulation of behavior on the basis of information provided by various sensory modalities, is functionally involved in cross-modal transfer, a cognitive process which fundamentally contributes to the development of abstraction and representational abilities (Rose, 1986; Rose & Ruff, 1987).

SUMMARY

The sensory systems of the human infant develop in an invariant sequence and in a competitive relationship amongst each other. This development reflects the experience-dependent maturation of various sensory areas of the posterior cerebral cortex. Over the first year, the mother provides different and more intense forms of stimulation in dyadic sociaffective transactions with the infant. In the first postnatal period, olfactory-gustatory stimulation is the predominant modality, with somesthetic-thermal inputs secondary. From the second through the ninth month, tactile stimulation predominates, with visual input secondary. At 10 months tactile decreases, and visual stimulation is heightened, and this in turn is followed by a period of auditory dominance. These events influence the programmed sequential growth of subcortical-olfactory, parietal-somesthetic, occipital-visual, and temporal-auditory connections into the orbitofrontal cortex.

Such structural maturational events allow for important functional advances. The infant can not only process higher intensities of information for each sensory modality, but he can also coprocess polymodal sensory stimulation. The transferring of information across sense systems enables him to recognize equivalence, to detect invariant features of an object even in the face of changing sensory input. A similarity of affective charge or arousal level may underlie this equivalence phenomenon. Cross-modal processing may therefore be responsible for the abstraction properties of internal representations. The right hemispheric orbitofrontal cortex and its connections with posterior cortical sensory areas, a site of the generation and storage of prototypical representations, is suggested to be essential to cross-modal processing.

24

The Development
of Increasingly Complex
Interactive Representations

Once infants have developed the brain architecture to enable memory, they can begin forming internal representations of elements of the external world and of experiences with these elements. The information captured in this form can now begin to functionally substitute for new information from the external world. By this I mean . . . in imagery is captured information with functional value for guiding acts to completion. Now such objects, which are represented in an enduring world of consciousness, can modulate energy dissipation without being physically present.

—Michael L. Schwalbe (1991)

At their core, the complementary working models of self and other have to do not so much with particular actions of thoughts as with expectations concerning the maintenance of basic regulation and positive affect even in the face of environmental challenge.

—L. Alan Sroufe (1989a)

At the level of the orbitofrontal cortex, representations of the external world are integrated with subcortical information regarding the internal visceroendocrine environment (Nauta, 1971). It is important to point out that, especially in infancy, representations of the external world also include representations of objects of the external social world, especially representations of interactions with the proximal social environment, that is, with the affectively regulating primary caregiver. In previous chapters I mentioned that it is now thought that object representations develop epigenetically through successive developmental stages

311

(Blatt et al., 1990), and that developmental gradations of representational capacity have important implications for affective development (Trad, 1986). I suggest that the very earliest maternal representations, in Mahler's autistic period, take the form of olfactory-tactile-thermal models. In the second through eighth-ninth month (Mahler's symbiotic period), these are supplanted by kinesthetic-dominant representations. At the onset of the practicing period visual models, "presymbolic" representations of the visual stimulation provided by the mother's emotionally expressive face, predominate. According to Bowlby (1973) internalized working models first emerge at about 12 months, the early practicing period. These inceptive internal working models of attachment are later reorganized in the middle of the second year into a highly complex "symbolic" representation, an enduring working model that contains auditory as well as visual, tactile, and olfactory components. As a result of his studies of the enduring effects of early sensory deficits on the capacity of children to form internal representations and experience affect, Freedman (1981) concludes that:

> The external object which we perceive as a whole is, in fact, the product of a synthetic operation. Its visual, acoustic, and somesthetic properties become internalized and establish representations independently of one another. (p. 863)

The early and the late phases of the practicing period are a critical time for the construction of affect regulating working models, as the orbitofrontal model generated in the earlier part of the period is modified and superceded by a more complex and efficient dual component model in the late practicing period. In this chapter I shall further discuss the function and content of the symbolic dynamic interactive representations that appear in the middle of the second year.

INTERACTIVE REPRESENTATIONS AS PSYCHOBIOLOGICAL REGULATORS

It is now clear that from earliest ages social interactions influence cognitive development (Perret-Clermont, 1980). In the last chapter I proposed that different types of sensory stimulation delivered to developing posterior cortical areas occurs in the context of an affective dyadic transaction. This stimulation influences the final growth and maturation, and therefore the functional capacity of the posterior cortical areas that process such modality-specific information. In light of Rose's (1986) conclusion that cross-modal processes, influenced by hedonic tone and arousal, contribute to the development of cognitive abstract representational abilities, dyadic, external psychobiological arousal regulation may allow for the creation of complex, internal, affect-laden abstract representations of the child's interaction with the mother.

This continues in practicing reunions, as cross-modal learning is facilitated by dyadic social referencing socioaffective transactions that create a psycho-biologically attuned arousal state in the mother and infant. Cognitive (focused attention) as well as affective (positive affect) transformational outcomes result from maternally regulated vitalizing reciprocity arousal amplifying transactions. Greenspan (1981) notes that infant arousal regulation is first performed by the responsive mother, then acquired by the infant. The psychobiological regulation of the ambulatory child's arousal level by the mother who allows him to securely move away from her in order to extract information from the environment in the context of juvenile play experiences (Fagen, 1981) and subsequently to freely return to her (Rosenblum, 1987) is thus instrumental to the development of self-regulation of both infant cognition and emotion. The importance of the develop-ment of arousal regulation to cognitive self-regulation is stressed by Sidman (1988):

> The infant who is able to regulate states of arousal so as to attend effectively may maintain this capacity for self-regulation so that attending and learning are easier in childhood. (p. 513)

In a similar conception Tucker (1992) concludes:

> The ability to participate in processes of play and affectional interaction may be a key determinant of both information flow and the brain arousal that help to shape developing neural networks. Furthermore, the experiences with self-regulation of arousal state and attentional mechanisms gained through early play and affective exchanges may form the foundation for continued development of attentional and cognitive skills. (p. 80)

These neural networks may specifically refer to orbitofrontal circuitries impli-cated in directed attention (King et al., 1989), as it is known that the right frontal area is involved in sustained attention (Whitehead, 1991; Wilkins, Shallice, & McCarthy, 1987). Neurobiological studies have revealed that this frontolimbic cortex is involved in a generalized arousal reaction (Kandel & Schwartz, 1985) and that orbitofrontal modulation of arousal onsets in late infancy (Bowden, Goldman, Rosvold, & Greenstreet, 1971). By the end of the practicing period this system can directly modulate both sympathetic ergotropic and parasym-pathetic trophotropic arousal.

Goldman-Rakic (1987b) emphasizes the adaptive regulatory function of pre-frontal internal representations. Representations of self interacting with the arousal regulating primary caregiver may be specifically internally coded in imprinted frontolimbic patterns of the two limbic circuits in response to varia-tions of the images of facial expressions of the external emotionally significant other. The unique functional capacities of this frontolimbic cortex suggest its maturation and activity is critical to the generation of Stern's (1985) self-regulating "generalized episodes of interactions that are mentally represented."

Hofer (1984a) demonstrates that internal representations of human relationships serve as "biological regulators," that internal experiences of a relationship as carried out in the minds of people can act to control physiological responses. In early ontogeny this function is initially mediated through the caregiver's psychobiological regulation of the infant's internal arousal state. Arousal level is known to be tightly coupled to the metabolic energy activity of the brain (Gonzalez-Lima & Scheich, 1985). In line with Hofer's suggestion that the mother acts as the regulator of the infant's developing autonomic nervous system, I have suggested that changes in stimulation emanating from the responsive caregiver's emotionally expressive face either energize the infant by triggering a neuropeptide induced activation of sympathetic energy-mobilizing function or de-energize the infant by a corticosteroid induction of parasympathetic energy-conserving activity.

This proposal dovetails with Schwalbe's (1991) model in which an external object can function to modulate the patterns of energy dissipation in the infant's brain and body. Schwalbe suggests that later in development the memorial internal representation of experiences with a modulating external object who "answers to impulses" can shape patterns of energy flow. Schwalbe concludes that the interaction of the infant's body with information derived from the mother is captured in the form of imagery, and the accessibility and retrievability of these representations in memory allows for the experience of "things going on in the head." Schwalbe's internal representations that modulate energy dissipation and are utilized to guide acts to completion are thus equated with Bowlby's internal working models that function as affect regulators and serve to generate coping strategies (Kobak & Sceery, 1988). Dynamic internalized working models are now conceptualized as mental representations that contain affective as well as cognitive components (Main et al., 1985).

The concept of mental representations has had a long history within psychoanalysis. The work of Kernberg (1976) has demonstrated the importance of the conception of internalized representations of the self affectively transacting with objects in the social environment as an explanatory mechanism of various psychopathological conditions that originate in very early development. Internal object relations are defined as mentally stored representations of the self directing affect toward an emotionally significant external object. According to Greenberg and Mitchell (1983):

> People react to and interact with not only an actual other but also an internal other, a psychic representation of a person which in itself has the power to influence both the individual's affective state and his overt behavioral reactions. (p. 10)

These conceptions based on clinical observations of adults have been supported by developmental psychoanalytic observations of infants. A major theme of contemporary developmental psychoanalysis is that the developing infant constructs an inner representational world, a model of the world that is based on his affective interactions with objects in the immediate social environment (Sandler & Rosenblatt, 1962). The representational construct is now visualized as a possible bridging concept between psychoanalysis and neuroscience (Hadley, 1983). In a recent critique of contemporary psychoanalytic theory, Shulman (1987) concludes that "the moorings of psychoanalytic thought lie of necessity in the study of natural (especially biological) *and* social processes" (p. 171). A primary investigatory focus of current object relations theories is on the nature and development of mental representations of the self and others and on the affective and cognitive processes associated with these representations (Westen, 1991).

THE ENCODING OF EXPECTATIONS IN RIGHT HEMISPHERIC DYNAMIC INTERACTIVE REPRESENTATIONS

Thus the representational concepts presently utilized in attachment and developmental psychoanalytic theory both stress the salience of both affective and cognitive elements. It is most important to point out that in his later work Piaget (1981) concluded, "there is no cognitive mechanism without affective elements" (p. 3). Conversely, Krystal (1974) argues that primitive cognitive contents may be part of every affect. A considerable body of evidence has accumulated which indicates that the generally accepted separation of mental life into cognition and affect is misleading (Basch, 1988). Changeux now asserts that "The connections existing between the limbic system and prefrontal cortex offer a material basis for relationships between the emotional and cognitive spheres" (Changeux & Dehacnc, 1989, p.98) and Sarter and Markowitsch (1985, p. 368) conclude that "emotions are part of the information represented in memory and that consequently affective and cognitive information are interwoven in retrieval." Kesner (1986) suggests this affect is associated specifically with orbitofrontal cortical functioning within an "expectancy-based memory system."

Recent cognitive research demonstrates that dynamic representations contain expectancy effects and code a temporal dimension in which "time goes forward" (Freyd, 1987). In terms of contemporary affect theory expectations are conceptualized as images amplified by excitement and enjoyment positive affect (Kaufman, 1989). The research of Stuss et al. (1982) demonstrates that orbitofrontal cortcx subserves memory and cognitive functions, and Thorpe et al. (1983) show that orbitofrontal association cortex categorizes and abstracts information, such as information embedded in the emotionally expressive face, and stores it in (episodic) memory. This cortex is activated during the mental generation of images of faces (Goldenberg et al., 1989), and images, now defined as thought representations with a sensory quality, are known to occur "when a person expects certain external stimuli" (Horowitz, 1983, p. 291). These expected external stimuli may specifically refer to socioemotional stimuli. Indeed, this may be a good definition of an emotion bias (Malatesta et al., 1989).

According to psychoanalytic object relations theory, representations of a template of the early significant other shape the child's "expectations of the interpersonal environment" (Horner, 1989). Beebe and Lachman (1988a) refer to the infant's utilization of representations of interiorized interaction which act as basic microstructures of "being with" another person: "the infant will represent the expectation of being matched by, and being able to match, the partner as well as the associated experience of participating in the state of another" (p. 15). Horowitz (1983) describes an "expectancy priming of certain schemata for matching with potential patterns." Interactive representations are generated in critical period social imprinting experiences that induce the formation of neuronal models of the socioemotional input provided by the imprinting object via an "experience-expectant mechanism" (Black & Greenough, 1986). This includes a coding of the expected affective input of a significant other. Pribram (1981, p. 107) defines neuronal models as neuronal configurations against which subsequent inputs are matched which form the sum of the organism's expectancies. Such models are inscribed in the prefrontal cortex, and are accessed in orbitofrontal appraisal (Pribram, 1987) processes.

This structure in the frontal lobes, cortex that is known to abstract selective features from a perceptual image and recombine the abstractions into models that guide decision-making and action (Pribram, 1981), therefore has the unique functional ability to produce "abstract representational units" of relational patterns that generate expectations regarding upcoming interpersonal interactions (Stern, 1989). Expectations are embedded in the orbitofrontal appraisal of patterns of affective facial displays that are predicted to occur in specific social interactions. This evaluative right prefrontal system is expanded in the hemisphere dominant for evaluating emotional expressions (Ahern et al., 1991), for perceiving and coding the emotional communicative content of nonverbal expressions from facial stimuli (Blonder, Bowers, & Heilman, 1991), for conceptually organizing facial emotion (Etcoff, 1984b), and for providing the gestalt-synthetic operations necessary for the cognitive representations of emotions (TenHouten, 1991). The orbitofrontal cortex, which contains "expectancy firing neurons" (Kubota & Niki, 1971) that generate "expectancy waves" (Fuster, 1985), is a central component of an "expectancy command circuit" (Panksepp, 1986). The socioaffective experience-dependent ontogenetic maturation of this cortical system which functions to appraise emotional stimuli and regulate emotional responses may underlie the assertion that "the typical pattern of emotional behaviors appears in a certain time sequence in infants only in an average, expectable environment" (Plutchik, 1983, p. 244).

The core of the earliest indelible internalized models of the self in relationship with an emotionally significant other, the substratum of self-identity, contains an expectation, a bias, that the primary attachment object will or will not remain available and accessible at times of hypo- or hyperstimulating affective stress. According to Ainsworth (1967), attachment is not in essence overt patterns of behavior, but rather is "internal," built into (imprinted in) the nervous system as a result of transactions with the mother, and expressed as "expectancies." Security of attachment is now thought to fundamentally relate to a physiological coding that "homeostatic disruptions will be set right" (Pipp & Harmon, 1987, p. 650). Lichtenberg (1989, p. 104) asserts that "The shadow that the nature of the early attachment casts over future relations is that, when in distress, the person will have an expectation of relief." Tronick (1989) concludes that as a result of dyadic affective miscoordination and interactive repair, the infant develops an expectation that relational disruptions are remediable and that negative affect will be transformed into positive affective experiences. Similarly, distress-relief sequences are thought to contribute to the development of social expectations (Lamb & Malkin, 1986) that are associated with emotional regulation (Thompson, 1990). Kobak and Sceery (1988) note that internal working models which define "styles of affect regulation" provide rules for regulating distress-related affect in the context of parental responsiveness to the child's signals of distress. As opposed to early practicing period forming presymbolic representations, more complex symbolic working models generated in the middle of the second year contain algorithms for regulating and recovering from stressful shame states.

Internal models are currently understood to be representations that enable the individual to form expectations and evaluate the interactions that regulate his attachment system. These models are guides for future interactions, and the term *working* refers to the individual's unconscious use of the model to interpret and act on new experiences (Crowell & Feldman, 1991). In discussing these internal models Rutter (1987) notes, "children derive a set of expectations about their own relationship capacities and about other people's resources to their social overtures and interactions, these expectations being created on the basis of their early parent-child attachments" (p. 449). Recent psychoanalytic theoreticians have conceptualized internal objects "as serving a kind of loose anticipatory image of what is to be expected from people in the real world" (Greenberg & Mitchell, 1983, p.11). Markus and Nurius (1986) refer to regulatory "self schemas," representations that are responsive to changes in the social environment, and which shape "expectations" and influence how information about the self is processed. Hofer (1984a) concludes that the regulating action of internal representations of object relationships on biologic systems lies in the generation of expectancies. Basch (1988) now refers to subcortical-cortical generated "patterns of affective expectations" that are a product of infant-caregiver transactions in the sensorimotor period which act as a "set" that colors all future socioemotional experiences. He also notes that the nature and intensity of the affect state determines the individual's behavioral reactivity—"affect is the gateway to action."

The unique structural connections of the orbitofrontal cortex allow for the individual to consider both complex sensory data and motivational and emotional factors prior to executing a motor act (Pandya & Yeterian, 1985). Fuster (1985, 1991) asserts that the structure-function of the prefrontal cortex accounts for its critical role in the temporal organization of behavior, in both retrospective and prospective future related functions involved in planning. Schwartz (1990) emphasizes the adaptive advantage of "the capacity to inscribe and retain neurobiologic records of survival-essential predictive relationships" (p. 122). Meltzoff (1990) asserts that a watershed transformation in higher cognitive functioning occurs at 18 months. This abrupt developmental shift allows the child to project into the future "what might be" and deduce from the past "what must have been" in advance of, and even in the absence of, external perceptual inputs. Meltzoff further remarks that the neural basis for this psychological shift is a mystery.

I suggest that the maturation of the connections between the prefrontal-limbic, frontal-motor, and posterior-sensory areas of the right hemisphere underlies this developmental advance. The middle of the second year marks an important point in time of the maturation of corticolimbic tracts (Kinney et al., 1988) and the auditory projection area, the visual association area of the occipital cortex, the anterior temporal lobes, and the anterior and posterior limbic areas of the cortex involved in mechanisms of memory and emotional activities (Rabinowicz, 1979). Sensorimotor components of affective interactive representations are inscribed and stored in the early developing nonverbal visuospatial-holistic right hemisphere (Geschwind & Galaburda, 1987; Tucker, 1986), known to be specifically impacted by early social experiences (Denenberg et al., 1978), in the first 1½ years, before the later maturation of the verbal analytic left cerebral cortex (Taylor, 1969). Piaget's "sensorimotor period," which spans 0–18 months, thus represents a critical period for the early maturation of the right hemisphere, the hemisphere dominant for "manipulo-spatial" ability (Gazzaniga & LeDoux, 1978) and "visuomotor" control (Bracewell, Husain, & Stein, 1990). This is confirmed in developmental neurological research. Children who suffer focal right cerebral hemisphere injury before the end of the first year show an enduring spatial cognitive deficit in the third year (Stiles-Davis, Sugarman, & Nass, 1985).

In current studies on hemispheric psychophysiology, Johnsen and Hugdahl (1991) demonstrate a right hemispheric superiority for associative learning of visual stimuli embedded in facial emotional expressions, and conclude that learned associations between emotional events are represented and stored in the right hemisphere. Kosslyn (1988) and Sergent (1989) suggest that this hemisphere plays a special role in processing visual imagery. Safer (1981) proposes that the right hemisphere is dominant for the processing and representation of emotional stimuli using imagery codes, while the left uses verbal codes:

> Imagery coding takes place for the feelings aroused by spontaneously produced facial expressions of emotion, the memory of the eliciting stimuli, and the memory of the responses occurring along with this emotional experience. (p. 87).

Complementing these experimental findings, Watt (1990), in the psychoanalytic literature, has recently offered multidisciplinary evidence to support the conclusion that the most critical units of representation of the right hemisphere are self-and-object images (as opposed to a lexical-semantic system of representation in the left hemisphere). Horowitz (1983) posits an image mode which precedes a lexical mode of representation, and refers to a heightening of one representational system over another. This right brain self-and-object image representational system matures and is in operation at around 18 months, the end of the first postnatal growth spurt (Epstein, 1978), before callosal systems of communication between the hemispheres occurs (callosal myelination does not even begin until the end of the first year; Galin, Johnstone, Nakell, & Herron, 1979; Salamy, 1978), and before the later maturing dominant verbal left hemisphere, which generates more verbally complex working models and verbally mediated affect states (Silberman & Weingartner, 1986), superimposes its imprint upon the physiological activity and information processing of the nonverbal right hemisphere (the left hemisphere does not become dominant until the third year; Levin, 1991).

SUMMARY

Developmental advances over the stages of infancy produce more complex interactive representations. Presymbolic representations, emerging at the end of the first year, are superceded by symbolic representations in the middle of the second. The increasingly abstract character of the latter results from cross-modal experiences that integrate all sensory (especially visual and auditory) modalities. These internalized object relations can more efficiently autoregulate the child's psychobiological states. Dynamic interactive representations encode expectancy effects, and this allows for an internal mechanism that appraises expected socio-emotional transactions. Such internal working models of relationships program styles of affect regulation, including the modulation of distress-related affects such as shame.

The functional advances of these representations depend upon the attainment of an experience-dependent structural maturation of an orbitofrontal system that regulates both cortical sensory and motor areas and subcortical limbic circuits. This event occurs at 15 to 18 months, the late practicing period. Symbolic interactive representations are stored specifically in the right hemisphere.

25

Orbitofrontal Influences on the Autonomic Nervous System

The great density of the cutaneous receptors in the face and the considerable variety of the patterns of contraction of the facial muscles suggest that the resulting patterns of neocortical excitations and hypothalamic-cortical discharges will match in diversity that of the emotional expression.

—Ernst Gellhorn (1964)

The hypothalamus plays a particularly important role in coordinating the endocrine, autonomic, and behavioral responses that assure survival of the individual (homeostasis) as well as survival of the species (reproduction). And since stress (or a stressor) is usually regarded as any condition or factor that disturbs the dynamic equilibrium (homeostasis) of the body, it has seemed reasonable to assume that hypothalamic circuitry mediates a number of adaptive responses initiated by such factors.

—L.W. Swanson (1991)

The orbitofrontal cortex, the major cortical source of direct connections with the diencephalic hypothalamus (Nauta, 1972), plays a critical role in influencing affective states via affect regulating interactive representations, since it acts to hierarchically control this major subcortical center which regulates both sympathetic and parasympathetic autonomic activities (Truex & Carpenter, 1964). It is well established that the hypothalamus is a locus of drive centers (Stellar, 1954), is critical to the expression of emotional behavior (Thatcher & John, 1977), and is the hub of the motivational systems (Hadley, 1989). In addition, its direct influence over central and peripheral catecholaminergic systems allows for its modulation of fundamental organismic arousal mechanisms. Scott (1958) has concluded that neural connections between the cortex and hypothalamus are established during the sensitive period for the development of social responses. The experience-dependent maturation of these connections in the practicing critical period underlies the observation that the infant's regulatory and reactive capabilities continue to develop after birth (Rothbart & Derryberry, 1982), and further elucidates the mechanism of "the regulation of affect in infancy" (Basch, 1988).

This frontolimbic structure represents the cortical system that is fundamentally involved in mediating the central autonomic manifestations of emotional behavior (Cechetto & Saper, 1987) and in regulating motivational states (Pandya & Yeterian, 1985). Although the orbitofrontal modulation of the sympathetic and parasympathetic components of the autonomic nervous system has been known for quite some time (Fuster, 1980; Kaada et al., 1949), the importance of this structure-function relationship is only now being appreciated (Neafsey, 1990). Its structural characteristics account for the extensive limbic and hypothalamic interconnections of the right cortex (Joseph, 1982), and its functional activity as a hemispheric regulator is responsible for the right cerebral regulation of autonomic activities (Heilman et al., 1977). In this chapter I extrapolate recent findings on autonomic activities, especially in the orbitofrontal cortex and the hypothalamus, to a deeper understanding of the dynamics of emotion processes.

THE CONTRIBUTIONS OF SUBCORTICAL AND CORTICAL ACTIVITIES TO FACIAL EXPRESSIONS OF EMOTION

According to Gellhorn, (1964) the generation of emotion involves proprioceptive facial-muscle stimulation that activates the hypothalamus. The centrality of facial feedback to the expression of emotion has since been stressed almost universally by the major contemporary affect theorists (e.g., Buck,1980; Ekman, 1984; Izard, 1971; Tomkins, 1962; Zajonc, 1985). For example, Izard (1971) contends that facial muscle feedback activates central neural activity in the limbic cortex, hypothalamus, and brain stem reticular system, which mediate emotion. Tomkins (1962) proposes that feedback from the face, which has a high density of "neural representations and firing," triggers changes in blood flow and temperature, and these physiological responses activate subcortical "affect programs." Zajonc (1985) presents evidence to support the postulate that facial actions in emotional expressions regulate the volume and temperature of the blood supply to brain areas. Recent experiments on the neuropsychology of emotion (Schiff & Lamon, 1989) have supported the idea that emotions can be aroused by unilateral facial muscle contractions; this induction occurs without conscious mediation. These psychological theories which stress the essential role of emotional facial action in the subjective experience of emotion have awaited a more precise characterization of the anatomical structural systems which mediate facially expressed affective function.

In a current influential text of clinical neurology, Adams and Victor (1989) refer to the "anterior frontothalamopontomedullary pathway" for emotional expression. In developmental studies on the effects of taste and smell on human facial responses Steiner (1979) concludes that facial expressions are mediated by the parasympathetic medullary nucleus of the solitary tract, and that this function is rerepresented in higher cortical structures. Neurons in the solitary nucleus are sensitive to gustatory stimulation (Travers & Smith, 1979; Sweazey & Bradley, 1989), and gustatory (Rolls et al., 1950) and olfactory (Tanabe, Yarita, Iino, Ooshima, & Takagi, 1975) sensory stimuli are known to be reprocessed at the orbitofrontal level. Indeed, facial motor control is considered to arise from the visceral nervous system (Rinn, 1984). The mature processing of facial information involves not only the activity of the previously discussed dopaminergic ventral tegmental circuit, but also the noradrenergic lateral tegmental circuit, which couples the orbitofrontal cortex with medullary catecholaminergic nuclei. The orbitofrontal cortex uniquely projects descending axons directly onto both A10 dopaminergic and A2 noradrenergic dendrites. This dual functioning orbitofrontal cortex, at the apex of both forebrain-midbrain limbic circuits, functions in emotion regulation by way of its direct connections with the hypothalamus and medullary nucleus of the solitary tract, which themselves are interconnected.

Facial skin is well supplied with receptors that are sensitive to the stretching and pressure changes that result from expressive movements (Norden, Hagbarth, Thomandu, & Wallin, 1984). The facial nerve, which innervates the skeletal muscles of the face and transmits this information directly terminates on the nucleus of the solitary tract (Beckstead & Norgren, 1979) as do visceral projections (Kalia & Mesulam, 1980), and this convergence may account for Izard's (1977) proposal that somatic feedback from the face plays a role in recruiting visceral activity. A2 noradrenergic neurons from this structure are known to terminate heavily on the facial motor nucleus (Vertes, 1990), in keeping with the fact that the accessory facial nucleus receives terminals from structures concerned with "the emotional control of facial musculature" (Truex & Carpenter, 1964). These connections, along with direct orbital-medullary connections, may underlie the observations that the anterior portion of the orbital gyrus includes part of the motor face areas and somatic sensory areas (Mizuno et al., 1968), and that stimulation of this cortex specifically produces eye and head movements (Pribram, 1987) and motor responses in the face (Sugar et al., 1948). Orbitofrontal functions may thus significantly contribute to the physiological expression of emotion that is electromyographically detected in the covert activity of facial muscles (Cacioppo, Martzke, Petty, & Tassinary, 1988; Dimberg, 1990).

Tomkins' and Zajonc's proposal that emotional facial activities are associated with vascular and temperature responses also imply orbitofrontal mediation, since vascular and thermal responses are regulated by this cortex (Delgado & Livingston, 1948). The function of the frontolimbic orbital cortex which processes information embedded in emotionally expressive faces (Thorpe et al., 1983), and which links up cortical sensory modalities and motor control networks (Tucker, 1992), elucidates the mechanism of facial regulation of internal affective phenomena. The maturation of the prefrontal regions of the right hemisphere in early infancy allows for the development of right cortical inhibitory control over subcortical facial displays (Rothbart et al., 1989), a prerequisite of the adaptive expression of emotion.

RECIPROCAL AND NONRECIPROCAL AUTONOMIC MODES

This prefrontal system, the only cortical structure that connects into the two limbic forebrain-midbrain circuits (Nauta & Domesick, 1982) and is hierarchically involved in the dual excitatory and inhibitory functional mechanisms of the limbic system (Stellar, 1982), acts as a central control of both the sympathetic and parasympathetic nervous systems (Fuster, 1980). Cortical frontolimbic structure is ideally situated to regulate emotion, since it is well established that "the physiological expression of emotion is dependent, in part, upon both sympathetic and parasympathetic components of the autonomic nervous system" (Truex & Carpenter, 1964, p. 431), and that "their dual activities are integrated into coordinated responses ensuring the maintenance of an adequate internal environment to meet the demands of any given situation" (p. 249). These components "arc frequently in competition and the final effect then depends upon the relationship between the momentary activity of the two systems" (Broverman ct al., 1968, p. 29). Hess (1954), in a classical conceptualization of autonomic regulation, proposed that the two branches of the ANS are antagonistic, reciprocally integrated circuits. The central tenet of autonomic reciprocity asserted that sympathetic and parasympathetic outflows are subject to tightly coupled reciprocal control, with increasing activity in one component associated with decreasing activity in the other.

In very recent revisions of the classical theory of autonomic control, Berntson, Cacioppo, and Quigley (1991) present evidence from various studies that demonstrates the existence of three elemental categories of autonomic control: a coupled reciprocal mode, a coupled nonreciprocal mode, and an uncoupled mode. In the first, increases in activity in one ANS division are associated with a decrease in the other; in the second, concurrent increases (coactivation) or concurrent decreases (coinhibition) occur in both components; in the third, responses in one division occur in the absence of changes in the other (Table 25.1). These authors point out that rostral brain areas modulate the three modes of autonomic control. The exact same results are found in current research on the psychophysiology of emotion induction. Grossman, Stemmler, and Meinhardt (1990) observe that the sympathetic and parasympathetic autonomic branches may manifest three patterns of interaction—reciprocal inhibition, mutual antagonism, and unilateral activity.

How do these patterns evolve? Hofer's work (1984a) demonstrates that the mother acts as a "hidden" psychobiological regulator of the child's developing autonomic physiology, and Taylor (1987) holds that the mother plays an important role in determining her infant's emerging patterns of "autonomic response specificity" (Lacey, Bateman, & Van Lehn, 1953). Thompson (1990) points out that parasympathetic systems, such as in the frontal lobes, develop more slowly than sympathetic systems. I posit that under optimal conditions the two branches, initially uncoupled, become progressively coupled in development, especially in the postnatally maturing orbitofrontal cortex. I also suggest that the adaptive changes of autonomic patterning that reestablish autonomic balance after socioemotional stresses may predominantly involve reciprocally coupled mechanisms. Berntson et al. (1991) conclude:

> Reciprocal modes can yield large directionally stable shifts, and are suited for well-defined adaptive adjustments to survival challenges. . . .One adaptive feature of reciprocal modes of control is a shift in the relative dominance of the two ANS divisions. (p. 473)

Scherer (1986) emphasizes that both ANS subsystems are involved in autonomic emotional arousal, but that their respective dominance, in the form of sympathetic predominant *ergotropic* arousal and parasympathetic predominant *trophotropic* arousal, may differentiate between specific emotions. This principle is

TABLE 25.1
Modes of Autonomic Control

Sympathic Response	Parasympathic Response		
	Increase	No Change	Decrease
Increase	Coactivation	Uncoupled sympathetic activation	Reciprocal sympathetic activation
No change	Uncoupled parasympathetic activation	Baseline	Uncoupled parasympathetic withdrawal
Decrease	Reciprocal parasympathetic activation	Uncoupled sympathetic withdrawal	Coinhibition

From Berntson et al. (1991). Reprinted by permission of the American Psychological Association.

important to the deciphering of distinct autonomic "signatures" associated with different emotions (Smith, 1989), and to the identification of the unique neural characteristics of discrete emotions (Izard, 1991). It also underscores the much overlooked important principle that just as arousal is now understood to relect multiple systems (Routtenberg, 1968; Thayer, 1989), emotion can not be understood as a single, unitary process. The structural system that physiologically mediates emotion, the limbic system, is composed of not one but two separate circuits (Nauta & Domesick, 1982). Lazarus (1991b) now concludes that any comprehensive theory of emotion must be a systems theory. General systems theory defines a system as a complex of components in mutual interaction (Bertalanffy, 1968). From a psychophysiological perspective, Schwartz (1982) asserts that emotional properties result from "complex interactions and organizations of its component processes" (p. 70).

These components may operate under unique and dissociable temporal parameters. For example, restraint stress, a potent elicitor of emotional responses, induces "striking differences in the temporal pattern of the ACTH and corticosterone responses, the latter one being usually delayed relative to its hypophysial counterpart" (Gaillet et al., 1991, p. 177). Earlier, I presented evidence to show that ACTH is a hormonal mediator of the sympathetic nervous system, while cortisol is a parasympathetic agent. Developmental studies also support the dual component model. Hofer's work (1983, 1984a) indicates that the affective components of attachment and separation involve multiple emotional systems that operate in different time frames. I interpret the acute separation stress response of protest, associated with increased activity and heart rate, to reflect a sympathetic-dominant state, while the slower forming despair response, accompanied by decreased activity and heart rate, denotes a parasympathetic-dominant state. The despair stress response is activated in the state of mourning, which Gellhorn (1964) postulates represents a state of parasympathetic dominance. Shame also represents a parasympathetic-dominant affective state (Buss, 1979; Schore, 1991). In other words, predominant excitatory sympathetic activity underlies high intensity high energy affective states, while dominant inhibitory parasympathetic function is reflected in low-keyed low energy emotional states.

Furthermore, both autonomic arousal components are proposed to be activated in enduring states of "unconscious affect," a phenomenon stressed in psychoanalytic conceptions of affect (Emde, 1980b; Pulver, 1971), which must be addressed in any overarching theory of emotion. Unconscious affect may represent a psychobiological pattern of "mutual antagonism," in which both autonomic branches are activated at enhanced levels during the induction of a negative emotion (Grossman et al., 1990), producing a chronic stressful state of contemporaneous heightened excitation and heightened inhibition. A chronic elevation of the two limbic circuits may characterize the psychobiology of repression (Schwartz, 1990) and may elucidate the well-known finding that individuals with a repressive personality style, who habitually repress all negative affects, are at risk for psychological and physical disorders (Bonanno & Singer, 1990). Coactivation of vagal and sympathetic divisions occurs in certain emotional states (Gellhorn, Cortell, & Feldman, 1941), such as in a classic defense reaction (Cannon, 1939). Gilbert (1989) concludes that "long-term states of defensive arousal may be (in part) mediated by the cortisol response" (p. 107). Berntson et al. (1991) note that: "novel or challenging environments— environments in which optimal or adaptive behavioral responses are unclear— may be more likely to evoke or promote coactivation of both the sympathetic and parasympathetic divisions than are familiar environments" (p. 483).

In early development, when both ANS components are maturing, an unpredictable environment defines a *stressful* environment. An infant encounters this in interactions with an unresponsive, clinically depressed mother. In such a situation the infant shows simultaneously low levels of motor activity (high parasympathetic inhibition) and elevated heart rate (high sympathetic excitation), hallmarks of a stressful response (Field et al., 1988). If this energetically inefficient psychological state is expressed over long periods of time in a critical period it becomes temperamentally expressed. Kagan, Reznick, and Snidman (1987) observe a pattern of high sympathetic arousal and elevated cortisol levels in a population of inhibited children who characteristically avoid unfamiliar people and contexts (socioaffective novelty) by the end of the second year of life. This may represent the origin of social phobias, which moreso than other phobias are caused and maintained by fears of negative evaluation (shame) (Zinbarg, Barlow, Brown, & Hertz, 1992). It may also be identical to a "braced readiness," a state of high but undischarged arousal described by Gilbert (1989), which he equates with "social anxiety." In this state a subordinate individual remains vigilant and ready for defensive activity in response to a conspecific (social) threat, specifically in case its (restrained, unconscious, aggressive?) behavior provokes hostility from a more dominant other. Indeed, heightened coactivation of the noradrenergic coeruleal and dopaminergic nigrostriatal systems may occur in classical anxiety (Zinbarg et al., 1992) disorders.

It is now accepted that affects reflect a person's internal state and have a hedonic (valenced) dimension and an arousal dimension (Russell, 1980). The arousal dimension has been equated with an intensity dimension (Diener et al., 1985). However, this model implies a unitary dimension of arousal, and does not reflect the known existence of multiple arousal systems and dual limbic circuits. Although arousal levels are heightened in different affective states, increased levels of energetic arousal will be found in different discrete emotions than increased levels of tense arousal (Thayer, 1989). Similarly, Tucker (1981) differentiates "phasic arousal," heightened in elation and reduced in depression, from "tonic activation," a substrate for anxiety. Energetic equated with phasic arousal may represent the underlying neurophysiological substrate of positive affectivity, a measure of general energy and pleasure (Watson & Clark, 1988). Active vs. passive arousal may also reflect the predominance of sympathetic, energy-expending ventral tegmental vs. parasympathetic, energy-conserving lateral tegmental catecholamine arousal systems.

Orbitofrontal projections to subcortical regions, known to mature in infancy (Johnson et al., 1976), are proposed to mediate its function in arousal modulation which onsets in late infancy (Bowden et al., 1971). The practicing phase thus represents a critical period for the structural growth and functional maturation of first, ventral tegmental dopaminergic ergotropic arousal components, and then, lateral tegmental noradrenergic trophotropic arousal systems. This accounts for the expansion of the affect array—the emergent adaptive capacity to experience the high intensity positive hedonic affect of elated states, and the ability to tolerate low arousal negative affect states, as in depression, loss, and shame. New combinations of coupled sympathetic and parasympathetic components allow for blendings of psychobiological states and the emergent expression of more complex emotions and more complex and permanent defensive organizations in the second half of the second year. These psychobiological mechanisms may explicate Izard's (1991) assertion that "emotions can become linked to or bonded with other emotions through learning and experience" (p. 192). Lane and Schwartz (1987) suggest that emotional development evolves through a series of stages culminating in the capacity to experience blends of feelings and finally blends of blends of feelings.

THE UNIQUE CONTRIBUTION OF PARASYMPATHETIC CONSERVATION-WITHDRAWAL TO EMOTIONAL FUNCTIONS

The two components of the centrally regulated autonomic nervous system are known to be distinct modular circuits (Hess, 1954) which control arousal expressions, with the catabolic sympathetic branch responsible for energy-mobilizing excitatory activity and heart rate acceleration, and the anabolic parasympathetic branch involved in energy-conserving inhibitory activity and heart rate deceleration (Porges, 1976). These dissociable autonomic functions may reflect the sympathetic biochemical stimulation of glycogenolysis and parasympathetic vagal stimulation of glycogenesis (Shimazu, 1971; Shimazu & Amakawa, 1968), known to be regulated by hypothalamic nuclei (Shimazu, Fukuda, & Ban, 1966). Glycogen is a readily mobilized fuel store, and in the mature brain it is localized not in neurons but in astrocytes (Ibrahim, 1975). These glial stores are modulated by monoaminergic neurotransmitters that trigger glycogenolysis (Pearce, Cambray-Deakin, & Murphy, 1985). Its "energetically advantageous" degradation into glucose (Stryer, 1981) occurs in intense states of emotional excitement and strenuous muscle activity, thereby allowing for increased blood glucose supply to the brain, heart, and lungs at the expense of the other viscera (Cannon, 1915/1953). On the other hand, the synthesis of glycogen, which is promoted by the glucocorticoid cortisol (Sie & Fishman, 1964; Stryer, 1981), an agent that regulates glucose metabolism, predominates in the resting well-fed organism (West & Todd, 1962). Horowitz (1983) asserts that the basic regulatory mechanisms of excitation and inhibition which have a biochemical/electrophysiological basis can be exerted in concert or in conflict.

Engel and Schmale (1972) postulate the existence of two structurally distinct biological defense systems, a sympathetic fight (aggression)—flight (fear) mechanism described by Cannon (1939), which involves increased activity of the sympathetic nervous system and active engagement with the environment, and a second regulatory mechanism of conservation-withdrawal, reflected in a predominance of parasympathetic activity and an unresponsiveness to the environment. Fight-flight is associated with catabolic metabolic changes, conservation-withdrawal with anabolic changes. Engel and Schmale suggest that these opposite patterns of physiological response correspond to the functioning of the ergotropic and trophotropic zones in the brainstem identified by Hess and Gellhorn. Furthermore, they present evidence that indicates that the psychobiological state of conservation-withdrawal can be triggered by psychological events. Indeed it is specifically ushered in by a failure of coping that had previously assured gratification and is accompanied by feelings of helplessness and hopelessness. Its adaptive function is highlighted by Taylor (1987):

> While helplessness and hopelessness are the affective responses to real or threatened object loss, conservation-withdrawal may represent a new level of regulation consequent to the loss of regulators within the preexisting object relationship. (p. 285)

Over the past century most of the work on the neurophysiology of emotions has focused almost exclusively on the activities of the sympathetic nervous system. As a rule, researchers have understudied the parasympathetic conservation-withdrawal mechanism and its contribution to low arousal emotion and passive coping. In very recent work, Powles (1992) characterizes this regulatory mechanism for maintaining homeostasis as being expressed in a "lowered metabolic rate", and as "inactive-disengaging, passively carried out, and passively experienced" (p. 213). Attachment researchers have observed that prolonged separations elicit infant passive coping mechanisms that instigate and maintain a state of conservation-withdrawal (Field & Reite, 1985). Henry and Stephens (1977) propose that specific emotional states are associated with the two autonomic/endocrine systems. According to these authors the sympathetic-adrenomedullary system is activated during active coping and supplies an accelerated metabolic rate and expenditure of energy in the body. Conversely, the pituitary adrenocortical system is activated in passive coping, and is endocrinologically expressed in cortisol secretion. This passive state which occurs in *helpless* stressful situations where active coping responses are unavailable (Kaufman & Rosenblum, 1969) represents a helpless depressed state of "distress without effort," which Lundberg and Frankenhaeuser (1980) note is characterized by elevated cortisol levels produced by the hypothalamo-pituitary-adrenal cortical system-activated conservation-withdrawal response.

The function of this parasympathetic adrenocortical system is thus heightened during shame triggered transitions from sympathetic to parasympathetic-dominant states. According to Powles (1992) the shift into conservation-withdrawal is from alert, powered up, and engaged to inhibited, unseen, withdrawn, and disengaged. The consequent onset of conservation-withdrawal, characterized by heart rate deceleration, low activity levels, and helplessness (McCabe & Schneiderman, 1985), is responsible for the typical withdrawal from significant objects (Lichtenberg, 1989) and helplessness and passivity (N.K. Morrison, 1985) seen in shame. Helplessness (Lundberg, 1980), submissiveness (Gilbert, 1989), avoidance learning (Ogren et al., 1981), and a depression of sensory detection activity in all sensory activities (Henkin, 1974) are known to be associated with cortisol release. Emotional states characterized by a decreased energy level are expressed in a lack of responsiveness in which the individual ceases to be active in attempting to reach personal goals (Duffy, 1941). Conservation-withdrawal, an inhibitory homeostatic regulatory process (Engel & Schmale, 1972), has been characterized as "a relative immobility, a quiescence, and an unresponsiveness to the environment" (Powles, 1992, p. 415), and as "adaptive for the 'exhausted' organism in replenishing energy stores and restoring physiological equilibrium" (Field, 1985b, p. 215).

Earlier, this physiological state was proposed to be mediated by orbitofrontal influences on the parasympathetic A2 noradrenergic system of the medullary solitary tract. The nucleus of the solitary tract is known to be densely interconnected into the hypothalamus (Saper et al., 1976) and thereby influences its function. This regulatory state may be biochemically expressed through orbitofrontal stimulation of hypothalamico-pituitary-adrenocortical corticosteroid levels (Hall & Marr, 1975; Kandel & Schwartz, 1985). Adrenal glucocorticoid hormones are known to play an important role in behavioral adaptation (Bohus, De Kloet, & Veldhuis, 1984), and glycogen synthesis, stimulated by cortisol (Hilz, Tarnowski, & Arend, 1963), accounts for the replenishing of energy stores. "It is very important that the glucocorticoids and other adrenal cortical hormones in their over-all effects put the tissues of an animal in better condition to withstand stress in general" (West & Todd, 1962, p. 1025). In this way the orbitofrontal association cortex, which is expanded in the right hemisphere (Falk et al., 1990), and which is the last evolving and most rostral component of the lateral tegmental limbic circuit, can act as an "extrapituitary mechanism in the regulation of cortisol secretion" (Fehm, Voigt, & Born, 1988) and override brain stem homeostatic mechanisms during periods of stress or emotional activity. In very recent work, Wittling and Pfluger (1990) have demonstrated that the cortical regulation of cortisol secretion in emotion-related situations is under primary control of the right hemisphere.

THE FUNCTIONAL IMPLICATIONS OF DUAL COMPONENT ORBITOFRONTAL INTERACTIONS WITH HYPOTHALAMIC NUCLEI

After extensive work on hypothalamic motivational systems, Stellar (1982) posits dual limbic excitatory and inhibitory mechanisms which determine hedonic balance "until some internal change in brain state biases responding to external stimuli in the positive or negative hedonic direction" (p. 397). Swanson (1991) finds that stresses induce biochemical switching in hypothalamic circuits. Gellhorn (1967) notes that in a state of sympathetic "tuning" of the hypothalamus, its sympathetic components are enhanced and parasympathetic lessened, while in parasympathetic tuning, hypothalamic parasympathetic reactivity is augmented and sympathetic reactivity reduced. The autonomic areas of the hypothalamus and brain stem are known to influence not only peripheral organs but the cerebral cortex as well, producing either sympathetic discharge and cortical excitation or parasympathetic discharge and reduced cortical activity. Similarly, Glassman and Wimsatt (1984) propose that the primary function of the hypothalamus is to serve as a source of an inhibitory or excitatory diffuse "bias" (tuning) on the cerebral structures that process sensorimotor information. The subcortical modulation of cortical activity may underly the observation that the microorganization of the cortex is constantly in a state of flux, and stability results from a balance of competing factors (Kaas, 1987).

Marder et al. (1987) have demonstrated that "a given neuronal circuit might easily express a variety of states, depending on the presence or absence of one or more peptides and amines" (p. 223). It is proposed that the hypothalamic neuroendocrine system is the source of these peptides, and the brain stem catecholamine nuclei the source of these bioamines. These concepts fit well with the earlier discussed effects of neuromodulators on the tone and operational states of the orbital frontolimbic cortex, that is, the subcortical *priming* of the prefrontal cortex. This mechanism may also be involved in the generation of unique patterns of catecholamine innervation that determine the known arousal differences between the two hemispheres (Levy et al., 1983).

Gellhorn also specifically mentions the role of orbital frontal cortex as an agent of cortical inhibition over hypothalamic activities. Fuster (1985) points out that stimulation of the (adult, mature) orbital cortex, which sends direct projections to nuclei of the hypothalamus and the brain stem which participate in movement, induces suppression of internal information and a variety of inhibitory phenomena in the motor and autonomic spheres. He also notes that the majority of autonomic effects produced by this stimulation "seem to be parasympathetic or the result of inhibitory influences on the sympathetic system' (Fuster, 1980, p. 94). This function may be specifically mediated by descending orbital axons which innervate the lateral hypothalamus (Nauta, 1972), known to be a parasympathetic structure. Activation of this region elicits profound bradycardia and quiet inactivity; conversely, cardiac acceleration is produced by activation of the ventromedial hypothalamus (Gellman, Schneiderman, Wallach, & LeBlanc, 1981), a sympathetic area which inhibits vagal activity and is involved in affective reactions. I would suggest that the cortical *tuning* of the different hypothalamic neuroendocrine centers is mediated by the two orbital systems. This allows for prefrontal (especially right) hemispheric regulation of the hypothalamico-pituitary-adrenocortical (Hall & Marr, 1975) and the sympatho-adrenomedullary systems (Euler & Folkow, 1958).

This dual component cortical system, at the supraordinate level of the hierarchically organized dual circuit limbic system, thus directly influences the two major endocrinological systems which release hormones into the circulation in response to both hypostimulating-low arousal (solitary) and hyperstimulating-high arousal (social) types of stresses in order to maintain internal homeostasis, and thereby plays a central role in determining what types of internal states the organism utilizes to respond to a particular environment. Contemporary psychoendocrinological (Mason, 1975; Tennes & Mason, 1982) and psychophysiological (Schwartz, 1982) approaches to the study of emotion both emphasize the importance of identifying the patterns of interaction of multiple component systems and processes. From a general systems theory perspective, Bertalanffy (1974) states that a small change in an anterior "higher" controlling center "may by way of amplification mechanisms cause large changes in the total system. In this way a hierarchical order of parts or processes may be established" (p. 1104). In a recent study of the cortical regulation of neuroendocrine function Wittling and Pfluger (1990) conclude that:

> The emotional dominance of the right hemisphere is not restricted to the regulation of subjective moods and emotional expression, but can also be found in the meta-control of fundamental physiological and endocrinological functions whose primary control centers are located in subcortical regions of the brain. (p. 260)

The adaptive orbitofrontal roles in homeostatic regulation and in passive and active coping mechanisms results from its function in integrating exteroceptive cortical sensory information with information from the internal visceroendocrine environment. It has been suggested that the nucleus of the solitary tract, like the immediately adjacent area postrema, (Fig. 4.16) contains a "weak" blood-brain barrier, and is therefore exposed to substances borne in the peripheral circulation (Gross, Wall, Pang, Shaver, & Wainman, 1990; Shapiro & Miselis, 1985) (see Fig. 25.1). Neural tissue which is sensitive to the internal environment is found

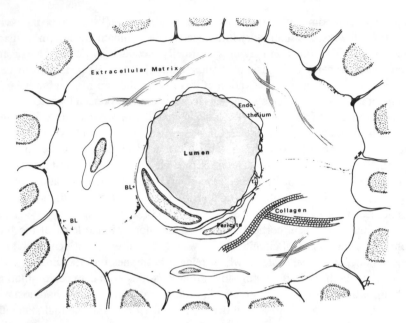

FIG. 25.1.   A "leaky" segment of the blood-brain barrier of the area
postrema. Compare to Fig. 11.2. From Dermietzel and Krause (1991).
Reprinted by permission of the publisher.

in the hypothalamus (Bronson, 1965), a highly vascularized structure (Fig. 10.1)
that contains "receptor regions for hormones and other changes in the internal environment important in motivated behavior" (Stellar, 1982, p.379). The
median eminence of the hypothalamus, excluded from the blood-brain barrier,
also monitors the contents of the blood. Furthermore, other hypothalamic areas
may be involved in this activty. For example, mature lateral hypothalamic activity is affected by internal sensory (homeostatic) stimuli such as alterations in the
physical composition of body fluids, e.g., a glucosensitivity (Anand, Chhina,
Sharma, Dua, & Singh, 1964), osmosensitivity (Cross & Green, 1959), and
thermosensitivity (Zajonc, et al.,1989), as well as external sensory influences.
The developmental fine-tuning of the functional features of these neurons occurs
in a postnatal "critical period" (Fisher & Almli, 1984) associated with a morphogenetic expansion of their dendritic fields (McMullen & Almli, 1981). This
modification of inputs into lateral hypothalamic neurons results in a functional
maturation in which the magnitude and complexity of responses evoked by
external sensory stimulation increases and internal stimulation decreases. Thus,
in addition to interoceptive influences, these neurons become more and more
influenced and modulated by specific exteroceptive, visual and auditory stimuli
(presumably by a parcellation process).

These data suggest that the postnatal fine-tuning of this structure is due to the synaptogenesis of postnatally growing descending orbital cholinergic axons (Johnson et al., 1976) on to simultaneously expanding lateral hypothalamic dendrites occurring in the same critical period. This allows for a monosynaptic connection between neurons in the deep layers of the prefrontal cortex and the lateral hypothalamus (Kita & Oomura, 1981), and for direct orbitofrontal-lateral hypothalamic (Luiten, Ter Horst, & Steffens, 1987) transmission of the multimodal input of all sensory areas of the (paricularly right hemispheric) maturing cortex which converges on orbital association columns to individual hypothalamic cells that control somatic metabolism. These conceptualizations are supported by Teitelbaum's (1971) assertion that the orbitofrontal cortex represents the cortical elaboration of more primitive homeostatic functions associated with the lateral hypothalamus.

Rolls functional data suggests that the selective responses of a group of hypothalamic neurons may be due to the "convergence of inputs from a number of different groups of neurons in the orbitofrontal cortex " (Thorpe et al., 1983, p. 109). Smith and Devito (1984) suggest that the point of transfer from psychological processing of newly acquired information to central autonomic control may occur in association cortex where multiple sensory modalities interact, specifically mentioning "direct inputs to the hypothalamus from portions of prefrontal cortex" (p. 61). As mentioned, connections between these structures are thought to occur during the critical period for socialization (Scott, 1958). Intriguingly, this developmental process may serve as a psychoneuroendocrinological mechanism by which socioaffective input generated in caregiver-infant transactions could directly and permanently influence ongoing neuroendocrine development. The orbitofrontal region, implicated in attachment functions (Steklis & Kling, 1985), sends direct axons to the hypothalamus, and such pathways "may be instrumental in affecting the alterations in hypothalamic regulatory functions that seem to accompany the disruption of attachment bonds" (Reite & Capitanio, 1985). A focus of current developmental psychoendocrinological research has been on the mechanism by which the mother's attitude toward the child becomes linked to the child's physiology, and on early postnatal experiences that might affect the permanent physiological functioning of neuroendocrine systems (Tennes & Mason, 1982). The ontogeny of this frontolimbic cortex, which Pribram (1981) characterizes as the apex of the hierarchy of control of autonomic functions, is critically influenced by early socioaffective transactions (object relations) that are responsible for the emergent function of "the central neural integration for the control of autonomic responses associated with emotion" (Smith & DeVito, 1984).

Hypothalamic circuits play an important adaptive role in endocrine, autonomic, and behavioral homeostatic functions (Swanson, 1991). The various hypothalamic nuclei, central limbic regulators of both the sympathetic energy-mobilizing and parasympathetic energy-conserving branches of the autonomic nervous system and the expression of emotional behavior, are themselves regulated by the orbitofrontolimbic cortex, the supraordinate cortical component of the limbic system that is involved in the adjustment and correction of emotional responses. It has long been known that higher centers in the brain regulate the hypothalamus, and that the neuroendocrine system is a hierarchy with higher centers regulating lower ones (Brownstein, 1989). It is through these structural relationships that behavior and experience that influence the hypothalamus come to alter the secretion of hypothalamic releasing factors and hormones (McEwen, 1989) (Fig. 25.2). The control of the somatic components of emotional processes by the hypothalamus is mediated by its release of various regulatory neuropeptides (e.g., corticotropin-releasing hormone, thyrotropin-releasing hormone, gonadotropin-releasing hormone, growth hormone releasing hormone) into the circulation that directly influence the synthesis and secretion of trophic hormones in the pituitary (e.g. ACTH, endorphins, thyrotropin, LH, FSH, growth hormone) as well as the activity of the central and peripheral nervous systems. Circulating hypothalamic regulatory peptides can influence these distantly separated sites since central autonomic systems contain receptor populations that overlap extensively with those of peripheral systems (Loewy & Spyer, 1990).

In very recent research, McGregor and Atrens (1991) have demonstrated that the orbitofrontal area of the prefrontal cortex modulates and is modulated by energy balance, and suggest that autonomic adjustments in relation to sensory input may be mediated by projections to the hypothalamus and autonomic centers in the brain stem (Krushel & van der Kooy, 1988). To expand upon this idea, neuronal populations within the hypothalamus are critical for the maintenance of energy balance (Atrens, Sinden, Penicaud, Devos, & LeMagnen, 1985), and prefrontal influences on the lateral and ventromedial nuclei are of particular importance, as it is known that lateral hypothalamic activity increases liver glycogenesis (through the vagus nerve), while ventromedial activity increases glycogenolysis (Brownstein, 1989). The regulation of glucose into the circulation is central to bodily and emotional processes, as plasma glucose is the major source of energy to the brain. This energy regulation may underlie the participation of hypothalamic systems in the regulation of the body's metabolic activity and in emotional processes. Glucose responsive neurons are found in the autonomic nucleus of the solitary tract (Mizuno & Oomura, 1984). The hypothalamic biasing of the cerebral cortex may be mediated by its control of glucose concentrations in the bloodstream, which are sensed by orbitofrontal neurons whose activity is modulated by glucose (McGregor & Atrens, 1991) and intensified during emotional behaviors (Yamamoto et al., 1984).

Fifty years ago Duffy (1941) asserted that energy shifts are the most basic and fundamental features of emotion. It has previously been suggested that patterns of energy transmissions represent the fundamental core of the attachment dynamic. Reite and Capitanio (1985) conceptualize affect as "a manifestation of underlying modulating or motivational systems subserving or facilitating social attach-

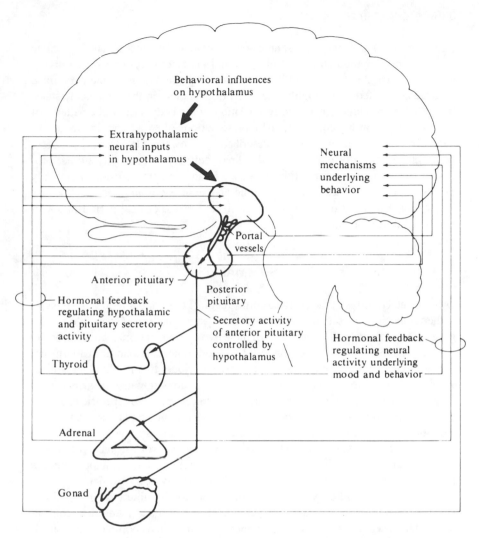

FIG. 25.2. Schematic representation of reciprocal interactions among hypothalamic, pituitary, thyroid, adrenal, and gonadal hormones. The labeled "behavioral influences on hypothalamus," though not anatomically identified, are suggested to be mediated by orbitofrontal-hypothalamic connections. From McEwen (1989). Endocrine effects on the brain and their relationship to behavior. In Siegel, Agranoff, Albers, and Molinoff (Eds.), *Basic neurochemistry* (4th ed., pp. 893–913). Reprinted by permission of Raven Press.

ments" (p. 248) and suggest that an essential attachment function is "to promote the synchrony or regulation of biological and behavioral systems on an organismic level" (p. 235). Tucker (1992) concludes representations at the paralimbic core are associated with "highly integrated information on the organismic state" (p. 100). The modulation and synchronization of the body's rhythmic patterns of energy dissipation by stored internal representations of experiences with attachment objects in the external world, described by Schwalbe (1991), may therefore be psychobiologically mediated by the direct delivery of cortically stored, processed, and activated information embedded in and emanating from emotionally expressive faces to various hypothalamic and brain stem autonomic nuclei via direct orbital connections which are established in the critical period of socioemotional development.

SUMMARY

Orbitofrontal regions of the cerebral cortex regulate the sympathetic and parasympathetic divisions of the autonomic nervous system that are responsible for the generation of emotion. The activities of these two components may be reciprocally coupled, nonreciprocally coupled, or uncoupled. These autonomic patterns are formed in the first 2 years, and permanently contribute to an individual personality''s unique style of emotional expression. The predominance of sympathetic versus parasympathetic operations determines the signature of specific emotions and the expression of active as opposed to passive coping responses to emotional stressors. The capacity to utilize reciprocal autonomic modes is adaptive in response to environmental challenges. On the other hand, extensive or chronic hyperactivation of both modes leads to enduring states of heightened unconscious affect, a precondition of susceptibility to psychological and physical disorders.

The important role of parasympathetic conservation-withdrawal in emotional functions has been overlooked in experimental research and theoretical conceptions. This energy-conserving, metabolically reduced psychobiological state is adaptive in circumstances that necessitate quiescence and an unresponsiveness to the environment. The conscious affective experience of shame is associated with an entrance into conservation-withdrawal.

Orbitofrontal projections are the major source of delivery of cortical information to the hypothalamus. Higher corticolimbic messages thereby hierarchically influence the activity of various nuclei within this lower limbic structure that are involved in drive, affect, motivational, and energetic functions. Of particular importance are the sympathetic ventromedial and parasympathetic lateral hypothalmic nuclei. Neuroendocrine release from these diencephalic sites reciprocally regulates higher cortical activities. Such interactions between higher and lower limbic functions account for the modulation and synchronization of the body's rhythmic patterns of energy dissipation by stored interactive representations.

26
The Regulation of Infantile
Rage Reactions

> *In rage the mobilization of energy is so great that one feels one will explode if one does not bite, hit, or kick something, or "act out the anger."*
>
> —Caroll E. Izard (1991)

> *By 18–19 months, we see a toddler who, when he does not get what he wants, does not necessarily respond with temper tantrums or other driven behavioral patterns. There is now a capacity to pause and make a judgment regarding what to do. The toddler can consider alternative behavioral patterns. Most 18–19-month-olds, for example, may pester mother, pull at her leg, but with one look at her, they can go back to her play area and wait for a while longer.*
>
> —Stanley I. Greenspan (1988)

The experience-dependent maturation of the dual orbitofrontal system's connections with subcortical sympathetic and parasympathetic limbic structures is essential to its adaptive affect regulating function. Brutkowski and Mempel (1961) propose that orbital areas are functionally concerned with "suppression of different kinds of motivated and affective responses mediated by hypothalamic mechanisms" (p. 2041). Descending cholinergic links of the limbic-forebrain midbrain circuits may represent Carlton's (1969) cholinergic inhibitory mechanism responsible for response suppression, a known orbitofrontal function (Wilcott, 1981). Of particular developmental importance is the suppression of the affective and motoric components of aggressive behavior.

The developmental emergence of the capacity to internally regulate rage reactions are explored in this chapter.

STRUCTURE-FUNCTION RELATIONSHIPS OF
REGULATED AND UNREGULATED RAGE

Recent psychological research now indicates that the autoregulation of aggression involves the operation of a self-regulatory mechanism operating at a preconscious level (Berkowitz, 1990). I propose that this mechanism refers specifically to the orbitofrontal inhibition of hypothalamic drive (Brutkowski, 1964; Rosenkilde, 1979). Indeed, neurobiological studies by de Bruin (1983, 1990) have revealed that this cortex is implicated in the suppression of aggression in dyadic encounters. This author reports that the orbitofrontal cortex exerts an inhibitory control over hypothalamic sites from which aggression can be elicited by electrical stimulation (Kruk, Van der Poel, & De Vos-Frerichs, 1979). Neurological studies with adult patients reveal that lesions in the right, but not left, orbitofrontal areas produce increased unregulated aggression and dramatic mood state alterations (Grafman, Vance, Weingartner, Salazar, & Amin, 1986). Aggressive behavior is a component of psychomotor epilepsy (Rodin, 1973); the orbitomedial frontal lobe is a prominent site of seizure activity (Tharp, 1972).

Ablation of this structure in animals after early infancy results in the release of the sympathetic and somatomotor responses of rage behavior (Kennard, 1945; Kolb, 1984) and an increase of aggressive interactions (Raleigh, Steklis, Ervin, Kling, & McGuire, 1979). The descending orbitofrontal tracts which emanate from cholinergic neurons in the deep layers of prefrontolimbic cortical columns may thus inhibit "septal rage" (Brady & Nauta, 1953) and ventromedial hypothalamic "fight" (aggression) reactions (Colpaert, 1975). Gilbert (1989) refers to a *stop* or *braking* of high arousal defensive states, and cites Carlton's (1969) work which indicates that acetylcholine neurochemically mediates the braking response pattern. Indeed, the orbitofrontal cortex is known to be a source of an inhibitory cholinergic pathway to the ventromedial hypothalamus (Ohta & Oomura, 1979). Sympathetic ventromedial hypothalamic neurons also develop in a postnatal critical period (Almli & Fisher, 1985), a time, it is suggested, when their dendrites receive frontolimbic axonal projections. The expression of "delayed aggressive behavior" (Zillman & Bryant, 1974) may thus be due to the orbitofrontal delayed response function and the prefrontal modulation of subcortical activity.

In terms of early socioemotional development, this system—whose ontogeny is influenced by shame socialization transactions—is critical to the automodulation of sympathetically driven, high drive, hyperaroused limbic states, such as those expressed in hyperaggressive and hypersexual behavior. Kaufman (1989) understands rage to be an inflation or magnification of anger affect, and Tomkins (1963) points out that anger is activated by any external or internal source of continuing high nonoptimal level of stimulation. The activation of high levels of energy-mobilizing sympathetic arousal (beyond the optimal activation band) is known to facilitate aggressive behavior (Zillman & Bryant, 1974), and aggres-

338

sion is asociated with a heightened activation of the ergotropic system (Blackburn, 1975). Rage represents a hyperactivation of the peripheral sympatho-adrenomedullary noradrenergic system. It is speculated that the lower levels of postnatal experience-dependent growth of descending orbitofrontal axons to subcortical sites (Johnson et al., 1976) would result in an inefficient orbital system of "vagal restraint" (Kaada et al., 1949) with a reduced functional capacity of stimulating the parasympathetic and inhibiting the sympathetic components (Fuster, 1980) of limbic function. Unmodulated rage also represents a hyperactivation of the subcortical components of the mesolimbic dopaminergic system. A histrionic-impulsive personality has been shown to biochemically manifest increased mesolimbic dopamine transmission during stress induced, under-controlled and impulsive acting out episodes (King, 1985). Elevated levels of mesolimbic (septal) dopamine have recently been found as a psychobiological separation response accompanying protest vocalizations in infant animals (Tamborski, Lucot, & Hennessy, 1990).

DEVELOPMENTAL SHAME EXPERIENCES AND THE MODULATION OF NARCISSISTIC RAGE

"Narcissistic rage" (Kohut, 1978b), the heightened frustration-triggered aggressive drive common in the practicing period of infancy (Parens, 1980), is equated with Bowlby's "bitter" separation protest as a response to a broken attachment tie, and Kagan's (1976) "separation protest," which peaks at 12 months and diminishes between 15–24 months. This robust phenomenon is also reported by Fox (1977) who observes an increase of protest from 8 to 15 months followed by a decrease thereafter. Izard (Shiller, Izard, & Hembree, 1986) finds that the dominant typical negative emotional response to brief separation of 13-month-old infants is anger (not sadness nor separation anxiety). At this age, the infant cannot yet autoregulate this state, as it propels him into extremely high levels of arousal beyond his active coping capacities. The initiation of the modulation of this negative/active affect during the late practicing/early rapprochement period (Settlage, 1977), the "rapprochement crisis" in which narcissistic rages and tantrums are used by the child in coercive and dramatic struggles with the mother (Mahler et al., 1975), is essential to further socioemotional maturation, since negative emotions such as experienced in fight responses place substantial energy demands on the organism (Zajonc et al., 1989), and a surplus of unneutralized aggression thwarts favorable development (Mahler, 1979).

In an earlier work, I proposed that an optimal resolution of this crisis involves both shame inducing and shame regulating interventions by the caregivers (Schore, 1991). The question of the interaction between shame and the affect associated with separation processes has been raised by Hofer (personal communication, July 16, 1991). It is known that shame generally inhibits the expression of any emotion (Tomkins, 1987) and the expression of emotion per se (Kaufman, 1992), and specifically opposes overt aggressive action and curbs "dangerous arousal" (Knapp, 1967). Although the origin of shame is dyadic and external, as maturation proceeds it is internalized. The mental image of the misattuned (disgusted) face of the mother engenders a rapid brake of ergotropic arousal, and therefore can be utilized as an internal inhibitory mechanism of a hyperaroused limbic rage state. This mechanism underlies the unique role of shame in emotion expression regulation (Buechler & Izard, 1983), especially the regulation of aggression. In an adaptive adjustment to this developmental challenge "there is a subsidence of the child's rages and of his external struggles with his mother for power" (Parkin, 1985, p. 147). Kohut (1978a) refers to the critical developmental achievement of the transformation of narcissistic rage into mature aggression. In a classic study of the early expressions of aggression within the first 2-years-of-life, Goodenough (1931) recognized a developmental transition from frustration-induced anger manifested in undirected energy, tantrums, and outbursts of motor activity into directed motor and language responses.

On the other hand, unregulated intense levels of shame may be a central component of enduring aggressive organizations which develop in the practicing period. Earlier it was suggested that maternal contempt—disgust plus anger—triggers humiliation and "shame rage" (H.B. Lewis, 1987). This is primarily transmitted nonverbally, specifically through exposure of the infant's gaze to the aggressive communications (Ellsworth, 1975) emanating from the mother's "terrifying eyes" (Peto, 1969) during her unmodulated states of narcissistic rage. The "fire of shame" that is generated in these imprinting experiences may last for long periods, since disgust motivates rejection and avoidance (Izard, 1991). Resultingly, the mother does not reengage with the child in order to regulate this painful negative affective state. The fundamental role of unregulated shame in physical child abuse is only now being understood (H. Krystal, personal communication, July 4, 1991). Kaufman (1989) asserts that "the organizing affects in physical abuse syndromes are shame and rage, conjointly magnified into explosive scenes" (p. 124). These transactions become imprinted and stored as prototypical interactive representations, and in the face of future stresses the internal image of the humiliating, contemptuous face would stimulate both parasympathetic trophotropic and sympathetic ergotropic arousal and produce a hyperaroused limbic state.

Izard (1991) emphasizes that disgust combined with anger creates the motivation to get rid of the object through attack and destruction, that this generates imagery about "harm, embarrassment, or defeat of the object of hostility," and that these dynamics are predominant in the generation of pathologically hostile behavior by aggressive personalities.

> The feeling of contempt toward a human being tends to depersonalize the target individual, to cause the person to be perceived as something less than human. It is

because of these characteristics that contempt can motivate murder and mass destruction of people. (p. 274)

The excessively impulsive, undermodulated state of blind rage is described by Horowitz (1992):

> Not thinking, all feeling. He wants to demolish and destroy persons who frustrate him. He is not aware of ever loving or even faintly liking the object. He has no awareness that his rage is a passion that will decline. He believes he will hate the object forever. (p. 80)

A deeper apprehension of the early life experiences that engender a personality organization that is susceptible to stress induced uncontrolled rage is obviously an important area of inquiry. Three decades ago Glueck and Glueck (1966) identified a cluster of predictors of potential delinquency in 2 year-old children. These included hostile or indifferent attachment to parents, vindictive destructiveness directed against others, physiological hyperactivity, parental alcoholism or criminality, and nonsubmissiveness of the child to parental authority. In very recent work on the developmental psychopathology of conduct disorder, Dodge and Somberg (1987) demonstrate that "hostile attributional biases" among aggressive boys are specifically exacerbated under conditions of threat to the self. Dodge (1993) suggests that early experiences of physical abuse, exposure to aggressive models, and insecure attachments lead a child to develop memory structures that contain a hostile world schema and an aggressive response repertoire. Later, when the child is presented with provocative stimuli, such as peer teasing, these structures lead him to attend to hostile cues and to engage in aggressive behavior.

The commission of violent acts by children is rapidly becoming one of the most serious problems facing American society. To my mind the essential problem of the human condition is not, as Freud supposed, psychoneurosis, nor even psychosis. Rather, I see the products of unregulated unconscious primary narcissism and humiliation-induced narcissistic rage in both children and adults as the major threat to the further development of our species.

NEGATIVISM AND THE DEVELOPMENT OF AUTONOMY

In optimal nonpathogenic socioaffective environments, the infant rarely is exposed to extended periods of parental rage and has access to the mother's affect regulating function. In such conditions there is a developmentally appropriate shift from the physical resistance of infancy to the emergence of negativism expressed in the semantic "no." Indeed this has been observed in the 15–18-month-old toddler, and has been interpreted as a change from energy-expending action to energy-conserving symbolic representation of action (Wenar, 1982).

(This transformation of function parallels the underlying experience-dependent transmutation of structure in the developing ANS from sympathetic energy-mobilizing to parasympathetic energy-conserving dominance.) Such a transition is adaptive in that intentional noncompliance is now thought to be crucial for the development of autonomy (Wenar, 1982) and for the expression of the child's developing "interpersonal influence strategies" (Kuczynski, Kochanska, Radke-Yarrow, & Girnius-Brown, 1987). The parents' emotional responsiveness is essential to this development. Lichtenberg (1989) notes that:

> the caregiver must empathically accept that it is to the child's advantage for the child to suspend the empathic linkage to the caregiver in order to formulate his or her own agenda and even at times to have a vigorously aversive reaction to interference with that agenda. (p. 174)

Wolf (1980) proposes that during this period of negativism the mother is both an ally who confirms the child's verbal-gestural refusal ("no") yet simultaneously an antagonist against whom self-assertion mobilizes healthy aggression. Izard (1991) points out that mild to moderate (regulated) anger is adaptive, in that it can be utilized in the psychological defense of the self.

These dyadic regulatory events are essential to the ongoing trajectory of an exploratory-assertive (Lichtenberg, 1989) motivational system and the capacity for symbolic play. Emde (1988) observes that the mother's signals to the child "by subtleties of glance and direction of looking" that "I will be available later" enables the child to continue exploratory play. Such transactions may also be relevant to a further elucidation of Mahler's inquiries into the child's struggle to develop a sense of autonomy and independent selfhood while continuing to maintain a sense of connectedness to the primary caregiver. Indeed, coping successfully with shame experiences has been suggested to facilitate the achievement of autonomy (Izard, 1991; Severino, McNutt, & Feder, 1987).

In Chapter 17 I discussed research which indicates that the development of autonomy in the 1½-year-old is strongly influenced by an intensified relationship with the father. Mahler et al. (1975) observe that in this period the father plays an indispensable role in the resolution of the child's emotional ambivalence towards the mother. The emotional accessibility of both parents is thus required for the full development of autonomous functioning in the developing child. The level of their conjoint involvement in the creation of an environment that facilitates the child's capacity for both independent action and affective interchange is alluded to in the sobering observation of the child psychologist, Burton White (1985):

> Whereas most families in this country today get their children through the first six to eight months of life reasonably well developed, I have come to the conclusion that relatively few families—perhaps no more than one in ten—manage to get their children through the age period from eight to thirty-six months as well educated and developed as they can and should be. (p. 105)

ORBITOFRONTAL REPRESENTATIONS AND THE
AUTOMODULATION OF RAGE

In his study of aggression in early childhood, Parens (1979) contrasts the forms and efficiencies of control utilized in the practicing and rapprochement phases. In the earlier practicing period, the child shows a partial or sporadic ability to inhibit hostile impulses; this function is present only in the physical presence of the mother. During rapprochement (onset around 18 months) inhibition further develops, and occurs even in the absence of the mother. He concludes that the progression from one phase to the next reflects the maturation of the child's inhibition of impulse, due to the of the internalization of this control function. This conclusion is mirrored in Schwalbe's (1991) observation that in the first two years "imagery begins to modulate impulsive behavior." Similarly, Kuczynski (Kuczynski, Kochanska, Radke-Yarrow, & Girnius-Brown, 1987) studying children as young as 1½ years, finds that defiance, in the form of poorly controlled anger, negative affect and tantrums, decreases significantly with age. Greenspan (1988) also describes at 18 months a decrease in temper tantrums as the toddler's response to not getting what he wants. Studies of the ontogeny of self-control reveal that delay/response inhibition in the presence of an attractive stimulus first appears at 18 months (Vaughn, Kopp, & Krakow, 1984).

The major emotional transformations in negativism and autonomy that occur at this time have been attributed to developmental neuropsychological events (Tucker, 1992). I propose that the ontogenetic progression in the maturation of "involuntary emotional control" based on the mechanism of "response inhibition" (Frijda, 1988) reflects the socialization stress induced experience-dependent structural transformation (rewiring) of the orbitofrontal cortex, a system governing internal inhibition (Velasco & Lindsley, 1965). This anatomical locus with its far reaching cortical and subcortical connections is equivalent to the frontal functional system which inhibits drive that has been described in the neurological literature (Stuss & Benson, 1987), and the controlling structure which maintains constancy by delaying "press for discharge" of aroused drives that has been described in the psychoanalytic literature (Rapaport, 1960). Its mature function is expressed in the braking mechanism of shame, which leads to inhibition and "drive restraint." Shame mechanisms can undergo elaboration and "gain representations as symbols that become signals" in a hierarchically organized system that can "delay, anticipate, and 'discharge' in fantasy" (Knapp, 1967, p. 533).

The developmental advance of this prefrontal system is specifically expressed in a more efficient delayed response function that underlies the cortically supported cognitive capacity of evocative memory, memory independent of immediate perception, required for more effective cortical autoregulation of subcortical activity. Blatt (Blatt, Quinlan, & Chevron, 1990) indicates this type of representation appears initially in "pictorial" from, and later in development in "more symbolic modalities." Early developing presymbolic representational capacity is vulnerable and susceptible to disorganization under stressful affective states (Greenspan, 1981), in contrast to later developing symbolic evocative memory which enables the child to tolerate greater disruptions in affective states (Trad, 1986) as experienced in the rapprochement crisis. Hofer (1990) concludes that "complex" mental representations enable the infant to endure temporary separations without full-scale separation (protest) responses.

This complex mental representation may include representations of caregiver-infant stress inducing and stress regulating transactions during the crisis, which if optimal instill an expectation that at some time subsequent to stress onset homeostatic regulation and distress-relief will occur. Wilson specifically notes that the experience of being with a self-regulating other can be incorporated into a generalized representation of interactions (Wilson et al., 1990). The adaptive function of stable self-and-object representations is now thought to be contained in their expression of the individual's efforts to cope with difficulties and crises (Stolorow & Atwood, 1979). I suggest that such interactive representations specifically encode "psychological variables that mediate or moderate autonomic reactivity to stress" (Allen, Blascovich, Tomaka, & Kelsey, 1991). The establishment of this more complex orbitofrontal internal working model allows for its function as a more effective strategy of affect regulation via its involvement in a reciprocally coupled mechanism of autonomic control, and the availability of this prefrontal cognitive set at times of interpersonal stress allows for the adaptive use of delay in the face of frustrated expectation (need).

The learning of adaptive stress regulating strategies is embedded in and influenced by late practicing "distress-relief sequences," which facilitate a transition from distress to quiet alertness (Lamb, 1981), "interactive repair" after dyadic misattunements which transform negative into positive affect (Tronick, 1989), and "reassurance signals," which occur after agonistic encounters (Gilbert & Trower, 1990). Relief is neurophysiologically expressed in the dimunition of sympathetic and activation of parasympathetic activity (Lazarus, 1991b), a pattern of reciprocal inhibition of one branch of the ANS over the other (Grossman, Stemmler, & Meinhardt, 1990). Distress-relief sequences, which are composed of sequential periods of sympathetic hyperaroused (Zillman & Bryant, 1974) distress (separation protest, narcissistic rage) followed by parasympathetic relief thus reflect a neurobiological shift of limbic system circuit predominance. Pine (1990) now concludes that as a result of particular experiences with a reliable caregiver the infant develops an expectation of relief which allows for delay in the face of need and acts to regulate inner states. This expectation of relief allows the child, when in distress, "to bridge the gap until reunion or restoration of the attachment" (Lichtenberg, 1989, p. 104). Prefrontal cortical structures are known to mediate the highest control of "bridging temporal gaps" (Fuster, 1991, p. 201).

Settlage (1977), a psychoanalytic infant researcher whose work focuses on this crisis period between developmental stages, observes that the ambitendent toddler oscillates between rages against the mother and approaches toward her during periods of distress. Her "quiet availability" during these reunions which follow misattunements are critical to the infant's emergent capacity to automodulate distress states. The mother's participation in interactive repair after these stressful agonistic dyadic encounters that expose her to the rage of her infant facilitates the further development of an adaptive structure to regulate negative affect. These phenomena may account for and explain the observation that the continued emotional availability and responsiveness of the mother (and now moreso than before the father) is essential to a healthy resolution of this developmental crisis (McDevitt, 1979; Settlage, 1977; Trad, 1986). The recent work of Greenberg, Kusche, and Speltz (1991) indicates that this availablity may specifically involve the parents' capacity to tolerate strong negative affect in the child and to have self-control over their own affect when responding to the child's ambitendencies. Thirty years ago, Tomkins (1963) proposed that negative affect is reduced when parents continue to maintain affective engagement with the child who is experiencing negative affect, and when parents communicate tolerance of negative affect in self and child. This is adaptive, since negative affects convey information about threat and lack of social success (Gilbert, 1992a). The importance of early negativity is emphasized by Bradley (1991), and the capacity to autoregulate negative affect, which evolves out of early maternal regulation of infant negative affect states, is stressed by Demos and Kaplan (1986).

The external regulation of intense negative affect states enables the structural differentiation and thereby functional development of the mature dual component orbitofrontal delayed response (Goldman, 1971) and memory and cognitive capacities (Stuss et al., 1982) that are responsible for the onset of evocative memory at 18 months (Fraiberg, 1969) and the emergence of more complex and efficient internal working models. The ontogenetic progression of evocative memory allows the child to evoke an image of a comforting other when the other is not physically present (Adler & Buie, 1979), thereby enabling the autoregulation of aversive hyperaroused rage and hypoaroused aloneness reactions. Greenspan (1979) offers the developmental observation that at 18 months, "In addition to his vastly improved capacities for dealing with his internal milieu . . . the child has a vastly enhanced capacity for experiencing the internal milieu" (p. 154). He further postulates, "the representational system, just as it organizes itself in order to perceive the external world, organizes itself to perceive sensation from the interior of the body" (Greenspan, 1990, p. 46). This allows the child to learn how emotion functions within himself and thereby essentially contributes to the burgeoning sense of autonomy and the capacity to remain secure when apart from the comforting caregiver. Winnicott (1958b) concludes that the vital "capacity to be alone" is supported by the intrapsychic presence of a mother who "temporarily identified with her infant and for the time being was interested in nothing else but the care of her infant" (p. 420).

Furthermore, this frontolimbic emergent function may mediate Freud's concept of mental imagery acting to delay drive gratification. Freud (1911/1958) originally conceived the functions of the reality ego to be the cognitive control of instinctual discharge, the delaying of gratification, the goal-direction of behavior in behalf of future gratification, and the capacity to face unpleasant reality. The late practicing onset of mature orbitofrontal functions of mediating between the external environment and the internal milieu (Mesulam & Mufson, 1982) and balancing internal desires with external reality (Jouandet & Gazzaniga), along with the ontogenetic development of orbital involvement in withholding non-reinforced responses and steering ongoing behavior to more reinforcing conse-quences (Rosenkilde, Bauer, & Fuster, 1981), and in modulating drive (Rosen-kilde, 1979) and motivational states (Pandya & Yeterian, 1985) are posited to be critical to the emergence of Freud's reality principle, a developmental achieve-ment which is accompanied by the control and restriction of affect (Suler, 1989).

> The ability to control motivational orientation in light of factors not present in the immediate environment, a capacity basic to the development of the reality princi-ple, must depend in part on maturation of the prefrontal lobes. (Bronson, 1963, p. 59)

The recent demonstration of the development of the frontal lobe in stages by the neuropsychologist Thatcher (1991), may thus underly the description of the development of the sense of reality in stages by the psychoanalyst Ferenczi (1913/1980) some 80 years ago.

SUMMARY

Neural connections between the cortex and hypothalamus are permanently estab-lished in the critical period for the development of social responses. The experience-dependent growth of orbitofrontal descending cholinergic axons to sites in the hypothalamus enables an automodulation of aggressive impulses. This corticolimbic inhibition of hypothalamic drive is manifest in the braking of ventromedial hypothalamic sympathetic ergotropic hyperarousal.

The development of this system is influenced by practicing period, caregiver shame inducing and especially shame regulating transactions. The external regu-lation of the infant's age-appropriate narcissistic rage (separation protest) allows for the maturation of an internal mechanism that transforms unmodulated rage into healthy aggression and that psychobiologically supports states of autono-mous functioning. The absence of such dyadic regulation, and an exposure to parental humiliation induced shame rage can have long-term pathological conse-quences for the emerging personality.

By the middle of the second year the dual component orbitofrontal cortex is capable of generating, storing, and activating stress regulating interactive representations. These complex representations contain algorithms of distress-relief that encode a reciprocally coupled mechanism of autonomic control. As a result the limbic system shifts from sympathetic to parasympathetic dominance. The establishment of this psychoneurobiological mechanism allows for access to evocative memory, the adaptive evocation of a stored representation of a comforting other in order to modulate the negative affect that accompanies and follows rage and aloneness reactions.

27 Affect Regulation and Early Moral Development

The task of parents is to teach their children to internalize values and to motivate children, in the absence of the parents, not to violate these standards, rules, and goals. What better way to prevent the child from doing this than by producing a strong emotion? The production of shame, even at normal levels, is an ideal device for instilling internalized values.
—Michael Lewis (1992)

In a previous publication (Schore, 1991), I offered the suggestion that the right hemispheric prefrontal affect regulator that performs an appraisal function is isomorphic to what has been termed in the psychoanalytic literature as the ego ideal, a controlling agency of the superego that originates at 18 months. This structural system is involved in temporal, delay, and postponement functions (Chasseguet-Smirgel, 1985) and in the autoregulation of the "early moral emotion" of shame (Emde, 1988). Its acting as a "pilot and guide for the ego" (Jacobson, 1954) enables ongoing socioemotional development by allowing for successful passage through the portal of the rapprochement affective crisis and the negotiation of socialization demands of the second year. This narcissistic component of the superego (Hartmann & Lowenstein, 1962) is composed of "a psychic representation of all the growth, maturation, and individuation processes in the human being" (Piers & Singer, 1953, p. 15). For the rest of the lifespan the ego ideal functions to regulate the maintenance of self-esteem (Blos, 1974).

According to Freud, the function of the internal monitoring superego was to regulate drive, that is, hyperstimulated aggression and sexuality. Towards this end, he emphasized guilt and the other component of the superego, the verbal elements of the conscience. Developmental researchers find that the affect of guilt appears at 36 months (Izard, 1978; Pine, 1980; Sroufe, 1979). Recent revisions of psychoanalytic theory have deemphasized oedipal Freudian contributions and highlighted preoedipal events in the formation of the personality. There is now substantial evidence that superego functions onset much earlier than Freud thought. This chapter focuses on the role of early forming, nonverbal shame in superego development, the emergence of empathic and altruistic behavior, and the contributions of neurobiological systems to moral functioning.

THE ROLE OF THE AFFECT OF SHAME IN THE EARLY DEVELOPMENT OF THE SUPEREGO

In current revisions of psychoanalytic theory the superego and not the ego is thought to modulate emotional expression and mood states (Jacobson, 1971; Kernberg, 1984; A. N. Schore, 1991; J. R. Schore, 1993). The superego affect of shame has been conceptualized as the affect that arises when a self-monitoring and evaluating process concludes that there has been a failure to live up to ego ideal images (Piers & Singer, 1953) (a failure of self expectations). The internal set of expectations that are part of the ego ideal form a "global gestalt" and the image of the ideal self has an "intensely visual" character (Wurmser, 1981). Fulfillment of the ideal results in an increase of self-esteem (pride), while a failure to meet the standards of the ideal (shame) results in a decrease in self-esteem (Turiell, 1967). Shame is a central affective component of low self-esteem (Josephs, 1989). In recent psychoanalytic conceptualizations self-esteem regulation is identified as a function of the superego system (Kernberg, 1984), and Nathanson (1987a) describes the superego as processing "minute gradations of self esteem."

Various authors (Erikson, 1950; Harter & Whitesell, 1989; Stipek, 1983) have pointed out that although the external evaluation of socialization agents is instrumental to the inceptive experiences of shame and pride in the second year, the internalization of values in the form of an ego ideal, a standard against which the self appraises itself, comes to allow for the self-generation of these "self affects." In discussing early moral development, Emde (1992) points out that from a motivational standpoint: "Pride exerts a positive pull, indicating that a standard or rule has been successfully applied in a given situation; shame exerts a negative push, indicating an experienced unpleasure (with a limpness) after carrying out a prohibited act" (p. 22). The visual origin of pride is referred to in Sartre's proposal that pride "reveals to me the Other's look and myself at the end of that look" (p. 261). Shame originates in the experience of being looked at by the other (Wright, 1991), subsequently is internalized as "the eye of the self gazing inward" (Morrison, 1987), and occurs in the context of a relationship with a significant person whose thoughts and feelings are valued (H. B. Lewis, 1971). Caregiver "reflections," indicators of parental mood and intention, "furnish images of a self that the child must strive to become and others that must never again be" (Wright, 1991, p. 273). In earlier chapters I emphasized the nonverbal nature of the "reflected appraisals" (Cooley, 1902) that become incorporated into an internal structural system that monitors self-standards.

Kagan (1979) demonstrates that internal standards are present early in ontogeny, and asserts (Kagan, 1981) that the child must be able to compare his behavior with a standard to experience the negative self-evaluation found in shame. In a recent review of social psychological studies of automatic and nonreflective (unconscious) self-regulatory processes, Schlenker and Weingold (1992) conclude:

> The self provides an evaluative orientation that can be distinct from the evaluative orientation of specific other people. Yet the judgment process itself is similar for audiences of self and others in that it involves observing, evaluating, and sanctioning conduct in relation to a particular set of prescriptions and standards. (p. 155)

M. Lewis (1992) points out that a major function of shame is to interrupt any action that violates either internally or externally derived standards or rules. Kaufman (1989) asserts that shame, specifically, is experienced by the child in response to norm violations, and Schneider (1977) emphasizes that shame plays an important role in the individual's system of values.

Shame is currently being studied experimentally as a "moral affect," and it is now thought that "Both the capacity to accurately interpret interpersonal events and the motivation to take reparative action are intimately related to emotional experiences commonly termed moral affect" (Tangney, 1991, p. 598). Self-evaluative emotions are considered to be required for self-regulation (Stipek, Gralinski, & Kopp, 1990). The establishment of a shame regulator was earlier proposed to derive from the internalization of late practicing period affect regulating interactive transactions, specifically representations of dyadic interactive repair and distress-relief sequences. The ego ideal, a "comforting modality of the superego" (Schechter, 1979) which first emerges at 18 months (Blos, 1974; Schore, 1991), may reflect the operation of a representational system that can mediate the evocation of the nurturing function of the maternal object, even in her absence (Solnit, 1982). The appearance of evocative memory at 18 months (Fraiberg, 1969) that enables the child to evoke an image of a comforting object (Adler & Buie, 1979) is thus essential to the incipient function of the autoregulatory superego.

THE EMERGENCE OF EMPATHY AND ALTRUISTIC BEHAVIOR

At 10 to 14 months children show the earliest form of an empathic reaction to the affective distress of another—agitation and general disturbance while seeking out the mother through visual contact (Radke-Yarrow & Zahn-Waxler, 1984).

The incipient capacity to respond with self-distress to the dist... feel another's psychological pain, is dependent upon dyadic s... experiences with an emotionally interacting mother in this criti... first step in the development of empathic capacities is important, is an esential prerequisite to later social and moral development Miller, 1987). It is not until 18 months that the child first exh... ...oral" prosocial altruistic behavior in the form of approaching persons in distress and initiating positive, other-oriented, affective and instrumental activities in order to comfort the other; simultaneously the child's own distress decreases (Radke-Yarrow & Zahn-Waxler, 1984). The child, now capable of internally appraising and regulating her own negative affect, such as shame distress, can act as a distress modulator, an affect regulator for others. The developmentally attained capacity to autoregulate self-oriented distress—feeling distress in response to a distressed other (Eisenberg, 1986)—is thus required for the capacity to demonstrate "other-oriented empathy" (Batson, 1990). Other-oriented empathy requires the capacities of taking another's perspective, reading the other's internal emotional experience, and being capable of experiencing a range of emotional states (Tangney, 1991).

Rozin and Fallon (1987) point out that Hoffman's (1975b) formulation of empathy presumes the development of role-taking abilities, person permanence, and a differentiated self-concept, and this formulation predicts a development of empathic responding that roughly matches the development of disgust. Empathy involves the ability to understand both self and others (Goldstein & Michaels, 1985), and the ability to tolerate, consciously experience, and not bypass one particular emotional state, the painful helpless state of shame, is central to the operation of other-oriented empathy, the moral affective capacity that facilitates altruistic and prosocial behavior (Batson et al., 1988). Social psychological studies demonstrate individuals can reliably be induced to experience embarrassment by having them imitate a child's behavior; in this shame state they are more likely to "seek the positive experience of helping someone in order to relieve the discomfort of their embarrassment" (Apsler, 1975, p. 145). Other-oriented empathy also mediates the important function of inhibiting interpersonal aggression (Feshbach & Feshbach, 1969; Miller & Eisenberg, 1988). These emergent functions are certainly essential goals of the socialization process of the second year of human life. Indeed, they represent an excellent definition of "socialization."

It should be kept in mind that in his earliest work Piaget (1932) argued that the development of moral judgment parallels the development of emotional understanding, and in his later work (Piaget, 1967) he considered the later phases of emotional development as identical to personality and moral development. Similarly, Kohlberg (1963) suggested that "moral behavior is relat... ties to the parents" (p. 302), and posited (Kohlberg, 1976) a h... theory of social-moral development which shows cross-cult... (Snarey, 1985). In his last works he presented a reformulated "m... theory in which a sociomoral self develops via an identification...

. ealization of the parents (Kohlberg & Diessner, 1991). In this reformulation he places more emphasis on affective processes, since the central moral disposition involves acting "in terms of the self's moral judgments and standards, and the capacity to feel guilt or shame for violation of these standards, and esteem for fulfilling them" (p. 236). This revised conceptualization bears striking similarity to psychoanalytic ego ideal characterizations.

Moral development thus begins in preverbal periods of infancy, earlier than generally thought. In fact, the practicing phase, from the end of the first through the middle of the second year, is a critical period in the early development of the superego. In current attachment theory, Bretherton (1985) stresses the involvement of internal working models in superego formation, while McDevitt (1979), from a developmental psychoanalytic standpoint, emphasizes the interaction between superego internalization and the resolution of the rapprochement crisis. This model of the superego as an affect regulator fits well with psychoanalytic conceptualizations of the ego ideal component of the superego which emerges at end of the practicing/beginning of the rapprochement stage and which contains an internalized set of expectations that are conveyed to the child (Wurmser, 1981). The ego ideal has recently become a focus of social cognition research (e.g., Ogilvie, 1987; Schlenker & Weingold, 1992). In agreement with this work on "possible selves" (Markus & Nurius, 1986), developmental cognitive research is characterizing the appearance, at 18 months, of the child's emergent capacity to represent what "might be" and to encode a contrast between an actual state of affairs and a possible one (Meltzoff, 1990).

NEUROBIOLOGICAL CONTRIBUTIONS TO MORAL BEHAVIOR

From the perspective of neurobiology, Bunge (1980a) advances the idea that "morality must have a biological root as well as a social one" (p. 181), a theme pursued in a recent book by Alexander (1987). In concurrence, Emde, a developmental psychoanalyst, in a recent study of early moral development (Buchsbaum & Emde, 1990), concludes that "propensities for moral development are strongly biological, but require facilitation and direction through accumulated experiences within the infant-caregiver relationship" (p. 131), and stresses the importance of caregivers who serve as "reparative agents." Vitz (1990) now emphasizes the importance of right hemispheric emotional-imagistic processes in moral development, and Kohut (1975) proposes the involvement of this cortex in empathic processes. Children with structural damage of this hemisphere are extremely poor at perceiving the emotional states of others (Voeller, 1986). Freud originally proposed that the function of the internal monitoring superego was to regulate drive, that is, hyperstimulated aggression and sexuality. The critical function of descending orbital cortical projections in drive modulation (Rosenkilde, 1979) and the suppression of aggression (DeBruin et al., 1983; Grafman et al., 1986) has been previously documented. In older classical neurological work, Kleist (1931, cited in Starkstein, Boston, & Robinson, 1988) considered the orbitofrontal cortex to be the center of emotional life, and to be implicated in ethical and moral behaviors. Pribram (1981) now concludes that frontolimbic function, manifested in increased internal control, is activated when the human turns inward to process the ethical considerations of one's behavior, and Frijda (1988) recently proposes that the elicitation and deeper processing of emotion "can extend the driving forces of emotion to the spheres of moral responsibility". (p. 357)

Twenty five years ago MacLean (1967) speculated that the prefrontal cortex and its limbic connections are the neural substrate for empathy. The association of a poor empathic capacity with orbital frontal damage has indeed been reported in a recent neuropsychological study (Martzke, Swan, & Varney, 1991). Other research indicates that prefrontal damage acquired early in life provides the neurological substrate for a permanent impairment of empathic, moral, and social behavior, all of which were "arrested at an immature stage" (Price, Daffner, Stowe, & Mesulam, 1990). Right frontal but not left frontal nor posterior lesioned adult patients have been observed to be deficient in moral judgment (Sorman, Wasserstein, & Zappulla, 1983). In a detailed neurological investigation, an adult patient with orbitofrontal pathology, when confronted with ethical dilemmas that required social judgment, usually chose the wrong action, often with disastrous consequences, suggesting to the authors that orbitofrontal dysfunction underlies sociopathic behavior (Eslinger & Damasio, 1985). A more recent neurological case report describes an acquired antisocial personality disorder associated with orbital frontal lobe damage (Meyers, Berman, Scheibel, & Hayman, 1992). Neuropsychological studies show that psychopathic personalities manifest a relative inability to develop empathic responses (Schalling, 1978). A study by Elliot (1978) on the neuropsychological concomitants of antisocial behavior also reported a significant prefrontal deficit in psychopathic subjects. Patients with orbital damage manifest an "interoceptive agnosia," an absence of any autonomic, affective response to emotional stimuli (Tranel et al., 1988), and an "amnesia for social knowledge" (Damasio & Tranel, 1988), and such deficits are thought to be responsible for "acquired sociopathy." These observations may underlie the finding that psychopaths label aroused states inappropriately because of poor discrimination of physiological changes (Schacter & Latane, 1964).

SUMMARY

The right hemispheric orbitofrontal affect regulator performs functions that are essential to the adaptive moral functioning of the individual. This frontolimbic structural system is identical to the ego ideal, described in the psychoanalytic literature as a component of the superego that emerges at 18 months. In current revisions of this theory, the superego is understood to modulate emotional expression and mood states, and the ego ideal functions to regulate self-esteem. The superego affect of shame arises when a self-monitoring process evaluates that there has been a failure to meet ego ideal expectations. This discrepancy results in a reduction of self-esteem. The ego ideal, a comforting modality of the superego, can access in evocative memory internal representations of the early nurturing, soothing, and shame regulating object.

At 18 months the child first exhibits moral prosocial altruistic behavior in the form of comforting—regulating the negative affect of—a distressed other. This other-oriented empathy is attained when the child is capable of reading her own as well as the other's negative internal state. Such a capacity necessitates the operation of an internalized shame regulator. These formulations suggest that moral development begins earlier than previously thought, and is much more of a visual than a verbal process.

The caregiver influences the trajectory of the child's developing moral capacities by shaping the neurobiological structural system that mediates such functioning. Neuropsychological and neurological studies suggest that the orbitofrontal cortex is centrally involved in empathic and moral behaviors. Structural deficits in this system are associated with sociopathic pathologies.

28 The Emergence of Self-Regulation

The mother initially provides an external regulating mechanism for many of the physiological mechanisms that the infant possesses but does not regulate itself. These effects are mediated by effects of the mother on the infant's neurobiological processes. At some point in development the infant becomes self-regulating through the development of internal regulatory mechanisms entrained to the stimuli that the mother provides.
—Gary W. Kraemer, Michael H. Ebert, Dennis E. Schmidt, and William T. Mckinney (1991)

Underlying the development of complex emotions is the maturation of the frontal region. Frontal lobe functions may be necessary for the integration of appraisal and emotion and for the generation of the responses necessary for successful coping. Planfulness, the ability to inhibit certain motor responses, and the ability to adopt nonegocentric perspectives are all frontal functions, and may be involved in the generation of complex emotions (e.g. shame, guilt, pride) that emerge during the second and third years of life, and in the regulation of emotional behaviors.
—Nathan A. Fox (1991)

Thirty years ago the late Russian neuroscientist Aleksandr Luria (1980) predicted that the solution of the "riddle of the frontal lobes" would be found in an explication of its "psychoregulatory" role.

There is no doubt that the introduction of various modern experimental neuropsychological techniques into the study of frontal lobe function and the interpretation of the results from the standpoint of modern ideas on self-regulating systems will shed fresh light on the functions of the frontal lobes and will enable the facts obtained to be fitted into a system of adequate scientific concepts. (p. 257; first published in Russian in 1962)

Indeed advances in neuroscience research have contributed much to our understanding of self-regulation. This adaptive function is now characterized as the operation of higher level processes which modulate the reactive states of the somatic, endocrine, autonomic, and central nervous systems (Derryberry & Rothbart, 1984). The prefrontal-orbital system, with its unique extensive subcortical and cortical connections, has been specifically implicated as a central mechanism of homeostatic regulation (Kolb, 1984).

In this chapter I present a fundamental ontogenetic principle of developing self-regulatory systems. I then discuss the adaptive role of shame in affect regulation, and propose a model of the regulation of self-esteem. Finally, I emphasize the importance of the adaptive capacity to internally switch psychobiological states in response to changes, or expected changes in the socioenvironment.

THE ONTOGENY OF SELF-REGULATION

The current rapidly expanding body of knowledge of regulatory systems and processes is being created not only by neuroscience but from many other disciplines. Self-regulatory constructs are now being utilized in a number of subdisciplines in psychology: personality, motivation/emotion, social psychology, clinical/abnormal, health psychology/behavioral medicine, and experimental psychology (Karoly, 1993). In addition, developmental psychologists are investigating the antecedents of self-regulation (Kopp, 1982; Zivin, 1979). In parallel to this, contemporary psychoanalysis, with its emphasis on the development of the capacity for the self-regulation of affect (Krystal, 1988), has been a primary source of heuristic ideas about the dyadic origin of self-regulation in infacy. Psychoanalytic theoreticians have expounded upon certain common principles of the ontogeny of self-regulation. Greenspan (1981) argues that the homeostatic regulation of the infant's arousal or excitation is first performed by the responsive mother, and then acquired by the infant. Kohut (1971) refers to the growth of psychological structures which continue to perform the drive-regulating, integrating, and adaptive functions that had previously been performed by the external object. Indeed, the essential experience and definition of the self are built out of internalized "selfobject" functions (Kohut, 1984). Sander (1977b) asserts that during development self-regulatory mechanisms are organized in relation both to endogenous activity and to the surrounding life support system.

Finally, in becoming internalized, adopted strategies which first characterized regulatory relationships with the interpersonal surround will now function as features of self-regulation and eventually characterize personality idiosyncrasy. (Sander, 1976, p. 312)

Though utilizing different disciplinary methodologies than developmental psychoanalysts, neuroscientists have converged upon similar ontogenetic principles. Joseph (1992) states that just as the mother originally had to determine what the baby's limbic system needed, now the child's mature brain must do the same. Based on extensive psychobiological research, Kraemer (1992) concludes: "If all goes well, the infant internalizes a dynamic, multimodal, temporal, and spatial sensory "image" of the regulatory systems of the caregiver that are tuned to caregiving" (p. 498). Tucker (1992) now holds that the mother's ability to modulate the infant's emotional expression is instrumental to the child's burgeoning capacity for self-regulation. Fox (1989) concludes that regulation of emotional distress emerges during the second year of life and involves the development of certain cognitive abilities. Notice a psychological function (right hemispheric affect regulation) which is externally regulated in one phase of infancy is internalized and autoregulated in the succeeding phase.

Other disciplines have converged on this essential principle that is fundamental to the growth of all living systems. In theoretical biological work, Goodwin (1982) asserts the general biological tenet that developing organisms "internalize" environmental forces by becoming appropriately structured in relation to them, and by incorporating an internal model of these exogenous signals develop adaptive homeostatic regulatory mechanisms which allow for stability in the face of external variation. In control theory research, Wonham (1976) proposes that regulation on the part of the organism, which maintains internal stability and output regulation and enables an effective response to external stimuli, depends on the formation of a dynamic model of the outside world. Wonham points out that this internal model principle applies to a very broad class of cybernetic situations including neurology (Oatley, 1972), psychology (Miller, Galanter, & Pribram, 1960), and general systems theory (Conant & Ashby, 1970). In a neurosociological model, Schwalbe (1991) points out that evolving dynamical systems that "co-evolve with their environments" form "internal representations of elements of the external world and of experiences with these elements." This internal mental imagery allows developing systems that are in continuous interaction with their environments to organize and regulate themselves, thereby enhancing their stability in response to environmental perturbations. In similar conceptualizations psychoanalytic theorists have defined internalization as a transformation of external regulations into internal ones (Hartmann & Loewenstein, 1962; Schafer, 1968), of external relations into internal ones (Loewald, 1962), and as a "taking in" of external others that enables the individual to refer to and experience others without their being physically present (Meissner, 1981). Furthermore, it is now thought that there are increasing levels of internalization (McDevitt, 1980) and a hierarchy of internalizing processes (Giovacchini, 1990).

Over 60 years ago, the Russian psychologist Vygotsky (1978), studying the basic mechanism underlying the internalization of higher psychological functions, posited the general developmental principle that all psychological processes appear first at an interpersonal and only later at an intrapersonal level. This process of internalization takes place within a "zone of proximal development". "The zone of proximal development defines those functions that have not yet matured but are in the process of maturation, functions that will mature tomorrow but are currently in an embryonic state" (p. 86). Learning experiences create this zone by arousing a "variety of internal developmental processes that are able to operate only when the child is interacting with people" (Vygotsky, 1978, p. 90). As a result "what the child can only do with the help of the adult today he will do on his own tomorrow." Thus an operation that initially represents an external activity is reconstructed and begins to occur internally, and in this way, all higher functions emerge as a result of social interaction.

This developmental axiom also applies to the emergence of an internal system of affect regulation: "Emotion is initially regulated by others, but over the course of early development it becomes increasingly self-regulated as a result of neurophysiological development" (Thompson, 1990, p. 371). An essential conclusion of this volume is that practicing phase-specific, external, interpersonal, caregiver-modulated arousal regulation, especially after stress-induced dyadic mismatches (attachment breaks), specifically influences the experience-dependent maturation of orbitofrontal structure which underlies and supports internal, intrapersonal regulatory functions subserved by prefrontal internal working models. The delayed response function, the functional output of orbitofrontal activity (Goldman, 1971), is known to be essential to the operation of internalized representational memory (Fuster, 1980), and representational memory is known to function as a behavioral regulator (Goldman-Rakic, 1987b). Current developmental psychological research supports the conclusion that the child internalizes both his role and aspects of the caregiver's role in the child-parent relationship (Sroufe & Fleeson, 1986). The developmental capacity to maintain mental representations is now thought to facilitate the establishment of satisfying interpersonal relationships (Bemesderfer & Cohler, 1983). I conclude that the experience-dependent psychoneurobiological maturation of arousal regulating cortical-limbic structure underlies the process of internalization and the transformation of external into internal regulation.

THE DYADIC DETERMINATION OF THE AUTONOMIC SET POINT

According to Schwalbe (1991) the emergence of the ability to form internal representations (imagery) allows for the creation of feedback channels which regulate patterns of energy dissipation in the brain. The functional capacity of visual imagery to elicit physiological changes (Zikmund, 1975) is mediated by corticolimbic modulation of various stress hormones, substances that prepare the organism for "energy changes" and activities to "reestablish homeostasis" (Joffe, Vaughn, Barglow, & Benveniste, 1985). Biologic homeostatic models character- ize regulatory mechanisms which maintain activity of a system around set points with specified ranges, thereby permitting the system to adapt to shifts in internal organismic needs and external stimuli by triggering feedback structures which inhibit or excite specific metabolic and physiologic processes (Jones, 1973). According to classical psychological arousal theory concepts, the set point is the optimal level of arousal required to sustain functional interactions; it is the point at which feedback mechanisms are set to operate, either in response to deficient or excessive stimulation, thereby restituting equilibrium (Pribram & McGuiness, 1975). Arousal, which reflects the activity of multiple ascending reticular sys- tems (Routtenberg, 1968), is known to be associated with changes in metabolic energy (Gonzalez-Lima & Scheich, 1985).

Nadel (1990) suggests that the maturation of brain systems is directly influ- enced by the amounts of early stimulation the developing organism is exposed to, and that "such experiences play a role in determining a 'set point' around which a given system fluctuates throughout life" (p. 623). As applied to the orbitofrontal affect regulatory system which directly influences two subcortical catecholamin- ergic systems, the set point may reflect the balance between sympathetic- excitatory, energy-mobilizing and parasympathetic-inhibitory, energy-conserving activity of the limbic system required for optimal emotional functioning and attachment (object relations) behavior. Indeed, the orbitofrontal modulation of energy balance (McGregor & Atrens, 1991) and regulation of set point (Kolb, Whishaw, & Schallert, 1977) have been experimentally demonstrated. In this differentiated system endogenous or exogenous variations from a reference stan- dard of autonomic balance (Grings & Dawson, 1978)—established in critical period imprinting transactions—trigger feedback functions which monitor its output and adjust its trajectory in accord with how it is interacting and coping with the environment. This allows the individual to access a stimulatory mechanism that increases or an inhibitory mechanism that decreases energy metabolism in response to stress (Bryan, 1990). Bryan notes that the net change in energy metabolism depends on the relative effects of these mechanisms acting simul- taneously, and that the dominance of one over the other depends on the particular individual and the nature of the stressful event.

Duffy (1941) proposed that change in energy level, occurring as an adjust- ment to external conditions, is the most basic characteristic feature of emotion. The excitation-inhibition concept, which views responsivity to environmental stimulation (autonomic reactivity) as requiring a continuous dynamic balance between excitatory and inhibitory neurophysiological systems, was first intro- duced by Pavlov (1927). Pavlov postulated that the "strength of the nervous system" was reflected in the ability to inhibit the buildup of excitation. Jackson

(1931) hypothesized that the ontogenetic termination of an early excitable stage of development was due to the later functional onset of a cortical inhibitory system. These classical notions are supported by the work of Hofer (1984b), who observes that the high resting heart rates of mid infancy are followed by a reduction in late infancy, reflecting the neural maturation of parasympathetic (vagal) restraint. On the basis of these findings I interpret the developmental decrease in elevated infant heart rate which begins at 13–15 months (Kagan, 1982) and the maturational increase in vagal tone (Porges & Fox, 1986) to reflect the parasympathetically-influenced final maturation of the orbitofrontal cortex.

These ideas fit well with Stuss' (1992) current model of the biological and psychological development of the executive functions of the frontal lobes. Development, a multistage process, culminates in a hierarchical system that processes information at different levels and monitors this output within a feedback loop:

> Incoming information is forwarded to a comparator which analyzes in a pattern-recognition format the incoming specific fact or group of facts. These comparator values have been developed through previous experience, modeling, and training. If there is no difference between the input and comparator values, no adjustment is necessary. If they are different, a change output is automatically triggered. (p. 10)

THE ADAPTIVE ROLE OF SHAME IN AFFECT REGULATION

The late practicing parasympathetic structural transformation underlies and supports the adaptive cortically regulated function of conservation-withdrawal, a primary regulatory process for organismic homeostasis (Engel & Schmale, 1972). Powles (1992) characterizes this state in which the inhibited organism passively disengages in order to attempt to become "unseen" as: "the organismic strategy . . . to conserve energies and strive to avoid attention, to foster survival by the risky posture of feigning death, to allow healing of wounds and restitution of depleted resources by immobility" (p. 213). In the parasympathetic-dominant affect state of shame, characterized by a sudden offset of sympathetic and an onset of vagal activity (MacCurdy, 1930), the deflated self, depleted of energy (Morrison, 1983) manifests withdrawal from significant objects (Levin, 1967) in order to protect against an anticipated loss of self-boundaries (H.B. Lewis, 1971). Inauguratory shame experiences in the second year occur in the context of a dyadic misattunement, and result from being looked at by the Other (Wright, 1991). Morrison (1987) emphasizes that ultimately the trigger of shame does not require the presence of an external person, that it may be internalized as "the eye of the self gazing inward."

This ubiquitous primary social emotion in which one is visible and not ready to be visible (Erikson, 1950) operates subtly in even the healthiest of human interactions (Kaufman, 1974) and is generated by the virtually constant monitoring of the self in relation to others (Scheff, 1988). Its unique potency as a negative affect is described by Tomkins (1963):

> Though terror speaks of life and death and distress makes of the world a vale of tears, yet shame strikes deepest into the heart of man. While terror and distress hurt, they are wounds inflicted from outside which penetrate the smooth surface of the ego; but shame is felt as an inner torment, a sickness of the soul. It does not matter whether the humiliated one has been shamed by derisive laughter or whether he mocks himself. In either event he feels himself naked, defeated, alienated, lacking in dignity or worth. (p. 118)

Morrison (1989) asserts that turning the potential control of shame inward is an important developmental step. The control (regulation) of shame, first externally performed by the caregiver, developmentally transforms into an internal psychobiological mechanism that reignites ANS sympathetic activity and arousal, thereby shifting the individual out of this aversive low energy state. The autoregulation of shame may depend on the internalization of the "mirroring" positive affect amplifying function of the maternal gleam. This mirroring function may amplify positive affect by means of an internalized "reflector" or "looking glass" self (Cooley, 1909/1962).

It is often overlooked that negative affects mediate important adaptive functions. Geller (1984) argues that successful adaptation in the sphere of emotionality requires the capacity to tolerate affects of formidable intensity, such as shame. In psychological research on affect, Izard (1971) argues that shame comes to play a central role in the regulation of all emotional expression, and therefore for more effective social interaction. Nathanson (1992) underscores its adaptive supra-affective function in describing shame as " . . . a biological system by which the organism controls its affective output so that it will not remain interested or content when it may not be safe to do so, or so that it will not remain in affective resonance with an organism that fails to match its patterns stored in memory" (p. 140). Utilizing clinical material various authors have pointed out the constructive function of shame in ego-protection (Mollon & Parry, 1984), in the differentiation of the self in the presence of dangerous self-other mergers (Spero, 1984), and in autonomy (Severino, McNutt, & Feder, 1987). This potent emotion that is generated by the virtually constant monitoring of the self in relation to others (Scheff, 1988) is associated with a termination of an object relating mode and a reduction in the motivation to merge with others in order to generate pleasurable affect, a capacity that is adaptive in various contexts which necessitate autonomous function. Broucek (1982) asserts: "In small, unavoidable 'doses', shame may enhance self and object differentiation and assist the individuation process because it involves acute awareness of one's separateness from the important other" (p. 370).

Moderate feelings of shame help the individual "monitor his relationship with the world" and act as signals to change (Potter-Efron, 1989) and self-correction (Kaufman, 1989). Kohut (1977) states that as a result of interactions with a regulating selfobject, the child experiences an "affect signal" instead of "affect spread." Rapaport (1953) asserts that "affect as signals are just as indispensable a means of reality-testing as thoughts" (p. 196). This signal shame (Fenichel, 1945; Levin, 1967; Meissner, 1986a) serves an adaptive regulatory function to the individual's sense of well being (Rizzuto, 1991). The ability to consciously experience the psychobiological state marked by shame is essential, since overt acknowledged shame allows for experiencing, dissipating, and transitioning out of the negative state, while bypassed shame avoids this state—which still exists and affects the self even if it not consciously attended to—and does not allow the individual the opportunity to take action to relieve this painful state. Izard (1991) states that repressed shame obviates self-repair, and refers to "the effort to repair and strengthen the self after experiencing intense shame" (p. 344).

The importance of regulating and thereby being able to tolerate shame throughout the lifespan from toddlerhood through adulthood becomes obvious in light of the fact that this affect state tends to linger for quite a long time until the subject recovers (Nathanson, 1987a) and spreads out from one specific content to all of 'inner reality' and hence to the entire function of expressing oneself (Wurmser, 1981). Internal shame regulation may be reflected in the diminution of the intensity of the "emotional tag" of the state-dependent activation of auto-biographical memory (Cimino, Verfaeillie, Bowers, & Heilman, 1991), especially historical painful memories that are "affectively imprinted" (Ciompi, 1991) with shame. Most importantly, however, it allows for the adaptive capacity of conservation-withdrawal, the passive coping mechanism that improves survival efficiency through inactive disengagement in order "to conserve resources" and to assure autonomy until environmental conditions are once again more compatible (Engel & Schmale, 1972).

THE DUAL COMPONENT REGULATION OF SELF-ESTEEM

In an earlier work (Schore, 1991) I offered a characterization of an internal dual component system which regulates the frequency, intensity, and duration of negative and positive affects and thereby modulates self-esteem. Self-esteem has been conceptualized as an "affective picture of the self," with high self-esteem connoting a predominance of positive affects and low self-esteem of negative ones (Pulver, 1970). Recent experimental studies have demonstrated that effective self-esteem regulation is characterized by a preponderance of positive self-representations (Power & Brewin, 1990). This dynamic self monitoring system regulates narcissistic affect, affect associated with internal self-representations, and acts to "maintain the structural cohesion, temporal stability and positive affective coloring of the self representation" (Stolorow & Lachmann, 1980, p. 10), a function formerly externally provided by regulating caregivers. Shame, an inhibitor of the positive affects of enjoyment and interest-excitement (Tomkins, 1963) is an affective component of low self-esteem (Josephs, 1989), while enjoyment-joy and interest-excitement affect invested in the self defines pride (Nathanson, 1987b), an indicator of high self-esteem. Low self-esteem, low expectations of success, and anticipated depression are known to activate increased cortisol production by the hypothalamo-pituitary-adrenocortical system (Price, 1982). Recent social psychological studies are also converging on the association of interpersonal affect regulation and self-esteem maintenance (Baumgardner, Kaufman, & Levy, 1989).

Infant researchers now report that "Maternal perception of oneself as a mother and the effective value (such as pride, shame) attached to the self-evaluation appear to be critical factors in maternal self-constructs" (McGrath, Boukydis, & Lester, 1993, p. 36). Maternal self-esteem is a primary determinant of the developmental outcomes of the infant, and is related to the efficacy of the mother's transactional attempts to influence her child's autonomic regulation. The infant's autonomic regulating system, which emerges at the end of the practicing period and is localized in the orbitofrontal cortex and its connections, monitors and controls the biphasic process of affect regulation. The functional output of this homeostatic system represents the activity of two dissociable psychobiological components, and the co-activity of these components mediates the dynamics of what Nathanson (1987b, 1992) calls the shame/pride axis. The attachment deactivator, a shame stimulator component, mediated by activation of the lateral tegmental limbic circuit, acutely brakes hyperaroused and hyperstimulated states, diminishes positive narcisisistic affective coloring of self-representations, contracts the self, lowers expectations, decreases self-esteem, active coping, interest and curiosity, interferes with cognition and increases overt consciously experienced shame, parasympathetic supported passive coping, blushing, gaze aversion, and depressive affect-toned mood. The second component, the attachment reactivator, a shame modulator, mediated by activation of the mesocortical ventral tegmental limbic circuit, reduces consciously experienced shame, negative affective self-representations, low-keyed depressive states and passive coping, and initiates self-comforting functions which enable recovery of sympathetic supported positive hedonic-toned mood and narcissistic affect, expansion of the self, and active stress coping capacities.

The functional operation of these components, reflected in specific patterns of physiological activity regulated by the two limbic neuromodulator circuits, is responsible for the generation of distinct psychobiological states. These circuits may act in a coupled reciprocal mode, a coupled nonreciprocal mode, or an uncoupled mode. Such potential relational patterns account for three modes of interaction—increased activity in one and decreased in the other, concurrent increases or decreases in both components, and responses in one subsytem in the absence of activation of the other. The confluence of their dissociable outputs is phenomenologically experienced as discrete emotions and enduring affect states—moods—that infuse and color distinctive internal states of consciousness, and that are externally expressed as discrete behavioral states. These states are ubiquitous background phenomena, and in daily life most switches between states produce minor bodily changes that occur just below the threshold of awareness and are marked by the conscious experience of mild, low intensity emotions. This state transition is usually seamless and contextually appropriate, but in conditions of socioemotional stress, the experience of intense emotion associated with major autonomic alterations punctuates and inaugurates a discontinuity in consciousness.

In light of the related principles of state-dependent learning of affectively charged information (Reus, Weingartner, & Post, 1979)—that retrieval of information is minimal when the subject's current state differs from that in which the information was acquired, and state-dependent recall (Bower, 1981)—that achieving a particular bodily state is necessary in order to access certain cognitions, switching between states allows for a full range of access to qualitatively different affectively laden autobiographical memories and various psychobiological motivations. For example, the operation of the attachment deactivator component suspends the behavioral state which drives attachment dynamics, while activity of the attachment activator re-initiates attachment motivation and drives the self into merger states which potentially generate positive affect. In an attachment deactivation predominant state, the self is motivated to withdraw inwardly, away from the view of social objects, and seeks to avoid direct gaze and face-to-face object relations. In an attachment reactivation motivational state, the self actively seeks reunion transactions in which it reveals and exhibits itself to an appraised emotionally meaningful social object in anticipation of a mirrored amplification of positive affect. Izard (1991) notes that in the experience of joy the object is seen as enhancing the self of the perceiver.

In addition to effects on attachment dynamics, these mechanisms also operate in shame-induced inactivation of high arousal, high interest exploratory-play behaviors. White (1960) asserts that shame is always associated with incompetence, and Broucek (1982) suggests inefficacy experiences may be the earliest releasers of shame. In relevant developmental research, Barrett and Zahn-Waxler (1987) constructed an experimental situation in which a young child was given a toy that fell apart after a few minutes of play. They then observed individual responses to this situation. In one typical response pattern one group of children showed a typical shame response—they averted gaze, their bodies seemed to collapse and they stopped movement, their thought processes appeared inhibited, and they remained impassive. Another group also averted gaze at the moment the toy surprisingly fell apart, but their bodies did not collapse. Rather than "disappearing" they attempted to focus attention not on themseles but on the toy which they then attempted to repair. This study demonstrates the induction of shame in an early competence failure and the operation in the latter type of child of an internalized shame regulator that adaptively reactivates interest and curiosity, increases expectations, and initiates active stress coping capacities. The resumption of activity in the mesocortical dopaminergic circuit neurochemically mediates the reappearance of exploratory behavior (Fink & Smith, 1980).

THE ADAPTIVE CAPACITY TO SELF-INITIATE PSYCHOBIOLOGICAL STATE TRANSITIONS IN RESPONSE TO SOCIOENVIRONMENTAL ALTERATIONS

As a result of its experience-dependent maturation, an emergent function of the mature dual component, dual process frontolimbic system is expressed in the middle of the second year—the homeostatic maintenance of sympathetic-parasympathetic limbic balance of autonomic-affective functioning. The resultant eurythmy of ergotropic arousal and tropotropic arousal can generally be sustained either in the presence or absence of social objects and for longer periods of time. This autonomic balance which specifies an optimal level of emotionality underlies an internal state of "regulatory equilibrium" (Sander, 1988) manifest in a mental state of "alert inactivity" (Beebe & Lachman, 1988a), which is equated with "alert wakefulness" (Gardner, 1969) and "interest" (Tomkins, 1963), and physiologically expressed as hyperfrontal "resting wakefulness" (Ingvar, 1979). In applying systems theory concepts to the elucidation of central nervous system processes in emotion, Schwartz (1982) proposes that emotional properties result from complex interactions and organizations of its component neurophysiological processes, and that the interaction of these components produces unique properties, such as self-regulation. Indeed, this dual component cortical-subcortical affect regulating system which mediates between the internal milieu and the external environment and which monitors, adjusts, and modifies emotional responses to both hypostimulating ("deprivational," "solitary") and hyperstimulating ("social") socioenvironmental stresses, allows for the adaptive preservation of a cluster of states that comprise self-identity and self-continuity in the face of continuously changing external environmental conditions. This stability is, in essence, a product of the adaptive capacity to appropriately and relatively fluidly autoregulate psychobiological state transitions in response to different types of environmental demands.

What do we know of the dynamics of such state shifts? State has been defined as "a constellation of relatively stable repeated patterns of motivational variables and patterns of self experience characterized by specific forms of activity, cognition, affect, and relatedness" (Lichtenberg, Lachmann, & Fosshage, 1992, p. 157). Distinct functional states are associated with specific forms of cognitve strategies and memory storage (Fischer, 1971), that is, with state-typical modes of information processing (Koukkou & Lehmann, 1983). Signal affects serve as stimuli that identify and augur a particular state transition, but in the absence of these unconsciously recognized stimuli an ongoing state persists. Lichtenberg et al. (1992) note however that: "When a transition from one state to another occurs, the new state acts to reorganize the prior behaviors, cognition, affect, and relatedness to resist changes to other states" (p. 157).

The phenomenon of state shifts has been extensively studied by Koukkou and

Lehmann (1983), and although they focus on dream and sleep phenomena they indicate that the psychophysiological mechanisms that mediate such shifts are common for mentation in a continuum of all states of consciousness. According to these authors a state shift corresponds to phasic EEG events and is experienced as a mental discontinuity. A shift from a lower to a higher functional state is associated with a higher level of vigilance and an orienting response.

> A state shift makes the material in the short-term store available for processing in a new, higher functional state, where it activates new associations, is treated with different more advanced cognitive strategies, and is then stored in the storage appropriate to the higher state. (p. 227)

This upward shift blocks access to material in lower storage spaces, a process that is equated with repression. Conversely, a downward state-shift, associated with decrease of vigilance, may bring some of the new context material which resides in the short-term store into a lower functional state. These authors emphasize the adaptive aspect of this transition:

> The temporary re-establishment of lower-order states with re-opened access to earlier memory stores and processing strategies, and the possibilities of shifts to other states with other stores and strategies, mean that the individual . . . has a wider spectrum of "solutions" available for tentative application to new problem material. (Koukkou & Lehmann, 1983, p. 228)

Most intriguingly, they underscore the adaptive nature of downward state shifts that renew access to older memory stores of "previous developmental stages."

The adaptive advantages of dynamic cycling between different types and levels of psychobiological states is echoed by other authors. Powles (1992) describes the fundamental biological principle that:

> All animate things cycle between activity and passivity: between the active out-reach for relationships and needed nourishment, security, and comfort, the active-engaging mode; and an active disengaging mode . . . Conservation-withdrawal has to be distinguished from an active disengagment from the environment, in which flight would be included. . . .its hallmarks are a relative immobility, a quiescence, and an unresponsiveness to the environment. (p. 415)

The ability to cycle back and forth between these organismic modes in response to environmental conditions increases survival efficiency. Chisolm (1990) defines adaptability in the face of socioecological stressors as: "the capacity of an organism to make a successful response to perturbations in its physical and social environments such that the next time it encounters that same perturbation, or one sufficiently similar, it can respond with less cost" (p. 240). This reduced "cost" may specifically be an optimization (Maynard Smith, 1978) of energy dissipation within the constraints of a specific environmental condition. "Perturbations" in the social environment refer to appraised changes in the socioaffective significance of an environmental signal. Novel challenging environments are thought to promote a nonreciprocal coactivation of both the sympathetic energy-mobilizing and parasympathetic energy-conserving divisions of the ANS (Berntson et al., 1991). Berntson notes that a successful response to an environmental perturbation may entail the adaptive use of a reciprocal mode of control in which the activity of one ANS component increases while the other simultaneously decreases. To ensure reduced cost, this adaptability must imply a parasympathetic-dominant mode. In support of this, Schmale and Engel (1975) conclude that conservation-withdrawal allows the organism to cope with stressful conditions with "as little involvement, cost or risk as possible", and to conserve resources until environmental conditions are more compatible (Schmale & Engel, 1972).

This flexible mechanism develops in the context of socioaffective learning experiences in which the mother acts as a "hidden" psychobiological regulator (Hofer, 1984a) of the energy-mobilizing sympathetic and energy-conserving parasympathetic components of the child's developing autonomic nervous system. The resultant imprinting of these critical period organismic-environmental transactions produces internal dynamic representations that program information about state transitions (Freyd, 1987) and generate cognitive expectations (Intraub & Richardson, 1989), and it is these cognitive-affective elements that encode reciprocal modes of ANS control that allow for a more efficient regulation of energy dissipation in subsequent socioaffective transactions. Tucker (1992) suggests that paralimbic networks that link increasingly sophisticated representations of the external context to an internal representation of the bodily state generate "anticipated sensory consequences" and appropriately respond to subtle and gross adaptive challenges. These networks are therefore responsible for what Edelman (1987) describes as the brain's creation of models of environment, images of "a context, which consists of the internal state of the animal (ultimately its brain state) as it responds to the appearance of certain objects and events in the world" (p. 295).

Schwalbe (1991) concludes that the development of more complex forms of self-organization in the first two years of life is mediated by the appearance of internal representations which shape spontaneous patterns of energy dissipation. These stored images come to automodulate processes of energy flow that support survival in a particular environment, and allow for: "the emergence of a human being who is resilient in the face of environmental perturbations, who has stable predispositions to act, and who can regulate the overt expression of these dispositions" (p. 279). This resilience involves an ability to tolerate signals of negative affect in environmental contexts where threat and lack of social success will interfere with the attainment of biosocial goals. Gilbert (1992a) describes: "internal evaluations of one's general energy level can feed into negative self-perceptions, sense of inferiority and incapacity, and predictions about obtaining future goals" (p. 169). Internal dynamic representations thus encode an appraisal of the organism's bodily state to generate energy in response to the challenge of a particular external context, that is an estimate of the individual's capacity to cope with a particular environmental situation. The adaptive character of such an appraisal system is stressed by Cacioppo and Berntson (1992): "With progressively higher organizational levels in evaluative mechanisms, there appears to be a general expansion in the range and relational complexity of contextual controls and in the breadth and flexibility of adaptive response" (p. 1026). In a paper on the evolution of frontal lobe structures, Goldberg (1987) emphasizes that the capacity to produce adaptive changes enables not only the ability to compete for survival, but also to surmount limiting environmental circumstances and to anticipate environmental contingencies. Orbital-limbic mechanisms that underlie "learned social contingencies" (Daigneault, Braun, & Whitaker, 1992) may thus specifically mediate the adaptive role of the limbic system in self-preservation (MacLean, 1958).

This orbital structural system, the cerebral system responsive to emotionally stressful stimuli, can now begin to bidirectionally autoregulate narcissistic affect, hypo- and hyper-aroused affect in response to an appraisal of hypo- or hyper-stimulating changes in the external environment. It thus functions to regulate emotional processes that result from "disrupting the relation between the person and the internal or external environment, when such relations are significant to the individual" (Campos, Campos, & Barrett, 1989, p. 395). Its emergence at the end of the practicing period is responsible for the function of emotions as "fundamental adaptational resources" (Lazarus, 1991b) which enable a successful transition through the stressful dyadic disruptions of the "rapprochement crisis" at the onset of the next critical period of socioemotional development. Plooij and van de Rijt Plooij (1989) refer to a hierarchical reorganization of the CNS at 18 months, which is expressed in the appearance of a new negative feedback control system, and Fox and Davidson (1984) describe a mechanism of affect regulation with the capacity for inhibition of distress, which first appears in the middle of the second year.

SUMMARY

By the middle of the second year the child of an emotionally responsive primary caregiver can access a mature frontolimbic system that can autoregulate ANS autonomic and endocrine functions, either in the presence or absence of the mother. The internalization of selfobject regulatory functions takes the form of an orbitofrontal neuronal representation of the affective experiences with the externally regulating caregiver. Practicing transactions permanently influence the determination of a set point that reflects the autonomic balance between the sympathetic and parasympathetic components of the ANS, and the reciprocal and nonreciprocal activities of the two limbic circuits. This homeostatic mechanism enables the child to more efficiently self-regulate affect, especially negative affect.

The affect of shame, associated with an entrance into the adaptive parasympathetic-dominant state of conservation-withdrawal, plays a central role in the regulation of all emotional expression, and thereby in effective social interaction. The ability to tolerate the conscious experience of this negative affect is essential to the development of the capacity for autonomous functioning. A model of a dual component affect regulator is presented. An attachment deactivator, a shame stimulator, initiates activity in the lateral tegmental limbic circuit, suspends attachment motivation, and induces withdrawal of the self. An attachment reactivator, a shame modulator, activates the ventral tegmental limbic circuit, triggers the seeking of object relations, and induces exhibition of the self. The adaptive capacity of such a system is expressed in the switching of psychobiological states in response to personally meaningful changes in the socioemotional environment.

V CLINICAL ISSUES

29 The Neurobiology of Insecure Attachments

Broadly speaking, it is an advantage to keep affects at a tolerable intensity, so that one's task of information processing is not interfered with.
—Henry Krystal (1988)

If infants characteristically must resort to increasingly severe and prolonged withdrawal states to regulate arousal, their attention and information-processing may be compromised.
—Beatrice Beebe and Frank M. Lachman (1988a)

In the fields of etiology and psychopathology [attachment theory] can be used to frame specific hypotheses which relate different family experiences to different forms of psychiatric disorder and also, possibly, to the neurophysiological changes that accompany them.
—John Bowlby (1978)

The development of a self-regulatory capacity requires an early experience with a regulating primary caregiver. The ontogenetic attainment of an efficient internal system that can adaptively autoregulate catecholaminergic generated arousal, and thereby affect, cognition, and behavior, is absolutely dependent upon the emotional responsiveness of the mother. Toward this end, access to her selfobject, psychobiological regulatory function is a fundamental prerequisite to the emergence of those homeostatic structural systems that are neurobiologically maturing during a critical period of infancy. As a result of an interactive history of psychobiological attunement, the motive force of the attachment process, the child forms a secure attachment with the caregiver. The "hidden" dyadic visuoaffective transactions that occur during reunions after incipient separations from the mother allow for essential neurohormonally induced energy transformations in the child's rapidly growing brain. These episodes of maternal arousal modulation enable the secure neo-mobile toddler to explore and thereby learn effective responses to the complex social and physical environment in which he is being reared. This secure attachment facilitates the transfer of regulatory capacities from caregiver to infant (Wilson et al., 1990). Over 20 years ago Ainsworth proposed that the quality of maternal sensitive responsiveness promotes the establishment of internalized controls (self-regulation) in the second year (Stayton, Hogan, & Ainsworth, 1971). Ten years later Main corroborated this by demonstrating that late in the second year, manifestations of internalized controls are found in securely attached as compared to insecurely attached infants (Londerville & Main, 1981).

What is the outcome of inconsistent or near nonexistent external regulation during the critical period? How do different patterns of maternal regulation qualitatively effect the nature of the attachment, and how do these influence the psychobiological maturation of the orbitofrontal cortex? In what way do these experiences shape the limitations of the individual's emerging regulatory capacities? These issues, broached in earlier chapters, are further elaborated in this one.

THE INTERACTIVE HISTORIES OF SECURE AND INSECURE ATTACHMENTS

The dyadic affective transactions of optimal and suboptimal caregiver-infant interactions have been well characterized (e.g., Ainsworth, 1985; Main & Solomon, 1986) and are now considered to engender "individual differences in attachment and personality development" (Bretherton, 1985, p. 14). Embedded in these very same early caregiver-infant experiences are the hidden psychobiological mechanisms which determine the emotional biases of the affective core that appear in the second year. This primordial central integrating biological structure functions to maintain positive mood and to regulate the infant's interactive behavior (Emde, 1983). According to Emde, early experiences in the caregiving relationship bias the infant's affective core with tendencies toward certain emotional responses. Malatesta et al. (1989) propose these emotion biases result from the fact that certain neurophysiological and neuroanatomical emotive circuits may become more readily activated than others, and Tronick et al. (1986) suggest that the affective core biases the infant's evaluation of a new situation and his interactive patterns even before the information arising from the situation is processed. In an earlier chapter I identified the dual limbic circuit orbitofrontal cortex as the site of the this system.

The question now is, how do early deprivations in empathic care (Weil, 1992) (in selfobject regulating experiences) influence the ontogenetic organization of the orbitofrontal system that is involved in attachment functions (Steklis & Kling, 1985), and that comes to maintain positive affect and regulate the infant's interactive behavior? A clue to the answer lies in the critical function of affect regulation with which the caregiver induces a secure attachment: "the baby will become attached to the caregiver who can help to modulate and to minimize the experience of negative affect and who maximizes and expands opportunities for positive affect" (Demos & Kaplan, 1986, p. 169). What happens to those infants who are not fortunate enough to have such an attachment experience? It is now thought that deprivations of essential experiences at critical phases of development are capable of skewing development (Meyersburg & Post, 1979). It is also now well established that "growth inhibiting environments" specifically impair the ontogeny of attachment and self-regulatory systems (Greenspan, 1981). This suggests to me that such essential experiences are affect regulating transactions, and that such environments afford less than optimal psychobiological attunement histories. These conditions retard the experience-dependent development of affect regulating structure-function relationships.

Developmental studies of individual differences in attachment, based on the observation of infant nonverbal behavior toward the caregiver in a structured separation-and-reunion situation, have repeatedly found three classifications: securely attached and two groups of insecurely attached infants, resistant and avoidant. (A third insecure group, a profoundly pathological insecure-disorganized/disoriented attachment pattern, has been recently [1986] discovered by Main and Solomon). The various attachment patterns refer to different "styles of maternal mutalization and regulation of infantile affect" (Nathanson, 1992, p. 233). Indeed, Gaensbauer demonstrates that these attachment groups express different patterns of regulation of emotions during separation and reunion (Gaensbauer, Connell, & Schultz, 1983; Gaensbauer & Mrazek, 1981). These groups thus represent the primordial expressions of unique and dissociable emotional biases in personality, reflecting different organizations of the biologically based affective core. Such biases are shaped by experiences with different types of affect regulating caregivers in the practicing period. The mother of the securely attached infant permits access to the child who seeks proximity at reunion and shows a tendency to respond appropriately and promptly to his or her emotional expressions (Ainsworth et al., 1978), thereby engendering an expectation in the secure infant that during times of stress the primary attachment object will remain available and accessible. Pipp and Harmon (1987) observe that security of attachment fundamentally relates to a physiological coding that homeostatic disruptions will be set right. On the other hand, mothers of insecurely attached infants have been shown to react to their infant's expressions of emotions and stress inappropriately and/or rejectingly (Egeland & Farber, 1984) and show minimal or unpredictable participation in the above mentioned affect regulating processes. Repeated failure to find comfort from an attachment figure engenders insecure attachments, impairs affect regulation, and leads to attachment activation, yet also induces anxiety, agitation, and anger (Bowlby, 1973).

Psychobiologically attuned practicing mothers of securely attached infants maintain the child's arousal within a moderate range that is high enough to maintain interactions (by stimulating the child up out of low arousal states) but not too intense as to cause distress and avoidance (by modulating high arousal states) (Brazelton et al., 1974; Stern, 1977). This entails her actively initiating and participating in not only mirroring-refueling (arousal amplifying) and shame socializing (arousal braking) transactions, but also in interactive repair (optimal arousal recovering) transactions after attachment breaks. Optimal arousal refers to the maintenance of autonomic balance between sympathetic ergotropic and parasympathetic trophotropic arousals. It is known that moderate levels of arousal (within the optimal activation band) are associated with positive affect and focused attention, while extreme levels of arousal (high or low) are related to negative emotion and distracted attention (Malmo, 1959). Brent and Resch (1987) have specifically observed this with practicing age infants.

Insecure-avoidant infants show no interest in an adult who is attempting to attract their attention, and exhibit little motivation to maintain contact. These infants characteristically do not appear distressed by the mother's departure nor happy at her return; at reunion they do not express distress or anger openly. However, there is evidence that they do experience anger during reunion episodes (Ainsworth et al., 1978; Sroufe, 1979). They actively avoid the mother, or in her presence ignore her by extensive use of gaze aversion, rather than seeking comfort from the interaction. It is now thought that this avoidance reflects an expectation of an unsatisfying and rejecting dyadic contact (Lamb & Esterbrooks, 1981). Reunited with the mother they actively turn away, look away, and seem deaf and blind to her efforts to establish communication (Main & Stadtman, 1981). Mothers of these infants typically experience contact and interaction with their babies to be aversive, actively block access to their proximity seeking (attachment) behavior, and respond to their child's emotional signals inappropriately or after long delays (Ainsworth et al., 1978). Main and Weston (1982) find that these mothers manifest a general aversion to physical contact and at times express an unverbalizable physical response of withdrawing, pushing the child away. This type of caregiver, when she rebuffs her infant, represents an assault from his haven of safety, and further, due to her aversion to physical contact, will not permit access to help him modulate environmentally induced stress, nor the painful emotions aroused by her behavior. Joseph (1992) describes:

> Some women (like some men) do not like to be touched, hugged, or cuddled. [T]his feeling of aversion is communicated via the right half of the brain. The child responds accordingly because of its own right brain perceptions. (p. 256)

Main and Stadtman (1981) point out that this produces a serious, deep, and nonverbal conflict which leads to the formation of a defensive process in which the infant "escapes" by actively shifting attention from the attachment figure and the entire conflict. These authors interpret avoidance as a mechanism to "modulate the painful and vacillating emotion aroused by the historically rejecting mother" (p. 293). Children designated avoidantly attached at 12 months show continuity in attachment organization; in later childhood, they cut off anger- and distress- related affective expressions to the mother, but express hostile emotion inappropriately in social relationships (Kobak & Sceery, 1988). At 6-years-of-age they continue to avoid the mother at reunion and have difficulty in discussing feelings or active coping strategies for dealing with separations (Main, Kaplan, & Cassidy, 1985). Interestingly, Arend, Gove, and Sroufe (1979) note that preschool children identified as insecure-avoidant at 18 months tend to be over-controlled and restrained.

In contrast, insecure-resisitant infants intermix proximity/contact seeking behaviors with angry, rejecting behaviors toward the mother at reunion; they are thus ambivalent. This type of mother has been found to permit access only inconsistently to the infant who seeks proximity at reunion. Due to the unpredictable nature of her emotional availability, even when she is present the infant is uncertain as to what to expect with regard to her being responsive to his or her signals and communication (Ainsworth, 1985, p. 778; Lamb & Easterbrooks, 1981). However, "in its heightened display of emotionality and dependence upon the attachment figure, this infant successfully draws the attention of the parent" (Main & Solomon, 1986). Additionally, during preseparation episodes they are often so preoccupied with the mother and with monitoring the mother's face that they can not play independently, since the mother appears not to function as a secure base for refueling, which enables practicing exploration. More than any other group, they show high separation distress and are notoriously difficult to comfort at reunion, indicators of high negative affectivity. This class of infants thus presents with "difficult temperament" (Thomas & Chess, 1982), the central attributes of which are tendencies to intense expressiveness and negative mood responses, slow adaptability to change, and irregularity of biological functions. Arend et al. (1979) find children earlier identified as insecure-resisitant infants to be undercontrolled and impulsive.

The characterization of insecure attachment patterns evolved from investigations of the emotional behaviors of 2- and 3-year-old children directed towards parents after longer, traumatic separations (Robertson & Robertson, 1971). Upon reunion, young children physically separated for a relatively short time appeared anxious, clingy, and easily angered; those separated for longer periods actively avoided the parent, backing away or turning away altogether. Bowlby (1973) labeled the acutely distressed phase, *protest,* the later more slowly developing phase of helplessness, *despair.* In animal studies of infant separations, Hofer (1984a) has concluded that acute onset protest responses involve different psychophysiological processes than chronic despair biological changes. Specifically, protest reactions are reflected·in agitation, vocalizations, crying, searching, and increased heart rate, while despair responses included social withdrawal, facial expressions of sadness, and decreased cardiac rate. We now know that protest reactions normally occur in response to even very brief separations. In a developmental psychological study of 13-month-old-infants, Izard (Shiller, Izard, & Hembree, 1986) finds that in a strange environment, a separation of as little as 3 minutes elicits a separation protest. Most interestingly, the dominant negative emotional response to brief separation at this age is anger, not sadness, and not "separation anxiety."

What's more, a recent developmental psychoanalytic observational study by Settlage et al. (1990) demonstrates that the attuned bond between the 16-month-old infant and mother can be degraded even when they are in close proximity and not physically separated. Maternal-instigated breaks in attunement (as in shame socializations) induce an infant distress state and trigger an infant appeal to enter into reunion transactions. This often overlooked principle has also been discovered in developmental neurobiological research. Primate experiments show that infants can undergo severe separation reactions even though their mothers are visually, but not psychologically, available (Rosenblum, 1987). These findings underscore the fallacy of many separation studies that assume that separation phenomena only occur with physical removal of the mother from the child over a period of time. I suggest that proximate separations are a common and potent phenomenon in early personality development, and that they are maintained by the mother's refusal to enter into mutual social referencing exchanges by blocking direct eye-to-eye visuoaffective contact with the distressed child. I further conclude that the psychobiological processes underlying proximate separation and reunion phenomena are isomorphic to those underlying longer physical separations and reunions. In both, there is a loss of the external regulating functions of the mother during a critical period of experience-dependent frontolimbic maturation. The child responds to this loss by communicating an appeal, an overt expression of the attachment need, which represents a request for maternal psychobiological arousal modulation. This communication reflects the existence of an expectation that the mother will respond to this affective transmission, that she will enter into a dyadic transaction. In other words the infant mentally predicts that the primary caregiver will be available, sensitive, and contingently responsive to the infant's internal stress state (an internalized working model of a secure attachment). If there is some delay in maternal regulation due to the mother's refusal to enter into a dyadic affect transaction, stress escalates beyond the child's coping capacity (self-regulation) and appeal becomes transformed into hyperexcitatory protest.

THE HIDDEN MISATTUNED AFFECT TRANSACTIONS OF INSECURE-AVOIDANT ATTACHMENTS

Infants manifesting insecure-avoidant patterns of attachment are dyadically involved with a primary caregiver who is consistently emotionally inaccessible. Tronick et al. (1982) describe a maternal pattern of interaction manifested in withdrawal, hesitancy, and reluctance to organize the infant's attention or behavior. These infants experience continual proximate separations, and like peers exhibiting despair responses to physical separation do not have access to maternal regulation of either sympathetic or parasympathetic states. Mothers of insecure-avoidant infants show very low levels of affect expression (Main, Tomasini, & Tolan, 1979), and their active blockade of the child's proximity seeking precludes the establishment of an effective dyadic regulatory system. These mothers neither stimulate the child up out of low arousal states (arousal induction) nor modulate high arousal states (arousal reduction). Insecure avoidant infants, unlike secure infants, do not stop experiencing anger once reunited with the mother (Shiller et al.,1986), but unlike insecure-resisitant children do stop expressing it. This suppressed anger may represent a muffled protest response accompanying the infant's frustrated proximity need as he encounters the "irritation, resentment, and sometimes outright anger" (Tracy & Ainsworth, 1981, p. 1343) and subsequent active blockade of the contact-aversive mother.

In pushing the child away, the mother induces a state of stressful hyperarousal reflected in negative affect and elevated heart rate. Indeed, the heart rate of these infants has been found to remain accelerated well into the reunion episode, "presumably because they were not comforted by the caregiver" (Donovan & Leavitt, 1985) who indeed triggered the stress. Infant-initiated contacts elicit not empathic care but parental aversion, behaviorally expressed not only in the caregiver wincing and arching away from the infant's approach, but also keeping the head at a different level from the infant's (Main, 1990), thereby precluding mutual gaze transactions. As a result of the deprivational stress accompanying the lack of access to the mother's regulatory function, rather than using dyadic mutual gaze to modulate the internal physiological disruptions (e.g., cardiac acceleration) underlying separation, they utilize averted (non-face-to-face) gaze, an arousal modulating mechanism which is known to lead to cardiac deceleration (Field, 1981). Gaze aversion and avoidance of (withdrawal from) the mother who herself withdraws from her infant is proposed to reflect a state of conservation-withdrawal, a primary regulatory process for organismic homeostasis (Engel & Schmale, 1972).

Depressed mothers exhibit frequent facial displays of negative affect (sadness, irritability, anger) and respond to the infant in a poorly timed, noncontingent manner (Tronick & Cohn, 1989). The infant of a mother with a unipolar depression shows less positive affect during an interaction with her (Cohn et al., 1986), and although the infant manifests withdrawal, gaze aversion, and reduced activity level, heart rate is elevated, indicating stress (Field et al., 1988). I interpret the adaptive function of this averting of the eyes to be the prevention of the registration of the disorganizing visuoaffective output of the caregiver's face. These maternal affective signals include not only unexpressive facial displays but at other times nonverbal aggressive communications (Ellsworth, 1975) emanating from the mother's "terrifying eyes" (Peto, 1969). Gaze aversion, an external manifestation of shame, allows the infant to escape and avoid processing this stress inducing message. When used as a preparatory set, the avoidant pattern precludes the vacillating affective distress and anger associated with directing the attachment need (the need for affect regulation) toward the psychologically unavailable mother. Ultimately, active mutual gaze, which mediates dyadic psychobiological attunement processes, is replaced by gaze aversion by both partners.

Beebe and Lachman (1988a) describe a stress-induced avoidance pattern of "inhibition of responsivity" associated with a total breakdown of the dyadic interaction. I propose that as a result of prolonged and repeated proximate separations from the contact-aversive, nonattuning mother, the hyperaroused distressed infant shifts from a sympathetic-dominant agitated distress state to a parasympathetic-dominant despair state. This very same transformation is described in Bowlby's (1969) classic work on sequential, biphasic responses to physical separation, which reveals an acute agitated protest phase that ultimately transitions into a chronic despair phase. In a primate experimental model, repetitive mother-infant separations lead to significant decreases in the protest response and the analog of human insecure-avoidant attachment (Suomi, Mineka, & DeLizio, 1983). The most probable mechanism involved in such a transformation, if it is to become permanent, is an extreme practicing period parcellation (experience-dependent selective elimination) of sympathetic ventral tegmental, and expansion of parasympathetic lateral tegmental innervation of orbitofrontal systems. Indeed, Izard et al. (1991) now report that insecure-avoidant infants have a relatively high level of parasympathetic tone. Joseph (1992) posits that the interaction of a noncuddling mother and a child who cannot respond appropriately to physical contact induces an atrophy of certain limbic nuclei in the infant's developing brain and a consequent social withdrawal and abnormal emotionality.

As a result, the infant develops a bias towards remaining in a state of unregulated conservation-withdrawal (Kaufman & Rosenblum, 1969), a parasympathetic dominant state characterized by heart rate deceleration, helplessness, and low levels of activity (McCabe & Schneiderman, 1985) when apart from the mother, yet in a state of unregulated hyper-parasympathetic and hyper-sympathetic agitation (due to a loss of orbital modulation of subcortical mesolimbic dopaminergic hyperactivity and ascending excitatory influences), reflected in heart rate acceleration and suppressed anger when the attachment need is activated in the presence of the stress inducing mother. Main and Solomon (1986) refer to this as a strategy of "defensive independence." It is suggested that when the infant is under the eye of the potentially aggressive mother, he maintains a psychophysiological state of "braced readiness." Gilbert and Trower (1990) describe this state as one in which an organism remains continuously ready to take defensive activity in case its behavior provokes hostility from a dominant conspecific.

The deprivation of the caregiver's regulation of either sympathetic or parasympathetic autonomic nervous system activity prevents the emergence of a system to cope with heightened levels of sympathetic arousal (Zillman & Bryant,

1974) and high nonoptimal levels of stimulation (Tomkins, 1963), which accompany the negative affect of anger.

> . . . an experience of distress or anger that combines intensity with duration, thereby producing a high density of negative affect, can cause the infant to retreat or avoid similar experiences in the future, either by overcontrolling the expression of distress or anger in order to prevent another punishing escalation, or by constricting activities to avoid the eliciting stimulus or stimulation. In either case, the infant is unable to remain in the situation and develop adaptive skills or strategies for dealing with the causes of distress or anger. (Demos, 1988, p. 35)

Furthermore, the caregiver's inability to stimulate or regulate the child's affect-arousal states ultimately leads to a deactivation of the infant's attachment system by defensively excluding from higher levels of processing (biasing against) socioemotional input that activates attachment behavior (Ainsworth, 1985) and prevents the conscious experiencing of elevated levels of sympathetic activity which accompany a positive state (Lipsitt, 1976), and the affects of interest and joy. Bowlby (1984) asserts that repeated and prolonged frustration of the attachment need produces an exclusion of emotions that activate the attachment system. Sroufe emphasizes the important point that although these infants no longer direct the need for contact towards the emotionally unavailable mother, the attachment need is not readily extinguished but goes "underground" (Sroufe, Fox, & Pancake, 1983). This split system may reflect that although higher level conscious processing is blocked, unconscious activation of the attachment need continues. Indeed, this may represent the incipient activation of "unconscious affect" (Pulver, 1971). Greenspan (1979), a developmental psychoanalytic researcher, concludes that the dynamic unconscious first emerges at 18 months, the practicing/rapprochement border.

By the end of the practicing period these children show a narrow range of stimulation that elicits a socioemotional response, a reduced capacity for internalized arousal modulation, diminished affect tolerance required for object relations, and a constriction, rather than an expansion of the affect array. A description of such an emerging personality is provided by Gaensbauer and Mrazek (1981). They observed an "affectively withdrawn" practicing female infant who manifested an impressive emotional flatness. The mother, herself identified as emotionally flat, was not able to perceive the needs of her infant, to whom she was "emotionally out of touch and unavailable." Positive as well as negative affective expressions were characteristically absent in the infant, even during reunion with the mother or approach of a stranger. As they get older, these "precociously independent" infants become highly emotionally dependent children who fail to develop autonomous function and are unable to seek direct emotional support in times of stress (Sroufe et al., 1983). Sroufe's observation that these infants become children who show a decreasing likelihood of contact seeking when emotional arousal increases may be explained by the fact that their limbic systems are parasympathetically dominated and geared to respond maximally to low levels of socioemotional stimulation. Psychophysiologically, the overcontrolled and restrained nature of insecure-avoidant typologies (Arend, Gove, & Sroufe, 1979) reflects a predominance of lateral tegmental over ventral tegmental limbic circuits. The resultant vagotonic pattern (Eppinger & Hess, 1915) reflects a parasympathetically biased, inhibitory, orbitofrontal affective core. This personality organization is susceptible to overcontrolled developmental psychopathologies (Lewis & Miller, 1990) and to overregulation disturbances (Emde, 1990).

In childhood, this anxiously inhibited, withdrawn personality utilizes an interactional style characterized as "moving away from the world" (Caspi, Elder, & Bem, 1988). As adults,

> These individuals prefer distance and are uncomfortable if others get too close. They do not like to be dependent on others nor for others to be dependent on them. They often find that their partners wish for them to be closer but this call to intimacy is frightening to them. They are often distrustful of others' motives and are sensitive to being hurt and/or controlled in relationships. They are least emotionally expressive and may be subject to strong shame. (Gilbert, 1992b, p. 21)

THE PSYCHOBIOLOGY OF INSECURE-RESISTANT ATTACHMENTS

On the other hand, infants showing insecure-resistant (insecure-ambivalent) patterns of attachment as a reaction to a mother who is physically present but emotionally inconsistently accessible, like those manifesting protest responses to longer physical separation, experience an unregulated hyperactivation of the sympathetic ventral tegmental limbic circuit. Tronick et al. (1982, p. 89) describe a type of mother who is "persistently engaging the infant even when the infant is looking away from her," and Spitz (1965) refers to a type of "psychotoxic" maternal care, manifest in an overdose of affective stimulation, that is dispensed by the mother who is concerned more with her own emotional needs than her infant's. Unlike the mother of the insecure-avoidant infant, she does successfully serve as a source of high intensity affective stimulation enabling the characteristic high arousal affects of the early practicing period. However, during these high arousal states this type of caregiver does not sensitively and appropriately reduce her stimulation, and thereby interferes with the infant's attempt to disengage and gaze avert in order to modulate ergotropic arousal, affect, and sympathetic supported cardiac acceleration. Field (1985a) notes that if the mother does not respond to the infant's dyadic affective cues of hyperarousal by diminishing her stimulation, especially during periods of infant gaze aversion, the child's aversion threshold may be exceeded. She thus does not alter the tempo or content of her stimulation in response to a monitoring of the infant's affective state; instead, she overloads him and interferes with his ability to assimilate new experiences. It is well known that the capacity of an organism to learn effective patterns of responses is negatively affected by heightened levels of arousal. Although she may be more responsive to protest than appeal, she may be inefficient in limit setting, regulated shame induction, and aggression socialization in the late practicing period.

Most importantly, this type of caregiver does not provide a socioaffective environment which is most conducive to the expansion of lateral tegmental catecholaminergic system in the late practicing period. It is logical to assume that the lower levels of postnatal growth of descending orbitofrontal axons to subcortical sites (Johnson et al., 1976) would result in an inefficient orbital system of "vagal restraint" (Kaada et al., 1949) with a reduced functional capacity of stimulating the parasympathetic and inhibiting the sympathetic components (Fuster, 1980) of limbic function. A resultant impaired orbital function of suppression of aggression (DeBruin et al., 1983) seen in the high levels of unregulated sympathetically-driven anger and distress of insecure-resistant infants may reflect a defective frontolimbic inhibitory influence on the sympathetic nervous system (Fuster, 1980) and may be due to an underrepresentation of the orbitofrontal inhibitory pathway to the sympathetic ventromedial hypothalamic nucleus (Ohta & Oomura, 1979) which influences fight-flight reactions (Colpaert, 1975).

This affect regulating system is thus biased towards the predominance of the sympathetic, excitatory dopaminergic ventral tegmental, over the parasympathetic, inhibitory noradrenergic lateral tegmental limbic circuit. As mentioned earlier, elevated levels of mesolimbic dopamine are expressed during infant protest vocalizations (Tamborski et al., 1990). The insecure-resistant undercontrolled and impulsive typology (Arend et al. 1979) is equated with a histrionic-impulsive personality who shows increased mesolimbic dopamine transmission (King, 1985). The heightened display of emotionality and inefficient capacity to regulate the high levels of anger and distress which characterizes these infants reflects a sympatheticotonically biased (Eppinger & Hess, 1915) affective core which poorly maintains positive mood in the face of stress. This psychobiological impairment may underly the observations that insecure-resistant infants manifest a physiological difficulty in coping with stress (Waters, Vaughn, & Egeland, 1980), and that 12–18 month-old infants characterized as anxiously attached show, at 3 to 4 years, a poor ability to recover from stressful experiences (Sroufe, 1984). They are therefore susceptible to undercontrolled developmental psychopathology (Lewis & Miller, 1990) and underregulation disturbances (Emde, 1990).

In a careful observational study of the "patterning of affective expressions" within an insecure-resistant infant-mother pair, Gaensbauer and Mrazek (1981) describe a "highly aroused" angry infant who expressed prolonged high intensity distress, tantrums, and anger during a separation from the mother. At reunion, the mother, characterized as immature with poor impulse control, was incapable of soothing her infant. Indeed, a behavioral micoanalysis of the reunion period showed the infant's anger to increase significantly upon reconnection with her; the child's anger was even higher than during separation. Although initially the toddler moved toward the mother, she soon aggresively resisted being held, which in turn provoked the mother into "teasing" the infant. (I have previously discussed the psychobiological effects of maternal shame-humiliation of the hyperaroused infant.) The mother's behavior frightened the child and intensified her screaming: she ran away from her and began to hit and spit in a provocative manner. Thus, the narcissistically injured mother's effort was not to soothe but to further arouse, to hyperstimulate the child into a state of narcissistic rage.

In late childhood, these ill tempered, hostile, dependent personalities become "explosive children" who utilize an interactional style described as "moving against the world" (Caspi, Elder, & Bem, 1987). In later adulthood,

> These individuals feel that they cannot get close enough to others and are very sensitive to cues of rejection or abandonment. They often worry that their partners and friends may leave or ignore them. Their needs for constant reassurance of their lovability and acceptance sometimes drives others away and can show up as clinginess, possessiveness, jealousy and other anxious forms of attachment and relating. They are more likely to be emotionally expressive. (Gilbert, 1992b, p. 21)

The evaluation and treatment of rage in childhood and adolescence is now being stressed (Mandoki, Sumner, & Matthews-Ferrari, 1992).

SUMMARY

Optimal dyadic interactions during the period of 10–12 to 16–18 months, the period in which attachment patterns are measured, facilitate the development of the self-regulatory functions of the anatomically maturing affective core. Access to the emotionally responsive mother engenders a secure attachment, an expectation that homeostatic disruptions will be set right. On the other hand, the mother's incapacity to act as the infant's psychobiological regulator specifically defines a growth inhibiting environment. Securely and insecurely attached infants express different patterns and capacities for affect regulation during proximal separations and reunions with the mother. The mother of the insecure-avoidant infant experiences contact with her infant to be aversive, and the child reacts to this by avoiding the painful and vacillating emotions aroused by her. The mother of the insecure-resistant toddler inconsistently allows contact at reunion, that is, she partially participates as an affect regulator. This is experienced by the child as an unpredictability, and interferes with leaving her in order to explore the surrounding environment.

A characterization of the hidden misattuned affect transactions of insecure attachments reveals important clues as to how early interactions with the caregiver produce long lasting limitations of the individual's future socioemotional functioning. What is avoided by the insecure-avoidant infant is disorganizing stimulation expected to emanate from the mother's face. An ongoing parasympathetic-dominant state psychobiologically supports a predisposition to gaze aversion and passive avoidance. As a result of these critical period experiences, the maturing limbic system of the insecure-avoidant infant is parasympathetically biased, resulting in an extensive utilization of lateral tegmental limbic circuit mediated states of conservation-withdrawal. This leads to a limited capacity to consciously experience intense positive or negative affect and to a susceptibility to overregulation disturbances. The insecure-resistant infant, on the other hand, remains in a mode of approach and active avoidance in response to a perception of the mother's face. This ambivalent infant struggles unsuccessfully to resist eye contact with the unpredictable caregiver. The insecure-resistant pattern reflects a sympathetically based, ventral tegmental limbic circuit dominance. Throughout the rest of the lifespan this personality manifests heightened expressions of intense emotionality and a susceptibility to underregulation disturbances.

30 The Clinical Psychiatry of Affect Dysregulation

[A]ll psychopathology constitutes primary or secondary disorders of bonding or attachment and manifests itself as disorders of self and / or interactional regulation.

—James S. Grotstein (1986)

In general, the inner experience of affect is congruent with the behavioral expression communicated to others; but one of the most interesting questions confronting psychoanalysts has to do with explaining clinical examples of the various ways in which affect regulation fails to develop normally, or becomes dissociated from adaptive behavior, from inner experience, and from communicative behavior.

—Myron A. Hofer (1990)

The developmental orientation, in fact, indicates a particular view about adaptation and pathology. What is not adaptive is a lack of variability in an individual who is faced with environmental demands necessitating alternative choices and strategies for change.

—Robert N. Emde (1988)

The recent upsurge in our knowledge of emotion and its development has important implications for the theoretical understanding of the genesis of all forms of psychopathology. There is now a consensus that emotional disorders must be formulated within a framework of a basic theory of emotion that emphasizes the functional value of emotions (Watts, 1992). The principles that specific emotions facilitate the preparation and sustenance for what must be done about the person-environment relationship (Lazarus, 1991b), and that affects serve the function of informing the individual who is tracking biologically relevant goals (Gilbert, 1992a) underscore the centrality of emotional behavior to adaptive functioning. In earlier chapters I have demonstrated that these cardinal properties of affective phenomena arise in the context of the relationship with the primary caregiver and have long enduring effects on the individual's emerging socioemotional capacities.

In particular, an essential adaptive capacity of a securely attached infant is that, when distressed by or during a separation, he or she can seek and be comforted at a reunion with a caregiver (Ainsworth et al., 1978). The mother of this infant responds in a timely manner to a broad range of affective experiences and correctly assesses her baby's affect, whether it is positive or negative (Haft & Slade, 1989). Tronick (1989) demonstrates that an infant who is exposed to sensitive and cooperative maternal interactive repair of dyadic misattunements consequently shows self-regulatory skills in the form of persistent efforts to overcome an interactive stress. Tronick also notes that the capacity for interactive repair contributes to the security of attachment. In securely attached practicing infants, stress-induced negative affect (distress) does not endure for long periods beyond the conditions that elicit them; rapid recovery to positively toned emotion is typical (Gaensbauer & Mrazek, 1981), reflective of efficient regulatory capacities. Later in childhood, the individual classified as securely attached in infancy actively and directly seeks and maintains contact with others when distressed, and finds this contact to be reassuring and effective in terminating distress. A cardinal feature of a "high-resilient" child and her or his parents is the capacity to fluidly transition from positive to negative back to positive affect (Demos, 1991). In fact, it is now thought that the ultimate indicator of attachment capacity is resilience in the face of stress (Greenspan, 1981).

Conversely, the mother of an insecurely attached baby reacts to her infant's expressions of emotions and stress inappropriately and/or rejectingly (Egeland & Farber, 1984). This infant shows "a greater tendency for negative emotional states to endure beyond the precipitating stimulus events" (Gaensbauer, 1982, p. 169). Thomas and Chess (1982) characterize an infant with "difficult temperament" as manifesting poor adaptability to environmental changes, negative mood when challenged, and extreme intensity of these reactions over time and different situations. Sroufe (1984) finds that an infant described as anxiously attached at 12 to 18 months (the span of the practicing period) specifically shows a poor capacity to recover from stressful experiences later in childhood. Indeed, the insecurely attached child tends not to seek contact when stressed, and fails to develop a capacity for autonomous (autoregulatory) functioning (Sroufe, Fox, & Pancake, 1983). Malatesta-Magai (1991) reports that the young child of a depressed mother shows (like the mother) a difficulty in moving back from a negative affect state to a positive affect of interest.

Earlier in this volume I contended that self-regulatory structural systems, essential to all aspects of the individual's internal and external functioning, mature during infancy, and that their development is a product of early dynamic socioenvironmental affect regulating interactions that shape the outcome of genetic predispositions. In this chapter I elaborate the thesis that affect dysregulating events in early development are the major contributor to various forms of developmental psychopathology. The developmental models outlined earlier suggest a number of heuristic hypotheses concerning the etiology and dynamics of several psychiatric syndromes.

INSECURE ATTACHMENT, AFFECT DYSREGULATION, AND DEVELOPMENTAL PSYCHOPATHOLOGY

During inceptive stressful separations the insecurely attached practicing toddler lacks access to the mother's affect regulatory functions. Her emotional accessibility at a reunion after a separation is essential for the modulation of stress and the reestablishment of the child's psychobiological attunement. The mother's poor responsiveness during reunion transactions has short- and long-term effects on the organization of brain structures involved in socioemotional functioning, and is therefore a critical factor in the generation of future pathology. It is now accepted that the effects of repeated separations are most debilitating when the reunion environment is not supportive (Coe et al., 1985). The sequelae of such events are deep-seated and long-enduring. Bretherton (1985) asserts that:

> . . . if an attachment figure frequently rejects or ridicules the child's bids for comfort in stressful situations, the child may come to develop not only an internal working model of the parent as rejecting but also one of himself as not worthy of help and comfort. (p. 12)

Kaufman (1989) proposes that failures of early attachment invariably become sources of shame. M. Lewis (1992) concludes that for the developing child a stress-filled environment is comparable to a shame-filled environment. Basch (1985) now argues that affect attunement experiences are instrumental to the establishment of a sensorimotor model for what will become the self-concept. If it is not present or is ineffective it may create "a sense of isolation and a belief that one's affective needs are generally somehow unacceptable and shameful" (p. 35).

Similarly, Beebe and Lachman (1988a) suggest that as a result of episodes of caregiver-infant "misregulation" or "misattunement," "the infant comes to expect that he cannot benefit from his mother's participation in the management of his affect-arousal states" (p. 19). Furthermore, these interactions are stored in memory "largely outside conscious awareness" as presymbolic representations.

> If they remain characteristic of the interaction, by the end of the first year they will be abstracted as prototypic. This composite prototype forms the basis for an emerging symbolic representation of self and object as misattuned (Beebe & Lachman, 1988b, p. 326).

This experience of being with a psychobiologically dysregulating other who initiates but poorly repairs misattunement is incorporated into an interactive representation, a working model of the self-misattuned-with-a-dysregulating-other. The same phenomenon is described by Balint (1968), who refers to the "basic fault," a deep and pervasive sense that there exists within a fault that extends widely to include "the whole psychobiological structure of the individual" (p. 22), and that is experienced as "a feeling of emptiness, being lost, deadness, and futility" (p. 19). This deficiency is due, according to Balint, to a discrepancy between the needs of the person as an infant and the capacity of people in his early environment to provide them. This formulation implies a defect in an internal structure.

What kind of psychoneurobiological mechanism might create the morphology of a basic fault? A fault is defined as a dislocation which breaks continuity, but, in electrical phenomena it also refers to a deflection or leak in a current due to abnormal connections of circuits. In earlier chapters I suggested that the experience-dependent imprinting of the two limbic circuits is influenced by the child's affective experiences in the first 2 years of life. Extensive dysregulating experiences during a critical period would permanently etch the forming frontolimbic circuitry, and this could induce a severe parcellation of, for example, ventral tegmental dopaminergic innervation patterns. According to Ebbesson (1980) parcellation is a Darwinian process, and it represents a rewiring that occurs in imprinting phenomena. Unmodulated, intense, and enduring negative affect states associated with early pathological object relations would induce an excessive elimination of mesocortical dopaminergic axons, and this circuitry would not therefore be available for future functions in reward (Thierry et al., 1978), exploratory behavior (Fink & Smith, 1980), and the regulation of affective responses (Tassin, 1987). This pathogenetic mechanism may fundamentally represent the unique role of evolutionary biology as a basic science for psychiatry (McGuire et al., 1992).

Emde (1983) asserts that the organization of the affective core, the system that regulates positive mood and interactive behavior, is influenced by early experiences in the infant-caregiver relationship. In a conceptualization very similar to this, Morris (1989) asserts that a primary function of self-regulatory activities in adults is to maintain positive emotional mood and eliminate or reduce the continued deterioration of negative mood states. He further suggests that mood parameters such as intensity, duration, and rate of decay (recovery) are related to neurophysiologic excitatory and inhibitory processes. On the other hand, failures of self-regulation, often involving preverbal processes, have been defined by Wilson et al. (1990) as:

(1) the failure to accomplish the earliest and ongoing psychobiological aims of regulating levels of stimulation, arousal, and interactive processes; (2) the emotional experiences that result from the flow of communicative actions or ties to objects needed to perform such functions; and (3) the early maladaptive representations of

self-in-interaction-with-other and their recurrent influence on later representations of self and other. (p. 152)

Hofer (1990) emphasizes the importance of explaining clinical examples of failures to develop adaptive affect regulation. In this pursuit, Grotstein (1986, 1990a, 1990b, 1991) is now integrating psychoanalytic and neurobiological data to propose that affect regulatory failures lie at the core of various "primitive" psychopathologies. Indeed, Grotstein (1986) proposes that all forms of psychiatric psychopathology are disorders of self-regulation involving "the failure of inherent internal control-regulators and/or external object and selfobject modulators" (p. 104).

Sroufe and Rutter (1984) define the primary goal of the emergent discipline of developmental psychopatholgy to be the identification and characterization of the "ontological process whereby early patterns of individual adaptation evolve into later patterns of adaptation" (p. 270). These authors propose that atypical patterns of self-regulation and affect expression are seminal to the later development of disorders of affect. A classification system in this perspective describes two broad dimensions of pathology, externalizing versus internalizing disorders, both of which reflect regulatory difficulties (Cicchetti & Toth, 1991). In a recent handbook of developmental psychopathology (Lewis & Miller, 1990) developmental disorders are divided into undercontrolled vs. overcontrolled psychopathology, a nosology that may reflect underregulation vs. overregulation affect regulatory disturbances (Emde, 1990). In accord with Eppinger and Hess' (1915) seminal studies of personality differences in the psychophysiological expression of emotional behavior, underregulation may be associated with a sympatheticotonic pattern, a dominance of a sympathetic reaction such as rapid heart beat, enlargened pupils, and excitable temperament in response to autonomic stress, while over-regulation may reflect a vagotonic pattern and a parasympathetic bias. These ANS patterns may underlie Gurrera's (1990) findings of distinct patterns of variations on multiple biological measures that differentiate "action-oriented" from "inhibited" personality prototypes.

PSYCHOPATHOLOGY IS OPERATIONALLY DEFINED AS A LIMITATION OF ADAPTIVE STRESS-REGULATING CAPACITIES

Early suboptimal attachment experiences produce pathomorphogenetic outcomes on the orbitofrontal cortex, the cortical system specifically involved in attachment functions (Steklis & Kling, 1985). Under optimal conditions of early development, this forebrain system in the deep prefrontal cortex functions to override brain stem homeostatic mechanisms during periods of emotional stress (van der Kooy et al., 1984). It is now known that the ontogeny of control systems is influenced by the particular environment in which development occurs (Bowlby,

1969), and that "growth-inhibiting environments" specifically impair the ontogeny of self-regulatory systems (Greenspan, 1981). A corpus of neurobiological studies shows that nascent structures supporting functions that emerge in postnatal critical periods of brain growth are vulnerable to harmful external agents or conditions (Almi & Finger, 1987; Dobbing & Smart, 1974; Jacobson, 1978). It is important to emphasize that these "harmful conditions" also include aberrations of the "social forces" that are responsible for the increase in brain weight during the postnatal period (Lecours, 1982). The "harmful external agent" described in the neurobiological literature is thus equated with the mother who provides "psychotoxic" maternal care characterized in the psychoanalytic literature (Spitz, 1965). In particular, a primary caregiver who does not participate in dyadic affect regulating (selfobject) functions that modulate levels of stimulation and arousal would create a socioaffective environment that generates frequent and enduring high levels of negative and low levels of positive affect in the developing child. A mother's inability to provide ample and modulated multimodal sensory information in a social context and to enter into symbiotic transactions precludes the genesis and amplication of infant joy and interest, positive affects that are necessary for the experience-dependent growth of postnatally developing brain areas. Izard (1991) points out that interest promotes brain development, and Tomkins (1962) posits that "absence of the affective support of interest would jeopardize intellectual development no less than destruction of brain tissue" (p. 343).

Referring to the extended postnatal ontogeny of prefrontal structures, Goldberg and Bilder (1987) conclude, "Critical periods for pathogenic influences might be prolonged in these more slowly maturing systems, of which the prefrontal cortex is exemplary" (p. 177). Delayed right frontal development is known to result in "poor social development" (Weintraub & Mesulam, 1983). Eslinger and Damasio (1985) conclude that the absence or dysfunction of the orbital and mesial cortices and their subadjacent white matter in infants and children leads to a pervasive developmental abnormality in social and affective behaviors. In an illuminating, in-depth, single case study, Price et al. (1990) demonstrate that early neurological damage to prefrontal areas produces permanent uncompensated deficits in social judgment and empathy that persists into adulthood (Price et al., 1990). Among these deficits is an impairment of adaptive maternal caregiving capacities. (See Tables 30.1 and 30.2, and Fig. 30.1 for a discussion of this case). The authors conclude that the permanent uncompensated deficits in this case reflect an impairment of prefrontal neural networks involved in the convergence of limbic inputs with processed information, and thereby the integration of thought with emotion. As a result the patient never acquired "self-governance" of behavior.

In line with the established principle that the early postnatally maturing right hemisphere is specifically impacted by early social experiences, Joseph (1988) asserts that

TABLE 30.1
Case History of Early Frontal Lobe Damage

At age 4 a child suffered a right frontal hematoma resulting from a car accident. Over the next year she began to exhibit temper outbursts when frustrated and became physically and mentally assaultive, a pattern that continued throughout her childhood. In her teen years she became sexually promiscuous and intermittently engaged in heavy drug usage. She had no sustained relationships. After high school graduation, although seemingly free of major depressive symptoms, she attempted suicide twice. At the time of the neurological evaluation she was 27-years-old, and was referred by a state social service agency for inappropriate behavior and negligent care of her 2 1/2-month-old infant. She underdressed the baby in inclement weather, fed her erratically, and left her unsupervised for lengthy periods of time. There were suspicions of physical assault.

Adapted from Price et al. (1990). Reproduced by permission of Oxford University Press.

TABLE 30.2
Neuropsychological Profile

Test		Score
WAIS		
Verbal IQ	78	Borderline
Performance IQ	83	Low average
Full Scale IQ	78	Borderline
Digit Span	6 forward/3backward	Mild inattention
Word Generation (F/A/S)	13/9/5	27th percentile
Stroop Interference	74 s/7 errors	51st percentile in time, no errors is norm
Trails B	99 s/0 errors	< 2nd percentile
3 words/3 shapes* (10 and 30 min delay)	6/6	Normal
Boston Naming Test	40/60 (46/60 with cues)	18th percentile
Hooper Visual Organization Test	26/30	Normal
Visual-Verbal Test	4/5	Normal

*This test is based on 3 simple designs and 3 words with low imagery value. Immediate incidental recall and recall after 10 and 30 min were intact (Weintraub & Mesulam, 1985).

In addition to the borderline IQ measures the patient shows an impairment on the Trail Making Test, Part B, which involves sustained effort and abstract reasoning. Tests of psychological development show a primitive level of social and moral reasoning, in which human interactions are viewed in physical, not psychological terms, and others are seen as avenues or obstacles of gratification. From Price et al. (1990). Reproduced by permission of Oxford University Press.

the developing organism is extremely vulnerable to environmental influences during infancy such that the nervous system and behavior may be altered dramatically in the adult. Interestingly, the right cerebral hemisphere seems to be more greatly affected. (p. 658)

In a neuropsychological and behavioral neurology study of children with right hemisphere structural damage, Voeller (1986) concludes that:

right-hemisphere dysfunction has a profound impact on a child's capacity to develop the ability to behave in an affectively appropriate fashion and to perceive the emotional states of other human beings. (p. 1008)

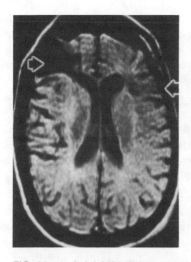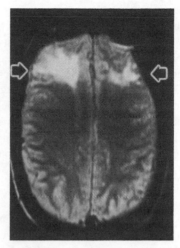

FIG. 30.1.   Axial MRI scans showing extensive damage confined to the frontal lobes. The left side of the head is on the right side of the scan. Frontal horn dilatation is present, greater on the left. An EEG taken some years earlier was normal. Neurological examination during the present evaluation was normal. From Price et al. (1990). Reprinted by permission of Oxford University Press.

The role of the right hemisphere dysfunction in psychiatric disorders is now being appreciated (Cutting, 1992).

The essential psychological and biochemical lesion of particular developmental disorders of the nonverbal (Krystal, 1978a) primitive (Gazzaniga, 1985) affect system is proposed to be found in developmentally interrupted, structurally unevolved, physiologically altered, orbitofrontal affect regulating appraisal systems located in the "primitive" (Tucker, 1992) right hemisphere that mediates the processing of "intrinsically more primitive emotions" (Semenza et al., 1986). Such prefrontolimbic structures that develop in the practicing period are inefficient in monitoring, adjusting, and rapidly modifying emotional reactions—especially "biologically primitive emotions" (Johnson & Multhaup, 1992) that color "primitive mental states" (Grotstein, 1980)—in response to stressful alterations of environmental stimuli. These systems inefficiently override brainstem homeostatic mechanisms during periods of stress, and therefore leave the individual susceptible to future "primitive emotional disorders" (Grotstein, 1990a). Gilbert (1992a) concludes that the primary source of human suffering is due to an "encapsulated appraisal system of primitive origin," and Guntrip (1968) refers to a "static internal closed system."

The functional limitations of such a system are described by Hopkins and Butterworth (1990): "Undifferentiated levels of development show relatively rigid but unstable modes of organization in which the organism cannot adapt responses to marked changes coming from within or without" (p. 9). From a developmental psychoanalytic perspective, Emde (1988) defines pathology as a lack of adaptive capacity, the incapacity to shift strategies in the face of environmental demands. In Chapter 28 I referred to the adaptive ability to self-initiate psychobiological state transitions in response to socioenvironmental alterations. The functional deficit of this capacity, a cardinal feature of all early forming developmental psychopathology, is uncovered when the prefrontal structural system is exposed in the future to stressful demands that exceed its physiological capacity—socioenvironmental challenges that call for alternative choices and strategies for change, that is, for adaptive capacities. Gilbert (1989) has offered interesting proposals regarding "the psychobiology of changing states"—a problem important to the deeper understanding of adaptive and maladaptive affect regulation. Unevolved developmental systems do not effectively internalize psychobiologically regulating selfobject functions, and so they continue to be dependent upon others as external selfobjects. One socioenvironmental change that would be traumatogenic to such individuals is the loss of a significant person who serves as a selfobject. Taylor (1987) concludes, "the withdrawal of people who are experienced as selfobjects may precipitate disturbances in psychological and/or biological regulation" (p. 248).

A fundamental postulate of contemporary clinical psychiatry holds that the major source of stress precipitating psychiatric disorders involves the affective response to a rupture or loss of a significant relationship (Kolb, 1977). Due to the "patterning of the nervous system" (p. 554), psychiatric patients show an inability to adapt internally to stress, and this is symptomatically expressed in a continuing activation or inhibition of organ systems in a manner inappropriate to the immediate environmental situation. Izard (1991) concludes that chronically tense emotion or frequent episodes of intense emotion are manifestations of psychopathology. Knapp (1992) concludes that "Emotional dysregulation, acute or chronic, localized or massive, is maladaptive, and when severe or sustained results in major forms of psychopathology" (p. 247). Oatley and Jenkins (1992) suggest that emotional disturbance may be a fundamental feature of every category of psychiatric diagnosis, and suggest that this dysfunction is presented in more intense and longer lasting emotional responses. These categories are classified in the Diagnostic and Statistical Manual of Mental Disorders, (DSM-III-R; American Psychiatric Association, 1987) and the underlying essential conception of this nosology is described by Spitzer and Endicott (1978): "Our approach makes explicit an underlying assumption that is present in all discussions of disease in disorder, i.e., the concept of organismic dysfunction" (p.370).

In very recent work on the concept of mental disorder, Wakefield (1992) asserts that *dysfunction* implies a failure of some naturally selected internal mechanism in the organism to perform a function for which it was designed by evolution. This dysfunction causes significant harm or negative consequences to the person under present environmental circumstances and according to present cultural standards. Such a conceptualization stresses the importance of locating and elucidating the structure-function relationships underlying psychiatric disorders. Wakefield's description fits well with the characterization of the social-emotional impairments associated with dysfunction of the orbitofrontal cortex, the cortical structure which hierarchically dominates the limbic system and is critically involved in the neurobiological mechanisms that support social (de Bruin, 1990; Kolb & Whishaw, 1990) and emotional (Rolls, 1986; Yamamoto et al., 1984) functioning.

In their detailed and comprehensive study of orbitofrontal pathology, Eslinger and Damasio (1985) describe a neurological case which demonstrates the dysfunctional effects of damage to such an internal mechanism. They demonstrate that impairments in adaptive motivational and complex social behaviors are found in orbitofrontal (but not dorsolateral) frontal lesions. (See Tables 30.3, 30.4, 30.5 and Fig. 30.2 for a discussion of this case.) Eslinger and Damasio conclude that the orbital cortex represents the structure on which such patterns are inscribed. They suggest that the dysfunction of this patient represents an impairment of the orbital systems that are involved in adaptive regulatory activites—the modulation of hypothalamic drives that are informed of environmental contingencies, and the activation of higher cortices by basic drives and tendencies. A frequently occurring but often unrecognized orbitomedial frontal syndrome, associated with personality change and poor social adjustment, has recently been reported (Malloy et al., 1993).

RECOVERY DEFICITS OF INTERNAL REPARATIVE MECHANISMS ARE FUNCTIONAL INDICATORS OF IMPAIRED AFFECT REGULATORY SYSTEMS

How can an affect regulatory dysfunction be operationally defined and clinically identified? Emotional traits are now thought to be most clearly exhibited under stressful conditions that tax the individual's adaptive capacities (Malatesta &

TABLE 30.3
Case History of an Orbitofrontal Ablation

At age 35, after a brief period of personality changes and visual disturbances, a large obritofrontal meningioma was diagnosed and surgically removed. Subsequent to a 3-month recovery period, this man returned to his accountant position. In contrast to his former organized personality patterns, his vocational behavior, though appropriate, became somewhat irresponsible and unreliable. His marriage deteriorated, and he was unable to hold a job. A month after his divorce he remarried; that marriage ended in divorce two years later. The profound changes in his personality included impairments of motivation and complex social judgment. Two years after surgery his neurological examination was normal except for bilateral anosmia (loss of smell). Eight years after the resection the personality changes remain stable and a follow-up neurological evaluation was done and presented in the following study.

Adapted from Eslinger and Damasio (1985). Reprinted by permission of Neurology, Advanstar Communications.

TABLE 30.4
Neuropsychological Test Scores

Intellect		
WAIS-R Verbal IQ	129	(97th; superior)
Performance IQ	135	(99th; very superior)
Shipley-Hartford Vocabulary Score	37/40	(superior)
	40/40	(superior)
Memory		
Wechsler Memory Scale**		
Quotient	143	
Digit Span (ACSS)	14.0	
Logical Memory (ACSS)	18.1	
Paired Associates (ACSS)	16.3	
Rey Auditory Verbal Learning (max: 15)		
Recall Trial 1	10	
2	8	
3	12	
4	14	
5	14	
Recognition	14	
Delayed Recall	11	
Benton Visual Retention Test (Adm. A, Form C)		
Correct	9	
Errors	1	
Rey-Osterrieth Complex Figure		
Copy	36/36	
Delayed Recall	32/36	

*Percentiles and interpretation in parentheses.
**Administered without visual reproductions subtest.

Note. See Table 30.5.

Wilson, 1988). The research of Cohen et al. (1982) demonstrates that difficult tasks which require greater effort most clearly reveal the deficits of psychiatric patients. In asserting the principle that meaningful neurophysiological correlates of psychopathology are most directly expressed under conditions of stressful challenge, Berman (1987) argues:

> An analogous situation in clinical medicine is that subtle weakness of a skeletal muscle may not be apparent in physical exam unless the muscle is challenged. Similaly, cardiac stress tests yield more information about cardiac function and reserve than do resting electrocardiograms. By analogy, "cortical stress tests" can be designed to challenge cerebral functional reserve and to test a specific hypothesis by imposing a selective physiological load on a cortical area of interest. (p. 1305)

The impairment of this psychophysiological adaptation mechanism in response to the challenge of a sudden alteration in the "average expectable environment" is

TABLE 30.5
Neuropsychological Test Scores

Language (Multilingual Aphasia Examination)		
Visual Naming	64	(89th)
Sentence Repetition	15	(89th)
Digit Repetition	10	(85th)
Word Fluency	49	(89th)
Oral Spelling	11	(70th)
Written Spelling	10	(39th)
Token Test	44	(89th)
Aural Comprehension of Words and Phrases	18	(71st)
Reading Comprehension of Words and Phrases	18	(59th)
BDAE Reading Comprehension of Sentences & Paragraphs	10	(Z + 2)
Writing to Copy	Normal	
Writing to Dictation	Normal	
Writing Spontaneously	Normal	
Dichotic Listening		
Right ear	98/110 (normal)	
Left ear	104/110 (normal)	
Visual Perception/Orientation/Construction		
Facial Recognition	43	(32nd)
Judgment of Line Orientation	30	(74th)
3-D Constructional Praxis		
Score	29	(intact)
Time	91 sec	
WAIS-R Block Design (ACSS)	16	(98th)
Gestural Praxis: Right Hand	10/10	
Left Hand	10/10	
Right-Left Orientation		
On Self	12/12	
On confrontation	8/8	
Geographic Orientation		
Deviation score	0	(normal)
Vector score	0	(normal)
Wisconsin Card Sorting Test		
No. categories achieved	6	
No. sorts	70	
No. errors	10	
No. perseverative errors	6	
No. trials to 1st category	4	

*Percentiles in parentheses.

Note. Notice the retention of the superior IQ scores. The Halstead-Reitan Battern shows average to superior ability in every subtest. The Wisconsin Card Soring Test, an instrument sensitive to frontal lobe functioning, is easily mastered. Notice the low score on a test of facial recognition. The MMPI is normal. Further evaluation showed that although he could solve artificial social problems in abstract form, real-life ethical situations failed to evoke patterns of social problem solving, and he manifests sociopathic behavior. The authors suggest that he possesses an impairment in the evocation of contextual (episodic) memories for social behavior and an ability to access internal automatic programs that propel him motivationally toward goals (see also Table 30.4). From Eslinger and Damasio (1985). Reprinted by permission of Neurology, Advanstar Communications.

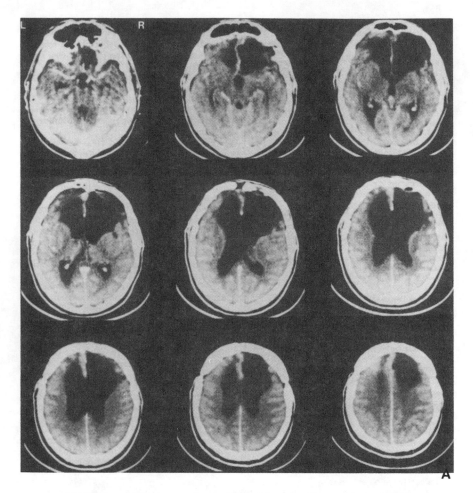

FIG. 30.2.   CT images and templates. A low-density area in both frontal lobes corresponds to the surgical resection. The resection involved
all of the orbital cortex on the right (areas 11, 12, and 25) and part of
the orbital cortex on the left. The right mesial cortex was also resected.
The left dorsolateral cortex is intact. Single photon emission tomogra-

thus expressed in the form of a functionally limited physiological reserve which
underlies an ineffective functional recovery mechanism to cope with states of
particular types of heightened emotional stress.

In a similar conceptualization, Putnam (1992) refers to the critical capacity to
maintain an appropriate psychobiological state in the face of destabilizing influences and the ability to recover from disruptions in state. In early childhood,
transitions between states and disruptions of ongoing states are modulated by

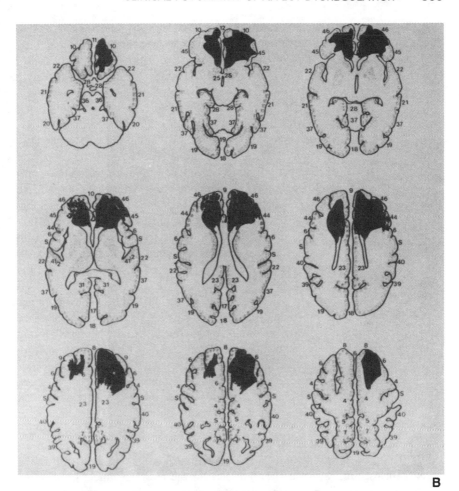

B

phy (not shown) indicates low cerebral blood flow in both frontal lobes, especially marked in the right hemisphere. Blood flow in the left dorsolateral frontal lobe is intact. From Eslinger and Damasio (1985). Reprinted by permission of Neurology, Advanstar Communications.

parents (Putnam, 1992). These experiences are imprinted into the hard wiring of the orbitofrontal cortex. A developmentally evolved orbitofrontal cortex regulates autonomic functioning (Fuster, 1980; Neafsey, 1990), and this output of a dual component prefrontal system is expressed in a capacity to maintain a reciprocal mode of autonomic control (Berntson et al., 1991). A dual circuit wiring of this frontolimbic structure allows for "switches" in prefrontal convergence zones (Oades & Halliday, 1987), and this enables the individual to shift back and forth from a balanced sympathetic-parasympathetic state, to motivational states of dominance of one circuit over another, and back to autonomic balance. On the other hand, pathological developmental functional deficits occur in the individual with a developmentally immature orbitofrontal cortex. A structurally defective system exhibits not only a sympathetic or parasympathetic bias of the set point, but also nonreciprocal coupling and a poor capacity to switch off one circuit and switch on the other. As a result, an individual with an "underregulation" disturbance (Emde, 1990) experiences difficulty in transitioning out of sympathetic-dominant states and in modulating parasympathetic states. Conversely, a person who manifests an "overregulation" disturbance has a problem shifting out of a parasympathetic trophotropic arousal and in modulating sympathetic, ergotropic arousal fueled states. This conception highlights the often unappreciated fact that there are two forms of stress system dysregulation, one associated with hyperactivation and hyperarousal, the other with hypoactivation and hypoarousal (Chrousos & Gold, 1992). The relationship between adequate and inadequate early empathic care and hyperaroused and hypoaroused states is a focus of the work of Weil (1992).

This stress-state recovery mechanism has previously been shown to ontogenetically evolve in practicing period reciprocal experiences with a caregiver who provides arousal and affect regulating interactive repair after stressful dyadic misattunements. In these interactions, the caregiver and child transition from positive to negative and back to positive affect (Demos, 1991). In reunions after attachment ruptures psychobiologically attuned mothers of securely attached infants act to re-regulate the child's arousal level back into a moderate range, that is within the optimal activation band, via actively initiating and participating in "distress-relief sequences" (Lamb, 1981), "interactive repair" (Tronick, 1989), and "reassurance" transactions after agonistic encounters (Gilbert & Trower, 1990). The growth facilitating, "good enough mother" acting as a "reparative agent" (Buchsbaum & Emde, 1990) allows for the reestablishment of affective communication after a reasonable period of time following a shame associated "failed affective communication" (Rizzuto, 1991), a stressful attachment break which she has instigated. This interval represents a delay period between the offset of and the resumption of the flow of a communicative tie to an anticipated maternal regulatory function, arousal regulation. This restoration of a secure emotional attachment is incorporated into an interactive representation (Wilson et al., 1990). Self-and-object representations specifically perform a "restitutive-reparative" function (Stolorow & Atwood, 1979).

The internalization of reparative distress-relief sequences which mediate interactive repair allows for the creation of a recovery mechanism that efficiently monitors and autoregulates the duration, frequency, and intensity of negative affect states. These specific caregiver stress regulating transactions, characterized in current developmental psychological and infant psychoanalytic studies, which occur in this critical period of corticolimbic maturation, directly influence the experience-dependent development of the catecholaminergic and cholinergic systems which are responsible for both arousal and the regulation of arousal. It was earlier argued that practicing maternal shame regulation reactivates opiate production and ventral tegmental dopaminergic arousal, thereby maintaining and preserving orbitofrontal mesocortical circuitry, known to be involved in the regulation of affective responses (Tassin, 1987). The transition from a nonobject relational state, such as a depressive shame state, back into the state that activates the reexpression of attachment and exploratory behaviors may specificy an important "recovery algorithm" (Schwalbe, 1991). This recovery algorithm may be coded within internal working models, which are now thought to define "styles of affect regulation" and to provide "rules for regulating distress-related affect" (Kobak & Sceery, 1988). Such representations also program information about state transitions (Freyd, 1987). This frontolimbic system is central to the operation of "emotion-focused coping," which regulates emotional distress that is described by Lazarus (1991b).

Since the activity of the orbitofrontal cortex, a cortical structure critically involved in homeostatic regulation (Kolb, 1984), is expressed in the delayed response function (Freedman & Oscar-Berman, 1986; Kubota & Niki, 1971; Mishkin, 1964; Rosenkilde, Bauer, & Fuster, 1981), and since delayed response underlies representational memory (Fuster, 1980), the ontogenetic attainment of a more efficient orbitofrontal dual limbic circuit supported delayed response will be reflected in a progressive developmental gradation of representational capacity (Trad, 1986). The maturation of this more complex cognitive-affective structure of the representational world occurs at the end of the practicing period, and its emergence is marked by the advent of evocative memory (Blatt, 1991). Jacobson (1983) asserts that there are "constraining timetables for crucial representational world developmental steps" (p. 55). Goldman-Rakic (1987a) argues that object permanence, the recognition that an object has continuity in time and space when not in view, depends on the capacity to form representations of the outside world. Psychoanalytic theoreticians have proposed that evocative memory enables the individual to evoke an image of a comforting object and the function of the maternal object, even in her absence (Adler & Buie, 1979). This "image" of the comforting object is specifically a multimodal image of the mother's face during interactive repair transactions.

> The unique configuration of the mother's face is a complex configuration that comes to represent the mother. Where there is any sense of threat, it becomes the one pattern that must be found, and nothing else will do. (Wright, 1991, p. 335)

In previous chapters, I described how orbitofrontal neuronal models which code representations of images of emotionally expressive faces mediate an affect regulating function. Indeed, representational capacities are critical to the regulation of behavior (Goldman-Rakic, 1987b). Hofer (1990) now concludes that "complex" mental representations enable the infant to modulate distress responses. Krystal (1978b) refers to self-representation and the capacity for self-care.

In marked contrast to this scenario, the mother of an insecurely attached infant does not instigate interactive repair nor does she initiate distress relief sequences. As a result the infant remains stuck fast in stressful unregulated disorganizing states of unmodulated negative affect. In the critical period of the imprinting of orbitofrontal circuits, this may be associated with the competitive elimination of mesocortical dopaminergic circuitry. Haracz (1985) suggests that plasticity of dopaminergic projections in postnatal periods is a potential site of developmental deficits. Indeed, this neurochemical system that innervates and serves as a trophic signal to the differentiation of frontolimbic cortex is critically involved in emotionality, regulation of affective responses, movements to motivational stimuli, and cognitive representational processes. Since the mesocortical dopamine system directly influences orbitofrontal maturation, any interference with this neurochemical system would produce an enduring impairment of orbitofrontal function. This would be manifest in an arrest in its developmental trajectory, and the vulnerability of the expansion of this catecholaminergic system into frontal areas would specifically occur during the practicing phase, a critical period of orbitofrontal maturation.

In line with a current suggestion that social deprivation and disruption of affiliative bonds causes changes in the number and nature of neurotransmitter receptors (van der Kolk, 1987), early unregulated traumatic socioaffective experiences could induce permanent alterations in mesocortical dopaminergic receptors. In light of the fact that dopamine-stimulated cAMP receptors play an essential role in affective, cognitive and neuroendocrine aspects of dopaminergic neurotransmission (Fremeau et al., 1991), these early changes will profoundly influence the individual's future adaptive functioning. Indeed, long-term changes in dopamine receptor function are noted to be produced by early social isolation (Lewis, Gluck, Beauchamp, Keresztury, & Mailman, 1990). Psychological trauma during a critical period of receptor amplification may cause receptor supersensitivity (Trendelenburg, 1963), and this may have long-lasting effects.

Van der Kolk (1987) also concludes that early social deprivation permanently alters opiate receptors: "There is . . . evidence that social isolation directly effects the number or sensitivity of brain opiate receptors [regulating pleasure], at least during critical stages of development" (p. 41). As previously mentioned, endorphinergic opiate receptor binding is elevated during early development (Maseda et al., 1983), and orbitofrontal areas contains the highest levels of opioids in the cortex (Steklis & Kling, 1985). Opiate reward functions are mediated by the ventral tegmental dopamine system (Bozarth, 1988). The less than optimal experience-dependent reduction of these receptors in the critical period of orbitofrontal development would have enduring limiting effects on the future function of this structure that is involved in the pleasurable qualities of social interaction (Panksepp et al., 1985). Weil (1992) argues that early deprivation of empathic care results in a chronic loss of pleasure. He also asserts that:

> the exposure of an infant to early traumatic emotional experiences (such as is afforded by chronic deprivation of empathic care) can result in the sensory-affecto-motor "emotional-instinctual recordings" of the experiences, for example, recordings of the chemical, neurotransmitter reactions of the limbic system within the instinctual brain. (p. 106)

In a very important recent study, Martin et al. (1991) report that permanent alterations in regional chemoarchitecture result from early social deprivation. A gross histological examination of the brain is unremarkable, but highly abnormal chemical patterns are found in the monoaminergic innervation of several subcortical and cortical areas. Among other findings, they specifically document an association between early environmental stress and a "significant" reduction in the number of dopaminergic neurons in the ventral tegmental area. These workers remark that they have preliminary evidence indicating a reduction of monoaminergic innervation of several unnamed cortical areas. They relate the resultant "abnormalities of social and affective function" to an impairment of integrated functions of interconnected subcortical and cortical systems, and specifically mention the glutamatergic projections of the cerebral cortex and midbrain dopaminergic groups. Martin concludes that early social and somatosensory deprivation may interfere with the expression of specific growth regulators and trophic molecules that are critical for the formation and stabilization of neurochemically distinct compartments of the postnatally maturing brain. No such studies have been done on the effects of early stress on the development of the lateral tegmental noradrenergic system, but long-term alterations in the subcortical and orbitofrontal components of this monoaminergic system should also be found. These changes would also reflect the well-established principle that loss of presynaptic catecholamine innervation is associated with functional supersensitivity of postsynaptic receptor sites (Snyder, 1979).

This early dyadic failure may play a significant role in an individual's susceptibility to later drug abuse, a disorder that reflects an impairment in the capacity for self-regulation (Khantzian, 1978). Wilson traces the etiology of addiction (dependence on exogenous opiates) to the inhibitory effects of early dyadic misattunements and negative affects on the psychobiological development of Emde's affective core. As adults, these personalities manifest socioemotional deficits in the form of difficulties in the temporal ordering of experiences, lack of planning, and poor impulse control and affect tolerance (Wilson, Passik, Faude, Abrams, & Gordon, 1989). Wilson concludes that "opiate addicts differ from normal subjects in manifesting a constellation of dynamics that implicate failures in self-regulatory functioning" (p. 397). Developmental disorders are also known to frequently manifest a dependence upon drugs (Krystal, 1988) that reflects an impairment in the capacity for self-regulation (Khantzian, 1978). Wurmser

(1987) concludes that drug abusers manifest shame sensitivity and utilize chemical substances as "auxilliary regulators." Knapp (1992) puts forth the idea that addictive drug use can be seen as self-medication in an effort to restore regulation. Putnam (1992) argues that alcohol abuse is utilized to suppress certain psychobiological states, and that "exogenous pharmacology" is substituted for "developmental deficiencies in state modulation." Ulman and Paul (1989) assert that drugs act as "addictive trigger mechanisms" that are used to arouse narcissistic fantasies and affects which provide relief from dysphoric states. These affect-laden fantasies are associated with early developing forms of grandiosity and omnipotence (R.B. Ulman, personal correspondence, November 2, 1992). In propounding a theory of "psychopharmacogenic recapitulation," Wieder and Kaplan (1969) suggest that drug users are attempting to reestablish early, self soothing, reparative affect states.

I surmise that this refers to a restitution of ventral tegmental-supported positive affect after a stressful negative affective state. Drugs abused by humans increase synaptic dopamine concentrations in the mesolimbic system (DiChiara & Imperato, 1988). Increased orbitofrontal metabolism reflecting altered dopamine activity occurs in cocaine craving and withdrawal (Volkow, Fowler, Wolf, & Hitzemann, 1991). Neurologic patients with orbitofrontal damage are known to be more overreactive to and more impaired by drugs and alcohol (Parker, 1990). The recent experimental demonstration that the stress-related activity of the hypothalamic-pituitary-adrenal axis specifically plays a critical role in the pathogenesis of psychostimulant addiction (Piazza et al., 1991) also implicates the orbitofrontal cortex that regulates this system (Hall & Marr, 1975). Piazza et al. conclude that a deregulation of corticosteroid secretion that sensitizes central dopamine systems is an important factor in susceptibility to drug-taking behavior.

"Developmental deficits," expressed in relational affect-transacting coping limitations or failures, are thus defects of "intrapsychic" reparative systems. These deficits arise from early trauma that occur during the critical period of right hemispheric frontolimbic growth. Earlier conceptions of trauma as traumatic activity that a child did or suffered are now being replaced by a more sophisticated concept of traumatic absence resulting in deficits (Lansky, 1992). Deprivation of empathic care creates a growth-inhibiting environment that produces immature, unevolved, physiologically undifferentiated orbitofrontal affect regulatory systems. These contain "pathological" interactive representations of the self-with-a-dysregulating-other (internalized working models of misattunement) and will be expressed in "impairments of cognitive-affective structures of the representational world" (Blatt, 1991, p. 450). Failures of self-regulation are expressed in early maladaptive representations of self-in-interaction-with-other (Wilson et al., 1990). In line with the observation that early developing undifferentiated representational capacity (unlike later developing differentiated evocative memory) is susceptible to disorganization under stressful affective states, orbital pathology will be revealed under these conditions. Indeed, in perhaps the most thorough neurological/neuropsychological study of orbitofrontal pathology, Eslinger and Damasio (1985) observe specific impairments in motivation and in the evocation of contextural memories that guide complex social behaviors. This implies an impairment of representational evocative memory and affective object constancy. As mentioned earlier, representational phenomena are now viewed as a bridging concept between psychoanalysis and neuroscience (Hadley, 1983).

THE NEUROCHEMISTRY OF AFFECT DYSREGULATING DEPRESSIVE STATES

In an informative recent article, Gabbard (1992) offers the observation that:

> Much of the polarization between the biological and psychodynamic perspectives arises from a failure to appreciate the complex relationships between psychosocial and neurophysiological factors in the etiololgy and pathogenesis of psychiatric disorders. (p. 991–992)

Seeking a path that might lead to a solution of this current, unresolved problem, Watt (1990) proposes that:

> an understanding of how biogenic amines link and regulate various corticolimbic connections could help bridge the current profound split between biological psychiatry and psychoanalytic psychology. (p. 521)

This volume attempts to illustrate that a developmental approach can go far to integrate what appear on the surface to be divergent data from the psychological and biological sciences. Toward this end, I have focused on the effects of socioenvironmental influences on catecholamines and neurohormones in early development, and on the action of these trophic agents in generating brain structure. In developmental neurochemical research Singer (1986b) suggests that in postnatal life experience-dependent processes rely both upon cortical sensory processing of information from the "outer" world, and on internally generated signals involving catecholamines from the reticular formation. We now know that during critical periods, monoamine neurotransmitters and neurohormones regulate the temporal framework of developmental brain growth as well as mediate the effects of external influences on this process (Lauder & Krebs, 1986). Monoaminergic neurotransmitters influence the ontogeny of cortical circuitry and have "complex, long-lasting effects on postsynaptic biochemical processes which might mediate developmental influences" (Foote & Morrison, 1991, p. 418). Critical period events which interfere with such processes are obvious scenarios of pathogenesis.

Indeed, these findings in the basic sciences are now being rapidly absorbed into the clinical sciences. Current research in biological psychiatry stresses the importance of bioaminergic and neuroendocrine dysfunction to the understanding of psychiatric disorders. Developmental neuroendocrinological studies show that modulated infant stimulation modifies developing neural processes specifically in the right hemisphere (Denenberg et al., 1978), the hemisphere that contains lateralized catecholamine systems which are the neurochemical substrates of arousal (Robinson, 1979) and that is dominant for the regulation of cortisol secretion (Wittling & Pfluger, 1990). This beneficial early experience leads to a permanent alteration of glucocorticoid receptors in the frontal cortex (Meaney et al., 1985) on glucocorticoid-sensitive neurons involved in terminating the adrenocortical stress response (Sapolsky et al., 1984), and thereby allows for the capacity of a relatively rapid return of corticosterone to baseline levels after exposure to a novel stimulus in later life (Hess, Denenberg, Zarrow, & Pfeifer, 1969). Deprivation of this early maternal stress modulation, on the other hand, is known to trigger an exaggerated release of corticosterone upon subsequent exposures to novelty (Stanton, Gutierrez, & Levine, 1988). Increased corticosteroid levels during infancy permanently reduce postnatal brain growth (DeKosky, Nonneman, & Scheff, 1982) and produce functional impairments of the directing of emotion into adaptive channels (Howard & Benjamins, 1975).

In order to function as a stress modulator for the infant the primary caregiver must be able to regulate her own affect with some efficiency. This capacity is severely impaired in a mother who is herself experiencing an affective disturbance. The most obvious example of this is a woman who is experiencing a postnatal depression (Pitt, 1968). Indeed, infant related stressors have recently been shown to be specific potent elicitors of postpartum depression (Hopkins, Campbell, & Marcus, 1987). The pathogenic effects of maternal depression on infant development (Cox, 1988; Melhuish, Gambles, & Kumar, 1988), including cognitive development (Cogill et al., 1986), and the enduring psychopathological sequelae associated with being parented by a depressed caregiver (Gordon et al., 1989) are well documented. In direct studies of the nonverbal dyadic interactions between infants and postnatally depressed mothers, Murray (1988) concludes that the caregiver's lack of interest and reactivity are the major contributors to the negative effects on shared affect, concentration, language development, and security of attachment. It is important to note that in many cases postnatal depression is not short-lived; in one study one half of a sample of depressed mothers remained so after one year (Cox, Rooney, Thomas, & Wrate, 1984). This means that these mothers are experiencing a significant disturbance of affect regulation while their infants are traversing the practicing period. This dysregulated state would initially preclude her from engaging in merger experiences that amplify positive affect in the infant, and later interfere with her acting as a shame regulator. The assertions by Basch (1985) that failures of affect attunement create a cognition that one's needs are shameful, and by Kaufman

(1989) that failures of attachment become sources of shame, have important implications for developmental psychopathologies. The pathological early experiences of various psychiatric affect disorders may include a failure of caregiver participation in dyadic shame regulation during the practicing critical period.

It is now accepted that disrupted mother-infant attachment promotes vulnerability to depressive pathology in childhood (Cytryn, McKnew, & Bunney, 1980) and later life (Akiskal & McKinney, 1975; Bowlby, 1982; Paykel & Hollyman, 1984), and that the "primitive, biologically based" (Broucek, 1982) "attachment emotion" (H.B. Lewis, 1980) of shame is a central component of severe depressive pathologies in both children (Izard & Schwartz, 1986) and adults (Gilbert, 1992a; H.B. Lewis, 1987; Nathanson, 1987a). Tomkins (1987) describes, "shame, if magnified in frequency, duration, and intensity such that the head is in a permanent posture of depression, can become malignant in the extreme" (p. 150). Recent research by Watson and Clark (1988) indicates that a lack of positive affectivity is perhaps more specific to depression than any other symptom. This finding may reflect unmodulated and heightened shame, an affect that uniquely acts as an inhibitor of positive affect (Tomkins, 1963) and is psychologically and neurologically more closely asociated with positive emotions than any other negative affect (Izard, 1991).

Multidisciplinary evidence is accumulating to show that there may be more than one type of psychobiologically dissociable depressive disorder. It is now thought that the nature of the individual's early attachment appears as a distinct determinant for future effects of psychopharmacological agents (Svensson, 1992). Nathanson (1992) asserts that unlike "guilt-loaded depression," "shame-loaded depression" is generally refractory to pharmacological treatment with tricyclic antidepressants but usually responsive to the monoamine oxidase group of antidepressants and the relatively new family of antidepressants represented by fluoxetine (Prozac). He concludes that the neurochemistry and the neurocircuitry of shame differs from that of guilt. Blatt's continuing empirical studies demonstrate two subtypes of depression: anaclitic, derived from an early disruption of the basic relationship with the mother, and introjective, a later forming more developmentally advanced type (Blatt et al., 1990). He posits that the former is associated with shame, the latter with guilt (S.J. Blatt, personal communication, October 2, 1991). Gilbert (1992a) suggests that shame is associated with the development of endogenous, as opposed to neurotic, depression.

Psychophysiologically, the basic state of depression is retardation, and agitation, if and when it occurs, is superimposed on this state of loss of energy. Furthermore, "depression may arise from either high arousal in punishment areas of the brain, low activity in reward areas or some combination" (Gilbert, 1992a, p. 40). Izard (1991) now advances the notion that depression may involve either an unbalanced dominance of the parasympathetic trophotropic system, or a simultaneous activation of trophotropic and ergotropic systems in which sympathetic hyperactivity produces inner and outer-directed anger (Izard, 1991). Both components of the autonomic nervous system are thought to be chronically activated in patient's exhibiting the anxiety and depression of a "melancholic" depression (Gold, Goodwin, & Chrousos, 1988a, 1988b; Wyatt, Protnoy, Kupfer, Snyder, & Engelman, 1971), a state that results from a "failure of adequate counterregulation" (Chrousos & Gold, 1992, p. 1247). Elevated concentrations of CRF, an agent that increases emotionality (Britton et al., 1982) and sympathetic nervous system activity (Brown et al., 1982b), are found in this subgroup of patients experiencing a major depression (Nemeroff et al., 1984). This group shows chronic corticotropin hypersecretion, an effect thought to be responsible for the adrenal gland enlargement found in certain depressed patients (Nemeroff et al., 1992). Conversely, decreased secretion of CRF occurs in a second form of depression (Gold et al., 1986; Vanderpool, Rosenthal, Chrousos, Wher, & Gold, 1991), as well as in chronic fatigue syndrome (Demitrack et al., 1991). Heightened and unregulated activation of the parasympathetic component of the ANS (and consequent low energy) in both of the depressive typologies would result in impaired corticosteroid dynamics. It is tempting to speculate that bypassed shame and narcissistic rage—humiliated fury are typical of the agitated depression of the former group, while intense overt experienced shame occurs in the latter.

Contact comfort was earlier proposed to be a component of the interactive repair of shame regulation which modulates shame-induced cortisol production, and the mother's failure to provide this regulatory function may etiologically underlie the observation that unregulated, especially bypassed shame exerts a detrimental force within the individual's intrapsychic life (M. Lewis, 1992). Indeed, clinicians have observed that bypassed shame is a fundamental component of suicidal crises (Lansky, 1992). Supporting the idea that shame dysregulation is a central defect of depressive disturbances, Gopelrud and Depue (1985) report that when stressed, adult psychiatric patients diagnosed with affective disorders show inadequate inhibitory regulation, manifest in slower behavioral recovery and prolonged recovery of cortisol levels. Young, Haskett, Murphy-Weinberg, Watson, & Akil, (1991) find that normal subjects manifest glucocorticoid fast-feedback inhibition, an effect mediated by the activity of higher brain centers. In contrast, depressed patients reveal decreased sensitivity of brain sites to steroid feedback. These studies support earlier findings that plasma cortisol is elevated in depressed patients (Board, Wadeson, & Persky, 1957), that cortisol hypersecretion is associated with the cognitive impairment of depression (Rubinow, Giold, Savard, & Gold, 1984), and that recovery from depression is accompanied by a decline of cortisol levels (Gibbons & McHugh, 1962).

In line with Gilbert's (1989) suggestion that the hypothalamo-pituitary-adrenal-cortical system is specifically involved in inducing and maintaining long-term states, adrenal alterations may be primarily responsible for persistent parasympathetic-dominant orbitofrontal states found in chronic depression. Gilbert also emphasizes that the neurophysiological and hormonal changes associated with affect arousal take time to reestablish a homeostatic state. Siever and Davis (1985) present a neurophysiological model of affect disorders in which the central pathology is a homeostatic defect of a biogenic amine neurotransmitter system, an impairment of an inhibitory affect regulatory system which is expressed in an inappropriate response to environmental stress, and a sluggish return of the system to basal activity following a perturbation. Dienstbier (1989) finds slow poststress sympathetic catecholamine-regulated arousal decline to be associated with poor coping ability and negative emotional response, and emphasizes the importance of fast recovery from heightened sympathetic arousal to both mental and physical health.

In developmental psychobiological research, Kraemer et al. (1991) show that despair, the depression-like response to mother-infant separation, is associated with significant changes in catecholamine levels, and conclude that despair may fundamentally reflect an inability to cope with the separation environment. Gilbert (1992a) hypothesizes that depressive personalities manifest a vulnerability in the limbic system that results from early experiences of loss/separation and inadequate parenting. In a similar conception, Gold et al. (1988a, 1988b) postulate that separations or losses early in life sensitize brain receptor sites, leading to a vulnerability to later recurrent depressions. I suggest that an inefficiency in regulating emotional homeostasis and in recovering from stressful alterations of environmental stimuli results from early critical period growth inhibiting experiences which permanently cause a limited capacity to produce a physiological reserve of orbitofrontal catecholamine receptors and thereby an impaired capacity to activate prefrontal metabolism which controls homeostatic equilibrium (autonomic balance) during periods of affective stress.

Altered prefrontal functioning has been reported in 11 to 17 month-old-infants of mothers with elevated depressive symptomatology. These children fail to exhibit the pattern of greater right frontal activity during a condition designed to elicit distress, maternal deprivation (Dawson et al., 1992). This hypothesis of an orbitofrontal impairment in depression is supported by Tucker's finding of a decrement of right frontal lobe activation and right hemisphere performance during depressed mood (Tucker, Stenslie, Roth, & Shearer, 1981), and Perris' observation of abnormal right frontal EEG function in depressed patients (Perris, Monakhov, VonKnorring, Botskarev, & Nikiforov, 1979). An association between depression and right hemispheric dysfunction has been found in both children (Brumback, Staton, & Wilson, 1980) and adults (Freeman, Galaburda, Cabal, & Geschwind, 1985; Kronfol, Hamsher, Digre, & Wazziri, 1978; Otto, Yeo, & Dougher, 1987).

THE NEUROCHEMISTRY OF DYSREGULATED MANIC STATES

Affect dysregulation is also a hallmark of Bipolar Disorders that involve manic episodes (DSM-IIIR; American Psychiatric Association, 1987). Manic depressive illnesses are currently understood to represent dysregulatory states (Klein,

Gittelman, Quitkin, & Rifkin, 1980). The developmental psychopathological precursor of a major disorder of underregulation can be demonstrated in the practicing period histories of infants of manic-depressive parents. Manic-depressive women show a high incidence of postpartum affective disorder (Baker, Dorzab, Winokur, & Cadoret, 1971), and a generalized disturbance in affect regulation, which is identifiable at 12 months and increases to prominence by 18 months (the span of the practicing period) has been found in infants of manic-depressive parents (Gaensbauer, Harmon, Cytryn, & McKnew, 1984). Problems in emotion regulation and aggression at 2 years have also been reported in children with a manic-depressive parent (Zahn-Waxler, McKnew, Cummings, Davenport, & Radke-Yarrow, 1984).

This practicing manifestation of affect dysregulation may represent the first expression of a vulnerability to later stress-triggered manic-depressive illness, a genetically linked affect disorder (Egeland et al., 1987; Hodgkinson et al., 1987). Egeland notes that the gene that confers a predisposition to this disorder encodes the structural gene for tyrosine hydroxylase, the enzyme that initiates dopamine biosynthesis. The genetic determinants of this dysfunction, perhaps involving the genetics of dopamine receptors (Vadasz, Laszlovszky, De Simone, & Fleischer, 1992), are first expressed in this postnatal period. It is now known that the human dopamine D1 receptor is encoded on chromosome 5 (Sunahara et al., 1990). I have earlier suggested that an amplification in the numbers of orbitofrontal D1 receptors occurs in the early practicing period. It is widely accepted that not all children with the genetic predisposition manifest the illness (Kuyler, Rosenthal, Igel, Dunner, & Fieve, 1980). I suggest that the necessary gene-environment condition is embedded specifically in practicing critical period transactions.

Noting the commonalities between elation as a basic practicing mood in infants and manic symptomatology in adults, Pao (1971) observes:

> . . . elation as a basic mood is characterized by an experience of elevated mood and exaggerated omnipotence which corresponds to the child's increasing awareness of his muscular and intellectual powers. Descriptively manic symptomatology is said to be comprised of an elevation of mood, increased activity (muscular as well as intellectual), and a grandiose concept of self. The similarity between the two is striking. (p.793)

Pao concludes that understanding Mahler's basic mood of practicing elation is relevant to, and revealing of, the genetic and dynamic elucidation of later states of pathologically elevated mood. Indeed, manic patients are described as being "on top of the world," experiencing expansive elated mood, grandiose mentation, increased motor activity, and boundless energy (Shopsin, 1979), and in a state of hyperarousal (Henry, Weingartner, & Murphy, 1971). Manic disorder has also been described in terms of a chronic elevation of the early practicing affect of interest-excitement; this causes a "rushing" of intellectual activity and a driving of the body at uncontrollable and potentially dangerous speeds (Izard, 1991).

In an early psychoanalytic attempt to understand mania, Abraham (1948) hypothesized that the initial and primary pathology of this disorder has its source in the first year of life in intense frustration and lack of gratification from the mother. Rochlin (1953) next proposed an etiology of the "labile narcissistic disorder" of depression and elation (manic-depressive disorder) with an origin in an early phase of primary narcissism. A seductive mother reinforces the primary narcissism, and attempts at disengagement from her elicits a narcissistic injury that triggers depression. Pao (1968) also conceptualized the depressive phase as a passive re-experiencing of a "narcissistic wound" which is "beyond words for description," and points out the importance of the nonverbal behavior of the patient in understanding mania. (The nonverbal affect of shame has been equated with narcissistic injury; Schore, 1991). Manic-depressives are notoriously irritable after mild frustration (Winokur & Tsuang, 1975), and such patients are readily provoked by seemingly harmless remarks, and react with rage to minor provocations (Shopsin, 1979). Shopsin also notes an inordinate lack of conscious shame in these individuals. Notice the inefficiency of a shame system to downregulate hyperaroused affect of elation or narcissistic rage.

Patients with bipolar affective disorders show severe impairments in interpersonal relationships. In the manic phase they display a type of "interpersonal hunger," which may be understood as an intense need for contact (attachment need activation). In the depressive phase the patient withdraws and shows an avoidant pattern in which he cannot sustain affective contact with significant others (Ludwig & Ables, 1974). I would point out the similarity of this to earlier discussed impaired attachment patterns which are outcomes of practicing misattunement and intense unmodulated shame induction. Specifically, the insecure-avoidant attachment shows commonality to the depressed phase of manic-depressive illness, while the insecure-resistant pattern shows homology to the manic phase. The bipolar nature of the illness reflects an essential defect in mechanisms involved in transitions between psychobiological states. A careful description of episodes of "switches" from depression into mania and mania into depression is reported by Bunney, Murphy, Goodwin, and Beorge (1972). Pao (1968) provides an interesting, carefully documented case history of the transitions of states in a bipolar patient.

I suggest that the biochemical lesion of manic states is localized in a structurally unevolved, physiologically altered orbitofrontal affect autoregulatory system which is inefficient in modulating stress-induced high arousal manic affect generated by an unrestrained, unregulated, hyperexcitatory sympathetic limbic system. Untreated "functional" manic patients may progress to an "organic" state of acute delirious mania (acute confusional state; Carlson & Goodwin, 1973) and display elevated expansive mood, inflated self-esteem, grandiosity, and psychomotor agitation. Mania is considered to represent a hypercatecholaminergic and hypocholinergic state (Malenka, Hamblin, & Barchas, 1989), and an interference with practicing phase growth of orbitofrontal descending cholinergic axons that modulate subcortical excitatory dopaminergic activity would produce a vulnerability to manic symptomatology. The research of Post (1977) suggests that stressful experiences occurring repetitively in early development will potentiate limbic catecholaminergic pathways; stressful events later in life reactivate these potentiated pathways. Thus, a psychopatholgical predisposition, an affect regulatory limitation, could later be stress-exposed, and manifest in a Jacksonian de-evolutionary loss of autonomic balance between an overactive ventral tegmental dopaminergic excitatory and an underactive lateral tegmental noradrenergic inhibitory system, a normal developmental state of the early practicing phase.

In support of this hypothesis, neuroendocrinological studies demonstrate that patients in the manic phase, like early practicing infants, show low levels of circulating corticosteroids (Bunney, Hartman, & Mason, 1965). Mania has been proposed to represent a hyperdopaminergic state, possibly related to a biochemical lesion of the mesocortical-prefrontal pathway which causes an imbalance with subcortical dopamine systems (Bakchine et al., 1989). Postnatally maturing dopaminergic projections are now considered to be potential sites of developmental defects (Haracz, 1985), and a role for mesolimbic dopamine receptors has been implicated in major affective disorders (Willner, Muscat, Papp, & Sampson, 1991). Gardner (1982) suggests that the pathophysiologic mechanism of this disorder involves an impairment of biogenic amine and opiate networks which produces an "altered regulatory system" exhibiting a "biased set point." Furthermore, in a recent neurological study, Starkstein, Boston, and Robinson (1988) now propose damage localized to the right hemispheric orbitofrontal cortex is associated with manic symptomatology. They conclude an altered asymmetric biogenic amine input to this prefrontal structure that modulates mood is responsible for the manic state.

SUMMARY

In the practicing critical period the onset of locomotion allows the toddler to physically separate himself from the mother in order to explore novel aspects of the larger environment, but this entails the deprivation of her availability for the regulation of his psychobiological functions for increasing amounts of time. These experiences can facilitate the growth of the child's adaptive self-regulatory systems if, and only if, he has access to her selfobject functions upon reconnection. The interactive dynamics that occur during reunions critically influence the permanent maturation of brain structures involved in homeostatic regulation. This emotional microenvironment is growth-promoting or growth-inhibiting, depending upon the caregiver's capacity to read her own and her child's affective state, and her ability to reinitiate dyadic affective transactions. Such interactions have a disproportionate influence on the development of an individual's vulnerability to future stress induced psychopathology. Actually, this characterization is imprecise; such fast acting, "hidden" events have far-reaching consequences because they imprint the hard-wiring of structures responsible for future socioemotional functioning for the rest of the lifespan.

The causal relationship between these early experiences and the genesis of predispositions to pathology is explained by the fact that the genetic systems that program the structural connections within the limbic system are extremely active during critical periods of infancy, and the activation of these genetic programs is sensitive and responsive to conditions in the external and thereby the internal environments. Such gene-environment interactions are potential sources of pathomorphogenetic alterations of frontolimbic dual-circuit hard-wiring that mark developmentally immature and defective limbic systems. Again, I emphasize that the external environment is a social environment, specifically contained in the dyadic interaction, and if psychotoxic it can literally induce increased synapse destruction in the internal environment of the child's growing brain.

The caregiver's dysregulating effect on the infant's internal state, and her poor capacity to psychobiologically regulate his negative affect, defines a pathogenetic influence, since such events interfere with the maturation of right hemispheric structural systems that mediate socioaffective self-regulation. The result is an organization that can not adaptively shift internal states and overt behavior in response to stressful external demands. The inability to adapt to stress and the continued activation or inhibition of internal systems that is inappropriate to a particular environmental situation essentially defines all psychiatric disorders. I believe that every type of early forming primitive disorder involves, to some extent, altered orbital prefrontal function. These impairments are most obvious under stressful and challenging conditions that call for behavioral flexibility and affect regulation. This adaptive capacity is psychobiologically mediated by frontolimbic switching mechanisms that allow the individual to uncouple and recouple the sympathetic and parasympathetic components of the autonomic nervous system in response to changing environmental circumstances. It is this specific ability that is compromised in pathological systems.

After a stress the reestablishment of autonomic balance between these components defines a recovery mechanism. The dynamic capacities and limitations of such a reparative system are forged in early dyadic interactive repair transactions that induce transitions out of disruptive states of affective distress. In situations where the caregiver routinely does not participate in reparative functions, the resulting unmodulated psychobiological dysregulation reflects a dysregulated brain chemistry. A chaotic biochemical alteration of catecholamines and hormones in this critical period could induce permanent modifications in the numbers and functional capacities of the frontolimbic receptors for these neuromodulatory agents, thereby causing long enduring defects in this structural system that are later uncovered during particular types of socioemotional stress. These events could account for the observation that patients with affective disorders manifest supersensitive catecholamine receptors in limbic structures.

Such structural deficits are expressed in impaired function, and this in turn is manifest in altered biochemical parameters of baseline-stress-baseline dynamics. Early cortisol dysregulation is an important factor in the etiology of a vulnerability to shame associated depressive disorders. Adults diagnosed with major depressive affective disorders, when stressed, show inadequate inhibitory regulation, biochemically expressed in chronically elevated cortisol levels and altered catecholamine metabolism, and behaviorally manifest in slower recovery of socioemotional functions. This symptomatic picture reflects an unmodulated hyperactivation of lateral tegmental, parasympathetic trophotropic arousal. Manic disorders, on the other hand, represent heightened activation of the ventral tegmental dopaminergic system that is unmodulated due to the deficient activity of a defective single circuit dominant orbitofrontal cortex.

31

The Developmental Psychopathology of Personality Disorders

If affect is primary, then affect must be our starting point in reexamining the nature and development of clinical syndromes.
—Gershon Kaufman (1989)

Synoptically, the borderline patient can be understood as one who is readily disposed to symptoms of primary dysregulation on the biopsychosocial continuum and, as a consequence, develops secondary symptoms in order to restore a compromised homeostasis. The borderline can be seen, furthermore, as containing "undigested" internal objects which have not been transformable into stable self or object representations.
—James S. Grotstein (1987)

Narcissistic personality disorder, a pathology of shame, is a disturbance of self-esteem regulation, the use of grandiose defenses against inadequate self-regard, but it is far more than that. It is at base a disturbance in the representation of self and of the relationship of self to others.
—John S. Auerbach (1990)

In Chapter 21 I proposed that the molding of temperamental traits into stable characteristics of personality results from the experience-dependent transformation of the orbitofrontal cortex that occurs during the practicing critical period. As a result of early experiences in the caregiving relationship, the infant's biologically organized affective core, the primordial central integrating structure of the nascent self located in the orbitofrontal cortex, becomes biased with tendencies toward certain emotional responses. These emotion biases in personality, which first appear in the second year of life, are neurobiologically mediated by an individual's prefrontal set to activate a particular neurophysiological/neuroanatomical emotive circuit. The prefrontal cortex is known to be involved in personality factors, and frontolimbic biases reflect an autonomic set point which expresses a predominance of one of the forebrain-midbrain limbic circuits, the ventral tegmental or lateral tegmental, in socioemotional functioning. The result is a predispositional emphasis on the activation of either excitatory or inhibitory limbic mechanisms, and this characterological feature of an individual personality is most observable under particular conditions that are appraised to be personally stressful.

The understanding of severe personality disorders (Kernberg, 1984), also known as primitive emotional disorders (Grotstein, 1990a), is an important focus of attention of present day clinical and theoretical psychopathologists. Both borderline and narcissistic personalities experience disordered affects and moods (Hartocollis, 1980). Unregulated shame and socioemotional psychopathology are fundamental clinical attributes of both of these personalities. In the last chapter I began to integrate the developmental ideas outlined throughout this volume into a model of the ontogeny of affect disorders. I now continue to expand the thesis that critical period dyadic failures of affect regulation lie at the core of developmental psychopathology, and apply this principle to the psychobiological etiology of the two major groups of personality disorders.

BORDERLINE PERSONALITY DISORDERS

Borderline personality disorders are clinically defined in terms of socioemotional pathology: an abnormality in maintaining social relationships, and an affective instability manifest in marked shifts from baseline mood to depression that is associated with a tendency to easily slip from a positive or neutral into a negative emotional state (DSM-III-R, American Psychiatric Association, 1987). Diagnostic research reveals that a large number of this group display a major affective disorder (Pope, Jonas, Hudson, Cohen, & Gunderson, 1983). Clinical studies characterize a syndrome-typical "abandonment depression" (Masterson, 1981), and experimental investigations of borderline personalities demonstrate a frequent expression of emotion and depressivity (Sundbom & Kullgren, 1992). An extremely inefficient capacity to regulate shame underlies this affective and characterological disturbance:

> Most of the defensive operations of borderline patients are reactions to their shameful self-consciousness among others. Borderline patients are exquisitely humiliation prone. They have a pronounced tendency to experience others as deliberately inflicting shame on them (Lansky, 1992, p. 37).

Borderline personalities are now being diagnosed in childhood (Cicchetti & Olsen, 1990; Robson, 1982), and throughout the lifespan they manifest "oscillations in attachment" (Melges & Swartz, 1989). Such children frequently present with neuropsychological problems that are associated with difficulties in social interaction and an inability to cope with stress (P. Kernberg, 1989). The deficits of neurocognitive development of these youngsters are identified and catalogued by Palombo (1987; 1993). Pine (1986b) postulates an etiological model of the "borderline-child-to-be," emphasizing a history of stress due to mismatched parenting, the evolution of developmental deficits, and the establishment of inefficient mechanisms for coping which become pathological defenses. The early experience of these children of neglect in the presence of the mother is associated with an inability to regulate an overwhelming "stimulus barage from within," an impaired taming of aggression, and a failure to develop positive self-esteem.

Grotstein (1986, 1987, 1990a) has reported extensive clinical studies of borderline adult patients. Utilizing a multidisciplinary, multilevel approach to interpret clinical data, he concludes that the fundamental pathology of these patients, who frequently manifest some form of neurobiological impairment, traces back to an early preverbal period in which an atmosphere of "mismatch" produces a failure of "good enough attachment and bonding" and "pathological identifications" to compensate for these altered attachments. His etiological speculations involve: . . "A sense of having been imprinted with and therefore bonded to a nonnurturing and / or impinging family environment and to a self that has varyingly modeled to its exigencies" (Grotstein, 1990a, p. 146). As a consequence of an inability to access a normal mother's "rheostat" function to modulate their affective experience, they experience a lifelong heightened vulnerability to shame and an "inability to self-regulate, to receive, encode, and process the data of emotional experience they arc subjected to" (Grotstein, 1990a, p. 157). Grotstein also notes that borderlines are not capable of transforming internal objects into "stable self or object representations" (1987, p. 374).

In a compatible model, Richman and Sokolove (1992) suggest that the etiology of borderline disorders lies in early experiences with a sustaining object that is unavailable. This results in a longstanding severe pathology in the capacity to evoke internalized images or memories as a source of self-soothing in the face of stress. These authors present experimental data that support the idea that borderlines have a deficit of positively toned representations and a developmentally lower capacity for object representations and evocative memory for affective object relationships. In earlier clinical work, Buie and Adler (1982) had proposed that due to a representational deficit, borderline personalities are unable to maintain a "holding introject," a positive internal soothing image of the loving object. Blatt (1991, p. 453) suggests that borderline pathology, manifest in an inability to "sustain an enduring sense of self and a sense of relatedness with significant others during stressful moments," is caused by an impairment of representational evocative memory. In line with all of these models which posit an early experience with a non-regulating primary caregiver, Wilson et al. (1990) report that clinically, borderline disorders present with an internalized representation of a pattern of interaction with a caregiver who manifests affective and self-regulatory limitations.

I understand the core socioaffective pathology of this type of personality disorder to result from a dyadic failure to successfully negotiate late symbiotic and early practicing merger experiences that amplify high arousal positive affect states. Brazelton and Cramer (1990) document that through the 4th month the mother learns how to prolong the baby's positive state, and this "control" gives her a feeling of being in close touch with him. At about 5 months, however, the typical infant "hatches", that is, he shows a new burst of interest in the environment. The fact that this is due to an experience-dependent maturation of the CNS is reflected in the shift in the electroencephalogram that is seen at this very time (Emde, Gaensbauer, & Harmon, 1976). The mother is now not as able to predict her child's behavior, and his increased gaze aversion elicits confusion and negative affect in the caregiver. This interference of the earlier intense reciprocity induce a feeling of being "deserted:"

> The rejection may revive old feelings of inadequacy or desertion from her own past. Such feelings of inadequacy or desertion may lead a mother to withdraw from her baby. . . .A parent who cannot tolerate independence will ignore and override this spurt in development of her baby. A mother with problems in her own life, who is under stress . . . will have difficulty in recognizing this stage of development and will need help in fostering it. If she cannot, the future cost may be great, for the baby will need to rebel or turn away even more forcefully later on. (Brazelton & Cramer, 1990, p. 119)

I suggest that these events describe the seminal pathogenic events of a dyadic matrix for the transmission of borderline disturbances.

Beginning in the symbiotic phase, a significant dyssynchronous disturbance of the dyad occurs when the mother, in a depressed state, is confronted with the stressor of a distressed child. During these incidences her active withdrawal (flight reaction from stress) from the infant is most intense and occurs precipitously and massively. Thus, during periods when the mother experiences a borderline abandonment depression, the borderline mother literally emotionally abandons the child, that is she totally ceases participating in selfobject psychobiologically affect regulating functions. This prevents the child from symbiotically merging with the mother in order to enter into structure-building affect amplifying mirroring experiences. In such a case, the child may direct this attachment need to the father:

> It seems that infants turn to their fathers when their mothers are overanxious or depressed. The infant reacts to the atmosphere of strain created by the mother's excessive anxiety, which the infant experiences as unpleasant and as unresponsive to his needs. The depressed mother is involved with herself, not with her child, leaving the infant feeling empty and dissatisfied. In these circumstances, if the

father is available, the infant turns to him for comfort, security, and pleasure. (Burlingham, 1973, p. 43)

In borderline histories, the father is not emotionally available.

Later in the practicing period the mother lacks empathy with and is therefore hyporesponsive to the infant's high arousal, elated states. Kohut (1984) refers to "the mother whose face does not light up at the sight of her child." (p. 21) Her lack of attunement deflates moments of practicing grandiosity, and this results in a rapidly emerging sense of low self-esteem, an attribute common to borderline personalities (Kernberg, 1975; Masterson, 1981). Indeed, this is further reinforced by her unavailability to upregulate the underaroused toddler who is in a state of shameful despair. It is now thought that the father serves a particularly important role in situations involving a severe empathic failure in the early mother child relationship. In such cases, according to Kohut (1971), the child must turn to him for the mirroring and idealization required for the development of a cohesive self. He reasons that if, in addition to the maternal empathic failure, the child now experiences disappointment in the father, if he or she doesn't find in him a source of reparation of maternally inflicted narcissistic wounds, then a serious disturbance in narcissism and self-pathology will ensue. I concur with this conception, and add that since neither caregiver acts as a psychobiological regulator, the child developing a borderline personality organization does not form a secure attachment to either the mother or the father.

In a longitudinal case study of a borderline boy from infancy through adolescence, Mahler and Kaplan (1977) observed that during the symbiotic period the child "strained away from his mother's body when she held him," and at 12 months, the practicing period, he crawled "rapidly away from the mother." The motive for this may lie in Pine's (1986b) assertion that the borderline child experiences an internal stimulus barage and unmodulated aggression. I suggest that this aggression is reactive to the rejecting mother, and the child attempts to cope with this by avoidant withdrawal from her. This withdrawal may be understood as a means of remaining inactive in order to reduce the disorganizing incoming stimulation. The abandonment depression reflects the infant's entrance into conservation-withdrawal; indeed, abandonment is a trigger for the onset of this state (Powles, 1992).

In Chapter 29 I suggested that an entrance into a state of conservation-withdrawal represents an attempt to cope with a contact-aversive, nonattuning mother, especially when she is expected to be in a state of affective (aggressive) dyscontrol. The infant remains in a parasympathetic-dominant state when apart from the mother; however sympathetic activity, though not as heightened, is simultaneously increased. When in the presence of the stress inducing mother, both trophotropic and ergotropic arousal may become even more intensified, and the resulting arousal level is certainly beyond the infant's regulatory capacities. At reunion, the infant hesitatingly seeks the mother's psychobiological regulation of this highly distressful state. This certainly represents an insecure pattern of attachment, perhaps an insecure-disorganized/ disoriented pattern described by Main and Solomon (1986). These authors observe the following reunion patterns in such high-risk, often abused infants:

> The impression in each case was that approach movements were continually being inhibited and held back through simultaneous activation of avoidant tendencies. In most cases, however, proximity-seeking sufficiently "over-rode" avoidance to permit the increase in physical proximity. Thus, contradictory patterns were activated but were not mutually inhibitory. (p. 117)

Over the course of the practicing period these dyadic experiences are imprinted into the limbic system and produce a permanent uncoupled nonreciprocal mode (Berntson et al., 1991) of autonomic control (see Chapter 25).

Importantly, due to the later maturation of the parasympathetic nervous system and the resultant cognitive advances of the late practicing period, the child's attempts to defensively cope with the stress inducing mother are more complex. With the additional maturation of the ANS, the child can now lock into two distinct, nonoverlapping dissociated psychobiological states of existence. According to Kernberg (1975) a major structural characteristic of the borderline condition is the utilization of "splitting defenses" that allow for the presence of mutually dissociated or split-off ego states. It is now thought that the cognitive preconditions for defensive splitting become established by the time the infant is between 12 and 18 months old (Gergely, 1992). Its function may be to avoid external or internal stimuli that could precipitate an unregulated hyperaroused or hypoaroused state. In a recent model, Cohen and Gara (1992) propose that borderline structure consists of two contrasting and opposing clusters of self. When one is challenged, the other is enacted, thus preventing the onset of severe disorganization. Due to the limitations of this dichotomous structure, the borderline is hesitant to enter into mutualistic, all-positive self states. I conclude that borderlines contain a negatively biased, impoverished lexicon of facial emotions stored in long-term memory representations, thereby producing a constriction of the affect array (Pine, 1980).

Stone (1988) has recently applied psychobiological principles to the understanding of borderline personality disorders. He focuses on the borderline's hyperirritability, a lowered threshold to emotional turbulence, manifested in exaggerated response and chaotic oscillations that promote altered forms of deregulation-regulation. This regulatory disturbance is behaviorally expressed in a "borderline tantrum" or "provocation and crash":

> In the tantrum or provocation-and-crash behavior . . . the response to certain stimuli is not only exaggerated but seems incapable of dying back to the baseline or relaxed level unless spiked still further to the peak or maximum tolerable level for the system. (p. 7)

He continues:

> This excess irritability might stem from a variety of factors, including decreased
> inhibition (viz., failure of frontal lobe dopaminergic tracts to exert their customary
> modulating influence in response to certain stresses) or increased excitability (viz.,
> from activation-states, set abnormally high within memory-modules oversensitized
> by various traumatic experiences in the past). (p. 10)

I suggest that the borderline's "provocation" rage state reflects an orbitofrontal
system that poorly modulates the excitatory ventral tegmental limbic circuit,
while the "crash" of the abandonment depression results from an inability to
regulate lateral tegmental circuit inhibition. The orbitofrontal hierarchical modulation of both circuits is inefficient, and this structural impairment is expressed
in recovery deficits of the repair of hyperaroused and hypoaroused negative
affective states. In support of this, a recent experimental study concludes that
borderlines have difficulty achieving "emotional restitution" and that "during
intense stress, borderline individuals may be unable to access their skills to
psychologically soothe themselves" (Sansone, Fine, & Mulderig, 1991).

As a result of this experience-dependent structural organization, not only
symbolic evocative representations but presymbolic representational capacities,
visuoaffective interactive representations that include face icons of the attuned,
regulating mother, never ontogenetically develop. The borderline's structure has
been characterized as a "stable instability," but when stressed by interactive
experiences that trigger hyperaroused rage or hypoaroused shame/despair, this
individual must rely upon earlier forming, less efficent kinesthetic-tactile representations for internalized affect regulation. Borderline personalities experience
rapidly shifting states, and this state transition may be sudden and traumatic.
Phenomenologically it is experienced as a precipitous entrance into a shame-
associated chaotic state, fascinatingly characterized by Grotstein (1990b, 1991)
as a descent into a "black hole." He suggests that this emotionally catastrophic
state of "nothingness" is usually prevented by self-regulation strategies. Gilbert
(1992b) refers to the patient falling into "the black hole of shame," an overwhelming, paralyzed state in which the mind goes blank, the head goes down,
and the capacity for speech is lost. The difficulty in verbalizing feelings reflects
"a problem of very early schema of the self which formed before language" and
results from "high levels of internal inhibition" (p. 128).

I understand these events to represent a major regulatory failure that triggers a
rapid psychobiological state transition, an implosion—a sudden shift from a
sympathetic high energy state to a parasympathetic low energy state. It is associated with a sudden dramatic shift from extreme hyperactivity to extreme hypoac-
tivity of the orbitofrontal cortex and a consequent loss of regulation of subcortical ergotropic and then trophotropic arousal. According to Grotstein, this clinical phenomenon is associated with a failure of a self-regulation strategy that

usually prevents this rapid state shift. I suggest that this defensive strategy that blocks the hypoactivation of the orbitofrontal cortex is a hyperactivation of the same region, one which is associated with extremely high levels of ergotropic arousal. This excessive hyperactivation is even further heightened by a particular condition that simultaneously triggers elevated sympathetic-ergotropic and parasympathetic-trophotropic arousal—humiliation (see Chapter 15). It is interesting to note that "expressed emotion," the communication of criticism and hostility by family members to chronic psychiatric patients, elicits heightened states of arousal and indeed schizophrenic relapse (Koenigsberg & Handley, 1986). Recent evidence indicates both that elevated activation of the orbital cortex is known to accompany hyperaroused states of pathological anxiety (Johanson et al., 1992; Tucker & Derryberry, 1992), and that hypofrontality is a cardinal finding in schizophrenia (Andreasen et al., 1992; Berman et al., 1992). During elevated states of ergotropic arousal humans experience a contraction and ultimate disappearance of nearby visual space (Fischer, 1971). Indeed, the mental states that occur at the peak of ergotropic and trophotropic arousal have been described as timeless and spaceless. These findings suggest that the state transition of the black hole phenomenon may represent a terrifying portal through which the borderline descends into psychotic states.

Interestingly, significant neurocognitive impairments are found in such patients (Burgess, 1992), and formal neuropsychological evaluations of borderline adults reveal deficits in the right parietal and frontal regions (Grotstein, 1987). The association areas of the parietal cortex are centrally involved in the processing of tactile (cutaneous) and kinesthetic (deep muscle and joint) sensation (Luria, 1980). Parietal areas in the right brain are involved in the maintenance of body image (Joseph, 1992). Orbital neurons receive afferent input from parietal (Cavada & Goldman-Rakic, 1989) areas that provide an image of the position of the body in space with respect to objects in the surrounding space (Hecaen & Albert, 1978). This allows for the prefrontal structure to play an essential role in "recording movements of the visual environment relative to the body" (Mucke et al., 1982). Due to the borderline's less than optimal experiences of maternal contact comfort in the symbiotic period, the growth of interconnections between the parietal and orbitofrontal cortices may be reduced. A stress on this system could produce a "functional disconnection syndrome." A sudden regulatory failure is expressed in an alteration in arousal levels and in a loss of kinesthetic function and thereby of a sense of the position of the body in space. This could produce a state of mental-physical disequilibrium and rapid postural collapse, as if one were rapidly spiraling downward into a black hole. According to Grotstein, (1991), patients suffering from primitive emotional disorders describe this catastrophic experiential phemonenon as "having no floor" and "falling over the abyss into the void." The phenomenological experience of the sympathetic to parasympathetic transition of shame has been described as a "spiraling downward" (Kaufman, 1989) and as a "leakage" through a drain hole in the middle of

one's being (Sartre, 1957). Sartre refers
universe" that leads to the feeling of "an (

NARCISSISTIC PERSON

Self-regulatory failure has also been propos(
er developmental psychiatric syndrome, n;
etiology of which is found specifically in d;
(Schore, 1991). This form of character dis(
present day American culture (Lasch, 1978),
features is essential to an understanding of
Experimental studies have shown that narc _____ ....waio caiivit affective
extremity and mood swings (Emmons, 1987), and mood regulation is excessively dependent upon external circumstances (Bach, 1977). The "affectomotor"
lability of these character disorders has been attributed to a regulatory impairment (Rinsley, 1989). A detailed characterization of the core pathology of these
disorders—an inefficient capacity to regulate narcissistic affect, especially
shame, the keystone affect of narcisssistic disorders—is outlined by this author
in a previous work (Schore, 1991). Developmentally impaired disorders of
"pathological narcissism" (Kernberg, 1975), manifest a pervasive pattern of
grandiosity, lack empathy, have an unreasonable expectation of entitlement, and
react to criticism with rage, shame, or humiliation (DSM-III-R, 1987). Kohut
(1971) notes that the specific pathological affective experiences of narcissistic
disorders "fall into a spectrum ranging from anxious grandiosity and excitement
on the one hand to mild embarassment and self-consciousness or severe shame,
hypochondria, and depression on the other" (p.200).

The fact that these individuals experience the intense positive affects that fuel
grandiose states indicates that, unlike borderlines, they have successfully
dyadically negotiated the symbiotic through early practicing periods. Late practicing shame transactions are central events in narcissistic pathogenesis. In support of this, Mahler and Kaplan (1977) speculate that the etiology of the narcissistic disorder of a 13-year-old girl involved the absence of practicing phase
refueling, and Masterson (1981) points out that narcissistic personalities must be
arrested before the development of the rapprochement crisis, since the deflation
of infantile grandiosity and omnipotence never occurs. The narcissistic state of
consciousness is one of hyperarousal associated with grandiosity (Bach, 1977).

It now appears there there are two classes of narcissistic disororders, an
"egotistical" type and a "dissociative" type (Broucek, 1982). The first form of
narcissistic personality, also described by Gabbard (1989) as the "oblivious
type," is self-absorbed, arrogant and aggressive, unabashedly self-aggrandizing
and attention demanding, insensitive to the reactions of others and overtly imper-
vious to their hurt feelings, and seemingly shameless. However, in response to a
humiliating event the egotistical "shameless" personality:

ealing with a shaming event and may refer to feeling embar-
out strong shame feeling, except for a brief jolt to the self—and
e shame experience by incessant, obsessive ideation about the role of
the shaming event. (Broucek, 1991, p. 7)

this affect cannot be regulated, it is routinely consciously avoided and
bypassed." Narcissistic personalities defend against feelings of self-contempt
and unworthiness by assuming an attitude of grandiosity and entitlement, which
is often accompanied by feelings of elation and contempt for others (Hartocollis,
1980). However, H.B. Lewis (1980) points out that "narcissistic personalities are
clearly suffering from shame and its brittle defense of grandiosity" (p. 63). It is
now thought that the continuous activation of the grandiose self in narcissistic
personalities minimizes the experience of depression (Masterson, 1981; Miller,
1979). Kohut (1978b) describes a personality structure with a poorly integrated grandiose self concept who is most prone to experience shame. Patients
diagnosed with such a disorder are known to experience a depression after a
narcissistic defeat or loss that shows "a predominance of shame over guilt"
(Bach, 1977).

These individual's are quick to experience narcissistic rage in response to a
narcissistic injury. Despite their overt behavior, their exquisite sensitivity to
humiliation may recapitulate early experience; clinical studies have suggested
that narcissistic personalities present a background with a parent who humiliates
the child "by harsh, continual, or massive exposure" (Johnson, 1987, p. 31).
Weil (1978) points out that maternal shame and rejection results in a particularly
hostile object relationship. This "shame-rage" or "humiliated fury" (H. B.
Lewis, 1985) or "self-righteous rage" (Horowitz, 1981) or "helpless rage" is
proposed to represent a shame-typical increase of parasympathetic limbic activity, but instead of a reduction of sympathetic excitation there is a contemporaneous unmodulated overexcited sympathetic ergotropic hyperarousal.

If shame dysregulation leads to heightened experiences of bypassed shame in
the egotistical narcissist, a vulnerability to overt shame characterizes the dissociative narcissist. This personality organization, also referred to as a "hyper-
vigilant type" (Gabbard, 1989), manifests low self-esteem, rejection sensitivity,
diminished energy and vitality, and is inhibited, shy, self-effacing, and avoids
being the center of attention. Consciously expressed self-devaluation exists side
by side with a subtle form of superiority and entitlement (Broucek, 1991).

These two personality types may evolve from different practicing dyadic
experiences and represent distinct psychobiological organizations. Spitz (1965)
describes a specific "wrong kind of mothering" dispensed by a narcissistic insecure mother who is concerned more with her own emotional needs than her
infant's. This type of "psychotoxic" maternal care is "the diametrical opposite of
emotional deprivation, namely a surfeit, an overdose of affective stimulation" (p.
753). Psychological studies have shown that overstimulation tends to be even

more aversive than understimulation (Goldberger, 1982). Regarding the egotistical personality type, Broucek (1991) offers the hypothesis that:

> Such individuals often are reared by "adoring," doting, narcissistically disturbed parents who have objectified the child and through their adoring gaze have projected onto the child aspects of their own idealized self; these parents have not only failed to find adequate support for the child's true sense of self but have also failed to provide enough realistic positive and negative evaluation to support some degree of tension between the actual self and the idealized self. (p. 60)

In a carefully documented single case study of pathological narcissism in childhood, Egan and Kernberg (1984) describe a boy who saw himself as "the center of the universe," with his parents "circling around him." The mother focused her own narcissism on her son, whom she viewed as "her appendage," and neither parent confronted nor disciplined the child. Although the mother was intrusive, controlling, and injurious to her son's self-esteem, she "could not tolerate it when he was sad" (p. 59).

I offer the following characterization of the critical practicing period interactive dynamics that shape this type of personality organization. This mother may successfully coordinate her needs and the childs' in the symbiotic phase, but as separation-individuation begins in the practicing period this may no longer occur. Rinsley (1989) points out that the mother of the narcissist rewards the child's growth toward separation-individuation, "but only and ultimately in relation to herself." When the child is in a grandiose state, mirroring of her narcissism, the mother is emotionally accessible, but may do little to modulate the positive hyperaroused state. On the other hand, when the infant is in a negative hyperaroused state, such as aggressive separation protest, she either fails to modulate it (in herself or in her child) or even hyperstimulates the infant into a state of dyscontrol. Most importantly, she can not attune to low arousal shame states in herself or in her child. The primary caregiver is therefore remarkably ineffective in regulating the infant up out of hypoaroused states that she herself triggers, such as occur in maternal shame-stress depletion of narcissistic affect. The observation that inconsistent attunement is an important element in the etiology of narcissistic disorders was first made by Kohut (1977). In a clinical reconstruction of a narcissistic patient's early history, he notes:

> On innumerable occasions she appeared to have been totally absorbed in the child—overcaressing him, completely in tune with every nuance of his needs and wishes—only to withdraw from him suddenly, either by turning her attention totally to other interests or by grossly or grotesquely misunderstanding his needs and wishes. (p. 52)

Thus, after a shame induced infant-caregiver misattunement, the infant too frequently encounters at reunion a narcissistically injured, aggressively teasing, and humiliating mother who rather than decreasing shame distress hyperstimulates the child into an agitated state of narcissistic rage. No caregiver acts to modulate shame, and this prevents the internalization and organization of a shame regulatory system in the child that can reduce hyperstimulated states and allow for recovery from hypostimulated states. The inner experience of the low arousal affect of shame therefore becomes associated with an expectation of a painful self-disorganizing internal state which can not be regulated, and therefore is consciously avoided or bypassed. Tomkins (1987) refers to:

> the paradox of one part of the self performing psychic surgery on another part of the self, so that the self which feels ashamed is totally and permanently split off and rejected by a judging self that has no tolerance for its more humble and hesitant self. (p. 152)

The caregiver's incapacity to mediate psychobiological state transitions in herself and her infant leads to a personality in which "haughty grandiosity, shyness, and feelings of inferiority (shame) may coexist without affecting each other" (Kernberg, 1975, p. 265). Recent social psychological research corroborates this; an experimental analysis of conceited, self-indulgent narcissistic personalities reveals a grandiosity-exhibitionism factor and a vulnerability-sensitivity factor (Wink, 1991). Grandiose and omnipotent fantasies allow these indiduals to maintain the illusion that they need nothing from others, that they can provide the source of their own emotional sustenance (Modell, 1975). This can only be done if shame is not admitted into consciousness, since shame, according to Sartre (1957), reveals that "I need the mediation of the Other in order to be what I am" (p. 288). Developmentally disordered narcissistic personalities, having had early experiences with an inefficient selfobject that impaired the development of affect autoregulation, continually deny their intense need for external selfobject regulation.

The early experience of the egotistical narcissistic personality is one of insecure-resistant attachment. The dyadic description offered by Gaensbauer and Mrazek (1981) in Chapter 29 represents a typical reunion transaction that generates future narcissistic pathology. In practicing transactions, this infant experiences prolonged states of unregulated hyperactivation of the ventral tegmental limbic circuit. Although the mother offers high arousal affective stimulation, she does not sensitively reduce this when the child disengages to gaze avert in order to modulate supra-heightened levels of arousal. She also is ineffective in limit setting, aggression socialization, and regulated shame induction. As a result of these critical period events, the maturing psychobiological affective core of this type of infant becomes sympathetically biased. In dealing with affective transactions, the emerging narcissistic personality tends to utilize physiologically heightened levels of arousal. This autonomic bias toward ergotropic arousal also accounts for the observed relationship between narcissism and sensation seeking

(Emmons, 1981). Since the practicing mother doesn't down regulate the toddler's hypersympathetic state the child does not evolve a reciprocal mode of autonomic control (Berntson et al., 1991). Rather this personality structure only has access to a coupled nonreciprocal mode; under stress there are concurrent increases in both the sympathetic and parasympathetic divisions. This orbitofrontal single circuit dominated organization cannot shift out of or reduce sympathetic activation when the parasympathetic component is activated. The result is an underregulation disturbance.

The dissociative narcissist, on the other hand, evolves an overregulation disturbance out of a practicing period avoidant attachment. The depressed, hypoarousing mother does not continue to provide sufficient positive vitality affects in mirroring transactions, nor shame recovery that reactivates the ventral tegmental circuit. This accounts for the low self-esteem and diminished energy and vitality of the dissociative narcissist. This individual is characterized by a parasympathetically-dominant limbic system, and an inability to adaptively shift out of low arousal shame states. As a result he or she is inhibited, shy, and avoids attention. The result is a "passive" narcissistic personality whose grandiosity is concealed behind a facade of shyness and compliance.

Both of these narcissistic types suffer from a developmental arrest of narcissism regulation that occurs specifically at rapprochement onset, and this is due to the failure to evolve a practicing affect regulatory system which can neutralize grandiosity, regulate practicing excitement, or modulate narcissistic distress. In early development caregivers serve as selfobjects, specifically to perform psychological functions "such as tension management and self-esteem regulation that the infant is unable to perform for himself" (Glassman, 1988, p. 601). It is now thought that selfobjects function as psychobiological regulators (Taylor, 1987), and this involves regulation of the immature functions of both the sympathetic and parasympathetic components of the ANS. These selfobject functions are specifically and exclusively unconscious, nonverbal, affect regulatory functions which stabilize self-structure against the hyperstimulated-explosive fragmenting or hypostimulated-implosive depleting potential of stressful levels of stimulation and affect. As mentioned earlier, if the child can not find such functions in the mother but can in the father, the pathogenesis may be somewhat ameliorated. Equally well, as Lansky (1992) demonstrates, a distant or humiliating father could exacerbate negative development.

An effective dual circuit orbitofrontal structural system to autoregulate mood and narcissistic affects, which is required for self-esteem homeostasis and for restoration and recovery of narcissistic equilibrium subsequent to affective stress and narcissistic injury, never ontogenetically evolves in either of the narcissistic personalities. Unlike borderline personalities, these individuals can access presymbolic representational capacities, but like the other group of primitive personality disorders, they do not evolve a capacity to access the symbolic representations that encode the reparative functions of evocative memory. These developmental phenomena may underlie Auerbach's (1990) contention that narcissistic personalities manifest a disturbance in the representation of self and of the relationship of self to others. The limitations of their regulatory capacities are summarized by Robbins (1993):

> With the the assistance of a symbiotic object, narcissistic personalities are able to maintain inner states of tension regulation, dependent satisfaction, and archaic self-esteem; they can approximate stable structures, defined as functions with a slow rate of change, and achieve rudimentary representational constancy. Sensorimotor-affective thinking is less pronounced than in borderlines, and as a result, impulse control tends to be better. Like borderlines, however, they cannot represent, sustain, and control basic affects such as love and rage. (p. 293)

The essential psychological lesion in these individuals is that they do not have the capacity to tolerate or recover from narcissistic injuries which expose distressing negative affect, especially hyperaroused affects like narcissistic rage and hypoaroused shame, while maintaining constructive engagement with others. The coping ability to affectively reconnect with an emotionally significant other after a shame-stress separation, and indeed to use the other to recover from shame associated narcissistic injury and object loss, has never effectively developed in these personality structures due to their early practicing experiences. Shame involves "awareness that one is in great danger of isolation, alienation, stigmatization, and ostracism from beneficent objects whose values and nurture are needs throughout the course of one's lifetime" (Grotstein, 1987, p. 355). The enduring presence of unregulated shame, either conscious or unconscious, leads to a resignation that one's defects are permanent and forever unalterable. Narcissistic disorders are thus disorders of the regulation of narcissistic affect, especially shame, the central affective experience of narcissism (Broucek, 1982; Kinston, 1983; A.P. Morrison, 1989), and their pathology is most observable during times of stress of narcissistic affect.

Despite this inefficient capacity to autoregulate distress, during periods of stress, when it may be more adaptive to communicate one's disorganized affective state to a significant other, they emotionally withdraw from object relations in order to protect against the unconsciously anticipated painful exposure of shame. Shame-prone narcissistic personalities are known to suffer from narcissistic injury triggered overwhelming internal self-shaming tendencies (A.P. Morrison, 1984) and repetitive oscillations of self-esteem, which necessitate "endless attempts at repair" (Reich, 1960). Bursten (1973) notes the task of the narcissistic repair mechanism is to rid the self of shame, an affect state which tends to linger for quite a long time until the subject recovers (Nathanson, 1987a), and which spreads out from one specific content to all of "inner reality" and thereby to the entire function of expressing oneself (Wurmser, 1981). When a narcissistically undesirable trait is suddenly exposed (to the self and/or the other), an uncontrolled escalating shame reaction occurs, and there is no adequate affect regulating mechanism for the personality to use to modulate or recover from this painful affective state. Without a system to actively cope with and thereby tolerate this potent affect, the immature, undeveloped, primitive narcissistic personalities avoids risk experiences which are potential points of shameful selfexposure.

SUMMARY

The two main groups of developmental personality disorders both share a common core pathology of a deficit in affect regulation. This dysfunction is most observable during socioemotional stress, and the adaptive limitations of a less than fully evolved limbic system are manifest in an inefficient capacity to flexibly cope with and then to recover from such stress. Because both borderline and narcissistic personality organizations do not developmentally evolve a dual circuit orbitofrontal system, neither has access to symbolic representations that can perform the important self-soothing, reparative functions encoded in evocative memory. They can not execute a reciprocal mode of autonomic control, an adaptive shift in the relative dominance of the two divisions of the autonomic nervous system that mediate emotional processes. Rather, due to a preponderance of shame-imprinted interactive representations of the self-in-interaction-with-a-misattuned-other, their ability to autoregulate affect is fundamentally impaired. Both of these primitive emotional disorders are particularly ineffective in regulating shame.

Up until recently a clear and comprehensible differentiation between these disorders has been difficult. This is due to the fact that most clinicians have focused on overtly expressed symptomatology and most theoreticians have speculated on internal structural dynamics, especially the cognitive aspects, of their intrapsychic functions. I suggest that a developmental perspective, especially of the dissociable interactive dyadic socioaffective conditions that contribute to their separate pathogenetic histories, is a powerful tool toward more deeply understanding the unique attributes and the essential biopsychopathology of these disorders. The dyadic dysjunctions between the caregiver and borderline-child-to-be are already apparent in the first 6 months, and this failure of the pair to traverse the challenges of the symbiotic period is manifest in their inability to form an affect communicating system. As a result, the dyad does not enter into cooperative and mutually attuned merger experiences that generate vitality affects which induce structural growth. Due to the primary caregiver's severely limited capacity to act as a selfobject, a psychobiological regulator of the infant's maturing nervous system, the attachment system poorly forms. This represents a deprivation of conditions that are necessary for the experience-dependent maturation of a frontolimbic system, and the result is a corticolimbic structure that can only utilize an uncoupled nonreciprocal mode of autonomic control, and thereby poorly regulate subcortical limbic activity. This develomental structural defect becomes permanent by the middle of the second year and is responsible for the later socioaffective impairments of borderline personalities.

On the other hand, narcissistic organizations signify a fairly successful dyadic adaptation through most of the first year. The crucial pathogenetic events of these disorders are played out in the practicing period, especially in affect transacting reunions that follow stressful inceptive separations within the dyad. Due to psychobiological regulatory failures the high levels of positive affect that fuel grandiose states are either underregulated or overregulated. An insecure-resistant attachment interaction is a source generator of egotistical narcissistic personalities who possess a sympathetic-dominant limbic system, while an insecure-avoidant one engenders dissociative narcissistic personalities who access parasympathetic-dominant autonomic nervous systems. Both contain a single circuit dominant orbitofrontal cortex that utilizes a coupled nonreciprocal mode of autonomic control, but the ventral tegmental limbic circuit dominates in the former, the lateral tegmental in the later. Both use presymbolic representations to regulate affect, and are therefore inefficient in psychobiologically switching off one curcuit and switching on the other, and both show recovery deficits. Neither can effectively regulate shame, and this is expressed in the enduring presence of unconscious bypassed shame in the former and conscious shame in the latter.

32

Vulnerability to Psychosomatic Disease

Psychobiological research and observational studies of infants are confirming that deficiencies in early object relationships result in developmental defects which reduce the individual's capacity to self-regulate essential psychobiological functions, thereby predisposing the individual to bodily disease.

—Graeme J. Taylor (1987)

[S]ocial relationships, or the relative lack thereof, constitute a major risk factor for health—rivaling the effects of well-established health risk factors such as cigarette smoking, blood pressure, blood lipids, obesity, and physical activity.

—James S. Howe, Karl R. Landis, and Debra Umberson (1988)

In the last chapter I discussed the interactive genesis of developmental psychopathology, specifically the early dyadic experiences that engender limitations of affect regulation in certain personality disorders. It has been known for some time that under stress these primitive disorders tend to exhibit psychosomatic illnesses. Almost 40 years ago, Schur (1955) proposed a theory of affect development in which he argued that the physiological responses that characterize infant states are progressively desomatized and replaced by more symbolic processes. When stressed, certain personalities regress to this undifferentiated "psychosomatic" phase of development, and these psychosomatic regressions were called "borderline states."

At the beginning of this volume I put forth the general principle that early regulatory experiences permanently influence the vulnerability of the individual to future pathologies. This refers to both psychological *and* physiological pathol-

431

ogy, that is, to alterations of mental and physical well being. The artificial distinction between psychological and organic pathology may have helped to classify diagnostic categories on the basis of overt discrete syndrome presentations, but it has, at the same time, seriously impeded a deeper appreciation of their covert causal mechanisms. The concept of disease has been a particularly difficult problem for psychiatry (Hafner, 1987), since an adequate definition of illness is a prerequisite to an elucidation of the concept of mental illness (Kendell, 1975). Towards this end, the theoretical understanding of disease processes is currently undergoing a revolutionary reconceptualization. In groundbreaking work on the psychobiology of disease, Weiner (1977, 1989) defines illness as an impairment or disorder in communication networks that is characterized by a disturbance in their regulation. Chrousos and Gold (1992) are now proposing that human disease states fundamentally involve a dysregulation of stress systems.

In this chapter I integrate current exciting advances in developmental psychobiology and psychoneuroimmunology—the study of the interactions among behavior, neural and endocrine function, and immune processes—with developmental psychoanalytic concepts of affect regulation in order to present a model of the dyadic etiology of a vulnerability to psychosomatic disease.

THE DEVELOPMENT OF PSYCHOSOCIAL-NEUROENDOCRINE-IMMUNE COMMUNICATIONS

In any discussion of the proximal causes of psychologically-induced impairments of organ function it is important to emphasize that in early development the functioning of the infant's immature organ systems is externally regulated by the mother. The mother's support of certain essential life-sustaining functions is so critical that the early infant has been referred to as an "external fetus" (Bostock, 1962). For example, her involvement is central to processes as basic as the infant's fluid balance regulation (Almroth, 1978) and temperature regulation (Schwartz & Rosenblum, 1983), life-sustaining functions that ultimately become autoregulated. From the moment of birth she also directly regulates the child's immune system, thereby serving as a protector against microbiological pathogenic agents that enter the infant's body. For some time into the postnatal period the infant's immature immune system cannot yet synthesize functional humoral antibodies and immunoglobulins in response to pathogens. Yet, in mammals, an evolutonary mechanism exists for such a critical purpose—these agents that confer resistance to disease are provided by the mother in breast feeding experiences. Human milk, for example, kills parasitic intestinal protozoa that cause enteric disease in children (Gillin & Reiner, 1983). Tronick, Winn, and Morelli (1985) describe this external regulatory phenomenon:

> Colostrum and following it mature milk. . . .provide cellular and humoral anti-pathogenic agents along with specific protective factors to the infant. The cellular components found in colostrum and milk include macrophages, lymphocytes, neutrophils, and other cells. (p. 300)

Head and Beer (1978) postulate that lymphocytes are incorporated into the suckling's tissues from maternal mammary exosecretions, and Lawrence (1980) suggests that maternal T and B lymphocytes induce immunological tolerance in the neonate.

The mother's essential external regulation of her child's developing immunological system continues as attachment systems form in later infancy, but now it may involve a different psychobiological mechanism. Attachment bonds fundamentally regulate physiological systems, and separations represent a loss of the mother's regulatory functions. Developmental psychobiological studies on early experience and immunity reveal that tactile stimulation during the preweaning period increases the antibody response (Solomon, Levine, & Kraft, 1968), and that animals handled in the neonatal period show an enhanced antibody response in adulthood (Raymond, Reyes, Tokuda, & Jones, 1986). Conversely, maternal deprivation before weaning is associated with lowered adult levels of immunoglobulins (Michaut et al., 1981). Primate studies show that mother-infant separations produce a suppression of cellular immune responses in the child (Laudenslager, Reite, & Harbeck, 1982). Specific psychobiological alterations in infant immune responses that are consequences of early maternal separation have been also reported by Coe, Wiener, Rosenberg, and Levine (1985). These authors observe that the stressful loss of the mother's modulating function elicits decreases in immunoglobulins and antibodies, and that this is accompanied by sustained pituitary-adrenal activation. The latter neuroendocrinological responses are specifically reflected in altered ACTH and elevated cortisol levels.

The co-alteration of both developing immune and developing neuroendocrine functions that results from a loss of external regulation in an early critical period is an important finding, since it may reveal clues as to how early experiences permanently influence the organism's invulnerability/vulnerability to psychophysiologically-altering pathology throughout the rest of the lifespan. Within the framework of dyadic affect communication, the primary caregiver's mature autonomic nervous system's neuroendocrine functions come to regulate the child's immature, developing immune system. Hofer (1984a) demonstrates that in early infancy the mother regulates the infant's developing autonomic nervous system. In this same period of infancy the maturation of the autonomic innervation of the organs of the immune system, the thymus, lymph nodes, and spleen, are taking place (Felten, Felten, Madden, Ackerman, & Bellinger, 1989). Infancy thus represents a critical period during which known bidirectional communications between the neuroendocrine and immune systems (Blalock, 1989) originate. Blalock and others are now laying the foundations of the new scientific discipline of neuroimmunoendocrinology. It is now recognized that both systems contain and use an identical set of signal molecules, (hormones, lymphokines, and monokines) for inter- and intrasystem communication and regulation. This biochemical integration of neuroendocrine and immune system circuits by common receptors and ligands allows for a "cross talk."

For example, T lymphocytes, which originate and mature in the thymus, destroy host cells with altered (or "nonself") surfaces and regulate immune reactions. They release the lymphokines interleukin and interferon, and both of these products of the immune system directly influence the neuroendocrine activity of the hypothalamo-pituitary-adrenal axis. Both elevate adrenal glucocorticoid levels (Besedovsky, Del Rey, & Sorkin, 1981; Lotze et al., 1985; Roosth, Pollard, Brown, & Meyer, 1986). Interleukin also activates hypothalamic corticotropin releasing factor (CRF), produced by hypothalamic paraventricular neurosecretory neurons (Berkenbosch et al., 1987; Sapolsky et al., 1987; Suda, Tozawa, Ushiyama et al., 1990). Receptors for interleukin are found in the human hypothalamus (Breder, Dinarello, & Saper, 1988). It also acts on pituitary cells (Bernton et al., 1987) to stimulate the release of ACTH and endorphins (Kehrer, Gaillard, Dayer, & Muller, 1986; Uehara, Gottschall, Dahl, & Arimura, 1987; Woloski et al., 1985).

Conversely, neuroendocrine hormones effect immunoregulatory functions. Glucocorticoids influence the immune response (Cohen & Crnic, 1982; Cupps & Fauci, 1982) and inhibit lymphokine synthesis (Wahl, Altman, & Rosenstreich, 1975). ACTH (Alvarez-Mon, Kehrl, & Fauci, 1985) and the opioid peptide beta endorphin modulate immune system activity (Brown & Van Epps, 1986; Gilman et al., 1982; Heijnen & Ballieux, 1986; Saland, Van Epps, Ortiz, & Samora, 1983). Lymphocytes contain receptors for both ACTH (Smith, Brosnan, Meyer, & Blalock, 1987) and beta endorphin (Hazum, Chang, & Cuatrecasas, 1979; Lopkor, Abood, Hass, & Lionetti, 1980). In addition, these cells also have receptors that bind monoamines, including circulating norepinephrine that is released by the sympathoadrenomedullary system (Hadden, Hadden, & Middleton, 1970).

On the basis of such phenomena, Blalock (1989) deduces that:

> the immune system may sense stimuli that are not recognized by the central and peripheral nervous systems. These stimuli have been termed noncognitive and include those things (i.e., bacteria, tumors, viruses, antigens, etc.) that would go unnoticed were it not for their recognition by the immune system. The recognition of such noncognitive stimuli by immunocytes is then converted into information, in the form of peptide hormones, lymphokines, and monokines, that is conveyed to the neuroendocrine system, and a physiological change occurs. Contrariwise, central and peripheral nervous system recognition of cognitive stimuli results in similar hormonal information conveyed to and recognized by hormone receptors on immunocytes and an immunologic change occurs. (p. 25)

Blalock's first point represents a bio-psychological mechanism by which bacterial and viral agents induce psychophysiological changes. Pathogens trigger the release of lymphokines by lymphocytes, and these in turn alter the activities of the hypothalamico-pituitary-adrenocortical and sympathoadrenomedullary activities of the ANS. This influences the communication between these components and between this subcortical system and the higher frontolimbic structures that connect into them. Right hemispheric cortical processes which are directly influenced by this subcortical component of the limbic system would especially be affected. As a result affective changes occur in response to these pathogens. For example, viral invasion of limbic structures (including the orbitofrontal cortex; Valenstein & Heilman, 1979), such as in encephalitis (Damasio & Van Hoesen, 1985) produces short-term deficits in memory and affect, and long-term defects in the form of personality change (Bannister, 1978).

Blalock's second proposal also has significant explanatory power and far-reaching ramifications. Cognitive stimuli recognized and processed by the central and peripheral (autonomic) nervous systems elicit hormonal changes. As mentioned earlier, the neuroendocrine system is a hierarchy with higher centers regulating lower ones (Brownstein, 1989). These higher centers reside in the cortex, the site where cognitive stimuli are processed. There is now extensive evidence that the cerebral cortex modulates immune functions (Neveu, 1988), specifically influencing the proliferation of lymphocytes (Neveu et al., 1986) and the activity of the mononuclear phagocytic system (Neveu et al., 1989). Neveu (1992) reports that the right hemisphere and not the left increases T lymphocyte cell functions. In fact, this group of researchers concludes that the immunomodulatory functions of the cortex depend upon the specific regions within the right cortex (Barneoud, Neveu, Vitiello, & LeMoal, 1987). Socioaffective stimuli are processed by the right hemisphere, which also regulates cortisol secretion in response to emotion-related situations (Wittling & Pfluger, 1990). Such hierarchical alterations in neuropeptides and corticosteroids in the brain circulation act on cells of the immune system, cells which travel in this vascular system. The changes in these neuroendocrine agents are sensed by local immunocytes, and this leads to an activation (or inactivation) of their unique self-protective functions. This conception fits well with the long established findings that a variety of psychological and environmental perturbations can affect the immune system (Coe et al., 1985) and that psychosocial context is a powerful determinant of immune reactions (Ader, 1981; Geiser, 1989).

A fundamental tenet of the emerging discipline of psychoneuroimmunology is that immune reactions occur within an internal neuroendocrine milieu that is sensitive to the organism's perception of and adaptation to events occurring in its external environment (Ader & Cohen, 1993). I suggest that the most potent of these environmental events are emotional transactions, and that Blalock's "cognitive stimuli" are specifically stimuli emanating from the emotionally expressive faces of other humans. More properly, they are right hemispheric cognitive-affective representations that are triggered by changes in socioaffective stimuli. In the earliest periods of an individual's life the emotionally expressive face of the mother is the predominant cognitive (-affective) stimulus. I have earlier shown that the multimodal socioemotional information that emanates from her face is integrated with information regarding the internal endocrine environment at the level of the orbitofrontal cortex. Frontocorticolimbic activation elicits biochemical changes in the parasympathetic lateral tegmental and sympathetic ventral tegmental limbic circuits. Such information is delivered from the orbit-ofrontal cortex directly to the hypothalamus, the major subcortical center which regulates the parasympathetic and sympathetic components of the ANS. Changes in hypothalamic neuroendocrinolgy then influence the secretory output of the adrenal and pituitary systems, and this in turn is sensed by receptors on the surface of cells of the immune system. Indeed, stimulation of hypothalamic areas increases anitbody levels (Besedovsky, Sorkin, Felix, & Haas, 1977; Fessel & Forsyth, 1963), and hypothalamic neuronal activity is observed to increase si-multaneously with spleen antibody synthesis (Besedovsky & Sorkin, 1977).

Felten et al. (1989) refer to "an integrated circuitry of cerebral cortex, limbic forebrain, hypothalamus and brain stem autonomic nuclei that can modulate immune reactivity in the periphery" (p. 382). The experience-dependent final wiring of the two limbic circuits occurs in the second year, and this is expressed in the maturation of direct orbitofrontal connections with the hypothalamus. An impairment of cortical structures that regulate the hypothalamus will have pro-found effects on not only mental but physical health, since the hypothalamus, a structure that regulates essential organismic functions, contains a direct pathway to the brain immune system that is influenced by emotional stress (Stein, Schia-vi, & Luparello, 1969). Lesions of the hypothalamus produce a disruption of T-cell immunity responses (Jankovic & Isakovic, 1973), a suppression of lym-phocyte stimulation (Keller et al., 1980) and antibody production (Korneva & Khai, 1964), and a decreased phagocytic activity of the reticuloendothelial sys-tem (Lambert, Harell, & Achterberg, 1981). Certain prefrontal lesions produce massive hypertrophy of the thymus and lymph nodes (Messimy, 1939).

MATERNAL PSYCHOBIOLOGICAL REGULATION AND THE DEVELOPMENT OF ADEQUATE AND INADEQUATE IMMUNOCOMPETENCE

What can be said of the origins of autoregulated psychoneuroimmunoen-docrinological function? The infant's attachment relationship with the mother permanently influences the development of the individual's future immune ca-pacities. The mother's affect regulating function during periods of infant distress is important, especially in light of the fact that early affective experiences are highly somatized (Krystal, 1974). This distress is biochemically expressed in heightened levels of circulating stress hormones, ACTH and corticosteroids, and diminished levels of endorphins. As mentioned earlier, the infant's glucocor-ticoid stress response is modulated by maternal cues (Stanton & Levine, 1990). The mother's regulating function allows for a rapid return of corticosteroids to baseline levels and a re-elevation of endorphin levels. The changes in the con-centrations of these hormonal agents are sensed by immunocytes, and the re-instigation of her regulatory functions after an emotional separation would terminate the suppression of the child's immune response. For example, beta endorphin enhances the generation of cytoxic T cells (Carr & Klimpel, 1986) and the lymphocyte proliferative response (Gilman et al., 1982), and augments the cytolytic activity and interferon products of natural killer cells (Mandler, Biddison, Mandler, & Serrate, 1986; Mathews, Froelich, Sibbitt, & Bankhurst, 1983). According to Weiner disease represents disturbed regulation. The mother's socioaffective response to the child's distress restores this regulation by directly influencing the infant's immune system. Indeed, the hormonal changes she induces as a result of her psychological interaction with her infant are the same ones that trigger his developing immunocompetence. These early regulatory events may provide an important context for the "conditioned modulation of immunity" (Ader & Cohen, 1993), and may contribute to the development of self-efficacy in coping with stressors on the immune system (Wiedenfeld et al., 1990).

This dyadic psychobiological mechanism ties together the child's adaptive recovery after "physical disease" to his adaptive recovery after "psychological disturbance." I have earlier presented arguments to show that dyadic reparative socioaffective transactions which provide comfort and arousal regulation in the short term, facilitate the creation of an autoregulatory recovery capacity to cope with future socioaffective stress in the long term. This coping mechanism includes the immunologically adaptive responses to the psychophysiological consequences of emotionally stressful stimuli. Neuroendocrine factors such as endorphins and cortisol also influence the growth of the neuronal components of developing limbic circuits during critical periods. Structurally, this is expressed in the growth of orbitofrontal connections with the hypothalamus, a linkage that occurs during the sensitive period for the development of social responses. The neuroendocrine output of the hypothalamus in turn influences the postnatal growth of brain stem and peripheral structures that innervate the thymus, lymph nodes, and spleen. This provides for a network which can communicate cortically processed information to subcortical and then to peripheral structures, thereby regulating the activity of such structures. In such a manner, complex, symbolic representations of the external world regulate alterations in neuroendocrine systems that affect the immune system. Information can also travel from the periphery to subcortical sites and back up to the cortex. The final maturation of cortical-neuroendocrine-immune connections allows for a system of bidirectional communication. This hierarchical conception of the nervous system is similar to the one proposed by Hughlings Jackson in the last century.

I suggest that Weiner's concept of disease specifically refers to an impairment of communication in this particular hierarchical network that causes a disturbance of organismic regulatory processes. This model has implications for the development of inadequate or limited recovery systems, and for the etiology of psychosomatic disorders. Many of the classical psychosomatic diseases involve autoimmune phenomena in their etiology (Geschwind & Behan, 1982; Solomon,

Amkraut, & Kaspar, 1974). I have earlier argued that the fundamental deficit of psychological disorders is an inefficient capacity to recover from a psychobiological stressor. Similarly, the core deficit of autoimmune-associated psychosomatic disorders is an inefficiency of immune functions to recover from a psychobiological stressor. In both, a *stressor* is any environmental perturbation that disrupts homeostasis, while the *stress response* is the set of neural and endocrine adaptations that are utilized to restore homeostasis. The inefficency of a mechanism to restore regulation is a common factor to all illness. Ader (1992) now refers to the "dysregulated immune system" of individuals with autoimmune disease, and advances the idea that autoimmune disease constitues a model in which to explore the role of learning in the maintenance of homeostasis.

What kind of early psychobiologically misattuned dyadic transactions might be involved in the genesis of psychosomatic diseases? Almost 50 years ago Spitz (1946) showed that infants suffering from hospitalism continued to demonstrate irreparable psychosomatic damage and a serious decreased resistance to disease. I suggest that if during early critical periods the mother does not supply, or only inconsistently supplies, regulatory, selfobject functions, the structurally organizing immune system will develop in a growth inhibiting environment. According to Reite and Capitanio (1985) disruptions in attachment are accompanied by hypothalamic dysfunction and disturbances in limbic activity are reflected in altered regulation of hypothalamic activity. Prolonged separations elicit a condition of passive coping in the infant. During this state of conservation-withdrawal activity level is decreased, pituitary adrenocorticotropin and adrenal cortical secretions are elevated, and the immune response is suppressed (Field & Reite, 1985). Thus, deprivation of maternal regulatory stress modulation leads to an exaggerated and prolonged release of ACTH and corticosteroids in the circulation, and such elevations would also be sensed by the immunocytic receptors for these hormones. Social isolation, the early deprivation of empathic care, causes a permanent reduction of brain opiate receptors (Bonnet, Hiller, & Simon, 1976), and this may include the opiate receptors on immunocytes of the brain circulation. As opposed to endorphin effects, ACTH suppresses interferon (Johnson et al., 1984) and glucocorticoids inhibit lymphokine production (Wahl, Altman, & Greengard, 1975). Continual high levels of corticosteroids decrease the circulating lymphocyte count and the size of the thymus and lymph nodes by inhibiting lymphocyte mitotic activity and increasing lymphocyte destruction (Ganong, 1973). Thymic involution is of course a hallmark of Selye's (1956) stress response. Very recent work shows that maturing lymphocytes in the thymus are induced to die by corticosteroid hormones secreted by the adrenal gland (Compton & Cidlowski, 1987; Raff, 1992). In developmental research, Coe et al. (1985) conclude: "Although the acute adrenal response may be adaptive for the separated infant, we have found that prolonged cortisol elevations induced by sustained separations can adversely affect the immune system" (p. 183).

What's more, these adverse effects may be permanent, and in future stressful situations limitations of immune responses may be evident. This may result from the effects of long-enduring elevated levels of glucocorticoids on the development of limbic circuits during their critical period of growth. Chronically elevated glucocorticoids disrupt cerebral energy metabolism (Sapolsky, 1987), and extended glucocorticoid exposure selectively causes neuronal cell death in "affective centers" in the limbic system (Kathol, Jaeckle, Lopez, & Meller, 1989). Glucocorticoids also are known to induce apoptotic cell death in lymphocytes (Compton & Cidlowski, 1986) and thymocytes (Wyllie, 1980). As mentioned previously, during infancy, increased corticosteroid concentrations in the circulation permanently reduce postnatal brain growth and produce functional impairments of the directing of emotion into adaptive channels. Such impaired capacities include psychoneuroimmunological responses to future psychosocial stressors. The course of autoimmune disorders is highly sensitive to such stressors, and T cell regulatory disturbances are seen in such autoimmune disorders as rheumatoid arthritis (Emery et al., 1987), multiple sclerosis (Rose et al., 1985), and systemic lupus erythematosus (Morimoto et al., 1980).

Practicing period events may thus significantly contribute to a vulnerability to later depression, which is known to adversely affect immune system function (Farrant & Perez, 1989). Depressed lymphocyte function typically occurs after bereavement (Bartrop et al., 1977), a time when plasma cortisol is elevated (Calabrese, Kling, & Gold, 1987) and the activity of natural killer cells is impaired (Irwin et al., 1987). The capacity to mount an immunocompetent defense against this stress is an essential component of the ability to recover from the psychophysiological disequilibrium caused by this stress. Depressive patients, who frequently develop psychosomatic illnesses in response to such a loss, exhibit slower behavioral recovery and prolonged cortisol levels in response to stress. This cortisol dysregulation would negatively influence the immune response. Studies show that an impaired immunological response is correlated with the severity of depressive symptoms (Irwin, Daniels, & Weiner, 1987), and that decrements in lymphocyte proliferative responses are found in patients suffering major depressive disorders (Schleifer et al., 1984).

EARLY PSYCHOBIOLOGICAL DYSREGULATION, IMPAIRED ORBITOFRONTAL DEVELOPMENT, AND THE VULNERABILITY TO PSYCHOSOMATIC DISEASE

In an important recent book, Taylor (1987) highlights the relevance of the psychobiological aspects of current developmental psychoanalytic theory to a deeper understanding of psychosomatic illness. Taylor presents multidisciplinary evidence to argue that deficiencies in maternal selfobject psychobiological regulating functions produce developmental defects that predispose the individual to bodily disease. He then applies the concept of disease as psychobiological dys-regulation to a number of classical stress-sensitive psychosomatic syndromes such as coronary artery disease, peptic ulcer, ulcerative colitis, anorexia, and bulimia. Indeed, Weiner's fundamental understanding that all physical disease represents a disturbance of regulation and Grotstein's penetrating insight that all psychopathology represents disordered self-regulation clearly indicate that a dif-ferentiation between physical and psychosomatic disease is meaningless and misleading.

According to contemporary psychoanalytic theory, the parental selfobject acts to "remedy the child's homeostatic imbalance" (Kohut, 1977, p. 85), and defi-ciencies in the early mother-infant relationship result in "a failure in the develop-ment of self-regulatory functions under the sponsorship of the selfobject" (Grot-stein, 1983, p. 178). This conceptualization is echoed in attachment theory: the disruption of attachment bonds in infancy leads to a regulatory failure and an "impaired autonomic homeostasis" (Reite & Capitanio, 1985). Recent neuro-biological findings suggest that the site of the developmental structural failure is specifically located in the postnatally maturing orbitofrontal cortex, the cerebral system that is directly involved in homeostatic regulation (Kolb, 1984). Due to the incomplete structural maturation of its connections with the cortex and sub-cortex, its capacity to generate affect regulating symbolic representations is limited. Without access to this more complex affect regulation, under stress, emotions are experienced as primitive, sensorimotor, undifferentiated bodily sensations, rather than complex blends of feelings with a signal function. Geller (1984) describes a dysregulation of affect intensity:

> A chronically elevated state of diffuse excitation can render an individual insensi-tive to significant alterations. When the nonspecific amplification which intensity provides exceeds a critical value, the threshold for irritability, agitation, upset, affect storms and outbursts is significantly lowered. Similarly, the diffuse and pervasive sense of being keyed up for action tends to interfere with the ability to gauge accurately the alarm signals indicating that one's stress quota has been reached. (p. 179)

Taylor (1987) presents clinical and experimental evidence to show that so-matic disorders are very common in borderline and narcissistic patients in whom emotion is undifferentiated and unregulated. He (along with Gilbert, 1989) has made the important observation of clear links between narcissistic personality disorders and the aggressive character of the Type A coronary-prone behavior pattern. High levels of anger and hostility are now understood to be the critical components of the Type A pattern (Dembroski et al., 1985). Taylor (1992) proposes that this may represent an impaired capacity for modulating narcissistic rage. Indeed, in Type A research, the aggressive aspect of this personality is revealed by experimentally exposing the subject to "harassment," that is, humili-ation (Suarez & Williams, 1992). Due to deficiencies in early object relationships, these disease-prone individuals exhibit a developmental arrest, manifest in the poor quality of their self and object representations. Taylor further observes that psychosomatic patients are alexithymic—their reactions to socioemotional stress are highly somatic and minimally verbal. This major disturbance in affective and symbolic functioning was first discovered in clinical work with psychosomatic patients (Nemiah & Sifneos, 1970).

The developmental arrest occurs in the orbitofrontal cortex, a cerebral structure that controls ACTH (Okinaka et al., 1960) and corticosteroid levels (Hall & Marr, 1975), especially in the right hemisphere that regulates cortisol secretion in emotion-related situations (Wittling & Pfluger, 1990). This structure is the major cortical component of the integrated cortical-subcortical circuit of the limbic forebrain, hypothalamus, and brain stem autonomic nuclei that modulates the immune response (Felten et al., 1989). Interestingly, this frontolimbic cortex which represents the apex of the hierarchy of control of autonomic functions (Pribram, 1981), which is particularly sensitive to visceral stress (Krushel & van der Kooy, 1988), and which directly innervates areas in the medulla that interconnect with cardiac, laryngeal, tracheobronchial, pulmonary, and gastrointestinal visceral organs (Kalia & Mesulam, 1980), has been proposed to be a potential anatomical substrate for psychosomatic disease (Mesulam & Mufson, 1982; Neafsey, 1990). In light of its central role in controlling the pituitary-adrenal axis, when this corticolimbic structure is not properly carrying out this function, corticosterone can persisit in brain systems at higher levels than appropriate. Prolonged states of conservation-withdrawal are known to increase the vulnerability of the organism to pathological factors (Taylor, 1987). Both Alexander (1950) and Szasz (1952) argued that chronic and localized parasympathetic excitation is responsible for many psychosomatic conditions.

Arteta (1951) implicates orbital activity in the origin of gastric ulcer, and this psychosomatic visceral pathology could reflect an inefficient regulation of the orbitofrontal "visceral forebrain system" that influences autonomic function (van der Kooy et al., 1984). Activation of this prefrontal cortex induces weight gain (McGregor & Atrens, 1988), and bulimia has been found to be associated with orbitofrontal dysfunction in patient's with a lesion at this site (Erb, Gwirtsman, Fuster, & Richeimer, 1989). In light of the facts that prefrontal afferents to the solitary nucleus play a significant role in modulating the baroreceptor reflex (van der kooy et al., 1984) and that prefrontal stimulation increases baroreflex sensitivity (Rinkel et al., 1947), the clinical finding of a "reset" of the baroreflex to maintain an elevated blood pressure in chronic hypertension (Ganong, 1973) may reflect orbitofrontal pathology. The work of Skinner (1988) suggests its involvement in stress-evoked cardiac vulnerability, and Hall, Livingstone, and Bloor (1977) find that orbital stimulation will produce focal myocardial necrotic lesions similar to that produced by injections of catecholamines into the coronary artery. Orbitofrontal cortex regulates subcortical corticosteroid production, and a dysregulation of this function could produce chronically elevated cortisol levels, known to be associated with early atherosclerosis (Troxler, Sprague, Albanese, & Thompson, 1977).

SUMMARY

Three streams of research are converging on the centrality of mutual connections between the nervous and immune systems—biological studies of the reciprocal interactions between the cellular components of these systems, developmental studies of the effects of early experience on later immunocompetent capacities, and clinical studies of the effects of psychological factors on the outcomes of particular diseases. The developing child's inceptive experiences with the socio-affective environment, embedded in the emotional relationship with the mother, induce both short-term physiological alterations and long-term structural modifications in his developing immune system. These primordial experiences imprint the cortical-subcortical neurophysiological mechanisms that mediates all later psychosocial influences on immunologic reactions.

In regulating the infant's autonomic functions, the caregiver influences the imprinting of the structures responsible for the communication between the neuroendocrine and immune systems. The hypothalamus which releases its neuropeptides into the circulation, and the organs of the immune system that deliver its cellular agents into the circulation, share an identical set of signal molecules. Connections between hypothalmic limbic areas and cortical frontolimbic areas of the right hemisphere allow for an integrated circuitry that can modulate and be modulated by peripheral immune activity. The patterning of these connections is affected by the infant's practicing perod affective transactions with the psychobiologically regulating mother. A relationship characterized by extensive misattunement and regulatory failures engenders an incomplete structural maturation of a dual circuit orbitofrontal cortex. The developmental failure of this system is responsible for future vulnerabilities to psychosomatic disease.

33 Psychotherapy of Developmental Disorders

The mortification suffered thirty years ago operates, after having gained access to the unconscious sources of affect, during all these thirty years as though it were a recent experience. Whenever its memory is touched, it revives, and shows itself to be cathected with excitation which procures a motor discharge for itself in an attack. It is precisely here that psychotherapy must intervene, its task being to ensure that the unconscious processes are settled and forgotten.

—Sigmund Freud (1900/1953)

Protracted empathic immersion in the feeling state of any patient, but particularly the narcissistic patient . . . will usually unveil deep and painful shame feelings. These may be difficult to detect because of the many defenses intended to cover over shame experiences . . . But their discovery, examination, and working through by the patient, and the ultimate realization that therapist and patient alike can accept them, represent a major curative factor in every successful treatment.

—Andrew P. Morrison (1989)

The analytic relationship heals by drawing into itself those methods of processing and regulating affect relied on by the patient for psychological survival and then transforming them. The mechanism of these transformations is the regulation of affect in a better way within the analysis than it was previously managed by the patient and the subsequent modification of what, in the classical language of structural change, might be called the patient's unconscious affect-regulating structures.

—Charles Spezzano (1993)

443

A deeper appreciation of the dyadic psychobiological mechanisms that facilitate or impede the development of structures that regulate socioemotional function is fundamental to a more comprehensive understanding of the mechanisms that underly the psychotherapeutic treatment of developmental disorders. Over the past 2 decades a dramatic shift in clinical technique has occurred (Kernberg, 1984; Kohut, 1977; Wolf, 1988), and the cause for this has been the rapidly increasing numbers of patients with early forming primitive disorders who are entering into psychological treatment. Such borderline and narcissistic personality disturbances were refractory to "classical" forms of verbal psychotherapy (and to pharmacological interventions), and this has necessitated a modification of preexisting techniques and the creation of different psychoanalytically-based treatment approaches. I have proposed that these "developmental arrests" (Stolorow & Lachman, 1980) are in essence pathologies of the affect regulating functions of the affective core of the self. In previous chapters I have suggested that psychopathology is defined as a limitation of adaptive stress-regulating capacities, and is manifest in the recovery deficits of internal reparative mechanisms to interpersonal stress. I have also argued that these functions are localized in the right brain.

The generation of models of psychotherapy has traditionally been based upon clinical observations of the socioemotional functioning of psychiatric patients. Now, however, research on emotional processes and on infant development is being used as a source for revisions of clinical paradigms (Dowling & Rothstein, 1989; Greenberg & Saffran, 1989). The groundshaking conceptual changes that are emerging from these developmental studies are altering the landscape of clinical approaches that are based on psychoanalytic theory. "Classical" psychoanalysis, conducted in 3 to 4 session per week, non face-to-face encounters, which utilizes the free associations of the patient and the verbal interpretations of the therapist as primary data, has been supplanted by psychoanalytic psychotherapy, which takes place in 1 to 2 face-to-face sessions per week and emphasizes the interactional affective transactions between patient and therapist. The newer developmental psychoanalytic principles are also being used to generate models for the short term treatment of psychopathological states.

Although many psychotherapeutic approaches are focusing more and more upon the treatment of developmental structural defects and the induction of structural changes, the precise nature of the structures involved is ill-defined. Similarly, the mechanisms by which the interpersonal relationship between the therapist and the patient alter the internal and external functioning of the patient are poorly understood. I suggest that such questions can be elucidated by utilizing our knowledge of the object relational-influenced development of the structures responsible for human socioemotional functioning. Information about the development of affect regulating brain structure, derived from neurobiology, must be incorporated into models of "psychological change." In a recent article on emotion and the psychoanalytic encounter, Knapp (1992) concludes, "Optimal regulation is a goal of maturation, including therapeutic maturation. Dysregulation is a therapeutic target" (p. 247).

In this chapter I contend that the principles that describe the early dyadic psychobiological mechanisms which shape the structural development of the right hemisphere and its self-regulating functions can generate heurisitic hypotheses about the treatment of developmental disorders of the self. I also apply the earlier outlined developmental principles of the regulation of primitive emotions, especially shame, to the psychotherapy of borderline and narcissistic patients. Then, I present ideas about the neurobiological characterization of the psychological structural changes that are induced in long-term psychotherapy. Finally, using concepts from contemporary nonlinear dynamic systems (chaos) theory, I offer a research model of the psychotherapeutic treatment of dysregulated psychodynamic state transitions.

UNCONSCIOUS OBJECT RELATIONS AS A FOCUS OF THE PSYCHOTHERAPEUTIC TREATMENT OF DEVELOPMENTAL DISORDERS

Kaufman, (1989) an affect theorist and psychotherapist, promulgates the obvious yet fundamental tenet that psychotherapy must mirror development by actively engaging the identical processes that shape the self. Basch (1988), a psychoanalytic theoretician and clinician, now asserts:

> Psychotherapy, as I see it, is applied developmental psychology. The therapist uses his or her knowledge of normal development to reach some conclusions about the reasons for a patient's malfunctioning and how one may enter the developmental spiral either to foster or reinstitute a more productive, or at least less destructive, developmental process. (p. 29)

Psychotherapy is currently conceptualized as being directed toward the mobilization of fundamental modes of development (Emde, 1990) and the completion of interrupted developmental processes (Gedo, 1979). The restoring into consciousness and reassessment of early internalized working models of attachment figures in the context of the therapist-patient relationship is now being suggested to be the essential task of psychoanalytic psychotherapy (Bowlby, 1988b). With an eye to psychoanalytic data, Bowlby (1973) proposes:

> In a person suffering from emotional disturbance it is common to find that the model that has the greatest influence on his perceptions and forecasts, and therefore on his feelings and behavior, is one that developed during his early years and is constructed along fairly primitive lines, but that the person may be relatively unaware of. . . .(p. 205)

The earliest sensorimotor models of self-and-other-in-interaction which organize strategies of affect regulation (Kobak & Sceery, 1988) are most resistant to change. Despite the fact that these models are concerned with homeostatic regulation and are not under conscious control, it has been claimed that they may account for many of the "puzzles of 'unconscious' or 'primary process' influences on later behavior" (Pipp & Harmon, 1987, p. 650). These sensorimotor models are equivalent to early-forming internalized object relations, unconscious representations of the self interacting with the social environment (Kernberg, 1976) whose function is the cornerstone of modern psychoanalytic conceptions of the mind. Kernberg (1988) now posits that unconscious, nonverbally communicated "units constituted by a self-representation, an object-representation, and an affect state linking them are the essential units of psychic structure relevant for psychoanalytic exploration" (p. 482).

According to contemporary psychoanalytic theory, the child creates a "template" of his early object relations with his or her significant other (Horner, 1989). Styles and patterns of early relationships become internalized and are reactivated in later relationships throughout life (Tyson, 1989). This conceptualization is echoed in current attachment theory. Templates that are built into an inner mechanism are created in inceptive attachment experiences, and these shape the individual's interpretation of interpersonal experiences and thereby his outwardly observable behavior (Ainsworth, 1967). From a neurobiological perspective, I have suggested that such patterns are stamped into developing frontolimbic circuitry during early critical period "template learning" (Staddon, 1983) experiences, thereby providing strategies of affect regulation for processing socioaffective information throughout the lifespan. These are stored in the right hemisphere whose most critical units of representation are self-and-object images (Watt, 1990). Such early object relations consist of attuned and misattuned affective transactions, and the resultant indelibly imprinted templates encode programs of affect regulation and dysregulation. Patterns that encode misattuned and unregulated socioaffective events, early pathological object relations that become unconscious, psychobiologically mediate psychiatric psychopathology.

Beebe and Lachman (1988a) suggest that critical episodes of caregiver-infant "misregulation" or "misattunement" are permanently stored in memory "largely outside conscious awareness" as prototypic presymbolic representations. The experience of being raised by a psychobiologically dysregulating (m)other who initiates but poorly repairs misattunement is incorporated into an interactive representation, a working model of the self-misattuned-with-a-dysregulating-other. These models are imprinted with painful and disorganizing negative affects that can not be intra- nor interpersonally regulated, and are therefore stored in "unconscious memory" (Hintzman, 1990). The right cortex is associated with a form of mental processing referred to as unconscious awareness (Joseph, 1992) and is dominant for the experiencing and expression of emotion (Josephs, 1988), for the processing of emotion-evoking stimuli without conscious awareness (Wexler et al., 1992), and for mediating pain endurance (Cubelli, Caselli, & Neri, 1984). Early enduring unmodulated painful emotional experiences interfere with the organization of a right cortical system that can regulate and thereby tolerate pain. Galin (1974) refers to a "functional commisurotomy" which underlies a hemispheric disconnection syndrome, and Watt (1986) describes the left hemisphere disconnecting itself from stressful, primitive, dystonic, and threatening affect-laden self-and-object images processed in the right hemisphere. In psychoanalytic terms, these become the split-off repressed parts of the self.

The right hemisphere is now thought to provide the structural substrate for episodic (Knapp, 1983) and autobiographical memory (Cimino et al., 1991).

> The earliest memories of each of us are richly registered in . . . nonverbal modes, which continue throughout life to extend their own range and refinement even as they are eventually overridden by the emergingly dominant verbal mode. . . . (McLaughlin, 1989, p. 112)

It is known that the cortical hemispheres contain separate, dissociable memory systems, and that nonverbal "well-kept secrets of the right hemisphere" may not be accessible to the left (Risse & Gazzaniga, 1978). Joseph (1982) refers to:

> . . . early emotional learning occuring in the right hemisphere unbeknownst to the left; learning and associated emotional responding may later be completely unaccessible to the language centers of the brain, even when extensive interhemispheric transfer is possible. (p. 243)

Tucker (1992) speaks of "highly organized networks in the left hemisphere that are unmatched in the right hemisphere, and not directly accessible to it" (p. 120). These ontogenetically programmed neuroanatomical properties may account for the well documented observation that experiences that occur during the first years of life are difficult to recall in later stages of development (Flavell, 1977).

The early maturing visuospatial right cerebral cortex (as opposed to the later developing lexical-semantic left cortex) which stores and processes self-and-object images has been suggested to be responsible for the manifestations of unconscious processes (Galin, 1974). Seventy years ago, in *The Ego and the Id*, Freud (1923/1961) speculated: " . . . thinking in pictures . . . approximates more closely to unconscious processes than does thinking in words, and it is unquestionably older than the latter both ontogenetically and phylogenetically" (p. 21). Freud's fundamental discovery of the expression of unconscious factors in normal and pathological processes, and his ideas about the relationship between primary and secondary processes are compatible with recent work which demonstrates that early acting nonconscious processes and representations precede and affect later acting processes applied to conscious representations (Marcel, 1983).

An essential tenet of Freud's approach to the treatment of psychopathology was that the unconscious needs to be made conscious. In a finding that has import to the understanding of this mechanism, a recent neuropsychological study points to "a role of orbitofrontal regions in controlling the allocation of attention to possible contents of consciousness" (Goldenberg et al., 1989). The anterior prefrontal areas of the right cortex perform an executive function in the operation of this hemisphere that is dominant for attentional processes (Heilman et al., 1977). Watt (1986) concludes:

> One is tempted to speculate that certain unconscious meaning schemas not available for left hemispheric articulation in words may have important foundations in the right frontal areas, and that the right frontal areas may be particularly critical for the regulation and overall organization of emotionally relevant plans and intentions. (p, 72)

In neurological research, Ardila (1984) demonstrates that the right, but not left prefrontal area is critically involved in memory for "remote facts belonging to the patient's past experience" (p. 183). Trevarthen (1990) notes that:

> Limbic structures of the hemispheres, reciprocally connected to the hypothalamus and brain stem reticular nuclei, enter into memory function in the neocortex and are essential for the transfer of learning between modalities as well as the retrieval of associations from memories. (p. 340)

The exploration of the early unconscious emotional memories of the patient is another cornerstone of psychoanalyic psychotherapies. Indeed, in psychoanalytic contributions, Gedo (1986) asserts that often what is most meaningful in life "is not necessarily encoded in words" (p. 206), and Bornstein (1993) contends that "affective responses may be a particularly useful tool for recovering unconscious memories in the clinical setting" (p. 342).

RIGHT HEMISPHERE-TO-RIGHT HEMISPHERE AFFECTIVE COMMUNICATIONS MEDIATE PSYCHOTHERAPEUTIC TRANSFERENTIAL TRANSACTIONS

Models of psychotherapy based on psychoanalysis, "the science of unconscious processes" (Brenner, 1980), focus on the recognition and retrieval of early affect-laden memories as they evolve in the transferential relationship between the therapist and patient. Freud (1915/1957) held that the work of psychotherapy is always concerned with affect. In this approach, affects, including unconscious affects (Pulver, 1971), are both "the center of empathic communication" and the "primary data," and "the regulation of conscious and unconscious feelings is placed in the center of the clinical stage" (Sandler & Sandler, 1978). The technique of free association is now understood as "following the tracks of nonverbal schemata," by loosening the hold of the verbal system on the associative process and giving the nonverbal mode the chance to drive the representational and expressive systems (Bucci, 1993). The patient's impairment in socioemotional functioning (self-pathology) is evaluated not only in terms of ongoing relationships between the patient and his external social environment, but in terms of his internalized object relations, that is, his particular internal representation of the self affectively interacting with objects, which guides these interactions. These internalized interactive representations, unconscious working models of affect regulation, are determined and evaluated as they are expressed in the socioaffective relationship between patient and therapist, especially during stress. Furthermore, the psychoanalytic therapist utilizes the therapeutic relationship as the primary vehicle through which pathological internal object relations, maladaptive internal working models coding insecure attachment patterns, may be transformed into adaptive models based on more secure attachment programs of affect regulation. The treatment of self-pathology, according to Kohut (1971, 1977), involves "transmuting internalization," the developmental process by which selfobject function is internalized by the infant and psychological regulatory structures are formed.

It is important to point out that this process is essentially an exploration of the patient's affective states, and that this is a dyadic venture in which the therapist serves an affect regulating selfobject function. In order for this to progress, the therapist must be experienced as being in a state of vitalizing attunement to the patient, that is, the crescendos and decrescendos of the patient's affective state must be in resonance with similar states of crescendos and decrescendos, crossmodally, of the therapist (E.S. Wolf, personal communication, September 29, 1991). The basic core of empathy consists of "the ability to sample other's affects . . . and to be able to respond in resonance to them" (Easser, 1974, p. 563). These resonances induce a state of "primary intersubjectivity" (Trevarthen, 1979). This creates an "intersubjective field," a system of differently organized, interacting subjective worlds (Stolorow, Brandchaft, & Atwood, 1987). The therapist's focus is on the empathic grasp of the experiential state of the patient, and his or her "mirroring" function (Kohut, 1971) allows for dyadic merger experiences and an amplification of positive affect. This shared "fusion state" (Rose (1972) generates dynamic "vitality affects" (Stern, 1985), the positive affects that drive an attachment bond and that are required to build self-structure. As a result the patient establishes an "archaic bond" with the therapist and thereby facilitates the revival of the early phases at which his psychological development has been arrested (Kohut, 1984). It is known that the emotional bond between the patient and therapist, manifested in the working alliance, promotes the exploration of the individual's internal experience and affective state (Bordin, 1979). This strongly felt bond enables the patient to confront inner states associated with frightening aspects of the self (Jaenicke, 1987).

The direct relevance of developmental mechanisms to the psychotherapeutic process derives from the commonality of socioemotional transactional processes in the caregiver-infant relationship and in the therapist-patient relationship. The methodology of the therapeutic interactional process involves an intense focus on emotional transactions in the transference—countertransference relationship (Racker, 1968), an unconscious dynamic between the therapist and patient. This process has long been held by psychoanalytic clinicians to mediate structural and characterological psychotherapeutic change. It is now thought that critical "cues" generated by the therapist, which are absorbed and metabolized by the patient, generate the transference (Gill, 1982), an "activation of existing units of internalized object relations" (Kernberg, 1980). In recent theorizing on the neurobiological underpinnings of this process, Watt (1986) proposes a "field effect" model, in which the activation of internalized object relations (unconscious, preverbal internal working models) is triggered by the patient's perception of aspects of the 'interpersonal field" that are external analogues of existing affect-laden self and object internal images (representations). More specifically, the transference crystallizes around perceived expressions of the therapist's personality, therapeutic style, and behavior—in particular his/her "facial expression" and "perceived tone of voice." Transference activation is intensified by "precipitating stresses in the environment that present some formal analog to the stored internal images" (p. 57), and the patient is especially sensitive to (biased towards) perceiving aspects of the treatment situation which resemble "the parent's original toxic behavior." The resulting affective distress, especially associated with painful shame experiences, may elicit unconscious defensive strategies rooted in practicing period insecure-avoidant and insecure-resistant attachment patterns that are invoked in order to selectively exclude (Bowlby, 1984) this intolerably painful affective material from consciousness.

The patient, according to Watt, is very "attuned" to alterations in the "bipersonal field" (Langs, 1976) which excite an emotional resonance within enduring internal object images (excitatory reverberations within the ventral and lateral tegmental forebrain-midbrain limbic circuits). This input generates "a series of analogical comparisons between distortions by the therapist ("misalliance") and the empathic failures and distortion of parents" (p. 61). Watt presents a number of persuasive arguments to show that the analogical cognition of the transference is organized by the analogical processing of the right hemisphere. This hemisphere is known to be involved in the expression and recognition of the affective, prosodic components of language (Ross, 1983), in the processing of unconscious information (Galin, 1974), and in affective nonverbal communication and the perception of facial expression (Benowitz et al., 1983). Indeed, Krause and Lutolf (1988) emphasize the importance of facial indicators of transference processes. Furthermore, this affectively charged information (socioaffective input) is cross referenced by the (anterior) right hemisphere across all sensory modalities—kinesthetic, somesthetic, visual, auditory, and tactile—so that a number of stimuli of different modalities can excite a resonance between present external object experiences and internal object images. In this process, a very basic aspect of human perception, the nondominant hemisphere is temporarily dominant over the left in processing nonverbal knowledge of current images of self and other. EEG studies have found that increased right hemispheric activation accompanies the emergence of strong affect during psychotherapy sessions (Hoffman & Goldstein, 1981).

In other conceptualizations, the transference process has been characterized as a selective bias in dealing with others that is based on previous early experiences and which shapes current expectancies (McLaughlin, 1981). The emotions evoked in the transference "hinge on the range and extent of expectations for different situations that are already a part of the patient's repertory" (Singer, 1985, p. 198). I suggest that attachment patterns discerned in treatment (secure, insecure-avoidant, and insecure-resistant), which reflect different expectations of external affect regulation, represent discrete stress-exposed transferential "modes." In response to stressful dyadic misattunements, the patient may attempt to seek, avoid, or resist emotionally transacting object relations with the psychotherapist. These three unconscious modes, which arise from dissociable dynamic orbitofrontal structural organizations of the right hemisphere which processes unconscious information, may fundamentally organize the three basic ways humans relate to each other: moving toward, moving away from, and moving against others (Horney, 1945).

The psychotherapeutic treatment of developmental disorders emphasizes the therapist's reception and response to a "special kind of communication that comes from the unconscious and is perceived unconsciously; this communication is reached through our countertransference feelings, aroused by the projective communication" (De Paola, 1990, p. 334). Freud (1913/1955) proposed that "everyone posseses in his own unconscious an instrument with which he can interpret the utterances of the unconscious of other people" (p. 320). Racker (1968) asserts, "Every transference situation provokes a countertransference situation" (p. 137). Countertransferential processes are currently understood to be manifest in the capacity to recognize and utilize the sensory (visual, auditory, tactile, kinesthetic, and olfactory) and affective qualities of imagery which the patient generates in the psychotherapist (Suler, 1989). Similarly, Loewald (1986) points out that countertransference dynamics are appraised by the therapist's observations of his own visceral reactions to the patient's material. He further suggests that the therapist's emotional investment and capacity to enter into the rapport of the transference-countertransference is a decisive factor in the curative process. This same mechanism may underly the conclusion of a recent experimental study that "the therapist's ability to form an alliance is possibly the most crucial determinant of his effectiveness" (Luborsky et al., 1985, p. 610). Emde

(1988) asserts that the therapist's emotional availability, defined as a sensitivity and responsiveness to a range of emotions, is essential to a "corrective emotional experience."

These principles are described by Hammer (1990) in a recent book, *Reaching the Affect*:

> My mental posture, like my physical posture, is not one of leaning forward to catch the clues, but of leaning back to let the mood, the atmosphere, come to me—to hear the meaning between the lines, to listen for the music behind the words. As one gives oneself to being carried along by the affective cadence of the patient's session, one may sense its tone and subtleties. By being more open in this manner, to resonating to the patient, I find pictures forming in my creative zones; an image crystallizes, reflecting the patient's experience. I have had the sense, at such times, that at the moments when I would pick up some image of the patient's experience, he was particularly ripe for receiving my perceptions, just as I was for receiving his. An empathic channel appeared to be established which carried his state or emotion my way via a kind of affective "wireless." This channel, in turn, carried my image back to him, as he stood open in a special kind of receptivity. (pp. 99–100)

To my mind, these observations are describing practicing-onset dyadic right hemispheric orbitofrontal-regulated nonverbal communications between patient and therapist. Hinze (1992) argues that a fundamental part of the psychoanalytic interaction consists of nonverbal communication signals between the two partners, resembling those exchanges between mother and infant. This essentially preverbal unconscious-preconscious communication between patient and therapist is proposed to reflect the exact same process that occurs in the infant-caregiver psychobiologically attuned state (Field, 1985a) in which a match occurs not between external behavioral (or verbal) events, but between the expression of internal states (Stern, 1985). As in early development the communicative exchange occurs between one person who possesses the capacity for symbolic representation and another who doesn't (Lichtenberg, 1989). Kohut (1977) describes an empathic merger between the selfobject function of a person with a highly developed psychic organization and another who posseses a rudimentary psyche. Psychotherapeutic interventions of dysfunctions of the infantile nonverbal affect system (Krystal, 1978a) rely more heavily on preverbal processes.

How are preverbal interactions expressed in the verbal exchanges of psychotherapy? Stern (1989) suggests that the "narrative" model is the verbal rendition of the nonverbal internal working models of regulation as told to oneself or to another. The advent of language brings about the capacity to begin to form an autobiographical history that ultimately evolves into the narrative life story a patient presents to a psychotherapist. Gilbert (1989) notes that the inner speech utilized in "the dialogues of the self" is not well coded in spoken linguistic form, that the "voices" of such internal dialogues are active and often charged with affect, and that psychoanalytic methodologies are constructed to articulate and understand the inner appraisal systems and meaning-making processes that are coded with affect. Wilson et al. (1990) propose:

> . . . the categorical, semantic meanings of linguistic utterances are not a fully reliable avenue to the psychological experience of the speaker. Rather, deeper structural factors that can be identified in narratives may provide better clues to any maladaptive "formats" at work under the surface. (p. 182)

Wilson asserts that these factors—metaphors that are meaningful and evocative and prosodic elements of language such as rhythm and tonality—directly influence psychobiological motivation. In more recent work, Wilson and Weinstein (1992b) propose that the metaphoric is created by the infusion of early affectivity, that it links early ideational and sensory organizations, and that the prosodic elements of language "can be a manifest form through which crucial material excluded from consciousness by primal repression can be glimpsed."

In referring to the importance of affective tone, Ross (1983) concludes that the right hemispheric regulated "affective components of language are probably, in the long run, far more influential in human discourse than the actual words one chooses" (p. 506). Vitz (1990) argues that narrative thought, expressed in intonation and emotion-associated images, represents "language in the service of right hemisphere cognition." The uncovering and exploration of early unconscious working models, stored in the right hemisphere which contains neural representations of prosodic contours, facial expression, and gestures (Blonder et al., 1991), performs a special role in establishing, maintaining, and processing personally relevant aspects of the individual's world (Van Lanker, 1991), contributes to the drawing of inferences from discourse (Beeman, 1993), and plays a dominant role in the comprehension of metaphor (Winner & Gardner, 1977), may thus be best guided by attending more to the affect-laden images embedded in language than to the semantic and lexical aspects of the patient's narrative presentations. This cortex, and not the linguistic left, is capable of determining and deducing not only what another person feels about what he or she is saying, but why and in what context he or she is saying it (Joseph, 1992). Over 50 years ago, Vygotsky (1988) concluded:

> The affective and volitional tendency stands behind thought. Only here do we find the answer to the final "why" in the analysis of thinking . . . A true and complex understanding of another's thought becomes possible only when we discover its real, affective-volitional basis . . . we complete the psychological analysis of any expression only when we reveal the most secret internal plane of verbal thinking-its motivation. (pp. 282–283)

THE ESSENTIAL ROLE OF SHAME DYNAMICS IN THE
TREATMENT OF DEVELOPMENTAL DISORDERS

The absolute necessity to attend to nonverbal affects, especially unconscious nonverbal affects, in the treatment of primitive disorders is underscored by the unique and overarching role of shame in all developmental psychopathologies. The early history of these patients is predominantly characterized by dyadic affect transactions that are infused with intense and lingering amounts of unregulated shame affect. These interactions are permanently imprinted in an enduring working model of the self-misattuned-with-a-self-dysregulating-other. Kaufman (1989) asserts that failures of early attachment invariably become sources of shame, and M. Lewis (1992) similarly concludes that impairments in the parent-child relationship leads to pathology through an enduring disposition to shame. As a result, these individuals do not evolve an efficient affect regulatory system to actively cope with and thereby tolerate the narcissistic pain of shame. They are thus vulnerable to depression, a narcissitic depletion of the self. The impairment of self-esteem homeostasis in these patients is posited to specifically define the "self-pathology" of these disorders as discussed by Kohut (1977) and Kernberg (1975). The fundamental goal of uncovering and working through shame, especially "bypassed" (H.B. Lewis, 1971) unregulated shame, in the psychotherapeutic treatment of developmental psychopathologies is now being urgently stressed (Basch, 1988; Broucek, 1991; Goldberg, 1991; Kaufman, 1989; Morrison, 1989; Nathanson, 1992; Schore, 1991).

Unregulated shame is thus equated with "bypassed shame," which is unconscious and therefore unrecognized shame, while regulated shame is equivalent to conscious, tolerated shame. Unregulated shame has been proposed to be a potent motive force which drives the process of repression (Kaufman, 1992; Wurmser, 1981). The avoidance of the recognition of shame "directly opposes derepression and the integration of unconscious material within the conscious ego" (Ward, 1972, p.63). In a recent experimental study, Davis (1987) concludes that repression is motivated, in particular, by affective experiences of heightened self-consciousness in which the self is exposed to a negative evaluation, specifically citing Miller's (1985) definition of shame. Shame has been shown to inhibit the expression of any specific emotion (Tomkins, 1987), and indeed the expression of emotion *per se* (Kaufman, 1992), and at continuous high levels produces a constriction of the affect array. Unrecognized and unaccepted shame is thus a growth-inhibitory force to emotional development, because it paralyzes the "self-generating" maturational drive. It therefore must be confronted, consciously recognized, and understood in psychotherapeutic interventions which attempt to facilitate growth and expansion of the self. The ability to tolerate the phenomenological pain experienced upon the emergence of repressed material (negative affect-laden cognition stored in unconscious episodic memory) is critical to the successful psychotherapeutic treatment of unconscious, early shame-dominated, misattuned, coping-ineffective internalized working models.

The core psychopathological lesion in these developmentally impaired individuals is that they do not contain a self-regulatory capacity to tolerate or recover from object relational-induced narcissistic injuries which expose distressing negative affect, especially hyperaroused rage and hypoaroused shame, while maintaining constructive engagement with others. Joffe and Sandler (1967) identify the essential defect of narcissistic disorders as "the existence of an overt or latent state of pain which constantly has to be dealt with by the ego, and the defensive and adaptive manoeuvers which are responses to it can assume pathological proportions"(p. 65). In referring to this work, Parkin (1985) specifies this mental pain as shame. Shame tolerance, the ability to consciously experience shame (narcissistic pain), which is a prerequisite to the establishment of core positive belief and self valuation, is extremely limited in "shame prone" narcissisitic and borderline personalities. Levin (1967) observes that:

> Intense reactions to shame are often seen in borderline and psychotic patients . . .
> Due to the intensity of their reaction of shame, these patients may use more extreme
> defenses such as withdrawal, excessive repression of thoughts, feelings and im-
> pulses, and repression of shame itself . . . Some of these patients appear to have a
> constitutional limitation in the ego's capacity to protect against shame through
> normal defensive measures. However, superimposed upon this basic limitation may
> be the effects of excessive shaming experiences in early life, leading to internaliza-
> tions which later manifest themselves through excessive internal shaming and
> through excessive anticipation of being shamed from without. (p. 272)

The developmental history of the early object relations of such patients may clarify the nature of the evolving transference relationship that unfolds between the patient and therapist. As in their earliest relationships, during times of emotional distress in treatment they defensively hide from, rather than turn to, a significant other, because they expect the other to be distant, unempathic, unavailable, and unresponsive during stress. They may also attack and devalue the other, who they experience as not soothing a narcissistic injury, but rather as stimulating narcissistic rage. The coping ability to reconnect emotionally at reunion with a significant other after a shame-stress disconnection, and indeed to use the other to recover from shame-associated narcissistic injury and object loss, never effectively developed in these personality structures. The patient's socio-affective transactions are guided by internalized working models of interactive misattunement, and these representations encode expectations of humiliating narcissistic assault from a primary object. This bias also operates in the patient's interpreting the input of the therapist, as the "analogical comparisons" between the distortions of the therapist and the distortions of the shaming parents excite an emotional resonance within enduring shame-imprinted internal self-and-object images. These dynamics become a major focus of treatment.

Narcissistic and borderline patients will specifically show an impaired ability to recover from transference breaks, especially between psychotherapy sessions, since they cannot regulate the enduring negative affect state (mood) triggered by and associated with the object during the separation. The inability to tolerate or regulate negative narcissistic affect, especially shame, while maintaining bidirectional object relations transactions may explain the severely restricted capacity of narcissistic patients to form a "classical" transference neurosis which involves an attachment relationship that persists in the face of dissappointment in drive gratification (Kron, 1971). It also may account for their inability to accept and internalize a classical transference interpretation due to its potential for inflicting traumatic narcissistic injury and shame (Josephs, 1989), and the often mentioned iatrogenic phenomenon of narcissistic patients suddenly aborting psychotherapy after a narcissistic insult (Kohut, 1968). Borderline patient's very often do not hear the "content of an interpretation" but instead feel instantly humiliated and react with rage and shame (Chessick, 1979).

Effective therapeutic interventions must focus on the mutual phenomenolgical explorations of the residues of "growth-inhibiting environments," defense systems, especially defenses that protect the defective self against shame depletion. In the very earliest psychoanalytic writings the major motive in defense was postulated to be the avoidance of shame:

> [By] means of my psychical work I have had to overcome a psychical force in the patients which was opposed to the pathogenic ideas becoming conscious. From these I recognized the universal characteristic of such ideas. They were all of a distressing nature calculated to arouse the affects of shame, of self-reproach and of psychical pain and the feeling of being harmed; they were all of a kind that one would prefer not to have experienced, that one would rather forget. From all this there arose, as it were, automatically the thought of defence. . . .(Breuer & Freud, 1893–1895, pp. 268–269)

In modern-day terms, these defenses prevent the individual from entering into dyscontrolled states which he can not autoregulate, especially the "dreaded state" of "shameful mortification" (Horowitz, 1992). The threatening word "shame", when presented tachistoscopically at levels beneath conscious awareness, primes the right hemisphere (Van Strien & Morpugo, 1992). Defensive operations eliminate from awareness aspects of the representational world that are colored with intensely negative affect (Stolorow & Atwood, 1979). Gilbert points out that defensive responses are associated with negative affects and that psychoanalytic defenses operate through the basic psychobiological systems of defense. Furthermore, he contends:

A person may be unable to explore and develop new, more flexible, internal cognitive representations and behaviors due to the ease of activation of the defense system. It is overcoming this stereotyped, defensive organization to certain cues and stimuli (which may be internal and/or external) that liberates the person from their shame and fear of humiliation, inhibited assertiveness or readiness to aggress. (P. Gilbert, personal communication, March 23, 1992)

Kohut (1984) asserts that defense-resistances perform specific self-preserving functions, and that strong resistances are mainly motivated by shame (1971).

In this process the therapist needs to be sensitive to the hidden expressions of the defenses against and the experience of this nonverbal affect. These become especially prominent at points of "intersubjective disjunctions" (Stolorow et al., 1987). Are there any preconditions in the therapy that increase the probability of such disjunctions? As a result of the empathic processes of the initial phase of treatment, the patient develops a positive anticipation of a continuing self-sustaining relationship with the therapist, and on the basis of this expectation of mirroring he or she engages in an open self-display of his or her affective inner world. The therapist's failure to do as expected is experienced as a non-confirmation that triggers shame (E.S. Wolf, personal communication, September 29, 1991). In a previous chapter I suggested a developmental model that serves as a prototype of all shame experiences. The individual, in a high energy state of excitement and elation, exhibits itself to a meaningful object. Despite an expectation of an attuned mutual amplification of positive affect, the self suddenly experiences a misattunement, triggering a shock-induced psychobiological state transition and a deflation of narcissistic affect. This object-induced energy depletion causes an impairment of self-cohesion and is phenomenologically experienced as a discontinuity.

Thus, the immediate, proximal internal event of any shame experience is an activated internal fantasy of a symbiotic attunement, of a motivation to move psychologically closer to the therapist who has become an emotionally significant object, but the external reality does not match this need and so the patient rapidly and reflexively withdraws from view of the therapist. Clinically this means attending to the patient's "nonverbal expressions of the self" such as turning the face away, gaze aversion, covering the face with the hands, or blushing. A break in eye contact at an emotionally significant moment may be experienced by the patient as a narcissistic injury. Postural changes are seen in slumping or seeming to shrink, as if hiding. It is also important to recognize the *language* of shame; rarely is the specific word used, and when it is it usually denotes a critical moment in a psychotherapy session (e.g., see Knapp, 1980). More commonly, the patient will speak of feeling foolish, ridiculous, pathetic, insignificant, worthless, etc., and will talk about being exposed or wishing to make himself invisible. Attendance to the nonverbal prosodic components of language have been previously mentioned. This is specifically conveyed in the variations in pitch, rhythm, and stress that convey emotion, interest, and background mood. In light of the fact that these patients with early forming character pathology are exquisitely sensitive to prosodic components of language, verbal interpretations may be accepted or rejected depending less upon content than upon the tone of the therapist's voice. Shame is known to be a major causal force of deficits in the capacity for internalization (Spero, 1984). It acts as a critical factor in the patient's capacity to internalize the therapist's empathic responses, and to identify with and introject his or her selfobject functions.

The working through of nonverbal defenses specific to shame is therefore essential to the effective psychotherapy of preverbal-onset developmental disorders, and the technique in this work is expressed in the dictum, "follow the Ariadne's thread of transference affects" (Brierley, 1937). Erikson (1950) has pointed out that two common defensive reactions of the shamed person are to hide (concealment) or to "destroy the eyes of the world" in a narcissistic rage. These defenses are highly developed in the "dissociative narcissist" and the "egotistical narcissist" (Broucek, 1982), respectively. The well known clinical phenomenon of the narcissistic patient's intense anger toward the therapist who fails to continually mirror his projected grandiosity (Rinsley, 1989) covers over the unrecognized, unconscious painful shame which was etiologically elicited in exactly this way. Morrison (1989) has provided convincing clinical evidence showing that shame which is "rapidly wiped out of consciousness" frequently underlies transference rage.

Interestingly, the psychotherapeutic exposure, confrontation, and uncovering of defenses which facilitates the breakthrough of repressed painful emotional distress into consciousness has been shown to be directly correlated with elevated corticosteroid levels (Sachar, MacKenzie, Binstock, & Mack, 1968), the physiological response identical to the conscious experiencing of shame. Clinicians have long recognized that crying is an emotional response that discharges painful affects. The relief that accompanies weeping has been suggested to involve limbic-hypothalamic mechanisms (McCrank, 1983). Inhibition of crying behavior in the sight of others is a major theme of early shame socialization. Its expression in the therapeutic environment, in the presence of a shame regulating, nonhumiliating therapist elicits an important psychobiological state transition associated with the working through of defenses against negative affect.

A major assumption of this work is that the more precise elucidation of the developmental process by which affect and affect regulatory systems evolve will be directly relevant to delineating the framework of a treatment approach specific to the pathologies of narcissistic affect. Indeed, the nature and the sequence of the critical object relational transactions of the therapy process should reflect the developmental process. Data outlined in earlier chapters suggest both that stress is necessary for further structural development and that stress is required to reveal structural deficits. The patient who constantly defends against experiencing and exhibiting conscious shame in the presence of an emotionally meaningful other must at some points experience it in the transferential relationship with the therapist. As mentioned, these moments are critical events in the ongoing interpersonal process of psychotherapy, as they are associated with breaks in the positive transference. In the same way as the bond between the infant-mother dyad was tested earlier at points of rapprochement "narcissistic" crises, the therapeutic relationship is "stress-tested" at exposed moments of the painful emergence of shame into consciousness, thereby vulnerably revealing the affect regulatory deficit. During the late-practicing/rapprochement-onset critical period, the mother and infant developmentally did not succeed in dyadically negotiating the shame-induced dysregulation. A failure of self-expectation and the ensuing intense internal physiological sensation of shame may trigger the state-dependent recall of the memory of this ontogenetic painful failure usually stored in a misattuned, coping-ineffective, insecure attachment working model. This internalized object relation, though usually unconscious, is activated and consciously expressed in the transference at these specific moments. At points of emotional bond rupture, the working alliance can effectively continue (not be defensively split) only if the unconscious painful shame dynamics beneath the narcissistic defenses are, initially in gradual small doses, sensitively identified and revealed. In this way the therapist acts as the shame-stimulating practicing mother who at selected moments withdraws her mirroring function and deactivates the grandiose self, thereby triggering a separation-induced stress response.

However, this defense analysis in itself is not a total corrective emotional experience to the developmental disorder. Patients can tolerate increasing amounts of conscious shame (narcissistic pain) under the aegis of the therapist who can serve as an external regulator of this painful affect. The therapist, in the same way as the attuned practicing mother, mediates affect regulatory selfobject functions for the patient, especially in disjunctive state transitions. This is specifically accomplished by the therapist's repeated demonstrated ability to consciously, and especially unconsciously, affectively resonate with the patient, allowing him or herself to stay emotionally connected with, and available to the patient during the oscillating separation and reunion periods of the dynamic transference that occur over the course of the therapeutic relationship. In order to do this the therapist must be able to tolerate the painful affect in him or herself. This requires that the clinician must recognize and deal authentically with the intersubjective shaming that occurs in the therapeutic session (C. Goldberg, personal communication, July 19, 1991). The "recognition and acceptance of the patient's shame lies at the heart of empathic listening in the analytic process." (Morrison, 1984, p.502). This process is extremely important during periods of stress which propel the patient into dysregulated affect—intense, spiralling shame states which are beyond his range of active coping and therefore beyond his capacity to resolve by himself. At this point of failure of narcissistic defenses against shame, narcissistic pain breaks through into consciousness. Much to his shame, the patient's intense attachment need is, at the same moment, reflected to himself and exposed to the significant other. Consequently, he feels the intense anxiety of needing another, of being forced into reunion, and experiences this need as a narcissistic injury.

As outlined earlier, the developmentally prototypical object relation of shame involves the induction of a sudden shock-induced deflation of narcissistic affect that is unexpectedly triggered by an emotionally significant object. In the etiological history of primitive disorders the ensuing hypoaroused depressed state was not regulated by the misattuned mother. Instead of helping the self to recover, she increased rather than decreased narcissistic distress. The internalized representation of these events contains an expectation that this environmental response will occur whenever the individual is stressed. Therefore, in this painful state, the disintegrating self reflexively protects itself against further deterioration by breaking attachment ties and hiding from unconsciously predicted and anticipated shame inducing self-disorganizing object transactions. Although it succeeds in hiding from the disorganizing object, during the separation it no longer has access to an external nor internal selfobject affect regulatory function. The attempt to narcissistically cope with the dysregulated affect state is doomed to failure, as the patient lacks the internal capacity to modulate the accelerating shame state. At this point the disorganizing personality becomes overwhelmed with intense feelings of helplessness and hopelessness.

These dynamics are heightened during moments of personal failure, as such stressful experiences expose the core psychological lesion of the failure to autoregulate depressive states. Exposed inefficacy is known to be a powerful stimulator of shame (Broucek, 1982; White, 1960). After such a failure of self-expectation the patient's unmodulated narcissistic rage may be directed internally toward the self, as in the early object relation with the humiliating caregiver, with intense internalized shaming of the self or what Nathanson (1992) calls an "attack self" shame mechanism. The inability to regulate the downward spiralling depressive state is manifested in overwheming internal self-shaming tendencies and rapidly de-escalating self-esteem. It is at these times that the patient's need for the therapist's selfobject function is most intense and most conscious. At these moments, the therapist must function as the attuned, shame modulating practicing mother who remains emotionally connected during decelerating hypoaroused states. During these critical transactions the therapist's active participation in dyadic shame affect regulation is essential to the treatment process. Nathanson (1992) stresses that:

> Therapeutic passivity—the decision to remain silent in the face of a humiliated, withdrawn patient—will always magnify shame because it confirms the patient's affect-driven belief that isolation is justified. (p. 325)

In a timely fashion the therapist subsequently reestablishes comforting and mirroring functions, thereby enabling the patient to recover from depressed low-keyed states, and facilitating a transition from negative/passive to positive/active mood. These transactions disconfirm the patient's expectation of humiliation and intensification of negative affectivty during periods of helpless self-exposure. The ability to internalize the therapist's shame modulating function is instrumental to metabolizing shame and restoring narcissistic balance, as well as to reinforcing the growth of the nascent reevolving structure which can autoregulate shame.

Increasing levels of experienced regulated shame serve an important socio-developmental function as the agent for the dilution of primary narcissism and narcissistic rage. As shame becomes less rejected from consciousness, it allows for the tranformation of primary into secondary narcissism, and explosive narcissistic rage into modulated, verbalized anger. At the same time the effects of unconscious shame on the blockage of affect are alleviated, leading to an expansion of the affect array. In general, fully experiencing affective responses is a prerequisite for "correcting distortions of the object world" (Greenberg & Safran, 1989). In particular, increased shame tolerance facilitates the acknowledgment and acceptance of earlier pain-associated attachment and dependency needs. The clinical import of this affect is that it is essential to the mechanism of repression, that it is a major force of inhibition of affect, cognition, and behavior. Shame, an affect that uniquely causes a "loss of words" (Izard, 1991) underlies alexithymia, "no words for feelings" (Krystal, 1988; Nemiah, Freyberger, & Sifneos, 1976; Rickles, 1986). When shame is unregulated and therefore chronic it interferes with the expression of almost all emotions, and this results in an alexithymic syndrome. Wilson et al. (1990) characterizes the alexithymic inability to articulate feeling states: "We suggest that some people will have a poorly developed lexicon for the description of some manifestations of self-regulatory failures—because they are not consciously accessible and are therefore out of awareness" (p. 189).

Shame also can bind individual affects (Kaufman, 1992) such as fear, distress, anger, and even positive affects. In other words, more developmentally advanced patients may manifest a "focal" alexithymic deficit in regard to specific affects that are "silenced" and cannot be identified and verbally labeled. The therapist helps the patient to recognize and then to label these affects, especially those associated with dreaded states of shameful mortification. In a "genuine dialogue" with the therapist, the patient raises to an inner word and then into a spoken word what he needs to say at a particular moment but does not yet possess as speech (Buber, 1957). This newly acquired verbal modulation of shame is facilitated by a verbal-cognitive understanding of its historical genesis, of "returning internalized shame to its interpersonal origin" (Kaufman, 1992), with an empathic focus on the child who experienced it.

The ultimate therapeutic goal however, is the development of an efficient ego ideal superego structure that can autoregulate stressful affect and self-esteem and stabilize narcissistic equilibrium, via identification with and internalization of the therapist's selfobject regulatory functions. This evolved psychic structure also allows the individual to seek affect regulation from valued others in times of intense emotional stress. In order to treat both the haughty grandiosity and shame-fueled inferiority of these patients the therapist must serve both the mirroring-frustrating and depression-regulating selfobject functions of the late practicing mother. Thus, both the shame stimulator and the shame modulator must be exposed to the treatment process to allow for the therapeusis of the defective shame regulator. Only then are the requirements met for Ward's (1972) description of the outcome of effective resolution of shame dynamics: "When in the course of therapy or growth a shame situation is faced and resolved there is a freeing up of vast amounts of energy that can be returned to the ego for other uses" (p. 63). Rakfeldt and Strauss (1989) observe a "low turning point" process that acts as a control mechanism in the course of a mental disorder. As a result of the regulation associated with this process, certain states can be maintained, and recovering patients now have available "freed energy" that allows them "novel opportunities for an active, more adaptive interchange and involvement with their environment" (p. 36).

The focus of superego-directed psychotherapy of narcissistic pathologies is thus on the disordered regulation of narcissistic affect. The ultimate goal of this treatment approach is a more integrated, functionally efficient affect regulating system which can allow the individual to tolerate the painful exposure of the self long enough to evolve a different affective equilibrium and to generate a new cognitive perception of the self, that is, the development of insight and the creation of revised internalized working models of the self. Affect regulatory dialogs mediated by a psychotherapist who is attuned to shame-associated inter-subjective breaches and dyadically repairs internal state dysregulations may induce literal psychic change. Affect tolerance, which allows for the experience of emotion to enter into consciousness, is equated by Krystal (1988) with the adaptive capacity to bear pain. This structural alteration may enable a functional advance—an increased capacity to experience shame and utilize it as a signal affect. Schneider (1977) points out that although shame reveals the limits of the self, this initially sudden painful self-consciousness, if tolerated, may put self-identity into perspective, and consequently confirm, shape, and enlargen it. "The immediate awareness in shame is often the sting of self-negation; a more sustained look reveals an underlying core of positive belief and self valuation" (p. 28).

DEVELOPMENTAL AFFECT THEORY AND THE MECHANISMS OF PSYCHOTHERAPEUTIC CHANGE

The therapist's attunement to the stress-exposed inefficient right frontolimbic socioaffective function of developmentally disordered borderline and narcissistic personalities is instrumental to the treatment of psychopathologies of the basic primitive affect system which is lateralized to the right hemisphere (Gazzaniga, 1985). Primitive emotions are associated with autonomic system functioning (Johnson & Multhap, 1992), and the right hemisphere is specialized for representation of autonomic emotional conditioning (Johnsen & Hugdahl, 1993). The psychotherapy of "primitive emotional disorders" (Grotstein, 1990a) (the disordered regulation of primitive affects) and the repair of "structural deficits" (Horner, 1991) of early right hemispheric attachment pathology (as opposed to later developing left hemispheric associated neurotic disorders) may specifically require a "right hemisphere-to-right-hemisphere interface between therapist and patient" (Miller, 1986). The treatment of impaired right brain affect regulation calls for a greater focus on the powerful nonverbal influences on the communications of primitive affects in the psychotherapeutic relationship.

This work necessitates the mobilization of primary process modes that are highly visual and are involved in the transmission of affect (Garfield, 1987). Indeed, the mirroring process, a cornerstone of psychotherapeutic treatment of preverbal onset narcissistic disorders (Kohut, 1971, 1977), as shown earlier, is a right hemisphere-right hemisphere transaction between infant and mother. The importance of visual-emotional processes to the construction of visuo-spatial right hemispheric internalized working models has also been detailed in previous chapters. The preeminent significance of the image of the human face to affective processes was also stressed earlier. In the first two years of life images of prototypical emotional faces are imprinted into enduring interactive representations that later unconsciously mediate affect regulation. A fundamental goal of inner psychotherapeutic exploration is to allow the individual to recognize, understand, and accept one's own "unknown face" (Joseph, 1992). Clinical observers have noted that early mental representations are specifically visually oriented (Giovacchini, 1981). Studying the reconstruction of preverbal experience, Anthi (1983) has concluded that historical visual imagery may be derivative of events of early phases of development. The effectiveness of tapping into visual imagery in the psychotherapy of shame disorders has been emphasized by Kaufman (1989). Similarly, the preverbal elements of language—intonation, tone, force, and rhythm—are "apt to stir up reactions derived from the early mother-child relationships" (Greenson, 1978). Structural growth of the self thus involves the psychotherapeutic activation of the interpersonal field, which induces the intensification of early forming internal states and allows for the appearance of right hemispheric, affect-imprinted multimodal internal working models, and the subsequent left hemispheric processing of this "unconscious" material.

The psychotherapist's establishment of a dyadic affective "growth promoting environment" influences the ontogeny of homeostatic self-regulatory systems (Greenspan, 1981). Towards this end, both positive and negative classes of affect need to be transacted and regulated in the therapist-patient relationship. I have earlier discussed the adaptive contribution of positive affect to the development of emotion regulating structures. This occurs in the context of infant play which transforms the early environment into an enriched one. Dyadic mirroring exchanges that amplify positive affect must also be part of the therapeutic environment. Emde (1992) is now presenting extensive multidisciplinary evidence that suggests that positive emotions need to be integrated into clinical theory. The essential importance of creating a "playground" in psychoanalytic therapy is currently being explored by Shor (1990) and Sanville (1991).

At the same time, dyadic transactions of interactive repair that reduce negative affect, especially after critical moments of shame-induced ruptures of the positive affective bonds of the therapeutic alliance, act as catalytic regulatory mechanisms that facilitate the development of a structural system that can homeostatically maintain positive and recover from negative affective states. Self-righting (Waddington, 1947), an embryological concept, describes an inherent tendency to recover or rebound from a developmental deficit with a developmental progression as a result of a positive change in an inhibiting external condition. Current treatment models of developmental disorders emphasize the principle that a focus on the disruption-restoration process (Wolf, 1988)—transference disruptions and their repair—is central to the curative process (Ornstein, 1990). Of special importance is the therapist's active involvement in arousal regulating "distress-relief sequences" (Lamb, 1981) and "reassurance" transactions (Gilbert & Trower, 1990), which "restore the interpersonal bridge" (Kaufman, 1992) after shame-stress induced dyadic mismatches. The working through of these shame dynamics allows for the establishment of an internal state of "quiet alertness" (Lamb, 1981) or "alert inactivity" (Beebe & Lachman, 1988), and this reestablishment of the affect of interest, particulary a benign interest focused toward the self, may be a requisite state for the development of insight. Indeed, shame reflects the intensification of trophotropic arousal, and heightened levels of trophotropic arousal are associated with meditative states (Fischer, 1971).

Pine (1986a) asserts that in early socioemotional development, much of the learning and growth toward higher order functioning take place in "quiescent periods" which occur in moments of delay following distress. In a recent work applying developmental principles to psychotherapy (1990), he concludes that as a result of transactions with a reliable caregiver, the child develops an expectation of relief, which he equates with trust. These experiences provide the "experiential glue of connection to the object" (p. 203). I would add that in longer term treatment the patient's ongoing interactive experience with an affectively interacting, affect regulating psychotherapist, especially after episodes of transference-countertransference stress (attachment breaks, or ruptures in the working alliance), may facilitate the transformation of an insecure into a secure attachment pattern. The ability to autoregulate affect allows for an advance in the individual's adaptive functions—a broadened affect tolerance, an expansion of the affect array, and an improved capacity to regulate psychobiological state transitions and to recover from disruptive affective states.

With regard to nonverbal affective communications within the therapist-patient dyad, classical psychoanalytic studies of child and adult patients with "primitive" developmental disorders have emphasized the importance of "projective identification" and "containment." Projective identification is defined as an early developmental interactive process between two individuals wherein largely unconscious information is projected from the sender to the recipient (Klein, 1946). The affect regulatory function of this mechanism was stressed by Bion's (1962) concept of "containment." Ideas concerning the interpersonal component of this ubiquitous mechanism have been advanced by Grotstein (1981) and also by Ogden (1979), who states, "Projective identification does not exist where there is no interaction between projector and recipient" (p. 14). In a later conceptualization, Ogden (1990) proposes that the infant projector induces a feeling state in the (maternal) other that corresponds to a state that the projector is unable to experience for himself. The recipient allows the induced state to reside within, and by reinternalizing this externally metabolized experience the infant gains a change in the quality of his experience. The developmental importance of projective identification and containment is described by Hamilton (1992):

> When children have strong affects that threaten to overwhelm them, they externalize their distress. The parent takes in the projected feeling and self-object state, contains it, modulates it, gives it meaning, and returns the transformed affect in the form of holding, a meaningful comment, or some other communication. The child can now accept the metabolized affect and self-object state as his own. He eventually takes in the containing process itself along with the transformed projections, identifies with it, and learns to contain his own affects to a large degree. (p. xiii)

Adler and Rhine (1992) conclude that projective identification involves the projection of affects associated with self and object representations. Furthermore, they suggest that the selfobject function of projective identification may be related to empathy and that it provides the opportunity for change in internal structure in psychotherapy.

For many patients the psychotherapeutic relationship creates, for the first time, an optimal socioemotional environment for the development of internal structures that efficiently regulate affect. In being psychobiologically attuned to and therefore matching the patient's unconscious internal state (Stern, 1985), instead of his verbal-behavioral state, the empathic therapist can enter into dyadic affect transactions with the patient and act as an affect regulator. The therapist's focus on nonverbal events is responsible for the use of visual imagery to identify primitive affective states. Activation of associative connections within the nonverbal system allows for the emergence of "warded off emotional schemata," discrete images of experiences that cannot be named (Bucci, 1993). As a result of the containing function of the therapist, the patient-therapist relationship can hold a negative affect in time, especially one triggered by a misattunement that induces shame in the patient, long enough to recognize it. The symbolic function of the therapist allows for the verbal description and communication of the affective experience, and naming it thereby gives it meaning. Due to the clinician's reparative function, the dyad reattunes and psychobiologically transitions from a negative into a positive affective state.

A clinical focus on unrecognized bypassed shame is important to the psychotherapy of affect dysregulations since this affect inhibits the expression of any emotion. This property is especially evident in alexithymic syndromes, since these patients are remarkably unaware of their feelings, have difficulty in talking about them, and have little emotional expression (Lesser, 1985). In the therapy process the inner state of "nameless shame" (Kohut, 1977), a total experience that forbids communication with words (Kaufman, 1974), must be described verbally. I have earlier shown that shame, when consciously experienced, represents a rapid psychobiological state transition from sympathetic predominant ergotropic arousal to parasympathetic predominant trophotropic arousal. In this way the shame mechanism can undergo elaboration and "gain representation as symbols that become signals" (Knapp, 1967, p. 533). Consequently, the patient's potentially self-disorganizing alexithymic experience—a distressing feeling without words—can now be represented at a "more mature level". That is to say, a presymbolic unshared and unregulated visceral affective experience is transformed into a shared and regulated symbolic affective experience. Taylor, who considers alexithymia to represent a disorder of affect regulation (personal communication, April 18, 1993), asserts that in psychoanalytic treatment,

> [A]ttention (is) given to repairing deficits in the patient's self-organisation, and to elevating chaotic impulses and inchoate emotions from a primitive sensorimotor level of experience to a mature representational level where they could be valued for their signal function and modulated through imaginal activity and communication with others. (1993, p. 12)

THE NEUROBIOLOGICAL CHARACTERIZATION OF PSYCHOTHERAPEUTICALLY INDUCED PSYCHIC STRUCTURAL CHANGES

In optimal early development, the child permanently internalizes the caregiver's regulatory function. Can this ontogenetic process be recreated over the course of a psychotherapeutic relationship? How is the therapist's affect regulating process "taken in" and what does the patient "identify with"? The treatment of early right hemispheric attachment pathology involves the socioaffective experience-dependent development in the patient of an internalized image of the therapist (Searles, 1987) that counters the one generated in interactions with an early "psychotoxic" mother (Spitz, 1965). Blatt (1992) now concludes that:

> . . . .it may be useful to view the therapeutic process, like psychological development more generally, as a process that involves a series of attachments and

separations—"gratifying involvements" and "experienced incompatibilities"—that facilitate and contribute to internalization and the development of more mature levels of psychological structures or schema. (p. 717)

Watt (1986) refers to the replacement of older internalizations with new internalizations based on the therapist's benign and more empathic responses to the patient's transferential expressions of dysphoric and distressing affect. A recent experimental study (Kantrowitz et al., 1989) of the facilitating effect of the matching process on psychoanalytic treatment indicates that the therapist's "characteristic style" provides a quality that was deficient in the patient, and that the patient's acquisition of the formerly missing attribute may be based on an internalization of an identification with the therapist. Ricks (1985), a developmental psychologist, suggests that the basic postulates of a representational model of attachment formed early in life can be changed through an especially strong emotional experience within a single relationship which disconfirms earlier postulates. The research of Geller (1984) indicates that patients' internalizations of the therapist range from an inert, static aggregate of part properties, to an elaborated representation of a vital, whole human being. The ability of the patient to evoke this latter "benignly influential" relatively stable cognitive-affective representation elicits a distinct and varied emotional experience, and allows for relief of pain, self-perceived growth, and autonomous self-regulation. In other words, the internalization of interactive repair transactions enables an expanded self-structure access to symbolic representations which encode the psychobiological state transitions that underlie evocative memory and self-comforting functions.

The emergence of these adaptive capacities reflects a further development of "psychic structure" in the patient. According to Bucci (1993) recoding within nonverbal emotional structures represents the theoretical goal of deep psychoanalytic treatment and the singular definition of successful outcome in psychoanalytic terms.

> The goal of treatment is building of the new referential strutures (i.e., insight), leading ultimately to change in the emotional structures themselves, that is, *structural change,* so that the world actually "looks different," "feels different," impulses operate differently, rather than simply being understood. . . .The construction of new emotional meanings in the therapeutic discourse parallels, in some respects, the development of emotional meanings in the early life of the child . . . In contrast to emotions per se, and in contrast to past events, *meanings,* including emotional meanings, are what humans are able to regulate and reconstruct. (pp. 43 and 44)

Advances in our understanding of the developmental neurobiology of corticolimbic regulatory structures now enables us to more precisely characterize the nature of such structural changes. An application of our knowledge of the affect regulating dyadic transactions that occur in a growth facilitating environment in early development may allow for its more precise recreation in a psychodynamic reparative relationship in later life. There is now general agreement that the massive growth of cortico-cortical connections with frontal regions begins in human infancy (Thatcher, 1991), that the maturation of the interconnections of prefrontal neurons is affected by environmental factors (Winson, 1985), and that limbic interconnections are influenced by the interaction the developing child has with its mediators (Gilbert, 1989). Imprinting experiences in infancy involve affective transactions between the mother's and the infant's cortex, especially in the right hemisphere that contributes to the development of reciprocal interactions within the mother-infant regulatory system (Taylor, 1987). Although these processes occur at their highest rates during early life, under proper conditions they may continue after a critical period. Recent neurobiological investigations indicate that adults retain certain capacities for plasticity. It is well established that central catecholaminergic neurons, including dopaminergic mesolimbic neurons, exhibit considerable regenerative capabilities (Reis, Ross, Gilad, & Joh, 1978). Prefrontal areas are known to continue maturing well into adulthood, perhaps throughout the lifespan. Affect regulatory dialogs mediated by a psychotherapist may induce literal structural change in the form of new patterns of growth of cortical-limbic circuitries, especially in the right hemisphere which contains representations of self-and-object images. These structural changes could allow for a more efficient right hemispheric representation of autonomic conditioning to facial emotional expressions (Johnsen & Hugdahl, 1993), orbitofrontal modulation of autonomic nervous system activity (Neafsey, 1990), and thereby more adaptive right cortical modulation of nonverbal communication and affect (Ross, 1985).

The outcome of an optimal psychotherapy relationship would be a dual limbic circuit orbitofrontal cortex that can adaptively transition between different psychobiological states. Efficient orbitofrontal activity is associated with a lower threshold for awareness of sensations of internal origin, that is, internal affective states (Goldenberg et al., 1989), a capacity essential to adaptive functioning. Basch (1988) now proposes that the aim of psychotherapy is more than symptom removal, rather, it can facilitate altering and reworking of "the patterns in the patient's nervous system" (p. 108) that govern how he or she processes socioemotional information. Most intriguingly, Watt (1986) proposes that the connections of the right frontolimbic cortex, a structure involved in homeostatic regulation, are specifically reworked in long term psychotherapy:

> . . . the importance of cortical-limbic connections, assimilated through experience in the regulation of emotion suggests the likelihood that what psychoanalysis has called "structural change" involves not only the changes in interhemispheric relations . . . but also significant changes in these sensorilimbic connections. (p. 68)

NONLINEAR DYNAMIC (CHAOS) THEORY AS A
MODEL FOR THE INVESTIGATION OF "HIDDEN"
NONVERBAL PROCESSES
OF PSYCHOTHERAPY

Psychoanalysis has been frequently criticized for its perceived failure to empirically test the critical hypotheses relating to its theory and therapy (Shulman, 1992), and such criticisms have been voiced from within the psychoanalytic community (Eagle & Wolitsky, 1985; Holzman, 1985; Wallerstein, 1986a) as well as from philosophers of science (Grunbaum, 1984). More and more attempts are now being made to address this issue, as psychotherapy research is finally beginning to be viewed as a fundamental area of study (Beutler & Crago, 1991; Horowitz & Stinson, 1991; Luborsky & Crits-Christoph, 1990; Sampson, 1992; Strupp, 1989; Wallerstein, 1986b; Weiss & Sampson, 1986). The bulk of such research, however, focuses upon the patient's verbal outputs as the primary data of the psychotherapeutic process. Often this material is represented in transcripts and not actual recordings of a patient's (and incidentally the therapist's) verbal behaviors. Such samples totally delete the essential "hidden" prosodic cues and visuoaffective transactions that are communicated between patient and therapist. I suggest that the almost exclusive focus of research on verbal and cognitive rather than nonverbal and affective psychotherapeutic events has severely restricted our deeper understanding of the dyadic therapy process. In essence, studying only left hemispheric activities can never elucidate the mechanisms of the socioemotional disorders that arise from limitations of right hemispheric affect regulation.

How can the crucial nonverbal aspects of transferential communications be both qualitatively and quantitatively investigated? How can the underlying mechanisms of psychopathology, the limitations of adaptive stress regulating capacities, be exposed in order to bring them into clearer focus of study? How can the induction of dynamic state transitions by clinical affect regulating transactions be experimentally demonstrated? What research design can be utilized to investigate the alterations in the nonverbal components of psychotherapy, and how can these be related to verbal interventions? And what type of methodology can incorporate measures of the affective and cognitive functions of not only the left and right cortical hemispheres, but also subcortical operations?

Chaos theory, used to describe neural information processing (Duke & Pritchard, 1991), brain function (Basar, 1990) and psychoanalytic models of mood and self-image (Abraham, Abraham, Shaw, & Garfinkel, 1990), is now being applied to the psychotherapy process. Very recent research is analyzing the chaotic dynamics of mental states and mental control (regulatory) processes that occur within an insight-oriented psychoanalytic psychotherapy session (Redington & Reidbord, 1992; Reidbord & Redington, 1992). The research paradigm of nonlinear dynamical analysis models complex patterns of state changes in autonomic nervous system activity and shows that autonomic functional dynamics (flows of heart rate) mark certain psychodynamic state changes. The property of chaos in such a system is related to the complexity or the dimensionality of the transitions among states, and dysfunction is defined as abnormality in the dimensionality of state transitions. The current state of a system evolves out of a sequence of preceding states, and a "trajectory" depicts the path taken by the system from one state to the next. These authors refer to the importance of pinpointing clinically meaningful moments during therapy that perturb the patient to change trajectories. In line with the essential assumption of chaos theory of the macroscopic sensitivity of chaotic phenomena to small changes in initial conditions, they suggest that mental states "may unfold in a dramatically different pattern following a miniscule interpersonal or intrapersonal perturbation" (p. 655).

Redington and Reidbord (1992) have examined the spontaneously occurring autonomic activity of a social phobic patient during a 50 minute psychotherapy session and illustrate that cardiac responses associated with psychologically meaningful events display chaotic dynamics. In perhaps their most significant finding, they identify a sequence of dissociable state trajectories with distinct onsets and offsets that unfold over the course of a session. A type I trajectory shows no apparent transitions and is associated with an unhealthy psychodynamic correlate. Types II through III represent sudden perturbations that result in changes (increases or decreases of heart rate), and type IV, a "wandering" trajectory, exhibits high dimensionality and adaptability. The transitions between trajectory types are clinically meaningful, as demonstrated by the finding that the arrival of the therapist perturbed the trajectory. The authors observe that, however, the most notable change in trajectory occurred as the patient dealt explicitly with a central psychodynamic issue—being admired and wanted versus being shunned and rejected by the therapist (shame dynamics). As this issue was discussed there was a sudden type III trajectory, a sharp deceleration of heart rate, and this reduction in cardiovascular arousal persisted throughout the remainder of the session. In the last part of the session "the patient had relaxed considerably, and was addressing a number of emotional issues in a calmer fashion " (p. 1001). They conclude that certain therapeutic interventions perturb patients from their "incarceration" in certain pathological mental states, leading to healthier trajectories during and after psychotherapy.

Reidbord and Redington (1992) have further investigated nonlineăr psychodynamics in a companion study of another patient, one diagnosed as a depressive and posttraumatic stress disorder. The arrival of the therapist shifted a baseline state in the midarousal range to a more "ballistic" trajectory and a higher heart rate, consistent with a startle response. With the additional data from this study, they are now beginning to characterize the various trajectory types of specific types of patients. Type I trajectories are brief in duration and homogeneous in terms of affective state and content. The patient tends to be avoidant of central feelings and issues, and appears overcontrolled. The authors suggest that this type corresponds to a pattern of "psychodynamic control, paid for by a constriction of affective range and topics of discussion, and a narrowing of attention" (p. 655). Type II has a "narrative" confessional quality, and the patient is slightly anxious and defensive. The greatest expression of overt affect occurs during type III trajectories, and these are clinically most variable. These two trajectories represent a less tightly controlled "search for expression in the face of troubling affect, a compromise position that balances affective expression and control" (p. 655). The onset of type IV trajectories coincides with therapist interventions and reflects lowered defenses and more genuine affective expression with a wider dynamic range of attention. These trajectories are longer in duration than the others. It is in this state that the patient experiences the most reflective introspective moments in therapy. Reidbord and Redington conclude that clinical findings during transitions may identify psychological mechanisms that have the capacity to change one's physiological state. They also assert that chaos represents a lifting of constraints on information processing. Most intriguingly, they report that in forthcoming research they plan to examine the dyadic interaction between patient and therapist in terms of the synchronization of two nonlinear dynamical systems.

I interpret these chaotic events to be psychobiological state transitions that occur during affective stress inducing and stress regulating transactions that take place in psychotherapy. As in infancy, these occur during discrete "central moments" (Pine, 1985) in the therapy session, critical times when chaotic dynamics are activated. I also suggest that these episodes of nonlinear psychodynamics are triggered by transferential communications, right hemspheric transmissions that are conveyed and received by visual and prosodic signals. These affective interactions represent critical nonverbal phenomena in the treatment of disorders of the regulation of primitive affect. The patient presents with characteristic object relational modes—easily accessible baseline states that reflect the operation of insecure avoidant or resistant strategies of affect regulation. These are especially expressed during initial engagements—reunions—with the psychotherapist, moments that are associated with expected psychobiological state transitions.

The early events in a psychotherapy session (or any human-human interaction) are highly influenced by the dyad's nonverbal transactions, and represent critical intervals of sensitivity to misattuned transactions that inflict narcissistic injuries and propel the patient into enduring non object relating dysregulated states. Such "hidden", fast-acting, unconscious dyadic transmissions can trigger entrance into "misattuned" and "defensive" or even "dreaded" dynamic states. If, on the other hand, the pair remain psychobiologically attuned throughout the reunion by creating a state of "mutually entrained central nervous system propensities" (Horner, 1985), if they can reestablish mirroring transactions that amplify positive affect, the patient and therapist will experience a transition into a less defensive state where they can jointly experience and explore states that are colored with negative affect. Confronting painful feelings and thoughts is known to decrease autonomic arousal (Pennebaker & Beall, 1986). This allows for an opportunity for state-dependent learning in states that are usually defended against and avoided. It is the therapist's verbally expressed affect regulating interventions, particularly those that induce comfort and reestablish states colored by positive affect that trigger entrance into a state of regulated affect expression. These phenomena may be demonstrated in changes in the amplitude of respiratory sinus arrythmia, an index of cardiac parasympathetic tone (Grossman et al., 1990).

In chaos research in the physical sciences, Jackson (1991) argues that "entrainment" of a dynamic system is a precondition to control of dynamic flows, and that this allows for "hierarchical systems to adapt to environmental changes" (p. 4839). Shinbrot, Grebogi, Ott, and Yorke (1993) now report that chaotic systems are extremely sensitive to small perturbations, and that these tiny feedback perturbations control trajectories in chaotic systems. These researchers experimentally demonstrate that small perturbations can be used both to stabilize regular dynamic behaviors and to direct chaotic trajectories rapidly to a "desired state". They also show that, using only tiny perturbations, one can switch between a rich variety of dynamical behaviors as circumstances change. Referring to "the advantage of chaos", they conclude that "Incorporating chaos deliberately into practical systems therefore offers the possibility of achieving greater flexibility in their performance" (p. 411). This principle of adaptivity also applies to the psychobiological functioning of the human mind (and indeed to all living systems). I have earlier presented multilevel evidence that indicates that the capacity to fluidly transition between various states allows for more complex modes of information processing and the generation of more complex symbolic representations. Putnam (1992) suggests that discrete behavioral states, reflecting enduring patterns of physiological and psychological variables, act as "nonlinear transforms for sensory information" (p. 99). He also concludes that as a result of state modulation by the external environment the developing individual is able to utilize "the ability to bring forth an appropriate behavioral state for a given situation" (1992, p. 101). Spezzano (1993) notes that:

> Repeated experiences of competent affect-regulation within the transference give the patient the material with which to construct a self-representation that sustains a sense of perceived affective competence. The conviction that one can competently regulate one's own affective life is a state of well-being. (p. 216)

SUMMARY

The knowledge gained from multidisciplinary research on socioemotional development can be applied to the problem of the treatment of various clinical manifestations of self-pathology. Psychotherapy represents the recreation of an optimal interpersonal environment which facilitates the growth of psychic structures that store and process social and affective information. Early forming representations of the self-interacting-with-a-misattuned-dysregulating-other become unconscious internalized object relations that mediate psychiatric psychopathology. Such representations are imprinted predominantly with painful primitive affect, which the developmentally impaired personality can not intrapersonally nor interpersonally regulate. Certain forms of external and internal affective input are therefore selectively excluded from conscious processing. These strategies of affect regulation must be recognized and addressed in the dyadic psychotherapeutic treatment of developmental disorders.

Affect, especially unconscious affect, is the focus of the psychoanalytically-oriented treatment of primitive emotional disorders. This affect is transacted between the therapist and patient in transference-countertransference communications. In such transactions the therapist becomes empathically and psychobiologically attuned to the patient's internal state. In the initial stages of treatment this allows for the creation of an intersubjective field in which positive vitality affects may be dyadically induced and amplified. This mirroring allows for the establishment of an affective attachment bond that supports a working alliance in which the two can explore the patient's internal world, especially his or her experiences with negative affect.

Unregulated, and therefore "bypassed" and unconscious, shame is a potent motive force that underlies repression. Early forming, nonverbal defenses are erected and maintained to specifically exclude this negative affect from consciousness. Its transformation into conscious shame then becomes a major treatment goal of the analysis and working through of defenses of the infantile nonverbal affect system. This occurs at points where, after a working alliance has been established, the therapist gradually and sensitively induces shame in the patient by not mirroring his or her grandiose expectations. Following these stressful relational ruptures, the therapist acts as a shame regulator, enabling the patient to recover from depressive states and to restore the narcissistic balance that underlies self-esteem homeostasis. The therapists's role in affect regulation contributes to the resolution of crisis states. Opportunities for dyadic interactive repair are expanded in longer term treatment. In the context of an extended relationship, interactive transactions can be internalized, allowing for the emergence of an adaptive mechanism that can, under periods of stress, be accessed for self-comforting.

The patient-therapist relationship acts as a growth promoting environment that supports the experience-dependent maturation of the right brain, especially those areas that have connections with the subcortical limbic structures that mediate emotional arousal. Structural change, an outcome of long-term psychological treatment, specifically involves the rewiring of the connections of the right frontolimbic cortex and the consequent replacement of toxic with more benign internal representations of the self. These events allow for the emergence of a system that can efficiently mediate psychobiological transitions between various internal states.

VI INTEGRATIONS

34

Right Hemispheric Language and Self-Regulation

[T]he nondominant right hemisphere can play a much more important role in children than in adults. . . .in the early period of the child's development the right hemisphere exerts a much greater influence on the course of speech processes than in older children and adults.
—Aleksandr Luria (1980)

The dialogical model takes as inputs the products of sensorimotor-intelligence, along with the infant's affect state and motivations to be with his primary caregivers in intimate ways. The output is language itself.
—John Dore (1985)

During the first year and more intensely during the second year, developmental process accounts for the formation of the child's self-regulatory capability. . . .Through identification with the mother, her regulatory interventions and the attitudes governing them are internalized and become part of the child's own regulatory functions.
—Calvin F. Settlage et al. (1990)

A deeper understanding and appreciation of the psychoneurobiological ontogeny of the orbitofrontal cortex, the critical control center of the affective core of the self that regulates affective and interactional function, may facilitate a reconciliation of "biological-neurophysiological" and "ontogenetic-sociocultural" mechanisms which is required by any general theory of emotions (Lazarus, 1991b). The experience-dependent development of this brain structure, which is intimately involved in the appraisal and regulation of socioaffective information, is relevant if not revealing to a general theory of socioemotional development, that is, to the

477

problem of how the developing child, whose social and emotional behaviors change over time, retains continuity. Alberts (1987) now concludes that a sequence of ontogenetic adaptations sustains continuity throughout the early stages of development, and that these adaptations involve constellations of adjustments on multiple levels of organization—physiological, anatomical, sensory, and behavioral. These ontogenetic adaptations represent the socioaffective experience-sensitive transmutations of the frontolimbic cortex which is involved in multi-level connections with various cortical and subcortical structures. The object relational influenced transformations of this system are responsible for the increasingly complex capacities of the right hemisphere to autonomously process socioemotional information. This phenomenon is proposed to be the mechanism underlying the observation that emotional development involves a sequential maturational progression in the quality and complexity of relatedness to others (Fairbairn, 1952).

The development of self-regulation is an important area of current developmental psychological research (Campos et al., 1989; Izard, 1990; Kopp, 1982). The cognitive processes of inhibition and delay are thought to be essential to this emergent capacity. Advances in symbolic abilities and the onset of speech have also been considered to play an important role in the ontogeny of internal regulatory capacities. The contributions of orbitofrontal inhibitory functions and of right hemispheric speech to self-regulation are discussed in this chapter. After this, I offer some ideas about the interpersonal origins of narrative thought, a concept developed by Spence (1982), a psychoanalytic theoretician. I then present a model that highlights the unique role of early shame-mediated socialization experiences in the genesis of representations of the "bad self". Finally, I discuss the affect regulating properties of another psychoanalytic construct, evocative memory.

INHIBITION, DELAY, AND SELF-REGULATION

The maturation of the orbitofrontal affect regulatory structural system which governs internal inhibition (Velasco & Lindsley, 1965) and performs a delayed response function (Freedman & Oscar-Berman, 1986; Mishkin, 1964; Niki, Sakai, & Kubota, 1972) is critical to the inauguratory emergence at the end of the practicing stage of the protoautoregulatory nascent self which supports autonomous function. At this juncture, the onset of the succeding rapprochement stage, for the first time thoughts and feelings persist beyond the situation in which they had their origin, and continue in the child's mind for longer periods of time (McDevitt, 1975). These enduring affects may represent the onset of true mood states and are associated with the appearance at this time of emotional biases in personality (Malatesta et al., 1989). These biases, in turn, are experienced as an individual's characteristic states of mind (Horowitz, 1987). At 18 months a major affective developmental change towards increasing emotional complexity occurs, which is reflected in the child's "increasing differentiation of his emotional life" (Mahler, 1980) and in her new ability to simultaneously experience blends of different emotions (Hyson & Izard, 1985). Extended periods of symbolic play, in which the child now attributes emotions and intentions to play-things—thereby more fully simulating his socioemotional interactions—also rapidly emerge at around 18 months (Leslie, 1987).

There is now general agreement that "control/delay/inhibition processes" are required for the expansion of the affect array (Pine, 1980). The regulation of complex emotional states involves a tolerance for a range of shifting affective states and the postponement of need gratification (Wilson et al., 1990). Kohut (1977) proposes that frustration experience-dependent transmuting internalizations initiate the maturation of regulatory structures which deal with uncomfortable emotions and which are necessary for "the tolerance of delays." As previously mentioned, neuropsychological research indicates that the delayed response function is the cognitive operation that underlies representational processes. This conclusion is also propounded by psychoanalytic workers: "The capacity to delay, to anticipate, to wait confidently, is developed along with, and through, the capacity to form and retain a reliable representation of the object" (J. Jacobson, 1983, p. 545). Greenspan (1979, p. 151) asserts that practicing age experiences of frustration are necessary to consolidate a capacity for delay and the use of mental representations. Both delay of gratification (Mischel & Underwood, 1974) and tolerance of frustration (Van Leishout, 1975) are considered to be functional derivatives of the ability to regulate emotional experience and expression. In developmental studies, self-control, defined as delay/response inhibition in the presence of an attractive stimulus, is first observed in 18-month-old children (Vaughn, Kopp, & Krakow, 1984). In a recent paper on the development of emotional regulation, Izard (1990) now concludes:

> This delay between the evaluation of the eliciting event and the onset of the expressive behavior becomes a doorway for regulatory processes. Perceptual and cognitive processes, which take time, can operate in this gap and hence influence subsequent emotion expression and emotion experience. (p. 493)

What is the nature of these intervening cognitive processes?

THE DIALOGIC ORIGIN OF EARLY SPEECH

It is important to emphasize that the child who attains this level of self-regulatory organization is still essentially preverbal, or more precisely neoverbal—the average 18-month-old has a vocabulary of only 22 words (Mussen et al., 1969). In a paper stressing the importance of early preverbal communication, Papousek et al. (1991) assert that: "Earlier impressions that cognitive and symbolic processes develop only in humans, following the acquisition of speech, has been corrected by recent findings in preverbal human infants and in animal research" (p. 115). Lazarus (1991a) points out that a corpus of developmental research indicates that:

> . . . children have much more understanding of the social and psychological rules of emotion than has hitherto been supposed, and that this understanding starts early, even before there has been language development and certainly before they can verbalize feeling rules. (p. 355)

The 1½-year-old toddler is thus capable of reception, expression, and self-regulation of complex emotions before the onset of emotion-descriptive language which does not first emerge until 20-months-of-age (Bretherton, McNew, & Beeghly, 1981). It is now accepted that early language learning represents the development of a communicational system rather than the unfolding of a formal system of syntax (Kaplan & Kaplan, 1970). With regard to the socialization changes over the practicing period, Schaffer and Crook (1980) conclude the nonverbal accompaniments of maternal verbalizations aimed at controlling, inhibiting and directing the behavior of 15-month-old infants carry the crucial communicative meaning. Mothers of 14-month-old toddlers utilize distinctive prosodic patterns to highlight affectively salient, meaningful events and to modulate the child's attention (Fernald & Mazzie, 1991). At the end of the second year children listening to adult commands have been shown to respond to the familiarity of particular single words and intonation rather than to syntactic framework and correct word order.

The child's participation in a network that communicates visuoaffective signals with the mother is firmly established by the end of the first year. Izard (1991) observes that long before the infant either comprehends or speaks a single word, it already has a remarkable repertoire of signals to communicate its internal states. Research studies indicate that even before children's first words emerge they adopt the particular tone of their native language (de Boysson-Bardies, Sagart, & Durand, 1984), and that when single words (Barrett, 1985) first appear they are used in combination with gestures (Greenfield & Smith, 1976) and occur within prosodic envelopes (Bloom, 1973). Dore (1985) describes a particular period from the end of the first year, when "protocommunications"— vocalizations accompanied by affectively salient tones, gestures, and facial expressions that signal internal affect states—first emerge, until later in the second year, when the child uses one word at a time. Dore observes that during this period (which exactly overlaps the practicing period) the child's nascent neoverbal abilities are primarily influenced by social and emotional factors. These specifically occur in dialogic "face engagements" in which the emotionally attuned mother shares in and articulates the child's emotional state. The tight coupling between the child's speech progress in the first two years and the mother-child interaction has been pointed out by other researchers as well (e.g., Olson, Bayles, & Bates, 1986; Rice, 1989). In a recent psychoanalytic conceptualization, Foster (1992) argues that intersubjective operations between the young child and the primary object involve a negotiation of consensual word meanings that describe particular internal states. Early language recognition/word meaning, organized around the object with whom and from whom the word meaning was learned, is a function of self and other experiencing the world together. In this way, language and object relations are inextricably linked. Wilson and Weinstein (1992b) point out that early word meanings encompass the psychophysiological senses that accompany a word.

Tomasello's (1988) work highlights the importance of dyadic joint attentional processes between the responsive mother and the child which provide important nonlinguistic scaffolding of early language learning. It has been proposed in earlier chapters that at the beginning of the practicing stage the mother plays a critical role in providing novel environmental stimuli to the infant in visuoaffective-communicating social referencing transactions that foster dyadic states of psychobiological attunement and joint visual attention. This dialogic process was suggested to facilitate opportunities for tactual-visual cross-modal transfer learning. In the early part of the first year infants demonstrate primitive capacities for auditory-visual integration (Humphrey, Tees, & Werker, 1979; Lawson, 1980), but with the maturation of visual and the ascendance of auditory capacities at the end of the first year visual-auditory cross-modal learning begins in earnest. Greenough and Black (1992) articulate the principle that information from a mature modality helps integrate and organize input from a newly developing modality. This developmental phenomenon is reflected in the appearance of Dore's multimodal protocommunications at the beginning of the practicing period.

In social referencing transactions the infant reads the mother's face for affective appraisals of salient interactions and events, and by the end of the practicing stage, the period of the emergence of single word speech, the infant increasingly attends to both the visual and auditory stimulation emanating from her emotionally expressive face. It is well known that visual information from faces is utilized in speech perception (Green & Kuhl, 1989), and the fundamental cross-modal nature of this phenomenon is expressed in McGurk and MacDonald's (1976) work on "hearing lips and seeing voices." Dore and Tomasello are describing the dyadic visuoauditory affective transactions in a Vygotskian zone of proximal deveopment which enhance cross-modal visual-auditory integrations that promote even more complex abstraction capacities. Furthermore, these dyadic phenomena may characterize Bruner's (1983) "language acquisition support system," the background communicative structures that exist between the caregiver and child that regulates cognitive, social, and emotional activities and potentiates the brain's hard wiring of Chomsky's (1965) "language acquisition device."

THE REGULATORY FUNCTIONS OF RIGHT HEMISPHERIC SINGLE WORD SPEECH

It should be pointed out that the 18-month toddler can use the semantic "no" (Spitz, 1957) and has been imputed to be able to conceptualize the self in terms of "good" and "bad" (Sander, 1975). In clinical neurological studies, Ross (1983) has shown that "the right hemisphere has dominant language functions involving the modulation of the affective components of language through prosody and emotional gesturing" (p. 505). In split brain research, Sperry, Zaidel, and Zaidel (1979) have demonstrated in adult cerebral commissurotomy patients that the right hemisphere is responsible for the generation of single words such as "no" and "good." Developmental psychological experiments indicate that children's single word speech represents an early important stage of language development. There is general agreement that single word utterances occur developmentally before syntax (Bloom, 1973), and Dromi (1986) has described "the one word period" as a stage of language development which occurs at around 18 months. Vygotsky (1988) has proposed, "The child's thought emerges first in a fused, unpartitioned whole. It is precisely for this reason that it must be expressed in speech as a single word" (p. 251).

I suggest that the experience-dependent maturation of the early developing affective-configurational right and not the later developing lexical-semantic left cerebral cortex is critically involved in the earliest manifestations of affect regulating socializing verbal communications and thought. This experience is embedded in the early affectively-focused language interactions between the child and the primary object which generate word meanings that attempt to verbally characterize internal (Foster, 1992) and psychophysiological (Wilson & Weinstein, 1992b) states. Infant studies now underscore the fact that the affective dimension is instrumental to the acquisition of meanings (Kaye, 1982). I would argue that the right hemisphere-to-right hemisphere dialogue is the primordial wellspring of the set of coherent systems of meanings that is acquired during development and that constitutes a personal narrative (Palombo, 1991). This early language thus represents "language in the service of right hemispheric cognition" that is associated with narrative thought (Vitz, 1990, p. 712). Vitz argues that narrative thought is expressed in intonation and emotion-associated images.

It is often overlooked that the right hemisphere also supports cognitive processing (Perecman, 1983) and verbal communication (Joanette, Goulet, & Hannequin, 1990). The right hemisphere is known to process perceptual wholes (Lezak, 1976), to contain neural representations of prosodic contours, gestures, and facial expressions (Blonder, Bowers, & Heilman, 1991), to establish personally relevant, familiar nonliteral language (Van Lanker, 1991), to contribute to the development of reciprocal interactions within the mother-infant regulatory system (Taylor, 1987), and to be dominant in the storage of self-and-object images (Watt, 1990) and autobiographical memory (Cimino, Verfaellie, Bowers, & Heilman, 1991). The maturation of this right cortical system is thus critical to "the development of self-regulation through private speech" (Ziven, 1979).

In a recent neuroanatomic study of the postnatal development of the orofacial motor speech region and Broca's area, Simonds and Scheibel (1989) demonstrate that:

> Dendrites in the presumptive motor speech zones on the right develop more preco-ciously than those on the left and seem more advanced during the perinatal period. Thereafter, developmental sequences are characterized both by growth spurts and resorption, until dendrite systems of the left hemisphere "catch up with" and begin to surpass those on the right by the fourth to sixth year. However, the speech zone on the right hemisphere continues to show robust development in distal segment patterns even as late as the sixth year. (p. 143)

These authors suggest that "the early structural primacy of right-sided dendritic systems" may be associated with "the right hemispheric role in emotional and prosodic components of language function."

Even more specifically, the developmental advances in language functions of the second year may represent the maturation of connections between the spe-cialized auditory cortical regions in the superior temporal gyrus and the orbito-frontal cortex (Benevento et al., 1977; Petrides & Pandya, 1988) (see Fig. 34.1). This information can now be delivered to and thereby influence the activity of the "paralimbic core of the brain" (Tucker, 1992) or the "core of the emotional system" (Ledoux, 1989). The orbitofrontal region, known to be involved in auditory-visual interactions (Fallon & Benevento, 1978), cognitive and memory functions (Stuss et al., 1982), and social behavior (de Bruin, 1990; Kolb & Whishaw, 1990), performs an exectutive role in the integration of right hemi-spheric operations. Temporal-right frontal connections have been implicated in a circuit that maintains prosodic information (Zatorre & Samson, 1991). As op-posed to the right orbitofrontal involvement in single word speech, the left dorsolateral prefrontal cortex is known to be activated in word fluency (Frith et al., 1991; Warkentin et al., 1991).

On the basis of these findings, I am suggesting that the auditory-visuoaffective dialectical process occurring in the second year is the specific source of narrative thought that is associated with autobiographic self-in-interaction-with-other ex-periences. The internal interactive representations of these transactions, stored in prosodically imprinted multimodal images, are heavily affectively charged. The advent of the earliest form of language brings about the capacity to begin to form an autobiographical history. The earliest form of this history of the self may be

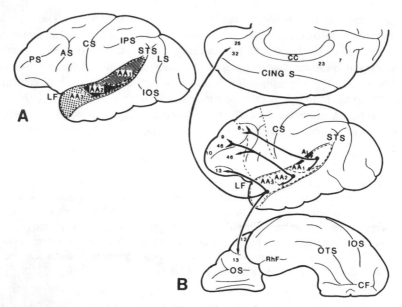

FIG. 34.1. Diagrams showing the three major subdivisions of the auditory association areas of the primate superior temporal gyrus (A), and their frontal lobe connections (B). Note the third-order auditory association area, AA3, connects with Areas 12 and 13 of the orbitofrontal cortex. From Pandya and Barnes (1987). Reprinted by permission of Lawrence Erlbaum Associates.

manifest in the developmental emergence of "imaginal dialogues" (Watkins, 1986), a fundamental part of the individual's narrative construction of the world according to Hermans, Kempen, and van Loon (1992). Stern (1989) concludes that "narrative-making may prove to be a universal human phenomenon reflecting the design of the human mind" (p. 174). Bruner (1986) postulates an early narrative form of thought is associated with autobiographic self-in-interaction-with-other experiences and is heavily affectively charged.

According to Palombo (1992) parental selfobjects regulate the child's affective experience and assist in the structuralization of meaning, thereby facilitating the creation of a coherent narrative and a cohesive self that remains stable over time. If this is not provided, the infant is exposed to overwhelming emotions that cannot be made meaningful and that are incorporated into enduring "incoherent narratives" that are associated with "dysfunctional states". In developmental neurobiological terms, the mother's emotional unavailability in the practicing critical period would interfere with the child's learning of emotion descriptive language (Bretherton et al., 1981) and impair the development of right hemispheric internalized single word speech (early narrative thought) to effectively self-regulate affect. By not providing opportunities for joint visual attention and cross-modal visual-auditory transfer, especially during and subsequent to episodes of affective stress, the mother does not participate in the operation of a language acquisition support system. Her lack of affective involvement thus produces a growth-inhibiting environment which severely retards the experience-dependent growth of right hemispheric temporal-frontal and frontal-subcortical connections that are necessary for the integrated functioning of the right cortex. Taylor (1987) describes:

> It is likely that the right hemisphere contributes to the development of reciprocal interactions within the mother-infant regulatory system, and when these are deficient the child may fail to develop a capacity for being "in tune" with himself. (p. 191)

Psychobiologically being "in tune" with oneself refers to the capacity to recognize, process, and regulate the internal visceral cues associated with the somatic components of emotion. According to Wilson, such a capacity is extremely inefficient in the "self regulatory failure" of alexithymia (Wilson et al., 1990). In more recent writings, Wilson concludes that:

> [S]o much of what is affectively charged, distorted, and expressed somatically is due to the fact that some of the most lasting emotional experiences derive from the preverbal, psychobiological, presymbolic phases of development. (Khantzian & Wilson, 1993, p. 274)

Mueller (1983), studying prosodic disturbances secondary to right hemispheric lesions, suggests that "alexithymia may represent a developmental disconnection syndrome" (p. 108). This diminished capacity to verbally express mood and emotion has been documented in commissurotomized patients who have reduced access to right hemisphere processing during verbal expression (TenHouten, Hoppe, Bogen, & Walter, 1986). In reviewing multidisciplinary studies, Taylor (1987) concludes that deficiencies in the early mother-infant relationship result in an alexithymic deficit associated with a limitation of symbolic function and an impaired capacity for self regulating emotional states and physiological functioning when under stress. I would add that such deficits result from a deprivation of dyadic experiences that engender word meanings that describe the infant's psychophysiological sensations (Wilson & Weinstein, 1992b). It is tempting to speculate that this relational environment also generates high levels of unregulated shame, and that shame, an affect that uniquely causes a "loss of words" (Izard, 1991) always accompanies alexithymic syndromes.

SHAME AND THE EMERGENCE OF THE "BAD SELF"

In the context of an optimally responsive socioemotional environment, "complex cognitive appraisal and coping become central to emotion experiences during the latter part of the first year and into the second year of life" (Fox, 1991, p. 870).

Beebe and Lachman (1988a) refer to the generation of representations of interiorized interactions which begin at the end of the first year and undergo a major
reorganization at 1½ years (the span of the practicing period). A fundamental
change in affect occurs in the middle of the second year. At 18 months the elated
mood of the practicing phase is supplanted by the depressive and fearful mood of
the rapprochement phase (Mahler et al., 1975). Also at about 18 months, a major
discontinuity in the development of mental abilities (Lewis, Jaskir, & Enright,
1986) is observed. This period represents the transition from Piaget's fifth stage
to the sixth and final stage of sensorimotor development. Such integrated
affective-cognitive advances allow for the emergence of symbolic evocative
memory which appears at this time. These complex multimodal interactive representation may contain auditory-prosodic and auditory-verbal as well as visual,
tactile, and proprioceptive components, that is, stored elements of the maternal
face vocalizing infant-directed single word expressions such as "no," "good,"
and "bad."

It is intriguing to note that the internal command in shame, a condition
involving a rapid depletion of positive narcissistic affect associated with internal
self representations, is "Stop. You are no good" (M. Lewis, 1992). The "bad
self" has recently been conceptualized to evolve from the magnification and
internalization of shame (Kaufman, 1989). Tangney, Wagner, Fletcher, & Gramzow (1992) propose that: "In shame, the object of concern is the entire self. The
"bad thing" is experienced as a reflection of a "bad self," and the entire self is
painfully scrutinized and negatively evaluated" (p. 670). In a similar conceptualization, Nathanson (1987), suggests that:

> The sudden unrelatedness accompanying shame-mediated sundering of the infant-
> mother communication dyad in the specific condition of maternal affective transfor-
> mation produces an experience of incompetence. . . .The resultant ideo-affective
> complex is what Klein (1957) termed "bad-me"; following the establishment of this
> linkage any experience of shame now brings with it images defining one as defec-
> tive, weak, or inadequate. (p. 38)

Nathanson (1992) further proposes that in response to early socialization experiences of humiliation and shameful rejection, the child constructs a lexicon of
self-related negative affect states characterized by a fusion of dissmell, disgust,
and shame. This experience is more complex than can be represented in the
child's beginning verbal language, which essentially utilizes global terms. Therefore, this fusion of affects and cognitions is described by the label "bad," and
these labels are carried forth into adulthood.

Watt (1990) describes a "developmentally early template" which contains a
self-image of a child as bad and naughty and an early object image of an angry
mother tied together by the affect of shame which can be activated in later
contexts. This interactive representation is stored as a right frontal engram:

an image of one's self as "bad boy" might consisit of the individual linking auditory information (mother's voice yelling), visual information (images of mother's angry face), somatosensory information (e.g., sensations of visceral upset and increased perspiration) . . . into an image of one's self as frightened, in trouble, and "bad", under the master organizing influence of painful [shame-amplified] affective valence. (p. 509)

In light of the principle that what is internalized are images or scenes that have become imprinted with affect (Kaufman, 1989), I propose that such representational images of self-in-interaction-with-other are imprinted in an "ideo-affective complex" with "nameless shame" (Kohut, 1977), an affect which gives rise to "identity imagery," pervades the whole self, and involves global self-evaluations (H.B. Lewis, 1971). These self-representations are stored in the right hemisphere which processes visual imagery (Robbins & McAdam, 1974) and unverbalizable patterns and perceptual wholes (Lezak, 1976), and contains a representational system based on self-and-object images (Watt, 1990). As previously mentioned the auditory perception of the single word "shame" primes the right hemisphere (Van Strien & Morpugo, 1992). These representations are also imprinted with the related low arousal emotion of disgust, another right hemispheric primitive affect (Davidson, 1992). Izard (1991) suggests that shame can become associated with visual and auditory stimuli, "events and objects even including one's own self" (p. 264). He also points out the adaptive central role that this negative affect plays in the regulation of all emotional expression, and therefore for more effective social interaction (Izard, 1971). The "bad self" thus serves an important regulatory function.

THE SELF-REGULATORY FUNCTIONS
OF EVOCATIVE MEMORY

A developmental progression of representational memory and inhibitory control occurs at 12 months (see earlier material), and again at 18 months in the form of emergent symbolic evocative memory and increased inhibitory capacity. Developmental gradations of representational ability, reflected in a progression of object constancy, are known to critically influence affective development and to allow the child to tolerate greater disruptions in affective states (Trad, 1986). Krystal (1988) refers to the evolution of affect tolerance which occurs during separation-individuation as being critical to the ontogeny of the self-regulation of affect. In developmental psychological studies, Kopp (Kopp, 1982; Vaughn, Kopp, & Krakow, 1984) demonstrates that self-regulation, the capacity to monitor and modulate behavior in order to adapt to the demands of the social and physical environment, is based on representational thought and evocative memory, and emerges at 18 months. Symbolic evocative memory is considered to be an indicator of affective (emotional) object constancy (Fraiberg, 1969).

The capacity of evocative memory enables the child to evoke an image of a comforting object (Adler & Buie, 1979), an adaptive function that contributes to self-regulation. This emergent ability represents an experience-dependent ontogenetic advancement over less complex affect regulating representations that elicit self-comfort. Earlier, due to the maturation of parietal and then occipital—orbital connections, representations of the mother's touch and then the visual image of her face provided this function. Now, with the addition of right parietotemporal—prefrontal connections, stored prosodic memories of her comforting voice can also be accessed in her absence. Putnam (1992) describes:

> It is not uncommon to find a stressed toddler repeating out loud some comforting phrase that his mother used to help him through other difficult experiences. Self-soothing behavior in young children may be an example of their naturally divided psychological organization as one "part" comforts another "part". (p. 102)

According to Putnam, the development of this capacity enables the child to recover from disruptions of state and to integrate sense of self across transitions of state. A further step of Vygotskian transformation leads to silent imaginal dialogues utilized under stress, an important function of 'the dialogical self" (Hermans et al., 1992).

The appearance of the stress regulating verbalizations of these internal thoughts is responsible for the development of self-regulation through private speech (Ziven, 1979). Such internal speech (thought) is initially language in the service of right hemisphere cognition (Vitz, 1990) and not later developing and more complex left hemispheric linguistic capacities. Most importantly to the development of the self, the language capacity involved in the child's recognition and understanding of one particular word—her own name—is also processed in the "non-dominant" [!] hemisphere. This particular word may be especially verbalized by the affect regulating caregivers in stress-comforting exchanges. The child's name is typically the first emotion word that the child learns (Bower, 1992). Behavioral neurology studies indicate that the right hemisphere is indeed specialized for the recognition of familiar personal names (Van Lancker & Klein, 1990). Schwalbe (1991) elaborates:

> language makes it possible to create elaborate self-representations. This begins with naming the self. A name allows us to integrate bits of imagery into a set of experiences that constitute an individual biography, thus giving us a sense of continuous identity. (p. 286)

When a child begins to use her or his own name she or he also acquires the ability to conceptualize the self in symbolic terms, as an abstract entity, and by doing so the image of the self becomes more firmly established (Joseph, 1992).

SUMMARY

Significant gains in self-regulation occur by the middle of the second year. These functional advances reflect the structural maturation of the right frontolimbic areas and the emergence of the more complex and efficient delay and inhibition operations that underlie regulatory capacities. This development is influenced by dyadic affectively-laden verbal transactions, a joint attentional process that scaffolds early language learning. The mother's socializing communications, used to inhibit and direct the toddler's actions, are expressed in prosodic patterns that highlight affectively salient events and modulate the child's attention. Such growth-facilitating events occur in the context of face engagements and are imprinted into the developing orbitofrontal-superior temporal circuitry that is involved in auditory-visual cross-modal learning. This intersubjective mechanism thereby serves as an enriched environment that generates single word speech.

In keeping with the principle that the right hemisphere develops before the left, the early language that appears in the second year represents the output of the right hemisphere. The socioaffectively-driven expansion of language in the service of right hemispheric cognition thus mediates the development of self-regulation through private speech, that is, thought. Thought originates in silent imaginal dialogs that represent the child's autobiographical narrative construction of his affective transactions with the world. Maternal stress regulating verbalizations are also internalized into the multimodal interactive representations that encode the self-caring functions of evocative memory. The child who is deprived of such affective communicational experiences in this critical period is in danger of developing the regulatory disturbance of alexithymia. Two highly affectively-charged words, "bad" and "good," play an important role in the continuing development of the self. The imprinting of shame affect accompanies the socialization injunction "bad," and these misattuned representations serve as a primary matrix for the "bad self." Another single word, the child's name, plays an important role in the ontogeny of the dialogical self.

35 The Dialogical Self and the Emergence of Consciousness

[I] suggest that this [cognitive shock produced by shame affect], this momentary lapse in the smooth, normal functioning of the organism, is a major factor in the development of the self. The difference between the infant before the moment of shame (the infant in the moment of alert activity, of interest, excitement, or enjoyment) and the infant suddenly unable to function, this difference may be registered by the infant as a significant experience calling attention to and helping to define the self.
—Donald L. Nathanson (1987a)

Emergence of an active self in the middle of the second year of life constitutes a central milestone and transition in the child's development.
—Michael Lewis (1982)

The core of the self lies in patterns of behavioral and affective regulation, which grant continuity to experience despite development and changes in context.
—L. Alan Sroufe (1989a)

Until fairly recently the self has been viewed as a metapsychological phenomenon that was not accessible to scientific investigation. Psychology's shift of focus away from overt behavior and onto covert cognitive, affective, and motivational mechanisms, as well as the productive explorations of internal representational processes by developmental psychology and neuroscience have legitimized and even emphasized the importance of a multidisciplinary study of the self. In the most recent conceptualizations it is now thought that a developmental perspective is vital to the understanding of how the self functions in regulating affect, motivation, and behavior (Cross & Markus, 1991). Wright (1991) now contends:

> From a systems point of view, psychological development has two major thrusts: the first is the development of ever more complex structures and systems from simpler ones; the second, a developing awareness of such structures, in particular, those structures in which the self is a participant. (p. 203)

In psychoanalysis the concept of the self as a superordinate structural entity has been a source of controversy (Meissner, 1986a) The greatest impetus in revising classical conceptualizations of the self has come from the seminal work of Kohut (1971, 1977). Contemporary psychoanalytic theorists using inter-disciplinary sources of information characterize the self, as differentiated from the ego, as "an active cognitive-affective structure or motivating system that records and organizes the memory of biologically activated bodily zones and the modes of relationships with others" (Sugarman & Jaffe, 1990, p. 118). These authors argue that this structural system, which originates in the mother-infant dyad, acts as a mediating center that is both receptive to incoming information as well as in confronting the environment, thereby functioning to maintain continuity across varied temporal and situational contexts. Self-schema become increasingly more differentiated and integrated over specific developmental stages via a hierarchical organization of subsystems that allows for emergent complex emotions, thoughts, and actions. Sugarman and Jaffe specifically emphasize that a transformation of the self-schema occurs at the time of the rapprochement crisis in the middle of the second year. In a similar conceptualization Blatt (1991) proposes that cognitive-affective schema are established in an interpersonal matrix and are "long-term, enduring psychological structures, modes of processing and organizing information, including affects, that provide templates that guide and direct an individual's interactions with the interpersonal and impersonal world" (p. 450). Blatt asserts that schema morphology becomes more complex over different developmental phases, as reflected in the emergence of evocative constancy at 16–18 months.

The complementarity of these psychological models of self-function with recent information on the functional properties of self-regulating structural systems being generated by neuroscience is striking. Very current developmental information on the ontogeny of structure-function relationships of self-regulatory systems is clarifying the fundamental "dialogic" nature of the self. The psychoneurobiological origins and properties of the dialogical self is the topic of this chapter.

THE ONTOGENY OF THE DIALOGICAL SELF AND THE PSYCHOSOCIAL ORIGIN OF CONSCIOUSNESS

Most present investigators would agree with Mead's (1934/1972) description, almost 60 years ago, of the ontogeny of the self:

> Self has a character which is different from that of the physiological organism proper, the self is something which has a development; it is not initially there at birth, but arises in the process of social experience and activity. That is, it develops in the given individual as a result of his relations to that process as a whole and to other individuals within that process. (p. 173)

According to current developmental psychoanalytic theory, the "psychological birth of the human infant," the emergence of the nascent self which supports autonomous function, occurs at the end of the practicing stage of separation-individuation (Mahler et al., 1975). Kohut (1971) refers to the growth of psychological structures which continue to perform the adaptive functions that had previously been performed by the external object. Indeed, the essential definition of the self is built out of the internalization of "selfobject" functions (Kohut, 1984). It is now accepted that the child internalizes aspects of the caregiver's role (Sroufe & Fleeson, 1986) and that the experience of being with a self regulating other is incorporated in an interactive representation (Wilson et al., 1990). At 18 months children begin to imitate what it would be like to be someone other than their own self—role taking—in pretending to be the mother (Meltzoff, 1990). In the middle of the second year the securely attached child is able to evoke the image of a comforting object, and Putnam (1992) describes a "divided" psychological organization in which one "part" of the self comforts another "part." In emphasizing the importance of evocative memory near the end of Piaget's sensorimotor period, Basch (1977), a psychoanalytic theorist, states:

> Figurative pre-thought, the act of interiorizing experience, and the act of evocative recall . . . separate self as an object from other objects . . . Only when the child is capable of objectifying his imaging activity can he become aware or both the activity of imaging and of himself as imager. This ability creates the "self" and a differentiation of objects that are not self or belong to the "outside world." (pp. 236–237)

These ideas are matched and confirmed from within psychology. It is now thought that distinguishing self from other seems to be a universal psychobiological principle (Lazarus, 1991b). Self-awareness is known to emerge in the second year (Kagan, 1981), and is now understood to derive from maturational events in the central nervous system (Kagan, 1986). At about 18 months the child first demonstrates the ability to recognize a picture of her own face, another manifestation of objective self-awareness, a property attributed to the functioning of the frontal lobes (Lewis, 1992). Objective self-awareness has been defined as "the awareness of oneself as an object of observation for others and, through identification with the observing others, taking oneself as an object of observation" (Broucek, 1982, p. 371). Lewis (1992) concludes, "The emergence of objectivity occurs somewhere around the middle of the second year of life and constitutes the final major structural feature of the self system" (p. 90).

Also at 18 months the child is capable of the conscious awareness of an affective event as a subjective experience belonging to the self (Basch, 1988). Self-consciousness, as demonstrated in mirror self-recognition reactions, is first observed around 18-months-of-age (Amsterdam, 1972), the same time at which "self-conscious emotion" appears (Lewis, 1992). Izard (1991) observes, "The heightened awareness of self and the exaggerated self-consciousness produced by shame tends to bring about more self-imaging" (p. 342). Not only is there an increase in the quantity of self-representational activities, but there is a qualitative change in the nature of these self-representations. In the experience of the "self-affect" (Harter & Whitesell, 1989) of shame, an emotion that originates in "social evaluation" (Stipek, 1983), there is a sudden shift in the direction of one's awareness, from subjective experience to awareness of self as object, from seeing the self from "out there" rather than from "in here" (Wright, 1991).

> When the child achieves objective self-awareness, the oscillations between sense of self (as indwelling) and objective self-awareness (as an outside looking-on experience) will become gradually regulated into a pattern unique to the individual. (Broucek, 1982, p. 371)

Dyadic shame and shame regulating events which mediate transitions between dissociable psychobiological states allow for the experience-dependent maturation of a system that can adaptively oscillate between different internal states, phenomenologically experienced as different states of awareness or consciousness. These states of consciousness range from hyperaroused ergotropic "ecstatic" states to hypoaroused trophotropic "meditative" states (Fischer, 1971).

This regulation may represent the emergent function of a structurally mature and integrated right hemisphere that is under the executive control of its frontal regions. It is now thought that this hemisphere mediates primary consciousness (Edelman, 1989) as well as "altered states" of consciousness (Frumkin, Ripley, & Cox, 1978; Goldstein & Stoltzus, 1973; Pagano & Frumkin, 1977). Frontal functions are involved in the generation of the self-conscious emotion of shame (Fox, 1991), and this affect is imprinted into interactive representations. Izard (1991) points out that most operations of consciousness involve some kind of representational process. The orbital frontolimbic cortex which has been demonstrated to be neuropsychologically involved in "appraisal," "evaluative" processes (Pribram, 1987), in controlling the allocation of attention to possible contents of consciousness (Goldenberg et al., 1989), may thus mediate the emergent capacity of consciousness, the awareness of the self's existence. These conclusions imply that although consciousness usually is thought to connote solely cognitive processes, the involvement of affective processes is an essential component. John (1962) proposes that consciousness is "ordered and colored by the affect and evaluation unique to, and a characteristic of, the experiencing organism" (p. 81). Pope and Singer (1976) emphasize the role of affect in the regulation of the stream of consciousness. Dore (1985) refers to "the identification of a kind of 'missing link' in explanations of symbolic consciousness; namely, the emotional link" (p. 56).

The social communicative role of consciousness is stressed by Barlow (1980), who posits the idea that consciousness arises in the relation between one individual and another. Consciousness is a product of that part of the brain that handles human relations, and is a property of a brain that is and has been in communication with other brains. Futhermore he asserts :

> One can, of course, be conscious when one is alone, but it is suggested that on these occasions one is rehearsing future discourse with an imagined individual. This is rendered plausible by the fact that our brains are certainly adept model-makers and the character and personality of parents and others must be amongst the most thoroughly modelled aspects of a person's environment. (p. 81)

According to Barlow an audience, as well as an actor, is necessary for consciousness.

EMERGENT PROPERTIES OF THE DIALOGICAL SELF

Social psychological research is now investigating the role of the self as an audience for one's behavior and is inquiring into the evaluative function of the self (Greenwald & Breckler, 1985; Schlenker & Weigold, 1992). The self is now being referred to as a "dialogical narrator" (Hermans et al., 1992). Moving in a similar direction, in very recent psychoanalytic work Wilson and Weinstein (1992b) contend that: "The dialogic nature of inner speech assumes two intrapsychic representations in an intimate involvement, which may eventually come to be so habitual that it is only experienced as syntonic self direction, not as recognizable inner conversation" (p.749). Gilbert (1989) refers to the emergent function of "dialogues of the self" as a form of internalized interaction in which appraisal systems, originally functioning interpersonally and subsequently intrapersonally, are accessed to receive messages and communications from within. Gilbert further proposes that the self is "the product of evolved properties of the psychobiological organization of human beings" (p. 321). Kohut (1984) postulated that critical self-maintaining experiences in early childhood result in an internalized sense of security that comes from feeling oneself "to be a human among humans." Evidence has been presented throughout the preceding chapters to demonstrate that the primary caregiver acts as a psychobiological regulator who attunes herself to the child's internal state by appraising his emotionally expressive displays. Through "reflected appraisals" in nonverbal dialogs with the child, she influences and selects the nature of internal states the emerging self can phenomenologically experience and thereby share with other human beings.

She also provides the essential function of modulating disruptions of states and, importantly, the transitions between states, thereby dispensing comfort to the distressed child.

In these dyadic transactions the mother's orbitofrontal evaluative system is used as a template for the imprinting of the child's developing frontolimbic cortex, which comes to integrate exteroceptive information with interoceptive autonomic information and to self-regulate affective processes. In this way the experience of being in an affective dialog with a self-regulating other is incorporated into a dynamic mental representation that contains information about transitions between states (Freyd, 1987), which is an internal representation of self-interacting-with-an-other that elicits a particular state in response to an appraisal of a particular environmental situation. Recall that the central psychoanalytic concept of an internal object relation is defined as a psychic representation of an internal other which is capable of influencing the individual's affective state (Greenberg & Mitchell, 1983). Upon the experience-dependent maturation of an orbitofrontal system that can generate such complex representations, the child can now access his own appraisal mechanism that assays information about his relationship to the socioemotional environment and generates central states responsible for an appropriate emotional expression. This allows for the development of self-modulation, the evocation of an appropriate psychobiological state for a given situation.

This system also displays the emergent function of evoking a self-comforting function that can modulate distressing psychobiological states and reestablish positively toned states. Izard (1991) depicts the adaptive capacity in which "feelings of discouragement or sadness may touch off imagery and thoughts of comforting oneself" (p. 14). Wilson and Weinstein (1992a) describe an internal dialog that enables the child to "transcend her immediate state" and to enhance "self-solace" capacities. The mature orbitofrontal cortex is uniquely involved in homeostatic regulation, motivational states, and social behaviors. Its adaptive role in adjusting and correcting emotional responses may be mediated by its capacity to shift between the two limbic circuits and transition between low and high arousal operational states and different states of consciousness in response to stressful alterations of external environmental conditions. The functional activity of this structure enables the dialogical self to maintain continuity across various situational contexts. According to Kohut (1971, 1977, 1984), continuity in space and time is a characteristic of a cohesive self.

The ability of the dialogical self to occupy a "multiplicity of positions" (Hermans, Kempen, & van Loon, 1992) may reflect the emergent capacity to adaptively switch between different psychobiological states associated with dissociable states of consciousness that are colored by different affects. The developmental attainment of a self-regulator has earlier been linked to the appearance, in the middle of the second year, of other-oriented empathy expressed in comforting an other in distress. The capacity to understand the inner state of distress of another self begins with an accurate appraisal of the other's face. The face is the "display board" of the affects and the bodily site where the self is most localized (Broucek, 1991). The ability to take on the perspective of a distressed other also requires the ability to shift from a neutral or positive into a negative state and to tolerate distress within the self in order to be aware of and thereby read one's own internal emotional experience. In order to offer comfort to another the self must have access to an internal self-comforting mechanism that can regulate negative affect and shift it back into a positive state.

Other-oriented empathy involves taking another's perspective, reading the other's internal emotional experience, and being capable of experiencing a range of emotional states (Tangney, 1991). These capacities may allow for the creation and operation of a "theory of mind" (Premack & Woodruff, 1978), in which an individual imputes mental states to self and to others and predicts behavior on the basis of such states. In the second year, infants are capable of communicating for the sake of a "meeting of minds" (Golinkoff, 1993). Indeed, Bretherton et al. (1981) present observational evidence that infants acquire a theory of mind in the course of the second year. Although this emergent ability onsets in the preverbal toddler, it is later in the third year that the child begins to acquire the verbal mental state terms of his language (Brettherton & Beeghly, 1982; Shatz, Wellman, & Silber, 1983). These data suggest that an intra- and interpersonally adaptive theory of mind is essentially nonverbal and that empathy involves not so much an awareness of another's cognitions as another's feeling state.

Empathy has been suggested to represent "a capacity that evolves with neuropsychological maturation and interpersonal interactions in the course of individual development" (Buie, 1981). This ontogenetic adaptation may specifically be dependent upon the maturation of a differentiated dual component prefrontal orbital cortex, a structural system that is critical to empathic function (Martzke et al., 1991; Price et al., 1990). This cortex is expanded in the enlarged prefrontal lobe of the right hemisphere, the hemisphere that is preferentially activated under stress conditions (Tucker et al., 1977), is essential to the perception of the communicative content of nonverbal expressions embedded in facial and prosodic stimuli (Blonder et al., 1991), is dominant for the processing of emotional information (Joseph, 1988), and is instrumental to the capacity of empathic cognition (Kohut, 1975) and the perception of the emotional states of other human beings (Voeller, 1986). Indeed, Mesulam and Geschwind (1978) have concluded that the self-system is more localized in the right rather than left brain.

A number of different disciplines are converging on a common conceptualization of the organization and functional role of the self. Developmental cognition studies suggest that the emergence of an active self, a central milestone in the child's development, occurs in the middle of the second year (Lewis, 1982). (Lewis' differentiation of this early emerging "existential" self from a later maturing "categorical" self may refer to early maturing right and later maturing left hemisphere systems). Current social cognition research formulates the self as active, forceful, and capable of change (Greenwald & Pratkanis, 1984). Lichtenberg (1989), a developmental psychoanalyst, now expands self-function to include motivational constructs: "The 'self' develops as an independent center for initiating, organizing, and integrating motivation" (p. 1). In his latest work he posits that: "Success in regulating smoothness of transition between states is a principal indicator of the organization and stability of the emergent and core self as well as caregiver success" (Lichtenberg et al., 1992, p. 162). The behavioral neuroscientists Grigsby and Schneiders (1991) now conclude that that the self is composed of a number of self-representations, each subserved by different but generally overlapping neural networks that include structures regulating affect. Based upon his developmental psychological research, Sroufe (1989a) asserts that in the second year there is a critical transition toward the emergence of an inner organization which includes a concept of self as action. He propounds the fundamental principle that the core of the self lies in patterns of affect regulation, and that this regulatory capacity is responsible for the maintenance of continuity despite changes in development and context. Putnam (1992), a psychiatric researcher, refers to the child's acquisition of the capacity to integrate sense of self across transitions of state . Schwalbe (1991), in neurosociological work, propounds the central tenet that "the earliest configuration of the self may establish a tremendously consequential trajectory for subsequent development" (p. 284).

These conclusions may elucidate the direction towards the solution of the central question posed at the beginning of this work on the development of emotional self-regulation, the problem of "how organized systems retain continuity while changing in response to developmental and environmental pressures" (Demos & Kaplan, 1986, p. 156). Indeed, a deeper understanding of the ontogeny of the self-regulation of affect may be the key to deciphering the fundamental problem of self organization, the origin of the self. Kaufman (1989) has recently suggested that an essential task of contemporary theory and research is the construction of a "science of the self" which elucidates "precise and accurate knowledge of how the self develops, functions, and changes" (p. 160). Perhaps more than any other natural phenomenon, the self and its emotionally imprinted states of consciousness can be most properly studied within the framework and paradigms of "state-specific sciences" (Tart, 1972).

SUMMARY

A number of different disciplines are now converging upon the scientific study of the self. Towards this end, an appreciation of its experience-dependent structural maturation and adaptive functions in early development can contribute important information concerning its role throughout the lifespan. As outlined in Chapter 28, access to maternal external psychobiological regulation allows for the expansion of an internal system that is capable of more complex self-regulatory function. There is now substantial evidence that such a system is functioning in the middle of the second year of human life. This cognitive-affective system mediates incoming environmental information, organizes internal information from activated bodily zones, initiates motivational processes, and actively directs appropriate modes of relationship with others. This description is similar, if not identical to the operations of the executive functions of the frontal regions of the right brain. Indeed, at the orbitofrontal level cortically processed exteroceptive information concerning the external environment is integrated with subcortically processed interoceptive information emanating from the visceroendocrine environment. By this mechanism the right frontolimbic system plays an essential adaptive role in emotional and motivational processes.

The emergent capacity of objective self-awareness implies the operation of a bipartite system that is capable of more than one state of consciousness. This system originates in a dialogical relationship with the primary object of the social environment. Her reflected appraisals and psychobiological regulation of the child's inner states are imprinted in interactive representations that encode programs for modulating transitions between states, that is between phenomonologically distinct states of consciousness. Access to a developmentally mature dual circuit orbitofrontal appraisal system that allocates attention to the contents of consciousness allows the individual to engage in an internal dialog for the purpose of adapting his internal state to a particular external condition. Affective signals, essential to this internal communicative process, color and therefore make recognizable different states of consciousness. The core of the self lies in patterns of affect regulation that integrate a sense of self across state transitions, thereby allowing for a continuity of inner experience.

36 Further Directions of Multidisciplinary Study

The various branches of neuroscience and psychology (individual and social) have one ultimate goal in common, i.e., the scientific understanding of behavior and mentation. No one branch of neuroscience, or of psychology, can attain that goal single-handed because the problem is a multilevel one, and this is because man exists on all levels.

—Mario Bunge (1980b)

The term "morphogenesis" denotes the generation of recognizable forms during growth and development, and this immediately implies the performance of physiological work: biosynthesis, the processing of genetic information, and the transport of building blocks large and small to their destination all require energy and come within the purview of bioenergetics. A deeper and more interesting nexus between bioenergetics and all aspects of developmental biology arises from the concept of biological order. . . .[This order] extends beyond the individual organisms to the structure of biological communities and human societies, and each level must be understood in terms that include energy, work, and information.

—Franklin M. Harold (1986)

[T]he regulatory systems are found on all levels of the organism's functioning, right from the genome up to psychological behaviors; thus they appear to be among the most general characteristics of the organism. Self-regulations seem to constitute at the same time one of the most universal characteristics of life and the most general mechanism to be found in both organic and cognitive behaviors.

—Barbel Inhelder (1971)

[T]he study of psychobiological states should become the cornerstone of psychological inquiry.

—Rob Neiss (1988)

499

An important conclusion of this work is that the study of the ontogeny of the self as a dynamic and integrated psychobiological and socioemotional system must be multilevel, mulitidisciplinary and must preclude a reductionist perspective, in that

> It . . . denies that the self can be understood on any single level of organization or existence, since the structures and processes that exist on any given level are ontologically tied to all other levels. . . .(Schwalbe, 1991, p. 290)

In a recent article in the *American Psychologist,* Cacioppo and Berntson, (1992) have exhorted investigators to move from a reductionistic to a multilevel integrative analysis of any particular psychological phenomenon. In such an approach "one considers not only the elements from two or more levels of analysis that bear on some phenomenon but also the relational features among these elements" (p. 1021). The latest theoretical models of development also stress the need for studying this process simultaneously along several interrelated dimensions ranging from the biological through the social levels (Hopkins & Butterworth, 1990). In fact, Hinde (1990) calls for "an integrated developmental science." And in neuroscience, the same principle is articulated by Bunge's (1980) systemic approach, in which a system is studied on its own level as well as a component of a supersystem and as composed of lower-level entities. Indeed, it is because certain problems cross a number of levels that they are claimed as targets of research of different disciplines. Bunge argues that only integration and not reduction can succeed in elucidating multidisciplinary problems (see Fig. 36.1).

The present multidisciplinary theoretical research has tied together developmental neuroscience, psychology, biology, chemistry, and psychoanalysis, to demonstrate that socioemotional development is specifically facilitated by caregiver infant affective communications. Earlier, in chapter 9, I suggested that these communications mediate dyadic psychobiological energy transformations, and that such reciprocal bioenergetic phenomona represent the essence of the attachment dynamic. These energy-transforming experiences are critical to the maturation of a structural system that is capable of automodulating patterns of organismic energy dissipation, the emergent functional activity of the psychobiological core of the self that underlies the self-regulation of affect. This conception fits well with nonlinear dynamic theory, which assigns the sources of new adaptive forms to the self-organizing properties of "systems that use energy in a particular configuration" (Thelen, 1989). In applying a systems approach to the study of developmental processes, Thelen calls for an integration of the different levels of description, and a coupling of the dynamics at the neural level to the dynamics at the behavioral level. Integrating biological and sociological developmental principles, Schwalbe (1991) has linked the "autogenesis of the self" with the "dynamic energy transformation regimes that coevolve with their environments." The psychobiologists Greenough and Black (1992) refer to a "hierarchy of environments": "At each level, nucleus, cytoplasm of the cell, adjacent cells, organs, multiorgan interactive systems, and organism, forces act back towards the expression of genes, and

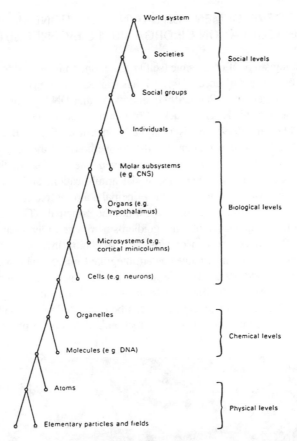

FIG. 36.1.   Supersystems and subsystems of a human being. From Bunge (1980b). From neuron to behavior and mentation: An exercise in level-manship. In Pinsker and Willis, Jr. (Eds.), *Information processing in the nervous system* (pp. 1–16). Reprinted by permission of Raven Press Ltd.

genetic specifications are manifest in structure" (p. 157). In a similar conceptualization, the developmental behavioral geneticists Scarr and Kidd (1983) assert that environmental forces "from the cellular to the social levels" affect developmental outcomes.

The multilevel research paradigm indicates directions for the further study of the development of self-regulatory systems. In this chapter I suggest that phenomena at the organelle and molecular levels are essential to an understanding of the processes of self-assembly, that is, the processes of development. Focusing on these levels highlights the essential contributions of bioenergetics—the study of the vital activities of living systems—to developmental theory, since the concept of biological energy coupling, the linkage between energy-yielding and energy-consuming processes, is an essential element in any integrated view of life (Harold, 1986).

THE DEVELOPMENT OF BRAIN MITOCHONDRIA AND
THE REGULATION OF ORGANISMIC BIOENERGETICS

In the continuing study of organismic (self) regulation, an increased focus should be placed upon events at the subcellular level. The mitochondrion (Fig. 36.2), contains "the other human genome" (Palca, 1990), and its circular DNA (Attardi et al., 1980), unique from the nucleus (Reich & Luck, 1966), utilizes its own genetic code (Barrell, Bankier, & Droiun, 1979) and is maternally inherited (Giles, Blanc, Cann, & Wallace, 1980). This dynamic organelle, the "powerhouse of the cell," is the critical site of the primary biological oxidations which generate cellular and thereby organismic energy. Organismic biosynthesis, signal amplification, and motion can only occur if adenosine triphosphate (ATP), the principal donor of free energy in biological systems, is continuously generated. In the brain the principal ATP energy-requiring functions are the maintenance of ionic gradients across cell membranes and neurotransmission. The major portion of biological oxidation involves a succession of oxidation-reduction systems arranged as an integrated linear chain in cellular mitochondria (West & Todd, 1962). The released energy "charges" the inner mitochondrial membrane, transforming the mitochondrion into a "biological battery."

A cell's concentration of mitochondria can be correlated with the its demand for metabolic energy in the form of ATP. Mitochondrial oxidative phosphorylation—

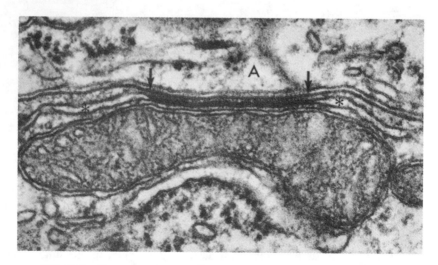

FIG. 36.2. Electron micrograph of a mitochondrion in a subsurface cistern just under the outer membrane of a neuron. The lumen of the cistern (asterisks) is very narrow along the junction of the cistern with the plasma membrane of the neuron (between arrows). The plasmalemma lies parallel to the cisternal membrane along this contact, and the gap between them contains a fuzzy material. Mitochondria are frequently applied to these subsurface cisterns, and cisterns are frequent in regions of the neuron plasmalemma opposite astrocytes (A). Reproduced from Henkart et al. (1976). *Journal of Cell Biology, 70,* 338–347, by copyright permission of the Rockefeller University Press.

the core of bioenergetics (Harold, 1986)—is a preeminent source of the aerobic production of the energy rich molecule of ATP, as it generates 32 of the 36 molecules of ATP that are produced when glucose is completely oxidized to H_2O and CO_2. During the ATP-generating process of respiration O_2 serves as the ultimate electron donor. The terminal component of this respiratory assembly is cytochrome oxidase, and it is this mitochondrial enzyme complex that is crucial to aerobic energy metabolism (Stryer, 1981; Wikstrom, Krab, & Saraste, 1981). The high respiratory capacity of the brain (Kety, 1961) is tightly coupled to oxidative phosphorylation in the mitochondrial respiratory chain (Kato & Lowry, 1973). The energetic capacity of neurons to sustain a broad range of activity levels is specifically related to the high concentration of mitochondrial cytochrome oxidase in these cells (Allman & Zucker, 1990). This mitochondrial enzyme is essential to oxidative glucose metabolism, and its distribution in the mature brain is now being mapped (Carroll & Wong-Riley, 1984; Horton, 1984). Cytochrome oxidase activity is known to be associated with increased metabolism (Humphrey & Hendrickson, 1983) and with the functional organization of the cerebral cortex (Allman & Zucker, 1990). Indeed, in current neurochemical research cytochrome oxidase is used as an endogenous metabolic marker for neuronal activity (Borowsky & Collins, 1989; Wong-Riley, 1989) (Figs. 36.3 a, b, and c).

It is clear that developmental changes in oxidative phosphorylation and the onset of the adaptive capacity to produce increasing amounts of biological energy are fundamental to an understanding of the ontogeny of structure-function relationships in the evolving brain. In early postnatal development the brain's production of energy is known to shift from anaerobic to predominantly aerobic oxidative metabolism, thereby enabling a significant increase in energy output (Himwich, 1951). Oxygen is now considered to be an essential gaseous nutrient that serves as the "engine of morphogenesis" (Forster & Estabrook, 1993). The fact that different areas of the brain develop at different rates is reflected in the

FIG. 36.3. Three types of mito-chondria in a neuron, classified by cytochrome oxidase activity level. Figure A shows a mitochon-drion with lightly reactive cyto-chrome oxidase reactivity. Figure B shows a substantial reactivty, and Figure C shows a moderately reactive mitochondrion. From Car-roll and Wong-Riley (1984). Quan-titative light and electron micro-scopic analysis of cytochrome oxidase-rich zones in the striate cortex of the squirrel monkey. *Journal of Comparative Neurol-ogy, 222.* Reprinted by permis-sion of Wiley-Liss, a division of John Wiley and Sons, Inc.

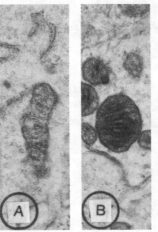

finding of regional differences in oxygen consumption (Himwich, Sykowski, & Fazekas, 1941). The postnatal transformation of energy production in various brain regions has been suggested to represent the physiological basis of developmental stage and critical period phenomena (Meier, Nolan, Bunch, & Schneidler, 1960). On a cellular level, it is at the stage of neuronal maturation, where anaerobiosis is replaced by aerobiosis, that mitochondria become numerous in the cytoplasm (Abood, 1969). Over the course of postnatal development the properties of brain mitochondria change significantly (Gregson & Williams, 1969), and cerebral respiratory capacities increase dramatically (Holtzman, Olson, Zamvil, & Nguyen, 1982). Clarke, Lajtha, and Maker (1989) point out that the size and function of brain mitochondria are known to change during maturation, that mature brain mitochondria have an unusually high affinity for oxygen, and that the heightened metabolic rate found in the adult brain is specifically due to high levels of mitochondrial respiration.

Electron microscopic studies show that both the number of mitochondria and the amount of inner membrane increase over the early stages of postnatal development of a brain region (Pysh, 1970) (Figs. 36.4 and 36.5). The nucleic acids of mitochondria are located on the inner membrane, and fission of these organelles

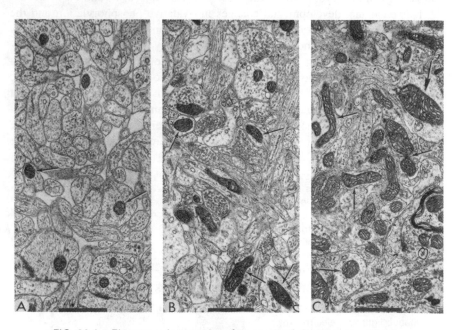

FIG. 36.4.   Electron micrographs of neuropil of developing rat brain (inferior colliculus) at several postnatal ages. (A) 7 days; (B) 14 days; (C) 35 days. The number of mitochondria (small arrows) can be seen to increase with postnatal age. Some mitochondria (large arrow) in 25-day and older neuropil are larger than those seen in younger animals. From Pysh (1970). Reprinted by permission of Elsevier.

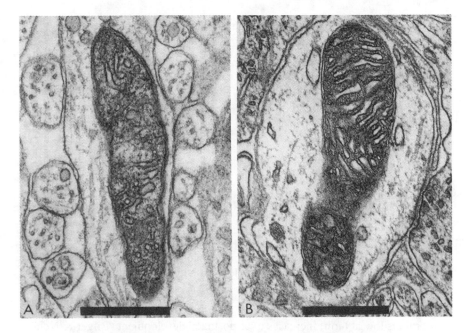

FIG. 36.5.   Electron micrographs of mitochondria from (A) 4-day-old and (b) 35-day-old neuropil. Neonatal mitochondria typically contain fewer cristae and more electron-lucent matrices than older mitochondria. From Pysh (1970). Reprinted by permission of Elsevier.

during "the period of rapid mitochondrial proliferation" (Fig. 36.6) may permanently define the mitochondrial complement of the neuron for the rest of its lifespan. Fission represents a mechanism for the generation of new mitochondria, and during such events the mitochondrial genome is replicated (Fawcett, 1981). This is followed by mitochondrial DNA-directed synthesis of elements of mitochondrial ribosomes and fewer than a dozen essential structural proteins that are components of the mitochondrial ATPase and cytochrome oxidase (Tzagoloff, Macino, & Sebald, 1979). Since the inner membrane is also involved in electron transport and oxidative phosphorylation these morphological changes accompany a functional change in the differentiating cell's future capacity for energy production. The amount of mitochondrial protein increases in the postnatal brain (Samson, Balfour, & Jacobs, 1960), and the protein synthesis of mitochondria in the immature brain is even greater (Klee & Sokoloff, 1964) and more responsive to environmental control than in adult brain (Roberts, Zomzely, & Bondy, 1970). Indeed, developmental neurochemical research demonstrates that there is an augmentation of mitochondrial energy metabolism in the developing brain. These studies show postnatal progressive increases in the rates of oxidative phosphorylation in infant brain mitochondria (Holtzman & Moore, 1975; Land, Booth, Berger, & Clark, 1977; Patel & Clark, 1981).

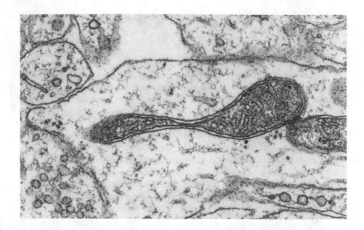

FIG. 36.6.   Dumbbell-shaped mitochondrial profiles commonly seen during period of known mitochondrial proliferation in postnatally developing neuropil. From Pysh (1970). Reprinted by permission of Elsevier.

The activity of cytochrome oxidase, an indicator of oxidative metabolism, in the brain is low at birth, increases over postnatal development (Bilger & Nehlig, in press; Brown, Crompton, & Wray, 1991; Chapelinsky, & Rodriguez de Lores Arnaiz, 1970; Gregson & Williams, 1969; Hallman, Mäenpää, & Hassinen, 1972; Klee & Sokoloff, 1967), and peaks during the developmental period of most rapid growth and maturation (Wong-Riley, 1989). The growth and differentiation of the fetal cortex proceeds in stages and is associated with increased cytochrome oxidase activity (Flexner, Flexner, & Strauss, 1941). This same pattern continues in postnatal cortical development. Excitatory sensory input, both visual and tactile, is required for the increases in cytochrome oxidase-driven oxidative metabolism in the developing cerebral cortex (Wong-Riley, 1979; Wong-Riley & Welt, 1980). The production and metabolism of glutamate, an amino acid that performs a regulatory role in excitatory phenomena (see earlier chapters), occurs within mitochondria (Abood, 1969). Mitochondria are especially concentrated in those regions of the neuron where excitatory events are most frequent (Abood, 1969), and in postnatal development are associated with the presynaptic and postsynaptic processes of developing synapses (Pysh, 1970). Studies of other developing brain areas indicate that during postnatal periods large numbers of mitochondria migrate from the perikaryon to the growing dendritic arbor (Altman, 1972; Landis, 1973). Investigations of neurons undergoing synaptogenesis in an early postnatal period reveal that high levels of cytochrome oxidase activity are found on the spines of growing dendrites which receive excitatory input (Mjaatvedt & Wong-Riley, 1988). These dendritic spines are sites of active synapse amplification (Miller, Rall, & Rinzel, 1985). Dendrites are known to have high levels of oxidative enzyme (Creutzfeldt, 1975) and cytochrome oxidase (Wong-Riley, 1989) activity (Fig. 36.7).

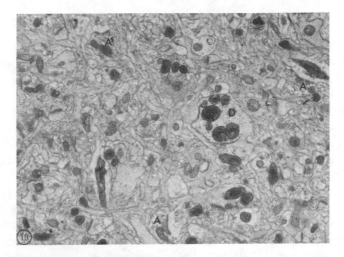

FIG. 36.7.   Mitochondria in cortical dendrites. A darkly reactive dendritic profile (D) is shown as are two lightly reactive (A) and a moderately reactive (A') axon terminal, all making asymmetrical axodendritic synapses. From Carroll and Wong-Riley (1984). Quantitative light and electron microscopic analysis of cytochrome oxidase-rich zones in the striate cortex of the squirrel monkey. *Journal of Comparative Neurology, 222.* Reprinted by permission of Wiley-Liss, a division of John Wiley and Sons, Inc.

In very recent work, age-related modifications of cytochrome oxidase have been observed in discrete brain regions (Curti, Giangare, Redolfi, & Benzi, 1990). Purves and LaMantia (1990) demonstrate that cytochrome oxidase-rich zones in the cerebral cortex increase in number in development, and propose that the pattern of these areas of high metabolic activity demarcates modular circuits. They further suggest that novel circuits are constructed in a critical period of postnatal life, that modular and processing units are added progressively during the period of brain growth and maturation, and that modular circuit formation wanes in the later stages of postnatal development. Indeed, they conclude that critical periods, "epochs in early life when the brain is particularly sensitive to the effects of experience" represent the normal duration of the construction of cytochrome oxidase-labeled circuits. I deduce that these experience-dependent developmental increases in mitchondrial oxidative metabolism in the postnatally developing brain (Land et al. 1977) underlie Schwalbe's (1991) description of energy transformation regimes that coevolve with their environments in early human infancy. Studies of this mitochondrial complex that is so central to oxygen metabolism have yet to be carried out in the postnatal orbitofrontal cortex.

A core developmental principle of this work is that the dialectic between the early social environment and the developing infant is transacted in the context of the mother's regulating the output and activity of the infant brain's regulatory neurohormones and hormones. These biochemical mediators of affective signals trigger an induction of energetic transmissions within the child's brain. The processing of these affective signals by the regulatory descending circuits of the orbitofrontal cortex then amplifies subcortical energy transformations, thereby causing shifts in internal motivational states. This affect is biochemically expressed in the activation of different central limbic catecholaminergic circuits that regulate the energy-mobilizing sympathetic and energy-conserving parasympathetic branches of the autonomic nervous system. In such a manner, emotion involves an internal adjustive change of energy level in response to an environmental situation (Duffy, 1941). A corollary principle stresses that during critical period social transactions the mother acts as a "hidden regulator" (Hofer, 1984a) of the energy-dependent differentiation of the infant's developing brain systems that regulate such energy transmissions and transformations. "Emotional refueling," defined in infant psychoanalytic research as exchanges of energy within the mother-infant dyad (Mahler et al., 1975), mediates the "psychological embryology" (Tucker, 1992) of structures that support ongoing emotional and cognitive development.

Extending these formulations even further, in the context of critical period face-to-face object relational interactions, the mother's "hidden" psychobiological regulation of the infant, referred to in the current psychoanalytic literature as "selfobject" regulatory function (Kohut, 1977), mediates alterations in a hierarchy of internal regulatory signals that directly exert trophic effects on the maturation of cellular and subcellular components of subcortical and cortical brain structures responsible for future socioaffective function, especially the energy-metabolizing mitochondrial populations of different monoaminergic neuronal systems and their target receptors in these developing regions. Mitochondrial populations of endothelial cells of "metabolically active capillaries" of the postnatal brain (Fig. 36.8), would be especially important, as these represent the site of the developing blood-brain barrier of a particular cortical region. These endothelial cells are unique—they contain five times as many mitochondria as other tissues of the body (Oldendorf & Brown, 1975), and this accounts for the large metabolic work capability of the blood-brain barrier (Old-

FIG. 36.8. Electron micrograph of mitochondria in a brain endothelial cell. Nucleus at left, vessel lumen at right, pinocytotic vesicles (open arrow) and a tight junction (closed arrow). Reprinted from Goldstein, Wolinsky, Csejtey, and Diamond (1975). Isolation of metabolically active capillaries from rat brain. *Journal of Neurochemistry, 25,* 715–717, with permission from Pergamon Press Ltd, Headington Hill Hall, Oxford OX3 OBW, UK.

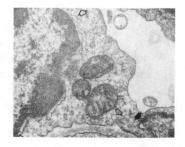

endorf, Cornford, & Brown, 1977) (see Fig. 36.9). Oldendorf notes that mito-chondrial function may assume importance in the function of the barrier, since monoamine oxidase, the major enzyme responsible for the catabolic inactivation of dopamine and noradrenaline (and serotonin), is found only in the outer mem-brane of mitochondria (Costa & Sandler, 1972). Indeed, this enzyme, located in the endothelial cells of cerebral microvessels, is now thought to play a role as a "biochemical blood-brain barrier" (Kalaria & Harik, 1987). Endothelial mito-chondria may represent the monoamine receptors that are associated with the "dynamic regulatory" functions of the blood-brain barrier (Cornford, 1985), a mechanism essential to local neuronal activity. I have earlier suggested that the innervation of cerebral microvessels by subcortical monoaminergic neurons is responsible for the regulation of local metabolic needs, that increased blood flow occurs as a result of postnatal imprinting experiences, and that the development of the regional blood-brain barrier is influenced by the stimulation emanating from the social environment.

This suggests that the child's relationship with the mother, the infant's bio-energetic transmissions that occur in critical period dyadic affective transactions, are an important determinant of the final differentiation of the mitochondria of a maturing cortical area. In an earlier chapter I suggested that the primary care-giver is the main source of environmental free energy that is sensed by the infant, and that these energies trigger catabolic energy-mobilizing processes. An appre-ciation of developmental bioenergetics, the scientific study of vitality (Harold, 1986), is a requisite to a deeper understanding of the genesis of "vitality affects" (Stern, 1985) and the mechanism of "vitalizing reciprocity" (Brent & Resch,

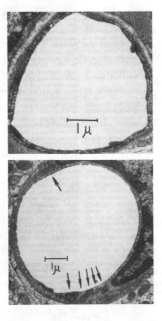

FIG. 36.9. (A) Capillary from rat muscle. Note the absence of mitochondria in the endothelial cell (B) Capillary from rat cere-bellum. The endothelial cell contains six mitochondria and very few pinocytotic vessicles. From Oldendorf and Brown (1975). Reprinted by permission of Williams and Wilkins.

1987). I propose that the psychoneurobiological mechanism of these phenomena involves the excitatory visual and tactile input that induces the cytochrome oxidase-driven increase in developing cortical oxidative metabolism described by Wong-Riley. How could this be mediated? I would argue that psychobiological activation of regulatory neurotransmitters and neurohumors, known to play key roles in the specification of critical periods by acting as internal "clocks" to coordinate the timing of developmental processes (Lauder & Krebs, 1986), also effect the differentiation of different types of brain mitochondria (Neidle, Van den Berg, & Grynbaum, 1969) in phylogenetically younger cortical regions (Leong, Lai, Lim, & Clark, 1984) that mature during infancy. These regulatory agents are identical to those discussed earlier.

A number of findings can be given to support this hypothesis. Purves and LaMantia (1990) conclude that "activity-driven trophic interplay" influences the postnatal construction of cytochrome oxidase-defined modular circuits, specifically mentioning BDNF (Leibrock et al., 1989), a neurotrophic factor for dopaminergic neurons (Hyman et al., 1991). Lauder and Krebs (1986) underscore the importance of thyroid hormones in the regulation of critical period phenomena, including neurite outgrowth in dopaminergic neurons, dendritic growth, and synaptogenesis. Proper levels of thyroid hormone are specifically required for the synthesis and degradation of dopamine in the postnatally developing brain. Thyroid hormones are known to be active agents in brain differentiation (Nunez, 1984) and to impact synaptogenesis and monoamine levels in the developing nervous system (Ford & Cramer, 1977). In contrast to adult brain, thyroxine stimulates protein synthesis in mitochondria from immature brain (Sokoloff & Klee, 1965). Neonatal and not adult brain mitochondria contain receptors for thyroid hormone, and it has been suggested that an early action of this hormone is to increase oxygen consumption and to effect oxidative phosphorylation (Sterling et al., 1978). It has also been demonstrated that during an early critical period of brain growth thyroid hormone increases glutamate levels (Cocks, Balazs, Johnson, & Eayrs, 1970). The excitatory input descibed by Wong-Riley could reflect the action of glutamate on developing mitochondria. In fact, in the brain, this amino acid is oxidized in the mitochondrial matrix in the tricarboxylic acid cycle (West & Todd, 1962; Rothman et al., 1992), an aerobic biochemical pathway that increases significantly in the postnatal brain (Balazs, 1971). The influence of thyroid hormone on monoamine systems may be permanent, as it is well established that this hormone increases the ability of catecholamine receptors to receive stimulation (Whybrow & Prange, 1981). Catecholamines are also known to have pronounced effects on cerebral oxidative metabolism (Berntman, Dahlgren, & Siesjo, 1978). Like thyroid hormone regulatory catecholamines have been shown to induce protein synthesis within biogenetically differentiating mitochondria of infant animals (Houstek et al., 1990).

Mitochondria can travel right up to the plasma membrane of the cell (see Fig. 36.2), a position where they could readily sense and respond to exogenous signals and primary messengers in the cellular environment. This is true for astroglial, endothelial (see Fig. 36.8), and neuronal (see Fig. 36.2) mitochondria. Henkart et al. (1976) note that subsurface cisterns containing mitochondria are frequently in regions where the neuronal plasma membrane directly oppose the astrocytic plasma membrane. This is an obvious site for communication between these two cell types. For example neurohormones such as monoamines could be taken up by the mitochondria and trigger glycogenolysis. Rosenbluth (1962) suggests that subsurface cisterns are involved in glycogenolysis. The end product of glycogenolysis is then used as a substrate for the pentose phosphate shunt, thereby inducing the biosynthesis of glycoproteins for the establishment of receptors at the surface of the neuron. Henkart et al. (1976) identify "a fuzzy material" between the membrane of the subsurface cistern and the plasma membrane (see Fig. 36.2). I deduce this material represents glycoproteins to be used in constructing synaptic complexes. "Free" postsynaptic-like densities, synaptic precursors, are known to be associated with surface cisterns (Spacek, 1982). The protein synthetic machinery of the mitochondrion, activated by the uptake of circulating thyroid hormone, may also contribute material to these synaptic structures, such as proteolipids that are encoded in mitochondrial DNA.

In the postnatally maturing orbitofrontal cortex, mitochondria, especially those of the local catecholaminergic axons and their receptors in the evolving microvasculature, represent a critical factor to the final maturation of this region. Mitochondrial protein (and phospholiplid) synthesis is required for the differentiation of these organelles, and this synthesis is responsive to "environmental control," especially to circulating thyroid hormone (Roberts et al., 1970). This regulatory agent is incorporated into mitochondria at a time when they are undergoing an anerobic-aerobic transformation. Mitochondrial thyroid uptake allows for adaptive structural and biochemical changes that enables them to cope with the changing oxygen levels in the local environment, and to utilize this oxygen for the more efficient aerobic production of ATP, the currency of biological energy.

In earlier chapters, I expanded upon Hofer's principle that the mother acts as a hidden regulator of the infant's biological control systems. I presented evidence to argue that in affective interactions, the mother induces hormonal alterations in the child's developing brain by regulating the infant's production of various hypothalamic releasing factors. For example, hypothalamic growth releasing hormone regulates the synthesis and secretion of growth hormone by the pituitary. It is now known that the level of maternal interaction influences both the infant's serum levels of growth hormone and the sensitivity of specific tissues to this hormone (Schanberg & Kuhn, 1980), and that severe maternal emotional deprivation leads to hypopituitarism and growth retardation (Powell, Brasel, & Blizzard, 1967). It seems most logical that the same principles would apply to other hypothalamic releasing hormones such as thyrotropin-releasing hormone. This agent stimulates the secretion of thyroid-stimulating hormone by the anterior pituitary, which in turn stimulates the release of thyroid hormones. Increased circulating levels of thyroid hormone would have a trophic effect on the mitochondria of differentiating areas of the postnatal cortex. This mechanism could mediate, at the organelle level, Schwalbe's dynamic energy transformation's that coevolve with their environments.

Other data also suggest that regulators within the mother-infant interaction directly influence the evolving structure-function relations of neonatal brain mitochondria. As previously mentioned in Chapter 13, excitatory neurotransmitters regulate postsynaptic calcium influx in developing neocortex (Yuste & Katz, 1991) and glutamate acting at NMDA receptors increases intracellular calcium in neurons (Burgoyne et al., 1988). Calcium ions regulate important neuronal functions, such as neurite elongation and growth cone movement (Cohan, Conner, & Kater, 1987) and neurotransmission at synaptic junctions (Erulkar, 1989). These ions are universally utilized as a messenger to couple cell surface signals to cell response (Rasmussen & Barrett, 1984), but prolonged, unregulated exposure to increased levels produces cell death (Farber, 1981), an effect seen in overactivation of excitatory amino acid receptors (Rothman & Olney, 1987). Calcium fluxes at the cell-surface are rapidly regulated by polyamines, agents important for cell growth and differentiation, and receptors for polyamines are found in the plasma membrane and subadjacent mitochondria (Koenig, Goldstone, & Lu, 1983). Jensen, Lynch, and Baudry (1989) demonstrate that an important action of polyamines is to specifically increase the rate of calcium uptake into neonatal brain mitochondria. As a result, during periods of rapid growth these mitochondria serve the important role of flexibly regulating calcium levels in the developing brain, damping down calcium increases to levels that promote growth and below levels that produce toxic effects. These authors also point out that the concentration of polyamines is particularly high during the postnatal period (Seiler & Lamberty, 1975), that polyamines increase pyruvate dehydrogenase activity in mitochondria (Damuni, Humphreys, & Reed, 1984), and that polyamines "might serve to regulate mitochondrial energy metabolism" (Jensen et al., 1989, p. 1179). Most intriguingly, Hofer (1984a) reports that the infant's production of ornithine decarboxylase, the enzyme catalyzing the rate-limiting step in polyamine synthesis, is externally controlled by the mother-infant relationship. I suggest that this could be mediated through the mother's regulation of the infant's glucocorticoid levels, since ornithine decarboxylase is induced by glucocorticoids (Cousin, Lando, & Moguilewsky, 1982), and corticosteroids are known to produce alterations in mitochondrial strucure and function (Kimberg, Loud, & Weiner, 1968).

When added to the data on the psychobiological induction of these neurohormones and neuropeptides presented in earlier chapters, this body of findings supports the proposal that socioaffective experience-dependent elicitation of internal chemical regulators of mitochondrial differentiation directly influences the observed postnatal changes in organelle morphology and function that underlie the transformation of energy production responsible for critical period phenomena. This developmental increase of bioenergetic capacities of populations of brain mitochondria supports brain growth, since this vital process is coupled to a source of energy (Harold, 1986). As with other critical period phenomena, the effects of these events are long-lasting. Mitochondria play an essential role not only in structural circuit formation (Purves & LaMantia, 1990) but also in neuronal functional activity in the mature brain (Wong-Riley, 1989). For example, studies reveal that the activition of the mitochondrial enzyme pyruvate dehydrogenase is essential to learning (Morgan & Routtenberg, 1981) and memory storage (Hock, Dingledine, & Wilson, 1984). The importance of mitochondrial activity to attachment phenomena is underscored in a study showing that in postnatal environments which reduce infant cytochrome oxidase synthesis, the mother's attempts to induce nursing of the newborn are not successful, and she ultimately rejects him (Kinnula & Hassinen, 1977). This multilevel conceptualization ties together the seemingly unrelated disciplines of cell biology, bioenergetics, neurochemistry, and developmental psychoanalysis.

REPARATIVE MECHANISMS AND STRESS PROTEINS

A deeper understanding of another self-regulatory phenomenon, the reparative response of the self during and following various socioaffective stresses, may also be elucidated by a multilevel perspective. It has been earlier suggested that the capacity of the dual innervated orbitofrontal cortex to shift between high and low arousal psychobiological states and sympathetic and parasympathetic modes in response to stressful environmental conditions may define a fundamental adaptive regulatory function. The transition into a quiescent, low energy-utilization state of conservation-withdrawal in response to certain hyperaroused, hyperenergetic stresses is adaptive in terms of replenishing energy stores and restoring physiological equilibrium. "The shift into this level is from tensional, alert, engaged, powered up, to withdrawn, atonic, inhibited, unseen, and disengaged: the organismic strategy is to conserve energy . . . to allow healing of wounds and restitution of depleted resources" (Powles, 1992, p. 213). The same psychobiological mechanism which optimizes "healing of wounds" is utilized not only in repairing stressful physical trauma that produce "tissue injury" but also in stressful psychological assaults against the self that produce "psychic" or "narcissistic injury" (Kohut, 1977).

The parasympathetic mechanism of conservation-withdrawal is biochemically expressed in elevated corticosteroid activity which increases glycogen synthesis (Sie & Fishman, 1964; Stryer, 1981), thereby replenishing energy stores and putting the tissues in better condition to withstand stress in general (West & Todd, 1962). Adrenal glucocorticoids play an essential role in behavioral adaptation (Bohus et al., 1984), and the failure to increase their concentrations in the circulation in response to stress is associated with potentially deleterious sequelae such as tissue damage (Munck, Guyre, & Holbrook, 1984). In the cortex this stress system is physiologically manifest in a decrease in cerebral blood flow and an inhibition of cerebral energy metabolism (Bryan, 1990). This could reflect the known modulation of the blood-brain barrier by pituitary-adrenal glucocorticoids (Long & Holaday, 1985). The experience-dependent maturation of orbital prefrontal areas is accompanied by a more efficient regulation of corticosteroid dynamics. These developments were previously shown to underlie long-enduring advances in reparative self-comforting and stress recovery functions. Earlier, I provided evidence that indicates that orbitofrontal activation of medullary noradrenergic populations induces corticosteroid release. The stimulation of this corticolimbic system uniquely influences hypothalamico-pituitary-adrenocortical corticosteroid levels (Hall & Marr, 1975; Kandel & Schwartz, 1985) and changes in sympathoadrenomedullary catecholamine release (Euler & Folkow, 1958). Timiras (1989) offers the intriguing suggestion that Seyle's adaptation syndrome, the response of the hypothalamo-pituitary-adrenocortical and sympathetic systems to stress at the organismic level, may reflect the response to stress at the cellular level, the activation of silent genes that produce stress ("heat shock") proteins (Leung et al., 1990; Morimoto, Tissieres, & Georgopoulos, 1990, Pelham, 1986).

It is now known that various forms of stress—drugs that effect monoamine activity, oxidative stress and a sudden elevation of temperature- induce a universal common pathway of transcription and translocation of particular genes that are not expressed under normal physiological conditions. The resultant production of stress proteins on cellular polysomes protects cells from the adverse consequences of heat and other stressors and confers an "ability of cells to survive following stress" (Miller, Raese, & Morrison-Bogorad, 1991). These proteins are also found in mitochondria (Mizzen, Chang, Garrels, & Welch, 1989). Stress proteins are actively produced by the brain during postnatal development (White, 1981). Brown (1983, 1985) reports that during periods of postnatal brain maturation, stress induces a heat shock protein with a molecular weight of 74,000 daltons. He asserts that stress protein synthesis specifically occurs as a "physiologically relevant phenomenon" in early postnatal development, and demonstrates that as infancy proceeds a higher heat stress is required to induce stress protein production in the maturing brain. I interpret this finding to represent a biochemical manifestation of the developmental increase in stress tolerance and coping over the infancy period.

In light of Timiras' hypothesis, the production of stress proteins in the limbic system, structures which show a high level of corticosteroid retention (McEwen et al., 1968), may be significant to this increase of stress regulating function. Glucocorticoids bind receptors on cell surfaces, and these receptors that act as regulators of intracellular events may subsequently be transported to the cell nucleus (Papamichail, Tsokos, Tsawdaroglou, & Sekeris, 1980) where they may activate genetic mechanisms. A recent study demonstrates that the steroid hormone receptor complex consists of the steroid receptor and heat shock proteins; binding of the steroid results in dissociation of the stress proteins and the transformation of the steroid receptor to an active DNA binding site (Tai et al., 1992). Timiras (1989) suggests that since heat activates the binding of corticosteroid receptor-complexes to DNA, this neuroendocrine mechanism may be involved in the action of cellular stress responses. Indeed, phasically activated brain glucocorticoid receptors are known to mediate homeostatic processes involved in the suppression of stress (deKloet, 1991). Glucocorticoid-sensitive neurons are involved in terminating the adrenocortical stress response (Sapolsky et al., 1984). Miller et al. (1991) concludes "the potential of certain cell types, in different brain regions, to elicit a stress response would be significant" (p. 2070). At the cellular level, a stressor is defined as a condition that exerts an effect upon the cell that disturbs its homeostatic balance beyond the cells ability to compensate for that disturbance (Nelson, 1980). The expression of stress proteins represent the cell's adaptive physiological response to environmental extremes. An inadequate response to a stressor may lead to structural damage to the cell; an adequate response may be the capacity to produce stress proteins that prevent or ameliorate such damage to the cell's membrane and protein systems.

Miller also notes that both dopamine and noradrenaline influence the stress response, and refers to a "catecholamine-mediated potentiation of the heat shock response in certain cell types" (p. 2069). It is also now established that both dopamine (Blanc et al., 1980; Claustre, Rivy, Dennis, & Scatton, 1986) and noradrenaline (Glavin, 1985) levels are altered under stressful conditions. Dunn (1988) concludes that "there is a global activation of cerebral dopaminergic systems in the brain to parallel the activation of noradrenergic systems during stress" (p. 200). Kalin and Carnes (1984) demonstrate that both catecholamines are released in response to stressful disruptions of the attachment bond. It is also known that the cerebral vasculature (which contains catecholamine receptors) responds to stress (Nemoto & Frankel, 1970), and that stress proteins are synthesized in the cerebral microvasculature (White, 1980, 1991). In fact, White demonstrates that the appearance of stress proteins coincides with the final maturation of brain capillaries and the blood-brain barrier.

I suggest that postnatal stress-inducing and stress-relieving caregiver-infant interactions will produce alterations of stress protein synthesis in hypothalamic neurosecretory, medullary noradrenergic, and ventral tegmental dopaminergic neurons and in their orbitofrontal receptors, especially in the orbitofrontal microvasculature that is being organized in this critical period. This may be biochemically mediated by effects on the pentose phosphate pathway, which is stimulated by catecholamines (Cummins et al., 1985), which protects against oxidative damage that occurs in the metabolism of catecholamines (Hothersall et al., 1982), which has high activity in the developing brain (O'Neill & Duffy, 1966), and which "serves as a reserve pathway for use under such stresses as the need for increased lipid synthesis, repair, or reduction of oxidative toxins" (Clarke et al., 1989, p. 552). Furthermore, these early experiences lead to irreversible effects, as they may determine the lifespan capacity of the cells in these areas of the limbic system that regulate the organismic dissipation of energy to withstand and recover from stress on the cellular level, and thereby stress on the organismic level.

In very recent work on the transduction of psychosocial stress into the neurobiology of psychiatric disorders, Post (1992) outlines a model by which such stressors lead to long-lasting changes in gene expression. He proposes that some of the consequent alterations in gene transcriptions may represent effects that are part of the primary pathological process, while others may represent "compensatory attempts at homeostasis." This suggests to me that too many studies assume that the biochemical alterations that accompany a particular disorder solely represent the pathological processes that underlie that disorder. Some of these changes represent the transcription of genes that code stress proteins, an adaptive response to a change in the reception of regulatory signals of an altered cellular environment. Illness, according to Weiner (1977, 1989) is characterized by a disturbance of regulation. Catecholamines perform an important role in the regulation of the brain microvasulature (Hartman & Udenfriend, 1972; Raichle et al., 1975) and microcirculatory homeostasis (Schayer, 1970). Cerebral endothelial cells assist in the integration of brain and body functions by transmitting metabolic and homeostatic information bidirectionally (Dermietzel & Krause, 1991). It is these endothelial cells of the brain microvasculature that produce stress proteins in response to trauma (White, 1980).

A major thesis of this volume is that socioaffective transactions between two individuals mediate psychobiological regulatory functions, both stress-inducing and stress-modulating. These changes occur at the molecular (stress protein) level, and effect function at the organelle, cellular, organ, and organismic levels. It is important to point out that the two limbic circuits, especially their catecholaminergic and vascular components, are the central sites of organismic damage and repair. This clearly implies that limbic activity—socioemotional function—is central to the individual's recovery mechanisms. Such a conceptualization may articulate the mechanism by which social connectedness provides protection and recovery from *physical* and *psychological* illness. It is now well established that "social support" modulates life stress and fundamentally influences the recovery from disease. A social support system is now being defined as "that subset of individual's total social network upon whom he or she relies for socioemotional aid, instrumental aid, or both" (Thoits, 1982, p. 148). Taylor (1987) asserts that the intervening mechanism by which social support effects illness involves "a direct effect on the individual's psychobiological functioning via the regulatory interactions within his social relationships" (p. 288).

I conclude that psychobiologically regulating self-selfobject transactions that are mediated by affective communications between the individual and the social environment, much of which are at the unconscious level, induce an alteration in brain stress protein synthesis. Furthermore, a primary site of the expression of stress proteins, the cell's adaptive physiological response to environmental extremes, is in the limbic system. This includes the hypothalamus, the central diencephalic system which regulates both the sympathetic and parasympathetic autonomic activities that underlie emotional and motivational functions. According to both Tomkins (1962) and Zajonc (1985) emotional expressions are associated with changes in blood flow and temperature in subcortical areas. Furthering these ideas, thermosensitive cells in the hypothalamus (Zajonc et al., 1989) would sense rapid temperature shifts associated with intense emotional transactions, and these shifts, if extreme enough, would trigger the local rapid production of heat shock proteins, proteins that play a fundamental role in stress response management. These proteins that act as a defense mechanism to protect susceptible cellular components and functions would also be activated in the corticolimbic components in the orbitofrontal cortex of the right hemisphere, the cortical system that regulates the autonomic nervous system (Neafsey, 1990). The stress-induced molecular alterations at this site account for its role in stress-regulating, reparative functions.

Furthermore, this model should also apply to the repair of cellular injury following brain trauma, that is to the particular individual's recovery from brain damage. Stress proteins that play an important role in cellular repair are produced at sites of brain tissue injury (Brown, Rush, & Ivy, 1989). Prefrontal dysfunction is a common accompaniment of various forms of brain injury. The 70-kDa stress protein is expressed in epilepsy (Vass et al., 1989), percussive brain injury (Tanno, Nockels, Pitts, & Noble, 1993), and focal cerebral ischemia (Kinouchi et al., 1993). The orbitomedial frontal lobe is a site of seizure activity (Tharp, 1972; Williamson et al., 1985). Orbitofrontal areas are particularly susceptible to hematomas, contusions, and intracerebral hemorrhages (Mattson & Levin, 1990), and disruptions of their connections with subcortical structures may be responsible for the disturbances of social awareness and the changes in perceiving the bond between the affective and cognitive aspects of the self which are frequently seen in brain injury (Prigatano, 1989). Frontal lobe damaged patients typically show emotional dysfunction in the form of an intolerance for stress, a difficulty in dealing with novel situations, and a defect in self-monitoring (Parker, 1990).

Object relational phenomena may be essential to the mechanism involved in recovery from brain injury. In a recent model of rehabilitation (Klonoff & Lage, 1991), the classically described catastrophic reaction experienced by neurologically impaired individual's is being interpreted as a reaction to narcissistic injury, a psychoanalytic concept of Kohut (1971). Klonoff and Lage further propose that individuals with a history of narcissistic problems that predate acquired brain injury exhibit a course of recovery marked by intensified problems in accepting and coping with brain injury. In another newer conceptualization, Bach-y-Rita (1990) is studying brain plasticity as a basis for recovery of function from brain injury. This author stresses that the creation of an affective bond between the rehabilitation therapist and the patient is essential. Other workers in the field of rehabilitation are also finding that using personally familiar (Holland, 1989) and individualized (Edelman, 1984) stimuli lead to more successful treatment of deficits after brain damage. It is commonly held that psychotherapy is not an effective treatment for brain injury. To the contrary, recent clinical studies are validating the efficacy of psychotherapy with brain-injured children (Leichtman, 1992) and adults (Langer, 1992). In groundbreaking work, Miller (1993) is now putting forth a rehabilitation therapy program that facilitates recovery of the "shattered self" that has sustained brain injury.

With regard to the psychoneurobiology of this recovery, the socioaffective stimulation embedded in psychotherapeutic, psychobiologically attuned mirroring transactions discussed in chapter 33 may directly influence the collateral sprouting of monoaminergic neurons. This idea is appealing, since it is known that central catecholaminergic neurons, including dopaminergic mesolimbic neurons, exhibit considerable regenerative capabilities (Reis et al., 1978). Even more intriguing, this stimulation may effect the activity of the monoaminergic receptors of the orbitofrontal endothelial cells. In chapter 11, I reported that Weibel-Palade bodies, cytoplasmic inclusions that are rare in the brain, are found in endothelial cells of the orbital cortex (Herrlinger, Anzil, Blinzinger, & Kronski, 1974) (see Fig. 11.10). These cytoplasmic components are the site of synthesis (Wagner, Olmsted, & Marder, 1982) of a coagulant that is released after vascular injury (Sakariassen, Bolhuis, & Sixma, 1979). It is tempting to speculate that this psychobiological mechanism may play an important role in the re-sealing of breaches of the blood-brain barrier and the recovery of the impairment of vascular permeability that accompanies all forms of brain pathology. Neurological studies of right hemispheric stroke patients indicate that a critical variable to recovery of function is the establishment of collateral circulation (Hier, Mondlock, & Caplan, 1983). In brain injury as in early life (Black et al., 1987) environmental conditions may influence the organization of the cortical vasculature.

MITOCHONDRIAL-NUCLEAR GENOME INTERACTIONS IN POSTNATAL BRAIN DEVELOPMENT

In a recent formulation of the induction of brain structure by experience, Greenough and Black (1992) pose the elemental developmental issue of "the manner in which the developing brain acquires its ability to guide the organism through the demands of a complex, changing environment" (p. 155). Gilbert (1989) concludes that the child goes through a process of continual inward transformation, and that ongoing social relationships penetrate into the structural dynamics of the individual's biological form. A major goal of this book has been to identify the operations that mediate this transformation. To recapitulate, the psychoneurobiological mechanism by which the social environment acts on the developing nervous system is embedded in dyadic transactions in which the psychobiologically attuned caregiver provides modulated socioaffective stimulation that mediates the "hidden maternal regulation" of the infant's endocrine and nervous systems. Of special importance are the hormonal changes in the infant elicited in maternal gaze transactions (Hoffman, 1987; Klaus & Kennell, 1976), since these monoaminergic neurotransmitters and neurohormones regulate the temporal framework of developmental brain growth (Lauder & Krebs, 1986). Both dopamine (Kalsbeek et al., 1987) and noradrenaline (Felten et al., 1982) are known to act as neurotrophic agents in the postnatal development of the cerebral cortex, and opiates (Bartolome et al., 1991) and steroid hormones (Beato et al., 1987) both directly regulate DNA synthesis. The activation and deactivation of monoaminergic systems by different dynamic patterns of dyadic object relations mediates the process by which the early postnatal environment experientially shapes genetic potential (Kendler & Eaves, 1986).

The expression of specific genes at particular times in development is thought to be associated with the onset of sensitive periods (Bateson & Hinde, 1987), and an increase in DNA synthesis has been observed during the growth spurt of the brain stem and cerebrum in the first two years of infancy (Benjamins & McKhann, 1981; Winick et al., 1970). It is important to emphasize that genetic systems occur both within the nucleus and within cytoplasmic mitochondria. The postnatal experience-sensitive maturation of these two cellular organelles that are involved in cellular metabolism may mediate critical periods of neuronal matura-tion (Lavelle, 1964). Lavelle concludes at the cellular level, the cytoplasmic architecture of individual neurons matures in stages.

Within the nucleus of developing brain cells, experience-dependent postnatal changes in nucleolar morphology result in increasing levels of metabolism (Buschmann & LaVelle, 1981). During early development circulating hormones produce alterations in the neuronal nucleolus (Cohen et al., 1984), a structure that contains a heat stress-sensitive function (Simard & Bernhard, 1967). The resultant amplification of ribosomal DNA (rDNA) (Kano, Maeda, & Sugiyama, 1976) in nucleolar organizer regions (McClintock, 1934; Ritossa & Spiegelman, 1965) allows for an intensification of ribosomal RNA production. Such a devel-opmental transformation of the cell nucleus supports an increased cellular capaci-ty for cytoplasmic RNA-driven protein synthesis, and this may significantly contribute to the critical period phenomena, since these periods are associated with heightened levels of RNA synthesis (Cummins et al., 1985). Nucleolar experience-dependent changes may also account for the observed increased di-versity of RNA synthesis that results from exposing the postnatally developing brain to environmental enrichment (Grouse et al., 1980).

In addition to the cell nucleus, gene-environment interactions also shape the genetic potential of the mitochondria of cells of the developing brain. There are 2 to 10 copies of maternally inherited mitochondrial DNA per mitochondrion within each cell (Robin & Wong, 1988), and this DNA (in collaboration with nuclear DNA) encodes the major subunits of cytochrome oxidase, the mito-chondrial complex that is essential to the cell's oxidative metabolism. Brain mitochondrial DNA may undergo an adaptive rearrangement during the transi-tion from anaerobic to aerobic conditions, so that it can now withstand the normal oxidative stress of higher oxygen tensions (Richter, Park, & Ames, 1988). Stress proteins, actively produced by the brain during postnatal develop-ment (White, 1981) and found in the outer membrane and matrix of mitochondria (Hartman, Hoogenraad, Condron, & Hoj, 1992; Jindal et al., 1989; Lubben et al., 1990; McMullin & Hallberg, 1987), may be involved in this adaptive pro-cess. How and when might they perform a stress protective role?

In postnatal critical periods new mitochondria are generated in a fission pro-cess (Pysh, 1970). This entails the generation of new nucleic acids, lipids and proteins, a process which involves products not only of the mitochondrial but also the nuclear genome. Basic studies of mitochodrial biosynthesis indicate that oxygen has an "assembly-inducing" effect on the components of cytochrome oxidase; in its presence products of the nuclear and mitochondrial genomes interact to form a complex (Woodrow & Shatz, 1979). Coordinated cellular activity allows for the import of proteins encoded on nuclear genes into new mitochondria. It is now thought that these imported proteins are physically associated with mitochondrial stress proteins in order to transport them into the mitochondrion (Ostermann, Horwich, Neupert, & Hartl, 1989; Prasad, Hack, & Hallberg, 1990; Sheffield, Shore, & Randall, 1990). These imported proteins ultimately combine with mitochondrial DNA products to form an inner membrane that contains mitochondrial ATPase and cytochrome oxidase, a system that can biophysically accommodate the aerobic generation of ATP (Tzagoloff et al., 1979). Cardiolipin, the most important lipid of this membrane, may be a prime repository of the essential fatty acids required for critical period brain growth (Innis, 1991). Stress proteins, known to participate in the assembly of biological membranes (Deshaies, Koch, & Schekman, 1988), may thus be involved in the capacity of differentiating brain mitochondria to adapt to the oxidation stress that occurs during the critical period transition from anaerobiosis to aerobiosis. It is now thought that alterations in membrane composition are specifically responsible for the capacity of an organism to physiologically adapt to a particular physical environment (Hazel & Williams, 1990).

Stress proteins may also contribute to the protection of the aerobic mitochondrial inner membrane, perhaps by inducing the synthesis of antioxidants such as manganese superoxide dismutase (Flohe, Laschen, Azzi, & Richter, 1977). Brain superoxide dismutase sharply increases in postnatal development (Kellogg & Fridovich, 1976), especially in regions with high catecholamine content (Ledig, Fried, Ziessel, & Mandel, 1982). It is often forgotten that molecular oxygen is potentially dangerous, since normal aerobic metabolism of brain cells produces oxygen free radicals that are known to be the most lethal substances to all biological systems (DiGuiseppi & Fridovich, 1984; Vercesi & Hoffmann, 1993). Intriguingly, NMDA receptor stimulation generates superoxide radicals (Lafon-Cazal, Pietri, Culcas, & Bockaert, 1993), and it is known that stress proteins protect neurons from damage by excitatory amino acids (Lowenstein, Chan, & Miles, 1991) and glutamate toxicity (Rordorf, Koroshetz, & Bonventre, 1991), and that mitochondrial activity effects the threshold for NMDA-mediated neuronal death (Simpson & Isacson, 1993).

Furthermore, mitochondrial differentiation may be centrally involved in apoptosis, a process that plays a crucial role in the early development and growth regulation of living systems (Gerschenson & Rotello, 1992). It has recently been discovered that an inner mitochondrial membrane protein, Bcl-2, prevents neuronal cell death by decreasing the generation of reactive oxygen species (Kane et al., 1993). The product of this proto-oncogene confers stress resistance upon differentiating cells (Tsujimoto, 1989) and blocks programmed cell death (Hockenberry et al., 1990). These latter authors conclude that "the main metabolic functions of the inner mitochondrial membrane, which include oxidative phosphorylation, electron and metabolite transport, are involved in the survival mechanism" (p. 336). Conversely, impairment of energy metabolism results in the excitotoxic neuronal death seen in neurodegenerative illnesses (Beal, 1992). The study of the dysfunction of mitochondrial energy production—defined as "defective ATP production due to enzymatic, transport, structural or *regulatory failure*" (Jones & Lash, 1993, p.1)—is rapidly becoming a very active area of research. The success or failure of the adaptive transformation of a brain cell's mitochondrial population may be a critical regulator of naturally occurring neuronal death (Hamburger & Oppenheim, 1982) and the regressive events of neurogenesis (Cowan et al., 1979) (and pathogenesis).

The importance of focusing research activities on to the developmental aspects of mitochondrial function is summarized by Aprille, Dransfield, and Joyal (1993):

> (Neonates) can be used to understand the normal sequence and regulation of biochemical events that enable (them) to make a successful transition to independent energy metabolism. More generally, the immediate postnatal period provides a useful model for investigating the regulation of oxidative phosphorylation; nature does the experiment for us, and we can simply compare the properties of isolated mitochondria at different stages of development. The perinatal transition is also a model system in which to study mechanisms that operate to protect cells in hypoxic versus normoxic states. Similarly, postnatal adaptation suggests a potential model for . . . mitochondrial biogenesis. Finally, (neonate) models can be used to evaluate unusual physiological conditions, various maternal and neonatal pathologies, and xenobiotic agents for effects on postnatal mitochondrial development and metabolic adaptation. (p. 429)

These mitochondrial developmental events may account for the observed differences in metabolic requirements between undifferentiated and differentiated neurons (Thurston & McDougal, 1969). Such bioenergetic adaptations may also influence the capacity of an individual neuron to prepare for synaptic contact (sites of intense mitochondrial activity) with not only other cells in its local microenvironment, but also with distant cells along a circuit that provides for a similar microenvironment. It is this interaction between cells in the same and different levels of the nervous system that accounts for the emergence of functions over the stages of brain development. The resultant connections occur specifically during critical periods, and the new capacities that appear as a result of these increased connections account for what Scott (1962) calls critical periods in behavioral development. Of particular importance is the development of bioenergetic processes in monoaminergic neurons and their endothelial receptors, since they, along with astroglia, are the essential cellular components of the blood-brain barrier, the system that delivers glucose, the basic metabolic substrate that supports all biosynthetic processes of the brain. Catecholaminergic nuclei in the brain stem make up not even 1% of the neurons in the CNS (Moore, 1982), yet this small number of cells has an enormous influence on the development and functioning of the billions of cells in the brain. The fact that each of these cells sends axons collaterals to multiple structures at different levels of the brain, and that one cell sends an axon over an enormous distance from the brain stem to the prefrontal cortex attests to the remarkably unique capacities of these master neurons. The reason for this remarkable capacity to reach and innervate distant sites may lie in the fact that these "exceptional" catecholaminergic neurons uniquely contain extremely high levels of enzymes of the hexose monophosphate shunt (Friede, Fleming, & Knoller, 1963), the metabolic pathway that mediates biosynthetic processes. This pathway, so prominent in postnatal brain development (Winick, 1974), is associated with critical period phenomena (Cummins et al., 1985) and is responsive to developmental stimuli (Guroff, 1980).

THE CELL BIOLOGY OF BRAIN MONOAMINE-MICROVASCULAR SYSTEMS

Although I have offered proposals concerning the trophic effects of mono-amines, I have not specifically suggested how they might regulate the various forms of brain microvasculatures and thereby the delivery and removal of essential metabolic substrates in different areas of the brain. Towards that end I offer the following speculations. The neuromodulatory role of biogenic amines is well established, yet the mechanism of their action is unresolved. One problem is the nature and number of receptors: How can the biochemical signals of a few million cells influence the activity of tens of billions of nonaminergic neurons in the cortex? Are there receptors on all of these cells, and if so how could such a small number of subcortical neurons deliver their biochemical signals to them? I have earlier reasoned that the endothelial cells of the brain vasculature, which constitute only 0.1% of the brain mass (Bar, 1980), are a critical site of the receptors of subcortically generated monoamines. Receptors on their luminal surfaces respond to circulating catecholamines secreted by the adrenal medulla, while receptors on their abluminal surface are sensitive to alterations in brain stem monoaminergic activity. The endothelial cells of the microvasculature are configured in tight junctions, and this single cell layer is responsible for the permeability characteristics of the blood-brain barrier. Endothelial mitochondria, which lie parallel to the luminal and abluminal cell surfaces, may represent a critical population of biogenic amine receptors. These mitochondria, which contain monoamine oxidase, the major enzyme system of monoaminergic catabolism, provide energy for the activity of the cell, including the energy required for cellular motion.

Brain capillaries are composed of contiguous endothelial cells separated by a tight junction (see Fig. 11.4), and in the brain microvasculature the two ends of the same endothelial cell completely surrounding the capillary lumen abut at a junction (see Fig. 11.2). These occluding junctions are the morphological basis for the blood-brain barrier, and it is known that agents that affect the permeability of the cerebral vasculature do so by causing leakages in the tight junctions. In a classical work on the effects of monoamines on vascular permeability, Majno and Palade (1961a) found that these agents cause endothelial openings along inter-cellular junctions, and speculate that the opening of a gap is due to the contraction of endothelial cells. This principle is now well established, and the molecular biology of endothelial contractile mechanisms and gap formation is now being worked out (Curry, 1992). Studying the effects of monoamines on blood-brain barrier mechanisms, Hardebo, Emson, and Owman (1979) proposed:

> The possibility should also be considered that the endothelium with its amine enzymes may not only serve a simple barrier function: the amine uptake and enzyme mechanisms may play a role in the function of the endothelial cells themselves, which may target structures for circulating and neurogenically released amines in, e.g. contractile processes. (p. 164)

Indeed, actin-like filaments anchored to the plasma membrane are found in endothelial cells of brain capillaries and postcapillary venules, suggesting that the elements necessary for contraction are present in these cells (Le Beux & Willemot, 1978). Activation of monoamine receptors in non-brain endothelial cells has been shown to reduce actin, induce a cytoskeletal reorganization and cell retraction, and increase the permeability of tight junctions (Rotrosen & Gallin, 1986).

Furthering these principles, I suggest that the major action of biogenic amines on brain microvasculature is on endothelial mitochondria whose energetic transductons influence the cell's contractile state. This results in an alteration of the tight junctions and thereby the permeability of the local blood-brain barrier, and the transient widening of the gap allows for the bidirectional exchange of substrates in and out of a specific brain region (Dermietzel & Krause, 1991). In this way, energy produced by cerebral mitochondria is used to transfer materials such as glucose across the blood-brain barrier, just as Oldendorf et al. (1977) suggest. Dopamine, noradrenaline, and serotonin and their different classes of receptors (associated with and without adenylate cyclase) differ in their capacity to influence the endothelial contractile state, and therefore in their capacity to regulate the opening of the tight junctions for various durations. (On the other hand, acetylcholine release by local cholinergic neurons could trigger release of endothelium-derived relaxing factor and nitric oxide by endothelial cells (Palmer, Ferige, & Moncada, 1987). Nitric oxide activity, (associated with guanylate cyclase and cyclic GMP) particulary enhanced in dendrites and axons closely apposed to intraparenchymal microvessels, is known to regulate the microcirculation and maintain resting cerebral blood flow by inducing vasodilation (Iadecola, 1993).

Such a mechanism regulates the amount of blood-borne glucose, the major substrate of neuronal and glial oxygen metabolism, that can enter and exit a brain region, and in this manner mediates the neuromodulatory function of bioamines. It is well established that biogenic amines play an essential role in microcirculatory homeostasis (Schayer, 1970), and that the blood-brain barrier regulates the transport of glucose from blood to brain (Fuglsang et al., 1988). Blood flow is known to correlate with changes in arousal levels (Obrist et al., 1975) and to be an indicator of regional oxidative metabolism (Raichle et al., 1976). Both regional blood flow and regional metabolism are known to be coupled to local synaptic activity

(Greenberg et al., 1979). The observed differences in capillary form and blood flow in different brain areas (Fenstermacher et al., 1988) would be a function of the unique patterns of catecholaminergic innervation of a local blood-brain barrier. Such patterns are responsible for specific cytoarchitectural structure-function relationships that are associated with the metabolic and therefore the information processing capacities of particular regions of the brain. This mechanism identifies Luria's (1973) structural systems in the subcortex and brainstem that maintain and regulate the tone of the cerebral cortex. "Cortical tone" may thus specifically refer to the tone of the cerebral microvasculature.

This proposal is supported by anatomical studies of prefrontal receptor populations. In the peripheral nervous system monoaminergic varicosities do not form specialized contacts on vascular elements (Devine & Simpson, 1967), and this same principle is thought to apply in the brain (Swanson, Connelly, & Hartman, 1977). Many dopaminergic varicosities in the deep layers of the orbitofrontal cortex lack a synaptic specialization, suggesting that dopamine exerts its effects at sites other than traditional neuronal presynaptic-axonal, postsynaptic-dendritic contacts (Seguela, Watkins, & Descarries, 1988) (see Fig. 11.8). On the basis of this finding, Descarries argues that these non-junctional dopaminergic varicosities act in a diffuse, long-lasting manner on vast neuronal ensembles implicated in 'state'-dependent activities. It is well established that the number of actively functioning cerebral capillaries (Mchedlishvili, 1964) and capillary permeability (Lorenzo, Fernandez, & Roth, 1965) may vary with the physiological state of the brain. At the end of the last century, Roy and Sherrington (1890) were the first to suggest a concept of intrinsic control of the circulation and propose that this is focally adapted to the region's metabolic and functional needs. We now know that the innervation of the brain's vasculatures by monoaminergic neurons operates as a regulator that responds to the local needs of brain regions (Hartman & Udenfriend, 1972). Dopamine produces a significant increase in blood flow in the frontal cortex, and this has been suggested to reflect the activation of specific receptors located on endothelium (Tuor et al., 1986). Noradrenergic axons in the frontal cortex also show a low incidence of "true" synaptic terminals (Lapierre, Beaudet, Demianczuk, & Descarries, 1973). The noradrenergic effects on cerebral blood flow have also been proposed to be mediated by endothelial receptors on the cerebral vasculature (Aubineau, Sercombe, Lusamvuku, & Seylaz, 1982). The nucleus of the solitary tract, site of medullary noradrenergic neurons, is now being referred to as the "gateway to neural circulatory control" (Andressen & Kunze, in press).

Vascular endothelial cells are strategically located at the critical interface between the extravascular tissue and the circulating blood. Once thought to be an inert layer of cells which simply line the blood vessels and separate these elements, the different populations of endothelial cells are now recognized as a complex organ of varied and essential capabilities. They perform distinct biological, chemical, and physiological functions at different vascular sites and in every individual organ—receptor binding, macromolecular permeability, stress responses, fluid transfer, interstitial transport, cell-cell interaction, cell locomotion, immune reactions, chemotaxis, eicosanoid biosynthesis, thrombosis, hemostasis, and hematopoiesis. In the brain their interaction with various central and peripheral bioaminergic and neuroendocrine systems supports all aspects of local and global central nervous system function, including the synaptic activities between neurons that underlies brain activity. The endothelial cells in limbic circuits are an essential element of a system that is responsible for the definitional circulatory changes that physiologically underlie the various discrete emotional states. The importance of an optimal microcirculation to the chemical and structural aspects of brain development is only now beginning to be appreciated (Casaer, 1993).

Even more specifically, I would speculate that there are morphological correlates of the different bioaminergic-vascular systems. Majno and Palade (1961b) reported that the site of action of serotonin is on the venous side of the vascular tree. Taking this idea further, different classes of serotonin receptors in the brain microcirculation may reside in the minute postcapillary venules, more permeable sites that display only limited tight junctions (Simionescu, Simionescu, & Palade, 1975). Different classes of dopamine receptors could occupy the endothelial cells of minute precapillary arterioles, and the various noradrenaline receptors could be represented on single-cell capillaries. Furthermore, these systems may appear in a regular ontogenetic fashion. For example, cortical serotonin receptors develop in an orderly ontogenetic sequence (Uzbekov, Murphy, & Rose, 1979). Like the catecholamines, serotonin neurons in the brainstem (raphe nuclei) project to small vessels in the brain (Reinhard, Liebman, Schlossberg, & Moskowitz, 1979), induce increased blood flow (Jacobs & Fornal, 1993), and have a modulatory effect on brain systems (Fornal & Jacobs, 1987) and neural information processing (Spoont, 1992). Although serotonin, by itself, produces little or no change in neuronal activity, when combined with an excitatory amino acid or electrical stimulation, it induces a neuronal state transition, a shift from a stable hyperpolarization state of neuronal inactivity to a new stable depolarized "plateau" state with tonic neuronal activity (Jacobs & Fornal, 1993).

Serotonin axons are capable of collateral sprouting (Azmitia, Buchan, & Williams, 1978), and the branching of serotonin axons in the cerebral cortex is thought to take place in postnatal stages of development (Aitken & Tork, 1988). Serotonergic axon terminals in the frontal cortex also exhibit mostly nonsynaptic terminals (Descarries, Beaudet, & Watkins, 1975). In addition, serotonin also shares other properties of the catecholamines—it stimulates the hexose monophosphate pathway in the neonatal cortex (Appel & Parrot, 1970), induces glycogenolysis (Quach et al., 1982), disaggregates brain polysomes (Weiss, Wurtman, & Munro, 1973), influences the differentiation of other neurons (Lauder & Krebs, 1986), and regulates neuronal architecture and sculpts connectivity (Haydon, McCobb, & Kater, 1984). Serotonin receptors coupled to adenylate cyclase are very frequent in newborn brains (Leysen, 1985). Importantly, in the period immediately after birth serotonin plays a critical role in very early neonatal experience (Giulian, McEwen, & Pohorecky, 1974). This bioamine is known to play an important role in sleep, thermoregulation, and appetitive behavior (Brownstein, 1981), prominent features of the neonatal repertoire.

Serotonin receptors are present in the orbitofrontal cortex (Arato et al., 1991). Goldman-Rakic et al. (1983) point out that in the prefrontal cortex, serotonin activity remains constant from birth through adulthood, while catecholamine activity steadily increases over the first 3-years-of-life. She also reports that prefrontal dopamine reaches peak concentration earlier in ontogeny than noradrenaline. I propose that the earliest activities of the orbitofrontal cortex, say in the first months of human life, are predominantly driven by serotonergic and not catecholaminergic systems. I have earlier argued that the maturation of ventral tegmental dopamine receptors precedes that of lateral tegmental noradrenergic receptors in the orbital cortex. I suggest that this pattern reflects the ontogeny of monoaminergic-vascular connections in particular orbitofrontal regions, and that these patterns determine the operations of the tight junctions of the local blood-brain barrier and thereby the metabolic activity of differentiating areas within this cortex. This in turn determines the activity of the cortical columns, and therefore the functional capacities of the orbitofrontal regions, including their essential role in affective processes.

THE ONTOGENY OF MONOAMINERGIC SYSTEMS
AND THE HIERARCHICAL DEVELOPMENT OF
DISCRETE PSYCHOBIOLOGICAL STATES

To my mind, development—the process of self assembly—may be fundamentally defined as the experience-dependent emergence of increasingly complex hierarchical self-regulatory systems in the brain which evolve out of a succession of specific gene-environment interactions embedded in a sequence of early infant-caregiver socioaffective environments. Changes in the external environment of the developing organism are paralleled by changes in the internal environment. As outlined in earlier chapters, the mother mediates the external environment of the child, and in dyadic affective transactions she psychobiologically influences the infant's production of hormones and neurohormones in the infant's developing nervous system. These same agents act on both nuclear and mitochondrial genomes, both of which are undergoing active transcription in the brain during a postnatal critical period. In this way she acts as a primary evolutionary agent of natural selection. Intracellular changes, especially in the nucleoli of developing hypothalamic neuroendocrine and functional groups of brain stem monoamine neurons and their orbitofrontal receptors, and mitochondrial changes in these same limbic cellular components, allow for the maturation of more extensive connections between the cortical and subcortical components of the limbic system, and thereby enable advances in socioemotional functioning.

During early critical periods, biogenic amines, regulators of the temporal framework of developmental processes (Lauder & Krebs, 1986), play a crucial role in the experience-dependent growth of brain structures and the consequent appearance of more complex emergent functions. These monoamines influence the ontogeny of cortical circuitry and have long-lasting effects on biochemical processes that mediate developmental influences (Foote & Morrison, 1991). It is now well established that a fundamental role of various monoaminergic agents in the brain is to regulate the metabolic activity on the CNS (Quach et al., 1978; 1982), and that increased metabolic activity is associated with arousal (Gonzalez-Lima & Scheich, 1985). Their actions on endothelial cells of the blood-brain barrier allow for circulating oxygen and glucose to be taken up into the local parenchyma, while their effects on astrocytes that line the barrier is to control the considerable respiratory capacities (Hertz & Schousboe, 1975) and glycogen metabolism (Lajtha, Maker, & Clarke, 1981) of these glial cells (Pearce et al., 1985). These metabolic events, in turn, supply the substrates for and thereby support the activity of synapses between local neurons. The major direct effect of the different monoamines is on these non-neuronal cells rather than on neurons themselves, and their neuromodulatory functions are expressed in their differing capacities to mobilize, in a coordinated fashion, varying levels of energy reserves for different classes of active neuronal environments. Authors investigating each and every known central aminergic system (dopamine, noradrenaline, adrenaline, serotonin, histamine) have found that all share a common involvement in arousal, vascular function, and energy metabolism, and that the diffuse projections of these neurons are well adapted to regulating the responsivity of large areas of the brain to inputs in a coordinated manner.

The fact that multiple forms of energetic arousal evolve in the brain is due to the existence of a maturational sequence of discrete monoaminergic systems. Each brain stem neuromodulatory aminergic system establishes territories of innervation in a caudal-to-rostral trajectory in the hindbrain, midbrain, and forebrain. Each system expresses a unique arousal-inducing capacity that is responsible for different state-dependent functional activities of higher brain regions. Particular neuromodulator bioaminergic inputs come to elicit unique "operational states" of specific neural networks that program numerous outputs (Marder et al., 1987). These inputs arise from the different classes of brain stem aminergic nuclei, and are identical to Luria's (1973) structural systems in the subcortex and brainstem that maintain and regulate the "tone" of the cerebral cortex. As development proceeds, a hierarchy of distinct aminergic-microvascular patterns account for dissociable "cortical tones" with unique metabolic characteristics that define specific psychobiological states. The mode of action of all biogenic amines is the generation of coordinated state transitions in the multicellular elements of a brain region. Individual functional states are associated with specific types of cognitive strategies and memory storage (Fischer, 1971), that is with unique modes of information processing. The functional state of a region determines the character and quality of its ability to process information, and the environmentally sensitive differential activation and inactivation of the same region by the various brain stem serotonergic, dopaminergic, and noradrenergic nuclei and their subcortical-cortical circuits would result in the induction of local functional states according to the demands of a changing environment. These psychoneurobiological developmental events drive the ontogeny of "basic psychological states of being that are developed in infancy and persist throughout life" (Ogden, 1990, p. 42).

The sequential appearance of more efficient central neural homeostatic systems in ontogeny reflects the experience-dependent increase of bidirectional connections between the prefrontal cortex with different subcortical monoaminergic systems and with maturing cortical systems that transmit more and more complex sensory (olfactory-gustatory, somesthetic, visual and then auditory) information about the environment. The formation of these circuits, especially in prefrontal areas that perform executive functions, allows for the hierarchical emergence of more complex brain states and the establishment of new internal dynamic representations (Freyd, 1987) that encode adaptive strategies to regulate the transitions between such states. Psychological states are coherent packages of cognitions, behaviors, and affects (Horowitz, 1987), and state transitions involve coordinated changes in patterns of arousal, energy level, motor behavior, cognitive processing, and affect (Putnam, 1992). In this manner the maturing brain shifts between different states that constitute essential components of motivational systems and provide the neural substrate of the internal and communicative aspects of affects (Hofer, 1990). The developmental advances in the ability to access an expanded array of internal states that supports more complex state-dependent information processing capacities are responsible for the appearance of emergent "higher" states of consciousness.

Such hierarchical advances in the "psychobiology of changing states" (Gilbert, 1989) are reflected in the appearance of affect regulating executive functions of the prefrontal areas of the right hemisphere, especially in the orbitofrontal areas that play a critical role in the establishing and maintenance of motivational states (Eslinger & Damasio, 1985; Pandya & Yeterian, 1985). Although the dominance of the information processing capacities of the early maturing right hemisphere is eventually superceded by the later developing left, it continues to perform its essential psychobiological functions throughout the lifespan. Koukkou and Lehmann (1983) observe that:

> Information received in early childhood is initially treated by inherent, built-in, basic strategies, but the continuously stored new information leads to the formation of new cognitive strategies, which are maintained and stored in newly developed functional states. New strategies are used to process the new information and to reprocess still accessible old information. (p. 226)

These authors conclude that brain stem aminergic systems are centrally involved in changes of functional brain states according to demands made by incoming information. Their work also demonstrates that state transitions occur not only in waking states but also during sleep, a time when "an individual will go repeatedly through previous developmental (ontogenetic) functional stages, using processing strategies and memory contents which are associated with earlier stages" (p. 226). They further conclude that during REM phases of sleep there is :

. . . increased access of the adult dominant (left) hemisphere to memory stored in the right hemisphere in early childhood, before functional left dominance was established, and the possibility of verbalization of material generated in the right hemisphere, which might be dominant during dreaming. (Koukkou & Lehmann, 1983, p. 228)

During REM sleep and dreaming cerebral blood flow is greatly increased in right temporal-parietal regions (Meyer, Ishikawa, Hata, & Karacan, 1987). REM is known to increase after a day in which the individual experiences emotionally stressful events (Hartmann, 1976). At the beginning of this century Freud (1900/1953), in *The Interpretation of Dreams*, posited that during dreaming salient early experiences are incorporated into adult waking life.

In later childhood this ontogenetic mechanism continues as the other prefrontal field, the nonlimbic dorsolateral prefrontal cortex interconnects with the noradrenergic domain of the locus coeruleus and the dopaminergic system in the substantia nigra, signaling the onset of integrated left hemispheric functioning. But preceding this, towards the end of the second year of human life the ventral tegmental dopaminergic and lateral tegmental noradrenergic limbic circuits complete their maturation. The functional transformation of the self-regulation of emotion and motivation that emerges at this time parallels the socioemotional experience-dependent transmutation of frontolimbic structure which generates a more efficient delayed response function. Delayed response function underlies representational memory (Fuster, 1980) and representational memory, involved in the mechanism of the regulation of behavior (Goldman-Rakic, 1987b), requires the collaborative processing of cortical and subcortical structures (Goldman-Rakic et al., 1990). These structural changes which occur within constraining timetables for crucial representational world developmental steps (Jacobson, 1983) are matched by a developmental gradation of representational capacities over the stages of infancy (Trad, 1986), thereby allowing for the expanding capacity to both generate and modulate new psychobiological states. In this manner, frontal paralimbic networks "link the increasingly sophisticated representations of the external context to an internal representation of the bodily state" (Tucker, 1992, p. 101), and in integrating information processed simultaneously by combinations of sensory modalities allow for more efficient autoregulation of bodily states even in the face of environmental perturbations. Representational and internalization capacities thus become more complex and more efficient as the information processing functions of the posterior right and the cognitive, affective, and memorial functions of the anterior right hemisphere mature, and as the growth of reciprocal connections between these areas allow for higher levels of integration.

Levin (1991) notes that, "With the further refinement of the system of the right cerebral hemisphere and limbic system (which have intimate connection with each other) it is known that affects are better regulated" (p. 194). The emergence in the second year of human life of an integrated right hemispheric multimodal information processing system that can generate interactive representations, which autoregulate affect by modulating autonomic nervous system patterns of organismic energy dissipation, enables the individual to more autonomously execute the organismic transformation and conservation of energy. Such an adaptive developmental advance is dependent upon the postnatal socioaffective experience-dependent maturation of connections between cortical and subcortical structures which mediate emotional functioning. Critical period dyadic experiences which subserve gene-environment interactions are imprinted into and influence the phenotypic maturation of the various brain systems that set the limits and ranges of the types of external and internal information the child's emotion regulating right hemisphere can process. This socioaffective information processing capacity is equated with the efficiency of the organism to enter into matter-energy transformations during interactions with the social environment, that is to enter into various basic types of dynamic low or high energy affective transactions with and without other humans. A personality's unique range of socioaffective experiences may define the individual's "affect array" (Pine, 1980), and the capacity to consciously experience a regulated affect may characterize "affect tolerance" (Krystal, 1988). These dimensions may in turn operationally define the "boundaries" of the self as a psychosocial system. Nathanson (1992) asserts that any increase in the potential for affective modulation confers upon the organism an increase in the potential for survival. Watt (1990) points out the important point that in contrast to the "dominant" left hemisphere, "The right hemisphere's total contribution to human adaptation has been, until recently, consistently undervalued and underassessed" (p. 494).

Throughout this volume I have offered numerous specific heuristic proposals regarding affect and its regulation. In totality, the body of this work suggests that in order for science to penetrate certain essential questions of human existence, multidisciplinary research at different levels of analysis should shift their focus of attention from the well-studied left hemipshere to the less-explored right hemisphere, from the posterior to anterior cerebral regions, from the outer surface to the under surface of the cortex, from the dorsolateral to the orbital prefrontal cortex, from cortical versus subcortical mechanisms to cortical-subcortical systems, from neurons to endothelial and astroglial cells, from cholinergic to monoaminergic neuronal populations, from nigral to ventral tegmental dopaminergic and locus coeruleus to medullary noradrenergic nuclei, and from nuclear genetic systems transmitted by Mendelian inheritance to mitochondrial systems governed by maternal inheritance. In parallel to this, investigators of emotional, cognitive, and behavioral functions should broaden their perspective to include underlying psychobiological states, and should overcome the bias of investigating verbal and conscious events and focus on the charting of the domain of nonverbal and unconscious phenomena.

SUMMARY

Regulatory systems exist at the physical, chemical, biological, and social levels of living systems. The self-assembly of hierarchical regulatory systems that allows for an adaptive capacity to cope with changing conditions in the surrounding physical and social environments is an essential characteristic of development. A series of early environments influences the activation of nuclear and mitochondrial genomic programs that encode the maturation of biological structures from the organelle to the organ level. An essential common property of all biological systems, including human systems, is that they exist within an immediate environment from which they receive matter and energy and to which they return matter and energy. Since the growth of the infant brain occurs only by virtue of being coupled to a source of energy, an appreciation of developmental bioenergetics is an absolute necessity to a deeper understanding of human development. In postnatal periods, the human social environment serves as a medium for essential energy transformations that are embedded in emotional transactions. These psychobiological interactions are essential to the individual's well-being throughout the lifespan, but during human infancy they are critical to the child's survival and future growth.

The dyadic relationship between the primary caregiver and her infant generates stimulation that regulates the neurohormonal and hormonal activity of the child's nervous system, especially its limbic components. Within the limbic system hypothalamic neuroendocrine centers and monoaminergic nuclei in the medulla and midbrain play a critical role in the maturation of evolving higher regulatory structures in the cortex, especially the frontolimbic cortex. The axonal processes of subcortical monoaminergic neurons ascend the neuraxis to establish new territories, and the action of their cellular product, the biogenic amines, is expressed at a critical site—the developing vasculature that will transport metabolic substrates into and out of the maturing brain regions. The developing blood-brain barrier, composed of endothelial cells with tight junctions, delivers the glucose that allows the local neurons and neuroglia to enter into the matter-energy transformations that sustain cell survival and function. The endothelial cell's population of mitochondria, which contain cytochrome oxidase, the enzyme complex responsible for the oxidative processes that generate biological energy in the form of ATP, is differentiating in the postnatal period. The final number, type, and functional capacities of mitochondria in various regional cellular populations are influenced by events in the postnatal external and internal environment. The activity of these mitochondria supports the functioning of the blood-brain barrier.

Molecular and physiological events that occur in the mitochondria and nucleoli of bioaminergic, neuroendocrine and endothelial cells are essential to critical period phenomena. The mitochondria of the endothelial cells contain an important population of monoaminergic receptors, as subcortically produced bioamines regulate the blood-brain barrier of the orbitofrontal cortex. Endothelial cells also represent the site of synthesis of stress proteins, biomolecules that confer an ability of cells to survive and cope with stress at the cellular level. The developing microvasculatures of the two circuits of the limbic system are thus a critical site for the emergence and future maintenance of socioemotional functioning. The postnatal experience-dependent maturation of monoaminergic-vascular systems in the frontolimbic cortex is the keystone of affect regulation, the modulation of psychobiological states.

37

A Proposed Rapprochement Between Psychoanalysis and Neurobiology

[M]ental states, as dynamic emergent properties of brain activity, become inseparably interfused with and tied to the brain activity of which they are an emergent property.

—Roger W. Sperry (1993)

Any psychological theory must, in addition to meeting the demands made by natural science, fulfill another major obligation. It must explain to us the things that we know, in the most puzzling fashion, through our "consciousness"; and since this consciousness knows nothing of [quantities of energy and neurones], our theory must also explain to us this lack of knowledge.

—Sigmund Freud (1887–1902/1954)

So science takes its coherence, its intellectual and imaginative strength together, from the concepts at which its lines cross, like knots in a mesh. Gravitation, mass and energy, evolution, enzymes, the gene and the unconscious—these are the bold creations of science, the strong invisible skeleton on which it articulates the movements of the world.

—Jacob Bronowski (1972)

The study of human emotion and social behavior, perhaps even moreso than any other problem confronted by science, highlights the absolute necessity of integrating the perspectives of various disciplines. By definition it directs us into a domain of the subjective, and in heightened states of emotion this phenomenological realm is dominated by an acute consciousness of interoceptive stimuli, dramatically emphasizing our fundamental biological origins. Perhaps more than any other, it was Freud who showed us that the disciplined and analytical study of emotion ineluctably leads us into an exploration of our most personal and least charted inner world. The inward journey prescribed by the psychotherapeutic technique he discovered is essentially concerned with encounters with affect. To my mind, contemporary psychoanalysis, whose area of study is now being described as "human emotional development and functioning" (Langs & Badalamenti, 1992), must be included and must include itself into the consortium of scientific disciplines that is inquiring into the basic nature of emotion. The recent appearance of an edited volume on psychoanalytic perspectives on affect represents such an effort (Shapiro & Emde, 1992).

It is well known that Freud's ideas about psychoanalysis were influenced by his neurological education (Amacher, 1965; Jeliffe, 1937), but it is generally less appreciated that he made important contributions to 19th-century neurology (L. Miller, 1991; Triarhou & del Cerro, 1985). These works were produced over the first 20 years of his professional life, and they included histological research on the movements of nucleoli in nerve cells (Freud, 1882), developmental investigations of the human embryonic nervous system (Freud, 1885), neuropathologic studies of the medulla oblongata (Darkschewitsch & Freud, 1886), and clinical works on aphasia (Freud, 1891) and infantile cerebral palsy (Freud, 1897). In 1895 he attempted to utilize what was then known about neurophysiology and biology to begin to construct a set of regulatory principles for psychological processes and a neuropsychological model of brain function. This endeavor to build a theory of mind based in natural science, *Project for a Scientific Psychology*, which included a neurophysiological model of affect generation, was never published in his lifetime, as in his subsequent development of psychoanalytic theory Freud attempted to expunge the neurophysiological and biological roots of his psychological model. Despite this, it is now thought that the ideas generated in this work, many of which were incorporated into the seventh chapter of *The Interpretation of Dreams*, represent the source pool from which he later developed the major concepts of his psychoanalytic model (McCarley & Hobson, 1977).

Fifty years later the psychoanalyst Heinz Hartmann (1939) attempted to commence a rapprochement between psychoanalysis and biology by proposing that adaptation is primarily a reciprocal relationship of the organism and its environment, and that development is a differentiation in which primitive regulatory factors are increasingly replaced or supplemented by more effective regulatory factors. Forty years after that Bowlby (1969) integrated then current biological findings into the corpus of psychoanalytic theory, and emphasized the importance of regulatory control systems that are open to influence by the environment in which development occurs. One hundred years after the inception of modern neurology and psychoanalysis workers from within psychoanalysis (e.g., Grotstein, Krystal, Stern, Emde, Lichtenberg, Taylor, Wilson, and Settlage) like those in various other disciplines are converging on the centrality of regulatory processes and structures.

At the beginning of this century Freud (1913/1955) suggested that:

> We have found it necessary to hold aloof from biological considerations during our
> psycho-analytic work and to refrain from using them for heuristic purposes, so that
> we may not be misled in our impartial judgment of the psycho-analytic facts before
> us. But after we have completed our psychoanalytic work we shall have to find a
> point of contact with biology; and we may rightly feel glad if that contact is already
> assured at one important point or another. (p. 181)

According to Sulloway (1979), Freud, the "biologist of the mind," "never abandoned the assumption that psychoanalysis would someday come to terms with
the neurophysiological side of mental activity" (p. 131). Are we now ready for
such a rapprochement? Writing in a prominent psychoanalytic journal, Reiser
(1985) notes a disturbing trend in which neurobiological data are being increasingly ignored by psychoanalysts, and psychoanalytic data dismissed by neurobiologists. And yet, a current influential text on developmental psychoanalysis
calls for a return to Freud's origination point:

> The scaffolding for a psychoanalytic theory of affect is provided by investigations
> of emotional expression and of the associated neuroendocrine, peripheral, and
> central nervous system processes, and studies dealing with the cognitive, behav-
> ioral, and linguistic dimensions of affects. (Tyson & Tyson, 1990, p. 136)

In very recent writings on the current status of psychoanalysis, Kernberg (1993)
argues that this discipline needs to identify itself as a science, and that the major
scientific breakthroughs in this theory require "an interdisciplinary environment." He sees contemporary psychoanalysis to be involved in:

> linking the biological, psychological, social, and cultural determinants of human
> behavior. . . . .Psychoanalysis increases an understanding, for example, of the early
> development of the human infant, affect theory, and the neuropsychology of memo-
> ry at its boundary with biological sciences. . . . .(p. 47)

These chapters have presented multidisciplinary evidence to argue that affect
regulation, the regulation of patterns of energy dissipation by internal images, is
a potent explanatory concept that clarifies and elucidates infant develomental,
affect, and memorial phenomena. Self-regulation, the modulation of subcortical
energetic processes by higher cortical activity, represents a potential contact
point between psychoanalysis and neurobiology.

It should be empasized, however, that the progression of psychoanalytic
thought on the questions originally defined by Freud has not been and still is not
a smooth or unbroken one. As a result of its losing sight of its point of origin, the
course of psychoanalytic theory in this century has been at times unsteady and
inconstant. Due to the loss of its moorings to the rest of science it has been an
easy target to the criticism that it is untestable (e.g., Nagel, 1959; Popper, 1962).
In 1981, Kline concluded that since psychoanalysis does not report observations

gathered under controlled conditions and does not provide constructs that are operational or hypotheses that are testable, it cannot be called a proper science. In neglecting and at times disclaiming its biological and neurological roots, the essential definitional concepts which lie at the very foundation of the most comprehensive and powerful psychological theory have been relegated to a secondary, dissociated status of "metapsychology." Into this domain that is "meta" or beyond psychology were placed poorly fitting and seemingly unresolvable remnants of psychoanalytic knowledge, to be put into storage until some vague later time. This repository specifically contains Freud's germinal concepts of the regulatory structures and energetic dynamics that characterize the psycho-neurobiological mechanisms of affect, attention, consciousness, and motivation. Due to advances in object relations theory and self psychology, the main body of psychoanalysis has moved dramatically forward in the last 20 years, however it has done so disconnected from a conceptual model which relates psychic (neuro-biological) structure to psychological function. The importance and the meaning of this fact is currently being debated (e.g., Basch, 1986; Stolorow & Atwood, 1979).

Indeed, from within the discipline various influential authors (Holt, 1967; G.S. Klein, 1976) drawing on Hartmann's (1939) and Rapoport's (1960) work on ego psychology have criticized Freud's idea of "quantity of energy" as being an antiquated concept steeped in 19th-century science, and have proposed that the earlier regulatory principles based on an energy concept should be scrapped altogether. Such a proposal was offered by Peterfreund and Schwartz (1971) who also asserted that:

> Because of its . . . fundamental conceptual divorce from biology and from all evolutionary time, current psychoanalytic theory is a very limited theory. It cannot develop an adequate learning theory nor an adequate theory of the psychoanalytic process, and it cannot be meaningfully linked to modern neurophysiology. (p. 85).

Yet in the exact same year, in a paper on psychic energy Applegarth (1971) argued:

> I believe that the core questions in psychoanalysis lie in the nature of psychic structures and the mechanism of their formation. Now it is true, of course, that the basic elucidation of these matters will lie with the neurophysiologists and neuroche-mists. (p. 398)

In an important treatise on the overlooked "Project," a neuroscientist in collaboration with a psychoanalyst (Pribram & Gill, 1976) have argued that the critics of the energy concept never referred to this seminal work which in actuality does contain an explicit concept that can be "meaningfully linked to modern neuro-physiology." Pribram and Gill conclude that psychoanalytic metapsychological conceptions are indeed neuropsychological in origin, and that energy and regulatory concepts are heuristic and need to be retained in psychological theory in order to further explicate affective and motivational phenomena. "The Project is specific in detail in how the neural structures that regulate behavior—i.e. the organism's motivational structures—come to be" (p. 48).

Contemporary neurobiological data may indeed offer a solution to a problem at the core of psychoanalytic metapsychology. In discussing the "Project," Basch (1975) explains that Freud conceptualized a brain whose primary function is to dissipate and allocate quantities of psychic energy derived from biological instinctual forces. This quantity of energy is also referred to as a "sum of excitation" or "quota of affect" (Freud, 1894/1962). In fact Freud proposed that the primary brain fundamentally acts as a "sympathetic ganglion" (1895/1966, p. 303). In a very recent work, Macmillan (1992) points out that every model of the mind conceived of by Freud is based on a mechanism that maintains a state of nonstimulation by disposing of excitation. Freud interpreted his clinical data in terms of one active excitatory process being repressed and maintained in the unconscious by an equally active conscious excitatory process. He always spoke in terms of an excitatory flow, and throughout his life never recognized the necessity for an independent central inhibitory process, despite the facts that an inhibitory role of the frontal lobes had been discussed in 1876 by Ferrier, and that the phenomenon of vagal inhibition had been demonstrated even earlier (Weber & Weber, 1845/1966).

In other words, Freud had overlooked the essential role of the energy-conserving parasympathetic branch of the autonomic nervous system and its reciprocal relationship to the energy-expending sympathetic component in the overall maintenace of organismic energy balance. I have earlier shown that this inhibitory system is represented in the orbitofrontal lobes, that vagal activity is regulated by these structures, and that an understanding of the phenomenon of conservation-withdrawal is critical to the elucidation of the mechanism that underlies conscious and repressed affects. Freud was correct in emphasizing the importance of internal bioenergetic events to psychological functioning; the science that was available to him still had to evolve for some time after his death in order to understand such events. There is now a tendency in the psychoanalytic literature to replace Freud's "energy model" with an "information processing model." This is misleading if not incorrect, since energetics and information processing are tightly coupled (Hockey, Gaillard, & Coles, 1986). Indeed, in contemporary bioenergetic theory, information is conceived of as "a special kind of energy required for the work of establishing biological order" (Harold, 1986, p. 475). Ciompi (1991) points out:

> the remarkable analogies that seem to exist between the effects of energy in physical and biological systems on the one hand, and of information in mental systems on the other. . . .(p. 102)

The processing of all forms of information by the brain, including that embedded in internal representations, occurs through transformations of metabolic energy. Studies of various types of human mental activity—imagining faces (Goldenberg et al., 1989), speech (Ingvar, 1983), reading (Ingvar & Schwartz, 1974), audio-visual stimulation (Mazziotta, Phelps, & Halgren, 1983), tactile perception (Seitz & Roland, 1992), and tactile learning (Roland et al., 1989)—show that information processing results in changes in the regional oxidative metabolism of the human brain (Roland, Eriksson, Stone-Elander, & Widen, 1987). Furthermore, I have presented a body of evidence in these chapters that demonstrates that the energy concept is absolutely heuristic. Indeed the progressive appearance of more efficient energy systems lies at the heart of development. I conclude that the extraordinary power of the concept of energy transformations derives from the fact that these fundamental phenomena occur on each and every level of organization of living systems, from the molecular to the societal.

Thermodynamic concepts are an essential feature of nonlinear dynamic theory, a powerful model that is now utilized at every level of scientific investigation. The growing postnatal brain, the physical matrix of the emerging human mind, is supplied with a continuous supply of energy through metabolic processes. A fundamental tenet of this theory states that the assembly of complex systems occurs under conditions of thermodynamic non-equilibrium (a directed flow of energy). This energy is utilized to facilitate the cooperativity of simpler subsystem components into a hierarchically-structured complex system that expresses the emergent functions of organizing and maintaining stability (Thelen, 1989). Two essential conclusions of this volume are that energy shifts are the most basic and fundamental feature of emotion, and that the energetic transactions embedded in the socioemotional interchanges between an adult and a developing brain indelibly shape the child's emerging capacity for self-organization. Bioenergetic conceptualizations thus need to be implanted into the central core of psychoanalytic and psychological theory, a position they now occupy in physics, chemistry, and biology. Thermodynamics are not only the essence of biodynamics, they are also the essence of neurodynamics, and therefore of psychodynamics.

At the present time, the linkages between psychoanalysis and developmental psychology are now cross-fertilizing both fields. Bowlby's attachment theory, an outgrowth of psychoanalysis, has become one of the primary paradigms generating developmental research. These data are now being reincorporated into psychoanalysis and are replacing many of its developmental concepts (Bowlby, 1984). In fact, a good argument can be made that, as much as clinical work with adults, multidisciplinary developmental studies are currently acting as a powerful catalyst to the rapidly expanding growth in psychoanalytic theory and practice. It is turning out that the "missing link" in psychoanalysis is the nonverbal affect transacting relationship between the developing human infant and the primary caregiver, since this serves as the matrix of the individual's emerging unconscious. Current developmental psychological findings on the dyadic genesis of unconscious working models are relevant to the origins of unconscious mental processes. Indeed, Freud's (1911/1958) seminal concept of the dynamic unconscious was embedded firmly within a developmental perspective. In discussing

the foundation of unconscious processes in the developmentally primitive incho-
ate infant mind, the developmental psychologists Fischer and Pipp (1984) note:
"A young infant functions in a fundamentally unconscious way, and unconscious
processes in an older child or adult are to be traced back to the primitive functioning of the infant or young child" (p. 88). These authors also conclude that
unconscious thought does not remain static during childhood but undergoes
systematic developments. Greenspan (1979), a developmental psychoanalytic
researcher, maintains that the dynamic unconscious first appears at 18 months.
Jung (1943, 1945) described the "collective unconscious" as an "image of the
world" that is the source of self-sufficiency, as it contains "all those elements that
are necessary for the self-regulation of the psyche as a whole" (p. 187).

In contemporary psychoanalytic conceptualizations, Freud's notion of repression is understood to represent the brain's capacity to recognize and filter affects
at an unconscious level (Thompson, Baxter, & Schwartz, 1992). Developmental
neurobiology can offer important clues as to the nature of the structures that
mediate unconscious thought and affect. I have argued that their emergence
reflects the maturation of the right brain, the hemisphere that is responsible for
the manifestations of unconscious processes (Galin, 1974). Neuropsychological
studies are now demonstrating the preeminent role of prefrontal paralimbic networks in the primitive nonverbal right hemisphere to the rapid, nonverbal appraisal of emotionally meaningful events, to the central regulation of whole brain
structure and function, and to the allocation of the contents of primary consciousness. There now appears to be an emerging consensus among emotion researchers that appraisal processing is essentially nonvolitional and unconscious
(Lazarus, 1993). This body of research affirms Freud's essential discovery that
unconscious psychic structures are the major sources of the primary forces that
drive human emotion, cognition, motivation, and behavior.

The unique contribution of contemporary psychoanalysis, "the science of
unconscious processes" (Brenner, 1980), to the study of development lies in its
emphasis upon and elucidation of critical early self-selfobject communications
that build psychic structure. These interactional regulatory processes are embedded within dyadic caregiver-infant object relations, and such socioaffective transactions characterize the form and dynamics of the "social forces" that influence
the maturation of structure within the infant brain in the first 2-years-of-life
(Lecours, 1982) and the process of "social contact" that acts upon the development of complex higher regulatory brain systems (Luria, 1980). The nature of
these interactions change over the stages of infancy, inducing morphological
consequences. The observation that the structural differentiation of the brain
occurs in developmental stages in early postnatal life verifies Freud's conceptualization of development as a sequence of stages. Current psychoanalytic literature
also focuses on the centrality of the permanent storage of these early interactions
as a primary source of the construction of an enduring internal psychic world of
self and object representations (Boesky, 1983; Sandler & Rosenblatt, 1962). An
individual's subjective representational world evolves "organically" from his

early encounter with critical formative experiences, conditions that include "the maturation of neurological structures" (Stolorow & Atwood, 1979). Object relations, a central concept in current psychoanalytic theory, refers to "the dynamic interplay between inner images of both self and other" (Horner, 1989, p. 29). These mental representations are cognitive-affective units that are composed of a self-representation, an object representation, and a linking affect (Kernberg, 1976).

This perspective has been recently integrated into developmental psychology (Kobak & Sceery, 1988). For example, Bretherton and Bates (1984) refer to the development of representations from 10 to 28 months, and Zeanah and Barton (1989) are studying internal representations of parent-infant relationships. Indeed, even current neuropsychological models are converging on the concept of interactive representations. In a very recent article published in the journal *Brain and Cognition*, Van Lancker (1991) cites evidence to show that "the ability to establish, maintain, and recognize personally relevant objects in the environment" is an important attribute of human behavior. This neuropsychological phenomenon "involves an affective interaction between subject and object" and the recognition of familiar objects requires a relationship and is accompanied by a "cognitive/affective inner state." The "establishing of a personally relevant universe" is "highly valuable to biological development and survival" and "appears early in ontogenesis."

Current developmental psychoanalytic models stress that internal representations of self and other evolve in hierarchical stages and encode templates which influence the child's expectations, perceptions, and behavior towards the interpersonal environment (Horner, 1989). A hierarchical model that delineates the epigenesis of self-organization has been proposed as a basis for developmental psychoanalysis (Gedo, 1991), and this model has been suggested to reflect the hierarchical organization of the brain (Levin, 1991). Indeed, a current edited volume presents a number of contributions on hierarchical concepts in psychoanalysis (Wilson & Gedo, 1993). A recent psychoanalytic conceptualization of structure formation echoes the work of Hughlings Jackson, an important influence on Freud's ideas (Fullinwider, 1983), especially on how complex structures develop from simpler structures. Over the course of development, structure becomes "increasingly complex and hierarchical, with every step in growth and complexity bringing about a further subordination and constraint of earlier structure and functions and the emergence of new functions" (Wright, 1991, p. 205).

Complementing these ideas, work from various disciplines has been presented to demonstrate that the experience-dependent maturation of a structure at the hierarchical apex of the limbic system which supports adaptive self-regulatory functions occurs in a particular period of infancy. The growth and differentiation of this corticolimbic system is directly influenced by the infant's object relations with the mother. This system is identical to a controlling structure, described in the psychoanalytic literature (Rapaport, 1960), that maintains constancy by delaying press for discharge of aroused drives. Neuropsychological investigations of the orbitofrontal cortex emphasize its role in the delayed response function (Goldman, 1971) and its essential contributions to the modulation of ascending excitatory influnces (Butter et al., 1970). This frontolimbic system which tracks emotionally relevant objects in the extrapersonal space (Mesulam, 1985) acts in an "evaluative" capacity (Pribram, 1987). It does so by performing match-mismatch comparisons in order to compute the affective significance of social stimuli, and this operation has also been described in psychoanalytic meta-psychological reconstructions. In psychoanalytic writings, Klein (1976) refers to a process of "perceptual-evaluative mismatch" that involves a comparison of perceptual input and a centrally generated pattern, and a comparison of the value judgments attached to these two patterns.

Although Freud was not the first to suggest that early events have an inordinate and permanent effect on all later functions of the individual, his work gave a powerful impetus to the concept. In contemporary psychoanalytic terminology, self-and-object representations with different affective colorings evolve from an individual's early experiences, and these enduring configurations are utilized to assimilate all later affective exchanges with social objects. In current developmental psychological models, attachment patterns are understood to be imprinted into internal working models that encode programs of affect regulation and guide the individual's future interpersonal interactions. A central thesis of this volume is that over the first 1½ years of life the infant's transactions with the early socioemotional environment indelibly influence the evolution of brain structures responsible for the individual's socioemotional functioning for rest of the life span. Such events occur in the context of a one-to-one relationship between the infant and the primary caregiver. In optimal circumstances the caregiver enters into an ongoing communicative relationship with the child in which she is accessible to enact various types of affect regulating functions. To be attuned to the child's internal states and the changes in these states takes a significant amount of empathic attention and emotional involvement on the part of the primary caregiver. Her participation in intimate face-to-face merger experiences generates and sustains sufficient levels of positive affect that trophically induce the growth of new connections between neurons. At a later point at the end of the first year the child reaches the stage where he/she attains the locomotor capacities to separate from the mother. Her involvement in dyadic social referencing transactions is the wellspring of the child's adaptive capacity to explore the environmental surround and to develop a secure attachment. As opposed to these optimal conditions, I have traced the long-term effects of the infant's misattuned affective interactions with a nonempathic caregiver. These insecure attachments are stored in neuronal templates in the limbic system, and are associated with a later vulnerability to various psychiatric and psychosomatic disorders.

The conclusions of this volume echo and amplify a recent "worrisome" concern expressed by Bretherton (1992) about the experimentally demonstrated increased risk of insecure attachments if day care, as typically provided in present American society, begins in the 1st year and is extensive in duration. In a series of studies Belsky is finding that extensive nonmaternal (and nonparental) care in this 1st year is a risk factor in the increased development of insecure patterns of attachment (Belsky & Rovine, 1988), and that insecure-avoidant infants with such care express more negative affect and engage in less object play in reunion episodes with the mother (Belsky & Braungart, 1991). Other research indicates that even infants in middle- and upper-middle-class families that use in-home baby-sitters for more than 20 hours per week display higher rates of avoidance on reunion with the mother and are more likely to be classified as showing an insecure attachment (Barglow, Vaughn, & Molitor, 1987). A link between early day care experience and subsequent levels of aggression and noncompliance is also being reported (Haskins, 1985). In an analysis of 13 studies of attachment and child care, Lamb et al. (1992) now concur with Belsky that elevated levels of insecure attachments are consistenly found in child care children. In a recent review article, Scarr and Eisenberg (1993) discuss the ongoing debate over the emotional outcomes of early entry into nonmaternal care and the meaning of the robust finding of elevated levels of aggression in children using center care.

I believe that such disturbing observations must be attended to very seriously. These studies are focusing on children from the latter half of the first and into the second year, a temporal interval that represents a critical period for the maturation of the corticolimbic strucures that mediate socioemotional and superego functioning for the rest of the lifespan. The assertion that infants are particularly vulnerable to the detrimental effects of poor quality child care during the first year (Gamble & Zigler, 1986) is in essence another expression of the critical period phenomenon—that the developing infant is maximally vulnerable to nonoptimal and growth-inhibiting environmental events during the period of most rapid brain growth (Dobbing & Sands, 1973). These early experiences with a suboptimal early environment result in the imprinting (Bowlby, 1969) of enduring insecure attachment patterns that are "built into the nervous system" (Ainsworth, 1967), and these continue to be accessed under emotionally stressful conditions in later childhood (Sroufe et al., 1983, 1984). It is now estimated that between 12 and 22% of this country's children are clinically maladjusted (National Plan for Research in Child and Adolescent Mental Disorders, 1990). The matter of caregiving, in not just the first few months but the first 2-years-of-life, is an essential problem for the future of human societies.

In an expansion and a revision of Freud's emphasis on the critical and enduring role of early emotional events, contemporary psychoanalytic developmental theory and research suggests that affects develop in an interpersonal context, and that the physical-structural organization of the psychobiological affective core of the self is critically affected by early experiences in the infant-caregiver relationship. The infant's affect-transacting object relations with the mother directly influence the development and organization of an increasingly complex psychic structure that is capable of adaptive self-regulation, and the maturation of this system in the second year is responsible for the emergence of autonomous emotional functioning. A major conclusion of this book is that affect regulation fundamentally underlies and maintains self-function, and that this process is essentially nonverbal and unconscious.

Again, developmental neurobiology corroborates these conclusions and specifies the nature and dynamic capacities of this emergent psychic structure. Towards the end of the second year of life, the functional appearance of the self-regulation of emotion and motivation parallels the socioemotional experience-dependent differentiation of a frontolimbic structural system in the right hemisphere. The experience-dependent transmutation of the orbitofrontal cortex is expressed in the growth and stabilization of its dense interconnections with both cortical and subcortical areas, and it is these pathways that account for its essential roles in the adaptive regulation of emotional behavior and motivational states. This prefrontal structure performs an executive function in the right cortex, the "minor" (!) hemisphere which is specifically impacted by early social experiences, which contains a representational system based on self-and-object images, and which modulates affect and nonverbal communication. The emergence of this system is instrumental to the maturation of Gazzaniga's basic primitive affect system that is lateralized in the right hemisphere, Krystal's infantile nonverbal affect system, Kohut's regulatory structures, Mesulam and Geschwind's self-system that is localized in the right brain, Emde's psycho-biological affective core that allows the nascent self to "understand others who are human," and indeed to the origin of the self.

References

Abelin, E. (1971). The role of the father in the separation-individuation process. In J.B. McDevitt & C.F. Settlage (Eds.), *Separation-individuation* (pp. 229–252). New York: International Universities Press.

Abood, L.G. (1969). Brain mitochondria. In A. Lajtha (Ed.), *Handbook of neurochemistry, Vol. 2* (pp. 303–326). New York: Plenum Press.

Abraham, F.D., Abraham, R.H., Shaw, C.D., & Garfinkel, A. (1990). *A visual introduction to dynamical systems theory for psychology.* Santa Cruz, CA: Aerial Press, Inc.

Abraham, K. (1948). Notes on the psychoanalytical investigation and treatment of manic-depressive insanity and allied conditions. In E. Jones (Ed.), *Selected papers of Karl Abraham* (pp. 137–156). London: Hogarth Press.

Adams, R.D. & Victor, M. (1989). *Principles of neurology* (4th ed.). New York: McGraw-Hill.

Ader, R. (1981). *Psychoneuroimmunology.* San Diego: Academic Press.

Ader, R. (1992). Behavioral responses to cyclophosphamide in animals with autoimmune disease. In N. Schneiderman, P. McCabe, & A. Baum (Eds.), *Stress and disease processes* (pp. 93–102). Hillsdale, NJ: Lawrence Erlbaum Associates.

Ader, R. & Cohen, N. (1993). Psychoneuroimmunology: Conditioning and stress. *Annual Review of Psychology, 44,* 53–85.

Adler, G., & Buie, D. (1979). Aloneness and borderline psychopathology: The possible relevance of child developmental issues. *International Journal of Psycho-Analysis, 60,* 83–94.

Adler, G., & Rhine, M.W. (1992). The selfobject function of projective identification. In N.G. Hamilton (Ed.), *From inner sources: New directions in object relations psychotherapy* (pp. 139–162). Northvale, NJ: Jason Aronson.

Agnati, L.F., Fuxe, K., Yu, Z.Y., Harfstrand, A., Okret, S., Wikstrom, A.-C., Goldstein, M., Zoli, M., Vale, W., & Gustafsson, J.-A. (1985). Morphometrical analysis of the distribution of corticotropin releasing factor, glucocorticoid receptor and phenylethanolamine-N-methyltransferase immunoreactive structures in the paraventricular hypothalamic nucleus of the rat. *Neuroscience Letters, 54,* 147–152.

Aguilera, G., Millan, M.A., Hauger, R.L., & Catt, K.J. (1987). Corticotropin-releasing factor receptors: Distributions and regulation in brain, pituitary, and peripheral tissues. *Annals of the New York Academy of Sciences, 512,* 48–66.

Ahern, G.L., Schomer, D.L., Kleefield, J., Blume, H., Rees Cosgrove, G., Weintraub, S., &

Mesulam, M-M. (1991). Right hemisphere advantage for evaluating emotional facial expression. *Cortex*, *27*, 193–202.

Ainsworth, M.D.S. (1967). *Infancy in Uganda: Infant care and the growth of love*. Baltimore: Johns Hopkins University Press.

Ainsworth, M.D.S. (1969). Object relations, dependency and attachment: A theoretical review of the infant-mother relationship. *Child Development*, *40*, 969–1025.

Ainsworth, M.D.S. (1985). Patterns of infant-mother attachments: Antecedents and effects on development. *Bulletin of the New York Academy of Medicine*, *61*, 771–791.

Ainsworth, M.D.S., Blehar, M.C., Waters, E., & Wall, S. (1978). *Patterns of attachment*. Hillsdale, NJ: Lawrence Erlbaum Associates.

Aitken, A.R., & Tork, I. (1988). Early development of serotonin-containing neurons and pathways as seen in wholemount preparations of the fetal rat brain. *Journal of Comparative Neurology*, *274*, 32–47.

Akert, K. (1964). Comparative anatomy of the frontal cortex and thalamocortical connections. In M. Warren & K. Akert (Eds.), *The frontal granular cortex and behavior* (pp. 372–396). New York: McGraw-Hill.

Akiskal, H.S., & McKinney, W.T. (1975). Overview of recent research in depression. *Archives of General Psychiatry*, *32*, 285–305.

Alberts, J.R. (1987). Early learning and ontogenetic adaptation. In N.A. Krasnegor, E.M. Blass, M.A. Hofer, & W.P. Smotherman (Eds.), *Perinatal development: A psychobiological perspective* (pp. 11–37). Orlando, FL: Academic Press.

Al-Damluji, S. (1988). Adrenergic mechanisms in the control of corticotrophin secretion. *Journal of Endocrinology*, *119*, 5–14.

Aldenhoff, J.B., Gruol, D.L., Rivier, J., Vale, W.W., & Siggins, G.B. (1983). Corticotropin releasing factor decreases postburst hyperpolarizations and excites hippocampal neurons. *Science*, *221*, 875–877.

Alexander, F. (1950). *Psychosomatic medicine*. New York: W. W. Norton.

Alexander, M.P., Benson, D.F., & Stuss, D.T. (1989). Frontal lobes and language. *Brain and Language*, *37*, 656–691.

Alexander, R.D. (1987). *The biology of moral systems*. Chicago: Aldine.

Allen, K.M., Blascovich, J., Tomaka, J., & Kelsey, R.M. (1991). Presence of human friends and pet dogs as moderators of autonomic responses to stress in women. *Journal of Personality and Social Psychology*, *61*, 582–589.

Allen, M. (1983). Models of hemispheric specialization. *Psychological Bulletin*, *93*, 73–104.

Allendorfer, K.L., Shelton, D.L., Shooter, E.M., & Shatz, C.J. (1990). Nerve growth factor receptor immunoreactivity is transiently associated with the subplate neurons of the mammalian cerebral cortex. *Proceedings of the National Academy of Sciences of the United States of America*, *87*, 187–190.

Allman, J. & Zucker, S. (1990). Cytochrome oxidase and functional coding in primate striate cortex: A hypothesis. *Cold Spring Harbor Symposia on Quantitative Biology*, *LV*, 979–982.

Allsopp, G., & Gamble, H.J. (1979). Light and electron microscopic observations on the development of the blood vascular system of the human brain. *Journal of Anatomy*, *128*, 461–477.

Almli, C.R. & Finger, S. (1987). Neural insult and critical period concepts. In M.H. Bornstein (Ed.), *Sensitive periods in development: Interdisciplinary perspectives* (pp. 123–143). Hillsdale, NJ: Lawrence Erlbaum Associates.

Almli, C.R., & Fisher, R.S. (1985). Postnatal development of sensory influences on neurons in the ventromedial hypothalamic nucleus of the rat. *Developmental Brain Research*, *18*, 13–26.

Almroth, S.G. (1978). Water requirements of breast-fed infants in a hot climate. *American Journal of Clinical Nutrition*, *31*, 1154–1157.

Altman, J. (1972). Postnatal development of the cerebellar cortex in the rat. II. Phases in the maturation of Purkinje cells and of the molecular layer. *Journal of Comparative Neurology*, *145*, 399–464.

Alvarez-Mon, A., Kehrl, J.H., & Fauci, A.S. (1985). A potential role for adrenocorticotropin in regulating human B lymphocyte functions. *Journal of Immunology*, *135*, 3823–3826.

Amacher, P. (1965). *Freud's neurological education and its influence on psychoanalytic theory*. *Psychological Issues*, *4*. (Monograph 16).

American Psychiatric Association. (1987). *Diagnostic and statistical manual of mental disorders (DSM III-R)* (3rd ed. rev). Washington DC: American Psychiatric Press.

Amsterdam, B. (1972). Mirror self-image reactions before age two. *Developmental Psychobiology*, *5*, 297–305.

Amsterdam, B., & Levitt, M. (1980). Consciousness of self and painful self-consciousness. *Psychoanalytic Study of the Child*, *35*, 67–83.

Anand, B.K., Chhina, G.S., Sharma, K.N., Dua, S., & Singh, B. (1964). Activity of single neurons in the hypothalamic feeding centers: Effects of glucose. *American Journal of Physiology (London)*, *207*, 1146–1154.

Anders, T.F. & Zeanah, C.H. (1984). Early infant development from a biological point of view. In J.D. Call, E. Galenson, & R.L. Tyson (Eds.), *Frontiers of infant psychiatry*, *Vol. 2* (pp. 55–69). New York: Basic Books.

Anderson, J.N. (1984). The effect of steroid hormones on gene transcription. In R.F. Goldberger & K.R. Yamamoto (Eds.), *Biological regulation and development: Hormone action*, *Vol. 3B* (pp. 169–232). New York: Plenum Press.

Andreasen, N.C., Rezai, K., Alliger, R., Swayze, V.W. et al. (1992). Hypofrontality in neuroleptic-naieve patients and in patients with chronic schizophrenia: Assessment with xenon 133 single-photon emission computed tomography and the Tower of London. *Archives of General Psychiatry*, *49*, 943–958.

Andressen, M.C., & Kunze, D.L. (in press). Nucleus tractus solitarius—Gateway to neural circulatory control. *Annual Review of Physiology*.

Anokhin, K.V., Mileusnic, R., Shamakina, I.Y., & Rose, S.P. (1991). Effects of early experience on c-fos expression in the chick forebrain. *Brain Research*, *544*, 101–107.

Antelman, S.M., & Caggiula, A.R. (1977). Norepinephrine—dopamine interactions and behavior. *Science*, *195*, 646–653.

Anthi, P.R. (1983). Reconstruction of preverbal experience. *Journal of the American Psychoanalytic Association*, *31*, 33–58.

Anthony, E.J. (1981). Shame, guilt, and the feminine self in psychoanalysis. In S. Tuttman (Ed.), *Object and self: A developmental approach* (pp. 191–234). New York: International Universities Press.

Aoki, C., & Siekevitz, P. (1988). Plasticity and brain development. *Scientific American*, *259*, 56–68.

Appel, S., & Parrot, B. (1970). Hexose monophosphate pathway in synapses. *Journal of Neurochemistry*, *17*, 1619–1626.

Applegarth, A. (1971). Comments on aspects of the theory of psychic energy. *Journal of the Ameriican Psychoanalytic Association*, *19*, 379–416.

Aprile, J.R., Dransfield, D.T., & Joyal, J.L. (1931). Developmental aspects of mitochondrial dysfunction. In L.H. Lash & P.D. Jones (Eds.), *Mitochondrial dysfunction* (pp. 428–437). San Diego, CA: Academic Press.

Apsler, R. (1975). Effects of embarrassment on behavior toward others. *Journal of Personality and Social Psychology*, *32*, 145–153.

Arato, M., Frecska, E., Tekes, K., & MacCrimmon, D.J. (1991). Serotonergic interhemispheric asymmetry: Gender difference in the orbitofrontal cortex. *Acta Psychiatrica Scandinavica*, *84*, 110–111.

Ardila, A. (1984). Right prefrontal syndrome. In A. Ardila & F. Ostrosky-Solis (Eds.), *The right hemisphere: Neurology and neuropsychology* (pp. 171–193). New York: Gordon and Breach.

Arend, R., Gove, F.L., & Sroufe, S.A. (1979). Continuity of individual adaptation from infancy to kindergarten: A predictive study of ego-resiliency and curiosity in preschoolers. *Child Development*, *50*, 950–959.

Arey, L.B. (1962). *Developmental anatomy* (6th ed.). Philadelphia: W.B. Saunders.

Arnold, A.P., & Breedlove, S.M. (1985). Organizational and activational effects of sex steroids on brain and behavior. *Hormones and Behavior*, *19*, 469–498.

Arnold, M.B. (1960). *Emotion and personality: Vol. 1. Psychological aspects*. New York: Columbia University Press.

Arnold, M.B. (1970). *Feelings and emotions*. New York: Academic Press.

Arnstein, A.F.T., & Goldman-Rakic, P.S. (1984). Selective prefrontal cortical projections to the region of the locus coeruleus and raphe nuclei in the rhesus monkey. *Brain Research*, *306*, 99–118.

Arteta, J.L. (1951). The neurological origin of peptic ulcer. Frontal-lobe lesions and gastric ulcer. *British Medical Journal*, *11*, 580.

Artola, A., & Singer, W. (1989). NMDA receptors and developmental plasticity in visual neocortex. In J.C. Watkins & C.L. Collingridge (Eds.), *The NMDA receptor* (pp. 153–166). Oxford: IRL Press.

Aslin, R. (1981). Experiential influences and sensitive periods in perceptual development: A unified model. In R.N. Aslin, J.R. Alberts, & M.R. Peterson (Eds.), *Development of perception: Psychobiological perspectives*, *Vol.2* (pp. 45–93.). New York: Academic Press.

Assef, S.Y., & Miller J.J. (1977). Excitatory action of the mesolimbic dopamine system on septal neurons. *Brain Research*, *129*, 353–360.

Attardi, G., Cantatore, P., Ching, E., Crews, S., Gelfand, R., Merkel, C., Montoya, J., & Ojala, D. (1980). The remarkable features of gene organization and expression of human mitochondrial DNA. In A.M. Kroon & C. Saccone (Eds.), *The organization and expression of the mitochondrial genome*, (pp. 103–119). Amsterdam: Elsevier/North Holland Biomedical Press.

Atrens, D.M., Sinden, J.D., Penicaud, L., Devos, M., & LeMagnen, J. (1985). Hypothalamic modulation of energy expenditure. *Physiology and Behavior*, *35*, 15–20.

Aubert, M., & Legros, J. (1970). Topographie des projections de la sensibilite viscerale sur l'ecorce cerebrale du chat. I. Etude des projections corticales du vague cervical chez le chat anesthesie au nembutal. *Archives of Italian Biology*, *108*, 423–446.

Aubineau, P., Sercombe, R., Lusamvuku, N.A.T., & Seylaz, J. (1982). Can the response to circulating vasoactive substances be initiated by endothelial receptors of cerebral arteries? In D.D. Heistand & M.L. Marcus (Eds.), *Cerebral blood flow: Effects of nerves & neurotransmitters Vol. 14* (pp. 47–56). New York: Elsevier.

Audet, M., Doucet, G., Oleskevich, S., & Descarries, L. (1988). Quantified regional and laminar distribution of the noradrenaline innervation in the anterior half of the adult rat cerebral cortex. *Journal of Comparative Neurology*, *274*, 307–318.

Auerbach, J.S. (1990). Narcissism: Reflections on others' images of an elusive concept. *Psychoanalytic Psychology*, *7*, 545–564.

Azmitia, E.C., Buchan, A.M., & Williams, J.H. (1978). Structural and functional restoration by collateral sprouting of hippocampal 5-HT axons. *Nature 274*, 374–376.

Babkin, B.P., & Kite, W.C., Jr. (1950). Cortical inhibition of gastric motility. *Journal of Neurophysiology*, *13*, 335–342.

Baca, G.M., & Palmer, G.C. (1978). Presence of hormonally-sensitive adenylate cyclase receptors in capillary-enriched fractions from rat cerebral cortex. *Blood Vessels 15*, 286–298.

Bach, S. (1977). On the narcissistic state of consciousness. *International Journal of Psychoanalysis*, *58*, 209–233.

Bach-y-Rita, P. (1990). Brain plasticity as a basis for recovery of function in humans. *Neuropsychologia*, *28*, 547–554.

Bailey, P., & Bremer, F. (1938). A sensory cortical representation of the vagus nerve. *Journal of Neurophysiology*, *1*, 405–412.

Bailey, P., & Sweet, W.H. (1940). Effects on respiration. blood pressure and gastric motility of stimulation of orbital surfaces of frontal lobes. *Journa of Neurophysiology*, *3*, 276–281.

Bakchine, S., Lacomblez, L., Benoit, N., Parisot, D., Chain, F., & Lhermitte, F. (1989). Manic-like state after bilateral orbitofrontal and right tempoparietal injury: Efficacy of clonidine. *Neurology*, *39*, 777–781.

Baker, M., Dorzab, J., Winokur, G., & Cadoret, R. (1971). Depressive disease: The effect of the postpartum state. *Biological Psychiatry*, *3*, 357–365.

Balazs, R. (1971). Biochemical effects of thyroid hormones in the developing rat. In D.C. Pease (Ed.), *Cellular aspects of neural growth and differentiation* (pp. 273–311). Berkeley and Los Angeles: University of California Press.

Balint, M. (1968). *The basic fault*. London: Tavistock.

Bandtlow, C.E., Meyer, M., Lindholm, D., Spranger, M., Heumann, R., & Thoenen, H. (1990). Regional and cellular codistribution of interleukin 1B and nerve growth factor mRNA in the adult rat brain: Possible relationship to the regulation of nerve growth factor synthesis. *Journal of Cell Biology*, *111*, 1701–1711.

Bannister, R. (1978). *Brain's clinical neurolgy* (5th ed). Oxford: Oxford University Press.

Bannon, M.J., & Roth, R.H. (1983). Pharmacology of mesocortical dopamine neurons. *Pharmacological Reviews*, *35*, 53–68.

Bar, T. (1980). *The vascular system of the cerebral cortex*. Berlin: Springer-Verlag.

Bar, T., & Wolff, J.R. (1972). The formation of capillary basement membranes during internal vascularization of the rat's cerebral cortex. *Zeitschrift fur Zellforschung und Mikroskopische Anatomie*, *133*, 231–248.

Barbas, H., & Pandya, D.N. (1989). Architecture and intrinsic connections of the prefrontal cortex in the rhesus monkey. *Journal of Comparative Neurology*, *286*, 353–375.

Barchas, P.R., & Perlaki, K.M. (1986). Processing of preconsciously acquired information measured by hemispheric asymmetry and selection accuracy. *Behavioral Neuroscience*, *100*, 343–349.

Bard, P. (1934). On emotional expression after decortication with some remarks on certain theoretical views. *Psychological Review*, *38*, 309–329.

Barglow, P., Vaughn, B., & Molitor, N. (1987). Effects of maternal absence due to employment on the quality of infant-attachment in a low-risk sample. *Child Development*, *58*, 945–954.

Barlow, H.B. (1980). Nature's joke: A conjecture on the biological role of consciousness. In B.D. Josephson & V.S. Ramachandran (Eds.), *Consciousness and the physical world* (pp. 81–94). Oxford: Pergamon Press.

Barneoud, P., Neveu, P.J., Vitiello, S., & Le Moal, M. (1987). Functional heterogeneity of the right and left cerebral cortex in the modulation of the immune system. *Physiology and Behavior*, *41*, 525–530.

Barondes, S.J. (1970). Brain glycomacromolecules and interneuronal recognition. In F.O. Schmitt (Ed.), *The neuroscience second study program* (pp. 747–760). New York: Rockefeller University Press.

Barrell, B.G., Bankier, A.T., & Drouin, J. (1979). A different genetic code in human mitochondria. *Nature (London)*, *282*, 189–194.

Barrett, K.C., & Zahn-Waxler, C. (1987, April). Do toddlers express guilt? Poster presented at the meetings of the Society for Research in Child Development, Toronto.

Barrett, M.D. (1985). *Children's single-word speech* (pp. 23–58). Chichester, England: Wiley.

Bartlett, F.C. (1967). *Remembering: A study in experimental and social psychology*. London: Cambridge University Press.

Bartolome, J.V., Bartolome, M.B., Harris, E.B., Pauk, J.S., & Schanberg, S.M. (1989). Regulation of insulin and glucose plasma levels by central nervous system beta endorphin in preweanling rats. *Endocrinology*, *124*, 2153–2158.

Bartolome, J.V., Bartolome, M.B., Lorber, B.A., Dileo, S.J., & Schanberg, S.M. (1991). Effects of central administration of beta-endorphin on brain and liver DNA synthesis in preweanling rats. *Neuroscience*, *40*, 289–294.

Bartrop, R.W., Lazarus, L., Luckhurst, E., Kiloh, L.G., & Penny, R. (1977). Depressed lymphocyte functions after bereavement. *Lancet*, *1*, 834–836.

Basar, E. (1990). *Chaos in brain function*. New York: Springer-Verlag.

Basch, M.F. (1975). Perception, consciousness, and Freud's "Project." *Annual of Psychoanalysis, 3*, 3–19.

Basch, M.F. (1976). The concept of affect: A re-examination. *Journal of the American Psychoanalytic Association, 24*, 759–777.

Basch, M.F. (1977). Developmental psychology and explanatory theory in psychoanalysis. *Annual of Psychoanalysis, 5*, 229–263.

Basch, M.F. (1985). Interpretation: Toward a developmental model. In A. Goldberg (Ed.), *Progress in self psychology* (pp. 33–42). New York: Guilford Press.

Basch, M.F. (1986). II Clinical theory and metapsychology: Incompatible or complementary? *Psychoanalytic Review, 73*, 261–271.

Basch, M.F. (1988). *Understanding psychotherapy.* New York: Basic Books.

Basch, M.F. (1992). *Practicing psychotherapy.* New York: Basic Books.

Bateson, P. & Hinde, R.A. (1987). Developmental changes in sensitivity to experience. In M.H. Bornstein (Ed.), *Sensitive periods in development: Interdisciplinary perspectives* (pp. 19–34). Hillsdale NJ: Lawrence Erlbaum Associates.

Bateson, P.P.G. & Reese, E.P. (1969). The reinforcing properties of conspicuous stimuli in the imprinting situation. *Animal Behavavior, 17*, 692–699.

Bateson, P.P.G., Rose, S.P.R., & Horn, G. (1973). Imprinting: lasting effects on uracil incorporation into chick brain. *Science, 181*, 576–578.

Batson, C.D. (1990). How social is an animal? The human capacity for caring. *American Psychologist, 45*, 336–346.

Batson, C.D., Dyck, J.L., Brandt, J.R., Batson, J.G., Powell, A.L., McMaster, M.R., & Griffitt, C. (1988). Five studies testing two new egoistic alternatives to the empathy-altruism hypothesis. *Journal of Personality and Social Psychology, 55*, 52–77.

Bauer, K. Fr., & Vester, G. (1970). Das elektronenmikroskopische Bild der Hirnkapillaren menschlicher Feten. *Fortschritte der Neurologie-Psychiatrie und ihrer Grenzgebiete, 38*, 269–318.

Bauer, P.J., & Mandler, J.M. (1992). Putting the horse before the cart: The use of temporal order in recall of events by one-year-old children. *Developmental Psychology, 28*, 441–452.

Bauer, R.M. (1982). Visual hypoemotionality as a symptom of visual-limbic disconnection in man. *Archives of Neurology, 39*, 702–708.

Baumgardner, A.H., Kaufman, C.M., & Levy, P.E. (1989). Regulating affect interpersonally: When low self esteem leads to greater enhancement. *Journal of Personality and Social Psychology, 56*, 907–921.

Beagley, W.K., & Holley, T.L. (1977). Hypothalamic stimulation facilitates contralateral visual control of a learned response. *Science, 196*, 321–322.

Beal, M.F. (1921). Does impairment of energy metabolism result in exitotoxic neuronal death in neurodegenerative illnesses? *Annals of Neurology, 31*, 119–130.

Bear, D.M. (1979). The temporal lobes: An approach to the study of organic behavioral changes. In M.S. Gazzaniga (Ed.), *Handbook of behavioral neurobiology, Vol. 2* (pp. 75–95). New York: Plenum Press.

Bear, D.M. (1983). Hemispheric specialization and the neurology of emotion. *Archives of Neurology, 40*, 195–202.

Bear, M.F., & Singer, W. (1986). Modulation of visual cortical plasticity by acetylcholine and noradrenaline. *Nature (London), 320*, 172–176.

Beato, M., Arnemann, J., Chalepakis, G., Slater, E., & Wilman, T. (1987). Gene regulation by steroid hormones. *Journal of Steroid Biochemistry, 27*, 9–14.

Beckstead, R.M., & Norgren, R. (1979). An autoradiographic examination of the central distributions of the trigeminal, facial, glossopharyngeal, and vagal nerves in the monkey. *Journal of Comparative Neurology, 184*, 455–472.

Beebe, B. (1986). Mother-infant mutual influence and precursors of self—and object representations. In J. Masling (Ed.), *Empirical studies of psychoanalytic theories, Vol. 2* (pp. 27–48). Hillsdale, NJ: The Analytic Press.

Beebe, B. & Lachman, F.M. (1988a). Mother-infant mutual influence and precursors of psychic structure. In A. Goldberg (Ed.), *Progress in self psychology, Vol. 3* (pp.3–25). Hillsdale, NJ: The Analytic Press.

Beebe, B., & Lachman, F.M. (1988b). The contribution of mother-infant mutual influence to the origins of self-and object relationships. *Psychoanalytic Psychology, 5*, 305–337.

Beebe, B., & Stern, D.N. (1977). Engagement-disengagement and early object experiences. In N. Freedman & S. Grand. (Eds.), *Communicative structures and psychic structures* (pp. 35–55). New York: Plenum Press.

Beeman, M. (1993). Semantic processing in the right hemisphere may contibute to drawing inferences from discourse. *Brain and Language, 44*, 80–120.

Beit-Hallahmi, B. (1987). Critical periods in psychoanalytic theories of personality development. In M.H. Bornstein (Ed.), *Sensitive periods in development: Interdisciplinary perspectives* (pp. 211–221). Hillsdale NJ: Lawrence Erlbaum Associates.

Belsky, J., & Braungart, J.M. (1991). Are insecure-avoidant infants with extensive day-care experience less stressed by and more independent in the Strange Situation? *Child Development, 62*, 567–571.

Belsky, J., & Rovine, M.J. (1988). Nonmaternal care in the first year of life and the security of infant-parent attachment. *Child Development, 59*, 157–167.

Bemesderfer, S., & Cohler, B.J. (1983). Depressive reactions during separation period: Individuation and self among children of psychotic depressed mothers. In H.L. Morrison (Ed.), *Children of depressed parents: Risk, identification and intervention* (pp. 159–188). New York: Grune & Stratton.

Benevento, L.A., Fallon, J., Davis, B.J., & Rezak, M. (1977). Auditory-visual interaction in single cells in the cortex of the superior temporal sulcus and the orbital frontal cortex of the macaque monkey. *Experimental Neurology, 57*, 849–872.

Benjamins, J., & McKhann, G.M. (1981). Development, regeneration, and aging of the brain. In G. Siegel, R.W. Albers, B.W. Agranoff, & R. Katzman, (Eds.), *Basic neurochemistry* (3rd ed., pp. 445–469). Boston: Little, Brown.

Benowitz, L.I., Bear, D.M., Rosenthal, R., Mesulam, M-M., Zaidel, E., & Sperry, R.W. (1983). Hemispheric specialization in nonverbal communication. *Cortex, 19*, 5–11.

Benton, D., & Brain, P.F. (1988). The role of opioid mechanisms in social interaction and attachment. In R.J. Rodgers & S.J. Cooper (Eds.), *Endorphins, opiates and behavioral processes* (pp. 217–235). Chichester, England: Wiley.

Berger, B., Febvret, A., & Goldman-Rakic, P.S. (1990). DARPP-32, a phosphoprotein enriched in dopaminoreceptive neurons bearing dopamine D1 receptors: Distribution in the cerebral cortex of the newborn and adult rhesus monkey, *Journal of Comparative Neurology, 299*, 327–348.

Berger, B., Gaspar, P., & Verney, C. (1991). Dopaminergic innervation of the cerebral cortex: Unexpected differences between rodents and primates. *Trends in Neurosciences, 14*, 21–27.

Berger, B., Trottier, S., Verney, C., Gaspar, P., & Alvarez, C. (1988). Regional and laminar distribution of the dopamine and serotonin innervation in the macaque cerebral cortex: A radioautographic study. *Journal of Comparative Neurology, 273*, 99–119.

Berkenbosch, F., Van Oers, J., Del Rey, A., Tilders, F., & Besedovsky, H. (1987). Corticotropin-releasing factor-producing neurons in the rat activated by interleukin-1. *Science, 238*, 524–526.

Berkowitz, L. (1990). On the formation and regulation of anger and aggression. *American Psychologist, 45*, 494–503.

Berman, K.F. (1987). Cortical "stress tests" in schizophrenia: Regional cerebral blood flow studies. *Biological Psychiatry, 22*, 1304–1326.

Berman, K.F., Torrey, E.F., Daniel, D.G., & Weinberger, D.R. (1992). Regional cerebral blood flow in monozygotic twins discordant and concordant for schizophrenia. *Archives of General Psychiatry, 49*, 927–934.

Bernard, C. (1930). Lecons sur les phenomenes de la vie communs aux animaux et aux vegetaux. In J.F. Fulton (Ed. and Trans.), *Selected readings in the history of physiology*. Springfield, IL: Thomas.

Berntman, L., Dahlgren, N., & Siesjo, B.K. (1978). Influence of intravenously administered catecholamines on cerebral oxygen consumption and blood flow in the rat. *Acta Physiologica Scandinavica, 104,* 101–108.

Bernton, E.W., Beach, J.F., Holaday, J.W., Smallbridge, R.C., & Fein, H.G. (1987). Release of
multiple hormones by a direct action of interleukin-1 on pituitary cells. *Science 238,* 519–
521.

Berntson, G.G., Cacioppo, J.T., & Quigley, K.S. (1991). Autonomic determinism: The modes of
autonomic control, the doctrine of autonomic space, and the laws of autonomic constraint.
Psychological Review, 98, 459–487.

Berntson, G.G., & Micco, D.J. (1976). Organization of brain stem systems (Theoretical Review).
Brain Research Bulletin, 1, 471–483.

Berretta, S., Robertson, H.A., & Graybiel, A.M. (1992). Dopamine and glutamate agonists stimulate neuron-specific expression of fos-like protein in the striatum. *Journal of Neurophysiology,
68,* 767–777.

Bertalanffy, L. von (1968). *General system theory foundations, development, applications.* New
York: George Braziller.

Bertalanffy, L. von. (1974). General systems theory and psychiatry. In S. Arieti (Ed.), *American
handbook of psychiatry, Vol. 1* (pp. 1095–1117). New York: Basic Books,.

Bertenthal, B., Campos, J., & Barrett, K. (1983). Self-produced locomotion: An organizer of
emotional, cognitive, and social development in infancy. In R. Emde & R.J. Harmon (Eds.),
Continuities and discontinuities in development. New York: Plenum Press.

Besedovsky, H., Del Rey, A., & Sorkin, E. (1981). Lymphokine-containing supernatants from Con
A-stimulated cells increase corticosterone blood levels. *Journal of Immunology, 126,* 385–387.

Besedovsky, H., & Sorkin, E. (1977). Network of immune endocrine interactions. *European Journal
of Immunology, 7,* 323–325.

Besedovsky, H., Sorkin, E., Felix, D., & Haas, H. (1977). Hypothalamic changes during the
immune response. *Clinical and Experimental Immunology, 27,* 1–12.

Beutler, L.E., & Crago, M. (Eds.). (1991). *Psychotherapy research: An international review of
programmatic studies.* Washington, DC: American Psychological Association.

Bever, T.G. (1975). Cerebral asymmetries in humans are due to the differentiation of two incompatible processes: Holistic and analytic. *Annals of the New York Academy of Sciences, 263,* 251–
262.

Bick, E. (1968). The experience of the skin in early object relations. *International Journal of Psycho-
Analysis, 49,* 484–486.

Bilger, A., & Nehlig, A. (in press). Quantitative histochemical changes in enzymes involved in
energy metabolism in the rat brain during postnatal development. I. Cytochrome oxidase and
lactate dehydrogenase. *International Journal of Developmental Neuroscience.*

Bion, W.R. (1962). *Learning from experience,* London: Heinemann.

Birch, H.G. (1962). Dyslexia and the maturation of visual function. In J. Money (Ed.), *Reading
disability.* Baltimore: Johns Hopkins University Press.

Bischoff, H-J. (1983). Imprinting and cortical plasticity: A comparative review. *Neuroscience and
Biobehavior Reviews, 7,* 213–225.

Bjorklund, A., Hokfelt, T., & Tohyama, M. (1992). *Handbook of chemical neuroanatomy.* New
York: Elsevier.

Black, J.E., & Greenough, W.T. (1986). Induction of pattern in neural structure by experience:
Implications for cognitive development. In M.E. Lamb, A.L. Brown, & B. Rogoff (Eds.),
Advances in developmental psychology, Vol. 4 (pp. 1–50). Hillsdale, NJ: Lawrence Erlbaum
Associates.

Black, J.E., Sirevaag, A.M., & Greenough, W.T. (1987). Complex experience promotes capillary
information in young visual rat cortex. *Neuroscience Letters, 83,* 351–355.

Blackburn, R. (1975). Aggression and the EEG: A quantitative analysis. *Journal of Abnormal
Psychology, 84,* 358–365.

Blakemore, C. (1974). Developmental factors in the formation of feature extracting neurons. In F.O. Schmitt & F.G. Worden (Eds.), *The neurosciences. Third study program*. Cambridge: MIT Press.

Blalock, J.E. (1989). A molecular basis for bidirectional communication between the immune and neuroendocrine systems. *Physiological Reviews, 69*, 1–32.

Blanc, G., Herve, D., Simon, H., Lisoprawski, A., Glowinski, J., & Tassin, J.P. (1980). Response to stress of mesocortico-frontal dopaminergic neurones in rats after long-term isolation. *Nature (London), 284*, 265–267.

Blasi, A. (1976). The concept of development in personality theory. In J. Loevinger & A. Blasi (Eds.), *Ego development: Conceptions and theories* (pp. 29–53). San Francisco: Jossey-Bass.

Blass, E.M. (1969). Thermoregulatory adjustments in rats after removal of the frontal poles of the brain. *Journal of Comparative Physiological Psychology, 69*, 83–90.

Blatt, S.J. (1991). A cognitive morphology of psychopathology. *Journal of Nervous and Mental Disease, 179*, 449–458.

Blatt, S.J. (1992). The differential effect of psychotherapy and psychoanalysis with anaclitic and introjective patients: The Menninger Psychotherapy Research Project revisited. *Journal of the American Psychoanalytic Association, 40*, 691–724.

Blatt, S.J., Quinlan, D.M., & Chevron, E. (1990). Empirical investigations of a psychoanalytic theory of depression. In J. Masling (Ed.), *Empirical studies of psychoanalytic theories, Vol. 3* (pp. 89–147). Hillsdale NJ: The Analytic Press.

Blonder, L.X., Bowers, D., & Heilman, K.M. (1991). The role of the right hemisphere in emotional communication. *Brain, 114*, 1115–1127.

Bloom, L. (1973). *One word at a time: The use of single word utterances before syntax*. The Hague: Morton.

Blos, P. (1974). The genealogy of the ego ideal. *Psychoanalytic Study of the Child, 29*, 43–88.

Blos, P. (1984). Sons and fathers. *Psychoanalytic Study of the Child, 32*, 301–324.

Blum, H.P. (1978). Symbolic processes and symbol formation. *International Journal of Psycho-Analysis, 59*, 455–471.

Board, F., Wadeson, R., & Persky,H. (1957). Depressive affect and endocrine function. *Archives of Neurology and Psychiatry, 78*, 612–620.

Boesky, D. (1983). Representations in self and object theory. *Psychoanalytic Quarterly, 52*, 564–583.

Bogen, J.E. (1969). The other side of the brain II. An appositional mind. *Bulletin of the Los Angeles Neurological Society, 34*, 135–162.

Bohlin, G. (1987). Infant's heart rate response to an approaching stranger. *Psychophysiology, 24*, 581 (abstract).

Bohus, B., De Kloet, E.R., & Veldhuis, H.D. (1984). Adrenal steroids and behavioral adaptation: Relationship to brain corticoid receptors. In D. Ganten & D. Pfaff (Eds.), *Adrenal actions on brain* (pp. 107–148). New York: Springer-Verlag.

Boll, T.J. (1974). Right and left cerebral hemisphere damage and tactile perception: Performance of the ipsilateral and contralateral sides of the body. *Neuropsychologia, 12*, 235–238.

Bonanno, G.A., & Singer, J.C. (1990). Repressive personality style: Theoretical and methodological implications for health and pathology. In J.L. Singer (Ed.), *Repression and dissociation* (pp. 435–470). Chicago: The University of Chicago Press.

Bondy, S.C., & Harrington, M.E. (1978). Brain blood flow: Alteration by prior experience to a learned task. *Science, 199*, 318–319.

Bondy, S.C., Lehman, R.A.W., & Purdy, J.L. (1974). Visual attention affects brain blood flow. *Nature (London), 248*, 440–441.

Bondy, S.C., & Morelos, B.S. (1971). Stimulus deprivation and cerebral blood flow. *Experimental Neurology, 31*, 200–206.

Bondy, S.C., & Purdy, J.L. (1976). Rapid changes in cerebral blood flow and initial visual experience in the developing chick. *Developmental Psychobiology, 9*, 31–38.

Bonnet, K.A., Hiller, J.M., & Simon, E.J. (1976). The effects of chronic opiate treatment and social isolation on opiate receptors in the rodent brain. In S. Archer, H.O.J. Collier, A. Goldstein, H.W.

Kosterlitz, E.J. Simon, H. Takagi, & L. Terenius (Eds.), *Opiates and endogenous opioid peptides* (pp. 335–343). New York: Elsevier/North Holland.

Bordin, E. (1979). The generalizability of the psychoanalytic concept of the working alliance. *Psychotherapy: Theory, Research and Practice, 16,* 252–260.

Borison, H.L., & Brizzee, K.R. (1951). Morphology of emetic chemoreceptor trigger zone in cat medulla oblongata. *Proceedings of the Society for Experimental Biology and Medicine, 77,* 38–42.

Bornstein, M.H. (1989). Sensitive periods in development: Structural characteristics and causal interpretations. *Psychological Bulletin, 105,* 179–197.

Bornstein, R.F. (1993). Implicit perception, implicit memory, and the recovery of unconscious material in psychotherapy. *Journal of Nervous and Mental Disease, 181,* 337–344.

Borod, J.C., & Koff, E. (1984). Asymmetries in affective facial expression: Behaviour and anatomy. In N.A. Fox & R.J. Davidson (Eds.), *The psychobiology of affective development* (pp. 293–323). Hillsdale, NJ: Lawrence Erlbaum Associates.

Borowsky, I.W., & Collins, R.C. (1989). Metabolic activity of brain: A comparison of regional capillary density, glucose metabolism, and enzyme activities. *Journal of Comparative Neurology, 288,* 401–413.

Bostock, J (1962). Evolutionary approaches to infant care. *Lancet i,* 1033–1035.

Bowden, D.M., Goldman, P.S., Rosvold, H.E., & Greenstreet, R.L. (1971). Free behavior of rhesus monkeys following lesions of the dorsolateral and orbital prefrontal cortex in infancy. *Experimental Brain Research, 12,* 265–274.

Bower, G.H. (1981). Mood and memory. *American Psychologist, 36,* 129–148.

Bower, G.H. (1992). How might emotions affect learning? In In S-A. Christianson (Ed.), *The handbook of emotion and memory: Research and theory* (pp. 3–31). Hillsdale NJ: Lawrence Erlbaum Associates.

Bowers, D., Blonder, L.X., Feinberg, T., & Heilman, K.M. (1991). Differential impact of right and left hemisphere lesions on facial emotion and object memory. *Brain, 114,* 2593–2609.

Bowlby, J. (1969). *Attachment and loss. Vol. 1: Attachment.* New York: Basic Books.

Bowlby, J. (1973). *Attachment and loss. Vol. 2: Separation, anxiety and anger.* New York: Basic Books .

Bowlby, J. (1978). Attachment theory and its therapeutic implications. In S.C. Feinstein & P.L. Giovacchini (Eds.), *Adolescent psychiatry: Developmental and clinical studies.* Chicago: University of Chicago Press.

Bowlby, J. (1981). *Attachment and loss. Vol. 3: Loss, sadness and depression.* New York: Basic Books.

Bowlby, J. (1982). Attachment and loss: Retrospect and prospect. *American Journal of Orthopsychiatry, 52,* 664–678.

Bowlby, J. (1984). Psychoanalysis as a natural science. *Psychoanalytic Psychology, 1,* 7–21.

Bowlby, J. (1988a). *A secure base* (2nd ed). New York: Basic Books.

Bowlby, J. (1988b). Attachment, communication, and the therapeutic process. In J. Bowlby (Ed.), *A secure base: Clinical applications of attachment theory.* London: Routledge.

Boyce, W.T., & Jemerin, J.M. (1990). Psychobiological differences in childhood stress response. *Development and Behavioral Pediatrics, 11,* 86–94.

Bozarth, M.A. (1986). Neural basis of psychomotor stimulant and opiate reward: Evidence suggesting the involvement of a common dopaminergic system. *Behavioral Brain Research, 22,* 107–116.

Bozarth, M.A. (1988). Opioid reinforcement processes. In R.J. Rodgers & S.J. Cooper (Eds.), *Endorphins, opiates and behavioral processes* (pp. 53–75). Chichester, England: Wiley.

Bozarth, M.A., & Wise, R.A. (1981). Intracranial self-administration of morphine into the ventral tegmental area of rats. *Life Sciences, 28,* 551–555.

Bozhovich, L.I. (1978). Stages in the formation of personality in ontogeny. *Soviet Psychology, 17,* 3–24.

Bracewell, R.M., Husain, M., & Stein, J.F. (1990). Specialization of the right hemisphere for visuomotor control. *Neuropsychologia, 28,* 763–775.

Bradbury, M. (1979). The blood brain barrier during the development of the individual and the evolution of the phylum. In *The Concept of a blood-brain barrier* (pp. 289–322). New York: Wiley.

Bradford, H.F. (1986). *Chemical neurobiology.* New York: W.H. Freeman.

Bradley, B.S. (1991). Infancy as paradise. *Human Development, 34,* 35–54.

Bradley, P., & Horn, G. (1981). Imprinting: A study of cholinergic receptor sites in parts of the chick brain. *Experimental Brain Research, 41,* 121–123.

Bradley, P., Horn, G., & Bateson, P. (1981). Imprinting: An electron microscopic study of chick hyperstriatum ventrale. *Experimental Brain Research, 41,* 115–120.

Bradshaw, J.L., & Nettleton, N.C. (1981). The nature of hemispheric specialization in man. *Behavioral and Brain Sciences, 4,* 51–91.

Bradshaw, J.L., & Nettleton, N.C. (1983). *Human cerebral asymmetry.* Englewood Cliffs, NJ: Prentice Hall.

Brady, J.V., & Nauta, W.J.H. (1953). Subcortical mechanisms in emotional behavior: Affective changes following septal forebrain lesions in the albino rat. *Journal of Comparative and Physiological Psychology, 46,* 339–346.

Brannan, I., Maker, H., & Karp, E. (1982). Norepinephrine stimulation of pentose cycle in rat brain prisms. *Research Communications in Chemical Pathology and Pharmacology, 38,* 509–512.

Brazelton, T.B., & Cramer, B.G. (1990). *The earliest relationship.* Reading: Addison-Wesley.

Brazelton, T.B., Koslowski, B., & Main, M. (1974). The origins of reciprocity: The early mother-infant interaction. In M. Lewis & L. Rosenblum (Eds.), *The effect of the infant on its caregiver* (pp. 49–77). New York: Wiley.

Breder, C.D., Dinarello, C.A., & Saper, C.B. (1988). Interleukin-1 immunoreactive innervation of the human hypothalamus. *Science, 240,* 321–324.

Breedlove, J.M. (1984). Androgen forms sexually dimorphic nucleus by saving neurons from programmed cell death. *Society for Neuroscience, 10,* 927 (Abstract).

Breese, G.R., Smith, R.D., Mueller, R.A., Howard, J.L., Prange, A.J., Lipton, M.A., Young, L.D., McKinney, W.T., & Lewis, J.K. (1973). Induction of adrenal catecholamine synthesizing enzymes following mother-infant separation. *Nature (London) New Biology, 246,* 94–94.

Breier, G., Albrecht, U., Sterrer, S., & Risau, W. (1992). Expression of vascular endothelial growth factor during embryonic angiogenesis and endothelial cell differentiation. *Development, 114,* 521–532.

Brenner, C. (1980). A psychoanalytic theory of affects. In R. Plutchik & H. Kellerman (Eds.), *Emotion: Theory, research, and experience, Vol. 1.* New York: Academic Press.

Brent L., & Resch, R.C. (1987). A paradigm of infant-mother reciprocity: A reexamination of "emotional refueling." *Psychoanalytic Psychology, 4,* 15–31.

Bretherton, I. (1985). Attachment theory: Retrospect and prospect. *Monographs of the Society for Research in Child Development, 50,* 3–35.

Bretherton, I. (1992). The origins of attachment theory: John Bowlby and Mary Ainsworth. *Developmental Psychology, 28,* 759–775.

Bretherton, I., & Bates, E. (1984). The development of representation from 10 to 28 months. In R.N. Emde & R.J. Harmon (Eds.), *Continuities and discontinuities in development* (pp. 229–261). New York: Plenum Press.

Bretherton, I., & Beeghly, M. (1982). Talking about internal states: The acquisition of an explicit theory of mind. *Developmental Psychology, 18,* 906–921.

Bretherton, I., McNew, S., & Beeghly, M. (1981). Early person knowledge in gestural and verbal communication: When do infants acquire a "theory of mind"? In M.Lamb & L. Sherrod (Eds.), *Infant social cognition* (pp. 335–373). Hillsdale, NJ: Lawrence Erlbaum Associates.

Breuer, J., & Freud, S. (1955). Studies on hysteria. In J. Strachey (Ed. and Trans.), *The standard edition of the complete psychological works of Sigmund Freud*. London: Hogarth Press. (Original work published 1893–1895).

Brewer, G.J., & Cotman, C.W. (1989). NMDA receptor regulation of neuronal morphology in cultured hippocampal neurons. *Neuroscience Letters, 99*, 268–273.

Bridges, K.M. (1932). Emotional development in early infancy. *Child Development, 3*, 324–341.

Brierley, M. (1937). Affects in theory and practice. *International Journal of Psycho-Analysis, 18*, 256–274.

Britt, M.D., & Wise, R.A. (1983). Ventral tegmental site of opiate reward: Antagonism by a hydrophilic opiate receptor blocker. *Brain Research, 258*, 105–108.

Britton, D.R., Koob, G.F., & Rivier, J. (1982). Corticotropin-releasing factor enhances behavioral effects of novelty. *Life Sciences, 31*, 363–367.

Broadbent, D.E. (1977). The hidden preattentive process. *American Psychologist, 32*, 109–118.

Broca, P. (1885). Data reported by P. Topinard. In A. Delabraye & E. Delabraye (Eds.), *Elements d'anthropologie generale*. Paris, France: Lecrosnier.

Brock, S.E., Rothbart, M.K., & Derryberry, D. (1986). Heart rate deceleration and smiling in 3 month old infants. *Infant Behavior and Development, 9*, 403–415.

Bronowski, J. (1972). *Science and human values*. New York: Harper and Row.

Bronson, G. (1963). A neurological perspective on ego development in infancy. *Journal of the American Psychoanalytic Association, 11*, 55–65.

Bronson, G. (1965). The hierarchical organization of the central nervous system: Implications for learning processes and critical periods in early development. *Behavioral Science, 10*, 7–25.

Bronson, G. (1974). The postnatal growth of visual capacity. *Child Development, 45*, 873–890.

Brooks, W.J., Petit, T.L., LeBoutillier, J. C., & Lo, R. (1991). Rapid alteration of synaptic number and post-synaptic thickening length by NMDA: An electron microscopic study in the occipital cortex of postnatal rats. *Synapse, 8*, 41–48.

Broucek, F. J. (1982). Shame and its relationship to early narcissistic developments. *International Journal of Psycho-Analysis, 63*, 369–378.

Broucek, F.J. (1991). *Shame and the self*. New York: Guilford Press.

Broverman, D.M., Klaiber, E.L., Kobayashi, Y., & Vogel, W. (1968). Roles of activation and inhibition in sex differences in cognitive abilities. *Psychological Review, 75*, 23–50.

Brown, G.C., Crompton, M., & Wray, S. (1991). Cytochrome oxidase content of rat brain during development. *Biochimica et Biophysica Acta, 1057*, 273–275.

Brown, I.R. (1983). Hyperthermia induces the synthesis of a heat shock protein by polysomes isolated from fetal and neonatal mammalian brain. *Journal of Neurochemistry, 40*, 1490–1493.

Brown, I.R. (1985). Modification of gene expression in the mammalian brain after hyperthermia. In C. Zomzely-Neurath & W.A. Walker (Eds.), *Gene expression in brain*. New York: Wiley.

Brown, I.R. (1991). Expression of heat shock genes (*hsp70*) in the mammalian nervous system. In L. Hightower & L. Nover (Eds.), *Heat shock and development* (pp.217–229). Springer-Verlag: Berlin.

Brown, I.R., Rush, S.J., & Ivy, G.O. (1989). Induction of a heat shock gene at the site of tissue injury in the rat brain. *Neuron, 2*, 1559–1564.

Brown, M.R., Fisher, L.A., Rivier, J., Spiess, J., Rivier, C., & Vale, W. (1982a). Corticotropin-releasing factor: Effects on the sympathetic nervous system and oxygen consumption. *Life Sciences, 30*, 207–219.

Brown, M.R., Fisher, L.A., Spiess, J., Rivier, C., Rivier, J., & Vale, W. (1982b). Corticotropin-releasing factor: actions on the sympathetic nervous system and metabolism. *Endocrinology, 111*, 928–931.

Brown, R., & Kulik, J. (1977). Flashbulb memories. *Cognition, 5*, 73–79.

Brown, R.M., Crane, A.M., & Goldman, P.S. (1979). Regional distribution of monoamines in the cerebral cortex and subcortical structures of the rhesus monkey: Concentrations and in vivo synthesis rates. *Brain Research, 168*, 133–150.

Brown, S.L., & Van Epps, A., (1986). Opioid peptides modulate production of interferon gamma by human mononuclear cells. *Cellular Immunology*, *103*, 19–26.

Brownstein, M.J. (1981). Serotonin, histamine, and the purines. In G.Siegel, R.W. Albers, B.W. Agranoff, & R. Katzman, (Eds.), *Basic neurochemistry* (3rd ed., pp. 219–231). Boston: Little, Brown.

Brownstein, M.J. (1989). Neuropeptides. In G. Siegel, B. Agranoff, R.W. Albers, & P. Molinoff (Eds.), *Basic neurochemistry* (4th ed., pp. 287–309). New York: Raven Press.

Bruce, V., & Young, A. (1986). Understanding face recognition. *British Journal of Psychology*, *77*, 305–327.

Brumback, R.A., Staton, R.D., & Wilson, H. (1980). Neuropsychological study of children during and after remission of endogenous depressive episodes. *Perceptual and Motor Skills*, *50*, 1163–1167.

Bruner, J. (1983). *Child's talk*. New York: W.W. Norton.

Bruner, J. (1986). *Actual minds, possible worlds*. Cambridge MA: Harvard University Press.

Brutkowski, S. (1964). Prefrontal cortex and drive inhibition. In J.M. Warren & K. Akert (Eds.), *The frontal granular cortex and behavior* (pp. 242–270). New York: McGraw-Hill.

Brutkowski, S., & Mempel, E. (1961). Disinhibition of inhibitory conditioned responses following selective brain lesions in dogs. *Science*, *134*, 2040–2041.

Bruyer, R. (1991). Covert face recognition in prosopagnosia: A review. *Brain and Cognition*, *15*, 223–235.

Bryan, R.M., Jr. (1990). Cerebral blood flow and energy metabolism during stress. *American Journal of Physiology*, *259*, H269-H280.

Buber, M. (1957). Elements of the interhuman. *Psychiatry*, *20*, 105–113.

Bucci, W. (1993). The development of emotional meaning in free association: A multiple code theory. In A. Wilson & J.E. Gedo (Eds.), *Hierarchical concepts in psychoanalysis* (pp. 3–47). New York: Guilford Press.

Buchanan, S.L., Powell, D.A., & Valentine, J. (1984). Cardiovascular adjustments elicited by electrical stimulation of frontal cortex in conscious rabbits. *Neuroscience Abstracts*, *10*, 614.

Bucher, K., Myers, R.E., & Southwick, C. (1970). Anterior temporal cortex and maternal behavior in the monkey. *Neurology*, *20*, 415.

Buchsbaum, H.K., & Emde, R.N. (1990). Play narratives in 36-month old children. Early moral development and family relationships. *Psychoanalytic Study of the Child*, *45*, 129–155.

Buck, R.W. (1980). Nonverbal behavior and the theory of emotion: the facial feedback hypothesis. *Journal of Personality and Social Psychology*, *38*, 811–824.

Buck, R.W., Parke, R.D., & Buck, M. (1970). Skin conductance, heart rate, and attention to the environment in two stressful situations. *Psychonomic Science*, *18*, 95–96.

Buechler, S., & Izard, C.E. (1983). On the emergence, functions, and regulation of some emotion expressions in infancy. In R. Plutchik & H. Kellerman (Eds.), *Emotion, theory, research, and experience*, *Vol. 3* (pp. 292–313). New York: Academic Press.

Buie, D. (1981). Empathy: Its nature and limitations. *Journal of the American Psychoanalytic Association*, *29*, 281–308.

Buie, D.H. & Adler, G. (1982). Definitive treatment of the borderline personality. In R. Langs, (Ed.), *International Journal of Psychotherapy*, *Vol. 9*. New York: Jason Aronson.

Bunge, M. (1980a). *The mind body problem: A psychobiological approach*. Oxford: Pergamon Press.

Bunge, M. (1980b). From neuron to behavior and mentation: An exercise in levelmanship. In H.M. Pinsker & W.D. Willis, Jr. (Eds.), *Information processing in the nervous system* (pp. 1–16). New York: Raven Press.

Bunney, W.R.E., Jr., Hartman, E.L., & Mason, J.W. (1965). Study of a patient with 48 hr manic-depressive cycles: II. Strong positive correlation between endocrine factors and manic defense patterns. *Archives of General Psychiatry*, *12*, 619–623.

Bunney, W.R.E., Murphy, D.L., Goodwin, F.K., & Borge, G.F. (1972). The "switch process" in manic-depressive illness. *Archives of General Psychiatry*, *27*, 295–302.

Burlingham, D. (1973). The preoedipal infant-father relationship. *Psychoanalytic Study of the Child*, *28*, 23–47.

Burgess, J.W. (1992). Neurocognitive impairment in dramatic personalities: Histrionic, narcissistic, borderline, and antisocial disorders. *Psychiatry Research*, *42*, 283–290.

Burgoyne, R.D., & Rose, S.P.R. (1980). Changes in glycoprotein metabolism in the cerebral cortex following first exposure of dark-reared rats to light. *Journal of Neurochemistry*, *34*, 510–517.

Burgoyne, R.D., Pearce, I.A., & Cambray-Deakin, M.A. (1988). *N* -Methyl-D-aspartate raises cytosolic calcium concentration in rat cerebellar granule cells in culture. *Neuroscience Letters*, *91*, 47–52.

Bursten, B. (1973). Some narcissistic personality types. *International Journal of Psycho-Analysis*, *54*, 287–300.

Burt, A., & Wenger, B.(1961). Glucose-6-phosphate dehydrogenase activity in the brain of the developing chick. *Developmental Biology*, *3*, 84–95.

Burton, L.A., & Levy, J. (1991). Effects of processing speed on cerebral asymmetry for left-and right-oriented faces. *Brain and Cognition*, *15*, 95–105.

Buschmann, M.B., T. & LaVelle, A. (1981). Morphological changes of the pyrmaidal cell nucleolus and nucleus in hamster frontal cortex during development and aging. *Mechanisms of Ageing and Development*, *15*, 385–397.

Bushnell, E.W. (1986). The basis of infant visual-tactual functioning—amodal dimensions or multimodal compounds? In L.P. Lipsett & C. Rovee-Collier (Eds.), *Advances in infancy research*, Vol. 4 (pp. 182–194). Norwood, NJ: Ablex.

Bushnell, E.W., Shaw, L., & Strauss, D. (1985). The relationship between visual and tactual exploration by 6-month-olds. *Developmental Psychology*, *21*, 591–600.

Bushnell, E.W., & Weinberger, N. (1987). Infants' detection of visual-tactual discrepancies: Asymmetries that indicate a directive role of visual information. *Journal of Experimental Psychology: Human Perception and Performance*, *13*, 591–600.

Buss, A.H. (1979). *Self consciousness and anxiety.* San Francisco: W.H. Freeman.

Butter, C.M., McDonald, J.A., & Snyder, D.R. (1969). Orality, preference behavior, and reinforcement value of nonfood object in monkeys with orbital frontal lesions. *Science*, *164*, 1306–1307.

Butter, C.M., Snyder, D.R., & McDonald, J.A. (1970). Effects of orbital frontal lesions on aversive and aggressive behaviors in rhesus monkeys. *Journal of Comparative and Physiological Psychology*, *72*, 134–144.

Butterworth, G.E. (1991). The ontogeny and phylogeny of joint visual attention. In A. Whiten (Ed.), *Natural theories of mind* (pp. 223–232). Oxford: Basil Blackwell.

Cacioppo, J.T., & Berntson, G.G. (1992). Social psychological contributions to the decade of the brain: Doctrine of multilevel analysis. *American Psychologist*, *47*, 1019–1028.

Cacioppo, J.T., Martzke, J.S., Petty, R.E., & Tassinary, L.G. (1988). Specific forms of facial EMG response index emotions during an interview: From Darwin to the continuous flow hypothesis of affect-laden information processing. *Journal of Personality and Social Psychology*, *54*, 592–604.

Cacioppo, J.T., Rourke, P.A., Marshall-Goodell, B.S., Tassinary, L.G., & Baron, R.S. (1990). Rudimentary physiological effects of mere observation, *Psychophysiology*, *27*, 177–186.

Cady, E.B., Dawson, M.J., Hope, P.L., Tofts, P.S., Costello, A.M., Delpy, D.T., Reynolds, E.O.R., & Wilkie, D.R. (1983). Non-invasive investigation of cerebral metabolism in newborn infants by phosphorous nuclear magnetic resonance spectroscopy. *Lancet*, *i*, 14th May, 1059–1062.

Cairns, R.B., Gariepy, J.L., & Hood, K.E. (1990). Development, microevolution, and social behavior. *Psychological Review*, *97*, 49–65.

Calabrese, J., Kling, M., & Gold, P. (1987). Alterations in immunocompetence during stress, bereavement, and depression,: Focus on neuroendocrine regulation. *American Journal of Psychiatry, 144*, 1123–1134.

Caley, D.W., & Maxwell, D.S. (1970). Development of the blood vessels and extracellular spaces during postnatal maturation of the rat cerebral cortex. *Journal of Comparative Neurology, 138*, 31–48.

Campbell, B.A., & Mabry, P.D. (1972). Ontogeny of behavioral arousal: A comparative study. *Journal of Comparative and Physiological Psychology, 81*, 371–379.

Campbell, P.S., Zarrow, M.X., & Denenberg, V.H. (1973). The effect of infantile stimulation upon hypothalamic CRF levels following adrenalectomy in the adult rat. *Proceedings of the Society for Experimental Biology and Medicine, 142*, 781–783.

Campos, J.J., Barrett, K.C., Lamb, M.E., Goldsmith, H.H., & Stenberg, C. (1983). Socioemotional development. In P.H. Mussen (Ed.), *Handbook of child psychology* (4th ed.,pp. 783–815). New York: Wiley.

Campos, J.J., Campos, R.G., & Barrett, K.C. (1989). Emergent themes in the study of emotional development and emotion regulation. *Developmental Psychology, 25*, 394–402.

Cannon, W.B. (1953). *Bodily changes in pain, hunger, fear, and rage: An account of recent researches into the function of emotional excitement* (2nd ed.) Boston: Charles T. Branford Co. (Original work published 1915).

Cannon, W.B. (1939). *The wisdom of the body.* New York: W.W. Norton.

Cannon, W.B., & Britton, S.W. (1925). Studies on the conditions of activity in endocrine glands. XV. Pseudoaffective medulliadrenal secretion. *American Journal of Physiology, 72*, 283–294.

Cannon, W.B., & de la Paz, D. (1911). Emotional stimulation of adrenal secretion. *American Journal of Physiology, 58,* 27–64.

Caplan, P.J., MacPherson, G.M., & Tobin, P. (1985). Do sex-related differences in spatial abilities exist? A multilevel critique with new data. *American Psychologist, 40*, 786–799.

Carlson, G.A., & Goodwin, F.K. (1973). The stages of mania: A longitudinal analysis of the manic episode *Archives of General Psychiatry, 28*, 221–228.

Carlson, M., Earls, F., & Todd, R.D. (1988). The importance of regressive changes in the development of the nervous system: Towards a neurobiological theory of child development *Psychiatric Development, 1*, 1–22.

Carlton, P.L. (1969). Brain-acetylcholine and inhibition. In T. Tapp (Ed.), *Reinforcement and behavior.* New York: Academic Press.

Carmon, A.J., & Benton, A.L. (1969). Tactile perception of direction and number in patients with unilateral cerebral disease. *Neurology, 19*, 525–532.

Caron, A.J., Caron, R.F., Caldwell, R.C., & Weiss, S.J. (1973). Infant perception of the structural properties of the face. *Developmental Psychology, 9*, 385–399.

Caron, A.J., Caron, R.F., & Myers, R.S. (1985). Do infants see emotional expressions in static faces? *Child Development, 56*, 1552–1560.

Carpenter, G. (1974). Mother's face and the newborn. *New Scientist, 61,* 742–744.

Carpenter, W.T., & Grune, P. (1982). Cortisol's effect on human mental functioning. *Journal of Clinical Psychopharmacology, 2*, 91–101.

Carr, D.J.J., & Klimpel, G.R. (1986). Enhancement of the generation of cytoxic T cells by endogenous opiates *Journal of Neuroimmunology, 12*, 75–87.

Carroll, E.W., & Wong-Riley, M.T.T. (1984). Quantitative light and electron microscopic analysis of cytochrome oxidase-rich zones in the striate cortex of the squirrel monkey. *Journal of Comparative Neurology, 222,*1–37.

Casaer, P. (1993). Old and new facts about perinatal brain development. *Journal of Child Psychology and Psychiatry, 34*, 101–109.

Caspi, A., Elder, G.H., Jr., & Bem, D.J. (1987). Moving against the world: Life-course patterns of explosive children. *Developmental Psychology, 22*, 303–308.

Caspi, A., Elder, G.H., Jr., & Bem, D.J. (1988). Moving away from the world: Life-course patterns of shy children. *Developmental Psychology*, *24*, 824–831.

Cavada, C. & Goldman-Rakic, P.S. (1989). Posterior parietal cortex in rhesus monkey: II. Evidence for segregated corticocortical networks linking sensory and limbic areas with the frontal lobe. *Journal of Comparative Neurology*, *287*, 422–445.

Ceccatelli, S., Villar, M.J., Goldstein, M., & Hokfelt, T. (1989). Expression of c-Fos immunoreactivity in transmitter-characterized neurons after stress. *Proceedings of the National Academy of Sciences of the United States of America*, *86*, 9569–9573.

Cechetto, D.F., & Saper, C.B. (1987). Evidence for a viscerotopic sensory representation in the cortex and the thalamus of the rat *Journal of Comparative Neurology*, *262*, 27–45.

Chance, M.R.A. (1962). An interpretation of some agonistic postures: The role of "cut-off" acts and postures. In *Evolutuonary aspects of animal communication. Symposium of the Zoological Society of London*, *8*, 71–89.

Changeux, J.P., & Dehaene, S. (1989). Neuronal models of cognitive function. *Cognition*, *33*, 63–109.

Chapanis, L. (1977). Language deficits and cross-modal sensory perception. In S.J. Segalowitz & F. A. Gruber (Eds.), *Language development and neurological theory* (pp. 107–120). New York: Academic Press.

Chapelinsky, A.B., & Rodriguez de Lores Arnaiz, G. (1970). Levels of cytochromes in rat brain mitochondria during postnatal development. *Biochimica et Biophysica Acta*, *197*, 321–323.

Chapple, E.D. (1970). Experimental production of transients in human interaction. *Nature (London)* *228*, 630–633.

Chasseguet-Smirgel, J. (1985). *The ego ideal*. London: Free Association Books.

Chavis, D.A., & Pandya, D.N. (1976). Further observations on corticofrontal connections in the rhesus monkey. *Brain Research*, *117*, 369–386.

Chess, S., & Thomas, A. (1986). *Temperament in clinical practice*. New York: Guilford Press.

Chessick, R. (1979). A practical approach to the psychotherapy of the borderline patient. *American Journal of Psychotherapy*, *33*, 531–546.

Chi, J.G., Dooling, E.C., & Gilles, (1977). F.H. Gyral development of the human brain. *Annals of Neurology*, *1*, 86–93.

Child, C.M. (1921). *The origin and development of the nervous system*. Chicago: University of Chicago Press.

Chisolm, J. (1990). Life-history perspectives on human development. In G. Butterworth & P. Bryant (Eds.), *Causes of development* (pp. 238–262). Hillsdale NJ: Lawrence Erlbaum Associates.

Chomsky, N. (1965). *Aspects of the theory of syntax*. Cambridge, MA: MIT Press.

Chrousos, G.P., & Gold, P.W. (1992). The concepts of stress and stress system disorders. Overview of physical and behavioral homeostasis. *Journal of the American Medical Association*, *267*, 1244–1252.

Chugani, H.T., & Phelps, M.E. (1986). Maturational changes in cerebral function in infants determined by [18]FDG positron emission tomography. *Science*, *231*, 840–843.

Chugani, H.T., Phelps, M.E, & Mazziotta, J.C. (1987). Positron emission tomography study of human brain functional development. *Annals of Neurology*, *22*, 487–497.

Chun, J.J.M., & Shatz, C.J. (1988). A fibronectin-like molecule is present in the developing cat cerebral cortex and is correlated with subplate neurons. *Journal of Cell Biology*, *106*, 857–872.

Chwalisz, K., Diener, E., & Gallagher, D. (1988). Autonomic arousal feedback and emotional experience: Evidence from the spinal cord injured. *Journal of Personality and Social Psychology*, *54*, 820–828.

Ciccheti, D. & Olsen, K. (1990). Borderline disorders in childhood. In M. Lewis & S.M. Miller (Eds.), *Handbook of developmental psychopathology* (pp. 355–370). New York: Plenum Press.

Cicchetti, D., & Toth, S.L. (1991). A developmental perspective on internalizing and externalizing disorders. In D. Cicchetti & S.L. Toth (Eds.), *Internalizing and externalizing expressions of dysfunction: Rochester symposium on developmental psychopathology, Vol. 2* (pp. 1–19.). Hillsdale, NJ: Lawrence Erlbaum Associates.

Cimino, C.R., Verfaellie, M,., Bowers, D., & Heilman, K.M. (1991). Autobiographical memory: Influence of right hemisphere damage on emotionality and specificity. *Brain and Cognition, 15,* 106–118.

Cintra, A., Fuxe, K., Harfstrand, A., Agnati, L.F., Wikstrom, A.-C., Okret, S., Vale, W., & Gustafsson, J.-A. (1987). Presence of glucocorticoid receptor immunoreactivity in corticotropin releasing factor and in growth hormone releasing factor immunoreactive neurons of the rat di- and telencephalon. *Neuroscience Letters, 77,* 25–30.

Ciompi, L. (1991). Affects as central organising and integrating factors. A new psychosocial/biological model of the psyche. *British Journal of Psychiatry, 159,* 97–105.

Ciriello, J., & Calaresu, F.R. (1980). Role of paraventricular and supraoptic nuclei in central cardiovascular regulation in the cat. *American Journal of Physiology, 239,* R137-R142.

Clark, A.S., & Goldman-Rakic, P.S. (1989). Gonadal hormones influence the emergence of cortical function in nonhuman primates. *Behavorial Neuroscience, 103,* 1287–1295.

Clark, A.S., MacLusky, N.J., & Goldman-Rakic, P.S. (1988). Androgen binding and metabolism in the cerebral cortex of the developing rhesus monkey. *Endocrinology, 123,* 932–940.

Clark, P., Jones, K.J., & La Velle, A. (1990). Ultrastructural and morphometric analysis of nucleolar and nuclear changes during the early growth period in hamster facial neurons. *Journal of Comparative Neurology, 302,* 749–760.

Clarke, D.D., Lajtha, A.L., & Maker, H.S. (1989). Intermediary metabolism. In G. Siegel, B. Agranoff, R.W. Albers, & P. Molinoff (Eds.), *Basic neurochemistry* (4th ed.,pp. 541–564). New York: Raven Press.

Claustre, Y., Rivy, J.P., Dennis, T., & Scatton, B. (1986). Pharmacological studies on stress-induced increase in frontal cortical dopamine metabolism in the rat. *Journal of Pharmacology and Experimental Therapeutics, 238,* 693–700.

Clavier, R.M., & Gerfen, C.R. (1979). Self-stimulation of the sulcal prefrontal cortex in the rat: Direct evidence for ascending dopaminergic mediation. *Neuroscience Letters, 12,* 183–187.

Cline, H.T., Debski, E.A., & Constantine-Paton, M. (1987). *N*- methyl-D-aspartate receptor antagonist desegregates eye-specific stripes. *Proceedings of the National Academy of Sciences of the United States of America, 84,* 4342–4345.

Clopton, J.P., & Winfield, J.P. (1976). Effect of early exposure to patterened sound on unit activity in rat inferior colliculus. *Journal of Neuroscience, 39,* 1081–1089.

Cocks, J.A., Balazs, R., Johnson, A.L., & Eayrs, J.T. (1970). Effects of thyroid hormone on the biochemical maturation of rat brain: Conversion of glucose-carbon into amino acids. *Journal of Neurochemistry, 17,* 1275–1285.

Coe, C.L., Wiener, S.G., Rosenberg, L.T., & Levine, S. (1985). Endocrine and immune responses to separation and maternal loss in nonhuman primates. In M. Reite & T. Field (Eds.), *The psychobiology of attachment and separation* (pp. 163–199). Orlando, FL: Academic Press.

Cogill, S.R., Caplan, H.L., Alexandra, H., Robson, K.M., & Kumar, K.M. (1986). Impact of maternal postnatal depression on cognitive development of young children. *British Medical Journal, 292,* 1165–1167.

Cohan, C.S., Conner, J.A., & Kater, S.B. (1987). Electrically and chemically mediated increases in intracellular calcium in neuronal growth cones. *Journal of Neuroscience, 7,* 3588–3599.

Cohen, B.D., & Gara, M.A. (1992). Self-structure in borderline personality disorder. *American Journal of Orthopsychiatry, 62,* 618–625.

Cohen, D.J., Shaywitz, E.E., Young, J.G., & Shaywitz, B. (1982). Borderline syndromes and attention deficit disorders of childhood. In K. Robson (Ed.), *The borderline child* (pp. 198–221). New York: McGraw-Hill.

Cohen, J.J., & Crnic, G.R. (1982). Glucocorticoids, stress and the immune response. In D.R. Webb (Ed.), *Immunopharmacology and the regulation of leukocyte function* (pp. 61–91). New York: Marcel Dekker.

Cohen, R.M., Weingartner, H., Smallberg, S.A., Pickar, D., & Murphy, D.L. (1982). Effort and cognition in depression. *Archives of General Psychiatry, 39*, 593–597.

Cohen, R.S., Chung, S.K., & Pfaff, D.W. (1984). Alteration by estrogen of the nucleoli in nerve cells of the rat hypothalamus. *Cell and Tissue Research, 235*, 485–489.

Cohen, S., & Syme, S.L. (1985). *Social support and health.* San Diego: Academic Press.

Cohn, J.F., Matias, R., Tronick, E.Z., Connell, D., & Lyons-Ruth, K. (1986). Face-to-face interactions of depressed mothers and their infants. In E.Z. Tronick & T. Field (Eds.), *Maternal depression and infant disturbance.* San Francisco: Jossey-Bass.

Collingridge, G.L., & Bliss, T.V.P. (1987). NMDA receptors—their role in long-term potentiation. *Trends in Neurosciences, 10*, 288–293.

Collins, R. (1981). On the microfoundations of macrosociology. *American Journal of Sociology, 86*, 984–1014.

Colpaert, F.C. (1975). The ventromedial hypothalamus and the control of avoidance behavior and aggression: Fear hypothesis versus response-suppression theory of limbic system function. *Behavioral Biology, 15*, 27–44.

Columbo, J. (1982). The critical period concept: Research, methodology, and theoretical issues *Psychological Bulletin, 91*, 260–275.

Compton, M.M., & Cidlowski, J.A. (1986). Rapid in vivo effects of glucocorticoids on the integrity of rat lymphocyte genomic deoxyribonucleic acid. *Endocrinology, 118*, 38–45.

Compton, M.M., & Cidlowski, A. (1987). Identification of a glucocorticoid-induced nuclease in thymocytes: A potental "lysis gene" product. *Journal of Biological Chemistry, 262*, 8288–8292.

Conant, R.C., & Ashby, W.R. (1970). Every good regulator of a system must be a model of that system. *International Journal of Systems Science, 1*, 89–97.

Conel, J. LeR. (1955). *The postnatal development of the human cerebral cortex. V. Cortex of the fifteen-month infant.* Cambridge, MA: Harvard University Press.

Cooley, C.H. (1902). *Human nature and the social order.* New York: Scribner's.

Cooley, C.H. (1962). *Social organization: A study of the larger mind.* New York: Schocken. (Original work published 1909).

Cooper, S.J. (1975). Anaesthetisation of prefrontal cortex and response to noxious stimulation. *Nature (London), 254*, 439–440.

Corbett, D., & Wise, R.A. (1980). Intracranial self-stimulation in relation to the ascending dopaminergic systems of the midbrain: A moveable electrode mapping study. *Brain Research, 185*, 1–15.

Cornford, E.M. (1985). The blood-brain barrier, a dynamic regulatory interface. *Molecular Physiology, 7*, 219–260.

Corter, C.M., & Fleming, A.S. (1990). Maternal responsiveness in humans: Emotional, cognitive, and biological factors. In P.J.B. Slater, J.S. Rosenblatt, & C. Beer (Eds.), *Advances in the study of behavior, Vol. 19* (pp. 83–136). San Diego: Academic Press.

Cortes, R., Gueye, B., Pazos, A., Probst, A., & Palacios, J.M. (1989). Dopamine receptors in human brain: autoradiographic distribution of D1 sites. *Neuroscience, 28*, 263–273.

Corwin, J.V., Leonard, C.M., Schoenfeld, T.A., & Crandall, J.E. (1983). Anatomical evidence for differential rates of maturation of the medial dorsal nucleus projections to prefrontal cortex in rats. *Developmental Brain Research, 8*, 89–100.

Coss, R.G., & Globus, A. (1978). Spine stems on tectal interneurons in jewel fish are shortened by social stimulation. *Nature, 200*, 787–790.

Costa, E., & Sandler, M. (1972). *Monoamine oxidase: New vistas.* New York: Raven Press.

Cotman, C.W., Monaghan, D.T., & Ganong, A.H. (1988). Excitatory amino acid neurotransmission: NMDA receptors and Hebb-type synaptic plasticity. *Annual Review of Neuroscience, 11*, 61–80.

Cotman, C.W., Monaghan, D.T. Ottersen, O.P., & Storm-Mathisen, J. (1987). Anatomical organization of excitatory amino acid receptors and their pathways. *Trends in Neuroscience, 10,* 273–280.

Cousin, M.A., Lando, D., & Moguilewsky, M. (1982). Ornithine decarboxylase induction by glucocorticoids in brain and liver of adrenalectomized rats. *Journal of Neurochemistry, 38,* 1296–1304.

Cowan, W.M., Fawcett, J.W., O'Leary, D.D.M., & Stanfield, B.B. (1979). Regressive events in neurogenesis. *Science, 225,* 1228–1235.

Cox, A.D. (1988). Maternal depression and impact on children's development. *Archives of Diseases in Childhood, 63,* 90–95.

Cox, J.L., Rooney, A., Thomas, P.F., & Wrate, R.W. (1984). How accurately do depressed mothers recall postnatal depression: Further data from a three year follow-up study. *Journal of Psychosomatic Obstetrics and Gynaecology, 3,* 185–189.

Coyle, J.T., & Axelrod, J. (1972). Tyrosine hydroxylase in the rat brain: Developmental characteristics. *Journal of Neurochemistry, 19,* 1117–1123.

Coyle, J.T., & Molliver, M.E. (1977). Major innervation of newborn rat cortex by monoaminergic neurons. *Science, 196,* 444–447.

Coyle, J.T., & Snyder, S.H. (1981). Catecholamines. In G.J. , R.W. Albers, B.W. Agranoff, & R. Katzman, (Eds.), *Basic neurochemistry* (3rd ed., pp. 205–217). Boston: Little, Brown.

Cragie, E.H. (1945). The architecture of the cerebral capillary bed. *Biological Reviews, 20,* 133–146.

Crawford, M.A., Hassam, A.G., & Stevens, P.A. (1982). Essential fatty acid requirements in pregnancy and lactation with special reference to brain development. *Progress in Lipid Research, 20,* 31–40.

Crespo, D., Viadero, C.F., Villegas, J., & Lafarga, M. (1988). Nucleoli numbers and neuronal growth in supraoptic nucleus neurons during postnatal development in the rat. *Developmental Brain Research, 44,* 151–155.

Creutzfeldt, O.D. (1975). Neurophysiological correlates of different functional states of the brain. In D.H. Ingvar & N.A. Lassen (Eds.), *Brain work. Alfred Benzon symposium VIII* (pp. 21–46). New York: Academic Press.

Crick, F. (1984). Function of the thalamic reticular complex: The searchlight hypothesis. *Proceedings of the National Academy of Sciences of the United States of America, 81,* 4586–4590.

Cross, B.A., & Green, J.D. (1959). Activity of single neurons in the hypothalamus: Effects of osmotic and other stimuli. *Journal of Physiology (London), 148,* 554–569.

Cross, S., & Markus, H. (1991). Possible selves across the life span. *Human Development, 34,* 230–255.

Crowell, D.H., Jones, R.H., Kapuniai, L.E., & Nakagawa, J.K. (1973). Unilateral cortical activity in newborn humans: An early index of cerebral dominance? *Science, 180,* 205–208.

Crowell, J.A., & Feldman, S.S. (1991). Mothers' working models of attachment relationships and mother and child behavior during separation and reunion. *Developmental Psychology, 27,* 597–605.

Cubelli, R., Caselli, M., & Neri, M. (1984). Pain endurance in unilateral cerebral lesions. *Cortex, 20,* 369–375.

Cummins, C.J., Loreck, D.J., & McCandless, D.W. (1985). Ancillary pathways of energy metabolism in mammalian brain: The pentose phosphate pathway and galactose metabolism. In R.C. Wiggins, D.W. McCandless, & S.J. Enna (Eds.), *Developmental neurochemistry* (pp. 160–179). Austin: University of Texas Press.

Cummins, R.A., Livesey, P.J., Evans, J.G.M., & Walsh, R.N. (1977). A developmental theory of environmental enrichment. *Science, 197,* 692–694.

Cummins, R.A., Livesy, P.J., & Bell, J.A. (1982). Cortical depth changes in enriched and isolated mice. *Developmental Psychobiology, 15,* 187–195.

Cunningham, E.T., & Sawchenko, P.E. (1988). Anatomical specificity of noradrenergic inputs to the paraventricular and supraoptic nuclei of the rat hypothalamus. *Journal of Comparative Neurology, 274,* 60–76.

Cupps, T.R., & Fauci, A.S. (1982). Corticosteroid-mediated immunoregulation in man. *Immunological Reviews*, *65*, 133–155.

Curry, F.E. (1992). Modulation of venular microvessel permeability by calcium influx into endothelial cells. *The Federation of American Societies for Experimental Biology Journal*, *6*, 2456–2466.

Curti, D., Giangare, M.E., Redolfi, I.F., & Benzi, G. (1990). Age-related modifications of cytochrome *c* oxidase activity in discrete brain regions. *Mechanisms of Ageing and Development*, *55*, 171–180.

Cuthbert, B.N., Vrana, S.R., & Bradley, M. (1991). Imagery: Function and physiology. In P.K. Ackles, J.H. Jennings, & M.G.H. Coles (Eds.), *Advances in psychophysiology* (Vol. 4, pp. 1–42). London: Kingsley.

Cutting, J. (1992). The role of right hemisphere dysfunction in psychiatric disorders. *British Journal of Psychiatry*, *160*, 583–588.

Cytryn, L., McKnew, D.H., & Bunney, W.E. (1980). Diagnosis of depression in children: A reassessment. *Americal Journal of Psychiatry*, *137*, 22–25.

Daigneault, S., Braun, C.M.J., & Whitaker, H.A. (1992). An empirical test of two opposing theoretical models of prefrontal functioning. *Brain and Cognition*, *19*, 48–71.

Damasio, A.R. (1979). The frontal lobes. In K.M. Heilman & E. Valenstein (Eds.), *Clinical neuropsychology* (pp. 360–412). London: Oxford University Press.

Damasio, A.R., & Tranel, D. (1988). Domain-specific amnesia for social knowledge. *Neuroscience Abstracts*, *14*, 1289.

Damasio, A.R., & Van Hoesen, G.W. (1985). The limbic system and the localisation of herpes simplex encephalitis. *Journal of Neurology, Neurosurgery, and Psychiatry*, *48*, 297–301.

Damasio, H. (1983). A computerized tomographic guide to the identification of cerebral vascular territories. *Archives of Neurology*, *40*, 138–142.

D'Amato, F.R., & Pavone, F. (1993). Endogenous opioids: A proximate reward mechanism for kin selection? *Behavioral and Neural Biology*, *60*, 79–83.

Damuni, Z., Humphreys, J.S., & Reed, L.J. (1984). Stimulation of pyruvate dehydrogenase phosphatase activity by polyamines. *Biochemical and Biophysical Research Communications*, *124*, 95–99.

Dareste, M.C. (1891). *Recherches sur la Production Artificielle des Monstruosites*. [*Studies of the artificial production of monsters*] Paris: C. Reinwald.

Darkschewitsch, L., & Freud, S. (1886). Uber die Beziehung des Strickkorpers zum Hinterstrang und Hinterstrangskern nebst Bemerkungen uber zwei Felder der Oblongata. [Studies of the medulla oblongata]. *Neurologisches Zentralblatt*, *5*, 121–129.

Darwin, C.B. (1965). *The expression of the emotions in man and animals*. Chicago: The University of Chicago Press. (Original work published 1872).

Darwin, F. (1888). *The life and letters of Charles Darwin*, 3 Vols. London: John Murray.

Davidson, J.M., Jones, L.E., & Levine, S. (1968). Feedback regulation of adrenocorticotropin secretion in "basal" and "stress" conditions: Acute and chronic effects of intrahypothalamic corticoid implantation. *Endocrinology*, *82*, 655–663.

Davidson, R.J. (1991). Cerebral asymmetry and affective disorders: A developmental perspective. In D. Cicchetti & S.L. Toth (Eds.), *Internalizing and externalizing expressions of dysfunction: Rochester symposium on developmental psychopatholgy*, Vol. 2 (pp. 123–154). Hillsdale, NJ,: Lawrence Erlbaum Associates.

Davidson, R.J. (1992). Anterior cortical asymmetry and the nature of emotion. *Brain and Cognition*, *20*, 125–151.

Davis, B.J., & Jang, T. (1988). Tyrosine hydroxylase-like and dopamine B-hydroxylase-like immunoreactivity in the gustatory zone of the nucleus of the solitary tract in the hamster: Light- and electron-microscopic studies. *Neuroscience*, *27*, 949–964.

Davis, P.J. (1987). Repression and the inaccessibility of affective memories. *Journal of Personality and Social Psychology*, *53*, 585–593.

Daw, N.W., Rader, R.K., Robertson, T.W., & Ariel, M,. (1983). Effects of 6-hydroxydopamine on visual deprivation in the kitten striate cortex. *Journal of Neuroscience, 3*, 907–914.

Dawson, G., Klinger, L.G., Panagiotides, H., Hill, D., et al., (1992). Frontal lobe activity and affective behavior of infants of mothers with depressive symptoms. *Child Development, 63*, 725–737.

de Boysson-Bardies, B., Sagart, L., & Durand, C. (1984). Discernible differences in the babbling of infants according to target language. *Journal of Child Language, 11*, 1–15.

de Bruin, J.P.C. (1990). Social behaviour and the prefrontal cortex. *Progress in Brain Research, 85*, 485–500.

de Bruin, J.P.C., VanOyen, H.G.M., & VandePoll, N.E. (1983). Behavioral changes following lesions of the orbital prefrontal cortex in male rats. *Behavioral Brain Research, 10*, 209–232.

De Carlos, J.M., & O'Leary, D.O.M. (1992). Growth and targeting of subplate axons and establishment of major cortical pathways. *Journal of Neuroscience, 12*, 1194–1211.

De Haan, E.H.F., Young, A.W., & Newcombe, F. (1987). Face recognition without awareness. *Cognitive Neuropsychology, 4*, 385–415.

deKloet, E.R. (1991). Brain corticosteroid balance and homeostatic control. *Frontiers in Neuroendocrinology, 12*, 95–164.

DeKosky, S.T., Nonneman, A.J., & Scheff, S.W. (1982). Morphologic and behavioral effects of perinatal glucocorticoid administration. *Physiology and Behavior, 29*, 895–900.

Delgado, J.M.R., & Livingston, R.B. (1948). Some respiratory, vascular and thermal responses to stimulation of orbital surface of frontal lobe. *Journal of Neurophysiology, 11*, 39–55.

Dell, P., & Olson, R. (1951). Projections thalamique corticales et cerebelleuses des afferences viscerales vagales. [Thalamic, cortical, and cerebellar projections from vagal visceral afferents]. *Comptes Rendue des Seances de la Societe de Biologie et des Filiales (Paris), 145*, 1084–1088.

Dembroski, T.M., MacDougall, J. M., Williams, R.B., Haney, T., & Blumenthal, J.A. (1985). Components of Type A, hostility and anger-in. Relationship to angiographic findings *Psychosomatic Medicine, 47*, 219–233.

Demitrack, M.A., Dale, J.K., Straus, S., et al. (1991). Evidence for impaired activation of the hypothalamic-pituitary-adrenal axis in patients with chronic fatigue syndrome. *Journal of Clinical Endocrinology and Metabolism, 73*,1224–1234.

Demos, V. (1988). Affect and the development of the self: A new frontier. In A. Goldberg (Ed.), *Progress in self psychology, Vol. 3.* Hillsdale, NJ: The Analytic Press.

Demos, V. (1991). Resiliency in infancy In T.F. Dugan & R. Coles (Eds.), *The child in our times: Studies in the development of resiliency.* New York: Brunner/Mazel.

Demos, V., & Kaplan, S. (1986). Motivation and affect reconsidered: Affect biographies of two infants. *Psychoanalysis and Contemporary Thought, 9*, 147–221.

Denenberg, V.H., Garbanti, J., Sherman, G., Yutzey, D.A., & Kaplan, R. (1978). Infantile stimulation induces brain lateralization in rats. *Science, 201*, 1150–1152.

Denenberg, V.H., & Zarrow, M.X. (1971). Effects of handling in infancy upon adult behavior and adrenocortical activity: Suggestions for a neuroendocrine mechanism. In D.N. Walcher & D.L. Peters (Eds.), *Early childhood: The development of self-regulatory mechanisms* (pp. 39–64). San Diego: Academic Press.

De Paola, H.F.B. (1990). Countertransference and reparative processes within the analyst. In L.B. Boyer & P.L. Giovacchini (Eds.), *Master clinicians on treating the regressed patient* (pp. 325–337). New York: Jason Aronson.

Depue, R.A., & Kleiman, R.M. (1979).Free cortisol as a peripheral index of central vulnerability to major forms of polar depressive disorders: Examining stress-biology interactions in subsyndromal high-risk persons. In R.A. Depue (Ed.), *The psychobiology of the depressive disorders: Implications for the effects of stress* (pp. 177–204). New York: Academic Press.

Dermietzel, R., & Krause, D. (1991). Molecular anatomy of the blood-brain barrier as defined by immunocytochemistry. *International Review of Cytology, 127*, 57–109.

Derryberry, D., & Rothbart, M.K. (1984). Emotion, attention and temperament. In C.E. Izard, J.

Kagan, & R.B. Zajonc (Eds.), *Emotion, cognition and behavior* (pp. 132–166). Cambridge, England: Cambridge University Press.

Descarries, L., Beaudet, A., & Watkins, K.C. (1975). Serotonin nerve terminals in adult rat neocortex. *Brain Research, 100,* 563–588.

de Schonen, S., Gil de Diaz, M., & Mathivet, E. (1986). Hemispheric asymmetry in face processing in infancy. In H.D. Ellis, M.A. Jeeves, F. Newcombe, & A.W. Young (Eds.), *Aspects of face processing* (pp. 199–209). Dordrecht: Nijhoff.

Deshaies, R.J., Koch, B.D., & Schekman, R. (1988). The role of stress proteins in membrane biogenesis. *Trends in Biochemical Sciences, 13,* 384–388.

Deskin, R., Seidler, F.J., Whitmore, W.L., & Slotkin, T. (1981). Development of beta noradrenergic and dopaminergic receptor systems depends on maturation of their presynaptic nerve terminals in the rat brain. *Journal of Neurochemistry, 36,* 1683–1690.

Devine, L.E., & Simpson, F.O. (1967). The fine structure of vascular sympathetic neuromuscular contacts in the rat. *American Journal of Anatomy, 121,* 153–175.

DeVoogd, T., & Nottebohn, F. (1981). Gonadal hormones induce dendritic growth in the adult avian brain. *Science, 214,* 202–204.

Dewsmedt, J.E. (1977). Active touch exploration of extrapersonal space elicits specific electrogenesis in the right hemisphere of intact right-handed man. *Proceedings of the National Academy of Sciences of the United States of America, 74,* 4037–4040.

Diamond, A. (1990). The development and neural bases of memory functions as indexed by the AB and delayed response tasks in human infants and infant monkeys. *Annals of the New York Academy of Sciences, 608,* 267–317.

Diamond, A., & Doar, B. (1989). The performance of human infants on a measure of frontal cortex function, the delayed response task. *Developmental Psychobiology, 22,* 271–294.

Diamond, A., & Goldman-Rakic, P. (1983). Comparison of performance on a Piaget object permanence task in human infants and rhesus monkeys: Evidence for involvement of prefrontal cortex. *Society of Neuroscience Abstracts, 9,* 641.

Diamond, M.C. (1976). Anatomical brain changes induced by the environment. In L. Petrinovich & J. L. McGaugh.(Eds.), *Knowing, thinking, and believing* (pp. 215–241). New York: Plenum Press.

Diamond, M.C. (1987). Sex differences in the rat forebrain. *Brain Research Reviews, 12,* 235–240.

Diamond, M.C., Johnson, R.E., & Ingham, C.A. (1975). Morphological changes in the young, adult and aging rat cerebral cortex, hippocampus and diencephalon. *Behavioral Biology, 14,* 163–174.

Diamond, M.C., Krech, D., & Rosenzweig, M.R. (1963). The effects of an enriched environment on the histology of the rat cerebral cortex. *Journal of Comparative Neurology, 123,* 111–120.

Diamond, R., & Carey, S. (1977). Developmental changes in the representation of faces. *Journal of Experimental Child Psychology, 23,* 1–22.

Diamond, S., Balvin, R., & Diamond, F. (1963). *Inhibition and choice.* New York: Harper & Row.

DiChiara, G., & Imperato, A. (1988). Drugs abused by humans preferentially increase synaptic dopamine concentrations in the mesolimbic system of freely moving cats. *Proceedings of the National Academy of Sciences of the United States of America, 85,* 5274–5278.

Diener, E., Larsen, R.J., Levine, S., & Emmons, R.A. (1985). Intensity and frequency: Dimensions underlying positive and negative affect. *Journal of Personality and Social Psychology, 48,* 1253–1265.

Dienstbier, R.A. (1989). Arousal and physiological toughness: Implications for mental and physical health. *Psychological Review, 96,* 84–100.

DiGuiseppi, J., & Fridovich, I. (1984). The toxicology of molecular oxygen. *CRC Critical Review of Toxicology, 12,* 315–342.

Dimberg, U. (1990). Facial electromyography and emotional reactions. *Psychophysiology, 27,* 481–494.

Dobbing, J. (1974). The later growth of the brain and its vulnerability. *Pediatrics, 53,* 2–6.

Dobbing, J., & Sands, J. (1973). Quantitative growth and development of human brain. *Archives of Diseases of Childhood, 48*, 757–767.

Dobbing, J., & Smart, J.L. (1974). Vulnerability of developing brain and behavior. *British Medical Bulletin, 30*, 164–168.

Dodge, K.A. (1993). Social-cognitive mechanisms in the development of conduct disorder and depression. *Annual Review of Psychology, 44*, 559–584.

Dodge, K.A., & Somberg, D.R. (1987). Hostile attributional biases among aggressive boys are exacerbated under conditions of threat to the self. *Child Development, 58*, 213–224.

Domesick, V.B., Stinus, L., & Paskevich, P.A. (1983). The cytology of dopaminergic and non-dopaminergic neurons in the substantia nigra and ventral tegmental area of the rat: A light- and electron-microscopic study. *Neuroscience, 8*, 743–765.

Donahue, S. & Pappas, G.D. (1961). The fine structure of capillaries in the cerebral cortex of the rat at various stages of development. *American Journal of Anatomy, 108*, 331–348.

Donovan, W.L., & Leavitt, L.A. (1985). Cardiac responses to mothers and infants in Ainsworth's strange situation. In M. Reite & T. Field (Eds.), *The psychobiology of attachment and separation* (pp. 369–387). Orlando, FL: Academic Press.

Dore, J. (1985). Holophrases revisited: Their "logical" development from dialog. In M.D. Barrett (Ed.), *Children's single-word speech* (pp. 23–58). Chichester, England: Wiley.

Dorner, G. (1980). Sexual differentiation of the brain. *Vitamins and Hormones, 38*, 325–381.

Dowling, S., & Rothstein, A. (1989). *The Significance of infant observational research for clinical work with children, adolescents, and adults.* Madison, CT: International Universities Press.

Dromi, E. (1986). The one-word period as a stage of language development: Quantitative and qualitative accounts. In I. Levin (Ed.), *Stage and structure: Reopening the debate* (pp. 220–245). Norwood, NJ: Ablex.

Drummond, P.D., & Lance, J.W. (1987). Facial flushing and sweating mediated by the sympathetic nervous system. *Brain, 110*, 793–803.

Duffy, E. (1941). An explanation of "emotional" phenomena without the use of the concept "emotion". *Journal of General Psychology, 25*, 283–293.

Duke, D., & Pritchard, W. (1991). *Measuring chaos in the human brain.* Singapore: World Scientific.

Dunn, A.J. (1988). Stress-related activation of cerebral dopaminergic systems. *Annals of the New York Academy of Sciences, 537*, 188–205.

Dunn, A.J., & Berridge, C.W. (1990). Physiological and behavioral responses to corticotropin-releasing factor administration: Is CRF a mediator of anxiety or stress responses? *Brain Research Reviews, 15*, 71–100.

Dunn, J. (1986). *The beginnings of social understanding.* Unpublished manuscript.

Dyson, S.E., & Jones, D.G. (1976). Some effects of undernutrition on synaptic development. A quantitative ultrastructural study. *Brain Research, 114*, 365–378.

Eagle, M.N., & Wolitsky, D.L. (1985). The current status of psychoanalysis. *Clinical Psychology Review, 5*, 259–269.

Easser, R. (1974). Empathic inhibition and psychoanalytic technique. *Psychoanalytic Quarterly, 43*, 557–580.

Ebbesson, S.O.E. (1980). The parcellation theory and its relation to interspecific variability in brain organization, evolutionary and ontogenetic development, and neuronal plasticity. *Cell and Tissue Research, 213*, 179–212.

Eckenstein, F. (1988). Transient expression of NGF-receptor-like immunoreactivity in postnatal rat brain and spinal cord. *Brain Research, 446*, 149–154.

Edelman, G. (1984). Assessment of understanding in global aphasia. In F.C. Rose (Ed.), *Progress in aphasiology.* New York: Raven Press.

Edelman, G.M. (1987). *Neural Darwinism.* New York: Basic Books.

Edelman, G.M. (1989). *The remembered present: A biological theory of consciousness.* New York: Basic Books.

Edelman, G.M. (1992). *Bright air, brilliant fire: On the matter of the mind.* New York: Basic Books.

Edelman, G.M., Gall, W.E., & Cowan, W.M (1987). *Synaptic function.* New York: Wiley.

Egan, J., & Kernberg, P.F. (1984). Pathological narcissism in childhood. *Journal of the American Psychoanalytic Association, 32,* 39–62.

Egeland, B., & Farber, E.A. (1984). Infant-mother attachment: Factors related to its development and change over time. *Child Development 55,* 753–771.

Egeland, J.A., Gerhard, G.S., Pauls, D.L., Sussex, J.N., Kidd, K.K. et al. (1987). Bipolar affective disorder linked to DNA markers on chromsome 11. *Nature (London), 325,* 783–787.

Ehlers, C.L., Frank, E., & Kupfer, D.J. (1988). Social zeitgebers and biological rhythms. *Archives of General Psychiatry, 45,* 948–952.

Eibl-Eibesfeldt, I. (1967). Concepts of ethology and their significance in the study of human behavior. In H.W. Stevenson, H.E. Hess, & H.L. Rheingold (Eds.), *Early behavior: Comparative and developmental approaches* (pp. 127–146). New York: Wiley.

Eichenbaum, H., Clegg, R.A., & Feeley, A. (1983). Re-examination of functional subdivisions of the rodent prefrontal cortex. *Experimental Neurology, 79,* 434–451.

Eisenberg, N. (1986). *Altruistic cognition, emotion, and behavior.* Hillsdale, NJ: Lawrence Erlbaum Associates.

Eisenberg, N., & Miller, P.A. (1987). The relation of empathy to prosocial and related behaviors. *Psychological Bulletin, 101,* 91–119.

Ekman, P. (1973). Cross-cultural studies of facial expression. In P. Ekman (Ed.), *Darwin and facial expression: A century of research in review* (pp. 169–222). New York: Academic Press.

Ekman, P. (1984). Expression and the nature of emotion. In K.R. Scherer & P. Ekman (Eds.), *Approaches to emotion* (pp. 319–343). Hillsdale, NJ: Lawrence Erlbaum Associates.

Ekman, P. (1993). Facial expression and emotion. *American Psychologist, 48,* 384–392.

Ekman, P., & Friesen, W.V. (1975). *Unmasking the face.* Englewood Cliffs, NJ: Prentice-Hall.

Ekman, P., & Friesen, W.V. (1986). A new pan-cultural facial expression of emotion. *Motivation and Emotion, 10,* 159–168.

Ekman, P., Levenson, R.W., & Friesen, W.V. (1983). Autonomic nervous system activity distinguishes between emotions. *Science, 221,* 1208–1210.

Ekstrom-Jodal, B., Elfverson, J., & Von Essen, C. (1982). Dopamine and the cerebral circulation. In D.D. Heistand & M.L. Marcus (Eds.), *Cerebral blood flow: Effects of nerves & neurotransmitters, Vol. 14* (pp. 137–142). New York: Elsevier.

Elliot, S.A. (1978). Neurological aspects of antisocial behavior in the psychopath. In W.H. Reed (Ed.), *A comprehensive study of antisocial disorders and behaviors* (pp. 146–189). New York: Brunner/Mazel.

Ellsworth, P.C. (1975). Direct gaze as a social stimulus: The example of aggression. In P.L. Pliner, L. Krames, & T. Alloway (Eds.), *Nonverbal communication of aggression* (pp. 53–75). New York: Plenum.

Emde, R.N. (1980a). Emotional availability: A reciprocal reward system for infants and parents with implications for prevention of psychosocial disorders. In P.M. Taylor (Ed.), *Parent-infant relationships* (pp. 87–115). Orlando, FL: Grune & Stratton.

Emde, R.N. (1980b). Towards a psychoanalytic theory of affect. In S.I. Greenspan & G.H. Pollock.(Eds.), *The course of life* (pp. 63–112). Washington, DC: U.S. Government Printing Office.

Emde, R.N. (1983). The pre-representational self and its affective core. *Psychoanalytic Study of the Child, 38,* 165–192.

Emde, R.N. (1988). Development terminable and interminable. I. Innate and motivational factors from infancy. *International Journal of Psycho-Analysis, 69,* 23–42.

Emde, R.N. (1989). The infant's relationship experience: Developmental and affective aspects. In A.J. Sameroff & R.N. Emde (Eds.), *Relationship disturbances in early childhood* (pp. 33–51). New York: Basic Books.

Emde, R.N. (1990). Mobilizing fundamental modes of development: Empathic availability and therapeutic action. *Journal of the American Psychoanalytic Association, 38,* 881–913.

Emde, R.N. (1992). Positive emotions for psychoanalytic theory: Surprises from infancy research and new directions. In T. Shapiro & R.N. Emde (Eds.), *Affect: Psychoanalytic perspectives* (pp. 5–44). Madison, CT: International Universities Press.

Emde, R.N., Campos, J.J., Reich, J., & Gaensbauer, T.S. (1978). Infant smiling at five and nine months: Analysis of heart rate and movement. *Infant Behavior and Development, 1,* 26–35.

Emde, R.N., & Gaensbauer, T. (1981). Some emerging models of emotion in human infancy. In K. Immelmann, G.W. Barlow, L. Petrinovich, & M. Main (Eds.), *Behavioral development. The Bielefeld interdisciplinary project* (pp. 568–602). Cambridge, England: Cambridge University Press.

Emde, R.N., Gaensbauer, T.J., & Harmon, R.J. (1976). *Emotional expression in infancy: A biobehavioral study.* Psychological Issues Monograph 37. New York: International Universities Press.

Emery, P., Gently, K.C., Mackay, I.R., Muirden, K.D., & Rowley, M. (1987). Deficiency of the suppressor inducer subset of T lymphocytes in rheumatoid arthritis. *Arthritis and Rheumatism, 30,* 849–856.

Emmons, R.A. (1981). Relationship between narcissism and sensation seeking. *Psychological Reports, 48,* 247–250.

Emmons, R.A. (1987). Narcissism: Theory and measurement. *Journal of Personality and Social Psychology, 52,* 11–17.

Encabo, H., & Ruarte, A.C. (1967). Non-primary sensory projections of the fronto-orbital cortical area in the cat. *Electroencephalography and Clinical Neurophysiology, 22,* 210–219.

Engel, G.L., & Schmale, A.H. (1972). Conservation-withdrawal: A primary regulatory process for organismic homeostasis. In *Physiology, emotion, and psychosomatic illness* (pp. 57–85). Amsterdam: Elsevier.

Engele, J., & Bohn, M.C. (1991). The neurotrophic effects of fibroblast growth factor on dopaminergic neurons in vitro are mediated by mesencephalic glia. *Journal of Neuroscience, 11,* 3070–3078.

Eppinger, H., & Hess, L. (1915). Vagotonia: A clinical study in vegetative neurology. *Journal of Nervous and Mental Disease, 20,* 1–93.

Epstein, H.T. (1978.). Growth spurts during brain development: Implications for educational policy and practice. In J.S. Chard & A.F. Mirsky (Eds.), *Education and the brain.* Chicago: University of Chicago Press.

Erb, J.S., Gwirtsman, H.E., Fuster, J.M., & Richeimer, S.H. (1989). Bulimia associated with frontal lobe lesions. *International Journal of Eating Disorders, 8,* 117–121.

Erikson, E. (1950). *Childhood and society.* New York: W.W. Norton.

Erulkar, S.D. (1989). Chemically mediated synaptic transmission: An overview. In G. Siegel, B. Agranoff, R.W. Albers, & P. Molinoff (Eds.), *Basic neurochemistry,* (4th ed., pp. 151–182). New York: Raven Press.

Erzurumlu, R.S., & Killackey, H.P. (1982). Critical and sensitive periods in neurobiology. *Current Topics in Developmental Biology, 17,* 207–240.

Escalona, S.K. (1963). Patterns of infantile experience and the developmental process. *Psychoanalytic Study of the Child, 18,* 197–244.

Escalona, S.K. (1973). Basic modes of social interaction: Their emergence and patterning during the first two years of life. *Merrill-Palmer Quarterly, 19,* 205–232.

Eslinger, P.J., & Damasio, A.R. (1985). Severe disturbance of higher cognition after bilateral frontal lobe ablation: Patient EVR. *Neurology, 35,* 1731–1741.

Etcoff, N.L. (1984a). Selective attention to facial identity and facial emotion. *Neuropsychologia, 22,* 281–295.

Etcoff, N.L. (1984b). Perceptual and conceptual organization of facial emotions: Hemispheric differences. *Brain and Cognition, 3,* 385–412.

Euler, U.S. von, & Folkow, B. (1958). The effect of stimulation of autonomic areas in the cerebral cortex upon the adrenaline and noradrenaline secretion from the adrenal gland in the cat. *Acta Physiologica Scandinavica, 42,* 313–320.

Fagan, J.F. (1976). Infants' recognition of invariant features of faces. *Child Development*, *47*, 627–638.

Fagan, J.F., & Singer, L.T. (1979). The role of simple feature differences in infant recognition of faces. *Infant Behavior and Development*, *2*, 39–46.

Fagen, R. (1977). Selection for optimal age-dependent schedules of play behavior. *American Naturalist*, *111*, 395–414.

Fagen, R. (1981). *Animal play behaviors*. New York: Oxford University Press.

Fagg, G.E., & Matus, A. (1984). Selective association of N—methyl aspartate and quisqualate types of L-glutamate receptor with brain postsynaptic densities. *Proceedings of the National Academy of Sciences of the United States of America*, *81*, 6876–6880.

Fagot, B.I., & Kavanagh, K. (1993). Parenting during the second year: Effects of children's age, sex, and attachment classification. *Child Development*, *64*, 258–271.

Fairbairn, W.R.D. (1941). A revised psychopathology of the psychoses and psychoneuroses. *International Journal of Psycho-Analysis*, *22*, 250–279.

Fairbairn, W.R.D. (1952). *An object-relations theory of the personality*. New York: Basic Books.

Fairman, D., Livingston, K., & Poppen, J.L. (1950). Skin temperature changes after unilateral and bilateral prefrontal lobotomy. In M. Greenblatt, R. Arnot, & H.C. Solomon (Eds.), *Studies in lobotomy* (pp. 380–385). Orlando, FL: Grune and Stratton.

Falk, D., Hildebolt, C., Cheverud, J., Vannier, M., Helmkamp, R.C., & Konigsberg, L. (1990). Cortical asymmetries in frontal lobes of Rhesus monkeys (*Macaca mulatta*). *Brain Research*, *512*, 40–45.

Fallon, J.H., & Benevento, L.A. (1978). Projections of lateral orbital cortex to sensory relay nuclei in the rhesus monkey. *Brain Research*, *144*, 149–154.

Fallon, J.H., & Loughlin, S.E. (1982). Monoamine innervation of the forebrain: Collateralization. *Brain Research Bulletin*, *9*, 295–307.

Fantz, R. (1963). Pattern vision in newborn infants. *Science*, *140*, 296–297.

Farber, J.L. (1981). Minireview: The role of calcium in cell death. *Life Sciences*, *29*, 1289–1295.

Farkas-Bargeton, E., & Diebler, M.F. (1978). A topographical study of enzyme maturation in the human cerebral cortex: A histochemical and biochemical study. In M.A.B. Brazier & H. Petsche (Eds.), *Architectonics of the cerebral cortex*. New York: Raven Press.

Farrant, J., & Perez, M. (1989). Immunity and depression. In J.G. Howells (Ed.), *Modern perspectives in the psychiatry of the affective disorders: Modern perspectives in psychiatry*, *Vol. 13*. New York: Brunner/Mazel.

Fast, I. (1984). *Gender identity*. Hillsdale, NJ: The Analytic Press.

Fawcett, D.W. (1981). *The cell* (2nd ed.). Philadelphia: W.B. Saunders.

Fehm, H.L., Voigt, K.H., & Born, J. (1988). Extrapituitary mechanisms in the regulation of cortisol secretion in man. In D. Hellhammer, I. Florin, & H. Weiner (Eds.), *Neurobiological approaches to human disease*. Toronto: Huber.

Feinman, S. (1982). Social referencing in infancy. *Merrill-Palmer Quarterly*, *28*, 445–470.

Feldman, S., Conforti, N., & Melamed, E. (1988). Involvement of ventral noradrenergic bundle in corticosterone secretion following neural stimuli. *Neuropharmacology*, *27*, 129–133.

Felten, D.L., Felten, S.Y., Madden, K.S., Ackerman, K.D., & Bellinger, D.L. (1989). Development, maturation and senescence of sympathetic innervation of secondary immune organs. In M.P. Schreibman & C.G. Scanes (Eds.), *Development, maturation, and senescence of neuroendocrine systems. A comparative approach* (pp.381–391). San Diego: Academic Press.

Felten, D.L., Hallman, H., & Jonsson, G. (1982). Evidence for a neurotrophic role of noradrenaline neurons in the postnatal development of rat cerebral cortex. *Journal of Neurocytology*, *11*, 119–135.

Fenichel, O. (1945). *The psychoanalytic theory of neurosis*. New York: W.W. Norton.

Fenstermacher, J., Gross, P., Sposito, N., Acuff, V., Pettersen, S., & Gruber, K. (1988). Structural and functional variations in capillary systems within the brain. *Annals of the New York Academy of Sciences, 529,* 21–30.

Ferenczi, S. (1980). Stages in the development in the sense of reality. In *First contributions to psycho-analysis.* London: H. Karnac. (Original work published 1913).

Ferguson, T.J., Stegge, H., & Damhuis, I. (1991). Children's understanding of guilt and shame. *Child Development, 62,* 827–839.

Fernald, A., & Mazzie, C. (1991). Prosody and forms in speech to infants and adults. *Developmental Psychology, 27,* 209–221.

Ferrier, D. (1876). *The functions of the brain.* London: Smith, Elder.

Feshbach, N.D., & Feshbach, S. (1969). The relationship between empathy and aggression in two age groups. *Developmental Psychology, 1,* 102–107.

Fessel, W.J., & Forsyth, R. (1963). Hypothalamic role in control of gamma globulin levels. *Archives of Allergy* (Abstract) 771.

Field, T. (1981). Infant arousal, attention and affect during early interactions. *Advances in infancy research, Vol. 4* (pp. 58–96). Norwood, NJ: Ablex.

Field, T. (1985a). Attachment as psychobiological attunement: Being on the same wavelength. In M. Reite & T. Field (Eds.), *The psychobiology of attachment and separation* (pp. 415–454). Orlando, FL: Academic Press.

Field, T. (1985b). Coping with separation stress by infants and young children. In T.M. Field, P.M. McCabe, & N. Schneiderman (Eds.), *Stress and coping* (pp. 197–219). Hillsdale, NJ: Lawrence Erlbaum Associates.

Field, T., & Fogel, A. (1982). *Emotion and early interaction.* Hillsdale, NJ: Lawrence Erlbaum Associates.

Field, T., Healy, B., Goldstein, S., Perry, S., Bendall, D., Schanberg, S., Zimmerman, E., & Kuhn, C. (1988). Infants of depressed mothers show "depressed" behavior even with non-depressed adults. *Child Development, 59,* 1569–1579.

Field, T., & Reite, M. (1985). The psychobiology of attachment and separation: A summary. In M. Reite & T. Field (Eds.), *The psychobiology of attachment and separation* (pp.455–479). Orlando, FL: Academic Press.

Fink, J.S., & Smith, G.P. (1980). Mesolimbocortical dopamine terminal fields are necessary for normal locomotor and investigatory exploration in rats. *Brain Research, 199,* 359–384.

Fischer, K.W., & Pipp, S.L. (1984). Development of the structures of unconscious thought. In K.S. Bowers & D. Meichenbaum (Eds.), *The unconscious reconsidered* (pp. 88–148). New York: Wiley.

Fischer, K.W., & Silvern, L. (1985). Stages and individual differences in cognitive development. *Annual Review of Psychology, 36,* 613–648.

Fischer, R. (1971). A cartography of the ecstatic and meditative states. *Science, 174,* 897–904.

Fisher, L.A. (1989). Central autonomic modulation of cardiac baroreflex by corticotropin-releasing factor. *American Journal of Physiology, 256,* H949-H955.

Fisher, R.S., & Almli, C.R. (1984). Postnatal development of sensory influences on labeled hypothalamic neurons of the rat. *Developmental Brain Research, 12,* 55–75.

Flavell, J.H. (1977). *Cognitive development.* Englewood Cliffs, NJ: Prentice-Hall.

Flexner, J.B., Flexner, L.B., & Strauss, W.L. (1941). The oxygen consumption, cytochrome and cytochrome oxidase activity and histological structure of the developing cerebral cortex of the fetal pig. *Journal of Cellular and Comparative Physiology, 32,* 355–368.

Flohe, L., Laschen, G., Azzi, A., & Richter, C. (1977). Superoxide radicals in mitochondria. In A.M. Michelson, J.M. McCord, & I. Fridovich (Eds.), *Superoxide and superoxide dismutases* (pp. 323–334). New York : Academic Press.

Fogel, A. (1982). Affect dynamics in early infancy: Affective tolerance. In T. Field & A. Fogel (Eds.), *Emotion and early interaction.* Hillsdale, NJ: Lawrence Erlbaum Associates.

Folkow, B., & Euler, U.S. von (1954). Selective activation of noradrenaline and adrenaline producing cells in the cat's adrenal gland by hypothalamic stimulation. *Circulation Research*, *2*, 191–213.

Fonnum, F., Soreide, A., Kvala, I., Walker, J., & Walaas, I. (1981). Glutamate in cortical fibers. *Advances in Biochemical Psychopharmacology*, *27*, 29–42.

Foote, S.L., & Morrison, S.H. (1987). Development of the noradrenergic, serotonergic, and dopaminergic innervation of the cortex, *Current Topics in Developmental Biology*, *21*, 391–423.

Ford, O.H., & Cramer, E.B. (1977). Developing nervous system in relation to thyroid hormones. In G.D. Grave (Ed.), *Thyroid hormones and brain development* (pp. 1–18). New York: Raven Press.

Forgas, J.P. (1982.). Episode cognition: Internal representations of interaction routines. *Advances in Experimental Psychology, Vol. 15*. New York: Academic Press.

Fornal, C.A., & Jacobs, B.L. (1987). Physiological and behavioral correlates of serotonergic single-unit activity. In N.N. Osborne & C.A. Fornal (Eds.), *Neuronal serotonin* (pp. 305–345). Chichester, England: Wiley.

Forssberg, H., Stokes, V., & Hirschfeld, H. (1992). Basic mechanisms of human locomotor development. In M. R. Gunnar & C.A. Nelson (Eds.), *Minnesota symposium on child psychology. Vol. 24, Developmental behavioral neuroscience* (pp. 37–73). Hillsdale, NJ: Lawrence Erlbaum Associates.

Forster, R.E., & Estabrook, R.W. (1993). Is oxygen an essential nutrient? *Annual Review of Nutrition, 13*, 383–403.

Foster, R.P. (1992). Psychoanalysis and the bilingual patient: Some observations on the influence of language choice on the transference. *Psychoanalytic Psychology*, *9*, 61–76.

Fowles, D.C. (1992). Schizophrenia: Diathesis-stress revisited. *Annual Review of Psychology, 43*, 303–336.

Fox, K., Sato, H., & Daw, N. (1989). The location and function of NMDA receptors in cat and kitten visual cortex. *Journal of Neuroscience*, *9*, 2443–2454.

Fox, N. A. (1977). The development of attachment on the Israeli kibbutz. *Child Development*, *55*, 1237–1260.

Fox, N.A. (1989). Psychophysiological correlates of emotional reactivity during the first year of life. *Developmental Psychology, 25*, 364–372.

Fox, N.A. (1991). If it's not left, it's right: Electroencephalography asymmetry and the development of emotion. *American Psychologist*, *46*, 863–872.

Fox, N.A., & Davidson, R.J. (1984). Hemispheric substrates of affect: A developmental model. In N.A.Fox & R.J. (Eds.), *The psychobiology of affective development* (pp. 353–381). Hillsdale NJ: Lawrence Erlbaum Associates.

Fox, N.A., & Davidson, R.J. (1986). Psychophysiological measures of emotion: New directions in developmental research. In C.E. Izard (Ed.), *Measuring emotions in infants and children*. Cambridge, England: Cambridge University Press.

Fox, N.A., & Fitzgerald, H.E. (1990). Autonomic function in infancy. *Merrill-Palmer Quarterly, 36*, 27–52.

Fox, P.T., Mintun, M.A., Raichle, M.E., Miezin, F.M., Allman, J.M., & Van Essen, D.C. (1986). Mapping human visual cortex with positron emission tomography. *Nature (London)*, *323*, 806–809.

Fox, T.O. (1975). Androgen- and estrogen- binding macromolecules in developing rat brain: Biochemical and genetic evidence. *Proceedings of the National Academy of Sciences of the United States of America, 72*, 4303–4307.

Fraiberg, S. (1969). Libidinal object constancy and mental representation. *Psychoanalytic Study of the Child, 24*, 9–47.

Frank, A. (1969). The unrememberable and the unforgettable: Passive primal repression. *Psychoanalytic Study of the Child, 24*, 59–66.

Franzen, E.A., & Myers, R.E. (1973). Neural control of social behavior: Prefrontal and anterior temporal cortex. *Neuropsychologia*, *11*, 141–157.

Fredrikson, M., Sundin, O., & Frankenhaeuser, M. (1985). Cortisol secretion during the defense reaction in humans. *Psychosomatic Medicine, 47*, 313–319.

Freedman, D.A. (1981). The effect of sensory and other deficits in children on their experience of people. *Journal of the American Psychoanalytic Association, 29*, 831–867.

Freedman M., & Oscar-Berman, M. (1986). Bilateral frontal lobe disease and selective delayed response deficits in humans. *Behavorial Neuroscience, 100*, 337–342.

Freeman, N.C.G., & Rosenblatt, J.S. (1978). The interrelationship between thermal and olfactory stimulation in the development of home orientation in newborn kittens. *Developmental Psychobiology, 11*, 437–457.

Freeman, R.L., Galaburda, A.M., Cabal, R.D., & Geschwind, N. (1985). The neurology of depression. *Archives of Neurology, 42*, 289–291.

Fremeau, R.T. Jr., Duncan, G.E., Fornaretto, M.G., Dearry, A., Gingrich, J.A., Breese, G.R., & Caron, M.G. (1991). Localization of D1 receptor mRNA in brain supports a role in cognitive, affective, and neuroendocrine aspects of dopaminergic neurotransmission. *Proceedings of the National Academy of Sciences of the United States of America, 88*, 3772–3776.

Freud, S. (1882). Uber den Bau der Nervenfasern und Nervenzellen beim Flusskrebs. [On the structure of nerve cells of the crawfish] *Sitzungsber Mathematik Naturwiss Cl Akademie Wissenschaftlich, 85*, 9–46.

Freud, S. (1885). Zur Kenntniss der Olivenzwischenschict. [On knowledge of the layers of the olivary nucleus] *Neurologisches Zentralblatt, 4*, 268–270.

Freud, S. (1891). *Zur Auffassung der Aphasien, eine kritische Studie. [On aphasia].* Leipzig: F. Deuticke.

Freud, S. (1897). Die infantile Cerebrallahmung. [Infantile cerebral palsy]. In *Nothnagel's Specielle Pathologic und Therapie.* Vienna: Holder.

Freud, S. (1953). The interpretation of dreams. In J. Strachey (Ed. and Trans.), *The standard edition of the complete psychological works of Sigmund Freud.* London: Hogarth Press. (Original work published 1900).

Freud, S. (1953). Three essays on the theory of sexuality. In J. Strachey (Ed. and Trans.), *The standard edition of the complete psychological works of Sigmund Freud.* London: Hogarth Press. (Original work published 1905).

Freud, S. (1954). *The origins of Psychoanalysis. Letters to Wilhelm Fliess, Drafts and notes: 1887–1902.* New York: Basic Books.

Freud, S. (1955). The claims of psycho-analysis to scientific interest. In J. Strachey (Ed. and Trans.), *The standard edition of the complete psychological works of Sigmund Freud.* London: Hogarth Press. (Original work published 1913).

Freud, S. (1955). Beyond the pleasure principle. In J. Strachey (Ed. and Trans.), *The standard edition of the complete psychological works of Sigmund Freud.* London: Hogarth Press. (Original work published 1920).

Freud, S. (1957). On narcissism: An introduction. In J. Strachey (Ed. and Trans.), *The standard edition of the complete psychological works of Sigmund Freud.* London: Hogarth Press. (Original work published 1914).

Freud, S. (1957). The unconscious. In J. Strachey (Ed. and Trans.), *The standard edition of the complete psychological works of Sigmund Freud.* London: Hogarth Press. (Original work published 1915).

Freud, S. (1958). Two principles of mental functioning. In J. Strachey (Ed. and Trans.), *The standard edition of the complete psychological works of Sigmund Freud.* London: Hogarth Press. (Original work published 1911).

Freud, S. (1961). The ego and the id. In J. Strachey (Ed. and Trans.), *The standard edition of the complete psychological works of Sigmund Freud.* London: Hogarth Press. (Original work published 1923).

Freud, S. (1962). The neuro-psychoses of defence. In J. Strachey (Ed. and Trans.), *The standard edition of the complete psychological works of Sigmund Freud.* London: Hogarth Press. (Original work published 1894).

Freud, S. (1964). An outline of psychoanalysis. In J. Strachey (Ed. and Trans.), *The standard edition of the complete psychological works of Sigmund Freud.* London: Hogarth Press. (Original work published 1940).

Freud, S. (1966). Project for a scientific psychology. In J. Strachey (Ed. and Trans.), *The standard edition of the complete psychological works of Sigmund Freud.* London: Hogarth Press. (Original work published 1895).

Freyd, J.J. (1987). Dynamic mental representations. *Psychological Review, 94,* 427–438.

Friauf, E., McConnell, S.K., & Shatz, C.J. (1990). Functional synaptic circuits in the subplate during fetal and early postnatal development of cat visual cortex. *Journal of Neuroscience, 10,* 2601–2613.

Fride, E., & Weinstock, M. (1988). Prenatal stress increases anxiety related behavior and alters cerebral lateralization of dopamine activity. *Life Sciences, 42,* 1059–1065.

Fridlund, A.J., Hatfield, M.E., Cottam, G.L., & Fowler, S.C. (1986). Anxiety and striate-muscle activation: Evidence from electromyographic pattern analysis. *Journal of Abnormal Psychology, 95,* 228–236.

Friede, R.L., Fleming, L.M., & Knoller, M. (1963). A comparative mapping of enzymes involved in hexosemonophosphate shunt and citric acid cycle in the brain, *Journal of Neurochemistry, 10,* 263–277.

Friedman, W.J., Olson, L., & Perrson, H. (1991). Cells that express brain-derived neurotrophic factor mRNA in the developing postnatal rat brain. *European Journal of Neuroscience, 3,* 688–697.

Frijda, N.H. (1988). The laws of emotion. *Amerian Psychologist, 43,* 349–358.

Frith, C.D., Friston, K.J., Liddle, P.F., & Frackowiak, R.S. (1991). A PET study of word finding. *Neuropsychologia, 29,* 1137–1148.

Frith, C.D., & Frith, U. (1991). Elective affinities in schizophrenia and childhood autism. In P. Bebbington (Ed.), *Social psychiatry: Theory, methodology and practice* (pp. 66–88). New Brunswick, NJ: Transactions.

Fritschy, J-M., & Grzanna, R. (1990). Distribution of locus coeruleus axons within the rat brainstem demonstrated by *Phaseolus vulgaris* leucoagglutinin anterograde tracing in combination with dopamine-beta-hydroxylase immunoflourescence. *Journal of Comparative Neurology, 293,* 616–631.

Frumkin, L.R., Ripley, H.S., & Cox, G.B. (1978). Changes in hemispheric lateralization with hypnosis. *Biological Psychiatry, 13,* 741–750.

Fuglsang, A., Lomholt, M., & Gjedde, A. (1988). Blood-brain transfer of glucose and glucose analogs in newborn rats. *Journal of Neurochemistry, 46,* 1417–1428.

Fullinwider, S. (1983). Sigmund Freud, John Hughlings Jackson, and speech. *Journal of the History of Ideas, 44,* 151–158.

Fulton, J.F. (1949). Cerebral cortex: The orbitofrontal and cingulate regions. In *Physiology of the nervous system* (3rd ed., pp. 447–467). New York: Oxford University Press.

Fusco, M., Polato, P., Vantini, G., Cavicchioli, L., Bentivoglio, M., & Leon, A. (1991). Nerve growth factor differentially modulates the expression of its receptor within the CNS. *Journal of Comparative Neurology, 312,* 477–491.

Fuster, J.M. (1980). *The prefrontal cortex: Anatomy, physiology, and neurophysiology of the frontal lobe,* New York: Raven Press.

Fuster, J.M. (1985). The prefrontal cortex and temporal integration. In A. Peters & E.G. Jones (Eds.), *Cerebral cortex. Vol. 4. Association and auditory cortices* (pp. 151–171). New York: Plenum Press.

Fuster, J.M. (1987). Single-unit studies of the prefrontal cortex. In E. Perecman (Ed.), *The frontal lobes revisited* (pp. 109–120). Hillsdale NJ: Lawrence Erlbaum Associates.

Fuster, J.M. (1991). The prefrontal cortex and its relation to behavior. *Progress in Brain Research, 87* 201–211.

Fuxe, K., Wikstrom, A-N., Okret, S., Agnati, L.F., Harfstrand, A., Yu, Z-Y., Granholm, L., Zoli, M., Vale, W., & Gustafsson, J-A. (1985). Mapping of glucocorticoid receptor immunoreactive neurons in the rat tel- and diencephalon using a monoclonal antibody against rat liver glucocorticoid receptor. *Endocrinology, 117*, 1803–1812.

Gabbard, G.O. (1989). Two subtypes of narcissistic personality disorder. *Bulletin of the Menninger Clinic, 53*, 527–532.

Gabbard, G.O. (1992). Psychodynamic psychiatry in the "decade of the brain". *American Journal of Psychiatry, 149*, 991–998.

Gabriel, M., Poremba, A.L., Ellison-Perrine, C., & Miller, J.D. (1990). Brainstem mediation of learning and memory. In W.R. Klemm & R.D. Vertes (Eds.), *Brainstem mechanisms of behavior* (pp. 269–313). New York: Wiley.

Gaensbauer, T.J. (1982). Regulation of emotional expression in infants from two contrasting caretaking environments. *Journal of the American Academy of Child Psychiatry, 21*, 163–171.

Gaensbauer, T. J., Connell, J.P., & Schultz, L. A. (1983). Emotion and attachment: Interrelationships in a structural laboratory paradigm. *Developmental Psychobiology, 19*, 815–831.

Gaensbauer, T.J., Harmon, R.J., Cytryn, L., & McKnew, D.H. (1984). Social and affective development in infants with a manic-depressive parent. *American Journal of Psychiatry, 141*, 223–229.

Gaensbauer, T.J., & Mrazek, D. (1981). Differences in the patterning of affective expression in infants. *Journal of the American Academy of Child Psychiatry, 20*, 673–691.

Gaillet, S., Lachuer, J., Malaval, F., Assenmacher, I., & Szafarczyk, A. (1991). The involvement of noradrenergic ascending pathways in the stress-induced activation of ACTH and corticosterone secretions is dependent on the nature of stressors. *Experimental Brain Research, 87*, 173–180.

Galaburda, A.M., LeMay, M., Kemper, T.L., & Geschwind, N. (1978). Right-left asymmetries in the brain. *Science, 199*, 852–856.

Galaburda, A.M., Rosen, G.D., & Sherman, G.F. (1990). Individual variability in cortical organization: Its relationship to brain laterality and implications to function. *Neuropsychologia, 28*, 529–546.

Gale, A., Lucas, B., Nissim, R., & Harpham, B. (1972). Some EEG correlates of face-to-face contact. *British Journal of Social and Clinical Psychology, 11*, 326–332.

Galenson, E., & Roiphe, H. (1976). Some suggested revisions concerning early female development. *Journal of the American Psychoanalytic Association, 24* (Suppl.), 29–57.

Galin, D. (1974). Implications for psychiatry of left and right cerebral specialization: A neuropsychological context for unconscious processes. *Archives of General Psychiatry, 31*, 572–583.

Galin, D. (1976). Hemispheric specialization: implications for psychiatry. In R.G. Grenell & S. Gabay (Eds.), *Biological foundations of psychiatry*. New York: Raven Press.

Galin, D., Johnstone, J., Nakell, L., & Herron, J. (1979). Development for the capacity of tactile information transfer between hemispheres in normal children. *Science, 204*, 1330–1332.

Gamble, T.J., & Zigler, E. (1986). Effects of infant day care: Another look at the evidence. *American Journal of Orthopsychiatry, 56*, 26–42.

Ganong, W.F. (1973). *Review of medical physiology*. Los Altos, CA: Lange Medical Publications.

Gardner, R.W. (1969). Organismic equilibration and the energy structure duality in psychoanalytic theory. *Journal of the American Psychoanalytic Association, 17*, 3–21.

Gardner, R. (1982). Mechanisms in manic-depressive disorder. *Archives of General Psychiatry, 39*, 1436–1441.

Garey, L.J., & Pettigrew, J. D. (1974). Ultrastructural changes in kitten visual cortex after environmental modification. *Brain Research, 66*, 165–172.

Garfield, D.A.S. (1987). The use of primary process in psychotherapy-III. Dramatization and the transmission of affect. *Psychotherapy, 24*, 217–224.

Garthwaite, G., & Garthwaite, J. (1986). Amino acid toxicity: Intracellular sites of calcium accumulation associated with the onset of irreversible damage to rat cerebellar neurones in vitro. *Neuroscience Letters, 71*, 53–58.

Gasanov, G.G. (1974). Emotions, visceral functions, and limbic system. In G.G. Gasanov (Ed.), *Emotions and visceral functions*. Moscow: Elm Press.

Gaspar, P., Berger, B., Febvret, A., Vigny, A., & Henry, J.P. (1989). Catecholamine innervation of the human cerebral cortex as revealed by comparative immunohistochemistry of tyrosine hydroxylase and dopamine-beta-hydroxylase. *Journal of Comparative Neurology*, 279, 249–271.

Gazzaniga, M.S. (1985). *The social brain: Discovering the networks of the mind*. New York: Basic Books.

Gazzaniga, M.S., & Le Doux, J.E. (1978). *The integrated mind*. New York: Plenum Press.

Gebber, G.L., & Snyder, D.W. (1970). Hypothalamic control of baroreceptor reflexes. *American Journal of Physiology*, 218, 124–131.

Gedo, J. (1979). *Beyond interpretation*. New York: International Universities Press.

Gedo, J. (1986). *Conceptual issues in psychoanalysis: Essays in history and method*. Hillsdale, NJ: The Analytic Press.

Gedo, J. (1991). *The biology of clinical encounters*. Hillsdale, NJ: The Analytic Press.

Gedo, J., & Goldberg, A. (1973). *Models of the mind*. Chicago: University of Chicago Press.

Geertz, H. (1959). The vocabulary of emotion: A study of Javanese socialization processes. *Psychiatry*, 22, 225–237.

Geiser, D.S. (1989). Psychosocial influences on human immunity. *Clinical Psychology Review*, 9, 689–715.

Gelb, L.A. (1989). Neuroscience, psychiatry, psychoanalysis—crisis and opportunity. *Journal of the American Academy of Psychoanalysis*, 17, 543–553.

Gelbard, H.A., Teicher, M.T., Faedda, G., & Baldessarini, R.J. (1989). Postnatal development of dopamine D1 and D2 receptor sites in the rat striatum. *Brain Research*, 490, 123–130.

Geller, J.D. (1984). Moods, feelings, and the process of affect formation. In C. Van Dyke, L. Temoshok, & L.S. Zegans (Eds.), *Emotions in health and illness: Applications to clinical practice* (pp. 171–186). Orlando, FL: Grune & Stratton.

Gellhorn, E. (1964). Motion and emotion: The role of proprioception in the physiology and pathology of emotions. *Psychological Review*, 71, 457–472.

Gellhorn, E. (1967). The tuning of the nervous system: Physiological foundations and implications for behavior. *Perspectives in Biological Medicine*, 10, 559–591.

Gellhorn, E. (1970). The emotions and the ergotropic and trophotropic systems. *Psychologische Forschung*, 34, 48–94.

Gellhorn, E., Cortell, R., & Feldman, J. (1941). The effect of emotion, sham rage and hypothalamic stimulation on the vago-insulin response. *American Journal of Physiology*, 132, 532–541.

Gellman, M., Schneiderman, N., Wallach, J., & LeBlanc, W. (1981). Cardiovascular responses elicited by hypothalamic stimulation in rabbits reveal a mediolateral organization. *Journal of the Autonomic Nervous System*, 4, 301–317.

Gergely, G. (1992). Developmental reconstructions: Infancy from the point of view of psychoanalysis and developmental psychology. *Psychoanalysis and Contemporary Thought*, 15, 3–55.

Gerschenson, L.E., & Rotello, R.J. (1992). Apoptosis: a different type of cell death. *The Federation of American Societies for Experimental Biology Journal*, 6, 2450–2455.

Geschwind, N., & Behan, P. (1982). Left-handedness—Association with immune disease, migraine, and developmental learning disorder. *Proceedings of the National Academy of Sciences of the United States of America*, 79, 5097–5100.

Geschwind, N., & Galaburda, A. M. (1987). *Cerebral lateralization: Biological mechanisms, associations, and pathology*. Boston: The MIT Press.

Giannitrapani, D. (1967). Developing concepts of lateralization of cerebral functions. *Cortex*, 3, 353–370.

Gibbons, J.L., & McHugh, P.R. (1962). Plasma cortisol in depressive illness. *Journal of Psychiatry Research*, 1, 162–171.

Gibson, E.J., & Spelke, E.S. (1983). The development of perception. In P.H. Mussen (Ed.), *Handbook of child psychology: Vol. 1. Cognitive development*. New York: Wiley.

Gibson, J.J. (1941). A critical review of the concept of set in contemporary experimental psychology. *Psychological Bulletin*, 38, 781–817.

Gibson, J.J. (1966). *The senses considered as perceptual systems*. Boston: Houghton-Mifflin.

Gilad, G., & Reis, D. (1979). Collateral sprouting in central mesolimbic dopamine neurons. *Brain Research, 160*, 17–36.

Gilbert, P. (1989). *Human nature and suffering*. Hove, Sussex: Lawrence Erlbaum Associates.

Gilbert, P. (1992a). *Depression: The evolution of powerlessness*. New York: Guilford Press.

Gilbert, P. (1992b). *Counselling for depression*. London: Sage Publications.

Gilbert, P. (1993). Evolution, behaviour and psychopathology: 1: Defense and safe(ty). Manuscript submitted for publication.

Gilbert, P., & Trower, P. (1990). The evolution and manifestation of social anxiety. In W.R. Crozier (Ed.), *Shyness and embarrassment* (pp. 144–177). New York: Cambridge University Press.

Giles, R.E., Blanc, H., Cann, H.M., & Wallace, D.C. (1980). Maternal inheritance of human mitochondrial DNA. *Proceedings of the National Academy of Sciences of the United States of America, 77*, 6715–6719.

Gill, M.M. (1982). *Analysis of transference*. New York: International Universities Press.

Gillan, F.D., & Reiner, D.S. (1983). Human milk kills parasitic intestinal protozoa. *Science, 221*, 1290–1292.

Gilman, S.C., Schwartz, J.M., Milner, R.J., Bloom, F.E., & Feldman, J.D. (1982). Beta endorphin enhances lymphocyte proliferative response. *Proceedings of the National Academy of Sciences of the United States of America, 79*, 4226–4330.

Giovacchini, P.L. (1981). Object relations, deficiency states, and the acquisition of psychic structure. In S.Tutman, C. Kaye, & M. Zimmerman (Eds.), *Object and self: A developmental approach* (pp. 397–427). New York: International Universities Press.

Giovacchini, P.L. (1990). Epilogue: Contemporary perspectives on technique. In L.B. Boyer & P.L. Giovacchini (Eds.), *Master clinicians on treating the regressed patient* (pp. 353–381). Northvale, NJ: Jason Aronson.

Giulian, D., McEwen, B.S., & Pohorecky, L.A. (1974). Altered development of the rat brain serotonergic system after disruptive neonatal experience. *Proceedings of the National Academy of Sciences of the United States of America, 71*, 4106–4110.

Gjone, R., & Setekleiv J. (1963). Excitatory and inhibitory bladder responses to stimulation of the cerebral cortex in the cat. *Acta Physiologica Scandinavica, 59*, 337–348.

Glassman, M. (1988). A test of competing psychoanalytic models of narcissism. *Journal of the American Psychoanalytic Association, 36*, 597–625.

Glassman, R.B., & Wimsatt, W.C. (1984). Evolutionary advantages and limitations of early plasticity. In C.R. Almli & S. Finger (Eds.), *Early brain damage, Vol. 1* (pp. 35–58). Orlando, FL: Academic Press.

Glavin, G.B. (1985). Stress and brain noradrenaline: A review. *Neuroscience and Biobehavioral Reviews, 9*, 233–243.

Glick, S.D., Meibach, R.C., Cox, R.D., & Maayani, S. (1979). Multiple and interrelated functional asymmetries in rat brain. *Life Sciences, 25*, 395–400.

Glueck, E.T., & Glueck, S. (1966). Identification of potential delinquents at 2–3 years of age. *International Journal of Social Psychiatry, 12*, 5–16.

Gold, P.W., Goodwin, F.K., & Chrousos, G.P. (1988a). Clinical and biochemical manifestations of depression: Relation to the neurobiology of stress, part I. *New England Journal of Medicine, 319*, 348–353.

Gold, P.W., Goodwin, F.K., & Chrousos, G.P. (1988b). Clinical and biochemical manifestations of depression: relation to the neurobiology of stress, part II. *New England Journal of Medicine, 319*, 413–420.

Gold, P.W., Loriaux, D.L., Roy A., et al. (1986). Responses to corticotropin-releasing hormone in the hypercorticolism of depression and Cushing's disease: pathophysiologic and diagnostic implications. *New England Journal of Medicine, 314*, 1329–1335.

Goldberg, C. (1991). *Understanding shame*. Northvale, NJ: Jason Aronson.

Goldberg, E., & Bilder, R.M. (1987). The frontal lobes and hierarchical organization of cognitive control. In E. Perecman (Ed.), *The frontal lobes revisited* (pp. 159–187). Hillsdale, NJ: Lawrence Erlbaum Associates.

Goldberg, E., & Costa, L.D. (1981). Hemisphere differences in the acquisition and use of descriptive systems. *Brain and Language, 14*, 144–173.

Goldberg, G. (1987). From intent to action: Evolution and function of the premotor systems of the frontal lobe. In E. Perecman (Ed.), *The frontal lobes revisited* (pp. 273–306). Hillsdale, NJ: Lawrence Erlbaum Associates.

Goldberg, L.I., Volkman, P.H., & Kohli, J.D. (1978). A comparison of the vascular dopamine receptor with other dopamine receptors. *Annual Review of Pharmacology and Toxicology, 18*, 57–79.

Goldberger, L. (1982). Sensory deprivation and overload. In L. Goldberger & S. Breznitz (Eds.), *Handbook of stress: Theoretical and clinical aspects* (pp. 410–418). New York: The Free Press.

Goldenberg, G., Podreka, I., Uhl, F., Steiner, M., Willmes, K., & Deecke, L. (1989). Cerebral correlates of imagining colours, faces and a map—I. SPECT of regional cerebral blood flow. *Neuropsychologia, 27*, 1315–1328.

Goldman, L., Coover, G.D., & Levine, S. (1973). Bidirectional effects of reinforcement shifts on pituitary adrenal activity. *Physiology and Behavior, 10*, 209–214.

Goldman, P.S. (1971). Functional development of the prefrontal cortex in early life and the problem of neuronal plasticity. *Experimental Neurology, 32*, 366–387.

Goldman, P.S., Crawford, H.T., Stokes, L.P., Galkin, T.P., & Rosvold, H.E. (1974). Sex-dependent behavioral effects of cerebral cortical lesions in the developing rhesus monkey. *Science, 186*, 540–542.

Goldman-Rakic, P.S. (1987a). Development of cortical circuitry and cognitive function. *Child Development, 58*, 601–622.

Goldman-Rakic, P.S. (1987b). Circuitry of the primate prefontal cortex and regulation of behavior by representational memory. In F. Plum & V. Mountcastle (Eds.), *Handbook of physiology, Vol. 5* (pp. 373–418). Bethesda, MD: American Physiological Society.

Goldman-Rakic, P.S. (1988). Topography of cognition: Parallel distributed networks in primate association cortex. *Annual Review of Neuroscience, 11*, 137–156.

Goldman-Rakic, P.S. (1992). Working memory and the mind. *Scientific American, 267*, 111–117.

Goldman-Rakic, P.S., & Brown, R.M. (1982). Postnatal development of monoamine content and synthesis in the cerebral cortex of rhesus monkeys. *Developmental Brain Research, 4*, 339–349.

Goldman-Rakic, P.S., Funahahi, S., & Bruce, C.J. (1990). Neocortical memory circuits. *Cold Spring Harbor Symposia on Quantitative Biology, LV*, 1025–1038.

Goldman-Rakic, P.S., Isseroff, A., Schwartz, M.L., & Bugbee, N.M. (1983). The neurobiology of cognitive development. In P.H. Mussen (Ed.), *Handbook of child psychology* (4th ed., pp. 281–344). New York: Wiley.

Goldsmith, H.H., & Campos, J.J. (1982). Toward a theory of infant temperament. In R.N. Emde & R. J. Harmon (Eds.), *The development of attachment and affiliative systems* (pp. 161–193). New York: Plenum.

Goldstein, A.P., & Michaels, G.Y. (1985). *Empathy: Development, training and consequences.* Hillsdale, NJ: Lawrence Erlbaum Associates.

Goldstein, G.W., & Betz, A.L. (1986). The blood-brain barrier. *Scientific American, 255*, 74–83.

Goldstein, G.W., Wolinsky, J.S., Csejtey, J., & Diamond, I. (1975). Isolation of metabolically active capillaries from rat brain. *Journal of Neurochemistry, 25*, 715–717.

Goldstein, L., & Stoltzus, N.W.. (1973). Psychoactive drug induced changes of interhemispheric EEG amplitude relationships. *Agents and Actions, 3*, 124–132.

Golinkoff, R.M. (1993). When is communication a "meeting of the minds"? *Journal of Child Language, 20*, 199–207.

Gonzalez-Lima, F., & Scheich, H. (1985). Ascending reticular activating system in the rat: A 2-deoxyglucose study. *Brain Research, 344*, 70–88.

Goodenough, F.L. (1931). Anger in young children. *Institute for Child Welfare Monographs*. Minneapolis: University of Minnesota Press.

Goodwin, B.C. (1982). Development and evolution. *Journal of Theoretical Biology, 97*, 43–55.

Goodwin, B.C. (1990). The causes of biological form. In G. Butterworth & P. Bryant (Eds.), *Causes of development* (pp. 50–63). Hillsdale NJ: Lawrence Erlbaum Associates.

Goplerud, E., & Depue, R.A. (1985). Behavioral response to naturally occurring stress in cyclothymia and dysthymia. *Journal of Abnormal Psychology, 94*, 128–139.

Gordon, D., Burge, D., Hammen, C., Adrian, C., Jaenicke, C., & Hiroto, D. (1989). Observations of interactions of depressed women with their children. *American Journal of Psychiatry, 146*, 50–55.

Gordon, H.W., & Galatzer, A. (1980). Cerebral organization in patients with gonadal dysgenesis. *Psychoneuroendocrinology, 5*, 235–244.

Gordon, S.L. (1989). The socialization of children's emotions: Emotional culture, competence, and exposure. In C. Saarni & P.L. Harris (Eds.), *Children's understanding of emotion* (pp. 319–349). Cambridge, England: Cambridge University Press.

Gorski, R.A., Harlan, R.E., Jacobson, C.D., Shryne, J.E., & Southam, A.M. (1980). Evidence for the existence of a sexually dimorphic nucleus in the preoptic area of the rat. *Journal of Comparative Neurology, 193*, 529–539.

Gospodarowicz, D., Brown, K.D., Birdwell, C.R., & Zetter, B.R. (1978). Control of proliferation of human vascular endothelial cells. *Journal of Cell Biology, 77*, 774–788.

Gospodarowicz, D., Chang, J., Lui, G.M., Baird, A., & Bohlen, P. (1984). Isolation of brain fibroblast growth factor by heparin-sepharose affinity chromatography: Identity with pituitary fibroblast growth factor. *Proceedings of the National Academy of Sciences of the United States of America, 81*, 6963–6967.

Gospodarowicz, D., Massoglia, S., Chang, J., & Fujii, D.K. (1986). Effect of fibroblast growth factor and lipoproteins on the proliferation of endothelial cells derived from bovine adrenal cortex, brain cortex and corpus luteum capillaries. *Journal of Cell Physiology, 136*, 121–136.

Gottfried, A., Rose, S.A., & Bridger, W.H. (1977). Cross-modal transfer in human infants. *Child Development, 48*, 118–123.

Gottlieb, G. (1961). Developmental age as a baseline for determination of the critical period for imprinting. *Journal of Comparative and Physiological Psychology, 54*, 422–427.

Gottman, J.M., & Fainsilber-Katz, L. (1989). Effects of marital discord on young children's peer interaction and health. *Developmental Psychology, 25*, 373–381.

Goy, R.W., Bercovitch, F.B., & McBriar, M.C. (1988). Behavioral masculinization is independent of genital masculinization in prenatally androgenized female rhesus macaques. *Hormones and Behavior, 22*, 552–571.

Grafman, J., Vance, S.C., Weingartner, H., Salazar, A.M., & Amin, D. (1986). The effects of lateralized frontal lesions on mood regulation. *Brain, 109*, 1127–1148.

Gray, J.A. (1982). *The neuropsychology of anxiety: An inquiry into the functions of the septo-hippocampal system*. New York: Oxford University Press.

Green, K.P., & Kuhl, P.K. (1989). The role of visual information in the processing of place and manner features in speech perception. *Perception and Psychophysics, 45*, 34–42.

Greenberg, J., Hand, P., Sylvestro, A., & Reivich, M. (1979). Localized metabolic-flow couple during functional activty. *Acta Neurolologica Scandinavica, (Suppl 72), 60*, 12–13.

Greenberg, J.R., & Mitchell, S.A. (1983). *Object relations in psychoanalytic theory*. Cambridge, MA: Harvard University Press.

Greenberg, L.S., & Safran, J.D. (1984). Hot cognition: Emotion coming in from the cold. A reply to Rachman and Mahooney. *American Psychologist, 44*, 19.

Greenberg, L.S., & Safran, J.D. (1989). Emotion in psychotherapy. *Cognitive Therapy and Research, 8*, 591–598.

Greenberg, M.T., Kusche, C.A., & Speltz, M. (1991). Emotional regulation, self-control, and psychopathology: The role of relationships in early childhood. In D. Cicchetti & S.L. Toth (Eds.), *Internalizing and externalizing expressions of dysfunction: Rochester symposium on developmental psychopatholgy, Vol. 2* (pp. 21–55). Hillsdale, NJ: Lawrence Erlbaum Associates.

Greenfield, P., & Smith, J. (1976). *The structure of communication in early language.* New York: Academic Press.

Greenough, W.T. (1986). What's special about development? Thoughts on the bases of experience-sensitive synaptic plasticity. In W.T. Greenough & J.M. Juraska.(Eds.), *Developmental neuropsychology* (pp. 195–221). Orlando, FL: Academic Press.

Greenough, W.T. (1987). Experience effects on the developing and the mature brain: Dendritic branching and synaptogenesis. In N.A. Krasnegor, E.M. Blass, M.A. Hofer, & W.P. Smotherman (Eds.), *Perinatal development: A psychobiological perspective* (pp. 195–221). Orlando: Academic Press.

Greenough, W.T., & Black, J.E. (1992). Induction of brain structure by experience: Substrates for cognitive development. In M. R. Gunnar & C.A. Nelson (Eds.), *Minnesota symposium on child psychology. Vol. 24, Developmental behavioral neuroscience* (pp. 155–200). Hillsdale, NJ: Lawrence Erlbaum Associates.

Greenough, W.T., Black, J., & Wallace, C. (1987). Experience and brain development. *Child Development, 58,* 539–559.

Greenough, W.T.,Carter, C.S., Steerman, C., & DeVoogd, T.J. (1977). Sex differences in dendritic patterns in hamster preoptic areas. *Brain Research, 126,* 63–72.

Greenson, R. (1978). *Explorations in psychoanalysis.* New York: International Universities Press.

Greenspan, S.I. (1979). *Intelligence and adaptation.* New York: International Universities Press.

Greenspan, S. I. (1981). *Psychopathology and adaptation in infancy and early childhood.* New York: International Universities Press.

Greenspan, S.I. (1988). The development of the ego: Insights from clinical work with infants and children. *Journal of the American Psychoanalytic Association, 36* (Suppl.), 3–55.

Greenspan, S.I. (1990). A developmental approach to pleasure and sexuality. In R.A. Glick & S. Bone (Eds.), *Pleasure beyond the pleasure principle* (pp. 38–54). New Haven, CT: Yale University Press.

Greenwald, A.G., & Breckler, S.J. (1985). To whom is the self presented? In B.R. Schlenker (Ed.), *The self and social life* (pp. 126–145). New York: McGraw-Hill.

Greenwald, A.G., & Pratkanis, A.R. (1984). The self. In R.S. Wyer & T.K. Srull (Eds.), *Handbook of social cognition, Vol. 3.* Hillsdale, NJ: Lawrence Erlbaum Associates.

Gregory, E. (1975). Comparison of postnatal CNS development between male and female rats. *Brain Research, 99,* 152–156.

Gregson, N.A., & Williams, P.L. (1969). A comparative study of brain and liver mitochondria from new-born and adult rats. *Journal of Neurochemistry, 16,* 617–626.

Grigsby, J., & Schneiders, J.L. (1991). Neuroscience, modularity and personality theory: Conceptual foundations of a model of complex human functioning. *Psychiatry, 54,* 21–38.

Grings, W.W., & Dawson, M.E. (1978). *Emotions and bodily responses.* New York: Academic Press.

Groenewegen, H.J., Berendse, H.W., Wolters, J.G., & Lohman, A.H.M. (1990). The anatomical relationship of the prefrontal cortex with the striatopallidial system, the thalamus and the amygdala: Evidence for a parallel organization. *Progress in Brain Research, 85,* 95–118.

Gross, P.M., Wall, K.M., Pang, J.J., Shaver, S.W., & Wainman, D.S. (1990). Microvascular specializations promoting rapid interstitial solute dispersion in nucleus tractus solitarius. *American Journal of Physiology, 28,* R1131-R1138.

Grossman, P., Stemmler, G., & Meinhardt, E. (1990). Paced respiratory sinus arrhythmia as an index of cardiac parasympathetic tone during varying behavioral tasks. *Psychophysiology, 27,* 404–416.

Grossman, S.P. (1967). *A textbook of physiological psychology.* New York: Wiley.

Grotstein, J.S. (1980). A proposed revision of the psychoanalytic concept of primitive mental states:

I. Introduction to a newer psychoanalytic metapsychology. *Contemporary Psychoanalysis*, *16*, 479–546.

Grotstein, J.S. (1981). *Splitting and projective identification*. New York: Jason Aronson.

Grotstein, J.S. (1983). Some perspectives on self psychology. In A. Goldberg (Ed.), *The future of psychoanalysis*. New York: International Universities Press.

Grotstein, J.S. (1986). The psychology of powerlessness: Disorders of self-regulation and interactional regulation as a newer paradigm for psychopathology. *Psychoanalytic Inquiry*, *6*, 93–118.

Grotstein, J.S. (1987). The borderline as a disorder of self-regulation. In J.S. Grotstein, J. Lang, & M. Solomon (Eds.), *The borderline patient: Emerging concepts in diagnosis* (pp. 347–383). London: The Analytic Press.

Grotstein, J.S. (1990a). Invariants in primitive emotional disorders. In L.B. Boyer & P.L. Giovacchini (Eds.), *Master clinicians on treating the regressed patient*.(pp. 139–163). Northvale, NJ: Jason Aronson.

Grotstein, J.S. (1990b). The "black hole" as the basic psychotic experience: Some newer psychoanalytic and neuroscience perspectives on psychosis. *Journal of the American Academy of Psychoanalysis*, *18*, 29–46.

Grotstein, J.S. (1991). Nothingness, meaninglessness, chaos, and the "black hole" III: Self- and interactional regulation and the background presence of primary identification. *Contemporary Psychoanalysis*, *27*, 1–33.

Grouse, L.D., Schrier, B.K., Letendre, C.H., & Nelson, P.G. (1980). RNA sequence complexity in central nervous system development and plasticity. *Current Topics in Developmental Biology*, *16*, 381–397.

Grunbaum, A. (1984). *The foundations of psychoanalysis: A philosophical critique*. Berkeley: University of California Press.

Guillaume, V., Conte-Devolx, B., Szafarczyk, A., Malaval, F., Pares-Herbute, N., Grino, M., Alonso, G., Assenmacher, I., & Oliver, C. (1987). The corticotropin-releasing factor release in rat hypophysial portal blood is mediated by brain catecholamines. *Neuroendocrinology*, *46*, 143–146.

Guillemin, R., Vargo, T., Rossier, J., Minick, A., Ling, N., Rivier, C., Vale, W., & Bloom, F. (1977). Beta endorphin and adrenocorticotropin are secreted concomitantly by the pituitary. *Science*, *197*, 1367–1369.

Guntrip, H. (1968). *Schizoid phenomena, object relations, and the self*. London: Hogarth Press.

Gur, R.C., Packer, I.K., Hungerbuhler, J.P., Reivich, M., Obrist, W.D., Amarnek, W.S., & Sackeim, H.A. (1980). Differences in the distribution of gray and white matter in human cerebral hemispheres. *Science*, *207*, 1226–1228.

Guroff, G. (1980). *Molecular neurobiology*. New York: Marcel Dekker.

Gurrera, R.J. (1990). Some biological and behavioral features associated with clinical personality types. *Journal of Nervous and Mental Disease*, *178*, 556–566.

Hadden, J.W., Hadden, E.M., & Middleton, E. (1970. Lymphocyte host transformation. 1. Demonstration of adrenergic receptors in human peripheral lymphocytes. *Journal of Cellular Immunology*, *1*, 583–595.

Hadjiolov, A.A. (1985). *The nucleolus and ribosome biogenesis*. New York: Springer.

Hadley, J. (1983). The representational system: A bridging concept for psychoanalysis and neurophysiology. *International Review of Psychoanalysis*, *10*, 13–30.

Hadley, J., (1989). The neurobiology of motivational systems. In J.L. Lichtenberg, *Psychoanalysis and motivation* (pp. 337–372). Hillsdale, NJ: The Analytic Press.

Hadley, J. (1992). Instincts revisited. *Psychoanalytic Inquiry*, *12*, 396–418.

Hadziselomovic, H., & Cus, H. (1966). The appearance of internal structures of the brain in relation to configuration of the human skull. *Acta Anatomica*, *63*, 289–299.

Hafner, H. (1987). The concept of disease in psychiatry. *Psychological Medicine*, *17*, 11–14.

Haft, W.L. & Slade, A. (1989). Affect attunement and maternal attachment: A pilot study. *Infant Mental Health Journal*, *10*, 157–172.

Hahn, W.K. (1987). Cerebral lateralization of function: From infancy through childhood. *Psychological Bulletin, 101*, 376–392.

Haith, M.M., Bergman, T., & Moore, M. (1979). Eye contact and face scanning in early infancy. *Science, 218*, 179–181.

Hall, R.E., & Marr, H.B. (1975). Influence of electrical stimulation of posterior orbital cortex upon plasma cortisol levels in unanesthetized sub-human primate. *Brain Research, 93, 367*–371.

Hall, R.E., Livingston, R.B., & Bloor, C.M. (1977). Orbital cortical influences in cardiovascular dynamics and myocardial structure in conscious monkeys. *Journal of Neurosurgery, 46*, 638–647.

Halliday, G., & Tork, I. (1986). Comparative anatomy of the ventromedial mesencephalic tegmentum in the rat, cat, monkey and human. *Journal of Comparative Neurology, 252*, 423–445.

Halliday, G.M., Li, Y.W., Joh, T.H., Cotton, R.G.H., Howe, P.R.C., Geffen, L.B., & Blessing, W.W. (1988). Distribution of monoamine-synthesizing neurons in the human medulla oblongata. *Journal of Comparative Neurology, 273*, 301–317.

Hallman, M., Mäenpää, P., & Hassinen, I. (1972). Levels of cytochromes in heart, liver, kidney and brain in the developing rat. *Experientia, 28*, 1408–1410.

Halpain, S., & McEwen, B.S. (1988). Corticosterone decreases ^{3}H glutamate binding in rat hippocampal formation. *Neuroendocrinology, 48*, 235–241.

Halpain, S., Girault, J.-A., & Greengard, P. (1990). Activation of NMDA receptors induces dephosphorylation of DARP-32 in rat striatal slices. *Nature (London), 343*, 369–372.

Hamburger, V., & Oppenheim, R.W. (1982). Naturally occurring neuronal death in vertebrates. *Neuroscience Commentaries, 1*, 39–55.

Hamilton, N.G. (1989). A critical review of object relations theory. *American Journal of Psychiatry, 146*, 1552–1560.

Hamilton, N.G. (1992). Introduction. In N.G. Hamilton (Ed.), *From inner sources: New directions in object relations psychotherapy*. Northvale NJ: Jason Aronson.

Hammer, E. (1990). *Reaching the affect: Style in the psychodynamic therapies*. Northvale, NJ: Jason Aronson.

Handa, Y., Nojyo, Y., Tamamaki, N., Tsuchida, A., & Kubota, T. (1993). Development of the sympathetic innervation to the cerebral arterial system in neonatal rats as revealed by anterograde labeling with wheatgerm agglutin-horseradish peroxidase. *Experimental Brain Research, 94*, 216–244.

Haracz, J.L. (1985). Neural plasticity in schizophrenia. *Schizophrenia Bulletin, 11*, 191–229.

Hardebo, J.E., Emson, P.C., & Owman, Ch. (1979). Barrier mechanisms to neurotransmitter monoamines at the blood-brain interphase. *Acta Neurolologica Scandinavica, (Suppl 72), 60*, 164–165.

Hardstaff, V.H., Jagadeesh, P., & Newman, P.P. (1973). Activity evoked in the orbital cortex from splanchic, vagal and cutaneous afferents. *Journal of Neurophysiology, 231*, 16P.

Hardy, S.G.P., & Holmes, D.E. (1988). Prefrontal stimulus-produced hypotension in the rat. *Experimental Brain Research, 73*, 249–255.

Harfstrand, A., Fuxe, K., Cintra, A., Agnati, L., Zini, I., Wikstrom, A., Okret, S., Yu, Z.Y., Goldstein, M., Steinbusch, H., Verhofstad, A., & Gustafsson, J. (1986). Glucocorticoid receptor immunoreactivity in monoaminergic neurons of rat brain. *Proceedings of the National Academy of Sciences of the United States of America, 83*, 9779–9783.

Harlow, H.F. (1958). The nature of love. *American Psychologist, 13*, 673–685.

Harlow, H.F. (1965). Total isolation: Effects on macaque monkey behavior. *Science, 148*, 666.

Harold, F.M. (1986). *The vital force: A study of bioenergetics*. New York: W.H. Freeman.

Harrelson, A., & McEwen, B. (1987). Steroid hormone influences on cyclic AMP-generating systems. *Current Topics in Membrane Transport, 31*, 217–247.

Harter, S., & Whitesell, N.R. (1989). Developmental changes in children's understanding of single, multiple, and blended emotion concepts. Ih *Children's understanding of emotion* (pp. 81–116). Cambridge, England: Cambridge University Press.

Hartley, E.J., & Seeman, P. (1983). Development of receptors for dopamine and noradrenaline in rat brain. *European Journal of Pharmacology, 91,* 391–397.

Hartman, B.K., & Udenfriend, S. (1972). The application of immunological techniques to the study of enzymes regualting catecholamine synthesis and degradation. *Pharmacological Reviews, 24,* 311–330.

Hartman, B.K., Zide, D., & Udenfriend, S. (1972). The use of dopamine *B*- hydroxylase as a marker for the central noradrenergic nervous system in rat brain. *Proceedings of the National Academy of Sciences of the United States of America, 69,* 2722–2726.

Hartman, D.J., Hoogenraad, N.J., Condron, R., & Hoj, P.B. (1992). Identification of a mammalian 10-kDa heat shock protein, a mitochondrial chaperonin 10 homologue essential for assisted folding of trimeric ornithine transcarbamoylase *in vitro. Proceedings of the National Academy of Sciences of the United States of America, 89,* 3394–3398.

Hartmann, E. (1976). *The functions of sleep.* New Haven: Yale University Press.

Hartmann, H. (1939). *Ego psychology and the problem of adaptation.* New York: International Universities Press.

Hartmann, H., & Loewenstein, R.M. (1962). Notes on the superego. *Psychoanalytic Study of the Child, 17,* 42–81.

Hartocollis, P. (1980). Affective disturbances in borderline and narcissistic patients. *Bulletin of the Menninger Clinic, 44,* 135–146.

Hasher, L., & Zacks, R.T. (1979). Automatic and effortful processes in memory. *Journal of Experimental Psychology: General, 108,* 356–388.

Haskins, R. (1985). Public school aggression among children with varying day-care experience. *Child Development, 56,* 689–703.

Hasselmo, M.E., Rolls, E.T., & Baylis, G.C. (1989a). The role of expression and identity in the face-selective responses of neurons in the temporal visual cortex of the monkey. *Behavioral Brain Research, 32,* 203–218.

Hasselmo, M.E., Rolls, E.T., Baylis, G.C., & Nalwa, V. (1989b). Object-centered encoding by face-selective neurons in the cortex in the superior temporal sulcus of the monkey. *Experimental Brain Research, 75,* 417–429.

Hatjis, C.G., & McLaughlin, M.K. (1982). Identification and ontogensis of beta-adrenergic receptors in fetal and neonatal rabbit myocardium. *Journal of Development Physiology, 4,* 327–338.

Hauscr, K.F., McLaughlin, P.J., & Zagon, I.S. (1989). Endogenous opioid systems and the regulation of dendritic growth and spine formation. *Journal of Comparative Neurology, 281,* 13–22.

Hauw, J-J., Berger, B., & Escourolle, R. (1975). Electron microscopic study of the developing capillaries of the human brain. *Acta Neuropathologica (Berlin), 31,* 229–242.

Haydon, P.G., McCobb, D.P., & Kater, S.B. (1984). Serotonin selectively inhibits growth cone motility and synaptogenesis of specific identified neurons. *Science, 226,* 561–564.

Hayne, H., Rovee-Collier, C., & Borza, M.A. (1991). Infant memory for place information. *Memory and Cognition, 19,* 378–386.

Haynes, H., White, B.L., & Held, R. (1965). Visual accommodation in human infants. *Science, 148,* 528–530.

Hazel, J.R., & Williams, E.E. (1990). The role of alterations in membrane lipid composition in enabling physiological adaptations of organisms to their physical environment. *Progress in Lipid Research, 29,* 167–227.

Hazum, E.K., Chang, K., & Cuatrecasas, P. (1979). Specific non-opiate receptors for beta endorphin. *Science, 205,* 1033–1035.

He, X., & Rosenfeld, M.G. (1991). Mechanisms of complex transcriptional regulation: Implications for brain development. *Neuron, 7,* 183–196.

Head, J.R., & Beer, A.E. (1978). The immunologic role of viable leukocytic in mammary exosecretions. In B.L. Larson (Ed.), *Lactation (Vol. IV): Mammary gland / human lactation / milk synthesis* (pp. 337–366). New York: Academic Press.

Heard, D.H., & Lake, B. (1986). The attachment dynamic in adult life. *British Journal of Psychiatry, 149*, 430–438.

Heath, R. G. (1964). Pleasure responses of human subjects to direct stimulation of the brain: Physiologic and psychodynamic considerations. In R.G. Heath (Ed.), *The role of pleasure in behavior* (pp. 219–243). New York: Harper and Rowe.

Hebb, D.O. (1949). *Organization of behavior*. New York: Wiley.

Hecaen, H. & Albert, M.L. (1978). *Human neuropsychology*. New York: Wiley.

Heck, G.L., Mierson, S., & DeSimone, J.A. (1984). Salt taste transduction occurs through an amiloride—sensitive sodium transport pathway. *Science, 223*, 403–405.

Heijnen, C.J., & Ballieux, R.E. (1986). Influence of opioid peptides in the immune system. *Institute of Advances in Health Sciences, 3*, 114–117.

Heilman, K.M., Schwartz, H., & Watson, R.T. (1977). Hypoarousal in patients with the neglect syndrome and emotional indifference. *Neurology, 38*, 229–232.

Heilman, K.M., & Van Den Abell, T. (1979). Right hemispheric dominance for mediating cerebral activation. *Neuropsychologia, 17*, 315–321.

Hellbrugge, T. (1960). The development of circadian rhythms in infants. *Cold Spring Harbor Symposia on Quantitative Biology, 25*, 311–323.

Hellige, J.B. (1990). Hemispheric asymmetry. *Annual Review of Psychology, 41*, 55–80.

Hellige, J.B. (1993). *Hemispheric asymmetry: What's right and what's left*. Cambridge, MA: Harvard University Press.

Hendry, I.A., & Iversen, L.L. (1971). Effect of nerve growth factor and its antiserum on tyrosine hydroxylase activity in mouse superior cervical sympathetic ganglion. *Brain Research, 29*, 159–162.

Henkart, M., Landis, D.M.D., & Reese, T.S. (1976). Similarity of junctions between plasma membranes and endoplasmic reticulum in muscle and neurons. *Journal of Cell Biology, 70*, 338–347.

Henkin, R.I. (1974). Effects of ACTH, adrenocorticoids and thyroid hormone on sensory function. In W.E. Stumpf & L.D. Grant (Eds.), *Anatomical neuroendocrinology* (pp. 298–317). Basel: Karger.

Henry, G.M., Weingartner, H., & Murphy, D.L. (1971). Idiosyncratic patterns of learning and word association during mania. *American Journal of Psychiatry, 128*, 564–574.

Henry, J.P., & Stephens, P.M. (1977). *Stress, health and the social environment*. New York: Springer-Verlag.

Herman, B.H., & Panksepp, J. (1978). Evidence for opiate mediation of social affect. *Pharmacological Biochemistry and Behavior, 9*, 213–220.

Hermans, H.J., Kempen, H.J.G., & van Loon, R.J.P. (1992). The dialogical self: Beyond individualism and rationalism. *American Psychologist, 47*, 23–33.

Herregodts, P., Velkeniers, B., Ebinger, G., Michotte, Y., Vanhaelst, L., & Hooghe-Peters, E. (1990). Development of monoaminergic neurotransmitters in fetal and postnatal rat brain: Analysis by HPLC with electrochemical detection. *Journal of Neurochemistry, 55*, 774–779.

Herrera, D.G., & Robertson, H.A. (1990). N-methyl-D-aspartate receptors mediate activation of the c-Fos proto-oncogene in a model of brain injury. *Neuroscience, 35*, 272–281.

Herrlinger, H., Anzil, A.P., Blinzinger, K., & Kronski, D. (1974). Endothelial microtubular bodies in human brain capillaries and venules. *Journal of Anatomy, 118*, 205–209.

Hertz, L., & Schousboe, A. (1975). Ion and energy metabolism of the brain at the cellular level. *International Review of Neurobiology, 18*, 141–211.

Herzog, J.M. (1980). Sleep disturbance and father hunger in 18-to 28-month-old boys: The Erlkonig syndrome. *Psychoanalytic Study of the Child, 35*, 219–233.

Hess, E. H. (1959). The relationship between imprinting and motivation. In M.R. Jones (Ed.), *Nebraska symposium on motivation* (pp. 44–77). Lincoln: University of Nebraska Press.

Hess, E.H. (1965). Attitude and pupil size. *Scientific American, 212*, 46–54.

Hess, E.H. (1973). *Imprinting: Early experience and the developmental psychobiology of attachment.* New York: Van Nostrand.

Hess, E.H. (1975). The role of pupil size in communication. *Scientific American, 233,* 110–119.

Hess, J.L., Denenberg, V.H., Zarrow, M.X., & Pfeifer, W.D. (1969). Modification of the corticosterone response curve as a function of handling in infancy. *Physiology and Behavior, 4,* 109–112.

Hess, W.R. (1954). *Diencephalon, autonomic and extrapyramidal functions.* Orlando, FL: Grune and Stratton.

Hier, D.B., Mondlock, J., & Caplan, L.R. (1983). Recovery of behavioral abnormalities after right hemispheric stroke. *Neurology, 33,* 345–350.

Hikosaka, K., Iwai, E., Saito, H., & Tanaka, K. (1988). Polysensory properties of neurons in the anterior bank of the caudal superior temporal sulcus of the macaque monkey. *Journal of Neurophysiology, 60,* 1615–1637.

Hildebrand, R. (1980). *Nuclear volume and cellular metabolism.* Berlin: Springer.

Hill, D.L., Mistretta, C.M., & Bradley, R.M. (1986). Effects of dietary NaCl deprivation during early development on behavioral and neurophysiological taste responses. *Behavioral Neuroscience, 100,* 390–398.

Hilz, H.W., Tarnowski, W., & Arend, P. (1963). Glucose polymerisation and cortisol. *Biochemical and Biophysical Research Communications, 10,* 492–502.

Himwich, H.E. (1951). *Brain metabolism and cerebral disorders.* Baltimore: Williams and Wilkins.

Himwich, H.E., & Fazekas, J.F. (1941). Comparative studies of the metabolism of infant and adult dogs. *American Journal of Physiology, 132,* 454–459.

Himwich, H.E., Sykowski, P., & Fazekas, J.F. (1941). A comparative study of excised cerebral tissues of adult and infant rats. *American Journal of Physiology, 132,* 292–296.

Himwich, W.A. (1975). Forging a link between basic and clinical research: Developing brain. *Biological Psychiatry, 10,* 125–139.

Hinde, R. (1990). Causes of social development from the perspective of an integrated developmental science. In G. Butterworth & P. Bryant (Eds.), *Causes of development* (pp. 161–185). Hillsdale, NJ: Lawrence Erlbaum Associates.

Hintzman, D.L. (1990). Human learning and memory: Connections and dissociations. *Annual Review of Psychology, 41,* 109–139.

Hinze, E. (1992). Die symmetrie in der Beziehung zwischen Analytiker und Analysand. [The symmetry in the analyst-analysand relationship]. *Jarbuch der Psychoanalyse, 29,* 9–28.

Hirano, A. (1974). Fine structural alterations of small vessels in the nervous system. In J. Cervos-Navarro (Ed.), *Pathology of microcirculation* (pp. 203–254). Berlin: de Gruyter.

Hock, D.B., Dingledine, R.J., & Wilson, J.E. (1984). Long-term potentiation in the hippocampal slice: Possible involvement of pyruvate dehydrogenase. *Brain Research, 328,* 1–10.

Hockenberry, D., Nunez, G., Milliman, C., Schreiber, R.D., & Korsmeyer, S.J. (1990). Bcl-2 is an inner mitochondrial membrane protein that blocks programmed cell death. *Nature (London) 348,* 334–336.

Hockey, G.R., Gaillard, A.W.K., & Coles, M.G.H. (1986). *Energetics and human information processing.* Dordrecht: Martinus Nijhoff.

Hodgkinson, S., Sherrington, R., Gurling, H., Marchbanks, R., Reeders, S., Mallet, J., McInnis, M., Petursson, H., & Brynjolfsson, J. (1987). Molecular genetic evidence for heterogeneity in manic depression. *Nature (London), 325,* 805–806.

Hofer, M. (1983). On the relationship between attachment and separation processes in infancy. In R. Plutchik & H. Kellerman (Eds.), *Emotion: Theory, research, and experience, Vol 2* (pp. 199–219). New York: Academic Press.

Hofer, M. (1984a). Relationships as regulators: A psychobiologic perspective on bereavement. *Psychosomatic Medicine, 46,* 183–197.

Hofer, M., A. (1984b). Early stages in the organization of cardiovascular control. *Proceedings of the Society for Experimental and Biological Medicine, 175,* 147–157.

Hofer, M.A. (1990). Early symbiotic processes: Hard evidence from a soft place. In R.A. Glick & S. Bone (Eds.), *Pleasure beyond the pleasure principle* (pp. 55–78). New Haven, CT: Yale University Press.

Hofer, M., & Barde, Y.-A. (1988). Brain-derived neurotrophic factor prevents neuronal death in vivo. *Nature (London), 331*, 261–262.

Hoffman, E., & Goldstein, L. (1981). Hemispheric quantitative EEG changes following emotional reactions in neurotic patients. *Acta Psychiatrica Scandinavica, 63*, 153–164.

Hoffman, H.S. (1987). Imprinting and the critical period for social attachments: Some laboratory investigations. In M.H. Bornstein (Ed.), *Sensitive periods in development, interdisciplinary studies* (pp. 99–121). Hillsdale, NJ: Lawrence Erlbaum Associates.

Hoffman, H.S., & Ratner, A.M. (1973). A reinforcement model of imprinting: Implications for socialization in monkeys and men. *Psychological Review, 80*, 527–544.

Hoffman, M.L. (1975a). Moral internalization, parental power, and the nature of parent-child interaction. *Developmental Psychology, 11*, 228–239.

Hoffman, M.L. (1975b). Developmental synthesis of affect anfd cognition and its implications for altruistic motivation. *Developmental Psychology, 11*, 607–622.

Hokin, M.R. (1969). Effect of norepinephrine on ^{32}P incorporation into individual phosphatides in slices from different areas of the guinea pig brain. *Journal of Neurochemistry, 16*, 127–134.

Holland, A. (1989, October). *Word-retrieval deficits in aphasia: Matching treatment to the problem.* Paper presented at the 27th Annual Meeting of the Academy of Aphasia. Santa Fe, NM.

Holson, R.R., Ali, S.F., & Scallet, A.C. (1988). The effect of isolation rearing and stress on monoamines in forebrain nigrostriatal, mesolimbic, and mesocortical dopamine systems. *Annals of the New York Academy of Sciences, 537*, 512–514.

Holt, R.R. (1967). Motives and thought: Psychoanalytic essays in honor of David Rapoport. *Psychological Issues, Nos. 18 / 19*, New York: International Universities Press.

Holtzman, D., & Moore, C.L. (1975). Respiration in immature rat brain mitochondria. *Journal of Neurochemistry, 24*, 1011–1015.

Holtzman, D., Olson, J., Zamvil, S., & Nguyen, H. (1982). Maturation of potassium-stimulated respiration in rat cerebral cortical slices. *Journal of Neurochemistry, 39*, 274–276.

Holzman, P.S. (1985). Psychoanalysis: Is the therapy destroying the science? *Journal of the American Psychoanalytic Association, 33*, 725–770.

Hopkins, B., & Butterworth, G. (1990). Concepts of causality in explanations of development. In G. Butterworth & P. Bryant, *Causes of development* (pp. 3–32). Hillsdale NJ: Lawrence Erlbaum Associates.

Hopkins, J., Campbell, S.B., & Marcus, M. (1987). Role of infant-related stressors in postpartum depression. *Journal of Abnormal Psychology, 96*, 237–241.

Horn, G., & McCabe, B.J. (1984). Predispositions and preferences. Effects on imprinting of lesions to the chick brain. *Animal Behavior, 32*, 288–292.

Horn, G., Bradley, P., & McCabe, B.J. (1985). Changes in the structure of synapses associated with learning. *Journal of Neuroscience, 5*, 3161–3168.

Horner, A.J. (1989). *The wish for power and the fear of having it.* Northvale, NJ: Jason Aronson.

Horner, A.J. (1991). *Psychoanalytic object relations therapy.* Northvale, NJ: Jason Aronson.

Horner, T. M. (1985). Subjectivity, intentionality, and the emergence of reality testing in early infancy. *Psychoanalytic Psychology, 2*, 341–363.

Horner, T.M. (1992). The origin of the symbiotic wish. *Psychoanalytic Psychology, 9*, 25–48.

Horney, K. (1945). *Our inner conflicts.* New York: W. W. Norton.

Hornik, R., Risenhoover, N., & Gunnar, M. (1987). The effects of maternal positive, neutral, and negative affective communications on infant responses to new toys. *Child Development, 58*, 937–944.

Horowitz, M.J. (1981). Self-righteous rage and the attribution of blame. *Archives of General Psychiatry, 38* 1233–1238.

Horowitz, M.J. (1983). *Image formation and psychotherapy*. New York: Jason Aronson.

Horowitz, M.J. (1987). *States of mind: Configurational analysis of individual psychology*. New York: Plenum Medical Book Company.

Horowitz, M. J. (1992). Formulation of states of mind in psychotherapy. In N.G. Hamilton (Ed.), *From inner sources: New directions in object relations psychotherapy* (pp. 75–83). Northvale, NJ: Jason Aronson.

Horowitz, M.J., & Stinson, C. (1991). University of California, San Francisco Center for the Study of Neuroses: Program on conscious and unconscious mental processes. In L. Beutler & M. Crago (Eds.), *Psychotherapy research: An international review of programmatic studies* (pp. 107–114). Washington, DC: American Psychological Association.

Horton, H.L., & Levitt, P. (1988). A unique membrane protein is expressed on early developing limbic system axons and cortical targets. *Journal of Neuroscience, 8*, 4653–4661.

Horton, J.C. (1984). Cytochrome oxidase patches: A new cyto-architectonic feature of monkey visual cortex. *Philosophical Transactions of the Royal Society London. Series B. Biological Sciences, 304*, 199–253.

Hosoya, Y., Sugiura, N. Okado., Loewy, A.D., & Kohno, K. (1991). Descending input from the hypothalamic paraventricular nucleus to sympathetic preganglionic neurons in the rat *Experimental Brain Research, 85*, 10–20.

Hothersall, J., Greenbaum, A., & McLean, P. (1982). The functional significance of the pentose phosphate pathway in synaptosomes: Protection against peroxidative damage by catecholamines and oxidants. *Journal of Neurochemistry, 39*, 1325–1332.

House, J.S. (1981). *Work, stress, and social support*. Reading, MA: Addison-Wesley.

Houstek, J., Kopecky, J., Baudysova, M., Janikova, D., Pavelka, S., & Klement, P. (1990). Differentiation of brown adipose tissue and biogenesis of thermogenic mitochondria in situ and in cell culture. *Biochimica et Biophysica Acta, 1018*, 243–247.

Howard, E. (1973). DNA content of rodent brains during brain maturation and aging, and autoradiography of postnatal synthesis in monkey brain. *Progress in Brain Research, 40*, 91–113.

Howard, E., & Benjamins, J.A. (1975). DNA, ganglioside and sulfatide in brains of rats given corticosterone in infancy, with an estimate of cell loss during development. *Brain Research, 92*, 73–87.

Howe, J.S., Landis, K.R., & Umberson, D. (1988). Social relationships and health. *Science, 241*, 540–545.

Hruska, R., & Silbergeld, E.K. (1980). Increased dopamine receptor sensitivity after estrogen treatment using the rat rotation model. *Science, 208*, 1466–1468.

Huang, Q., Zhou, D., Chase, K., Gusella, J.F., Aronin, N., & DiFiglia, M. (1992). Immunohistochemical localization of the D1 dopamine receptor in rat brain reveals its axonal transport, pre- and postsynaptic localization, and prevalence in the basal ganglia, limbic system, and thalamic reticular nucleus. *Proceedings of the National Academy of Sciences of the United States of America, 89*, 11988–11992.

Hubel, D. H., & Wiesel, T. N. (1970). The period of susceptibility to the physiological effects of unilateral eye closure in kittens. *Journal of Physiology* (London), *206*, 419–436.

Humphrey, A.L., & Hendrickson, A.E. (1983). Background and stimulus induced patterns of high metabolic activity in the visual cortex (area 17) of the squirrel and macaque monkey. *Journal of Neuroscience, 3*, 345–355.

Humphrey, K., Tees, R.C., & Werker, J. (1979). Auditory-visual integration of temporal relations in infants. *Canadian Journal of Psychology, 33*, 347–352.

Hunt, J. McV. (1965a). Intrinsic motivation and its role in development. In D. Levine (Ed.), *Nebraska symposium on motivation*. Lincoln: University of Nebraska Press.

Hunt, J.McV. (1965b). Traditional personality theory in light of recent evidence. *American Scientist, 53*, 80–96.

Huntley, G.W., Benson, D.L., Jones, E.G., & Isackson, P.J. (1992). Developmental expression of brain derived neurotrophic factor mRNA by neurons of fetal and adult monkey prefrontal cortex. *Developmental Brain Research, 70*, 53–63.

Huston, J.P. (1982). Searching for the neural mechanism of reinforcement (of "stamping-in"). In B.G. Hoebel & D. Novin (Eds.)., *The neural basis of feeding and reward* (pp. 75–83). Brunswick, ME: Haer Institute for Electrophysiological Research.

Huttenlocher, P.R. (1979). Synaptic density in human frontal cortex—developmental changes and effects of aging. *Brain Research, 163*, 195–205.

Huttenlocher, P.R. (1990). Morphometric study of human cerebral cortex development. *Neuropsychologia, 28*, 517–527.

Huttenlocher, P.R., & de Courten, C. (1987). The development of synapses in striate cortex of man. *Human Neurobiology, 6*, 1–9.

Huttenlocher, P.R., de Courten, C., Garey, L.J., & Van der Loos, H. (1982). Synaptogenesis in human visual cortex: Evidence for synapse elimination in normal development. *Neuroscience Letters, 33*, 247–252.

Hyden, H. (1943). Protein metabolism in the nerve cell during growth and function. *Acta Physiologica Scandinavica, 6*, (Supplement 17), 1–136.

Hyman, C., Hofer, M., Barde, Y-A., Juhasz, M., Yancopoulos, R.M., Squinto, S.P., & Lindsay, R.M. (1991). BDNF is a neurotrophic factor for dopaminergic neurons of the substantia nigra. *Nature (London), 350*, 230–232.

Hyson, M.C., & Izard, C.E. (1985). Continuities and changes in emotion expressions during brief separation at 13 and 18 months. *Developmental Psychology, 21*, 1165–1170.

Iadecola, C. (1993). Regulation of the cerebral microcirculation during neural activity: Is nitric oxide the missing link? *Trends in Neuroscience, 16*, 206–214.

Iadecola, C., Lacombe, P.M., Underwood, M.D., Ishitsuka, T., & Reis, D.J. (1987). Role of adrenal catecholamines in cerebrovasodilation evoked from brain stem. *American Journal of Physiology, 252*, H1183-H1191.

Ibrahim, M.Z. (1975). Glycogen and its related enzymes of metabolism in the central nervous system. *Advances in Anatomical and Embryological Cell Biology, 52*, 1–85.

Immelman, K., & Suomi, S.J. (1981). Sensitive phases in development. In K. Immelman, G.W. Barlow, L. Petrinovich, & M. Main (Eds.), *Behavioral development. The Bielefeld interdisciplinary project* (pp. 395–431). Cambridge, England: Cambridge University Press.

Ingvar, D.H. (1979). "Hyperfrontal" distribution of the cerebral grey matter flow in resting wakefulness; on the functional anatomy of the conscious state. *Acta Neurolologica Scandinavica, 60*, 12–25.

Ingvar, D.H. (1983). Serial aspects of language and speech related to prefrontal cortical activity: A selective review. *Human Neurobiology, 2*, 177–189.

Ingvar, D.H. (1985). "Memory of the future": An essay on the temporal organization of conscious awareness. *Human Neurobiology, 4*, 127–136.

Ingvar, D.H., & Schwartz, M.S. (1974). Blood flow patterns induced in the dominant hemisphere by speech and reading. *Brain, 97*, 273–288.

Inhelder, B. (1971). The sensory-motor origins of knowledge. In D.N. Walcher & D.L. Peters (Eds.), *The development of self-regulatory mechanisms* (pp. 141–155). New York: Academic Press.

Innis, S.M. (1991). Essential fatty acids in growth and development. *Progress in Lipid Research, 30*, 39–103.

Insel, T.R., Miller, L., & Gelhard, R.E. (1990). The ontogeny of excitatory amino acid in the rat forebrain. I. N-Methyl-D aspartate and quisqualate receptors. *Neuroscience, 35*, 31–43.

Intraub, H., & Richardson, M. (1989). Wide-angle memories of close-up scenes. *Journal of Experimental Psychology: Learning, Memory, and Cognition, 15*, 179–187.

Irwin, M., Daniels, M., Smith, T.L., Bloom, E., & Weiner, H. (1987). Impaired natural killer cell activity during bereavement. *Brain Behavior and Immunity, 1*, 98–104.

Irwin, M., Daniels, M., & Weiner, H. (1987). Immune and neuroendocrine changes during bereavement. *Psychiatric Clinics of North America, 10*, 449–465.

Irwin, M., Hauger, R.L., Brown, M., & Britton, K.T. (1988). CRF activates autonomic nervous system and reduces natural killer cytotoxicity. *American Journal of Physiology, 255*, R744–R747.

Isen, A.M. (1990). The influence of positive and negative affect in cognitive organization: Some implications for development. In N.L. Stein, B. Leventhal, & T. Trabasco (Eds.), *Psychological and biological approaches to emotion*. Hillsdale, NJ: Lawrence Erlbaum Associates.

Iversen, S.D. (1977). Brain dopamine systems and behavior. In L.L. Iversen, S.D. Iversen, & S.H. Snyder (Eds.), *Drugs, neurotransmitters and behavior: Vol. 8. Handbook of psychopharmacology*. New York: Plenum Press.

Ixart, G., Alonso, G., Szafarczyk, A., Malaval, F., Nouguier-Soule, J., & Assenmacher, I. (1982). Adrenocorticotropic regulations after bilateral lesions of the paraventricular or supraoptic nuclei in Brattleboro rats. *Neuroendocrinology, 35*, 270–276.

Izard, C. E. (1971). *The face of emotion*. New York: Appleton-Century-Crofts.

Izard, C.E. (1977). *Human emotions*. New York: Plenum.Press.

Izard, C.E. (1978). On the ontogenesis of emotions and emotion-cognition relationships in infancy. In M. Lewis & L. Rosenblum (Eds.), *The development of affect* (pp. 389–413). New York: Plenum Press.

Izard, C.E. (1979). *The maximally discriminative facial movement coding system (max)*. New York: Plenum Press.

Izard, C.E. (1990). Facial expressions and the regulation of emotions. *Journal of Personality and Social Psychology, 58*, 487–498.

Izard, C.E. (1991). *The psychology of emotions*. New York: Plenum Press.

Izard, C.E., & Haynes, O.M. (1988). On the form and universality of the contempt expression: A challenge to Ekman and Friesen's claim of discovery. *Motivation and Emotion, 12*, 1–16.

Izard, C.E., Hembree, E.A., & Huebner, R.R. (1987). Infants' emotion expressions to acute pain: Developmental change and stability of individual differences. *Developmental Psychology, 23*, 105–113.

Izard, C.E., Porges, S.W., Simons, R.F., Haynes, O.M., Hyde, C., Parisi, M., & Cohen, B. (1991). Infant cardiac activity: Developmental changes and relations with attachment. *Developmental Psychology 27*, 432–439.

Izard, C.E., & Schwartz, G.M. (1986). Patterns of emotion in depression. In M. Rutter, C.E. Izard, & P.B. Read (Eds.), *Depression in young people: Developmental and clinical perspectives* (pp. 33–70). New York: Guilford Press.

Jackson, E.A. (1991). Controls of dynamic flows with attractors. *Physical Review A, 44*, 4839–4853.

Jackson, J. Hughlings (1879). On affections of speech from diseases of the brain. *Brain, 2*, 203–222.

Jackson, J. Hughlings (1931). *Selected writings of John Hughlings Jackson, Vols. I and II*. London: Hodder and Stoughton.

Jacobs, B.J., & Fornal, C.A. (1993). 5HT and motor control: A hypothesis. *Trends in Neurosciences, 16*, 346–352.

Jacobson, C.D., Shryne, J.E., Shapiro, F., & Gorski, R.A. (1980). Ontogeny of the sexually dimorphic nucleus of the preoptic area. *Journal of Comparative Neurology, 193*, 541–548.

Jacobson, E. (1954). The self and the object world. *Psychoanalytic Study of the Child, 9*, 75–127.

Jacobson, E. (1964). *The self and the object world*. New York: International Universities Press.

Jacobson, E. (1971). *Depression*. New York: International Universities Press.

Jacobson, J. G. (1983). The structural theory and the representational world: Developmental and biological considerations. *Psychoanalytic Quarterly, 52*, 543–563.

Jacobson, M. (1978). *Developmental neurobiology* (2nd ed). New York: Plenum Press.

Jaenicke, C. (1987). Kohut's concept of cure. *Psychoanalytic Review, 74*, 537–548.

James, H. (1960). Imprinting with visual flicker: Evidence for a critical period. *Canadian Journal of Psychology, 14*, 13–20.

James, W. (1922). What is an emotion? In K. Dunlap (Ed.), *The emotions* (pp. 11–30). Baltimore: Williams and Wilkins. (Original work published 1884).

Jankovic, B.D., & Isakovic, K. (1973). Neuroendocrine correlates of immune response. *International Archives of Allergy and Applied Immunology, 45*, 360–384.

Jeliffe, S. (1937). Sigmund Freud as a neurologist: Some notes on his earlier neurobiological and clinical neurological studies. *Journal of Nervous and Mental Disease, 85*, 696–711.

Jensen, J.R., Lynch, G., & Baudry, M. (1989). Allosteric activation of brain mitochondrial Ca^{2+} uptake by spermine and by Ca^{2+}: Developmental changes. *Journal of Neurochemistry, 53*, 1173–1181.

Jindal, S., Dudani, A.K., Singh, B., Harley, C.B., & Gupta, R.S. (1989). Primary structure of a human mitochondrial protein homologous to the bacterial and plant chaperonins and to the 65-kilodalton mycobacterial antigen. *Molecular and Cellular Biology, 9*, 2279–2283.

Joanette, Y., Goulet, P., & Hannequin, D. (1990). *Right hemisphere and verbal communication*. New York: Springer.

Joffe, L.S., Vaughn, B.E., Barglow, P., & Benveniste, R. (1985). Biobehavioral antecedents in the development of infant-mother attachment. In M. Reite & T. Field (Eds.), *The psychobiology of attachment and separation* (pp. 323–349). Orlando, FL: Academic Press.

Joffe, W.G., & Sandler, J. (1967). Some conceptual problems involved in the consideration of disorders of narcissism. *Journal of Child Psychotherapy, 2*, 56–66.

Johanson, A., Smith, G., Risberg, J., Silfverskiold, P. et al. (1992). Left orbital frontal activation in pathological anxiety. *Anxiety, Stress, and Coping: An International Journal, 5*, 313–328.

Johanson, C.E. (1989). Ontogeny and phylogeny of the blood-brain barrier. In E.A. Neuwelt (Ed.), *Implications of the blood-brain barrier and its manipulation* (pp. 157–198). New York: Plenum.

John, E.R. (1962). Some speculations on the psychophysiology of the mind. In J. M. Scher (Ed.), *Theories of the mind* (pp. 80–121). New York: The Free Press of Glencoe.

Johnsen, B.H., & Hugdahl, K. (1991). Hemispheric asymmetry in conditioning to facial emotional expressions. *Psychophysiology, 28*, 154–162.

Johnsen, B.H., & Hugdahl, K. (1993). Right hemisphere representation of autonomic conditioning to facial emotional expressions. *Psychophysiology, 30*, 274–278.

Johnson, H.M., Torres, B.A., Smith, E.M., Dion, L.D., & Blalock, J.E. (1984). Regulation of lymphokine (interferon gamma) production by corticotropin. *Journal of Immunology, 132*, 246–250.

Johnson, M.H., Bolhuis, J.J., and Horn, G. (1985). Interaction between acquired preferences and developing predispositions during imprinting. *Animal Behavior, 33*, 1000–1006.

Johnson, M.K., & Multhaup, K.S. (1992). Emotion and MEM. In S-A. Christianson (Ed.), *The handbook of emotion and memory: Research and theory* (pp. 33–66). Hillsdale NJ: Lawrence Erlbaum Associates.

Johnson, S.M. (1987). *Humanizing the narcissistic style*. New York: W.W. Norton.

Johnson, S.W., Seutin, V., & North, R.A. (1992). Burst firing in dopamine neurons induced by *N*-methyl-D-aspartate: Role of electrogenic sodium pump. *Science, 258*, 665–667.

Johnson, T.N., Rosvold, H.E., Galkin, T.W., & Goldman, P.S. (1976). Postnatal maturation of subcortical projections from the prefrontal cortex in the rhesus monkey. *Journal of Comparative Neurology, 166*, 427–444.

Johnston, M.V. (1985). Neurotransmitters. In R.C. Wiggins, D.W. McCandless, & S.J. Enna (Eds.), *Developmental neurochemistry* (pp. 193–224). Austin: University of Texas Press.

Jones, B.E., Halaris, A.E., & Freedman, D.X. (1979). Innervation of forebrain regions by medullary noradrenaline neurons, a biochemical study in cats with central tegmental tract lesions. *Neuroscience Letters, 10*, 251–258.

Jones, D.G., & Smith, B.J. (1980). The hippocampus and its response to differential environments. *Progress in Neurobiology, 15,* 19–69.

Jones, D.P., Lash, L.H. (1993). Introduction. Criteria for assessing normal and abnormal mitochondrial function. In L.H. Lash & D.P. Jones (Eds.), *Mitochondrial dysfunction* (pp. 1–7). San Diego, CA: Academic Press.

Jones, E. (1948). Anal-erotic character traits. In E. Jones (Ed.), *Papers on psychoanalysis* (pp. 413–437). London: Bailliers, Tindall, & Cox.

Jones, E.G., & Powell, T.P.S. (1970). An anatomical study of the converging sensory pathways within the cerebral cortex of the monkey. *Brain, 93,* 793–820.

Jones, M.T., Gilhan, M.B., Greenstein, B.O., Abraham, R.R., Dornhorst, A., Beckford, U., Holmes, M.C., Lin, J. H., Torrellas, A., Bowery, N.G., Direnzo, G., & Knowles, F. (1982). The role of neurotransmitters and glucocorticoid hormones in the control of adrenocorticotrophin secretion. In M. Motta, M. Zanisi, & F. Piva (Eds.), *Pituitary hormones and related peptides* (pp. 281–303). London: Academic Press.

Jones, R.W. (1973). *Principles of biologic regulation: An introduction to feedback systems.* New York: Academic Press.

Jones, S.S., Collins, K., & Hong, H.-W. (1991). An audience effect on smile production in 10-month-old infants. *Psychological Science, 2,* 45–49.

Jones-Gotman, M., & Zatorre, R.J. (1993). Odor recognition memory in humans: Role of right temporal and orbitofrontal regions. *Brain and Cognition, 22,* 182–198.

Jonides, J., Smith, E.E., Koeppe, R.A., Awh, E., Minoshima, S., & Mintum, M.A. (1993). Spatial working memory in humans revealed by PET. *Nature (London), 363,* 623–625.

Jonsson, G., & Kasamatsu, T. (1983). Maturation of monoamine neurotransmitters and receptors in cat occipital cortex during postnatal critical period. *Experimental Brain Research, 50,* 49–458.

Joo, F., & Toth, I. (1975). Brain adenylate cyclase: Its common occurrence in the capillaries and astrocytes. *Naturwissenschaften, 62,* 397–398.

Jork, R., Lossner, B., & Matthies, H. (1982). Dopamine and glycoprotein synthesis in rat hippocampus. In C.A. Marsan & H. Matthies (Eds.), *IBRO monograph series, Vol. 9: Neuronal plasticity and memory formation* (pp. 359–365). New York: Raven Press.

Joseph, R. (1982). The neuropsychology of development: Hemispheric laterality, limbic language, and the origin of thought. *Journal of Clinical Psychology, 38,* 4–33.

Joseph, R. (1988). The right cerebral hemisphere. Emotion, music, visual-spatial skills, body-image, dreams, and awareness. *Journal of Clinical Psychology, 44,* 630–673.

Joseph, R. (1992). *The right brain and the unconscious: Discovering the stranger within.* New York: Plenum Press.

Josephs, L. (1989). Self psychology and the analysis of the superego. *Psychoanalytic Psychology, 6,* 73–86.

Jouandet, M., & Gazzaniga, M.S. (1979). The frontal lobes. In M.S. Gazzaniga (Ed.), *Handbook of behavioral neurobiology, Vol. 2* (pp. 25–59). New York: Plenum Press.

Joyce, E.M., & Iversen, S.D. (1979). The effect of morphine applied locally to mesencephalic dopamine cell bodies on spontaneous motor activity in the rat. *Neuroscience Letters, 14,* 207–212.

Jung, C.G. (1943). *Two essays on analytical psychology.* Cleveland and New York: Meridian Books. (Reprinted 1945).

Juraska, J.M. (1984). Sex differences in developmental plasticity in the visual cortex and hippocampal dentate gyrus. *Progress in Brain Research, 61,* 205–214.

Juraska, J.M. (1986). Sex differences in developmental plasticity of behavior and the brain. In W.T. Greenough & J.M. Juraska (Eds.), *Developmental neuropsychobiology* (pp.409–422). Orlando, FL: Academic Press.

Kaada, B.R. (1960). Cingulate, posterior orbital, anterior insular and temporal pole cortex. In H.W. Magoun (Ed.), *Neurophysiology* (pp. 1345–1372). Baltimore: Waverly Press.

Kaada, B.R., Pribram, K.H., & Epstein, J. (1949). Respiratory and vascular responses in monkeys from temporal pole, insular orbital surface, and cingulate gyrus. A preliminary report. *Journal of Neurophysiology, 12,* 347–356.

Kaas, J.H. (1987). The organization of neocortex in mammals: Implications for theories of brain function. *Annual Review of Psychology, 38,* 129–151.

Kagan, J. (1971). *Change and continuity in infancy.* New York: Wiley.

Kagan, J. (1976). Emergent themes in human development *American Scientist, 64,* 186–196.

Kagan, J. (1979). The form of early development. *Archives of General Psychiatry, 36,* 1047–1054.

Kagan, J. (1981). *The second year: The emergence of self-awareness.* Cambridge, MA: Harvard University Press.

Kagan, J. (1982). Heart rate and heart rate variability as signs of a temperamental dimension in infants. In C.E. Izard (Ed.), *Measuring emotions in infants and children* (pp. 38–66). Cambridge, MA: Cambridge University Press.

Kagan, J. (1986). Presuppositions in developmental inquiry. In L. Cirillo & S. Wapner (Eds.), *Value presuppositions in theories of human development* (pp. 63–78). Hillsdale, NJ: Lawrence Erlbaum Associates.

Kagan, J., Reznick, J. S., & Snidman, N. (1987). Temperamental variation in response to the unfamiliar. In N.A. Krasnegor, E.M. Blass, M.A. Hofer, & W.P. Smotherman (Eds.), *Perinatal development: A psychobiological perspective* (pp. 421–440). Orlando, FL: Academic Press.

Kagan, J., Reznick, J. S., & Snidman, N. (1990). The temperamental qualities of inhibition and lack of inhibition. In M. Lewis & S.M. Miler (Eds.), *Handbook of developmental psychopathology* (pp. 219–226). New York: Plenum Press.

Kalaria, R.N., & Harik, S.I. (1987). Blood-brain barrier monoamine oxidase: Enzyme characterization in cerebral microvessels and other tissues from six mammalian species, including human. *Journal of Neurochemistry, 49,* 856–864.

Kalaria, R.N., Stockmeiser, C.A., & Harik, S.I. (1989). Brain microvessels are innervated by locus ceruleus noradrenergic neurons. *Neuroscience Letters, 97,* 203–208.

Kalia, M., Fuxe, K., & Goldstein, M. (1985). Rat medulla oblongata. II. Dopaminergic, noradrenergic (A1 and A2) and adrenergic neurons, nerve fibers, and presumptive terminal processes. *Journal of Comparative Neurology, 233,* 308–332.

Kalia, M., & Mesulam, M.-M. (1980). Brain stem projections of sensory and motor components of the vagus complex in the cat: II. Laryngeal, tracheobronchial, pulmonary, cardiac, and gastrointestinal branches. *Journal of Comparative Neurology, 193,* 467–508.

Kalia, M., Schweitzer, P., Champagnat, J., & Denavit-Saubie, M. (1993). Two distinct phases characterize maturation of neurons in the nucleus of the tractus solitarius during early development: Morphological and electrophysiological evidence. *Journal of Comparative Neurology, 327,* 37–47.

Kalin, N.H., & Carnes, M. (1984). Biological correlates of attachment bond disruption in human and nonhuman primates. *Progress in Neuropsychopharmacological and Biological Psychiatry, 8,* 459–469.

Kalivas, P.W., Duffy, P., & Latimer, L.G. (1987). Neurochemical and behavioral effects of corticotropin-releasing factor in the ventral tegmental area of the rat. *Journal of Pharmacology and Experimental Therapeutics, 242,* 757–763.

Kalivas, P.W., Duffy, P., & Barrow, J. (1989). Regulation of the mesocorticolimbic dopamine system by glutamic acid receptor subtypes. *Journal of Pharmacology and Experimental Therapeutics, 251,* 378–387.

Kalsbeek, A., Buijs, R.M., Hofman, M.A., Matthijssen, M.A.H., Pool, C.W., & Uylings, H.B.M. (1987). Effects of neonatal thermal lesioning of the mesocortical dopaminergic projection on the development of the rat prefrontal cortex. *Developmental Brain Research, 32,* 123–132.

Kalsbeek, A., Voorn, P., Buijs, R.M., Pool, C.W., & Uylings, H.B.M. (1988). Development of the dopaminergic innervation in the prefrontal cortex of the rat. *Journal of Comparative Neurology, 269*, 58–72.

Kandel, E.R., & Schwartz, J. H. (1985.). *Principles of neural science* (2nd ed.). New York: Elsevier.

Kane, D.J., Sarafian, T.A., Anton, R., Hahn, H., Gralla, E.B., Selverstone Valentine, J., Örd, T., & Bredesen, D.E. (1993). Bcl-2 inhibition of cell death: decreased generation of reactive oxygen species. *Science, 262*, 1274–1277.

Kano, Y., Maeda, S., & Sugiyama, T. (1976). The location of ribosomal cistrons (rDNA) in chromosomes of the rat. *Chromosoma, 55*, 37–42.

Kantrowitz, J. L., Katz, A.L., Greenman, D.A., Morris, H., Paolitto, F., Sashin, J., & Solomon, L. (1989). The patient-analyst match and the outcome of psychoanalysis: A pilot study. *Journal of the American Psychoanalytic Association, 37*, 893–919.

Kaplan, E.L., & Kaplan, G.A. (1970). The prelinguistic child. In J. Eliot (Ed.), *Human development and cognitive processes*. New York: Holt, Rinehart and Winston

Kaplan, H.A., & Ford, D.H. (1966). *The brain vascular system*. Amsterdam: Elsevier.

Karoly, P. (1993). Mechanisms of self-regulation: A systems view. *Annual Review of Psychology, 44*, 23–52.

Kashiwayanagi, M., Miyake, M., & Kurihara, K. (1983). Voltage-dependent Ca^{2+} channel and Na^+ channel in frog taste cells. *American Journal of Physiology, 244*, C82-C88.

Kathol, R.G., Jaeckle, R.S., Lopez, J. F., & Meller, W.H. (1989). Pathophysiology of HPA axis abnormalities in patients with major depression: An update. *American Journal of Psychiatry, 146*, 311–317.

Kato, T., & Lowry, O.H. (1973). Enzymes of energy-converting enzymes in individual mammalian nerve cell bodies. *Journal of Neurochemistry, 20*, 151–163.

Katz, D.M., & Karten, H.J. (1979). The discrete anatomical localization of vagal aortic afferents within a catecholamine containing cell group in the nucleus tractus solitarius. *Brain Research, 171*, 187–195.

Katz, R.J. (1988). Endorphins, exploration and activity. In R.J. Rodgers & S.J. Cooper (Eds.), *Endorphins, opiates and behavioral processes* (pp. 249–267). Chichester, England: Wiley.

Kaufman, G. (1974). The meaning of shame: Toward a self-affirming identity. *Journal of Counseling Psychology, 21*, 568–574.

Kaufman, G. (1989). *The psychology of shame*. New York: Springer.

Kaufman, G. (1992). *Shame: The power of caring*. Boston: Schenkman

Kaufman, I.C., & Rosenblum, L.A. (1967). The reaction to separation in infant monkeys: Anaclitic depression and conservation-withdrawal. *Psychosomatic Medicine, 40*, 649–675.

Kaufman, I.C., & Rosenblum, L.A. (1969). Effects of separation from mother on the emotional behavior of infant monkeys, *Annals of the New York Academy of Sciences, 159*, 681–695.

Kavanau, J. L. (1990). Conservative behavioural evolution, the neural substrate. *Animal Behavior, 39*, 758–767.

Kaye, K. (1982). *The mental and social life of babies: How parents create persons*. Chicago: The University of Chicago Press.

Kebabian, J., W. & Caine, D.B. (1978). Multiple receptors for dopamine. *Nature (London), 277*, 93–96.

Keck, P.J., Hauser, S.D., Krivi, G., Sanzo, K., Warren, T., Feder, J., & Connolly, D.T. (1989). Vascular permeability factor, an endothelial cell mitogen related to PDGF. *Science, 246*, 1309–1312.

Kehrer, P.H., Gaillard, R.C., Dayer, J.-M., & Muller, A.F. (1986). Human interleukin 1 beta stimulates ACTH release from rat pituitary cells in a cAMP and prostaglandin E2 independent-manner (Abstract). *International Congress of Neuroendocrinoly* (p. 107). San Francisco.

Kellaway, P. (1989). Introduction to plasticity and sensitive periods. In P. Kellaway & J.L. Noebels (Eds.), *Problems and concepts in developmental neurophysiology* (pp. 3–28). Baltimore: Johns Hopkins University Press.

Keller, S.E., Stein, M., Camerino, S.J., Schleifer, S.J., & Sherman, J. (1980). Suppression of lymphocyte stimulation by anterior hypothalamic lesions in guinea pigs. *Cellular Immunology*, *52*, 334–340.

Kelley, A.E., & Stinus, L. (1984). Neuroanatomical and neurochemical substrates of affective behavior. In N.A. Fox & R.J. Davidson (Eds.), *The psychobiology of affective development*. Hillsdale NJ: Lawrence Erlbaum Associates.

Kellogg, E.W., III & Fridovich, I. (1976). Superoxide dismutase in the rat and mouse as a function of age and longevity. *Journal of Gerontology*, *31*, 405–408.

Kemp, A.A., & Haude, R.H. (1979). Visual field-cerebral hemisphere differences in perception of visual nonverbal stimuli. *Perceptual and Motor Skills*, *48*, 1127–1131.

Kendell, R.E. (1975). The concept of disease and its implications for psychiatry. *British Journal of Psychiatry*, *127*, 66–81.

Kendler, K.S., & Eaves, L.S. (1986). Models for the joint effect of genotype and environment on liability to psychiatric illness. *American Journal of Psychiatry*, *143*, 279–289.

Kennard, M.A. (1945). Focal autonomic representation in the cortex and its relation to sham rage. *Journal of Neuropathology and Experimental Neurology*, *4*, 295–304.

Kennedy, C., Grave, G.D. Jehle, J. W., & Sokoloff, L. (1972). Changes in blood flow in the component structures of the dog brain during postnatal maturation. *Journal of Neurochemistry*, *19*, 2423–2433.

Kernberg, O. (1975). *Borderline conditions and pathological narcissism*. New York: Jason Aronson.

Kernberg, O. (1976). *Object relations and clinical psychoanalysis*. New York: Jason Aronson.

Kernberg, O. (1980). *Internal world and external reality*. New York: Jason Aronson.

Kernberg, O. (1984). *Severe personality disorders: Psychotherapeutic strategies*. New Haven, CT: Yale University Press.

Kernberg, O. (1988). Object relations theory in clinical practice. *Psychoanalytic Quarterly, 57*, 481–504.

Kernberg, O. (1993). The current status of psychoanaysis. *Journal of the American Psychoanalytic Association, 41*, 45–62.

Kernberg, P. (1984). The psychological assessment of children with borderline personality organization. Presented to the American Psychoanalytic Association, New York.

Kertesz, A., Polk, M., Black, S.E., & Howell, J. (1992). Anatomical asymmetries and functional laterality. *Brain*, *115*, 589–605.

Kesner, R.P. (1986). Neurobiological views of memory. In J. L Martinez & R.P. Kesner (Eds.), *Learning and memory. A biological view* (pp. 399–438). New York: Academic Press.

Kesner, R.P., & Conner, H.S. (1973). Effects of electrical stimulation of limbic system and midbrain reticular formation upon short and long term memory. *Physiology and Behavior*, *9*, 271–279.

Kestenberg, J. (1985). The flow of empathy and trust between mother and child. In E.J. Anthony & G.H. Pollack (Eds.), *Parental influences in health and disease* (pp. 137–163). Boston, MA: Little Brown.

Kety, S.S. (1961). Sleep and the energy metabolism of the brain. In G.E.W. Wolstenholme & M. O'Connor (Eds.), *The nature of sleep* (pp. 375–385). London: Churchill.

Khantzian, E. (1978). The ego, the self and opiate addiction. *International Review of Psycho-Analysis*, *5*, 189–198.

Khantzian, E.J., & Wilson, A. (1993). Substance abuse, repetition, and the nature of addictive suffering. In A. Wilson & J.E. Gedo (Eds.), *Hierarchical concepts in psychoanalysis* (pp. 263–283). New York: Guilford Press.

Kimberg, D.V., Loud, A.V., & Wiener, A. 1968). Cortisone-induced alterations in mitochondrial function and structure. *Journal of Cell Biology*, *37*, 63–76.

Kimura, D. (1992). Sex differences in the brain. *Scientific American*, *267*, 119–125.

Kimura, H., Naito, K., Nakagawa, K., & Kuriyama, K. (1974). Activation of hexose monophosphate pathway in brain by electrical stimulation in vitro. *Journal of Neurochemistry*, *23*, 79–84.

King, R. (1985). Motivationl diversity and mesolimbic dopamine: An hypothesis concerning temperament. In R. Plutchik & H. Kellerman (Eds.), *Emotion: Theory, research and experience, Vol. 3*. New York: Academic Press.

King, V., Corwin, J. V., & Reep, R.L. (1989). Production and characterization of neglect in rats with unilateral lesions of ventrolateral orbital cortex. *Experimental Neurology, 105*, 287–299.

Kinney, H.C., Brody, B.A., Kloman, A.S., & Gilles, F.H. (1988). Sequence of central nervous system myelination in human infancy. II. Patterns of myelination in autopsied infants. *Journal of Neuropathology and Experimental Neurology, 47*, 217–234.

Kinnula, V.L., & Hassinen, I. (1977). Effect of hypoxia on mitochondrial mass and cytochrome concentrations in rat heart and liver during postnatal development. *Acta Physiologica Scandinavica, 99*, 462–466.

Kinouchi, H., Sharp, F.R., Hill, M.P., Koistinaho, J., Sagar, S.M., & Chan, P.H. (1993). Induction of 70-kDa heat shock protein and hsp70 mRNA following transient focal cerebral ischemia in the rat. *Journal of Cerebral Blood Flow and Metabolism, 13*, 105–113.

Kinsbourne, M., & Bemporad, B. (1984). Lateralization of emotion: A model and the evidence. In N.A. Fox & R.J. Davidson (Eds.), *The psychobiology of affective development* (pp. 259–291). Hillsdale, NJ: Lawrence Erlbaum Associates.

Kinston, W. (1983). A theoretical context for shame. *International Journal of Psycho-Analysis, 64*, 213–226.

Kita, H., & Oomura, Y. (1981). Reciprocal connections between the lateral hypothalamus and the frontal cortex in the rat. *Brain Research, 213*, 1–16.

Klaus, M.H., & Kennell, J. H. (1976). *Maternal-infant bonding: The impact of early separation or loss on family development*. St. Louis: C.V. Mosby.

Klee, C.B., & Sokoloff, L. (1964). Mitochondrial differences in mature and immature brain. Influence on rate of amino acid incorporation into protein and responses to thyroxine. *Journal of Neurochemistry, 11*, 709–716.

Klee, C.B., & Sokoloff, L. (1967). Changes in D (-)—beta-hydroxybutyric dehydrogenase activity during brain maturation in the rat. *Journal of Biological Chemistry, 242*, 3880–3883.

Kleeman, J. A. (1966). Genital self-discovery during a boy's second year. *Psychoanalytic Study of the Child, 21*, 358–392.

Klein, D.F., Gittelman, R., Quitkin, F., & Rifkin, A. (1980). *Diagnosis and drug treatment of psychiatric disorders: Adults and children* (2nd ed.). Baltimore: Williams & Wilkins.

Klein, G.S. (1976). *Psychoanalytic theory: An exploration of essentials*. New York: International Universities Press.

Klein, M. (1946). Notes on some schizoid mechanisms. *International Journal of Psycho-Analysis, 27*, 99–110.

Klein, M. (1957). *Envy and gratitude*. London: Tavistock.

Kline, P. (1981). *Fact and fantasy in Freudian theory*. London: Methuen.

Klinnert, M.D. (1984). The regulation of infant behavior by maternal face expression. *Infant Behavior and Development, 7*, 447–465.

Klonoff, P.S., & Lage, G.A. (1991). Narcissistic injury in patients with traumatic brain injury. *Journal of Head Trauma Rehabilitation, 6*, 11–21.

Knapp, A.G., Schmidt, K.F., & Dowling, J. E. (1990). Dopamine modulates the kinetics of ion channels gated by excitatory amino acids in retinal horizontal cells. *Proceedings of the National Academy of Sciences of the United States of America, 87*, 767–771.

Knapp, P.H. (1967). Purging and curbing: An inquiry into disgust, satiety and shame. *Journal of Nervous and Mental Disease, 144*, 514–544.

Knapp, P.H. (1980). Free association as a biopsychosocial probe. *Psychosomatic Medicine, 42*, 197–219.

Knapp, P.H. (1983). Core processes in the organization of emotions. In M.B. Cantor & M.L. Glucksman (Eds.), *Affect: Psychoanalytic theory and practice*. New York: Wiley.

Knapp, P.H. (1992). Emotion and the psychoanalytic encounter. In T. Shapiro & R.N. Emde (Eds.), *Affect: psychoanalytic perspectives* (pp. 239–264). Madison, CT: International Universities Press.

Kobak, R.R., & Sceery, A. (1988). Attachment in late adolescence: Working models, affect regulation, and representations of self and others. *Child Development, 59*, 135–146.

Koenig, H., Goldstone, A., & Lu, C.Y. (1983). Polyamines regulate calcium fluxes in a rapid plasma membrane response. *Nature (London)*, *305*, 530–534.

Koenig, H.L., di Giamberardino, L., & Bennett, G. (1973). Renewal of proteins and glycoproteins of synaptic constituents by means of axonal transport. *Brain Research*, *62*, 413–417.

Koenigsberg, H.W., & Handley, R. (1986). Expressed emotion: From predictive index to clinical construct. *American Journal of Psychiatry*, *143*, 1361–1373.

Kohlberg, L. (1963). Moral development and identification. In H.W. Stevenson (Ed.), *Child psychology, NSSE yearbook*, Pt. 1. Chicago: University of Chicago Press.

Kohlberg, L. (1976). Moral stages and moralization: The cognitive-developmental approach. In T. Lichona (Ed.), *Moral development and behavior: Theory, research, and social issues*. New York: Holt, Rinehart, and Winston.

Kohlberg, L. & Diessner, R. (1991). A cognitive-developmental approach to moral attachment. In J. L. Gewirtz & W. M. Kurtines (Eds.), *Intersections with attachment* (pp. 229–246). Hillsdale NJ: Lawrence Erlbaum Associates.

Kohle, S., & Vannucci, R. (1977). Glycogen metabolism in fetal and postnatal rat brain: influence at birth. *Journal of Neurochemistry*, *28*, 441–443.

Kohsaka, S., Takamatsu, K., Aoki, E., & Tsukada, Y. (1979). Metabolic mapping of chick brain after imprinting using 2—[^{13}C] deoxyglucose technique. *Brain Research*, *172*, 539–544.

Kohut, H. (1968). The psychoanalytic treatment of narcissistic personality disorders. *Psychoanalytic Study of the Child*, *28*, 86–113.

Kohut, H. (1971). *The analysis of the self*. New York: International Universities Press.

Kohut, H. (November, 1975). Discussion of *"Split brains and psychoanalysis"* by K.D. Hoppe. Meeting of the Chicago Institute of Psychoanalysis, Chicago, IL.

Kohut, H. (1977). *The restoration of the self*. New York: International Universities Press.

Kohut, H. (1978a). Thoughts on narcissism and narcissistic rage. In P. Ornstein (Ed.), *The search for the self*. New York: International Universities Press.

Kohut, H. (1978b). Forms and transformation of narcissism. In P. Ornstein (Ed.), *The search for the self*. New York: International Universities Press.

Kohut, H. (1984). *How does analysis cure?* Chicago: University of Chicago Press.

Kolb, B. (1974). Dissociation of the effects of lesions of the orbital or medial aspect of the prefrontal cortex of the rat with respect to activity. *Behavioral Biology*, *10*, 329–343.

Kolb, B. (1984). Functions of the frontal cortex in the rat: A comparative review. *Brain Research Reviews*, *8*, 65–98.

Kolb, B. (1989). Brain development, plasticity, and behavior. *American Psychologist*, *44*, 1203–1212.

Kolb, B., & Milner, B. (1981). Performance of complex arm and facial movements after focal brain lesions. *Neuropsychologia*, *19*, 491–503.

Kolb, B., & Nonneman, A.J. (1975). Prefrontal cortex and the regulation of food intake in the rat. *Journal of Comparative and Physiological Psychology*, *88*, 806–815.

Kolb, B., & Whishaw, I.Q. (1990). *Fundamental of human neuropsychology* (3rd ed). New York: W.H. Freeman.

Kolb, B., Whishaw, I.Q., & Schallert, T. (1977). Aphagia, behavior sequencing and body weight set point following orbital frontal lesions in rats. *Physiology and Behavior*, *19*, 93–101.

Kolb, L.C. (1977). *Modern clinical psychiatry*. Philadelphia: W.B. Saunders.

Kolodny, E. (1984). A postulated role for metal hydrolases in developing brain. *Discussions in Neuroscience*, *1*, 89–91.

Kopin, I.J. (1985). Catecholamine metabolism: Basic aspects and clinical significance. *Pharmacological Reviews*, *37*, 303–364.

Kopp, C.B. (1982). Antecedents of self-regulation: A developmental perspective. *Developmental Psychology*, *18*, 199–214.

Korn, H. & Massion, J. (1964). Origine et topographie des projections vagales sur le cortex anterieur chez le chat. [Origin and topography of vagal projections on the anterior cortex of the cat] *Comptes.Rendues d'Academie de la Science, Paris, 259,* 4373–4375.

Korn, H., Wendt, R., & Albe-Fessard, D. (1966). Somatic projection to the orbital cortex of the cat. *Electroencephalography and Clinical Neurophysiology, 21,* 209–226.

Korneva, E.A., & Khai, L.M. (1964). Effect of destruction of hypothalamic areas on immunogenesis. *Federal Proceedings Transactions, 23,* (Supplement) T88.

Kosslyn, S.M. (1988). Aspects of a cognitive neuroscience of mental imagery. *Science, 240,* 1621–1626.

Kostovic, I. (1990). Structural and histochemical reorganization of the human prefrontal cortex during perinatal and postnatal life. *Progress Brain Research, 85,* 223–239.

Kostovic, I., Lukinovic, N., Judas, M., Bogdanovic, N., Mrzljak, L., Zecevic, N., & Kubat, M. (1989). Structural basis for the developmental plasticity in the human cerebral cortex: The role of the transient subplate zone. *Metabolism and Brain Disease, 4,* 17–23.

Kostovic, I., & Rakic, P. (1990). Developmental history of the transient subplate zone in the visual and somatosensory cortex of the macaque monkey and human brain. *Journal of Comparative Neurology, 297,* 441–470.

Kostovic, I., Skavic, J., & Strinovic, D. (1988). Acetylcholinesterase in the human frontal associative cortex during the period of cognitive development: Early laminar shifts and late innervation of pyramidal neurons. *Neuroscience Letters, 90,* 107–112.

Koukkou, M., & Lehmann, D. (1983). Dreaming: The functional state-shift hypothesis. A neuropsychophysiological model. *British Journal of Psychiatry, 142,* 221–231.

Kovach, J. K. (1970). Critical period or optimal arousal? Early approach behavior as a function of stimulus, age and breed variables. *Developmental Psychology, 3,* 73–77.

Kraemer, G.W. (1992). A psychobiological theory of attachment. *Behavioral and Brain Sciences, 15,* 493–541.

Kraemer, G.W., Ebert, M.H., Schmidt, D.E., & Mckinney, W.T. (1991). Strangers in a strange land: A psychobiological study of infant monkeys before and after separation from real or inanimate mothers. *Child Development, 62,* 548–566.

Kraicer, J., & Milligan, J. V. (1970). Suppression of ACTH release from adenohypophysis by corticosterone: an *in vitro* study. *Endocrinology, 87,* 371.

Krause, R., & Lutolf, P. (1988). Facial indicators of transference processes within psychoanalytic treatment. In II. Dahl & H. Kachele (Eds.), *Psychoanalytic process research strategies.* New York: Springer-Verlag.

Krause, R., Steimer, E., Sanger-Alt, C., & Wagner, G. (1989). Facial expression of schizophrenic patients and their interaction partners. *Psychiatry, 52,* 1–12.

Kron, R. E. (1971). Psychoanalytic complications of a narcissistic transference. *Journal of the American Psychoanalytic Association, 19,* 636–653.

Kronfol, Z., Hamsher, K.D., Digre, K., & Wazziri, R. (1978). Depression and hemispheric functions: Changes associated with unilateral EEG. *British Journal of Psychiatry, 132,* 560–567.

Kruk, M.R., Van der Poel, A.M., & De Vos-Frerichs, T.P. (1979). The induction of aggressive behavior by electrical stimulation in the hypothalamus of male rats. *Behaviour, 70,* 292–321.

Krushel, L.A., & Van der Kooy, D. (1988). Visceral cortex: Integration of the mucosal senses with limbic information in the rat agranular insular cortex. *Journal of Comparative Neurology, 270,* 39–54.

Krystal, H. (1974). The genetic development of affects and affect regression. *The Annual of Psychoanalysis, 2,* 117–145.

Krystal, H. (1978a). Trauma and affects. *Psychoanalytic Study of the Child, 33,* 81–116.

Krystal, H. (1978b). Self representation and the capacity for self care. *The Annual of Psychoanalysis, 6,* 209–246.

Krystal, H.(1988). *Integration and self-healing: Affect-trauma-alexithymia.* Hillsdale, NJ: The Analytic Press.

Kubota, K., & Niki, H. (1971). Prefrontal cortical unit activity and delayed cortical unit activity and delayed alternation performance in monkeys. *Journal of Neurophysiology, 34*, 337–347.

Kuczynski, L., Kochanska, G., Radke-Yarrow, M., & Girnius-Brown, O. (1987). A developmental interpretation of young children's noncompliance. *Developmental Psychology, 23*, 799–806.

Kuyler, P.L., Rosenthal, L., Igel, G., Dunner, D.L., & Fieve, R.R. (1980). Psychopathology among children of manic-depressive patients. *Biological Psychiatry, 15*, 589–597.

Lacey, J.I., Bateman, D.E., & Van Lehn, R. (1953). Autonomic response specificity. *Psychosomatic Medicine, 15*, 8–21.

Lafon-Cazal, M., Pietri, S., Culcasi, M., & Bockaert, J. (1993). NMDA-dependent superoxide production and neurotoxicity. *Nature, 364*, 535–537.

Lajtha, A.L., Maker, H.S., & Clarke, D.D. (1981). Metabolism and transport of carbohydrates and amino acids. In G.J. Siegel, R.W. Albers, B.W. Agranoff, & R. Katzman, (Eds.), *Basic neurochemistry* (3rd ed. pp. 329–353). Boston: Little, Brown.

Lamb, M.E. (1981). The development of social expectations in the first year of life. In M.E. Lamb & L.R. Sherwood (Eds.), *Infant social cognition: Empirical and theoretical consequences* (pp. 155–175). Hillsdale, NJ: Lawrence Erlbaum Associates.

Lamb, M.E., & Esterbrooks, M.A. (1981). Individual differences in parental sensitivity: Origins, components, and consequences. In M.E. Lamb & L.R. Sherwood (Eds.), *Infant social cognition: Empirical and theoretical consequences*. Hillsdale, NJ: Lawrence Erlbaum Associates.

Lamb, M.E., & Malkin, C.M. (1986). The development of social expectations in distress-relief experiences: A longitudinal study. *International Journal of Behavior and Development, 9*, 235–249.

Lamb, M.E., Sternberg, K.J., & Ketterlinus, R. (1992). Child care in the United States. In M.E. Lamb, K. Sternberg, C.P. Hwang, & A.G. Broberg (Eds.), *Child care in context* (pp. 207–222). Hilsdale, NJ: Lawrence Erlbaum Associates.

Lambert, P.L., Harell, E.H., & Achterberg, J. (1981). Medial hypothalamic stimulation decreases the phagocytic actiivity of the reticuloendothelial system. *Physiological Psychology, 9*, 193–196.

Land, J. M., Booth, R.F.G., Berger, R., & Clark, J. B. (1977). Development of mitochondrial energy metabolism in rat brain. *Biochemical Journal, 164*. 339–348.

Lander, A.D. (1987). Molecules that make axons grow. *Molecular Neurobiology, 1*, 213–245.

Landis, S.C. (1973). Ultrastructural changes in the mitochondria of cerebellar Purkinje cells of nervous mutant mice. *Journal of Cell Biology, 57*, 782–787.

Lane, R.D., & Schwartz, G. (1987). Levels of emotional awareness: A cognitive-developmental theory and its application to psychopathology. *American Journal of Psychiatry, 144*, 133–143.

Lane, R.D., Novelly, R., Cornell, C., Zeitlin, S., & Schwartz, G. (1988). Asymmetric hemispheric control of heart rate. *Psychophysiology, 25*, 464.

Lang, P.J. (1979). A bio-informational theory of emotional imagery. *Psychophysiology, 16*, 495–512.

Langer, K.G. (1992). Psychotherapy with the neuropsychologically impaired adult. *American Journal of Psychotherapy, 46*, 620–639.

Langs, R. (1976). *The bipersonal field*. New York: Jason Aronson.

Langs, R., & Badalamenti, A. (1992). The three modes of the science of psychoanalysis. *American Journal of Psychotherapy, 46*, 163–182.

Langsdorf, P., Izard, C.E., Rayias, M., & Hembree, E.A. (1983). Interest expression, visual fixation, and heart-rate changes in 2- to 8-month-old infants. *Developmental Psychology, 19*, 375–386.

Lankford, K.L., DeMello, F.G., & Klein, W.L. (1988). D_1-type dopamine receptors inhibit growth cone motility in cultured retina neurons: Evidence that neurotransmitters act as morphogenetic growth regulators in the developing central nervous system. *Proceedings of the National Academy of Sciences of the United States of America, 85*, 2839–2843.

Lansky, M.R. (1992). *Fathers who fail: Shame and psychopathology in the family system.* Hillsdale NJ: The Analytic Press.

Lapierre, Y., Beaudet, A., Demianczuk, N., & Descarries, L. (1973). Noradrenergic axon terminals in the cerebral cortex of the rat. II. Quantitative data revealed by light and electron microscope radioautography of the frontal cortex. *Brain Research, 63,* 175–182.

Larsen, R.J., & Diener, E. (1987). Affect intensity as an individual difference characteristic: A review. *Journal of Research in Personality, 21,* 1–39.

Lasch, C. (1978). *The culture of narcissism.* New York: W.W. Norton.

Lash, L.H., & Jones, D.P. (1993). *Mitochondrial dysfunction.* San Diego, CA: Academic Press.

Laudenslager, M.L., Reite, M., & Harbeck, R. (1982). Suppressed immune response in infant monkeys associated with maternal separation. *Behavioral and Neural Biology, 36,* 40–48.

Lauder, J. (1983). M. Hormonal and humoral influences on brain development. *Psychoneuroendocrinology, 8,* 121–155.

Lauder, J. M., & Krebs, H. (1986). Do neurotransmitters, neurohumors, and hormones specify critical periods?. In W.T. Greenough & J. M. Juraska (Eds.), *Developmental neuropsychobiology* (pp. 119–174). Orlando, FL: Academic Press.

Lavelle, A. (1964). Critical periods of neuronal maturation. *Progress in Brain Research, 9,* 93–96.

Lavelle, A. (1973). Levels of maturation and reactions to injury during neuronal development. *Progress in Brain Research, 40,* 161–166.

Lawicka, W., Mishkin, M., Kreiner, J., & Brutkowski, S. (1966). Delayed response deficit in dogs after selective ablation of the proreal gyrus. *Acta Biologica Experimentales, 26,* 309–322.

Lawrence, R.A. (1980). *Breast feeding: A guide for the medical profession.* London: Mosby.

Lawson, K.R. (1980). Spatial and temporal contiguity and auditory-visual integration in infants. *Developmental Psychology, 16,* 195.

Lazarus, R.S. (1968). Emotions and adaptation: Conceptual and empirical relations. In W. Arnold (Ed.), *Nebraska symposium on motivation* (pp.175–200). Lincoln: University of Nebraska Press.

Lazarus, R.S. (1991a). Cognition and motivation in emotion. *American Psychologist, 46,* 352–367.

Lazarus, R.S. (1991b). Progress on a cognitive-motivational-relational theory of emotion. *American Psychologist, 46,* 819–834.

Lazarus, R.S. (1993). From psychological stress to the emotions: A history of changing outlooks. *Annual Review of Psychology, 44,* 1–21.

Lazarus, R.S., & Smith, C.A. (1988). Knowledge and appraisal in the cognition-emotion relationship. *Cognition and Emotion, 2,* 281–300.

Le Beux, Y.J., & Willemot, J. (1978). Actin-like filaments in the endothelial cells of adult rat brain capillaries. *Experimental Neurology, 58,* 446–454.

Lecours, A.R. (1982). Correlates of developmental behavior in brain maturation. In T.G. Bever (Ed.), *Regressions in mental development: Basic phenomena and theories* (pp. 267–298). Hillsdale, NJ: Lawrence Erlbaum Associates.

Ledig, M., Fried, R., Ziessel, M., & Mandel, P. (1982). Regional distribution of superoxide dismutase in rat brain during postnatal development. *Developmental Brain Research, 4,* 333–337.

LeDoux, J. E. (1989). Cognitive-emotional interactions in the brain. *Cognition and Emotion, 3,* 267–289.

LeDoux, J. E. (1992). Information flow from sensation to emotion: Plasticity in the neural computation of stimulus value. In M. Gabriel & J. Moore (Eds.), *Neurocomputation and learning: Foundation of adaptive networks.* Cambridge, MA: MIT Press.

LeDoux, J.E., Thompson, M.E., Iadecola, C., Tucker, L.W., & Reis, D.J. (1983). Local cerebral blood flow increases during auditory and emotional processing in the conscious rat. *Science, 221,* 576–578.

Lee, D.N., & Aronson, E. (1974). Visual proprioceptive control of standing in human infants. *Perception and Psychophysics, 15,* 529–532.

Leibrock, I., Lottspeich, F., Hohn, A., Hofer, M., Hengerer, B., Masiakowski, P., Thoenen, H., & Barde, Y.-A. (1989). Molecular cloning and expression of brain-derived neurotrophic factor. *Nature (London)*, *341*, 149–152.

Leichtman, M. (1992). Psychotherapeutic interventions with brain-injured children and their families: II. Psychotherapy. *Bulletin of the Menninger Clinic*, *56*, 338–360.

LeMay, M. (1982). Morphological aspects of human brain asymmetry: An evolutionary perspective. *Trends in Neuroscience*, *5*, 272–275.

Lenz, H.J., Raedler, A., Greten, H., & Brown, M.R. (1987). CRF initiates biological reactions within the brain that are observed in response to stress. *American Journal of Physiology*, *252*, R34–R39.

Leonard, C.M. (1969). The prefrontal cortex of the rat. I. Cortical projections of the mediodorsal nucleus. II. Efferent connections. *Brain Research*, *12*, 321–343.

Leong, S.F., Lai, J.C.K., Lim, L., & Clark, J.B. (1984). The activities of some energy-metabolising enzymes in nonsynaptic (free) and synaptic mitochondria derived from selected brain regions. *Journal of Neurochemistry*, *42*, 1306–1312.

Leshner, A.I. (1978). *An introduction to behavioral endocrinology*. New York: Oxford University Press.

Leslie, A.M. (1987). Pretence and representation: The origins of "theory of mind". *Psychological Review*, *94*, 412–426.

Lesser, I.M. (1985). Current concepts in psychiatry: Alexithymia. *New England Journal of Medicine*, *312*, 690–692.

Lester, E.P. (1983). Separation-individuation and cognition. *Journal of the American Psychoanalytic Association*, *31*, 127–156.

Leung, E.H.L., & Rheingold, H.L. (1981). Development of pointing as a social gesture. *Developmental Psychology*, *17*, 215–220.

Leung, T.K.C., Rajendran, M.Y., Monfries, C., Hall, C., & Lim, L. (1990). The human heat-shock protein family. *Biochemical Journal*, *267*, 125–132.

Levin, F.M. (1991). *Mapping the mind*. Hillsdale, NJ: The Analytic Press.

Levin, S. (1967). Some metapsychologfical considerations on the differentiation between shame and guilt. *International Journal of Psycho-Analysis*, *48*, 267–276.

Levine, S. (1985). A definition of stress? In G.P. Moberg (Ed.), *Animal stress* (pp. 51–69). Bethesda, MD: American Physiological Society.

Levine, S., Goldman, L., & Coover, G.D. (1972). Expectancy and the pituitary-adrenal system. In *Physiology, emotion, and psychosomatic illness*, CIBA Foundation Symposium, 8 (pp. 281–296). Amsterdam: Elsevier.

Levine, S., Haltmeyer, G.C., Karas, G.G., & Denenberg, V.H. (1967). Physiological and behavioral effects of infantile stimulation. *Physiology and Behavior*, *2*, 55–59.

Levine, S., & Treitman, D.M. (1969). Determinants of individual differences in the steroid response to stress. In E. Bajusz (Ed.), *Physiology and pathology of adaptation mechanisms* (pp. 171–184). Oxford: Pergamon.

Levitt, P., Rakic, P., & Goldman-Rakic, P. (1984). Region-specific distribution of catecholamine afferents in primate cerebral cortex: A flourescence histochemical analysis. *Journal of Comparative Neurology*, *227*, 23–36.

Levy, A.P., Tamargo, R., Brem, H., & Nathans, D. (1989). An endothelial cell growth factor from the mouse neuroblastoma cell line NB 41. *Growth Factors*, *2*, 9–19.

Levy, J., Heller, W., Banich, M. T., & Burton, L. A. (1983). Are variations among right-handed individuals in perceptual asymmetries caused by characteristic arousal differences between hemispheres? *Journal of Experimental Psycholology: Human Perception and Performance*, *9*, 329–359.

Lewis, D.A., Foote, S.L., Goldstein, M., & Morrison, J. H. (1988). The dopaminergic innervation of monkey prefrontal cortex: A tyrosine hydroxylase immunohistochemical study. *Brain Research*, *449*, 225–243.

Lewis, D.A., Foote, S.L., & Cha, C.I. (1989). Corticotropin-releasing factor immunoreactivity in monkey neocortex: An immunohistochemical analysis. *Journal of Comparative Neurology, 290*, 599–613.

Lewis, D.A., & Lund, J. S. (1990). Heterogeneity of chandelier neurons in monkey neocortex: Corticotropin-releasing factor and parvalbumin-immunoreactive populations. *Journal of Comparative Neurology, 293*, 599–615.

Lewis, D.A., & Morrison, J. H. (1989). Noradrenergic innervation of monkey prefrontal cortex: A dopamine-beta-hydroxylase immunohistochemical study. *Journal of Comparative Neurology, 282*, 317–330.

Lewis, H.B. (1971). *Shame and guilt in neurosis.* New York: International Universities Press.

Lewis, H. B. (1980). "Narcissistic personality" or "Shame-prone superego mode". *Comparative Psychotherapy, 1*, 59–80.

Lewis, H. B. (1985). Depression vs. paranoia: Why are there sex differences in mental illness? *Journal of Personality, 53*, 150–178.

Lewis, H. B. (1987). Shame and the narcissistic personality. In D.L. Nathanson (Ed.), *The many faces of shame* (pp. 93–132). New York: Guilford Press.

Lewis, M. (1982). Origins of self-knowledge and individual differences in early self-recognition. In J. Suls (Ed.), *Psychological perspectives on the self. Vol 1* (pp. 55–78). Hillsdale, NJ: Lawrence Erlbaum Associates.

Lewis, M. (1992). *Shame: The exposed self.* New York: The Free Press.

Lewis, M., Jaskir, J., & Enright, M. (1986). Development of mental abilities in infancy. *Intelligence, 10*, 331–354.

Lewis, M., & Miller, S.M. (1993). *Handbook of developmental psychopathology.* New York: Plenum Press.

Lewis, M., Sullivan, M.W., Stanger, C., & Weiss, M. (1989). Self-development and self-conscious emotions. *Child Development, 60*, 146–156.

Lewis, M.H., Gluck, J. P., Beauchamp, A.J., Keresztury, M.F., & Mailman, R.B. (1990). Long-term effects of early social isolation in *Macaca mulatta* : Changes in dopamine receptor function following apomorphine challenge. *Brain Research, 513*, 67–73.

Lewontin, R.C. (1978). Adaptation. *Scientific American, 239*, 212–230.

Leysen, J.E. (1985). Characterization of serotonin receptor binding sites. In A.R. Green (Ed.), *Neuropharmacology of serotonin* (pp. 79–116). Oxford: Oxford University Press.

Lezak, M. (1976). *Neuropsychological assessment.* New York: Oxford University Press.

Lichtenberg, J.D. (1983). *Psychoanalysis and infant research.* Hillsdale, NJ: The Analytic Press.

Lichtenberg, J.D. (1989). *Psychoanalysis and motivation.* Hillsdale, NJ: The Analytic Press.

Lichtenberg, J.D., Lachmann, F.M., & Fosshage, J.L. (1992). *Self and motivational systems: Toward a theory of psychoanalytic technique.* Hillsdale, NJ: The Analytic Press.

Lichtenstein, H. (1961). Identity and sexuality. A study of their interpersonal relationships in man. *Journal of the American Psychoanalytic Association, 9*, 179–260.

Lidov, H.G.W., Molliver, M.E., & Zecevic, N.R. (1978). Characterization of the monoaminergic innervation of immature rat neocortex: A histoflourescence analysis. *Journal of Comparative Neurology, 181*, 663–679.

Lim, R., Mitsunobu, K., & Li, W. (1973). Maturation-stimulation effect of brain extract and dibutryl cyclic AMP on dissociated embryonic brain cells in culture. *Experimental Cell Research, 79*, 243–246.

Lindvall, O., Bjorklund, A., & Divac, I. (1977). Organization of mesencephalic dopamine neurons projecting to neocortex and septum. *Advances in Biochemical Psychopharmacology, 16*, 39–46.

Lindvall, O., Bjorklund, A., Moore, R.Y., & Stenevi, U. (1974). Mesencephalic dopamine neurons projecting to the neocortex. *Brain Research, 81*, 325–331.

Lindvall, O., Bjorklund, A., & Skagerberg, G. (1984). Selective histochemical demonstration of dopamine terminal systems in rat di- and telencephalon: New evidence of dopaminergic innervation of hypothalamic neurosecretory nuclei. *Brain Research, 306*, 19–30.

Lipovits, Z. & Paull, W.K. (1989). Association of dopaminergic fibers with corticotropin releasing hormone (CRH)-synthesizing neurons in the paraventricular nucleus of the rat hypothalamus. *Histochemistry, 93*, 119–127.

Lipsitt, L. P. (1976). Developmental psychology comes of age: A discussion. In L.P. Lipsett (Ed.), *Developmental psychology: The significance of infancy*. Hillsdale, NJ: Lawrence Erlbaum Associates.

Livingston, R.B. (1967). Reinforcement. In C.G. Quarton, T. Melnechuck, & F. O. Schmidt (Eds.), *The neurosciences: A study program* (pp. 568–576). New York: Rockefeller University Press.

Lobb, H. (1965). Vision versus touch in form discrimination. *Canadian Journal of Psychology, 19*, 175–187.

Loewald, H.W. (1962). Internalization, separation, mourning and superego. *Psychoanalytic Quarterly, 31*, 483–504.

Loewald, H.W. (1970). Psychoanalytic theory and psychoanalytic process. *Psychoanalytic Study of the Child, 25*, 45–68.

Loewald, H.W. (1978). Instinct theory, object relations, and psychic structure formation. *Journal of the American Psychoanalytic Association, 26*, 493–506.

Loewald, H.W. (1986). Transference-countertransference. *Journal of the American Psychoanalytic Association, 34*, 275–287.

Loewy, A.D., & Spyer, K.M. (1990). *Central regulation of autonomic functions*. New York: Oxford University Press.

Loh, H.H., & Smith, A.P. (1990). Molecular characterization of opioid receptors. *Annual Review of Pharmacology and Toxicolology, 30*, 1230–147.

Loizou, L.A. (1972). The postnatal ontogeny of monoamine-containing neurons in the central nervous system of the albino rat. *Brain Research, 40*, 395–418.

Londerville, S., & Main, M. (1981). Security of attachment, compliance, and maternal training methods in the second year of life. *Developmental Psychology, 17*, 289–299.

Long, J.B., & Holaday, J.W. (1985). Blood-brain barrier: Endogenous modulation by adrenal-cortical function. *Science, 227*, 1580–1583.

Lopkor, A., Abood, L.G., Hass, W., & Lionetti, F.J. (1980). Stereoselective muscarinic acetylcholine and opiate receptors on human phagocytic leukocytes. *Biochemical Pharmacology, 29*, 1361–1371.

Loren, I., Bjorklund, A., & Lindvall, O. (1976). The catecholamine systems in the developing brain: Improved visualization by a modified glyoxylic acid-formaldehyde method. *Brain Research, 117*, 313–318.

Lorente de No, R. (1983). Studies on the structure of the cerebral cortex. I. The area entorhinalis. *Journal of Psychological Neurology, 45*, 381–438.

Lorenz, K.Z. (1970). *Studies in animal and human behavior*. Cambridge, MA: Harvard University Press.

Lorenzo, A.V., Fernandez, C., & Roth, L.J. (1965). Physiologically induced alteration of sulfate penetration into brain. *Archives of Neurology, 12*, 128–132.

Lossner, B., Jork, R., & Matthies, H. (1981). Dopamine induced changes in L-fucose incorporation into proteins of rat hippocampus and corpus striatum during postnatal development. *Pharmacology, Biochemistry and Behavior, 15*, 705–709.

Lossner, B., & Rose, S.P.R. (1983). Passive avoidance training increases fucokinase activity in right forebrain base of day old chicks. *Journal of Neurochemistry, 41*, 1357–1363.

LoTurco, J.J., Blanton, M.G., & Kriegstein, A.R. (1991). Initial expression and endogenous activation of NMDA channels in early neocortical development. *Journal of Neuroscience, 11*, 792–799.

Lotze, M.T., Frana, L.W., Sharrow, S.O., Robb, R.J., & Rosenberg, S.A. (1985). In vivo administration of purified human interleukin 2. I. Half-life and immunologic effects of the Jurkat cell line-derived interleukin 2. *Journal of Immunology, 134*, 157–166.

Lowenstein, D.H., Chan, P.K., Miles, M.F. (1991). The stress protein response in cultured neurons: Characterization and evidence for a protective role in excitotoxicity. *Neuron, 7*, 1053–1060.

Loy, R., & Miller, T.A. (1980). Sexual dimorphism in extent of axonal sprouting in rat hippocampus. *Science, 208*, 1282–1284.

Lubben, T.H., Gatenby, A.A., Donaldson, G.K., Lorimer, G.H., & Viitanen, P.V. (1990). Identification of a groES-like chaperonin in mitochondria that facilitates protein folding. *Proceedings of the National Academy of Sciences of the United States of America, 87*, 7683–7687.

Luborsky, L., & Crits-Cristoph, P. (1990). *Understanding transference: The CCRT Method*. New York: Basic Books.

Luborsky, L., McLellan, A., Woody, G.E., O'Brien, C.P., & Auerbach, A. (1985). Therapist success and its determinants. *Archives of General Psychiatry, 42*, 602–611.

Ludwig, A.M., & Ables, M.F. (1974). Mania and marriage: The relationship between biological and behavioral variables. *Comparative Psychiatry, 15*, 411–421.

Luiten, P.G.M., Ter Horst, G.J., & Steffens, A.B. (1987). The hypothalamus, intrinsic connections and outflow pathways to the endocrine system in relation to the control of feeding and metabolism. *Progress in Neurobiology, 28*, 1–54.

Lund-Anderson, S. (1979). Transport of glucose from blood to brain. *Physiological Reviews, 59*, 305–352.

Lundberg, U. (1980). Catecholamine and cortisol excretion under psychologically different laboratory conditions. In E. Usdin, R. Kvetnansky, & I.J. Kopin (Eds.), *Catecholamines and stress*. New York: Elsevier.

Lundberg, U., & Frankenhaeuser, M. (1980). Pituitary-adrenal and sympathetic-adrenal correlates of distress and effort. *Journal of Psychosomatic Research, 24*, 125–130.

Luque, J. M., de Blas, M.R., Segovia, S., & Guillamon, A. (1992). Sexual dimorphism of the dopamine- B -hydroxylase-immunoreactive neurons in the rat locus ceruleus. *Developmental Brain Research, 67*, 211–215.

Luria, A. R. (1973). *The working brain*. New York: Basic Books.

Luria, A.R. (1976). *The nature of human conflicts*. New York: Liveright. (Original work published 1932).

Luria, A. R. (1980). *Higher cortical functions in man* (2nd ed.). New York: Basic Books.

Lynch, G.S. (1970). Separable forebrain systems controlling different manifestations of spontaneous activity. *Journal of Comparative and Physiological Psychology, 70*, 48–59.

Lynd, H.M. (1958). *On shame and the search for identity*. New York: Harcourt Brace.

Maccoby, E.E., & Jacklin, C.N. (1974). *The psychology of sex differences*. Palo Alto: Stanford University Press.

Maccoby, E.E., & Martin, J. (1983). Socialization in the context of the family: Parent-child interaction. In P.H. Mussen & E.M. Hetherington (Eds.), *Handbook of child psychology, socialization, personality, and social devlopment*, (4th ed., pp. 1–101). New York: Wiley.

MacCurdy, J. T. (1930). The biological significance of blushing and shame. *British Journal of Psychology, 21*, 174–182.

MacFarlane, A. (1977). *The psychology of childbirth*. Cambridge, MA: Harvard University Press.

MacLean, P.D. (1949). Psychosomatic disease and the "visceral brain": Recent developments bearing on the Papez theory of emotion. *Psychosomatic Medicine, 11*, 338–353.

MacLean, P.D. (1954). The limbic system and its hippocampal formation: Studies in animals and their possible application to man. *Journal of Neurosurgery, 11*, 29–44.

MacLean, P.D. (1958). The limbic system with respect to self-preservation and the preservation of the species. *Journal of Nervous and Mental Disease, 127*, 1–11.

MacLean, P.D. (1967). The brain in relation to empathy and medical education. *Journal of Nervous and Mental Disease, 144*, 374–382.

MacLusky, N.J., Naftolin, F., & Goldman-Rakic, P.S. (1986). Estrogen formation and binding in the cerebral cortex of the developing rhesus monkey. *Proceedings of the National Academy of Sciences of the United States of America, 83*, 513–516.

Macmillan, M. (1992). Inhibition and the control of behavior: From Gall to Freud via Phineas Gage and the frontal lobes. *Brain and Cognition, 19*, 72–104.

Mahler, M. (1968). Adaptation and defense in statu nascendi. *Psychoanalytic Quarterly, 37*, 1–21.

Mahler, M.S. (1979). Notes on the development of basic moods: The depressive affect. In *The selected papers of Margaret S. Mahler* (pp. 59–75). New York: Jason Aronson.

Mahler, M. S. (1980). Rapprochement subphase of the separation-individuation process. In R. Lax, S. Bach & J.A. Burland (Eds.), *Rapprochement: The critical subphase of separation-individuation* (pp. 3–19). New York: Jason Aronson.

Mahler, M. S., & Kaplan, L. (1977). Developmental aspects in the assessment of narcissistic and so-called borderline personalities. In P. Hartocollis (Ed.), *Borderline personality disorders* (pp. 71–95). New York: International Universities Press.

Mahler, M., Pine, F., & Bergman, A. (1975). *The psychological birth of the human infant.* New York: Basic Books.

Maier, V., & Scheich, H. (1983). Acoustic imprinting leads to differential 2-deoxy-D-glucose uptake in the chick forebrain. *Proceedings of the National Academy of Sciences of the United States of America, 80,* 3860–3864.

Main, M. (1990). Parental aversion to infant-initiated contact is correlated with the parent's own rejection during childhood. In K. Barnard & T.B. Brazelton (Eds.), *Clinical infant reports: Touch* (pp. 461–495). Madison CT: International Universities Press.

Main, M., Kaplan, N., & Cassidy, J. (1985). Security in infancy, childhood and adulthood: A move to the level of representation. *Monographs of the Society for Research in Child Development, 50,* 66–104.

Main, M., & Solomon, J. (1986). Discovery of an insecure-disorganized / disoriented attachment pattern. In T.B. Brazelton & M.W. Yogman (Eds.), *Affective development in infancy.* Norwood, NJ: Ablex.

Main, M., & Stadtman, J. (1981). Infant response to rejection of physical contact by the mother: Aggression, avoidance and conflict. *Journal of the American Academy of Child Psychiatry, 20,* 292–307.

Main, M., Tomasini, L., & Tolan, W. (1979). Differences among mothers judged to differ in security. *Developmental Psychology, 15,* 472–473.

Main, M., & Weston, D.R. (1981). The quality of the toddler's relationship to mother and to father: Related to conflict behavior and the readiness to establish new relationships. *Child Development, 52,* 932–940.

Main, M., & Weston, D.R. (1982). Avoidance of the attachment figure in infancy: Descriptions and interpretations. In C.M. Parkes & J. Stevenson-Hinde (Eds.), *The place of attachment in human behavior.* New York: Basic Books.

Mains, R.E., Eipper, B.A., & Ling, N. (1977). Common precursor to corticotropins and endorphins. *Proceedings of the National Academy of Sciences of the United Strates of America, 74,* 3014–3018.

Majno, G., & Palade, G.E. (1961a). Studies on inflammation. The effect of histamine and serotonin on vascular permeability: An electron microscopic study. *Journal of Biophysical and Biochemical Cytology, 11,* 571–607.

Majno, G., & Palade, G.E. (1961b). Studies on inflammation. II. The site of action of histamine and serotonin on the vascular tree: A topographic study. *Journal of Biophysical and Biochemical Cytology, 11,* 608–633.

Makara, G.B. (1985). Mechanisms by which stressful stimuli activate the pituitary-adrenal system. *Federation Proceedings, 44,* 149–153.

Makara, G.B., Stark, E., Karteszi, M., Palkovitz, M., & Rappay, G. (1981). Effect of paraventricular lesions on stimulated ACTH release and CRF in stalk-median eminence of the rat. *American Journal of Physiology, E240,* 441–446.

Malatesta-Magai, C. (1991). Emotional Socialization: Its role in personality and developmental psychopathology. In D. Cicchetti & S.L. Toth (Eds.), *Internalizing and externalizing expressions of dysfunction: Rochester symposium on developmental psychopatholgy, Vol. 2* (pp. 203–224). Hillsdale, NJ: Lawrence Erlbaum Associates.

Malatesta, C.Z., Culver, C., Tesman, J.R., & Shepard, B. (1989). The development of emotion expression during the first two years of life. *Monographs of the Society for Research in Child Development, 54*, 1–103.

Malatesta, C.Z. & Wilson, A. (1988). Emotion cognition interaction in personality development: A discrete emotions, functionalist analysis. *British Journal of Social Psychology, 27*, 91–112.

Malenka, G.B., Hamblin, M.W., & Barchas, J. D. (1989). Biochemical hypotheses of affective disorders and anxiety. In G. J. Siegel, B.W. Agranoff, R.W. Albers, & P.B. Molinoff, (Eds.), *Basic neurochemistry* (4th ed., pp.877–891). New York: Raven Press.

Malloy, F.P., Bihrle, A., Duffy, J., & Cimino, C. (1993). The orbitomedial frontal syndrome. *Archives of Clinical Neuropsychology, 8*, 185–201.

Malloy, P. (1987). Frontal lobe dysfunction in obsessive-compulsive disorder. In E. Perecman (Ed.), *The frontal lobes revisited* (pp. 207–223). Hillsdale, NJ: Lawrence Erlbaum Associates.

Malmo, R.B. (1959). Activation: A neurophysiological dimension. *Psychological Review, 66*, 367–386.

Mandal, M.K., Tandon, S.C., & Asthana, H.S. (1991). Right brain damage impairs recognition of negative emotions. *Cortex, 27*, 247–253.

Mandler, J. M. (1990). Recall of events by preverbal children. *Annals of the New York Academy of Sciences, 608*, 485–503.

Mandler, J.M. (1992). How to build a baby: II. Conceptual primitives. *Psychological Review, 99*, 587–604.

Mandler, R.N., Biddison, W.E., Mandler, R., & Serrate, S.A. (1986). Beta endorphin augments the cytolytic activity and interferon production of natural killer cells. *Journal of Immunology, 136*, 934–939.

Mandoki, M.I., Sumner, G.S., & Matthews-Ferrari, K. (1992). Evaluation and treatment of rage in children and adolescents. *Child Psychiatry and Human Development, 22*, 227–235.

Marcel, A.J. (1983). Conscious and unconscious perception: An approach to the relations between phenomenal experience and perceptual processes. *Cognitive Psychology, 15*, 238–300.

Marder, E.E., Hooper, S.L., & Eisen, J. S. (1987). Multiple neurotransmitters provide a mechanism for the production of multiple outputs from a single neuronal circuit. In G.M. Edelman, W.E. Gall, & W.M. Cowan (Eds.), *Synaptic function* (pp. 305–327). New York: Wiley.

Marin-Padilla, M. (1970). Prenatal and postnatal ontogenesis in the human motor cortex: A Golgi study. I. The sequential development of the cortical layers. *Brain Research, 23*, 167–183.

Markowitsch, H.J. (1988). Anatomical and functional organization of primate prefrontal cortical system. In H.D. Steklis & J. Erwin (Eds.), *Comparative primate biology, Vol. 4, Neuroscience.* New York: Alan Liss.

Marks, L.F. (1978). *The unity of the senses: Interrelations among the modalities.* New York: Academic Press.

Markus, H., & Nurius, P. (1986). Possible selves. *American Psychologist, 41*, 954–969.

Martin, E., Kikinis, R., Zuerrer, M., Boesch, Ch., Briner, J., Kewitz, G., & Kaelin, P. (1988). Developmental stages of human brain: An MR study. *Journal of Computer Assisted Tomography, 12*, 917–922.

Martin, J. B. (1977). *Clinical neuroendocrinology.* Philadelphia: Davis.

Martin, J.H. (1989). *Neuroanatomy: Text and atlas.* New York: Elsevier.

Martin, J. T. (1978). Imprinting behavior. Pituitary-adrenocortical modulation of the approach response. *Science, 200*, 565–567.

Martin, L.J., Spicer, D.M., Lewis, M.H., Gluck, J. P., & Cork, L.C. (1991). Social deprivation of infant rhesus monkeys alters the chemoarchitecture of the brain: 1. Subcortical regions. *Journal of Neuroscience, 11*, 3344–3358.

Martzke, J., Swan, C.S., & Varney, N.R. (1991). Posttraumatic anosmia and orbital frontal damage: Neuropsychological and neuropsychiatric correlates. *Neuropsychology, 5*, 213–225.

Maseda, C.E.G., Aguado, E.G., Mena, M.A., & de Yevenes, J. G. (1983). Ontogenetic development of beta endorphin immunoreactivity in rat brain regions. *Neuroscience Letters, 14*, (Supplement) 5237.

Mason, J. W. (1968). A review of psychoendocrine research on the sympathetic adrenal medullary system. *Psychosomatic Medicine, 30*, 631–653.

Mason, J. W. (1975). Emotion as reflected in patterns of endocrine integration. In L. Levi (Ed.), *Emotions: Their parametrics and measurement* (pp. 143–181). New York: Raven Press.

Masterson, J. F. (1981). *The narcissistic and borderline disorders.* New York: Brunner/Mazel.

Masur, E.F. (1983). Gestural development, dual-directional signaling, and the transition to words. *Journal of Psycholinguistic Research, 12*, 93–109.

Mathews, P.M., Froelich, C.J., Sibbitt, W.L. Jr., & Bankhurst, A.D. (1983). Enhancement of natural cytoxicity by B—endorphin. *Journal of Immunology, 130*, 1658–1662.

Matthews, R.T., & German, D.C. (1984). Electrophysiological evidence for excitation of rat ventral tegmental area dopaminergic neurons by morphine. *Neuroscience, 11*, 617–626.

Mattson, A.J., & Levin, H.S. (1990). Frontal lobe dysfunction following closed head injury. A review of the literature. *Journal of Nervous and Mental Disease, 178*, 282–290.

Mattson, M. (1988). Neurotransmitters in the regulation of neuronal cytoarchitecture. *Brain Research Review, 13*, 179–212.

Mattson, M.P., & Kater, S. (1987). Calcium regulation of neurite elongation and growth cone motility. *Journal of Neuroscience, 7*, 4034–4043.

Maurer, D., & Salapatek, P. (1976). Developmental changes in the scanning of faces by young infants. *Child Development, 47*, 523–527.

Mayes, L., & Zigler, E. (1992). An observational study of the affective concomitants of mastery in infants. *Journal of Child Psychology & Psychiatry & Allied Disciplines, 33*, 659–667.

Maynard Smith, J. (1978). Optimization theory in evolution. *Annual Review of Ecolological Systems, 9*, 31–56.

Mazur, A., Rosa, E., Faupel, M., Heller, J., Leen, R., & Thurman, B. (1980). Physiological aspects of communication via mutual gaze. *American Journal of Sociology, 86*, 50–74.

Mazziotta, J.C., Phelps, M.E., & Halgren, E. (1983). Local cerebral glucose metabolic response to audiovisual stimulation and deprivation: studies in human subjects with positron CT. *Human Neurobiology, 2*, 11–23.

McCabe, B.J., & Horn, G. (1988). Learning and memory: Regional changes in N-methyl-D-aspartate receptors in the chick brain after imprinting. *Proceedings of the National Academy of Sciences of the United States of America, 85*, 2849–2853.

McCabe, B.J., & Horn, G. (1991). Synaptic transmission and recognition memory: time course of changes in N- methyl-D-aspartate receptors after imprinting. *Behavioral Neuroscience, 105*, 289–294.

McCabe, P.M., & Schneiderman, N. (1985). Psychophysiologic reactions to stress. In N. Schneiderman & J.T. Tapp (Eds.), *Behavioral medicine; The biophysical approach* (pp. 99–131). Hillsdale, NJ: Lawrence Erlbaum Associates.

McCalden, T.A., Benjamin, H., & Eidelman, H. (1976). Cerebrovascular response to infused noradrenaline and its modification by a catecholamine blocker. *Neurology, 26*, 987–991.

McCarley, R.W., & Hobson, A.J. (1977). The neurobiological origins of psychoanalytic dream theory. *American Journal of Psychiatry, 134*, 1211–1221.

McClearn, G.E. (1970). Genetic influences on behavior and development. In P.H. Mussen (Ed.), *Carmichael's manual of child psychology, Vol. 1* (pp. 39–76). New York: Wiley.

McClearn, G.E., & DeFries, J.H.C. (1973). *Introduction to behavioral genetics.* San Francisco: W.H. Freeman.

McClintock, B. (1934). The relation of particular chromosomal element to the development of the nucleoli in Zea mays. *Zeitschrift fur Zellforschung und Mikroskopische Anatomie, 21*, 294–328.

McCobb, D.B., Haydon, P.G., & Kater, S.B. (1985). Dopamine: An additional regulator of neurite outgrowth in Helisoma. *Society of Neuroscience Abstracts, 11*, 761.

McConnell, S.K., Ghosh, A., & Shatz, C.J. (1989). Subplate neurons pioneer the first axon pathway from the cerebral cortex. *Science, 245*, 978–981.

McCrank, E.W. (1983). Commentary on "Crying behavior in the human adult". *Integrative Psychiatry, 1*, 98–99.

McCulloch, J., Savaki, H.E., & McCulloch, M.C. (1982). The distribution of alterations in energy metabolism in the rat brain produced by apomorphine. *Brain Research, 243*, 67–80.

McDevitt, J. B. (1975). Separation-individuation and object constancy. *Journal of the American Psychoanalytic Association, 23*, 713–742.

McDevitt, J. B. (1979). The role of internalization in the development of object relations during the separation-individuation phase. *Journal of the American Psychoanalytic Association, 27*, 327–343.

McDevitt, J. B. (1980). The role of internalization in the development of object relations during the separation-individuation phase. In R.F. Lax, S. Bach, & J. A. Burland (Eds.), *Rapprochement: The critical subphase of separation-individuation* (pp. 135–149). New York: Jason Aronson.

McEwen, B.S. (1988). Steroid hormones and the brain: Linking "nature and nurture". *Neurochemical Research, 13*, 663–669.

McEwen, B.S. (1989). Endocrine effects on the brain and their relationship to behavior. In G. Siegel, B. Agranoff, R.W. Albers, & P. Molinoff (Eds.), *Basic neurochemistry* (4th ed., pp. 893–913). New York: Raven Press.

McEwen, B.S., Weiss, J.M., & Schwartz, L.S. (1968). Selective retention of corticosterone by limbic structures in rat brain. *Nature (London), 220*, 911–912.

McGlone, J. (1980). Sex differences in human brain asymmetry: A critical survey. *Behavorial and Brain Sciences, 3*, 215–264.

McGrath, M., Boukydis, C.F.Z., & Lester, B.M. (1993). Determinants of maternal self-esteem in the neonatal period. *Infant Mental Health Journal, 14*, 35–48.

McGregor, I.S., & Atrens, D.M. (1988). Enhanced weight gain following electrical stimulation of the sulcal prefrontal cortex in rats. *Neuroscience Letters, 30* (Supplement) S98.

McGregor, I.S., & Atrens, D.M. (1991). Prefrontal cortex self-stimulation and energy balance. *Behavorial Neuroscience, 105*, 870–883.

McGregor, I.S., Menendez, J.A., Atrens, D.M., & Lin, H.Q. (1991). Prefrontal cortex alpha 2 adrenoreceptors and energy balance. *Brain Research Bulletin, 26*, 683–691.

McGuire, M.T., & Troisi, A. (1987). Physiological regulation-deregulation and psychiatric disorders. *Ethology and Sociobiology, 8*, 9S-25S.

McGuire, M.T., Marks, I., Neese, R.M., & Troisi, A. (1992). Evolutionary biology: A basic science for psychiatry? *Acta Psychiatrica Scandinavica, 86*, 89–96.

McGurk, H., & MacDonald, J. (1976). Hearing lips and seeing voices. *Nature (London), 264*, 746–748.

Mchedlishvili, G.J. (1964). Vascular mechanisms pertaining to the intrinsic regulation of the cerebral circulation. *Circulation, 30*, 597–610.

McIllwain, H. (1966). *Biochemistry of the central nervous system.* Boston: Little, Brown.

McLaughlin, J. (1981). Transference, psychic reality and countertransference. *Psychoanalytic Quarterly, 50*, 639–644.

McLaughlin, J. (1989). The relevance of infant observational research for the analytic understanding of adult patients' nonverbal behaviors. In S. Dowling & A. Rothstein (Eds.), *The significance of infant observational research for clinical work with children, adolescents, and adults* (pp. 109–122). Madison, CT: International Universities Press.

McMullen, N.T. & Almli, C.R. (1981). Cell types within the medial forebrain bundle: A Golgi study of preoptic and hypothalamic neurons in the rat. *American Journal of Anatomy, 161*, 323–340.

McMullin, T.W., & Hallberg, R.L. (1987). A normal mitochondrial protein is selectively synthesized and accumulated during heat shock in *Tetrahymena thermophila*. *Molecular and Cellular Biology, 7*, 4414–4423.

Mead, G.H. (1972). *Mind, self, and society.* Chicago: University of Chicago Press. (Original work published 1934).

Meador, K.J., Loring, D.W., Lee, G.P., Brooks, B.S., Nichols, F.T., Thompson, E.E., Thompson,

W.O., & Heilman, K.M. (1989). Hemisphere asymmetry for eye gaze mechanisms. *Brain, 112,* 103–111.

Meaney, M.J., Aitken, D.H., Bodnoff, S.R., Iny, L.J., Tatarewicz, J.E., & Sapolsky, R.M. (1985). Early postnatal handling alters glucocorticoid receptor concentrations in selected brain regions. *Behavorial Neuroscience, 99,* 765–770.

Meaney, M.J., Dodge, A.M., & Beatty, W.W. (1981). Sex-dependent effects of amygdaloid lesions on the social play of prepubertal rats. *Physiology and Behavior, 26,* 467–472.

Mears, C. (1978). Play and development of cosmic confidence. *Developmental Psychology, 14,* 371–378.

Meehl, P.E. (1975). Hedonic capacity: Some conjectures. *Bulletin of the Menninger Clinic, 39,* 295–307.

Meier, G.W., Nolan, C.Y., Bunch, M.E., & Scheidler, C.H. (1960). Anoxia, behavioral development, and learning ability. *Psychological Monographs, 74,* 1–45.

Meissner, W.W. (1981). *Internalization in psychoanalysis.* New York: International Universities Press.

Meissner, W.W. (1986a). *Psychotherapy and the paranoid process.* Northvale, NJ: Jason Aronson.

Meissner, W.W. (1986b). Can psychoanalysis find its self? *Journal of the American Psychoanalytic Association, 34,* 379–400.

Melges, F.T., & Swartz, M.S. (1989). Oscillations of attachment in borderline personality disorder. *American Journal of Psychiatry, 146,* 1115–1120.

Melhuish, E.C., Gambles, C., & Kumar, R. (1988). Maternal mental illness and the mother-infant relationship. In R. Kumar & I.F. Brockington (Eds.), *Motherhood and mental illness. Vol. 2: Causes and consequences.* London: Wright.

Meltzoff, A.N. (1990). Towards a developmental cognitive science. The implications of cross-modal matching and imitation for the development of representation and memory in infancy. *Annals of the New York Academy of Sciences, 608,* 1–31.

Menetrey, D., & Basbaum, A.I. (1987). Spinal and trigeminal projections to the nucleus of the solitary tract: A possible substrate for somatovisceral and viscerovisceral reflex activation. *Journal of Comparative Neurology, 255,* 439–450.

Messer, D., & Vietz, P. (1984). Timing and transitions in mother-infant gaze. *Infant Behavior and Development, 7,* 167–181.

Messimy, R. (1939). Les effets, chez le singe, de l'ablation des lobes prefrontaux. [The effects, in the monkey, of the ablation of the prefrontal lobes] *Revues Neurologiques, 71,* 1–37.

Mesulam, M.-M. (1985). Patterns in behavioral neuroanatomy: Association areas, the limbic system, and hemispheric specialization. In M. Mesulam (Ed.), *Principles of behavioral neurology.* Philadelphia: F.A. Davis.

Mesulam, M.-M., & Geschwind, N. (1978). On the possible role of neocortex and its limbic connections in the process of attention in schizophrenia: Clinical cases of inattention in man and experimental anatomy in monkey. *Journal of Psychiatric Research, 14,* 249–259.

Mesulam, M.-M., & Mufson, E.J. (1982). Insula of the old world monkey. I. Architectonics in the insulo-orbito-temporal component of the paralimbic brain. *Journal of Comparative Neurology, 212,* 1–22.

Meyer, J.S. (1985). Biochemical effects of corticosteroids on neural tissues. *Physiological Reviews, 65,* 946–1020.

Meyer, J.S., Nomura, F., Sakamoto, K., & Kondo, A. (1969). Effect of stimulation of the brain-stem reticular formation on cerebral blood flow and oxygen consumption. *Electroencephalography and Clinical Neurophysiology, 26,* 125–132.

Meyer, J.T., Ishikawa, Y., Hata, T., & Karacan, I. (1987). Cerebral blood flow in normal and abnormal sleep and dreaming. *Brain and Cognition, 6,* 266–294.

Meyers, C.A., Berman, S.A., Scheibel, R.S., & Hayman, A. (1992). Case report: Acquired antisocial personality disorder associated with unilateral left orbital frontal lobe damage. *Journal of Psychiatry and Neuroscience, 17,* 12–125.

Meyersburg, H. A., & Post, R. M. (1979). An holistic developmental view of neural and psychological processes: A neurobiologic-psychoanalytic integration. *British Journal of Psychiatry, 135,* 139–155.

Michaut, R-J., Dechambre, R-P., Doumerc, S., Lesourd, B., Devillechabrolle, A., & Moulias, R. (1981). Influence of early maternal deprivation on adult humoral immune response in mice. *Physiology and Behavior, 26,* 189–191.

Miller, A. (1979). Depression and grandiosity as related forms of narcissistic disturbance. *International Review of Psychoanalysis, 6,* 61–75.

Miller, A. (1981). *The drama of the gifted child.* New York: Basic Books.

Miller, A.J., McKoon, M., Pinneau, M., & Silverstein, R. (1983). Postnatal synaptic development of the nucleus tractus solitarius (NTS) of the rat. *Developmental Brain Research, 8,* 205–213.

Miller, E.K., Raese, J.D., & Morrison-Bogorad, M. (1991). Expression of heat shock protein 70 and heat shock cognate 70 messenger RNAs in rat cortex and cerebellum after heat shock or amphetamine treatment. *Journal of Neurochemistry, 56,* 2060–2071.

Miller, G.A., Galanter, E., & Pribram, K.H. (1960). *Plans and the structure of behavior.* New York: Henry Holt.

Miller, J.P. (1965). The psychology of blushing. *International Journal of Psycho-Analysis, 46,* 188–199.

Miller, J.P., Rall, W., & Rinzel, J. (1985). Synaptic amplification by active membrane in dendritic spines. *Brain Research, 325,* 325–330.

Miller, L. (1986). Some comments on cerebral hemispheric models of consciousness. *Psychoanalytic Review, 73,* 129–144.

Miller, L. (1991a). On *Aphasia* at 100: The neuropsychodynamic legacy of Sigmund Freud. *Pschoanalytic Review, 78,* 365–378.

Miller, L. (1991b). *Freud's brain: Neuropsychodynamic foundations of psychoanalysis.* New York: Guilford Press.

Miller, L. (1993). *Psychotherapy of the brain-injured patient: Reclaiming the shattered self.* New York: W.W. Norton.

Miller, P.A., & Eisenberg, N. (1988). The relation of empathy to aggressive and externalizing / antisocial behavior. *Psychological Bulletin, 103,* 324–344.

Miller, S. (1985). *The shame experience.* Hillsdale, NJ: The Analytic Press.

Milner, B. (1968). Visual recognition and recall after right temporal lobe excision in man. *Neuropsychologia, 6,* 191–209.

Milner, B., & Taylor, L. (1972). Right hemisphere superiority in tactile pattern recognition after cerebral commissurotomy: Evidence for nonverbal memory. *Neuropsychologia, 10,* 10–15.

Mischel, W., & Underwood, B. (1974). Instrumental ideation in delay of gratification. *Child Development, 45,* 1083–1088.

Mishkin, M. (1964). Perseveration of central sets after frontal lesions in monkeys. In J.M. Warren & K. Akert (Eds.), *The frontal granular cortex and behavior* (pp. 219–241). New York: McGraw-Hill.

Mitchell, J.B., & Meaney, M.J. (1991). Effects of corticosterone on response consolidation and retrieval in the forced swim test. *Behavioral Neuroscience, 105,* 798–803.

Mizukami, S., Nishizuka, M., & Arai, Y. (1983). Sexual difference in nuclear volume and its ontogeny in the rat amygdala. *Experimental Neurology, 79,* 569–575.

Mizuno, N., Sauerland, E.K., & Clemente, C.D. (1968). Projections from the orbital gyrus in the cat. I. To brain stem structures. *Journal of Comparative Neurology, 133,* 463–476.

Mizuno, Y., & Oomura, H. (1984). Glucose responding neurons in the nucleus tractus solitarius of the rat: In vitro study. *Brain Research, 307,* 109–116.

Mizzen, L.A., Chang, C., Garrels, J.I., & Welch, W.J. (1989). Identification, characterization, and purification of two mammalian stress proteins present in mitochondria, grp 75, a member of the hsp 70 family and hsp 58, a homolog of the bacterial groEL protein. *Journal of Biological Chemistry, 264*, 20664–20675.

Mjaatvedt, A.E., & Wong-Riley, M.T.T. (1988). Relationship between synaptogenesis and cytochrome oxidase activity in Purkinje cells of the developing rat cerebellum. *Journal of Comparative Neurology, 277*, 155–182.

Modell, A.H. (1975). A narcissistic defense against affects and the illusion of self-sufficiency. *International Journal of Psycho-Analysis, 56*, 275–282.

Molliver, M.E., & Kristt, D.A. (1975). The fine structural demonstration of monoaminergic synapses in immature rat neocortex. *Neuroscience Letters, 1*, 305–310.

Mollon, P., & Parry, G. (1984). The fragile self: Narcissistic disturbance and the protective function of depression. *British Journal of Medical Psychology, 57*, 137–145.

Money, J., Hampson, J.G., & Hampson, J.L. (1957). Imprinting and the establishment of gender role. *Archives of Neurology and Psychiatry, 77*, 333–336.

Money, J., & Ehrhardt, A. (1968). *Man, woman, boy, and girl*. Baltimore: Johns Hopkins University Press.

Monrad-Krohn, G.H. (1924). On the dissociation of voluntary and emotional innervation in facial paresis of central origin. *Brain, 47*, 22–35.

Moorcroft, W.H. (1971). Ontogeny of forebrain inhibition of behavioral arousal in the rat. *Brain Research, 35*, 513–522.

Moore, R.Y. (1982). Catecholamine neuron systems in brain. *Annals of Neurology, 12*, 321–327.

Moore, S.D., & Guyenet, P.G. (1983). An electrophysiological study of the forebrain projection of nucleus commissuralis: Preliminary identification of presumed A2 catecholaminergic neurons. *Brain Research, 263*, 211–222.

Mora, F., Avrith, D.B., & Rolls, E.T. (1980). An electrophysiological and behavioral study of self-stimulation in the orbitofrontal cortex of the rhesus monkey. *Brain Research Bulletin, 2*, 111–115.

Mora, F., & Cobo, M. (1990). The neurobiological basis of prefrontal cortex self-stimulation: A review and an integrative hypothesis. *Progress in Brain Research, 85*, 419–413.

Moran, M.A., Mufson, E.J., & Mesulam, M.-M. (1987). Neural inputs into the temporopolar cortex of the rhesus monkey. *Journal of Comparative Neurology, 256*, 88–103.

Morecraft, R.J., Geula, C., & Mesulam, M.-M. (1992). Cytoarchitecture and neural afferents of orbitofrontal cortex in the brain of the monkey. *Journal of Comparative Neurology, 323*, 341–358.

Morgan, B.L., & Winick, M. (1980). Effects of environmental stimulation on brain N—acetylneuraminic acid content and behavior. *Journal of Nutrition, 121*, 425–423.

Morgan, B.L., & Winick, M. (1981). The subcellular localization of administered N—acetylneuraminic acid in the brains of well fed and protein restricted rats. *British Journal of Nutrition, 46*, 231–238.

Morgan, D.G., & Routtenberg, A. (1981). Brain pyruvate dehydrogenase: Phosphorylation and enzyme activity altered by training experience. *Science, 214*, 470–471.

Morgan, J.I., & Curran, T. (1988). Calcium as a modulator of the immediate-early gene cascade in neurons. *Cell Calcium, 9*, 303–311.

Morgan, J.I., & Curran, T. (1989). Calcium and proto oncogene involvement in the immediate-early response in the nervous system. *Annals of the New York Academy of Sciences, 568*, 283–290.

Morimoto, C., Reinherz, E.L., Schlossman, S.F., Schur, P.H., Mills, J.A., & Steinberg, A.D. (1980). Alternatives in immunoregulatory T cell subsets in active systemic lupus erythmatosus. *Journal of Clinical Investigation, 66*, 1171–1177.

Morimoto, R.I., Tissieres, A., & Georgopoulos, C. (1990). *Stress proteins in biology and medicine*. Cold Spring Harbor, NY: Cold Spring Harbor Laboratory.

Morris, W.N. (1989). *Mood: The frame of mind*. New York: Springer-Verlag.

Morris, R.G.M., Anderson, E., Lynch, G.S., & Baudry, M. (1986). Selective impairment of learning and blockade of long-term potentiation by an *N*—methyl-D-aspartate antagonist, AP-5, *Nature (London)*, *319*, 774–776.

Morrison, A.P. (1983). Shame, ideal self, and narcissism. *Contemporary Psychoanalysis, 19*, 295–318.

Morrison, A.P. (1984). Working with shame in psychoanalytic treatment. *Journal of the American Psychoanalytic Association, 32*, 479–505.

Morrison, A.P. (1987). The eye turned inward: Shame and the self. In D.L. Nathanson (Ed.), *The many faces of shame* (pp. 271–291). New York: Guilford Press.

Morrison, A.P. (1989). *Shame, the underside of narcissism*. Hillsdale, NJ: The Analytic Press.

Morrison, J.H., Molliver, M.E., & Grzanna, R. (1979). Noradrenergic innervation of cerebral cortex: Widespread effects of local cortical lesions. *Science, 205*, 313–316.

Morrison, N.K. (1985). Shame in the treatment of schizophrenia: Theoretical considerations with clinical illustrations. *Yale Journal of Biology and Medicine, 58*, 289–297.

Morrison, R.S., Sharma, A., De Vellis, J., & Bradshaw, R.A. (1986). Basic fibroblast growth factor supports the survival of cerebral cortical neurons in primary cultures. *Proceedings of the National Academy of Sciences of the United States of America, 83*, 7537–7541.

Mounoud, P. (1982). Revolutionary periods in early development. In T.G. Bever (Ed.), *Regressions in mental development: Basic phenomena and theories*. Hillsdale, NJ: Lawrence Erlbaum Associates.

Mount, H., Quirion, R., Chaudieu, I., & Boksa, P. (1990). Stimulation of dopamine release from cultured rat mesencephalic cells by naturally occurring excitatory amino acids: Involvement of both *N*—methyl D-aspartate (NMDA) and non-NMDA receptor subtypes. *Journal of Neurochemistry, 55*, 268–275.

Mountcastle, V.B. (1978). An organizing principle for cerebral functioning: The unit module and the distributed system. In G.M. Edelman & V.B. Mountcastle (Eds.), *The mindful brain* (pp. 7–50). Cambridge, MA: MIT Press.

Mrzljak, L., Uylings, H.B.M., Kostovic, I., & Van Eden, C.G. (1988). Prenatal development of neurons in the human prefrontal cortex: I. A qualitative Golgi study. *Journal of Comparative Neurology, 271*, 355–386.

Mrzljak, L., Uylings, H.B.M., van Eden, C.G., & Judas, M. (1990). Neuronal development in human prefrontal cortex in prenatal and postnatal stages. *Progress in Brain Research, 85*, 185–222.

Mucke, L., Norita, M., Benedek, G., & Creutzfeldt, O. (1982). Physiologic and anatomic investigation of a visual cortical area situated in the ventral bank of the anterior ectosylvian sulcus of the cat. *Experimental Brain Research, 46*, 1–11.

Mueller, J. (1983). Neuroanatomic correlates of emotion. In L. Temoshok, C. Van Dyke, & L. S. Zegans (Eds.), *Emotions in health and illness*. New York: Grune and Stratton.

Muller, H.F. (1985). Prefrontal cortex dysfunction as a common factor in psychosis. *Acta Psychiatrica Scandinavica, 71*, 431–440.

Munck, A., Guyre, P.M., & Holbrook, N.J. (1984). Physiological functions of glucocorticoids and their relation to pharmacological actions. *Endocrinological Reviews, 5*, 25–44.

Murphy, C.M. (1978). Pointing in the context of a shared activity. *Child Development, 49*, 371–380.

Murray, L. (1988). Effects of postnatal depression on infant development: Direct studies of early mother-infant interactions. In R. Kumar & I.F. Brockington (Eds.), *Motherhood and mental illness. Vol.2: Causes and consequences*. London: Wright.

Mussen, P.H., Conger, J.J., & Kagan, J. (1969). *Child development and personality*. New York: Harper and Row.

Nadel, L. (1990). Varieties of spatial cognition. Psychobiological considerations. *Annals of the New York Academy of Sciences, 608*, 613–626.

Nagel, E. (1959). Methodological issues in psychoanalytic theory. In S. Hook (Ed.), *Psychoanalysis, scientific method, and philosophy: A symposium* (pp. 38–56). New York: New York University Press.

Nakamura, S., Kimura, F., & Sakaguchi, T. (1987). Postnatal development of electrical activity in the locus ceruleus. *Journal of Neurophysiology, 58,* 510–524.

Nakamura, S., Tepper, J.M., Young, S.J., Ling, N., & Groves, P.M. (1982). Noradrenergic terminal excitability: Effects of opioids. *Neuroscience Letters, 30,* 57–62.

Nakano, Y., Oomura, Y., Nishino, H., Aou, S., Yamamoto, T., & Nemoto, S. (1984). Neuronal activity in the medial orbitofrontal cortex of the behaving monkey: Modulation by glucose and satiety. *Brain Research Bulletin, 12,* 381–385.

Natale, M., Gur, R.E., & Gur, R.C. (1983). Hemispheric asymmetries in processing emotional expressions. *Neuropsychologia, 21,* 555–565.

Nathanson, D.L. (1987a). A timetable for shame. In D.L. Nathanson (Ed.), *The many faces of shame* (pp. 1–63). New York: Guilford Press.

Nathanson, D.L. (1987b). The shame/pride axis. In H.B. Lewis (Ed.), *The role of shame in symptom formation.* Hillsdale, NJ: Lawrence Erlbaum Associates.

Nathanson, D. L. (1992). *Shame and pride: affect, sex, and the birth of the self.* New York: W.W. Norton.

National plan for research on child and adolescent mental disorders. (1990). (DHHS Publication No. ADM 90-1683). Washington, DC: U.S. Government Printing Office.

Nausieda, P.A., Koller, W.C., Weiner, W.J., & Klawans, H.L. (1979). Modification of postsynaptic dopaminergic sensitivity by female sex hormones. *Life Sciences, 25,* 521–526.

Nauta, W.J.H. (1964). Some efferent connections of the prefrontal cortex in the monkey. In J.M. Warren & K. Akert (Eds.), *The frontal granular cortex and behavior* (pp. 397–407). New York: McGraw Hill.

Nauta, W.J.H. (1971). The problem of the frontal lobe: A reinterpretation. *Journal of Psychiatric Research, 8,* 167–187.

Nauta, W.J.H. (1972). Neural associations of the frontal cortex. *Acta Neurobiologica Experimentales, 32,* 125–140.

Nauta, W.J.H. (1979). Expanding borders of the limbic system concept. In T. Rassmussen & R. Marino (Eds.), *Functional neurosurgery* (pp. 7–23). New York: Raven Press.

Nauta, W.J.H., & Domesick, V.B. (1982). Neural associations of the limbic system. In A.L. Beckman (Ed.), *The neural basis of behavior* (pp. 175–206). New York: SP Medical and Scientific Books.

Neafsey, E.J. (1990). Prefrontal cortical control of the autonomic nervous system: Anatomical and physiological observations. *Progress in Brain Research, 85,* 147–166.

Neidle, A., Van den Berg, C.J., & Grynbaum, A. (1969). The heterogeneity of rat brain mitochondria isolated on continuous sucrose gradients. *Journal of Neurochemistry, 16,* 225–234.

Neiss, R. (1988). Reconceptualizing arousal: Psychobiological states in motor performance. *Psychological Bulletin, 103,* 345–366.

Nelson, C.A. (1987). The recognition of facial expressions in the first two years of life: Mechanisms of development. *Child Development, 58,* 889–909.

Nelson, C.A., & Ludemann, P.M. (1989). Past, current, and future trends in infant face perception research. *Canadian Journal of Psychology, 43,* 183–198.

Nelson, C.A., Morse, P.A., & Leavitt, L.A. (1979). Recognition of facial expressions by seven-month old infants. *Child Development, 50,* 1239–1242.

Nelson, D.H. (1980). The adrenal cortex: Physiological function and disease. In L. Smith (Ed.), *Major problems in internal medicine.* Philadelphia: Sanders.

Nemeroff, C.B., Krishnan, K.R.R., Reed, D., Leder, R., Beam, C., & Dunnick, N.R. (1992). Adrenal gland enlargement in major depression; A computed tomographic study. *Archives of General Psychiatry, 49,* 384–387.

Nemeroff, C.B., Widerlov, E., Bisette, G., Walleus, H., Karlsson, I., Eklund, K., Kilts, C.D.,

Loosen, P.T., & Vale, W. (1984). Elevated concentrations of CSF corticotropin-releasing factor-like immunoreactivity in depressed patients. *Science, 226,* 1342–1344.

Nemiah, J.C., & Sifneos, P.E. (1970). Affect and fantasy in psychosomatic disorders. In O.W. Hill (Ed.), *Modern trends in psychosomatic medicine, Vol. 2 (*pp. 26–34). London: Butterworth.

Nemiah, J.C., Freyberger, H., & Sifneos, P.E. (1976). Alexithymia: A view of psychosomatic process. In O.W. Hill (Ed.), *Modern trends in medicine, Vol. 3 (* pp. 430–439). London: Butterworth.

Nemoto, E.M., & Frankel, H.M. (1970). Cerebrovascular response during progressive hyperthermia in dogs. *American Journal of Physiology, 218,* 1060–1064.

Neveu, P.J. (1988). Cerebral neocortex modulation of immune functions. *Life Sciences, 42,* 1917–1923.

Neveu, P.J. (1992). Asymmetrical brain modulation of the immune response. *Brain Research Reviews, 17,* 101–107.

Neveu, P.J., Barneoud, P., Georgiades, O., Vitiello, S., Vincendeau, P., & LeMoal, M. (1989). Brain neocortex modulation of the mononuclear phagocytic system. *Journal of Neuroscience Research, 22,* 392–394.

Neveu, P.J., Taghzouti, K., Dantzer, R., Simon, H., & LeMoal, M. (1986). Modulation of mitogen-induced lymphoproliferation by cerebral cortex. *Life Sciences, 38,* 1907–1913.

Newman, D.B., & Liu, R.P.C. (1987). Nuclear origins of brainstem reticulocortical systems in the rat. *American Journal of Anatomy, 178,* 279–299.

Newman, P.P., & Wolstencroft, J.H. (1959). Medullary responses to stimulation of orbital cortex. *Journal of Neurophysiology, 22,* 516–523.

Nichols, M.E.R., & Cooper, C.J. (1991). Hemispheric differences in the rates of information processing for simple non-verbal stimuli. *Neuropsychologia, 29,* 677–684.

Nieuwenhuys, R. (1985). *Chemoarchitecture of the brain.* Berlin: Springer-Verlag.

Nieuwenhuys, R., Voogd, J., & van Huijzen, Chr. (1981). *The human central nervous system: A synopsis and atlas* (2nd ed. rev.). New York: Springer-Verlag.

Niki, H., Sakai, M., & Kubota, K. (1972). Delayed alternation performance and unit activity of the caudate head and medial orbitofrontal gyrus in the monkey. *Brain Research, 38,* 343–353.

Nishizuka, M., & Arai, Y. (1983). Regional difference in sexually dimorphic synaptic organization of the medial amygdala. *Experimental Brain Research, 213,* 422–426.

Noebels, J.L. (1989). Introduction to structure-function relationships in the developing brain. In P. Kellaway & J.L. Noebels (Eds.), *Problems and concepts in developmental neurophysiology* (pp. 151–160). Baltimore: Johns Hopkins University Press.

Noison, E.L., & Thomas, W.E. (1988). Ontogeny of dopaminergic function in the rat midbrain tegmentum, corpus striatum and frontal cortex. *Developmental Brain Research, 41,* 241–252.

Nonneman, A.J., Corwin, J.V., Sahley, C.L., & Vicedomini, J.P. (1984). Functional development of the prefrontal system. In S. Finger & C.R. Almli.(Eds.), *Early brain damage, Vol. 2* (pp. 138–153). Orlando, FL: Academic Press.

Nonneman, A.J. & Whishaw, I.Q. (1982). Asymmetry in the cerebral hemisphere of the rat, mouse, rabbit, and cat: The right hemisphere is larger. *Experimental Neurology, 78,* 348–359.

Nordeen, E., Nordeen, K., Sengelaub, D., & Arnold, A.P. (1985). Androgens prevent normally-occuring cell death in sexually dimorphic spinal nucleus. *Science, 229,* 671–673.

Norden, M., Hagbarth, K.E., Thomandu, L., & Wallin, U. (1984). Microneurographic recordings from the trigeminal and facial nerves. *Electroencephalography and Clinical Neurophysiology, 59,* 59.

Norman, A., Earl, C., & Bird, M.M. (1991). The effects of dopamine on neurites and growth cones of mammalian spinal cord neurons *in vitro. Journal of Anatomy, 176,* 260.

Nosaka, S. (1984). Solitary nucleus neurons transmitting vagal visceral input to the forebrain via a direct pathway in rats. *Experimental Neurology, 85,* 493–505.

Nosaka, S., Yamamoto, T., & Yasunaga, K. (1979). Localization of vagal cardioinhibitory preganglionic neurons within the rat brain stem. *Journal of Comparative Neurology, 186,* 79–92.

Novey, S. (1961). Further considerations on affect theory in psychoanalysis. *International Journal of Psycho-Analysis, 42,* 21–31.

Nunez, J. (1984). Effects of thyroid hormones during brain differentiation. *Molecular and Cellular Endocrinology, 37*, 125–132.

Oades, R.D., & Halliday, G.M. (1987). Ventral tegmental (A10) system: Neurobiology. 1. Anatomy and connectivity. *Brain Research Reviews, 12*, 117–165.

Oatley, K. (1972). *Brain mechanisms and mind*. London: Thames and Hudson.

Oatley, K., & Jenkins, J.M. (1992). Human emotions: Function and dysfunction. *Annual Review of Psychology, 43*, 55–85.

Obrist, W.D., Thompson, H.D., Wang, H.S., & Wilkinson, W.E. (1975). Regional cerebral blood flow estimated by [133]xenon inhalation. *Stroke, 6*, 245–256.

Ogden, T.H. (1979). On projective identification. *International Journal of Psycho-Analysis, 60*, 357–373.

Ogden, T.H. (1990). *The matrix of the mind*. Northvale NJ: Jason Aronson.

Ogilvie, D.M. (1987). The undesired self: A neglected variable in personality research. *Journal of Personality and Social Psychology, 52*, 379–385.

Ogren, S-O., Archer, T., Fuxe, K., & Eneroth, P. (1981). Glucocorticoids, catecholamines and avoidance learning. In K. Fuxe, J-A. Gustafsson, & L. Wetterberg (Eds.), *Steroid hormone regulation of the brain* (p. 355–375). Oxford: Pergamon Press.

Ohman, A. (1986). Face the beast and fear the face: Animal and social fears as prototypes for evolutionary analyses of emotion. *Psychophysiology, 23*, 123–145.

Ohman, A., Dimberg, U., & Ost, L.G. (1985). Animal and social phobias: Biological constraints on learned responses. In S. Reiss & R. Bootzin (Eds.), *Theoretical issues in behavior therapy* (pp. 123–175). New York: Academic Press.

Ohta, M., & Oomura, Y. (1979). Inhibitory pathway from the frontal cortex to the hypothalamic ventromedial nucleus in the rat. *Brain Research Bulletin, 4*, 231–238.

Ojemann, G., Fried, I., & Mateer, C. (1980). Organization of visual function in human nondominant cortex. *Neuroscience Abstracts, 6*, 418.

Okinaka, S., Ibayashi, H., Motohashi, K., Fujita, T., Yoshida, S., & Ohsawa, N. (1960). Effect of electrical stimulation of the limbic system on pituitary-adrenocortical function: Posterior orbital surface. *Endocrinology, 67*, 319–324.

Oldendorf, W.H., & Brown, W.J. (1975). Greater number of capillary endothelial cell mitochondria in brain than in muscle. *Proceedings of the Society for Experimental Biology and Medicine, 149*, 736–738.

Oldendorf, W.H., Cornford, M.E., & Brown, W.J. (1977). The large apparent work capacity of the blood-brain barrier: A study of the mitochondrial content of capillary endothelial cells in brain and other tissues of the rat. *Annals of Neurology, 1*, 409–417.

Olds, J., & Milner, P. (1954). Positive reinforcement produced by electrical stimulation of septal area and other regions of rat brain. *Journal of Comparative and Physiological Psychology, 47*, 419–427.

Oliverio, A., Castellano, C., & Puglisi-Allegra S. (1984). Psychobiology of opioids. *International Review of Neurobiology, 25*, 277–337.

Olson, G.M. (1981). The recognition of specific persons. In M.E. Lamb & L.R. Sherrod (Eds.), *Infant social cognition: Empirical and theoretical considerations* (pp. 37–59). Hillsdale, NJ: Lawrence Erlbaum Associates.

Olson, L., & Fuxe, K. (1972). Further mapping out of central noradrenaline neuron systems: Projections of the 'subcoeruleus' area. *Brain Research, 43*, 289–295.

Olson, S.L., Bayles, K., & Bates, J.E. (1986). Mother-child interaction and children's speech progress: A longitudinal study of the first two years. *Merrill-Palmer Quarterly, 32*, 1–20.

Onada, N., Imamura, K., Obata, E., & Iino, M. (1984). Response selectivity of neocortical neurons to specific odors in the rabbit. *Journal of Neurophysiology, 52*, 638–652.

O'Neill, J.J., & Duffy, T.E. (1966). Alternate metabolic pathways in newborn brain. *Life Sciences, 5*, 1849–1857.

Onesti, S.T., Strauss, R.C., Mayol, B., & Solomon, R.A. (1989). The effects of norepinephrine depletion on cerebral blood flow in the rat. *Brain Research, 477*, 378–381.

Ongini, E., Caporali, M.G., & Massotti, M. (1985). Stimulation of dopamine D-1 receptors by SKF 38393 induces EEG desynchronization and behavioral arousal. *Life Sciences, 37*, 2327–2333.

Ongini, E., & Trampus, M. (1992). Modulation of sleep and waking states by D-1 receptors. *Journal of Psychopharmacology, 6*, 61–67.

Oppenheim, R.W. (1980). Metamorphosis and adaptation in the behavior of developing organisms. *Developmental Psychobiology, 13*, 353–356.

Oppenheim, R.W. (1981). Ontogenetic adapations and retrogressive processes in the development of the nervous system and behavior: A neuroembryological perspective. In K. Connolly & H.F.R. Prechtl (Eds.), *Maturation and development: Biological and psychological perspectives* (pp. 73–109). Philadelphia: J.B. Lippincott.

Ornstein, P.H. (1990). Case discussion: The self psychology perspective. In E.M. Plakun (Ed.), *New perspectives on narcissism.* Washington DC: American Psychiatric Press.

Oster, H. (1981). "Recognition" of emotional expression in infancy? In M.E. Lamb & L.R. Sherrod.(Eds.), *Infant social cognition: Empirical and theoretical considerations* (pp. 85–125). Hillsdale, NJ: Lawrence Erlbaum Associates.

Ostermann, R., Horwich, A.L., Neupert, W., & Hartl, F.-U. (1989). Protein folding in mitochondria requires complex formation with hsp60 and ATP hydrolysis. *Nature (London) 341*, 125–130.

Otto, M.W., Yeo, R.A., & Dougher, M.J. (1987). Right hemisphere involvement in depression: Towards a neuropsychological theory of negative affective experiences. *Biological Psychiatry, 22*, 1201–1215.

Owman, C., & Rosengren, E. (1967). Dopamine formation in brain capillaries—an enzymatic blood-brain barrier mechanism. *Journal of Neurochemistry, 14*, 547–550.

Oyama, S. (1979). The concept of the sensitive period in developmental studies. *Merrill-Palmer Quarterly, 25*, 83–103.

Pagano, R., & Frumkin, L. (1977). The effect of transcendental meditation on right hemispheric functioning. *Biofeedback and Self-Regulation, 2*, 407–415.

Paivio, A. (1973). Psychophysiological correlates of imagery. In F. McGuigan & R. Schoonover, *The psychophysiology of thinking* (pp. 263–295). New York: Academic Press.

Palca, J. (1990). The other human genome. *Nature (London), 249*, 1104–1105.

Palkovits, M., & Zaborszky, L. (1977). Neuroanatomy of central cardiovascular control. Nucleus tractus solitarius: Afferent and efferent connections in relation to the baroreceptor reflex arc. In W. De Jong, A.P. Provoost, & A.P. Shapiro (Eds.), *Hypertension and brain mechanisms* (pp. 9–34). Amsterdam: Elsevier.

Palmer, R.M.J., Ferige, A.G., & Moncada, S. (1987). Nitric oxide release accounts for the biological activity of endothelium-derived relaxing factor. *Nature (London), 327*, 524–526.

Palombo, J. (1987). Selfobject transference in the treatment of borderline neurocognitively impaired children. In J.S. Grotstein, J. Lang, & M. Solomon (Eds.), *The borderline patient: Emerging concepts in diagnosis* (pp. 317–345). Hillsdale, NJ: The Analytic Press.

Palombo, J. (1991). Bridging the chasm between developmental theory and clinical theory: Part I. The Chasm. Part II. The Bridge. *The Annual of Psychoanalysis, 19*, 151–193.

Palombo, J. (1992). Narratives, self-cohesion, and the patient's search for meaning. *Clinical Social Work Journal, 20*, 249–270.

Palombo, J. (1993). Neurocognitive deficits, developmental distiortions, and incoherent narratives. *Psychoanalytic Inquiry, 13*, 85–102

Pandya, D.N., & Barnes, C.L. (1987). Architecture and connections of the frontal lobes. In E. Perecman (Ed.), *The frontal lobes revisited* (pp. 41–72). Hillsdale, NJ: Lawrence Erlbaum Associates.

Pandya, D.N., Seltzer, B., & Barbas, H. (1988). Input-output organization of the primate cerebral cortex. In *Comparative Primate Biology, Vol IV: Neurosciences* (pp. 39–80). New York: Allen Ardis.

Pandya, D.N., & Yeterian, E.H. (1985). Architecture and connections of cortical association areas. In A. Peters & E.G. Jones (Eds.), *Cerebral cortex. Vol. 4. Association and auditory Cortices* (pp. 3–61). New York: Plenum Press.

Panksepp, J. (1986). The anatomy of emotions. In R. Plutchik & H. Kellerman (Eds.), *Emotion: Theory, research, and experience Vol. 3* (pp. 91–124). Orlando, FL: Academic Press.

Panksepp, J. (1991). Affective neuroscience: A conceptual framework for the neurobiological study of emotions. In K. Strongman (Ed.), *International reviews of studies in emotions* (Vol. 1, pp. 59–99). New York: Wiley.

Panksepp, J. (1992). A critical role for "affective neuroscience" in resolving what is basic about emotion. *Psychological Review, 99,* 554–560.

Panksepp, J., Siviy, S., & Normansell, L. (1984). The psychobiology of play. Theoretical and methodological perspectives. *Neurosciences and Biobehavioral Reviews, 8,* 465–492.

Panksepp, J., Siviy, S. M., & Normansell, L. A. (1985). Brain opioids and social emotions. In M. Reite & T. Field (Eds.), *The psychobiology of attachment and separation* (pp. 3–49). Orlando, FL: Academic Press.

Pao, P. (1968). On manic-depressive psychosis. *Journal of the American Psychoanalytic Association, 16,* 809–832.

Pao, P. (1971). Elation, hypomania, and mania. *Journal of the American Psychoanalytic Association, 19,* 787–798.

Papamichail, M., Tsokos, G., Tsawdaroglou, N., & Sekeris, C.E. (1980). Immunocytochemical demonstration of glucocorticoid receptors in different cell types and their translocation from the cytoplasm to the cell nucleus in the presence of dexamethasone. *Experimental Cell Research, 125,* 499–510.

Papez, J.W. (1937). A proposed mechanism of emotion. *Archives of Neurology and Psychiatry, 38,* 725–743.

Papousek, H., & Papousek, M. (1979). Early ontogeny of human social interaction: Its biological roots and social dimensions. In M. von Cranach, K. Foppa, W. Lepenies, & D. Ploog (Eds.), *Human ethology: Claims and limits of a new discipline.* New York: Cambridge University Press.

Papousek, H., & Papousek, M. (1984). The evolution of parent-infant attachment: New psychological perspectives. In J.D. Call, E. Galenson, & R.L. Tyson (Eds.), *Frontiers in infant psychiatry, Vol. II* (pp. 276–283). New York: Basic Books.

Papousek, H., Papousek, M., Suomi, S.J., & Rahn, C.W. (1991). Preverbal communication and attachment: Comparative Views. In J.L. Gewirtz & W. M. Kurtines, *Intersections with attachment* (pp. 97–122). Hillsdale, NJ: Lawrence Erlbaum Associates.

Parens, H. (1979). *The development of aggression in early childhood.* New York: Jason Aronson.

Parens, H. (1980). An exploration of the relations of instinctual drives and the symbiosis/separation-individuation process. *Journal of the American Psychoanalytic Association, 28,* 89–114.

Parker, R.S. (1990). *Traumatic brain injury and neuropsychological impairment.* New York: Springer-Verlag.

Parkin, A. (1985). Narcissism: Its structures, systems and affects. *International Journal of Psycho-Analysis, 66,* 143–156.

Passingham, R.E. (1972). Non-reveral shifts after selective prefrontal ablations in monkeys (*Macaca mulatta*). *Neuropsychologia, 10,* 41–46.

Patel, T.B., & Clark, J.B. (1981). Mitochondrial / cytosolic carbon transfer in the developing rat brain. *Biochimica et Biophysica Acta, 677,* 373–380.

Patel, S.N., & Stewart, M.G. (1988). Changes in the number and structure of dendritic spines 25h after passive avoidance training in the domestic chick, *Gallus domesticus. Brain Research, 449,* 34–46.

Patel, S.N., Rose, S.P., & Stewart, M.G. (1988). Training induced dendritic spine density changes are specifically related to memory formation processes in the chick, *Gallus domesticus. Brain Research, 463,* 168–173.

Pavlov, I.P. (1927). *Conditioned reflexes.* New York: Oxford University Press.

Paxinos, G., & Watson, C. (1982). *The rat brain and stereotaxic coordinates*. New York: Academic Press.

Paykel, E.S., & Hollyman, J.A. (1984). Life-events and depression—a psychiatric view. *Trends in Neuroscience, 9*, 478–481.

Payne, J.K., & Horn, G. (1982). Differential effects of exposure to an imprinting stimulus on 'spontaneous' neuronal activity in two regions of the chick brain. *Brain Research, 232*, 191–193.

Payne, J.K., & Horn, G. (1984). Long-term consequences of exposure to an imprinting stimulus on 'spontaneous' impulse activity in the chick brain. *Behavavioral Brain Research, 13*, 155–162.

Pearce, B., Cambray-Deakin, M.A., & Murphy, S. (1985). Glial glycogen stores are regulated by alpha-adrenergic receptors. *Biochemical Society Transactions, 13*, 232–233.

Pelham, H.R.B. (1986). Speculations on the function of the major heat shock and glucose-regulated proteins. *Cell, 46*, 959–961.

Penfield, W. (1968). Engrams in the human brain. *Proceedings of the Royal Society of Medicine, 61*, 831–840.

Penman, R., Meares, R., & Milgrom-Friedman, J. (1983). Synchrony in mother-infant interaction: A possible neurophysiological base. *British Journal of Medical Psychology, 56*, 1–7.

Pennebaker, J., & Beall, S.K. (1986). Confronting a traumatic event: Toward an understanding of inhibition and disease. *Journal of Abnormal Psychology, 92*, 274–281.

Perecman, E. (1983). *Cognitive processing in the right hemisphere*. New York: Academic Press.

Perkel, D.H., & Perkel, D.J. (1985). Dendritic spines: Role of active membrane in modulating synaptic efficacy. *Brain Research, 325*, 331–335.

Perner, J. (1991). *Understanding the representational mind*. Cambridge, MA: MIT Press.

Perret-Clermont, A-N. (1980). *Social interaction and cognitive development in children*. Academic Press: London.

Perrett, D.I., Rolls, E.T., & Caan, W. (1982). Visual neurons responsive to faces in the monkey temporal cortex. *Experimental Brain Research, 47*, 329–342.

Perris, C., Monakhov, K., VonKnorring, L., Botskarev, V., & Nikiforov, A. (1979). Systemic structural analysis of the EEG of depressed patients. *Neuropsychobiology, 4*, 207–228.

Peterfreund, E., & Schwartz, J.T. (1971). Information, systems and psychoanalysis: An evolutionary biological approach to psychoanalytic theory. *Psychological Issues, Nos. 25 / 26*. New York: International Universities Press.

Peters, A., Palay, S.L., & Webster, H. (1991). *The fine structure of the nervous system: The neurons and supporting cells*. New York: Oxford University Press.

Peto, A. (1969). Terrifying eyes: A visual superego forerunner. *Psychoanalytic Study of the Child, 24*, 197–212.

Petrides, M., & Iversen, S.D. (1976). Cross-modal matching and the primate frontal cortex. *Science, 192*, 1023–1024.

Petrides, M., & Pandya, D.N. (1988). Association fiber pathways to the frontal cortex from the superior temporal region in the rhesus monkey. *Journal of Comparative Neurology, 273*, 52–66.

Petrovich, S.B., & Gewirtz, J.L. (1985). The attachment learning process and its relation to cultural and biological evolution: Proximate and ultimate considerations. In M. Reite & T. Field (Eds.), *The psychobiology of attachment and separation* (pp. 259–291). Orlando, FL: Academic Press.

Pettigrew, J.D., & Kasamatsu, T. (1978). Local perfusion of noradrenaline maintains visual cortical plasticity. *Nature (London), 271*, 761–763.

Pfaff, D.W. (1982). Neurobiological mechanisms of sexual motivation. In D. W. Pfaff (Ed.), *The physiological mechanisms of motivation* (pp. 287–317). New York: Springer Verlag.

Phelps, C.H. (1972). Barbiturate-induced glycogen accumulation in brain. An electron microscopic study. *Brain Research, 39*, 225–234.

Phillips, A.G., & Le Piane, F.G. (1980). Reinforcing effects of morphine microinjection into the ventral tegmental area. *Pharmacology, Biochemistry, and Behavior, 12*, 965–968.

Phillips, A.G., Le Piane, F.G., & Fibiger, H.C. (1983). Dopaminergic mediation of reward produced by direct injection of enkephalin into the ventral tegmental area of the rat. *Life Sciences*, *33*, 2520–2511.

Phillips, P., Kumar, P., Kumar, S., & Waghe, M. (1979). Isolation and characterization of endothelial cells from rat and cow brain white matter. *Journal of Anatomy*, *129*, 261–272.

Piaget, J. (1932). *The moral judgment of the child*. New York: Harcourt, Brace and World

Piaget, J. (1967). *Six psychological studies*. New York: Random House.

Piaget, J. (1981). *Intelligence and affectivity: Their relationship during child development*. Palo Alto: Annual Reviews.

Piaget, J., & Inhelder, B. (1956). *The child's conception of space*. London: Routledge and Keegan Paul.

Piazza, P.V., Maccari, S., Deminiere, J-M., Le Moal, M., Mormede, P., & Simon, H. (1991). Corticosterone levels determine individual vulnerability to amphetamine self-administration. *Proceedings of the National Academy of Sciences of the United States of America*, *88*, 2088–2092.

Pickel, V.M., Chan, J.H.-L., Joh, T.H., & Beaudet, A. (1983). Vagal afferents and serotonergic terminals form synapses with catecholaminergic neurons in rat area postrema. *Neuroscience Abstracts*, *9*, 1127.

Piers, G., & Singer, M. (1953). *Shame and guilt*, New York: W. W. Norton.

Pine, F. (1980). On the expansion of the affect array: A developmental description. In R. Lax, S. Bach, & J.A. Burland (Eds.), *Rapprochement: The critical subphase of separation-individuation* (pp. 217–233). New York: Jason Aronson.

Pine, F. (1981). In the beginning: Contribution to a psycho-analytic developmental psychology. *International Review of Psycho-Analysis*, *8*, 15–34.

Pine, F. (1985). *Developmental theory and clinical process*. New Haven, CT: Yale University Press.

Pine, F. (1986a). The "symbiotic phase" in light of current infancy research. *Bulletin of the Menninger Clinic*, *50*, 564–569.

Pine, F. (1986b). On the development of the "borderline-child-to-be". *American Journal of Orthopsychiatry*, *56*, 450–457.

Pine, F. (1990). *Drive, ego, object, and self*. New York: Basic Books.

Pipp, S., & Harmon, R.J. (1987). Attachment as regulation: A commentary. *Child Devopment*, *58*, 648–652.

Pitt, B. (1968). 'Atypical' depression following childbirth. *British Journal of Psychiatry*, *114*, 1325–1335.

Plomin, R. (1983). Developmental behavioral genetics. *Child Development*, *54*, 252–259.

Plomin, R., Rende, R., & Rutter, M. (1991). Quantitative genetics and developmental psychopathology. In D. Cicchetti & S.L. Toth (Eds.), *Internalizing and externalizing expressions of dysfunction: Rochester symposium on developmental psychopatholgy, Vol. 2* (pp. 155–202). Hillsdale, NJ: Lawrence Erlbaum Associates

Plooij, F.X., & van de Rijt-Plooij, H.H.C. (1989). Vulnerable periods during infancy: hierarchically reorganized systems. Control, stress, and disease. *Ethology and Sociobiology*, *10*, 279–296.

Plutchik, R. (1980). *Emotion: A psychoevolutionary synthesis*. New York: Harper & Row.

Plutchik, R. (1983). Emotion in early development: A psychoevolutionary approach. In R. Plutchik & H. Kellermen (Eds.), *Emotion, theory, research, and experience* (pp. 221–257). New York: Academic Press.

Pollard, H., Llorens, D., Boneet, J.J., Costentin, J., & Schwartz, J.C. (1977). Opiate receptors on mesolimbic dopaminergic neurons. *Neuroscience Letters*, *7*, 295–299.

Pope, H.G., Jonas, J.M., Hudson, J.I., Cohen, B.M., & Gunderson, J.G. (1983). The validity of DSM-III borderline personality disorders. *Archives of General Psychiatry*, *40*, 23–30.

Pope, K.S., & Singer, J.L. (1976). Regulation of the stream of consciousness: Toward a theory of ongoing thought. In G. Schwartz & D. Shapiro (Eds.), *Consciousness and self regulation: Advances in research, Vol. II* (pp. 101–138). New York: Plenum.

Popper, K.R. (1962). *Conjectures and refutations: The growth of scientific knowledge*. New York: Basic Books.

Porges, S.W. (1976). Peripheral and neurochemical parallels of psychopathology: A psychophysiological model relating autonomic imbalance to hyperactivity, psychopathy, and autism. *Advances in Child Development and Behavior, 11*, 33–65.

Porges, S.W. (1984). Heart rate oscillation: An index of neural mediation. In M.G.H. Coles, J.R. Jennings, & J.A. Stern (Eds.), *Psychophysiological perspectives: Festschrift for Beatrice and John Lacey.* New York: Van Nostrand Reinhold.

Porges, S.W., & Fox, N.A. (1986). Developmental psychophysiology. In M. Coles, E. Donchin, & S.W. Porges (Eds.), *Psychophysiology.* New York: Guilford Press.

Porrino, L.J., Crane, A.M., & Goldman-Rakic, P.S. (1981). Direct and indirect pathways from the amygdala to the frontal lobe in rhesus monkeys *Journal of Comparative Neurology, 198,* 121–136.

Porrino, L.J., & Goldman-Rakic, P.S. (1982). Brainstem innervation of prefrontal and anterior cingulate cortex in the rhesus monkey revealed by retrograde transport of HRP. *Journal of Comparative Neurology, 205,* 63–76.

Porter, K.R., & Bruni, C. (1959). An electron microscopic study of the early effects of 3′-Me-DAB on rat liver cells. *Cancer Research, 19,* 997.

Posner, M.I. (1980). Orienting of attention. *Quarterly Journal of Experimental Psychology, 32,* 3–25.

Posner, M.I., & Petersen, S.E. (1990). The attention system of the human brain. *Annual Review of Neuroscience, 13,* 25–42.

Post, R.M. (1977). Clinical implications of a cocaine-kindling model of psychosis. In H.L. Klawans (Ed.), *Clinical neuropharmacology, Vol. 2.* New York: Raven Press.

Post, R.M. (1992). Transduction of psychosocial stress into the neurobiology of recurrent affective disorder. *American Journal of Psychiatry, 149,* 999–1010.

Potter-Effron, R.T. (1989). *Shame, guilt and alcoholism: Treatment issues in clinical practice.* New York: The Haworth Press.

Powell, G.F., Brasel, J., & Blizzard, R. (1967). Emotional deprivation and growth retardation simulating idiopathic hypopituitarism: 1. Clinical evaluation. *New England Journal of Medicine, 276,* 1271–1278.

Power, M.J., & Brewin, C.R. (1990). Self-esteem regulation in an emotional priming task. *Cognition and Emotion, 4,* 39–51.

Power, R.F., Mani, S.K., Codina, J., Conneely, O.M., & O'Malley, B.W. (1991). Dopaminergic and ligand-independent activation of steroid hormone receptors. *Science, 254,* 1636–1639.

Power, T.G., & Chapieski, M.L. (1986). Childrearing and impulse control in toddlers: A naturalistic investigation. *Developmental Psychology, 22,* 271–275.

Powles, W.E. (1992). *Human development and homeostasis.* Madison, CT: International Universities Press.

Pradhan, S.N., & Pradhan, S. (1980). Development of central neurotransmitter systems and ontogeny of behavior. In H. Parvez & S. Parvez (Eds.), *Biogenic amines in development* (pp. 641–662). Amsterdam: Elsevier/North Holland Biomedical Press.

Prasad, T.K., Hack, E., & Hallberg, R.L. (1990). Function of the maize mitochondrial chaperonin hsp60: Specific association between hsp60 and newly synthesized F1-ATPase alpha subunits. *Molecular and Cellular Biology, 10, 3979–3986.*

Prechtl, H.F.R. (1982). Regressions and transformations during neurological development. In T.G. Bever (Ed.), *Regressions in mental development: Basic phenomena and theories* (pp. 103–116). Hillsdale, NJ: Lawrence Erlbaum Associates.

Premack, D., & Woodruff, G. (1978). Does the chimpanzee have a theory of mind? *Behavioral and Brain Sciences, 4,* 515–526.

Pribram, K.H. (1981). Emotions. In S.B. Filskov & T.J. Boll (Eds.), *Handbook of clinical neuropsychology* (pp. 102–134). New York: Wiley.

Pribram, K.H. (1987). The subdivisions of the frontal cortex revisited. In E. Perecman (Ed.), *The frontal lobes revisited* (pp. 11–39). Hillsdale, NJ: Lawrence Erlbaum Associates.

Pribram, K.H. & Gill, M.M. (1976). *Freud's 'Project' re-assessed.* New York: Basic Books.

Pribram, K.H., & McGuiness, D. (1975). Arousal, activation and effort in the control of attention. *Psychological Review, 82*, 116–149.

Price, B.H., Daffner, K.R., Stowe, R.M., & Mesulam, M.M. (1990). The comportmental learning disabilities of early frontal lobe damage. *Brain, 113*, 1383–1393.

Price, D.J., & Blakemore, C. (1985). Regressive events in the postnatal development of association projections in the visual cortex. *Nature (London), 316*, 721–723.

Price, V.A. (1982). *Type A behavior pattern: A model for research and practice*. New York: Academic Press.

Prigatano, G.P. (1989). Work, love, and play after brain injury. *Bulletin of the Menninger Clinic, 53*, 414–431.

Pritchett, D.B., & Roberts, J.L. (1987). Dopamine regulates expression of the glandular-type kallikrein gene at the transcriptional level in the pituitary. *Proceedings of the National Academy of Sciences of the United States of America, 84*, 5545–5549.

Pulver, S.E. (1970). Narcissism. The term and the concept. *Journal of the American Psychoanalytic Association, 18*, 319–341.

Pulver, S.E. (1971). Can affects be unconscious? *International Journal of Psycho-Analysis, 52*, 347–354.

Purves, D., & LaMantia, A.-S. (1990). Construction of modular circuits in the mammalian brain. *Cold Spring Harbor Symposia on Quantitative Biolology, LV*, 445–452.

Purves, D., & Lichtman, J.W. (1980). Elimination of synapses in the developing nervous system. *Science, 210*, 153–157.

Purves, M.J. (1972). *The physiology of the cerebral circulation*. Cambridge, England: Cambridge University Press.

Putnam, F.W. (1992). Discussion: Are alter personalities fragments or figments. *Psychoanalytic Inquiry, 12*, 95–111.

Pysh, J.J. (1970). Mitochondrial changes in rat inferior colliculus during postnatal development: An electron microscopic study. *Brain Research, 18*, 325–342.

Quach, T.T., Rose, C., & Schwartz, J.C. (1978). [^{3}H] Glycogen hydrolysis in brain slices: Responses to neurotransmitters and modulation of noradrenaline receptors. *Journal of Neurochemistry, 30*, 1335–1341.

Quach, T.T., Rose, C., Duchemin, A.M., & Schwartz, J.C. (1982). Glycogenolysis induced by serotonin in brain: Identification of a new class of receptor. *Nature (London), 298*, 373–375.

Rabacchi, S., Bailly, Y., Delhaye-Bouchard, N., & Mariani, J. (1992). Involvement of the N—methyl D-aspatate (NMDA) receptor in synapse elimination during cerebellar development. *Science, 256*, 1823–1825.

Rabinowicz, T. (1979). The differentiate maturation of the human cerebral cortex. In F. Falkner & J.M. Tanner (Eds.), *Human growth, Vol. 3, Neurobiology and nutrition* (pp. 97–123). New York: Plenum Press.

Racker, H. (1968). *Transference and countertransference*. New York: International Universities Press.

Radke-Yarrow, M., & Zahn-Waxler, C. (1984). Roots, motives, and patterns in children's prosocial behavior. In E. Staub, D. Bar-Tal, J. Karylowski, & J. Reykowski (Eds.), *Development and maintenance of prosocial behavior* (pp. 81–99). New York: Plenum Press.

Raff, M.C. (1992). Social controls on cell survival and cell death. *Nature (London), 356*, 397–400.

Raichle, M.E., Eichling, J.O., & Grubb, R.L. (1974). Brain permeability of water. *Archives of Neurology, 30*, 319–321.

Raichle, M.E., Grubb, R.L., Gado, M.H., Eichling, J.O., & Ter-Pogossian, M.M. (1976). Correlation between regional cerebral blood flow and oxidative metabolism. *Archives of Neurology, 33*, 523–526 .

Raichle, M.E., Hartman, B.K., Eichling, J.O., & Sharpe, L.G. (1975). Central noradrenergic regulation of cerebral blood flow and vascular permeability. *Proceedings of the National Academy of Sciences of the United States of America, 72*, 3726–3730.

Raisman, G., & Field, P.M. (1973). Sexual dimorphism in the neutropil of the preoptic area of the rat and its dependence on neonatal androgen. *Brain Research, 54*, 1–29.

Rakfeldt, J., & Strauss, J.S. (1989). The low turning point. A control mechanism in the course of mental disorder. *Journal of Nervous and Mental Disease, 177*, 32–37.

Rakic, P., Bourgeois, J.-P., Eckenhoff, M.F., Zecevic, N., & Goldman-Rakic, P. (1986). Concurrent overproduction of synapses in diverse regions of the primate cerebral cortex. *Science, 232*, 232–235.

Raleigh, M.J. (1977). *The orbital frontal cortex and monkey social behavior*. Unpublished doctoral dissertation, University of California, Berkeley.

Raleigh, M.J., & Steklis, H.D. (1981). Effects of orbitofrontal and temporal neocortical lesions on the affiliative behavior of vervet monkeys (*Cercopithecus aethiops sabaeus*). *Experimental Neurology, 73*, 378–389.

Raleigh, M.J., Steklis, H., Ervin, F.R., Kling, A.S., & McGuire, M.T. (1979). The effects of orbitofrontal lesions on the aggressive behavior of vervet monkeys (Cercopithecus aethiops sabaeus). *Experimental Neurology, 66*, 158–168.

Ramon y Cajal, S. (1960). *Etude sur la neurogenese de quelques vertebres (L. Guth, trans. Studies on vertebrate neurogenesis)*. Springfield, IL: Thomas. (Original work published 1929).

Rapoport, D. (1953). On the psychoanalytic theory of affects. *International Journal of Psycho-Analysis, 34*, 177–198.

Rapoport, D. (1960). The structure of psychoanalytic theory. *Psychological Issues, Monograph 6*. New York: International Universities Press.

Rashid, N.A., & Cambray-Deakin, M.A. (1992). N -Methyl-D-aspartate effects on the growth, morphology and cytoskeleton of individual neurons in vitro. *Developmental Brain Research, 67*, 301–308.

Rasmussen, H., & Barrett, P.Q. (1984). Calcium messenger system: An integrated view. *Physiological Reviews, 64*, 938–984.

Rauschecker, J.P., & Marler, P. (1987). Cortical plasticity and imprinting: Behavioral and physiological contrasts and parallels. In J.P. Rauscheker & P. Marler (Eds.), *Imprinting and cortical plasticity: Comparative aspects of sensitive periods* (pp. 349–366). New York: Wiley.

Raymond, L.N., Reyes, E., Tokuda, S , & Jones, B.C. (1986). Differential immune response in two handled inbred strains of mice. *Physiology and Behavior, 37*, 295–297.

Redington, D.J., & Reidbord, S.P. (1992). Chaotic dynamics in autonomic nervous system activity of a patient during a psychotherapy session. *Biological Psychiatry, 31*, 993–1007.

Redmond, D.E., & Huang, Y.H. (1979). Current concepts. 2. New evidence for a locus—coeruleus—norepinephrine connection with anxiety. *Life Sciences, 25*, 2149–2162.

Reep, R.L., & Winans, S.S. (1982). Afferent connections of dorsal and ventral agranular insular cortex in the hamster, *Mesocricetus auratus*. *Neuroscience, 7*, 1265–1288.

Reese, T.S., & Karnovsky, M.J. (1967). Fine structural localization of a blood-brain barrier to exogenous peroxidase. *Journal of Cell Biology, 34*, 207–217.

Regard, M., & Landis,T. (1989). Beauty may differ in each half of the eye of the beholder. In I. Rentschler, B. Herzberger, & D. Epstein (Eds.), *Beauty and the brain* (pp. 243–256*)*. Basel: Birkhauser Verlag.

Reich, A. (1960). Pathologic forms of self-esteem regulation. *Psychoanalytic Study of the Child, 15*, 215–234.

Reich, E., & Luck, D.J.L (1966). Replication and inheritance of mitochondrial DNA. *Proceedings of the National Academy of Sciences of the United States of America, 55*, 1500.

Reidbord, S.P., & Redington, D.J. (1992). Psychophysiological processes during insight-oriented therapy: Further investigation into nonlinear psychodynamics. *Journal of Nervous and Mental Disease, 180*, 649–657.

Reinhard, J.F., Liebman, J.E., Schlossberg, A.J., & Moskowitz, M.A. (1979). Serotonin neurons project to small blood vessels in the brain. *Science, 206,* 85–87.

Reis, D.J., Ross, R.A., Gilad, G., & Joh, T. (1978). Reaction of central catecholaminergic neurons to injury: Model systems for studying the neurobiology of central regeneration and sprouting. In C. Cotman (Ed.), *Neuronal Plasticity* (pp. 197–226). New York: Raven Press.

Reiser, M.F. (1985). Converging sectors of psychoanalysis and neurobiology: Mutual challenge and opportunity. *Journal of the American Psychoanalytic Association, 33,* 11–34.

Reisert, I., Han, V., Lieth, E., Toran-Allerand, D., Pilgrim, C., & Lauder, J. (1987). Sex steroids promote neurite outgrowth in mesencephalic tyrosine hydroxylase immunoreactive neurons *in vitro. International Journal of Developmental Neuroscience, 5,* 91–98.

Reite, M., Kaufman, I.C., Pauley, J.D., & Stynes, A.J. (1974). Depression in infant monkeys: Physiological correlates. *Psychosomatic Medicine, 36,* 363–367.

Reite, M., & Capitanio, J.P. (1985). On the nature of social separation and attachment. In M. Reite & T. Field.(Ed.), *The psychobiology of attachment and separation* (pp. 223–255). Orlando, FL: Academic Press.

Reivich, M., Sokoloff, L., Ginsberg, D.M., Kennedy, C., Shapiro, H., & Greenberg, J. (1977). Regional metabolism of the brain. In K.J. Zulch (Ed.), *Brain and heart infarct* (pp. 58–72). Berlin: Springer-Verlag.

Renner, M.J., & Rosenzweig, M.R. (1987). *Enriched and impoverished environments.* New York: Springer.

Reppert, S.M., Duncan, M.J., & Weaver, D.R. (1987). Maternal influences on the developing circadian system. In N.A. Krasnegor, E.M. Blass, M.A. Hofer, & W.P. Smotherman (Eds.), *Perinatal development: A psychobiological perspective* (pp. 343–256). Orlando, FL: Academic Press.

Rescorla, R. A. (1981). Simultaneous conditioning. In P. Harzem & M.D. Zeiler (Eds.), *Advances in the analysis of behavior Vol. 2.* New York: Wiley.

Retzinger, S.R. (1989). *Marital conflict: The role of emotion.* Unpublished manuscript.

Reus, V.I., Weingartner, H., & Post, R.M. (1979). Clinical implications of state-dependent learning. *American Journal of Psychiatry, 136,* 927–931.

Rheingold, H.L. & Eckerman, C.O. (1979). The infant separates himself from his mother. *Science, 168,* 78–83.

Ricardo, J.A., & Koh, E.T. (1978). Anatomical evidence of direct projections from the nucleus of the solitary tract to the hypothalamus, amygdala, and other forebrain structures in the rat. *Brain Research, 153,* 1–26.

Rice, M. (1989). Children's language acquistion. *American Psychologist, 44,* 149–156.

Riche, D., de Pommery, J., & Menetrey, D. (1990). Neuropeptides and catecholamines in efferent projections of the nuclei of the solitary tract in the rat. *Journal of Comparative Neurology, 299,* 399–424.

Richfield, E.K., Young, A.B., & Penney, J.B. (1989). Comparative distribution of dopamine D-1 and D-2 receptors in the cerebral cortex of rats, cats, and monkeys. *Journal of Comparative Neurology, 286,* 409–426.

Richman, N.E. & Sokolove, R.L. (1992). The experience of aloneness, object representations, and evocative memory in borderline and neurotic patients. *Psychoanalytic Psychology, 9,* 77–91.

Richter, C., Park, J-W., & Ames, B.N. (1988). Normal oxidative damage to mitochondrial and nuclear DNA is extensive. *Proceedings of the National Academy of Sciences of the United States of America, 85,* 6465–6467.

Richter-Landersberg, C., & Dukain, D. (1983).. Role of glycoprotein in neuronal differentiation. *Experimental Cell Research, 149,* 335–345.

Rickles, W.H. (1986). Self psychology and somatization: an integration with alexithymia. In A. Goldberg (Ed.), *Progress in self psychology, Vol. 2* (pp. 212–226). New York: Guilford Press.

Ricks, M.H. (1985). The social transmission of parental behavior: Attachment across generations. *Monographs of the Society for Research in Child Development, 50,* 211–227.

Riegel, K.F. (1976). The dialectics of human development. *American Psychologist, 31,* 689–700.

Riesen, A.H. (1961). Stimulation as a requirement for growth and function in behavioral development. In D.W. Fiske & S.R. Maddi (Eds.), *Functions of varied existence* (pp. 57–80). Homewood, IL: Dorsey.

Riess, A. (1978). The mother's eye: For better and for worse. *Psychoanalytic Study of the Child, 33,* 381–409.

Rinkel, M., Greenblatt, M., Coon, G., & Solomon, H. (1947). Relation of the frontal lobe to the autonomic nervous system in man. *Archives of Neurology and Psychiatry, 58,* 570–581.

Rinkel, M., Solomon, H., Rosen, D., & Levine, J. (1950). Lobotomy and urinary bladder. In M. Greenblatt, R. Arnot, & H.C. Solomon (Eds.), *Studies in lobotomy* (pp. 370–379). Orlando, FL: Grune and Stratton.

Rinn, W.E. (1984). The neuropsychology of facial expression: A review of the neurological and psychological mechanisms for producing facial expressions. *Psychological Bulletin, 95,* 52–77.

Rinsley, D.B (1989). *Developmental pathogenesis and the treatment of borderline and narcissistic personalities.* Northvale, NJ: Jason Aronson.

Risau, W. (1986). Developing brain produces an angiogenesis factor, *Proceedings of the National Academy of Sciences of the United States of America, 83,* 3855–3859.

Risberg, J., & Prohovnik, I. (1983). Cortical processing of visual and tactile stimuli studied by non-invasive rCBF measurements. *Human Neurobiology, 46,* 744–754.

Riskind, J.H. (1984). They stoop to conquer: Guiding and self-regulatory functions of physical posture after success and failure. *Journal of Personality and Social Psychology, 47,* 479–493.

Risse, G.L., & Gazzaniga, M.S. (1978). Well-kept secrets of the right hemisphere: A carotid amytal study of restricted memory transfer. *Neurology, 28,* 950–953.

Ritossa, F.M., & Spiegelman, S. (1965). Localization of DNA complementary to ribosomal RNA in the nucleolar organizing region of Drosophila melanogaster. *Proceedings of the National Academy of Sciences of the United States of America, 53,* 737–745.

Rizzuto, A-M. (1991). Shame in psychoanalysis: The function of unconscious fantasies. *International Journal of Psycho-Analysis, 72,* 297–312.

Robbins, T.W., & Everitt, B.J. (1982). Functional studies of the central catecholamines. *International Review of Neurobiology, 23,* 303–365.

Robbins, K.L., & McAdam, D.W. (1974). Interhemispheric alpha asymmetry and imagery mode. *Brain and Language, 1,* 189–193.

Robbins, M. (1993). The psychopathological spectrum and the hierarchical model. In A. Wilson & J.E. Gedo (Eds.), *Hierarchical concepts in psychoanalysis* (pp. 284–308). New York: Guilford Press.

Roberts, S., Zomzely, C.E., & Bondy, S.C. (1970). Protein synthesis in the nervous system. In A. Lajtha (Ed.), *Protein metabolism of the nervous system* (pp. 14–35). New York: Plenum Press.

Robertson, H.A., Peterson, M.R., Murphy, K., & Robertson, G.S. (1989). D1-dopamine receptor agonists selectively activate striatal c-fos independent of rotational behavior. *Brain Research, 503,* 346–349.

Robertson, J., & Robertson, J. (1971). Young children in brief separation: A fresh look. *Psychoanalytic Study of the Child, 26,* 264–315.

Robertson, P.L., Dubois, M., Bowman, P.D., & Goldstein, G.W. (1985). Angiogenesis in developing rat brain: An in vivo and in vitro study. *Developmental Brain Research, 23,* 219–223.

Robin, E.D., & Wong, R. (1988). Mitochondrial DNA molecules and virtual number of mitochondria per cell in mammalian cells. *Journal of Cell Physiology, 136,* 507–513.

Robinson, R.G. (1979). Differential behavioral and biochemical effects of right and left hemispheric infarction in the rat. *Science, 205,* 707–710.

Robison, G.A., Butcher, R.W., & Sutherland, E.W. (1971). *Cyclic AMP.* New York: Academic Press.

Robson, K. (1967). The role of eye-to-eye contact on maternal infant attachment. *Journal of Child Psychology and Psychiatry, 8,* 13–25.

Robson, K. (1982). *The borderline child.* New York: McGraw-Hill.

Rochat, P. (1983). Oral touch in young infants: Responses to variations of nipple characteristics in the first months of life. *International Journal of Behavior and Development, 6,* 123–134.

Rochlin, G. (1953). The disorder of depression and elation. *Journal of the American Psychoanalytic Association, 1,* 438–457.

Rodin, E.A. (1973). Psychomotor epilepsy and aggressive behavior. *Archives of General Psychiatry, 28,* 210–213.

Rodriguez-Tebar, A., Dechand, G., & Barde, Y.-A. (1990). Binding of brain-derived neurotrophic factor to the nerve growth factor receptor. *Neuron, 4,* 487–492.

Roiphe, H., & Galenson, E. (1984). Infantile origins of disturbances in sexual identity. In J.D. Call, E. Galenson, & R. L. Tyson (Eds.), *Frontiers in infant psychiatry, Vol. 2* (pp. 435–440). New York: Basic Books.

Roitblat, H.L. (1982). The meaning of representation in animal memory. *Behavioral Brain Science, 5,* 353–406.

Roland, P.E. (1985). Cortical organization of voluntary behavior in man. *Human Neurobiology, 4,* 155–167.

Roland, P.E., Eriksson, L., Stone-Elander, S., & Widen, L. (1987). Does mental brain activity change the oxidative metabolism in the human brain? *Journal of Neuroscience, 7,* 2373–2389.

Roland, P.E., Eriksson, L., Widen, L., & Stone-Elander, S. (1989). Changes in regional oxidative metabolism induced by tactile learning and recognition in man. *European Journal of Neuroscience, 1,* 3–18.

Rolls, E.T. (1976). *The brain and reward.* New York: Pergamon Press,.

Rolls, E.T. (1986). Neural systems involved in emotion in primates. In R. Plutchik & H. Kellerman (Eds.), *Emotion: Theory, research, and practice Vol. 3* (pp. 125–143). Orlando, FL: Academic Press.

Rolls, E.T., Baylis, G.C., Hasselmo, M.E., & Nalwa, V. (1989). The effect of learning on the face selective responses of neurons in the cortex in the superior temporal sulcus of the monkey. *Experimental Brain Research, 76,* 153–164.

Rolls, E.T., & Cooper, S.J. (1974). Anesthetization and stimulation of the sulcal prefrontal cortex and brain-stimulation reward. *Physiology and Behavior, 12,* 563–571.

Rolls, E.T., Yaxley, S., & Sienkiewicz, Z.J. (1990). Gustatory responses of single neurons in the caudolateral orbitofrontal cortex of the macaque monkey. *Journal of Neurophysiology, 64,* 1055–1065.

Roosth, J., Pollard, R.B., Brown, S.L., & Meyer, W.J. III. (1986). Cortisol stimulation by recombinant interferon alpha 2. *Journal of Neuroimmunology, 12,* 311–316.

Rordorf, G., Koroshetz, W.J., & Bonventre, B.V. (1991). Heat shock protein protects cultured neurons from glutamate toxicity. *Neuron, 7,* 1043–1051.

Rose, G. (1972). Fusion states. In P.L. Giovacchini (Ed.), *Tactics and techniques in psychoanalytic theory* (pp. 137–169). New York: Jason Aronson.

Rose, J.E., & Woolsey, C.N. (1948). The orbitofrontal cortex and its connections with the mediodorsal nucleus in rabbit, sheep and cat. *Research Publications of the Association of Nervous and Mental Disease, 27,* 210–232.

Rose, L.M., Ginsberg, A.H., Rothstein, T.L., Ledbetter, J.A., & Clark, E.A. (1985). Selective loss of a subset of T helper cells in active multiple sclerosis. *Proceedings of the National Academy of Sciences of the United States of America, 82,* 7389–7393.

Rose, S.A. (1984). Developmental changes in hemispheric specialization for tactual processing in very young children: Evidence from cross-modal transfer. *Developmental Psychology, 20,* 568–574.

Rose, S.A. (1986). Abstraction in infancy: Evidence from cross-modal and cross-dimension transfer. In L.P. Lipsett & C. Rovee-Collier (Eds.), *Advances in infancy research, Vol. 4* (pp. 218–229). Norwood, NJ: Ablex.

Rose, S.A. (1990). Cross-modal transfer in human infants. What is being transferred? *Annals of the New York Academy of Sciences, 608*, 38–47.

Rose, S.A., Gottfried, A.W., & Bridger, W.H. (1978). Cross-modal transfer in infants: Relationship to prematurity and socioeconomic background. *Developmental Psychology, 14*, 643–652.

Rose, S.A., Gottfried, A.W., & Bridger, W.H. (1981). Cross-modal transfer and information processing by the sense of touch in infancy. *Developmental Psychology, 17*, 90–98.

Rose, S.A., Gottfried, A.W., & Bridger, W.H. (1983). Infant's cross-modal transfer from solid objects to their graphic representations. *Child Development, 54*, 686–694.

Rose, S.A., & Ruff, H.A. (1987). Cross-modal abilities in human infants. In J.D. Osofsky (Ed.), *Handbook of infant development* (2nd ed., pp. 318–362). New York: Wiley.

Rose, S.P.R. (1981). From causation to translations: What biochemists can contribute to the study of behavior. In P.O.G. Bateson & P.H. Klopfer (Eds.), *Perspectives in ethology, Vol. IV*. New York: Plenum Press.

Rose, S.P.R. (1989). Glycoprotein synthesis and postsynaptic remodelling in long-term memory. *Neurochemistry International, 14*, 299–307.

Rosenblum, L.A. (1987). Influences of environmental demand on maternal behavior and infant development. In N.A. Krasnegor, E.M. Blass, M.A. Hofer, & W.P. Smotherman. (Eds.), *Perinatal development: A psychobiological perspective* (pp. 377–395). Orlando, FL: Academic Press.

Rosenbluth, J. (1962). Subsurface cisterns and their relationship to the neuronal plasma membrane. *Journal of Cell Biology, 13*, 405–421.

Rosenkilde, C.E. (1979). Functional heterogeneity of the prefrontal cortex in the monkey: A review. *Behavorial and Neural Biology, 25*, 301–345.

Rosenkilde, C.E., Bauer, R.H., & Fuster, J.M. (1981). Single cell activity in ventral prefrontal cortex of behaving monkeys. *Brain Research, 209*, 375–394.

Rosenzweig, M.R., Bennet, E.L., & Diamond, M.C. (1972). Brain changes in response to experience. *Scientific American, 226*, 22–29.

Rosenzweig, M.R., & Leiman, A.L. (1968). Brain functions. *Annual Review of Psychology, 19*, 55–98.

Ross, E.D. (1983). Right-hemisphere lesions in disorders of affective language. In A. Kertesz (Ed.), *Localization in neuropsychology* (pp. 493–508). New York: Academic Press.

Ross, E.D. (1985). Modulation of affect and nonverbal communication by the right hemisphere. In M. Mesulam (Ed.), *Principles of behavioral neurology* (pp. 239–259). Philadelphia: F.A. Davis.

Rosselli-Austin, L., Hamilton, K.H., & Williams, J. (1987). Early postnatal development of the rat accessory olfactory bulb. *Developmental Brain Research, 36*, 304–308.

Rosvold, H.E. (1972). The frontal lobe system: Cortical-subcortical interrelationships. *Acta Neurobiologica Experimentales, 32*, 439–460.

Rothbart, M.K., & Derryberry, D. (1981). Development of individual differences in temperament. In M.E. Lamb & A.L. Brown (Eds.), *Advances in developmental psychology, Vol. 1* (pp. 37–86). Hillsdale, NJ: Lawrence Erlbaum Associates.

Rothbart, M.K., & Derryberry, D. (1982). Theoretical issues in temperament. In M. Lewis & L.T. Taft (Eds.), *Developmental disabilities: Theory, assessment, and intervention* (pp. 383–400). New York: SP Medical and Scientific Books.

Rothbart, M.K., Taylor, S.B., & Tucker, D.M. (1989). Right-sided facial asymmetry in infant emotional expression. *Neuropsychologia, 27*, 675–687.

Rothman, D.L., Novotny, E.J., Shulman, G.I., Howseman, A.M., Petroff, A.C., Mason, G., Nixon, T., Hanstock, C.C., Prichard, J.W., & Shulman, R.G. (1992). ^{1}H-[^{13}C] NMR measurements of [4-^{13}C] glutamate turnover in human brain. *Proceedings of the National Academy of Sciences of the United States of America, 89*, 9603–9606. .

Rothman, S.M., & Olney, J.W. (1987). Excitotoxicity and the NMDA receptor. *Trends in Neuroscience, 10*, 299–302.

Rotrosen, D., & Gallin, J.I. (1986). Histamine type I receptor occupancy increases endothelial cytosolic calcium, reduces F-actin, and promotes albumin diffusion across endothelial mono- layers. *Journal of Cell Biology, 103*, 2379–2387.

Routtenberg, A. (1968). The two-arousal hypothesis: Reticular formation and limbic system. *Psychological Review, 75*, 51–80.

Rovee-Collier, C.K., & Fagen, J. W. (1981). The retrieval of memory in early infancy. In L.P. Lipsitt (Ed:), *Advances in infancy research, Vol. 1*. Norwood, NJ: Ablex.

Rowan, R.A., & Maxwell, D.S. (1981). Patterns of vascular sprouting in the postnatal development of the cerebral cortex of the rat. *American Journal of Anatomy, 160*, 247–255.

Roy, S.C., & Sherrington, C.S. (1890). On the regulation of the blood supply of the brain. *Journal of Physiology (London), 11*, 85–108.

Rozin, P., & Fallon, A.E. (1987). A perspective on disgust. *Psychological Review, 94*, 23–41.

Rubin, R.T., Poland, R.E., Lasser, I.M., Winston, R.A., & Blodgett, N. (1987). Neuroendocrine aspects of primary endogenous depression. I. Cortisol secretory dynamics in patients and matched controls. *Archives of General Psychiatry, 44*, 328–336.

Rubinow, D.R., Gold, P.W., Savard, R., & Gold, P.W. (1984). Cortisol hypersecretion and cognitive impairment in depression. *Archives of General Psychiatry, 41*, 179–183.

Rubinow, D.R., Post, R.M., Gold, P.W. et al. (1984). The relationship between cortisol and clinical phenomenology of affective illness. In R.M. Post & J.C. Ballenger (Eds.), *Neurobiology of mood disorders*. Baltimore: Williams & Wilkins.

Ruch, T.C., & Shenkin, H.A. (1943). The relation of area 13 on orbital surface of frontal lobes to hyperactivity and hyperphagia in monkeys. *Journal of Neurophysiology, 6*, 349–360.

Ruijter, J.M., Baker, R.E., de Jong, B.M., & Romijn, H.J. (1991). Chronic blockade of bioelectric activity in neonatal rat cortex grown in vitro: Morphological effects. *International Journal of Developmental Neuroscience, 9*, 331–338.

Russell, J.A. (1980). A circumplex model of affect. *Journal of Personality and Social Psychology, 36*, 1152–1168.

Russell, M.J. (1976). Human olfactory communication. *Nature (London), 260*, 520–522.

Rutter, M. (1987). Temperament, personality and personality disorder. *British Journal of Psychiatry, 150*, 443–458.

Sachar, E.J., Mackenzie, J. M., Binstock, W.A., & Mack, J.E. (1968). Corticosteroid responses to the psychotherapy of reactive depressions. II. Further clinical and physiological implications. *Psychosomatic Medicine, 30*, 23–44.

Sachs, E. Jr., Brendler, S.J., & Fulton, J.F. (1949). The orbital gyri. *Brain, 72*, 227–240.

Sackheim, H.A., & Gur, R.C. (1983). Facial asymmetry and the communication of emotion. In J.T. Cacioppo & R.E. Petty (Eds.), *Social psychophysiology: A sourcebook* (pp. 307–352). New York: Guilford Press.

Safer, M.A. (1981). Sex and hemisphere differences in access to codes for processing emotional expressions and faces. *Journal of Experimental Psychology: General, 110*, 86–100.

Sakariassen, K.S., Bolhuis, P.A., & Sixma, J.J. (1979). Human blood platelet adhesion to artery subendothelium is mediated by Factor VIII-von Willebrand factor bound to the subendothelium. *Nature (London), 279*, 636–638.

Salamy, A. (1978). Commissural transmission: Maturational changes in transmission. *Science, 200*, 1409–1411.

Saland, L.C., Van Epps, D.E., Ortiz, E., & Samora, A. (1983). Acute injections of opioid peptides into the rat cerebral ventricle: A macrophage-like cellular response. *Brain Research Bulletin, 10*, 523–528.

Sameroff, A.J. (1989). Principles of development and psychopathology. In A.J. Sameroff & R.N. Emde (Eds.), *Relationship disturbances in early childhood* (pp. 17–32). New York: Basic Books.

Sameroff, A.J., & Emde, R.N. (1989). *Relationship disturbances in early childhood*. New York: Basic Books.

Sampson, H. (1992). A new psychoanalytic theory and its testing in research. In J.W. Barron, M.N. Eagle, & D.L. Wolitsky (Eds.), *Interface of psychoanalysis and psychology* (pp. 586–604). Washington, DC: American Psychological Association.

Samson, F.E., Jr., Balfour, W.M., & Jacobs, R.J. (1960). Mitochondrial changes in developing rat brain. *American Journal of Physiology, 199,* 693–696.

Sananes, C.B., Gaddy, J.R., & Campbell, B.A. (1988). Ontogeny of conditioned heart rate to an olfactory stimulus. *Developmental Psychobiology, 21,* 117–134.

Sander, L.W. (1975). Infant and caretaking environment. In E.J. Anthony (Ed.), *Explorations in child psychiatry* (pp. 129–166). New York: Plenum Press.

Sander, L.W. (1976). Epilogue. In E.N. Rexford, L.W. Sander, & T. Shapiro (Eds.), *Infant psychiatry.* New Haven: Yale University Press.

Sander, L.W. (1977). Regulation of exchange in the infant caretaker system: A viewpoint on the ontogeny of structures. In N. Freedman & S. Grand (Eds.), *Communicative structures and psychic structures* (pp. 13–34). New York: Plenum Press.

Sander, L.W. (1980). New knowledge about the infant from current research: Implications for psychoanalysis. *Journal of the American Psychoanalytic Association, 28,* 181–198.

Sander, L.W. (1988). The event-structure of regulation in the neonate-caregiver system as a biological background for early organization of psychic structure. In A. Goldberg (Ed.), *Progress in self psychology, Vol. 3* (pp. 64–77). Hillsdale, NJ: The Analytic Press.

Sandler, J. (1987). *From Safety to superego.* London: Karnac.

Sandler, J., & Rosenblatt, B. (1962). The concept of the representational world. *Psychoanalytic Study of the Child, 17,* 128–145.

Sandler, J., & Sandler, A-M. (1978). On the development of object relationships and affects. *International Journal of Psycho-Analysis, 59,* 285–296.

Sanghera, M.K., Rolls, E.T., & Roper-Hall, A. (1979). Visual responses of neurons in the dorsolateral amygdala of the alert monkey. *Experimental Neurology, 63,* 610–626.

Sansone, R.A., Fine, M.A., & Mulderig, J.K. (1991). An empirical examination of soothing tactics in borderline personality disorder. *Comprehensive Psychiatry, 32,* 431–439.

Sanville, J. (1991). *The playground of psychoanalytic therapy.* Hillsdale, NJ: The Analytic Press.

Saper, C.B. (1982). Convergence of autonomic and limbic connections in the insular cortex of the rat. *Journal of Comparative Neurology, 210,* 163–173.

Saper, C.B., Loewy, A.D., Swanson, L.W., & Cowan, W.M. (1976). Direct hypothalamo-autonomic connections. *Brain Research, 117,* 305–312.

Sapolsky, R.M. (1987). Glucocorticoids and hippocampal damage. *Trends in Neurosciences, 10,* 346–349.

Sapolsky, R.M., & Eichenbaum, H. (1980). Thalamocortical mechanisms in odor-guided behavior. II. Effects of lesions of the mediodorsal thalamic nucleus and frontal cortex on odor preferences and sexual behavior in the hamster. *Brain Behavior and Evolution, 17,* 276–290.

Sapolsky, R.M., Krey, L.C., & McEwen, B.S. (1984). Glucocorticoid-sensitive neurons are involved in terminating the adrenocortical stress response. *Proceedings of the National Academy of Sciences of the United States of America, 81,* 6174–6177.

Sapolsky, R.M., Rivier, C., Yamamoto, G., Plotsky, P., & Vale, W. (1987). Interleukin-1 stimulates the secretion of hypothalamic corticotropin-releasing factor. *Science, 238,* 522–524.

Sarter, M., & Markowitsch, H.J. (1984). Collateral innervation of medial and lateral prefrontal cortex by amygdaloid, thalamic, and brain-stem neurons. *Journal of Comparative Neurology, 224,* 445–460.

Sarter, M., & Markowitsch, H.J. (1985). Involvement of the amygdala in learning and memory. A critical review, with emphasis on anatomical studies. *Behavioral Neuroscience, 99,* 342–380.

Sartre, J-P. (1957). *Being and nothingness.* London: Methuen.

Sauerland, E.K., Knauss, Y., Nakamura, Y., & Clemente, C.D. (1967). Inhibition of monosynaptic and polysynaptic reflexes and muscle tone by electrical stimulation of the cerebral cortex. *Experimental Neurology, 17*, 159–171.

Saunders, N.R. (1977). Ontogeny of the blood-brain barrier. *Experimental Eye Research, 25*, 523–550. (Supplement).

Savasta, H., Dubois, D.A., & Scatton, B. (1986). Autoradiographic localization of D1 dopamine receptors in the rat brain with (^{3}H)SCH 23390. *Brain Research, 375*, 291–301.

Sawchenko, P.E. (1987). Evidence for a local site of action for glucocorticoids in inhibiting CRF and vasopressin expression in the paraventricular nucleus. *Brain Research, 403*, 213–224.

Sawchenko, P.E., & Swanson, L.W. (1982). Immunocytochemical identification of neurons in the paraventricular nucleus of the hypothalamus that project to the medulla or to the spinal cord in the rat. *Journal of Compartive Neurology, 205*, 260–272.

Saxby, G.P., & Bryden, M.P. (1985). Left visual-field advantage in children for processing visual emotional stimuli. *Developmental Psychology, 21*, 253–261.

Scaife, M., & Bruner, J.S. (1975). The capacity for joint visual attention in the infant. *Nature (London), 253*, 265–266.

Scarr, S. & Kidd, K.K. (1983). Developmental behavior genetics. In P.H. Mussen (Ed.), *Handbook of child psychology* (4th ed). New York: Wiley.

Scarr, S., & Eisenberg, M. (1993). Child care research: Issues, perspectives, and results. *Annual Review of Psychology, 44*, 613–644.

Schaal, B. (1986). Presumed olfactory exchanges between mother and neonate in humans. In J. LeCamus & R. Campon (Eds.), *Ethologie et psychologie de l'Enfant*. Toulouse: Privat.

Schacter, D.L., & Moscovich, M. (1984). Infants, amnesics, and dissociable memory systems. In M. Moscovich (Ed.), *Infant memory* (pp. 173–216). New York: Plenum.

Schacter, S., & Latane, B. (1964). Crime, cognition, and the autonomic nervous system. In M.R. Jones (Ed.), *Nebraska symposium on motivation*. Lincoln: University of Nebraska Press.

Schafer, R. (1968). *Aspects of internalization*. New York: International Universities Press.

Schaffer, H.R. (1984). *The child's entry into a social world*. London: Academic Press.

Schaffer, H.R., & Crook, C.K. (1980). Child compliance and maternal control techniques. *Developmental Psychology, 16*, 54–61.

Schaffer, H.R. & Emerson, P.E. (1964). The development of social attachments in infancy. *Monographs of the Society for Research in Child Development, 29*, (3, whole No. 94).

Schalling, D. (1978). Psychopathic behavior: Personality and neuropsychology. In R.D. Hare & D. Schalling (Eds.), *Psychopathic behavior: Approaches to research*. Chichester, England: Wiley.

Schanberg, S.M., & Kuhn, C.M. (1980). Maternal depression: an animal model of psychosocial dwarfism. In E. Usdin, T.L. Sourkes, & M.B.H. Youdim (Eds.), *Enzymes and neurotransmitters in mental disease* (pp. 373–393). New York: Wiley.

Schapiro, S. (1968). Some physiological, biochemical, and behavioral consequences of neonatal hormone administration: Cortisol and thyroxine. *General Comprehensive Endocrinology, 10*, 214–228.

Schapiro, S., & Vukovich, K.R. (1970). Early experience effects upon cortical dendrites: A proposed model of development. *Science, 167*, 292–294.

Schayer, R.W. (1970). Biogenic amines and microcirculatory homeostasis. In J.J. Blum (Ed.), *Biogenic amines as physiological regulators* (pp. 239–251). Englewood Cliffs, NJ: Prentice-Hall.

Schechter, D. (1979). The loving and persecuting superego. *Contemporary Psychoanalysis, 15*, 361–379.

Scheff, T.J. (1988). Shame and conformity: The deference-emotion system. *American Sociological Review, 53*, 395–406.

Scheflen, A.E. (1981). *Levels of schizophrenia*. New York: Brunner / Mazel.

Scheibner, T., & Tork, I. (1987). Ventromedial mesencephalic tegmental (VMT) projections to ten functionally different cortical areas in the cat: topography and quantitative analysis. *Journal of Comparative Neurology, 259*, 247–265.

Scheiss, M.C., Joels, M., & Shinnick-Gallagher, P. (1988). Estrogen priming affects active membrane properties of medial amygdala neurons. *Brain Research*, *440*, 380–385.

Schenkenberg, T., Dustman, R.E., & Beck, E.C. (1971). Changes in evoked responses related to age, hemisphere and sex. *Electroencephalography and Clinical Neurophysiology*, *30*, 163–164.

Scherer, J. (1967). Electrophysiological aspects of cortical development. *Progress in Brain Research*, *22*, 480–489.

Scherer, K.R. (1986). Vocal affect expression: A review and a model for future research. *Psychological Bulletin*, *99*, 143–165.

Scherer, K.R. (1993). Neuroscience projections to current debates in emotion psychology. *Cognition & Emotion*, *7*, 1–41.

Schiff, B.B., & Lamon, M. (1989). Inducing emotion by unilateral contraction of facial muscles: A new look at hemispheric specialization and the experience of emotion. *Neuropsychologia*, *27*, 923–935.

Schiff, S.R. (1982). Conditioned dopaminergic activity. *Biological Psychiatry*, *17*, 135–154.

Schleifer, S., Keller, S., Meyerson, A., Raskin, M., Davis, K., & Stein, M. (1984). Lymphocyte function in major depressive disorder. *Archives of General Psychiatry*, *41*, 484–486.

Schlenker, B.R., & Weigold, M.F. (1992). Interpersonal processes involving impression regulation and management. *Annual Review of Psychology*, *43*, 133–168.

Schmale, A.H., & Engel, G.L. (1975). The role of conservation-withdrawal in depressive reactions. In E.J. Anthony & T. Benedek (Eds.), *Depression and human existence*. Boston: Little, Brown.

Schmidt, R.H., Bjorklund, A., Lindvall, O., & Loren, I. (1982). Prefrontal cortex: Dense dopaminergic input in the newborn rat. *Developmental Brain Research*, *5*, 222–228.

Schneider, C. (1977). *Shame, exposure and privacy*. Boston: Beacon Press.

Schneiderman N., & McCabe, P.M. (1985). Biobehavioral responses to stress. In M.Field, P.M. McCabe, & N. Schneiderman (Eds.), *Stress and coping* (pp. 13–61). Hillsdale, NJ: Lawrence Erlbaum Associates.

Schofield, S.P.M., & Everitt, B.J. (1981). The organisation of catecholamine-containing neurons in the brain of the rhesus monkey (*Macaca mulatta*). *Journal of Anatomy*, *132*, 391–418.

Schore, A.N. (1991). Early superego development: The emergence of shame and narcissistic affect regulation in the practicing period. *Psychoanalysis and Contemporary Thought*, *14*, 187–250.

Schore, J.R. (1993, Number 11). Women, the superego and shame. *Psychiatric Times*, pp. 41–42.

Schultz, W., & Romo, R. (1990). Dopamine neurons of the monkey midbrain: Contingencies of responses to stimuli eliciting immediate behavioral reactions. *Journal of Neurophysiology*, *63*, 607–617.

Schumacher, M. (1990). Rapid effects of steroid hormones: An emerging concept in neuroendocrinology. *Trends in Neuroscience*, *13*, 359–362.

Schur, M. (1955). Comments on the metapsychology of somatization. *Psychoanalytic Study of the Child*, *10*, 119–164.

Schwalbe, M.L. (1991). The autogenesis of the self. *Journal of the Theory of Social Behavior*, *21*, 269–295.

Schwartz, A. (1990). On narcissism: An (other) introduction. In R.A. Glick & S. Bone (Eds.), *Pleasure beyond the pleasure principle* (pp. 111–137). New Haven: Yale University Press.

Schwartz, G.E. (1982). Psychophysiological patterning and emotion revisited: A systems perspective. In C.E. Izard (Ed.), *Measuring emotions in infants and children* (pp. 67–93). Cambridge, England: Cambridge University Press.

Schwartz, G.E. (1990). Psychobiology of repression and health: A systems approach. In J. L. Singer (Ed.), *Repression and dissociation* (pp. 405–434). Chicago: The University of Chicago Press.

Schwartz, G.G., & Rosenblum, L.A. (1983). Allometric influences on primate mothers and infants. In L. Rosenblum & H. Moltz (Eds.), *Symbiosis in parent-young interactions*. New York: Plenum Press.

Schwartz, M., Creasey, H., Grady, C.L., DeLeo, J.M., Frederickson, H.A., Cutler, N.R. et al.

(1985). Computed tomographic analysis of brain morphometrics in 30 healthy men, aged 21 to 81 years. *Annals of Neurology, 17,* 146–157.

Schwartz, M.L., & Goldman-Rakic, P.S. (1984). Callosal and intrahemispheric connectivity of the prefrontal association cortex in rhesus monkey: Relation between intraparietal and principal sulcal cortex. *Journal of Comparative Neurology, 226,* 403–420.

Scott, J.P. (1958). Critical periods in trhe development of social behavior in puppies. *Psychosomatic Medicine, 20,* 42–54.

Scott, J.P. (1962). Critical periods in behavioral development. *Science, 138,* 949–958.

Scott, J.P. (1979a). *Critical periods.* New York: Academic Press.

Scott, J.P. (1979b). Critical periods in organizational processes. In F. Falkner & J.M. Tanner (Eds.), *Human growth, Vol. 3, Neurobiology and nutrition* (pp. 223–241). New York: Plenum Press.

Scott, W.A. (1969). Structure of nature cognitions. *Journal of Personality and Social Psychology, 12,* 261–278.

Searles, H. (1963). The place of neutral therapist-responses in psychotherapy with the schizophrenic patient. In *Collected papers on schizophrenia and related subjects* (pp. 626–653). London: Hogarth Press.

Searles, H. (1987). The development in the patient of an internalized image of the therapist. In J.S. Grotstein, J.Lang, & M. Solomon (Eds.), *The borderline patient: Emerging concepts in diagnosis.* London: The Analytic Press.

Segalowitz, S.J., Unsal, A., & Dywan, J. (1992). Cleverness and wisdom in 12-year-olds: Electrophysiological evidence for late maturation of the frontal lobe. *Developmental Neuropsychology, 8,* 279–298.

Seguela, P., Watkins, K.C., & Descarries, L. (1988). Ultrastructural features of dopamine axon terminals in the anteromedial and the suprarhinal cortex of adult rat. *Brain Research, 442,* 11–22.

Seiler, N., & Lamberty, U. (1975). Interrelations between polyamines and nucleic acids: Changes of polyamine and nucleic acid concentrations in the developing rat brain. *Journal of Neurochemistry, 24,* 5–13.

Seitz, R.J., & Roland, P.E. (1992). Vibratory stimulation increases and decreases the regional blood flow and oxidative metabolism: A positron emission tomography (PET) study. *Acta Neurolologica Scandinavica, 86,* 60–67.

Seligman, M.E.P., & Hager, J.E. (1972). *Biological boundaries of learning.* New York: Appleton-Century-Crofts.

Seltzer, B., & Pandya, D.N. (1989). Frontal lobe connections of the superior temporal sulcus in the rhesus monkey. *Journal of Comparative Neurology, 281,* 97–113.

Selye, H. (1956). *The stress of life.* New York: McGraw Hill.

Semenza, C., Pasini, M., Zettin, M., Tonin, P., & Portolan, P. (1986). Right hemisphere patients' judgements on emotions. *Acta Neurologica Scandinavica 74,* 43–50.

Semmes, J. (1968). Hemispheric specialization: A possible clue to mechanism. *Neuropsychologia, 6,* 11–26.

Sergent, J. (1987). Information processing and laterality effects for object and face perception. In G. W. Humphreys & M.J. Riddoch (Eds.), *Visual object processing: A cognitive neuropsychological approach.* Hillsdale, NJ: Lawrence Erlbaum Associates.

Sergent, J. (1989). Image generation and processing of generated images in the cerebral hemispheres. *Journal of Experimental Psychology: Human Perception and Performance, 15,* 170–178.

Sesack, S.R., & Pickel, V.M. (1992). Prefrontal cortical efferents in the rat synapse on unlabeled neuronal targets of catecholamine terminals in the nucleus accumbens septi and on dopamine neurons in the ventral tegmental area. *Journal of Comparative Neurology, 320,* 145–160.

Settlage, C.F. (1977). The psychoanalytic understanding of narcissistic and borderline personality disorders: Advances in developmental theory. *Journal of the American Psychoanalytic Association, 25,* 805–833.

Settlage, C.F., Curtis, J., Lozoff, M., Silberschatz, G., & Simburg, E.J. (1988). Conceptualizing adult development. *Journal of the American Psychoanalytic Association, 36*, 347–369.

Settlage, C.F., Rosenthal, J., Spielman, P.M., Gassner, S., Afterman, J., Bemesderfer, S., & Kolodny, S. (1990). An exploratory study of mother-child interaction during the second year of life. *Journal of the American Psychoanalytic Association, 38*, 705–731.

Seutin, V., Verbanck, P., Massotte, L., & Dreese, A. (1990). Evidence for the presence of N-methyl-D-aspartate receptors in the ventral tegmental area of the rat: An electrophysiological study. *Brain Research, 527*, 147–150.

Severino, S., McNutt, E., & Feder, S. (1987). Shame and the development of autonomy. *Journal of the American Academy of Psychoanalysis, 15*, 93–106.

Shapiro, T., & Emde, R.N. (1992). *Affect: psychoanalytic perspectives*. Madison, CT: International Universities Press.

Shapiro, R.E., & Miselis, R.R. (1985). The central neural connections of the area postrema of the rat. *Journal of Comparative Neurology, 234* 344–364.

Shatz, M., Wellman, H., & Silber, S. (1983). The acquisition of mental verbs: A systematic investigation of the first reference to mental states. *Cognition, 14*, 301–321.

Sheffield, W.P., Shore, G.C., & Randall, S.K. (1990). Mitochondrial precursor protein: Effects of 70-kilodalton heat shock protein on polypeptide folding, aggregation, and import competence. *Journal of Biological Chemistry, 265*, 1069–1076.

Sheng, M., & Greenberg, M.E. (1990). The regulation and function of c-*fos* and other immediate early genes in the nervous system. *Neuron, 4*, 477–485.

Sheridan, P. (1979). Estrogen binding in the neonatal cortex. *Brain Research, 178*, 201–206.

Sherrod, L.R. (1981). Issues in cognitive-perceptual development: The special case of social stimuli. In M.E. Lamb & L.R. Sherrod (Eds.), *Infant social cognition: Empirical and theoretical considerations* (pp. 11–36). Hillsdale, NJ: Lawrence Erlbaum Associates.

Sherry, D.F., & Schacter, D.L. (1987). The evolution of multiple memory systems. *Psychological Review, 94*, 439–454.

Sherwood, V.R. (1989). Object constancy: The illusion of being seen. *Psychoanalytic Psychology, 6*, 15–30.

Shibasaki, T., Yamauchi, N., Hotta, M., Imaki, T., Oda, T., Ling, N., & Demura, H. (1991). Brain corticotropin-releasing hormone increases arousal in stress. *Brain Research, 554*, 352–354.

Shiller, V.M., Izard, C.E., & Hembree, E.A. (1986). Patterns of emotion expression during separation in the strange-situation procedure. *Developmental Psychology, 22*, 378–382.

Shimazu, T. (1971). Regulation of glycogen metabolism in liver by the autonomic nervous system. IV. Activation of glycogen synthetase by vagal stimulation. *Biochimica et Biophysica Acta, 252*, 28–38.

Shimazu, T., & Amakawa, A. (1968). Regulation of glycogen metabolism in liver by the autonomic nervous system. II. Neural control of glycogenolytic enzymes. *Biochimica et Biophysica Acta, 165*, 335–348.

Shimazu, T., Fukuda, A., & Ban, T. (1966). Reciprocal influences of the ventromedial and lateral hypothalamic nuclei on blood glucose level and liver glycogen content. *Nature (London), 210*, 1178–1179.

Shimizu, H., Creveling, C.R., & Daly, J. (1970). Stimulated formation of adenosine $3',5'$-cyclic phosphate in cerebral cortex: Synergism between electrical activity and biogenic amines. *Proceedings of the National Academy of Sciences of the United States of America, 65*, 1033–1040.

Shinbrot, T., Grebogi, C., Ott, E., & Yorke, J.A. (1993). Using small perturbations to control chaos. *Nature (London), 363*, 411–417.

Shipley, M.T. (1982). Insular cortex projection to the nucleus of the solitary tract and brain stem visceromotor regions in the mouse. *Brain Research Bulletin, 8*, 139–142.

Shopsin, B. (1979). Mania: Clinical aspects, rating scales and incidence of manic-depressive illness. In B. Shopsin (Ed.), *Manic illness* (pp. 57–104). New York: Raven Press.

Shor, J. (1990). *Work, love, play: Self repair in the psychoanalytic dialogue*. Los Angeles: Double Helix Press.

Shulman, D.G. (1992). The quantitative investigation of psychoanalytic theory and therapy: A bibliography 1986–1992. *Psychoanalytic Psychology, 9*, 529–542.

Shulman, M.E. (1987). On the problem of the id in psychoanalytic theory. *International Journal of Psycho-Analysis, 68*, 161–173.

Sidman, M. (1988). Infant attention: What processes are measured? *Cahiers de Psychologie Cognitive / European Bulletin of Cognitive Psychology, 8*, 512–516.

Sie, S.-S., & Fishman, W.H. (1964). Glycogen synthetase: Its response to cortisol. *Science, 143*, 816–819.

Siegfried, J. (1965). Topographie de projections corticales du nerf vague chez le chat. [Topography of the cortical projections of the vagal nerve in the cat]. *Helvetica Physiologica Acta, 19*, 269–278.

Siever, L.J., & Davis, K.L. (1985). Overview: Toward a dysregulation hypothesis of depression. *American Journal of Psychiatry, 142*, 1017–1031.

Silberman, E. K. & Weingartner, H. (1986). Hemispheric lateralization of functions related to emotion. *Brain and Cognition, 5*, 322–353.

Simard, R., & Bernhard, W. (1967). A heat-sensitive cellular function located in the nucleolus. *Journal of Cell Biology, 34*, 61–71.

Simerly, R.B., Swanson, L.W., & Gorski, R.A. (1985). The distribution of monoaminergic cells and fibers in a periventricular preoptic nucleus involved in the control of gonadotropin release: Immunohistochemical evidence for a dopaminergic sexual dimorphism. *Brain Research, 330*, 55–64.

Simionescu, M., Simionescu, N., & Palade, G.E. (1975). Segmental differentiation of cell junctions in the vascular endothelium. The microvasculature. *Journal of Cell Biology, 67*, 863–886.

Simon, H. (1974). How big is a chunk? *Science, 183*, 482–488.

Simon, H., Scatton, B., & LeMoal, M. (1980). Dopaminergic A10 neurons are involved in cognitive function. *Nature (London), 286*, 150–151.

Simonds, R.J., & Scheibel, A.B. (1989). The postnatal development of the motor speech area: A preliminary study. *Brain and Language, 37*, 42–58.

Simonoski, K., Murphy, R.A., Rennert, P., & Heinrich, G. (1987). Cortisone, testosterone, and aldosterone reduce levels of nerve growth factor messenger ribonucleic acid in L-929 fibroblast. *Endocrinology, 121*, 1432–1437.

Simpson, J., & Isacson, O. (1993). Mitochondrial impairment induced by 3-nitropropionic acid reduces the threshold for NMDA-mediated neuronal death in the rat striatum. *Experimental Neurology, 121*, 56–72.

Singer, J.L. (1985). Transference and the human condition: A cognitive-affective perspective. *Psychoanalytic Psychology, 2*, 189–219.

Singer, W. (1986a). The brain as a self-organizing system. *European Archives of Psychiatry and Neurological Sciences, 236*, 4–9.

Singer, W. (1986b). Neuronal activity as a shaping factor in postnatal development of visual cortex. In W.T. Greenough & J.M. Juraska (Eds.), *Developmental neuropsychobiology* (pp. 271–293). Orlando, FL: Academic Press.

Sirotin, B.Z. (1961). Electrophysiological study of reception from certain internal organs in man. Report I. Impulses from receptors of the resected stomach and small intestine. *Bulletin of Experimental Biology and Medicine U.S.S.R., 50*, 873–877.

Siviy, S.M., Kritikos, A., Atrens, D., & Sheperd, A. (1989). Effects of norepinephrine infused in the paraventricular hypothalamus on energy expenditure in the rat. *Brain Research, 487*, 79–88.

Skinner, B.F. (1953). *The behavior of organisms: An experimental analysis*. New York: Appleton-Century Crofts.

Skinner, B.F. (1989). *Recent issues in the analysis of behavior*, Columbus, OH: Merrill.

Skinner, J.E. (1988). Regulation of cardiac vulnerability by the frontal cortex: A new concept of Cannon's cerebral defense mechanism. In G.C. Galbraith, M.L. Kietzman, & E. Donchin (Eds.),

Neurophysiology and psychophysiology: Experimental and clinical Applications (pp. 68–80). Hillsdale, NJ: Lawrence Erlbaum Associates.

Smiley, J.F., Williams, S.M., Szigeti, K., & Goldman-Rakic, P.S. (1992). Light and electron microscopic characterization of dopamine-immunoreactive axons in human cerebral cortex. *Journal of Comparative Neurology, 321*, 325–335.

Smith, C.A. (1989). Dimensions of appraisal and physiological response in emotion. *Journal of Personality and Social Psychology, 56*, 339–353.

Smith, C.G. (1981). *Serial dissection of the human brain*. Baltimore-Munich: Urban & Scwarzenberg.

Smith, H.M. (1960). *Evolution of chordate structure*. New York: Holt, Rinehart, and Winston.

Smith, E. M., Brosnan, P., Meyer, W.J., & Blalock, J.E. (1987). An ACTH receptor on human mononuclear leukocytes: relation to adrenal ACTH-receptor activity. *New England Journal of Medicine, 317*, 1266–1269.

Smith, O.A., & DeVito, J.L. (1984). Central neural integration for the control of autonomic responses associated with emotion. *Annual Review of Neuroscience, 7*, 43–65.

Snarey, J.R. (1985). Cross-cultural universality of social-moral development: a critical review of Kohlbergian research. *Psychological Bulletin, 97*, 202–232.

Snider, W.D., & Johnson, E.M. Jr. (1989). Neurotrophic molecules. *Annals of Neurology, 26*, 489–506.

Snyder, S.H. (1979). Receptors, neurotransmitters, and drug responses. *New England Journal of Medicine, 300*, 465–472.

Socarides, C.W. (1982). *Homosexuality*. New York: Jason Aronson.

Sogon, S., & Masutani, M. (1989). Identification of emotion from body movements: A cross-cultural study of Americans and Japanese. *Psychological Reports, 65*, 35–46.

Sokoloff, L., & Klee, C.B. (1965). The effects of thyroid on protein synthesis in brain and other organs. *Association for Research in Nervous and Mental Disease, 43*, 371–386.

Solnit, A.J. (1982). Developmental perspectives on self and object constancy. *Psychoanalytic Study of the Child, 32*, 201–217.

Solomon, G.F., Amkraut, A.A., & Kasper, P. (1974). Immunity, emotions and stress, with special reference to the mechanisms of stress effects on the immune system. *Annals of Clinical Research, 6*, 313–322.

Solomon, G.F., Levine, S., & Kraft, J.K. (1968). Early experience and immunity. *Nature (London), 220*, 821–822.

Sommerville, J. (1986). Nucleolar structure and ribosome biogenesis. *Trends in Biochemical Science, 11*, 438–442.

Sonnenberg, J.L., Mitchelmore, C., MacGregor-Leon, P.F., Hempstead, J., Morgan, J.I., & Curran, T. (1989). Glutamate receptor agonists increase the expression of FOS, Fra, and AP-1 DNA binding activity in the mammalian brain. *Journal of Neuroscience Research, 24*, 72–80.

Sorman, P., Wasserstein, J., & Zappulla, R. (1983). *Cerebral correlates of cognitive regression and parallels with schizophrenic thought processes*. Paper presented to the International Neuropsychological Society Meeting, Mexico City.

Spacek, J. (1982). "Free" postsynaptic-like densities in normal adult brain: Their occurrence, distribution, structure and association with surface cisterns. *Journal of Neurocytology, 11*, 693–706.

Spear, N.E. (1978). *The processing of memories: Forgetting and retention*. Hillsdale, NJ: Lawrence Erlbaum Associates.

Specht, L.A., Pickel, V.M., Joh, T.H., & Reis, D.J. (1981). Light-microscopic immunocytochemical localization of tyrosine hydroxylase in prenatal rat brain. II. Late ontogeny. *Journal of Comparative Neurology, 199*, 255–276.

Spemann, H. (1938). *Embryonic development and induction*. New Haven: Yale University Press.

Spence, D.P. (1982). *Narrative truth and historical truth: Meaning and interpretation in psychoanalysis*. New York: W.W. Norton.

Spence, J.T., & Helmreich, R. (1978). *Masculinity and feminity: Their psychological dimensions, correlates, and antecedents*. Austin: University of Texas Press.

Spencer, W.G. (1894). The effect produced upon respiration by faradic excitation of the cerebrum in the monkey, dog, cat and rabbit. *Philosophical Transactions of the Royal Society of London, 185b*, 609–657.

Spero, M.H. (1984). Shame: An object-relational formulation. *Psychoanalytic Study of the Child, 39*, 259–282.

Spero, M.H. (1993). The concept of iconic mental representation as anticipated by the talmudic term *De'mut De'yukon. Psychoanalysis and Contemporary Thought, 16*, 233–296.

Sperry, R.W. (1993). The impact and promise of the cognitive revolution. *American Psychologist, 48*, 878–885.

Sperry, R.W., Zaidel, E., & Zaidel, D. (1979). Self recognition and social awareness in the deconnected minor hemisphere. *Neuropsychologia, 17*, 153–166.

Spezzano, C. (1993). *Affect in psychoanalysis: a clinical synthesis*. Hillsdale NJ: The Analytic Press.

Spitz, R. (1946). Hospitalism: A follow-up report. *Psychoanalytic Study of the Child, 1*, 53–74.

Spitz, R.A. (1957). *No and yes—On the beginnings of human communication*. New York: International Universities Press.

Spitz, R. A. (1958). On the genesis of superego components. *Psychoanalytic Study of the Child, 13*, 375–404.

Spitz, R.A. (1965). *The first year of life: A psychoanalytic study of normal and deviant development of object relations*. New York: International Universities Press.

Spitzer, R.L., & Endicott, J. (1978). Medical and mental disorder: Proposed definition and criteria. In R.L. Spitzer & D.F. Klein (Eds.), *Critical issues in psychiatric diagnosis* (pp. 15–39). New York: Raven Press.

Spoont, M.R. (1992). Modulatory role of serotonin in neural information processing: Implications for human psychopathology. *Psychological Bulletin, 112*, 330–350.

Spyer, K.M. (1989). Neural mechanisms involved in cardiovascular control during affective behavior. *Trends in Neuroscience, 12*, 506–513.

Squatrito, S., Galletti, C., Maiali, M.G., & Battaglini, P.P. (1981). Cortical visual input to the orbito-insular cortex in the cat. *Brain Research, 221*, 71–79.

Squire, L.R. (1986). Mechanisms of memory. *Science, 232*, 1612–1619.

Squire, L.R. (1987). *Memory and brain*. New York: Oxford University Press.

Sroufe, L.A. (1979). Socioemotional development. In J. Osofsky (Ed.), *Handbook of infant development* (pp. 462–516). New York: Wiley.

Sroufe, L.A. (1984). Infant-caregiver attachment and patterns of adaptation in preschool: The roots of maladaptation and competence. In M. Perlmutter (Ed.), *Minnesota symposium on child psychology. Vol. 6* (pp. 41–84). Hillsdale, NJ: Lawrence Erlbaum Associates.

Sroufe, L.A. (1989a). Relationships, self, and individual adaptation. In A.J. Sameroff & R.N. Emde (Eds.), *Relationship disturbances in early childhood* (pp. 70–94). New York: Basic Books.

Sroufe, L.A. (1989b). Relationships and relationship disturbances. In A.J. Sameroff & R.N. Emde (Eds.), *Relationship disturbances in early childhood* (pp. 97–124). New York: Basic Books.

Sroufe, L.A., & Fleeson, J. (1986). Attachment and the construction of relationships. In W. Hartup & Z. Rubin (Eds.), *The nature and development of relationships* (pp. 51–71). Hillsdale, NJ: Lawrence Erlbaum Associates.

Sroufe, L.A., Fox, N.E., & Pancake, V.R. (1983). Attachment and dependency in developmental perspective. *Child Development, 54*, 1615–1627.

Sroufe, L.A., & Rutter, M. (1984). The domain of developmental psychopathology. *Child Development, 55*, 17–29.

Sroufe, L.A., & Wunsch, J.P. (1972). The development of laughter in the first years of life. *Child Development, 43*, 1326–1344.

Staddon, J.E.R. (1983). *Adaptive behavior and learning*. Cambridge, England: Cambridge University Press.

Stallcup, W., Beasley, L., & Levine, J. (1985). Antibody against nerve growth factor-inducible large external (NILE) glycoprotein labels nerve fiber tracts in the developing rat nervous system. *Journal of Neuroscience, 5*, 1090–1101.

Stam, C.J., de Bruin, J.P.C., van Haelst, A.M., van der Gugten, J., & Kalsbeek, A. (1989). Influences of the mesocortical dopaminergic system on activity, food hoarding, social-agonistic behavior, and spatial delayed alternation in male rats. *Behavorial Neuroscience, 103*, 24–35.

Stanfield, B.B. (1984). Postnatal reorganization of cortical projections: The role of collateral elimination. *Trends in Neuroscience, 7*, 37–41.

Stanton, M.E., Gutierrez, Y.R., & Levine, S. (1988). Maternal deprivation potentiates pituitary-adrenal stress responses in infant rats. *Behavioral Neuroscience, 102*, 692–700.

Stanton, M.E., & Levine, S. (1990). Inhibition of infant glucocorticoid stress response: Specific role of maternal cues. *Developmental Psychobiology, 23*, 411–426.

Stanton, M.E., Wallstrom, J., & Levine, S. (1987). Maternal contact inhibits pituitary-adrenal stress response in preweanling rats. *Developmental Psychobiology, 20*, 131–145.

Starkstein, S.E., Boston, J.D., & Robinson, R.F. (1988). Mechanisms of mania after brain injury: 12 case reports and review of the literature. *Journal of Nervous and Mental Disease, 176*, 87–100.

Stayton, D.J., Hogan, R., & Ainsworth, M.D.S. (1971). Infant obedience and maternal behavior: The origins of socialization reconsidered. *Child Development, 42*, 1057–1069.

Stearns, S.C. (1982). The role of development in the evolution of life histories. In J.T. Bonner (Ed.), *Evolution and development*. New York: Springer-Verlag.

Stechler, G.S., & Carpenter, G. (1967). A viewpoint on early affective development. In J. Hellmuth (Ed.), *The exceptional infant, Vol 1*. New York: Brunner/Mazel.

Stein, M., Schiavi, R.C., & Luparello, T.J. (1969). The hypothalamus and immune process, *Annals of the New York Academy of Sciences, 164*, 464–472.

Steindler, D.A. (1981). Locus coeruleus neurons have axons that branch to the forebrain and cerebellum. *Brain Research, 223*, 367–373.

Steiner, J.E. (1979). Human facial expressions in response to taste and smell stimulation. *Advances in Child Development and and Behavior, 13*, 257–295.

Steklis, H. D., & Kling, A. (1985). Neurobiology of affiliative behavior in nonhuman primates. In M. Reite & T. Field.(Ed.), *The psychobiology of attachment and separation* (pp. 93–134). Orlando, FL: Academic Press.

Stellar, E. (1954). The physiology of emotion. *Psychological Review, 61*, 5–22.

Stellar, E. (1982). Brain mechanisms in hedonic processes. In D.W. Pfaff (Ed.), *The physiological mechanisms of motivation* (pp. 377–407). New York: Springer-Verlag.

Sterling, K., Lazarus, J.H., Milch, P.O. Sakurada, T., & Brenner, M.A. (1978). Mitochondrial thyroid hormone receptor: Localization and physiological significance, *Science, 201*, 1126–1129.

Stern, D. N. (1974). Mother and infant at play: The dyadic interaction involving facial, vocal, and gaze behavior. In M. Lewis & L. Rosenblum (Eds.), *The effect of the infant on its caregiver* (pp. 187–213). New York: Wiley.

Stern, D. N. (1977). *The first relationship*. Cambridge, MA: Harvard University Press.

Stern, D. N. (1983a). Early transmission of affect: Some research issues. In J. Call, E. Galenson, & R. Tyson.(Eds.), *Frontiers of infant psychiatry* (pp. 52–69). New York: Basic Books.

Stern, D. N. (1983b). Implications of infancy research for psychoanalytic theory and practice. In L. Grinspoon (Ed.), *Psychiatry update*. Washington: American Psychiatric Press.

Stern, D. N. (1985). *The interpersonal world of the infant*. New York: Basic Books.

Stern, D.N. (1989). The representation of relational patterns: Developmental considerations. In A.J. Sameroff & R. N. Emde (Eds.), *Relationship disturbances in early childhood* (pp. 52–69). New York: Basic Books.

Stern, D.N. (1990). Joy and satisfaction in infancy. In R.A. Glick & S. Bone (Eds.), *Pleasure beyond the pleasure principle* (pp. 13–25). New Haven: Yale University Press.

Sternberg, S. (1969). The discovery of processing stages: Extension of Donders' method. In W.G. Kester (Ed.), *Attention and performance II* (pp. 276–315). Amsterdam: North-Holland.

Steward, O. (1983). Polyribosomes at the base of dendritic spines of central nervous system neurons—Their possible role in synapse construction and modification. *Cold Spring Harbor Symposia on Quantitative Biology, 48*, 745–759.

Stewart, J., de Witt, H., & Eikelboom, R. (1984). Role of unconditioned and conditioned drug effects in the self-administration of opiates and stimulants. *Psychological Review, 91*, 251–268.

Stewart, M.G., Csillag, A., & Rose, S.P.R. (1987). Alterations in synaptic structure in the paleo-striatal complex of the domestic chick, *Gallus domesticus*, following passive avoidance training. *Brain Research, 426*, 69–81.

Stewart, P.A., & Hayakawa, E.M. (1987). Interendothelial junctional changes underlie the developmental "tightening" of the blood-brain barrier. *Developmental Brain Research, 32*, 271–281.

Stiles-Davis, J., Sugarman, S., & Nass, R. (1985). The development of spatial and class relations in four young children with right-hemisphere damage: Evidence for an early spatial constructive deficit. *Brain and Cognition, 4*, 388–412.

Stinus, L., Koob, G.F., Ling, N., Bloom, F.E., & LeMoal, M. (1980). Locomotor activation induced by infusion of endorphins into the ventral tegmental area: Evidence for opiate-dopamine interactions. *Proceedings of the National Academy of Sciences of the United States of America, 77*, 2323–2327.

Stipek, D. (1983). A developmental analysis of pride and shame. *Human Development, 26*, 42–54.

Stipek, D.J., Gralinski, J.H., & Kopp, C.B. (1990). Self-concept development in the toddler years. *Developmental Psychology, 26*, 972–977.

Stockard, C.R. (1921). Developmental rate and structural expression: An experimental study of twins, "double monsters," and single deformities and their interaction among embryonic organs during their origins and development. *American Journal of Anatomy, 28*, 115–275.

Stoller, R.J. (1968). *Sex and gender. Volume 1.* New York: Jason Aronson.

Stolorow, R.D., & Atwood, G.E. (1979). *Faces in a cloud: Subjectivty in psychoanalytic theory.* New York: Jason Aronson.

Stolorow, R.D., Brandchaft, B., & Atwood, G. (1987). *Psychoanalytic treatment: An intersubjective approach.* Hillsdale, NJ: The Analytic Press.

Stolorow, R.D., & Lachmann, F.M. (1980). *Psychoanalysis of developmental arrests.* New York: International Universities Press.

Stone, E.A. (1975). Stress and catecholamines. In A.J. Friedhoff (Ed.), *Catecholamines and Behavior. Neuropsychopharmacology* (pp. 31–72). New York: Plenum.

Stone, E.A., Bonnet, K., & Hofer, M.A. (1976). Survival and development of maternally deprived rats: Role of body temperature. *Psychosomatic Medicine, 39*, 242–249.

Stone, M.H. (1988). Toward a psychobiological theory on borderline personality disorder: Is irritability the red thread that runs through borderline conditions? *Dissociations, 1*, 2–15.

Strauss, M.S. (1979). Abstraction of prototypical information by adults and 10 month old infants. *Journal of Experimental Psychology: Human Learning and Memory, 5*, 618–632.

Streri, A. (1987). Tactile discrimination of shape and intermodal transfer in 2-to-3-month old infants. *British Journal of Developmental Psychology, 5*, 213–220.

Strom, G., & Uvnas, B. (1950). Motor responses of gastrointestinal tract and bladder to topical stimulation of the frontal lobe, basal ganglia and hypothalamus in the cat. *Acta Physiologica Scandinavica, 21*, 90–104.

Strupp, H.H. (1989). Psychotherapy: Can the practitioner learn from the researcher? *American Psychologist, 44*, 717–724.

Stryer, L. (1981). *Biochemistry* (2nd. ed). San Francisco: W. H. Freeman.

Stuss, D.T. (1992). Biological and psychological development in executive functions. *Brain and Cognition, 20*, 8–23.

Stuss, D.T., & Benson, D. F. (1983). Frontal lobe lesions and behavior. In A. Kertesz (Ed.), *Localization in neuropsychology* (pp. 429–454). New York: Academic Press.

Stuss, D.T., & Benson, D. F. (1986). *The frontal lobes.* New York: Raven Press.

Stuss, D.T., & Benson, D. F. (1987). The frontal lobes and control of cognition and memory. In E. Perecman (Ed.), *The frontal lobes revisited* (pp. 141–158). Hillsdale NJ: Lawrence Erlbaum Associates.

Stuss, D.T., Kaplan, E.F., Benson, D.F., Weir, W.S., Chiulli, S., & Sarazin, F.F. (1982). Evidence for the involvement of orbitofrontal cortex in memory functions: An interference effect. *Journal of Comparative Physiological Psychology, 96*, 913–925.

Suarez, E.C., & Williams, R.B. (1992). Interactive models of reactivity: The relationship between hostility and potentially pathogenic physiological responses to social stressors. In N. Schneiderman, P. McCabe, & A. Baum (Eds.), *Stress and disease processes* (pp. 175–195). Hillsdale, NJ: Lawrence Erlbaum Associates.

Suberi, M., & McKeever, W.F. (1977). Differential right hemispheric memory storage of emotional and non-emotional faces. *Neuropsychologia, 15*, 757–768.

Suda, T., Tozawa, F., Ushiyama, T., et al. (1990). Interleukin-1 stimulates corticotropin-releasing factor gene expression in rat hypothalamus. *Endocrinology, 126*, 1223–1228.

Sugar, O., Chusid, J.G., & French, J.D. (1948). A second motor cortex in the monkey. *Journal of Neuropathology and Experimental Neurology, 7*, 182–189.

Sugarman, A., & Jaffe, L.S. (1990). Toward a developmental understanding of the self schema. *Psychoanalysis and Contemporary Thought, 13*, 117–138.

Suler, J.R. (1989). Mental imagery in psychoanalytic treatment. *Psychoanalytic Psychology, 6*, 343–366.

Sullivan, R.M., Shokrai, N., & Leon, M. (1988). Physical stimulation reduces the body temperature of infant rats. *Developmental Psychobiology, 20*, 225–235.

Sullivan, R.M., Wilson, D.A., & Leon, M. (1988). Physical stimulation reduces the brain temperature of infant rats. *Developmental Psychobiology, 20*, 237–250.

Sulloway, F.S. (1979). *Freud, biologist of the mind: Beyond the psychoanalytic legend.* New York: Basic Books.

Sumal, K.V., Blessing, W.W., Joh, T.H., Reis, D.J., & Pickel, V.M. (1983). Synaptic interactions of vagal afferents and catecholaminergic neurons in the rat nucleus tractus solitarius. *Brain Research, 277*, 31–40.

Sunahara, R.K. et al. (1990). Human dopamine D_1 receptor encoded by an intronless gene on chromosome 5. *Nature (London), 347*, 80–83.

Sundbom, E., & Kullgren, G. (1992). Multivariate modelling and the Defence Mechanism Test: a comparative study of defensive structures in borderline, other personality disorders and schizophrenic disorder. *Acta Psychiatrica Scandinavica, 86*, 379–385.

Suomi, S.J. (1981). The perception of contingency and social development. In M.E. Lamb & L.R. Sherrod (Eds.), *Infant social cognition: Empirical and theoretical considerations* (pp. 177–203). Hillsdale, NJ: Lawrence Erlbaum Associates.

Suomi, S.J., Mineka, S., & DeLizio, R.D. (1983). Short- and long-term effects of repetitive mother-infant separations on social development in rhesus monkeys. *Developmental Psychology, 19*, 770–786.

Sutton, R.E., Koob, G.F., LeMoal, M., Rivier, J , & Vale, W. (1982). Corticotropin releasing factor produces behavioral activation in rats. *Nature (London) 297*, 331–333.

Suzuki, H., & Azuma, M. (1977). Prefrontal neuronal activity during gazing at a light spot in the monkey. *Brain Research, 126*, 497–508.

Svensson, T.H. (1992). A psychopharmacologist's view of attachment. *Behavorial Brain Sciences, 15*, 493–541.

Svrakic, D.M. (1985). Emotional features of narcissistic personality disorder. *American Journal of Psychiatry, 142*, 720–724.

Swanson, L.W. (1982). The projections of the ventral tegmental area and adjacent regions: A combined flourescent retrograde tracer and immunoflourescence study in the rat. *Brain Research Bulletin, 9*, 321–353.

Swanson, L.W. (1991). Biochemical switching in hypothalamic circuits mediating responses to stress. *Progress in Brain Research, 87*, 181–200.

Swanson, L.W., Connelly, M.A., & Hartman, B.K. (1977). Ultrastructural evidence for central monoaminergic innervation of blood vessels in the paraventricular nucleus of the hypothalamus. *Brain Research, 136*, 166–173.

Swanson, L.W., & Hartman, B.K. (1975). The central noradrenergic system. An immunoflourescence study of the location of cell bodies and their efferent connections in the rat utilizing dopamine-b-hydroxylase as a marker. *Journal of Comparative Neurology, 163*, 467–506.

Swanson, L.W., & Sawchenko, P.E. (1980). Paraventricular nucleus: a site for the integration of neuroendocrine and autonomic mechanisms. *Neuroendocrinology, 31*, 410–417.

Swanson, L.W., Sawchenko, P.E., Rivier, J., & Vale, W.W. (1983). Organization of ovine corticotropin-releasing factor immunoreactive cells and fibers in the rat brain: An immunohistochemical study. *Neuroendocrinology, 36*, 165–186.

Sweazey, R.D., & Bradley, R.M. (1989). Responses of neurons in the lamb nucleus tractus solitarius to stimulation of the caudal oral cavity and epiglotis with different stimulus modalities. *Brain Research, 480*, 133–150.

Szasz, T.A. (1952). Psychoanalysis and the autonomic nervous system. *Psychoanalytic Review, 39*, 115–151.

Szekely, A.M., Barbaccia, A., Alho, H., & Costa, E. (1990). In primary cultures of cerebellar granule cells the activation of N-methyl-D-aspartate-sensitive receptors induces c-fos mRNA expression. *Molecular Pharmacology, 35*, 401–408.

Tabakoff, B., Groskopf, W., Anderson, R., & Alivisatos, S.G.A. (1974). "Biogenic" aldehyde metabolism. Relation to pentose shunt activity in brain. *Biochemical Pharmacology, 23*, 1707–1719.

Tabin, J.K. (1985). *On the way to the self: Ego and early Oedipal development*. New York: Columbia University Press.

Tai, P.-K. K., Albers, M.W., Chang, H., Faber, L.E., & Schreiber, S.L. (1992). Association of a 59-kilodalton immunophilin with the glucocorticoid receptor complex. *Science, 256*, 1315–1318.

Takahashi, Y., Satoh, K., Sakumoto, T., Tohyama, M., & Shimizu, N. (1979). A major source of catecholamine terminals in the nucleus tractus solitarii. *Brain Research, 172*, 372–377.

Tamborski, A., Lucot, J.B., & Hennessy, M.B. (1990). Central dopamine turnover in guinea pig pups during separation from their mother in a novel environment. *Behavorial Neuroscience, 104*, 607–611.

Tamis-LeMonde, C., & Bornstein, M.H. (1987). Is there a "sensitive period" in human mental development? In M.H. Bornstein (Ed.), *Sensitive periods in development: Interdisciplinary perspectives* (pp. 163–187). Hillsdale, NJ: Lawrence Erlbaum Associates.

Tanabe, T., Yarita, H., Iino, M., Ooshima, Y., & Takagi, S.F. (1975). An olfactory projection area in orbitofrontal cortex of the monkey. *Journal of Neurophysiology, 38*, 1269–1283.

Tangney, J.P. (1991). Moral affect: The good, the bad, and the ugly. *Journal of Personality and Social Psychology, 61*, 598–607.

Tangney, J.P., Wagner, P., Fletcher, C., & Gramzow, R. (1992). Shamed into anger? The relation of shame and guilt to anger and self-reported aggression *Journal of Personality and Social Psychology, 62*, 669–675.

Tanno, H., Nockels, R.P., Pitts, L.H., & Noble, L.J. (1993). Immunolocalization of heat shock protein after fluid percussive brain injury and relationship to breakdown of the blood-brain barrier. *Journal of Cerebral Blood Flow and Metabolism, 13*, 116–124.

Tart, C.T. (1972). States of consciousness and state-specific consciousness. *Science, 176*, 1203–1210.

Tassin, J.P. (1987). Dopamine and mental illness: And what about the mesocortical dopamine system? *Behavorial and Brain Sciences, 10*, 224–225.

Taylor, D. C. (1969). Differential rates of cerebral maturation between sexes and between hemispheres. *Lancet*, July, 140–142.

Taylor, G. (1987). *Psychosomatic Medicine and Contemporary Psychoanalysis.* Madison, CT: International Universities Press.

Taylor, G. (1992). Psychosomatics and self-regulation. In J.W. Barron, M.N. Eagle, & D.L. Wolitzky (Eds.), *The interface of psychoanalysis and psychology.* Washington, DC: American Psychological Association.

Taylor, G.J. (1993). Clinical application of a dysregulation model of illness and disease: a case of spasmodic torticollis. *International Journal of Psycho-Analysis, 74*, 1–12.

Teitelbaum, P. (1971). The encephalization of hunger. In E. Stellar & J.J. Sprague (Eds.), *Progress in physiological psychology* (pp. 319–350). San Diego: Academic Press.

TenHouten, W.D. (1991). Mind, self, image, emotion, and brain in the thought of George Herbert Mead. *Journal of Mental Imagery, 15*, 157–159.

TenHouten, W.D., Hoppe, K.D., Bogen, J.E., & Walter, D. (1986). Alexithymia: An experimental study of cerebral commisurotomy patients and normal control subjects. *American Journal of Psychiatry, 143*, 312–316.

Tennes, K., Downey, K., & Vernadakis, A. (1977). Urinary cortisol excretion rates and anxiety in normal 1-year-old infants. *Psychosomatic Medicine, 39*, 1178–187.

Tennes, K.H., & Mason, J.W. (1982). Developmental psychoendocrinology: an approach to the study of emotion. In C.E. Izard (Ed.), *Measuring emotions in infants and children* (pp. 21–37). Cambridge, England: Cambridge University Press.

Ter Horst, G.J., De Boer, P., Luiten, P.G.M., & van Willigen, J.D. (1989). Ascending projections from the solitary tract nucleus to the hypothalamus: A *Phaseolus vulgaris* lectin tracing study in the rat. *Neuroscience, 31*, 785–797.

Termine, N.T., & Izard, C.E. (1988). Infants' responses to their mothers' expressions of joy and sadness. *Developmental Psychology, 24*, 223–229.

Thach, B.T., & Wiffenbach, J.M. (1976). Quantitative assessment of oral tactile sensitivity in preterm and term neonates, and comparison with adults. *Developmental Medicine and Child Neurology, 18*, 202–212.

Tharp, B.R. (1972). Orbital frontal seizures. An unique electroencephalographic and clinical syndrome. *Epilepsia, 13*, 627–642.

Thatcher, R.W. (1991). Maturation of the human frontal lobes: Physiological evidence for staging. *Developmental Neuropsychology, 7*, 397–419.

Thatcher, R.W. (1992). Cyclic cortical reorganization during early childhood. *Brain and Cognition, 20*, 24–50.

Thatcher, R.W., & John, E.R. (1977). Neurophysiology and emotion. In R.W. Thatcher & E.R. John (Eds.), *Functional neuroscience 1. Foundations of cognitive processes* (pp. 117–134). New York: Lawrence Erlbaum Associates.

Thatcher, R. W., Walker, R. A., & Giudice, S. (1987). Human cerebral hemispheres develop at different rates and ages. *Science, 236*, 1110–1113.

Thayer, R.E. (1989). *The biopsychology of mood and arousal.* New York: Oxford University Press.

Thelen, E. (1989). Self-organization in developmental processes: Can systems approaches work? In M. Gunnar & E. Thelen (Eds.), *Systems and development. The Minnesota symposium in child psychology, Vol.22* (pp. 77–117). Hillsdale, NJ: Lawrence Erlbaum Associates.

Thierry, A.M., Tassin, J.P., Blanc, G., & Glowinski, J. (1976). Selective activation of the mesocortical DA system by stress. *Nature (London), 263*, 242–244.

Thierry, A.M., Tassin, J.P., Blanc, G., & Glowinski, J. (1978). Studies on mesocortical dopamine systems. *Advances in Biochemical Psychopharmacology, 17*, 205–216.

Thierry, A.M., Deniau, J.M., Herve, E., & Chevalier, G. (1980). Electrophysiological evidence for non-dopaminergic mesocortical and mesolimbic neurons in the rat. *Brain Research, 201*, 210–214.

Thierry, A.M., Chevalier, G., Ferron, A., & Glowinski, J. (1983). Diencephalic and mesencephalic efferents of the medial prefrontal cortex in the rat: Electrophysiological evidence for the existence of branched axons. *Experimental Brain Research, 50*, 275–282.

Thierry, A.M. Godbout, R., Mantz, J., & Glowinski, J. (1990). Influence of the ascending mono-aminergic systems on the activity of the rat prefrontal cortex. *Progress in Brain Research, 85*, 357–365.

Thoenen, H. (1991). The changing scene of neurotrophic factors. *Trends in Neuroscience, 14*, 165–170.

Thoits, P.A. (1982). Conceptual, methodological, and theoretical problems in studying social support as a buffer against life stress. *Journal of Health and Social Behavior, 2*, 145–159.

Thomas, A., & Chess, S. (1982). The reality of difficult temperament, *Merrill-Palmer Quarterly, 28*, 1–20.

Thomas, M.R., & Calaresu, F.R. (1974). Localization and function of medullary sites mediating vagal bradycardia. *American Journal of Physiology, 226*, 1344–1349.

Thompson, J.M., Baxter, L.R., & Schwartz, J.M. (1992). Freud, obsessive-compulsive disorder and neurobiology. *Psychoanalysis and Contemporary Thought, 15*, 483–505.

Thompson, R.A. (1990). Emotion and self-regulation. *Nebraska symposium on motivation* (pp. 367–467). Lincoln: University of Nebraska Press.

Thor, K.B., & Helke, C.J. (1988). Catecholamine-synthesizing neuronal projections to the nucleus tractus solitari of the rat. *Journal of Comparative Neurology, 268*, 264–280.

Thorpe, S.J., Rolls, E.T., & Maddison, S. (1983). The orbitofrontal cortex: Neuronal activity in the behaving monkey. *Experimental Brain Research, 49*, 93–115.

Thrane, G. (1979). Shame and the construction of the self. *Annual of Psychoanalysis, 7*, 321–344.

Thurston, J.H., & McDougal, D.B. Jr. (1969). Effect of ischemia on metabolism of the brain of the mouse. *American Journal of Physiology, 216*, 348–352.

Timiras, P.S. (1989). Neuroendocrine models regulating lifespan. In M.P. Schreibman & C.G. Scanes (Eds.), *Development, maturation, and senescence of neuroendocrine systems. A comparative approach* (pp. 275–288). San Diego: Academic Press.

Titchener, E.G. (1916). *A textbook of psychology*. New York: Macmillan.

Tofts, P., & Wray, S. (1985). Changes in brain phosphorous during the post-natal development of the rat. *Journal of Physiology (London), 359*, 417–429.

Tolpin, M. (1986). The self and its selfobjects: A different baby. In A. Goldberg (Ed.), *Progress in self psychology, Vol.2* (pp. 115–128). New York: Guilford Press.

Tomasello, M. (1988). The role of joint attentional processes in early language development. *Language Sciences, 10*, 69–88.

Tomkins, S. (1962). *Affect / Imagery / Consciousness: Vol. 1 The Positive Affects*. New York: Springer.

Tomkins, S. (1963). *Affect / Imagery / Consciousness: Vol. 2. The Negative Affects*. New York: Springer.

Tomkins, S. (1979). Script theory: Differential magnification of affects. In: H.E. Horowitz & R.A. Dienstbier (Eds.), *Nebraska symposium on motivation*. Lincoln: University of Nebraska Press.

Tomkins, S. (1984). Afffect theory. In P. Ekman (Ed.), *Approaches to emotion*. Hillsdale, NJ: Lawrence Erlbaum Associates.

Tomkins, S. (1987). Shame. In D.L. Nathanson (Ed.), *The many faces of shame* (pp. 133–161). New York: Guilford Press.

Tooby, J., & Cosmides, L. (1989). Evolutionary psychology and the generation of culture, Part I. Theoretical considerations. *Ethology and Sociobiology, 10*, 29–49.

Toran-Allerand, D. (1978). Gonadal hormones and brain development: Cellular aspects of sexual differentiation. *American Zoologist, 18*, 535–565.

Toran-Allerand, D. (1983). Sex steroids and the development of mouse hypothalamus *in vitro*. III. Effects of estrogen on dendritic differentiation. *Developmental Brain Research, 7*, 97–101.

Townsend, J.B., Ziedonis, D.M., Bryan, R.M., Brennan, R.W., & Page, R.B. (1984). Choroid plexus blood flow: Evidence for dopaminergic influence. *Brain Research, 290*, 165–169.

Tracy, R.L., & Ainsworth, M.D.S. (1981). Maternal affectionate behavior and infant-mother attachment patterns. *Child Development, 52*, 1341–1343.

Trad, P.V. (1986). *Infant depression*. New York: Springer-Verlag.

Tranel, D., Damasio, A.R., & Damasio, H. (1988). Impaired autonomic responses to emotional and social stimuli in patients with bilateral orbital damage and acquired sociopathy. *Neuroscience Abstracts, 14*, 1288.

Travers, J.B., & Smith, D.V. (1979). Gustatory sensitivities in neurons of the hamster nucleus tractus solitarius. *Sensory Processes, 3*, 1–26.

Travers, S.P., Pfaffmann, C., & Norgren, R. (1986). Convergence of lingual and palatal gustatory neural activity in the nucleus of the solitary tract. *Brain Research, 365*, 305–320.

Trendelenburg, U. (1963). Supersensitivity and subsensitivity to sympathomimetic amines. *Pharmacological Reviews, 15*, 225–276.

Trevarthen, C. (1979). Communication and cooperation in early infancy: A description of primary intersubjectivity. In M.M. Bullowa (Ed.), *Before speech: The beginning of interpersonal communication*. New York: Cambridge University Press.

Trevarthen, C. (1989). Development of early social interactions and the affective regulations of brain growth. In C. von Euler & H. Forssberg (Ed.), *The neurobiology of early infant behavior*. New York: MacMillan.

Trevarthen, C. (1990). Growth and education of the hemispheres. In C. Trevarthen (Ed.), *Brain circuits and functions of the mind* (pp. 334–363). Cambridge, England: Cambridge University Press.

Triarhou, L.C., & del Cerro, M. (1985). Freud's contribution to neuroanatomy. *Archives of Neurology, 42*, 282–287.

Tronick, E.Z. (1989). Emotions and emotional communication in infants. *American Psychologist, 44*, 112–119.

Tronick, E.Z., Cohn, J., & Shea, E. (1986). The transfer of affect between mothers and infants. In T.B. Brazelton & M.W. Yogman (Eds.), *Affective development in infancy* (pp. 11–25). Norwood, NJ: Ablex.

Tronick, E.Z., & Cohn, J.F. (1989). Infant-mother face-to-face interaction: Age and gender differences in coordination and occurrence of miscoordination. *Child Development, 60*, 85–92.

Tronick, E.Z., Ricks, M., & Cohn, J.F. (1982). Maternal and infant affective exchange: Patterns of adaptation. In T. Field & A. Fogel (Eds.), *Emotion and early interaction*. Lawrence Erlbaum Associates: Hillsdale, NJ.

Tronick, E.Z., Winn, S., & Morelli, G.A. (1985). Multiple caretaking in the context of human evolution: Why don't the Efe know the Western prescription for child care? In M. Reite & T. Field (Ed.), *The psychobiology of attachment and separation* (pp. 293–322). Orlando, FL: Academic Press.

Troxler, R.G., Sprague, E.A., Albanese, R.A., & Thompson, A.J. (1977). The association of elevated plasma cortisol and early atherosclerosis as demonstrated by coronary angiography. *Atherosclerosis, 26*, 151–162.

Truex, R., & Carpenter, B. A. (1964). *Strong and Elwyn's human neuroanatomy* (5th ed). Baltimore: Williams and Wilkins Company.

Tsujimoto, Y. (1989). Stress resistance conferred by high level of bcl-2 protein in human B lymphoblastoid cells. *Oncogene, 4*, 1331–1336.

Tsumoto, T., Hagihara, K., Sato, H., & Hata, Y. (1987). NMDA receptors in the visual cortex of young kittens are more effective that those of adult cats. *Nature (London), 327*, 513–514.

Tucker, D.M. (1981). Lateral brain function, emotion, and conceptualization. *Psychological Bulletin, 89*, 19–46.

Tucker, D.M. (1986). Neural control of emotional communication. In P. Blanck, R. Buck, & R. Rosenthal, (Eds.), *Nonverbal communication in the clinical context*. Cambridge, England: Cambridge University Press.

Tucker, D.M. (1992). Developing emotions and cortical networks. In M. R. Gunnar & C.A. Nelson (Eds.), *Minnesota symposium on child psychology. Vol. 24, Developmental behavioral neuroscience* (pp. 75–128). Hillsdale, NJ: Lawrence Erlbaum Associates.

Tucker, D.M., & Derryberry, D. (1992). Motivated attention: Anxiety and the frontal executive functions. *Neuropsychiatry, Neuropsychology, and Behavioral Neurology, 5*, 233–252.

Tucker, D. M., Roth, R. S., Arneson, B. A., & Buckingman, V. (1977). Right hemisphere activation during stress. *Neuropsychologia, 15*, 697–700.

Tucker, D.M., Roth, D.L., & Bair, T.B. (1986). Functional connections among cortical regions: Topography of EEG coherence. *Electroencephalography and Clinical Neurophysiology, 63*, 242–250.

Tucker, D.M., Stenslie, C.E., Roth, R.S., & Shearer, S.L. (1981). Right frontal lobe activation and right hemisphere performance: Decrement during depressed mood. *Archives of General Psychiatry, 38*, 169–174.

Tucker, D. M., & Williamson, P. A. (1984). Asymmetric neural control in human self-regulation. *Psychological Review, 91*, 185–215.

Tulkin, S.R., & Kagan, J. (1972). Mother—infant interaction in the first year of life. *Child Development, 43*, 31–42.

Tulving, E. (1972). Episodic and semantic memory. In E. Tulving & W. Donaldson (Eds.), *Organization of memory*. New York: Academic Press.

Tuor, U.I., Edvinsson, L., & McCulloch, J. (1986). Catecholamines and the relationship between cerebral blood flow and glucose use. *American Journal of Physiology, 251*, H824-H833.

Tuor, U.I., Simone, C., & Bascaramurty, S. (1992). Local blood-brain barrier in the newborn rabbit: Postnatal changes in alpha aminoisobutyric acid transfer within medulla, cortex, and selected brain areas. *Journal of Neurochemistry, 59*, 999–1007.

Turiell, E. (1967). An historical analysis of the Freudian conception of the superego. *Psychoanalytic Review, 54*, 118–140.

Turkewitz, G., & Kenny, P.A. (1982). Limitations on input as a basis for neural organization and perceptual development: A preliminary theoretical statement. *Developmental Psychobiology, 15*, 357–368.

Turner, A.M., & Greenough, W.T. (1985). Differential rearing effects on rat visual cortex synapses. I. Synaptic and neuronal density and synapses per neuron. *Brain Research, 329*, 195–203.

Tyler, S.K., & Tucker, D.M. (1982). Anxiety and perceptual structure: Individual differences in neuropsychological function. *Journal of Abnormal Psychology, 91*, 210–220.

Tyson, P. (1989). Two approaches to infant research: A review and integration. In S. Dowling & A. Rothstein (Eds.), *The significance of infant observational research for clinical work with children, adolescents, and adults* (pp. 3–23). New York: International Universities Press.

Tyson, P., & Tyson, R.L. (1990). *Psychoanalytic theories of developmen*. New Haven: Yale University Press.

Tzagoloff, A., Macino, G., & Sebald, W. (1979). Mitochondrial genes and translation products. *Annual Review of Biochemistry, 48*, 419–441.

Uehara, A., Gottschall, P.E., Dahl, R.R., & Arimura, A. (1987). Interleukin-1 stimulates ACTH release by an indirect action which requires endogenous corticotropin releasing factor *Endocrinology, 121*, 1580–1582.

Ulman, R.B., & Paul, H. (1989). A self-psychological theory and approach to treating substance abuse disorders: The "intersubjective absorption" hypothesis. In A. Goldberg (Ed.), *Progress in self psychology, Vol.6* (pp. 129–156). Hillsdale NJ: The Analytic Press.

Ungerstedt, U. (1971). Stereotaxic mapping of the monoamine pathways in the rat brain. *Acta Physiologica Scandinavica*, (Supplement 367) 1–48.

Unsicker, K., Krisch, B., Otten, U., & Thoenen, H. (1978). Nerve growth factor-induced fiber outgrowth from isolated rat adrenal chromaffin cells: Impairment by glucocorticoids. *Proceedings of the National Academy of Sciences of the United States of America*, 75, 3498–3502.

Uylings, H.B.M., & van Eden, C.G. (1990). Qualitative and quantitative comparison of the prefrontal cortex in rat and in primates, including humans. *Progress in Brain Research*, 85, 31–62.

Uzbekov, M.G., Murphy, S., & Rose, S.P.R. (1979). Ontogenesis of serotonin "receptors" in different regions of rat brain. *Brain Research*, 168, 195–199.

Vaccari, A., Brotman, S., Cimino, J., & Timiras, P.S. (1977). Sex differentiation of neurotransmitter enzymes in central and peripheral nervous systems. *Brain Research*, 132, 176–185.

Vadasz, C., Baker, H., Fink, S.K., & Reis, D.J. (1985). Genetic effects and sexual dimorphism in tyrosine hydroxylase activity in two mouse strains and their reciprocal F1 hybrids. *Journal of Neurogenetics*, 2, 219–230.

Vadasz, C., Kobor, G., Kabai, P., Szrika, J., Vadasz, I., & Lajtha, A. (1988). Perinatal anti-androgen treatment and genotype affect the mesotelencephalic dopamine system and behavior in mice. *Hormones and Behavior*, 22, 528–539.

Vadasz, C., Laszlovszky, I., De Simone, P.A., & Fleischer, A. (1992). Genetic aspects of dopamine receptor binding in the mouse and rat brain: An overview. *Journal of Neurochemistry*, 59, 793–808.

Vale, W., Spiess, J., Rivier, C., & Rivier, J. (1981). Characterization of a 41-residue ovine hypothalamic peptide that stimulates secretion of corticotropin and beta-endorphin. *Science*, 213, 1394–1397.

Valenstein, E.S. (1973). *Brain control*. New York: Wiley.

Valenstein, E.S., & Heilman, K.M. (1979). Emotional disorders resulting from lesions of the central nervous system. In K. M. Heilman & E. Valenstein (Eds.), *Clinical neuropsychology* (pp. 413–438). Oxford University Press: New York.

Vallortigara, G. (1992). Right hemisphere advantage for social recognition in the chick. *Neuropsychologia*, 30, 761–768.

Valverde, F., & Facal-Valverde, M.V. (1988). Postnatal development of interstitial (subplate) cells in the white matter of the temporal cortex of kitten: A correlated and electron microscopic study. *Journal of Comparative Neurology*, 269, 168–192.

van der Kolk, B.A. (1987). *Psychological trauma*. Washington, DC: American Psychiatric Press.

van der Kooy, D., McGinty, J.F., Koda, L.Y., Gerfen, C.R., & Bloom, F.E. (1982). Visceral cortex: A direct projection from prefrontal coretex to the solitary nucleus in rat. *Neuroscience Letters*, 33, 123–127.

van der Kooy, D., Koda, L.Y., McGinty, J.F., Gerfen, C.R., & Bloom, F.E. (1984). The organization of projections from the cortex, amygdala, and hypothalamus to the nucleus of the solitary tract in the rat. *Journal of Comparative Neurology*, 224, 1–24.

Vanderpool, J., Rosenthal, N., Chrousos, G.P., Wher, T., & Gold, P.W. (1991). Evidence for hypothalamic CRH deficiency in patients with seasonal affective disorder. *Journal of Clinical Endocrinology and Metabolism*, 72,1382–1387.

Van der Vlugt, H. (1979). Aspects of normal and abnormal neuropsychological development. In M.S. Gazzaniga (Ed.), *Handbook of behavioral Neurobiology, Vol. 2* (pp. 99–117). New York: Plenum Press.

Van Eden, C.G., Kros, J.M., & Uylings, H.B.M. (1990). The development of the rat prefrontal cortex. Its size and development of connections with thalamus, spinal cord and other cortical areas. *Progress in Brain Research*, 85, 169–183.

Van Eden, C. G., & Uylings, H.B.M. (1985a). Cytoarchitectonic development of the prefrontal cortex in the rat. *Journal of Comparative Neurology, 241*, 253–267.

Van Eden, C.G., & Uylings, H.B.M. (1985b). Postnatal volumetric development of the prefrontal cortex in the rat. *Journal of Comparative Neurology, 241*, 268–274.

Van Eden, C.G., Uylings, H.B.M., & Van Pelt, J. (1984). Sex-differences and left-right asymmetries in the prefrontal cortex during postnatal development in the rat. *Developmental Brain Research, 12*, 146–153.

Van Lancker, D. (1991). Personal relevance and the human right hemisphere. *Brain and Cognition, 17*, 64–92.

Van Lancker, D., & Klein, K. (1990). Preserved recognition of familiar personal names in global aphasia. *Brain and Language, 39*, 511–529.

Van Leishout, C.F.M. (1975). Young children's reactions to barriers placed by their mothers. *Child Development, 46*, 879–886.

Van Strien, J.W., & Morpugo, M. (1992). Opposite hemispheric activations as a result of emotionally threatening and non-threatening words. *Neuropsychologia, 9*, 845–848.

Van Wimersma Greidanus, T., B. & De Wied, D. (1977). The physiology of the neurohypohyseal system and its relationship to memory processes. In A.M. Davison (Ed.), *Biochemical correlates of brain structure and function* (pp. 215–248). New York: Academic Press.

Vass, K., Berger, M.L., Nowak, T.S., Welch, W.J., & Lassman, H. (1989). Induction of stress protein hsp70 in nerve cells after status epilepticus in the rat. *Neuroscience Letters, 100*, 254–259.

Vaughn, B.E., Kopp, C.B., & Krakow, J.B. (1984). The emergence and consolidation of self-control from eighteen to thirty months of age: Normative trends and individual differences. *Child Development, 55*, 900–1004.

Velasco, M., & Lindsley, D.B. (1965). Role of orbital cortex in regulation of thalamocortical electrical activity. *Science, 149*, 1375–1377.

Vercesi, A.E., & Hoffmann, M.E. (1993). Generation of reactive oxygen metabolites and oxidative damage in mitochondria: Role of calcium. In L.H. Lash & P.D. Jones (Eds.), *Mitochondrial dysfunction* (pp. 256–265). San Diego, CA: Academic Press.

Vertes, R.P. (1990). Fundamentals of brain stem anatomy: A behavioral perspective. In W.R. Klemm & R.P. Vertes (Eds.), *Brainstem mechanisms of behavior*, (pp. 33–103). New York: Wiley.

Vitz, P.C. (1990). The use of stories in moral development. *American Psychologist, 45*. 709–720.

Voeller, K.K.S. (1986). Right-hemisphere deficit syndrome in children. *American Journal of Psychiatry, 143*, 1004–1009.

Volkow, N.D., Fowler, J.S., Wolf, A.P., & Hitzemann, R. et al. (1991). Changes in brain glucose metabolism in cocaine dependence and withdrawal. *American Journal of Psychiatry, 148*, 621–626.

Von Essen, C. (1974). Effects of dopamine on the cerebral blood flow in the dog. *Acta Neurologica Scandinavica, 50*, 38–52.

Von Hungen, K., Roberts, S., & Hill, D.F. (1974). Developmental and regional variations in neurotransmitter-sensitive adenylate cyclase in cell-free preparations from rat brain. *Journal of Neurochemistry, 22*, 811–819.

Vygotsky, L.S. (1978). *Mind in society*. Cambridge, MA: Harvard University Press.

Vygotsky, L.S. (1988). Thinking and speaking. In R.W. Rieber & A.S. Carton (Eds.), *The collected papers of L.S. Vygotsky, Vol. 1* (pp. 39–288). New York: Plenum Press.

Waddington, C. (1947). *Organizers and genes*. Cambridge, England: The University Press.

Waddington, J.L., & O'Boyle, K.M. (1987). The D1 dopamine receptor and the search for its functional role: from neurochemistry to behavior. *Reviews of Neuroscience, 1*, 157–184.

Wagner, D.D., Olmsted, J.B., & Marder, V.J. (1982). Immunolocalization of von Willebrand protein in Weibel-Palade bodies of human endothelial cells. *Journal of Cell Biology, 95*, 355–360.

Wagner, H., & Fine, H. (1981). A developmental overview of object relations and ego psychology. In L.Saretsky, G.D. Goldman, & D.S. Milman (Eds.), *Integrating ego psychology and object relations theory* (pp. 3–20). Dubuque, IA: Kendall/Hunt.

Wahl, S.W., Altman, L.C., & Rosenstreich, D.L. (1975). Inhibition of *in vitro* lymphokine synthesis by glucocorticosteroids. *Journal of Immunology, 115*, 476–486.

Wakefield, J.C. (1992). The concept of mental disorder: On the boundary between biological facts and social values. *American Psychologist, 47*, 373–388.

Walaas, S.I., Aswad, D.W., & Greengard, P. (1983). A dopamine- and cyclic AMP- regulated phosphoprotein enriched in dopamine-innervated brain regions. *Nature (London), 301*, 69–71.

Walden, T.A., & Baxter, A. (1989). The effect of context and age on social referencing. *Child Development, 60*, 1511–1518.

Walden, T.A., & Ogan, T.A. (1988). The development of social referencing. *Child Development, 59*, 1230–1240.

Wallerstein, R.S. (1986a). Psychoanalysis as a science: A response to new challenges. *Psychoanalytic Quarterly, 55*, 414–451.

Wallerstein, R.S. (1986b). *Forty-two lives in treatment: A study of psychoanalysis and psychotherapy.* New York: Guilford Press.

Walsh, R.N., & Cummins, R.A. (1975). Mechanisms mediating the production of environmentally-produced brain changes. *Psychological Bulletin, 82*, 986–1000.

Wang, S.C., & Borison, H.L. (1950). The vomiting center. *Archives of Neurology, 63*, 928–941.

Ward, H. P. (1972). Shame—A necessity for growth in therapy. *American Journal of Psychotherapy, 26*, 232–243.

Warkentin, S., Risberg, J., Nilsson, A., Karlson, S., et al. (1991). Cortical activity during speech production: A study of regional cerebral blood flow in normal subjects performing a word fluency task. *Neuropsychology and Behavioral Neurology, 4*, 305–316.

Watanabe, M. (1992). Frontal units of the monkey coding the associative significance of visual and auditory stimuli. *Experimental Brain Research, 89*, 233–247.

Waters, E., Vaughn, B., & Egeland, B. (1980). Individual differences in infant-mother attachment relationships at age one: Antecedents in neonatal behavior in an urban, economically disadvantaged sample. *Child Development, 51*, 208–216.

Watkins, J.C., & Evans, R.H. (1981). Excitatory amino acid transmitters. *Annual Reviews in Pharmacology and Toxicology, 21*, 165–204.

Watkins, M. (1986). *Invisible guests: The development of imaginal dialogues.* Hillsdale, NJ: The Analytic Press and Lawrence Erlbaum Associates.

Watson, C. (1977). *Basic human neuroanatomy, An introductory atlas* (2nd ed). Boston: Little, Brown.

Watson, D., & Clark, L.A. (1988). Positive and negative affectivity and their relation to anxiety and depressive disorders. *Journal of Abnormal Psychology, 97*, 346–353.

Watt, D.F. (1986). Transference: A right hemispheric event? An inquiry into the boundary between psychoanalytic metapsychology and neuropsychology. *Psychoanalysis and Contemporary Thought, 9*, 43–77.

Watt, D.F. (1990). Higher cortical functions and the ego: Explorations of the boundary between behavioral neurology, neuropsychology, and psychoanalysis. *Psychoanalytic Psychology, 7*, 487–527.

Watts, F.N. (1992). Applications of current cognitive theories of the emotions to the conceptualization of emotional disorders. *British Journal of Clinical Psychology, 31*, 153–167.

Weber, E.F.W., & Weber, E.H.W. (1966). Experiments by which it is proved that when stimulated with a rotary electro-magnetic apparatus the vagus nerves slows down and, to a considerable extent, interrupt the heart beat. In J.F. Fulton (Ed.), *Readings in the history of physiology* (2nd ed.). Springfield, IL: Thomas. (Original work published 1845).

Weber, S.L., & Sackeim, H.A. (1978). The development of functional brain asymmetry in the regulation of emotion. In N.A. Fox & R.J. Davidson (Eds.), *The psychobiology of affective development* (pp. 325–351). Hillsdale, NJ: Lawrence Erlbaum Associates.

Weil, A.P. (1978). Maturational variations and genetic-dynamic issues. *Journal of the American Psychoanalytic Association, 26*, 461–491.

Weil, J.L. (1992). *Early deprivation of empathic care*. Madison CT: International Universities Press.

Weinberg, J., Krahn, E.A., & Levine, S. (1978). Differential effects of handling on exploration in male and female rats. *Developmental Psychobiology, 11*, 251–259.

Weinberger, D.R., Luchins, D.J., Morihisa, J., & Wyatt, R.J. (1982). Asymmetrical volumes of the right and left frontal and occipital regions of the human brain. *Annals of Neurology, 11*, 97–100.

Weiner, H. (1977). *Psychobiology and human disease*. New York: Elsevier.

Weiner, H. (1989). The dynamics of the organism: Implications of recent biological thought for psychosomatic theory and research. *Psychosomatic Medicine, 51*, 608–635.

Weintraub, S., & Mesulam, M.-M. (1983). Developmental learning disabilities of the right hemisphere. *Archives of Neurology, 40*, 463–468.

Weis, S., Haug, H., Holoubek, B., & Orun, H. (1989). The cerebral dominances: Quantitative morphology of the human cerebral cortex. *International Journal of Neuroscience, 47*, 165–168.

Weiss, B.F., Munro, H.N., Ordonez, L.A., & Wurtman, R.J. (1972). Dopamine: Mediator of brain polysome disaggregation after L-dopa. *Science, 177*, 613–616.

Weiss, B.F., Wurtman, R.J., & Munro, H.N. (1973). Disaggregation of brain polysomes by L-5-hydroxytryptophan: Mediation by serotonin. *Life Sciences*, 411–416.

Weiss, J., & Sampson, H. (1986). *The psychoanalytic process: Theory, clinical observation and empirical research*. New York: Guilford Press.

Weiss, J., Kohler, W., & Landsberg, J.-W. (1973). Increase of the corticosterone level in ducklings during the sensitive period of the following reponse. *Developmental Psychobiology, 10*, 59–64.

Weiss, M.L., & Hatton, G.I. (1990). Collateral input to the paraventricular and supraoptic nuclei in rat. II. Afferents from the ventral lateral medulla and nucleus tractus solitarius. *Brain Research Bulletin, 25*, 561–567.

Weiss, P.A. (1969). The living system: Determinism stratified. In A. Koestler & J.R. Smythies (Eds.), *Beyond reductionism*. Boston: Beacon Press.

Wenger, M.A. (1950). Emotion as a visceral action: An extension of Lange's theory. In M.L. Reymert (Ed.), *Feelings and emotions* (pp. 3–10). New York: McGraw-Hill.

Wenar, C. (1982). On negativism. *Human Development, 2*, 1–23.

Werner, H. (1957). The concept of development from a comparative and organismic point of view. In D. Harris (Ed.), *The concept of development* (pp. 125–148). Minneapolis: University of Minnesota Press.

West, E.S., & Todd, W.R. (1962). *Textbook of biochemistry* (3rd ed). New York: Macmillan.

West, M.J., & King, J.A. (1987). Settling nature and nurture into an ontogenetic niche. *Developmental Psychobiology, 20*, 549–562.

Westen, D. (1991). Social cognition and object relations. *Psychological Bulletin, 109*, 429–455.

Wexler, B., Schwartz, G., Bonano, G., Warrenburg, S., Jammer, L., & Michaelis, J. (1989, May). *Unconscious processing of emotional stimuli*. Paper presented at the 142nd annual meeting of the American Psychiatric Association, Washington, D.C.

Wexler, B.E., Warrenburg, S., Schwartz, G.E. & Janer, L.D. (1992). EEG and EMG responses to emotion-evoking stimuli processed without conscious awareness. *Neuropsychologia, 30*, 1065–1079.

Whishaw, I.Q., & Kolb, B. (1989). Tongue protrusion mediated by spared anterior ventrolateral cortex in neonatally decorticate rats: Behavioral support for the neurogenetic hypothesis. *Behavioral and Brain Research, 32*, 101–113.

Whishaw, I.Q., Tomie, J-A., & Kolb, B. (1992). Ventrolateral prefrontal cortex lesions in rats impair the acquisition and retention of a tactile-olfactory configural task. *Behavorial Neuroscience, 106*, 597–603.

White, B. (1985). *The first three years of life*. Englewood Cliffs, NJ: Prentice Hall.

White, F.P. (1980). Differences in proteins synthesized *in vivo* and *in vitro* by cells associated with the cerebral microvasculature: A protein synthesized in response to trauma? *Neuroscience, 5,* 1793–1799.

White, F.P. (1981). The induction of 'stress' proteins in organ slices from brain, heart, and lung as a function of postnatal development. *Journal of Neuroscience, 1,* 1312–1319.

White, R. (1960). Competence and the psychosexual stages of development. In M.R. Jones (Ed.), *Nebraska symposium on motivation*. Lincoln: University of Nebraska Press.

Whitehead, M.C. (1993). Distribution of synapses on identical cell types in a gustatory subdivision of the nucleus of the solitary tract. *Journal of Comparative Neurology, 332,* 326–340.

Whitehead, R. (1991). Right hemisphere superiority during sustained visual attenton. *Journal of Cognitive Neuroscience, 3–4,* 329–331.

Whybrow, P.C., & Prange, A.J. (1981). A hypothesis of thyroid-catecholamine -receptor interaction. *Archives of General Psychiatry, 38,* 106–113.

Wiedenfeld, S.A., O'Leary, A., Bandura, A., Brown, S., Levine, S., & Raska, K. (1990). Impact of perceived self-efficacy in coping with stressors on components of the immune system. *Journal of Personality and Social Psychology, 59,* 1082–1094.

Wieder, H., & Kaplan, E. (1969). Drug use in adolescents: Psychodynamic meaning and pharmacogenic effect. *Psychoanalytic Study of the Child, 24,* 399–431.

Wiener, B., & Graham, S. (1989). Understanding the motivational role of affect: Life-span research from an attributional perspective. *Cognition and Emotion, 3,* 401–419.

Wiesenfeld, A., & Klorman, R. (1978). The mother's psychophysiological reactions to contrasting affective expressions by her own and an unfamiliar infant. *Developmental Psychology, 14,* 294–304.

Wiggins, R. C. (1985). Critical periods in development: Editorial and historical perspectives. In R.C. Wiggins, D.W. McCandless, & S.J. Enna (Eds.), *Developmental neurochemistry* (pp. 3–7). Austin: University of Texas Press .

Wikstrom, M., Krab, K., & Saraste, M. (1981). *Cytochrome oxidase*. London: Academic Press.

Wilcott, R.C. (1981). Medial and orbital cortex and the suppression of behavior in the rat. *Physiology and Behavior, 27,* 237–241.

Wilkins, A.J., Shallice, T., & McCarthy, R. (1987). Frontal lesions and sustained attention. *Neuropsychologia, 25,* 359–365.

Williams, G.C. (1966). *Adaptation and natural selection*. Princeton, NJ: Princeton University Press.

Williamson, P.D., Spencer, D.D., Novelly, R.A., & Mattson, R.H. (1985). Complex partial seizures of frontal lobe origin. *Neurology, 18,* 497–504.

Willner, P., Muscat, R., Papp, M., & Sampson, D. (1991). Dopamine, depression and antidepressant drugs. In P. Willner & J. Scheel-Kruger (Eds.), *The mesolimbic dopamine system: From motivation to action* (pp. 387–410). Chichester, England: Wiley.

Willner, P., & Scheel-Kruger, J. (1991). *The mesolimbic dopamne system: From motivation to action*. Chichester, England: Wiley.

Wilson, A., & Gedo, J.E. (Eds.). (1993). *Hierarchical concepts in psychoanalysis*. New York: Guilford Press.

Wilson, A., Passik, S.D., Faude, J., Abrams, J., & Gordon, E. (1989). A hierarchical model of opiate addiction. Failure of self-regulation as a central aspect of substance abuse. *Journal of Nervous and Mental Disease, 177,* 390–399.

Wilson, A., Passik, S.D., & Faude, J.P. (1990). Self-regulation and its failures. In J. Masling (Ed.), *Empirical studies of psychoanalytic theory, Vol. 3* (pp. 149–213). Hillsdale, NJ: The Analytic Press.

Wilson, A., & Weinstein, L. (1992a). An investigation into some implications for psychoanalysis of Vygotsky's perspective on the origin of mind, Part I. *Journal of the American Psychoanalytic Association, 40,* 524–576.

Wilson, A., & Weinstein, L. (1992b). Language and the psychoanalytic process: Psychoanalysis and Vygotskian psychology, Part II. *Journal of the American Psychoanalytic Association, 40*, 725–760.

Wilson, D.A., Willner, J., Kurz, E.M., & Nadel, L. (1986). Early experience alters brain plasticity. *Behavioral Brain Research, 21*, 223–227.

Wilson, R.S. (1983). The Louisville twin study: developmental synchronies in behavior. *Child Development, 54*, 298–316.

Winick, M. (1974). Cellular growth during normal and abnormal development. In W. Himwich (Ed.), *Biochemistry of the developing brain, Vol. 2* (pp. 199–226). New York: Marcel Dekker.

Winick, M. (1976). *Malnutrition and brain development.* New York: Oxford University Press.

Winick, M., & Noble, A. (1965). Quantitative changes in DNA, RNA and protein during prenatal and postnatal growth in the rat. *Developmental Biology, 12*, 451–466.

Winick, M., Rosso, P., & Waterlow, J. (1970). Cellular growth of cerebrum, cerebellum, and brain stem in normal and marasmic children. *Experimental Neurology, 26*, 393–400.

Wink, P. (1991). Two faces of narcissism. *Journal of Personality and Social Psychology, 61*, 590–597.

Winner, E., & Gardner, H. (1977). The comprehension of metaphor in brain-damaged patients. *Brain, 100*, 717–729.

Winnicott, D.W. (1958a). Mind and its relation to the psyche-soma. In *Through paediatrics to psycho-analysis.* London: Hogarth Press.

Winnicott, D.W. (1958b). The capacity to be alone. *International Journal of Psycho-Analysis, 39*, 416–420.

Winnicott, D.W. (1965). *The family and individual development.* London: Tavistock.

Winnicott, D.W. (1966). From dependence towards independence in the development of the individual. In *The maturational processes and the facilitating environment* (pp. 83–92). New York: International Universities Press.

Winnicott, D.W. (1971). Mirror-role of mother and family in child development. In *Playing and reality.* New York: Basic Books.

Winnicott, D.W. (1986.). *Home is where we start from.* New York: W.W. Norton .

Winokur, G., & Tsuang, T. (1975). Elation vs. irritability in mania. *Comprehensive Psychiatry, 15*, 435–436.

Winson, J. (1985). *Brain and psyche: The biology of the unconscious.* Garden City, NY: Anchor.

Wise, R.A. (1983). Brain neuronal systems mediating reward processes. In J.S. Smith & J.D. Lane (Eds.), *The neurobiology of opiate reward processes* (pp. 406–437). New York: Elsevier/North Holland Biomedical Press.

Wise, R.A. (1988). The neurobiology of craving: Implications for the understanding and treatment of addiction. *Journal of Abnormal Psychology, 97*, 118–132.

Wise, R.A., & Rompre, P.-P. (1989). Brain dopamine and reward. *Annual Review of Psychology, 40*, 191–225.

Wise, S.P., & Herkenham, M. (1982). Opiate receptor distribution in the cerebral cortex of the rhesus monkey. *Science, 218*, 387–389.

Wittling, W., & Pfluger, M. (1990). Neuroendocrine hemisphere asymmetries: Salivary cortisol secretion during lateralized viewing of emotion-related and neutral films. *Brain and Cognition, 14*, 243–265.

Wolf, E.S. (1980). On the developmental line of selfobject relations. In A. Goldberg (Ed.), *Advances in self psychology* (pp. 117–132). New York: International Universities Press.

Wolf, E.S. (1988). *Treating the self: Elements of clinical self psychology.* New York: Guilford Press.

Wolff, J.R. (1979). Some morphogenetic aspects of the development of the central nervous system. In K. Immelmann, G.W. Barlow, M. Main, & L. Petrinovich (Eds.), *Behavioral development. The Bielefeld interdisciplinary project* (pp. 164–190). Cambridge, England: Cambridge University Press.

Wolff, J.R., & Bar, T. (1972). "Seamless" endothelia in brain capillaries during development of the rat's cerebral cortex. *Brain Research, 41*, 17–24.

Wolff, P.H. (1987). *The development of behavioral states and the expression of emotion in early infancy.* Chicago: University of Chicago Press.

Woloski, B.M., Smith, E.M., Meyer, W.J. III, Fuller, G.M., & Blalock, J.E. (1985). Corticotropin-releasing activity of monokines. *Science, 230*, 1035–1037.

Wong-Riley, M.T.T. (1979). Changes in the visual system of monocularly sutured or enucleated cats demonstrable with cytochrome oxidase histochemistry. *Brain Research, 171*, 11–28.

Wong-Riley, M.T.T. (1989). Cytochrome oxidase: an endogenous metabolic marker for neuronal activity. *Trends in Neuroscience, 12*, 94–101.

Wong-Riley, M.T.T., & Welt, C. (1980). Histochemical changes in cytochrome oxidase of cortical barrels after vibrissal removal in neonatal and adult mice. *Proceedings of the National Academy of Sciences of the United States of America, 77*, 2333–2337.

Wonham, W.M. (1976). Towards an abstract internal model principle. *IEEE Transactions of Systems, Man, and Cybernetics, SMC-6*, 735–740.

Woo, C.C., & Leon, M. (1987). Sensitive period for neural and behavioral response development to learned odors. *Developmental Brain Research, 36*, 309–313.

Woo, T.V., Beale, J.M., & Finlay, B.L. (1991). Dual fate of subplate neurons in a rodent. *Cerebral Cortex, 1*, 433–443.

Woodrow, G., & Shatz, G. (1979). The role of oxygen in the biosynthesis of cytochrome c oxidase of ‾yeast mitochondria. *Journal of Biological Chemistry, 254*, 6088–6093.

Wright, K. (1991). *Vision and separation: Between mother and baby.* Northvale NJ: Jason Aronson.

Wurmser, L. (1981). *The mask of shame.* Baltimore: Johns Hopkins University Press.

Wurmser, L. (1987). Flight from conscience: Experiences with the psychoanalytic treatment of compulsive drug abusers Part two: Dynamic and therapeutic conclusions from the experiences with psychoanalysis of drug users. *Journal of Substance Abuse Treatment, 4*, 169–174.

Wyatt, R.J., Protnoy, G., Kupfer, D.J., Snyder, F., & Engelman, K. (1971). Resting catecholamine concentrations in patients with depression and anxiety. *Archives of General Psychiatry, 24*, 65–70.

Wyllie, A.H. (1980). Glucocorticoid-induced thymocyte apoptosis is associated with endogenous endonuclease activation. *Nature (London), 284*, 555–556.

Yakovlev, P. I., & Lecours, A. R. (1967). The myelogenetic cycles of regional maturation of the brain. In A. Minkow (Ed.), *Regional development of the brain in early life.* Oxford: Blackwell.

Yamamoto, T., Oomura, Y., Nishino, H., Aou, S., Nakano, Y., & Nemoto, S. (1984). Monkey orbitofrontal neuron activity during emotional and feeding behaviors. *Brain Research Bulletin, 12*, 763–769.

Yang, G., & Koistinaho, J. (1990). Age-related increase in c-Fos expression in the sympathetic neurons in the rat cervical ganglian. *Brain Research, 533*, 338–343.

Yarita, H., Iino, M., Tanabe, T., Kogure, S., & Takagi, S.F. (1980). A transthalamic olfactory pathway to orbitofrontal cortex in the monkey. *Journal of Neurophysiology, 43*, 69–85.

Yasui, Y., Itoh, K., Kaneko, T., Shigemoto, R., & Mizuno, N. (1991). Topographical projections from the cerebral cortex to the nucleus of the solitary tract in the cat. *Experimental Brain Research, 85*, 75–84.

Yates, F.E., & Moran, J.W. (1974). Stimulation and inhibition of adrenocorticotropin release. In E. Knobil & W. Sawyer (Eds.), *Handbook of physiology: Sec. 7 Endocrinology: Vol. 4, The pituitary gland (Part 2)* (pp. 367–404). Washington, DC: American Physiological Society.

Yokote, H., Itakura, T., Nakai, K., Kamel, I., Imai, H., & Komai, N. (1986). A role of the central catecholamine neuron in cerebral circulation. *Journal of Neurosurgery, 65*, 370–375.

Young, E.A., Haskett, R.F., Murphy-Weinberg, V., Watson, S.J., & Akil, H.A. (1991). Loss of glucocorticoid fast feedback in depression. *Archives of General Psychiatry, 48*, 693–699.

Young, J.Z. (1964). *A model of the brain.* New York: Oxford University Press.

Young, S.T., Porrino, L.J., & Iadarola, M.J. (1991). Cocaine induces striatal c-fos immunoreactive proteins via dopaminergic D1 receptors. *Proceedings of the National Academy of Sciences of the United States of America, 88,* 1291–1295.

Younger, B.A., & Cohen, L.B. (1983). Infant perception of correlations among attributes. *Child Development, 54,* 858–867.

Younger, B.A., & Cohen, L.B. (1986). Developmental changes in infant perception of correlations among attributes. *Child Development, 57,* 803–815.

Yuste, R., & Katz, L.C. (1991). Control of postsynaptic Ca^{2+} influx in developing neocortex by excitatory and inhibitory neurotransmitters. *Neuron, 6,* 333–344.

Zafra, F., Hengerer, B., Leibrock, J., Thoenen, H., & Lindholm, D. (1990). Activity dependent regulation of BDNF and NGF mRNAs in the rat hippocampus is mediated by non-NMDA glutamate receptors. *EMBO Journal, 9,* 3545–3550.

Zagon, I.S., & McLaughlin, P.J. (1988). Endogenous opioid systems and neurobehavioral development. In R.J. Rodgers & S. J. Cooper (Eds.), *Endorphins, opiates and behavioral processes* (pp. 287–309). Chichester, England: Wiley.

Zagon, I.S., McLaughlin, P.J., Weaver, D.J., & Zagon, E. (1982). Opiates, endorphins and the developing organism: A comprehensive bibliography. *Neuroscience Biobehavioral Review, 6,* 439–479.

Zahn-Waxler, C., McKnew, D.H., Cummings, M., Davenport, Y.B., & Radke-Yarrow, M. (1984). Problem behaviors and peer interactions of young children with a manic-depressive parent. *American Journal of Psychiatry, 141,* 236–240.

Zajonc, R.B. (1965). Social facilitation. *Science, 149,* 269–274.

Zajonc, R.B. (1984). On primacy of affect. In K.R. Scherer & P. Ekman (Eds.) *Approaches to emotion* (pp. 259–270). Hillsdale, NJ: Lawrence Erlbaum Associates.

Zajonc, R.B. (1985). Emotion and facial efference: A theory reclaimed. *Science, 228,* 15–21.

Zajonc, R.B., Murphy, S.T., & Inglehart, M. (1989). Feeling and facial efference: Implications of the vascular theory of emotion. *Psychological Review, 96,* 395–416.

Zarrow, M.X., Campbell, P.S., & Denenberg, V.H. (1972). Handling in infancy: Increased levels of hypothalamic corticotropin releasing factor (CRF) following exposure to a novel situation. *Proceedings of the Society for Experimental Biology and Medicine, 141,* 356–358.

Zatorre, R.J., Jones-Gotman, M., Evans, A.C., & Meyer, E. (1992). Functional localization and lateralization of human olfactory cortex. *Nature, 360,* 339–340.

Zatorre, R.J., & Samson, S. (1991). Role of the right temporal neocortex in retention of pitch in auditory short-term memory. *Brain, 114,* 2403–2417.

Zeanah, C.H., & Barton, M.L. (1989). Introduction: Internal representations and parent-infant relationships. *Infant Mental Health Journal, 10,* 135–141.

Zelazo, P.R. (1982). The year-old infant: A period of major cognitive change. In T.G. Bever (Ed.), *Regressions in mental development: Basic phenomena and theories* (pp. 47–79). Hillsdale, NJ: Lawrence Erlbaum Associates.

Zhang, X., Fogel, R., & Renehan, W.E. (1992). Physiology and morphology of neurons in the dorsal motor nucleus of the vagus and the nucleus of the solitary tract are sensitive to distension of the small intestine. *Journal of Comparative Neurology, 323,* 432–448.

Zikmund, V. (1975). Physiological correlates of visual imagery. In P. Sheeman (Ed.), *The function and nature of imagery* (pp. 355–387). New York: Academic Press.

Zillman, D., & Bryant, J. (1974). Effects of residual excitation on the emotional response to provocation and delayed aggressive behavior. *Journal of Personality and Social Psychology, 30,* 782–791.

Zinbarg, R.E., Barlow, D.H., Brown, T.A., & Hertz, R.M. (1992). Cognitive-behavioral approaches to the nature and treatment of anxiety disorders. *Annual Review of Psychology, 43,* 235–267.

Ziven, G. (Ed.). (1979). *The development of self-regulation through private speech.* New York: Wiley.

Subject Index

A

Adaptation syndrome, 211, 226, 514

Adaptive capacities, *see also Ontogenetic adaptation*
of brain-stem systems, 276
conservation-withdrawal, 328-329
of cross-modal transfer, 307
of emotions, 110, 287
expanded affect array, 327
facial expressions, 75
immunological response to stress, 437
of interactive repair, 245-247, 344
mitochondrial developmental changes, 521
of negative affects, 345, 361
orbitofrontal role, 35, 225, 229, 269-282, 293, 331, 528
of parcellation, 253-258
reciprocal modes of autonomic control, 324
regulation of state transitions, 276, 282, 365-368, 472, 495, 529
of representational memory, 177, 313, 487-488
secure attachment, 387
of shame in affect regulation, 241, 360-362

Addiction, 403-404

Adenosine triphosphate (ATP), 16, 502-503, 511, 520, 531

Adenylate cyclase, 119, 133, 138, 142, 152-154, 183, 223, 251, 276, 525

Adrenal gland, 140-141, 215, 223-224, 226, 296, 329, 408, 434, 436, 438, 513, 522

Adrenocortical function, 216, 223, 227, 243, 328-329, 406, 515

Adrenocorticotrophic hormone (ACTH), 137-140, 145, 216, 223, 226, 253, 325, 334, 433-434, 436, 438, 441

Affect array, 32-33, 327, 381, 420, 454, 461, 464, 479, 530

Affect signal function, 210, 365, 440, 462, 466

Affect, theory of, 285-301

Affect tolerance, 381, 403, 462, 464, 487, 530

Affective core, 279-280, 374-375, 382-384, 389, 403, 415, 426, 444, 477, 541-542

Aggression, *see also Rage*
autoregulation of, 338
day care and infant, 541
defense system, 328
empathy and, 351
gender differences in, 266
hypothalamus and, 338
maternal response to infant, 343
mature, relation to narcisstic rage, 339, 342
orbitofrontal cortex and, 41, 338
right hemispheric lesion and, 338
superego and, 348, 352
unmodulated, and development, 339

Alexithymia, 461, 485, 489

649

Author Index